TORONTO
A Literary Guide

Greg Gatenby

McArthur & Company
Toronto

Canadian Cataloguing in Publication Data

Gatenby, Greg
    Toronto: a literary guide

Includes index
ISBN 1-55278-073-2

1. Literary landmarks – Ontario – Toronto – Guidebooks. 2. Toronto (Ont.) – Tours. I. Title.

PS8087.G37 1999   917.13'541044   C98-933097-4
PR9187.G37 1999

Composition and Design by Michael P. Callaghan
Maps and digital processing by Moons of Jupiter, Inc. (Toronto)
Cover Design by Scott Richardson
Printed in Canada by Best Book Manufacturers

McArthur & Company
322 King Street West, Suite 402
Toronto, ON, M5V 1J2

10 9 8 7 6 5 4 3 2 1

This book is for my mother,

Margaret Helen O'Connor, my first Torontonian

CONTENTS

ABBREVIATIONS:

apt.: apartment
c.:circa
c.: century
CanLit: Canadian Literature
G&M: *Globe and Mail*
M&E: *Mail & Empire*
ms: manuscript
UCC: Upper Canada College
UofT: University of Toronto
WWI: World War One
WWII: World War Two

A word about newspapers: dailies in Toronto were continually modifying their names. Thus the *Star* has variously been the *Toronto Star*, the *Toronto Daily Star*, and the *Toronto Evening Star*. For the sake of clarity, I have chosen to cite the newspapers by the names Torontonians used or would have used when buying the paper at a kiosk: *Star, Mail, World, News, Globe, Empire,* and *Telegram*. To save space, I have condensed the *Mail and Empire* to *M&E*. The *M&E* merged with the *Globe* in 1936 to form the *Globe and Mail*, abbreviated to *G&M* throughout the *Guide*.

INTRODUCTION

My formal research for this book began in 1978 at a dinner I had with Morley Callaghan. At the dinner Morley casually mentioned to me that he had shared a reminiscence with William Butler Yeats during one of Yeats's visits to Toronto. Having been raised to believe that I lived at the edge of the civilized world where no one as important as Yeats would deign to visit, I was stunned to learn from Morley that Yeats had been to Toronto not once, twice, or thrice—but four times. And visits by someone as internationally renowned as Yeats were hardly unusual, according to Callaghan. They were the norm. Yes, he told me, the city had certainly been a buttoned-up, straight-laced place, but that did not mean it was empty of readers. So with the name of Yeats before me, I set out to uncover exactly when he and others had come, and why, and what they had written concerning our fair city. That search inevitably led to questions about where native Torontonians had lived. Twenty-one years later, my researches are far from finished, but I wanted to begin to share with Torontonians the discoveries I had made, and this *Guide* is the distillation of those disclosures.

As well as informing you about the homes of authors who are famous in our time (Atwood, Davies, Hemingway, and Faulkner, for example) and what books they wrote there, I hope to surprise you with stories of passion, corruption, greed, and generosity involving the famous and the yet-to-be-famous.

The schools attended by authors are frequently cited so that those readers who attend—or attended the same schools—can bask in the associated glory. And the *Guide* documents for the first time public visits to Toronto by some of the most prominent names in world literature.

The origins of this book can be traced, in fact, to school, to a moment in my Grade 12 history class when I asked my teacher why we were going to spend yet another term studying the American Civil War. Important as that event may have been to the Americans, I was curious as to why we spent no time studying Canadian history. My teacher commiserated with my question, but was also embarrassed by it, and mumbled something about doing what the Ministry of Education told him to do. There were no instructions to teach Canadian history, he said, while there were instructions that two terms had to be given over to the American conflict. As a 17-year-old, I lacked the wit and knowledge to rebut such an answer, but amorphous as my nationalist feelings were, they were nevertheless real, and the inadequacy of my teacher's response has stuck in my craw ever since.

This is a guide to authors in Toronto rather than a comprehensive literary history. The latter would require several volumes, whereas I wanted to write a book that would appeal to both the non-specialist interested in just the high points of our literary past as well as to those needing a deeper and detailed knowledge of where authors lived and worked.

To keep the book to a manageable length, I have had to make some hard editorial choices: this is a history of authors who have published at least one book of adult fiction, poetry or drama published between the founding of the city in 1793, and 1993. The exceptions are unapologetically subjective.

Those who regret that this *Guide* is not also a history of book publishing or retailing must have stronger arms than the rest of us, because to do justice to any one of those fields would have easily doubled this book's length. Also, this is a guide to places where authors lived, worked, and went to school. It is not a dictionary of Toronto places as they have been described in the literary imagination of its writers. The compilation of such a compendium is probably beyond the research abilities of any single historian, and would easily quadruple the extent of the book you are holding in your hands.

As a general rule, I have cited authors by the names they used on the title pages of their books. Thus "Mark Twain" and not "Samuel Clemens."

My research has uncovered some general truths which the careful reader might find helpful to have in the back of his or her mind while following the walking tours proposed in subsequent chapters. For example, because many authors then, as now, are poor, they tended to rent small flats rather than buy houses which meant that they found it easier to move frequently. It is not uncommon for some authors to have had more than 30 Toronto addresses. The Depression played its part, and in tracing an author's whereabouts through the city directories, I found it was frequently the case that they would have stable address-es until 1929. After the stock-market crash, however, many authors seemed to change rooms with every new moon, either because they found a place down the road that was a couple of dollars cheaper a week to rent—or because they were one step ahead of the bailiff. Both World Wars also forced families to break apart, and the financial rollercoaster of the post-war period also led to frequent moves by much of the population.

Women writers were especially hard to trace because, until recently, they often pub-lished under their maiden names but lived their public and legal lives under their hus-band's name. Unless I found a newspaper profile or book jacket that told me author Mary Jones was also Mrs. John Smith, for example, I found it nearly impossible to find where Mary Jones lived, because only Mr. Smith would be listed in directories. Fortunately, after more than two decades of looking, I can happily state that I have uncovered the addresses of a number of women writers, and in some cases even their years of birth and death are here established for the first time.

Another facet of our cultural past which is poorly documented and thus not suffi-ciently applauded is the role played by women's organizations. They were responsible for bringing a number of eminent writers to Toronto (e.g., Sinclair Lewis and John Cowper Powys) but much more importantly, they provided ready and willing audiences for literary events and were one of the keys in the maintenance of a literary culture. While they could also be bastions of tiresome primness and dictatorial propriety, these women's organizations, by their ongoing interest in writers—including, or even espe-cially Canadian writers—became pillars of whatever public literary events and discourse existed in Toronto up to approximately 1970.

Newspapers have also played a singular role in our literary history. As much as pos-sible I have documented the journalistic affiliations of the creative writers mentioned in this book, in part because such an extensive correlation is so at odds with our own time. And discussion of newspapers is pertinent because it has been my experience that most people today are unaware of how much newspapers have changed their attitudes to authors from what those attitudes were in the 1940s and before. For example, in the good old days, it was normal for book reviews to comprise no more than half a broadsheet page one day a week (the sections edited by William Arthur Deacon being noble deviations from the rule). Reviews were generally 500 words or less—often much less—and pictures of book jackets or of authors almost non-existent. Clearly in our own time, book pages are more numerous, better designed, and feature longer reviews.

However, we do not compare well when one examines how creative writers were considered "news" by newspapers. Until the 1950s, it was common for visits by eminent literary authors to be given page-one treatment. Even on the second day of an author's visit, a subsequent report of what he had to say (for it was almost always a "he") may have fallen to page two or three, but it was still regarded as important and newsworthy. When the author gave a speech (readings alone were uncommon until the 1960s), newspapers reported on the speech, again treating the event as news, and placing the story in the news section of the paper accordingly. The society columns also reported on the parties and receptions attended by the author. And the editorial pages frequently featured editorials which were simultaneously welcome-notices as well as intelligent commentaries on the author's literary output.

Now, the ignorant or the cynical have been known to remark at this point that Toronto gave such prominent coverage to the visits (or deaths) of authors because there was so little else to report. We can forgive such a view because its utterers have been raised in a colonial culture and, sadly, know no better. The fact is Toronto newspapers had as many gruesome murders, conniving politicians, armed bank robberies, and foreign wars to report on as they do today, yet for more than a century (c. 1850-c. 1960) the visit of a distinguished novelist (and occasionally even a poet) was almost always a front-page item in Toronto.

A word is in order about the inclusion of authors whom time seems to have forgotten. There seem to me many reasons why they should be included. First, our time has no monopoly on good taste. Authors once famous but now dismissed as unimportant may become highly acclaimed again in subsequent generations.

Second, a literary guide that includes only those authors who are fashionable or deemed important at the time of its publication will soon find itself dated, because tastes and standards are constantly changing.

Third, they deserve inclusion because, even if they will never be famous or critically celebrated again, they were well regarded in their own time. If we are to better understand that time (and thereby better understand from where we ourselves have come), we had better come to terms with those whom the age deemed important.

Fourth, no history is complete with just the sagas of its heroes or leaders. Generals are nothing without their troops, and in this book I have attempted to remind the reader that authors such as Mazo de la Roche or E.J. Pratt did not spring from a void but were surrounded by a community of writers, editors, publishers, and booksellers, all of whom practised as professionals and rose well above the level of the amateur.

Fifth, just because you have not heard of an author does not mean that he or she is not a highly regarded figure. We all have blind spots.

When making choices about which lesser-known author to include or exclude, I have always given preference—all other aspects being equal—to the author who was born or who died in Toronto. Preference was also shown for authors who ran for, and sometimes were even elected to, public office. I did this for two reasons. First, because the number of such authors came as a surprise to me and I thought it might to other readers. And second because at a time when most politicians at all levels continue to believe the arts count for next to nothing, it is salient to remember there was a time in our history when politicians read more than polls.

The origins, explanations, and caveats now out of the way, do let me lead you on a series of literary tours of Toronto neighbourhoods. Be astounded to discover that you may have lived in the house of a famous poet, or down the street from an acclaimed dramatist, or just around the corner from an important novelist.

See the houses lived in by authors you have long associated with the city (although you were never quite sure where they *actually* lived): Morley Callaghan, Mazo de la Roche, Ernest Thompson Seton, E.J. Pratt, Margaret Atwood, Michael Ondaatje, Robertson Davies, Gwendolyn MacEwen, Hugh Garner, Charles G.D. Roberts, Timothy Findley, Northrop Frye, Marshall McLuhan, Alexander Muir, Marian Engel, Irving Layton, Dennis Lee, and Raymond Souster.

Discover the homes of authors you never suspected once lived in Toronto: Mordecai Richler, Ernest Buckler, W.O. Mitchell, Lucy Maud Montgomery, Wyndham Lewis, Willa Cather, Margaret Laurence, William Faulkner, Nellie McClung, Algernon Blackwood, Ross MacDonald, Stephen Leacock, Marshall Saunders, Douglas Coupland, Farley Mowat, William Gibson, Jane Urquhart, Susanna Moodie, Don DeLillo, Alice Munro, Leon Edel, Brian Moore, Derek Mahon, Pierre Salinger, Arthur Hailey, Robert Ross, and Ernest Hemingway.

And finally, stand before Massey and other halls where some of the greatest names of 19th- and 20th-century literature have spoken to large and appreciative Toronto audiences—names such as Bertrand Russell, Winston S. Churchill, Mark Twain, Oscar Wilde, Rudyard Kipling, G.K. Chesteron, John Masefield, Arthur Conan Doyle, Theodore Dreiser, J.B. Priestley, Rex Stout, Brendan Behan, Thomas Mann, Vladimir Nabokov, Walt Whitman, Ralph Waldo Emerson, Langston Hughes, Vita Sackville-West, Aldous Huxley, Henry James—and yes, William Butler Yeats.

Toronto

A Literary Guide

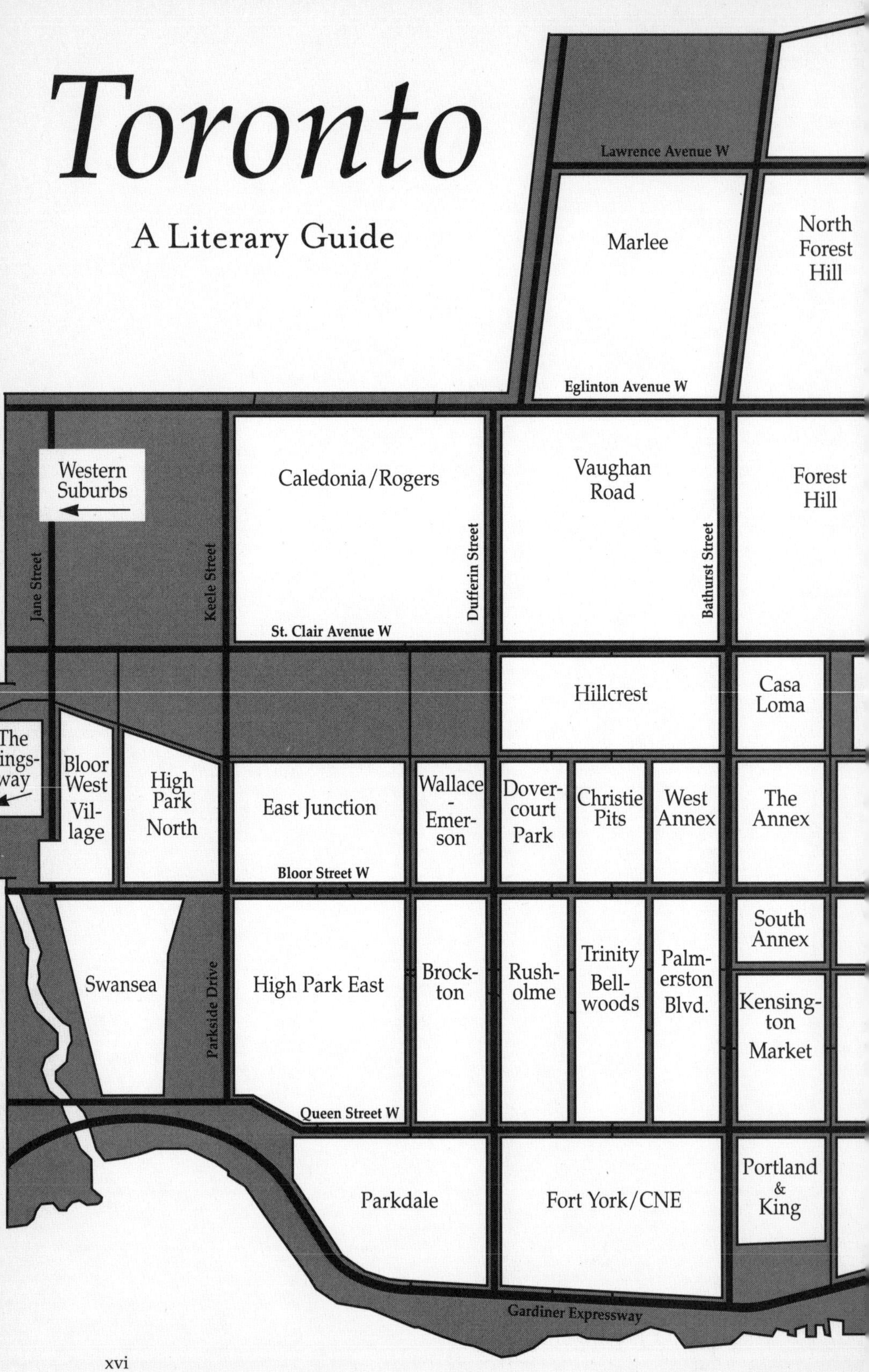

Lawrence Avenue W

Marlee

North Forest Hill

Eglinton Avenue W

Western Suburbs ←

Caledonia/Rogers

Vaughan Road

Forest Hill

Jane Street

Keele Street

Dufferin Street

Bathurst Street

St. Clair Avenue W

Hillcrest

Casa Loma

The Kingsway ←

Bloor West Village

High Park North

East Junction

Wallace-Emerson

Dovercourt Park

Christie Pits

West Annex

The Annex

Bloor Street W

Swansea

Parkside Drive

High Park East

Brockton

Rusholme

Trinity Bellwoods

Palmerston Blvd.

South Annex

Kensington Market

Queen Street W

Parkdale

Fort York/CNE

Portland & King

Gardiner Expressway

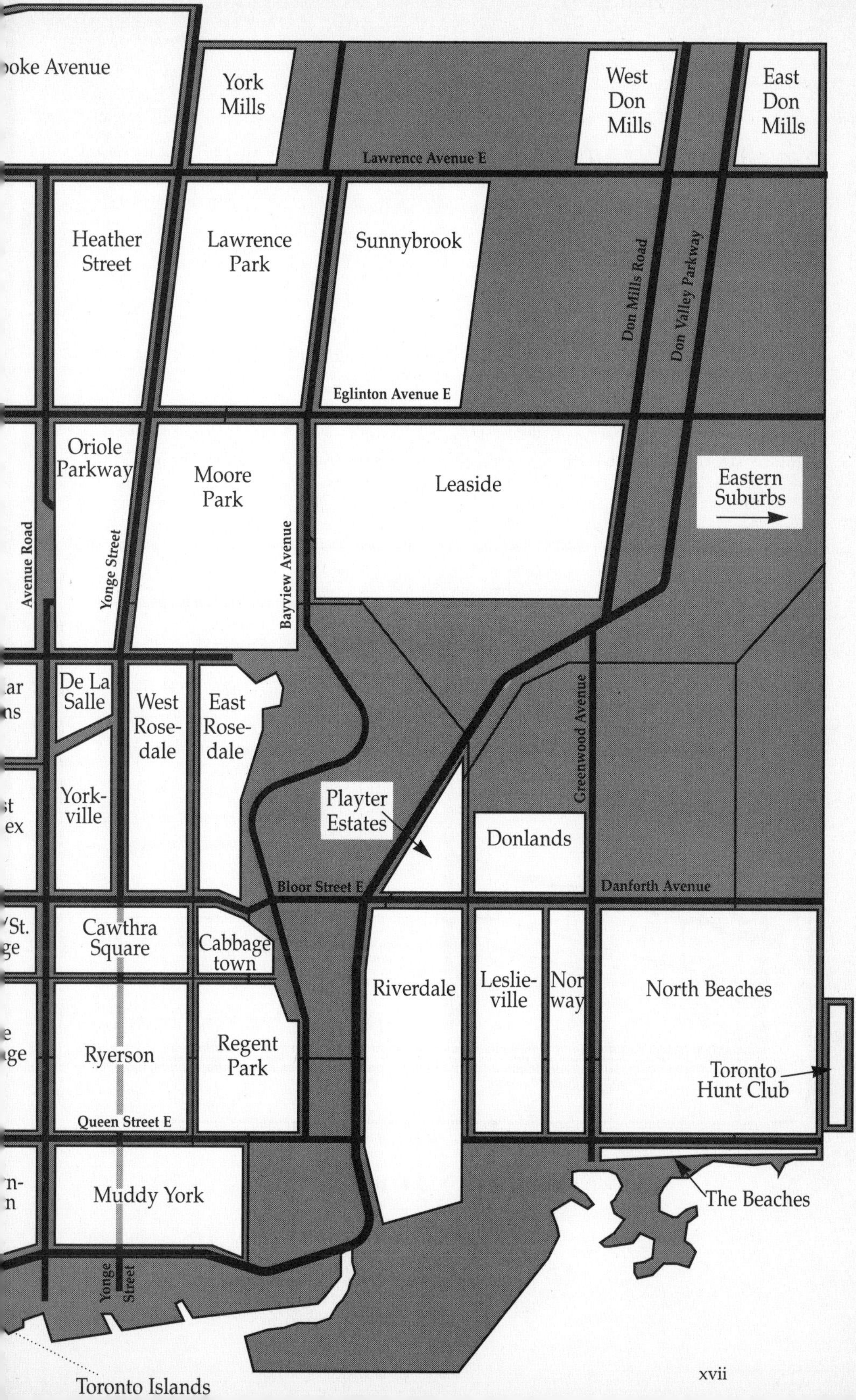

oke Avenue

York
Mills

West
Don
Mills

East
Don
Mills

Lawrence Avenue E

Heather
Street

Lawrence
Park

Sunnybrook

Don Mills Road

Don Valley Parkway

Eglinton Avenue E

Oriole
Parkway

Moore
Park

Leaside

Eastern
Suburbs
→

Avenue Road

Yonge Street

Bayview Avenue

ar
ns

De La
Salle

West
Rose-
dale

East
Rose-
dale

Greenwood Avenue

st
ex

York-
ville

Playter
Estates

Donlands

Bloor Street E

Danforth Avenue

St.
ge

Cawthra
Square

Cabbage
town

Riverdale

Leslie-
ville

Nor
way

North Beaches

e
ge

Ryerson

Regent
Park

Toronto
Hunt Club

Queen Street E

n-
n

Muddy York

The Beaches

Yonge
Street

Toronto Islands

KEY TO MAPS

As each tour in this book represents a portion of Toronto, and the maps provided are meant to display the streets mentioned in the text, I have taken the liberty of asking the designer to keep the maps as simple as possible for the sake of clarity.

The start of each tour is indicated by a star ⭐ as in the sample map below. Each map is oriented top to North.

The main perimeter streets are given in full, e.g. Front Street East, Queen Street East, Pariament Street or Gardiner Expressway.

Neighbourhood streets are given strictly by name, with bold lines representing main arteries. Narrow lines represent side streets. East, West, North and South are noted E. W. N. S.

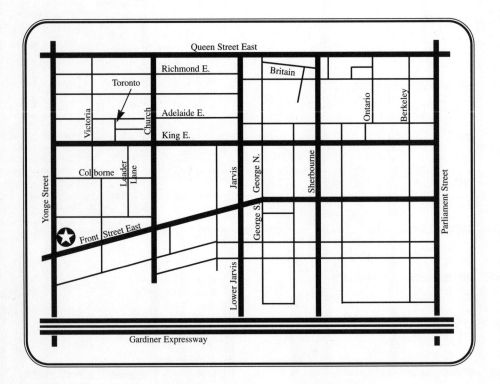

Maps are NOT to scale

(maps for the last three tours — the Toronto Islands, West Suburbs, and East Suburbs — have not been provided)

Sic transit gloria mundi

MUDDY YORK

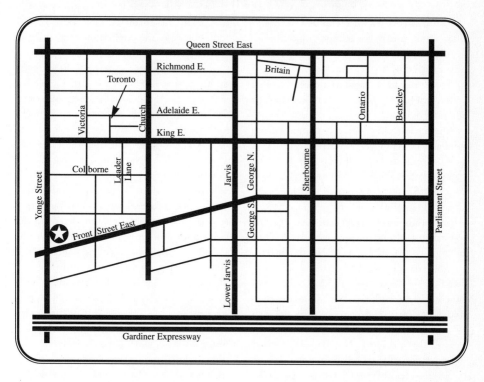

The tour begins at the northeast corner of Front Street East and Yonge Street.

A long wooden pier, thrusting deep into the Toronto harbour, once stood where the Hummingbird Centre is now located. The dip in the land immediately to the west of the Hummingbird marks the former shoreline of the port. Sailing vessels and steamers moored at this spot well into the 19th c., and from those ships affluent passengers disembarked and crossed Front Street to enter the North American Hotel. The hotel was located where the LePage Building now stands at **33 Yonge Street.** Among the tenants of the building are Random House of Canada and Alfred A. Knopf Canada, which between them have published a number of well-known Canadian authors, including novelists Carol Shields and Mordecai Richler.

One well-to-do passenger who stayed at the North American Hotel was Charles Dickens (1812-70). He arrived in Toronto on Wednesday evening, May 4, 1842, on the steamboat *Transit* from Niagara, and departed two days later at noon on Friday, May 6 via the steamer *City of Toronto*, bound for Kingston, Ontario. The North American Hotel, sometimes referred to as "The American Hotel" or "The American House," had accommodation for 150 guests and a large dining hall capable of seating up to 200. The hotel's room tariff was two dollars per day, including meals—among the more expensive rates in Toronto, a town with high hopes for growth and a population at the time of approximately 13,000.

Despite what some books on Toronto would have you believe, Dickens never read in Toronto—indeed, made no public appearance whatsoever, apart from attending one, possibly two, private dinners held in his honour. Based on his published account of the city, he obviously made a walkabout of the main streets, and it seems he was able to do so anonymously, or at least without bother, for neither he nor the newspapers make any mention of his being harassed by fans.

This is not to say he was ignored. But it is important to recall that Dickens was only 30 when he arrived, and, while he was a best-selling author, his apotheosis into literary godhead had not yet happened. He was a popular author, nevertheless. By 1842 he had published *The Pickwick Papers* (1837), *Oliver Twist* (1838), *Nicholas Nickleby* (1839), *The Old Curiosity Shop* (1841), and *Barnaby Rudge* (1841) —had published so much, in fact, that he was exhausted, and decided to recuperate by taking a five-month tour of North America in the first half of 1842. Although he was feted at his stops in the USA, Dickens saw much that he did not like about America and Americans, and one can hear the sigh of relief in his journal and letters as he crosses the border at Niagara and is once again on soil of the British Empire.

After a few days at Niagara (which he quite enjoyed), he set sail for Toronto. One of the reasons there may have been no public reception for Dickens was that Toronto at the time had no Lieutenant-Governor. The year before, Upper and Lower Canada had been united under one Governor General, and there was no representative of the Queen permanently resident in Ontario until Confederation. Another reason may have been, quite simply, that Dickens did not want a ceremonial welcome. But the most likely reason is that no one knew he was coming. Within days of his arrival in the States he had been deluged with dinner invitations, and to save his sanity he soon made a policy of declining almost all of them, and to prevent such invitations from even being issued, he seems to have kept his exact arrivals and departures to himself. The Toronto newspapers of the day tell us that once they had learned of his appearance "all the leading persons in the city left their cards at his hotel," inviting him to dinner or to tea. But in this city he made an exception to his no-formal-dinner rule, choosing to accept the invitation of the Chief Justice, John Beverley Robinson.

Robinson's dinner party was held at the domicile that had been his home since his marriage in 1817. The building had been constructed just after the War of 1812 on the lot between Queen and Richmond streets, its western border abutting John Street— where the CITY/Bravo building now stands. Toronto building historian Lucy Booth Martyn said of it, "Beverley House faced south to the lake and had a centre hall plan. A gravel drive swept in a long curve to the front door and a sundial on a square stone stood on the lawn. A high brick wall enclosed the property, except on Richmond Street where the front gates were set in a wrought-iron fence above a low wall. A tiny stream ran along the west side of the house, while on the east side a garden—vegetables, berry bushes, and roses—flourished. The library contained ceiling-high walnut bookshelves and a high carved desk. Three-corner chairs and a big sofa were covered with bright red damask, matching the window drapes." It was here that Dickens met Robinson, Mrs. Robinson, and a few of Robinson's friends hastily assembled for the occasion. As the doyen of the Family Compact, Robinson is unlikely to have invited anybody but those who were in agreement with his extreme politics, and because the Farmers' Revolt of 1837 was still fresh in their minds, Robinson's company was not shy about sharing with Dickens the merits of their autocracy and the demerits of those who preferred responsible government. This dinner party, then, was undoubtedly the source for Dickens's much-quoted line (taken from a letter to a friend in England) that "the wild and rabid Toryism of Toronto, is, I speak seriously, *appalling.*"

When Charles Dickens returned to England, he wrote a book about his travels, *American Notes*. The candour of his remarks caused howls of outrage, not least in Toronto where the gentry felt their hospitality had been betrayed by the matters on which he chose to focus. Almost half of Dickens's brief description of Toronto refers to the murder of a man by an Orange Lodge fanatic. It was frequently difficult to tell apart the Orangemen of Toronto from the city's oligarchy, and Dickens was not the only literary visitor repulsed by their public and shameless displays of hate and prejudice. Even royal visitors later found the ferocity of the Orange banners and welcoming arches beyond the pale, and refused to step ashore until they were removed.

On a more positive note, Dickens was clearly impressed to find such distinguished shops in this outpost of Empire. The main street to which he refers in the quotation below is King Street—which would not cede its place as the city's principal thoroughfare until later in the century with the ascendancy of the Eaton's and Simpson's department stores on Yonge Street. And "the first stone of a new college" to which Dickens also refers is the beginning of what became the Queen's Park campus of the UofT: "The country round this town being very flat is bare of scenic interest; but the town itself is full of life and motion, bustle, business, and improvement. The streets are well paved, and lighted with gas, the houses are large and good; the shops excellent. Many of them have a display of goods in their windows, such as may be seen in thriving county towns in England; and there are some which would do no discredit to the metropolis itself. There is a good stone prison here; and there are, besides, a handsome church, a court-house, public offices, many commodious private residences, and a Government observatory for noting and recording the magnetic variations. In the College of Upper Canada, which is one of the public establishments of the city, a sound education in every department of polite learning can be had, at a very moderate expense: the annual charge for the instruction of each pupil, not exceeding

nine pounds sterling. It has pretty good endowments in the way of land, and is a valuable and useful institution.

"The first stone of a new college had been laid but a few days before by the Governor-General. It will be a handsome, spacious edifice approached by a long avenue which is already planted and made available as a public walk. The town is well-adapted for wholesome exercise at all seasons, for the footways in the thoroughfares which lie beyond the principal street are planked like floors, and kept in very good and clean repair.

"It is a matter of deep regret that political differences should have run high in this place, and led to most discreditable and disgraceful results. It is not long since guns were discharged from a window in this town at the successful candidates in an election, and the coachman of one of them was actually shot in the body, though not dangerously wounded. But one man was killed on the same occasion; and from the very window whence he received his death, the very flag which shielded his murderer (not only in the commission of his crime, but from its consequences), was displayed again on the occasion of the public ceremony performed by the Governor-General, to which I have just adverted. Of all the colours in the rainbow, there is but one which could be so employed: I need not say that flag was orange. The time of leaving Toronto for Kingston is noon."

The North American Hotel was also where the St. George's Society held its meetings. The Club was dedicated to the promotion of things English. At a dinner here in 1838, Captain Frederick Marryat, one of the earliest important literary visitors to the city, made a notorious toast that was quoted throughout the continent, and vilified across the United States.

Captain Marryat (1792-1848) earned his rank in the British navy, and his literary reputation for his novels of adventure. Before his arrival in Toronto, he was already well known for the bestsellers *Peter Simple* (1834) and *Mr. Midshipman Easy* (1836), and his later works only augmented his international fame. He travelled from England to this continent with the intention of writing a book about his experiences. As it happened, not one but two books emerged: the inevitable travel account known as *The Diary in America* (a six-volume opus published in 1839) and a young adult novel, *The Settlers in Canada* (1844).

Marryat was arriving in Toronto just months after William Lyon Mackenzie had tried to topple the government in an armed insurrection. Although the revolt had failed, it had not failed by much, and those in power were shaken by how close they had come to political demise, possibly even death. Their anxiety was not diminished by the flight of Mackenzie and his men to the USA, for the rebels had merely camped on the other side of the border at Niagara (on Navy Island) and it seemed a real possibility to the gentry of Toronto that, once rearmed, he might attack again. To the Americans, however, Mackenzie was a hero. They identified with his attempt to throw off the British yoke, and applauded his many statements regarding the right of men to vote for their leaders. He was given not only asylum in the USA, but sustenance and small amounts of military aid, much of it shipped to the Navy Island camp by a steamboat called the *Caroline*. To the Family Compact and its cronies in Toronto, this American support of a rebel leader was an outrage. Exasperated by weeks of what they perceived to be American taunts, a group of Canadian soldiers under a Captain Drew sneaked across the Niagara River on December 30, 1837. They rowed to the berth of the *Caroline*, cut loose her lines, towed her into the middle of the river, set her on fire, and then set her adrift. According to some accounts, she actually soared over the Falls, a mighty conflagration—and political statement—that no one would miss. The illegality of this action was bad enough, but far worse was the murder of an American, killed during the fracas to cut the steamer free. The American government would demand immediate redress, while the British government said the action of her soldiers was authorized under international law. Tensions between the USA and UK (and therefore Canada) grew to a level not seen since the War of 1812, and escalated over the next few years to the point that Dickens actually debated with himself in 1841 whether it was safe to travel to this side of the pond.

It is against this background that one can start to understand how deliberately provocative Marryat was when he rose in the banquet room of the North American Hotel in April 1838, as the guest of honour at the St. George's Club dinner, and proposed a toast to "Captain Drew and his brave comrades who cut out the *Caroline*." These approving comments travelled like electricity throughout the border states, and many American newspapers called for Marryat to be burned in effigy, for his books to be torched, and for far worse torments to his person. As he wrote to his mother on May 11, "I am not in very great favour with the Yankees here on the borders, in consequence of my having drank the health of those who cut out the *Caroline* when at Toronto. It was put in the papers, as everything is that I do or say, and a great deal more that I do *not* do or say; and they declared they would lynch me if they got hold of me."

In 1839, back in England, he wrote about Toronto, then just a town of a few thousand souls: "Toronto, which is the present capital and seat of government of Upper Canada, is, from its want of spires and steeples, by no means an imposing town, as you view it on entering the harbour. The harbour itself is landlocked, and when deepened will be very good. A great deal of money has been expended by the English government upon the Canadian provinces, but not very wisely. The Rideau and Welland canals are splendid works; they have nothing to compare with them in the United States; but they are too much in advance of the country, and will be of but little use for a long period, if the provinces do not go ahead faster than they do now. One half the money spent in making good roads through the provinces would have done more good, and would have much increased the value of property . . . The minute you put your foot on shore, you feel that you are no longer in the United States; you are at once struck with the difference between the English and the American population, systems, and ideas. On the other side of the lake you have much more apparent property, but much less real solidity and security. The houses and stores at Toronto are not to be compared with those of the American towns opposite. But the Englishman has built according to his means—the American, according to his expectations. The hotels and inns at Toronto are very bad; at Buffalo they are splendid—for the Englishman travels little; the American is ever on the move. The private houses of Toronto are built, according to the English taste and desire of exclusiveness, away from the road, and are embowered in trees; the American, let his house be ever so large, or his plot of ground however extensive, builds within a few feet of the road, that he may see and know what is going on. You do not perceive the bustle, the energy, and activity at Toronto that you do at Buffalo, nor the profusion of articles in the stores; but it should be remembered that the Americans procure their articles upon credit, whilst at Toronto they proceed more cautiously. The Englishman builds his house and furnishes his store according to his means and fair expectations of being able to meet his acceptances."

99 Yonge Street, just up the road, was the home address for the most important writers' organizations in the late 1930s and throughout the forties. The Canadian Literature Club, the Writers Club, the Canadian Authors' Association, and the PEN Club shared quarters on one of the upper floors. Their space encompassed a room large enough to accommodate readings over the years by some noted authors, including Roger Lemelin, Wilson MacDonald, Nellie McClung, and Arthur Stringer.

The great Scottish poet Hugh MacDiarmid (1892-1978) has a tiny connection to **109 Yonge**. In the building that used to stand here, noted Canadian painter Aba Bayefsky had a studio. He told me it was not uncommon for Barker Fairley to drop into this studio, and the two men would chat while each painted at an easel. One day, Fairley brought along Hugh MacDiarmid who was in the area paying a visit to his daughter in Georgetown. Also joining the party was a mutual friend, Humphrey Milnes. Milnes, a scholar and literary translator, had succeeded Fairley as chair of the German dept. at the the UofT. While Bayefsky and Fairley painted MacDiarmid's portrait, Milnes, who had been astute enough to bring along a tape recorder, asked MacDiarmid to read some poems. Bayefsky recalls that among the works MacDiarmid read was his most famous poem: "A Drunk Man Looks on at the Thistle."

Friends of MacDiarmid in the UK soon learned that the portraits had been painted and bought the Bayefsky painting for the National Gallery of Scotland. To his surprise, Bayefsky learned in 1972 that his painting had been used on a portrait stamp celebrating MacDiarmid's 80th birthday. In fact, he learned of its use only after MacDiarmid, with whom he had continued to correspond, sent him a letter with the very stamp on the envelope. Bayefsky wrote the Royal Mail asking if he might have an unfranked example for his files. The philatelic authority replied he could—as long as he remitted one Canadian dollar for its purchase.

Take Adelaide Street East to **Victoria Street**. Nearby were the three earliest Toronto addresses of John Wilson Bengough: **55 Victoria Street** in 1873; **No.66** from 1874-75; and **No.78** in 1874. Bengough (1851-1923) was born in Toronto but was raised in Whitby. At the age of 20 he returned to Toronto to make his fortune. A stint at the *Globe* as a reporter convinced him that he would be better off as his own boss and in May 1873, while living on

Victoria Street, he launched his own magazine, *Grip* (named in honour of the raven in *Barnaby Rudge*). He was clearly inspired by Thomas Nast's editorial cartoons against the Tammany Hall Ring in *Harper's*, and *Grip* was illustrated throughout by Bengough himself. A magazine of current events, the periodical quickly became famous for its unsparing coverage of the Pacific Scandal, and was a factor in the downfall of Sir John A. Macdonald's government. Bengough remained editor and chief illustrator until late 1892. In addition to collections of his editorial cartoons, he published poetry and tried his hand more than once at poetic dramas.

It was also while living on Victoria Street that Bengough began his famous chalk-talks. Today we would call these illustrated lectures. Essentially, they involved Bengough speaking at a lectern and illustrating his points with cartoons drawn on a large blackboard. His first talk was given at the Music Hall on March 20, 1874, and the chalk-talks remained popular (and lucrative) for almost 50 years—he gave them across Canada, as well as throughout the USA, UK, and Australia, a phenomenal record.

Another editor of a humorous journal was Knox Magee (1877-1934) who published his short-lived magazine, *The Moon*, out of **48 Adelaide Street East** from 1902-3. In the two years previous, he had published a couple of novels: *With Ring of Shield* (1900) and *Mark Everard* (1901), no small feat given his age, and the fact that he had just graduated from University College. When *The Moon* folded from want of patronage, Magee worked as an editor at *Saturday Night* for a few years before returning to Winnipeg. Despite much looking, I could not determine where he lived in Toronto.

Yet another comic magazine, *Punch in Canada*, has a connection to this area. Its editor, Charles Dawson Shanly (1811-75), was born and raised in Ireland but came to Upper Canada with his parents in 1836. He had early hopes as a poet, but the reality of earning a living saw him assume the editorship in Montreal of a new venture, *Punch in Canada*, modelled on its famous British namesake. Editing the magazine meant he had to write much of its copy—satirical copy mocking politicians and the Governor General's retinue. Shanly also contributed most of the poems and cartoons. When the seat of government moved in 1850 from Montreal to Toronto, the magazine had to move with it, because Shanly was a civil servant and it was his salary as assistant secretary in the Dept. of Public Works which subsidized the magazine (although it is doubtful his bosses were aware they were paying for their own pillorying). However, something was lost in the transfer and the magazine soon folded after its arrival in our metropolis. Unable to find regular employment for his journalism talents after seven years in Toronto, Shanly went to the States in 1857 where he had success both as a writer and as a cartoonist. Among other accomplishments, he had a hand in the creation of *Vanity Fair*, and for some time was its editor. The only address I could find for Shanly were lodgings he shared with an actor at what is today **168 Adelaide Street East** from c. September 1849 to c. 1851. The *Punch in Canada* office was on the northwest corner of Yonge and Melinda Streets.

A couple of blocks to the north is **100 Richmond Street East** where, from 1972-76, on the second floor, Josef Skvorecky and his wife, Zdena, managed the operations of 68 Publishers, their press devoted to Czech authors and books banned by the Communist authorities. Just paces away is **104 Richmond Street East** where Tomson Highway (b.1951) wrote his play *The Sage, the Dancer and the Fool* while he lived here from October 1983 to June 1985.

Another small publishing house which had its base nearby was House of Anansi. Under Ann Wall and novelist James Polk (b.1939), the press had its editorial offices and warehouse at **35 Britain Street** from 1973-88. One of their neighbours was the writer and translator Alberto Manguel (b.1948). When he first arrived in Toronto in the fall of 1982 he lived in a small flat at **151 George Street** (near the corner with Britain) until the autumn of 1983. Here he wrote book reviews for the *G&M* and for *Books in Canada*. Also while in this flat he was commissioned by director Richard Rose to write *The Kipling Play*, later workshopped at Necessary Angel Theatre and at Stratford. Manguel has since be-come one of the better-known Canadian writers of his generation, writing a novel, *News From a Foreign Country Came* (1991), and several works of non-fiction with huge international sales and acclaim; among them: *The Dictionary of Imaginary Places* (1987) and *A History of Reading* (1996).

A block or so to the east is the intersection of Richmond and Sherbourne where one of the most famous actresses of the 19th c. was born. Clara Morris (c. 1847-1925) was the child of a scullery maid and a cab driver. In later years Clara recalled the flights from the bailiff and the skipping out on rent: "We had to flit so often—suddenly, noiselessly. Often I was gently roused from my sleep at night and hastily dressed—sometimes simply wrapped up without being dressed, and carried through the dark to some other place of refuge, from—what? When I went out into the main business streets I had a tormenting barège veil over my face that would not let me see half the pretty things in the shop windows, and I was quick to notice that no other little girl had a veil on."

It was only after Clara's mother had had three children that she discovered that her husband was a bigamist. Upon separating, the mother assumed her maiden name of Morrison. Economics forced her to give up two of her children for adoption but she kept her eldest child, Clara. Mother and daughter then moved to Cleveland and a life of hard poverty. To help their income, Clara went to work at fourteen as an extra and then bit player at a Cleveland theatre. By 1870 she had arrived in New York (her

Clara Morris as "Jane Eyre" c.1870

stage-name now shortened to Morris) where her first role harvested a standing ovation and instant celebrity. "Thereafter, season followed season until she was known throughout the United States as the most prominent if not the greatest emotional actress of the American stage." Her roles ranged from Lady Macbeth in Shakespeare's tragedy to Jezebel in Dion Boucicault's melodrama. We get a glimmering of her power to seduce an audience from one of the New York theatre critics in 1885: "The wet eyes, the sobs . . . the hysterical tremor like a little wave of electricity that went through the house . . . Nothing like it when Bernhardt or Modjeska plays *Camille*. Why? I give up. Criticism has wrestled with that condition in and out of season—how she can play upon all sensibilities, and sweep as with supernatural fingers the whole gamut of emotions, passes critical knowledge."

Clara Morris was not only a gifted actor, she was smart, and knew when to quit. Her forte was the melodrama, and as the taste of theatre-goers shifted slowly but inevitably to more realistic fare, she chose that time to curtail her appearances until she had effectively retired from the boards by the late 1890s. It was then she began to indulge her love of writing, composing articles for the major magazines, and penning three volumes of her theatrical memoirs. Moreover, she wrote a novel for children, five novels for adults, and a collection of short stories called *A Silent Singer* (1899).

Clara's hold on the New York imagination was strong. When she died, she was one of the few actors ever to receive an obit on the front page of the *New York Times*. More interesting, perhaps, is that even two years after her death, a Clara Morris item still rated front-page treatment in the *New York Times*: her sister had been discovered in 1927 in abject poverty by a court-appointed executor of the Clara Morris estate. The old woman lived in Hell's Kitchen. Crippled with rheumatism, the sister, who had never met her famous sibling since the family rupture in Toronto, inherited all of Clara's assets, a figure amounting to a small fortune.

The city directories for the period corresponding to Clara's years in Toronto give only one address for her wastrel father: "lives on Caroline Street near Duchess Street" (1846-47). Both roads have undergone name changes. Caroline is now Sherbourne Street, and Duchess is now Richmond Street East. My search for a more specific address yielded nothing.

Walk east on Richmond to **Ontario Street** and then proceed south to **No.11**. When novelist Hugh Garner (1913-79) was six years old, he left his native England with his mother for Toronto. She came with the intention of rejoining a husband who had sailed to the New World in advance to find work. Unfortunately, when she arrived in July 1919, Hugh's mother discovered her husband was living with another woman. She immediately began divorce proceedings, but rather than return to Britain

decided to remain in Toronto. She and her sons moved to their first home at this site. Hugh was enrolled at nearby Duke Street Public School, since demolished. They remained at this address until April 1920.

Our most easterly stop on this tour is **Berkeley Street**. Go south on Berkeley to **No.26**, formerly the home of Toronto Free Theatre and now the alternative performing space of Canadian Stage Company. Toronto Free was the idea of playwright and former Stratford dramaturge Tom Hendry. Tired of the Stratford management's failure to engage with Canadian playwrights, and anxious to make his own contribution to the explosive off-Yonge theatre scene in Toronto, he took advantage of a government works scheme known as LIP (Local Initiatives Program) and obtained a grant for a theatre that would concentrate on presenting new Canadian work in non-traditional venues. Because the expenses of the theatre were covered by the LIP grant, he did not have to let box-office revenue affect his choice of plays. In fact, because he had seen at Stratford how hard it was to get box-office revenue from plays which were not well known, he convinced the granting body to let him make admission free, thereby potentially opening the plays to a huge audience who otherwise could not afford to, or, due to uninterest, would not attend. Thus, the Theatre was Free in both senses of the word: free of charge, and free of artistic constraint.

Because of his background in accounting Hendry was determined to see the Free Theatre run with proper administration, and it became a model for the other alternative theatres in Toronto. Hendry was convinced by the granting bodies to take on others as co-directors. So playwrights Martin Kinch and John Palmer rounded out the triumvirate which was at the helm when the theatre opened in 1972 in what had been the coal-gas plant of the Consumers Gas Company. Constructed in the late Victorian age, it was going to be razed but was saved by the wreckers themselves. Greenspoon Brothers, hired to demolish the building, thought it too attractive to destroy, so they bought it—with the intention of making it an arts centre. Toronto Free Theatre was their first tenant. The theatre opened formally on June 19, 1972, with a production of Tom Hendry's *How Are Things with the Walking Wounded?* Of the subsequent dramas premiered in the first season, Carol Bolt's *Gabe* (a play about Gabriel Dumont) remains the most renowned. The next season's highlight was *Clear Light* by Michael Hollingsworth, a play made legendary due to very public police threats to close the production and arrest the actors on obscenity charges. Other writers who had premieres here in later years include Larry Fineberg, Martin Kinch, John Palmer, Hrant Alianak, Anne Chislett, and Erika Ritter. A second, smaller theatre was added in 1977, and in 1988 Toronto Free Theatre merged with Bill Glassco's CentreStage theatre at the St. Lawrence Centre to form the unique two-building company known as Canadian Stage.

Walk back north to King Street and west to Jarvis Street. At the intersection, on the southwest corner stands the majestic St. Lawrence Hall, **157 King Street East**. By the 1840s the city fathers were conscious of the fact they lacked a public building reflecting the grandeur and sophistication of the emerging city. On a less ethereal note, they lacked a suitable building for up-market lectures, soirees, and classical musical concerts. So when a huge fire in 1849 forced reconstruction of the area, the fathers seized the moment to erect a multi-purpose edifice which would be a focus of public life befitting the city's needs and image of itself. When it opened in 1850, the building was an instant hit with the public, who thronged to hear great divas like Adelina Patti and Jenny Lind, or to listen to speeches by nation-builders Sir John A. Macdonald and George Brown. But within a mere quarter-century, its top rank was taken away by the Horticultural Pavilion in Allan Gardens, and by the Grand Opera

House to the west. The building fell into appalling disrepair, but thanks to a campaign led by Eric Arthur, it was restored as a City centennial project in 1967.

St. Lawrence Hall was used occasionally by the Ontario Literary Society, a little-documented organization founded in 1856. It was responsible for bringing an impressive variety of literary speakers to the city—particularly throughout the 1860s. Among the authors who spoke in the Hall at the Society's behest were Ralph Waldo Emerson, Grace Greenwood, Joseph Howe, Bayard Taylor, and Father of Confederation and poet, Thomas D'Arcy McGee.

Emerson (1803-82), of course, is regarded as one of the pioneer philosophers in America. The death of his wife happened to coincide with his own intensifying doubts about the Christianity on which he had been raised, and after many troubling years of philosophical questioning he resolved many of his quandaries with a system of thought he called Transcendentalism. At the same time, he was writing the poems that would lead to him being regarded as one of the most important writers in the United States. Emerson liked Toronto, as we know from his diary. His lecture at St. Lawrence Hall on January 27, 1860, titled "Manners and Morals," was the second of three he gave in the city over a six-year period.

The only documented public visit to Toronto by noted politician Joseph Howe took place on June 28, 1851, when he raced to the city to salvage his plans for an inter-colonial railway as one of the steps towards Confederation. He gave a speech which was covered in the newspapers as though royalty had spoken. There were so many column inches given over to his remarks that "column yards" would be more appropriate. Today Howe is commemorated as the leading politician of Nova Scotia in the Victorian era, but it should not be forgotten that he was proud of his poetry. He also had the wit to publish Thomas Chandler Haliburton's *The Clockmaker, or the Sayings and Doings of Sam Slick,* as part of his belief in the necessity of fostering a Canadian literary culture.

Thomas D'Arcy McGee (1825-68) is yet another Father of Confederation who spoke in St. Lawrence Hall. While he did give political speeches here, his more popular addresses were those on literary topics. He was such a renowned and respected orator that he stands alone in his era as a man capable of attracting an audience—and praise—from those who detested his politics but savoured his lectures on authors and books. On September 17, 1858 (within a year of his immigration to this country from Ireland via the USA), he gave an advertised discourse on "The Political Morality of Shakespeare's Plays" which the *Globe* said drew "one of the largest audiences ever gathered together" at the Hall. "He was frequently interrupted by bursts of applause, evidencing the complete influence his eloquence had attained over his hearers." A measure of his ability to cross party and ethnic prejudices was his invitation to be a major speaker at the Hall's celebration of the Robbie Burns Centennial in 1859. Although he published only one book of poetry in his lifetime, another poet, Mary Anne Sadlier, gathered his verse and published the collection in New York in 1869. McGee was assassinated outside his home in Ottawa in 1868.

The current St. James' Cathedral (northwest corner of **King Street East** and **Church Street**) is the fifth church on this spot. Previous incarnations burned. Authors overtly connected with the church are the bestselling maritime novelist Douglas Reeman (b.1924) who was married here to a Toronto woman he met—at his reading at Harbourfront. Poet and cleric Robert Norwood (1874-1932) gave an advertised public sermon from the pulpit in 1926. And Rev. James Edward Ward, long associated with St. Stephen's on Bellevue Avenue, was made the Canon of St. James in 1940.

One of the earliest literary descriptions of the cathedral was provided by Amelia Matilda Murray (1795-1884), a maid of honour to Queen Victoria. Murray, an abolitionist, travelled to North America in 1854 to see slavery first hand, and on her way back to England stopped in Toronto for a few days and found herself quite taken with the city. Soon after, back in Britain, she was told categorically that no member of the royal court could publish a political book. Rather than remain silent, however, she quit her appointment to the Queen and wrote a number of books, including *Letters from the United States, Cuba and Canada* (1856): "The cathedral here is a pretty new church, in style, early perpendicular. It was built by a young architect from England, of the name of Cumberland, and is very creditable to his taste. The eastern termination is an apse rather than a chancel. I thought the windows particularly good, and they will be beautiful when a little painted glass is introduced. . . . "

F.W. Cumberland also designed the Mechanics' Institute which used to lie

Thomas D'Arcy McGee

immediately to the north of the cathedral on the northeast corner of **Church Street and Adelaide Street**. The word "mechanic" as used in the first half of the 19th c., had a much broader meaning than it does today. Then it referred to any skilled tradesman, and the Mechanics' Institutes were first formed in Britain by religious communities and benevolent societies as places where working men could go to read newspapers, magazines, books, and to attend lectures. Part of the motivation of the Institute founders was to keep the men out of taverns and thus presumably out of trouble. But equally as powerful a motive was the belief that people were spiritually improved by reading and education, as long as the reading material was of a pure, moral character, of course. The idea of the Mechanics' Institute was carried to Toronto with British immigration to the province. The first meeting of what was called a Mechanics' Institute was held in Toronto as early as 1830. By the middle of the century, as the population of the city swelled, the compelling need was recognized for a large edifice to handle the Institute's expanded needs. As historian William Dendy noted, "The Mechanics' Institute not only lacked the traditional religious and aristocratic associations of most other public institutions, it was already best known as a semi-public lending and reference library, while the new building was to include a music hall that could be used as a concert hall or a ballroom as a potential source of income. In the end, Cumberland chose not to emphasize any specific function by choices of style or detail, but to stress the more general public character of the organization." Cumberland's handsome building was razed in

1949 and the site was used as a parking lot for the next 30 years.

The music hall of the Mechanics' Institute (referred to simply as "The Music Hall" in books and newspaper advertisements of the time) was approximately 76 feet long and 56 wide, "with a coved and frescoed ceiling rising 35 feet to a central dome, and was lit on the Adelaide Street façade by three tall windows. At the west end, there was a curved musicians' gallery supported on twisted, almost-Gothic columns of cast iron; at the east end there was a stage framed by Corinthian columns like a triumphal arch. The walls of the hall were painted with large panels in the fashionable Neo-Rococo style. The dome was also painted with figures representing the Muses and the entire ceiling, with its framing pattern of plaster beams must have resembled (with simpler details) the elaborate ceiling that Cumberland and Storm designed for the Osgoode Hall library."

The cost of finishing the building was borne by the public purse, and it seems the taxpayers paid for the books as well, for the number of books continued to grow. Indeed, in the absence of public libraries, membership in the Mechanics' Institute was the only way to borrow books or use the reference room. By the 1880s the need for a public library was finally admitted, and in 1883 the Institute became the first building of the city's new public library system. The

Mechanics' Institute, Adelaide and Church Streets, 19th c. view

Music Hall was converted to a reading room, but the building remained the principal library in town until Chief Librarian James Bain convinced Andrew Carnegie to pay for the construction of the Central Reference Library at College and Beverley in 1906.

Some authors of note gave readings or talks at the Music Hall. Under the auspices of the Ontario Literary Society, Ralph Waldo Emerson gave two addresses, as part of his third and final visit to Toronto: on January 5, 1863, his talk was "Classes of Men" and on the following night he spoke about "Talent and Genius." An author equally famous at the time was the British novelist Charles Kingsley (1819-75), author of *Westward Ho!*, who lectured in 1874 about Westminster Cathedral. His address was delivered in the evening so his audience was predominantly adult (described in the newspapers as large and fashionable)—which may be why he seems to have said nothing about his still-popular book for children, *The Water-Babies* (1863).

More popular than either of these writers was Artemus Ward. His real name was Charles F. Browne (1834-67). Ward was a phenomenon of the century in that his humour—which used to leave audiences from San Francisco to Europe rolling in the aisles—leaves modern readers scratching their heads in bewilderment. Yet scholars agree his platform style, his humour, and his delivery were the single largest influences on Mark Twain's approach to public speaking. But where Twain emphasized the foibles of human nature, Ward emphasized the peculiarities of dialect. This is not to say Artemus Ward was merely a stand-up comedian. His talks, published in several books, rise above topical humour, and can still be be amusing in spots once one gets the hang of the idiosyncratic spelling meant to reproduce either dialect or hayseed lexicography. His talk to a capacity house in the Music Hall on October , 1862, was immensely popular, according to the newspaper.

Thomas D'Arcy McGee spoke at the Music Hall on at least three occasions. On January 29, 1862, he gave a talk on Sir Walter Scott, and the critic of the *Leader* ran out of superlatives to describe McGee's remarks. The *Globe* was no less enthusiastic about a lecture McGee gave on February 3, 1862: "Mr. McGee's lecture on 'The Life and Genius of John Milton' was on Monday night delivered to a large and intelligent audience in the Mechanics' Institute. It is almost unnecessary to say that all were highly gratified in the manner in which the learned gentleman dealt with his subject. Mr. McGee was eloquent as usual, and his astute and searching criticism spoke not only of an attentive reading of John Milton's works, but also of extensive acquaintance with the poetic literature ancient and modern." This lecture had been billed as his Farewell from the public lecture platform, but like a good opera diva's, his Farewell lasted for several years. In 1866 he was back at the Music Hall to address another capacity house on "A Visit to Oxford."

My best educated guess as to the former whereabouts of Paul Kane's studio is **100 King Street East**. The street numbers and buildings have been completely changed several times since Kane (1810-71), best known for his mid-century paintings and sketches of more than 80 Canadian Indian tribes, worked in this block of King (in the 1850s, for example, the even-numbered buildings were on the south side of the street). Despite close examination of the maps, directories, and town lots, I can conclude only that the studio where he painted was in the block between Church and Toronto streets on the north side of King. Knowing where Kane painted is of some literary importance because one of the earliest eminent literary visitors to Toronto, William Henry Giles Kingston, made a point of visiting Kane here.

Kingston (1814-80) is still read and studied, especially as an author of once hugely popular books for boys, although he wrote both fiction and non-fiction for adults. How popular he was with younger readers can be gauged from an 1884 poll of two thousand schoolboys in England. When asked to name their favourite author, 223 cited Dickens, but not far behind in second place (with 179 votes) was W.H.G. Kingston. The others, who were not even close, were, in descending rank, Walter Scott, Jules Verne, Captain Marryat, R.M. Ballantyne, H. Ainsworth, and in tenth place, William Shakespeare.

Kingston came to Canada as part of a honeymoon tour of North America in 1853. Like any decent writer, he mined the trip for use in a book, published not long after he returned to England as *Western Wanderings* (1856). Apart from his descriptions of Toronto, part of which are quoted below, he was a draughtsman of some skill, and we have from his pen a picture of the city as it appeared when he was a visitor from October 22-29, 1853. A month before, he had spent some days in Toronto while on his way from Montreal to the western reaches of the province. By going all the way to Manitoulin Island he was being very adventuresome indeed. Georgian Bay and its villages were not part of the usual tourist itinerary at mid-century, and neither transportation nor accommodation were comfortable by European standards. In Toronto, he stayed in a hotel at **36 Colborne Street**, next to a hotel later owned by the British writer Algernon Blackwood (see below, in this tour).

Kingston is worth quoting at some length because, as a widely travelled author, he brought a deep perspective, hemispheric context, and a large reservoir of worldly knowledge to what he saw. He is also worth quoting because he clearly liked the city a lot—both as it was, and as it would be. He was specific in his portrayal, so that when reading him we see, hear, and almost smell what the city was like more than from any other literary visitor during Victoria's reign.

Here is what he wrote when he first beheld Toronto in September, 1853, from the deck of a steamboat, and then from onshore: "Toronto faces south-east; and from the north side of the city, a very narrow tongue of land, with a line of trees on it, springs out, and sweeping round to the south and west, forms a breakwater in front of the city, with a long, spacious bay or lagoon inside; thus creating a most perfect and valuable natural harbour. Vessels and boats, with white sails, moving inside this fringe of wood, had a very picturesque appearance; and the blue water and clear sky, the bright sun and sparkling atmosphere, made everything look doubly beautiful. Beyond rose the city on a gentle slope, backed by a dark pine-forest, some hundred and twenty feet above the water. On the southwest end of the point is a lighthouse, rounding which we entered the harbour, having passed, on our right, a fine stone edifice with a large dome, the provincial lunatic asylum; the new Church-of-England University, Trinity College; and an extensive stone pile, formerly the House of Assembly, and now converted to the use of the University of Toronto . . . Our surprise was very great, and very agreeable, to find ourselves in a large, handsome, admirably-laid-out city; the streets wide, long, and straight, running at right angles to each other, and with many fine public buildings and stores and private houses in them; and with shops, which, in size, elegance, and the value of their contents, may vie with those of any city in England, except, perhaps, London and Liverpool. It is especially free from the narrow, dirty lanes to be found in nearly all the cities of the Old World, and even in Quebec and Montreal, and the old French towns of Canada; while all the outlets to the harbour are broad and spacious, and allow an ample scope for the erection of fine quays and wharves, which London might well envy . . . In speaking of Toronto as a very handsome city, it must be understood rather that it contains all the requisites for becoming one. As yet it is young; its prosperity is of late years, and it contains many of the imperfections of youth; but so rapid has been its progress, and so rapid will it, I think, continue, that those imperfections

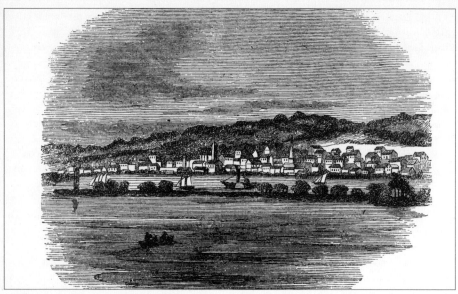

W.H.G. Kingston's own drawing of Toronto as seen from the deck of a steamboat, 1853

which I speak of today may, in another year or so, have completely vanished. Though in many of the streets there are rows of handsome brick and even granite buildings; in their near propinquity are to be found small and shabby houses of plank; though the streets are broad, many of them are undrained, unmacadamized, and full of holes and ruts, while a narrow plank-causeway affords the only means by which passengers on foot can traverse them. This footway, however, is throughout the city kept in good repair and clean, so that in the wettest weather a dry walk can always be found.

"The soil on which the city is built is of a fine sandy nature, and in the streets, left in their primitive condition, the hot sun in summer creates masses of dust, which the wind wantonly blows into thick and disagreeable clouds . . . The weather when we landed was hot and sultry, though in the open air it was in no way oppressive. As soon as we had breakfasted and dressed, we chartered a cab to carry ourselves and our card cases, and drove off to leave a packet of letters of introduction. Our vehicle was remarkably like a modern London cab in shape; but it had leather curtains at the sides, and the doors were taken off to allow a freer circulation of air . . . In the course of our drive, we went two or three miles along Yonge Street, and for the greater part of the distance there were few spaces unbuilt on. We were amused with the mode in which the shopkeepers exhibit their rivalry, each trying to outvie the other in the size of the letters with which his calling and the goods he has to dispose of are notified, either over his shop-door or at the side of his house.

"A magnificent day induced us to accept the kind invitation of a friend to drive with him along the banks of the Humber, and, at two o'clock, we started in a Canadian wagon. Now a Canadian wagon has four wheels like an English one but here the similarity ends; for there are two seats; and it is, in fact, a very comfortable phaeton, though for a reason I cannot comprehend, the front axle is not made to turn . . . The ground on the sides was not as much cultivated as I expected to find it. The primeval forests had been felled long ago; a few patriarchal trees alone remaining to speak of former days; but a new growth had sprung up in many places, and had already attained a considerable height. In other places, tall trees were standing, but branchless, burnt and charred; in others, black stumps alone . . . As we drove, the horse shied a little, and no wonder if he had been raised in the backwoods; for, from a cutting below us, rapidly there hissed, puffing by, a locomotive, with panting breath dragging after it a long line of railway carriages bound for the shore of Lake Simcoe."

On his return visit, in late October 1853, Kingston was again impressed: "Toronto, on this our second visit, strikes us as far larger and handsomer than it appeared at first. After Hamilton it looks very large, and it is much larger than Detroit, and not much inferior to Buffalo in size.

"I called during our stay on all the principal publishers and booksellers in the city . . . When Mrs. Jameson wrote [her book about Canada] Toronto contained one small bookshop in which stationery, bandboxes, and I believe pill-boxes were sold, I think also boys' kites; indeed, nearly every article of paper in common use, the stock of books being very small and of a very ordinary description. Now there are five or six large booksellers' shops, equal to any in the larger towns of England.

Three or more of them are publishers also . . . As the case stands at present, although there is a very large reading public in Canada, every day increasing with the extension of education, as well as by the increase of population, the British author enjoys from it not the slightest benefit. With all new works, they supply themselves almost exclusively from the States, and only such British works as the American publishers do not think it worthwhile to pirate are imported from England . . . All the booksellers I had the pleasure of conversing with were men of excellent education and deportment, fully equal to their brethren in England."

After extensive and detailed descriptions of the principal buildings of the city, Kingston recounts how he was taken to see Paul Kane by a local man of means, George Allan: "At an early hour next morning, Mr. Allan called to accompany us to Paul Kane's studio in King Street . . . He had now for some time been residing quietly in Toronto where he had married a wife, and was engaged in painting a series of views illustrative of Indian life and scenery. We found

King Street East (Yonge to Church) in 1846. The street would have looked much as this when W.H.G. Kingston paid a visit to the studio of Paul Kane at 53 King Street East in 1855. This illustration was first published in the *London Illustrated News*, January 30, 1847.

our way up a steep, high stair to an apartment at the top of the house, more like a poet's chamber than a painter's studio, where we found the artist at work. His appearance, though roughish from the style of life he had led, much prepossessed me in his favour, and still more did his manners which were truly pleasing and courteous . . . He works hard but steadily; refuses to sell any of his pictures, for he has now a sufficient private fortune for his support. His great ambition is to make a perfect collection illustrative of Indian life."

Kingston was clearly enamored of Kane, and while his many observations on Kane's work lack political correctness when referring to the Indians, they form a unique document concerning a painter whom Toronto has yet to honour sufficiently. After several more pages of admiration for the city, Kingston concluded his paean with a remark almost ingenuous in its charm: "I do not wish to overflatter Toronto, but in speaking thus of it I believe that I am only giving what is fairly its due."

Across the street at **37 King Street East** is the regal mass of the King Edward Hotel, opened in 1903. The hotel is affectionately referred to by locals as the "King Eddie." Until the Royal York Hotel debuted in 1929, the King Eddie had no rivals, and even with the competition of the Royal York, this hotel continued to attract much of the carriage trade. Its Crystal Ballroom could seat up to 2,000 people and on more than one occasion accommodated that many people for literary events. The following is a partial list of the authors who have stayed at the King Edward while in town to make formal public appearances:

Walter Allen
John Kendrick Bangs
Ralph Bates
Henri Bordeaux
Rupert Brooke
John Buchan
Susan Buchan

Louis Ferdinand Céline
G.K. Chesterton
Leonard Cohen
Ralph Connor
Noel Coward
Arthur Conan Doyle
Theodore Dreiser
Edgar Guest
Elbert Hubbard
Rudyard Kipling
Alexander Knox
Arthur Marchmont
Anne Marriott
Nellie McClung
Gilbert Parker
Isaac Bashevis Singer
E.B. White

The hotel's large public rooms were always popular with publishers and authors who used it frequently for the annual National Book Fair. These fairs were begun by the Canadian Authors' Association to introduce the country's books and authors to Canadians living in the Toronto area. In a country which has always worshipped American and British culture and which has regarded the neglect of—or even disdain for—our own culture as a badge of erudition and sophistication, the act of promoting Can-adian writers was daring, brave, and, ultimately, successful. The first Canadian Book Week was held at Simpson's department store in 1921 but soon switched to the King Eddie, and the event was held annually until 1935, when the stresses of the Depression forced the organizers to include a much heavier percentage of foreign books. The last Book Fair seems to have been held in 1956.

The Canadian Club and the Empire Club are primarily businessmen's luncheon clubs where celebrities in various fields give talks. Around the start of the 20th c. the Canadian and Empire Clubs gradually abandoned the Café Royale, the Temple Café, and McConkey's Restaurant as the venues for their luncheon meetings in favour of the King Edward. In the following list of writers who have given readings or lectures at the King Edward, most of the authors appeared under the aegis of either the Book Fairs or of one of the Clubs:

Beverley Baxter
John Buchan
Susan Buchan
Bennett Cerf
Ralph Connor
Mazo de la Roche
William Arthur Deacon
Erle Stanley Gardner
John Murray Gibbon
Wilfred Grenfell
Grey Owl
Frederick Philip Grove
Edgar Guest
John Gunther
Elbert Hubbard
Howard Angus Kennedy
Basil King
Margaret Lawrence
Vachel Lindsay
Wilson MacDonald
Lucy Maud Montgomery
Gilbert Parker
Mary Pickford
E.J. Pratt
J.B. Priestley
Burton Rascoe
Charles G.D. Roberts
Laura Salverson
Maurice Samuel
B.K. Sandwell
Elizabeth Sprigge
Kathleen Strange
Henry Van Dyke
Pierre van Paassen
Israel Zangwill

The King Edward was probably the hotel where Agatha Christie stayed for about one week in 1922 to nurse her ill husband. The couple had been travelling as part of a round-the-world expedition with a Major Belcher when, as Christie wrote, "[my husband] managed the journey the next day as far as Toronto, but once there he collapsed completely, and it was out of the question for him to continue of the tour . . . I called in a doctor advised by the hotel, and he pronounced that Archie had congestion of the lungs, must not be moved, and could not be fit for any kind of activity for at least a week. Fuming, Belcher made his departure and I was left, with hardly any money, alone in a large, impersonal hotel, with a patient who was by now delirious . . . It was a terrible time, and I am only glad now that I have forgotten the desperation and the loneliness."

Another famous literary guest who stayed here for non-literary reasons was Somerset Maugham. He was a guest of the hotel for an indeterminate period in December 1912, probably stopping over in Toronto on his way to New York from Manitoba. He had spent some weeks in the prairies collecting material for his play *The Land of Promise*, a dramatic work which was quite popular in Britain and the USA (there were two silent film versions and a talkie rendition as well), but the play was not liked in our nation for what was regarded as its stereotyping of Canada.

Less than a block from the King Edward Hotel was the Café Royale, **14 King Street East**. Even after the King Eddie was opened and flourishing, the Canadian and Empire Clubs occasionally made use of the Café Royale, apparently attracted by its ambiance. On October 18, 1915, author and politico Nellie McClung gave a speech at this address to the members of the Canadian Club. What is amusing to note about this speech is that McClung was the only politician in Canada at the time for whom the Club could charge an admission fee and be sure of a full house. When other politicians spoke, the admission charge was waived. She certainly had a full house, and this marked one of the few occasions in its early history when the Canadian Club allowed women to sit in the audience.

Just three weeks later, the Canadian Club welcomed the American novelist Winston Churchill. Churchill (1871-1947) is little read today, but in the first half of his career he was certainly better known than the British politician and author of the same name. The American Churchill's visit was considered so important the Toronto newspapers reported it on page one, and ran major editorials discussing the literary merits of his fiction.

Running north from the King Edward Hotel is **Toronto Street**, once one of the handsomest blocks in the metropolis, but thanks to the insensitivity of urban planners and developers, is now just another thoroughfare with a couple of old buildings left to remind us of what used to be. A house formerly located at **10 Toronto Street** was the home of Sir James David Edgar from 1864-65. At the time of his death Edgar (1841-99) was the Speaker of the House of Commons. When he was not practising politics, he practised law in Toronto, and wrote poetry for publication.

Another lawyer-politician connected to this street is our first prime minister, Sir John A. Macdonald. He was the senior partner in the firm of Macdonald, Marsh— whose offices were at **No.25** in the early 1890s. One of the young women who worked in that law office was the poet Gertrude Bartlett (1876?-1942). In 1891, she married an English artist and left Toronto for Montreal. Where she lived in Toronto is unknown. In 1932 she published her first book which brought together a number of poems that had appeared in leading journals such as *Atlantic Monthly* and *Saturday Night*. *The New York Times* reviewed the book and said of it, "Not only is Miss Bartlett sensitive in a marked degree to every lyric nuance, but these lights and shades are transferred to her printed page with a pastel delicacy."

In behind the King Edward Hotel is **Colborne Street**. The British novelist Algernon Blackwood (1869-1951), the master of the mystery story, became the owner of a pub-hotel at **42 Colborne** for about half a year beginning in November 1891. Unfortunately, the north half of the street has been razed, but in character and appearance was identical to the buildings that remain on the south side of the street. Although the *World* misspelled Blackwood's name, it considered the change of hotel ownership a news event and wrote, "Amongst business men downtown, no establishment has for years been better known than the Hub Café off Leader Lane. This well-frequented hotel has has now changed hands, Mr. W. Bingham having sold out the business to two young Englishmen, Mr. A. Blackmore and Mr. J.P. Pauw."

Blackwood, in his early twenties and painfully naïve, was living in Toronto because his father had unceremoniously dumped him in the city two years before with the hope that his son, without parents and England around to distract him, might finally decide what he wanted to do with his life. The father was relatively well-off, and gave Blackwood a more than decent annual allowance. However, much of this capital was quickly milked from him by confidence tricksters who could smell his innocence from miles away.

In his amusing memoir, *Episodes Before Thirty* (which I highly recommend to anyone who likes to laugh), he relates how a fellow English emigrant was trying to talk him into investing what little money he had left: "He proceeded to describe his 'scheme'—to buy a small hotel which, owing to its bad name, was going cheap; to work up a respectable business and a valuable goodwill; then to sell out at a top price and retire with a comfortable fortune. Kay was twenty-three, two years my senior; to me, then, he seemed an experienced man of business, almost elderly. The scheme took my breath away. It was very tempting. The failure of the dairy farm had left me despondent; I felt disgraced; the end of life, it seemed, had come. I was ready to grasp at anything that held out hopes of a recovery of fortune. But an hotel! I hesitated. 'I know nothing about running an hotel,' I objected.

"'Neither do I—yet,' was the sanguine answer, 'but we can learn. It's only common sense and hard work. We can hire a good manager and engage a first-class cook.'

"'How many rooms are there?'

"'Only thirteen. It's the bar where we shall make the money.'

"'The bar—!'

"'There are two bars, one on the main street and another on the back. Billy Bingham has made the place too hot to hold him. His licence is to be withdrawn. He's got to get out. We can get his licence transferred to us all right, if we promise to make the place respectable. We'll have good food, a first-rate lunch counter for the business men, we can let the big rooms for club dinners and society banquets, and there's a 100 per cent profit, you know, on liquor. We'll make the Hub the best 'joint' in the town. All the fellows will come. A year will do it. Then we'll sell out . . . . '

"I was not listening. The word 'liquor'—I had never touched alcohol in my life—made such a noise in my mind that I could hear nothing else. 'My father,' I mentioned in a faint voice, 'is a public man at home. He's a great temperance reformer. He speaks and writes against drink. He's brought me up that way. It would be a terrible shock to him if his son made money out of a bar. . . . '

"'He need never know anything about it,' came the answer at once. 'Why should he? Our names needn't appear at all. We'll call ourselves the *Hub Wine Company, Limited*. My head was swimming, my mind buzzing with conflicting voices as we walked down King Street to inspect the premises. I ached to re-establish my position. The prospect of a quick recovery of fortune was as sweet a prize as ever tempted a green youth like myself. My partner, too, this time would be a 'gentleman,' a fellow my father might have invited to dine and play tennis; it was my appalling ignorance of life that gave to his two years' seniority some imagined quality of being a man much older than myself, and one who knew what he was about. . . .

"We strode down King Street together, past the corner of Yonge Street, below the windows of the hated Temperance and General Life Assurance Company where I had licked stamps, and on towards the Hub Hotel. The Toronto air was fresh and sweet, the lake lay blue beyond, the sunlight sparkled. Something exhilarating and optimistic in the atmosphere gave thought a happy and sanguine twist. It was a day of Indian summer, a faint perfume of far-distant forest fires adding a pleasant touch to the familiar smell of the cedar-wood sidewalks. A mood of freedom, liberty, great spaces, fine big enterprises in a free country where everything was possible, of opportunities seized and waves of fortune taken on their crest—I remember this mood as sharply still, and the scent of a wood-fire or a cedar pencil recalls it as vividly still, as though I had experienced it last week.

"I glanced at my companion. I liked him, trusted him. There was a light in his frank blue eyes. He was a good heavyweight boxer too. The very man, I felt, for a bold enterprise of this sort.

"Turning down a narrow side street, the Hub blocked the way, a three-storey building with a little tower, clean windows, and two big swinging doors. It ran through to a back street where there was another entrance.

"'Here it is,' said Kay, in the eager, happy voice of a man who has just inherited a family mansion and come to inspect it. 'This is the Hub where we shall make our fortune. . . . '

"The Hub Wine Company, camouflaging the saloon business of two foolish young idiots, passed through its phases towards the inevitable collapse . . . To me it was a six months' horror. The impulsive purchase was paid for dearly. It was not only the declining business, the approaching loss of my small capital, the prospect of presently working for some farmer at a dollar a day and green tea—it was not these things I chiefly felt. It was, rather, the fact that I had taken a step down-hill, betrayed some imagined ideal in me, shown myself willing to 'sell my soul' for filthy lucre. The price, though not paid in lucre, was certainly paid in mental anguish, and the letters from home, though patient, generously forgiving, even understanding, increased this tenfold. . . . "

Blackwood and his partner were forced to flee Toronto under cover of darkness, thereby escaping angry creditors. They hid at a friend's cabin north of Toronto for a few months before Blackwood eventually returned to Britain where he began what became a remarkable literary career.

Leader Lane leads south to Wellington and across Berzcy Park to Front Street East. For most of the 19th c. **Front Street** marked the water's edge, and followed the shoreline of Lake Ontario. **64 Front Street East** was the address of The Steamboat Hotel, a portrait of which survives (renamed the City Hotel), by a miracle, in the famous picture *Toronto's Fish Market* by W.H. Bartlett. The Scottish novelist John Galt (1779-1839) lived in the hotel on two occasions in the 1820s—making him the earliest literary resident of the city. His stays in Toronto, amounting to almost nine months, preceded by several years the later Toronto visits of Anna Jameson and Captain Marryat, the next literary notables to spend appreciable time in Toronto.

Galt's first stop was for about two months when he arrived in Toronto c. December 1825 as an agent for the Canada Company. This organization had been formed in 1824 at Galt's instigation as a complicated device by which to grant financial restitution to the Upper Canada colonists who had suffered damages during the War of 1812. In essence, Galt hoped to sell the province's huge, unsold lot of Crown land to a company that would then re-sell the land in subdivided parcels to new immigrants. It would be the company's task to find these immigrants and convince them to travel to the New World. The purpose of his first residency was to scout for appropriate property for the Canada Company to buy.

After approximately two months he returned to Britain and, paperwork completed, came back to Canada to commence the populating of the newly acquired properties. He founded the towns of Goderich and Guelph, and the town of Galt was also named in his honour. History confirms that John Galt did an excellent job as chief administrator of the Canada Company, but the Board of Directors, with no knowledge of the difficulties he

The *Fish Market* by W.H. Bartlett showing the City Hotel, formerly the Steamboat Hotel, 1841

faced in a trackless land, felt his expenses were excessive and recalled him to London in 1829. In the decade left to him he wrote furiously (although he had been publishing before and during his Canadian adventures), but his health deteriorated. Plans to return to Canada, a land that clearly fired his imagination, had to be abandoned because of his sickness.

John Galt's second stay at the Steamboat was relatively long—about seven months. He arrived on December 12, 1826, and made the inn his base while he travelled between Muddy York and the various land parcels held by the company. Ultimately, he built a permanent home for himself in Burlington in July 1827. Galt briefly described the Toronto hotel in his *Autobiography* as well as in his novel *Bogle Corbet* (1831), a tale about an immigrant coming to Upper Canada. In the memoir he wrote, "In a small, new town, accommodations were not easily found, but I obtained at last a room of about ten feet square for an office, for which I paid a dollar a week . . . I was obliged in the meantime, to stay at a tavern myself . . . The reader is probably acquainted with the manner of living in the American hotels, but without experience he can have no right notion of what in those days was the condition of the best tavern in York. It was a mean, two-storey house, and being constructed of wood, every noise in it resounded from roof to foundation." In his novel, Galt was slightly more loquacious. Bogle Corbet reports, "The Steamboat Hotel, a raw, plank-built house, with a double veranda, fronts the harbour. The guests consisted of certain permanent boarders and accidental travellers who, with visitors, their friends, all mess at one common table. On this occasion the dinner-party consisted of seventeen, the majority of whom, being inhabitants of the province, had generally that peculiar lassitude of manner about them which I had remarked in the passengers by the steamboat. They consumed the viands in silence, with an earnestness that betokened the sincerity of their appetites."

One of the handsomest bookshops in Toronto is Nicholas Hoare Books at **49 Front Street East**. Opened on October 20, 1990, the shop frequently hosts in-store readings by distinguished writers. Those who have read here include Margaret Atwood, Russell Banks, David Malouf and Michael Ondaatje. In recent years it has co-sponsored a popular brunch-with-authors series at the King Edward Hotel that mixes well-known authors with those who are up-and-coming.

The final stop on this tour is the Hummingbird Centre, formerly the O'Keefe Centre, **1 Front Street East**, opened to the public in late 1960. It has very few literary connections. Indeed, the motivation behind its construction was typically colonial for the time. As its first general manager, Hugh Walker, wrote in his history of the space, "We had given the architects our priorities in the following order: Broadway musicals, international artists, ballet and opera, symphony and, lastly, plays." Six months after the Centre opened, the *Star* was boasting in a headline "We Now Rate As a No.1 City For Broadway Tryouts and National Show Tours." Not all of Toronto was preening, however, at the thought that our highest theatrical worth was measured by being a tryout town for American musicals. In a remarkably prescient editorial penned just after the Centre opened, Herbert Whittaker, the long-serving theatre critic of the *G&M*, commented, "In our enjoyment of the grandeur which the O'Keefe Centre has bestowed upon us, we must not lose sight of what must be recognized as the more indigenous theatre and its problems. There is a big danger that Toronto might sit smugly back as a road town, complacently accepting whatever New York managements send out to us. With the grosses being chalked up by the O'Keefe box-office, this town could well settle down smugly as a teacher's pet of Broadway."

Paradoxically, the most important event to affect Canadian culture ever produced here took place mostly in the lobby of the

Hummingbird, not in the theatre itself. This was the Canadian Conference of the Arts, May 4-6, 1961. Opening remarks were made by Arthur Gelber, Alan Jarvis, Claude Bissell, and Northrop Frye, followed by a poetry reading by Irving Layton, Gilles Hénault, Anne Hébert, Jay Macpherson, Earle Birney and Leonard Cohen.

Irving Layton talking to Anne Hebert while at the CAA Conference

G&M, May 5, 1961

The following day there were panel discussions featuring vigorous exchanges between those on stage and the audience. The panels were organized by artistic discipline. For example, the visual arts panel had Harold Town, Alex Colville, and Isamu Noguchi, with Alan Jarvis as moderator. The literary panelists were Mordecai Richler, Hugh MacLennan, and George Lamming, with Arnold Edinborough in the chair. This was inventive programming, taking advantage of the temporary residence in Toronto at the time of both Lamming and Richler. The following day there were more panels, with writing represented by Morley Callaghan, Anita Malik, Yves Theriault, and George Lamming (again). The event closed

with a keynote speech by the British philosopher and poet Sir Julian Huxley.

Star columnist, Robert Fulford, reported on the reading held on opening night: "The poetry reading was far more successful than anyone expected. It was put in the concourse at the west side of the building. A few score chairs were arranged, a microphone was set up, and it was thought that the spiral staircase would accommodate anyone else who turned up. But the poetry lovers filled both chairs and stairs and then overflowed onto the floor above, by the dozens. Some stood leaning over the staircase, looking down, as if contemplating suicide. Others lay on the floor. A few women were seen kneeling, as if in prayer. Sometimes the poets read badly (a monotone is standard poetic equipment, apparently) but no one except the odd actor really minded. That part of the conference, at least, was a rousing success."

Those who attended the conference were in agreement that the liveliest panels were those dealing with the performing or applied arts: theatre and architecture particularly. The newspaper coverage unwittingly shows that all of the panels expressed concern for the physical drabness of cities, especially Toronto, and this conference was the first in Canada to propose that a percentage of the cost of construction of large buildings be devoted to artistic embellishment for the same building. Like many productive congresses, the value of this one was intangible but real. It served the purpose of having the arts—and the problems of artists in Toronto—taken seriously by the media and by politicians. It seems to have galvanized many performing artists and arts administrators into organizational action. And, as with any good conference, it allowed dozens of participants to meet face to face, often for the first time. At a time in Canada when artists rarely travelled beyond their own towns, this was no small accomplishment.

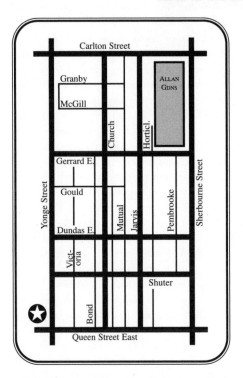

The tour begins at the northeast corner of Queen Street East and Yonge Street.

Walk two blocks east along **Queen Street** to Church Street. Our first stop is the Metropolitan United Church, **56 Queen Street East**, one of the three cathedral-sized churches abutting Church Street from which that road takes its name (St. Michael's and St. James' being the others). At least two noted authors have spoken to assembled crowds in this building: Daniel Berrigan in the seventies; Kurt Vonnegut Jr. in the nineties. But the most important literary visitors associated with this building did not speak here at all. Rather, one was asked by the church's congregation not to speak, and the other, Pierre van Paassen (1895-1968), in 1916 had a change of heart.

Watson Kirkconnell (1895-1977) was a poet, translator, academic—and rabid anti-communist who missed no chance to speak about the reds under beds and the international communist conspiracy, a stance that won him passionate friends in the usual places and passionate enemies in the usual places. The Christian Social Order Group, attached to the Metropolitan Church, was the only organization I encountered ever to cross Kirkconnell. In 1943, the Group asked the organizers of a Church Friendship League rally being held in Varsity arena to block Kirkconnell's appearance as the keynote speaker. They failed, but their effort was unique—enough to merit mention in a Toronto daily. Kirkconnell ended his days maintaining that fluoridation of our drinking water was a commie plot to destroy our precious bodily fluids and organs.

Pierre van Paassen's connection to the church is more profound. He arrived in Canada from Holland as a young man, and studied theology at the UofT in order to become a Methodist minister, eventually combining apprentice pastorships in remote areas with classroom work in Toronto. He had been so busy studying for his clerical collar—and learning English—that he claimed he had scarcely noticed that WWI had started. Like everyone else, he believed the war would be over in weeks. However, by 1916, as he explained in his memoir, he felt he had to make a moral decision: "In the spring of 1916 occurred a crisis of conscience which shook me to the depths of my being and radically changed my course through life: I abandoned all thoughts of the ministry. Although it is true, *que l'on revient toujours à ses premières amours*, and that some years later I resumed my studies in the theological school of the Reformed Church of France, I then left dogmatics severely alone. Having reached the conclusion—not without a deep sense of loss and disillusionment—that centuries of theology have brought us not one step nearer to the solution of the mystery of our existence, I took up the study of the history of religion with special emphasis on the origins of Christianity. . . .

"As I see it now my mistake in 1916 was that I took the Christian gospel too seriously. When I returned to Toronto from the north, I was invited to follow a course that would lead in quick order to a commission as a military chaplain. I declined on the grounds that in spite of my sympathy for Britain's stand, her cause did not seem to warrant desertion from the Militia Christi. I decided to take the side of the conscientious objectors. . . . True, the Sunday evening meetings in Toronto's Labour Temple under the chairmanship of the president of the typographical union, James Simpson, a later socialist mayor of the city, were more than once disrupted by invading bands of war veterans and super patriots who indiscriminately and howlingly decried all present as slackers, cowards, defeatists, paid agents of the Kaiser, and so on. . . . In the end, it was before the argument that the war was 'a righteous war' that I capitulated. Two serious-minded elderly citizens, Newton W. Rowell, the leader of the Liberal opposition in the Ontario parliament, and Justice John J. Maclaren of the provincial supreme court, persuaded me to look upon the struggle with Germany as the war to end all wars.

"The two men sat with me in a small room in the back of the Metropolitan Church in Toronto from nine in the evening till far into the night trying to show me the error of my ways. They readily granted that war was evil, that it was Christianity's most grievous sin. But the war was on. It could not be stopped till a decision had fallen one way or another. 'If evil is to be done, however much we detest it, let it be done quickly! . . . Help us to put an end to war for all time to come! . . . This war is waged for liberty, in the defence of weak nations, and to set the whole world free. . . .'

"I was no match for two such dedicated and learned Christian gentlemen. I had also grown thoroughly disgusted, I must say, with being stopped in the streets by women who insisted on pinning a white feather, the badge of craven cowardice, on my clothes. I stood six feet two in my stockings at the time, and looked most fit for the service to these militant females. I could not begin an argument each time a woman halted me to ask: 'Why aren't you in uniform?'"

Another clergyman-author was Ian Maclaren who spoke at Cooke's Presbyterian Church, **88 Queen Street East** (northwest corner of Mutual) in 1896. The church was built in 1891 but demolished in the 1960s. It was a handsome building, famous for the music concerts held there because of its excellent pipe organ. It was also the place where Ian Maclaren (1850-1907) chose to speak on his second visit to Toronto. His first was to a packed house of 5,000 people at Massey Hall on October 19, 1896, and the wily lecture agent, Major Pond, who was travelling with Maclaren, seeing the chance for a second lucrative payday, booked Maclaren for a return engagement a few weeks hence. Such was the novelist's popularity that, on his return on November 9, 1896, he almost sold out Cooke's Church (despite a hefty admission charge) which could easily seat 2,000 people.

The popularity of this author separates us more than any other from the sensibility of our Victorian ancestors. Matthew Arnold, Mrs. Humphry Ward, Wilkie Collins—these Victorian authors (and Toronto visitors) are still in print, and read. However, what our forebears saw in Maclaren is not easy to decipher. Revere him, though, they certainly did. The advance press coverage was huge, with daily reminders of his arrival appearing in the papers well in advance. The *World* rhapsodized: "A man of more interesting personality, pleasing appearance, and greater charm than the famous author of *Beside the Bonny Brier Bush* possibly has never spoken to a Toronto audience. This evening in Cooke's Church will be the last opportunity offered you of hearing Ian Maclaren and no doubt the church will be crowded to its utmost capacity. Fifteen hundred 50-cent tickets are on sale at Nordheimer's for those who wish to avoid the crush at the doors." The *Globe's* report on the lecture at **88 Queen** was equally rhapsodic. It approvingly quoted the chairperson introducing Maclaren to the audience as saying that the task was "the greatest honour in his life."

WITH THE GLOBE'S COMPLIMENTS TO "IAN MACLAREN.

Globe, October 19, 1896, p. 1

No other literary author appears to have spoken at Cooke's Church, and the reason Ian Maclaren seems to have been the exception was that he was a Presbyterian minister. In fact, his real name was John Watson. He reserved "Ian Maclaren" for his fiction, while using his own name for his religious writings. The latter were not conventional at all—they even brought him under suspicion of heresy for some time.

Walk north on the east side of **Church Street** towards Shuter. The building that housed Toronto's first Labour Temple still stands at **167 Church Street**. The Labour Temple was the administrative home of early unions and labour organizations, and it had a hall for large meetings occasionally used for talks by individual speakers. At least two authors spoke here on literary subjects. One was the poet J.L. Hughes. The other was W.J. Alexander (1855-1944), whose lecture to the Labour Party Forum on March 13, 1921 was "The Evolution of Literature." The speech was given extensive coverage the next day in the *M&E* which quoted him as saying, for example, that "much of what was regarded as romantic fiction was but the expression of a desire to bring about great social changes in the conditions of the people." Later on, he also remarked, "The modern newspaper and periodical was a tremendous factor in influencing public opinion. If the press of a country were dominated by a few individuals who sought to dictate any policy from purely selfish motives, it would be a menace to the community."

Alexander has always struck me as the ideal kind of academic. He had the vast respect of his colleagues at the UofT where he was the head of the English dept. for many years. He was known across the continent for the intelligence of his publications and the diligence of his scholarship. Yet he frequently spoke at real-world occasions such as this, never speaking down to his audience—in fact, giving the impression that he enjoyed these encounters with the general public as much as his quotidian life in the ivory tower.

The next intersection is **Shuter Street. 142 Shuter** was the first residence in Toronto of Isabella Valancy Crawford (1850-87) and her mother who took rooms here for about a year in 1876. Isabella had moved to Toronto to pursue her dream of being one of the first Canadian authors to survive solely by her creative writing. This determination is praiseworthy, of course, but what makes Crawford such an attractive figure is that she actually succeeded at making a living, strictly by her pen, albeit one full of economic stresses. She was no sooner unpacked at the Shuter Street boarding house (which by a miracle still survives), than she marched to the Mechanics' Institute nearby at Adelaide and Church to obtain a reader's card. Her poems began appearing in the Toronto newspapers shortly after she moved into this address. Though Isabella's talent was rated higher in England than it ever was in her lifetime in her home town, two Torontonians later did much to rescue her reputation here. John Garvin published her *The Collected Poems* in 1905 (with an Introduction by poet Ethelwyn Wetherald), and his wife, Katherine Hale, published a biographical-critical study of Crawford in 1923 as part of the *Makers of Canada* series.

There is something fitting about John Garvin (1859-1935) writing the first book about Crawford because while finishing his undergraduate studies at the UofT from 1884-87, he boarded at nearby **118 Shuter**—which also still stands. He would later become one of the great champions of Canadian authors, and the editor of an early and influential anthology of writing by Canadian poets.

William A. Sherwood (1859-1919) was better known as a painter than a poet, but write he did, and writers often sat for his portraits (Pauline Johnson and Alexander McLachlan among them). In 1901 he boarded at **81 Shuter**, and the following year moved practically next door to **No.77** where he remained until 1903.

Before reaching Massey Hall, we pass **Bond Street**. The poet Albert Smythe (1861-1947) lived at **12 Bond** from 1905-7, little suspecting that his son, Conn Smythe, would later build Maple Leaf Gardens nearby. The St. Michael's Choir School is based at **66 Bond Street** and at least two authors, poet Paul Dutton (b.1945) and mystery writer James Powell, were students of the institution. Almost next door at **No.70** were the offices of Macmillan of Canada (referred to by senior employees somewhat pompously as St. Martin's House, after the headquarters in England). The firm was founded in 1905 and moved into this building in 1910. In the early years, Macmillan leased office space here to other publishers (Collins, for example), but soon it was one of the most important, if not the most important publisher of Canadian authors in the country, and it used every inch of this space as well as the adjoining warehouse. Macmillan's editorial rise began in 1921 under Hugh Eayrs who, incredibly, was appointed C.E.O. when he was only 26 years old. He, together with his colleague and then successor John Morgan Gray, published some of the most famous names in Canadian literature of the time, including Morley Callaghan, Charles G.D. Roberts, E.J. Pratt, Mazo de la Roche, W.S. Wallace, and Lorne Pierce. A later editor, Douglas Gibson (who is now publisher of McClelland and Stewart), would become famous for his care of such Macmillan

Isabella Valency Crawford

authors as Robertson Davies and Alice Munro. For some years now, roughly corresponding to its departure from these premises in the late 1980s, Macmillan has been inactive as a publisher of literary fiction, and the recent sale of the firm has led to the demise of the name.

Nearby is Mackenzie House, **82 Bond Street**. The house was constructed in 1859 and was lived in by newspaper publisher William Lyon Mackenzie from 1859 until he died in 1861. Mackenzie was the leader of the Rebellion of 1837. Heritage Toronto has reclaimed the house as a museum, and it is well worth a visit because, through careful attention to historical detail, it gives an excellent sense of how the upper middle-class lived in the middle of the 19th c. In 1950, one of the weekend guides at Mac-kenzie House was Scott Symons (b.1933), then in the last year of high school and later one of Toronto's more notorious novelists. He told me, "I came to have a strong sense of William Lyon Mackenzie. Indeed, I used to sit in his Mayoral chair in between tourist visitors. I read a lot. And pondered the fact that a lot of the pioneer material on display there was loaned from the Perkins Bull collection. I decided that Mackenzie was a Yankee-style loudmouth who belonged best in the USA. I haven't changed my mind much since."

Return to **Shuter Street**. The last domicile in Toronto of Nicholas Flood Davin (1843-1901) was **24 Shuter** (razed). He lived here from c. 1879 until the middle of 1880. Little is known about Davin's life before he arrived in Canada in July 1872, except that he was born in Ireland, and later worked as a journalist in London on some of the best newspapers. As soon as he landed in Toronto, a friend from the old country got him a job at the *Globe*, but he quit the post in 1875 to freelance. At the same time, he studied law and was called to the bar in 1876. Although he rarely practised as a lawyer, for some reason he took on the defence of the man charged with shooting George Brown, a Father of Confederation. Davin lost that case.) Like many converts, Davin was a passionate immigrant, and he had barely arrived in Canada before he was making public speeches lauding our country's superiority over the United States (that he seems never to have visited the USA did not interfere with his assessment of its worth). Yet he never forgot where he was born, and in 1877 published *The Irishman in Canada*, a book still read with enthusiasm by historians and followers of the Irish diaspora. The book, however, may have been written primarily as an elaborate strategy to win election to Parliament the following year as a Tory in a riding thick with Irish immigrants. The riding had voted Liberal for years, and Davin still lost the seat—but only by a few votes, a display of electoral fortitude not lost on Sir John A. Macdonald and his patronage-mongers. They rewarded Davin with a number of town lots in Saskatchewan, a part of the country to which he had been aching to move. He left Toronto in July 1880, and not long afterwards he was on the prairies where he sold some of the town lots in order to finance the start of a local Tory newspaper, the *Regina Leader*. All of Davin's rhetorical skills, entrepreneurial chutzpah, and an ability to write fetchingly and mellifluously coalesced in the early years of the paper and the journal was a singular success. He even put the big-city eastern papers to shame by scoring a spectacular scoop: the night before Louis Riel was to be hanged, he interviewed the otherwise inaccessible prisoner by entering the prison dressed as a priest bent on giving solace to the condemned man.

Two years later, Davin finally won election to the House of Commons, the first of what would be three terms, representing his western riding as a backbencher. There, his garrulous skills found a natural home, and in the thrust and parry of debate he was always able to hold his own. But despite success at the ballot-box, his personal life began to disintegrate, mostly due to the drink. In 1901, he shot himself in a hotel room in Winnipeg.

On the other side of **Shuter Street** (although its official address is **178 Victoria Street**) is the great bulk of Massey Hall, originally known as Massey Music Hall, opened in 1894. A gift of Hart Massey in memory of his son Charles (who had died aged only 36), the auditorium was the first in Toronto able to accommodate properly large touring companies of musicians. Neither St. Lawrence Hall nor the Music Hall in the Mechanics' Institute were sufficiently spacious to handle major choirs or symphony orchestras, so there certainly was a clear need for a large performing space. Actually, the city did have such spaces, but they were called theatres—such as the Grand Opera House. However, no proper Methodist would be caught dead entering such a wicked, sinful hovel as a theatre, no matter how pure the music on stage. This is why Massey Hall originally had no proscenium arch—so that it would not be "confused" with a theatre. Hart Massey boasted that in his entire life he had never stepped inside a theatre.

While the primary purpose was the presentation of music, it was always intended that lecturers would occasionally grace its stage. In an era before microphones, good acoustics were essential in such a building, and we must always be thankful to Hart Massey for having the wit to indulge his architect in this regard. To this day, the Hall is world-renowned for its acoustic aliveness.

Many authors spoke here. The following is a complete list (as far as I could establish) of creative writers who have spoken from the Massey Hall stage:

Sholem Asch
Hilaire Belloc
J.W. Bengough
Anthony Burgess
Hall Caine
G.K. Chesterton
Sir Winston S. Churchill
Robertson Davies
Arthur Conan Doyle

W.H. Drummond
Howard Fast
Sir Philip Gibbs
Sir Wilfred Grenfell
Grey Owl
Richard Halliburton
Maurice Hindus
Anthony Hope
Douglas Hyde
Jerome K. Jerome
Watson Kirkconnell
Emil Ludwig
Ian Maclaren
André Malraux
Thomas Mann
John Masefield
Nellie McClung
Arthur Miller
David Christie Murray
Max O'Rell
J.B. Priestley
Bertrand Russell
Lincoln Steffens
Timothy D. Sullivan
Margaret Truman
Pierre van Paassen
Gilles Vigneault
Israel Zangwill

Just up the road at **215 Victoria Street**— and almost backing onto the Macmillan offices—were the editorial offices of McClelland and Stewart from 1920 until the house moved to Scarborough in 1954 (although the executive offices had previously been transferred in 1948 to 228 Bloor Street West). For most of this period, M&S was run by John McClelland, father of the legendary Jack. The house was founded in 1906 as McClelland and Goodchild, then became McClelland, Goodchild and Stewart, and then John McClelland and George Stewart alone owned the company when Frederick Goodchild departed in 1918. Before it moved to **215 Victoria**, M&S had offices at 42 Adelaide Street West (c.1906-13) and then at 266 King Street West (1914-19), but as the firm expanded it needed more space, so soon moved into the less-crowded regions of Victoria Street at the northern edge of the then business district.

Under John McClelland, the house did original literary publishing of some notable Canadian names. Among them: Arthur Stringer, Stephen Leacock, Beverley Baxter, Peter Donovan, Lucy Maud Montgomery, Bliss Carman, Marshall Saunders, Marian Keith, Laura Salverson, and Ralph Connor. Authors who worked at these offices include Donald French (who was long a vice-president) and poet Colleen Thibaudeau.

Dundas Street East used to be known as Cruikshank Street in the 1860s and 1870s when playwright and actor Denman Thompson (1833-1911) lived at **No.12** from 1868 until c. 1873. Thompson came to Toronto from the USA in 1854 to work at the Royal Lyceum and he remained in the city until around the time of Confederation, the most popular comic actor in town. He married here and all his children were born in Toronto. A contemporary account notes that he played "a round of characters that included Irishmen, Negroes, and Yankees . . . His favourite roles were Myles na Coppaleen in *Colleen Bawn*, Uncle Tom in *Uncle Tom's Cabin*, and Salem Scudder in the *Octoroon*."

C. 1868 he is said to have returned to the States to try a new career—train robber. A reward was put on his head. He deemed it wise to hide out in Toronto until the authorities south of the border lost interest. Eventually they did. As a comedian he was still in demand all over the continent, and by the mid-1870s he found he could travel safely to leading theatres across America. It was in this period that he wrote *Josh Whitcomb*, a play about a simple but wise and warm-hearted farmer. The play, with Denman Thompson himself playing the lead, became one of the greatest successes of 19th c. American theatre. The role became his only job for the rest of his life, and it made him a great deal of money (six-figure amounts—annually). He returned to Toronto with the play throughout the 1880s, and his biographer claims that on his first trip back to the city, now a rich man, he took out ads in the Toronto newspapers asking those to whom he owed money to meet him at the theatre because he wished to make full restitution. As might be expected there were many claimants, and many of those were false, but he was such a soft touch for a hard-luck story that he gave money even to those who had no right to it.

North of Dundas on **Yonge Street** are a varying number of porno (or, if you prefer, erotic) bookstores. Today their fare is predictable, but in the 1960s a few of these stores offered a bizarre mix of soft-core skin mags and leading-edge literary magazines and books. The literary material first appeared when Nick Drumbolis started to work in 1973 at the Olympia Bookstore, **589 Yonge Street**—one of several Yonge Street porn outlets controlled by Bookazine Enterprises. The shops made so much profit, and the owners were so rarely in the stores that Drumbolis, now one of Canada's most respected antiquarian book dealers, was able to use a small percentage of the profits to bring into Canada an astounding selection of small-press books and literary periodicals that no other Toronto bookshops would carry—either because the material was considered aesthetically too marginal, or because it cost too much to import, or both. After a year, Drumbolis was promoted to the managership of Reid's Bookstore, **329 Yonge Street**. Here he expanded the display of books and writing by literary authors from Canada, San Francisco, New York, London, France, Germany, and Italy to an impressive degree, although I must confess, it was always a bit strange to have to pass rows of *Big Boobs Magazine* in order to get to the esoteric poetry titles at the back. One of the people hired by Drumbolis to work in the store at **No.329** was Richard Shuh. Within a few years, Shuh would leave **329 Yonge** to start his own antiquarian business, Alphabet Books, originally in Toronto but for many years now based in Port Colborne,

Ontario. Shuh is internationally known in the trade today as a dealer in the finest, and rarest, 20th c. literary material. Another bookman who worked as a sales clerk in the Yonge Street porn (and poetry) shops was Steven Temple, now one of the city's most highly regarded antiquarian booksellers. Yet another was Richard Bachmann now owner of Different Drummer Books in Burlington, Ontario. The stores collapsed shortly after one of the owners was murdered in what some called a gangland hit.

A few paces to the north is **363 Yonge**, the original location of The Book Cellar, opened in 1961. The store was popular with many authors, in part because it was open evenings until ten o'clock, highly unusual at the time. Another spot that was popular was Bassell's Restaurant at **No.387**. From 1974-75, one of its waitresses was Wendy Lill (b.1950), who later became one of the leading playwrights of our country, and who now sits as a Member of Parliament in the House of Commons.

The Margaret Eaton School and Theatre at **415 Yonge Street** has been replaced, alas, by an anonymous office building. The School, formerly located in a good-looking, temple-like structure on Bay Street just south of Bloor, had to move from Bay Street in the summer of 1925 because Bay Street was being widened and the school building was in the way. The Eatons then purchased the former YMCA Building at **415 Yonge** and rehabilitated the structure considerably in order to make it suitable for the needs of the girls who were to be given a special education in the dramatic arts and athletics.

Part of the renovation included the transformation of the space formerly known as Association Hall into a 750-seat theatre renamed the Margaret Eaton Hall. The School and Hall continued to operate until 1940. In that year the pedagogical functions were assumed by the UofT. But the Hall was used for many years thereafter by the CBC as a studio (frequently by Andrew Allan for his legendary broadcasts of radio plays) until the entire building was demolished and replaced by the bland edifice there now.

The Margaret Eaton Hall was frequently used for concerts, and without question the most famous musician ever to perform on its stage was Maurice Ravel. His only Toronto appearance took place on its boards in 1928. Both the Association Hall and the Margaret Eaton Hall were also used for readings and talks by notable authors, including:

> W.J. Alexander
> J.W. Bengough
> Pauline Johnson
> Vachel Lindsay
> David Christie Murray
> George Russell ("A.E.")
> Mrs. Humphry Ward
> John Wexley

Noted authors also spoke at the Carlton United Church which used to stand on the southeast corner of Yonge and Carlton Streets. Both Watson Kirkconnell and Nellie McClung were invited to speak from the pulpit, and the underrated English author Vera Brittain (1893-1970) gave a talk here in 1946 on post-war conditions in Europe.

Doctor and novelist John Price-Brown (1844-1938) had his surgery and residence together at **37 Carlton Street** from 1893 until 1910. After graduating from the UofT in medicine in 1869, he practised in Galt before returning to Toronto c.1892. Among his popular novels were *The Mac's of '37: A Story of the Canadian Rebellion* (1910). Very much his own man, Price-Brown felt competent to design an entire wing of the Toronto Western Hospital, much to the chagrin of the town's architects. And no doubt he was an influence on his more famous granddaughter, novelist Gwethalyn Graham (1913-65), author of *Earth and High Heaven*, winner of the Governor General's Award in 1944.

Poet Robert Zend (1929-85) lived in this area when he first arrived in Canada from Hungary. He made his home at **92 Granby Street** from July 1957 to September 1959. His books *From Zero To One* (1973) and *Beyond Labels* (1982) were written in Hungarian here and later translated into English by the author with assistance from Canadian writers.

Austin Clarke (b.1934) owned **62 McGill** from 1981-97. Since his arrival in Toronto from Barbados in 1955, Clarke has been one of the leading black spokespersons of the city. Between 1968 and 1974 he was abroad much of the time, serving as writer-in-residence at leading American universities such as Yale and Duke. Then followed a period of reacquaintance with Barbados, first as its cultural attaché in the USA, and then as counsellor to the Prime Minister. By 1977 he was again living full-time in Toronto. Books written at his McGill Street home include *Nine Men Who Laughed* (1986), *Proud Empires* (1986), *In This City* (1992), *There Are No Elders* (1993), *The Austin Clarke Reader* (1996), and *The Origin of Waves* (1997)

21 McGill has been famous in our time as a women's club with many ups and downs. Interestingly, the building began life in the 19th c. also as a woman's club: The Young Woman's Christian Guild Hall. One of the most famous authors to speak here was Charlotte Perkins Gilman (1860-1935), referred to in one authoritative reference text as "the preeminent intellectual in the women's movement at the turn of the century." Gilman first came to national attention in the USA as a poet with her volume *In This Our World* (1893). This was followed five years later by her magnum opus, *Women and Economics*, a scathing analysis of women's place in the status quo, combined with recommendations for action to improve the lot of women. Her only appearance in Toronto took place on November 9, 1904, and, despite the radicalism of her politics and proposed reforms, she was treated seriously by the newspapers both before and after the speech.

Another eminent author to speak here was Langston Hughes (1902-67), king of the Harlem Renaissance, who in 1943, during the first of two visits to Toronto, gave a speech titled "Soviet Literature" to an open meeting of the Society for the Study of Russia. Both the *Star* and the *G&M* carried brief news items announcing the lecture. By the time Langston Hughes was here the building had become the YWCA, as it was when B.K. Sandwell (1876-1954) spoke on "Our Adjunct Theatre" in 1914.

Anson Gard (1849-1925) seems to have had only one address in Toronto: **353 Church Street** between 1909 and 1916. Born in Ohio, he came to Canada (Montreal) around 1900 following some business scandals in the States. Once here, he dove headlong into writing about the Dominion, with books such as *The Yankee in Quebec* (1901), and *The Hub and the Spokes: The Capital and Its Environs* (Ottawa, 1904). After adventures in the mining towns of the north, he settled in Toronto and wrote, for example, *Silverland and Its Stories* (1909). From Toronto he seems to have returned to the USA where his death in Bowling Green, Kentucky, in 1925 was considered important enough to merit an obituary in the *New York Times*.

A few authors have connections to nearby **Gerrard Street East**. Kathryn Colquhoun (1873-1952) was born in Hamilton but after working as a teacher, and then as book illustrator in New York, she moved to Vancouver. Perhaps because she was writing plays, and Toronto had at least two theatres where her writing might be produced, she moved here in 1938 and stayed until 1940, living for most of that time at Willard Hall, **20 Gerrard East**. Her poetry appeared as part of the Ryerson Poetry Chapbook Series, and in a number of American anthologies.

Fantasy novelist Guy Gavriel Kay (b.1954) lived in a flat at **No.40** from 1980-83 where he wrote *The Summer Tree* (1984), the first novel of his *Fionavar Tapestry* trilogy. **No.78** was where the artist and writer Michael Tims (b.1946) was living c. 1968 when, to make money, he co-authored (with another visual artist) a deliberately trashy novel called *Lena*. Each wrote an alternating chapter after agreeing on the basic direction of the plot. The book was first published in Toronto by Taurus Press. Rather than offer a royalty, Taurus bought the copyright outright from the authors for a few hundred dollars. The prissy Toronto of the time was scandalized by the novel, and the police aided its sales by seizing some copies from bookstores. The book was later published in New York by Grove Press, but the authors received no payment since they had signed away their copyright. To hide his identity, Tims published the fiction under the name A.L. Bronson, but for some reason his friends recalled the name as A.A. Bronson, "so I thought it must be a good commercial name" he told me, and it is the name he has used publicly ever since, most especially when he was one-third of the celebrated artist-triumvirate known as General Idea.

Continuing south on **Church Street**, we pass Ryerson Polytechnic University on the right (whose literary connections I will discuss in a moment), and on the east side of the street we pass **No.325$^{1}/_{2}$**. This bedsitter was where mystery novelist Howard Engel (b.1931), creator of the popular detective Benny Cooperman, lived from 1959-64.

In December 1899, when Emily Murphy returned from Europe with her husband where he had been invited to preach, they settled into **287 Church Street** in Toronto. Her exact movements are unclear at this period, but her stay at **287 Church** seems to have lasted until c. October 1901 when she and her family moved to Wright Avenue near High Park. If this sequence is correct, that means she put the finishing touches to her first book, *The Impressions of Janey Canuck Abroad* (1902) while living at **287 Church.** She was certainly writing articles and reviews for magazines and newspapers at this address. Murphy would eventually move to western Canada where she published large amounts of fiction and non-fiction. She was very much an *engagé* writer, and her political experience led her to become the first female magistrate in the British Empire. Her right to sit in legal judgement, however, was chal-

lenged almost immediately on the grounds that she was not, under the law, a person. Only men were deemed "persons" according to British common law. So she, writer Nellie McClung, and three other women led a legal attack to have women declared "persons," a trial process that took thirteen years to resolve. They finally won the case only after it was reviewed by the Privy Council in England which, at the time, was the court of final appeal in the Commonwealth.

The undistinguished main entrance to Ryerson Polytechnic University is near **50 Gould Street**. Just beyond the entrance, standing like a war ruin after the London Blitz, is the façade of one of the buildings which originally stood on the site: the Toronto Normal School—an odd-sounding name for what we now call a teachers' college. It was opened in 1852. The grounds around here amounted to a seven-acre park, and early visitors to Toronto often refer to the pleasant walk up Church Street to the well-tailored grounds of the school. In essence, the Normal School was dedicated to teacher training while the adjacent Model School to the north (opened in 1855; razed) provided student-teachers with children on whom to practise (or inflict) their pedagogical skills. Both schools were founded by Egerton Ryerson as the linchpins of the Ontario education system he devised. While the Model School was nothing special architecturally, the Normal School certainly was, with its tripartite façade and Italianate cupola. Its loss was accentuated—almost laughably so—by the blandness of what took its place in the early 1960s.

A number of authors have affiliations with the Normal School. Authors who taught here include James L. Hughes, O.J. Stevenson, A.J. Williamson, and Sydney H. Preston. More were students: Robert Barr, Luella Creighton, E.H. Dewart, Sara Jeannette Duncan, Mabel Dunham, John Garvin, James L.Hughes, A.D.Watson, and Flos Jewell Williams.

Robert Barr would later write a novel based on his time at the school, *The Measure*

Toronto Normal School, Gould Street, 19th c. etching

of the Rule (1907). His pen name, Luke Sharp, was taken from an undertaker with premises close by, and during his studies here he roomed at **248 Church Street**. He later went on to great fame and fortune in London. He founded *The Idler,* an influential English monthly (1892-1911), with Jerome K. Jerome, and was part of a literary circle that included Arthur Conan Doyle and Rudyard Kipling. His own novels and short stories were much admired by the British critics, and his humorous writing remains an undiscovered country to most Canadians.

Authors who taught full-time at Ryerson Polytechnic include Constance Beresford Howe, Graeme Gibson, Eric Wright, and George Swede. The full-time students have been Keith Ross Leckie, Des McAnuff, Ken Mitchell, Karen Mulhallen, Robert J. Sawyer, Peter Such, Guillermo Verdecchia, and Richard B.Wright.

Just south of Ryerson at **115 Bond Street** is St. George's Ukrainian Church, formerly Holy Blossom Synagogue. The edifice before you was finished in 1897 and incorporated a lecture hall in addition to the usual temple. At least three creative writers gave publicly advertised talks at Holy Blossom before the congregation closed the synagogue in 1937, moving to larger premises in the north end of the city. They were American playwright Elmer Rice (who earlier in his life had spent part of his honeymoon in Toronto), American poet and anthologist Louis Untermeyer, and the American novelist and journalist John Spivak. The visits of all three men were considered front-page news.

105 Bond Street has been the home of Doubleday Canada since June 1948. For some years now, the house has published noted Canadian authors of fiction, including Tomson Highway and Evelyn Lau. Through its acquisition of Seal paperbacks it counts many other well-known Canadian literary names in its backlist.

Return to **Church Street**. The first address in Toronto for Duncan McKellar (1865-99) was **239 Church Street** in 1888. He had moved to Toronto a year before when he joined the reportorial staff of the *News*. These are rooms he probably shared with Peter McArthur, an important Canadian editor who went on to substantial fame and influence in New York. McArthur wrote an affectionate Introduction to a posthumous collection of McKellar's poems after the young man had died of tuberculosis. According to McArthur, McKellar never lost his sense of humour. "In his last illness he was visited by a boyhood friend who had entered the ministry. With the solicitude appropriate to his calling, the young clergyman ventured to ask: 'Have you made your peace with God?' With the slow smile with which we were all so familiar, and with no irreverence, the dying poet-artist replied, 'I was not aware that we had quarrelled.'" While living at this address, McKellar had moved from the *News* after his friend E.E. Sheppard had been forced from the paper. He joined Sheppard in his new enterprise, a magazine known as *Saturday Night*. At the weekly he acted as assistant editor, drama critic, and poetry editor. McKellar provided many of the thumbnail illustrations that graced the early issues of the magazine. He was accomplished enough a draughtsman that with C.W. Jeffreys he founded the Art Students' League which evolved into the Graphic Arts Society. He moved to New York where his talents were welcomed and promised much, but his fatal illness never allowed him the chance to flower fully.

Novelist and literary publisher Barry Callaghan (b.1937) lived at **193 Church** from the spring of 1973 until May 1976. 1976 was also the year he began Exile Editions, one of the finest exclusively literary presses in Canada (he had founded *Exile* magazine in 1972).

Jarvis Street between Queen and Carlton has some literary associations worth noting. The City's first librarian, James Bain (1842-1908) lived at **138 Jarvis** in 1873. Writer Susie Frances Harrison ("Seranus") had rooms at **No.183** in 1887.

In 1948, believing that if he was going to succeed as a writer he had to work at the task full-time, Hugh Garner quit his day job, sent his wife back to her parents, and moved into the Warwick Hotel at **202 Jarvis**, a hotel more accustomed to renting rooms by the hour than by the week. In his autobiography, he continues, "During the week or so I lived at the Warwick I entered a short story contest run by *Maclean's* magazine, entering 'One, Two, Three Little Indians.' The stories had to be sent in under a pseudonym, so I combined the names of the hotel and the street, using the pen-name 'Jarvis Warwick.' It was a pseudonym I was to use many times in later years, when more than one of my articles and stories appeared together in a magazine, and I also used it as the author's name of a novel I wrote a couple of years later, *Waste No Tears*.

"'One, Two, Three Little Indians' did not win a prize in the *Maclean's* contest, though ironically I'll bet that it has been reprinted, broadcast and telecast, translated and everything else more than the total of *Maclean's* short story winners in the history of the magazine. To this moment, the story has been revived thirty-six times, on radio, television, in anthologies and textbooks in Canada, the United States, Great Britain and West and East Germany.

"When the contest results were announced and I found I had not won a prize, I went over to *Maclean's* where I met W.O. Mitchell, then the fiction editor. We had never met before, but when I told him I was the author of the Indian story he sat me down in his office and said, 'I don't know what the hell was wrong with the judges, but in my estimation it was one of the best stories we received. Even after the prizes were announced I tried to get it printed in the magazine anyhow, but the editor turned thumbs down.' . . . Bill Mitchell showed me a chit attached to the manuscript of the Indian story which he had circulated among the other editors. Including Pierre Berton, John Clare and others, and they had all scribbled favourable comments about the story and agreed with Bill that the magazine should print it. Though Mitchell did his best to get the magazine to publish it, he finally had to mail it back to me.

"I moved from the Warwick Hotel to a rooming house at the corner of Bay and Grosvenor Streets, now long since torn down. . . . "

Another pioneer female writer would have been the neighbour of "Seranus" when she was on Jarvis: novelist Sara Jeanette Duncan (*The Imperialist*) had her home at **No.239** from 1886-87. When novelist W.O. Mitchell (*Who Has Seen the Wind*) moved to Toronto in 1948 to become the fiction editor at *Maclean's*, one of his first addresses was the Westminster Hotel, **240 Jarvis**. He and his wife, Merna, recalled living there for some months until a cottage offered by a friend opened on Ward's Island in the following spring.

William Henry Withrow was born in Toronto in 1839, making him one of the earliest people actually born in the city to become a creative writer. He received training as an architect but preferred the ministry, and was ordained in 1864 in the Methodist persuasion. Rising through the ranks of the church, he was appointed to the Metropolitan Church on Queen Street for a while. However, it was his literary work that makes him worth our attention. He helped to forge an early Canadian point of view about literary matters. The *Dictionary of Canadian Biography* discusses his influence this way: "In 1872 the book committee of the Wesleyan conference had expressed the need for a Methodist magazine in Canada and the suggestion was endorsed in 1874 . . . Withrow was appointed editor . . . It contained articles on the education of women, exploration in Africa, and current topics . . . as well as poetry, a book review and religious and missionary news. The first issue's contents set a pattern that would be followed broadly until the *Magazine* ceased publication in 1906. Withrow was also a major contributor, as he would continue to be in future. He stated his objectives succinctly: the *Magazine* was to be 'an exponent of the religious and intellectual life of our rapidly extending Church . . . to furnish wholesome reading for Christian households and to foster the growth of a sound native literature in our young Dominion.'" Withrow himself wrote novels with a strong religious bent. Of more historical importance was his textbook, co-authored with G. Mercer Adam, *Canadian History and Literature* (1887), one of the earliest attempts in English Canada to state that there was a canon worth documenting, reading, and studying. Given that there were compatriots one hundred years later who still denied the importance of Canadian literature, the optimism—and determination—of Withrow and Adam seems a marvel to behold. Withrow lived at **240 Jarvis** (in a house that antedated the Westminster Hotel) from 1877-89, and then at **244 Jarvis** from 1890 until he died at this address in 1908.

His neighbour at **No.246**, Ezra Hurlburt Stafford (1865-1912?), probably ended his days here—he disappears from the record in 1912 but I could find no obits. He had lived on Jarvis since 1904. Earlier, being a physician at the Lunatic Asylum, he had had to live at the hospital at 999 Queen West for some years, although he is listed at **266 Jarvis** in 1886 and 1887. Stafford was a frequent contributor of poems and stories to Canadian and American magazines, and it was while living here that he wrote most of his fiction that was issued between covers.

William Hume Blake (1861-1924) is yet another author called to the bar who never really practised. Today he remains best-known as the fine translator of Louis Hémon's novel *Marie Chapdelaine*, but he published *belles lettres* of his own, including *Brown Waters and Other Sketches* (1915) which had later editions, one with a Foreword by Vincent Massey, and another with a Foreword by John Buchan. Blake also did an excellent translation of another Quebec novel, *Chez nous* by Adjutor Rivard. In 1888-89 he resided at **252 Jarvis**, but spent the next year at **No.271**. One of his longest domiciles was a block away at **171 Mutual Street** (1891-1905).

A founder of the Arts and Letters Club, writer August Bridle (1869-1952), roomed at **281 Jarvis Street** in 1904. An even older literary pioneer, poet Archibald Lampman (1861-99), lived at **No.283** from May to August 1882. Lampman, regarded as one of the best of our 19th c. lyricists, had just graduated from Trinity College on Queen West and was using this address as a base from which to find a good job. Nothing good appeared, so with heavy heart, he began teaching in Orangeville.

Another poet connected to this address is Laura Elizabeth McCully (1886-1924). Later in life she was a leading campaigner for women's rights, but from 1886 to 1889 she was just a babe, for **No.283** was where she was born and passed her infancy.

The mansion at **314 Jarvis Street** was once the home of Dr. Charles Sheard, the chief of the Toronto Board of Health, and the man generally credited with leading the successful campaign to rid Toronto of smallpox. His wife, Virna (c. 1865-1943) began to write poems and tales initially just for her children. Then, when 27, she began to submit her work to periodicals and soon found a ready market. Not long afterwards, especially because of her novels for adults, she became a nationally known literary figure. Death came by heart attack at this house.

One of the children to whom she told her stories was a son who inherited a share of this mansion. Indeed, the house was subdivided, and he lived here with his bride, and then, as of 1953, with his daughter Sarah for the first three months of her life. She too became a nationally known novelist. Her first book, *Almost Japanese* (1985), had great success commercially and critically in Canada and the USA, and her later books have maintained that standard.

In 1948, Hugh Garner, just before he moved to the Warwick Hotel, "took a taxi downtown. When the cab-driver asked me where I wanted to go, I told him to take me to the Walsingham Hotel on **[321] Jarvis Street**, a comfortable hostelry owned by an old friend, Mr. Freeman, in which I'd lived for a couple of happy, carefree months nine years

before when I'd first joined the artillery, and for a time after returning from the war. I stayed at the Walsingham for a week or two, and then for reasons which now escape me, but were no doubt connected with my lack of money, I moved down the street. . . ."

John McCrae (1872-1918), author of "In Flanders Fields," a poem known wherever English is spoken, studied medicine at the UofT after obtaining his BA in Natural Sciences in 1894. It would seem that he shared rooms with his brother at **329 Jarvis** from 1894 until he got his Bachelor of Medicine degree in 1898, after which time he did his residency at the Toronto General Hospital. Certainly John McCrae is listed at **No.329** for the years 1896, 1897, and 1898.

For at least part of the time (1881) he was an editor at the *Globe*, E.W. Thomson (1849-1924) lived at **No.334**. He might have stayed longer, but the boom in land sales in Winnipeg was like a siren call, and he abandoned journalism to run off to Manitoba to be a surveyor. That job lasted only weeks because he had no sooner arrived than the bust followed the boom, and he re-turned to Toronto (and a new address) with his tail between his legs.

From here, it is necessary to return to the foot of **Pembroke Street**. An early champion of Canadian authors, and the man who organized the first reading by Canadian writers in Toronto was Frank Yeigh (1861-1935). In 1883 he roomed at **10 Pembroke**.

Across the road at **No.17** lived one of the most important 19th c. Toronto novelists, Ernest Thompson Seton (1860-1946). Seton was raised in a large family with an abusive father. When the Setons arrived in Toronto from Lindsay in 1871, they were so poor they had to live in one of the city's worst neighbourhoods. But by 1872 they were able to move up to **137 Mutual Street**, and two years after that to the solidly middle-class **17 Pembroke Street** where Ernest remained until he left for England on June 12, 1879.

Seton was well-regarded in his lifetime—and is still respected today—for his animal stories, tales that combine remarkable detail with good narrative technique. There were two Toronto places where he first fell in love with animals: the Island, and the Don Valley, with the latter being the more important and the one he discovered while living on Pembroke, as his biographer notes: "It was on one of these 'far tramps' up the Don Valley in the summer of 1874 that Seton found his private paradise. Although the City of Toronto had straddled the Don Valley in its lower reaches, farther north the city's rim coincided with the Necropolis and St. James Cemetery. Beyond these was a wilderness of ravines and forest richly inhabited by wildlife. Each Saturday, Seton's explorations led him deeper and deeper into these woods until one day he found himself in a small heavily wooded ravine carved by one of the Don's tributary streams. Here, against the hillside, he built a crude cabin, using discarded cedar fenceposts for the walls, and brushwood, clay and grass laid over poles for the roof—as Yan does in *Two Little Savages*.

Ernest Thompson Seton, self-portrait, 1879

"Then, in a curious foreshadowing of his life on the prairie ten years later, having built a shelter for himself that utilized the basic pioneer techniques, he began playing Indian there instead. He became the lone member of a mighty Indian band, silently skulking through the forest tracking game. He stripped off his clothes so that the sun would turn his skin bronze, made himself moccasins and put feathers in his hair. He was supremely happy in his secret paradise . . . While the snow lay on the ground in the winter of 1874-75, the cabin on the Don held little allure, but when spring came again, Seton returned every Saturday afternoon to continue his fantasy."

In 1969, a city park was created near where the cabin was built and named Ernest Seton Thompson Park in his honour.

Seton was actually driven from his house on **Pembroke Street** by a father so obsessed with money and religion that the author's account of his dismissal from home, more than a century later, is still shocking: "One day, after I had been home long enough to recover from the immediate effects of the voyage, my father called me into his study. He took down his cash book, a ponderous and aged volume, opened it at E, and then made one of his characteristic speeches:

"'Now, my son, you are twenty-one years of age; you have attained to years of manhood if not of discretion. All the duties and responsibilities which have hitherto been borne for you by your father, you must now assume for yourself. I have been prayerfully rememberant of your every interest, and I need hardly remind you that for all that is good in you, you are, under God, indebted to your father—and of course, to some extent, your mother also.

"'For this, you must feel yourself under a bond of gratitude that will strengthen rather than weaken as life draws near the goal that all should keep in view. You owe everything on earth, even life itself, to your father; reverent gratitude should be your only thought. While it is hopeless that you should ever discharge this debt, there is yet another to which I must call your attention at once.'

"He now pointed to page after page in the cash book—the disbursements that had been made for me since my birth. There they were, every item with day and date perfect—unquestionably correct—even the original doctor's fee for bringing me into the world was there. The whole amount was $537.50.

"'Hitherto,' said he, with traces of emotion at the thought of his own magnanimity, 'I have charged no interest; but from this point on, I must add the reasonable amount of 6 per cent per annum. This I conceive to be a duty I owe to myself as well as to your own sense of duty and manhood; and I shall be glad to have you reduce the amount at the earliest possible opportunity.'

"I was utterly staggered. I sat petrified. Most men consider that they owe their sons a start in life. My father thought that his father owed that to him; but his case, he felt, was different."

Poet E.A. Lacey (1938-95) returned to Canada from Thailand for medical care following an accident which had caused him severe head injuries. Eventually he was admitted to Queen Elizabeth Hospital for treatment, but they could do nothing for him and he was discharged on August 12, 1994, to a welfare rooming house at **41 Pembroke.** It was here he died of a heart attack on June 21, 1995. Lacey's friend, poet Fraser Sutherland, scattered Lacey's ashes on Lake Ontario as directed by Edward's will.

James L. Hughes (1846-1935) was one of the leading educationists in the province and for many years was the director of all school inspectors in Toronto. He had a public profile such as no educator has in our time. He frequently made speeches on school topics, but since he also published seven books of poetry he was considered a leading man of Toronto letters, and often gave discourses on CanLit. He was occasionally invited to be the master of ceremonies for visiting literary luminaries at their readings and lectures. From 1875-78 he made his home at **No.77.**

Right across the street was a house that was home to two writers at different times. The mystery writer James Powell (b.1932), who was born in Toronto, said in a letter from his home in the States that when he was about 11 his parents had separated and he initially lived with his mother: "We then moved to **78 Pembroke Street** where my mother ran a rooming house. I continued to attend St. Peter's until the end of the school year when I entered St. Michael's School on Bond Street. As I recall, that was the beginning of Grade VI. I believe we remained on Pembroke Street for more than a year. We then moved to a smaller rooming house on Moss Park Place which I understand vanished beneath a public housing development a long time ago. Before I finished Grade VIII I was living with my father in various rooming houses on Jarvis, Shuter, and George Street." Not long after, he and his father moved again to an unspecified address including a rooming house on Mutual between Queen and Shuter. "In my early years, there were, as there were with anyone growing up in Toronto when I did, the Royal Ontario Museum in winter and the Riverdale Zoo or Centre Island in the summer . . . Outside of Sundays, it was the Central Library on College and movie theatres. At one time I could recite all the movie theatres from the Brighton on Roncesvalles to the Empire on Queen beyond Parliament. The Bluebell and the Eclipse on Parliament were favourites. But I think I spent more time in the Regent at Sherbourne and Queen than any other . . . I grew up in Toronto fully expecting to spend my life there and am, in fact, still a bit surprised that it hasn't turned out that way (I am still a Canadian citizen). As a result, whenever I come across a Toronto reference I usually make a note of it. For example, in Bea Lillie's autobiography *Every Other Inch A Lady* I discovered that thirty-five years before I lived on George Street so did she, and in the same block (across from the Duke of York schoolyard) and perhaps even the same house."

Certainly the same house, **78 Pembroke Street**, was also the home of another Toronto writer who settled in the USA, Norman Reilly Raine (1895-1971). The creator of Tugboat Annie, although born in Pennsylvania, came to Toronto when quite young and served with the Canadian Army throughout WWI. The biographical material available on Reilly is thin and contradictory. For example, one source says he worked as an assistant editor at *Maclean's* following the war, but the city directories list his occupation as a purser in the Canadian Merchant Marine until 1922, and only after that date is he cited as a journalist. He seems to have left Toronto in 1929, and by the mid-thirties he was working in Hollywood. Throughout the twenties he had been writing stories for *Saturday Evening Post* and the other slicks, and it was in that decade that he concocted his most famous character, Tugboat Annie. The character became more famous than her creator, especially thanks to two feature films (1933 and 1940) inspired by the lady. He penned a play and a novel that were also made into motion pictures, but in Los Angeles he was really only known as a screenwriter. He won an Academy Award for the filmscript of the 1937 movie *The Life of Emile Zola*. He lived at **78 Pembroke** from 1919 until 1923.

Marian Engel (1933-85) and Howard Engel (b.1931) were husband and wife when they lived at **No.116** from 1964-65. Neither had yet published a book at this stage of their lives. Novelist Joyce Marshall (b.1913) was working as a freelance journalist when she lived at **No.118** in 1937. Her first novel, *Presently Tomorrow*, appeared in 1946.

At the north end of **Pembroke Street** is a good view of Allan Gardens. The first five acres of the park were the gift in 1858 of George William Allan who owned this and much of the surrounding land in the 19th c. The City purchased the remaining five acres, giving the park its current scale. The Gardens have some surprising literary connections.

Toronto has only two life-sized bronze statues of authors: Winston S. Churchill in Nathan Philips Square (and, let's be honest, it was erected not to honour the writer but the statesman); the other is the poorly sited tribute to the Scottish poet Robert Burns in the east end of Allan Gardens. Toronto author John Imrie led the drive to erect the statue which he boasted would be the first in Canada dedicated to Burns. In 1899, Imrie printed a plea for funds and eventually convinced the many Scottish immigrants where their duty lay. The statue was sculpted by Edinburgh artist D.W. Stevenson. The pedestal and panels were done locally by the McIntosh Marble and Granite Co., Toronto. At 3:30 p.m. on Monday, July 21, 1902, there was a grand unveiling of the statue. Dignitaries made the usual noises while the 48th Highlanders Band and Chorus sang "There was a Lad Was Born in Kyle" and later, "A Man's a Man for a' That."

Sixty years later, Milton Acorn chose this spot as the place to bring poetry to the people. He had been reading his verses at the Bohemian Embassy, but the Marxist in him was bothered that only a bourgeois audience was hearing his work. So, in late June 1962, he began to read poems and excerpts from his journal in the shadow of Robbie Burns. Quite why there was a plainclothes policeman nearby has never been clear, but Milton had only been reading for a few minutes before the cop asked him to stop, and ordered Acorn's few listeners to disperse. Other poets might have obliged the policeman, but not feisty Milton. So he was given a ticket for reading poetry in a park. Outraged at this violation of free speech, he gathered the Bohemian Embassy crowd at a meeting later in the week (the effete bourgeoisie sometimes have their uses, it seems) and together they concocted a group known as Interpoet which, Gandhi-like, was going to indulge in civil disobedience and, damn it, read poems aloud in Allan Gardens.

The following Sunday, Milton and Interpoet went to the foot of the Burns statue, set down their soapbox, and, one after the other, stood on it and read poetry. By the next

Sunday, the press had caught up to the story and were on hand to document Metro's Finest handing out tickets left and right to the poets. The newspapers gave the issue prominent placement, and as a result, on following Sundays, up to a thousand people came out to see the poets being harassed every week by the police. Among the most frequently ticketed were Acorn, Joe Rosenblatt, Tom Arnett, and Stephanie Nynych.

This foolish business is worth noting because it marked an important change in Toronto's demeanour. The police behaviour represented the old, strict rectitude of dour Toronto, the city that lived in dread of any pleasure and in fear of anyone who dared to flout the law. But the newspapers of the day realized the *zeitgeist* had changed, and in their news stories they ridiculed the police. Worse, from the point of view of the old guard, the newspapers were sarcastic, even withering in their editorials, lambasting the municipal politicians for not acting promptly to put an end to the matter. Tellingly, the bylaws did allow religious preaching in the parks. In other words, psalms good, poems bad. As the summer wore on, the police ticketing continued and the city council, reflecting the dichotomy of the old and new city, actually debated the moral turpitude associated with poets reading their work in parks, and voted, predictably, to do nothing.

The issue ended in mid-August when the poets, no longer able to afford the fines they were given in magistrates' court, stopped reading. But, while they lost the battle, they won the war. Without question, they helped to permanently lighten Toronto's demeanour.

Allan Gardens from its beginning was intended to have a pavilion suitable for musical events. The first pavilion, dating from 1861, while roofed was actually tent-like, in that it was open at the sides and thus open to the elements. This made it unusable for concerts in winter but extremely popular in summer when, in the days before air conditioning, all other theatrical spaces had to close (and churches, too, were like saunas). The Horticultural Society presented the concerts to raise money to care for its flowers and plants, but the Society soon realized it needed a properly enclosed theatre in order to gain control over tickets and admissions. Therefore in 1879 it unveiled (approximately where the palmhouse is now) the second "Horticultural Pavilion." The Society gave the building this name with the hope that by referring to the space as a pavilion (rather than a theatre) Methodists and others who abjured theatres would attend the concerts, as well as promenade among the adjoining glass-enclosed conservatories full of leaves and blossoms. The nomenclature sleight-of-hand worked, and people attended in droves. As for the hall itself, architectural historian William Dendy gives a good detailed picture of the interior: "The hall was the central element of the scheme—far larger than the two conservatories planned to the north and south—and was built first. Measuring 76 feet by 137, and entered from the east, it included a permanent stage and two green-rooms along the west side. There was seating on the main floor and in the two galleries above: the first ran around the north, east and south sides of the hall; the second was only on the east side. There were also exterior promenade galleries around both these levels, from which the doors opened to the interior galleries. The interior could seat 2,100 but the number could be stretched to 3,000 if all of the interior and exterior galleries were used. Standards of audience comfort were variable in the period, and the seating that was provided varied from armchairs for the highest-price tickets to stools for extra places in the balconies." The interior was lit by gas until 1896, when electricity was introduced. A fire in June 1902 completely destroyed the concert hall and the adjoining flower and plant emporium.

From its opening the second Horticultural Pavilion became the preferred place to present readings and talks by eminent authors—especially writers who could draw a large audience and thereby enrich the producers. Not every author had a sold-out house, but many did, and given that the capacity of the hall was three thousand people, even a 50 per cent house represented a huge audience for a literary lecture by today's standards. The creative writers who spoke at the Horticultural Pavilion were:

> George Washington Cable
> Florence Marryat
> Bill Nye
> Max O'Rell
> James Whitcomb Riley
> Mark Twain
> Oscar Wilde

Twain and Wilde, of course, are the most important names on that list. Twain (1835-1910) actually read here on two occasions. He and novelist George Washington Cable (1844-1925) were doing a reading tour of the United States in 1884 and Twain insisted

Promotional photo from North American reading tour which featured Mark Twain and George Washington Cable, 1884

that Toronto be part of the tour for a couple of reasons: first, he knew it would offer a big payday (he received a percentage of the gate), and second, because he was desperate to find some way to outwit the Canadian book pirates. The worst of these were the Belford Brothers of Toronto. In the flush of nationalism following Confederation, the Belfords and others argued that British copyright law no longer applied in Canada (then, as now, our federal politicians forgot about books when formulating national policy). In the absence of any enforceable copyright law in Canada, a few Toronto publishers felt free to print copies of best-sellers published in the USA and sell them in Canada. This deprived the authors of royalties on sales of their books in this country—annoying to the Americans admittedly but, given our small population, hardly ominous. However, it wasn't long before the Belford Brothers of Toronto began advertising their pirated editions in American magazines and newspapers for sale to American customers. In some cases, bestsellers were being offered to Americans by the Belfords at one-tenth the cost of the legitimate American edition. The public, not concerned with the niceties of copyright, merely wanted the cheapest price and so began buying the Belford editions in huge quantities. Sales were made, at first, via the post, but later were made directly to the public via American bookshops willing to turn a blind eye to the illegal editions they were selling. Naturally, the authors did not receive a penny from the copies sold this way—and Twain was the most vocal American in protesting against this outrage. He never did succeed in having his own government treat the matter with dispatch, and Twain personally spent a small fortune hiring lawyers in the USA, UK, and Canada trying to devise legal means of halting the pirates' activity. One group of lawyers suggested that if he were resident on British Empire soil at the time *Huckleberry Finn* was published, then it might qualify for protection. His correspondence of 1884 shows that while he was on the reading tour he badgered his publishers to guarantee that there be no delays in the book's publication date, so as to ensure that his Toronto reading date coincided with the book's official appearance. The frantic scheduling was all to no avail; the legal advice was wrong and the Belfords continued to pirate.

The first stop of Twain and Cable in Toronto was actually a two-night engagement: December 8 and 9, 1884. Cable was a Cajun author whose readership has almost completely disappeared today, but he was very popular in his day, especially in the southern U.S. Twain miscalculated in thinking Cable would be popular in the northern states and Canada as a partner on the bill. In Toronto, at least, Cable was given a polite reception, but it is clear from reading the newspaper accounts that almost everyone would have been happier if only Samuel Clemens had taken the stage.

The *Mail* gave an eyewitness account of Mark Twain's first appearance in Toronto: "The advent of Mark Twain on the platform was the signal for a storm of applause. In personal appearance he has altered little within the past few years. His shock of hair is greyer if anything than of yore, but the lugubrious expression of his countenance, his awkward gestures, and his slow, nasal drawl are still there. He commenced with a sketch of Mississippi life from *The Adventures of Huckleberry Finn*—'King Sollermunn.' His next two readings were taken from *A Tramp Abroad*." In an interview with a *Globe* reporter after the reading, Twain was asked how he reconciled this reading tour with his vow that he would never go on the lecture platform unless driven there by want of bread. He replied, "Well, I'd kept that vow so long—fifteen years or so—that I thought it time to break it and make a better one." The *World* reported that "the audience these two drew last night was large enough to fill the Horticultural Pavilion and respectable enough to include most of the best people of the town." On the following night, both authors read different selections, and again, the Pavilion was sold out. Twain wrote to his wife from Toronto's Rossin House Hotel where he was staying, "Tonight a noble hall to talk in and an audience befitting it. Both of us had a gorgeously good time."

The Twain-Cable tour was organized by Major J.B. Pond, the greatest lecture impresario of the 19th c. This is worth noting because he recognized that Toronto—again—would be one of only a few cities where authors could make a (possibly profitable) unscheduled return engagement a few months hence. Twain and Cable did return for a one-night stand two months later on February 14, 1885. Newspaper reports suggest the Pavilion was quite crowded for this February 1885 appearance, but Pond's receipt book suggests only half the house was sold, a fate that befell the authors in every city to which they made unscheduled return engagements—it became readily apparent that even a writer as famous as Twain had returned too soon after his initial success.

Another lecture impresario at that time, Richard D'Oyly Carte, doubled as a theatre producer. In New York he was having success with the Gilbert and Sullivan opera *Patience*, a satire of the Aesthetic Movement. Included in the opera is a lead character obviously based on Oscar Wilde. D'Oyly Carte wanted to tour *Patience* to other cities on the continent, but he realized for the tour to be profitable he needed to make North Americans more aware of Wilde and his ideas about aesthetics. What better way to do this than lure Wilde himself to these shores with a lucrative lecture tour? Wilde (1854-1900) accepted D'Oyly Carte's offer, and in 1882 undertook a tour scheduled to last a year, visiting scores of cities and towns. One of those cities was Toronto.

At noon on Victoria Day, May 24, 1882, Oscar Wilde arrived at the Grand Trunk Station on Front Street and was pleasantly surprised to find a welcoming committee. In most other places, only one or two people were on hand to escort him to his lodgings. Ordinarily for a young, rising star of the British literary scene, such a small reception would be the norm. But the large Irish population of Toronto, already familiar with the political poetry of Wilde's mother, Speranza, was determined to show Oscar that Toronto was special—and loyal to the sons of Erin. The delegation accompanied him to the Queen's Hotel (later replaced by the Royal York Hotel). Because of the national holiday, the streets were full of people, the public events many, and the weather pleasant with clear skies.

No sooner had Wilde registered than he was whisked away for a sightseeing tour of the town. Then, just after three o'clock, he was taken to the Lacrosse Grounds to watch a game between an Indian team from the St. Regis reserve near Cornwall and the Toronto Lacrosse Club. Wilde was not a sports fan and one can only assume the Lieutenant-Governor (who was Wilde's unofficial host) assumed that he might want to see something peculiarly Canadian during his stay. Despite his aversion to sports, Oscar seems genuinely to have enjoyed himself, watching the game intently from the Royal Box, and refusing to notice the many people who were watching him.

In the early evening he had dinner with unnamed hosts at the Toronto Club, and then he attended a ball in his honour at Government House. The next day, after spending the morning writing letters, he went to the annual exhibition of the Ontario Society of Artists where he discovered Homer Watson, a painter whose career he furthered not only with praise but with introductions to the right people in London. He then toured the UofT where he was openly impressed by the façade and portal of University College.

That evening he lectured in the Grand Opera House, 9 Adelaide Street West. His topic was "Art Decoration," advertised as "the practical application of the principles of the Aesthetic Theory to Exterior and Interior House Decoration, with observations upon Dress and Personal Ornaments."

Reading between the lines of the newspaper coverage, my sense is that Torontonians had a confused response to Wilde—at least before he gave his first lecture. On the one hand, some wanted to mock him because he was unashamedly espousing new dress and new architecture while simultaneously criticizing current homes and dress. They also wanted to mock him because Gilbert and Sullivan and a certain coterie in London thought Wilde laughable. And if London thought him laughable, well, we here in Toronto could be just as up-to-date as London and would also find him silly. On the other hand, enough Torontonians knew not everyone in London thought Wilde absurd, and those Torontonians wanted to be as up-to-date as the progressive Londoners. As well, and this becomes obvious when reading the newspaper coverage that came after he had lectured, Toronto had lots of people who were willing to make up their own minds about the man, regardless of what others said. This ability to ignore the madding crowds, for example, showed itself again when Toronto gave Matthew Arnold a very different and more intelligent reception in 1884 than he had received in the USA. And that independence of thought was generally visible in the extensive news reports that accompanied Wilde's Toronto visit.

The *Mail* admitted as much in its lead paragraph reviewing the Grand lecture: "It is probable that the desire to see the young leader of the aesthetic movement was stronger in its influence to attract a large audience than the desire to hear his lecture. At all events the Grand Opera House was filled last evening by a very select audience, and doubtless when Mr. Wilde lectures on Saturday afternoon next, as has been announced, the desire to hear him will supersede in influence the desire to see him." The *News*, in a page-one story, actually apologized for its inadequacy to do justice to the speech:

"In this condensed report of the lecture it has been impossible to reproduce the beautiful language used, or to furnish a full and adequate idea of the lecturer's meaning in many passages." The *Globe's* report was equally serious and ultimately most complimentary, with the reporter finally admitting that "Mr. Oscar Wilde is not such a fool as he looks." Only the *Telegram* dissented, mounting from the beginning an attack that can only be described as vicious. In one report it actually pretended to interview Oscar, as if he were a girl, calling him "Miss Wilde" throughout the report. The newspaper's coverage was so malicious it seems to have been counter-productive and resulted in augmented interest in his presence.

The lecture at the Horticultural Pavilion was added to the author's itinerary at the last minute—probably because the Grand Opera House lecture sold out and there was still demand for tickets. He went to Brantford on Friday, May 26, 1882, as originally scheduled, and then returned by train to Toronto the next morning to speak on "The House Beautiful" at 2:30 pm in Allan Gardens. Once again, a large crowd, this time mostly women, assembled to hear Oscar. The stage was so covered with flowers that the lower half of his body was hidden from view. Much of what Wilde said that day is, regrettably, still true: "I suppose that the poet will sing and the artist will paint regardless whether the world praises or blames. He has his own world and is independent of his fellow-men. But the handicraftsman is dependent on your pleasure and opinion . . . Your people love art but you do not sufficiently honour the handicraftsmen. Of course, those millionaires who can pillage Europe for their pleasure need have no care to encourage such; but I speak here for those whose desire for beautiful things is larger than their means. I find that one great trouble all over is that your workmen are not given to noble designs. You cannot be indifferent to this, because art is not something which you can take or leave. It is a necessity of human life . . . " Later, commenting on clothing, he said, "Perhaps one of the most difficult things for us to do is to choose a notable and joyous dress for men. There would be more joy in life if we could accustom ourselves to use all the beautiful colours we can in fashioning our own clothes . . . "

Following the lecture, Oscar went to the home of Henry Pellatt (who had not yet built Casa Loma), then returned to Government House for a *musicale*, followed by a private dinner with the Lieutenant-Governor and his family. Before the night was over, he sat for a bust by the Toronto sculptor Frederick Dunbar. The bust was exhibited shortly afterwards in Toronto but its subsequent fate is unknown. It is very likely lingering in an attic somewhere in Toronto, awaiting discovery.

When Oscar Wilde conquered Toronto, he was just 27 years old.

OSCAR WILDE, BARD OF THE ÆSTHETES: "SON OF SPERANZA."

Earliest announcement of Oscar Wilde's pending visit to Toronto

The Irish Canadian, February 9, 1882

REGENT PARK

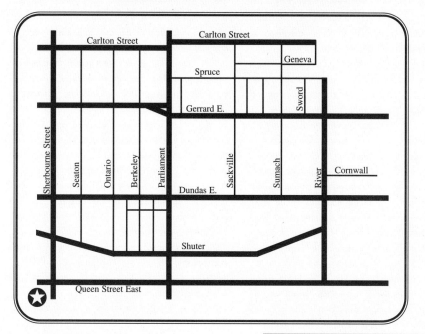

The tour begins at the northeast corner of Sherbourne Street and Queen Street East.

The noted wildlife painter and author Arthur Heming (1871-1940) published his first book in 1907, although he had illustrated a book of tales by W.A. Fraser in 1905. He illustrated all of his own books which he continued to publish until late in his life. From 1908-12 he lived at **183 Sherbourne Street**.

Poets Roo Borson (b.1952) and Kim Maltman (b.1950) lived as a couple at **281 Sherbourne** from 1982-83. By coincidence, this address was where Arthur Conan Doyle stayed a century earlier when he first came to Toronto. The creator of Sherlock Holmes was in town to lecture at Massey Hall on November 26, 1894. The house on Sherbourne belonged to Dr. Latimer Pickering, a friend of Doyle's from their days together in Edinburgh. Pickering's wife, Annie, was also a physician, one of the

Toronto Meets British Novelist

Globe announcement of Conan Doyle lecture at Massey Hall, May 15, 1922

first women doctors in the city. A Doyle biographer believes that Doyle "probably based his story 'The Doctors of Hoyland' on what he knew of the Pickerings." Conan Doyle was introduced to the audience at Massey Hall by Goldwin Smith, an appropriate choice, for the Sage of the Grange had given Doyle the first positive review of his work published anywhere in the world— a fact Doyle never forgot. The newspapers gave the talk extensive coverage in advance, including a line drawing of the author, a rare privilege in the 19th c. Press reports describe the turnout as "a very large audience" yet one newspaper said about 1,500 paid admission, a large number to be sure but, still, one that would leave two-thirds of the hall empty. Following the Doyle appearance, there were published complaints about the high cost of admission and speculation that many more would have attended had the cost of admission been more affordable. The next day, Doyle did a quick tour of the city, then continued his lectures around the continent.

Poet David Fujino (b.1945) lived at **No.321** from 1979-81. This building was also where novelist and television broadcaster Daniel Richler (b.1956) lived from April 1984 to 1989 (apt. 507) and where he wrote the first drafts of his novel *Kicking Tomorrow* (1991).

Theodore Goodridge Roberts (1877-1953), younger brother of the more famous Charles G.D. Roberts, moved to Toronto in 1934 and bought a house at **351 Sherbourne** just a few blocks from his brother's residence at Sherbourne and Wellesley. By the time he arrived in Toronto, he had published all of the adventure novels and poetry which garnered him substantial attention in his own lifetime but which sit unread today. He was sufficiently well-regarded by his contemporaries that in the year he moved to Toronto he was elected a Fellow of the Royal Society in Canada. He moved to Ottawa in 1939.

Carlton Street is the next major intersection. The American novelist William Dean Howells (1837-1920) stayed at his father's house, **171 Carlton Street**, for about one week in early October 1879 during a family visit. This handsome row of homes was typical of the upscale housing spawned in this area by the development of Allan Gardens. It was certainly an address appropriate for the senior Howells's occupation: he was the American Consul-General in Toronto. His son was recognized by Lowell, Longfellow, and others of the American literary pantheon as their natural successor. While it is true he was regarded as one of the most important writers in America from his early middle-age onwards, his status as an editor was even higher, for he published not only the older literary lions, but also younger writers such as Mark Twain and Henry James. Howells was also the first important author to applaud the shift to realism in American fiction. Because of his high political connections, William Dean Howells was able to keep a watch on his father's career. Just before the old man moved to Toronto from another post, his son wrote to him on June 2, 1878: "I fancy you will find many agreeable people also in Toronto. I have given a letter of introduction to a nice young fellow who has just gone from St. Johns, N.B. to take charge of *Belford's Monthly* at Toronto. His name is Stewart, and he has a house in the same block with you." Indeed he did. George Stewart (1848-1906) moved to Toronto from Montreal in May 1878 and made his home at **179 Carlton**. His connection to the Belford Brothers lasted for only a year or so, because they refused to pay him royalties on a book he had written. The Belfords claimed (and the courts upheld their claim) that Stewart wrote the book as an employee. He left Toronto to find more congenial employers back in Quebec (Graeme Mercer Adam then took over the editor's chair at *Belford's Monthly*).

Stewart's departure was Toronto's loss, because Stewart had shown himself to be a literary editor of singular determination.

In 1867 he had founded *Stewart's Literary Quarterly Magazine*, a periodical which published only Canadian authors—a remarkable gesture for the time, made even more so by his unusual commitment to celebrating Quebec writers (in translation) as well. After his Toronto years, he continued to promote Canadian authors by writing profiles, brief histories, and critical assessments about them for magazines in the UK and USA. He was a constant traveller to London and big cities in the States where he was friends with many of the chief figures of the book trade (Matthew Arnold, for example, arranged for him to be made an honorary member of the Athenaeum Club). How he maintained his passion for Canadian writing in the face of so much indifference at home remains a marvel. Despite valiant efforts, he died in poverty—and from grief at the sudden passing of his wife. As the *Dictionary of Canadian Biography* remarks, "His letters, stamps, and books were sold to pay creditors. His dream of living by and for good literature had foundered in a society more interested in commerce than in culture."

Short-story writer Roger Burford Mason (1943-98) was installed at **240 Seaton** from April 1989 to November 1997. This was a fruitful place for him to work, as he explained to me in a letter: "I finished 'Bees' here, and wrote and published my second collection *The Beaver Picture* (Hounslow, 1992). At this address I also wrote *Print and Be Damaged* (1994), a memoir of my private press business in the 1970s; *Somewhere Else* (1996), a collection of travel pieces in Europe and North America; *Travels in the Shining Island* (1997), a biography of Rev. James Evans who invented the Cree syllabary which enable the Cree to read books printed in their own language; *Roy Vernon Sowers: A Life in Rare Books* (1997), the biography of one of North America's most erudite and quirky rare book dealers; and *A Grand Eye For Glory: A Life of Franz Johnston* (1998), the first biography of the mostly-unsung founder-member of the Group of Seven."

Roger came to Canada from Britain in 1988. When I asked him what the city meant to him, he replied, "I love Toronto for its rich literary life—festivals everywhere, competitions, book prizes galore—where else does it happen? And I am grateful that, coming here, I was able to extend the tentative writer's life I was attempting in the UK into a real life where writing could provide an income of sorts, some occasional notoriety in the public prints, and a wide network of friends and acquaintances who share these interests. Maybe there are too many of us, and the quality is commensurately thin—but rather that than a narrow, enclosed literary landscape where the singing birds whistle to, and only to, each other and the door opens to admit a new bird so infrequently that its hinges squeak and grind."

Cartoonist and poet J.W. Bengough had a home at **19 Seaton Street** between 1877 and 1880, a period in which he was busy travelling the country giving his famous chalk-talks: humorous lectures augmented by his illustrations drawn on a handy blackboard.

A block to the east is **Ontario Street**. The remarkable Richard T. Lancefield (1854-1911) was a bookseller, author, and thief. Brought to Canada from England he was raised in Hamilton where, in the 1870s, he opened a bookshop and lending library with his brother. The enterprise seems to have faltered, and by 1883 Lancefield had moved to Toronto where, undaunted, he remained involved in the book business, including the fight for a decent Canadian Copyright Act. At the end of the decade Lancefield returned to Hamilton as the city's first public librarian. By all accounts he did an excellent job. Perhaps "accounts" is not the word I want here, for it seems Lancefield's well-disguised addiction to gambling led him to embezzle the accounts and it was not until 1902 that his deceit was unveiled. Interestingly, he was such a charmer that the public's outrage was directed against the library's board of directors for its want of due diligence rather than against the perpetrator. Friends repaid the missing amounts as far as those could be established (Lancefield destroyed the account books which would have been the main evidence against him) and the man was never charged. He kept a low profile in Toronto for several years thereafter. During his first stint in the city he lived at two addresses encountered on this tour. One of them was **430 Ontario** in 1886.

For some years George Henry Doran (1869-1956) was one of three or four most important publishers in the United States—important not only because of the size of his publishing house and the money it made but as well because of the authors (Canadian, British, and American) he introduced to the USA market. Yet few Canadians seem to know that this titan of the book trade was born and raised in Toronto and that, at the end of his life, he returned to the city to live out his final years. His infancy and childhood were spent on a few of the streets we will encounter on this tour. The first address I could find for the Doran family was **274 Ontario** where they lived from 1874-79. The family also lived on the next road east, at **208 Berkeley Street** from 1880-82.

The Dorans were living at **328 Berkeley** when young George quit school to enter publishing, an incident he describes in his memoirs: "One Saturday morning as I was walking up Yonge Street . . . I passed an imposing looking publishing house and bookstore. I discovered at its door a placard reading 'Smart Boy Wanted.' Undaunted, I dared the challenge and presented myself as a potential candidate for the vacancy . . . Upon returning to my home I reported the event of the day to my mother. She was most sympathetic and greatly relieved that my first contact in business promised to be rather closely allied to the professional. The position for which I had applied was in a company bearing the formidable name of the Toronto Willard Tract Depository Limited. In reality, it was the business of one S.R. Briggs, a forceful man in his early forties who had made and lost one or two fortunes in the wholesale lumber business. Whether he turned to religion for solace because his newly acquired deep religious convictions interfered with his lumber business, or because of distress at failure, I never could discover. But the fact remained that he had become a religious zealot, almost a fanatic. . . .

"In those days religious publishing was of considerable importance, for everybody was religious. On Sunday mornings and evenings the streets of Toronto were crowded by thousands of our ultimate customers wending their respective ways cheerfully and devotedly to their several churches . . .

"To meet the business growth the staff was not greatly increased. Our working-hours were, but our pay envelopes gave no evidence of undue inflation . . . These were the days before the great department stores, so individual shops were numerous and relatively prosperous. Good bookshops were to be found in every town of more than one thousand inhabitants. Toronto, with a population of about 150,000 had at least a score of real bookstores owned and operated by highly intelligent booksellers. Toronto was the headquarters of book distribution of the entire Dominion, hence it was the greatest publishing centre in Canada. Thus it attracted representatives from the leading publishing houses of Great Britain and the United States. As I grew older I was enabled to make contacts with these ambassadors from greater courts; to get an enlarged vision of the potentialities of publishing. However, the atmosphere of a big little city in an enormously great but thinly populated country was really metropolitan. We seemed to touch the world at many angles. As individuals we could not be specialists; we were obliged to learn every part of a business . . . The lumberman was really a great merchant. He brought to the minutiae of a business of comparatively small units a breadth of view and the scope of a large industry. So we never thought of ourselves as small or insignificant. We developed commercial precocity and courage."

Between Ontario and Berkeley Streets can be found a former home of the highly regarded American poet and novelist Paulette Jiles (b.1943). She reminisced in a letter, "I lived at **213 Carlton Street** for a couple of years, 1970, 1971, and at that time Cabbagetown was a wonderful area. I loved it. It was a real neighbourhood. There were trees in the yard of the apartment building that hung very close to my window. Streetcars went by outside. I wrote 'Heat Lightning' and 'Garbage Pickup' there, two poems in *Celestial Navigation* (1984). My novel, *The Late Great Human Road Show* (1986), is formed entirely around Cabbagetown, and all the street characters (Sam, and Man-With-No-Nose, and partially, Roxanna, and the street kids) were all taken from real street people in the area that I used to see every day, and all the streets and houses mentioned in the book are descriptions taken from real streets and houses. And the old Riverdale Zoo, that's all accurate, or at least as it was in 1971. A lot has changed, of course. At the time I was freelancing for CBC Radio Public Affairs, and I used to come home late at night in a taxi from editing like a mad person for hours in the Jarvis Street editing rooms, and it would always seem like the city had been evacuated. I loved Toronto. I still do. It's a very special city. But I don't live in cities very well, and so moved out, and went north, back to the landscape. When I come back to Toronto I am lucky to have good friends to stay with who live in the central part of the city, and I wander around and have a good time, and go back and look at Cabbagetown places, and enjoy myself. When I lived there, I was poor and kind of harassed, and trying to learn my way around, but mostly they are all very good memories."

Charles (1837-80) was the eldest of the Belford Brothers, printers who, by their piracy, infuriated Mark Twain and other bestselling American authors whose books they published without permission or payment. The first address I could find for

Charles Belford was **262 Parliament Street,** where he lived from 1862-65. The three Belford brothers came here from Ireland in 1857. Charles immediately entered into newspaper work (he was the first editor of the *Mail*) and Conservative politics. In 1876 he went into the publishing business with his brothers, if publishing is the term to describe the blatant theft of text and royalties from foreign writers. Under the mess of our copyright laws at the time, what they did was legal although obviously unethical. It must be said in their defence, however, that the American publishers who cried foul at the Belfords' actions were doing the same thing to English authors in the USA.

Some of the Belford Brothers' profits were put into the production of a handsome literary magazine, *Belford's Monthly*, and the publishing of a few books by Canadian authors. By 1878, however, Charles Belford was in ill health, and he retired from the business. Within a couple of years he was dead from exhaustion.

Spruce Street runs east from Parliament just south of Carlton. When novelist Barbara Gowdy (b.1950) moved into **19 Spruce** in 1997, she was not aware the area was popular in the wee hours of the morning with unsavoury characters. She was not long in looking for new accommodation. Nonetheless, in the year or so she was at this address she managed to write much of her novel *The White Bone* (1998).

No.82 was the first home in Toronto for the Milne family after they arrived in Toronto in 1913. One of the children, W.S. Milne (b.1902) would later become an English teacher at Northern Secondary by day, and by night a specialist in playwriting and drama production. All of the one-act plays he wrote himself were performed in Canada, several of them during the Dominion Drama Festivals. For *Saturday Night, Canadian Forum, Billboard*, and other magazines he wrote many articles documenting the progress of the Little Theatre movement in

Canada—for decades, the only outlet for Canadian authors of plays. He and his family lived at **82 Spruce** until 1922. Death came for him in 1979.

When Mavor Moore (b.1919) lived at **147 Spruce** from 1976-78, he was writing less and doing much of the unthanked but necessary leg work for the flourishing of arts organizations in this country. He joined the Canada Council (becoming its Chair in 1979). Also while living here he was elected the founding Chair of the Guild of Canadian Playwrights, a body which later evolved into today's Playwrights' Union of Canada.

Crossing Spruce near its middle is **Sackville Street**. The first domicile of ex-librarian Richard Lancefield during his "honest years" in Toronto was **317 Sackville Street**. This was his home from 1883-85.

In 1976, when he lived at **336 Sackville**, the public and critical reaction to David French's play *One Crack Out* was so disappointing to him that he gave serious thought to abandoning the theatre altogether. However, director Bill Glassco commissioned him to write a new translation of Chekhov's *The Seagull*, and he worked on that translation while living at this address for about one year.

Novelist and anthologist Sarah Sheard, after a *wanderjahr* in Europe, made a brief occupation of rooms at **No.365** in 1973, but did no writing here that has been published. By coincidence, the same house was the home of novelist and distinguished children's author Tim Wynne-Jones (b.1948). He returned to Toronto in 1974 after an aborted career as a rock musician, this time with a new bride and baby. After short stays all over the map, they finally settled into this row house. Tim elucidated in a letter: "I worked in publishing for the first year or two, down at 35 Britain Street where lots of little presses were holed up: Anansi, James Lorimer, and Peter Martin Associates (later PMA Books) for whom I worked as a designer.

"I wrote my first major published manuscript, *Odd's End*, which won the [$50,000] Seal First Novel Award, at **365 Sackville Street** in Cabbagetown . . . I was inspired to write the novel having just finished my M.V.A. at York University and wanting to have nothing more to do with the visual arts world! I set the book in Nova Scotia, as far away from Toronto as I could afford to get on a rented typewriter (a Corona, by the way, which jumped every time I pressed the return button—those were the bad old days) . . . My next book, *The Knot*, was set in Cabbagetown, though, by then, we had moved."

At the invitation of the Ontario College of Art, the American poet Burton Raffel (b.1928) moved to Toronto to be Senior Tutor. At the time, it seemed like a good idea he told me, and he happily moved into **No.374**, little suspecting that he was walking into a maelstrom and battle among teachers, administration, board, and province such as the College had never seen before or has seen since. Burton referred to it in a letter as "a brawling, divisive, unpleasant year." He then joined the faculty of York University and taught there for three more years. He told me that while his Toronto academic memories are not his greatest, he will always have a soft spot for the city because it was here he met his wife, Elizabeth Clare Raffel. They have since collaborated on a couple of novels, *Founder's Fury* (1988) and *Founder's Fortune* (1989).

Novelist M.T. Kelly (b.1947), winner of the Governor General's Award for his novel *A Dream Like Mine*, now lives in a fine house in the Annex. But from 1981-82 his economic circumstances were such that he lived in a less than salubrious room at **275 Carlton Street**. While here, he worked on his play *The Green Dolphin*, first performed at Theatre Passe Muraille.

Flos Jewell Williams (b.1893) moved to Calgary in 1915 and it is in the farmlands and oilfields of the west where most of her novels are set. In her lifetime, the books were given polite reviews in Toronto newspapers, but since her undated death, her work has disappeared from the literary radar—at least in eastern Canada. She passed her infancy and youth at **415 Carlton Street**, remaining here until c. 1910.

When the distinguished American novelist Don DeLillo (b.1936) moved to Toronto in the fall of 1975, he and his wife installed themselves at **417 Carlton** and remained at this address until June 1976, when they moved to Ottawa Street near Yonge. During his stay in Cabbagetown, DeLillo informed me, he wrote all of his novel *Players* (1977). It was not until he wrote *The Names* (1982), however, that Toronto appears meaningfully in his fiction.

At the east end of Carlton Street is a lane that runs south along the brim of the Don Valley. As you stand here admiring the bucolic scene along the riverbank and the dale, be aware that more than a century ago, on this very spot, once stood a man who conversed with vampires.

The great 19th c. English actors Henry Irving and Ellen Terry came to Toronto with their stage manager Bram Stoker (and about 75 other stage crew) in February 1884 as part of a North American tour. The principals of the troupe were invited to join a local expedition of the Toronto Toboggan Club. The newspaper accounts do not cite the actual location of the outing, but a toboggan slide was once located at this point in the Riverdale ravine and so this seems the most likely spot. Ellen Terry and Bram Stoker (1847-1912) had never seen a toboggan before, and were exhilarated by the slide, and especially by the downhill speed they attained. Stoker apparently had trouble keeping his balance, and frequently fell off the toboggan, tumbling and somersaulting down the hillside, flapping his arms like a bird—or, as some say, like a bat—because Bram Stoker was the author of *Dracula* (1897), the famous novel about the undead. As you imagine the white snow on the hillside here, scare yourself a little by picturing Count Dracula's creator standing where you now stand, dressed in his black winter clothes, his cape flourished menacingly, his arms akimbo and raised, and you do not know, as his unblinking gaze momentarily seizes yours whether he is about to descend to the depths—or fly away.

Follow the lane to the next street south, **Geneva Avenue**. Facing you is **45 Geneva**, the home of man of letters Alberto Manguel (b.1948) from December 1983 to spring 1994. This house was a good place for Manguel to work for he wrote a number of popular and well-received books at this address, including his novel *News From a Foreign Country Came* (1991). Among the anthologies he compiled here were *Canadian Mystery Stories* (1991), *Dark Arrows: Chronicles of Revenge* (1985), *Evening Games: Chronicles of Parents and Children* (1986), *The Gates of Paradise: An Anthology of Erotic Fiction* (1993), *Meanwhile in Another Part of the Forest: Gay Stories from Alice Munro to Yukio Mishima* (1994), and *Other Fires: Short Fiction by Latin American Women* (1986). Alberto once told me, "Toronto is the best of imaginary places because it doesn't overwhelm you with its presence. It allows you to build upon it, and to invent your own stories for its landscape."

Geneva terminates at **Sumach Street**. When Bernard McEvoy (1842-1932) came to Canada from England he had hoped to work as a bridge engineer on a huge railway construction project. But he no sooner arrived than the government reneged on its promise to build the line, and McEvoy was forced to fall back on his writing skills to support his family. He settled in Toronto c. 1889 and lived at **293 Sumach Street** until 1893 when he then moved to **484 Ontario** for about three more years. During most of this period he worked as a reporter at the *M&E*. In his Toronto years he wrote and published poems which were highly regarded at the time, far above the usual newspaper verse in quality. One of the books, *Away from Newspaperdom and Other Poems* (1898) was illustrated by the noted Canadian painter G.A. Reid. In 1902 he moved to Vancouver where he worked at the *Province* until he died, boasting until the end that he was the oldest working daily journalist in the world.

Novelist Douglas Coupland (b.1961) was living in B.C. planning a career for himself as a visual artist when he was invited to Toronto to work as a fact checker and occasional writer on a new magazine about to be founded by a Toronto business magnate. Coupland (*Generation X* (1994); *Shampoo Planet* (1992); *Girlfriend in a Coma* (1998)) arrived in Toronto on Labour Day, 1988. He remained in the city for only a year, but it was a year that would prove pivotal—because it was while living in this city that he decided to abandon a visual arts career and become a novelist. For the first six months of his stay he had a flat at **295 Sumach**.

The first novel featuring the lesbian sleuth Helen Keremos was written by Eve Zaremba (b.1930) when she lived in a two-room cottage at **30 Sword Street** (razed). Since then Zaremba has written half a dozen Keremos mysteries, and with each book, her Canadian and international audience grows.

The noted science fiction author S.M. Stirling (b.1954) is now a resident of the USA. In 1987, however, he moved to a co-op flat on the fifth floor at **50 Cornwall Street**, a most fertile address for him as an author (when he married in 1990, he moved into apt. 803). Here he wrote *Marching Through Georgia* (1988), *The Cage* (1989), *Under the Yoke* (1989), *The Stone Dogs* (1990), *The Forge* (1991), and *Shadow's Sun* (1991) among others. Why he left Toronto in 1995 may be gleaned from a comment he made to me about the city: "Toronto is an ideal city for a writer—except for the cost of living! The libraries, bookshops, the congenial and stimulating company of my peers, and the fact that you can find out *anything* make it a continual delight—and distraction."

Near the south end of River Street is the area that was well known to novelist Hugh Garner. In his autobiography, he discussed in unsentimental tones his many abodes in this area and the area immediately to the south of this tour: "Most of Cabbagetown was eradicated after WWII and replaced by government-subsidised housing known as Regent Park North and Regent Park South. I used an amalgam of Wascana Avenue and Blevins Place, a couple of blocks north of it running east from Sumach, as 'Timothy Place' in my novel *Cabbagetown*.

"It's not quite coincidental that so many of the houses I lived in during my childhood have since been torn down . . . Houses I lived in on Sumach and Ontario Streets have gone too. Other houses I lived in on Steiner Street, Metcalf, Wellesley, Berkeley and other 'inner city' streets have either been torn down or have been completely forgotten by me."

CAWTHRA SQUARE

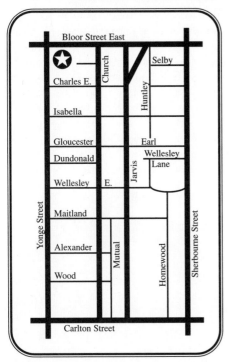

The tour begins at the southeast corner of Yonge Street and Bloor Street East.

O n Bloor East, where shops now stand, there once was a mix of modest and grand homes. **85 Bloor Street East** was the home for a few months of Sigmund Freud's colleague and biographer Ernest Jones (1879-1958) immediately after Jones arrived in Toronto in September 1908. In his first letter to Freud he told the Master that he found Toronto delightful, a sentiment that would rapidly devolve to loathing by the time he quit us some years later.

The 19th c. numbering of houses has changed so much along the blocks of Bloor immediately east of Yonge that being specific about current equivalents is risky. Suffice it to say that Sir Daniel Wilson (1816-92), poet, scientist, and long-time President of the UofT lived in a grand mansion on the

south side of Bloor East near Church from 1856-81. A neighbour would have been the boy Hector Charlesworth and his family. Charlesworth (1872-1945) later wrote three charming books of memoirs about his many years as one of the leading arts journalists in Canada. In one of them, *Candid Chronicles* (1925), he reminds us that Toronto once stopped at Bloor: "I remember vividly my first arrival in Toronto one bright autumn day in 1876 when I had just turned four years old. It was in the old, domed train shed, which still forms part of Union Station, and I have still the picture of my father . . . running along the platform to help my mother down with the babies. It was, so far as I know, the occasion of my first ride in a hack; and the vehicle drew up in front of a little house on the south side of a hot road on which the yellow sand lay deeply rutted. This was on **Bloor Street East** on the northern fringe of what was then the city of Toronto. It seemed strange to me to be told that while I stayed in my own front yard I was in Toronto, but that if I broke rules and crossed the road, I would be in another place, Yorkville."

Writer Marjory MacMurchy had a rather grand home at **133 Bloor East** from 1904-15. One of her house guests was novelist, dramatist, and old friend Sara Jeannette Duncan. Duncan stayed at the MacMurchy household from January 1-10, 1915, during the rehearsals and premiere of her play *His Royal Happiness* at the Princess Theatre. On another occasion, another guest was her friend Nellie McClung. In fact, the first public reception ever held for McClung in Toronto was hosted by MacMurchy at this home in late November 1910.

The historical novelist Carrie Holmes MacGillivray (d.1949) was resident at **155**

Bloor East from 1937 until her death. She loved Ontario history. A long-time employee of the Archives of Ontario, she dealt in her fiction with the province's past. When she died, William Arthur Deacon approvingly quoted Dorothy Dumbrille as saying that MacGillivray's *The Shadow of Tradition* "deserves a much better circulation than it achieved. Fortunately it is now in a second edition."

St. Paul's Anglican Church, **227 Bloor East**, has a modest lecture hall tucked in behind the main building. At least three authors have given public lectures here: Ralph Connor, Toyohiko Kagawa, and B.K. Sandwell.

Return to **Jarvis Street**. Historian and poet Edgar McInnis (1899-1973) lived longer at **611 Jarvis** than at any other of his Toronto addresses. He made this his home from 1935-47. He was a Rhodes Scholar at the UofT (where he won the Jardine Prize for poetry in 1922) and while at Oxford he won the Newdigate Prize for his verse writing. Sensitivity to language distinguishes his many books on history and international relations, and accounts in part for why his work was read by many outside of the academic world as well as by those in it.

Politician True Davidson (1901-78) always regarded herself as a poet above all else, and published her work during her earliest years as an adult. While struggling to make a living as a teacher, she lived at **581 Jarvis** from 1934-38. E.E. Sheppard, once the editor of the *News* and then the founding editor of *Saturday Night*, lived at **No.578** from 1890-1907.

Near here is the end of **Charles Street East**. The father of forensic science in Ontario and published poet, William Hodgson Ellis (1845-1920) lived at **99 Charles East** for the last four years of the 1870s. Across the street at **No.98** was a building known as La Plaza Apartments. In apt. 2, poet and literary historian Katherine Hale (1878-1956) passed two decades, 1933-52, during which she wrote a number of books,

including *The Island and Other Poems* (1934), *This Is Ontario* (history, 1937), and *The Flute and Other Poems* (1950). Hale supported herself throughout the Depression by giving public lectures on an astonishing variety of literary topics. She chose her venues well, for newspaper reports always describe the lectures as well-attended or full. Peregrine Acland (1891-1963), author of the novel *All Else Is Folly*, praised by Bertrand Russell and Ford Madox Ford, also had a flat in this building from 1924-25. **98 Charles East** was E.E. Sheppard's home for several years: apt. 5 from 1908-22 to be specific.

James Bain

James Bain (1842-1908) became the city's first librarian in 1883 and held the post until his death. Bain directed the development of the entire library system. He is given high marks by today's librarians for the job he did. But he is also to be thanked for so diligently seeking out Canadiana at a time when the material was still available and affordable, and few other libraries bothered. He sought historical

74

manuscripts, documents, ephemera as well as books—books of history, travel, exploration, politics, as well as a collection of Canadian fiction and poetry unsurpassed in the world. His home from 1886 until 1906 was **90 Charles East**.

Poet Miriam Waddington (b.1917) lived in apt. 7 of **632 Church Street** from 1940-45 as she explained in her memoir: "In 1940, a year after our marriage, my husband and I moved into a three-room apartment on the top floor of an old limestone building on the corner of Church and Charles in Toronto. We fell in love with the gabled roof and slanted ceilings, and most especially with the large gravelled area surrounded by a brick wall outside our living room door." At the time, Waddington worked as a translator and then editor for *Magazine Digest* just long enough to realize that she wanted to do something else with her life. So she enrolled at the School of Social Work at the UofT, which proved an eye-opener: "During my field work with the Toronto Public Welfare Department, which operated with untrained and often uneducated workers, I came into contact for the first time in my life with real poverty; unmarried mothers, women with husbands or sons in jail, syphilitics in the last stage of paresis, retarded parents who couldn't cope with their children, chronic tubercular patients and their families. It shook me to the depths of my being."

Another important 19th c. literary figure who lived in this small area was J.W. Bengough (1851-1923). In 1873, Bengough had founded the humour magazine *Grip*, where he published many of his cartoons, a few of which were so wickedly on target about the Pacific Scandal that historians agree they had a hand in bringing down the government of John A. Macdonald. When Toronto-born Bengough was ensconced at **No.66** from 1905-11, he was still giving his famous chalk-talks across the continent to large and very appreciative audiences. In essence, chalk-talks were humorous speeches interrupted by his own illustration of his remarks on a nearby blackboard. Throughout his life he also wrote and published poems, and at this address he published his last book of verse, *In Many Keys* (1902). One of the few historical plaques in Toronto dedicated to a cultural figure is found at this address.

The Charlesview, an apartment-hotel at **No.55**, is where novelist Stephen Vizinczey (*In Praise of Older Women*) usually stayed when he visited Toronto. He lived there for the spring and summer of 1980, and had another lengthy stay from November 1985 to May 1986. During this latter stop Vizinczey (b.1933) rewrote and expanded many of the essays and reviews in his book *Truth and Lies in Literature* (1986). When novelist Josef Skvorecky (b.1924) and his wife, Zdena, owners of 68 Publishers, landed in Toronto their first address was this same apartment-hotel. They remained here throughout February and March 1969 before heading to the USA for a few months. They returned to this address in September 1969. It was their home until May 1970.

The inventor of the word "cyberspace" and one of our pre-eminent science fiction writers, William Gibson (b.1948), came to Toronto from the USA in 1967 and lived in this city until 1971. He confessed to me that he could recall only two of his addresses from that period, and one of those was **23 Isabella Street** "where I lived in a rented room in 1968, in a memorable row of very decrepit Victorian houses." Later in his letter he stated, "Virtually everything in Toronto that might have become serious nostalgia-fodder for me—the original Pilot Tavern, say—was either torn down or cleaned up beyond recognition by 1972. The only part of the city that retains a special magic for me is Kensington Market (where I never lived)."

Next to nothing is known of the early biography of novelist Annie Gregg Savigny (d.1901). And even though she was very prominent in Toronto as a woman of letters, so little was—is—really known about her that she may have been only 53 when she died, not 75 as some believed. All of her fiction for adults and juveniles is set in Toronto. Biographical data concerning her less-celebrated husband are more readily available, and it is by tracking his addresses that we know Annie Gregg lived at **43 Isabella** in 1888 and 1889. While living here she published her second novel, *A Romance of Toronto* (1888). The last ten years of her life were spent at **No.49**.

One of Canada's best poets, Earle Birney (1904-95), forced out of his Hazelton Avenue flat because the landlord did not permit children, moved into the ground-floor rooms of an old house at **No.45 Isabella** in December 1942. With his wife and new child he remained here until he went overseas to fight in WWII on May 5, 1943. In July 1945, his war duty done, he returned to his family at this address, but by September he had resigned his teaching post at the UofT and moved to Montreal to work for the CBC.

Lionel Stevenson (1902-73) was a *wunderkind* as a student, getting his PhD from the University of California at the age of 23, at the time the youngest person in that university's history to receive a doctorate. A native of Edinburgh, he came to Canada as a young child, settling with his parents on the west coast where he got his BA. He decided to come to Toronto for his master's degree and lived at **50 Isabella** throughout the 1922-23 academic year. His first two books were volumes of his own poetry, published by Ryerson Press. But after that, he published immensely popular biographies that combined scholarly accuracy with ease of comprehension. Among these books were *The Showman of Vanity Fair* (a life of Thackeray; 1947) and *The Ordeal of George Meredith* (1945). For approximately the last 29 years of his life he was a senior professor at Duke University and yet was known across the continent as one of the leading theorists of

literary biography. He had several friends in Toronto and made frequent trips to the city, during which he was sometimes called on to give public talks.

When novelist Grace Irwin (b.1907) lived at **No.72** from the summer of 1925 until May 1927, her mother insisted that Grace continue to study at Parkdale Collegiate. A good thing, too, because just one semester later, Grace won so many prizes and scholarships, the *Star* ran her picture on the front page, (December 4, the day the news was announced), along with a long caption documenting her academic achievements. Mother and daughter returned to the west end of the city in 1927, and Grace has lived there ever since.

BRILLIANT PARKDALE STUDENT

Grace Irwin as she appeared on the front page of the *Star*, December 4, 1925

Novelist Ethel Chapman (c. 1900-76) lived for almost half her life in apt. 25 at **81 Isabella**: 1939-74. She was an early female graduate in Home Economics at the University of Guelph and one of her first jobs was going across the country teaching farm wives and daughters about nutrition and healthy cooking. By 1927 she had switched to journalism as a profession but continued to concentrate on domestic matters in her writing. Her first novel appeared in 1922 and her last just the year before she moved to this apartment. Thereafter, for reasons unknown, she published no more creative writing.

Although associated by most readers with the west coast, poet Phyllis Webb (b.1927) moved to Toronto from Montreal in 1965 to work in the Public Affairs Department of the CBC as a program organizer in both radio and TV. She remained here for four years, and one of her accomplishments in radio was creating the long-running program "Ideas." Her first two years in Toronto were spent in apt. 34 at **83 Isabella**. She wrote to me, "Toronto has always meant, apart from the CBC, and even including writers I worked with or met at CBC, friendship with other writers who have been important to me. For instance, I met Timothy Findley in 1965 when he was still doing radio work, both as an actor and radio script writer . . . It means memories of ferry trips to Ward's island . . . Toronto took over my affections from Montreal [only] after I left Toronto."

The novelist and painter Wyndham Lewis maintained a studio at **86-A Isabella** from June 1941 until June 1943. This locale was close to his home at the Tudor Hotel on Sherbourne Street, discussed in the Cabbagetown tour.

Sometimes regarded as one of our more underrated poets of mid-century, R.G. Everson (1903-92) spent his last two Toronto years, 1930-31, boarding at **No.93**. A native of Burlington, Everson graduated from the UofT in 1927 (E.J. Pratt was his English professor), then went to Osgoode. Although admitted to the bar in 1930 he never practised but rather worked as a freelance writer before joining a PR firm.

He eventually settled in Montreal. His most important books were published between 1957 and 1970, although serious book collectors would love to get their hands on the pulp fiction he wrote for American publishers in the twenties and thirties to help make ends meet. He was married in Parkdale United Church on April 15, 1931, after which he and his bride moved to Muskoka.

Fiction writer Joyce Marshall (b.1913) had one of her longest stretches at one Toronto address in apt. 304 of **105 Isabella**; she was here from 1968-80. During this time she put the finishing polish to her short-story collection *A Private Place* (1975). This building was also the residence of mystery writer Anthony Quogan (b.1937) shortly after he arrived in Toronto from his native Britain (after landing in Canada he had roomed at the YMCA while apartment-hunting). His mystery writing did not start until he was at other addresses.

Joyce Marshall photographed in Toronto c. 1940

Barbara Gowdy (b.1950) lived in apt. B at **67 Gloucester** from September 1976 to February 1977. Then she moved to **No.60** (apt. 704) and remained there until September 1977. At the time she was not writing fiction. Rather, she was editing the novels of others at Lester & Orpen Dennys.

She had started to work there in 1974 and eventually rose to the rank of managing editor before quitting in 1979 to write her own books.

Pulp writer Thomas Kelley (1905-82) became nationally famous when he published *The Black Donnellys* (1954), and cemented his notoriety with *The Vengeance of The Black Donnellys* (1956). But prior to these successes he had written untold numbers of books and articles as a result of a blizzard, as he explained in an article: "With the wind whistling along Toronto's Yonge Street on a February day in 1937, I stepped before the window of a millinery store to dodge an oncoming snow-swirl. My eyes fell upon the heads of several window mannequins, adorned with hats of various styles. That did it. 'Heads,' I thought. 'Heads without bodies that have lived for centuries. Such an idea could be made into a whale of a yarn.' The next moment I was hurrying to my small apartment, determined to think up some literary gem. I had no way of knowing that during the years ahead I was to write and sell more than seven hundred stories, an output of more than eight million words." It took him 11 days to write by longhand the 60,000 words of his story. He sent it to *Weird Tales*, and they sent him 500 dollars, a miraculous sum during the Depression. Kelley was hooked, and as a result the world was subsequently blessed with *Riders of the Plains*, *Bad Men of Canada*, *Wicked Women of Canada*, *Deadshot Riders*, *Fast on the Draw*, and *Six-Shooters at Sundown* among many other books published under his own name and at least 30 pseudonyms. It remains to be determined when he arrived at **86 Gloucester**, but he was definitely there from 1978-80 when awkward personal circumstances forced him to move.

Susan Frances Harrison (1859-1935), who published under the pseudonym "Seranus," lived at **94 Gloucester** from 1889-92. She became one of the first Canadian authors of either sex to read her work in public in Toronto. The *Mail* reported on November 20, 1891: "Mrs. Harrison is to be congratulated on the success of her reading last Monday, and the invited guests who were present owe to the Modern Language Club of Toronto University a debt of gratitude for a delightful afternoon. This flourishing club has frequently discussed Canadian literature, but it has not hitherto had the opportunity of listening to one so gifted as 'Seranus' in poetry, prose and elocution . . . The example of the Modern Language Club will, it is to be hoped, be imitated by those who desire to widen the acquaintance of Canadians with their own literature, which, it would almost seem, must first win recognition abroad in order to be appreciated at home." She was a master of the villanelle, and at this reading gave voice to some of the poems that appeared in her collection *Pine, Rose and Fleur-de-lis* (1891). She also wrote novels.

Susan Frances Harrison

Thomas Stinson Jarvis (1854-1926), I trust, would have bid "Good morning" to Seranus since he lived just across the street at

No.89 from 1889-91. A criminal lawyer, he put his experience with law-breakers to good use with his first novel, *Geoffrey Hamstead*, published by a major American house in New York in 1890 (while he was living on Gloucester). The murder mystery is set in Toronto, and the book was said to have been the most widely reviewed novel that year in the USA. Jarvis seems to have stopped counting after the 163rd review arrived in the mail. The book's incredible success induced him to throw over his law practice, move to the States and lead a leisurely life of travel and occasional book-writing.

Three authors lived at **100 Gloucester Street.** Earle Birney, mentioned above, returned to Toronto in the late summer of 1936, having accepted a teaching job at the UofT, determined to carry on the Trotskyite Revolution. He was not married to the woman he had been living with in Europe, and in prissy Toronto that just would not do, so, as he told me one day, "we got single rooms across the street from each other on Gloucester Street. Back then, it was almost a depressed street. What we were trying to do was get one room in the same house. But we couldn't. So we got rooms with front windows so we could sort of signal across the street." He seems to have lived here until the following summer.

By the late 1950s Birney's rooming house had been replaced by a high-rise. Apt. 1104 of **100 Gloucester** was Peregrine Acland's final address in Toronto. He lived here from 1960 until his death in May 1963. Acland (*All Else Is Folly*) had been a major with the 48th Highlanders in WWI and was given the Military Cross. At the Battle of the Somme he was severely wounded. Following the first war he worked in advertising in New York, and later Toronto. I wasn't able to ascertain if he was in the city when one of his poems was read at the unveiling of the Queen's Park statue dedicated to the 48th Highlanders. During WWII he was on the private staff of Prime Minister Mackenzie King.

The science fiction writer Garfield Reeves-Stevens lived in apt. 911 in this same building from 1974-77. It was here that he wrote for the first time as a professional, contributing to the first volume of *The Friendship of Edna McCann*. He was one of five "Ednas."

In the block of **Church Street** between Gloucester and Dundonald, at **No.592,** lived one of Ireland's most important living poets, Derek Mahon (b.1941). He wrote in a letter: "I spent six months in Toronto, October 1966 to March 1967, in the course of my American wander-years, and lived at two addresses: first, by myself, in a tiny room on Prince Arthur [street number unknown], then, sharing with two others, at Gloucester Mansions on Church Street . . . During the six months in Toronto I had three jobs in succession: in the UofT Bookstore, as a night telephonist in the CBC offices, and teaching English to immigrants in a Canadian Government programme. I spent nearly the entire time in Toronto itself, with one weekend in Montreal. There were no exciting visits to the Arctic Circle or anything like that; no outdoors stuff at all, except trudging around in the ice and snow. I had no literary contacts—never, at the time, met Kildare Dobbs or Barry Callaghan, for example—though I once glimpsed Pierre Berton (whom I'd seen on TV) in the lobby of, I think, the Royal York Hotel, where I'd just got a haircut. What took me to Canada I can't now recall, or why I stayed six months, because I knew virtually nobody and had no particular reason to be there. Maybe that was it: I didn't really know *where* I wanted to be at that point in my life, so I might as well be on the moon. I'm sorry if this sounds uncomplimentary; but you know yourself how Toronto strikes some visitors. I never gave it a chance, of course . . . I apologize for the appallingly negative tone of this letter, which has more to do with me than with Toronto; and I'm happy, for all our sakes, that the city is so much more fun now than it was thirty years ago."

Novelist and *Star* book columnist Philip Marchand (b.1946), while pursuing his bachelor's degree at St. Michael's College, lived in the same building at about the same time.

Poet James L. Hughes (1846-1935) lived at **47 Dundonald Street** from 1908 until his death at this address at the venerable age of 89 in 1935. A mere five years before, Hughes had set tongues wagging throughout the city when he married a woman about 50 years his junior. In case anyone missed the gossip, the *Star* ran a prominently placed photo of the lusty old gent with his comely bride on its front page. As an educationist, Hughes was regarded as strongly progressive by his contemporaries. For over 40 years he had been the supervisor of all school inspectors in the city, and for those four decades led an unsuccessful effort to have corporal punishment banned from the schools. He was also opposed to exams. At his death, every school in the city flew its flag at half-mast out of respect for his years of dedication to improved schooling, and the obituaries focused on his fame as a pedagogue throughout the USA and Canada.

When novelist and broadcaster Daniel Richler moved from Montreal to Toronto in the summer of 1981, he settled at **49 Dundonald** and remained there until the early months of 1984. While living at this address he worked at radio station CFNY and then, in 1983, began working in TV by hosting "The New Music" at CITY. His first novel was published in 1991.

An as-yet-to-be ascertained address on **Dundonald Street** was also the run-down, rooming-house home for some months in the 1970s of the talented but mentally ill novelist Juan Butler (1942-81). Man of letters Douglas Fetherling recalled visiting Butler at this time: "In the foyer was a crudely lettered sign imploring the residents in broken English to please flush the communal toilet. When one visited Juan there of an evening to talk about writing, the conversation would be punctuated by an horrendously loud thwack! coming from the room immediately above, followed by a light shower of plaster dust from Juan's ceiling. The space overhead was occupied by a man who enjoyed lying abed while trying to kill cockroaches with a ten-foot bullwhip."

Barbara Gowdy, encountered a few pages back, lived in the third-floor (rear apartment) of **64 Wellesley Street East** from January to September 1976. Across the road at **No.85** Winnipeg native Candace Cael Carman lived with her new husband (they were married in Toronto City Hall) in apt. 904 from October 1, 1985 until July 1988. While here she wrote most of the short stories and poems which have been published in magazines (her two poetry books were published in 1980 and 1981). Considering the insect-welcome she had, it is a wonder she stayed: "My introduction to Toronto was a black rain of cockroaches falling upon me as I pulled the old wallpaper off the wall in the new Toronto highrise apartment.

"I came to call Toronto the City of Infinite Gray. Each day of winter brought a new gray—a different shade, tint, or tone. The dramatic shifts of prairie weather were absent in this southern clime. The summers seemed luxurious, the foliage almost tropical. I wrote home about the Garden of Eden.

"My writing, art, and photography are collections of experiences—the visceral elements that stimulate me in this urban environment. I am a collector. Toronto is a collector. We have something in common. Toronto is not home, although it feels more like home than where I grew up. It is a dynamic transit point, a crossroads and the magic of the crossroads surrounds it."

Apt. 3 of **91 Wellesley East** was the earliest Toronto address of John de Navarre Kennedy (b.1888). He moved to this flat in 1921 shortly after arriving in Toronto from B.C. to become a partner in a Bay Street law firm. Kennedy authored *In the Shadow of the Cheka* (1935), a popular espionage thriller written on a bet that he could not write a bestseller about a country (Russia) he had never visited. He wrote one other novel, a clever mystery *Crime In Reverse* (1939), as well as other books including the not-so-exciting *History of the Department of Munitions and Supply* (1950).

483 Church Street, between Wellesley and Maitland, has been the address since 1986 of This Ain't The Rosedale Library, a bookshop popular with those seeking leading-edge fiction by small presses, and books of special interest to gays and lesbians. The store was named "as a smart-ass response to the Toronto social scene," according to Charlie Huisken (b.1949), one of the founders. He is quick to emphasize that the store's name is not intended as a slight against librarians. As it happens there is no Rosedale Library. Authors who have worked as sales clerks in the store at this location include Lisa Downe and Gillian Anderson.

Poet Earle Birney lived and worked briefly in rooms at **484 Church** in 1987, and bestselling novelist Charles Templeton (b.1915) did likewise in 1959. Elizabeth Rhett Woods (b.1940) wrote her first novel, *The Yellow Volkswagen* (Simon & Schuster, 1971), when she lived at **489 Church** between November 1968 and March 1970. Douglas Fetherling (b.1949) fondly recalled in one of his memoirs his visits to this address: "Elizabeth Woods was about ten years older than I was, tall and slender with a strong face and straight dark hair that hung down to her waist. She had been, briefly, one of the volunteers who flitted in and out of the Anansi basement . . . She invited me to her small apartment upstairs over a shop on the east side of Church Street between Wellesley and Maitland (almost the entire west side being vacant land in those days). . . . One announced oneself at the apartment—two small bedrooms, a tiny living room, and a kitchen with a dangerously slanting floor—by pulling a string that dangled down from the unenclosed summer porch, activating a small cowbell that hung on a nail upstairs . . . It had been, I believe,

Liz's destiny since adolescence in Prince George, B.C., to preside over some sort of salon, and she had quickly made **489 Church** (a different building stands there now) into a sort of all-night drop-in centre for poets and performers . . . One was Patrick Lane, who had known Liz in high school, and would come by whenever he was in Toronto on poetry business and regale us with stories of logging and hunting and working on fire crews. And it was at **489 Church** that I first became aware that Juan Butler . . . was in fact slipping into madness."

Thus far, Toronto-born novelist Eliza Clark (b.1963) has not written about her hometown. The American South, as she says, is the place that speaks to her heart and imagination. Nonetheless, she has been nominated for both the Trillium Award and the Stephen Leacock Award (for her novel *Miss You Like Crazy*, 1991). From August 1981 until September 1986 her home was **36 Maitland Street**.

Sound and concrete poet bill bissett (lower case spelling at his request; b.1939) lived in rooms at **54 Maitland Street** in 1991, and because the grass is always greener on the other side of the street, he moved in 1993 to **55 Maitland** where he remained for approximately another year. The short-story writer and novelist Peter McGehee (1956-91) passed his last six years at this same address. The Arkansas-born writer moved to Toronto in 1983 and is remembered primarily for his novel *Boys Like Us* (1991), written here. The novel's protagonist is a homosexual and the book touches on the impact of AIDS on the gay community. According to his friends, McGehee little knew when writing the novel that he would die from the disease, aged 35.

Buddies In Bad Times, the theatre at **12 Alexander Street,** was originally known as Toronto Workshop Productions. Created by stage-director George Luscombe, TWP is generally considered the first alternative theatre in Toronto, i.e., the first offering non-commercial fare as part of an ongoing schedule. TWP had its beginnings in donated space at 47 Fraser Avenue in Parkdale, where Luscombe (1926-99), heavily influenced by Joan Littlewood's Theatre Workshop in England, hoped to produce an ensemble of actors trained intensely in the thespian arts and prepared to do *engagé* theatre by left-of-centre playwrights. The company moved to Alexander Street in 1967 where it endured a disastrous fire, and a never-ending battle with debt and creditors, and occasionally hostile reviewers. But no one ever doubted Luscombe's integrity or commitment, and he had just enough spectacular artistic successes to make even his fiercest critics admit that he had greatly enlivened the Toronto arts environment. Luscombe resigned as Artistic Director in 1986. His ensemble approach to theatre-making, wherein the playwright is just one among many and not *primus inter pares*, meant, of course, that he was never popular with playwrights. They tended to work with him once, but found the experience so draining, they rarely repeated it. Yet, despite all the pain, TWP produced some of the finest moments in Toronto theatre in the last decades of the 20th c.

Poet Richard Outram was married in April 1957 in what was then his home at **26 Alexander Street**, and he lived here throughout most of 1957. Radio playwright Lister Sinclair also lived briefly on this street, at **No.31** in 1981. Sports writer and fiction writer Scott Young (b.1918) took a bachelor apartment in this same building following the breakup of his marriage in 1959. He lived here until he remarried in 1961. While living here, he continued as a *G&M* columnist by day. By night he wrote the non-fiction text to

accompany photos by Gilbert Milne; the resulting book was published in 1960 as *HMCS*.

Horace Brown (1908-96) was widely known to the media and to the general public as a constantly re-elected municipal politician. Yet he considered himself a writer above all else. Brown did write poetry, but published rather more fiction of the commercial variety, mostly in the thirties. From 1971-94 he lived at **No.40**.

For the last three years of the fifties, novelist Peregrine Acland (*All Else Is Folly*), discussed previously, resided in apt. 417 of **No.51**. He made his living at this time as a copywriter at MacLaren Advertising. Poet Earle Birney, also met before on this tour, lived in suite 908 of this same building. His domicile began in September 1973 and continued to August 1974, when he departed for extensive travel abroad. He kept the apartment, however, and it was his home after he returned to Toronto in May 1975 until he moved to Balliol Street in July.

During his Alexander Street sojourn Birney made a remarkable series of three LP albums with the internationally acclaimed Toronto percussion group Nexus, an exemplary combination of poetry and music. He also went through a personal renaissance, finding new love and inspiration with his new spouse Wailan Low. It was her inspiration that led him to write some of his best love poems in this apartment, and it was her acceptance into Osgoode Hall that prompted him to take her on a round-the-world tour. In fact, he was not in Canada when his *Collected Poems* was published, a boxed set of two handsomely cased volumes such as no other poet in this country had ever received.

John Charles Dent

Radio broadcaster Lister Sinclair occupied apt. 116 of **No.51** for the first three years of the seventies while he toiled at the CBC. Another author encountered elsewhere on this tour, Stephen Vizinczey, also inhabited an apartment at **51 Alexander** from November 1962 to September 1963.

John Charles Dent (1841-88) lived at **84 Alexander Street** from 1878-80, longer than at most of his other Toronto addresses. Dent, born in England, had come to Canada with his parents when still quite young. They settled in Brantford where Dent trained to be a lawyer. Like Morley Callaghan and other authors, he was called to the bar but never practised, preferring journalism and fiction to legal fact. He went to London and somehow began working immediately for the *Daily Telegraph*, a leading paper, but nowhere near as highbrow then as it is now.

By the early 1870s Dent had moved to the States, where he wrote for the *Boston Globe*. Goldwin Smith had been following Dent's career. When Smith decided to give financial backing to John Ross Robertson's new newspaper, the *Telegram*, he lured Dent back to Toronto as the *Telegram*'s first editor-in-chief. Within a year, Dent had switched to the *Globe* where he worked until 1880, when the thought of being a book writer finally won him over. In the eighties, Dent produced two remarkable histories, the more important being the four-volume *Canadian Portrait Gallery* (1880-81), a biographical study of hundreds of standouts in our history. The book remains essential reading for anyone studying our past.

J.C. Dent also published fiction, most famously *The Gerrard Street Mystery and Other Weird Tales* (1888). The *Dictionary of Canadian Biography*, in summing up his life, decreed that "In his time Dent was assailed by critics of all political stripes who were far from accepting his interpretation of Canadian history and whose criticisms, on the whole, were quite well taken. Dent, however, published several stout volumes, as they did not, and over the years his views tended to win out. Thus, as a popularizer of a point of view, his achievement was a great one."

James L. Hughes, cited above, lived in many places in this neighbourhood. Two of them were **70 Wood Street** from 1871-72, and **86 Wood** in 1873. The only professional golfer included in this *Guide* is Launcelot Servos (dates unknown). The sole address I could find for him was **91 Wood Street** where he lived 1938-39. During this short stay he published *Frontenac and the Maid of the Mist* (1938), a novel set during the epoch when the Frenchman ruled Canada. While reviewing *Practical Instruction in Golf* (1939), another book by Servos, the distinguished editor Lorne Pierce attested from personal knowledge that Servos designed golf courses in Florida, captured more than 200 course records, and gave more than 75,000 lessons—some of them to Pierce.

Wood Street terminates at **Mutual Street**. When Vancouver native Lesley Krueger (b.1954) moved to Toronto in 1978, her first dwelling was **305 Mutual** and it continued as her home until 1980. She first published fiction in the same book that featured Rohinton Mistry's debut: *Coming Attractions 4* (1986).

The last domestic address I could locate for the poet and pioneer feminist Laura McCully (1886-1924) was a rooming house at **309 Mutual** in 1920. The obituaries stated that she died after a long illness, but we now know that

Laura McCully

she had been suffering from paranoid schizophrenia since 1917. In the years up to 1923, the disease seemed to have come in bursts, although as the years wore on the periods of clarity were shorter and shorter. She was probably living in this rooming house on Mutual when *Bird of Dawn and Other Lyrics*, her second book of poetry, was published in December 1919. She was admitted to the Hospital for the Insane in 1923 and never left.

Near where Mutual Street meets Carlton can be found **116 Carlton Street**. From 1873-87 this was the domicile of John McCaul—indeed, he died at this address. McCaul had been raised in a well-to-do family in Ireland who ensured that he had a first-class education. When Upper Canada College was seeking a new principal in 1838, the Archbishop of Canterbury himself recommended McCaul for the post. Immediately after his arrival in Toronto in 1839, he entered comfortably the world of the Family Compact, although unlike most members of the Compact, McCaul was actually qualified for his job. Within five years he left UCC in order to head the new university being founded in Toronto. When that college became the UofT in 1849 McCaul was the obvious and popular choice to be its first president.

He brought to the cultural life of pioneer Toronto the same high standards that he exercised at the University. From a literary point of view, his finest contribution was the editing of *The Maple Leaf: or Canadian Annual, a Literary Souvenir*. There were three annual numbers published. Each issue was really a book, twelve inches in height by eight inches in width. The typesetting and design are classical and attractive, and the volumes were interspersed with engraved plates of literary figures and scenes. All of the contributors were Canadian, and most were based in Toronto. Turning the pages of *The Maple Leaf* is an extraordinary experience. Its production is generous by the standards of our time. To think that it was produced between 1846 and 1848 when Toronto was still a town with mud for streets is to be genuinely in awe of the accomplishment, and it is a wonderful testament to McCaul's belief that books (and education) had to be—could be—as fine as those produced even in the imperial capital. Before living at **No.116**, McCaul had resided at **74 Carlton Street** from 1850-72.

Cavernous as it is, Maple Leaf Gardens, **60 Carlton Street**, has been used for speeches and talks by a few authors. One such speaker was Sir Winston Churchill.

Sir Winston spoke in Toronto on four occasions: 1900, 1901, 1929, and 1932. The last date was originally planned for Simpson's Arcadian Court, but the organizers, sensing a big payday, seriously miscalculated Churchill's drawing power, and switched his lecture to the Gardens. As it happened, he spoke to a few thousand people (estimates range from three to seven thousand), a formidable number for any lecturer, but still an audience dwarfed by the ten thousand empty seats surrounding them in the arena.

The demands of his North American lecture tour allowed him only 48 hours in Toronto on this occasion, but he did put aside his usual speech to deliver one written for the Toronto engagement, his only Canadian stop: "Canada and the Empire." Toronto had always been kind to Churchill. After his first appearance in late 1900 to a packed house at Massey Hall, his tour manager arranged for him to come back a few weeks later in 1901 to regale audiences with stories of his daring escape and exploits in the Boer War. The Hall was packed again.

Some measure of Churchill's power as an orator can be gleaned by learning that, disgusted with the inadequacy of the public-address system in Maple Leaf Gardens, he dispensed with the microphone after just one sentence, and spoke without amplification for the rest of the night. He was heard clearly by everyone in the hockey emporium.

About 5,000 people turned out to hear the Soviet authors Ilya Ehrenburg (1891-

1967) and Konstantin Simonov (b.1915) when they spoke in the Gardens on June 14, 1946. They were joined on stage by Major-General Galaktionov, the editor of *Pravda*, who was travelling with them (whether as colleague or warden is unclear). We know from Ehrenburg's journals that he reluctantly toured the continent only because he had been ordered to do so by Stalin. Stalin commanded him to reiterate pledges of Soviet peaceful intentions—a bid to dispel fears of the Red Menace which had come flying out of the closet in the west with the end of WWII.

It was the bad luck of the Soviet trio to land in Canada immediately on the heels of the Gouzenko revelations. As a result, the Toronto newspapers were very aggressive in their questioning of the writers, and Ehrenburg, clearly fatigued by the tone, and the long trip, responded in kind. Here is a typical riposte as recounted by the *Star* on its front page: "The famous 'iron curtain' which stretches across Europe from Albania to the Baltic is of a material softer than iron; it is a smoke screen thrown out by a section of the U.S. press. This statement was made in Toronto today by Ilya Ehrenburg, noted Russian writer and war correspondent. 'The curtain is there,' he declared, 'but it is not on our side of the stage . . . It is not we who are publishing the wild statements that another war is inevitable. It is not we who are constructing secret weapons. It is not we who speak of upholding democracy and then give our support to Franco.'"

Flora Macdonald Denison (1867-1921) was not only a poet, but a dress designer of quite high local renown, and a trailblazing feminist. When she decided that her marriage was a failure after eight years, she left her husband, taking her child with her. Through a combination of fortitude and savvy, she not only survived but flourished and somehow even managed to elude most of the murmuring and social-cutting which Toronto would ordinarily have inflicted upon such a homebreaker. In her will, she left her son Merrill (1893-1975) Bon Echo, a large country estate she had purchased. Her son grew up to become the most important playwright of his generation in Canada. He, in turn, donated Bon Echo to Ontario. Thus was born the provincial park of the same name, famous for its ancient Indian pictographs. From 1902-10, they lived at **52 Carlton Street**. For the next three years they lived at **No.22**. And finally, in 1914, she is listed in the directories at **146 Carlton**. Earlier, in 1897, she and Merrill had lived around the corner at **454 Church Street**.

After Earle Birney had his heart attack in March 1987, he spent five months at Toronto General Hospital and three more at Queen Elizabeth Hospital. His wife, Wailan Low, was determined that she would look after him at home for as long as possible, and so she bought a condominium, no.1201, at **130 Carlton Street**. Earle arrived here in November 1987 and this was his home until he died in 1995.

Constance Davies Woodrow (1899-1937) spent the last nine years of her sadly abbreviated life in apt. 5 of **142 Carlton**. Although she was born in England, Toronto had been her home since childhood. By day she worked as a sales clerk at Britnell's Bookstore and by night she translated and wrote poetry. The literary historian Vernon Rhodenizer termed "excellent" her translation of Georges Bugnet's novel *Nipsya* (New York, 1929), and her two books of poetry were warmly received: *The Captive Gypsy* (1926) and *The Celtic Heart* (1929).

Return to **Jarvis Street**. The old buildings just to the north of Carlton on the west side of Jarvis have been home to two institutions with literary associations. The first was Havergal College, a private school for Anglican girls of the evangelical branch of the faith. The men, led by Samuel Blake, who founded and built the school, were adamant about their religion (as an historian of the school points out): "By naming the new evangelical girls' school Havergal, after the inspirational British poet Frances Ridley Havergal, they emphasized the Wycliffe/

Ridley/Havergal connection . . . To say that High and Low Anglicans in Toronto tended to look askance at one another would be a distinct understatement. It is believed that Samuel Blake regarded the Bishop Strachan School as positively papist."

The first building of the school opened in September 1894 at **350 Jarvis**, but almost immediately, the need for more rooms and more play area became apparent. Until a new building could be constructed, the school rented **No.346** and **No.348** in 1897 and physically connected them. Then, in 1898, there was the grand opening of the new main school-building, **354 Jarvis**. Authors who attended Havergal at this location include Muriel Denison, Rica Farquharson, Gwethalyn Graham, Elizabeth Sprigge, and Ruth Massey Tovell.

"Northfield," the handsome house just to the north of **No.354**, was purchased by the school in 1913 to provide yet more classrooms. Northfield had been constructed in 1846 for Oliver Mowat (later to become premier of Ontario) and he so named it because, when he moved in, there was nothing but fields north of the house. By WWII, Havergal had abandoned this site for newer, larger premises on Avenue Road near Lawrence. The Air Force used Northfield during the hostilities, but after the war, all of the school buildings were sold to the CBC, and inadequate as the facilities were for the job, the complex of structures became the headquarters of the CBC until it, too, moved to newer, larger premises at 250 Front Street West in1991.

Authors who were on salary from the CBC at this Jarvis building include Andrew Allan, Tony Aspler, Adrienne Clarkson, Nathan Cohen, Patricia Joudry, Derek Mahon, Fletcher Markle, Mavor Moore, John Reeves, Lister Sinclair, Robert Weaver, Phyllis Webb, and Robert Zend.

The most important literary show in the history of the CBC was, without doubt, "Anthology" which ran weekly on the radio network out of these Jarvis Street studios from October 19, 1954 to September 28, 1985. The program was created by Robert Weaver, and he remained its guiding light for most of its 31 years. The program was a compelling mix of old and new voices, and an intelligent blend of fiction, poetry, belles lettres, and interviews.

In more recent years the pre-eminent literary radio program has been "Writers and Company," hosted by Eleanor Wachtel. Unlike "Anthology" which concentrated on Canadian writers, Wachtel's program is concerned with eminent foreign creative writers.

The 400 block of **Jarvis Street** lent itself to peripatetic times in authors' lives. For example, novelist Joyce Marshall roomed at **No.400** in 1939 and at **No.404** in 1940. *Saturday Night* founder and novelist E.E. Sheppard was at **No.406** for a few months in 1888. Crime novelist Howard Engel had a furnished room at **No.410** in 1958, while poet Anne Cimon inhabited **No.412** for some months in 1979. Man of letters Hector Charlesworth boarded at **No.423** in 1895 while science fiction maven Judith Merril had a flat at **No.433** over the academic year 1974-75. Mazo de la Roche never lived anywhere for very long until her last years; she spent 1902-3 at **No.469**. There was a marvellous picture once of the House of Anansi crew standing and seated on the front steps of **No.471**, its home from 1970-73. Included in the photo were Dennis Lee, Shirley Gibson, Dale Zieroth, and Ann Wall. To show how quickly our history can be lost, no institution or person now knows where the negative or even a print of the photo can be found.

Lloyd Roberts (1884-1966), son of Sir Charles G.D. Roberts, showed an early promise as a lyricist in his own right that was, unfortunately, never fulfilled. Among his poetry volumes are *England over the Seas* (1914), *Along the Ottawa* (1927), and *I Sing of Life* (1937). His personal life was complicated. When he was 59, he abandoned his wife and job in Ottawa to move to Toronto in order to try to make a career as a professional literary writer—and to live with a young nurse. To subsidize his writing, he purchased **No.486** and managed it as a boarding house. The boarding-house operation seems never to have flourished, but at least Lloyd had the solace of seeing his father almost every day— Sir Charles lived a couple of blocks away at Wellesley and Sherbourne. By 1945 Lloyd was living in Jamaica and did not return to Toronto until the end of his life when he developed Alzheimer's disease. He died on January 25, 1966.

Crime novelist and art-book writer Ruth Massey Tovell (1889-1961) was born at **No.515** in the home of her grandfather Hart Massey. She and her parents soon moved across the street into **No.486** (the same house Lloyd Roberts would later buy) and stayed at this address until the turn of the century. Tovell (*The Crime in the Boulevard Raspail*, 1932) was not the first crime writer based in Toronto, but she was certainly a pathfinder among Canadians working in the genre.

Jarvis Collegiate, the oldest secondary school in Toronto, has gone through many transmogrifications since its birth in 1807. At that time it was called the Home District Grammar School and had an enrolment of five students. By 1825 it was called the Royal Grammar School. Its evolution into what we would consider a high school took place in 1871 when it became the Toronto High School and moved into new premises at **361 Jarvis Street**. The enrolment was still relatively small: 150 pupils in all grades. The school became a collegiate just two years later, and then adopted the name Jarvis Street Collegiate Institute in 1890. In 1923, it moved to its current location at **No.495**, and now boasts of an enrolment of around 1,500. Authors who attended Jarvis Collegiate at either No.361 or at No.495 include:

Victor Coleman
Ralph Cunningham
Merrill Denison

Timothy Findley
Maida Parlow French
Ann Ireland
Edith Summers Kelley
Marjory MacMurchy
Laura Elizabeth McCully
Sarah Sheard
Charles H.J. Snider
Flos Jewel Williams

Noted authors who have lectured at the school include E.J. Pratt, Basil King, Arthur Stringer, and Charles G.D. Roberts.

The editor, poet, and journalist Samuel Thompson died in 1886 at **518 Jarvis**, where he had been living for about two years. Arriving from London, England, as a young man, Thompson (b.1810) originally settled in Nottawasaga, but in 1837 walked the entire distance to Toronto seek his fortune. The printing trade captured his fancy, and soon he was working with Henry Rowsell's bookselling and printing business. Coming from a poor background, he realized more than most the economic difficulties placed in the way of learning, so in 1855 he led efforts to found a free lending library. In 1883 when the Toronto Public Library was formed, he believed he was the front-runner for the post of chief librarian. However, on the grounds that he was too old, the job was given to a younger man, James Bain. As a consolation prize, Thompson was offered the job of heading the Yorkville branch of the library system, and, needing the money, he accepted. The money, then as now, was never much, and at the end of his life it appears he was just able to keep his family afloat. Those who love Toronto history are well advised to read the autobiography Thompson published in 1884, *Reminiscences of a Canadian Pioneer*. His powers of observation were acute, his lack of self-pity is affecting, and his prose attractive and occasionally humorous.

Novelist and journalist E.E. Sheppard (1855-1924) lived at **520 Jarvis** in 1889 and then moved the next year to **578 Jarvis**, his home until 1908. He had just published his third novel when he moved to Jarvis. His Stetsoned appearance in this decade was rather different from the dress of other Toronto gentlemen, as writer Douglas Fetherling makes clear: "E.E. Sheppard, though Canadian, had gone to Bethany College in Virginia . . . In the days before the Civil War, Bethany had been the favourite school for the errant sons of the Southern slave-holding aristocracy. Later Sheppard moved west and is said to have worked for a time as a stagecoach driver on the frontier. Back in Toronto in the 1880s, he cultivated a southwestern appearance, with free-falling mustachios and the sort of long linen duster favoured by drovers and outlaws. He used the Spanish honorific *Don* as his pseudonym. He took great sport in, and drew deep reader response from, reviewing the sermons preached from every pulpit in the city. He reviewed them not as theology but as theatre, which is doubtless what they were."

Playwright John Herbert (*Fortune and Men's Eyes*) occupied apt. 427 of **550 Jarvis** from 1967 to 1971, at which point he moved to Paris where he wrote more plays. While living at this address, Herbert simultaneously rented a studio at 529 Yonge Street. In the studio he produced plays under the banner of the Garret Theatre. One of the people he invited to direct at the Garret was a young man cutting his teeth in the world of the playhouse: Ken Gass. When Herbert knew he would be quitting his home and his studio for Paris in 1971, he gave Ken Gass all of his theatre equipment, facilitating slightly the opening of Gass's new theatre on Dupont Street, Factory Theatre Lab. Herbert returned to **550 Jarvis** in 1986 (apt. 614) and remained until 1995. During this period he wrote only two plays: *Broken Antique Dolls*, and *The Merchants of Bay Street*. The market rates of the rents in the building eventually forced Herbert to move to a co-op, where the rent is scaled to the tenant's income.

The under-appreciated fiction writer Raymond Knister (1899-1932) moved to Toronto at the beginning of September 1926 in order to be closer to the likely outlets for publication of his work. He first lived at **574 Jarvis** and found the address conducive to his work. A number of his short stories were purchased by the *Star Weekly*, and he was quickly embraced as an important young talent by the Toronto literary world, including Morley Callaghan, Merrill Denison, Bertram Brooker, and Mazo de la Roche. Also while living here he met his bride-to-be. Two weeks after arriving, he moved to 1544 King Street West, but was back at his Jarvis Street flat by November 11. This was his home until he was married

PRAISED BY WALPOLE

RAYMOND KNISTER, Canadian novelist, whose book, "White Narcissus," was singled out for commendation by the eminent British novelist, Hugh Walpole, in his recent Toronto address.

Globe, February 8, 1930

on June 18, 1927. During this brief but important era, he continued to write fiction and have it published in magazines. As well, he began the compilation of the anthology which would come to be known as *Canadian Short Stories* (1928), now regarded as the first important critical salute to a discipline in which Canadians have long felt they excelled. To this address can also be ascribed the beginnings of Knister's important novel, *White Narcissus*, published as a major event in London, New York, and Toronto in 1929.

At the end of his undergraduate years at the UofT, David Lewis Stein (b.1937), fiction writer and urban-affairs specialist at the *Star,* shared (1961-63) part of the apartment of Srul and Dorothy Glick at what was **587 Jarvis Street.** David wrote to me, "Friday nights at the Glicks became institutions. Srul had become a music producer for CBC radio and people such as Walter Buchinski, Bill Aide and even Glenn Gould used to come to eat Dorothy's great food and to play and sing. And writers such as me . . . used to read from works in progress. It was a wonderful time . . . I think the house we shared on Jarvis Street was the beginning of one of the longest-running musical and literary salons in the city."

Pierre Berton (b.1920) first came to Toronto from the Yukon when he was 11 years old. His mother, Laura Berton (1878-1967), later the author of the popular *I Married the Klondike* (featuring a preface by Robert Service), in 1931 had finished a novel. Berton writes, "I don't think it occurred to my mother that she could mail it to a publisher in Toronto. At any rate, she had no intention of doing that. We would all go to Toronto, and she would take the novel personally to one of the big houses . . . When we reached Toronto, we moved into my Aunt Florrie's house, a two-storey building of yellow brick at **[98] Huntley Street.** Like so much else, bricks were new to me. So were the big stone mansions on nearby Jarvis Street.

"When we first arrived in Toronto I felt almost as if I had come from another planet . . . In those days, Toronto really was Hogtown: most people considered it the dullest community in Canada. The time would come when I would agree. But to me in 1931, it was wonderland. Everything was so new, everything was different—from the orange Honey Dew signs that winked on and off to the policeman who stood in the middle of the main intersections twirling stop-and-go signs. (Traffic lights were just beginning to appear.)

"It was the small, every day discoveries that made the sharpest impact. I had never seen a milk bottle before; the milk in Dawson came round in beer bottles. I had never seen or tasted a toffee apple. I had never *heard* of roller skates. Ice cream tasted different, for it was made with real cream, not canned milk . . . Even the school was different. I was enrolled in what was called the Junior Fourth at Rosedale Public, where all the boys wore berets on their heads. My mother was charmed at that old-world fashion, but I thought they looked like sissies. Within a month I had bowed to peer pressure and was wearing a beret of my own . . .

"Lucy too had few friends. She was no longer my kid sister, tagging along behind me because my parents insisted that I look after her and include her in my circle of friends. There was no circle of friends, and so she became my best and only friend and constant companion, not out of duty but out of real need. We depended on each other, hiking off to school hand in hand and facing the terrifying traffic on Bloor Street together. Our parents bought us roller skates as part of our new education, and we spent almost every afternoon and most Saturday mornings skating together up and down Jarvis Street, once the classiest boulevard in Toronto. It still retained the old sandstone sidewalks, which were so much smoother and easier to skate on than concrete. No doubt this was considered very high class before the ladies of the night appropriated it as their own. When the snow fell, my parents also gave us ice skates and we skated together in the Lacrosse Park—or, I should say, stumbled about on the ice. It sounds odd—two kids from the frozen North who had to learn to skate on the Outside. But there wasn't a smooth pond or stream in all of the Klondike; the rivers were a tangle of ice blocks; and the rink at Dawson had long since burned down. I never learned to skate properly and though I went to the YMCA regularly didn't learn to swim. I had been taught to fear the water, and I still feared it, even in the Y pool. I was especially afraid to tumble in head first and dreaded the instructors who tried to train me. To this day, I can't dive." The Toronto adventure ended in May 1932 when the Berton family returned to Dawson.

Cartoonist, poet, and public speaker J.W. Bengough (1851-1923) lived at **44 Huntley Street** longer than at any other address in his life: 1884-1903. While he was already a nationally known figure by the time he moved here, it was while living on Huntley that he published most of the books by which we know him today. These include his two volumes of poetry and his far more popular *The Up-to-Date Primer: A First Book of Lessons for Little Political Economists* (1896) composed entirely of words of no more than one syllable. He attended the unveiling of the Burns monument in Allan Gardens and listened as his dedicatory poem about the statue was read aloud to the Burns-rapt throng. This residency coincided with his teaching of Elocution at Knox College.

34 Huntley was James Macdonald Oxley's home from 1902-6. Oxley began adult life as a lawyer but after five years switched to backroom politics and writing fiction (apparently there is a difference). His feature articles on a variety of historical topics appeared in leading U.S. publications such as *Scribner's, Harper's, Cosmopolitan*, and *Atlantic Monthly*. In addition, he translated literary material, including Eugene Sue's *L'Orgueil* in its entirety, but it is as the author of well

over two dozen novels for boys that he is best remembered. His fictions were sold around the world, and had their widest circulation when they appeared regularly in the *Boy's Own Paper*. Almost all of his novels are set in Canada, and deal with male rites of passage: boy struggles against the dangers of the world and then triumphs. He may have come to Toronto in 1899 for treatment of the tuberculosis which ultimately killed him.

For the last quarter-century of his life, Father James Dollard (1872-1946) was the parish priest of Our Lady of Lourdes church at **11 Earl Street**. Born in Ireland, it was only after he came to Canada that he decided to take Holy Orders. After ordination, he served at other pastorates in Toronto, but in 1921 he found his real home at this handsome church. The building was constructed in 1886. Dollard was renowned across Canada as a powerful and effective orator and when he spoke from the pulpit the Masses were always filled to overflowing. His fame as a speaker may have been national, but his fame as a poet was international. Joyce Kilmer was an admirer, and an Irish newspaper in New York declared it obvious that he was read around the world wherever an Irish person breathed. Three volumes of verse survive: *Irish Mist and Sunshine* (1901), *Poems* (1910), and *Irish Lyrics and Ballads* (1917). He also wrote a collection of short stories.

Curiously, another important religious figure and poet also once called this street home. William Patrick McKenzie (1861-1942) was educated at UCC, the UofT, and Knox College. After graduating from the UofT in 1884, but before entering Knox c. 1888, he worked for some years as a reporter for the *Mail*, and travelled to the prairies to cover the Riel Rebellion. He was ordained in 1889 as a Presbyterian minister. He then immediately left for further theological study in New York State, following which he became the pastor of a Presbyterian church in Avon, New York

(1891-94). It was probably during a return visit to Toronto in 1891 that he first encountered Christian Science. It appears that he went with some friends to The Sharon House, **526 Sherbourne Street**, to listen to a young woman, Daisette Stocking, talk about her new-found faith. McKenzie,

William Patrick McKenzie, frontispiece to his book *Voices and Undertones* (New York and Toronto, 1998)

intrigued, began to read Christian Science books intently, and kept up such a correspondence with Ms. Stocking that he married her in 1901. As his interest in the new religion intensified, he made regular trips back to Toronto to attend Christian Science Sunday services. Later, he became a reader at these Toronto services. By 1904, he had severed his ties with Presbyterianism and had embraced Christian Science completely. The following year, he returned to Toronto to live—to **20 Earl Street**.

Through all of this religious activity, McKenzie had continued to write verse. His first poetry book was published in 1887, and his ninth in 1930. Indeed, it was one of his poems which brought him to the attention of Mary Baker Eddy, the founder of the faith (and eventually led to his final departure from Toronto at the end of 1906). *The Christian Science Journal* recounts, "To the amazement of some longtime Scientists, Mrs. Eddy made Mr. McKenzie a First Member of The Mother Church . . . even before she had met him. Why she would do so can perhaps be seen in a letter she wrote to him a few days before, 'Your poem in our *Journal* is like the song of the redeemed, and the smiles and tears of the new-born for the milk of the Word. It touched my heart of hearts.'" At Mary Baker Eddy's behest, McKenzie quickly rose through the ranks of the Church, and she even asked for his help "in the arrangement of various editions of her *Manual of the Mother Church*"—the sacred document containing the tenets to which all Christian Science churches throughout the world must subscribe. By the thirties, McKenzie was one of the most significant members of the faith. He was on the Board of Directors, 1932-42, and was Chairman of the Board on two occasions. He also served a number of terms as President of the Mother Church in Boston.

Wellesley Hospital, I am sure, has treated many authors throughout the years, but to me its most surprising literary patient has to be Moss Hart (1904-61). Hart was in Toronto overseeing the tryout-run of the Broadway-bound *Camelot* when, on October 14, 1960, he suffered a heart attack in his hotel room. He was rushed by ambulance to Wellesley. Probable contributing factors to his coronary thrombosis were the death of his father the week before—and the massive rewrites he and the producers felt the musical still required. The show had opened in Toronto on October 1, but Hart was still in town two weeks later making severe cuts and changes. The Broadway opening had already been postponed by a fortnight.

Moss Hart was not lonely in Wellesley Hospital—for, incredibly, the show's lyricist, Alan Jay Lerner, had been admitted just a few days earlier, suffering from ulcer troubles. Both men returned to the show at the O'Keefe Centre within days, and *Camelot* went on to become one of the most successful Broadway musicals ever. No doubt, as he lay in his hospital bed here, Moss recalled with a wry smile the title of the play for which he won the Pulitzer Prize in 1937: *You Can't Take It with You.*

The noted translator William Hume Blake (*Maria Chapdelaine*) lived at **99 Homewood Avenue** from 1883-87. Victorian poet and educationalist James L. Hughes lived at **77 Homewood** from 1878-79, while about 120 years later, sound poet bill bissett lived at **No.60** from 1994-97.

Two important women playwrights have lived on **Homewood**. Betty Jane Wylie (b.1931) moved here because she found success unexpectedly stressful. A number of her titles in various editions were published within the same 12 months and as she explained, "I had four promotion trips in one year: three in Canada and one in the States. The result was that I spent six months without an income because, while my expenses were paid by the publishers, I had no time to write and generate new income . . . I decided to try to cut my losses and expenses. I sold my co-op and began to get rid of a lifetime of accumulated possessions.

"I jumped into a high-rise in the heart of the red-light district: **40 Homewood Avenue**, where I rented a one-bedroom box [apt. 2403] from an actor I knew because it had a great pool. I wrote *Successfully Single* there and in Bermuda. I also wrote the play *Double Vision*, commissioned by Theatre Direct." She arrived in June 1985 and then departed Toronto from here in January 1987.

Erika Ritter (b.1948) had been living at **1 Homewood** for only a few months when her play *Winter 1671* premiered at the St. Lawrence Centre in 1979. By 1981 she was living elsewhere in the city.

Poet and CBC producer George Jonas (b.1935) made his home at **392 Sherbourne Street** from 1968-72. While here he wrote many of the poems which appeared in his second volume, *The Happy Hungry Man* (1970). Just a few years later, he would publish (with his then-wife Barbara Amiel) his bestselling *By Persons Unknown* (1977).

Emily Carr (1871-1945) is one of the country's most famous painters, yet like many visual artists active in Canada in the first decades of the 20th c. she also published creative writing. Her best-known fiction is *Klee Wyck* (1941), a collection of short stories awarded the Governor General's Award.

While Carr is quite rightly thought of as a west-coast artist, her time in Toronto, although brief, was to have a powerful effect on all of her subsequent work. In 1927, thanks to writer Marius Barbeau, she was invited by the National Gallery in Ottawa to show some of her art in an exhibition devoted to British Columbian artists. She jumped at the chance, knowing that the trip would finally allow her to stop over in Toronto and meet the Group of Seven.

She arrived in Toronto by train on November 13, 1927, and checked into the Tuxedo Hotel at **504 Sherbourne**, an inn whose specialty was accommodating itinerant single women. The next day she was taken to the Studio Building on Severn Street where the members of the Group painted. She met first with A.Y. Jackson and some of the students he was teaching. As her biographer notes, "They had tea, and sweets were passed around on the tops of cake tins. Carl Schaefer—then a student—has recalled that Emily 'appeared jolly and so pleased to meet us,' and was 'enthusiastic about what was going on in Toronto.' She viewed Jackson's three canvases of Indian villages in the Upper Skeena and felt they had something her work lacked: rhythm and poetry. So impressed was she by Jackson's Indian pictures that she felt 'a little beaten at my own game.' . . . Two days later, under a bleak November sky, she picked her way through the slush of Severn Street and climbed the Studio Building stairs to the third floor to call on Lawren Harris. On that day her ideas about art wholly changed.

"Emily had been anxious for the meeting. Harris's *Above Lake Superior*, as reproduced in Housser's book, had impressed her as 'an austere formal picture of great depth and dignity.' Now she hoped to see more. Miss Buell, her guide, led her into the bare, grey-walled studio. The distinguished-looking grey-haired artist greeted her kindly, in a quiet and gentlemanly manner. Emily sat down on his sofa, and as he pulled out painting after painting for her to see, she hardly said a word. She was 'like a dumb-founded fool,' leaving Miss Buell to do all the talking. Nothing she had seen before—in England, in France, anywhere—had touched her so deeply, 'right to the very core.' Gibb's work in Paris had been strange and new, but Harris's was 'a revelation, a getting outside of oneself and finding a new self in a place you did not know existed.' His pictures were a radical departure from the prettiness of England and the modernity of France. They struck deep 'into the vast lovely soul of Canada; they plumbed to her depths, climbed her heights and floated into her spaces.' On Thursday, the seventeenth of November 1927, she had an epiphany.

"Back in her hotel room she could not sleep. 'Two things had hold of me with a double clutch. Canada and Art. They were tossing me round & tearing me.' Between bursts of crying, she wrote in the journal she had begun a week earlier: 'Oh, God, what have I seen? Where have I been? Something has spoken to the very soul of me, wonderful, mighty, not of this world.'"

The rest of her week in Toronto was a whirl of studio visits, gallery hopping, and obligatory social calls. On November 21 she left for Ottawa, her mind still ablaze from her encounters with the Group, especially Harris. And, not to be overlooked in assessing the trip's importance is this: for a painter—for a woman—who was regarded by her neighbours back home as an eccentric, in Toronto she was treated as a professional equal. George

Woodcock has also remarked that the trip was crucial for Carr because it "introduced her to artists who saw with eyes like hers."

Her duties in Ottawa and Montreal seemed to drag on and on, for she was aching to return to Toronto and see more paintings by, and have talks with, Lawren Harris. A week later she was back in the city, again staying at the Tuxedo Hotel. She telephoned Harris almost immediately, and he "invited her to dine at his home that evening. They talked little. Harris played a symphony on his orthophonic and Emily—absorbing the glorious sounds that filled the room, along with his paintings—was carried off into another world.

"Two days later she was once again sitting on the sofa in Harris's large grey studio, looking at *Above Lake Superior* and revelling in the other canvases he brought out for viewing. Sensing her enthusiasm, Harris talked a great deal about his work. He showed her the different ingredients he put into his paint to give his colour vibration and explained the technique of rubbing raw linseed oil into the canvas before applying the paint. But most important, he discussed his religion and how it was linked closely to his art . . . Emily found much of what Harris told her about Theosophy appealing: the role of the artist as teacher and high priest; the call to create a new Canadian art; and especially the artist's relationship to God through nature. She had long ceased to be satisfied by conventional religion and had not attended the Reformed Episcopal Church of her family regularly since her return from England in 1904. Harris's ability to convey the spirituality of nature in his painting impressed her greatly, and she was open to any teaching that would enable her to achieve his level of consciousness. She wanted to get hold of something in his work that hers lacked—the 'bigness lying behind it.' She did not want to paint like him. Their temperaments—his 'calm' and hers 'all turbulence and eruption'—prohibited that. But Emily felt that, given a chance, she too could bring the Divine spirit of nature into her painting. She longed to return to her totems and 'wrestle something out for myself, to look for things I did not know of before, and to feel and strive and earnestly try to be true and sincere to the country and to myself.' Aware of the great impression his work and his ideas had made on Emily, Harris encouraged her to find her own way in expressing her material.

"The meeting in Harris's studio, on the thirteenth of December, was by sheer coincidence Emily's fifty-sixth birthday and it was 'a wonderful birthday treat.' In retrospect it became much more than that to her. Not only had she found a person whose painting she admired, who was sympathetic to her difficulties, but through Harris she was moved to explore the spiritual significance of her own work. 'I guess that long talk in Lawren Harris's studio was the pivot on which turned my entire life.'" By December 21, 1927, Carr was back in B.C.

Novelist Shirley Faessler (1915-97) operated her house at **576 Sherbourne Street** as an actors' and artists' boarding house for several years after she purchased it in 1953. In 1967 she started to write short stories, and had the pleasant surprise of seeing the first three of them published in *Atlantic Monthly*. Other tales appeared in *Tamarack Review* and in anthologies edited by John Metcalf. At the urging of her publishers, she then wrote a novel, *Everything in the Window* (1979), a book greeted with less warmth than her short stories. She then published nothing until 1988 when *A Basket of Apples and Other Stories* was published to mild acclaim. Unfortunately, by this point, her health was deteriorating, and she wrote no more. All of her writing was done at this address.

Our final stop on this tour is the southwest corner of Sherbourne and Selby Streets, a nondescript spot at the best of times, yet in its way, remarkable. Within a stone's throw of this corner can be found addresses of seven important authors, including some of the most famous ever to live in Toronto.

Before you stands the Selby Hotel, **592 Sherbourne**. Prior to its being a hotel, it was the home of Charles Horace Gooderham. Among his many children was Grace Adel (1885?-1975), the author of at least two books for children, one of which, *Friendly Feet* (192?), contains historically significant poems about growing up in this house. Because she never married, I assume she continued to live here until her mother sold the building in 1910. Where she lived after that I could not determine.

The edifice was opened as a residential hotel in 1913 with the Selby name. When Ernest Hemingway decided to return to Toronto from Paris in August 1923, he stayed at the Selby for about a month while he and his wife went apartment-hunting, and he settled into his new job at the *Star*. Or, at least, into a job at the *Star*. Unfortunately, the editor who had induced Hemingway to return by promising him a features position had been shuffled aside. In his place was a martinet of the old school who felt Hemingway should be taken down several pegs. Instead of interviewing celebrities during the day, or working on major stories, Hemingway was handed assignments more suitable for a cub reporter, or jobs that took him far from Toronto for days on end—the very thing he had been promised would not happen since his wife was about to give birth. His first visit to Toronto in 1920 had been ecstatic. The second, thanks to his boss at the *Star*, became a nightmare.

Twenty years later, Wyndham Lewis lived at the Selby for a few weeks after a fire on February 15, 1943 forced him to flee the Tudor Hotel across the street (**No.559**) where he had been living. Lewis return to his rooms at the Tudor once the smoke and fire damage had been repaired.

Another resident for just a few weeks was the Italian-American fiction writer Arturo Vivante (b.1923). He spent a long summer in Toronto in 1941, the first half of it in the Selby, an experience he relates in the largely autobiographical story "The Stream," published in *The New Yorker* in 1958. The Vivante family, Jewish refugees to England from Italy in 1938, were interned during WWII. When Arturo reached the age of 16 he too was interned, but by that point, the British were shipping enemy aliens to Canada for the duration. A family friend, the actress and monodramatist Ruth Draper, during a Red Cross tour of Canada, stopped in Ottawa and met Mackenzie King. She told him of the absurdity of Arturo's incarceration, and the very next morning he was released, free to travel to Toronto, and somehow find his way in the world.

Poet David Wevill's stay at the Selby was in the same year (1941) and also for reasons having to do with the fighting. Wevill (b.1935) and his family had been living in Japan where his father worked for Canadian Pacific, at the time doing formidable business in the Far East. With the outbreak of war they slowly worked their way back to Canada and stayed at the hotel for a few weeks while the parents shopped for a house elsewhere in town.

In mid-1940, during the time that Wyndham Lewis lived at the Tudor Hotel and the Selby Hotel, a 37-year-old journalist from Kingston and his wife had moved into second-floor rooms at **2 Selby Street**. They had come to the big city so that he could write his first book, a commissioned grade-eight textbook called *Shakespeare for Young Players*, all of which was written at this address. The young man and his bride did not recognize Lewis or realize he was a neighbour. And it is a harmless pleasure to picture Wyndham Lewis passing the younger writer every day in the street without realizing who he was to become. He became—he was—Robertson Davies. Davies was also resident here when he was appointed the literary editor of *Saturday Night*. He and his wife Brenda remained here until about the middle of 1941.

2 Selby Street, by coincidence, was also the home of the distinguished poet A.G. Bailey (1905-97) when he was studying for his doctorate at the UofT. The school records for this period are less than perfect, but it seems he lived in rooms here from May 1931 to May 1932. If so, he had just published his second book of poems, *Tao* (November 1930). While in Toronto, Bailey supplemented his income by working as a journalist for the *M&E*.

Short-story writer E.W. Thomson (*Old Man Savarin and Other Stories*) made his home at **7 Selby** from 1882 until he fled Canada for a short-lived, self-imposed exile in the States in 1891. During most of this period on Selby he was the chief editorial writer of the *Globe*. It was also a decade wherein he became close friends with Archibald Lampman. He even wrote an editorial in the *Globe* exhorting the federal government "to recognize and foster Canadian genius by promoting men like Lampman to higher positions in the civil service."

British Columbia playwright Charles Tidler wrote in a letter: "First time I came to Toronto was in 1968 to dodge the draft. I was there for three days only, stayed at **12 Selby Street**, and then returned to Indiana to live underground for a year."

CABBAGETOWN

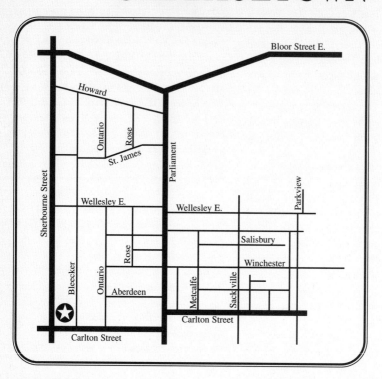

The tour begins at the northeast corner of Sherbourne Street and Carlton Street.

When the poet Robin Mathews first moved to Toronto to pursue his PhD at the UofT in 1958, he and his wife settled into an apartment at **433 Sherbourne Street**. They remained here for about a year, during which time he wrote for *Canadian Forum, Varsity*, taught television playwriting at the Central YMCA, and began the formal development of his nationalist critique which would bring him so much controversy throughout the 1970s.

Novelist Ethel Chapman (d.1976) had her home in apt. 22 of **No.435** for most of the later Depression years. Chapman was an early female graduate of the agricultural college that later became the University of Guelph, and most of her early career was spent criss-crossing Canada teaching nutrition and healthier cooking to farm and country women. In 1927 she became an editor of *The Farmer's Magazine*. Her three novels reflect her professional experience. Two of them, *The Homesteaders* (Ryerson, 1936) and her best-known, *With Flame of Freedom* (1938) were written at this address. The distinguished novelist Barbara Gowdy (b.1950) also lived in this building. From September 1977 to February 1978 she dwelt in apt. 3 while working as an editor at the book publishing house Lester & Orpen Dennys.

Edward Hartley Dewart (1828-1903) spoke of the need for a Canadian literature and a Canadian literary culture before there was a Canada. In 1864, three years before Confederation, he published *Selections From Canadian Poets*, the first anthology of Canadian work ever published. The book is important not only for being the first, but as well for the confidence which exudes from Dewart's choices and declarations. For example, in his Introduction, he uttered truths whose validity have not changed: "A national literature is an essential element in the formation of a national character." Critic Mary Lu Mac-Donald makes a compelling argument for scholars to pay more attention to Dewart as a poet in his own right. Regardless, he deserves our applause for the seriousness and diligence with which he helped to establish the idea of Canadian Literature, and to construct the first canon against which others could react. From 1874-89, he lived at **No.439**. During those years his job was editing the Methodist journal *The Christian Guardian*. His last years (1890-1903) were spent at **515 Sherbourne** but they were hardly quiet. In 1898, he ran unsuccessfully for the Ontario Legislature, and he was one of the principals in the extremely heated debates over whether Victoria College should federate with the UofT. Dewart's position prevailed, and the Methodist college moved from Cobourg to Toronto in 1892.

Fiction writer Shirley Faessler (1915-97) spent her last four years in poor health at the Fudger House Nursing Home—it has usurped Dewart's former residence at **No.439**. For decades, Faessler lived further up the street on the west side and it was there she wrote her internationally acclaimed short stories.

In between the time the site was Dewart's home and our time, the building was used for meetings of the American Women's Club. Without doubt the Club's most eminent literary speaker was Sinclair Lewis, who gave his first speech in Canada here on April 12, 1921.

Nomi Berger, a successful writer of commercial fiction for women, wrote two of her novels while living from 1984-91 at **545 Sherbourne**: *So Many Promises* and *Dreams to Keep*. Novelist Matthew Trill (b.1887) worked as the Queen's Park reporter for the *World* while living in Toronto for a couple of years c. 1915. When his novel *The Stranger*

Within appeared in 1935, it received excellent reviews, but after that, silence. And his place and time of death are unknown.

559 Sherbourne was the site of the Tudor Hotel, the home of Wyndham Lewis (1882-1957) from 1940-43. It is a commonplace among some Canadians to nod knowingly and state with great authority that Lewis had a special hate for the country generally, and the city in particular. Unfortunately, in my opinion, these savants seem more intent on denigrating where they live than in seeing his declarations in context. While it is indisputable that Lewis made disparaging remarks about the city, it bears remembering that he was one the most misanthropic authors of the 20th c. He made withering, hurtful remarks about every place he lived and about almost everyone he knew. In that context, his quoted assessments of Toronto are neither better than—nor worse than—other places. There are those who feel honour accrues to Toronto because it is disparaged by Lewis in his autobiographical novel *Self Condemned*. Setting aside the colonial mindset that relishes any attention paid by someone from the imperial centre, no matter how negative, the fact is that by the end of the novel the protagonist of *Self Condemned* decides Toronto is actually the best city for him in which to remain and prosper. He weighs Toronto's merits and demerits against those of other, more famous centres, and adjudges that, for all its faults, Toronto is the place he should remain.

Lewis came to North America in August 1939 because he felt his talent was insufficiently recognized in Britain and he believed the New World would be more open to his work. In his dreams he was going to sweep through the continent, accumulating lucrative commissions for portraits. Unfortunately, the United States remained relatively indifferent to his genius. Because he had been born on his father's yacht in Canadian waters off Nova Scotia, Lewis was able to claim Canadian citizenship—and thus easy access to the country after the outbreak of war. He came to Toronto from America because he thought the city might be a better source for art commissions. How much he looked forward to Toronto can be gleaned from a letter he sent to an intimate in the UK in December 1940: "After the winter of my discontent in the long and chilly shadow of that statue of Liberty, I feel as if I had come up out of a coalmine or a dungeon into fresh air again. All I need is one more heave, and, to change to equestrian metaphor, I shall be in the saddle. . . ." He also came here because he mistakenly believed it would be easier to transfer money from his British bank account to Canada than it would be to the neutral USA. It seems to have been only after they settled in Toronto that Lewis and his wife realized civilian women were not allowed to travel to England because of the war. Further, to their dismay, they learned the British Government forbade any transfers of funds out of the country for the duration of the war. What was supposed to have been a trip of a few months now became an enforced stay of years.

He arrived in Toronto on November 11, 1940 and by November 20 was installed in suite 11-A at the Tudor Hotel. ("It is an apartment hotel—14 bucks a week. One big room, kitchen and bathroom.") A misanthrope, yes, but no fool, Lewis had an almost immediate grasp of Toronto's complexity, comprehending its Caledonian rectitude but wildly misjudging its wish for annexation: "The city is said to be the most American of Canadian cities; but it is a mournful Scottish version of America (union with which it yearns for dismally). However, outside the business classes there are a number of pleasant people here; and anywhere I can find work is a good place to me . . . the Scotch swamped the original French and English [and] with their asphyxiating godliness set up a reign of terror for the toper and the whoremaster, which makes life curiously difficult for the person who likes a couple of

mild cocktails a day—Do not let this rather sombre picture deter you however from paying the place a visit . . . Not far away are places of terrific beauty: and Hart House has to be seen to be believed. I also listened to a Czech refugee play Johann Sebastian Bach the other day as well as I have ever heard it done."

Throughout his stay, he struggled for portrait commissions, and progressively alienated the affection of almost everyone who tried to assist him in some way. One of the exceptions was Lorne Pierce, editor-in-chief of Ryerson Press. Pierce had the wit to ask Lewis to write a book on democracy. Lewis replied with *Anglosaxony: A League That Works* (1941). It is an interesting book which went completely unreviewed in the Toronto press for reasons which remain elusive. Noting the lack of reviews, Lewis wrote to his publisher, "A prominent bookseller, unsolicited, took me aside the other day and said: 'If I might venture to give a little advice, another time if I thought of publishing, it would be much better to have it published in New York or London' . . . I am sure you are better acquainted than I am with your compatriots peculiarities: but perhaps you have not fathomed the depth of their distrust for anything Canadian (that is one of the things that made success so difficult for the Canadian School of Painters [Group of Seven]) . . . It is a very important fact: if you cannot break their attitude you will never have any more artists or writers here. Or so it seems to me."

Another figure spared Lewis's wrath was A.Y. Jackson, whose work Lewis praised in one of five contemplative essays he wrote while in Toronto—four of them were published in *Saturday Night*. He also had kind words for Morley Callaghan's writing. And it would seem he began to write *Self Condemned* in Toronto, even though it was not published until 1954.

There is some vagueness about Lewis's writing in Toronto because it is unclear how much of it was lost during the fire of

February 15, 1943, that drove the hotel residents into the street and into record cold. One person was killed in the fire, but the wing where Lewis lived seems to have been left relatively unscathed. Curiously, in its front-page coverage of the fire, the *Star* ran a photo, not of the burning hotel, but of Wyndham Lewis, noting in its headline that "Novelist-Artist Loses Valuable Paintings and Unfinished Manuscripts." The *Telegram's* pictures, in fact, are the only known photos of the hotel in any condition. Until the building was repaired some weeks later, the Lewises occupied the Selby Hotel across the road. Lewis returned to the burnt-out Tudor, its charred ruins an unhappy symbol reflecting what he felt was his own condition as an artist. Fortunately, a position was offered him at Assumption College in Windsor, and four months after the fire, in June 1943, Wyndham Lewis left Toronto.

For four of the five years that John Cornish (b.1914) lived in Toronto (1948-52), his home was established at **579 Sherbourne**. He sorted mail for the Post Office in the evenings, and wrote his first novel, *The Provincials* (1951), during the day at the former Central Library at College and St. George. He published short stories as well as other novels, one of which, *Olga* (1956), won a $5,000 prize from *Maclean's*. His most famous novel is *Sherbourne Street* (1968), a tragicomedy with much of its narrative set on this street.

Ernest Thompson Seton home on Howard Street as portrayed in *Canadian Magazine*, January, 1908

For some reason, next-to-no writers lived on **Bleeker Street**. The most notable—and that was not for long—was the poet Albert E.S. Smythe (1861-1947) whose home was at **85 Bleeker** from 1912-17. Bleak, of course, is one of the words that comes to mind when contemplating the urban planning disaster known as St. Jamestown. A Torontonian walking through

this development-horror does not even have the satisfaction of knowing that someone went to jail for this outrage. Most of the houses where authors once lived were demolished to make way for these high-rises. Incredibly, at the time, the destruction was called progress.

The most famous resident of **Howard Street** was Ernest Thompson Seton (1860-1946). Since he fled the family home on Pembroke Street a few years before, his mother and father had moved to this part of the city. Seton returned to Toronto from western Canada in order to work on what he hoped would be his first book. "On January 31, 1885, I landed in Toronto and put up at the paternal domicile, **86 Howard Street**. I felt that my first duty was to complete arrangements and polish my notes on *The Birds of Manitoba*, preparing it for publication. I thought I could complete this in one month.

"I worked with intense concentration at my desk, twelve to eighteen hours a day, putting my notes together for the volume. But the work increased as I went on. Instead of rounding it up in one month, August came and I was far from finished. Meanwhile, the home government was giving me some strong hints about setting out on my own. So, bitterly laying aside my chosen job, on September 16 [1885] I boarded the steamer Chicora for Rochester where I changed to the railway, and landed in New York . . . ."

Howard Street terminates at the St. James Cemetery. Authors buried in these grounds include Graeme Mercer Adam, Anna Durie, Sir James David Edgar, Sir John Hagarty, Thomas Guthrie Marquis, James Lewis Milligan, Marjory Pickthall, and Sir Daniel Wilson.

Hereward Cockin (1854-1917) was one of the authors who participated in the city's first group reading by Canadian authors in 1892 (along with Duncan Campbell Scott, Wilfred Campbell, Pauline Johnston, *et al.*). A graduate of Oxford, he had come to Canada in the late 1870s. For an indeterminate time he worked for Goldwin Smith as an associate editor of *The Week*. In 1889 he also wrote for E.E. Sheppard at *Saturday Night* (although Sheppard soon got rid of him because his style was too "literary"). Eventually he moved to Guelph, where he died. While Cockin lived at **60 St. James Avenue**, he wrote the poetry book *Gentlemen Dick o' The Greys* (1889) which was so popular it had four printings in less than twelve months after publication.

Nearby is the northern remnant of **Rose Avenue**. Novelist Rich-ard Wright (b.1937) told me that apt. 702 of **135 Rose** was the first space he lived in without having to share with other people. This was his home in 1965 and 1966, but in the latter year he and his new wife were going to have baby, and they had to leave what was then an adults-only building. It would be a few years yet before he wrote his remarkable first novel, *The Weekend Man*. Franco-Manitoban author Paul Savoie (b.1946) also lived in

this building. In a letter, he elaborated, "Between June 1988 and May 1989 I lived in St. Jamestown on **135 Rose Avenue** where I sublet a cheap apartment . . . My stay there was extremely productive even though often punctuated by loud screams in the middle of the night (these were usually the result of 'bad trips' by drug users in the surrounding apartment complexes). While at this address I was fortunate enough to be named Writer-in-Residence at the Metro Reference Library, which took care of my financial problems for most of the year. I completed *Cosmic Picnic* and did substantial work with Marie-Lynn Hammond on *Mimi's Bar & Grill*. I wrote *Bois Brulé* which was recently published by Les Editions du Noroit. I also collaborated with several writers (Ayanna Black, Dore Michelut, Anne-Marie Alonzo, Lee Maracle) on a book of Renga poetry, *Linked Alive*."

"Ernscliffe," the apartment building at **197 Wellesley Street East** (corner of Sherbourne) has been home to three authors, the most famous being Sir Charles G.D. Roberts (1860-1943), who may have chosen this address partly out of nostalgia

Senior Staff of the *Canadian Poetry Magazine*, meeting c.1939: left to right are Charles G.D. Roberts, E.J. Pratt, Pelham Edgar, and Nathniel Benson.

because this was the area in which he had lived more than 40 years earlier (see Ontario Street below). Roberts moved into a third floor apartment in May 1925, shortly after his triumphal return to Canada from a long residence in England. In 1926 he moved to a fifth-floor flat and remained there until he died in November 1943. While resident in this building, Roberts discovered a second wind and produced noteworthy poetry books, including *The Vagrant of Time* (1927) and *The Iceberg and Other Poems* (1934). In 1935 he was knighted for his services to literature. Most of his poetry is out of fashion today, but his animal stories are still read with pleasure around the world. Along with Ernest T. Seton, he established a Canadian way of telling the animal story, from "inside the fur and the feathers," as Margaret Atwood has phrased it, that is followed by writers in this country right up to the present.

Poet Wilson MacDonald (1880-1967) also lived at **197 Wellesley East** from 1927-34: apt. 54 for the first three years and apt. 62 for the last four. He would occasionally visit Roberts by walking down the hall, but MacDonald felt unjustly eclipsed in fame by the older poet and the visits were said to be more polite than intimate. MacDonald is a tough character to gauge. Many people dismiss him as a bad poet, but he was better than most others of his generation. His aggression in selling his own work evokes titters or dismissive pooh-poohing from those who are easily shamed by commerce or ignorant of the man's desire to live solely by his pen. While others sat on their rears waiting and complaining about invitations to give readings that never arrived, MacDonald was out hustling for readings anywhere that would pay. But his pride clearly came across as arrogance to a lot of people, and his struggle to survive as a poet in Canada would occasionally cause his comments to transcend the critical and appear tiresomely bitter. When he was not talking about himself, MacDonald was usually sagacious or prescient. Take, for example, his comments about Toronto's

urban planning failures as of 1927 when he was living in The Ernscliffe: "Toronto has failed to make the most of her opportunities. There is the matter of the great park in the east end which might have been purchased some years ago for $10,000, and later for $100,000, but which now would cost $2,000,000. The buildings in Toronto are often haphazard and poor. Bloor Street should be made into one of the noblest of thoroughfares. And then the opportunity given by the Lake is being neglected. There is no reason why the railway could not be run underground, and a fine boulevard and parkway built over it. Instead of that there is the meretricious dazzle of Sunnyside and its bright lights. Such an amusement park should be inland. Even Chicago, with its fame for ugliness has a magnificent system of parks along the many miles of its lakefront. And the last great tragedy for Toronto would be to put a bridge over to the Island, refting seclusion from it—its most beautiful possession." *Plus ça change. . . .*

Novelist Joyce Marshall (b.1913) shared an apartment in The Ernscliffe for some months in 1943 with Joan Montgomery—who not long afterward became Mrs. Charles G.D. Roberts.

Afua Cooper (b.1957) wrote her children's book of poems *Red Caterpillar on College Street*, not on College, but on **Wellesley Street East: No.200** to be precise. Part of her adult poetry collection, *Memories Have Tongue* (1992), was also written at this address. Before he published his award-winning science fiction novels, Robert J. Sawyer (b.1960) lived in apt. 1002 at **240 Wellesley East.**

Kansas-born Peter Donovan (b.1884) came to Quebec to become a priest but changed his mind in order to become a writer in Toronto. He was well known to the book trade for his columns and reviews in *Saturday Night* in the early years of the century (1909-20) when he was the magazine's literary editor. The British-Canadian newspaper tycoon, Lord Beaverbrook, at the suggestion of Beverley Baxter, lured Donovan away to London in 1920 to work at the *Daily Express*. Some of Donovan's light essays were collected and published, just before he left town, as *Imperfectly Proper* (1920). A more substantial contribution to our literary culture was his novel *Late Spring* (1930) set entirely in Toronto (called Yorkton in the book). In 1911-12 he had rooms at **251 Wellesley East**. Then, for some reason he moved to the High Park area, only to return to **249 Wellesley East** in 1916, where he stayed until his departure for the UK in late 1920.

The internationally celebrated Czech-language novelist Josef Skvorecky (b.1924) lived in apt. 717 of **260 Wellesley East** throughout 1970-71, and then moved literally next door to apt. 719 and remained there from 1971-73. The altitude must have agreed with him, because he wrote, in Czech, three complete books here, all of which were later translated and published to

Josef and Zdena Skvorecky, summer 1970, at their home, 260 Wellesley Street East

acclaim around the world: *Miracle in Bohemia*, *Sins for Father Knox*, and *The Swell Season*. One of his neighbours in this building from 1971-72 was playwright Ken Gass (b.1945), founder of Factory Theatre Lab. Before it was a high-rise tower, **268 Wellesley East** was the home of John D. Robins (1884-1952), humour essayist, fishing fanatic, professor of English at Victoria, and a big influence on both Northrop Frye and E.J. Pratt.

Although Des McAnuff (b.1952) did write and publish a couple of plays, including *Leave It to Beaver Is Dead* (1976), he is now best known as a leading director of feature films and on Broadway. His film credits include *Cousin Bette* (starring Jessica Lange), and his New York hits include *The Who's Tommy*, which ran for two and a half years on the Great White Way. His first address on his own after leaving the family nest was **280 Wellesley East** from 1974-75.

Ontario Street used to run uninterruptedly through Wellesley up to Howard and it was on that stretch, near St. James Avenue, that Charles G.D. Roberts lived from October 1883 until almost a year later. He had come to Toronto to edit *The Week* for Goldwin Smith, but he found the workload so arduous and draining that he resigned, amicably, in early 1884 in order to support himself as a freelancer while still having sufficient free time to write poetry. To stretch his budget further, he rented part of his accommodation to the novelist Edmund Collins (1855-92). It must have been economic necessity alone which drove Roberts to choose to live so far from the offices of *The Week* (located near King and Yonge). The distance is even longer when one learns that, to save money, he walked to and from work every day except Sunday.

Poet David McFadden (b.1940) told me, "In early 1985 I moved out of the Annex to a seventh floor apartment at the Hugh Garner Co-op at **550 Ontario Street**, with a sunroom/studio that commanded a splendid view of Cabbagetown and St. Jamestown.

While there I finished both *Gypsy Guitar* (1987) and *A Trip Around Lake Ontario* (1988). At the end of the film version of *A Trip Around Lake Ontario* you can see me typing away in that studio. I moved from the Hugh Garner in spring 1988."

William Arthur Deacon is, in our time, an unfortunately overlooked hero of Toronto's literary life. This is foolish, really, because he is undeniably one of the most important literary figures of the 20th c. in our city. From May 29, 1922, when he was hired by *Saturday Night* to be the first full-time professional book reviewer in the history of Canada, he became the quiet comptroller of CanLit, the man who wrote weekly columns extolling his colleagues to write better, to have confidence in their abilities, and to be proud of their talents. Yet he was never afraid to admonish them in print when they were silly in their boostering, or too grandiose in their claims. Reading Deacon, especially his weekly news-and-views column in the *G&M* known as "The Fly Leaf," I accumulated the sense that he enjoyed playing the role of the self-effacing coach who gave advice, but then was happy—even proud—to watch others gather most of the glory.

Fred Paul, the editor of *Saturday Night*, employed Deacon on the recommendation of B.K. Sandwell. Fresh from Winnipeg where he had been raised, Deacon had come to Sandwell's attention because of the intelligence of the articles he had penned for such outlets as the *New York Times Book Review* and Henry Canby's *Literary Review* in the *New York Post*. Also, Sandwell must have been impressed by Deacon's love of Canada, obvious between the lines of almost every word he wrote. As one biography notes, "In his years in the west, he had established and consolidated for himself a powerfully idealized view of Canada's destiny from which he never wavered . . . In the twenties, in his years at *Saturday Night*, he was the right man in the right place at the right time. He was international in his intellectual interests

and totally Canadian in his emotional loyalties. When the two came in conflict in his work, he chose nationalistically and was convinced that it was in the best interests of Canada, its culture, its readers and its writers to do so." When he and his wife arrived in Toronto in May 1922, they moved into **530 Ontario Street**, their home for the next two years.

Flos Jewell Williams (b.1893) taught at Rose Avenue School when she lived at **5 Rose Avenue** from 1913-15. This was her last address in Toronto, as she married in 1915 and moved to Calgary. There she wrote novels set in her adopted province. This house was also the home of detective-fiction author John Lawrence Reynolds (b.1940), as he explained in a letter: "I lived in Toronto from June 1985 to December 1987. My wife and I purchased a home at **5 Rose Avenue**, one of six in a beautifully restored terrace in Cabbagetown.

"The structure was originally built c. 1880 and restored during the height of the Cabbagetown boom about a century later.

"My first novel, *The Man Who Murdered God*, was written at **5 Rose Avenue**. I had a neat writing room with a word processor set in a two sided window alcove on the second floor overlooking the intersection of Rose Avenue and Winchester Street. While the inspiration for the novel occurred in Hamilton and the setting was Boston, many of the characters were derived from residents of Cabbagetown. For example, the character of Mattie O'Brien originated with a neighbour who had once been a popular model and, in her forties, was earning a living as a real estate agent.

"In fact, the immediate area generated a wonderful cast of characters I expect to draw upon in the future. I know of no neighbourhood in Toronto, or perhaps anywhere else in Canada that provides such an astonishing range of socio-economic groups. Where else could one's neighbours include street people who measure time between bottles of cheap sherry, homeowners whose real estate is well into seven figures, sullen public housing residents who drove black souped-up Firebirds as though they were the drug-dealing equivalents of North Carolina bootleggers, and party hosts who bragged about their four-seater Jacuzzis and two-seater Mercedes?

"We moved from Toronto back to Burlington for an opportunity to avoid dog droppings on the sidewalk and vagrants sleeping in our backyard, and to enjoy the blessings of silence. Besides, we made an almost unconscionable amount of money on our two-year investment in the Toronto property, enabling us to move several rungs up the status ladder in house-proud Burlington.

"Yet not a day goes by when the writer in me doesn't miss the vitality of that area. I still steal an hour or two periodically to drive through the area or walk along Parliament Street assessing the prosperity of local merchants. Restaurants such as Brasserie les Artistes, La Plume and Le Petit Café are little jewels of dining pleasure and value. Allan Gardens is as rich in human drama as New York's Central Park. And I always wanted to do something literary with the lives of the prostitutes who gather at the Carlton-Ontario intersection, but I was never able to overcome the constraints of being a married WASP male and the laws against communication with prostitutes. Besides, I was afraid that if I approached a hooker with a proposition of paying her to talk to me about herself, she would consider me a particularly bizarre category of pervert.

"Aside from the above, I have mixed opinions of Toronto from a writer's perspective. Its best attribute—unparalleled safety for a city so large and complex—makes it less appealing to me as a writer of crime novels; I simply can't imagine dastardly events occurring there on a large scale. (Jack Batten set his first crime novel in Toronto, and structured the plot around a garbage collection scam—could there be a more appropriate villain for Toronto than an unscrupulous garbage collector?)

"I also believe it has generated a literary in-group with the usual incestuous aspects, but since I am not a part of it I am in no position to judge. It's also become far too expensive for many writers to reside in the central area, and the suburbs of Mississauga and Markham are as arid as any in the world, it seems. So where is a writer to live?"

One block south of Winchester and Rose is **Aberdeen Avenue. No.4** was the final Toronto address of Ernest Thompson Seton. The street was formerly called Carlton Avenue. His stay here was not long (as he explains below), in that he moved from here to Port Credit—a crucial move because it was in Port Credit that he finally had the time to write the stories that would comprise his first widely available book and launch his spectacular career. To please his mother, he made frequent trips to the family home, and certainly would have visited this address every Sunday until he finally left the city: "I arrived again at Toronto in January [1887] and put up at my parents' home. I did a little bird collecting up the Don and in the Toronto Marsh.

"My mother was very unwilling for me to go back to New York. She wondered if I could not carry on my work in Toronto.

"Then my brother Joseph made a suggestion. He was inclined to buy a tract of wild land outside of Toronto, and develop it into a summer resort. He gave me the chance of being the resident manager. It would furnish outdoor life among the wild things, and I could have a little cabin-studio in which to do my artwork. Thus it came about that in May 1887 my brother bought an eighty-six acre farm on Lake Ontario, a mile from Port Credit, and adjoining the resort of Lorne Park . . .

"It was here that I met the animal heroes whose histories are the basis of my stories, 'The Springfield Fox,' 'Molly Cottontail,' 'Dabbles the Coon,' 'Bannertail the Grey Squirrel,' 'Why Does the Chickadee Go

Crazy Twice a Year?,' 'The Song of the Golden-Crowned Thrush,' and, in less degree, many others.

"But more and more I was possessed of the thought that this was not my world. 'If I am to be an animal painter, I must break away—make a sudden, complete break.'

"The opportunity was brusquely put up to me by a business crisis. The Lorne Park Company, whose land adjoined ours, was bitterly hostile, and were able to do us much mischief. My brother's financial condition compelled him to sell out at a loss. The end of 1889 saw the mortgage foreclosed, and my last visit to our Park was on April 21, 1890. I got nothing out of the venture financially, but the experience, including the material for the above stories, was worth much.

"I had, however, bought some Toronto real estate. This I managed to sell for $1,800. With $450 of this, I paid my father a last installment, in full, of all his claims for educating and bringing me up. Then, with my steamer ticket and $1,200 cash, I set out for the East, arriving in London, England, June 11, 1890."

Cross Parliament Street and go south one block to **Carlton Street**. The man many regard as our finest playwright, George F. Walker (b.1947), established his home in a second-storey walkup apartment at **212 Carlton Street** from 1980-86. During this period he wrote one of his best-known dramas, *Criminals in Love*, which premiered at Factory Theatre Lab in 1984 as the first play at the theatre's new location on Adelaide Street. The drama has been successfully revived to continued acclaim. Other plays written and produced during his time at this address were *The Art of War* (1984), *Better Living* (1986), *Science and Madness* (1982), and *Theatre of the Film Noir* (1981). The latter won five Doras, including Best New Canadian Play. In the early part of his Carlton Street stint he took a few months off to serve as playwright-in-residence at the New York Shakespeare Festival, where the Manhattan debut of *Zastrozzi* took place in 1981. Other

Sarah Anne Curzon

cities around the world were also mounting Walker plays: among them Sydney, Australia; Edmonton; Seattle; Vancouver; San Francisco; London, England; Ottawa.

Any female who has attended university in Toronto will want to pause and offer a nod of thanks before **274 Carlton Street**, for this was once the address (1873-75) of Sarah Anne Curzon (1833-98), the playwright who did more than anyone to shame the UofT into opening its doors to women. Although she did not publish her satirical drama *The Sweet Girl Graduate* until 1882, a play mocking the university's claims that women lacked the intellectual capacity to study at the college level, she was already active as a journalist in championing women's rights when she lived here. She was a pioneer in educating the readers of her newspaper and magazine columns about female suffrage, access to higher education, and property rights equal to men. She was an important and vocal supporter of Dr. Emily Stowe's efforts to found the Women's Medical College (finally opened in 1883). And with another leading feminist, Mary Agnes Fitzgibbon, Curzon co-founded in Toronto the Women's Canadian Historical Society.

A block east of Parliament Street running north from Carlton is **Metcalfe Street**. Poet Dale David Zieroth (b.1946) had digs from August 1969 until June 1970 at **34 Metcalfe,** where he wrote many of the poems published in his first two books, *Mindscapes* (1971) and *Clearing* (1973). He worked in the CBC Radio Archives building on Sumach Street during this period. Playwright John Gray (*Billy Bishop Goes To War*) arrived in Toronto in 1975 and settled at once into **37 Metcalfe** for about 18 months. Then he moved next door to **No.39** and stayed there for a few months before quitting Cabbagetown for the west Annex. One of the reasons Gray had come to Toronto was to be an associate director of Theatre Passe Muraille, and to oversee the premiere of his new play, *18 Wheels*. While living on Metcalfe he also composed music for the dramas of other writers, such as *1837* by Rick Salutin.

Fantasy novelist O.R. Melling (b.1956) made her home at **38 Winchester Street** from 1980-81. Exactly one century earlier the humorist and poet Sydney Preston dwelt at **66 Winchester** for a couple of years. Melling had also resided at **No.115** over 1964-65. An even briefer residency was that of the country's most famous communist poet, Joe Wallace (1890-1975). He was at **No.139** for only a few months in 1938.

The English biographer and crime novelist Tim Heald (b.1944), who had lived in Toronto in the late seventies, wrote to me to say that "in 1982 I had some spare cash for the only time in my life . . . so we decided to 'do' North America, starting at the Epcot Centre and winging up to Toronto in our huge Chevy wagon before crossing to Santa Fe, New Mexico, where we were based through the winter and following spring. We couldn't face another Canadian winter! This time we rented **151 Winchester Street**, hard by the famous ice cream store, and spent the summer. I wrote the first draft of my non-fiction *Networks* as well as some journalism

mainly for England. I used to get inspiration from walking around that excellent cemetery [The Necropolis] or the children's zoo. And everyone ate a lot of ices. We met everyone all over again and Derrick Murdoch and I got the Crime Writers of Canada up and rolling after drinks on the roof of the Park Plaza. (I have a feeling that this glorious episode in my literary history has been the subject of some revisionism among the crime writers of Canada but luckily it is a matter of record because Derrick sent a note to *Red Herrings*, the official newsletter of the English Crime Writers, proclaiming the fact.) . . . What did Toronto mean? Easy. A sense of perspective. It was so refreshing to find a world where nobody had heard of all the boring household words around London and where there was a new stock of people who were 'world famous in Canada.' It was great to be taken at face value, whatever that was, and made to feel welcome and wanted and apart from a couple of brief and surprising moments, unresented. I wouldn't like to settle in Toronto for good perhaps because it's too far from my own roots, but perhaps if I'm honest because it does seem in the last analysis a bit parochial. London, too, is parochial, but it's my parish and also more people come through. (We see almost as many of our Canadian friends now as we did when we lived in TO, whereas we saw hardly any of our Brit friends in Toronto.) But for me and my family our Toronto years were exciting and stimulating, a chance to make a lot of good friends and to absorb a quite distinct and different culture. I liked—and like—the city a lot. I even came to like the CN Tower."

Salisbury Avenue is the next block north of Winchester. **41 Salisbury** was Jack Batten's base from June 1980 to July 1987. While making this his home, he wrote a number of his more than 30 books of fiction and non-fiction, including his best-known mystery novel, *Crang Plays the Ace* (1987). Other published works composed here on his Olivetti electric typewriter include *In Court* (1982), *On Trial* (1988), and *Judges* (1986).

Salisbury is intersected by the northern end of **Sackville Street**. When playwright Tomson Highway (b.1951) decided to settle in Toronto, his first place of abode was **399 Sackville**. He was here from October 1978 to February 1979. Little did he suspect that his neighbours were a couple of very well-known Canadian cultural figures. Adrienne Clarkson (b.1939) had abandoned novel writing by the time she moved to **409 Sackville** in 1975 so that she could devote herself full-time to broadcasting. Her companion, the novelist and polemicist John Ralston Saul (b.1947), joined her at this address in 1979, and it was here that he packed the jungle kits and desert supplies he needed for the research trips undertaken before writing his novel *Baraka* (1983). Drafts of the novel were also penned at this address. Clarkson and Saul moved to a house in the Yorkville area in 1980.

Don Bailey (b.1942) was sent to prison for armed robbery in the 1960s, and when he was released in August 1969, he drifted to the Christian Resource Centre and its writing circle at **297 Carlton Street**. Around November 1969, he moved into a room at **412 Sackville Street** and it was his home until May 1970. By chance, Bailey was interviewed by the *G&M* for an article on people who lived alone in rooms: "Take Don Bailey. He's 27, highly articulate and is attempting to work his way up as a freelance writer. He earns an average of $100 a month from the various publications, including an article in *Saturday Night* that he strings for but out of that must come $8 a week for a room at 412 Sackville Street—'I really like the room. I used to pay $24 a week at one place and $17 at another'—as well as provide himself with meals, clothes and other essentials.

"When you've got to shave it as close as that you don't do a lot of the things that you like doing—like drinking beer—unless you can do them for nothing,' he smiles. 'And obviously, I don't get haircuts,' he adds with a laugh as he shakes an unruly mop of nondescript brown hair . . .

Don Bailey as seen in his room, 412 Sackville Street, for a profile in the *Globe*, April 16, 1970

"Mr. Bailey also put his finger on the most soul-destroying aspect of rooming-house life—the loneliness. 'I don't think I've ever had a landlord who knew my name or who wanted to know my name. They don't want to become involved with you and neither do your neighbours, so you end up feeling like a very isolated human being. I can imagine what that does to you over a number of years." In an article for *Canadian Forum*, he elaborated on why he chose Sackville Street: "I got a small room in the Don Vale district. It was close to the Christian Resource Centre and perhaps there was a certain security in that. It was an insecure time. A time spent trying to find something. Direction. A meaning. All through that I continued to work during the day repairing cameras, a trade I'd learned years before and at night I drifted more and more often down to the Centre." Not long afterwards, he did find direction, and published his first book in 1971. Now he is a nationally known short-story writer and novelist (*In The Belly of the Whale*, 1974) based in Winnipeg.

One of Canada's most beloved poets, Al Purdy (b.1918), moved to **435 Sackville Street** in the fall of 1964 to join his wife, Eurithe, who was attending Teacher's College on Carlaw Avenue. They lived in a small flat on the top floor of the house which, at the time, had been subdivided into many small apartments. Regarding this time Al wrote to me in his telegraphic style, "We lived on Sackville Street in Cabbagetown, just two or three blocks from Riverdale Zoo and the Toronto Crematorium. I used to wander in graveyard and zoo sometimes. In summer of 65 I went to the arctic, returning to work on poems in *North of Summer* at that apartment. In fact, I remember turning the light out for sleep in winter after return, and thinking of that title, *North of Summer*, so much like a child's conception of the north. I used to walk to Parliament for groceries, passing the Winchester Hotel at corner of Winchester and Parliament. There were a liquor and beer store close to

that corner and the bums used to hit you up for a quarter to buy something."

The novelist Michael A. Gilbert (b.1945) lived for about half a year at **489 Sackville** after he separated from his wife in 1983. Earlier he had lived around the corner, as he explained in a letter: "I moved . . . from Kitchener-Waterloo in July of 1973 to **373 Wellesley Street East**. In 1976, I moved across the street to **386 Wellesley Street East**. While there I wrote *How to Win an Argument* (1979), and [my first novel] *Office Party* (Simon & Schuster, 1981) . . . For me, Toronto is a small town. I grew up in New York City, and Toronto is quieter, calmer, cleaner, safer, and more peaceful. It has many of the good aspects of a major urban centre without New York's fear and squalor. I find it a good place to work."

Hereward Cockin, met above on St. James Street, lived at **1 Parkview Avenue** (found at the eastern terminus of Wellesley Street) from 1891-94. He then sold the house to another writer, the novelist and poet James Miller Grant (1853-1940). Grant lived here until 1906, when he transferred to an address up the street, **No.16**, which remained his home until he died. Almost all of Grant's published writing was penned at one or the other of these addresses. His work appeared under the name Grant Balfour, and comprises an odd mix as indicated by the titles: *The Mother of St. Nicholas* (1899) was followed by *The Bride of Death* (1904?). In 1901 he published the patriotic-sounding poetry book *Canada My Home* (which sold 15,000 copies by 1912) and yet could describe himself to the Canadian historian Henry Morgan as "a Briton to his fingertips; considers it an honour to remain a subject of Great Britain, and to strengthen it to the full extent of his ability."

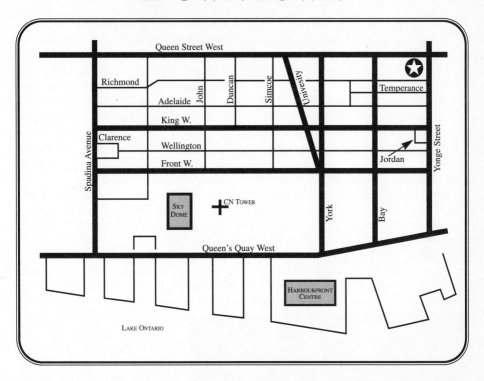

The tour begins on the southwest corner of Yonge Street and Queen Street West.

The Hudson's Bay Company building which currently occupies the corner of Queen and Yonge was originally constructed in 1896 by the Robert Simpson Company as its flagship store. In 1930, with Eaton's College Street about to open, and the Royal York Hotel to the south drawing record numbers, the management of Simpson's worried they were going to lose all of the lucrative lunch trade to these famous rivals. So they spent lavishly and opened the largest restaurant in the city, a spectacular Byzantine hall suitable, of course, for dining, but also for ballroom dancing—and for lectures. The official address of Arcadian Court was **176 Yonge Street**.

Arcadian Court never seriously rivalled Eaton Auditorium as a lecture hall, in part because the latter was purpose-built for such programming, and in much larger part because Eaton's had a full-time theatre management team charged with keeping the theatre booked with the best musical and literary talent of the day. Nevertheless, some distinguished authors gave public addresses in the Simpson hall. They include:

Basil King
Wyndham Lewis
Madge Macbeth
Wilson Macdonald
Nellie McClung
Alice Duer Miller
Blair Niles
E.J. Pratt
Thomas Raddall
Ernest Raymond
Charles G.D. Roberts
Wilhelmina Stitch

Rex Stout
Hugh Walpole

One of the most important writers of Africa—an assessment expressed by Africans themselves—lived in Toronto for some months early in the 20th c. Sol Plaatje (1876-1932) was born near Kimberley, in the Orange Free State. After the Boer War, he founded newspapers aimed at black readers and in the editorials expressed the frustrations and hopes of his nation—efforts which made his name prominent throughout the country. When the forerunner of the African National Congress was founded in 1912, Plaatje was easily elected to its executive. Within a few years he had written his most famous novel, *Mhudi*, described by the *Encyclopedia of Post-Colonial Literatures* as "the first South African epic, not only because it was the first epic written after the unification of the country, but, more importantly, because

it articulated the idea of 'South Africaness' as a common identity opposed to the divisiveness of tribalism and ethnicity." He also published a Setswana translation of Shakespeare, but most of his other writing, believed to be voluminous, has been lost.

Plaatje came to Toronto near the start of a year-long tour of North America he made from October 1921 to October 1922. He was in Toronto by November 12, 1921, and remained in the city almost three months—until January 31, 1922. The few letters of his that survive from this period give his address as the Kent Building, **156 Yonge Street**, the offices of an African-Brotherhood organization. He certainly used it as his office, but I have not been able to determine the addresses of the various families with whom he stayed.

He was very much taken with Toronto and with Canadians. To a friend back home he wrote, "I fell head over heels in love with the Canadians with their kindly manners and peculiar accents." He was busy giving sermons and speeches, meeting with people high and low and he proudly mentioned, "last Sunday I had in my audience Mr. Justice Coatsworth of the Supreme Court. He and his family came to shake hands and congratulate me on my sermon. I went to dinner with his son." His audiences included both whites and blacks. As the newspaper *Negro World* reported, "The best index of the impression stamped by his speeches and sermons on the minds of thinking Canadians is that the White Canadian brotherhood has undertaken, at a cost of $7,000, to print his African translation of the Fellowship Hymnbook." The same paper announced that local black community groups had rallied to buy him a $1,500 pipe organ to take home to his church

Sol Plaatje, photographed in Canada, probably in Toronto, c. 1920-21; identity of the young girls unknown.

hall in Kimberley. His biographer notes, "although neither gift ever in fact materialized, Plaatje never forgot the warmth of his reception in Toronto, and over the next few months [in the USA] he was to uphold it as an example for other communities to emulate."

The American Government was reluctant to let Plaatje into the States. They stalled his visa application on bureaucratic grounds but it is obvious the State Department was wary of what he might say. The Canadian Government had no such qualms. In fact, as he wrote to W.E. Du Bois (the famed civil rights activist in the States), the Canadian Government had just given him a Canadian passport—not knowing or caring that the South African Government had denied him one. Like any author, he also couldn't help bragging to Du Bois, "of the 600 books I brought with me to Canada, nearly 400 sold, 2/3 of them to coloured people, and they are still selling."

When author Alan Paton (*Cry the Beloved Country*) died recently, Nobel laureate Nadine Gordimer stated Paton was one of the five rocks on which South African literature was built. She then named the other four—and Sol Plaatje was one of them.

Newspaper Alley

The area immediately south of here was—for approximately one hundred years—Newspaper Alley, a small strip centred around King and Yonge into which were crammed the editorial offices and even the printing plants of all of the city's newspapers. The air must have been redolent with printer's ink. Pause and imagine the noise of the hustle and bustle of small trucks shuttling back and forth delivering as many as five editions, six days a week, of these newspapers. The cafés and restaurants would have been full of reporters and editors, many of them dreaming of being published as novelists or poets. Some of them actually wrote books rather than dream

about them. The sense of competition between papers and the craving for a scoop is palpable even when reading the microfilmed editions a century later. For one heady period of a quarter century (1894-1919) when the city's population was in the low hundreds of thousands, it was blessed with six daily broadsheet newspapers, and each of them devoted space at least once a week to book reviews. As well, all of them interviewed major authors when they came to town, and usually all but the *Telegram* put those interviews on the front page.

Many writers cited in this *Guide* worked for one or more of the newspapers. Many more writers were occasional freelance contributors, but space restrictions require that only those who were on salary can be listed.

The *News* began life in 1880. It really came into its own when its editor, the novelist E.E. Sheppard (1855-1924) bought the paper and, by hiring some of the best authors and journalists available, made it clear that good writing would be a hallmark of the journal. Unfortunately, within a few years of buying the paper and making it the journalism sensation of Canada, he was successfully sued for libel and the legal costs forced him to sell in 1887. Undeterred, he soon started another periodical: *Saturday Night*. Without Sheppard, the *News* was never the same, and it finally died in 1919. From 1883-1902 it was based at **106 Yonge Street**. In the next decade it was based at **116 Yonge** and from 1912 until its demise its home was **107 Bay Street**. Authors who worked for the *News* included:

William Allison
Augustus Bridle
John A. Currie
Rica Farquharson
Watson Griffin
Norah Holland
John David Logan
Marjory MacMurchy
Laura Elizabeth McCully
Duncan McKellar

Jesse Edgar Middleton
B.K. Sandwell
E.H. Stafford
Matthew Trill

The *Empire* was a morning paper founded in 1889 as the official voice of the John A. Macdonald faction of the Conservative party in Toronto. It began life at **8 King Street East**, spent a year at **2 John Street**, and from 1892-95 was based at **42 Adelaide Street West**—when it merged with the *Mail*.

The *Mail*, also a Conservative morning paper, had been started even earlier—in 1872—to support Macdonald's policies but was quickly abandoned by the party for not agreeing with the prime minister on all major issues. It then had a series of owners. Eventually it found proper backers who constructed the Mail Building in 1880 (at the northwest corner of King and Bay Streets), an architectural gem in the heart of the city, and the first building to be regarded as a sky-scraper in Toronto. When Sir John A. Macdonald died, the two Tory papers merged in 1895 as the *Mail & Empire* and as such continued to publish until 1936. The most important literary figure employed here was William Arthur Deacon (1890-1977). He had been working at *Saturday Night*. However, the playwright Fred Jacob, the *Mail*'s literary editor, died suddenly of a heart attack in 1928, and Deacon was promptly hired as his replacement. On the book page, Deacon introduced the characteristics that would become his trademark: a lead review accompanied by several brief reviews, and a column of literary and publishing news and gossip. It was, in other words, with this platform that he became the single most important book editor in the history of Canada.

From its beginning, the *Mail*—and then the *M&E*—were based at **52 King Street West**. Authors who worked for either the *Mail*, the *Empire,* or the *Mail & Empire* included:

A.G. Bailey
Charles Belford

Nathaniel Benson
John A. Currie
Nicholas Flood Davin
William Arthur Deacon
Frederick Dixon
Katherine Hale
Susie Frances Harrison
Fred Jacob
Peter McArthur
Franklin Davey McDowell
Bernard McEvoy
Owen McGillicuddy
Anne Merrill
Jesse Edgar Middleton
Guy Morton
Francis Pollock
Colin Sabiston
E.E. Sheppard

In 1936, the *Mail & Empire* merged with the *Globe* to become the *Globe & Mail*. The *Globe*, the city's oldest surviving newspaper, was started in 1844 (daily as of 1853). Founded by George Brown as a Liberal party vehicle, it bore the personality of its publisher more than any other until the advent of John Ross Robertson at the *Telegram*. For example, Brown refused to allow any report or reviews of theatrical productions in his newspaper—refused even to allow ads for the theatre.

During most of the latter half of the 19th c. it was based at **26 King Street East** but in 1890 it moved to new premises at **64 Yonge Street** (corner of Melinda Street). The melding with the *M&E* required a new home, which was found at **140 King Street West** in 1938 and it remained at that address until 1974 when it moved to its current location, **444 Front Street West.**

William Arthur Deacon kept his job as literary editor and remained in the position until 1960. His place was taken by William French who brought a different bearing on the position. With his longer reviews (occasionally published throughout the week, not just on Saturdays) and national distribution, he was the most influential reviewer in the country until the late 1980s.

Authors who worked for either the *Globe* or the *Globe & Mail* included:

Ralph Allen
Jean Blewett
John Clare
Joseph E. Collins
Nicholas Flood Davin
John Charles Dent
Sara Jeanette Duncan
James D. Edgar
John Mebourne Elson
Douglas Fetherling
John Norman Harris
Susie Frances Harrison
Vernal House
James Hogg Hunter
Charles C. Jenkins
Lois Reynolds Kerr
Newton MacTavish
Owen McGillicuddy
Anne Merrill
Guy Morton
Colin Sabiston
Robert Sellar
Christine Slater
Charles Templeton
E.W. Thompson
Pierre van Paassen

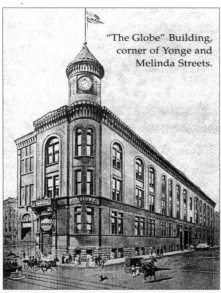

"The Globe" Building, corner of Yonge and Melinda Streets.

The *Star* began life in shaky circumstances in 1894 and it was some time before its future was secure. Most observers date that moment to the arrival of Joseph Atkinson, who shook up the Canadian newspaper world as no editor or publisher has since. The *Star*'s first office was **114 Yonge Street** until 1897, when it operated from **26 Adelaide Street West**. By 1901 it was back on **Yonge** at **No.109** until 1904. In 1906 it was housed in generous quarters at **18 King Street West** and remained there until 1929 when a much larger edifice was constructed for it at **80 King Street West**. This was its headquarters until a move to its current location at **1 Yonge Street** in 1972.

The most famous authors ever to have worked for the *Star* are Ernest Hemingway and Morley Callaghan. Other novelists, poets, and playwrights included:

Ralph Allen
Ron Base
Fred Bodsworth
Augustus Bridle
Nathan Cohen
Victor Coleman
Kildare Dobbs
Wilfred Eggleston
John Mebourne Elson
Rica Farquharson
Douglas Fetherling
Sylvia Fraser
Hugh Garner
Vancy Kaspar
Roy MacSkimming
Philip Marchand
Douglas Marshall
John Herries McCulloch
Owen McGillicuddy
Guy Morton
David Lewis Stein
Peter Taylor
Charles Templeton
Pierre van Paassen
Jon Edgar Webb
Frances Shelley Wees
Leon Whiteson

The *Telegram* (known to locals as the *Tely*) was begun by John Ross Robertson with financial assistance from Goldwin Smith as a liberal paper in 1877. However, Robertson was very much his own man and more conservative in outlook, so he and Smith split within a year or so of the newspaper's founding. At this time Robertson also lost his editor, John Charles Dent, who would later publish *The Gerrard Street Mystery* as well as several signal books of Canadian history.

The *Telegram's* first address was **67 Yonge Street**, but after two years it moved to **55 King Street West** (southwest corner of King and Bay, opposite the *M&E*) where it prevailed until the turn of the century. Its address was then **81 Bay Street** until 1923 when it moved again, this time to **233 Bay Street**. Its final years were spent at **444 Front Street West** from 1964-71.

The *Tely* was the least literary of all the Toronto dailies. However, Robertson had an affection for the history of Toronto, unusually passionate for the time, and his contributions to the study of the city's past have never been exceeded. After Robertson, various owners kept the journal Anglo-philiac, conservative, and more downmarket than up. Which makes Barry Callaghan's reign (1966-71) as editor of its literary pages anomalous. Elsewhere I have described Bill Deacon as the most influential book editor in Toronto history and his length of tenure and national reach make that description unassailable. But Callaghan's contribution was singular, for he exploded the traditional dull look of our book pages, introducing as regular components line caricatures of authors by "Annesley," succinct literary essays often in lieu of reviews, interviews notable for their candour, and reviews by eminent foreign writers whom no other book editor in Toronto had dared to ask. He also published on the book page important poetry by major figures from around the world (unheard in Toronto) and printed it with seductive design and in eye-catching typefaces. Other creative writers on the *Telegram* payroll included:

Ralph Allen
Nathaniel Benson
Nathan Cohen
Albert Munday
Phil Murphy
Charles H.J. Snider
Susan Swan
Scott Symons
Eva-Lis Wuorio
Scott Young

The *World* came into existence in 1880 and after foundering for about a year (it had begun life as a liberal paper, but turned conservative) it became famous for the uniqueness of its design (it is by far the easiest paper to read). It was also the first journal in Toronto to publish a Sunday edition, and the success of the *Sunday World* was what later inspired Joseph Atkinson to establish the *Star Weekly* as the *Star's* competitive equivalent. Its first permanent home was **18 King Street East**, and then, in 1883 it set up shop at **83 Yonge Street** where it remained until 1910. **40 Richmond Street West** was its final home when it died in 1921.

For a while, the noted author Albert E.S. Smythe was editor of the *World*. Other authors on its staff included:

Dora Conover
Flora Denison
John Mebourne Elson
Hubert Evans
Rica Farquharson
Donald G. French
James Haverson
John David Logan
Laura McCully
Franklin Davey McDowell
Archibald McKishnie
Roy Mitchell
Matthew Trill

Now that the reader has some sense of how rich this area was in newspaper publishing, the location of two important magazines with strong literary aspects may not seem so unusual. *The Week*, founded by Goldwin Smith in 1883, and edited in its first months by Charles G.D. Roberts, was published at **5 Jordan Street**, a lane running south from King, one tiny block west of Yonge. The magazine was an amalgam of poetry, essays, reviews, and articles on politics, science, and culture. Regular literary contributors included Bliss Carman, W.W. Campbell, Sara Jeanette Duncan, Susie Frances Harrison, Archibald Lampman, Canon F.G. Scott, and Ethelwyn Wetherald. It remained here until its demise in 1896. The magazine is also interesting to us now because it was the first to have a woman (S.F. Harrison) as its musical editor, and then literary editor. A literary biographer comments, "It was at this time while Mrs. Harrison was its literary editor that a new writer climbed those dingy stairs. 'A tall dark young woman,' says Mrs. Harrison, 'one whom most people would feel was difficult, almost repellent in her manner. But her work charmed me, though I had to tell her . . . that we didn't pay for poetry.'" The rejected writer was Isabella Valancy Crawford.

The other magazine with a literary bent founded in 1887 in this area was *Saturday Night*. The founder, novelist E.E. Sheppard, was forbidden to edit a daily newspaper as a result of a libel suit he lost, so he made an end-run around the court decision by starting a weekly newspaper. Those who know *Saturday Night* only as today's glossy magazine will not know that it was published, literally, on Saturdays as a newspaper aimed at the high society of Toronto. Even in the first number, issued from offices in the Grand Opera House at **9 Adelaide Street West**, it published fiction, including excerpts from one of Sheppard's own novels. The entire first issue sold out in a day. As did many subsequent numbers.

Sheppard was a charismatic editor, in that, just as he had done at the *News*, he attracted the brightest of the younger artists into his fold. Walter C. Nichol, Kit Coleman,

Hector Charlesworth, Pauline Johnston, and J.W. Bengough are just a few of the writers whose first or early writings appeared in the pages of *Saturday Night*. But by 1906, Sheppard was burned out and fed up with Canada. He moved to California and converted to Christian Science.

Once Sheppard was gone, the magazine became more traditional and coasted until 1932—although it did hire William Arthur Deacon in 1922, thereby giving the start to, as he described it, his long career as "the first full-time, professional book reviewer that Canada had ever seen." It was thanks to Deacon that the periodical in 1925 began to publish a huge literary supplement of up to 24 pages—never as frequently as Deacon wanted, but a breakthrough in the extent of book coverage nonetheless.

B.K. Sandwell became editor in 1932 and immediately raised the journalism standard of the paper and expanded its horizon to include all of Canada, not just Toronto. He hired a young Robertson Davies in 1940 as his literary editor. To many observers, Sandwell's reign was the finest in the history of the periodical. By 1951, however, he was an old man, and the fatigue showed. He resigned and the newspaper in that year became a magazine, a format it has kept to this day.

Saturday Night moved to **26 Adelaide Street West** in 1896 and remained there until 1912. It then moved into **73 Richmond Street West**, its home until 1962 when it began a head-spinning series of address changes.

Bay Street south of Front Street has no literary connections. Immediately north of Front, however, from 1861-64 lived one of the first professional creative writers in Toronto, James McCarroll (1814-92). Through political patronage, he became Surveyor of the Port of Toronto in 1854, although he was a good enough flautist that he went on concert tours. He was also the music critic for two Toronto newspapers. He had been publishing creative writing in magazines for years but it was not until the

1860s that he published his first books: a collection of humorous sketches and two plays. In 1889 he published his first volume of verse. By this time he was a resident of New York. The *Dictionary of American Biography* says that "at the time of his death he was negotiating the sale of patents upon his inventions: an improved elevator, and a fire-proof wire gauze." He was represented in all of the important Canadian anthologies of his time, and his death merited an obituary in the *New York Times*.

Bay crosses **King Street** near here and is a convenient place to detour to see **31 King Street West**, once the location of McConkey's Restaurant and Banquet Rooms, the preeminent place to dine for the *haute monde* of Toronto in the decade after 1900. Some eminent authors made public addresses at McConkey's, in part because the city was short of appropriate venues for such affairs: the St. Lawrence Hall had fallen on hard times, the Horticultural Pavilion was not available, and the "opera houses" were either engaged or too large.

McConkey's, 31 King Street West

Among the authors who spoke here were William Henry Drummond, Elbert Hubbard, Alfred Noyes, Sir Gilbert Parker, Sir Charles G.D. Roberts, and Cy Warman. But the most famous by far was Rudyard Kipling (1865-1936).

The poet and fiction writer of Empire, Kipling made a few visits to Canada but his only time in Toronto was a two-day stop in 1907. On October 17, 500 people stretched in a line along King Street past Bay in order to obtain tickets for Kipling's speech the following night. Three policemen were needed to help keep order in the queue. The media coverage in advance, during, and after his talk was awesome and came close to displacing the record for coverage held by Matthew Arnold. Newspapers treated his visit on their front pages, on their editorial pages, in their editorial cartoons, on their news pages, and in the society columns. There was much murmuring about why his hosts, the Canadian Club, had not rented a larger space so that many more could hear him, and the answer to the question remains a mystery. Although some of the editorials challenged his stand on "Asiatic immigration to the colonies," most of the newspaper reports were unusually flattering. An example is the lead of the report in the *News*: "Other visitors from the big world beyond Toronto have crowded the banqueting hall where the Canadian Club entertains its guests; other visitors have awakened louder applause but it remained for Rudyard Kipling to draw so near to the hearts of the members that they crowded round him at the end to shake his hand—and that without an introduction. It was not needed. They had known him before, or felt they did, when he had expressed, as no one else, the thoughts of their everyday lives. . . ." *The World* was more level-headed: "Never had the Canadian Club a more popular or distinguished guest. He spoke briefly, not to exceed twenty minutes. Indeed, the local celebrities spoke at greater length. Mr. Kipling talks very slowly. There is a little

MR. KIPLING LISTENING TO THE "RECESSIONAL"

MR. KIPLING'S LAUGH

Sketches of Rudyard Kipling at the Canadian Club

Star, front page illustrations, October 19, 1907

pause between syllables, and a perceptible pause after every word. His voice is not strong, and he makes no pretence at eloquence. But his articulation is clear and distinct, with just a suggestion of what we are accustomed to call 'the English accent,' and he speaks to the point. No time was wasted in local references or conventional compliment . . . To a friend last night he stated that Toronto was the most loyal city within the British empire.' The *Star* remarked that the dinner 'was well advanced when the guest of the evening arrived. There was a tremendous ovation in his honour when he walked into the main dining hall . . . The crowd rose and cheered and cheered again . . . When Mr. Kipling arose [to speak] it was some minutes before he could get a hearing. The applause and the ovations, the *Jolly Good Fellow* and the *Cheers*, kept him standing at attention for several minutes." The speech itself was Kipling's usual exhortation to Canada to take a leading role—within the Empire, naturally—in solving its problems and conveying its solutions to the other colonies. Nonetheless, it made a deep impression on the locals, and even a wise old journalist like J.S. Willison, Editor of the *News*, was seduced into thinking the usual was the unusual. He wrote in his lead editorial, "There is an eager, biting quality in his sentences and the stamp of an original mind is over them all. He may have said nothing that was very new or very profound to those who have read his books and have caught the turn and temper of his writing. But he spoke as only Kipling speaks. . . ." Well, from our vantage, it is hard to imagine Kipling speaking as anyone else, but such was the man's sway.

The *Globe* report included an extraordinary account of how Kipling's day was spent, forcing one to marvel at his patience: first, he was driven through Rosedale, and then calls were made at the private schools of St. Andrews and Upper Canada College where he spoke to the principals and boys—and was "accorded a hearty reception." At the UofT he spoke to the professors in a body. Next came City Hall and an encounter with the mayor, and then another visit, this time to meet the Chief Justice. The entire exercise took three hours. The *Globe* quoted Mr. Kipling as saying it was "most enjoyable."

The National Club at **303 Bay Street** hosted two dinners for Sir Gilbert Parker (1862-1932). The first was held on April 6, 1896 and the second about two years later. His friend, the novelist Robert Barr (1850-1912), also happened to be visiting at the same time and both men made what the newspapers termed "witty speeches."

The eminent Scottish novelist Eric Linklater (1899-1974) was in Toronto in October 1958 to coordinate his researches for a corporate history of the Rio Tinto Zinc company (from its offices then at **No.335**) which he had been commissioned to write. He abandoned the book the following year because the deeper he dug, the less he liked what he saw regarding environmental and other abuses by the company. By coincidence the UK edition of his latest novel was being published in Canada, so he lingered to help with publicity. At a publisher's party, someone mentioned to him that Scottish letters

The Grand Opera House, from *Canadian Illusrated News*, August, 1874. Amoung authors associated with this building were Bram Stoker, Oscar Wilde, Sarah Bernhardt, and Dion Boucicault.

seemed to be in a lull. "No young Boswells?" he was asked. "No Johnsons," he retorted.

Linklater found Canada beautiful, and the people friendly—but abstemious to the point of absurdity as he wrote to his wife on October 17, 1958: "In Toronto I had nothing much to do except meeting and talking to people. I arrived on the eve of their Thanksgiving Day . . . We sat down to Thanksgiving dinner which consisted of 2½ pounds of rather tough turkey and *iced water*. Nothing else to drink. Nothing . . .

"My Canadian publishers again took charge of me on my last day in Toronto. I was led, like a dancing bear, from bookshop to bookshop, at each of which I had to inspect their shelves and talk nicely to a large number of people—then I was delivered to the Canadian Broadcasting Corporation for a television interview . . . After the television, I attended a publisher-and-booksellers' dinner in my honour. Again a great deal to eat—and iced water to drink. I answered questions for three-quarters of an hour—they were all very kind and friendly—and so was I. I was indeed. On iced water . . . "

Adelaide Street West crosses near here. **No. 9** was once the home of one of the most beautiful Victorian theatres ever built in Canada, the Grand Opera House. Opened in 1874, it was erected to eclipse the Royal Lyceum Theatre nearby on King Street. The Grand seated more than two thousand people. (Readers should be wary of the Victorians' use of the word "opera." Opera houses on this continent rarely produced opera. Rather, the term was used to describe almost any theatrical performance, including vaudeville.) The legendary impresario Ambrose Small bought the Grand Opera House in 1903, and, according to Hector Charlesworth, "it lost its ancient glory from the very day Small entered its doors as proprietor, and never recovered it." Small would later become infamous as the man who sold this and other theatres for almost two million dollars in 1919. He immediately deposited more than half of the funds, and then

instantly disappeared forever. Mysteriously, the deposited sum remained untouched. The Grand closed forever in 1927.

Well before Small's ownership, the Grand Opera House featured some of the biggest theatrical names of the age—a few of whom also wrote novels or their own plays. One of them continues to frighten people witless.

Millions of vampire fans are unaware that Bram Stoker (1847-1912) wrote *Dracula* (1897) relatively late in his life and would much have preferred to be remembered by history as one of the greatest theatrical managers of all time. His innovations and his importance are summarized neatly by one of his best biographers: "Stoker was the first to number expensive seats which made advance booking advantageous. He stopped the practice of the house staff's upgrading customers' seats and pocketing the difference. Instead of the box office issuing complimentary tickets, he did so personally and had them printed on cardboard to resemble invitations to elite social events. By advertising upcoming plays, Stoker's management made possible the financial projections necessary to plan, promote and sell a season—rather than a show a night. In truth, his business acumen helped to mold the modern theatre."

He worked for Sir Henry Irving, the most celebrated actor of his day and a man who spent lavishly, often imprudently, on his productions in his London theatre. In order to pay the mounting debts, Stoker created the idea of the "road show" whereby the Irving troupe (including Ellen Terry, one of the most eminent actors of the era) would travel by their own train throughout North America presenting both classics and melodramas. The operation was so massive that two boxcars were required just to hold the wigs. And the labour involved was fantastic: arriving in a town in the morning, Irving, Terry, and Stoker would meet the press and dignitaries while the crew erected and adjusted the sets to meet the limitations of the local theatre (or what passed for a theatre). If there was time, the cast would re-block and rehearse their moves due to the changed circumstances of the performing space, and then would be expected to perform at their peak. Immediately after the production, the crew would strike and pack the set, and everyone would board the train, and set off for the next town to repeat the process, day after day after day—for months. No wonder they looked forward to large cities with real theatres such as Toronto where the audiences were sufficiently large that they could remain for up to a week.

Bram Stoker accompanied Henry Irving on all eight North American tours, five of which included Toronto. It was in Stoker's nature to withdraw to the shadows while Henry Irving and Ellen Terry shone in the limelight, so unfortunately Stoker does not appear in any Toronto newspaper coverage of the Irving retinue visits. And paper programs and posters from that era have largely disappeared. However, a few survive, and one of them documents his presence in the city. All five of the Irving company visits took place at the Grand and spanned the years 1884-1900. Robertson Davies noted in a history of Victorian theatre in Toronto that "even players so high above commonplace criticism as Henry Irving and Ellen Terry, when they travelled on this continent, stayed at separate hotels so that there could be no suspicion that they were associated other than as artists."

Two other dramatic stars who played the Grand, Sarah Bernhardt and Dion Boucicault, also did creative writing of their own. The first four of Sarah Bernhardt's (1845-1923) many productions in Toronto between 1881 and 1910 took place in this theatre. It was during her third visit, October 29-30, 1891, that the inimitable journalist Kit Coleman talked her way into the Divine Sarah's dressing room at the Grand for an interview and came out of the meeting her friend—and came out as well with a real rarity, a drawing of the actress backstage *en déshabillé*. Towards the end of her career, Bernhardt, who had already penned some plays, began to write novels which were published to polite but muted response.

Dion Boucicault (1820-90) is a playwright important to American theatre especially, in that he led the dramatists' group

---

Thursday Evening and Saturday Matinee—Shakespeare's Comedy in Five Acts,

MUCH ADO ABOUT NOTHING
Benedick—Mr. Henry Irving.   Beatrice—Miss Ellen Terry.

Friday Evening, Oct. 10th—Shakespeare's Tragedy in Five Acts,
HAMLET
Hamlet—Mr. Henry Irving.   Ophelia—Miss Ellen Terry.

Saturday Night—Farewell Performance, when will be presented Casimer Delavigne's Play in Five Acts,
LOUIS XI
Adapted and arranged by Dion Boucicault.
Louis XI.   —   —   —   Mr. Henry Irving.

Mr. H. J. Loveday..Stage Manager
Mr. J. H. Palser (American tour)..................................Business Manager
Mr. Bram Stoker...Acting Manager
Mr. Marcus R. Mayer..Agent

Rare Grand Opera House programme, October 8, 1884, showing Bram Stoker (near bottom) as Acting Manager which lobbied Congress successfully for the copyright protection of playwrights. His own plays were hugely popular, and, because of its suggested attack on slavery, his drama *The Octoroon* (1859) caused great commotion and became his best-known work. He has been credited with writing more than 150 plays. As an actor he was renowned for his skill and insight, and again is historically important for almost single-handedly elevating the stage portrayal of the Irishman above that of the

Sarah Bernhardt in her dressing room, Grand Opera House, after the third act of La Tosca
Mail, October 31, 1891

buffoon. Robertson Davies rated Boucicault highly and described him as "that genius of melodrama. [His] skilled contrivances of plot are cloaked under picturesque scenes and characters that first-rate actors were glad to sink their teeth into and make their own . . . It was Boucicault who said that good plays are not written, but rewritten, and although this cannot be taken as a general truth, he proved its applicability to the sort of sure-fire, well-contrived melodrama he himself put on the stage and in which he played leading roles." He first played the

Grand Opera House in February 1884 for three nights and returned in November of the same year for a week-long run.

390 Bay Street was the site of the Temple Café which, despite its informal name, was rather an elegant restaurant. If McConkey's was not available, the Temple Café was a satisfactory second choice for meetings of the Canadian Club at the start of the 20th c. At least three novelists gave addresses here, all of them knights: Sir Wilfred Grenfell, Sir Gilbert Parker, and Sir Rider Haggard. Haggard (1856-1925) was the author of the hugely popular *King Solomon's Mines* and *She* (from which the expression "She Who Must Be Obeyed" originates) among many other novels. His arrival in Toronto in mid-April 1905 was front-page news and came at the tail end of a two-month tour of the USA. During his speech he asked questions of his audience that, a century later, continue to bear asking? "Why do you allow so much emigration to go to the United States? . . . Why do you not make yourselves better known?" Haggard continues to have fans among serious literary authors. Graham Greene was a devoted reader (he instructed Anthony Burgess "Haggard has to be read entire"), and Margaret Atwood devoted a third of her PhD thesis to Rider Haggard.

Nearby is **Temperance Street** where in 1848 Jesse Ketchum built a Temperance Hall at **No.21** (after which the street was named in 1850). It was here that Ralph Waldo Emerson gave a lecture to a packed house on December 22, 1858 during his first of three visits to Toronto. He spoke on the rise of America and the "Law of Success." He was shaken by a question posed at the end of his remarks. A contemporary reporter noted, "Emerson lectured in Toronto the night previous to his lecture [in Hamilton] and having uttered some heresies, a pious bookseller named Geikie was moved to put a question to him, fearing that some of the audience might go away thinking less of the Bible than they ought. Emerson's answer, the Toronto papers say, was not consoling to Geikie and the pious, but was applauded by the audience. Speaking of this, Emerson said it was the first instance in which he had been interrogated in that way, and that it was best to make no reply, but that he did it at the request of Dr. McCaul, [the Master of Ceremonies]. 'My idea of the Lyceum,' he said, 'is that I shall there speak what I like without question, and that others shall have like freedom.'"

The *Methodist Magazine* was based at **30-36 Temperance Street** in the early 1890s when the 20-year-old British writer Algernon Blackwood (1869-1951) began his literary career at this very spot. In his amusing memoir, he notes: "I served my first literary apprenticeship on the *Methodist Magazine*, a monthly periodical published in Toronto, and before that licked stamps in the back office of the Temperance and General Life Assurance Company, at nothing a week, but with the idea of learning the business, so that later I might bring out some English insurance company to Canada . . . It was the three months in the insurance office that caused me to accept eagerly the job on the *Methodist Magazine* at four dollars a week and the reaction helped to make the work congenial if not stimulating . . . Dr. Withrow, editor of the leading Methodist magazine, and of various Christian Endeavour periodicals for children and young people, was a pleasant old gentleman, who went about in a frock coat and slippers . . . I still hear him giving me my first and only lesson how to write. His paraphrase of 'fatal facility' stays with me: 'Fluency means dullness, unless the mind is packed with thought.' It stays with me because the conversation led to my asking if I might write an article for the monthly on the subject of Buddhism. Behind it lay an ever keener desire to write something on Hegel, whose philosophy I felt certain was based on some personal experience of genuine mystical kind.

"'From what point of view?' he asked, his forehead puckering with amazement.

"That of belief,' I said, my mind bursting with an eager desire to impart information, if not also to convert.

"'He passed his hand across his forehead, knocking the spectacles off. Then, catching them with a fumbling motion which betrayed his perturbation, he inquired:

"'But, of course, Mr. Blackwood, not your *own?*'

"The voice, the eyes, the whole attitude of the body made me realize he was prepared to be shocked, if not already shocked.

"'Yes,' I replied truthfully, 'my own. I've been a Buddhist for a long time.'

"He stared for some time at me without a word, then smiled a kindly, indulgent, rather sceptical smile. 'It would be hardly suitable,' he mentioned, as I felt his whole being draw away from me as from something dangerous and unclean.

"Possibly, of course, he did not believe me; I am sure he prayed for me. Our relations seemed less cordial after that; he read most carefully every word I wrote in his magazine and children's pages, but he never referred to the matter again."

Another writer of about the same age who lived in a rooming-house somewhere on this short street (the exact number is unknown) was William Wilfred Campbell (1858-1918). Campbell is considered by scholars as one of the "Confederation Poets," that group of writers who, flushed with the birth of new country, were passionate in expressing their love of the Canadian landscape and its legends.

Poet and *Descant* magazine editor Karen Mulhallen (b.1942) wrote to me about a job she took at **66 Temperance** to supplement her income while in grad school 1963-64: "I supported myself as a Bell Telephone Emergency Operator, going each evening to Temperance Street where, festooned with headphones, I took calls from people on the verge, and stayed with them until I could get help to them. I would leave Temperance Street in the dark of the night and take a Bay bus up to my one room (bachelor) apartment, and then read Milton's *Paradise Lost* or Spenser's *Faerie Queene* in the dead of the night, the choking terrified voices, the suicides, the victims still in my headphones."

The next street north is **Richmond Street West**. At **No.80** poet Leo Kennedy (b.1907) worked for an advertising agency when he lived in Toronto 1934-39. His residences during this period remain a mystery. For a man who published only one volume of verse, his reputation is rather substantial. That is because eminent literary people such as E.J. Pratt, W.E. Collins, and F.R. Scott thought so highly of it—and said so in print and in publishing hallways. The Italian-American storyteller Arturo Vivante (b.1923) spent a long summer in Toronto in 1941, the latter half of which was lived in a room at **No.85**. His Toronto experience was only lightly fictionalized in the story "The Stream," first published in *The New Yorker* in 1958 and later reprinted in several collections. Playwright Tomson Highway (b.1951) kept rooms from October 1983 to June 1985 at **No.104,** where he wrote his apprentice plays which led soon after to *The Rez Sisters* and other hits.

By heading south on Sheppard we can find our way to **152 Adelaide Street West** where the pioneer writer Susanna Moodie (1803-85) lived with her daughter, Katie, and son-in-law from 1869-71 and again in 1885. She died here. Her sister Catherine Parr Trail (1802-99), also a writer, made extended visits to her relatives at this address from time to time.

Alexander Somerville (1811-85), Scottish-born soldier and author, related in his *Autobiography of a Workingman* (1848) how he was given 100 lashes for daring to publish a letter in which he told the authorities that he and his fellow soldiers were discomfited by the extreme force they were ordered to use to control protesters of the Reform Bill. Newspapers, politicians, and the public were outraged at his punishment, and a public subscription raised £300 on his behalf. In fact, he claimed with some justification that

his whipping led to the abolition of that form of punishment in the military. He quit the army and began a career as a freelance journalist and pamphleteer. In 1858 he emigrated to Canada, settling first in Hamilton, where he was the first editor of *Canadian Illustrated News*. In this country he wrote several books and acted as a correspondent for British periodicals. By 1873 he was in Toronto editing a church newspaper but that job ended a scant two years later when the journal folded. He struggled to make a living as a freelancer but towards the end of his life was reduced to the severest poverty, finally living in a shed behind **106 York Street**, living on porridge and the kindness of strangers. He died, derelict, in the shed on June 17, 1885.

One of the earliest literary visitors to Toronto was Richard Henry Dana (1815-82), author of the American classic novel *Two Years Before the Mast*. He came here after a trip to Niagara in 1845. In his journal for July 17 he noted, "The sail across Lake Ontario was delightful; the afternoon clear, a steady cool breeze, and a spacious, pleasant boat. The passage took us three hours and we reached Toronto at 6:30. Put up at McDonald's and after tea rode, in an open carriage, to the barracks where S. and I heard the tattoo and a full band playing at the officers' mess.

"July 18: Friday: After breakfast, walked to the barracks and saw the end of a parade and heard some music from the band which was remarkably good. Went over the Government House which is now deserted, the seat of government being removed to Montreal. It is a spacious building with wide entries and suites of high rooms; but stripped of all ornament and furniture and a bar is kept at one end of the reception room. The Parliament Houses are now only used for a college and a Courts of Law. We walked through the town which is much larger than I supposed, and having the appearance of increase and of great business. I should think it was as large and as busy as Hartford." He was correct. Both cities had populations of approximately 15,000 at this time. The barracks to which he refers were the Stanley Barracks at the CNE. His hotel, properly spelled as "MacDonald's" was located at what is today **95 King West**.

Just to the west of this hotel was the Royal Lyceum Theatre, at what is today **No.101**. The theatre was built in 1848 and was set quite far back from the street, so the approach to the entrance through an arched gate on King became known as Theatre Lane. The Royal Lyceum was the first purpose-built theatre in Toronto and as such became home to the performances of the Philharmonic Society, touring musicians and actors, and the stock company of local impresario and director John Nickinson. Like all theatres of the age it was a frequent victim of fire, and following an especially damaging blaze in 1874 it was completely rebuilt and then reopened as the Royal Opera House, seating about 1,500. Another fire a decade later ended its use as a theatre. Later a warehouse, it was demolished in 1940.

The noted Irish playwright and actor John Brougham (1810-80) had a very successful week's run at the Royal Lyceum in 1855. Another actor-playwright, Graves Simcoe Lee (1828-1912), was not so internationally acclaimed, but merits mention here because his play *Fiddle, Faddle, and Foozle* was the first Canadian play to be performed in Toronto—at the Royal Lyceum in 1853.

The final actor turned playwright to note in association with the Royal is Denman Thompson (1833-1911), whose fame near the end of his life knew no bounds on this continent. Born in the States, he was hired by Nickinson in 1854 to play comic roles in his Toronto productions and Thompson remained here until 1867, the most popular actor in the city. According to the *Oxford Companion to Canadian Theatre* he was "charged in 1868 with complicity in American express-train robberies [but] he hid in Toronto where an offered reward found no takers and where, on his return to the stage

in 1871, enthusiastic crowds greeted him with undiminished affection." In 1874 while recuperating from an illness in Pittsburgh, he wrote his first full-length play, *Josh Whitcomb*. He took the leading role and starred in theatres in the States and Canada for the next 11 years, playing to full houses and rave reviews. In 1886 he premiered his next play, *The Old Homestead*, much along the same lines as the first, and just as applauded. Tastes certainly change. A contemporary encyclopedia account describes his work in these amazing terms: "Josh Whitcomb, the plain, warm-hearted and simple New England farmer as enacted by Mr. Thompson, has long been recognized as one of the distinct and masterly creations of the American stage . . . The essential attributes of its success are its naturalness and fidelity to truth." Such terms are unlikely to be used today but, that distinction aside, it is worth noting that one of the most popular playwrights of the 19th c. began and fostered his career at 101 King West.

Man of letters and theatre critic Hector Charlesworth lived in the thick of the newspaper and theatrical worlds when he lived at **113 King West** from 1900-1.

On the south side of King, between York and University Avenue (approximately today's **167-173 King**) was the Princess Theatre. Originally, the site was occupied by the Thomas Pianoforte Manufactory. But in 1889 it was modified to become the Academy of Music, complete with a small art gallery and a large performing space, the first in town to be lit entirely by electricity. The spot has tremendous significance for Canadian writing because it was here, on January 16, 1892, that Frank Yeigh organized the first group reading by Canadian authors in the history of the country. An account by the *World* gives the flavour of the contemporary reaction: "It was a great success, the Young Liberal's Club Evening of Canadian Authors; still, they made one mistake and that was in not getting a larger hall than the gallery of the Ontario Society of Artists. The room was crowded to excess; even ladies had to stand and numbers were turned away.

"President Frank Yeigh was in the chair, and opened with an address, in which he deplored the Canadian habit of neglecting our authors and leaving it to the Americans to discover them and appropriate them. He thought that Canada had a literary class and that she needs to encourage it to gain for herself a distinct individuality . . . Mr. William Wilfred Campbell, 'The Poet of the Lakes,' read a prose sketch of his General Bain of Sandy Beach. It is a very humorous sketch of an odd freak of character, exactly such as the solitude of the backwoods produces, and it lost none of its humour in Mr. Campbell's quiet yet effective tones. . . . Mrs. Harrison, well known under her pen name 'Seranus,' read her sketch of French-Canadian life, 'In the Valley of the St. Eustache.' For lack of time it had to be condensed, but it was most effective . . . Then came Mr. Hereward K. Cockin, the genial editor of the *English-Canadian*, with his well-known favourite, 'Gentleman Dick o' the Grays.' It was applauded and he retired in favour of Mr. W.D. Lighthall of Montreal who read a chapter from *The Young Seigneur*, a glowing picture of an ideal Canada . . . The second part was opened by Miss E. Pauline Johnson with her 'Cry from an Indian Wife,' a sympathetic rendering of the sorrow of a widow of a warrior at Cut Knife Creek. It was enthusiastically received, so enthusiastically that the author had to reappear and recite her wildwood poem, 'My Bark Canoe.' After her recall, Mr. Duncan Campbell Scott, 'one of our trio of Ottawa poets,' as the president said, read his powerful and sombre tale 'Veronica.' Miss Helen Merrill recited her poem

'Regret.' The Minister of Education now addressed the audience briefly, congratulating it on the success of the evening. Then in conclusion Mr. Campbell recited his now famous poem 'The Mother.' As he read the intensely sympathetic rendering of yearning mother-love, the room became as silent as the tomb. With its intense fire of feeling the poem made an impression that attested to its worth. This closed a delightful evening."

The evening was special in many ways. This night at the Academy of Music, in effect, launched Pauline Johnson's career. The audience reaction to her reading was not lost on Yeigh and he quickly organized prompt return engagements for her in Toronto—visits profitable to both of them. In fact, he suggested to her that she should compose a new poem suitable for public reading. It was for the next Toronto reading that she wrote her most celebrated work, "The Song My Paddle Sings." The evening was also special because it marked the first time, after a half-century of visits to Toronto by foreign writers, that Canadian-born authors were being feted by the press and the public.

The Academy of Music was rebuilt in 1895 and renamed the Princess Theatre. It was while playing here in 1901 in a melodrama he had written himself (one of more than a

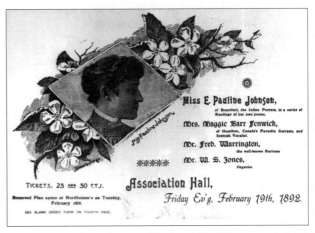

Playbill for Pauline Johnson's February 19th, 1892, engagement in Toronto

hundred credited to him) that actor-dramatist Hal Reid (1873-1920) discovered a child-actor named Gladys Smith. He encouraged her mother to foster her career on the stage. The mother agreed, the child soon moved to the States, and adopted the stage-name Mary Pickford. The rest is film history. Actress Sarah Bernhardt also played this theatre twice (1891 and 1910). Late in her career she tried her hand at both fiction and drama—which, unlike Pickford, we know with certainty she wrote herself. The novelist Sara Jeanette Duncan (1861-1922) had the pleasure of being the first Canadian woman ever to have a major production in Toronto. Her play, *His Royal Happiness*, was premiered in this theatre in January 1915.

In 19th c. Toronto there were two grand hotels. Royalty stayed at The Queen's, the forerunner of the Royal York. But a happy second choice for most people (and authors) was the Rossin House, once located at **91 York Street**. Among the writers who resided here while in town for public events were George Washington Cable, Edward J. Chapman, Sir Winston Churchill, Wilkie Collins, Wilfred Eggleston, Frederick Philip Grove, Anthony Hope, Henry Wadsworth Longfellow, Ian Maclaren, Florence Marryat, Max O'Rell, and Mark Twain.

Longfellow was in town for only one night as part of a flying visit he was making to Niagara and Quebec. It is one of the ironies of Canadian literary history that the man who wrote *Evangeline*, one of the most identifiably "Canadian" poems to foreigners, never visited Acadia, and can hardly be said to have visited Canada, his stay was so short. Toronto made little impression on him, understandable given the brevity of his stay, and because he was agitated by what he had gone before—as he wrote in his journal of 1862: "June 9th: Niagara is too much for me; my nerves shake like a bridge of wire; a vague sense of terror and unrest haunts me all the time. My head swims and reels with the ceaseless motion of the water. June 10th: . . . Leave Niagara for Toronto after dinner

today. After supper, take a stroll through the main street of Toronto [King Street] with E. Then to bed in our gloomy Castle of Otranto, called the Rossin House."

Near here is a spot linked to the American novelist William Dean Howells (1837-1920). Howells was so famous in his day that his face appeared on cigar boxes (as a sign of quality) and he remains compulsory reading for anyone wanting to understand American letters in the Victorian age. His father was a political appointee in the diplomatic service, and when his Consulship in Toronto looked shaky, the son had a large hand in securing the Toronto post for his father, as he explained in his book *My Mark Twain*: "When my father was consul at Toronto during [Chester] Arthur's administration, he fancied that his place was in danger, and he appealed to me. In turn I appealed to Clemens, bethinking myself of his friendship with [former President Ulysses S.] Grant and Grant's friendship with Arthur. I asked him to write Grant in my father's behalf, but No, he answered me, I must come to Hartford and we would go to New York together and see Grant personally . . . We went to find Grant in his business office . . . He was very simple and very cordial . . . When I stated my business he merely said, Oh no, that must not be; he would write to Mr. Arthur; and he did so that day; and my father lived to lay down his office, when he tired of it, with no urgency from above." Howells came to Toronto to visit his father on at least two occasions. The last was June 28 to July 18, 1882 when he stayed with his father in his house at **146 Wellington Street West**.

The Queen's Hotel was located around the corner at **100 Front Street West**. This block of Front was originally comprised of a few row houses built in 1843 which were soon linked to make the first Knox College. The Presbyterians moved about seven years later and the premises became Sword's Hotel, and a few more years after that the Revere House—where writer Susie Frances

Harrison ('Seranus') was born. In 1862, it was renamed The Queen's Hotel. Re-modelling made it *the* hostelry, the first in Toronto to have an elevator, a business phone, and (most marvellous to behold!) running water in the rooms. In 1928, eclipsed by this time by the King Edward Hotel which had opened in 1903, the Queen's was razed to make way for the Royal York Hotel (same address). The list of authors who have slept at this address while in Toronto to make public speeches or readings is impressive:

Sholem Asch
Beverley Baxter
Brendan Behan
William Black
Phyllis Bottome
Lewis Browne
John Buchan
Winston S. Churchill
Ralph Connor
E.M. Delafield
George Doran
Ilya Ehrenburg
John Erskine
Philip Gibbs
A.P. Herbert
Maurice Hindus
Frances Parkinson Keyes
Alexander Knox
Stephen Leacock
Sinclair Lewis
Marquis of Lorne
Emil Ludwig
André Malraux
Erika Mann
Klaus Mann
Thomas Mann
Vladimir Nabokov
Gilbert Parker
Mary Pickford
J.B. Priestley
Elmer Rice
Rafael Sabatini
Gerald Savory
Robert Sherwood

Konstantin Simonov
Osbert Sitwell
Lillian Smith
Mickey Spillane
Rex Stout
T.D. Sullivan
John Van Druten
Mrs. Humphry Ward
Walt Whitman
Oscar Wilde
William Butler Yeats

The Royal York Hotel, unlike its predecessors on this site, was frequently used for public lectures. Both the Canadian and Empire Clubs abandoned the King Edward as a site for their famous luncheon talks almost as soon as the Royal York opened its doors. Other organizations also hosted testimonial banquets and straight readings here. Among the literary folk who gave talks open to the public at the Royal York were:

Sholem Asch
Isaac Asimov
Beverley Baxter
John Buchan
Winston S. Churchill
Thomas B. Costain
Mazo de la Roche
Monica Dickens
Lloyd Douglas
Walter Duranty
Rosita Forbes
Gratien Gélinas
John Murray Gibbon
Richard Gordon
Wilfred Grenfell
Grey Owl
Arthur Guiterman
Maurice Hindus
Howard Angus Kennedy
Frances Parkinson Keyes
Watson Kirkconnell
Stephen Leacock
Ludwig Lewisohn
William Douw Lighthall
Klaus Mann

Nellie McClung
A.A. Milne
Nicholas Monsarrat
J.B. Priestley
Thomas Raddall
Charles G.D. Roberts
B.K. Sandwell
Marshall Saunders
Arthur G. Street
Arthur Stringer
Pierre van Paassen
Edward A. Weeks

One could write a book comprised only of stories dealing with the authors associated with this hotel and their reception in Toronto. However, space restrictions limit me to focusing on just one figure, George Henry Doran (1869-1956).

A Toronto native, Doran left school at 14, having answered an ad in a Yonge Street window that read "Wanted, Smart Boy." At two dollars a week he began to work at the Willard Tract Depository, a religious book distributor and publisher. He was apt at learning the Canadian end of book business but felt there was a larger world awaiting him. So, at 23, he left for Chicago where he joined the Fleming Revell firm, another evangelical publisher, but one substantially larger than Willard. Within a year he was made a vice-president of the American house, and that rank, coupled with his Canadian knowledge, helped him to bring a fellow ex-Torontonian, Ralph Connor, and his first novel *Black Rock*, into the Revell fold. Connor described Doran's role in helping him become the first Canadian to make a million dollars solely from royalties: "In the publishing house of the Fleming H. Revell Company of Chicago, there was an enterprising young clerk who was developing a nose for books, George H. Doran by name, a Canadian by birth and a bookman by the gift of God. He had followed the chapters in the *Westminster Magazine* and came to Macdonald with an offer for *Black Rock* which, though it was now too late to copy-

right in the United States, he was eager to publish. Macdonald accepted his offer and thus I first came into touch with George H. Doran who became eventually one of the three greatest publishers in America and one of the best and closest friends I have ever made during my life . . . Before a year had passed, Jim MacDonald and George Doran's faith in me had been more than justified. *Black Rock* had gone some hundreds of thousands while with *The Sky Pilot*, which followed during the succeeding year, and *The Man From Glengarry*, two years later, the total issue was estimated by my publishers as over five million copies."

Doran became an American citizen in 1896. Nearing 40, he thought the time was ripe to start his own business. He made a deal with Hodder & Stoughton, at the time one of the world's largest publishers of religious as well as general books, to be their sole distributor in North America. He set up shop in Toronto as George H. Doran Company in 1908, but as part of a long-planned strategic move shifted operations to New York City in 1909, taking contracts for, and the goodwill of Ralph Connor with him. Almost immediately, he knew success in this new huge market. His first bestseller was Connor's *The Foreigner*, followed afterwards by a distinguished mix of American and British authors such as Aldous Huxley, Mary Roberts Rinehart, Frank Swinnerton, Stephen Vincent Benet, Hugh Walpole, Somerset Maugham, and Arnold Bennett. He also hired a young editor named John Farrar, who would later found his own eminent firm, Farrar, Strauss & Giroux. By 1927 the world of fiction was changing and Doran, uncomfortable with the raw realism that was gaining hold, and starting to feel his age, merged with a former rival to form the largest publishing house in America at that time, Doubleday Doran & Company. Unfortunately, the corporate marriage was not a good one and Doran was soon gone from the executive suite. In 1934 he retired from the trade (a wealthy man) and wrote his memoirs, *Chronicles of Barabbas*, an autobiography that shocked almost everyone who read it at the time for the frankness with which he discussed the quick as well as the dead.

His autumn years were spent in the easy climate of the southwestern USA, but with the approach of his 80th birthday he made the decision to move back to Toronto. As a home he chose a multi-room suite at the Royal York Hotel. The *G&M* described him as "Tall, straight as a ramrod, ruddy-faced and wearing a goatee and neatly trimmed moustache, he was a striking figure as he strode through the lobby of the Royal York Hotel. His room was packed with books and cabinets containing collector's items in letters from some of the most famous of the world's men and women of letters. Intimate secrets and confidences were contained in these exchanges, some saved from his days as a publisher, some of them more recent notes that indicated the wide correspondence he had maintained with such people as H.L. Mencken and Aldous Huxley . . . His room was the mecca of a lot of book lovers and many younger Canadian authors."

The eastern boundary of Harbourfront starts at the foot of York Street and proceeds west to Bathurst. However, the literary programs of Harbourfront have all taken place within a small compass of buildings including the Premier Dance Theatre in the Queen's Quay Terminal, the DuMaurier Theatre Centre, and the Brigantine Room in the York Quay Centre. The addresses are, respectively, **207**, **231**, and **235 Queen's Quay West.**

The federal government opened the park in June 1974 with exhortations to the public to speak up about what should be done with the hundred acres of derelict waterfront property. In the meantime, to entice people back to an area of the city they had almost forgotten existed, the government spent a fortune on consultants, one of whom recommended the resurrection of the

Bohemian Embassy, a 1960s coffee house legendary for being open every night of the week and as the place where famous writers and folk musicians got their starts. Thus, in the first week of June 1974, the BoEm was reborn, complete with its programming schedule featuring one night for jazz, one night for comedy, one for folk music, one for classical music, and one night reserved for poetry readings. John Robert Colombo was hired to select the authors, ensure their arrival and payment, and act as M.C. From the beginning, the readings were quite well attended, even though they featured local authors only (there was no budget at the time for travel or hotel, and the honoraria were absurdly modest). The failure of Harbourfront to gain political favour with the Province or City meant the federal government was fast losing interest in paying large subsidies to maintain the programming with which the site had been launched. So, as part of a massive sweep of cuts, Colombo's services were terminated. Indeed, the entire poetry program was going to be cancelled until your humble scribe (who had been working at the Centre since March 1975 in an administrative position) suggested that he could take on the management of the readings as part of his regular duties. The Harbourfront directors pondered this possibility for about ten seconds. But since this was about nine seconds more than they usually gave to poetry in a year, their patience was taxed and rather than debate the matter further, they agreed to my being the steward of the readings.

At first, momentum and my own ignorance kept the program as it had been: one published author reading for about half an hour, followed by an army of neophytes who could read for five minutes each during what was called the Open Mike portion of the evening. When it became apparent that the Open Mike was not a proving ground for serious novices but rather a versified version of Hyde Park Corner, the Open Readings were dropped in favour of second and even third published authors on a bill.

Until 1978, the readings were entirely Canadian. But in that year unusual circumstances arose allowing me to invite, at no charge to the program, a couple of foreign authors, George MacBeth of Great Britain and American novelist John Cheever. The success of their readings and the comments of the audience led me to believe that, after more than a decade of having heard nothing but Canadian voices, the time had come for a judicious blend of Canadian and foreign authors—as long as a Canadian was determining the balance. The program has operated under that principle ever since.

Around this same time I began to feel frustrated that marvellous authors were appearing at Harbourfront and yet the majority of Torontonians did not know the program existed or, because of the way literature is taught in our schools, were afraid of formal encounters with writers and writing, were afraid that they might appear stupid or not know what was going on, or that there might be a test. So, noting the success of what was then the Festival of Festivals in inducing people to watch Bulgarian and other films they would never otherwise peruse, I scheduled a gathering of writers for October 1980, optimistically calling it the First International Festival of Authors. From the beginning, the Festival was promoted and programmed as an adjunct of the weekly reading series. One of the authors booked for the first Festival was a Polish poet, Czeslaw Milosz, whom next to no one in Toronto had heard of—until ten days before the Festival when he won the Nobel Prize. It continues to amaze me how many people over the next week refreshed their memories and told me how they had been admiring Milosz's work—for years. The Festival was a great hit with the public, the media, and the participating authors. It has been presented annually ever since.

In the 1980s and early 1990s the Harbourfront Reading Series also presented festivals of poetry and of short stories, but cuts to funding put paid to those after just a few years.

At last count, more than 3000 authors, from about 100 countries, have appeared on the Harbourfront stage. The list of writers who have won the Governor General's Award, the Booker Prize, and the Pulitzer, totals well over a hundred. And at least twelve Nobel laureates have read at Harbourfront—ten of them before they won the Prize.

The smallest audience ever was one person. He came to hear a Danish author read in Danish. Because the man had paid for his admission, he was entitled to the reading, and the author happily complied. The largest audience was nearly 4000 people. They filled every seat (and then some) in Massey Hall, which was rented for a double bill of Anthony Burgess and Robertson Davies.

Take Lower Simcoe Street north to Simcoe via the Convention Centre walkways. Roy Thompson Hall at **60 Simcoe Street** occupies a site where two handsome buildings were constructed in sequence as the official residence of the Lieutenant-Governor of Ontario. A surprising number of British aristocracy in Canada (usually here as representatives of the monarch) published creative writing. The best known is John Buchan (1875-1940), author of the still-famous *The Thirty-Nine Steps*. As Lord Tweedsmuir, he was our Governor General from 1935-40, and was a frequent visitor to this city. (When royalty or the Governor General came to town, it was not uncommon for the Lieutenant-Governor to have to quit his home and find shelter elsewhere until the bigwigs left.)

Another Toronto visitor as Governor General (1854-61) was Sir Edmund Walker Head (1805-68), who was not only a published poet, but a grammarian of note. His *Shall and Will* was published in London in 1856.

The Marquis of Lorne, governor general from 1878-83, had written poetry since he was a boy and had published an important volume with Macmillan by 1875. As a literary man he counted Tennyson and Longfellow among his friends. Born in 1845 as John Douglas Sutherland Campbell, the ninth Duke of Argyll, he married Princess Louise,

Marquis of Lorne,
Canadian Illustrated News, November 26, 1870

Queen Victoria's favourite daughter, in 1871. After he returned to England he wrote a number of books about Canada, all of them favourable. But a full dozen years before he came to this country in an official capacity, he visited Canada in May 1866 on his way back from the tropics. He had this to say about Toronto: "The weather at Toronto was cold, raw, and wet and the town looked too dull for words. There is some good land about, one hears; but beyond the town, we saw only the wretched looking white pines, leaning here and there and everywhere, as if too much blown about ever to think of holding themselves straight again. The Torontoites were all talking of the proposed North American federation; and most of them were seemingly in its favour." He felt better about the city during his later official

annual visits and it was in Toronto that he initiated the politicking needed to establish the Royal Society of Canada and the Royal Canadian Academy of Art. He was also responsible for shaming Ottawa into creating a National Gallery.

Sir Francis Bond Head (1793-1875) was the Lieutenant-Governor from 1835-37. As a politician he was hopeless but as a writer he showed more talent. He published travel writing all his life, and one book was so popular it went through six printings at least. He was a frequent contributor to the *Quarterly Review,* and in his autumn years back in England he published volumes on a wide range of topics As the *Dictionary of Canadian Biography* notes, "Had Francis Bond Head never come to Upper Canada he would still be remembered as a minor and rather engaging member of the gallery of 19th-century English literary eccentrics."

Lady Byng (1870-1949) was wife of a very popular Governor General (1921-26), Lord Byng. As Marie Evelyn Moreton (her maiden name) she published two romantic novels and, as Lady Byng, an autobiography. She returned to Canada in 1940 for the duration of the war. The Lady Byng Trophy, named in her honour, and first presented by her in 1925, is given annually to the NHL's most gentlemanly player.

The first building at **60 Simcoe** was constructed in 1798 as the home of the Chief Justice but was purchased after the War of 1812 for use as Government House. It lasted until a major fire in 1862. The second Government House was built on the ashes of the old in 1870 and it endured until razed in 1912. Chorley Park on Roxborough Drive in Rosedale was then built to house the official representative of the sovereign until it, too, was demolished in 1959—one of the grossest acts of civic vandalism in a city, sadly, where far too many demolitions vie for that distinction.

One marvellous building that escaped the wrecker's ball, thanks to the singular generosity of Mr. Ed Mirvish, is the nearby

Royal Alexandra Theatre, **260 King Street West**. A surprising number of playwrights have doubled as actors on its stage. Among them:

> Maurice Colborne
> Ruth Draper
> Alexander Knox
> Sinclair Lewis
> Michael MacLiammor
> Mary Pickford
> Cornelia Otis Skinner

In addition, some major dramatists have supervised the rehearsals for premieres in this theatre and as a result were here to take their bows on opening night. Among them were Jean Basile, Noel Coward, Mazo de la Roche, Rolf Hochhuth, Gerald Savory, Robert Sherwood, Lilian Smith, and John Van Druten.

For many years, immediately to the west, lay the original Upper Canada College at **300 King Street West**. Stephen Leacock is the best-known graduate of the school at this location and it was here that he returned to teach and to live. Other writers attached to the institution when it was on King include William Wilfred Campbell, John McCaul, William Patrick Mackenzie, Arthur Rankin, George Rankin, and B.K. Sandwell.

Walking north on **Duncan Street** we pass **No. 72** where poet Norah Holland (1876-1925) lived from 1889-90. Near where Duncan crosses Adelaide can be found a couple of addresses where the once-popular writer Isabella Valancy Crawford lived: **214 Adelaide Street West** was her home from 1882-83, and she returned in 1885 to live next door at **No. 216** for about twelve months. She certainly liked Adelaide Street West—she lived at **No. 180** in 1884.

More than a dozen authors can be linked to **John Street** over the decades. As noted in the Muddy York tour, Charles Dickens was a visitor to John Beverley Robinson's house near the corner of **John and Queen Streets**. The house was razed in 1913 when the property was purchased by the Methodist (later United) Church. The Church needed expanded premises for its administration and for its large publishing program, and between 1913 and 1915 constructed the Wesley Building to house its offices, printing plant, editors, and retail book room. The façade of the edifice still features gargoyles reading books. The book publishing arm, known as the Ryerson Press, flourished for several decades under Lorne Pierce, but by 1971 the house had fallen on hard times. As a result, the United Church sold the press to a large American conglomerate, little prepared for the national outcry which greeted this loss of a legendary Canadian firm. The sale went ahead, but it sparked a Royal Commission on the nature and future of Canadian book publishing. Many of the Commission's recommendations were adopted as policy by the government, and remain in place to this day.

The building was also sold in 1971 and for some years was home to a wide variety of artists (such as Michael Snow) and artists' organizations (such as A Space). In 1985, the building was transformed by television impresario Moses Znaimer, and it is now the base of his TV empire which includes CITY-TV and the arts channel BRAVO.

Stephen Leacock was reported by early biographers to have lived on John Street but I could find no documentation to that effect. Among the more important authors who certainly made this thoroughfare their home were Newton MacTavish (1875-1941), editor and man of letters, who resided at **No. 218** for the first three years of the 20th c. James David Edgar (1841-99) was a poet—and Speaker of the House of Commons at his death. He lived at **No. 183** for a couple of years at the beginning of the 1870s and at **No. 147** from 1873-74. His son Pelham, born in 1871, lived with him, naturally, at these same addresses. Pelham grew up to be the mentor of such literary stalwarts as E.J. Pratt and Northrop Frye.

The last address in Toronto I could find for William Henry Fuller (fl.1870-90) was **156 John Stree**t, where he lived in 1879 and again from 1881-86 (he also lived at **No.179** from 1873-74). He is included in this *Guide* because I admire his *chutzpah* in writing an opera on a Canadian theme as early as 1880 and actually seeing it produced. *HMS Parliament, or The Lady Who Loved a Government Clerk* was a satire of our first prime minister and his policies—hardly promising material for a successful comedy one would have thought. And yet, as the *Oxford Companion to Canadian Theatre* has noted, "It opened in Montreal on 16 Feb. 1880 to laudatory reviews. One critic praised the performance as one that 'may not ineptly be considered as marking a new departure in the theatrical world as far as Canada is concerned.' The play was toured . . . playing mainly in eastern Canada . . . The play's success encouraged Fuller to continue his career as a playwright but further success eluded him." He wrote two other musicals while living at this address.

When she was a girl, Mazo de la Roche (1879-1961), author of the *Jalna* novels, lived at **No.113** for about two years in the mid-1880s.

Isabella Valancy Crawford (1850-87) was a remarkable woman and an excellent writer. As one critic has succinctly noted, she "is one of the first poets whose work really matters to the development of the Canadian literary imagination. This was recognized in her own lifetime—though in England rather than Canada—and the recognition has continued, even from critics and poets who find her Victorian manner uncongenial." The same critic remarks on the absurd vulnerability of our literary history: "Crawford seems to have retained hardly any manuscripts of her published work, and paradoxically this has led to the loss of the few novels and stories that were well known in her own day. The periodicals in which they appeared have not survived, and we know only the titles of these works."

Crawford was born in Ireland in 1850 and brought to Canada by her parents when she was six. Her father, it seems, was an alcoholic and an embezzler, occupations which led to a gradual but sure decline in the family fortunes. By the time she was 20 she was publishing her writing in magazines across the continent, and was determined to make a career as a creative writer in Canada. This was a difficult goal at the time for a man, given the poverty of paying markets—but was an absolutely extraordinary decision for a woman, given the prejudices of the day. As her biographer remarks, "Isabella had no income now other than what she made from her writing. That she was able to survive on the proceeds in a city that had no social service says a lot for her ingenuity and resourcefulness."

Following the death of her father, she moved to Toronto with her mother in 1876, living with her in a variety of boarding houses, some of which (on Adelaide Street West) are cited above. It seems Canadian magazines and book publishers were not interested in her work because for the next trio of years her only publications were abroad. Thereafter, a few Toronto newspapers printed her work with some regularity but, as I have noted elsewhere in the *Guide*, magazines like *The Week* did not pay anything for poems, and being a professional who needed cash, she refused to have anything to do with them. The only book she published, *Old Spookses' Pass* (1884), sold a mere 50 copies while she was alive. Now, of course, the book is an expensive but necessary rarity for any serious collector of Canadiana.

Crawford seemed to make enough money that she could live modestly but not in poverty. By December 1885, she could afford to rent the entire third floor of **285 King Street West** (southwest corner of King and **John**). "From the back of the flat she looked down on a sea of factories and train tracks while the east afforded a view of distant chestnut trees and the mansions of the wealthy. The north window gave out onto King Street, the city's busy main thoroughfare . . . Finally, beyond the west window and visible only to her mind's eye, lay the wilderness she loved." Mother and daughter seemed to their friends to be quite happy here. Isabella decorated the apartment to her own exotic taste and was able to indulge a love of cooking which strict landladies at previous residences had forced into dormancy. Throughout 1886 she continued to write prose as much as poetry and her prospects seemed good. And then, at this address, in early February 1887, while preparing for bed, she was struck down by a heart attack, apparently without warning, and died in her mother's arms. She had just turned 37 years of age.

It is important when assessing Isabella Valancy Crawford not to overestimate her work because we confuse role with writing. But relegation of Crawford to the status of minor poet just won't do either. Because without intending to, she became a material trailblazer, showing all Canadian authors, especially women, that it was possible to be a proud, professional creative writer in a city that too often thought the vocation befitted only foreigners. For that alone, much less the genuine merit of her writing, she deserves wider recognition among her compatriots.

Roy Mitchell (1884-1944) has long been regarded as one of the fathers of indigenous theatre in Toronto. As early as 1908 he was directing Canadian plays at the Arts and Letters Club over the old Adelaide Street Court House. He was the first Artistic Director of the Hart House Theatre doing exciting work with plays no other theatre in town would touch. As the years pass, his importance in the history of drama in Canada is becoming more evident. From 1905-11 he lived at **14 John Street**. Did he know that the playwright Charles W. Bell lived in the same house from 1897-99?

Bell (1876-1938) has one of the most remarkable biographies I encountered in my 21 years of research on this book. At his peak he was a nationally famous lawyer, an internationally popular playwright, an athletic champion, and a hugely popular Member of Parliament.

Born in Hamilton into a well-to-do family, Bell was sent by his father to Trinity College in 1892 to get his undergraduate degree (BA 1896). From Trinity he went to Osgoode Hall for legal studies and he was called to the bar in 1899. He then set up his own practice and worked in Toronto until 1903 out of offices at 18 King Street West. At this point he returned to Hamilton, but Toronto was a frequent business and personal destination. Most young lawyers find their days full just dealing with the demands of the profession. But it seems Bell was writing plays even while studying for the bar (he later happily allowed that writer and barrister E.D. Armour had been his most influential teacher). Charles Bell's success in both fields was rapid and outstanding. He was soon known as one of the best criminal lawyers in Canada, specializing in murder cases. In those days, trials for capital crimes were always front-page news, in part because there were few appeals of guilty verdicts—and punishment by hanging soon followed any conviction. Bell was so associated with murder trials that he finally wrote a book, *Who Said Murder?* (1935), reminiscing about his most celebrated murder cases. The book manages to be quite humorous in places, and by revealing unknown details of investigations and his strategies for defence of the accused, it became a bestseller. He manages to be convincingly modest about the fact that the first 13 accused killers he defended were all acquitted.

At the same time, his plays were becoming better known in New York—and then in Toronto, on the rebound: "I began to write plays away back about 1900. In the first few years of my law practice I was far too busy chasing the elusive dollar, but I always itched to get at it. My first attempt at a play was called *The Prince of Zanzibar*. I tried for two years to get it placed but no one on this side [i.e., Canada] would look at it. So finally I sent it to some literary brokers in England who with commendable enterprise, but I am afraid, doubtful wisdom had it translated

CHAS. W. BELL

The author of "Up in Mabel's Room," Chas. W. Bell, shown ABOVE, will address a meeting of the Young Men's Canadian Club, to be held at the Carls-Rite on Monday night. Mr. Bell is a member of the federal parliament, and a distinguished barrister in addition to being a playwright of repute.

Star, October 27, 1928

into German and actually sold it in that country where it failed miserably. I have no doubt it deserved it too. First efforts usually do, but to the young writer such matters are tragedies. From my own experience I should say that there are three requisites for any success at authorship. The first is courage, the second is courage and the third is courage. I kept on anyhow and in 1905 another play was produced called *The Heart of a Charlatan*. It concerned some of the absurdities of patent medicine fakers and was put on by a stock company at the Old Savoy where it did fairly well so that I was encouraged to go on . . . I had absolutely no training in the art and could write for no market in Canada as there was none. There was

then no Hart House in Canada to set standards and encourage budding authors or actors of the drama."

By 1913, major producers (including fellow Torontonian Edgar Selwyn) were pleading for the rights to his work. At the opening of his play *Her First Divorce* in 1913 on Broadway, the *New York Tribune* wrote: "It is to be hoped that New York will for once not live up to its more or less well-earned reputation of being unable to recognize a 'good thing' in the playhouse. Here is one of the best things of a long theatrical season, coming with ripples of laughter, provoked by legitimate comedy, by clever lines, and ingeniously planned situations, not be the broader methods of barely distinguished farce." This success was followed by ten other Broadway appearances of his plays, including comedies, a melodrama, and a farce. One play, *Parlour, Bedroom, Bath*, ran on Broadway non-stop from December 1917 until the following September and was later made into a film with Buster Keaton in the starring role (1931). By 1920, Bell was asked if he would write a musical. When he protested that he did not know how to write tunes—or lyrics—the producer said he had a couple of up-and-coming brothers standing by who could do just that if Bell would only come up with the idea for a musical, write "the book" and supervise the dialogue. He agreed. The musical was called *A Dangerous Maid*. And the names of the brothers whose careers were just starting to rise?: George and Ira Gershwin. George later took one of the tunes originally written for *A Dangerous Maid* and renamed it "Four Little Sirens" in his 1924 hit *The Primrose*.

Given this talent for writing what is generally dismissed as lighter fare, it is instructive to note the playwrights Bell most admired: "Among the older playwrights I love Sheridan best. His joyousness never fails nor his charm. Among the modern Pinero has, I think, the finest grace of expression, Wilde the most wonderful sparkle, and Ibsen the greatest power of construction. I like Shaw in spots, but his everlasting cleverness tires me, great though he is."

Bell first ran for Parliament in 1925 and won by "an astounding majority of 12,000 votes. He joked that he won because 'they [the voters]' didn't know me very well." He was elected in the two following federal elections but would not run in 1935. "If you want to be constructive, the House of Commons is the dullest grind I know of. It's miserable indeed compared to the glory of battle in a criminal case, and that in turn is dull compared with the delights of the theatre."

Although based in Hamilton late in life, Bell was a constant presence in Toronto not only as a public speaker but in the Toronto dailies. Even his nomination to the Tory candidacy in 1925 was a serious news story in our papers. Whenever he gave a speech here, it was usually well-covered in advance and then reported with dispatch. So Toronto mourned, too, when one of its former citizens passed away on February 8, 1938. The *G&M* ran its obituary on the front page.

The first block south of King Street on the east side of Spadina brings us to Clarence Square, an occasion for a pleasant detour. Novelist Ann Ireland (b.1953) lived at **9 Clarence Square** from 1980 to 1983 and while here wrote about half of the novel *A Certain Mr. Takahashi*, which won the $50,000 Seal Best First Novel Award. Pioneer author Susanna Moodie (1803-85) lived with her children at various Toronto addresses in her last years, including **14 Clarence Square** in 1880. Novelists Marian Engel and Howard Engel were still married when they lived at **16 Clarence Square** between 1965-68. In the square itself is a park-bench with a plaque commemorating novelist Mort Forer (d.1981). The Toronto Parks Dept., in conjunction with ACTRA, as recently as 1984 had hoped to make Clarence Square a landmark wherein all of the great writers of the city's past would be honoured by oak trees and plaqued benches. Apart from the memorial to Forer, the plan seems never to have taken root.

Marian Engel with her children William and Charlotte in Clarence Square, c. 1967.

Moving towards the Lake, we pass **161 Spadina Avenue** where novelist, publisher, and controversial historian James Bacque (b.1929) spent the first year of his life until his parents moved northwards. Arthur Heming (1870-1940), better known as a painter than as a writer, but interesting in both fields nonetheless, lived briefly at **No.79** in 1913.

PORTLAND & KING

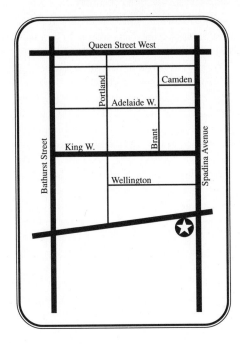

The tour begins at the southwest corner of Spadina Avenue and Front Street West.

Today this is an ugly intersection where torrents of cars mock the needs of pedestrians. But for many years, this was a beautiful spot: Lake Ontario came up to Front Street itself, and near where the *G&M* buildings now stand once stood a large, handsome house in a five-acre, park-like setting. Although the house fronted onto Wellington Street, it is easier to discuss it as part of Spadina. The house belonged to Robert Jameson, a member of the Family Compact. His accomplishments, as with so many members of the Compact, were so minor that he is remembered today for only two reasons: first, for Jameson Avenue named after him, and second, and much more importantly, because he married Anna, née Murphy, one of the most amazing women to visit 19th c. Canada.

Anna Jameson (1794-1860) was born in Dublin and married Robert in 1826. They were an ill-matched couple and marriage only revealed their incompatibility. However, in an age when divorce was socially scandalous, they maintained the pretence they were happily married, although for years they were separated by Robert's patronage postings abroad, including his 1833 appointment as Attorney General of Upper Canada. While he sipped tea and gossiped with his cronies at this outpost of Empire, Anna, ignoring most of the strictures imposed on women, established herself in London as a formidable writer of art history, and an adroit author of literary travel books. She became a friend of the Brownings, of Lady Byron, and during her travels on the Continent became an intimate of Goethe's niece, and through that connection, came to know the great man himself. Against such heady and sophisticated company, the allure of Muddy York seemed bereft. Nonetheless, she travelled to Toronto in December 1836. She came because her husband pleaded, may even have ordered her to do so. But possibly she came to negotiate an increase in the money which Robert sent her as an allowance, or, more generously, possibly because she wanted to try, one last time, to make the marriage work.

The timing of her arrival in mid-winter was unfortunate. It had taken her eight days to travel from New York to Toronto. Despite the fact that she felt she had alerted her husband to her time of arrival, no one met her at the docks, and wading through ankle-deep mud and slush, she made her way to Jameson's rooms, only to find the house-fires unlit and the servants unprepared for her arrival. The city was not making a good first impression. And the society people to whom she was soon introduced exacerbated her ill-will by their inflexibility, dullness, and conservatism so at odds with the exciting world she knew back home. She wrote that Toronto was "a little, ill-built town on low land at the bottom of a frozen bay, with one very ugly church without tower or steeple, some Government offices built of staring red brick in the most tasteless, vulgar style imaginable, three feet of snow all around—I did not expect much, but for this I was not prepared."

Talbotype photograph of Mrs. Jameson c. 1846

When she arrived, Jameson's mansion was still under construction in the block between Front and Wellington streets on the west side of **Spadina Avenue**. Anna's architectural criticism of it is actually more revealing about the state of her marriage: "The new house which he is building from the plans I have seen must be a nice, comfortable little place. I remarked that there was no arrangement made for any friend who might stray this way, but I thought the omission characteristic." They moved into the new house in late February 1837, coincident with Robert's appointment as Vice-Chancellor of the province—an appoint-

ment which made Anna now feel he had exhorted her to come to Toronto primarily for the sake of appearances. As the winter stretched on beyond anything she had known in Europe, she wrote, "The place, the society are so detestable to me, my own domestic situation so painful that to remain here would be death to me."

Her options for escape seemed non-existent, but, so singular were her ambitions, as soon as the snow melted she made arrangements to undertake a massive trip, mostly by bateaux and by canoe, to Lake Erie, Lake Huron, Manitoulin Island, and Lake Simcoe, and to travel to many places where she was likely to be the first white woman, certainly the first genteel white woman, ever to visit. Her voyages into the Canadian wilderness exhilarated her, and her description of the Canadian countryside and its inhabitants in her book *Winter Studies and Summer Rambles* are in acute contrast to her scathing remarks about Toronto and its gentry. Standing today at the corner of Front and Spadina, one can look south and in our imagination join Anna when she writes with clear euphoria on August 13, 1837: "At 3 o'clock in the morning, just as the moon was setting on Lake Ontario, I arrived at the door of my own house in Toronto, having been absent on this wild expedition just two months." Not long afterward, she left Toronto for good, never to see Robert Jameson again, her marriage a demonstrated failure but the fiction of its success maintained for propriety. Still, she must have been shocked when, after Robert died in 1854, she was informed that in his will he had not left her a single penny. Friends rallied to her aid and raised sufficient funds to allow her to keep writing.

The Jameson house passed to other owners who named it Lyndhurst. After them, in 1867, it became Loretto Abbey, a day and residential school run by nuns. The distinguished French-Canadian novelist Germaine Guèvremont (1896-1968), sent to Toronto by her parents primarily to learn English, boarded here as a student for the academic year 1908-9.

Retracing our steps to **Wellington Street West** we note **No.374** where poet David Fujino lived in the mid-seventies. At **No.382** Edward Douglas Armour lived at the end of the 19th c. Armour was a distinguished lawyer, the founder and first editor of *Canadian Law Times*, and a man who also published poetry. In addition to *Law Lyrics* (1918), he was proud of his *Odes From Horace* (1922).

Walking west to the northeast corner of Adelaide and Bathurst we find the current home (and recently purchased premises of Factory Theatre Lab). More than most alternative theatres in Toronto, Factory's existence has always seemed on a knife edge due to a chronic shortage of funds and occasional executive battles. But of late, the founding father of Factory Theatre, Ken Gass, has returned to its helm and with the assistance of playwright George Walker he has put the theatre in the financial black and on firm ground artistically.

On **Portland Street** we pass **No.97** where E.S. Caswell lived in the latter half of the 1880s, and then **No.117** to which he moved in 1890 and stayed for a decade. While living here Caswell was doing the reading and writing necessary for his influential poetry anthology, *Canadian Singers and Their Songs* (1902), the first in Canada to feature photos of the contributors. The book had a long life, including two revised editions.

A couple of blocks to the east is **47 Brant Street**, the site of E.J. Hathaway's home (1873-74). His previous residence had been around the corner at **41 Camden Street**. Hathaway (1871-1930) had a lifelong interest in Toronto history. His only book was *Jesse Ketchum and His Times*, but he is included in this *Guide* because he was the first writer to make a concentrated study of the city's literary past. He published his results in newspaper or magazine articles, which meant that he could only lightly touch upon his subject. Nonetheless, he clearly enjoyed informing his readers about Toronto's rich literary traditions and tales, and was tireless in mildly castigating the authorities for not celebrating that richness with historical plaques and appropriate statues and other civic signs of honour. *Plus ça change, plus c'est la même chose.*

1837 drawing by Anna Jameson of the Toronto shoreline, as seen from the mouth of the Humber, looking east to the faint lighthouse on Gibraltar Point, Toronto Island

THE GRANGE

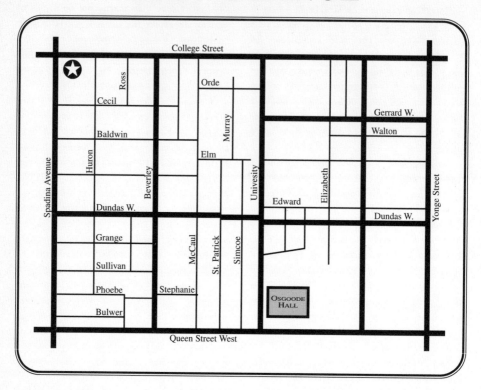

The tour begins at the southeast corner of College Street and Spadina Avenue.

The under-rated poet Gerry Shikatani (b. 1950) lived at **413 Spadina Avenue** with his parents from 1950 to 1958. At **No.401** Eldon Garnet (b. 1946), today better known as the artist who created some of the city's best-known public sculptures (such as the monument to the Chinese railway workers near Skydome), was writing poetry when he lived here 1977-79. Although he is most often regarded as a western writer, poet Patrick Lane (b. 1939) has lived in Toronto for many extended stretches. One of those took place in **No.383** in 1972 when he had a room here.

Grossman's Tavern at **379 Spadina Avenue** is where the first and only People's Poet Award was presented to Milton Acorn at a legendary ceremony in 1970. That year, several poets (who felt Milton Acorn should have been the obvious winner) were further appalled that the Governor General's Award had been given, not to Gwendolyn MacEwen whom they might grudgingly have admitted was a worthy alternative, but to George Bowering, at the time seen by them as little more than a lapdog of American prosody. To right what they thought was a serious wrong, they organized a very public presentation of an alternative literary medal to Milton Acorn at Grossman's, his favourite watering hole. Eli Mandel and Joe Rosenblatt led the drive to make the event a success, and cash donations were received from some of the best—and best-known—poets in the land: Leonard Cohen, Earle Birney, Irving Layton, and John Glassco among them. By the time the actual presentation took place on the evening of May 16, 1970 the event was a national *cause célèbre* and the tavern was packed with authors from several cities as well as Toronto, including Layton, Mandel, Rosenblatt, Al Purdy, R.G. Everson, Avi Boxer, and Stephanie Nynych. The night proved of more enduring importance for two other authors who were also in attendance at this salute to Acorn. Although they had read each other's work, they had never met until the night of this presentation. Later, they became a couple and have lived together ever since. Their names were Graeme Gibson and Margaret Atwood.

The Paramount Tavern, a rough, blue-collar bar was located at **No.337**. Here the prize-winning novelist and children's author Tim Wynne-Jones (playing rhythm guitar and singing vocals) fronted a rock-and-roll band called Boogie Dick for about six months. But his budding musical career was undone in 1970, unwittingly enough, by another noted novelist, Jack Batten, then a reporter for the *G&M*. Wynne-Jones described the scene in a letter: "I painted my face paisley in those days and wore robes. The band included an electrified sewing machine and an electric baseball bat called a 'vunt' which I had the honour to swing, fending off things thrown by the audience. Pop cans made a satisfyingly psychedelic sound when I got good wood on them. There were guitar pick-ups nailed onto the bat. We played the Paramount for several months before Jack Batten 'discovered' us and wrote an Entertainment Section front-page article . . . in which he quoted us, correctly, griping about the club and the management. We got fired that same day. In fact, the manager of the Paramount blockaded the doorway, making it incredibly difficult to get our equipment out . . . It was that kind of band. The Paramount is now an LCBO."

The building at **287 Spadina** has gone through many transmogrifications. It began life on August 18, 1921 as the Standard Theatre, described as "one of the finest Yiddish theatres in North America." The bills ranged from trashy melodramas to European classics in translation, including Shakespeare. Occasionally the Standard was used for lectures in Yiddish, but, while I am sure there must have been more, I have been able to discover only one lecture on its stage by a Yiddish creative writer: H. Leivick (1886-1962) gave a reading from his work on November 5, 1933. His name may not mean much to most people today, but his appearance in Toronto was considered important enough that the *Star* gave his appearance front-page treatment accompanied by a photo. The playwright and critic Oscar Ryan (1904-88) spoke—in English—from the same stage to the Young Communist League in 1928. The Standard Theatre fell on hard times and became the Victory Burlesque, the last of the old-style strip joints (complete with bored, three-piece band and bodacious ladies with pasties). Recently, as Chinatown has spread to Spadina, it has known life as a Chinese-language cinema.

217 Spadina Avenue was the last Toronto address of Graeme Mercer Adam, a native of Scotland who arrived in Toronto in 1858 when he was nineteen. Adam arrived in town with a job offer from a small Toronto book business in his pocket. Within two years he was a partner in the firm, which changed its name to reflect his status: Rollo and Adam. They published the *British American Magazine*, a handsome periodical which was among the first to publish Canadians in a journal intended for international circulation. By 1866, Adam headed his own book publishing company, and was aggressive in printing Canadian authors. In 1872, with the financial and moral backing of Goldwin Smith as well as the Canada First Movement, he launched the magazine *Canadian Monthly*. Its nine-inch high by six-inch wide format featured elegant typesetting, a two-column design, and each issue contained an amalgam of informed political commentary, poetry, reviews of books on many topics, translations, memoirs, and a compelling mix of essays in the humanities.

The Toronto Reference Library makes the magazine available in hard copy to serious readers, and more than a century later, much of its contents still make for fascinating reading. Alas, Adam's nationalist zeal was too far ahead of his colonized market. He lost a lot of money, and was forced to sell the magazine to the Rose-Belford firm a decade later. He did have financial success, however, with the primary-school readers that he prepared for the education department of the province, and one of his history primers had a sale of more than 100,000 copies. His main contribution to our imaginative literature was a novel, *Algonquin Maiden* (1886), which he wrote with noted author Ethelwyn Wetherald. But by far his most important book was *Prominent Men of Canada*, an invaluable record still regularly used by historians. Despite all that he had done for Canada and Canadian letters, Adam felt that to make a living doing work of the highest literary quality he had to move to America—which he did in 1892. He emigrated to New York from this, his last Toronto residence. He died in the USA, but his body was returned to Toronto for interment in St. James Cemetery.

One block north of Queen Street is **Bulwer Street**, alleged to have been named for Bulwer-Lytton, the hugely popular Victorian novelist who is mocked today by people who have never read him as the author of the line "It was a dark and stormy night." Such people might be less quick to mock if they read him, of course, or if they knew he was also the author of the line "The pen is mightier than the sword." Such a literary street, alas, has no creative writers associated with it. The same cannot be said of **Sullivan Street**.

Poet Elizabeth Rhett Woods (b.1940) occupied an apartment on the top floor of **82 Sullivan** from 1971-72 and while here wrote part of her book *Gone* (1972). She sublet one room for some months in 1972 to Patrick Lane (b.1939) during one of his Toronto idylls. Novelist Barbara Gowdy

(b.1950) worked at **No.78** as an editor at Lester & Orpen Dennys from 1974-79. L&OD was a medium-sized house specializing in Canadian and foreign contemporary novelists. It quickly established for itself an enviable reputation at home and abroad, but financial challenges led to its demise.

Margaret Atwood and Graeme Gibson moved from their farm in Alliston back to Toronto in 1980 and bought **No.73**, where they lived (apart from a year in Edinburgh when Graeme was part of a writers' exchange) until 1985. From a literary viewpoint, this was a fruitful address for Atwood in particular (although it should be noted that she had an office at 82 Manning where much writing was done as well). While living here she finished *Just Stories*, wrote all of *Bodily Harm*, part of *The Handmaid's Tale*, all of *Murder in the Dark*, assembled *Second Words*, edited *The Oxford Book of Canadian Poetry in English*, and wrote most of the stories in *Bluebeard's Egg* and *Interlunar*. When F.R. Scott and other Montreal writers asked a few authors in Toronto to assume leadership of the PEN Canadian Centre, the initial meetings to organize the re-establishment of PEN were held at this address with Atwood and Gibson as hosts. By coincidence, this house was also Ken Adachi's home from 1956-61. Adachi (1928-89) was the book columnist of the *Star* for much of the 1980s and the author of *The Enemy That Never Was* (1976), a history of Japanese-Canadians.

Novelist and publisher Barry Callaghan (b.1937) also wrote novels, short stories, and poetry just two doors away at **No.69** from 1983-90. He was justly famous at this time for the lavishness of his parties at which scores of writers would be present. A combination of circumstances induced Callaghan to move. His father, Morley, died in 1990 and left his house to Barry. Around the same time (while Callaghan was out of town), moronic thieves, as if they were followers of Charles Manson, thought they could cover their tracks after looting **No.69** by setting fires to, and ransacking each floor of the house. Quick action by neighbours and the fire department saved the building, but most of the contents were destroyed. Barry produced a superb long essay about the incident (later published in his *A Kiss Is Still a Kiss*, 1995), one of the few positive aspects to emerge from an otherwise horrendous experience.

Novelist Susan Swan (b.1945) wrote her first book, *Unfit for Paradise* (1981), while living in a second-floor apartment at **No.30** from 1978-82. She was still doing performance art in this period, and had also begun writing her first novel, *The Biggest Modern Woman of the World* (1983).

Sullivan crosses **Huron Street**. **35 Huron** was home to the indomitable Bishop Richard Evans (1841-1921). As a child in London, Ontario, he worked as a newsboy, and then as a trapeze artist. These jobs led to music-hall singing which apparently qualified him to work in a bank, his next position. While working in the bank, he had a major epiphany and returned to the fold of the Mormon church, becoming one of its priests when he was only 21. It was at this point, c. 1908, that he established a pastorate of the Church of Latter Day Saints in Toronto and moved into **No.35**. However, around the time he left this address (c. 1917) he experienced another, even bigger epiphany which instructed him to break from the Mormons and establish his own religion—The Christian Brotherhood. He appointed himself bishop, and weathered the charges that he stole substantial funds from his previous church. The year 1918 saw his *The Songs, Poems, Notes and Correspondence* published. The book contains a poem titled "The Old Maids Convention" which sounds terribly patronizing until you learn that it was actually commissioned by the organizers of The Old Maids Convention held in Toronto May 14, 1909.

Grange Avenue intersects with Huron. At **4-B Grange Avenue** novelist Howard Engel (b.1931) gave birth to his famous sleuth, Benny Cooperman, while he lived here with his novelist wife, Janet Hamilton (1951-98) from 1977-79. Howard dates the birth as January 1979.

Howard Engel at 287 Spadina Avenue near Dundas Street, 1988.

Walking north on Huron through China-town, we arrive at **Baldwin Street**. The Governor General's Award-winning novelist John Steffler (b.1947), who was raised on a farm just north of Toronto, explained what the Baldwin Street area meant to him: "When my family moved north of Steeles in 1948 the area was still very rural. I went to a one-room school . . . and shared with my schoolmates the natural conviction that people from 'the city' were a different species altogether. Kids from Toronto—occasionally one would stray into our territory—seemed to live divorced from the physical world, in a realm of comic books, movies, new clothes, and slick mannerisms. We liked to contrive ordeals for them in barnyards, build traps along forest paths where bent saplings would whisk them into the air by their ankles, underscoring the point that the countryside had its own complexities and perils. I resented Toronto.

"Later, in high school, waiting for the school bus each morning on German Mills Road, I looked to ¹e south and literally watched the city marching my way. Tall apartments had taken over Don Mills. A railway had gone in beside John Street. Hydro transmission towers were striding over the fields like the alien invaders in H.G. Wells' *War of the Worlds*. Land prices and taxes were going up. Everyone was selling, moving away.

"I thought of Toronto as a kind of nuclear explosion, the reverse of the one that destroyed Hiroshima. Whereas the Americans' bomb had vaporised people and houses, laying bare the ancient topography, Toronto was the city's revenge, an explosion of people and buildings that obliterated the countryside. Toronto wiped out my home.

"It annexed me. I moved downtown and went to UofT. I found that I preferred the very centre of the city, in Chinatown, Little Italy, Kensington Market. I identified with the immigrants. Rural traditions seemed still to be strong in them. They were more like my old neighbours, the ruined farmers of Milliken, than the prosperous English Torontonians (those ultimate aliens) had ever been.

"I was putting myself through university, living on about $25.00 a week. I got my clothes from Grossman's Jobbers at [20] Baldwin St. just east of Beverley (torn down long ago). The clothes in Mr. Grossman's store would have filled miles of racks if he'd arranged them on hangers. He solved the storage problem by sorting hⁱ⁻ stock according to garment type and piling it on the floor. His trouser pile was the size of a hay stack and had a ladder against it to reach the loose, newer pairs scattered on top.

"Mr. Grossman had been collecting clothes for so long that the piles had developed historical strata like limestone. Three or four feet down you hit the 1940's; five or six feet down brought you to the 30's. Below that it was hard to tell. The weight of the upper layers was transforming the bottom of the pile into the textile equivalent of coal. Mr. Grossman would climb the ladder and toss down a pair of Levi stay-pressed jeans. Good as new, he'd call. We would have disputes. I wasn't interested in modern crap. It was the 1930's and 20's tweeds I was after, the kind with pleats and button flies, that were tightly embedded three or four decades down. Mr. Grossman would suffer me to excavate only so far, disrupting his lifetime's work. I was often forced to abandon heartbreaking specimens, real F. Scott Fitzgerald bags, having uncovered a cuff or waistband but being unable to pull them free without ripping them.

"Pants were fifty cents a pair. I had a double-breasted chalk stripe suit, a long tweed overcoat. Maybe I wanted to look like my father in photos from his youth, in his city phase, or like the guys my mother always described swarming out of the street car windows in front of the dog racing track at Ulster Stadium on Billings Avenue. The city had seemed to belong to them.

"I tunnelled into Mr. Grossman's piles of clothes like a mole. Maybe I wanted to burrow right down out of the new city and find myself back on the gravel roads to Markham and Unionville surrounded by farms, long before the earth-movers had started their work.

"Living in Newfoundland I now have another perspective on Toronto. There's no question that it's Canada's urban centre. The most envied and hated place. People are afraid of it like a foreign power or a ride in a rocket ship. It is forging its own economy and its own high speed habits without any regard for the hinterland. In a sense it has already swallowed Canada whole, since so much of the time we see ourselves and the rest of the nation reflected through the eyes of the Toronto media.

"Always the first question a Newfoundlander will ask you is where you're from. If you say Ontario, he'll overlook the subtlety of your reply and ask if you miss living in

Toronto. In his eyes Toronto contains at least Ontario, and 'Ontario' is just sanitized jargon for that most hated centre of smugness and privilege: Upper Canada.

"And so I find myself defending the bloody place. Boasting about its ethnic mix. And wishing I could get back more often for a quick day or two, for the films and galleries, the bookstores and food. And I insist I don't mind its being the centre of publishing and TV. We need a cultural clearing house of some kind, and it might as well be TO. And I'm glad to have a Toronto publisher because its distribution is good.

"And some day soon I'm going to have to move back to the vicinity of Toronto to deal with my ancestral demons that lie buried on its fringe."

Susanna Moodie as portrayed in H.J. Morgan's book *Types of Canadian Women (Toronto, 1903)*

30 Baldwin Street was the home of Susanna Moodie's daughter and son-in-law in 1879. She came to stay with them for several weeks centred around Christmas and New Year's Day while recovering from a lengthy illness. One of the holiday callers to the home was a scientist and a poet himself, Edward Chapman (1821-1904). Susanna wrote to her sister, "he asked me for a copy of a little poem of mine, 'The Canadian Herd Boy,' as he wished to recite it at a lecture he was going to give next week." She happily complied.

Nicholas Flood Davin (1840-1901) had just quit George Brown's *Globe* to work at the *Mail* when he was living at **No.83** in 1876. At the same time, he was finishing his legal studies, and was called to the bar on February 18, 1876. On top of that, he was writing essays, poetry, and plays, much of which was published in the same year. And somehow he found the time to research and write *The Irishman in Canada* (1877) assessed by an important critic as "generally acknowledged to be his most important contribution to Canadian letters." Even though he did not practise much law (because he was so busy writing), Davin took on the defence of the man who shot and killed George Brown at Brown's home—coincidentally nearby (at 186 Beverley Street).

At **123 Huron Street**, novelist Nino Ricci (b.1959) wrote much of his second novel, *In a Glass House* (1993), a sort-of sequel to his award-winning and international success, *Lives of the Saints* (1990). Ricci had been living in Florence for about a year when he returned to Toronto to live at this address in August 1989. He remained until June 1991.

When Joseph Opatoshu (1887-1954) made his first of two visits to Toronto, his arrival was front-page news. Unfortunately, one of the reporters he had to endure was the bombastic R.E. Knowles, who began his profile of the Yiddish writer, "It is delightful—and should not be surprising—to meet and talk with a brilliantly intellectual Jew." The rest of the article is the usual mush of Knowles's arch attitude and baroquely phrased questions. Nonetheless, to his credit, he did convey the news that Opatoshu was in town to deliver a public lecture, "The Decline of World Literature," on December 2, 1934, at the hall on **24 Cecil Street**. At least one other literary author spoke at this venue, known as the Norman Bethune Centre: Wilson Macdonald read his poems as part of a one-day bookfair held on December 8, 1962.

No.27 was Stanley Ryerson's home (1911-12) immediately after he was born. While best known as an historian and very public Marxist, he had a creative side expressed by his cartoons and one play. The poet and Public School Inspector for the Province, James L. Hughes (1846-1935), established a home at No.34 from 1884-86. Across the street at No.35 painter and poet W.A. Sherwood (1859-1919) had a garret in 1895.

A "terrific little apartment at 160 Huron Street" was playwright Wendy Lill's last home in Toronto c. 1976-77. Lill (b.1950), who now sits in the House of Commons, wrote to me: "I knew a lot of film types at the time and theatre people but was very much on the margins; working as a cocktail waitress to make ends meet and trying all different kinds of writing; never showing anybody anything . . . just being in my twenties, trying everything, living dangerously, looking for love in all the wrong places . . . I loved Toronto—was a really free-wheeling young woman in Toronto and I loved it until one day I woke up and decided I had to get out of town if I was ever going to really get anything going in my life." She certainly did. Her plays are regularly produced across Canada and around the world, and she is the winner of ACTRA Awards for her radio writing. Her stage play, *The Occupation of Heather Rose*, won the Governor General's Award in 1987. Science fiction writer and anthologist Judith Merril (1923-97) also had lodgings in this building. She installed herself in apt. 30 from 1977-81, and then returned to live on the same street (at No.183) from 1988-92—the second tenure particularly appropriate since she was now living in the shadow of the new library building housing the superb SF collection named after her.

A few paces away, at No.164, fiction writers Ann Ireland (b.1953) and Toby Maclennan (b.1939) shared an apartment. It was to be at least two years before Ireland began the first draft of her first novel that won the Seal $50,000 Prize.

The next road to the west is Ross Street. No.34 was the final home of the Dora Hood Book Room from 1962 until it closed in 1968. It was Canada's most famous antiquarian bookshop, in part because it really was an excellent store and Dora Hood really knew her business—and in part because she was the only antiquarian dealer in Canada to write her memoirs. That more of them do not is a shame, for I have often found them to have extensive knowledge about writers which they are happy to share with anyone (buyer or not), who appears genuinely interested. The playwright and actor Tommy Tweed lived above the store from 1963 until he died in 1971.

Arthur Beverley Baxter (1891-1964) grew up in Toronto but made his name in Britain, first as an editor of newspapers and later as a popular Member of Parliament. He wrote novels and plays and late in life was well regarded in England as a drama critic. His first four years on earth were spent at the family home at 222 Beverley Street. The Street was named after John Beverley Robinson who owned property at its foot. As far as I know there is no family connection, via the name "Beverley" to the Baxters.

When British novelist Hall Caine (1853-1931) came to Toronto to give a reading at Massey Hall in 1898, he stayed for a few days at No.193, the home of his publisher in Canada, G.N. Morang. If book sales are a gauge (and in the trade they are) Caine was once as popular as Dickens in England but his star has fallen far since then. He had been to Toronto about three years before as part of a cross-Canada tour to lobby for changes to our Copyright Act that hurt British authors.

Anne Langton (1804-93) was ignored as a writer for almost a century, but the explosion in Canadian studies—and in women's studies—in the 1970s (and since) has seen her star rise higher than ever. Her best-known book is *A Gentlewoman in Upper Canada*. One of the pleasures of reading Langton is her constant goodwill. There is none of the self-pity that sometimes creeps into the journals of other middle- and upper-class immigrants to Ontario. She was a spinster who chose to live with her brother John and his family after the death of their parents. Her brother was elected to the Legislative Assembly in 1851, which meant that they had to live where the government was sitting. Eventually he joined the civil service as an accountant, and became the first auditor of Ontario. His career culminated with his appointment as the nation's first Auditor-General at Confederation. In other words, in contrast to their pioneer settlement, their circumstances in Toronto were comfortable. Anne died while living with her brother's family at **123 Beverley**, where they had been since 1890. Between 1885-89 they had lived at **115 Beverley**.

Playwright and novelist Rachel Wyatt (b.1929) lived at **No.98** in the first half of the 1980s. During that time she would have had a most pleasant view of the Grange, long the home of Goldwin Smith (1823-1910).

The Grange was built in 1817, making it one of the oldest surviving buildings in the city. Smith came to Toronto from England (after a short stop at Cornell) as one of the best-known writers and polemicists of his day. In 1875 he married the widow Harriet Boulton, who had been living in the Grange for some years. Smith was highly respected in Toronto but not necessarily loved. Thanks to Mrs. Boulton's money he was financially independent and thus was capable of being frank when expressing his views—views which were often at odds with the dominant orthodoxy. He wrote voluminously: letters to the editors of British, American, and Canadian newspapers, articles (signed and unsigned) for magazines in several countries, and books that were internationally reviewed. He started his own

magazines and in them he wrote about literary matters, religious topics, and certainly about the overtly political. His loan to John Ross Robertson allowed the latter to start the *Telegram*. And he not only founded *The Bystander*, a magazine examining issues free of party blinkers, he wrote almost every article in each number. In 1883 Smith started *The Week*, a liberal intellectual journal, and he was prescient enough to hire Charles G.D. Roberts as its first editor. The energy needed for all this publishing activity, coupled with a colonized public, led Goldwin Smith to write a lament that has a disturbingly contemporary ring: "In the field of periodical literature, what chance can our Canadian publishers have against an American magazine with a circulation of a hundred and fifty thousand, and a splendour of illustration such as only a profuse expenditure can support? The idea that Canadian patriotism will give preference to the native product is not borne out my experience."

Goldwin Smith on the steps of the Grange in 1907.

Benjamin Disraeli, the former Prime Minister of England, detested Goldwin Smith, and modelled a pompous character upon Smith in one of his later novels, *Lothair*. Smith foolishly abetted sales of the book by complaining about the ill treatment. An expert on Disraeli's fiction comments: "From the commercial point of view, *Lothair* was the most successful of all Disraeli's novels to date. The first edition was exhausted in two days, and eight editions were produced in 1870 . . . So great was the public identification with Lothair and Corisande, the hero and heroine, that horses, songs, dances and ships were named after them. Sales were considerably assisted by a letter from Disraeli's old enemy Goldwin Smith, publicly identifying himself as the Oxford professor of chapter XXIV, 'of advanced opinions on all subjects, religious, social and political.' 'The Oxford Professor's letter is doing its work well,' wrote Longman to Disraeli, 'so much so that we shall print again as soon as I have your corrections.' In the United States, Lothair was no less successful. One publishing company attempted to steal a march on its rivals by having the novel telegraphed across the Atlantic, and was deterred only by the cost. Fifteen thousand copies were sold on the first day of publication, and it was said that no book had been so popular since *Uncle Tom's Cabin*."

Smith made pleasant alterations to the Grange, most notably the addition of the library on the west side. He added the stone porch, but otherwise the exterior of the building looks much as it did almost two hundred years ago. The interior was restored with remarkable attention to historical detail and the home now operates as a museum-adjunct to the Art Gallery of Ontario (which accounts for the Grange having the same address as the AGO, **317 Dundas West**, even though the Grange is not visible from Dundas). Eminent authors, when visiting Toronto between 1875 and 1910, were happy to visit Goldwin Smith, either for tea, dinner, or if especially intimate friends, as

houseguests. Among the latter was Matthew Arnold in February 1884. Poet Sir Edwin Arnold was also a houseguest in November 1891. Mrs. Humphry Ward came for tea, and the famous English literary biographer John Morley (after whom Morley Callaghan was named) came for dinner.

Old Hollywood movies often feature a newsboy shouting "Extra! Extra! Read all about it!" Although I spent a lot of time looking at newspapers on microfilm, I never encountered such an "Extra" edition—except once, and that once was when Goldwin Smith died. All of the newspaper streated his passing as if a monarch had died—there were extensive front-page articles as well as lead editorials praising his life and contributions to Toronto.

The Grange would have been visible to another writer and just as fierce a polemicist, Robin Mathews (b.1931). He lived at **80 Beverley** from 1959-60 while working at the UofT on a PhD. In between his studies, he wrote poems continuously, wrote essays for *Canadian Forum*, taught TV playwriting at the central Y, and read plays submitted to CBC. In a letter to me he stated: "I found the University of Toronto amazingly complacent and stuck on itself—which is one of the reasons I didn't complete the PhD . . . I sat through the seminar N. Frye conducted on criticism and developed my unchanging aversion to the arrogance, colonial-mindedness, vanity, and ignorance he had about Canadian literature, and the fawning nature of many of his students." Later in his letter he remarked, "I had a great time in Toronto because there was lots to love and lots to hate, and I didn't give a hoot for its self-importance and absolutely perpetual (which it never stops) social, artistic, political, personal, pathological climbing. I still find Toronto absorbing and interesting. . . ."

In his delightful memoir of literary Toronto in the 1960s, *Travels by Night* (1974), poet Douglas Fetherling recounts how a surprising number of poets managed to be associated with **No.52**. "When I returned, Sandy

Stagg had found Liz [Woods], Bill [Howell] and the rest of us the perfect place to live, **52 Beverley Street**, one of the Victorian terrace houses, steps from Queen. The rent (there was no lease) was $250, which was more than we were accustomed to paying but then it was a big old place. Pat Lane had come back to town and he and Joe Rosenblatt . . . had helped the residents move in. People drew lots for rooms. I got one *in absentia* and when I saw it for the first time, found it being slept in by Jim and Phillip and Jim's Swedish girlfriend, with traces of previous occupation by Erling Friis-Bastaad, another poet of that place and time (who subsequently moved to the Yukon). Bill took over the attic of the house and made it into a studio: the first he'd ever enjoyed."

Running east from Beverley near this spot is **Stephanie Street** where novelist Richard B. Wright had an unusual housing arrangement from 1958-60 as he explained in a letter, "I lived for three years in an area that I always found fascinating, the McCaul-Queen area. I understand that Queen West is now a trendy, artsy area but in those days (the late fifties) it was working class. I lived at **15 Stephanie Street**, now the site of the Municipal Baths. The Baths were there in those days too, but I lived in a room above them . . . That little rinkydink building that is now 15 Stephanie was put up in the early sixties. The one I lived in was a two storey edifice, probably built around the turn of the century or at least before 1920. The entire second floor was an enormous apartment . . . It wasn't a particularly distinguished place, but it was certainly a few notches above the bland little thing they have there now." Richard mentioned to me in a telephone conversation that he worked as a lifeguard part-time at the Baths, and occasionally was hired to clean them. The area in behind the Baths has recently been refurbished and makes for an interesting stroll down to Queen Street.

Nearby at **256 Queen Street West** is Pages Bookstore (opened 1979), one of the favourites of many Toronto poets and fiction writers because of its singular stock and learned staff. This shop is one of the few that survives from the heady period c. 1975-85 when this strip of Queen between Simcoe and Spadina featured more than 40 bookshops selling new or antiquarian titles. Indeed, most city planners would agree that the clientele attracted to such a concentration of bookshops leads to the very downfall of the stores. The well-educated bookshop customers attract upscale restaurants and expensive fashion boutiques with high profit margins and a better ability to pay larger rents than the bookstores can. An example of a store driven out by the skyrocketing rents demanded of a trendy area is Bakka, the first science fiction bookshop in Canada and now the oldest one in the world. It opened at **282 Queen West** in 1972 and remained at this address until it moved to 598 Yonge in 1998. Any major SF author within three light years of the store was a willing participant in the store's many autographings. And three Toronto authors who have achieved substantial international success in this field were once sales clerks in the store: Tanya Huff (b.1957), Michele Sagara (b.1963), and Robert J. Sawyer (b.1960). Not far from this site is a lovely shop owned by a man often referred to as the Dean of antiquarian dealers in Toronto: David Mason Books, **342 Queen Street West**.

Walk back east along Queen Street to **McCaul Street**. Prize-winning playwright Allan Stratton (b.1951) resided in Village by the Grange at **No.73** for the last three years of the 1980s and during that time wrote the play *Bag Babies*. He remains best known for his earlier *Nurse Jane Goes to Hawaii* which has had more than 100 different productions across the country.

The Ontario College of Art and Design at **100 McCaul** is a post-secondary institution noted for schooling some of the most famous artists in the country. A few of the College's graduates or teachers have also turned their hand to publishing their creative writing.

Among published authors who attended OCAD are Selwyn Dewdney, Estelle Kerr, J.E.H. MacDonald, Claire Mowat, Isabelle Hope Muntz, Lydia Palij, Burton Raffel, Ernest Thompson Seton, and Phyllis Brett Young.

Near the north end of McCaul, **Orde Street** crosses. **No.9** was Mary Pickford's home from 1900 to c. 1907 (when she wasn't on the road). Pickford (1893-1979) was born around the corner on University Avenue. One of the greatest stars of Hollywood's silent era, she was known as "America's Sweetheart" even though she was a Canadian. Her millions of fans wanted her to remain forever the waif she portrayed in her films—hard to do when entering middle age. As her career began to wane, a novel, *The Demi-Widow*, was published under her name in 1935. Whether she wrote the book herself, or just dictated it, or simply affixed her name to the labour of some hack in the publicity department of the film studio is unknown—all three possibilities have been suggested. There is little doubt though that she dictated and edited her memoirs published in 1955, so she may indeed have had a large hand in the novel.

Just to the north of Orde Street is **College Street**. In a gentler age, **135 College Street** was the Royal Conservatory of Music, a handsome building which stood where the glass anonymity of the Ontario Hydro Building is now plopped at the corner of College and University. On at least one occasion, an organization in the pre-microphone age took advantage of the good acoustics of the RCM's recital hall to host a public literary lecture. Elbert Hubbard spoke in Toronto on many occasions, but one of his first was on March 21, 1901, when he gave a speech here titled "Roycroft Ideals." Authors who studied music here include Watson Kirkconnell and Pierre Salinger.

Novelist Selwyn Dewdney (1909-79) had rooms at **32 Murray Street** from 1930-31 while finishing his undergraduate degree. Murray Street descends to Elm and eventually **St. Patrick Street**.

Sir Beverley Baxter, met with earlier on this tour, resided with his parents at **98 St. Patrick Street** from 1895-1908. In his witty autobiography (1935), Baxter reminisces about his years while at this address: " . . . all this while the world was speeding up as if it could not reach quickly enough the precipice that was waiting at the end of the path. Electric trams had succeeded the horse-drawn ones, the two-wheel bicycle had come to bark our shins on the rough roads of progress, telephones had linked up far apart people who had nothing to say to each other, motor cars had appeared to terrorise the horses and to rob us of the use of our legs, a little English doctor named Crippen was journeying to Canada when a message travelled through the air to his ship, and from that moment his collar became a noose, but history had been made.

"Millionaires were multiplying in America and already it could be seen that the U.S.A. would never know depression again. Toronto had become a vast city with miles of such beautiful homes that no one to this day can account for the incomes necessary to support them. The curse of Scotland, in the form of golf, had reached us and wonderful clubs sprang up to lure the business man from his task.

"My voice had altered to a pleasing, but undistinguished tenor. I sang in one church after another as a paid soloist and performed in amateur opera. I fancied myself in love a dozen times and accumulated $400 in cash.

"Desiring to impress a certain young lady I decided to join the Royal Canadian Yacht Club, but found to my dismay that there was a waiting list for at least three years. It was possible, however, to buy a life membership for $400. It was the only money I had, the accumulation of my savings and the basis of a future competence.

"I bought the life membership. The girl married some other fellow.

"I wrote short plays and organised the Toronto Musical and Dramatic Society to perform them—loyally backed and financed by Mr. Nordheimer. I wrote innumerable short stories and sent them to every magazine in America. To the credit of the Post Office authorities, let it be recorded that not one manuscript was lost. Every one was returned safely.

"I was brought back to Nordheimer's head office and made assistant sales manager at $3000 a year. I wrote a full-length play and had it accepted by a New York management. A few days before production the management failed and my play, among other effects, was seized by the bailiffs. On reading the play the bailiffs returned it to me unconditionally."

Science fiction author Michelle Sagara (b.1963) wrote about her writing: "I started writing seriously—which means, in effect, for publication—in 1987, and I wrote my first published novel at **80 St. Patrick Street**. I remember when it was first rejected—by the same editor who later purchased it—because I came into the lobby and the package was sitting on the floor; it wouldn't fit into the mailbox, so it had just been left there. I wrote *Into the Dark Lands*, *Children of the Blood*, *Lady of Mercy*, and *Chains of Darkness, Chains of Light* there."

181 Simcoe Street was the home of the *Canadian Courier* from 1915-20, a noble experiment in combining essays, stories, and news articles with profiles of cultural and political figures.

When Sir John Hawkins Hagarty (1816-1900) died at his residence, **229 Simcoe Street**, the passing was treated as a major

Notable English Personalities Return to Native Land

Beverley Baxter, Canadian-born journalist who was editor of the London Express and is now a figure in the English film industry as well as English politics, arrived yesterday in Toronto with his Canadian wife. They are seen entering the Westminster Hotel.

Mail & Empire, September 28, 1935

news story by all the dailies. He had retired from the Bench in 1897 as the Chief Justice of Ontario. In addition to writing legal decisions, he penned hundreds of occasional verses which frequently appeared in one of the few outlets in Toronto in the 1840s for creative writing: *The Maple Leaf, or Canadian Annual: A Literary Souvenir*. The three issues of *The Maple Leaf* (1846-48) were twelve inches high by eight inches wide and featured handsome typefaces and even better design. Along with its many engraved plates of literary figures and scenes, it would be called lavish today but given the period can only be called outstanding. According to poet Samuel Thompson, "each volume appeared about Christmas day, and was eagerly looked for." Literary historian Mary Lu MacDonald states (with convincing evidence in support of the claim) that Hagarty was one of the three best-known poets in Canada in the second quarter of the 19th c. He had lived at this address since 1872.

Another Establishment figure who published poetry was Edward Chapman (1821-1904), who came from Britain to Toronto in 1853 to assume the post of Professor of Geology at University College, a post he retained until 1889 when he transferred to the Engineering School. Chapman was one of the most important geologists of the Victorian age in Canada, combining scientific research across the country with an admirable desire to make the field better known and accessible to the layman. His volume of poems, *A Song of Charity*, was published in in 1857. He boarded at **No.238** from 1890-92. His last address before returning to the UK in 1895 was nearby at **65 St. Patrick Street**.

Charles G.D. Roberts was never so poor as when he lived at **No.286 Simcoe** in November and December 1884. Earlier in the year he had quit as editor of Goldwin Smith's *The Week* and was trying to make a career as a freelance. By the end of the calendar year he was having to face the fact that he could not make such a career pay in Canada. He was so strapped for cash he had

to write to his father-in-law for a loan to cover the cost of his board. And by Christmas he had barely enough for the train ticket that took him back to his home in the Maritimes. He would not return to Toronto until 1925, but then, it would be in triumph—as a Canadian hero, knighted for his services to poetry, his return allotted page-one status in the newspapers.

481 University Avenue (at Dundas) has been the home of two publishing giants. From 1934-82 it was the editorial centre of the Maclean Hunter magazine empire. And since 1987, the head offices of McClelland and Stewart have been located here. Novelists and poets who worked full-time at *Maclean's* (as opposed to only freelancing) include Ralph Allen, Fred Bodsworth, John Clare, Pierre Berton, Charles Templeton, Eva-Lis Wuorio, and Scott Young. Other authors have worked for various trade magazines owned by Maclean Hunter. Among them are Arthur Hailey, Fraser Sutherland, and M.T. Kelly.

Where **555 University Avenue** used to stand is a tablet and statue marking the spot as the birthplace of Mary Pickford, silent movie star and alleged novelist.

Around the corner at **87 Elm Street** the Toronto Poorhouse was located, and it was here that one of the most famous Toronto eccentrics of the 19th c. passed away. Sir John Smyth (c.1792-1852) came to the city when he was 23 from a farm somewhere in the province—he was always evasive about where. Once settled in the city, he tried to make a living as a land agent and he has a footnote in our economic history because he was a pioneer railroad speculator—unfortunately, about half a century ahead of his time in that regard. But it was as a poet that he gained renown in his lifetime. We may scoff today at the simplicity of his verses, but in the 1830s it was considered remarkable that anyone in Muddy York would aspire to do publicly what all right-thinking people knew was done properly only in Britain. Moreover, unlike many later

Canadian writers who tried to pretend they were resident in the Lake District even as snowdrifts blocked their windows, Sir John celebrated the local scene. He was probably introduced to the famous writer Captain Marryat during the latter's visit to Toronto in 1838, because Marryat included one of Smyth's poems in his *A Diary in America* (1839). Of course, there is nothing like foreign applause to make Torontonians swoon over one of their own, and Marryat's imprimatur elevated Smyth from local oddity to literary celebrity. In 1841 he published his first book, *Select Poems,* and it received rave review. The success seemed to go to his head, because from around 1840 he appointed himself a baronet, no longer worked at a paying job, but rather wrote only poems, and soon found himself in the poorhouse, literally. The poorhouse was known politely as The House of Industry. Somehow he lost the use of his legs, but rather than be a shut-in, he had a small wagon constructed and pushed himself about town. The House of Industry was going to be razed by the Forces of Progress. But thanks to vocal opposition, led by writers Pierre Berton and Margaret Atwood, the building was saved.

40 Elm Street did not survive the wrecking ball. For decades its medium-sized auditorium was rented by outside groups to present various speakers—a few of them quite distinguished literary figures. The building had various names in the first half of the 20th c., including Elm Street Methodist Church, but the most commonly used was Hygeia Hall, and its main purpose was to address issues of social purity and hygiene— code used at the time in newspapers and by the public to describe venereal disease and pregnancy out of wedlock. Foreign authors who gave talks here include John Erskine (*The Private Life of Helen of Troy*), Emma Goldman (lectures on Tolstoy, Chekhov, and Ibsen among others) the Baroness Orczy (*The Scarlet Pimpernel*), and Thornton Wilder (*The Bridge Of San Luis Rey*). Canadian

talks included a rare public appearance by Frederick Philip Grove, and an early appearance by F.R. Scott. The most unusual appearance by my reckoning was that of Louis Ferdinand Céline (1894-1961). Céline (whose real name was Dr. Louis Ferdinand Destouches) was photographed in front of this building as part of a group of doctors touring North America in 1925 at the behest of the League of Nations. The group stayed at the King Edward Hotel and spent three days in the city. Céline made no appearances or speeches as a literary figure, so the event is but a footnote in our literary history, but then, by such events are our histories enlivened and spiced.

Algernon Blackwood (1869-1951), the British novelist, seems to have lived at **29 Elm Street** for the entire length of his stay in Toronto, 1890-92. His autobiography is engagingly frank (and often humorous) about his unhappy encounters with Toronto swindlers. He had been sent here by his father to grow up, be a man, and decide what he wanted to do with his life. A sheep with too much money, the wolves soon fleeced him. But what shines through his account is an affection for the city and the many friends he made here, and an amused wonder that he survived the perils into which his own stupidity placed him.

The Arts and Letters Club, by definition, is a literary landmark. It was founded in McConkey's Restaurant in 1908 by some of the leading artists in Toronto, including Lawren Harris (of the Group of Seven), A.S. Vogt (founder of the Mendelssohn Choir), and novelist Augustus Bridle (1869-1952). The emblem of the Club was designed by another member of the Group of Seven, J.E.H. MacDonald. The first meetings were held in the garret rooms of the Court House, 57 Adelaide East. Membership grew to the point that the Club needed larger quarters and in 1920 it moved to **14 Elm Street**. The building had been constructed in 1891 for the St. George's Society, formed to celebrate things English, but it had fallen on meagre times and the real estate deal was convenient for both clubs. The Arts and Letters has seen visits by thousands of authors, hundreds of whom have been members, and it would take a separate book to list them. However, a few visitors deserve special citation.

The first time women were allowed into the Club during the dinner-hour was in 1921 when Nellie McClung gave a speech. It is hard to imagine such a noted feminist author speaking here otherwise. Her talk attracted some of the top women authors in Toronto: Marshall Saunders, Katherine Hale, Lucy Maud Montgomery, and Marjory Mac-Murchy among them, and Emily Pankhurst, the famous suffragette, who happened to be in town, came as well.

Authors who gave formal speeches open to the general public include Beverley Baxter, Thomas B. Costain, Basil King, Sir Henry Newbolt, and Sir Charles G.D. Roberts. Informal talks were given, usually at lunches, by Christopher Morley, J.B. Priestley, A.A. Milne, Hugh Walpole, Bliss Carman, John Buchan (in 1924—before he returned to Canada to be Governor General), G.K. Chesterton, Arthur Stringer, Philip Gibbs, and Duncan Campbell Scott.

The Club today is not as vital as it once was. Of course, the places where artists can be entertained in congenial, simpatico surroundings have mushroomed since the Club moved to this address. And today there is much less homogeneity among leading artists, so their interests and passions and excitements are far more variegated than they were in the Club's heyday. Nonetheless, when reading the history of the Club, there is something stirring about noting the comfortable intercourse between and among the artists of different disciplines. They had a sense of community which we lack. While their gazes may not have been as international as today's top Toronto artists, their world was replete with cross-disciplinary ventures and projects we would do well to emulate.

Just north of Elm on the west side of **Yonge Street** is **360 Yonge**, the residence of Edgar Selwyn (1875-1944) in 1879 and 1880. Selwyn, although born in the USA, came to Toronto as a very young child with his parents and this was their first home. In a 1925 newspaper interview during a return visit, Selwyn told the reporter that his show-business career began in Toronto when he put on a show "in a shed with pins as admission money." At what point he left Toronto is unknown, but it would seem to have been when he was about 15. He moved to New York where he quickly became a matinee

Edgar Selwyn photographed in Hollywood, c.1920

idol, and then the author of plays in which he appeared, and then the producer of those plays. He moved into motion pictures and in 1916 co-founded a new film company with another producer named Goldfish. Each man donated a syllable from his last name to form the name of the new company —and thus was the Goldwyn (later MGM) film colossus begun. Sam Goldfish so liked the company name he legally had his own name changed to that of their firm. Selwyn left Hollywood on amicable terms and returned to New York where, in addition to writing 35 plays, he became one of the most successful producers in Broadway history. His first play, in fact, was an adaptation of a novel by a fellow former-Torontonian, Sir Gilbert Parker, and it's probable that he first read *Pierre and His People* while living here. Perhaps because of the stock-market crash, he returned to Hollywood in 1929 where he worked in several executive capacities on many MGM movies. Ever the showman, he went back to the sound stage in 1931 and directed Helen Hayes in her sound film debut, *The Sin of Madeleine Claudet*. The film won her an Oscar.

Just to the north is **Walton Street** where another Hollywood giant (and possible novelist) once lived. Mary Pickford's family was based at **No.17** from 1896-97, and the following year a little further west at **No.81**. Walton ends at **Elizabeth Street**. Near here is **184 Elizabeth**, Ernest Thompson Seton's first home when the ten-year-old moved to Toronto with his family in April 1870. Seton (1860-1946) is one of Canada's greatest animal storytellers, and his works have influenced hundreds of Canadian authors. When the Setons settled here, they were on the northern edge of a developing slum known as The Ward. His biographer describes the home's appearance: "It was serviced by a well in the backyard and a privy behind the house, for though piped water, sewers, gaslights and indoor plumbing were available in the better part of the city, it would be another twenty-five years before they came to Elizabeth Street."

The Seton home was next to the public school he attended. Seton describes his schoolmates: "Our daily associates were newsboys, Negroes, and the toughest youngsters I had ever met, including some jailbirds. Their common talk was of successful robberies that they had taken part in, or fights in which they had used a knife with effect. Rarely did I hear a sentence of their speech that was fit for publication."

While living on **Elizabeth Street**, Seton had his first adventure with drawing and writing. On a bet, he had wood-engraved some letters, and became fascinated by the process: "Woodcuts of letters led to an interest in type. The principal newspaper in Toronto was the *Globe*. Back of the *Globe* office on King Street was an open lot, littered over with the offscourings of the pressroom. Rummaging through these, I picked up quantities of type that had been thrown out by accident, or because they were damaged. I set to work to assemble a complete font. I made a little box with thirty-two compartments, and in this sorted my type, both capitals and lower case in the same bin. The last six bins were for periods, commas, etc. With my font assembled I soon made a wooden frame in which to set up the type, and, nothing daunted, announced that I would now publish *The Toronto Times*, intended to imitate and surpass *The London Times*.

"Ink I made by beating the soot out of some old stove pipes and grinding it up with water and a flat stone on a board. My roller was eighteen inches of broom shank, wrapped in the middle with muslin. My newsprint was grocer's paper. I now set about writing my copy. I set it up, and, as nearly as I remember, the first edition was limited to six copies. The editorials were short epigrammatic attacks on my teachers. The news was brief records of misbehaviour on the part of my schoolmates. Among the 'correspondence' were some like this:

"'Yes, the disease you describe is known as mullygrubs or cranks. The best remedy is birch oil, applied twice daily on the bare behind.'

"The general literature department was about two by four inches.

"I can recall only one item; it referred to three of my school rivals as follows:

> Miller is an ass;
> Harris is another;
> If Smith looks at the donkey's foal
> He'll see his little brother.

"There were so many disputes and feuds raised by my first issue that publications was temporarily suspended. Then a fire in the workshop where I held my plant destroyed the whole equipment. The experience I got in the venture stood me in good stead, and in later years I made many woodcuts for a work on *Birds*. But I lost interest in wood engraving when the photoengraving process was invented. By this, in the aftertime, I made thousands of illustrations from my line drawings."

Just how much this part of Toronto has changed can be gleaned from reading Seton's description of the area around his home: "Not far, a quarter mile from our home was Queen's Park, one hundred acres of virgin forest preserved but little changed. Farther north were the grassy hills of Seaton Village and Wells' Hill where, not long before, a mountain lion had been killed."

Walking north on University Avenue we come to **Gerrard Street West** where, at **12 Gerrard West**, E.H. Dewart lived from 1866-69, his first permanent address in Toronto Dewart (1828-1903) is well known to students of our literature as the compiler of the first anthology of Canadian verse, *Selections from Canadian Poets* (1864). His book was used as a textbook well into the 20th c., a strong compliment to its worth. What is not so well known is that Dewart was a very good poet himself. Historian Mary Lu MacDonald describes his volume *Songs of Life* (1869) as "one of the neglected masterpieces of early Canadian writing. Given the poetic conventions of his day and his deep religious convictions, the poems nonetheless compel a reader's attention. The forms are varied, he eschews the then-popular singsong rhyme schemes, and he handles iambic pentameter with great assurance." One of the other important literary figures of Victorian Toronto, John Charles Dent (1841-88) had a home next door at **No.14** in 1882. Dent wrote parts of his important books on Canadian history while he lived here, but given the address and of more literary sig-

John McCrae (right) and his brother Thomas at High Park, Toronto, October 25, 1893

nificance is his novel *The Gerrard Street Mystery and Other Weird Tales* (1888), the first mystery ever set in Toronto.

Elizabeth Street ends at **College Street**. Immediately on the left can be seen the oldest surviving buildings of Toronto General Hospital, **101 College Street**. Too many authors died or were born here to list—but one who worked here deserves mention: John McCrae, the author of "In Flanders Fields." After graduating with a gold medal from the medical college of the UofT, he interned at this hospital 1898-99 and probably lived here for about a year. While completing his internship he wrote poems and stories published in several journals, including *Saturday Night*.

East of this site, at **No.31**, was the first location of Bishop Strachan School. Two of its most celebrated graduates who studied at this location were poet Marjory Pickthall (1883-1922) and the pioneer feminist author Emily Murphy (1868-1933), who published extensively under the pen name Janey Canuck. She boarded at the school from September 1883 until June 1887. Another creative writer, Byrne Hope Sanders, wrote the first biography of Murphy and in it claimed Emily Murphy "found here . . . more opportunities to increase her understanding and love of words. Her school books, meticulously cared for, show how through her innate appreciation she went far beyond the customary routine of the classes. Look at her volume of Browning's *Poems*, and see how every page is underscored with notes—not in the fashion of those who want quick information for class recital, but with a devotional sense . . . There is ample evidence that she was an excellent student, and went with ease to the top of her class . . . A photograph taken when she was seventeen shows a proud tilt to her chin, and a calm confidence in her candid eyes. About her that is the Alexander Manning Medal for general proficiency—a beautiful jewel set on a silver dog-collar and presented by the Mayor of Toronto."

The most important literary address on this block of **College Street** is, lamentably, not open to the public: the Eaton Auditorium, **1 College Street**. The Auditorium was part of the Art Deco masterpiece, "Eaton's College Street," a gigantic project born of the Eaton family's belief that the downtown centre was moving north and they wanted to move with it. To that end, in the Roaring Twenties they initiated plans for construction of a huge store and office complex. Unfortunately, only the first stage of the landmark was opened because of cost overruns—and the reality of the Depression. Despite its restricted development, in the words of architectural historian William Dendy, "the fine finish of the completed sections made it a credit to the company and an ornament to Toronto . . . The ultimate showplace of the entire store was the suite of public rooms on the seventh floor which opened on March 26, 1931, five months after the October 30, 1930 opening of the rest of the building. Arranged like the first-class reception rooms on one of the great French ocean liners of the period, the seventh floor included an acoustically superb concert hall (the Eaton Auditorium), a restaurant (the Round Room) . . . and a ticket/reservations area . . . [The architect] had control over everything, from the furniture and architectural detail to the table linen, silver and china—even to the uniforms of the ushers and waitresses."

The seating capacity of the Auditorium was variable but was usually set at one thousand. For lunch or evening programs that were worthy (but drew smaller houses), the Round Room was easily convertible for concerts or lectures, and could accommodate up to four hundred. Readings and talks by authors took place usually in the Auditorium because Eaton's was excellent at promoting events in its buildings and the houses were large or completely sold out. Between 1931 and 1971 many of the most famous and some of the most popular writers of the era stood on this stage. Some remain household names; the others who are now out of fashion nonetheless harvested serious attention in their time and may do so again.

Space does not allow elaboration on more than a few individual programs, but so that the reader can contemplate the richness of the literary past of this site, here is a list of the creative writers who spoke here:

Beverley Baxter (five times)
Phyllis Bentley (two times)
Don Blanding
Hector Bolitho
Phyllis Bottome
Vera Brittain
Lewis Browne
Bennett Cerf (two times)
Ilka Chase
Clemence Dane
Bonamy Debree
O. Douglas
John Drinkwater
Rosita Forbes
Oliver St. John Gogarty
Wilfred Grenfell
Katherine Hale
Richard Halliburton
Bertita Harding
Rockwell Kent
Emily Kimbrough (two times)
Sinclair Lewis
Madge MacBeth
André Malraux
Erika Mann
Bruce Marshall
André Maurois
Nellie McClung
Christopher Morley
Edward J. O'Brien
J.B. Priestley
John D. Robins (two times)
Rafael Sabatini
Vita Sackville-West
Marshall Saunders
Vincent Sheean
Cornelia Otis Skinner
Robert J. Stead
Rex Stout

Sigrid Undset
Pierre van Paassen
Hugh Walpole
Edward A. Weeks
William Butler Yeats
Stefan Zweig

From the literary point of view, the last two on the list are among the most compelling. Stefan Zweig (1881-1942) was a German author whose excellence in several fields of writing catapulted him at a young age into the authorial Valhalla of Europe. A fierce critic of the Nazis, he fled Germany in 1934, choosing to settle first in England and then, in 1940, in Brazil where, despondent and far from friends, he died by his own hand. He spoke here on February 27, 1939. Interviewed by a *Star* reporter, he said he was happy to be in Canada as part of a lecture tour of the continent because "it's like coming to a sanatorium or rest home. Here all is peace and quiet. In Europe one cannot concentrate. But it will end—either by war or by understanding. I hope it will be the latter . . . England's triumph is her language. With it she has conquered half the world, and every year she conquers more and more countries in the peaceful way of language." All of the Toronto newspapers gave unusually hefty advance coverage to his coming and all reported on his speech—the *G&M* on page one. Immediately following his talk in the Auditorium, he moved to the adjacent Round Room for a reception by the Toronto chapter of the Canadian Authors' Association. More than 300 book people were present, including E.J. Pratt, Charles G.D. Roberts, Pelham Edgar, and Nat Benson. On behalf of Toronto writers, Pratt formally conferred on Zweig a presentation copy of George Wrong's book *The Canadians*. William A. Deacon, the *G&M's* veteran book critic, reported, "Seldom has a visiting writer impressed a Toronto audience with his simple greatness as did Stefan Zweig whose lecture was profound in thought, simple in diction. The most internationally famous of living writers was personally friendly, unassuming, dignified without stiffness, and a loyal, tolerant upholder of truth as the basis of art. Here was a man, clear of isms, who proved himself an idealist without distorting the realities. He is one celebrity who must come again."

William Butler Yeats's reading on November 23, 1932 in the Eaton Auditorium marked his fourth and last visit to Toronto. Curiously, it seems to have been the most poorly attended, although it received at least as much advance publicity in the newspapers as his other talks in 1904, 1914, and 1920. The bills announced that he would speak on "The Irish National Theatre," (the Abbey Theatre was due to arrive in Toronto a few months later). The *M&E* reported, "His beautiful blurred Irish speech made up in charm what it lacked in clarity. Some of his words were lost due to inflection but one would not have guessed that the most lyrical voice of dreamy Ireland proceeded from a body so tall and robust, a mind so logical. The fall of Parnell, Mr. Yeats said, convinced him that the National Movement must be promoted through channels other than political; and the stage was chosen because the Irish were not a book-reading people. Until the founding of the National University twenty-three years ago, there was no seat of higher education for Catholics. Actors and playwrights, to create the national drama, were drawn from all classes of the people.

"Mr. Yeats traced the careers of Lady Gregory, J.M. Synge and others, naming Sean O'Casey as the greatest genius produced by the movement. Many happily chosen anecdotes about such celebrities were relished by the many Toronto literary people present. The speaker stressed the importance of the subsidy of £1,000 a year which the theatre has received under both Cosgrave and De Valera Governments.

"Half an hour at the conclusion of the lecture was devoted to answering questions which the speaker said were 'the most sensible questions I have been asked on this side of the Atlantic.' During his replies he alluded with admiration to the 'heroic intensity' of James Joyce's *Ulysses*, and called Shaw 'one of the greatest public men in the world,' tactfully evading discussion of his famous quarrel with Shaw."

At this point, Yeats left the platform, not having been told that it was *de rigueur* in Toronto to play "God Save The King" after every public performance and speech. When he realized what had happened, he was visibly upset, informing the organizers that he intended no slight to the monarchy and was angry that he had not been given the chance to remain on stage. Reasonable people understood this, but the *Telegram*, rabid in its anglophilia, and regarding any criticism of ties to England as a sign of disloyalty, and having essentially ignored Yeats until then, the next day headlined a report on the incident "Irish Poets Quits Platform Before 'The King' Is Upset." The bias of the newspaper was most transparent in its description in the report of the National Theatre: "All night the lecturer had been treading thin ice. The Irish National Theatre, better known as the Abbey Theatre, had been founded by him and a band of kindred spirits, in those dark days following the Parnell tragedy when Ireland sounded sunken, bereft of pride, and forever doomed to indignity at the hands of a corrupt political machine. The Abbey Theatre was formed with the hope of rebuilding national pride. It built on intense nationalism, which has found expression in a series of riots and rebellions which have come to a head under the De Valera regime in a frank demand for republican independence and economic war with England."

The two pillars of French letters who spoke here, André Malraux (1901-76) and André Maurois (1885-1967), did so within a couple of years of each other. Malraux's remarks were given entirely in French with an interpreter by his side, so his audience was not large. He came here in 1937 to give a report on the progress of the war in Spain. His reception in the press was intelligent, even fulsome, the *Star* favouring him with a major page-one interview. Much more attention was devoted, however, to Maurois. His first talk in April 1939 was extensively promoted and covered. To prove that writers are not always perfect, it is worth noting that Maurois said from the stage, "I am no prophet but I don't think there will be war in Europe. Not since England and France have taken a firm stand in regard to aggression in Poland. I don't think there will be war, for it would mean such wholesale destruction." WWII, of course, began the same year.

In January 1940 he returned, and the advance publicity was even more extensive than it had been for his first visit. The audience was larger too. Eight hundred people had paid to hear him speak in 1939, but in 1940 extra chairs had to placed at the back of the theatre and even on stage to accommodate the more than 1,200 war-shocked people who wanted to hear inspiring words from this member of the French Academy. That he was completely fluent in English certainly augmented his popularity.

We leave this building to head south on the west side of **Yonge Street**. As we descend we pass some of the early locations of the Albert Britnell Bookshop—until its recent demise the oldest bookstore in Toronto. Britnell's was not always a sedate operation. Albert Britnell owned the garish Mammoth Bookstore at **248 Yonge Street**. Other Yonge Street locations for his bookstores (under various names) have included **Nos.241, 250, 263, 265, 815**, and **880**, as well as the original store at **No.240**, opened in 1893. The store at **No.765**, for so long a fixture on our literary scene, was opened on May 26, 1928 and closed on March 28, 1999. The first W.H. Smith Bookstore in Canada opened at **No.224** with great fanfare on September 29, 1950 and made an impact on the Toronto book world by hosting occasional lunches, open to the general public, with eminent visiting writers (almost

always novelists) such as Nicholas Monsarrat and Monica Dickens. An unusual bookstore that remains in operation near here is The World's Biggest Bookstore at **20 Edward Street**. When it opened in 1980 its claim to the title was already in dispute—a controversy which only served to make the public more aware of the store, of course.

At **Queen Street** turn right and proceed a few steps in a westerly direction. Where the non-descript entrance to the Eaton Centre is now located one of the majestic buildings of Victorian Toronto once stood. **26 Queen Street West** was the address of Shaftesbury Hall, the first permanent headquarters of the YMCA in Toronto, opened in 1873. In addition to offices, a library, rooms for single men, and a gymnasium, it contained a large auditorium able to seat about 600 people. The hall was occasionally used for talks by visiting authors. Among the more notable who spoke here were Sir Edwin Arnold, Matthew Arnold, Nicholas Flood Davin, Bret Harte, George MacDonald, and Max O'Rell.

SHAFTESBURY HALL.

MR. R. D'OYLY CARTE has the honor to announce two lectures only, in this city, by the distinguished poet, critic and essayist, Mr.

MATTHEW ARNOLD

on the following dates.

Tuesday Afternoon, Feb. 12th,

Subject—*"Literature and Science."*

Wednesday Evening, Feb. 13th,

Subject—"*Numbers, or the Majority and the Remnant.*"

Tickets, with reserved seats $1.00. On sale at Nordheimer's Music store, beginning Friday morning, Feb. 8th. Afternoon lecture at 3 o'clock. Evening at 8.

World, February 13, 1884

More coverage was given to the Matthew Arnold visit by the Toronto press than has ever been given to any other author in the history of the city. Arnold (1822-88), still famous for his poem "Dover Beach," gave two speeches here: "Literature and Science" on the afternoon of February 12, 1884, and "Numbers, Or the Majority and the

Remnant" on the evening of February 13. Tickets were one dollar. "His audiences were good; better, it was thought, than he could have expected in any English city of comparable size on two successive days. . . . " The newspapers outdid themselves in the intelligence with which they discussed his imminent arrival, and the perspicacity with which they debated the import of his remarks. All of the dailies printed at least one editorial on what Arnold had to say during his visit and the high seriousness with which they wrestled with his ideas is attractive to behold. This is even more remarkable than it might seem at first glance, because most of the newspapers ultimately disagreed with his position on many philosophical issues, and they were particularly threatened by what they felt was his far drift from the anchorage of Christianity. That said, their reaction to this drift, indeed to all of his arguments, was not hysterical but respectful. In all, ten editorials, a further ten lengthy articles, and five syndicated essays—all focused on Arnold—

were published in Toronto within the five days of his visit. Arnold, naturally, was not blind to this reaction. Having just finished a lecture tour in the USA, where he had been frequently vilified, he was immediately struck by the difference in temperament of the citizenry here, and appreciative of the respect shown to his work and his person. He stayed at the Grange during his visit as the guest of Goldwin Smith.

George MacDonald (1824-1905) was almost as popular a literary visitor in Toronto as his friend Matthew Arnold, albeit one of a different artistic bent. MacDonald was famous in his day for his Christian allegories and novels celebrating Scottish life, but he is remembered fondly today for his famous book for children, *At the Back of the North Wind* (1871). He is not as forgotten an author as some might think. Margaret Atwood, for example, devoted a third of her Harvard doctoral thesis to his writing. MacDonald's lecture on Robbie Burns was delivered here April 1, 1873.

The YMCA new building (also known as Shaftesbury Hall) as seen in *Canadian Illustrated News*, November 23, 1872

A mere five weeks previously, the American author Bret Harte (1836-1902), internationally acclaimed for his western tales (*The Luck of Roaring Camp*), had spoken at Shaftesbury Hall to a full house. All his life, Harte believed that his writing was too urbane, too sophisticated for his compatriots to appreciate and he felt he would have to move to Europe in order to find the audience he deserved. He did finally settle in England, but not without singling Toronto out for special praise. He wrote to his wife on February 26, 1873: "At Toronto the audience waited for me for an hour and a half as I flew towards them in a special train (an engine and a single car) which I telegraphed ahead for, and in which I dressed myself, at the rate of seventy miles an hour—the most rapid and unsatisfactory toilette I ever made . . . They were so well pleased with me at Toronto—an English audience, and, I fancied, quite a pleasant forecast of the reception I should meet abroad—that I made an arrangement to return in the latter part of March . . . I had a long talk with a prominent Canadian publisher at Toronto and have entered into a contract to prepare a complete edition of my works in one volume."

Our final stop on this tour is Osgoode Hall, **130 Queen Street West**, where several authors of fiction, poetry, or drama also studied law. The architectural history of Osgoode is complicated, but suffice to say the oldest part of the building (the eastern third of the façade) was constructed in 1829, the western wing in 1844, and the central portion in 1857. It has been my experience that many Torontonians have never entered the building, fearing that it is reserved for those either in robes or in chains. Quite the contrary. It has a handsome interior by any standard. The library cannot be used by the public—but can be viewed from the doorway, and is a bibliophile's dream. Some of the courtrooms are actually Minoan in their colour schemes, especially Courtroom Number Four, and are most impressive. Certainly literary visitors such as William Dean Howells found them so: "[Osgoode] is a beautiful structure, faced with a freestone which is easy to work. The pavements of the courts are templated with little squares of blue, purple, red and yellow stones. The rotunda is finished in perfect taste, and the whole edifice in this respect presents a contrast with our public buildings not pleasant to the American. The room of the library of the Toronto Law Society is particularly fine." Literary figures who studied here include:

Sol Allen
Edward D. Armour
Jack Batten
Charles W. Bell
William Hume Blake
Arthur S. Bourninot
Morley Callaghan
James Cawdell
Brian Doherty
R.G. Everson
James Haverson
Wilfrid Heighington
Thomas Stinson Jarvis
William Henry Kerr
George Allen Kingston
Judy LaMarsh
Tom MacInnes
George Allan Mackenzie
William Henry Moore
Patrick Slater
Thomas B. Stewart
Morley Torgov

SOUTH ANNEX

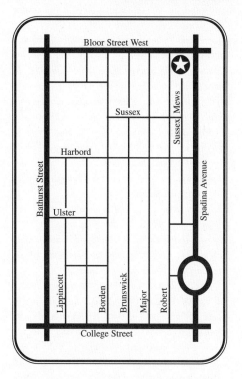

The tour begins at the southwest corner of Bloor Street West and Spadina Avenue.

The YM-YWHA Community Centre at **750 Spadina Avenue** was—for one year—the home of the legendary Contact Reading Series, the city's first effort to present contemporary Canadian and American poets in a relatively well-publicized program of appearances. The Series began elsewhere—in 1957 at the Greenwich Gallery on Bay Street (made available for readings by the generosity of art dealer Av Isaacs). After three years, the organizers, poets Raymond Souster and Kenneth McRobbie, were wooed by this YM-YWHA, which apparently had dreams of emulating the famous and distinguished readings presented since 1939 by its counterpart at the 92nd Street Y in New York. In just one programming year the following authors read here:

October 16, 1960: Leroi Jones [Amiri Baraka]
November 19, 1960: Louis Zukofsky
December 10, 1960: George Johnston
January 21, 1961: Cid Corman
February 25, 1961: Margaret Avison and Phyllis Gotlieb
March 25, 1961: Jacques Godbout and Yves Prefontaine
April 29, 1961: Theodore Enslin

This is an impressive list, especially given the limited resources of the organizers and the literary conservatism of the city at that time. Moreover, these authors were still developing their reputations. Today they are regarded as major figures in 20th c. poetry. However, Souster and McRobbie found that they had different goals and manners of working than their hosts at the Y, so they parted amicably from the organization, and authors appearing under the Contact aegis returned to the Isaacs Gallery for its next season of readings.

722 Spadina Avenue was the home of Edgar McInnis (1899-1973), who lived here in the late 1920s when he returned from his Rhodes scholarship at Oxford. While McInnis is known today as having been one of Canada's finest historians, he had early dreams of being a poet. He won the Newdigate Prize for Poetry in 1925 at Oxford, and later in life published books of poems inspired by his experiences as an artillery officer in WWI.

The Dora Hood Book Room was one of the most famous antiquarian shops in Canadian history, in part because Dora Hood made a specialty of Canadiana (especially Canadian history), at a time when the numbers of people who might be customers were much smaller than today, and in part because she wrote a touching personal memoir of her founding and administration of the shop, *At the Side Door*. The store was located at **No.720** from 1927 until 1962, when it moved to 34 Ross Street. Hood sold the business to the former UofT librarian W. Stewart Wallace, whose reference books on Canadian authors and history remain icons to which all historians of our culture happily genuflect out of respect for their importance. Another formidable reference-book author, John Robert Colombo, recounts an interesting experience at the shop: "Prices were higher and the stock was strictly Canadiana at Dora Hood's Book Room then located on Spadina Avenue. The mail-order service was presided over by Dora Hood, the author of a biography of Davidson Black, the discoverer of Peking Man, and the retired librarian W. Stewart Wallace. I bought a small book from Dr. Wallace. He was immediately suspicious of me when I mentioned that I was a student. 'I'm enrolled at University College,' I explained. 'I live in the Sir Daniel Wilson Residence.' He looked uncertain. 'My house is Wallace House.' Not until I uttered that piece of information did I realize that the man who was standing in front of me, wearing a dark suit and bow tie on a hot day, was the house's namesake. If he felt surprise, he never showed it."

Professor W.J. Alexander (1855-1944) lived at **No.712** from 1890 to 1893, his first address in Toronto. He had just started to teach English at University College. Within a few years, well before the mid-point of his career, he was one of the most eminent scholars in Canada. An extraordinary teacher, he was also extraordinary in publicly declaring a scholarly interest in contemporary literature and, most amazingly, an interest in Canadian authors. The UofT's annual Alexander Lectures, named in his honour, have attracted as speakers some of the finest literary critics from around the world.

A quick aside onto **Sussex Avenue**, west of Spadina, is worth a detour at this point. **No.59** was the first Toronto home of Colin Sabiston (1893-1961), originally from Orangeville, who toiled for most of the city's dailies but ended his days as the music and drama critic of the *G&M* (his wife was its visual arts critic). His one novel, *Zoya*, was published in London to fine reviews in Canada. Bibliomane and thief Richard T. Lancefield (whom we meet several times on these Annex tours) lived at what used to be **No.62** in 1889. Mazo de la Roche, the author of the famous *Jalna* series, lived at **No.68** in 1905, long before she published her first novel. Mazo lived in no place for very long; we discuss her at length during the tour of Yorkville.

With his new bride, novelist David Helwig moved to an attic apartment in a house once located at **684 Spadina Avenue**. It was here that he wrote the first draft of his famed novella *The Streets of Summer*.

For about six years **No.672** was the home of Frank Yeigh (1861-1935) and his wife, Kate Yeigh (1856-1906). At his death, Frank Yeigh was described by the newspapers as an "eminent historian," but he was always more interested in writing than researching. After dabbling in newspaper journalism, he worked for some time as the private secretary of the premier of Ontario. Later still he worked for a variety of organizations, including the Ontario Shorthand Writers Society, all the while penning freelance articles and lecturing frequently on Canadian topics. In the words of a biographer, "he was part of Toronto's smart professional writers' set, well connected in society, and extremely commercially minded." He merits inclusion in this book, however, for two reasons. First, when he ran for the presidency of the Young Men's Liberal Club of Ontario, one of his planks was a commitment to greatly amplify the party's nationalist policy. Elected, he delivered on his promise—in part by organizing in Toronto a gala reading by Canadian novelists and poets—the first in the history of the country. On January 16, 1892, some of the best-known writers of the day gathered at the Academy of Music to read to an audience so large that, as the newspapers noted, even ladies had to stand in the aisles.

The second reason Yeigh is included in this *Guide* has to do with the first: one of the authors on the bill that night was unknown to almost everyone except Frank Yeigh. Pauline Johnson had been invited to read because Yeigh had known her from his youth in Brantford, and because he had sufficient showman's instincts to realize that her Indian heritage and physical good looks would add cachet to the program. In fairness, let us also note that he sincerely liked her writing. Pauline Johnson almost stole the show, and Frank Yeigh quickly arranged for her to make subsequent solo appearances in Toronto, appearances that were so successful she began a new career as a recitalist of her own work on stages across the country and in Britain.

This Spadina address was the first Toronto home of Kate Yeigh who moved here with her husband immediately after their wedding in 1892. A year before, when she was Kate Westlake, she had written an anonymous dime-novel based on the recent death of Sitting Bull, and had sold it to an American publisher for what was then a small fortune: $500. Her later and more respectable writing took the form of contributions to *Saturday Night* and other leading periodicals, although she did write one more novel, *A Specimen Spinster* (under her married name), notable today for its humour and its wry commentary on the social condition of women.

St. Vladimir's Ukrainian Institute at **620 Spadina Avenue** was home to novelist Janice Kulyk Keefer (b.1952) during her first two years (1970-72) as an undergrad at the UofT.

The curves in the street at this point are known locally as Spadina Crescent. The circular space was originally intended as a park, but the property was sold to Knox College in 1873 and two years later the edifice (whose rear looms before us—the south end of the Crescent provides the better view) was opened as the official college of the Presbyterian Church where all students attended classes and some lived in residence. Among the authors who pursued Divinity

Knox College, in a wood engraving printed 1873

studies here were Ralph Connor (1884-87), William Patrick McKenzie (1886-89), and William T. Allison (1900-1). As well, students with Presbyterian affiliation could use the residence. John McCrae, the author of "In Flanders Fields," lived here while studying Medicine from about 1888 until 1892.

In 1917, the largest publicly attended funeral in the history of the city up to that point (and possibly ever) was held for Francis Stephens Spence (1850-1917). Such an outsized display merely confirmed the affection Torontonians held for Spence. When he died on March 8, the *Globe*, the *Star*, the *World*, and the *News* gave his death front-page treatment, and he was the subject of glowing panegyrics on the editorial pages. The ceremonies began from his home, **554 Spadina Avenue**. The City Hall flag flew at half-mast in his honour, and on the day they learned of his death, the city's politicians did no business at all, adjourning immediately in respect to his memory. The Board of Control, the entire City Council, and all Civic Departmental heads attended the funeral *en masse*. Before the funeral itself, a memorial service open to the public was held at Massey Hall, then with a seating capacity of around 5,000. Yet there were not enough seats to accommodate the thousands of mourners. Who was this man?

Although born in Donegal, F.S. Spence came to Canada when young, and after a stint as a teacher, tried his hand at journalism, although he soon found his true calling in the struggle against the traffic in "beverage alcohol." Spence was a Prohibitionist such as the city had never seen, and he devoted most of his adult life to fighting the demon rum. To do this, he ran for public office and was elected to many terms as a city councillor. When not preoccupied with his temperance work, he busied himself with urban matters, overseeing the creation of the Toronto Harbour Board, for example, or pushing for public ownership of hydro. In addition to writing many books and

pamphlets on the merits of abstinence from alcohol, he wrote a book of poetry which time has forgotten with the same ease it has forgotten his fame. Today it is easy to giggle or sneer at fanaticism such as Spence's. But the level of attention given to his death is testimony to the widespread desperation of many of our forebears when confronted by the massiveness of the drinking problem—and their widespread failure to link the prevalence of drunkenness with the social and economic causes behind it. The temperance brigades were the Victorian and Edwardian equivalents of the folks today who believe that all one has to do to solve a social ill is "Just say no." Spence lived in this house from 1905-17, longer than at any of his many other Toronto addresses. Indeed, he died here, and it was to this house that hundreds of wreaths were sent, and to which the leading members of the Establishment came to pay their last respects.

From 1970-72 poet Joe Rosenblatt lived at **No.550 Spadina Avenue** and this home in particular Rosenblatt generously offered as a "crash pad" to poets visiting the city with few or no funds for hotel accommodation.

"The northernmost residence on the west side of the avenue above College, just where it starts to encircle Knox College, is a mansard-roofed brick structure which today houses an undertaking establishment. The garden which originally flanked the house to the south has long since disappeared and its site is occupied by an addition to the main building, a structure in which the business of the institution is conducted. That old garden is still fresh in the memory of this oldster who, as a very little boy, made it his playground. There were mignonettes and sweet peas there, pansies and forget-me-nots. But most vividly through the mists of memory come back little clusters of that shyest and daintiest of flowers, the bleeding-heart—bleeding-heart, and the golden glory of huge sunflowers at the bottom of the garden." This sylvan description of his grandparents' home at **510 Spadina Avenue** is by novelist Gordon Hill Grahame. Remarkably little is known about Grahame. While we know that he was a cousin of Kenneth Grahame (author of the children's classic *Wind in the Willows*), we don't know when he was born, when he died, where he died, or where he spent his boyhood in Toronto. In his memoir he writes so lovingly about **No.510** that one has the impression that if it wasn't his formal home, he spent so much time there it might as well have been. He admits that his mother "was a woman who could never be settled for any length of time without seeking pastures new. I was bedded in more different establishments during my early childhood and adolescence than the most indiscriminate call-girl," including unspecified houses on Sussex Avenue and Washington Avenue. Grahame's memoir is too little known—which is a shame because he is excellent at bringing back the sounds and sights of the quotidian Toronto of more than a century ago.

Grahame published four novels but it was his first which was his bestselling and most notorious—and which, paradoxically caused him the greatest embarrassment. Magazine historian Fraser Sutherland recounts that in 1922 the British publisher Hodder & Stoughton had teamed with *Maclean's* magazine "to sponsor a $2,500 competition for an original Canadian novel. The winner was Gordon Hill Grahame's *The Bond Triumphant*, which was split into five sections and sent to be illustrated by C.W. Jeffreys. In this tame historical romance about French Canada in 1661, Bishop Laval was portrayed as a bigot. When the 1 July issue appeared, there was an outcry from French and English Catholics, and considerable kerfuffle over an illustration depicting the hero, Etienne, sitting on a bench with his arm around a girl in a nun's habit, although in the text the girl was a volunteer, not a religious sister. Though not offended himself, the [publisher] ordered the galleys withdrawn. This created an anomalous 15 July issue that listed the book

in a table of contents—in a section printed prior to his decision—but had the chapter replaced with a short story by Archibald McKishnie.

"With the 15 August issue came the statement 'The story was taken entirely on the judgement of, and awarded first prize by, a committee of literary experts outside our organization. It is absolutely contrary to the principles and policies upon which Maclean's Magazine has been built up to publish partisan material which would hurt any reputable body of citizens in the Dominion'. . . . The always Orange Toronto *Telegram* bought the book's serial rights," and, of course, the censorship only served to make the book itself a bestseller.

The Waverley Hotel at **No.484** was home to poet Milton Acorn (1923-86) from 1970 to 1977. In the public mind he is associated with this address more than any other. According to his friend James Deahl, Acorn was constantly changing his rooms at the Waverley because he was convinced the rooms were bugged, or were about to be bugged by the RCMP. To throw the Mounties off the scent Acorn would change rooms at unpredictable moments. Despite the fact that he lived here for so many years (and he kept a writing room here until 1981), he paid a daily rate rather than a cheaper weekly or monthly rate because, he told friends, he was never sure if he were going to stay at the hotel or have to leave town suddenly. Acorn was seen frequently storming up and down Spadina, chomping on a cheap cigar and murmuring curses *sotto voce* at phantom enemies. In the 1970s when I first knew him, it was still a pleasure to stop and chat with him on Spadina—often in front of the Waverley itself. But by the end of his life he was, alas, so irascible that I—and most others who had known him—would cross the street to avoid him if we saw him hurtling in our direction.

The American novelist Elmore ("Dutch") Leonard called me one night in the 1980s from his home near Detroit and said that in honour of the fierce affection we held for

College Street looking east towards Spadina Avenue, 1911

our respective major-league baseball teams (the Toronto Blue Jays and Detroit Tigers were fighting for the league championship) he was going to set the start of his next novel in Toronto. Indeed, the bad guy was going to hail from the city. Dutch wanted me to describe a cheap residential hotel where his villain was likely to live, and after a moment's thought, I suggested the Waverley. He then asked me to describe the hotel. I did for no more than a minute—at which point he told me he got the picture. Based on that brief conversation, he penned a chillingly accurate description of the bad guy's home—without ever having seen it—and the results are the opening pages of his novel *Killshot*.

The Lord Lansdowne School at **33 Robert Street** is clearly no architectural threat to the Taj Mahal. In a previous existence, it was merely Lansdowne School, the primary school of poet Joe Rosenblatt and writer Gordon Hill Grahame. At some point, the school was raised to the peerage, and from 1955-63 was the public school of poet Gerry Shikatani.

The forced evacuation of Japanese-Canadians from our west coast in 1942 is widely regarded today as a shameful part of our history, the morality of the action seen in black and white. However, a few souls were willing to declare that the situation was rather more grey than that, and first among the detainees to take this stance was poet Takeo Nakano (b.1903). Born in Japan, he arrived in Canada in 1920, worked at a sawmill near Vancouver, and even returned to Japan in 1930 to marry. Although he then returned to this country with his new wife, he kept his savings in a bank, not in Vancouver, but in Japan. When war was declared, he was forcibly separated from his wife and child, and while justly aggrieved at the illegality and racism inherent in his internal deportation to what were, in effect, P.O.W. camps, he was honest enough a writer to note that most of his fellow detainees were just as racist as his jailors and were completely committed to a Japanese victory in WWII. In November 1943, he was released from internment on condition that he be employed at an essential war-time task—in his case, working amid the stink of offal at Canada Packers in Toronto. The job was hardly pleasant, but living, as of early

1944, at **117 Robert Street** was certainly better than living behind double rows of high barbed-wire fence such as he had known at his former address in northern Ontario. Nakano's poems, primarily in the tanka form, have been published to acclaim around the world. He lived in this house until 1949.

Disgraced librarian Richard T. Lancefield, perhaps fleeing from his demons, or perhaps just short of cash, lived in many Annex area residences—**No.120** was his abode in 1908.

The Newfoundland author Percy Janes (1922-99) disappeared from the literary radar screen in his later years, but in 1970, when his novel *House of Hate* was published, he was very much seen as a coming challenge to the old-guard authors. The paperback edition of the novel features a flattering Introduction by none other than Margaret Laurence. Following a career in the navy, Janes enrolled at Victoria College, and during the 1947-48 academic year made his home at **No.128**.

The American writer Valerie Miner (b.1947) once lived in Toronto, doing so from 1970 to 1971 at **163 Robert Street**. The street was also briefly home to the *enfant terrible* of 1970s CanLit, Scott Symons (b.1933). Since he fled Canada for Morocco, Symons has made few return visits; but on two occasions he called **No.171** home: one occasion was a stay of about four months' duration in 1985 (when he finished the writing of his novel *Helmet of Flesh*), and he also lived here for most of 1989.

Before crossing Harbord Street we should note that **89 Harbord Street** was home for many years in the 1970s and 80s to the Abbey Bookstore, subsequently transposed to Paris where it has been active in promoting English-Canadian authors to the French. Before it was the Abbey, writer Andreas Schroeder lived there for a year, beginning in May 1968. He had just arrived from the west with, as he wrote to me, "every expectation that my 'Toronto experience'

would put me through the literary sound barrier in double quick time." In the second-floor apartment overlooking the street he wrote his first book of poems, *The Ozone Minotaur*.

Abbey Books, 89 Harbord Street, residence of poet Andreas Schroeder, 1968-69

We return to **Robert Street**, heading north. Novelist Eve Zaremba is slowly developing a solid reputation among aficionados of crime novels. Three of her Helen Keremos mysteries (featuring an openly lesbian detective) were written while Zaremba resided at **No.208** from 1986 to 1997—Zaremba's longest stay at any of her Toronto homes to date.

Franklin Davey McDowell (1888-1965), when he first touched down in Toronto in 1916, roomed at **No. 223** before moving elsewhere within the year. McDowell would later become a senior in the Toronto literary establishment of mid-century. His first novel won the Governor General's Award in 1939, and, as a public relations manager for Canadian National Railways, he was unfailingly generous to fellow authors in dispensing rail passes.

The ground-floor flat at **No.240** was the final home of the inimitable poet Gwendolyn MacEwen (1941-87). She was born in Toronto, and lived in—or within a few bus stops of—the Annex for most of her life. By the time she arrived at this address in 1983, her life had taken several turns for the worse, physically and spiritually. She was far from helpless, but the alcoholism she had battled for years was in its final ascendancy, and her love affairs with men seemed to be more ruinous than ever. Perhaps as compensation, she became especially attached to the many abandoned cats in the alley behind her new home. In her wonderful book *Shadow Maker*, MacEwen's biographer, Rosemary Sullivan, writes: "She bought cat food and every day changed and replenished the food and water supply in Coca-Cola boxes she set out for the strays. She found there were at least two or three other people, 'my shady accomplices' she called them, who were doing the same. Together they kept the stray cats fed and removed the stiff little corpses of the ones who died. Gwen also built a small shelter of several storeys at the bottom of her garden for the cats, which, of course, made her unpopular with the neighbours who wanted to be rid of the pestilence." Among her neighbours at the time was the writer Aviva Layton who was taken by the neatness of MacEwen's housekeeping. Sullivan reports Layton as saying, "She had covered the chest in which she kept her books with a bit of embroidery and placed it under a shelf so that it was easy to slip books into it, but would have been hard to remove them . . . On the white walls she had her poster from the production of [her play] *The Trojan Women* and the broadside of her "Loch Ness Monster" poem, and had strategically placed her few icons . . . But what most astonished Layton was Gwen's desk: 'It was about three inches by two and a half, the size of a postage stamp. I, who was doing nothing, had a desk the size of Bloor Street messed with papers

and books. And there was Gwen turning out this marvellous stuff, and I remember saying, "Gwen, I've got a spare desk." No. She explained why she wanted that tiny desk, the pencils and pens just so, and not a crumpled paper.'"

A.J.M. Smith, in Toronto, presents poet and novelist Gwendolyn MacEwen with Michigan State's A.J.M. Smith award for poetry for her book *Armies of the Moon*
Star, May 10, 1973

While living here, MacEwen had some important professional triumphs: in 1984-85 she was writer-in-residence at the University of Western Ontario, and in the autumn of 1986 she was appointed to the same position at the UofT. Her last book, *Afterworlds*, published the year she died here, is a mixture of old work and new writing on new topics. Like much of her life, it is an admixture of soaring optimism and love, bleakest despair and pain.

As I write this *Guide*, Grace Irwin (b.1907) is the longest lived of our novelists. She spent the first three years of her life at **No.286**. For many years she was both a teacher at Humberside Collegiate and an author of sophisticated, Christian novels. Today, in her nineties, she is long retired as a teacher, but continues to write fiction particularly popular with religious people, and still relishes the performance of her duties as an ordained pastor.

At the age of 18, Paul Quarrington moved from the suburbs to **302 Robert** when starting his studies at the UofT. Like any undergraduate worthy of the name, he did not come home *every* night, but did use this address as his base from 1971 to 1973.

286 Major Street was the home of M.T. Kelly, novelist, poet, and author of the play *Green Dolphin*, which he conceived when he lived here 1982-83. Across the street at **No.281** writer Janet Hamilton (1951-98) lived almost twenty years (from 1979 until her death) with her husband, novelist Howard Engel. Although she published only one novel, *Sagacity* (1981), there were—and are—select admirers of its experimental technique and celebration of Canadian history. Howard Engel (b.1931) is one of the country's best-known crime novelists, but for some time he was the producer of CBC Radio's most important literary program, the much missed "Anthology."

270 Major Street was home for a couple of years in the early 1890s to Albert E.S. Smythe, the poet, Theosophist, and father of the very unpoetical Conn Smythe who built Maple Leaf Gardens. The next house south (**No.268**) has very strong literary connections. Fiction author Aviva Layton lived here with her novelist husband, Leon Whiteson, from 1984 to 1985. The following year, they rented the house to Leon and Connie Rooke. Rooke (b.1934) is a highly regarded novelist and short-story author, and Connie was for many years the editor of the literary journal *The Malahat Review*. Their stay in Toronto was intended for a year only, so they moved on, but not before giving the keys to Michael Ondaatje (b.1943) and his companion Linda Spalding (b.1943), who

also lived here for another year (1986-87). While resident at this address Ondaatje worked on his breakthrough novel, *In the Skin of a Lion*, and did some early work on his even more successful *The English Patient*.

The dramatist Charles Tidler (b.1946) is most often thought of as a product of the west coast, but he has also lived in Toronto— the city was his first stop when he arrived in Canada fleeing the Vietnam draft, and he lived in Toronto again from October 1983 to April 1984. Relatively brief as the second stay was, it was fruitful: he oversaw the production of his play *The Farewell Heart* at Tarragon, and wrote most of a radio play for the CBC, and all of a new full-length play for the stage. Part of this second Toronto stint was spent at **No.249**.

Martyn Burke (b.1942) has been directing most of his energies to successful television documentaries and screenplays of late, but he was writing fiction and for TV when he lived at **No.231** for two years starting in 1972.

Sussex Avenue is nearby. At the northeast corner of Sussex and Major is **84 Sussex Avenue**, built in 1885. From 1970-73, this was the home of "new press," the house founded by Dave Godfrey, Roy MacSkimming, and James Bacque to publish intensely Canadian non-fiction as well as literary texts. Jim Bacque wrote to me that "new press from the first was a venture in faith. Maclean Hunter sensed the enterprise and bought in very early, enabling us to grow into the second largest Canadian publishing house inside three years. That was our *annus mirabilis*. But we were doing it mainly on borrowed money, and when interest rates rose steeply because of the oil crisis, the press was doomed. It was sold for a dollar to Jack Stoddart in 1974." Greg Hollingshead, winner of the Governor General's Award for Fiction in 1995, lived in this house during its new press days (while studying for an MA in English at the UofT). Poet and *Maclean's* magazine critic John Bemrose lived here briefly at that time as well.

"new press" at 84 Sussex Avenue, c. 1971. At fence are, left to right, Mike Spurgeon, John Bemrose, Christina Hartling, James Bacque, Marilyn Field-Marsham, Carol Orr, Roy MacSkimming; balcony: David Lewis Stein, Peter Maher, Ingrid Cook, Dave Godfrey and Frank Paci

Refocusing on **Major Street**, we note that the poet Joe Rosenblatt (b.1933) lived at **No.185,** longer (1943-51) than at any other Toronto address. He described it as the "major street" of his teenage years. In a letter he continued, "The Major Street Fish Market used to be [near] there and sold the best fresh water fish in the city next to, of course, my uncle's fishstore on Baldwin Street . . . Right next door is my favourite bakery, Harbord Bakery, which has been there for decades— since I was a kid. From my house on Major Street I managed to meander through the city (I would walk for miles) . . . I attended Central Technical School 1949-50, failed grade ten and kept on drifting in life.

Just as her novelist father was attracted to the Annex area, so too is poet Maggie Helwig. From 1986 to 1990 she lived at **No.177**.

Continue south on Major to College Street. Turn west and continue until you reach **Brunswick Avenue**, one of the most literary streets in the history of Toronto where at least 50 creative writers have lived over the past century or more. Only one other street of about equal length (Huron Street) can claim more. However, few of the authors who lived on Brunswick did so for long. It seems to be a street that attracts writers when they are in transition rather than in a mood to settle.

One of the pleasures of **Brunswick Avenue** is that the streetscape has changed relatively little in over a century—except where it intersects with College Street. Doctor's Hospital, of course, accounted for the razing of many old buildings. One of them may have been the Labour League Mutual Benefit Society once located at **No.7**. This venue was popular with Jewish speakers, and on October 1, 1945, one of the greatest, the acclaimed Yiddish novelist Joseph Opatoshu (1887-1954), visiting from New York, gave a speech to the officers of the Canadian Jewish Congress and to anyone else who cared to listen. Opatoshu is still considered by many knowledgeable folk as second only to Isaac Bashevis Singer in the pantheon of Yiddish authors. William Arthur Deacon, the literary critic at the *G&M* during the middle years of the 20th c., attended the lecture even though he knew beforehand he would not understand a word. He reported that Opatoshu "read an essay in Yiddish. I noted the poetic rhythms of his vigorous prose and was pleased to hear a subsequent speaker use the word *lyrical*. Remarks from Professor Leopold Infeld revealed that Mr. Opatoshu had been comparing Hebrew and Greek cultures. Dr. Infeld used the words 'one of the most beautiful addresses I ever heard in my life.'" Infeld, a celebrated mathematician, was a friend of Albert Einstein's—indeed, was his collaborator on many projects and theoretical papers. Infeld was also a novelist, and for many years a resident of Toronto.

For some reason, the houses at the southern end of Brunswick have been anathema to authors. But once we arrive at the 100 block the residencies start to fly thick and fast. However, before examining those, there are a couple of addresses nearby on **Ulster Street** deserving a moment's notice. The first of these is **No.32** where Sarah Anne Curzon's son lived—and where she died. Curzon (1833-98) is important in our history for many reasons. She was a pioneer, with Dr. Emily Stowe, in founding the Toronto Women's Literary Club, which, despite its name, was not so much literary but rather the first organization in Canada devoted solely to advancing women's rights. She was also a founder of the Women's Canadian Historical Society in 1895. As an author, she is important because Canadian history was the prime source of her writing at a time when too many of her compatriots believed real art lay solely in other domains. Her major work, for example, was *Laura Secord, the Heroine of 1812: A Drama and Other Poems* (1887). Furthermore, she was adamant in proving that a woman could write professionally in the fields dominated in Canada by men. Coinciden-tally this same house accommodated novelist Henry Kreisel (1922-91) during his fourth undergraduate year at the UofT (1944-45). At the start of WWII, Kreisel was mistaken for the enemy and interned for 18 months before he was released in 1941. He lived in Toronto six years before moving to Alberta where he wrote, among other books, the minor classic, *The Rich Man*.

131 Brunswick Avenue was home to Arthur Phelps from 1909-11. Phelps (1887-1970) was well-known in his day for his many broadcasts on national radio, an oddity at the time for someone who was both a famed professor of English, a poet, and a Methodist minister. He lived in Toronto just long enough to get a BA in 1913 from Victoria College. For two (and possibly more) of his undergraduate years he lodged at this address. Two doors further north (**No.135**) the writer Janice Kulyk Keefer also spent two undergraduate years (1972-74) rooming here while she attended University College, and wrote the first draft of her poetry book *White of the Lesser Angels* (1986).

Award-winning Jamaican writer Olive Senior has lived on and off in Toronto since c. 1990. One of her earliest addresses in the decade was **No.137**. Crossing the street and heading in the direction of Bloor Street we encounter **No.214** where poet Maggie Helwig resided in the mid-1980s for a couple of years. The novelist Adele Wiseman (1928-92), author of *The Sacrifice* (Governor General's Award for Fiction, 1956) as well as *The Crackpot* (1974), spent approximately the last two years her life at **No. 224**. This stretch of the street has also been the home since 1977 of David French (b.1939), one of the nation's most popular playwrights. Another playwright, Erika Ritter, made her home at **No. 257** from 1974 to 1975. The peripatetic Maggie Helwig appears again at **No.287**, where she lived from 1985-86. Karen Mulhallen is the long-time editor of one of Canada's best literary periodicals, *Descant*, now well into its third decade of publishing. In the top-floor apartment of **No.314** (1966-67) she wrote part of the elegy to her father which appears in her book *Modern Love*.

Moving west along the south side of Bloor, we pass **501 Bloor Street West**, home of Book City, the most popular store for new books in the Annex region since the founding of the shop in 1976 by Frans Donker. The store has expanded into a chain of four sites across Toronto and all of them feature a combination of intelligently selected remainders mixed with an assortment of new literary titles in a decor that is winningly unkempt. A few of the former sales clerks at **No.501** have since published novels themselves, among them André Alexis, Philip Kreiner, and Derek McCormack.

At **294 Borden Street** lived Larry Fineberg, a playwright whose dramas caused outrage and excitement in the 1970s. Indeed, in 1972 alone, the year Fineberg moved to Toronto from his native Montreal, three of his plays were produced by Factory Theatre Lab and Toronto Free Theatre. Regrettably Fineberg (b.1945) seems to have stopped writing drama. He lived here from 1979 to 1981.

The author, and authors' friend, Franklin Davey McDowell, whom we have met twice before on this tour, lived at **No.233** from 1919 to 1925. The next house immediately to the south (**No.231**) was the home in 1984 of fantasy author Guy Gavriel Kay (b.1954). A few doors down, at **No.190**, the poet and novelist Dionne Brand lived from 1986-87, and wrote some of the poems that appeared in her book *No Language Is Neutral* (1990), nominated for the Governor General's Award. **166 Borden Street** was briefly home in 1936 to the Rosenblatt family, with young Joe, the poet-to-be, in tow.

A little further south is **Ulster Street. 64 Ulster** was occasionally the habitat of American novelist Howard Norman (b.1949). He stayed here in spring 1976 before beginning his summer travels to the Canadian north (the source of some of his best books), after which he returned to this address for more months. He later used this same address as his base during his subsequent explorations of our country 1977-80, his stays here varying from days to several weeks at a time.

Return to Borden and continue south to College Street. Go west along College Street, then turn north onto **Lippincott Street**. At. **No.68** you are standing before the 1953-55 home of the witty poet and very serious professor of philosophy Francis Sparshott (b.1926). **No.167** was occupied from 1950-52 by Chusaburo Ito (b.1910), a renowned haiku poet who emigrated to Canada from Japan in 1927. Fiction writer Matt Cohen lived at **No.178** at the beginning of the 1980s, putting the finishing touches to his

novel *Flowers of Darkness* (1981). William T. Allison (1874-1941) lived at **No.184** for the last three years of the 19th c. while attending the UofT. Allison, who passed his boyhood in Toronto, later became a poet, and then an educator of national renown. He was an early and vital influence on William Arthur Deacon (the most important book reviewer we've ever had in this country), when Deacon was a young man in Winnipeg. Allison was Professor Emeritus of English at the University of Manitoba—but much more than an academic, he was, in Deacon's words, "the pioneer voice of books in western Canada. Five days a week he published a short review in the *Tribune*, and a long one on Saturdays . . . Doctor Allison's real contribution was that he publicized thousands of books that his community would not otherwise have heard of." For one year at least (1898) Allison would have passed Francis Pollock in the street because Pollock (b.1876) lodged at **188 Lippincott** in 1898, also an undergrad at the UofT. Pollock, for most of his life, was an apiarist and maker of mead, but the bees left him enough time to write both commercial fiction as well as literary novels, among the latter being *Jupiter Eight* (1936). This book is set in Toronto and features a Toronto mystery writer named Derrock, who, given the era, makes some observations that were brave and prescient and, shame on Toronto, disturbingly contemporary to our ears : "He had been accustomed to abuse his city as his friends did. All the sporting set, all the arty crowd vilified it as one of their staples of conversation. The sportsman vilified it because it did not sufficiently resemble Chicago or Havana; the artist because it did not sufficiently resemble Paris and Munich. They called it a half-grown city, a nest of Methodists and Orangemen, of Puritans and Pharisees, who had not yet learned that Queen Victoria was dead. They called it a rube town, a hick town, an overgrown tank-town with half a million people who confused DADA with Santa Claus. Derrock had called it all of these things himself. But now he perceived how entirely he had been wrong. All that was bunk."

The English poet John William Lewthwaite (b.1880) lived in Toronto from 1911 until at least 1934. He served with the Canadian Expeditionary Force in WWI, but apart from the fact that he worked as a cleaner at the CNR, the only other fact I could discover about him was that he boarded at **No.210** for about two years, 1924-25. Further north at **No.240** the novelist Peter Such (b.1939) lived from 1989 until 1997 but published little creative writing. The same cannot be said of poet George Swede (b.1940), who wrote about **No.325**, "This was the house in which I grew much as a poet. Most of the work that was to appear in my first collection, *Unwinding* (1974) was written here."

Finally, as I noted in my Introduction, I was surprised in my research for this book to discover how many authors with Toronto connections were elected to political office or made serious runs for office. I say surprised because so few writers in my own lifetime are formally *engagé* in this way. One of the exceptions is playwright Wendy Lill (b.1950) who sits, as I write this, as a federal Member of Parliament. Toronto was her home from 1968 to 1976. In the city directories for that period her occupation was listed as "waitress at Bassell's Restaurant," a once-famous Toronto eatery. However, when she moved to **No.372** in 1975-76, her talent was finally recognized—and she was listed for the first time as "writer."

Go west one block on Bloor Street to **Bathurst Street**. Walk south on **Bathurst** on the east side. At **No.783** is a Catholic school now known as Loretto. It was formerly known as St. Dominic's, and before that, when mystery writer James Powell (b.1932) and Barry Callaghan (b.1937) went there, it was called St. Peter's. By whatever name, the school has produced few writers.

Speaking of poverty of literary graduates, only two creative writers of any note as far as I have been able to determine attended Central Technical School (**No.725**)—and

Joe Rosenblatt, by his own admission, dropped out of grade 10 here (the other author was Robert Mirvish who attended night school). However, in the 1920s, the school had a wonderful auditorium (since lost to the school's expansion) which was sometimes rented to outside groups for readings and lectures. Among the celebrity authors who gave public talks here were:

> Bliss Carman
> John Drinkwater
> Rosita Forbes
> Basil King
> Chief Buffalo Long Lance
> Hugh Walpole

One of the most respected rare-book librarians ever produced in Canada is also a bibliographer of poets—and himself a poet of some accomplishment. While residing at **No. 583** from 1977-79, Bruce Whiteman (b.1952) unleashed a torrent of verse that had been a long-time distilling. Here he published his first three volumes, including the fetchingly titled *The Sun at Your Thighs the Moon at Your Lips*. This was his last residence in Toronto. From here he moved to McMaster, where he began his impressive library career, later moving to McGill, and then U.C.L.A.

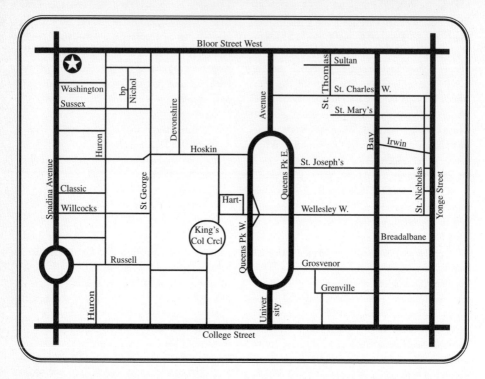

The tour begins at the southeast corner of Spadina Avenue and Bloor Street West.

At **709 Spadina Avenue** Ross Macdonald (1915-83) and Margaret Millar (1915-94) lived for more than a long academic year (September 1938 to July 1940) and it was a crucial address—to his history particularly—because it was here that he decided to become an author. Macdonald, whose real name was Kenneth Millar, is generally regarded as one of the triumvirate who catapulted detective fiction into the realm of serious literature (Dashiell Hammett and Raymond Chandler being the other two). He lived here while studying to become a high-school teacher at the Ontario Faculty of Education, located around the corner at **371 Bloor Street West**. Years later, Macdonald described his origins as a writer while living on Spadina: "In early June of 1939, in Toronto, I was a student

teacher with no money and a very pregnant wife. I left Margaret at home one afternoon in order to hear Lord Tweedsmuir deliver a high school graduation address. Lord Tweedsmuir was the Governor General of Canada at that time, but the reason I went to hear him was that he was also John Buchan, the author of *The Thirty-Nine Steps*.

"He turned out to be a small, bright-eyed Scot who wore the mantle of empire easily. At the climax of his speech he told the graduating seniors the old story of the race between the hare and the tortoise. But he told it with a difference. The hare fooled around a good deal while the slow dependable tortoise stuck to the course and never even looked up. Still the hare won easily. Lord Tweedsmuir drew the moral that the race is not always to the slow.

"About this time, I won a typewriter on a radio quiz show and started immediately to write for publication. I like to think that the Governor General inspired me; but like most other would-be writers I drew on more mundane sources of inspiration. Though I had a teaching job waiting in the fall at my old high school in Kitchener, Margaret and I had nothing to live on between June and September. My wife's approaching confinement and the prospective hospital bill made the situation urgent.

"If I had been a genuine hare, I'd have dashed off a detective novel in about three weeks, sent it to the biggest publisher in New York, and got an immediate acceptance by telegram. (A year or so later Margaret did just that.) I aimed lower, at tortoise level, writing a flock of short stories and sketches for quickly available markets, most of which were so-called Sunday school papers paying a cent a word. I made over a hundred dollars the first few weeks, and with this blessed wad of cash ransomed my wife and infant daughter out of the Women's College Hospital. I was a pro."

On another occasion, he talked about another, vital source of writing income: "My main market was the Toronto political and literary weekly, *Saturday Night*. I lightly bombarded the editor, B.K. Sandwell, with verses and humorous sketches, and my first few realistic stories. *Saturday Night* came out on Saturday morning, and we used to walk up to Bloor Street to see if anything of mine had been printed that week. Payment was just a cent a word, but the early joys of authorship were almost as sweet as sex. I felt as if Toronto, that unknown city of stone, had opened an eye and looked at me, then relapsed into her dreams of commerce." To augment his income, Macdonald sold articles and witty tidbits to *Saturday Night* for several years, even after he had moved to the United States.

Many of these were anonymous contributions to a column called "The Passing Show."

Ross Macdonald returned to Toronto on several occasions on private visits, and all his life kept abreast of Canadian literary fiction. When asked, for example, about Robertson Davies, he said, "I don't know Robertson Davies, but I greatly enjoy his writing. I always have. We were, so to speak, together on *Saturday Night* in the old days. He joined *Saturday Night* a year or two after I did and I thought he was a great wit and I still do. Now, of course, he's more than that—he's a very good novelist and a great literary critic too." But he reserved his highest praise for Morley Callaghan: "He was the Canadian writer who had the most influence on me . . . Callaghan was the one we all most admired

Detail showing Kenneth Milla/Ross Macdonald (centre, sitting on concrete block, eyes closed) with fellow students and staff of the O.C.E. graduating class, 1939. Photo taken at 371 Bloor Street West.

and wanted to emulate. He wasn't exactly a crime writer, or what you might call a member of the hard-boiled school, but his style belonged in that category. I think it had a great influence on me. I still have an enormous admiration for his work."

References to Toronto are peppered throughout Macdonald's fiction. Writing about *The Barbarous Coast*, Macdonald said of the hero, "I'm not and never was George Wall, the angry young Canadian lost in Hollywood. But I once lived as George did, on Spadina Avenue in Toronto." And the city figures most prominently in what many consider Ross Macdonald's finest novel, *The Galton Case*. The last chapters of that book are set in or near Toronto.

Kenneth Millar visited the city often enough to be able to contrast its psyche from when he lived here to its transformation in the 1970s: " . . . Toronto, I like it now, but at that time it was pretty much a buttoned-up and closed-down city and it just didn't have the spirit of life that it has now. It was a vast provincial capital that hadn't realized itself, but I believe it's doing that now."

Margaret Millar wrote distinguished but under-valued fiction under her married name rather than a pseudonym. She wrote no fiction until she and her husband left **No.709** for Kitchener, Ontario. Some of her novels, though, are set in Toronto, and two of them have as the hero Inspector Sands of the Toronto Police Department.

Over the decades **687 Spadina Avenue** has been an important address, the home of three very different writers. Richard T. Lancefield (1854-1911) lived in the large house that was once here from 1910-11. After running a variety of printing and book businesses in Hamilton, he moved to Toronto c.1884. Five years later he returned to Hamilton to become the city's first public librarian. He not only established the Hamilton library system as one of the best in the country but was, as well, an articulate campaigner for copyright reform to protect Canadian writers and one of the nation's earliest advocates of social liberation for women. Unfortunately, he was also a gambling addict. In February 1902, his embezzlement of substantial library funds was exposed, and he fled (but not before destroying the library's ledgers and the board's minutes) to Toronto. It is a measure of the affection with which he was regarded that his friends arranged for all of the major losses to be covered, and he was never charged with any offence. Indeed, the newspapers of Hamilton reserved most of their outrage for the library board and its negligence as an overseer. Lancefield, disgraced nevertheless, lived out his years quietly in Toronto at a variety of addresses in the Annex, of which this was his last.

In contrast, this was the first Toronto home of Frances Shelley Wees (1902-82) who moved into apt. 7 in the 1930s. She published more than 20 books, most of them crime novels, and most of those (unusually for the time, according to some) set in Toronto. They were Canadian bestsellers, but her writing was also welcomed by several major American publishers and magazines, including *Ladies Home Journal*. Wees began her writing career in Alberta and knew so little about the business that she sent her first detective novel to Curtis, Brown, the famed literary agency, believing it was a publishing house. But ignorance cuts both ways. Curtis, Brown, noting the Alberta postmark, assumed the author was an Eskimo, and sold the novel to eminent houses in New York and London on that basis. The confusion was eventually sorted out, and Wees continued to publish her novels to acclaim and success around the world.

Playwright John Herbert (b.1926), internationally famous for his drama *Fortune and Men's Eyes*, rented a first-floor studio at **No.687** in 1956. During the four years he lived here, he continued his theatre studies at the New Play Society and his dance studies with Boris Volkoff.

Novelists Dave and Ellen Godfrey rented **671 Spadina Avenue** from the UofT in the

1960s. Dave and his friend, the poet Dennis Lee, frustrated by the failure of most Canadian publishing houses to show any interest in new Canadian novelists and poets, decided in 1967 to start their own company, House of Anansi Press, and agreed to use the Godfrey's residence as the base of operations. The press was named for the spider god of Africa, presumably because Godfrey had just returned from that continent and its mythology was fresh in his mind. The basement of this house was converted into an office, but books, and then boxes, and then boxes and boxes of books soon spawned and worked their way up the stairs, eventually, according to eye witnesses, reaching the garret. The press was quickly the most exciting in the country, publishing the first, or nearly first books of authors who today are in our pantheon: Margaret Atwood, Graeme Gibson, George Bowering, Roch Carrier, Matt Cohen, Marian Engel, and Michael Ondaatje, as well as founders Dennis Lee and Dave Godfrey. Anansi's impact was as unexpected as that of a volcano erupting overnight on a landscape which for decades had been little more than flat plain. Critic George Woodcock wrote that "something unprecedented happened to Canadian publishing and even to Canadian writing when Anansi came on the scene." And the press's combination of daring and critical success quickly inspired other writers across the country to establish their own publishing houses. Dennis Lee was the sole editorial director during Anansi's third year while Dave Godfrey was abroad on sabbatical. However, when Godfrey returned in 1969, he made it clear he wanted the press to publish more nationalist material and he also wanted writers James Bacque and Roy MacSkimming added to the editorial board. Dennis Lee pointed out that the firm lacked the resources to accommodate so many editors, so Godfrey, MacSkimming, and Bacque formed a new firm, called "new press" while Lee continued to run Anansi. Both firms operated side by side relatively amicably at **671 Spadina**, until the University decided in 1970 that they were in violation of the zoning laws and asked them to leave.

Among the authors during this era who resided at Anansi for periods ranging from weeks to months were Douglas Fetherling (who lived in the attic), Greg Hollingshead, and Russell Marois (who, rumour has it, lived in the basement next to the furnace).

In 1909 and 1910, author Patrick Slater (1880-1951) resided in the house formerly at **669 Spadina Avenue** while he practised law on Bay Street. As "John Mitchell," he wrote the highly respected novel *The Yellow Briar*. His life turned tragic years later when he accused himself of theft from clients, was tried, jailed, disbarred, and ruined.

Kate and Frank Yeigh moved in 1899 to **667 Spadina Avenue** from their home just a few houses north. Kate was one of the first women in Canada to become, indeed, to insist that she be allowed to become a professional journalist at a time when most newspapers would not even allow a female onto the newsroom floor. She died here in 1906 and all of the Toronto newspapers ran major obituaries. A third printing of her novel *A Specimen Spinster* was announced just prior to her death and the book apparently had similar success in the USA and UK. Frank Yeigh remarried in 1908, and lived here until 1912.

651 Spadina Avenue was the site of a residential and day school for middle-class girls, Glen Mawr School, and on the social scale was considered just a notch below Havergal, Bishop Strachan, and Branksome Hall. Among the authors who attended classes here were Dorothy Livesay and Katherine Hale. Livesay (1909-96) explained in one of her chronicles how she first came to the school: "When we settled in Toronto's Annex, I spent my first year at St. Mildred's School, run by Anglican sisters. Then my mother heard about Glen Mawr, a small boarding school on Spadina Avenue near Hoskin, where the principal, Miss Gertrude Stuart, emphasized the arts—music, painting, drama, and the history of art. For the first term I was put into the fourth form, very timid with my classmates but determined to please my teachers and to shine. As a result, after Christmas I was promoted to the lower fifth . . . "

For about two years (1889-90) the short block immediately north of Harbord Street on the east side also contained the home of Tom MacInnes, a man with a colourful biography who wrote some interesting poems. Born in Dresden, Ontario, he received a BA from the UofT in 1889. He then proceeded to Osgoode Hall and was called to the bar in 1893 but never practised. By 1896, he was in British Columbia, working on the Bering Sea Claims Commission, but not content with that he dove headlong into the Yukon Gold Rush by becoming an officer with the special police force established at Skagway to control the prospectors. Two years later, he worked for his father as a private secretary, no small task in that his father was the Lieutenant-Governor of B.C. Two years onwards yet again, he was working on the B.C. Salmon Fisheries Commission, all the while learning to speak Cantonese from the many Chinese immigrants based in the province. His fluency and knowledge of Chinese culture was such that he was asked by Ottawa to formally investigate the 1907 anti-Oriental Riots in B.C. In 1910, he actually wrote several bills for the House of Commons, including the Canadian Immigration Act, and the Anti-Opium Act. Filled with wanderlust, by 1916 he was living in Canton, China, where, with a series of bluffs, lies, and outrageous daring, he convinced the Governor of Canton to allow him to supervise the destruction of much of the city and the construction of a Toronto-like urban transit system. Once the system was built, he stayed as its general manager until 1922, when civil wars forced him to return to Canada. Over the next decades he lived in genteel poverty, and the poorer he became the quicker he was to take offence at alleged slights from friends. Nonetheless, his poems increasingly attracted the praise of connoisseurs. Whenever he could, he visited Toronto, staying, sometimes for weeks at a time, with thick-skinned admirers such as E.J. Pratt, Charles G.D. Roberts, and William Arthur Deacon. Deacon, an astute judge, rated MacInnes a finer lyric poet than either G.D. Roberts or Bliss Carman.

633½ Spadina Avenue was the penultimate Toronto address of gambler and librarian Richard T. Lancefield (see above). He lived here in 1909, one of his many Annex addresses during his decade of disgrace.

More authors have lived on **Huron Street** than any other in Toronto, in part because of its proximity to the classrooms of the UofT. But not all literary residents of **Huron Street** (at least, the part covered by this tour) were students. Far from it. Stephen Leacock once bragged that he had lived at 40 rooming houses on this street alone. Alas, not one of those Leacock addresses has been found. In fact, it is very possible he never lived on Huron at all—his remark being merely symbolic.

Our first real address on **Huron** on this tour, **No.212**, was the home of a writer who never attended university: Mazo de la Roche. She had been living with her parents on a farm in Bronte when her father died, liberating the women from the last of his follies. Thanks to a family friend, Mazo's lifelong companion, Caroline Clement, was offered a job in the Ontario Civil Service, an act of patronage that allowed Mazo to continue writing without having to get a day job of her own. Mazo, her mother, and Caroline abandoned the Bronte farm and moved to **212 Huron** in 1915. In her autobiography, Mazo described the moving day: "What must be done now was to prepare for the removal. Our furniture must be taken out from store, our personal belongings packed.

"On the day when we set out for Toronto we stopped at the house of the breeder. My mother went in and selected a puppy. She returned with him in her arms. She was elated, flushed, her eyes shining. We had come prepared with a little box to put him in. He was not a pretty puppy but a skinny little fellow with a horrified yellow eye. The Scottie looked him over with smug appraisal. We tucked him into his box and fastened the lid. Ever since my mother's nervous breakdown of years ago she could not bear the thought of travelling by train. Never again in her lifetime did she enter a train. So we must make the long drive by carriage and pair. Motor cars had already displaced horses, so that it was not easy to hire them, but we discovered a livery where they were available, and so set out. The carriage was piled high with our belongings. A clock in their midst began to strike, its note in the open sounding new and strange. The puppy would not settle down in his box but yelped distractedly till we were forced to take him out of it. Then he began to scramble about, in a frantic effort to obliterate himself he found a place at last on top of the clock, but again it struck and so terrified him that he fell off, down the mountainside of luggage between the wheels and on to the road. When, fearing the worst, we looked round, we discovered him trotting determinedly after us. He knew that, strange as we were, we belonged to him. What a contrast in that road, as it then was, to the stream of traffic that rages over it today! Then we stopped at a grassy spot, beneath a chestnut tree, to open our hamper and eat our lunch. The driver fed and watered his horses. We had tea at an inn by the way, and it was almost dark when we stopped in front of the house where our furniture, in chaos, has already been delivered . . . My health by slow degrees improved. I turned again to writing others of the Explorers of the Dawn Series. I became a member of several literary clubs." Mazo lived at **212 Huron** until the summer of 1916.

Mazo was a neighbour and friend in passing of Leonora McNeilly (b.1900?) who lived at **No.242** from 1909-42. Biographical facts about McNeilly are scarce on the ground. On one occasion she was reported to be a "political playwright" but otherwise, references to her plays make no mention of their content. Canadian playwrights had next-to-no professional outlets for their work in this city until the 1950s, and so were ruefully grateful whenever a play was mounted. McNeilly's one-act plays were presented in the 1930s at Hart House Theatre, once as part of a bill with Nat Benson and Mazo de la Roche. She also wrote short stories. In 1945 she moved to **16 Willcocks Street** and remained there until 1950.

A nearby cross-street is **Russell**, home to three book authors over the years. John Imrie (1846-1902), popular poet and publisher of *The Scottish Canadian* and anthologies of Scottish-Canadian verse, lived at **3 Russell Street** for half a decade, 1878-83. Half a decade later, Thomas Stinson Jarvis (1854-1926) lived at **No.19** for about a year. By 1888 Jarvis was already thinking of moving to the States. He was part of the great Jarvis clan that dominated much of 19th c. life in the city. His father made the interesting choice of sending the son to Europe rather than to university, believing that travel would teach him more than classwork. Jarvis went rather further afield than Europe, and his first book, *Letters From East Longitudes* (1875), documents his travel in the middle east. He returned to Toronto to study at Osgoode and article under Sir Oliver Mowat. He practised criminal law and his experiences in this field helped him with the writing of his first novel, a mystery published in New York but set in Toronto, titled *Geoffrey Hampstead* (1890), said to have been the most widely reviewed book in the USA in the year of publication. In 1891 he abandoned Law and moved to the USA to pursue a full-time literary career as a novelist and freelance writer of articles on yachting, his sporting passion.

Poet, translator, and rabid anti-Communist Watson Kirkconnell described in his memoir how he came to live in—and then leave—this street: "A brief spasm of concentrated music study came in the winter of 1919-20. I was just back in Lindsay after some weeks in a military hospital in London,

England, and was being fattened up by a solicitous mother. Presently I learned that Francis Coombs, a voice teacher at the Toronto Conservatory of Music, now came to Lindsay one day a week to instruct local pupils. Soon after I had enrolled with him, he gave me such a sales talk on a musical future that I was persuaded to move to Toronto, where I could get two lessons a week and practice long hours every day in the soundproof practice rooms at the Conservatory. He even inflated my ego by prophesying an operatic career in New York. Soon I was ensconced in a top-floor bedroom at **36 Russell Street**, and was dividing my time between the Conservatory and the Toronto Public Library. Lieder and oratorio were mixed seductively in with scales and exercises and all went merry as a marriage bell. But it was too good to last. Spanish influenza, at the end of the great post-war epidemic, struck me down, and pleurisy followed. With my chest heavily buttered with Antiphlogistine, I listened to a medical verdict that I would have to go home and recuperate for a long time. Thereafter, a chronic ethmoid and antrum infection gave rise to annoying and unpredictable bouts of laryngitis. Any vocal career had clearly gone down the drain. The dream had been exhilarating while it lasted, but I was wide awake again." Kirkconnell learned languages as some people collect stamps. He published translations of poetry from more than fifty languages as early as 1928, and long before multiculturalism became a mantra of politicians he published in 1935 a book called *Canadian Overtones*, an anthology of his translations of poems written by Canadians in seven languages other than French and English.

Willcocks Street, like so many others in this area, has been completely transformed in character by the razing of houses to make way for huge university buildings. In the good old days, however, a few writers lived on the east end of **Willcocks** when its appearance was more like that of the streetscape west of Spadina. For instance, poet Colleen Thibaudeau (b.1925) was resident at **No.5** from September 1947 to June 1948 while taking French classes at University College from Robert Finch and a creative writing course from Norman Endicott. During the following summer months she worked at the University Library alongside another summer student and budding poet: Margaret Avison. **No.16** was Leonora McNeilly's home in the late 1940s.

The Rev. Archer Wallace used to live at **No.24** in the early 1940s. Wallace was a bestseller in an area that attracts little scholarly notice: religious writing. In 1954, he was able to boast that over a million copies of his books had been sold. He wrote fiction mostly for young adults but some of his more than 20 books were aimed at adults. Wallace also has the distinction of being the first editor to buy creative writing by the great detective novelist Ross Macdonald (when Macdonald was just Kenneth Millar, a grad student at the UofT in 1939). Archer was editor of a number of United Church periodicals, and desperate for funds, Macdonald wrote stories suitable for *The Canadian Girl* or *The Canadian Boy*. Thanks to Wallace's purchases of Macdonald's material, Kenneth was able to pay the hospital bill for the recent birth of his daughter.

The poet and occasional music critic of the *Star*, Ronald Hambleton (b.1917) lived at **No.35** in 1944 while working in the editorial offices of the Maclean Hunter empire. The UofT Faculty Lounge at **No.45** is home to a lounge named in honour of Barker Fairley (1887-1986), poet, artist, and German professor extraordinaire. The Club also displays some of Fairley's paintings.

New College at **300 Huron Street** has taught only a handful of authors since its relatively recent founding. The two best-known writers who pursued studies here are poets J.A. Wainwright (b.1946) and Janis Rapoport (b.1946). When Mavis Gallant was writer-in-residence at the UofT from 1983-84 her office was at New College. Dennis Lee had the same job 1978-79 and likewise had an office in this college. One of the houses (**No.298**) destroyed to make way for New College had been a rooming house, one room of which had been the home of fiction writer and civic-affairs journalist David Lewis Stein (b.1937). David was living in this rooming house during his fourth year at University College. When the day came to leave the premises, the owner and tenants held a grand farewell party with a sledge hammer and took turns making the wreckers' job easier.

Augustus Bridle (1869-1952) roomed at **303 Huron Street** in the years 1912-13 while an associate editor at the *Canadian Courier*. After graduating from the UofT, Bridle had taught school. Then, bored with teaching, he became a reporter, first for the *News*, and then in 1923 he was named book review and drama editor of the *Star*. Shortly afterwards he published his first novel, *Hansen*. Bridle had considerable status in Toronto, in part because of his huge commitment of energy to choral concerts, and in part because of his seminal role in the founding of the Arts and Letters Club. In fact, his funeral was held at the Club, a rare honour.

John P. Clare (1911-91) also worked at the *Star*. He was one of its war correspondents in 1944. Earlier, from 1936-40, while a copy-editor and reporter at the *G&M*, he lived at **No.310**. After the war he worked for *Maclean's*, assuming the managing editorship in 1949. Three years later he became editor in chief of *Chatelaine*. In the meantime, he was writing short stories with regularity for magazines that were known in the trade as "the slicks": *Saturday Evening Post* and *Collier's* being two in which he appeared. His satirical novel *The Passionate Invaders* was published by Doubleday in New York in 1965.

Tomi Nishimura (b.1915) came to Canada in 1936. I suspect she was interned during WWII because the earliest address I can find for her dates from 1953. Then, and for five more years she lived at **28 Classic Avenue** which ends at Huron near here. She has

been one of the most respected contributors to the haiku and tanka poetry societies of this country.

When Thomas Guthrie Marquis died in 1936 at his home at **35 Classic**, his passing was a page-one story in Toronto and the subject of newspaper editorials lamenting his death. The *Star's* editorial offers a touching summation of the man and his career: "Thomas Guthrie Marquis is dead, an old and almost forgotten man who was in his youth one of Canada's greatest hockey and football stars; in his prime, one of Canada's greatest historians . . . Mr. Marquis was in the book world most of his life, as a writer of histories and school textbooks (some in collaboration with Agnes Maule Machar), as an editor of other people's writing, and as a novelist . . . [His] enthusiasms reached throughout English literature and English history—especially Canadian history. In his death Canada loses one of those best versed in her historic past and who did most to make it known."

It would be pleasant to believe that Marquis stopped on the street and exchanged literary news and views with his neighbour from 1933-35, Ernest Buckler. Buckler (1908-84) would later be regarded as the author of the Canadian classic *The Mountain and The Valley* (1952). Indeed, because of the pervasive success of that book, he is so associated with the Maritimes it is easy to forget he lived in Toronto as a young man for a number of years. He might have stayed in Toronto had ill health not forced him to return to the family farm. After graduating from the UofT with an MA in 1930, he worked for half a decade at the Manufacturer's Life Insurance Company as an actuarial mathematician. **No.37** was his last address in Toronto.

Return to Huron Street. **328 Huron Street** was the home of two novelists at different times. Beaumont Cornell (1892-1958) lived here from 1916-17. The mystery writer Margaret Millar (1915-94) had rooms here 1934-35 while attending the

UofT. Gambling addict, thief, and librarian Richard T. Lancefield (1854-1911) hid out at **No.352** for the years 1887-88.

Poet and magazine historian Fraser Sutherland (b.1946) wrote to me: "From May to September 1968 I was summer reporter at the *Globe and Mail*, which was then located on King St. West, just east of the now-vanished Lord Simcoe Hotel and from Ed Mirvish's pseudo-Edwardian establishments for playgoing and dining (Royal Alexandra Theatre, Ed's Warehouse). I lived on Huron Street in a Campus Co-op building (the number currently not available without my spending hours within the icy tomb in which most of my papers are housed), the very street on which Stephen Leacock had, he said, once lived in 40 rooming houses. In any event, the mostly-deserted Co-op was across from St. Thomas's Church. As a reporter, I crisscrossed the city in Co-op cabs (no connection with Campus Co-op) dredging up the usual cub-reportorial dreck: federal election campaign meetings, courts, automotive casualties and once, a fruitless quest for Martin Luther King's assassin, then thought to be skulking around Toronto. On the staff, but much senior to me, were the friendly Michael Valpy and Don Newman, later of the CBC; Clark Davey, later publisher of the *Montreal Gazette*, was my boss. One of my few by-lines concerned a party the theatre director George Luscombe gave for a pack of U.S. draft dodgers and deserters. Half my summer was spent spinning out corporate minutiae for the *Globe's Report on Business*.

"From May to September 1969 I was back in Toronto, this time at the *Toronto Star* which, since Hemingway had once worked there, I thought to be a necessary part of my writer's apprenticeship. The *Star* was also then on King St. West. One fellow-cub reporter was Mark Starowicz, later producer of the CBC's 'The Journal'. Eric Malling, later a host of the CBC's 'Fifth Estate', like me had emigrated from Carleton University's School of Journalism, but was clawing his way somewhere further up on the ladder. I lacked their ambition. This time I lived at **354 Huron St**. in an upstairs room of a small red-brick house owned by a tolerant, bunlike little German lady named Mrs. Kader, just across the street from where they would soon be driving piles for that hideous behemoth, the Robarts Library. Just north, and mysteriously down an alley, was Coach House Press. At the corner of Huron and Bloor was of course Rochdale College, founded by Dennis Lee, among others. Even then I thought how insane it was to house an experiment in counter-culture and alternative education inside a towering high-rise.

"At the end of Summer 1969 I was laid off from the *Star* and descended a few pecks in the journalistic order by joining Maclean-Hunter Business Publications, located in that architectural frog squatting on the corner of Dundas Street and University Avenue which now houses McClelland & Stewart. I ended up at *Canadian Travel Courier* . . . Its only redeeming feature was that it once sent me to Bulgaria. While I was at 481 University Ave. I met fellow Carleton University graduates: I and an Ottawan named Terrance MacCormack started a friendship which led to our founding the literary magazine *Northern Journey* in Fall 1971; another fellow M-H sufferer, a Torontonian, was David McDonald, and he, too, later became involved in the magazine, as did Craig Campbell, then a taxi driver who used my rooming house for what he called his "piss stops." In April 1970 I was fired from *Canadian Travel Courier*, though I was given the option of moving to another magazine. Instead, I quit and soon left for Europe. As M.T. (Terry) Kelly, who also toiled for the organization at one point, has memorably said, 'Getting fired from Maclean-Hunter was like getting bounced from a leper colony.'"

Huron crosses **Sussex Avenue** near here. Despite the ugly looming of Robarts, most of the places with literary connections have survived. Poet and novelist Michael Ondaatje had rooms in **No.18** in 1964 while studying for his B.A. at the UofT. Little did he know that in just a few years he would be returning regularly to this area as a member of the Coach House Press editorial board (see below).

At the southwest corner of Huron and Sussex is another unattractive building, **No.21**, which now houses university offices but which used to be an apartment building—home to a surprising number of important literary folk. John Garvin (1859-1935) lived in apt. 47 from 1917-20 while consolidating his position as a senior VP of a large stock-and-bond trading firm. Garvin's importance lies in the anthologies he compiled of Canadian poets and in his tireless promotion of Canadian authors. He lived here with poet and influential book reviewer Katherine Hale (1878-1956), whom he married in 1912. Novelist and translator Joyce Marshall (b.1913) lived in apt. 43 in 1955, one of many places of short duration she occupied in that decade.

This address was the last of the influential but too little known John Sutherland (1919-56). Sutherland had been forced to leave his studies at Queen's University because of tuberculosis and, although he spent three years in a sanatorium, the disease never really left him. He tried to get his B.A. again in 1941, this time at McGill, but once more ill health forced him to retire. It was at this point that he began *First Statement*, a mimeographed magazine of only a few pages and a circulation of less than one hundred, yet now seen to be one of the most important magazines in Canadian literary history. After a few issues Irving Layton and Louis Dudek joined as editors but John Sutherland was very much editor-in-chief. I got a sense of Sutherland's editorial dominance when, as a young man, I first spoke to Layton about Sutherland. There were very few people of whom Layton spoke in hushed terms, but Sutherland was a man who inspired respectful, even awed tones from Irving. *First Statement*'s importance lies partially in its aggressive stance that American poetry offered appropriate models

John Sutherland with his dog "Louie," 1995 at the University of Toronto campus

or lessons for Canadians—not the polite, British work that seemed to be favoured by those at its rival, *Preview*. Poet and literary historian Bruce Whiteman, in a tribute to Sutherland, highlights other facets that make Sutherland so vital: "He was, for ten years at least, at the very centre of the modernist movement in Canadian poetry, as midwife and conscience, as psychopomp, interpreter, and disciplinarian . . . From the first, Sutherland was interested in a kind of poetry that would deal realistically with the experience of Canadians in the world of the time. He recognized the value of earlier Canadian poetry—recognized it but rejected most of its assumptions as incommensurate with the world he knew . . . Many of the writers with whom Sutherland became associated and who published in the pages of *First Statement* were also dedicated to adopting a poetic language that would be equal to the expression of this realistic aesthetic . . . including Layton, whom Sutherland thought of primarily as a short story writer, and who married [Layton's] sister Betty."

By 1944 the extent and design of *First Statement* had greatly improved, and it was then that Sutherland decided to publish a series of chapbooks alongside the magazine. The poets he published are now regarded by many commentators as among the most important of mid-century Canada: Irving Layton, Miriam Waddington, Patrick Anderson, Raymond Souster, and Anne Wilkinson. Sutherland merged his magazine with his old rival, *Preview*, in 1945 and the resulting periodical was called *Northern Review*, with Sutherland still at the helm. The magazine died with him in 1956. His widow wrote to me, "John and I moved to Toronto in January 1955, and he began to attend the UofT and work for a B.A. In the late summer of 1955 he fell ill, and his symptoms were interpreted as a recurrence of the TB of the kidney. He entered the sanatorium at Weston [Toronto], and stayed there for about three months, then decided it wasn't doing much good, and came home again. A further medical examination revealed a tumour . . . We moved to Toronto for practical reasons. John had been unable to make money out of writing and publishing, and had indeed never expected to do so. His various part time jobs brought in very little. (He never made enough money to file an income tax return in all his life.) In Montreal he had become recognized as an authority on Canadian writing and had been invited to lecture at Sir George Williams (now Concordia) and at the Thomas More Institute, but could not obtain a permanent job at any university without a degree of some kind. St. Michael's College at the UofT offered him free tuition and a small scholarship allowance (I think it was $100 a month). They were of course influenced by his recent conversion to Catholicism and the reflection of his new sympathies in the magazine. We moved in January 1955 and John started work at the university right after the Christmas break. He completed his

year in a single term, and was given credit for the time he had spent at Queen's and McGill. I believe that he was considered to have completed the third year, and that he would have obtained his B.A. degree in 1956 (however, he fell ill in 1955 and never returned to the university). There was some suggestion that he would then go on to take an M.A. and perhaps to lecture at the UofT at the same time, or at any rate to join the staff when he obtained the M.A., but there was no firm undertaking on either side about this. However, the setup seemed promising—and that was why we moved. I'm afraid that John was slightly prejudiced against Toronto, though not in any serious way. 'Toronto the Good,' and so on.

"We arrived in January 1955 and went to stay in a rooming-house where Paul Almond (then in his 20s, working in television) lived. He engaged a furnished room for us with a miniature frigidaire and electric ring. We put our furniture in store and stayed there for a month or so while we looked for an apartment. I cannot remember the address of this place, but we liked it. Paul Almond lived there alone, in wild disorder, with a tame skunk.

"In February (?) 1955 we moved into a three-room apartment at **21 Sussex Avenue**— a nice old building. We stayed there until John died in September 1956. I left Toronto before the end of that year."

29 Sussex Avenue has been the home of poet David Knight (b.1926) since 1960, and just a few years later he sublet a small apartment in his house to Dennis Lee (b.1939), from August 1965 to June 1966. Lee put the time to good use: he wrote much of his first poetry book for adults, *Kingdom of Absence* (1967), at this address, and here began two of his most famous books for children, *Alligator Pie* and *Nicholas Knock*. David Knight's highly regarded books were all written while he lived here, including his novel *Farquharson's Physique* (1971) and poetry volume *The Army Does Not Go Away* (1969). In addition, he established his own imprint out of this house. Founded in 1982, Child Thursday Press has published over 40 poets to date.

Another Maritimer who made this area his home was poet and critic A.G. Bailey (1905-97) of New Brunswick, who studied for his M.A. and PhD at the UofT. During the 1932-33 academic year he lived at **No.35**. Yet another author associated with the Atlantic region is novelist Percy Janes (1922-99), author of the highly regarded *House of Hate* (many veteran readers think it is the best novel ever to come out of Newfoundland). Janes, originally from Corner Brook, travelled to Toronto to obtain a B.A. at Victoria College. He lived at **No.56** during the academic year 1946-47. The year before, the same house had been home to Norman Ward (1918-90), who was also pursuing master's and doctoral studies. Ward won the Leacock Medal for Humour in 1960 for his book *Mice in the Beer*.

Return to **Huron Street** to **No.375**, the last home of Daniel Clark (1835-1912). He came to Ontario from England in 1847 and had a colourful youth. When only 15 he had set off for the California gold fields via Central America on a tramp ship, and found enough gold to at least pay his way back to Ontario. On his return he became serious about his medical studies—and he no sooner graduated in 1864 than joined the Union Army and saw action in several battles as a volunteer surgeon. While the guns and scalpels were flying, he somehow found time to write a mix of critical articles, medical literature, and original creative writing. Among the monographs he published were "Canadian Poetic Literature" and "Heavysege and His Poetry." His novel, *Josiah Garth*, dealt with the Farmer's Revolt of 1837. For thirty years (1875-1905) he was superintendent of the Provincial Lunatic Asylum at 999 Queen Street West (his home was on the grounds), after which he moved to **Huron Street** where he died in 1912.

St. Thomas's Church at **No.383** has hosted a number of poetry readings over the years. This was the only place I ever heard the noted Canadian poet Robert Finch (1900-95) give a reading to the general public (as opposed to unadvertised readings intended solely for the university community). Another literary connection to this church is a tad unusual. In July 1906, T.E. Hulme (1883-1917) came to this country and worked his way across Canada by labouring on farms and in lumber camps. After eight months he returned to Britain healthier, mentally and physically, than ever. As his biographers note, however, little is known about this Canadian period except that he stopped in Toronto for some weeks and "while in Toronto he attended religious services in St. Thomas's Church which was Anglo-Catholic . . . The rector remembered his visits with pleasure. His interest in religious philosophy dates from this time and while he was brought up an Anglican, he never firmly embraced any orthodox religious creed although he was most sympathetically inclined towards both Roman Catholicism and Anglo-Catholicism. Any conversion of a religious kind that he may have undergone was brought about, not by reading or persuasion, but by the realization, while in Canada, of man's cosmic insignificance." By way of aside, it's worth pointing out that Hulme, who is widely regarded as the father of Imagism, always maintained that the idea for Imagist poetry —that is, poetry based on "the hard, dry image"—came to him when he lived in Canada, inspired by the hard, dry prairies where he had been a farm labourer. "The first time I ever felt the necessity or inevitableness of verse, was in the desire to reproduce the peculiar quality of feeling which is induced by the flat spaces and wide horizons of the virgin prairie of Western Canada." Hulme was killed in the trenches of WWI.

John Steffler (b.1947), poet and novelist (his *The Afterlife of George Cartwright* won the *Books in Canada* First Novel Award for 1992), has been resident in Newfoundland for most of his creative writing life so it is easy to forget that he was born in Toronto. Just prior to the beginning of his undergrad studies at the UofT, he moved in 1967 into a rooming house at **No.414** and stayed here for two years until the building was condemned, then razed. Among the places he lived over the next months were **12 Sussex Avenue** and then **388 Huron Street**, where he stayed until he left Toronto in September 1971. While at this latter address he started to write poetry which won prizes and later appeared in his earliest collections.

Poet Ludwig Zeller (b.1927) lived in Oakville for three years and one day—he is specific about the number because it struck him appropriately as a kind of jail sentence. He escaped in August 1978 and returned to Toronto to live at **No.392**. It was his full-time home until 1994 when he decided to spend winters in Mexico. During this fruitful Toronto period he published much (including *The Marble Head and Other Poems*, 1987; and *To Saw the Beloved to Pieces Only When Necessary*, 1990) and consolidated his position as one of the world's leading surrealist poets and collagists.

Muriel Denison (1885-1954) lived with her father at **No.395** from 1913-15. Denison had lived on the prairies as a young girl and had been allowed to ride with the Mounties, experiences she would put to use when writing her famous series of Susannah novels. The books were made even more famous in 1939 when Shirley Temple starred in *Susanna of the Mounties,* a film based on the first title in the series. Others included *Susanna of the Yukon* (1937) and *Susanna Rides Again* (1940). These books were translated into Danish, Dutch, Finnish, French, Norwegian, and Swedish. It may surprise some readers to learn that one of the biggest fans of the Susannah books is Timothy Findley. In 1988 he wrote in the *Hungry Mind Review*, "When I was a boy I feasted on Ernest Thompson Seton, Muriel Denison, and Charles G.D. Roberts. I did so because—uniquely, it so happens—they laid before me my landscape, my people, and its animals in ways that drew me further into that landscape and closer to the people and animals that I loved."

E.A. Lacey (1938-95) is a poet few have heard of, but among initiates he commands respect. In the 1960s he became the first openly homosexual poet in Canada—at a time when such a declaration guaranteed notoriety for his person and obscurity for his verse. Earlier, he had been a legendary figure as an undergrad at University College. In that conservative era he seemed positively outlandish, going, for example, on a hunger strike to protest an abstruse residence rule. On another occasion he was reported to have sat in the university library wearing a piece of sod on his head along with a sign saying *Do not water the grass*. But his writing in the university magazines impressed sophisticated readers, and a small group of them (including Dennis Lee and Margaret Atwood) put together sufficient funds to publish his first volume. During his third year at U.C., 1957-58, he roomed at **No.397**.

401 (rear) Huron Street has been the site of various incarnations of one of Canada's most famous literary presses, Coach House Books (formerly known as Coach House Press). The press was founded in 1964 as a design-printing operation by art-school dropout and printer Stan Bevington in the coach house at the rear of 317 Bathurst Street. Stan told me the press would probably have remained there had the area not been designated for slum clearance in 1968. At the embryonic stages of the house, the principal advisers to Stan were people with whom he had studied at the UofT, especially Dennis Reid. Around the same time that Stan was looking for a new home for the press, Dennis Lee recruited him as a "Resource Person" for the newly founded Rochdale College. It was Dennis Lee who suggested that Stan camp out in the old coach house to the rear of **401 Huron** (immediately south of Rochdale) until appropriate space could be found for the press in the basement of Rochdale proper. However, administrative developments at Rochdale were erratic, and space in the Rochdale building never was found for the press, so its temporary quarters in the coach house on Huron became permanent.

The first book to bear the Coach House imprint was *Man in a Window*, a volume of poetry by Wayne Clifford, a UofT student and friend of Reid's. The book features illustrations by Reid, who is now the Chief Curator at the Art Gallery of Ontario, and the model for the photos used as the basis of his illustrations was Janet Amos, who has gone on to become one of the leading actors and artistic directors in Canadian theatre. The book was printed in March 1965, but because the principals were still learning the publishing business, distribution difficulties meant the book was not available until several weeks later. The second Coach House title appeared only after more than a year had elapsed. In July 1966 *LSD Leacock* by Joe Rosenblatt hit the shelves. As Dennis Reid recalled, 1966 "was a busy year. The coach house had become the focus not only of the old UofT gang but of an increasing number of artists and designers from OCA. And there were more writers showing up. Stan met Victor Coleman late in 1964 at a party at Earle Birney's house and we decided to ask Victor, with his knowledge of the small press and literary network, to help us with the marketing and distribution of *Man in a Window*. We met bp Nichol around the same time . . . Scott Symons, with whom I'd taken a Canadian decorative arts course the previous year, was often around. Instead of a literary salon, the model was the sort of weekly newspaper/job-printer where Stan had worked in Alberta, a place that centred the community." Bevington, Clifford, and Reid are now considered the founding triumvirate of Coach House.

By the time the press moved to its current location, it had already published volumes by George Bowering, bp Nichol, Roy Kiyooka, and Michael Ondaatje (*Dainty*

Coach House Books. This photograph shows the façade on bp Nichol Lane, with bp Nichol's poem implanted in the street's pavement, April 14, 1997.

Monsters, his first book). The move to Huron Street only served to attract more visual artists and writers to the press, by now under the editorial direction of Victor Coleman. The presence of so many painters accounts for the design attractiveness of the books from this period, and innovative typesetting, binding, and printing were early hallmarks of Coach House titles. In the mid-1970s Coleman left, and an editorial committee took his place. The committee members were Nichol, Ondaatje, Frank Davey, David Young, Rick/Simon, David McFadden, Sarah Sheard, Robert Wallace, Dennis Reid, and Stan Bevington, with Nichol and Davey very much the most dominant editors. Nichol's death in 1988 seemed to mark the beginning of a spiritual disintegration at the house, a demise that ended with the bankruptcy of the press in 1996. Coleman and Bevington, however, were convinced that with a rethinking of the purpose of the operation, and distribution of literary texts via computer, the business could be made viable. Together they created Coach House Books from the ashes of what had been Coach House Press. For those who don't have computers, or who prefer to own what the Coleman calls "the fetish item formerly known as the book" Coach House Books will still make printed bound pages available. The actual coach house of Coach House Books backs onto **bp Nichol Lane**, named in honour of the poet shortly after his death in 1988.

At **410 Huron Street** we stand before a building once the home of True Davidson, one of the most recognized politicians in the history of the city. With her flamboyant hats and her tart tongue Davidson (1901-78) was instantly visible wherever she went, and, until her last election, was hugely popular with the voters in East York—where she was mayor for several terms. What is not so well known is that True (short for Gertrude) always regarded herself as a writer first (especially a poet) and a politician second. She wrote and published verse from adolescence,

and as a young woman wrote and directed plays. Long before she entered politics, she was general factotum in the Canadian headquarters of the publisher J.M. Dent. Dent had its own building, Aldine House at **224 Bloor West,** which probably accounts for why she was living on Huron in 1927. Later she worked as the lead researcher for historian and author Perkins Bull.

When O.J. Stevenson (1869-1950) moved to Toronto for half a dozen years to become Head of the English Dept. at the UofT Schools, he lived in a series of nearby homes, including **No.424** in 1912. Stevenson published a few books of poetry but his literary influence was felt far more through the Shakespeare and poetry texts he edited for use in the province's secondary schools. At a more personal level, his influence was also felt by his quiet championing of Canadian authors. In 1916, for instance, Stevenson was appointed Chair of the English Dept. at the University of Guelph, a position he kept for the rest of his working life. As William Arthur Deacon noted in his obituary of Stevenson, "Under his direction one Canadian writer was brought annually to the college to deliver a set lecture to faculty and students and to talk informally with the senior students. It was a unique experience in the 1930s to address an audience of a thousand persons on Canadian writers and their work and to know that everybody present followed with educated intelligence everything that was being said." Would that Canadian authors had such champions in our universities today.

Another "Newfoundland novelist," Percy Janes (1922-99), lived on this street while pursuing graduate studies. He lived at **No. 428** from 1948-49. Janes's novel *House of Hate* (1970) was considered a powerful debut.

The UofT Schools (a primary and secondary school) and the Faculty of Education (a post-graduate school) share a building with **371 Bloor Street West** as a mailing address. Authors who attended UTS as students include crime novelist Jack Batten (b.1932),

E.K. Brown (1905-51), Greg Hollingshead (b.1947), Dennis Lee (b.1939), Douglas LePan (1914-98), Lydia Millet (b.1968), Mavor Moore (b.1919), Raymond Souster (b.1921) and Scott Symons (b.1933).

Authors who learned to be teachers at the Faculty of Education include Nat Benson (1903-66), Herman Buller (1923-96), Selwyn Dewdney (1909-79), H. Gordon Green (b.1912), M.T. Kelly (b.1946), Ross Macdonald (1915-83), Frank Paci (b.1948), and Peter Such (b.1939). Gordon Green's only extended stayed in Toronto was the period from January 5 to April 30, 1946 that he spent studying here—although all of his time was not given over to educational concerns because, as he wrote to me, "while there I wrote much of my novel *A Time to Pass Over* published by Morrow in the U.S. and McClelland and Stewart in Canada. I was also writing for the *Star Weekly*, *Reader's Digest*, and other periodicals while there. Boarded somewhere on Dufferin."

However, the author I most associate with the Faculty of Education is Bert Case Diltz (1894-1992), who was Dean of the College from 1958-63. Earlier, and incredibly, he had been the only teacher of English teachers there since 1931, meaning, in effect, that he single-handedly trained every high-school teacher of English in the province between 1931 and 1958. Anyone who went to school in Ontario in the Diltz decades (and he lived to be 98) undoubtedly had to study at least one of the many textbooks he wrote or edited. Historian Robin Harris rightly notes that, "with the possible exception of W.J. Alexander, whose *Shorter Poems* (1924) and *Short Stories and Essays* (1928) remained prescribed texts in the senior high school grades in the mid-1950s, no one had a greater influence on English studies in the Ontario schools in the 1930s, 1940s and 1950s than Professor Diltz." He also published volumes of his own modest poetry as well as a novel, *Barnardo Boys* (1982). A man whose career curiously foreshadowed that of Diltz was O.J. Stevenson (see previous page),

who, from 1910-15, taught English to the students at UTS while also teaching Methods of English Instruction to the teacher candidates. And like Diltz, he edited or wrote several textbooks that were standard in Ontario (in his case during the early decades of the century) and he also published volumes of modest verse.

The Faculty of Ed was also used on a couple of occasions for authorial talks advertised to the general public. Marshall Saunders, author of the bestselling novel *Beautiful Joe*, for instance, gave a talk to the Canadian Business Women's Club on March 3, 1914. It is worth remembering that a business group invited a novelist to address them (talks by novelists to formal gatherings of business people are not common in our time) and the early date by which business women had formed their own organization.

Another author who gave a speech here that was open to the general public was the poet and painter George Russell (1867-1935), usually known by his *nom de plume* "A.E." The Irish patriot made two visits to Toronto and both were big front-page stories at the dailies. The first talk was delivered on February 24, 1928, and his topic was "Some Personalities in Irish Literature." As a close friend of the leading figures of the Celtic Renaissance he was more than qualified to give such a speech. The *Star* rhapsodized in its lead editorial: "George W. Russell's lecture last night will be unforgettable by those who heard it—certainly by all those who have even a strain of Irish in them.

"As the lecturer recited verses by Yeats or his own lines on his two fellow poets who met tragic deaths—with his fine head tilted back and rocking to the music of the words spoken in slightly plaintive monotone, one could imagine the spell that was wrought by some ancient bard on the hill of Tara in olden days. And Russell wrought a spell on his audience last night.

"It is interesting to find that this distinguished visitor speaks English as it is spoken by those who speak it best in Toronto. His English would be no different had he spent his life in this city, but there is a musical quality in his voice and a leisure of enunciation quite his own."

Across the road, on the east side of Huron is **341 Bloor Street West**, originally constructed as Rochdale College but now a home for seniors. Rochdale, opened in 1968, and named after the English town where the principles and rules of the cooperative movement were most perceptively defined, was the creation of a small but determined band, poet Dennis Lee among them. They were seeking a place where free education could be conducted among free thinkers. The ideals were noble but the administration was erratic. There were many exploiters of the utopian ambitions of the place. Rochdale, as originally envisioned, did not last more than a couple of years. Before it was taken over by bikers and freeloaders, however, it shook staid Toronto to its roots and did much to inform young people that there was more to existence than roast beef dinner and a job for life in a bank. It was in the nature of Rochdale that the residents abhorred forms, so lists of who lived there really depend on the memories of the residents. My census of writers who lived there for more than a few nights includes Giles Blunt, Matt Cohen, Victor Coleman, Robert Fones, Dennis Lee, Judith Merril, Kenneth Radu, and Jane Urquhart—but I am sure there must have been more. The playwright David French, while living in the Annex had a job as a janitor at Rochdale, but he had no intercourse with the artistic community there, and it is equally unlikely that they knew he was then writing one of his best known plays, *Leaving Home*.

Tiny **Washington Avenue** crossing Huron near this point has housed many writers since the 19th c. Celebrated Canadian poet Margaret Avison (b.1918) lived in **No.2** from 1961-63. It was while living here that she experienced the last in a chain of epiphanies which led to her formal conversion to Christianity on January 4, 1963. Unbeknownst to her, three decades earlier, the same building was novelist Gordon Hill Grahame's home for a couple of years. Poet and poetry publisher David Knight, whom we met on Sussex Avenue above, lived in a small apartment at **No.6** from 1956-58 until he was married, at which point he moved across the street into **No.5** and house-sat for a colleague on sabbatical, 1959-60.

Poet Katharine Hale (1878-1956) and her husband John Garvin, (1859-1935), moved from an apartment on Sussex Avenue to the more upscale Russell Hill Road and then back down to **13 Washington Avenue**, where they rented an apartment for the years 1926-27, following which they leased **No.9** for the years 1928-32. In my researches I sometimes came across veiled suggestions that Garvin devoted so much time to the promotion of Canadian literature that it affected his daytime job as a wheeler-dealer in finance. If true, variances in his income might account for these relatively frequent address changes and, as the real-estate people say, significant changes in location. Hale's reputation as a poet was near its peak when she lived on Washington. In 1929, her stature was such that no one thought it odd that she be one of the keynote attractions at a highly publicized reading by members of the Canadian Literature Club at Convocation Hall, on November 5, 1929. Sharing the bill with her were bestsellers Ralph Connor, Robert Norwood, E.J. Pratt, and Marshall Saunders. A year later she would share poetry judging duties with poets of the calibre of Charles G.D. Roberts, E.J. Pratt, and Constance Davies Woodrow. And in the fall of 1931 she gave a series of six well-promoted public talks on modern literature at the Heliconian Club, sponsored by the wife of the Lieutenant-Governor. This series of lectures was but one among many that she gave to a wide variety of organizations in the 1920s and 1930s. Hale is an interesting case in taste—why, for example, was she so popular in her day and now is almost unknown? Is it because her work was mere reportage, as soon out of date as last month's newspaper? No, her writing is better than that. Was it old-fashioned and sentimental? No, in fact she was seemingly relentless in promoting the modern to the conservative Toronto readers who loved to look backwards for the exposition of the eternal verities. Was her literary stature due to her personal connections? In my opinion, those connections helped her become established— but no more. She came from a well-to-do family in Galt. In fact, when Raymond and Vincent Massey were orphaned, it was Katherine Hale's mother who raised the boys. Hale was comfortable moving among the wealthy, and Mazo de la Roche biographer Ronald Hambleton argues persuasively that it was only exclusively from her friendship with Hale that Mazo de la Roche obtained any verisimilitude about the rich in her Jalna novels. Hale's writing, and her place in our cultural history deserve more analysis than she has received to date—an easy assessment to make because no one has published any focused research or analysis about her anywhere in Canada.

Margaret Avison made an extended stay in an apartment (at the back of the second floor) **10 Washington Avenue** for the first half of the 1950s. It was while here that she put the finishing touches to her first book, *History of Ontario* (1951), curiously not a poetry book, but a textbook,. Coincidentally, this same house was where playwright Mavor Moore lived when he was born in Toronto in

Amelia W. Garvin
(Katherine Hale)

1919 (just one year later than Avison). His family remained here for about a decade. His mother, Dora, became one of the most famous theatre directors in Canadian history, and one group of the country's leading awards in theatre, "The Doras," are named after her.

Poet Karen Mulhallen wrote to me, "I decamped to **19 Washington Avenue** in July of 1976 and lived there very happily until December of 1986 when I moved on Christmas eve to a house on Markham Street. On Washington Avenue I completed and finally published *Sheba and Solomon* and also edited and published two anthologies, *Tasks of Passion: Dennis Lee at Mid-Career*, as well as *Views from the North: An Anthology of Travel Writing*. I also continued to edit and publish *Descant* magazine."

Kingston-born Alice Chown (1866-1949) was an important pioneer feminist and, like many of her passion, was also a proselytizer for international peace. She worked at a trade union college in New York for a decade before returning to Toronto in 1927 to form the women's section of the League of Nations Society. She was so committed to the League that she was a delegate on occasion to the League's deliberations in Geneva. Ever hopeful, she accepted the title of Honorary President of the United Nations Society in 1945. In addition, she was, from her earliest years, a fighter for women's right to vote, and once that right was obtained, for other women's rights. She penned an autobiographical novel, *The Stairway*, published in Boston in 1921. In 1934 she had rooms at **21 Washington Avenue.**

Go north to Bloor Street and east two blocks to to **St. George Street**, one of the main thoroughfares of the UofT, and long a home for student residences, especially those attached to University College, the oldest college of the university federation. However, before citing authors who lived in residence, we must note some of the other addresses south of Bloor with authorial associations.

John Morgan Gray (1907-78) was born in Toronto and attended the UofT but did not graduate. The failure to finish did not hurt his advancement in the world. After serving as a senior Intelligence Office with the Canadian Army in WWII, he returned to Canada to become the head of Macmillan of Canada. His timing was good, in that the war had raised new national feeling in Canada and Gray was anxious to publish and celebrate the best Canadian writing. Not as dynamic, perhaps, as Jack McClelland, his friendly competitor, he was nonetheless an important advocate of the Canada Council and of Canadian culture generally at a time when artists needed sober business people speaking on their behalf. As an author he had a plain style masking a droll sense of himself and the world, this most especially apparent in his wonderful autobiography, *Fun Tomorrow* (1978). He published just enough fiction and literary biography to make us realize, as Lovat Dickson has said, "what Canadian writing lost to Canadian publishing when he opted for a career as a publisher." Shortly after he joined Macmillan in 1930 he moved to **126 St. George Street** and lived there until 1932.

His house was one of many razed to make way for Robarts Library, a building whose interior is a masterpiece for ease of use, and whose exterior is one of the most glaring examples (among many contenders, unfortunately) of the UofT's architectural insensitivity to its neighbours and its neighbourhood. Actually, what is generally referred to as the Robarts Library (or more commonly as "Fort Book" by locals) is, in fact, three buildings. The most southerly houses the Thomas Fisher Rare Book Library at **120 St. George**, constructed like the other two in 1973. Fisher boasts the finest collection of rare books in the country. The holdings include half a million tomes ranging from second millennium B.C. cuneiform tablets, through incunabula, an impressive selection of Shakespeare folios and quartos, up to an inimitable collection of Canadian fiction, poetry, and drama. In all, the UofT Library system has about nine million books, the vast majority housed in the Robarts building. While the general public cannot wander the stacks, they can have free reference access to any book in the system simply by asking. This is in stark contrast to almost all other large libraries in the world. The third building in the complex is the library school, now known as the Faculty of Information Studies, **140 St. George Street**.

Lawren Harris (1885-1970), as a member of the Group of Seven, thought of himself as a painter foremost but he was also proud enough of his writing to publish *A Book of Verse* (M&S, 1922). As a child, following the death of his father, Harris was brought by his mother to his new home at **No.123**, and this remained his home address until 1904, although he boarded at St. Andrew's College after 1899.

The house immediately to the south, **No.121**, was Sir Daniel Wilson's home from 1882-89. Wilson (1816-92) was a big man on campus—the biggest, for a while, given that he was president of University College 1880-87, and of the entire University 1887-92. His presidency overlapped with some of the most cantankerous moments in the history of the institution. Because of previous run-ins with Egerton Ryerson, he was deeply distrustful of Ryerson the man and of the Ryerson who advocated a Methodist college sharing university funding within a federation. Wilson also opposed women being admitted to the university for fear that mingling the sexes when their hormonal levels were high was dangerous to the pursuit of a proper education. He was president in 1890 when University College caught fire. The building was gutted, the library completely destroyed. Wilson was also no friend of Canadian culture. He felt no obligation to hire Canadians over apparently equally qualified foreigners. And although when younger he had penned some flattering reviews of Canadian authors, in old age he regarded almost all Canadian writers as unworthy of serious criticism. My reasons for including him in this book are his book of poems (1875) and his *Chatterton, A Biographical Study* (1899). Wilson also lived at **No.46** from 1890-92. The largest residence at the UofT's main campus is named in his honour.

Poet Earle Birney's first residence in Toronto was a room at the chapter house of his fraternity Zeta Psi at **No.118**. He arrived here in September 1926 on a graduate scholarship. By delicious irony, the house, long razed, sat on the current site of the Thomas Fisher Rare Book Library where his papers have been deposited.

From 1948-52, while a student at University College, Morley Torgov (b.1928) lived at the Pi Lamda Phi frat house at **No.115**. After graduation, he practised law during the day and wrote gentle satirical novels at night. In 1994 he won the Leacock Medal for Humour for his *A Good Place to Come From* (1974).

Sidney Smith Hall at **No.100** has echoed with at least two important literary speeches. Jorge Luis Borges (1899-1986) gave a public lecture (in English), "Tales and The Fantastic" in Room 2217 at 4:30 p.m. on March 1, 1968. This was the Argentine master's only visit to Toronto and sadly was not recorded, although the CBC had the opportunity to do so. It declined on the grounds that Borges did not have a good speaking voice. John Robert Colombo, then a young poet, wrote a personal essay for *Canadian Forum* about listening to, and meeting Borges on this occasion. In the middle of the essay he inserted a tiny editorial critical of the university. His admonishments,

alas, are still relevant: "The Department [of Hispanic Studies] should be praised for inviting Borges, but the University should again be criticized for allowing yet another important visitor to come and go without public announcement. The University happens to be the cornerstone of Toronto's intellectual and cultural life, such as it is, but apparently the University authorities feel no obligation to publicize their attractions off the campus. It's irritating to have to learn, purely by chance, that a man of Borges' stature is visiting one's own city." The other world-famous literary speaker in this Hall was Nobel Laureate Czeslaw Milosz (b.1911), who gave a lecture "Science Fiction and the Coming of the Anti-Christ" in Room 2118 on October 22, 1970 at 4:15 p.m.

Mrs. Byron Walker, wife of the head of the Bank of Commerce, used to live at **No.99**, and on May 16, 1908 she held a reception at her home in honour of the visiting English novelist who was always referred to, and published as, Mrs. Humphry Ward (1851-1920). Ward was quite well connected: she was the niece of Matthew Arnold, the mother-in-law of George Trevelyan, and the aunt of Julian and Aldous Huxley. Her most famous novel, *Robert Elsmere* (1888), had sold well from the beginning, but after it was reviewed by William Gladstone (a man who found time to write astute literary criticism even while he was the Prime Minister of Great Britain) the book became an international bestseller. Mrs Humphry Ward's visit was page-one news in Toronto. She was in town primarily to give a speech at Association Hall. Some measure of the regard in which she was held can be gleaned from the *News'* coverage of the Walker reception: "[It] was one of the most interesting social events ever held in Toronto. Nearly all of the most distinguished members of the Church, the Law, and other professions, including Art, Literature and Journalism, in town, at present, attended, and most of them met and had some conversation with the guest of honour." The newspaper report then proceeds to list, over six column inches,

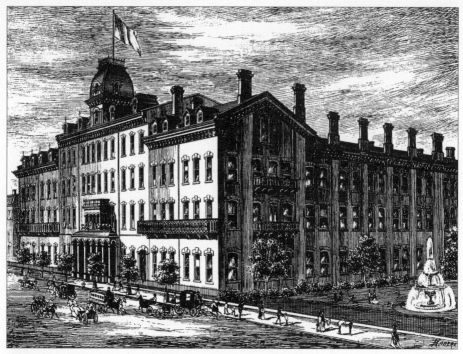

Queen's Hotel, *Canadian Illustrated News*, February 13, 1875

the eminences who attended. Lovers of sartorial detail will want to know that "Mrs. Ward's gown was of cornflower blue satin Duchesse veiled with mauve chiffon, with silver passementerie, a beautiful scarf of Limerick lace fastened with diamond stars, lappets of real lace and blue wheat ears in her hair; a diamond necklace and spray were also worn." Such attention to details of dress was obligatory in social columns in Toronto for over a century. Ward, who was staying at the Queen's Hotel, had hardly any time to herself during this visit. J.L. Hughes, poet and school inspector, drove Mrs. Ward and her daughter around the city for two hours shortly after their arrival and just before the Walker reception, and then hosted his own party for her on the following evening. She was entertained at a large luncheon hosted by Mrs. George Denison and then took afternoon tea at the Grange with Goldwin Smith, and gave a second lecture (on adventure playgrounds) at the Evangelia Settlement Hall on River Street. All this within two days. At her lecture at Association Hall she was introduced by the Lieutenant-Governor, "who made a short speech in warm praise of the beauties and resources of Ontario, asking Mrs Ward to remember this Province as the greatest in the British Empire even after she had journeyed through the Western Provinces . . . When Mrs Ward reached the platform she was presented with a bunch of roses from the Toronto members of the Canadian Women's Press Club." The lady then began her lecture by discussing "man in contact with the primal forces in nature as depicted in letters." She adroitly and diplomatically concluded her talk by gracefully quoting a sonnet of Charles G.D. Roberts. In the middle of her speech she gave an assessment of her literary contemporaries, which is fascinating for whom she ranked highly: "Among modern writers Mrs. Ward gave a high place to Ian Maclaren, to Hardy, to Mary Wilkins, to Owen Wister, to Barrie, to Tolstoi, to Bjornstein, and to Pierre Loti. Pierre Loti's *Iceland Fisherman* she placed at the very head of the list, and the next place was given to Barrie's *A Window in Thrums*." For her talk at the Evangelia Settlement Hall her gown was "of leaf-green satin veiled with black chiffon with a deep Paisley border, the bodice was embroidered in gold and a pearl necklace and magnificent sables were also worn, her hat was of black crinoline with black and white ostrich plumes and she carried a bouquet of Richmond roses." Before she left Toronto, Mrs. Ward had the satisfaction of seeing three of the town's dailies rhapsodize about her on their editorial page while her every utterance and move were reported extensively by all newspapers.

Ward's own responses to the city were generally favourable. She had just come to Toronto from a stay with the Governor General in Ottawa, so her sense of quotidian existence was, shall we say, a mite distorted. To her husband, she wrote on May 18th from the Queen's Hotel: "Toronto is less exciting [than Ottawa], though pleasant. We lunched yesterday with Colonel George Denison, a great Loyalist and Preferentialist, much in with Chamberlain. He cut Goldwin Smith twenty years ago!—so it was piquant to go from him to the Grange." Two days earlier she had written to her spouse: "Toronto seems to be a vast place—much more attractive than Montreal, and much better paved. Mr. James Hughes has been driving us about in the afternoon, and we got the same impression of tree-shaded avenues, of houses as at Washington [D.C.]—the trees in about the same shade of green. But there is a touch of grace & distinction in Washington which Toronto misses, & the main building, the Parliament House—a wretched performance in Canadian Gothic—won't do after the Capitol, though it stands well among fine trees. But the town is rich and spacious and green, & seems to be very conscious of a great and industrial future." Sir William Van Horne gave the Royal Suite at the Queen's to Mrs. Ward and her daughter for free, and then, when they were set to leave for the west, he made them the gift of a private deluxe railway car in which to travel across Canada.

The poet R. G. Everson (1903-92) was held in high regard while he was alive and is still considered an important, if not quite top-rank poet of mid-century in Canada. He graduated in arts from the UofT in 1927 and then studied at Osgoode Hall. In his final undergrad year he lived at **93 St. George Street**. The same literary assessment can be made of Ron Everson's contemporary, A.G. Bailey (1905-97), who had digs at **No.86** during his final year of doctoral studies, 1933-34.

No.85, Whitney Hall, has been University College's women's residence since 1931, and was home away from home at various times for students (later authors) Margaret Millar, Karen Mulhallen, Elizabeth Brewster, Colleen Thibaudeau, Germaine Guèvremont, and Mary Quayle Innis

The men's residence at one time was the former home of Sir Daniel Wilson near **No.73**. Then the residence named after him was constructed on the site. Among the authors who have lived here while studying at the UofT are John Robert Colombo, Matt Cohen, Jack MacLeod (who was don of Wallace House while pursuing his PhD), David Helwig, E.A. Lacey, Earle Birney, Roy MacSkimming, James Reaney, Hugh Kenner, and David Lewis Stein. David wrote to me about how uptight this residence was, even as late as 1957: "Toward the end of my second year, I was told I would not be allowed to return to Sir Dan the following year. What happened was this: Mike Rasminski . . . and I were very active at Hillel House, the Jewish students centre on the campus. Both of us were on the executive. We had been at some Hillel affair and then had gone out to celebrate some political victory, most likely over the restrictions the Orthodox faction wanted to impose, and we had gotten quite drunk. We were riding a bicycle very noisily around the quad in the early hours of the morning. A don came out and told us to stop and I told him he was a sanctimonious bastard and to stop bothering us. [His] dignity was offended and he complained. Rasminski

Undergraduate editorial board of UofT 1944 yearbook including Hugh Kenner (back row, far right)

and I were told we could finish out the year since we were close to exams but we would not be allowed to come back in the fall."

When Henry Van Dyke came to Toronto to speak in 1919, he stayed at the home of Sir Robert Falconer, **69 St. George Street**. Van Dyke (1852-1933) was first a minister of the cloth, and then, following an appointment by Woodrow Wilson, a minister of the USA to Holland and Luxembourg. Just as religion pervaded the lives of North Americans at the beginning of the 20th c. in a manner that is almost inconceivable to us today, so too were the poems, stories, plays, and essays of Van Dyke soaked in formal religion. His work found a large following in his time, and in his old age he had the pleasure of seeing his collected works published in a uniform set of 17 volumes. In Toronto, he made three appearances in 1919. The first was a speech to the Empire Club on October 25, unusual for the time in that women were permitted to attend. "Dr. Van Dyke ingratiated himself with his audience by hoping that the ladies would not feel inconvenienced by the rule that forbade smoking. After the laughter had subsided he said he had visited Canada every year for forty years . . . 'What a glorious thing it has been that these great nations have dwelt together so long, not in dull unanimity, but in real solid concord,'

he explained. He dwelt on the long borderline along which he had fished, hunted and camped, and which required no protection." The highlight of his visit, though, was a sermon he gave at Convocation Hall on October 26. Forty minutes before he was due to deliver his talk, the hall was packed with admirers, while more than three thousand others formed a queue (reaching to College Street!) hoping that by some miracle they might get in. There were so many people struggling to be admitted that Van Dyke himself had to try several crowded doorways before he could gain entrance.

How much a conventional man of his time Van Dyke was can be garnered from his third talk in Toronto. The *Star* reported his remarks this way, "'Women ought to stay women and men ought to try to be men,' was the statement of Dr. Henry Van Dyke in an address to the annual dinner of the University Women's Club on Saturday. In times of stress, he said, it was quite all right for women to engage in men's pursuits, but it would be nothing short of a calamity if women's education were to take her away from her God-given sphere of home-making and the care of children." Van Dyke was invited by the UofT to give a sermon again in 1924, but tellingly perhaps, the University Women's Club did not take advantage of this second visit to have him speak.

Marshall Saunders's (1861-1947) first residence in Toronto was **No. 66** in 1914. The city remained her home until her death. Although she published more than two dozen books, fairly or unfairly she remains known for only one: *Beautiful Joe* (1893). The book, an autobiography of a beaten dog, remains in print more than a century later, and in its long life has sold millions of copies in a score of languages. It is interesting to note in her *Canadian Who's*

Who entry that she credited T.H. Rand, her father's best friend in their native Nova Scotia, with deciding her writing career for her—a remark she meant in a positive, flattering way. Rand, a poet and educator, had also moved from the Maritimes to Toronto and had lived essentially around the corner from Saunders's first home here.

Brian Doherty (1906-74) is recalled today as the founding father of the Shaw Festival at Niagara-on-the-Lake, but in the 1930s he was celebrated in the Toronto papers as the author of a play on Broadway that excited the New York critics. He had written the play, *Father Malachy's Miracle*, while studying at Osgoode. Curiously, the play was not produced in Toronto until two years after the Broadway run, when a Montreal troupe brought a production to the Eaton Auditorium—for one day only. Despite his success on Broadway, Doherty continued to practise law. He kept his toe in theatrical waters by producing Toronto appearances by such notables as John Gielgud and Michael Redgrave. In the early 1950s he had a large hand in the creation of TV station CHCH, and then in the late 1960s gave almost all his attention to the Shaw Theatre project. As an undergraduate, he spent the academic year 1928-29 at the Psi Upsilon fraternity at **No.65**. Almost two decades later, poet Douglas Lochhead (b.1922) joined the same frat and lived here 1945-48.

Knox College's current location at **59 St. George Street** is but the latest in a series beginning with a downtown site, and later and more famously, at Spadina Crescent. Novelist Philip Kreiner lived in residence here from 1973-75. Poet Earle Birney (1904-95) also lived here, albeit briefly, in 1927, after living at a frat house up the street at **No.118**. Why Birney moved into Knox is an illustrative tale. During a long talk we had about his Toronto years, he unwittingly revealed for me ways in which Toronto had changed: "I wasn't very alert or concerned about Canadian literature when I first came down here. I came down here to take an M.A. and do some work on Chaucer . . . I was here for only 8 months, 1926-27 . . . I didn't run with literary people. I didn't run with anybody; I was very poor and I just worked in the goddam library. After seven months I got my M.A. and lit out back to the West . . . I lived in one of the smartest fraternities, one of the wealthiest fraternities on the campus. This is because I was a sort of an unwanted ward from a poor branch of this fraternity out in B.C. . . . I came down to Toronto and I came automatically to the fraternity house here because it had already been arranged that I got a room for practically nothing, provided that I'd do a little coaching of some of the undergrads in spare moments. So I moved in. This house is one of the old brick houses on St. George Street. So, I lived there for about, I guess, 2 months and I was enjoying it so long as I didn't have to mix too much socially because these guys were well-heeled—these were all undergrads and they were all wonderful guys, they had lots of money . . . the fraternity was just bouncing all the time, whether it was the jazz or whether it was the music and the big billiard table, and hellish big brawls. But the thing that fascinated me was that I couldn't completely move into this [world], I didn't have the money. But I was a dancer when I was young, I loved dancing, ballroom dancing, and I found that I could go to the deb dances for free as long as I could dress, as long as I had a tux. So, the boys outfitted me properly. Dock shoes and the whole works, all these fancy clothes I'd never had before. On loan but they fitted me because they wanted me to go to these parties because I danced pretty well, and that's what the girls wanted, a guy who could dance well. So I went to places with stag lines . . . when there was a big deb dance party the father of the girl who was debbing would invite several fraternities *en bloc* and they would all come and form a big stag line in the centre of the ball room and we'd stand there until they saw a girl that interested them and we'd cut in, especially if it was a brother you could always cut in on a brother or you could try to cut in on one of the rival fraternity boys. So, you got there in a limousine, and you had this wonderful food and drink. So this is what kept me, I think, staying in the house—that, and the fact that I was living there very cheaply. One day I met a guy I had known out in British Columbia. He wasn't a fraternity brother or anything, he was just a guy down taking a higher degree in music and he was the leading young pianist of Vancouver and I was delighted to see him. He was a poor Jewish boy. He got a scholarship and was doing well and so forth. So I said, 'Come on in to the house and have some tea.' So we went in. There were some comrades around, I introduced him to a few brothers. It was fine. After supper that night I was called in to the room of the guy who of all our brothers was in charge. And he said, 'I understand that you were entertaining a friend this afternoon.' I said yes. 'Did you know he was Jewish?' he asked. I said, 'Of course!' He said, 'But did you know that the constitution doesn't allow us to entertain Jews? It's in our charter, you know?' I was so angry that I walked right out and hunted up a guy I knew who was living in Knox College and who had asked me before. He said, 'I've got a room for two and the other bed is empty.' So I moved in with him. Never went back to that fraternity and never had anything to do with fraternities since."

Because he was the son of a Presbyterian minister, playwright and legendary radio producer Andrew Allan (1907-74) had much-reduced residence charges at this address, even though he studied at other colleges as an undergraduate from 1927-30. Allan was candid about his undergrad conduct: "At the University of Toronto in the late 1920s my life was torn three ways: by theatre, by newspaper, and by academic studies. Academic studies lost, hands down. My academic career was marked by an exquisite lack of distinction. Theatre was represented by the University College Players' Guild, and by Hart House Theatre—which, in those days, although on the campus, was not part of the university. Newspaper was represented by the *Varsity*, the undergraduate daily, on which I started as a reporter, proceeded to masquerade as Drama Editor, and finally became boss Editor. For a drama man to achieve the top of the mast-head was by no means usual. Your drama man was held to live on Parnassus, with neither taste nor talent for the market-place."

After reading a news item in which a local minister had pontificated that the university was teaching atheism Allan penned what he intended to be an ironic editorial saying of course the university was teaching atheism since everyone was acting like an atheist all the time anyway. The Student Council suspended all publication of the *Varsity* at once, and the daily newspapers, led by the *Star*, attacked the *Varsity* and the university for seeming to abet this godlessness. "There were red faces in the provincial cabinet," according to Allan, "red faces on the faculty, the Caput, and the University Senate. Headline readers decided the [*Varsity*] editor had declared himself an atheist. There were thunderings from pulpits, and heart-searchings in farmhouse kitchens . . . The results of what I had thought to be a harmless piece of irony had stunned me. My sense of balance was restored, fortunately, by an afternoon in the study of the Dean of the Faculty of Arts, Alfred Tennyson DeLury, who was also the head of the Department of Mathematics, had been a friend of Yeats and Lady Gregory and many other famous Dubliners of the Celtic Renaissance, and had one of the best collections of Irish literature in North America. He also had a delicious sense of humour and of humanity. That afternoon he let me see how funny the whole thing was—and for that I love to remember him."

Thanks to Claude Bissell, President of the UofT, poet Earle Birney was greatly helped out of a bad patch in mid-career. In 1965, after a twenty-year absence from Toronto, Birney was appointed by Bissell to be the first writer-in-residence in the history of the institution. Part of Birney's time was to be spent at the Scarborough campus, and part at an office at **No.49**. He kept the position and this office until moving to Waterloo in the summer of 1967.

The northwest corner of **St. George Street** and **College Street** is filled with a stately building, originally the main reference library of Toronto and now the UofT Bookstore. Northrop Frye worked for the summer of 1928 (between his first and second years at Vic) in the bowels of this building putting labels onto incoming new volumes. As his biographer has noted, "the job was menial but meant that he could finance the next year as well as buy himself a new suit . . . The library job was consummately tedious and despite its utter simplicity, he never developed any skill at it. Still he managed to squirrel away new books that interested him, the most important of which was Denis Saurat's 1924 book *Blake and Modern Thought*. Frye later repudiated it but it awoke his interest in Blake." Novelist Carolyn Llewellyn (*The Masks of Rome*) worked as a reference librarian here 1972-73.

Another important university residence is Devonshire House located at **3 Devonshire Place**, sandwiched between Trinity and Massey Colleges. Among the authors who made this their home while studying at the UofT were Kenneth Kirkwood, Evan Vere Shute, W.W.E. Ross, Leslie H. Reid, and Hugh Kenner.

Kirkwood (1899-1968) got a B.A. in 1922—after which he immediately went to Turkey on behalf of the Student Christian Movement, an organization which ran an excellent bookshop (called the SCM Bookroom) for many years in the seventies and eighties on the ground floor of what used to be Rochdale College. Within a few years, he had joined the Dept. of External Affairs and rose to high stations. His posts included being our Ambassador to Egypt and our High Commissioner to Pakistan and to New Zealand. With Arnold Toynbee he co-authored a book on Turkey, and on his own wrote a number of titles, including several books of poetry. His final undergraduate year was spent in South House in Devonshire Place.

Dr. Evan Shute (1905-78) was a pioneer in the therapeutic use of Vitamin E, and with his brother, also a doctor, founded the Shute Institute in London, Ontario. Shute's early passion for Vitamin E meant that he was frequently at odds with his colleagues, but no shrinking violet, he confronted and challenged them in medical circles and in the press without remorse. Yet he still found time, under the pseudonym Vere Jameson, to publish poetry books and several books for children. For the six years (1921-27) he attended the UofT (M.B. 1927) he lived entirely in South House. The Imagist poet Eustace Ross (1894-1966) graduated with first-class honours in chemistry and mineralogy in 1915 after living in residence in South House during his undergraduate era. His room rent for the entire period was ten dollars a month.

Leslie Reid's studies in Forestry were interrupted by service in WWI. After the war he obtained his degree and then worked for the Ontario government's forestry branch. During his sylvan studies he also found plenty of time to act and write. He wrote a play which may have been the first to be produced at Hart House, but it is his novels (all published by Dent) for which he accrued the most renown. One, *The Rector of Maliseet* (1927), is a creepy tale of two ministers who live 700 years apart. He resided in North House for the three academic years covered by 1919-22.

Hugh Kenner (b.1923), a native of Peterborough, obtained his B.A. from the UofT in 1945, and the following year, while studying for his master's degree, lived in South House. Within another year he published his first book, *Paradox in Chesterton* (1947), soon to be followed by *The Poetry of Ezra Pound* (1951), the tome that gained him worldwide acclaim from fellow academics.

The Oxford Companion to Twentieth Century Literature in English notes that Kenner is "widely considered the pre-eminent critical commentator on literary Modernism."

Massey College, across the street at **No.4**, had novelist Robertson Davies (1913-95) as its driving force and founding Master when it opened in 1963. He remained Master until 1981, firmly determining the character and customs of this graduate college. Among authors who worked at Massey College while UofT writers-in-residence were Margaret Laurence, Dorothy Livesay, Fletcher Markle, W.O. Mitchell, and Margaret Atwood. Nobel literature laureate Czeslaw Milosz (b.1911) gave his first poetry reading in Toronto at Massey on October 21, 1970. Poets Douglas LePan and Robert Finch were senior fellows of the College, and Finch actually lived in an apartment in the college for several years after its founding. He donated the wonderful grisaille which dominates the Junior Common Room. Poet Douglas Lochhead (b.1922), also a senior fellow, was the founding Librarian of Massey College and held that post until 1975.

The English novelist and critic Walter Allen (1911-95) is hardly well known here but his fans are intense in their defence of his literary merits. He came into his own as a novelist in the Depression, writing stories of working-class life in Birmingham that attracted high praise. He was also internationally distinguished as a critic, publishing seminal studies of George Eliot, Joyce Cary, and Arnold Bennett, and standard histories such as the monumental *The English Novel*. He was kind enough to write me in 1992, while in serious ill health, about his Toronto connections: "I first met Toronto, albeit obliquely, when as a very young man I was on my way to the University of Iowa to take up an appointment as a visiting lecturer in English in the summer school. I sailed on a Canadian Pacific liner to Montreal, and in Montreal railway station, where I was to get the train to Chicago, I was baffled to hear references in conversations overheard to a place called

Tirana, which I associated with Albania. In the end I realized that Toronto was what was meant. I reported this in a book I wrote ten years or more ago called *As I Walked Down New Grub Street*. The book was reviewed by a Canadian weekly, I think *Saturday Night*, and the reviewer, quite wrongly, thought this to denote a British attitude to Canada that was patronizing and superior.

"In fact, my memories of Toronto couldn't be more pleasant. I first visited it in 1967 when I was on a lecture tour of North America . . . I saw it on that first visit as a typically American city. My second, and first real visit was in 1970 when I was a Visiting Professor of English at the University of Toronto summer school. I lived for five or six weeks at Massey College. I found that Toronto was nothing like any city in the United States but was *sui generis*; if it reminded me of anywhere else it was of Edinburgh, however different in appearance. I suppose I mean that I thought its values predominantly Scottish rather than American or English. I also found that it was a cosmopolitan city with excellent restaurants. I discovered the joys of the Park Plaza Hotel. It was there, in the restaurant one night, I ran into a Canadian friend I had last seen ten years before in London, Alan Fraser, now dead, but very well-known in Canada at that time."

Devonshire starts at **Hoskin Avenue**. Halifax-born David Manners (1900-98) was enrolled in the School of Forestry nearby and gave **16 Hoskin** as his Toronto address for the years 1921-23. He seems not to have graduated, no doubt due to his extra-curricular involvement with acting. Under his real name, Rauff de Ryther Acklom, he appeared in nearly every production of Hart House Theatre in its first years, but by late 1923 he was working professionally in New York. His greatest fame as an actor came, however, from movies under his new stage-name, David Manners. His most famous role was that of Jonathan Harker, the clean-cut hero who defeated Bela Lugosi in the famous 1931 version of *Dracula*. He also played romantic

Dracula (Bela Lugosi) disagreeing with the literary appraisal of Jonatan Harker (David Manners). From the movie *Dracula* (1931). Manners, a novelist from Toronto, played the romantic lead in several other films.

leads opposite such stars as Katharine Hepburn (in her movie debut, *A Bill of Divorcement*, 1932), Barbara Stanwyck, and Loretta Young, and worked under such famous directors as Frank Capra and George Cukor. At the height of his success in 1936, Manners, fed up with Hollywood, abandoned the silver screen. Instead, he set up an exclusive, 1,000-acre guest ranch in the California drylands for writers and actors who needed a contemplative retreat from the showbiz grind and the public glare. While running the ranch, he made occasional returns to the Toronto and New York stages, and also began to write fiction. He published two novels to modest acclaim, both of them set in Canada; *Convenient Season* (1941) and *Under Running Laughter* (1942).

Wycliffe College is based at **5 Hoskin Avenue** and Trinity College was moved to **No.6** in 1923. Both are slim in literary con-

nections when compared to University College or Victoria College, but nonetheless some notable authors are associated with them.

Trinity College at **6 Hoskin Avenue** was originally founded by Bishop Strachan as a reaction to the secularization of the UofT in the middle of the 19th c. Strachan was a fanatic who believed in the God-given right of the Anglican Church to a preferred position in secular matters, and he was determined that the Church of England have a university in Toronto to call its own. Trinity was originally located on Queen Street West (appropriately at Strachan Avenue) but, undone by the sheer costs of running a postsecondary institution, the school eventually amalgamated with its old rival, the secular UofT, and moved to its current location in 1925. Over the years, about half a dozen notable literary authors have studied at the new Trinity. Many of them were in residence. And a few grads even returned to teach. Among the latter was Philip Child (1898-1978). A native of Hamilton, Child did part of his undergrad work at the old Trinity but lectured in English at the new campus from 1925-26, and again from 1942 until he retired. Today he is remembered as the author of the novel *The Village of Souls* (1933), although his thriller about Nazi fifth-columnists, *Blow Wind, Come Wrack* (1945), was a popular serial before it was published under his pseudonym of John Wentworth. Child won the Governor General's Award for Fiction for his later novel *Mr. Ames Against Time* (1949). This book also won the Ryerson Fiction Award, as did his earlier novel *Day of Wrath* (1945).

Novelist Austin Clarke (b.1932) first came to Canada from Barbados in 1955 in order to study Economics and Political Science at Trinity. He stayed for two years during which time he wrote poems that won an undergraduate literary prize. Only later would he turn his hand to the fiction for which he has become so renowned. At the time, he was eager, "as members of my generation were, to read economics and political science. For in it we expected to find all the answers to the multitude of social and economic problems—none of us had pondered for a moment upon the psychological and cultural problems—by studying and then using methods and methodologies of systems which were by definition inappropriate to our political and economic constitutions. But the glamour spread itself over the irrelevancies of this education. . . ."

Broadcaster, diplomat, and novelist Adrienne Clarkson (b.1939) attended Trinity as Adrienne Poy in the late 1950s (she lived in the Trinity women's residence, St. Hilda's, at 44 Devonshire Place). Novelist Michael Ignatieff (b.1947) was enrolled from 1965-69 and lived in the men's residence for his first three years. Carolyn Smart (b.1952), a poet, lived with her parents while taking classes from 1969-73. Novelist Scott Symons (b.1933) is yet another writer who did not get a degree in English. His was in Modern History (B.A. 1955). Novelist and publisher James Bacque (b.1929) was at Vic for his first year, worked for a year, and then switched to Trinity for the last two years of his undergrad degree (B.A. 1952). Carolyn Llewellyn (b.1948), a novelist now living in the USA, graduated in 1972.

Novelist Dave Godfrey (b.1938) touched down briefly at Trinity as an undergraduate before flying elsewhere for his B.A. and further degrees. He returned to Toronto around 1967 in order to teach English full-time at Trinity, and within no time he and Dennis Lee were plotting the creation of an exciting publishing house devoted to important new national voices. The press became, of course, House of Anansi.

Dorothy Livesay (1909-96) began her studies in Modern Languages in 1927 at Trinity and graduated in 1931, having won the Jardine Poetry Prize in only her second year, the same year in which her first book of verse, *Green Pitcher*, was published to enviable reviews. As with many people, her university years were filled with the joys of assertive ignorance and freshly discovering what had been known for aeons. She also learned about Marxism at college, something that would seriously flavour her thinking for the rest of her life. In one of her memoirs, she recollected, "By the age of eighteen at Trinity College I protested vigorously at having to take R.K.—Religious Knowledge. Actually there turned out to be a lot of ferment among the theological students concerning 'The Historical Jesus.' A series of lectures at Trinity on new archaeological finds did much to support the concept developing in my mind of 'a real and human Jesus,' not a mysterious godhead. And then, on the *Varsity* newspaper where I worked as a cub reporter there exploded the dismissal of our editor, Andrew Allan, for daring to state that 'eighty per cent of the student body is atheistic.' All these challenges to 'received opinion' (including those of John S. Mill himself) prepared the way for my acceptance, by my fourth year, of the theories of dialectical materialism." Later, she described her hardcore introduction to Marxist thinking: "In my fourth university year my academic standing collapsed completely because I got in with a group of young people who were centred around a professor of Economics who had come over from Holland—Otto Van der Sprenkel, a very brilliant man. He had a way of gathering students into his apartment and talking only about the new literature and new politics. He had been to Russia and we had great arguments about why he wore silk pyjamas because if he was communist he ought to wear cotton!

"This was my first encounter with the ideas of communism—he did it to all of us! Jim [Livesay's best friend] and Otto had a prolonged affair that year. They eventually went to Europe that next summer . . . That summer before I went to Paris was the end of innocence—politically speaking as well as emotionally and physically. But it would take a long time—months and years—before the bourgeois literary world I had grown up in would brush off and leave me naked, stripped, a most vulnerable young woman making gestures of repudiation but finding it hard to change herself psychically." A bronze bust of Dorothy Livesay was unveiled in 1989 and is located around the corner at the George Ignatieff Theatre at 15 Devonshire Place.

Wycliffe College across the street at **5 Hoskin Avenue** was also founded (in 1877) as an Anglican college, but one intended to emphasize the Reformation aspects of Anglicanism as opposed to the religiously conservative stance of Trinity. A number of prominent people in the 1870s in Toronto, deeply affected by the Oxford Movement as well as by the revival of evangelical Christianity, wanted their vision of Anglican doctrine taught to future clergy of the Church and so raised the funds necessary to create Wycliffe. The College moved to Hoskin c. 1892. Almost from the beginning, Wycliffe adopted the wise policy of renting rooms to both theologs and students who majored in other subjects on the grounds that future clergy should always be in contact with people of the quotidian world—which accounts for why some of the following authors, who were not divinity students, found themselves resident at this address.

Although Selwyn Dewdney (1909-79) is now best known for his important work in preserving and celebrating Ontario petroglyphs, he was a novelist of some accomplishment. For the first three years of his undergraduate degree (B.A. 1931) he lived in residence at Wycliffe.

During his first year, Stephen Leacock roomed at Wycliffe in the academic year 1887-88 while enrolled at University College. Next to nothing is known about this period of Leacock's life because he was generally silent about it in his autobiographical writing, and because the university records are barren for this era. We do know that his marks were excellent but his finances poor, so the following year, even though he was allowed to enter third year studies—in effect, skipping a grade, an extraordinary event at any university—he could not afford to return. With wonderfully characteristic humour, Leacock "reminisced" about this first year at Varsity in his book, *My College Days*: "When I look back upon the men and things of my college days and compare them with the college days of those who are now undergraduates, I stand appalled at the contrast.

"What strikes me most in looking back to the college life of my time is the extraordinary brilliance, the wonderful mental powers of the students of those days. In my time there were men at college, especially in the year above me, who could easily have discovered, had they cared to, the Newtonian Laws of Motion and the Theory of Light.

"This, I think, was particularly noticeable in the very year when I happened to be a freshman. The fourth year, the graduating class, of that moment represented a galaxy of intellectual capacity which was probably

205

unparalleled in the history of the human mind. I state this in positive terms because I myself witnessed it. I knew, or at any rate, I saw and heard these very men. It will always remain with me as a source of gratification till I die, that it was my lot to enter college at the very time when the fourth year represented an exaltation of the intellect never since equalled.

"The deplorable change which has since happened was already, I fear, setting in during my own college days. The third year and the second year men, when they came to graduate, although infinitely in advance of anything I have since known, stood for a range of mentality far below that of the first graduating class that I remember. More than that, I am compelled to admit that the classes which followed immediately upon my own year, were composed of the very dregs of the human intelligence, and betokened an outlook and a point of view more fitted for the nursery than the class room.

"Nor is the change that I observe only in the students. The professors whom I see about me today, ordinary, quiet men, with the resigned tranquillity that betrays the pathos of intellectual failure, how can I compare them with the intellectual giants to whom I owe everything that I have forgotten. The professors of my college days were scholars, vast reservoirs of learning into whose depths one might drop the rope and bucket of curiosity—to bring it up full to the brim with the limpid waters of truth. Plumb them? You couldn't measure their learning! Impossible. It defied it. They acknowledged it themselves. They taught, not for mere pecuniary emolument—they despised it—but for the sheer love of learning. And now when I look about me at their successors, I half suspect (it is a hideous thought) that there is a connection between their work and their salaries."

The most famous literary resident of Wycliffe College was William Faulkner (1897-1962) who lived on an upper floor of this building from September 21, 1918 until December 8 of the same year. He shared his room with four other men. Faulkner was here because he wanted to be a pilot and fight with the Canadians against the Germans in WWI. He had also wanted to escape his native Oxford, Mississippi. There he had proposed marriage to a childhood sweetheart only to see her acceptance of his proposal overruled by her father. Worse, his rival for the girl's affections then proceeded to propose marriage to her and the rival's offer was approved by both daughter and father. Humiliated, Faulkner craved escape from the wagging tongues of his small town. He applied to be a pilot with the American Air Force but was rejected on the grounds that he was too small (Faulkner was not much bigger than a jockey). Now doubly rejected— and mortified—he grabbed at a chance to come to Toronto for pilot training. Initially he thought one had to be a Canadian to enter our air service. To augment his "Canadian" credentials, he tried to learn a British accent, obtained false papers claiming he was the son of an English vicar, and even changed his name. In the United States, and to his family, he was "Billy Faulkner." But feeling that Canadians were more elevated, he thought William would sound better than Billy. And because he noticed we spelled words like harbour and colour with the letter u, he added that letter to his family name to make it seem more elegant, more Canadian. I doubt the recruiting officer was fooled, but Faulkner's nationality seems never to have been an issue with our air force. He arrived in Toronto in early July 1918 to report to Jesse Ketchum School, then used as a depot for recruits. Once given a uniform, a medical check-up, and an introduction to military rules, he was shipped to the camp and aerodrome at Long Branch (the site is now in Mississauga) for basic training.

Basic training completed, he was transported again on September 21 to Wycliffe College whose rooms had been seconded to the air force for use by officer cadets for the duration. Here he studied machine gunnery, engine repair, and the basics of navigation and flight. If his classroom drawings of the Jenny airplane (Curtiss JN-4) he was hoping to fly are any gauge, he was an excellent student. Unfortunately for Faulkner, the war ended before he was ever allowed into a military aircraft, even as a passenger. The wheels of the military turn slowly, so even though peace was declared on November 11, he was not demobilized until weeks later when he left Toronto to return to Mississippi.

William Faulkner photographed on the back campus of University College, Toronto, November 18, 1918.

Some men might have regarded this experience as a waste of half a year. But for Faulkner, the six months in Toronto were absolutely seminal. For not only did he establish for himself an identity that was overwhelmingly positive and in accord with his family's traditional aspirations, it was in Toronto that he started to write fiction. Before Canada, the thought of being a storyteller never seems to have crossed his mind. In Oxford he had written poetry and had toyed with the idea of being a commercial artist. After Canada, his career path was set in only one direction, and he fulfilled that career (to near-perfection), as one of the finest novelists of the century and as a winner of the Nobel Prize for literature in 1949.

For some time now I have maintained that Faulkner became a fiction writer in Toronto in two senses. The first is in his letters home. He wrote almost daily to close members of his family. Reading the correspondence one becomes aware that shortly after his arrival he described his accomplishments and progress with tiny exaggerations that soon become outright fabrications, then evolved into real whoppers and reached maturity, of sorts, as complete fiction. For example, two days after the Armistice he told his mother that he was just about to get his pilot's licence—hardly possible given that he would need at least another half-year's study to procure his wings. To a friend he bragged that he had taken a plane on a solo flight in Toronto and had crashed through the roof of a hangar only to end up hanging in its rafters. When he returned to his family they were stunned to see him walking with a cane and a limp. The injury was due, he told them, to a flying accident during his training—and he faked the limp for years afterward. Silly as these white lies were, they illustrate how Faulkner was learning to re-shape events for dramatic purposes.

The other sense in which he wrote fiction, naturally, was the formal: his very first short story is set in the Leaside aerodrome where he and his fellow students would have been taken on day-trips to study aviation engines. The story is called "Landing in Luck." And in his two best novels, *The Sound and The Fury* and *Absolom, Absolom!*, while the campus and buildings ostensibly belong to Harvard, it is much more likely that he modelled them on the UofT campus with which he was far more familiar.

William Wilfred Campbell (1858-1918), one of the most important Confederation Poets, attended Wycliffe 1882-83 and then moved to the States for further theological studies. A decade later he would collaborate with Archibald Lampman and Duncan Campbell Scott in creating a *belles lettres* column known as "At The Mermaid Inn" for the *Globe*.

Immediately south of Wycliffe College is the Hart House complex, given to the university by the Massey family to accommodate the non-academic needs of male undergraduates—a healthy mind in a healthy body being the dominant thought behind its construction. The Masseys were Methodists, for whom the theatre was the devil's playground. So there was surely a keen element of rebellion against the father in the decision of both Vincent and Raymond to work in theatre. Raymond Massey, who went on to great international acclaim as a stage and film actor, once told an interviewer that it was years before he could face the thought of his stern father seeing him on the West End stage (even in a play by Shakespeare), his guilt about working in the theatre was that strong. This father-son conflict may also account in part for why a theatre was not part of the original plans for Hart House. Nonetheless, the complex and the theatre opened in 1919. The theatre was one of the best-equipped for its time anywhere in the world, and for the first decades of its life was run as a professional theatre with little connection to the university. If they were lucky, students might be called on to be spear-carriers, but otherwise, the operation used only career actors under a series of noted artistic directors. Poet Robert Finch (1900-95) was old enough to attend productions from the beginning and reminded a journalist in 1984 that it was a very fashionable institution. Its only other theatrical competitors were the Royal Alexandra and Princess. "Going to plays at Hart House was the smart thing to do, people subscribed for the season. Everyone who was anyone in Toronto came in a car . . . [and] evening dress was *de rigueur*. The ushers were beautifully dressed young society women or young men in black tie."

The first Artistic Director was Roy Mitchell (1884-1944). *The Oxford Companion to Canadian Theatre* describes him as a "member of a Canadian avant-garde that included Lawren Harris, Arthur Lismer and Bertram Brooker. Mitchell represents the most prophetic voice in Canadian theatre history, anticipating the work of Antonin Artaud, Tyrone Guthrie, Peter Brook and Jerzy Growtowski in Europe as well as developments in Canadian theatre of the 1960s." Along with the Massey brothers, Mitchell was determined to include Canadian content in his seasons, and from the second year onwards, the theatre incorporated at least one play by a Canadian author. Thus, for example, Merill Denison's *Brothers in Arms* premiered in the 1920-21 season, a work that continues to be revived into our own time. It's vital to remember that this theatre was effectively the only place in Toronto where a Canadian playwright had any chance of getting a professional production of his or her work. We will never know how many dramas about Canadian life were never written or staged because local playwrights knew there was little point in proceeding when there was only one theatre—doing one local play per annum—willing to present their work.

In its history, the boards of Hart House Theatre have been trod by some esteemed foreign playwrights who came either to speak or to oversee new productions of their work—or both. Among them were Harley Granville-Barker, G. Wilson Knight, Lennox Robinson, John Van Druten, and Denis Johnston.

Roy Mitchell wrote several books on dramatic subjects, none more important than his *Creative Theatre* (1929), still regarded as an important text by serious theatre people all over the world. Alas, finding scant sympathy for his artistic vision in Toronto, Mitchell left the city for New York in 1927. Twenty years later, the UofT assumed formal control of the space, and by appointing Robert Gill as director made it clear that Hart House Theatre was changing direction—that it was going to be a home for student productions and training, rather than be just another professional stage.

In addition to presenting plays, Hart House has hosted an amazing number of readings or talks by weighty literary figures. Here is a list of some of the better-known:

W.H. Auden
Bliss Carman
Leonard Cohen
Mazo de la Roche
Allan Ginsberg
P.D. James
Watson Kirkconnell
Irving Layton
Wilson MacDonald
Gwendolyn MacEwen
Thomas Mann
Nicholas Monsarrat
Frederick Pohl
E.J. Pratt
Thomas Raddall
B.K. Sandwell
Duncan Campbell Scott
F.R. Scott
Osbert Sitwell
Lionel Stevenson
Kathleen Strange
William Butler Yeats

The above list could almost be doubled were I to add the list of participants at the international poetry festival held at Hart House October 26 to November 1, 1975—the first literary festival that included prominent foreign authors ever held in Toronto. Among the foreign stars on that occasion were Yehuda Amichai, D.J. Enright, Robert Creeley, Thom Gunn, Seamus Heaney, A.D. Hope, Octavio Paz, and Diane Wakoski. The Canadian celebrities included Margaret Atwood, Anne Hébert, Irving Layton, and Al Purdy.

Many of the Alexander Lectures have been delivered at Hart House. The great Henry James scholar and biographer Leon Edel (1907-97) wrote in a letter: "My second visit [to Toronto] of about a fortnight was, when in 1956, I was invited to deliver the Alexander lectures. By this time I was a full prof at New York University and had published E.K. Brown's posthumous *Willa Cather* (which I finished) and the first volume of my five-volume life of James. I stayed in rooms at the University and gave five lectures on 'Literary Biography' which came out as a book and is still in print. I revised it in recent years and it is now known as *Writing Lives*. I worked on these lectures as a guest in a UofT residence and delivered them at Hart House on five successive days."

Hart House is joined to University College by the Peace Tower. Immediately under the tower is an arch into which has been carved the famous villanelle by John McCrae "In Flanders Fields."

Books dealing with Toronto's past state without contradiction that the front portal of University College at **15 King's College Circle** is the most frequently illustrated architectural detail in the city's history. The structure was designed by one of Toronto's most famous firms, Cumberland and Storm, and was built in 1856-59. A fire in 1890 destroyed the middle tower and its huge bell, as well as all of the eastern wing, most of the interior, all of the library, and every book in it. Rather movingly, people and libraries from around the world responded to the disaster by sending money and duplicate books from their collections so that a new library could be reconstituted quickly. As W.S. Wallace later pointed out, "Before the fire the University had boasted a collection of no more than 33,000 volumes, many of which were antiquated classical texts and theological treatises; within two or three years these had been replaced by a library of over 50,000 volumes, chosen for the most part with a view to their usefulness in a modern university. There had been, of course, losses which it was difficult or impossible to replace. A magnificent edition of Audubon's *Birds*, now virtually unobtainable, and a valuable collection of works on Greek and Latin epigraphy gathered by [Dr. John] McCaul, went up in smoke. But, on the whole, one might almost hazard the opinion that, so far as the Library was concerned, the fire of 1890 was a blessing in disguise."

Standing today in the middle of the front quadrangle and looking directly at University College one can see, apart from towering elms, almost exactly what someone over a century ago would have seen. Also standing here, we should try to imagine the bursting pride that must have been felt by those who lobbied so hard and so long for a government-supported, non-denominational, post-secondary institution. After what must have been many—and vicious—arguments with clerics and conservatives (who saw the formal separation of church from education as diabolical), the creation of such a massive yet handsome building, in a city still small, must have been cause for tremendous satisfaction.

The earliest literary visitor to comment on this building was a giant of American 19th c. letters, William Dean Howells (1837-1920). As a 23-year-old out of work, Howells had jumped at the invitation of a publisher to undertake a roving tour of eastern Canada and publish his impressions. No fool, he also sold his observations to a couple of newspapers back in his native Ohio. Unfortunately, no complete copy of his Canadian reportage exists. Nonetheless, enough survives of his July 27, 1860 report in the *Cincinnati Gazette* to give a sense of how impressed he was by the city generally and by U.C. in particular: "It is the glory of these northern cities to look down their shady avenues, out upon the cool and glittering expanses of lake, and one might be tempted to endure their fierce winter for the fair summer's sake. . . .

"I did the churches last evening, and had them off my conscience. The Canadian Parliament no longer meets at Toronto, and there remained chiefly Osgoode Hall and the University. In the former building the Court of Queen's Bench is held, and all of the Government offices of Toronto are located there. It is a beautiful structure . . .

You approach the University through a noble avenue of pines, cedars, locusts and willows. The College stands in the midst of beautiful grounds on which the forest trees still stand in picturesque groves, shadowing the winding, undulating walks and drives. The building is of white sandstone, and in the Elizabethan style—gabled, and spired, and towered, quaint in detail, and stately in general effect. It is said to be the finest structure of the kind in the New World; and, indeed, it is hard to conceive any which could surpass it in beauty. It is newly finished but its air of newness does not detract from its grandeur, though I confess that as I walked through its sounding and arched aisles and noted a 'modern improvement' in the shape of a coil of hose, I felt my finer feelings somewhat shocked. There cannot be any doubt that the hose would prove extremely useful in case of a fire.

"The Museum of the University is very complete, from the head of a mummy down through all the branches of stuffed, natural history, to the toe of a bat. There is a fine library, and lecture rooms uncounted. The provincial lunatic asylum is near the University; but as one meets insanity at large everywhere, I did not care to look at it here in confinement. I chose rather to pause in the University grounds, and see two cannon captured at Sebastopol. They were presented to Toronto by the fond motherland, and Toronto is mounting them on two sandstone blocks in sight of her University. (The reader will notice here that I am virtuous enough to refrain from allusion to teaching the young how to shoot—so natural is the connection.) Both pieces were spiked. They are immense in size and in bore—being as large round as a flour barrel, and of the calibre of 'The Mount Vernon Papers.' I suppose they appeared grim enough when belching flame and death into the allied camp; but here they looked singularly peaceful, and yawned idly at the gate, where a small boy was flattening his nose against the paling.

"I thought the college avenue a mile in length as I went up; but coming back hungry to dinner, I found it two miles long. The reader may average it as he pleases. It is odd, this effect that hunger will have upon us."

Many other writers have made complimentary remarks about University College but their words have about them the odour of people saying what they are expected to say. Matthew Arnold, however, went far beyond polite commentary when he was in Toronto in 1884. He said that the façade was one of the finest he had ever seen.

Just the year before, the novelist known as Ralph Connor spoke about the entrance to U.C. more viscerally: "In 1883 we graduated from the university. How large a place that institution had made for itself in my heart I never knew till after I had written my last examination. I walked out through the door under the noble Gothic arch and made my way onto the beautiful green in front. Then I turned and looked at the noble building, one of the finest on the continent. It was a perfect day in early May, the trees in Queen's Park were at their best. I was suddenly stricken with an acute homesickness. It was a shock to remember that the varsity was no longer mine, I was no longer of it. I belonged to the great mob outside. I walked slowly down that green toward the School of Science and turned once more to look at the scene before me. There lay the campus, vividly green, the scene of many a hard rugby battle, and beyond it the university, calm, grandly magnificent with its fine old façade of Gothic mullioned windows, every window tricked out with its funny-faced gargoyles, the whole new softened with green splashes of ivy. No longer mine. I lay down with my face on the greensward, homesick and desperately lonely. For the first time I understood the heart of the old Hebrew prophet when he sang: 'Thy saints take pleasure in her stones,/Her very dust to them is dear.' I had not dreamed, till that moment, how dear stones and dust could be."

The list of authors who have studied or taught at University College is certainly impressive. A partial tally includes the following authors who are discussed elsewhere in the *Guide*:

W.J. Alexander
Jack Batten
Walter Bauer
Earle Birney
Hermann Boeschenstein
Arthur Bourinot
E.K. Brown
Matt Cohen
John Robert Colombo
Ralph Connor
Norman Duncan
Pelham Edgar
George Elliott
Barker Fairley
Robert Finch
Lawrence Garber
John Garvin
W.G. Hardy
Lawren Harris
David Helwig
Robert Smith Jenkins
Janice Kulyk Keefer
Edith S. Keefer
E.A. Lacey
Wilmot B. Lane
Douglas LePan
Edgar McInnes
Marie McPhedran
Margaret Millar
Karen Mulhallen
Michael Ondaatje
Frank Prewett
James Reaney
W.W.E. Ross
Gerry Shikatani
David Lewis Stein
Orlando J. Stevenson
Thomas Brown Stewart
Arthur Stringer
Colleen Thibaudeau
Morley Torgov
James L. Tucker

W. Stewart Wallace
Robert Weaver
William Henry Withrow

Among the literary authors who visited, gave readings, or spoke at University College are Henri Bordeaux, Bliss Carman, A.D. Hope, Isaac Bashevis Singer, Anthony Trollope, and Vladimir Nabokov.

Trollope (1815-82), author of the famous Barsetshire novels (e.g., *Barchester Towers*) was in town from October 5-7, 1861, and although generally unimpressed by the city, was deeply impressed by the same two edifices about which W.D. Howells had waxed so flatteringly. In his volume *North America* (1862), Anthony Trollope wrote, "From Prescott we went on by the Grand Trunk Railway to Toronto, and stayed there for a few days. Toronto is the capital of the province of Upper Canada, and I presume will in some degree remain so in spite of Ottawa and its pretensions. That is, the law courts will still be held there. I do not know that it will enjoy any other supremacy, unless it be that of trade and population. Some few years ago Toronto was advancing with rapid strides, and was bidding fair to rival Quebec, or even perhaps Montreal. Hamilton, also, another town of Upper Canada, was going ahead in the true American style; but then reverses came in trade, and the towns were checked for a while. Toronto, with a neighbouring suburb which is a part of it, as Southwark is of London, contains now over 50,000 inhabitants. The streets are all parallelogramical, and there is not a single curvature to rest the eye. It is built down close upon Lake Ontario; and as it is also on the Grand Trunk Railway it has all the aid which facility of traffic can give it.

"The two sights of Toronto are the Osgoode Hall and the University. The Osgoode Hall is to Upper Canada what the Four Courts are to Ireland. The law courts are all held there. Exteriorly little can be said for Osgoode Hall, whereas the exterior of the Four Courts in Dublin is very fine; but as an interior the temple of Themis at Toronto beats hollow that which the goddess owns in Dublin. In Dublin the Courts themselves are shabby, and the space under the dome is not so fine as the exterior seems to promise that it should be. In Toronto the courts themselves are, I think, the most commodious that I ever saw, and the passages, vestibules, and hall are very handsome. In Upper Canada the common law judges and those in Chancery are divided as they are in England; but it is, as I was told, the opinion of Canadian lawyers that the work may be thrown together. Appeal is allowed in criminal cases; but as far as I could learn such power of appeal is held to be both troublesome and useless. In Lower Canada the old French laws are still administered.

"But the University is the glory of Toronto. This is a Gothic building and will take rank after, but next to the buildings at Ottawa. It will be the second piece of noble architecture in Canada, and as far as I know on the American continent. It is, I believe, intended to be purely Norman, though I doubt whether the received types of Norman architecture have not been departed from in many of the windows. Be this as it may the college is a manly, noble structure, free from false decoration, and infinitely creditable to those who projected it. I was informed by the head of the College that it has been open only two years, and here also I fancy that the colony has been much indebted to the taste of the late Governor, Sir Edmund Head. . . .

"The streets in Toronto are framed with wood, or rather planked, as are those of Montreal and Quebec; but they are kept in better order. I should say that the planks are first used at Toronto, then sent down by the lake to Montreal, and when all but rotted out there, are again floated off by the St. Lawrence to be used in the thoroughfares of the old French capital. But if the streets of Toronto are better than those of the other towns, the roads round it are worse. I had the honour of meeting two distinguished members of the Provincial Parliament at dinner some few miles out of town, and, returning back a short while after they had left our host's house, was glad to be of use in picking them up from a ditch into which their carriage had been upset. To me it appeared all but miraculous that any carriage should make its way over that road without such misadventure. I may perhaps be allowed to hope that the discomfiture of those worthy legislators may lead to some improvement in the thoroughfare."

An even more famous visitor to University College was Vladimir Nabokov (1899-1977). His widow wrote to me that her husband gave a lecture once a year at the UofT "for several years" but to date I have been able to locate only two lectures, both given in 1950 (the papers of the Dept. of Slavic Studies for this period were thrown away). The first lecture I could find was as part of a series on Eastern Europe presented by the Slavic Studies dept. Titled "Triumphs and Tribulations of Russian Writers" it was given by Nabokov at five o'clock on February 1 in Room Eight of University College. The second lecture was called "Chekhov, His Mind and Matter" and was delivered on October 25 at the same time and place as the first. Part of the *Varsity*'s report on this lecture stated, "Illustrating his points by means of a detailed analysis of one of Chekhov's incomparable short stories, 'The Lady With A Dog,' written in 1899, professor Nabokov emphasized that the pre-revolutionary Russian novelist was successful only as a writer of short stories. He suggests that Chekhov was unable to retain more than just a 'patchy vividness' of life which could not be retained long enough to be reproduced in a novel." Nabokov never wrote about Toronto—unless his comments were among the letters he undoubtedly exchanged with his university hosts, and which they, for reasons that remain unfathomable, never gave to the University Archives.

At the southern end of the front quadrangle lies the domed vastness of Convocation Hall, construction of which was begun in

Poetry Night: At Convocation Hall, under the auspices of the *Canadian Poetry Magazine*, November 24, 1937. Top left to right: Lord Tweedsmuir, Charles G.D. Roberts. Second row, left to right: Wilson MacDonald, E.J. Pratt, Bertram Brooker, and Katherine Hale.

G&M, November 20, 1937

1904, paid for entirely, not by the university or government, but by the Alumni. The formal street address is **31 King's College Circle**. Space constrictions permit a discussion of only a very few of the events which featured authors. However, to give the reader an idea of how popular a literary venue it has been, here is a partial list of novelists, poets, and playwrights who have appeared on its stage (several authors appeared on more than one occasion):

Beverley Baxter
Louis Bromfield
John Buchan
William F. Buckley
William S. Burroughs
Paul Claudel
Ralph Connor
E.M. Delafield
Rosita Forbes
Buckminster Fuller
Allen Ginsberg

Wilfred Grenfell
Katherine Hale
Vaclav Havel
Watson Kirkconnell
R.D. Laing
Stephen Leacock
John Le Carré
Wilson MacDonald
Peter McArthur
Lucy Maud Montgomery
Emily Murphy
Henry Newbolt
Robert Norwood
Alfred Noyes
Arthur Phelps
E.J. Pratt
Charles G.D. Roberts
B.K. Sandwell
Siegfried Sassoon
Marshall Saunders
Frederick G. Scott
Isaac Bashevis Singer
Arthur Stringer
Henry Van Dyke
Elie Wiesel
Tom Wolfe

This list would be easily doubled were one to include the authors featured by the UofT Bookstore Reading Series. That program began using this venue in the late 1980s.

One of the first important literary occasions at Convocation Hall (featuring more than a single author) was March 31, 1920, a Benefit Night for Bliss Carman, the Canadian poet lying ill (and poor) at Saranac Lake, New York. Siegfried Sassoon, on a lecture tour of North America, was persuaded by his host, Pelham Edgar, to give a speech rather than a reading even though he had not been warned beforehand that a speech was expected of him. Thanks to the help of his fellow poet Frank Prewett, who was living in Toronto at the time, Sassoon was able to cobble together an address that seemed to please the crowd. Good colonials that they were, the organizers placed Sassoon's name in huge type, and that of popular Canadian writer Peter McArthur,

also on the bill, in barely legible type in the newspaper ads for the event.

Canadians fared rather better on November 24, 1937 at a Benefit organized by E.J. Pratt and the Canadian Authors' Association for *The Canadian Poetry Magazine* of which Pratt was the editor. The Governor General, Lord Tweedsmuir (a.k.a., John Buchan, author of *The Thirty-Nine Steps* and other novels) spoke first and gave a speech on the nobility of poetry. The hall was filled to capacity. Buchan was followed to the lectern by poets Charles G.D. Roberts, Wilson MacDonald, and E.J. Pratt, each of whom read for six minutes. Then came the presentation of the first Governor General's Awards for Literature (Buchan had been asked by Pelham Edgar to help finance the awards but was snubbed by Buchan and offered only the use of his title. Thus, there was no cash attached to the award in its first years). Bertram Brooker stepped forward to receive his medal for fiction. Interestingly, the medal for poetry was given not for a book but rather for a single poem—and the poetry award was named, not after the Governor General, but after Seranus, the *nom de plume* of poet Susie Frances Harrison, a lady we shall encounter from time to time in this *Guide*. George Herbert Clarke was this first winner of the poetry prize. Brooker was not invited to read his work, presumably because of time pressures. Clarke was allowed to read only the latter half of the winning poem before an unnamed singer sang Healey Willan's setting of two poems by Norah Holland. Katherine Hale and Nathaniel Benson then read short extracts from their work, and Montreal novelist Leslie Gordon Barnard, President of the Canadian Authors Association, concluded the event with an appeal for subscribers and donations. "O Canada" was played to mark the end of the evening, but, because this was Toronto, not one of the 1,500 people present sang.

Poet and playwright Paul Claudel's visit was page-one news when he arrived in Toronto on November 7, 1928. He was in town to receive an Honorary Doctor of Letters degree from the UofT at a special convocation called to accommodate his availability. At the time Claudel (1868-1955) was the Ambassador of France in Washington. His writing has always carried more weight in Latin countries than in ours, so it is striking to note that Hart House Theatre had already produced one of his plays years before this, his only visit to the city. Also worth noting is the cosmopolitan perspicacity of the university in even thinking of conferring the degree, much less in actually doing so. Another dramatist, Canadian Merrill Denison, wrote a contemporary account of Claudel's remarks for the *Star* in the flowery and deferential style used at the time by the newspaper when interviewing famous writers: "Who but a Frenchman (and a Frenchman graced not only with the endowments of the diplomat but those of the poet and playwright as well) could state that Canadians are a race of poets? And in making the extraordinary statement to do it in such a connection as to guarantee its reception as a compliment by the least literary amongst us.

"From many visitors an opinion that Canadians were a race of poets would come as a searing insult; from M. Claudel's it is but an expression of deep insight and the discovery of hidden and unappreciated qualities by a man gifted in searching beneath the surface of things to interpret their true nature. He could not have known that his visit to the city coincided with the annual throes of Canadian Book Week and turned the compliment out of deference to his fellow (if unknown to him) authors, because we interviewed him shortly after his arrival in the city and while he was still resting from his journey at Sir William Mulock's residence where he and his daughter, Mademoiselle Reine, are guests during their stay in Toronto . . . M. Claudel replied, not deprecatingly but emphatically, 'You do not translate your poetry into words, but into deeds. In a young country it is better to make

poetry in actions than in words. I have seen your great powerhouses at Niagara Falls. Great simple buildings where all that energy is translated. They are very beautiful. Very impressive. The turbines! There you have revolving poetry . . . You are building up a young country; do not worry too deeply about interpreting it. You are expressing yourselves in another medium than literature, but you are expressing yourselves.' The fact that he had made a short visit to the university where he called on members of the French department, seemed justification to ask the inevitable interviewing question of this continent. We had the grace not to couch it in the form, 'How do you like our city?' but asked instead if he found the atmosphere of the local university similar to colleges he had visited in the States. We asked the question because one so often hears that Toronto is becoming Americanized, and M. Claudel is French and so could not greatly care.

"'I have seen but little of it,' he answered, 'but it seemed to me that it had a distinctly different flavour. It is more English in its atmosphere. And I was glad to learn the position of importance occupied by the Department of French. It was most gratifying.

"'You must understand,' he hastened to tell us, 'that I am not altogether ignorant of your city or your university. I have learned a great deal of it through my friend Mr. Vincent Massey whom I know in Washington. I think he is a very pleasant man and it was through his good offices and because of him that I am here in Toronto today.'" After the convocation ceremonies on November 7, Claudel gave a speech in French to the Alliance Française in the old Physics Building of the UofT. That building, razed in the 1970s, had a large and comfortable auditorium occasionally used for literary readings such as Claudel's. Other authors who gave readings in the Physics Building were William Butler Yeats and W.H. Drummond, author of the *habitant* poems. Claudel also gave a speech in English to the Empire Club at the King Edward Hotel on November 8.

Stephen Leacock (1869-1944) spoke twice at Convocation Hall. The first occasion was on January 13, 1912 when, in an address on the relationship of university values to citizenship, he unwittingly unveiled attitudes showing that the more things change, the more they are the same: "We are exposed to the striking force of material considerations; our young men see the dominant importance of the main chance. Thus the relations made between individuals is on a mechanical basis only. They are established by purely business connections. They are reduced to one of purchase-and-sale.

"Our tendency is to measure with the yardstick or the hundred cents that make our dollar. We feel that a millionaire ought to be made a baronet; we regard a merchant prince with more reverence than a scientist or philosopher. 'If he be wise, why has he never made any money?' is the universal attitude. And it is this apotheosis of the businessman who, because of his success, is regarded as knowing everything that constitutes our greatest menace."

To get to the east side of Queen's Park, walk along College Street and then proceed north on University Avenue. The street mandorla that surrounds the provincial parliament buildings is known as Queen's Park Crescent. Where the legislature now stands was the first home of the Toronto lunatic asylum. No more need be said about that coincidence.

At one time, Queen's Park Crescent, from College to Bloor, was lined with large and beautiful homes of the city's wealthiest people. Most of those houses have been replaced with hideously anonymous buildings housing the staff of various ministries but just enough of the original homes

remain to hint at what a spectacular neighbourhood this must have been. Many of them had coach houses, and it is in one such coach house found at **39 Queen's Park Crescent East** that Marshall McLuhan (1911-80) founded his Centre for Culture and Technology in 1963. McLuhan is one of the most famous professors in any discipline ever to teach at the UofT. His importance, however, remains more controversial than most. While the influences on his thinking were many, he himself was always quick to cite James Joyce as the literary fountainhead of his ideas on media and communication. While working at this address he published some of his best-known books, including *The Medium is the Message* (1967) and *War and Peace in the Global Village* (1968). Worth noting

The Watsons are greeted by Professor McLuhan on their arrival at the University of Toronto   *UofT Staff Bulletin*, October 3, 1968

is that the first two people hired by McLuhan to work at this address were creative writers Wilfred and Sheila Watson. They collaborated with McLuhan in the team-teaching of three graduate courses and also in graduate English classes at St. Michael's College.

Painter and poet Lawren Harris (1885-1970) lived at **63 Queen's Park Crescent** from c. 1919 until 1929. Harris did no painting at this address—that was done at the large studio building, still standing, at 25

Severn Street. But he did write, and while resident here McClelland and Stewart published his poetry book *Contrasts* (1922). In that same year, the third Group of Seven exhibition was held at the Art Gallery of Toronto. Vincent Massey, amateur actor, generous sponsor of the arts, and later Governor General of Canada, lived in a large house at **No.71** for several years. The most famous of his literary houseguests, at least as far as I have been able to find, was John Drinkwater, here for a few days in early March 1921 to speak at the auditorium of Central Technical School under the auspices of the University Women's Club.

The principal address today for Victoria College is **73 Queen's Park Crescent**. Vic just surpasses University College for the honour of having graduated the highest number of people who became published creative writers. Despite the similarity in numbers, there were essential differences between the colleges. For one, as the list below shows, Victoria was more congenial to women than any other college on campus. Women had been enrolled since the 1880s, and Annesley Hall, Vic residence for women, still stands, a century-old testimonial to the College's relative progressiveness. Female professors were hired to teach at Vic before they were elsewhere in the University. This fact may explain the higher number of women writers affiliated with the College. Thanks to Pelham Edgar, the College was not above employing Canadian writers—of either sex (recall that E.J. Pratt, hired by Edgar to teach English, had never taken any English courses whatsoever). This was a radical policy in a university that, to its eternal shame, was one of the last in the country to formally acknowledge the existence of Canadian literature and encourage its study at the doctoral level. And Vic was always perceived as slightly more "unbuttoned" (as the Germans say)—more congenial than other colleges to real or pretending bohemians.

Here is a partial list of authors who studied or taught at Victoria College:

Luke Allan
Margaret Atwood
Margaret Avison
James Bacque
Ethel Granger Bennett
Ethel Hume Bennett
Nathaniel Benson
Kathleen Coburn
Don Coles
Dora Conover
Luella Creighton
Donald Creighton
True Davidson
Wayland Drew
Pelham Edgar
R.G. Everson
Northrop Frye
Ethel Kirk Grayson
Janet Hamilton
W.G. Hardy
Greg Hollingshead
Percy Janes
George Johnston
Lois Reynolds Kerr
David J. Knight
Dennis Lee
Louis MacKay
Jay Macpherson
Jesse Edgar Middleton
Richard Outram
Desmond Pacey
Walker Percy
Arthur Phelps
Marjory Pickthall
Lorne Pierce
E.J. Pratt
Kenneth Radu
John D. Robins
Patrick Slater
Francis Sparshott
Allan Stratton
Pierre Van Paassen
Ian Young

One of the few authors never to visit Toronto who deserves inclusion in this *Guide* has a ghostly connection to Victoria College. In his memoirs, Pelham Edgar (1871-1948), the much-loved Chair of the English Dept. for many years, told of an encounter he had around the turn of the century during one of his visits to the London salon of Wilfred and Alice Meynell, the British poets who had tried to rescue their compatriot, the opium-addicted writer Francis Thompson: "If it was an evening visit, Francis Thompson was unfailingly there. I confess that I could never get very far with him. He responded readily enough to the theme of cricket at Lords. When I played Boswell and asked him if he was at all interested in Canadian poetry he said he knew nothing about it except for Carman's *Vagabondia* which he thought good but not first rate. I realized that he had had a Vagabondia of his own that went far deeper.

"When I left on that evening, Wilfred Meynell saw me out of the door, and on the landing told me the whole story of Thompson's life which now can be read in Everard Meynell's record. It was a grim and revealing narrative, and all the more exciting because I received it from the source, and before it was disclosed to the world.

"On another evening, Ezra Pound was a fellow visitor. As we walked away together he said he had gone there less on Mrs. Meynell's account than because he wanted to see Francis Thompson at close quarters. A fact perhaps worth mentioning is that he asked me to have him appointed my assistant in French at Victoria College! An odd addition to our staff that would have been, for I have a strong suspicion that the 'miglior fabbro' of T.S. Eliot's dedication would have been a misfit despite his sporadic brilliance." It is truly heart-stopping to contemplate how Victoria College might have changed, how English-language literature would certainly have changed, had Pelham Edgar hired the impecunious Pound.

Margaret Atwood (b.1939) is unquestionably the College's most famous literary graduate. She enrolled in 1957, a wide-eyed kid from Leaside Collegiate: "I was intimidated by almost everything at University. Red lipstick and pearl button earrings intimidated

me; so did black turtleneck sweaters . . . I always suspected there was something, some secret, that other people knew and I didn't." She soon made the acquaintance of Dennis Lee (b.1939), another freshman, and both took classes from, among others, poet Jay Macpherson (b.1931) and the phenomenal critic Northrop Frye (1912-91). Later in life, Atwood reflected on the faculty and its approach: "I thought at the time that the attitude towards the study of English at Vic—that it was supposed to make you somehow not only brighter but better, and that it should be undertaken in a spirit of friendliness and mutual cooperation—was the norm for English departments. I've found since that it's the exception."

Wayland Drew (1932-98), whose novel *The Wabeno Feast* (1973) has its many champions, is an author most often associated with our North and with the wilderness but not with Toronto. Yet, as he said in a letter, he enjoyed Toronto—at least when he was a student at Vic: "From September 1953 till May 1957 I lived in Ryerson House, Victoria College, 89 Charles Street West. I began writing there, helped by several patient teachers, Millar MacLure foremost among them, and encouraged by Bob Weaver of *The Tamarack Review*, who bought my first story.

"I have many happy memories of Toronto in the '50s. It was a far kindlier place. When I arrived at Victoria College there were still trees on Bloor Street, in front of the old mansions which had by then become women's residences. Both trees and houses are long gone, of course, as are other landmarks I recall affectionately—Palmer's Drugstore, the building at the corner of Bay and Charles where I worked in the '60s for the Department of Education, the Bay-Bloor Hotel, the original Pilot, and the Reference Library at St. George and College where I researched and wrote portions of *The Wabeno Feast*. Fortunately Britnell's, a real bookstore, is still there.

"Since the early '70s I've had no significant ties with the city and my separation has widened as Toronto has fattened and sprawled, each year becoming more a symbol of our ecological peril. It is now just another world-class basket case, and I visit as infrequently as possible."

David Knight and Dennis Lee were two Vic grads who returned to teach at their alma mater. Knight (b.1926) is especially proud of the word "teacher" because, as he wrote to me, "I was every grade of University teacher from Lecturer to full Professor during thirty-six years in which I managed to survive (even if barely, sometimes!) *while never publishing a scholarly word*. I taught." Dennis Lee was a Lecturer from 1963-67, dates which correspond with his co-founding of House of Anansi. Louis MacKay (b.1901) had a brilliant career as an English undergrad, capped when he was named the Ontario Rhodes Scholar of 1925. As if he were not busy enough that year, he also oversaw production of his three-act play, *The Freedom of Jean Guichet*, at Hart House Theatre. MacKay had written the play originally in French and then translated it into his mother tongue, English. After he returned from Oxford, MacKay taught at U.C., and then moved on to various universities in Canada and the States. As a creative writer, he seems to have abandoned plays for poetry; he published a book of verse in 1938 and another in 1948.

Marjorie Pickthall (1883-1922), once one of the most famous writers in Canada, was for a time an assistant librarian at Victoria College. When her father died in 1910, she was forced for the first time in her life to get a job. Friends intervened with Vic and arranged for the library post for her. Viola Pratt was happy to have known Pickthall as a woman and as a writer, but Viola also told me that Pickthall was "no good as a librarian, I must say. When we used to go for books and I saw her, I always thought of that line from Browning, 'She merely looked with her large eyes on me.' She just didn't know anything at all about books." This inadequacy may account for why Pickthall's friends encouraged her in 1912 to leave Victoria College and devote herself full-time to a writing career.

E.J. Pratt is the writer most commonly associated with Vic. He arrived at the College in September 1907 from his native Newfoundland to study theology. How he was able to afford the trip is amusing: "I and another fellow belonging to Bell Island concocted a brew made out of cherry bark and the tops of spruce and some sarsaparilla and, I must say that at the time, though it was very unconventional, a pretty strong lacing of rum, and we sold quite a number of bottles at a dollar, and two of us got up to Toronto with a hundred and fifty dollars and that paid all our expenses practically for the year in tuition, and food and lodging. Well, we never repeated the experiment because we were afraid to go back to Newfoundland for a long time."

At the time, Victoria College still lacked a men's residence, so Pratt roomed with buddies, first on St. George Street and then on Charles Street West. It is interesting to note the similarity of his experience as an undergraduate student with that of Atwood half a century later. One of Pratt's best friends reported, "He was probably the most brilliant, certainly the most unusual student of his time at Victoria. He had, at the outset at least, the almost naïve conviction that his courses would open doors not only to knowledge—facts, data, enlightenment—but to *truth*. I think it can be said that Ned Pratt set out on a kind of *quest*, which had as its goal nothing less than Truth—with a capital T!" From the beginning he found his theology classes tiresome and largely irrelevant to his own religious struggles, and so he began to write more and more poetry, although he never majored in English. But his drift is reflected in the new college friends he made at the time, among them William Arthur Deacon (later to be the great book critic of the *G&M*), and especially poet Arthur ("Art") Phelps, a fellow theologue who shared Pratt's disinclination to the ministry and his attraction to the literary.

Money was always in short supply when Pratt was an undergraduate and never more so than the winter of 1909 when he could afford only two small meals a day, "one of which was provided him as a part-time waiter in Simpson's [department store] restaurant on Yonge Street. So destitute was he, in fact, that, on learning of his plight, a group of his better-off classmates banded together to make a collection of funds on his behalf. Greatly embarrassed at being the subject of a charitable campaign and vigorously protesting his self-sufficiency, he refused at first to accept the well-meaning gift, but eventually agreed to a private and unpublicized bestowal." He also supplemented his income by reading regularly to the blind for twenty-five cents an hour. Memories of these indigent times no doubt account for his legendary hospitality to students and writers. Spontaneous banquets for an entire class were not uncommon, and many were the famous authors from abroad who stayed at his house or dined at his table. In an interview, his patient wife, Viola, explained how she met Pratt—and how he met Pelham Edgar: "It wasn't until my final year that I was invited to a wedding and met him. We both came back on the streetcar together and that's how we met. After I graduated, Pelham Edgar, my favourite teacher, started a group for graduates who wanted to continue with their English study. I asked Pelham if I could bring Ned along. Ned hadn't taken English at all, but that's how the friendship between Pelham and Ned started and eventually led to Ned teaching English at Victoria. Pelham had a marvellous way of spotting potential in people." Pratt had been ordained as a minister and was reluctantly preaching in churches in and around Toronto when Edgar made the momentous decision, over the objection of colleagues, to hire Pratt as an English professor even though he had not on paper a single qualification for the job. One of the students taught by Pratt became his most fervent admirer: Northrop Frye. In 1958 Frye offered the highest praise of his former teacher: "As long as Canada's culture can remember its origin, there will be a central place in its memory for the poet in whom it found its tongue." The College offered praise of its own when it decided in 1964, shortly after Pratt's death, to name its new library in his honour.

Nearby Northrop Frye Hall was named (1983) while Frye was still very much alive, and in his later years he had an office in the eponymous building. It seems too incredible to be true but when Frye first arrived at Vic from the Maritimes in 1929, the university considered his secondary-school education to have been so deficient he was permitted to enrol only in the three-year Pass course, not the envied four-year Honours program. Even worse, he was admitted only "on probation." One presumes the Admission Officer's doubts were soon dispelled. Four of Frye's teachers were also writers we encounter throughout this *Guide*: Donald Creighton, Pelham Edgar, Kathleen Coburn, and J.D. Robins. Frye's biographer, John Ayre, noted that "Robins, who was part black, worked his way out of a poor family in Kingsville, Ontario, as a railroad porter and labourer, eventually earning a PhD from the University of Chicago in German Philology. While he taught the college's difficult courses in Old

Northrop Frye (left) with Barry Callaghan at launch party for Morley Callaghan's *Wild Old Man*, 1988

English, Robins had a fascination for folk literature which was then considered academically eccentric in North America. He did not publish many scholarly papers and was looked down upon by professors at other colleges. But despite fits of deep gloom he was probably the most popular teacher at Vic. He had a welcome tendency to wander off topic in his undergrad courses by reciting folk literature including Paul Bunyan and Uncle Remus tales which he told with appropriate black dialect inflections. Though Frye's own later interests in

Pat Hume (left) [successor to Robertson Davies as Master of Massey College] and Davies at Massey College, 1982

literature were academically orthodox, it was Robins who presented to him the scrappy sub-culture of ballads and folk tales which was not blessed by academe but yet needed a place."

Frye lived in residence as an undergrad and never had much money. He dined at cheap Chinese restaurants and walked whenever and wherever he could. On one Saturday night, he and a friend thought it would be a lark to walk the length of Bloor Street. When they reached Jane Street, then the western border of the City, they about-faced and strode to the eastern edge of town and then marched back to Vic, arriving at dawn. "When they returned to residence, Knight remembers curling up in a heap in a shower stall and putting his feet under a stream of hot water, but Frye seemed unaffected."

After postgraduate studies and an unhappy period as an itinerant cleric, Frye joined the English dept. at Vic in 1939. In less than a decade he published *Fearful Symmetry*, the study of Blake that won him international applause and alerted the world to his singular mind. *Anatomy of Criticism* (1957) confirmed him as one of the greatest literary critics of the century, and although several important books

then followed, he was personally proudest of his magnum opus, *The Great Code* (1982), his analysis of the relationship between the Bible and western literature.

Robertson Davies and Northrop Frye seemed never to have been more than respectful acquaintances but to me they shared an important characteristic: while they were both conscious, even wry, about their passive ability to intimidate students and graduates alike, they were essentially shy, and welcomed any honest person willing to engage them in adult conversation. Neither had any patience with pretenders, although both were polite to a fault. Frye's private utterances could even be quite salty, always a surprise coming from such man who cultivated the appearance of a mild-mannered parson. And although Frye had spent his entire life within academe, he was not blind to its stupidities and would, without much provocation, regale friends with examples of institutional or professorial idiocy. As a teacher, his influence on his literary students was varied but legendary, although never as oppressive as his detractors are fond of claiming. But his effect on authors as diverse as Margaret Atwood, Jay Macpherson, and James Reaney is quite transparent. Before he was through with Vic, he had been Chair of its Dept. of English, and then was the College's Chancellor.

A few visiting authors gave public readings or talks in the old main building of Victoria College. Duncan Campbell Scott gave the keynote address to the Poetry Society of Canada on the 22nd of April, 1925. And Lawrence Binyon (1869-1943), the English art historian and poet, gave a public lecture, "The Essential Elements of Poetry," on November 13, 1926.

Women writers who lived in Annesley Hall (just to the north of Northrop Frye Hall) at **95 Queen's Park Crescent** are few in number and not particularly renowned or even respected in our time, with the exception of Jay Macpherson and Kathleen Coburn. Margaret Addison Hall at **140 Charles Street West** can count Jay Macpherson as well among its one-time residents, along with prize-winning fiction writer Elizabeth Hay (b.1951). While Margaret Atwood lived in a rooming house at **108 Charles Street West** she wrote her first novel. It remains unpublished at the author's insistence. What has been published that she wrote at this address is the short story "The War In The Bathroom" (in *Dancing Girls*, 1977). Marjorie Pickthall also had a room at **No.102** in 1911 when she worked at the Vic Library. A shared room at **No.92** was E.J. Pratt's home from 1908-10. Mystery writer Gail Bowen (b.1942) also lived at this address. She wrote in a letter, "In 1960 my parents moved to Port Hope [from Toronto], and I started at the University. During my university years I lived at **92 Charles Street West** which was right across from Victoria College. That's where Joanne [the sleuth in her novels] lives when she attends the UofT and where she and her eventual husband, Ian, first drink Chianti, eat spaghetti, argue politics and have sex (is there a pattern here?). I also used **92 Charles Street West** as the home for Adelaide Farlinger in my first book, *1919: The Love Letters of George and Adelaide*."

Burwash Hall, the men's residence of Victoria College (with an attached dining hall suitable for literary lectures), has been the home of writers Don Coles, Wayland Drew, Northrop Frye, and David J. Knight. One resident here (albeit only briefly) was Japanese novelist Toyohiko Kagawa (1888-1960). He stayed in an upper room of Burwash in May 1936 during his second and last visit to Toronto (he had been here in 1931 as part of the world convention of the YMCA). Kagawa was a Christian minister and writer based in Tokyo. In addition to his clerical duties, he travelled across Japan on behalf of the poor, helping them to unionize, establish credit unions, and, when possible, convert to temperance and even to Christianity. After his return from post-grad studies at Princeton, he published his bestselling autobiographical novel, *Face to Face with Death*. Despite the fact that he published more than 100 books (fiction, poetry, non-fiction) he is still regarded as a reputable literary author by the standard reference books in his native country. His 1936 arrival in Toronto as part of a continental lecture and sermon tour earned front-page treatment in the *Star*, partly because, I suspect, in that nervous, pre-war era he publicly declared that he would not be a combatant.

The British poet Alfred Noyes (1880-1959) made his first of three visits to Toronto in 1914. On April 3 of that year he spoke to the Canadian Club in the afternoon, and then lectured in Burwash Hall on "Poetry and Peace" in the evening. Noyes was a fervid anti-Modernist in most matters, including art, and his remarks were warmly welcomed by the conservative audience. The *Star* journalist reporting on the event (over several column inches) noted this among Noyes's *bon mots*: "The four greatest words of poetry ever written were 'In the beginning, God.' It is not an advantage, said Noyes, to substitute the words *life force* for *God*, or even the words *Bernard Shaw*."

Poet and music critic Ronald Hambleton (b.1917) lived at **No.67** from January 1945 to May 1948 during which time he started the nine-inch by six-inch magazine *Reading*, described by periodical historian Fraser Sutherland as "an early, worthwhile attempt at a magazine of arts criticism." Hambleton had just been fired from Maclean Hunter for having dared to recommend a Jew for a job at the magazine where he worked. Financially, the dismissal was awkward for him, as he would later explain in his autobiography: "It was spring, 1945. Our son was then six months old, and we had just bought a ten-roomed house on Charles Street West for five thousand dollars with five hundred of it borrowed from an aunt for down payment, and I had already signed a contract for the decorating of the huge living room; the rough alterations I had done myself.

"The house had been a rabbit warren of a rooming house, but by agreement we allowed the third-floor tenant, Madge Parkhill, to stay when she pleaded with a tear in her eye and an extra five dollars in her rent envelope that raised her legally-frozen rent of twenty-five dollars a month to an illegal black market under-the-counter inflated rent of thirty. How was I to know that twenty years later while I was doing my research on the hidden life of Mazo de la Roche, it would come to light that Miss Parkhill had been an office-mate of Mazo de la Roche's cousin, and was to give me many important leads?

"Our other tenant, until we sold the house to Walter Yarwood, one of Painters Eleven, was Len Peterson who moved in the fall and whose typewriter resounded through the house sometimes more than twenty-four hours a day, or so it seemed.

"With a house that size, often permeated—to use a phrase of Robertson Davies—with the 'faint, contemptuous smell of coal-gas,' and needing much renovation, I could not be without work for long. Without hesitation, I flung myself once again into harness, by presenting myself to Mark Napier, Creative Head of the J. Walter Thompson Company, advertising agents.

"I doubt that my lack of vocation would have meant dismissal if it had not been for the literary magazine *Reading*, founded early in 1946 by Allan Anderson, then with the Wartime Prices & Trade Board; Lister Sinclair; and myself. Our idea was to cover all aspects of the writing field, with new poetry, fiction, and criticism; and regular monthly departments called 'Reading about Books,' 'Reading about Radio,' and so on. The publication office was our front room at **67 Charles Street West**, and on the mast-head the names of the three editors rotated each month. The magazine lasted just long enough to use up the three editors.

"In the year following the war, there were many shortages, including paper, hence the first issue was delayed a month while we scrambled around for something to print it on. At last, Everready Printers 'remembered' that they had some paper in their basement. As Sinclair wrote in our first editorial, 'We need not catalogue in detail our humiliating descent from Eggshell paper (as originally planned) through English Finish, S. C. Book, Novel News and many others down to Economy Book which as you can see for yourself is precariously balanced on the thin border line that divides paper from raw wood pulp. How anyone, even a printer, could forget that he had a ton of the most precious material in the world lying in his shop . . .! We snatched it up. As you can see, it is not by any means Eggshell; it is scarcely even paper, but it serves its purpose . . .'

"Most of the elegant literary duties were shared amongst us, though Alice Sinclair acted as Business Manager, and I also took on the job of production and advertising salesman. Most publishers I approached for ads were quite ready to help.

"The first issue contained new work by P. K. Page, Earle Birney, Raymond Souster, Robert Greer, Morley Callaghan, A. J. M. Smith, Fletcher Markle, G. B. Harrison, Len Peterson, Mavor Moore, and Gerald Noxon. Succeeding issues were no less studded with names well-known today in the writing field: Pierre Berton, Eric Nichol, R. S. Lambert, Ralph Gustafson, and Anne Wilkinson (whom we, like so many others, claim to have 'discovered.' It is a fact that we were the first to publish her gnomic verse).

"As for the authors writing in our monthly departments, only Earle Birney writing from Vancouver spotted anything odd about their names, which were all taken from the English folk song "Widdicome Fair." We had contributions from Jan Stewer, William Brewer, and Peter Gurney, while holding in reserve Peter Davy, Daniel Whiddon, Harry Hawke and Uncle Tom Cobbleigh!

"In the April issue, which appeared of course in March (unlike the January issue, which appeared in February) I, writing as William Brewer, wrote a severe criticism headed 'What's Wrong with Commercial Radio?' The identities of our house names were not top secret, but they were not generally known; yet Mark Napier immediately tagged me as William Brewer. When he was firing me, the first thing he said was 'You mustn't think it's because of your connection with *Reading*.' Naturally that became exactly what I did think, and I was probably right . . . The name *Reading* was suggested by Fletcher Markle. When by late April it seemed certain that we could not afford to keep going, he suggested we re-name the magazine 'Folding,' because fold it did, when we tried to become too big too fast, or at all. A clever-sounding man whose name I have wiped from my memory approached us one day with what seemed to be a firm offer to buy the name *Reading* from us for ten thousand dollars. We would have taken five! . . . Hundred! Blinded by the notion that we were worth money, we took the suggestion of a magazine promoter to print not our usual 500 copies, but several thousand, less than which the distributing company he represented would not handle from coast to coast. It did in fact appear on newsstands. Simpson's even featured the magazine on their back-page advertisement in all three newspapers, and stocked the magazine on their racks in a prominent place, but John Porter, of the advertising department, who had encouraged us by giving way to my per-

suasion, told me that they had never before had such a poor response to any product pictured for sale. The returns came in like the tide at Fundy.

"We had resolved from the outset to pay all our contributors, a policy then unheard of among literary magazines, our rates being equal to those paid by *Maclean's* magazine, roughly four cents a word, and fifty cents a line for poetry. All contributors were, however, invited to forgo payment, as an extra contribution to the magazine, and some did. When *Reading* turned into 'Folding,' we paid all contributors, and refunded money to subscribers, some of whom sent it back.

"The three founders had to bear the financial loss, $475.24 each. For me, it was the equivalent of two months salary from J. Walter Thompson, which of course I was not to receive any more following my dismissal."

Before he lived on Charles, Hambleton lived for about a year at **4 St. Thomas Street** which intersects near this point. Actor and playwright Tommy Tweed (1908-71) resided briefly at **No.6**, but our main goal on this small thoroughfare is **No.22**, which began life as the Windsor Arms Hotel. One of its most famous literary residents was the great biographer and Henry James expert Leon Edel (1907-97), a man usually associated with Montreal, not Toronto, in his connection with Canada. Yet he had been paying frequent visits to the city from his youth, and, then he actually lived here: "I have had three periods of residence in Toronto—not prolonged but sufficient to give me an in-depth sense of its life and manners.

"In 1939 I took a job with the Canadian Press (I had been in journalism all through the Depression) and J.F.B. Livesay, the Canpress head, stipulated that I spend some time in Toronto before starting work in the New York Bureau. I arrived in Toronto January 1 and stayed into the spring when I went to Montreal for a stint there. I knew Toronto before that having had various weekends with friends during the years I lived in Montreal. You are probably too young to have a picture in your mind of the old and effaced Toronto—those silent muffled Sundays when the view of Bloor during a blizzard from my window at the Windsor Arms (which has since been remodelled into its present state) was like one of Morrice's paintings of old Canada. I had many friends and a lively time in the journalistic and CBC world. But with my literary writings and academic connections I also saw much of the scholarly and writing part of Toronto —E.K. Brown in particular and through him met E.J. Pratt and others. Callaghan I had known during 'that summer' in Paris—not very well; I was introduced to him by Buffy Glassco, then a young faun. In the long snow-filled evenings I did a lot of writing and worked on my edition of James's failed plays (published ten years later, after the war)."

Peregrine Acland (1891-1963), author of the remarkable WWI novel *All Else Is Folly*, had an apartment in the Windsor Arms in 1922. Grey Owl was a reluctant resident of the hotel. The producers of a 1937 documentary film on the pseudo-Indian, fed up with his drunken binges at the Ford Hotel when he came to Toronto to see rough footage and help with the editing, finally forced him to stay at the Windsor Arms in July because at that time it did not have a liquor licence.

Around the corner on **Bloor Street West**, just a few steps from the top of St. Thomas Street, were some authorial homes. At what was **207 Bloor West**, for example, Flora Macdonald Denison, the suffragette, writer, and mother of Merrill Denison, died in 1921 on a visit to a friend's house. The Colonnade at **131 Bloor West**, contains a number of attractive apartments in which at least four authors have resided. Novelist Joy Fielding (b.1945) made her home here from 1975-77. As she was arriving she may have seen novelist Sylvia Fraser leaving. Her dates at this address are 1965-75. In Penthouse 9 Fraser wrote her first novel *Pandora* (1972) and another novel, *The Candy Factory* (1975). Poet George Jonas (b.1935)

lived here too in the 1970s, while poet Ronald Hambleton lived here in the late 1980s.

113 Bloor Street West was where Sir James David Edgar (1841-99) had his home from 1878 until he died. His death was the major news story on the front pages of all Toronto dailies, not because he was a published poet but because he was Speaker of the House when he passed away—although all of the obituaries did highlight his literary career. His son Pelham (1871-1948) lived here until his marriage in late 1893, after which he went on to become one of the most popular teachers of English in the history of Victoria College, and friend and supporter of several Canadian authors of note. In his memoir, Pelham Edgar described his years at this address, and in so doing describes a scene almost shocking in its difference from what prevails today: "Between our house and Avenue Road there were no buildings on the south side of Bloor Street and lower Queen's Park was equally unencumbered. We could pitch our [cricket] wickets where we would and the bumpiness of the crease was accepted as a law of nature . . . In winter we would bob-sleigh from the top of the St. Mary Street hill to St. Alban's [Wellesley] Street, and a few years later a toboggan slide was reared high on the hill where Victoria College now stands, which gave a free run to Bloor Street. So light was street traffic in those days that if we wished to venture further afield we could take our bob-sleighs to the top of the Avenue Road hill and have a run down to the CPR tracks, or better still to Gunther's hill and swing down the present Poplar Plains Road, with small risk of encountering pedestrians or horsedrawn traffic on the way."

Morley Callaghan told a lovely story about himself and Hemingway in late 1923 or early 1924 walking along these blocks. The anecdote deserves retelling here. "I remember our last conversation before he went away. When we met in the afternoon, he asked me if I had a copy of his *Three Stories and Ten Poems*.

I hadn't. At that time there was a little book-store at Bay and Bloor Streets where Hem-ingway had left some copies. 'Let's walk up there,' he said. It was a long walk and we loafed along slowly, absorbed in our conver-sation. I remember we were talking about the great Russian Dostoyevsky, and I said, 'The way he writes—it's like a forest fire. It sweeps indiscriminately over everything.'

"'That's pretty good,' he said, ponder-ing. Then he stopped on the street. 'You know Harry Greb,' he said, referring to the wonderful middleweight champion with the windmill style. 'Well, Dostoyevsky writes like Harry Greb fights,' he said. 'He swarms all over you. Like this.' And there on the street he started shadow boxing.

"We got his little book from the book-shop, then walked over to Yonge and Bloor for a coffee. He wrote in the book, 'To Callaghan, with best luck and predictions,' and while he was doing it I said wryly that now he was going away it looked as if I was losing my reading public of one—him. 'No,' he said. 'Remember this. There are always four or five people in the world who are interested in good new writing. Some mag-azines are starting up in Paris,' and he sounded like a bishop and again I believed I only needed to wait."

"On his last day at the *Star*, I went down to the *Weekly* and walked in boldly to say goodbye to him. I remember he was sitting with the three top writers of the *Star Weekly*: Greg Clark who was his friend, Charlie Vining and Fred Griffin. As I approached Hemingway to say goodbye, these three men looked at me in surprise for they didn't even know me.

"'Write and let me know how you're doing and as soon as you get anything done shoot it to Paris,' he said. 'I'll tell them about you.'

"'I've got your address.'

"'Care of the Guaranty Trust. That's right.'

"As I shook hands with him my face was burning for I knew the others were looking at me in some wonder."

Returning to St. Thomas Street, which crosses an even smaller **Sultan Street**, nov-elist, critic, and *animateur* Augustus Bridle (1869-1952) roomed at **No.16** while a reporter for the *News*.

Toronto poet Bernard Freeman Trotter (1890-1917) was killed in action in France in WWI. Only 26 when he died, his poems were gathered and published posthumously. His father taught at McMaster University when it was located on Bloor Street West. Trotter had just enrolled at the UofT when he joined the call to arms. Earlier (1893-95) he had spent his boyhood at **66 Charles Street West.**

James Bain (1842-1908) has been called the Father of Canadiana, and he is worthy of the title. He came from Scotland to Toronto in 1846 with his parents, because his father had been hired to manage the Hugh Scobie bookshop. Ten years later the father opened his own bookstore and Bain dropped out of school to learn the business in his father's employ. After working for a number of book firms in Toronto and London, Bain applied to be Toronto's first public librari-an when the City decided in 1882 to inau-gurate a free public library—the first city in Canada to do so (up to that time the Mech-anics' Institutes fulfilled most library func-tions). Two other competitors for the post were authors we shall meet throughout this *Guide*: Graeme Mercer Adam and John Charles Dent. Bain won the job, although there must have been many days when he wondered why he bothered. A century ago, the city fathers starved the library for funds, and one year the board actually had to sue the city for its operating monies. Bain, intent on creating more branches, constructing a main reference library, and building a collection of Canadian documents and books, grew tired of the excuses from philistine local politicians and instead approached Andrew Carnegie for money. Carnegie, a fellow Scottish immigrant, was philanthropic with some of his wealth, and focused his dona-tions on temples to music and the construction of libraries (he donated to over 2,800 before he died). It is thanks to Carnegie, for example, that the Central Reference Library at College and St. George was erected in 1909. You will note from his dates, alas, that Bain did not live to see the opening of that building. But he did have the satisfaction of knowing that, via extraordinary sleuthing and dogged digging, he had compiled one of the greatest collections of early Canadian documents in the country, and a collection of Canadian literature that was the envy of every library in the land. Historian Donald Jones offered another reason that contributed to the size and importance of the collection: "To a large extent, it was because of their admiration for him that so many celebrated families of old Toronto decided to donate their family papers to his library. The Baldwin family, in particular, were so generous with their gifts that the library eventually named its principal collection of rare books and early Canadiana 'The Baldwin Room'." When Bain was first hired by the City to be its first Librarian, he moved to **No.59 Charles Street West** and remained here until 1885.

Near **1170 Bay Street**, just south of Bloor, stood the majestic Margaret Eaton School of Literature and Expression. Opened in 1907, it was called "the most beautiful public building in the city of Toronto." The school was the brainchild of a single woman, Mrs. Emma Scott Raff, a teacher at Victoria College who believed at the turn of the century that more attention should be given to the role of the spoken word in education, that such attention would enhance the mental and physical health of girls and augment their artistic sensibilities. Her zeal attracted many supporters and students, and, soon after establishing her school in 1901, she found she needed enlarged facilities. Timothy Eaton agreed to be her patron, and in return for funding the purchase of land and construction of a new school at this address, the enterprise was renamed in honour of his wife. Given its pedagogic orienta-

tion, we should not be surprised that the recital theatre was one of the most attractive rooms in an already handsomely appointed edifice. The space turned out to be pivotal. *The Oxford Companion to Canadian Theatre* dates the beginning of the little theatre movement in Toronto to Mrs. Scott Raff's productions of Celtic Renaissance plays here. As well, it was used for readings and talks by noted visiting authors, most notably William Butler Yeats (1865-1939). Yeats spoke here on Friday, February 13, 1914, during the second of what would ultimately be four trips to Toronto. All of the daily newspapers gave the visit extensive coverage. The *Star* reporter noted "Mr. Yeats is tall, slim and slightly stooped. The pallor of a thin refined face is enhanced by a heavy mop of straight black hair, streaked here and there with grey. Deep set, dark eyes look out from behind almost invisible eyeglasses. Finely cut sensitive lips alternately smile and set themselves. He spoke in a rich musical chant, intoning his phrases like a high priest, and, moving his thin, finely shaped hand with long listless fingers like the conductor of an orchestra, to the rhythm of his sentences. And yet he claimed to be an unemotional, analytical, pitiless observant artist. His address was ostensibly 'The Theatre and Beauty' but it was not long before he was launched on a discussion of the underlying questions of beauty and art." The *World* described the audience as "representative of Toronto's highest scholastic culture" and "distinguished."

Across the street is the entrance to the flagship store of Indigo Books and Music, although the official address is **55 Bloor Street West**. The store plays host to author events in several disciplines, including occasional readings by poets and fiction writers. The café in the Indigo store itself has become a popular spot for meeting fellow booklovers. The store encourages customers to browse, have a coffee, and peruse books and magazines at their leisure.

Albert E.S. Smythe (1861-1947) lived in a house approximately near what is today

1132 Bay Street from 1897 to 1904. At this time, he was heavily involved in fostering Theosophy in Toronto and in furthering his journalism career. Later, he would become one of the best-known newspapermen in Canada, and serious critics would call him one of the best poets in the nation.

The address of **44 Charles Street West**, if not the building, has been home to three authors. Fiction writer Beaumont Cornell (1892-1958) was here in 1913, the same house where Montreal novelist Trevor Ferguson (b.1947) lived when he discovered the joys of literature: "I lived in the city from September 1964 to March 1965. For part of that time I worked as an usher at the Royal Alexandra Theatre (in footman's clothes; I turned seventeen that winter) and for all of that time I spent every evening at the Bohemian Embassy on St. Nicholas Street. I was living at **44 Charles St. West**, which is an affluent monolith today, but at the time was one of a row of rooming houses ($8.00 a week). When I quit the Royal Alex, even that rent became untenable, and I moved into the Embassy gratis, and later into a house on Davenport, also gratis, a few doors west of Spadina. I lived in the basement of a house shared by UofT students whose sensibilities had been mortified by someone living on the street. So they gave me a home and I remain grateful.

"I was too young to be writing publishable manuscripts, but I was writing. Impressed by Al Purdy-adjudicated readings at the Embassy, I explored poetry, but stuck to prose. That winter was pivotal for I relinquished picking guitar for a greater passion and one that I have not put down: writing fiction. Departed for the northwest both to earn an honest living while developing as a writer, and as a reaction against literary groupings."

After his heart attack in 1973, poet Earle Birney (1904-95) returned to Toronto and lived for a few weeks at the Andorra Hotel on Charles Street East before moving into apt. 921, belonging to his final companion, Wailan Low, at **30 Charles Street West**. The unit was too small for two people, so they moved to Alexander Street in September.

St. Nicholas Street terminates near here. **No.85** was the first home of A-Space, an artists' co-op founded in 1970. In 1974, poet Victor Coleman (b.1944) assumed control of the literary program and quickly made A-Space *the* place for readings, especially by authors interested in sound and concrete poetry or in alternative means of literary expression. The building still stands, although now converted to other uses. The ground floor was a wonderful counter-culture café whose profits were used to subsidize the arts activities focused on the second-floor loft-like gallery and reading area. The list of authors who read here between 1974 and 1978 is impressive by any standard and simply remarkable for such a short period of operation. In the history of the city the A-Space readings under Coleman's aegis have been surpassed in number only by the UofT and Harbourfront. A-Space continues to operate as a multi-faceted gallery, but once Coleman left, the literary whoosh went out of its sails. Authors who read here include:

Kathy Acker
Robert Amos
Michael Andre
Rafael Barreto-Rivera
Wade Bell
Bill Berkson
bill bissett
Robin Blaser
E.D. Blodgett
George Bowering
David Bromige
A.A. Bronson
Nicole Brossard
William S. Burroughs
Penny Chalmers (Penn Kemp)
Paul Chamberland
Henri Chopin
Bob Cobbing
Victor Coleman
Robert Creeley
Gary Michael Dault

Frank Davey
Fielding Dawson
Constance de Jong
Christopher Dewdney
Pier Giorgio Di Cicco
Edward Dorn
Raoul Duguay
Robert Duncan
Paul Dutton
Brian Fawcett
Robert Fones
Four Horsemen
Maxine Gadd
Dwight Gardiner
Eldon Garnet
General Idea
Gerry Gilbert
John Giorno
Artie Gold
Bill Griffiths
Joan Haggerty
ASA Harrison
Bobbie-Louise Hawkins
William Hawkins
Bernard Heidsieck
Kati Hewko
Dick Higgins
Gladys Hindmarch
David Hlynsky
Michael Hollingsworth
Chris Hurst
Bill Hutton
Hans Jewinski
George Johnston
D.G. Jones
Hugh Kenner
Valerie Kent
Crad Kilodney
Roy Kiyooka
August Kleinzahler
Pat Lowther
Daphne Marlatt
John Bentley Mays
Toby MacLennan
Steve McCaffery
David McFadden
Wayne McNeil
Thomas Meyer

Opal L. Nations
Al Neil
bp Nichol
Michael Ondaatje
Joel Oppenheimer
O(we)n So(u)nd
Robert Sward
David UU
Tom Vietch
Fred Wah
Anne Waldman
Darien Watson
Lewis Warsh
John Wieners
Jonathan Williams
Douglas Woolf
David Young

The Rendezvous Bookshop was located near the junction of Charles Street West and Yonge, at **734 Yonge Street**. The store had no particular literary significance—except for one author who worked there: Jane Urquhart (b.1949). She told me, "I discovered poetry in two places. The first was the old Central Library on College Street where I sometimes went to avoid school. The second was the Rendezvous Bookshop on Yonge Street just below Bloor where I worked as a part-time clerk when I was sixteen and seventeen. The latter carried a tiny selection of small press titles and I would sometimes purchase one or two volumes with my take-home pay which was, I believe, about ten dollars a week. I was occasionally sent on errands to the old Book Cellar on Bay Street and there I was able to glimpse some of the *Poets Themselves*. I was, of course, myself writing secretly but would never have had the nerve to bring this fact to anyone's attention."

No doubt an occasional customer in the store (whom Urquhart may have even served without knowing him) was the playwright John Herbert (b.1926) whose apartment was the entire third floor of **730 Yonge Street** from 1965-67. It was in this loft-like space that he wrote his most famous play, *Fortune and Men's Eyes*.

Adeline Teskey (d.1924) wrote several novels that were popular in her day. She is usually regarded as a Welland author, but a combination of epilepsy and strokes left her health so fragile that she spent the last twelve years of her life in an infirmary at **21 St. Mary Street**. Across the street at **No.22**, the man of letters B.K. Sandwell had lodgings in 1890. Coleridge scholar Kathleen Coburn lived at the same address from 1941-54.

The world-renowned Hungarian poet George Faludy moved to Toronto in 1967 but did not settle into apt. 1608 at **25 St. Mary Street** until 1975. He remained here until he returned to his native country in 1989. While ensconced here he wrote a number of books including at least three collections of poetry in English translation: *East and West* (1978), *Learn This Poem of Mine By Heart* (1983), and *Selected Poems* (1985). He also wrote *Letters to Posterity* (1978) in Hungarian, and had the pleasure of seeing his *Collected Works* appear in Hungarian in 1980. Playwright Ken Gass (b.1945) had an apartment in this same building from 1968-69. Apt. 1901 was the home of Phil Murphy (b.1925), author of the novel *Summer Island* (1984), a fictional recreation of his boyhood on Ward's Island.

Dramatist Dora Conover (1897-1985), whose plays were produced at Hart House with some regularity before it abandoned professional productions for students, lived at **No.68** for half a decade (1923-28). As an undergraduate from 1960-61, poet Dennis Lee had a room in Stephenson House at **No.80**.

Elmsley Hall, part of St. Michael's College, at **No.81**, has hosted visits by some remarkable authors. On February 10, 1971, for example, the Canadian Seminar in Irish Studies managed to gather W.H. Auden, Buckminster Fuller, and Marshall McLuhan onto the same panel to open their public conference. Noted Yeats biographer Norman Jeffares was moderator. The next afternoon at three o'clock Auden read to about 600 people under absurd circumstances in the same building: the microphone failed to work properly and no one bothered to close the doors, so students changing classes noisily and constantly interrupted the reading. Despite these hazards, auditors of the reading say it was deeply moving.

Renowned Irish playwright and literary biographer Denis Johnston (1901-84) made two visits to Toronto, the first in 1970 to give a public lecture devoted to other Irish playwrights and their witticisms. In that lecture he presciently predicted that Brian Friel would prove to be the best playwright of the next generation in Ireland.

Writers who were students at the University of St. Michael's College (as it is known officially) include:

Barry Callaghan
Morley Callaghan
Hugh Hood
David Manicom
Philip Marchand
Thomas O'Hagan
Frank Paci
James Powell
Christine Slater
John Sutherland

Among the literati who taught here, the most famous, of course, is Marshall McLuhan (1911-80). He joined the faculty in 1946, partly because of the presence of Etienne Gilson, the French philosopher, from whom McLuhan still hoped to learn much and because "he planned to start a magazine, recognizing that it 'might function well in Toronto by reason of the very hostility of the environment.'" McLuhan remained on the faculty until the year before he died. His first home was on St. Joseph Street, but in the fall of 1951, with an expanding family, he moved to a larger home, since razed, at **81 St. Mary Street**, and stayed here until 1955. As his biographer Terrence Gordon has noted, "Across the road, the yellow brick wall of St. Michael's College playing field stretched to the western end of the street, stopping beside the only house on the south side—No.81. This

Left to right: John McGoren, W. H. Auden, A.N. Jeffares, Buckminster Fuller, Marshall McLuhan formerly opened the seminar in Celtic Studies at St. Michael's College, February 10, 1971

situation allowed McLuhan to boast with a measure of truth that his family was installed in a large house with two acres of land in downtown Toronto."

Walking south on Bay Street to get to the south side of the St. Michael's campus, we pass **Irwin Avenue.** Playwright Michael Hollingsworth (b.1950) lived in the ground-floor apartment at **No.43** from 1974 to 1977. It was while living here that he recovered from the trauma of having seen his play *Clear Light* (1973) busted by the Morality Squad on the grounds of alleged obscenity, one of the last, ludicrous gasps of the old stuffy Toronto to suppress any artistic expression that wasn't conventional. More importantly, it was also here that Hollingsworth began to experiment with a theatrical amalgam of text, video, and music which have almost become his trademark. Out of these experiments, he formed Video Cabaret International, and at various theatres in Toronto, most recently with Factory, has used these techniques in his grand project of Canadian history plays, known collectively as *The History of the Village of Small Huts.*

13 Irwin was the home for three years of writer Flora MacDonald Denison (1867-1921) and her better-known son Merrill Denison (1893-1975) at the turn of the century. Not long after her arrival in Toronto as a young woman, Flora worked in the women's fashion department of Simpson's, a job that brought her into regular contact with the fashion sweatshops on Spadina Avenue. Appalled by the treatment of women in these places, her labour education accelerated and her activism quickened. She quit Simpson's to run her own very successful dress and seamstress shop yet found time in the same period to work with Dr. Augusta Stowe-Gullen and others to form the Canadian Women's Suffrage Association of which she eventually became president. Earlier, she had written a novel, based on the life of her sister, a psychic; the paranormal was a lifelong interest of Flora. And she wrote a regular column on labour matters for the *World,* one of—if not the first—in Toronto devoted to that topic. You get an idea of her fire and determination when you learn that she moved temporarily to Detroit to give birth to her son solely as a protest against Ontario's refusal to educate women as doctors, much less as obstetricians (women doctors were legal in Michigan). She was a devout admirer of Walt Whitman, and at her summer home in Bon Echo she attracted others who strove to live what they perceived as Whitmanesque ideals. This, in turn, led her to a belief in Theosophy, a belief shared by dozens of the leading Toronto visual artists and writers of the first half of the 20th c., most of whom happily spent time in the natural splendour of Bon Echo. She had lines from Whitman's poem *Song of Myself* carved into a huge granite cliff-face on the property. At her death, the Bon Echo estate passed to Merrill, who gave the property to the Province of Ontario in 1959 for use as a provincial park. Merrill Denison is generally regarded as the first important playwright of the 20th c. in English-Canada.

8 St. Joseph Street is certainly worthy of a pause and minute's contemplation, for it was here that one of the most famous novels set in Toronto was written. Its author, Hugh Garner (1913-79), explained in his autobiography how he, just returned from WWII, came to write: "Just before New Year's, 1946, I rented a room in a rooming house on Toronto's St. Joseph Street, and bought myself notepaper, a fountain pen (there were no ballpoints then), and a pencil. I didn't buy myself the most necessary tool of all, an eraser, nor did I own either a dictionary or a Roget's Thesaurus. I also signed up with the Department of Veterans Affairs for a three-month course in Co-operative Management. The course would give both myself and my wife a small income during the winter, would give me the time on evenings and weekends to write a novel, and it seemed right up my alley after managing a co-operative grocery store seven years before.

"On New Year's Day, 1946, I printed with my fountain pen the title, *Cabbagetown*, at the head of a blank sheet of notepaper,

and under it, 'By Hugh Garner.' The book I began to write that day was to become a veritable monkey on my back for the next four years.

"I decided to write a partially autobiographical novel, in the third person, using as my protagonist a boy and young man my own age, and beginning it the day he left the East End technical high school on his sixteenth birthday. Though I hadn't been living in Cabbagetown myself while attending high school, but in the Riverdale district across the Don River, I had remained quite close to the people of Cabbagetown, having prewar male friends who lived there, and going out with Cabbagetown girls. Our gang during the years 1936 to 1939 had hung around in Riverdale Park, which straddles the Don River and separates Cabbagetown and the district north of it from Riverdale to the East, and half the gang lived on Cabbagetown and Moss Park streets while the other half, including myself, lived in Riverdale.

"I sensed too that 'Cabbagetown' was a more colourful name for a neighbourhood than Riverdale; it was still a collection of slum streets as it had been during my childhood when I did live in it, and was much the better title for a novel.

"I did two things during the next three months: I wrote an eight hundred page hand-printed novel, and took off forty pounds of fat I'd acquired in the navy and in drinking up my ninety days' leave pay and my war service gratuities after being discharged from the navy the previous October. During the three months while I wrote the book I did no drinking at all, for I never do when I'm writing. I wrote a chapter every evening in pencil after deciding to make my chapters fifteen pages long, and on weekends I corrected the previous week's work in ink . . . My protagonist, Ken Tilling, lived on a street I lived on as a small boy, Wascana Avenue. He shared some of the jobs I had held at his age, took some of the boxcar trips to Western Canada that I had taken, hung around with a gang in Riverdale Park, and finally went off to fight in Spain in 1937. I made him about my size, gave him my personality, but that was all. Other than that he is a fictional figure. His alcoholic mother is completely fictional (my own mother never took a drink in her whole life), his girl friend Myrla Patson is also completely fictional, as are all the other characters in the novel. Incidentally, and to answer once and for all a question about Myrla I am sometimes asked, I never knew a girl from Cabbagetown who became a prostitute, though no doubt there were some, as there are girls who go into prostitution from all city neighbourhoods and not only slums.

"Ernest Hemingway once said that the best parts of his books were the parts he had made up himself, and not the true parts. I believe this is true, and though 'truth may be stranger than fiction' it's not half as interesting.

"*Cabbagetown* and the Co-operative Management course both came to an end in late March, 1946. I read an ad in the Employment Wanted column of a newspaper placed there by a North Toronto housewife who wanted to take on typing jobs at home. I called her up, told her I had a book manuscript which needed typing, and she and her husband came down to see me. We came to an agreement on fee, $65, which was a good bit of money in those days."

As Garner's biographer, Paul Stuewe, has noted, the determination he first showed at **No.8** not to drink while yet writing ferociously "established a pattern Garner would, with few deviations, follow for the remainder of his writing career. Although he discovered that he could write journalistic pieces and commercially oriented short stories while indulging his usual moderate to heavy drinking habits, his more serious fiction was written during rigidly enforced periods of almost complete abstinence."

Around the corner from 8 St. Joseph is **630 Yonge Street**, the first location of a legendary bookshop called Longhouse. The store was founded in 1972 by two women, Beth Appeldoorn and Susan Sandler, who shared a deep affection for, and commitment to, Canadian books and authors. At a time when most observers thought it was madness to base a business solely on the sale of Canadian titles, these women believed that the business could only grow. The back room of the shop became a favourite spot for authors to visit, and professionals in the book trade were always assured of a cup of coffee, an informative chat, and the chance usually to meet others, including prominent authors, who had also dropped in for a quick visit. The store was a success from its first day, and one reason for that success was the wise decision to create a mail-order business for CanLit. Universities and others around the world who were discovering Canadian writers found it trying and sometimes impossible to obtain books from Canadian publishers, so Longhouse stepped in and almost singlehandedly met the needs of the foreign buyers—indeed, played a role in educating those buyers about new authors and new books. The shop moved to new premises at **626 Yonge** in 1984. Appeldoorn and Sandler sold the business in 1988 to bookseller John Sime. He moved the shop to the Annex, 497 Bloor Street West, where it, sadly, petered out of existence in 1995.

St. Nicholas Street crosses near here. A few steps south (before returning to St. Joseph Street) will bring you to **7 St. Nicholas Street**, home of the legendary Bohemian Embassy from 1960-66. The coffee house was started by television comedian Don Cullen and operated seven nights a week. Located over a garage, it was reached by a narrow flight of stairs that opened onto a brick-walled box that could house, in a pinch, up to 120 people. To circumvent Toronto's strict by-laws regarding restaurants, Cullen called the Embassy a social club: he charged a yearly membership of fifty cents and a separate admission for each event after that. The police always suspected that the site was a den of drugs, sex-crazed beatniks, and most invidiously of all, espresso coffee—a dead giveaway to its commie, subversive, white-slave leanings. Folksingers such as Ian Tyson and Sylvia Fricker were regulars at the club, but with the passing of time, its greatest claim to fame remains the authors who were regularly attracted by its literary collegiality—and to its poetry readings, either as audience or as reader: Milton Acorn, Margaret Atwood, David Donnell, Gwendolyn MacEwen, Padraig O Broin, Al Purdy, Joe Rosenblatt, Phyllis Webb, Ian Young and sean o'huigin (then known as John Higgins he doubled as the daytime caretaker). Cullen hired other poets to manage the literary program and choose a writer who would headline the weekly poetry night, although an open mike followed every headline reading. Victor Coleman ran the program for about a year, as did George Miller. John Robert Colombo assumed these duties in the Embassy's last years on St. Nicholas Street (and re-assumed them when the club was re-born in 1974 at Harbourfront). He summed up the original Embassy's importance to poetry by declaring, "It was also a force that led to the formation of a listening public."

Novelist Hugh Hood (b.1928) shared a basement apartment at **22 St. Joseph Street** from 1951-53. From 1875-77 **No.36** was the home of Sir James David Edgar (1841-99) and his son, Pelham (1871-1948). The latter we have encountered many times in this *Guide* as one of the most influential professors of English ever at the UofT and an important advocate of Canadian authors to Canadians. His father is not so well known, but deserves some notice. He was elected to the House of Commons on several occasions, was chief Liberal Party whip during the Canadian Pacific Scandal, and most famously was Speaker of the House from 1896 until he died. But he is cited here because his literary work is too often ignored. In 1863, he was the president of the Ontario Literary Society, a sadly understudied organization which brought to

Toronto to lecture some of the biggest names of mid-Victorian, North American letters, including Ralph Waldo Emerson (three times), Thomas D'Arcy McGee, Artemus Ward, and Bayard Taylor. While in Parliament he led the ongoing battle for copyright protection of Canadian authors. And he published books of poetry: *The White Stone Canoe: A Legend of the Ottawa* (1885) and *This Canada of Ours and Other Poems* (1893); the title poem was written to honour Confederation. While living at this address, he continued to write poetry, and served as the chief backroom strategist in Toronto for Prime Minister Alexander Mackenzie's Liberal government.

When Marshall McLuhan first came to Toronto in 1946 to teach at St. Michael's College, he availed himself of the faculty housing and settled with his family into **91 St. Joseph Street**, just a short walk from his office. McLuhan stayed in this house until the fall of 1951. One of the few plaques in Toronto dedicated to a literary figure was unveiled by the Historical Board in 1990; it stands outside what was McLuhan's office for several years at **No.96**. At the time, he was still trying to find a publisher for his non-traditional cultural criticism. Another famous literary critic, Hugh Kenner, lived with the McLuhans at this address for the summers of 1947 and 1948.

If the lines "I think that I shall never see/ A poem lovely as a tree" are among your favourites, you will want to note that their author, Joyce Kilmer, made his only appearance in Toronto near here. On February 25, 1916, Kilmer (1886-1918) gave a public reading of his work in the auditorium of St. Joseph's College, then located in the block surrounded by Wellesley, Bay, Grosvenor, and Queen's Park Crescent East. The official address at the time was at 89 St. Alban's Street. The College grounds and buildings were sold *en masse* to the Ontario government and the Macdonald block and other massively undistinguished provincial buildings now sit on the site. The name "St. Alban's Street" was changed to "Wellesley Street West," although the proper street address of the Macdonald block is **900 Bay Street**.

Just to the south of where St. Joseph's used to sit, tiny **Breadalbane Street** culminates at Bay Street. Three authors have called **89 Breadalbane** home. Poet Robert Finch (1900-95) lived here from 1958-63. Another talented poet and translator, Kenneth McRobbie (b.1929), during his short residency in Toronto (1959-60), kept a room in this building. And when Lister Sinclair (b.1921) first came to Toronto in 1942 to pursue grad studies in Math at the UofT, he lived in apt. 503 for about a year, and then, after he was married, he lived in apt. 406 until 1946. During this era he joined the CBC team being assembled by Andrew Allan in Toronto that would elevate radio drama to new heights. Initially, Sinclair only acted in these dramas, but he soon found writing original plays and adaptations very much to his liking. For some decades he was the host of the CBC radio program "Ideas."

On the west side of **Bay Street**, south of Breadalbane, the American novelist Willa Cather lived at the home of her best friend, Isabelle McClung, married to the famed violinist Jan Hambourg, whose family bestrode the Toronto music scene like a Colossus for the first half of the century. The official address was **38 St. Vincent Street**, one of the many smaller streets absorbed when the city chose to make **Bay Street** a fast thoroughfare for traffic (the little bends in Bay Street today are the only legacies of those former diminutive streets). The Hambourg home, were it standing, would be immediately south of the Mowat building, and would be numbered something akin to **880 Bay Street**.

Willa Cather (1873-1947) and Isabelle had been passionate friends when they lived in the USA, and Willa was devastated when Isabelle announced to her, without any forewarning, that she was about to marry an internationally acclaimed musician and move with him to Toronto. Eventually the two women reconciled, and Willa came to Toronto for a visit in October 1917 and stayed with the Hambourgs for about two weeks. She spent most of the summer of 1919 with them as well, but her longest stay was of five months: April to August 1921. During this last visit she finished her novel *One of Ours* (1922).

Unfortunately, Cather insisted in her will that her personal papers be destroyed or embargoed, so it is difficult to ascertain what else she wrote during her stays here. But it seems she enjoyed working in Toronto because she was anonymous—until Sinclair Lewis came to town. Lewis, believing he was paying Toronto—and Cather—a compliment, told his audience that he was proud to be appearing in the same town in which Willa Cather was currently resident. The next day, the press landed on the Hambourg doorstep and her picture (and presence in Toronto) were all over the front page of the *Star*. As one of her biographers noted, "it looked as if her life would be wrecked by dinner parties, luncheons, and teas. She finally convinced all the well-intentioned people that they could best show their interest in her work by letting her alone to write, and Isabelle came to her rescue to fend off the lion hunters so that she could get on with the novel." Although they had corresponded, it seems Lewis and Cather had never met until Toronto. She quickly forgave his *gaffe*, and they became lifelong friends. Critic E.K. Brown, who was living in Toronto during these years, wrote one of the first important book-length assessments of Cather. It is likely he also knew the Hambourgs, and it was Brown's opinion that "the time was to come when [Jan] Hambourg would sit for a not wholly unflattering portrait as Louie Marsellus in [Cather's novel] *The Professor's House*. Jan and Isabelle left Toronto to live in Europe shortly after Cather's final departure from the city.

It's possible that Hector Charlesworth tipped his hat to Miss Cather as he passed her on the street because his residence (at what would now be **832 Bay Street**) from 1904-21 overlapped with her extended visits to the Hambourgs. Charlesworth (1872-1945) was the first high-profile drama critic in the history of the city, writing theatre reviews for the both *Saturday Night* and the *World* in the 1890s. His move to this address in 1904 coincided with his appointment to the *M&E*, firstly as its leading arts commentator and then as the city editor until 1910. In that year he became associate editor of *Saturday Night* and was promoted editor in 1925. Silly people remember Charlesworth only for his ongoing feud with, and negative comments on, the Group of Seven. But whatever his error in assessing the worth of the Group, he was a sophisticated critic. He did what he could to help talented Canadian artists but did not shy from tempering the boosterism that crept into other's well-meaning but misguided estimates of Canadian talent. His many books of memoirs strike some literary historians as having little merit, but I find them unique, often amusing entrees to the mindset of Toronto artists and consumers from epochs long before our own. Hector Charlesworth lived at this address longer than at any other.

Grosvenor Street is only two blocks long but has been the address of half a dozen authors. When playwright and theatre administrator Tom Hendry (b.1929) moved to Toronto in 1951 he stayed in a rooming house at **No.12** for half a year while working for the British Book Service. Donald Jack (b.1924) has won the Leacock Medal for Humour three times—no one has won it more—and his novels about the rapscallion Bandy have huge followings. He was born in England, but as he explained to me: "I came to Canada in December 1951, and arrived in Toronto on December 4, 1951. The first place I lived in the city (after a few days in the Y on College Street along with hosts of other eager immigrants) was at **21 Grosvenor Street** north of College where I had an overheated bedsitter. It was my first taste of Canadian central heating, and boy did I love being cooked after living in unheated English and Scottish houses for 26 years. I'd expected to be frozen in freezing Canada; instead I was never so warm in my whole life.

"My first impressions of Toronto were rather a shock. When I emerged from Union Station that wet and muddy December morning I was astonished to find that the streets were made of wood. Good God, what kind of a city was this where Yonge Street, the main street, was made of wood. I was only slightly less reassured when I learned that the condition was temporary while they were building the Subway. But, shades of Muddy York. Rather more colourful was the experience of walking up that same Yonge Street and being stopped by a Swedish-accented lumberjack who flashed a roll of bills the same size as his horny hand and enquired the way to the nearest 'joy house'. (I gave him directions to the CNE.) But it was delightful. It was just the way I'd visualized Canada from all my mother's stories (she was born in PEI)."

Kathryn Colquhoun (1873-1952) was a poet, playwright, and journalist who was published in British, American, and Canadian anthologies of poetry. She was living at **No.30** in 1942. Writer Thomas O'Hagan (1855-1939) moved mysteriously in and out of town—and travelled the world—as though he were a spy. One of his last residences was **No.33** in 1937. The year before, the *Globe* ran a sad story detailing how O'Hagan had sat ignored and unknown at the closing banquet of the Book Fair in the King Edward Hotel. The room was filled with everybody who was anybody in writing and publishing in Toronto and "while the 350 lovers of books and literature were dining, Dr. O'Hagan arrived. For a time he sat in a far corner of the foyer. Men and women passed him by, said never a word. Finally, though, came Hugh S. Eayrs, executive member of the Association of Canadian Bookmen. He gave a friendly greeting, wanted to know if

O'Hagan wouldn't 'come in.' The O'Hagan face wrinkled in a smile. 'Why no thanks,' he said, 'I'll just sit upstairs to hear what's going on.' . . . All about him talk flowed on Scholar and *littérateur*, he was unrecognized." *Sic transit gloria mundi.*

The fine Imagist poet Eustace Ross (1894-1966), just returned in 1919 from fighting overseas, moved into rooms at **59 Grosvenor Street** and remained until 1924 by which time had begun his lifelong employ at the Dominion Magnetic Observatory in Agincourt. Another good poet, Robert Finch (1900-95), kept rooms at **No.78** from 1933-36 while he was teaching French at University College and writing poems that would see him win the Governor General's Award within a decade.

Grenville Street, one block south, although shorter than Grosvenor, has been home to even more writers. The final home (1896-98) of pioneer feminist author Sarah Anne Curzon (1833-98) was at **No.15**. Only in her last hours did she leave this address to stay with her son on Ulster Street where she died.

Painter and writer Wyndham Lewis (1882-1957) had his artist's studio at **22 Grenville Street** from November 1940 until June 1941. It was here that one of the few photographs of Lewis in Toronto was taken, showing him working on his commissioned portrait of J.S. McLean.

Patricia Joudry (b.1921) also lived at this address from c. 1947 to 1957 during which time she wrote many plays for CBC radio and television and her first plays for the stage, including *Teach Me How to Cry*, produced at Hart House in 1956, a production that won the Dominion Drama Festival prize for Best Canadian Play. Another important award was one she shared in 1957 with novelist Gabrielle Roy: The Woman of the Year Award in Literature and Art.

Lawren Harris and J.E.H. Macdonald were not the only famous painters to also publish their creative writing. Renowned wildlife artist Arthur Heming (1870-1940) published three books about our wilderness and its animals which he illustrated himself. Curiously, they were all published in the USA, not Canada. **No.64** was his home and studio for the first four years of the Depression. A *Star Weekly* profile describes how Heming lived and worked at this address: "Mr. Heming's studio-apartment in Toronto could well be taken as a pattern by the most meticulous housewife. There is a place for everything and everything is always in its place. Beyond that, it caters to comfort. There is nothing stiff about the place. The large book-lined studio shows the artistry of well-placed lamps—lamps made to his own order and which reveal to best advantage the beauty of his paintings . . . Other writers would do well to pattern themselves after Mr. Heming. Before writing a book he first skeletonizes it. For this he uses a large easel containing about half a hundred hooks. The hooks are in even rows and each is clearly numbered in rotation. Under each hook is a paper clasp, and as each numbered hook represents a chapter in the book-to-be, it is very obvious that the manuscript in each clasp was for the chapter corresponding to the number under which it was filed. Many of them were marked as complete. 'I always collect the material for my book first,' says Mr. Heming. 'I work chapter by chapter. All the information I want for each chapter is carefully sorted out and hung under its proper hook. Then, when I am all ready to write the book, I am all equipped and I can go straight ahead with it.'"

Poet James Reaney (b.1926) lived at **No.70** from 1947-49 during his final undergrad years at University College. Reaney cut quite a figure on campus, renowned for the singularity of his dress, for his ceaseless work as a creative writer, and for his involvement with extra-university endeavours such as major literary magazines and CBC book shows (younger readers may not be aware that there was a time when the CBC devoted entire programs to Canadian books and writers). In 1947 he also became famous for his short story "Box Social," whose publication in a university magazine caused such an uproar across the university that the controversy was reported on in the mainstream media. But it was his poems that gained him the highest reputation while he lived at **No.70**. They were published in most of the major magazines of the day, and, most amazingly of all, in 1949 he became one of the youngest winners ever of the Governor General's Award for his volume *The Red Heart*. When Reaney moved to take a job in Winnipeg, his room (and the seven dollars per month rent) were taken over by poet Colleen Thibaudeau (b.1925), who remained here until her wedding day, December 29,

1951. She married James Reaney. During her stay at this address she wrote poems, but sustained herself by working in the publicity dept. at McClelland and Stewart. Colleen maintains that she started working there on the same day that Jack McClelland did. Both she and Reaney were members of Norman Endicott's creative writing class at the UofT, a class that included Phyllis Gotlieb, Mort Forer, and Bob Mirvish.

Women's College Hospital at **No.76** was officially opened on February 22, 1936 by Governor General Lord Tweedsmuir (1875-1940), better known as John Buchan the novelist. Before it was a hospital, **No.76** was a rooming house and it housed poet Robert Finch (1900-95) for the years 1933-35.

Our final stop on this tour is **22 College Street** where once stood Foresters' Hall, the Toronto headquarters for the fraternal International Order of Foresters. During the 1920s and 1930s its auditorium was rented for literary events. Among the authors who gave public talks here were Ralph Bates, Stephen Leacock, John Cowper Powys, Patrick Slater, and Albert E.S. Smythe, and in 1922 it was the site of a major tribute to Norman Duncan.

James Reaney, Freshman, 1944, standing on front steps of University College

KENSINGTON MARKET

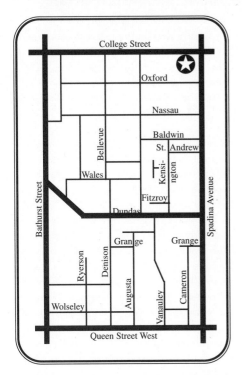

The tour starts at the southeast corner of Spadina Avenue and College Street.

In his charming memoir, *Episodes Before Thirty*, the British novelist Algernon Blackwood (1869-1951) recounts how, as a young man sent to Canada by his father to learn something of the world, he was hoodwinked out of most of his capital by the sharp practice of a local farmer. The farmer convinced Blackwood that with a combination of his capital and the farmer's knowledge they could make a fortune, and to the painfully naïve Blackwood it seemed a great idea. Once their company was established, however, the farmer continually found that if he could only get just a little more cash from Blackwood then the operation would yet be a success. Into the black hole of the farmer's greed Blackwood willingly poured his savings. Of course, the writer was being

fleeced, but he refused to believe the obvious because the farmer, "Alfred Cooper, was a delightful fellow . . . fitting my ideal of a type I had read about—the fearless, iron-muscled colonial white man who fought Indians." One gets a sense of poor Blackwood's exploitation on reading how the company set up shop at **291 College Street** in 1891: "The Islington Jersey Dairy, Messrs Cooper and Blackwood, started business with a retail office in College Street, a number of milk carts bearing out names in black lettering upon a yellow background . . . The upper floors of the building in College Street we furnished, letting bedrooms at a dollar a week to young Englishmen, clerks in offices, and others. I engaged an old, motherly Englishwoman, Mrs. 'iggins, with a face like a rosy apple, to 'do' for us—she made the beds and cooked the breakfast—while her pretty daughter, in cap and apron, was our dairymaid. The plan did not work smoothly—the dairymaid was too pretty, perhaps; Mrs Higgins too voluble. Complaints came from all sides; the lodgers, wildish young fellows in a free and easy country, made more promises than payments. One wanted a stove, another a carpet in his bedroom, another complained about his bed. I had my first experience of drink and immorality going on under my very eyes . . . Trouble, though mercifully of another kind—spread then to the customers. The milk began to go sour; it was too rich; it wouldn't keep; the telephone rang all day long . . . At dinner parties my hostess would draw me aside. 'The milk, I'm afraid, Mr. Blackwood,' she would murmur softly, 'was sour again this morning. Will you speak about it?' I spoke about it—daily—but Alfred Cooper's only comment was, 'Say, have you got a bit more capital? That's what we really want.' . . . Six months later the firm of Cooper and Blackwood dissolved partnership, Blackwood having got the experience and Cooper having got—something quite as useful but more marketable."

Backtrack to **Spadina Avenue.** The Labour Lyceum at **No.346**, although primarily a hall for union meetings and addresses on issues affecting organized workers, was host to talks by at least two celebrated literary folk: Emma Goldman and Joseph Opatoshu. Goldman, who was living in Toronto at the time, gave a lecture titled "Youth In Revolt" on April 4, 1937. Opatoshu (1887-1954) was a distinguished Yiddish novelist, considered by many to be second in stature in that language only to Isaac Bashevis Singer. His speech, "Palestine and Soviet Russia," was delivered December 2, 1934, during his first visit to Toronto, an event considered important enough that it was given page-one treatment by one of the leading newspapers. This temple to Labour was also the second-last refuge of scoundrels. Pierre Van Paassen, the legendary journalist and novelist recounts in one of his memoirs the treatment he and others received when, in 1916, they chose to be conscientious objectors on the grounds that war itself was a crime against humanity. "I must say that on the whole the churchmen and the civil authorities showed great tolerance and forbearance when I began to debate the question publicly. True, the Sunday evening meetings in Toronto's Labour Temple under the chairmanship of James Simpson, a later socialist mayor of the city, were more than once disrupted by invading bands of war veterans and super patriots who indiscriminately and howlingly decried all present as slackers, cowards, defeatists, paid agents of the Kaiser and so on. These ruffians, finding it easier to beat an opponent into unconsciousness than reason with him, got into the habit of reinforcing their catcalls and epithets with rubber truncheons and chunks of lead pipe. As long as we stayed inside the hall, we had police protection. No sooner did we come outside than we, not the rowdies, were deemed to have disturbed the peace. We got it in the neck from both sides, from the veterans *and* the cops."

Continuing south, we pass **No.196** where G. Mercer Adam lived (1890-91), and at **No.184** we behold yet another of his addresses on **Spadina** (1885 to 1889).

176 Spadina was the home for three years of Jean Graham (d.1936) a poet and journalist—indeed, when she died she was described as one of Canada's best-known journalists. In the last decades of her life she worked as an editor at *Saturday Night*, the *Canadian Courier*, and *Canadian Home Journal*. Hector Charlesworth, describing E.E. Sheppard and the beginnings of *Saturday Night*, wrote (in what he surely intended to be a compliment) that "Mr. Sheppard had considerable editorial assistance from a gifted woman who could write like a man, the late Jean Graham . . . Universally popular, Miss Graham by preference chose the type of work usually performed by men and scorned feminine assignments." Her list of residences in Toronto is depressingly long, revealing changes of address almost every year of her life. Her three-year stay at this address (1931-33) was one of her longest anywhere.

At Queen Street West turn west and walk to **Ryerson Avenue.** Walk north on **Ryerson** and at the northwest corner of Ryerson and Wolseley Street is the current home of Theatre Passe Muraille, the apotheosis of alternative theatre in Toronto, indeed, English Canada. The theatre began in Rochdale College in 1968 under artistic director Jim Garrard but was almost invisible until 1969 when the company produced *Futz* at the Central Library Theatre. With what was regarded as risible stupidity even then, the police charged the players with obscenity after each performance, thereby guaranteeing that the rest of the run would sell out. Artistic direction of Passe Muraille thereafter passed through a number of hands until Paul Thompson became boss in the very early seventies and breathed into the place his commitment to collective theatre and Canadian history. By this point it was ensconced in a big, beautiful, black box on Terauley Street (razed to make way for the Eaton Centre), where some of its earliest artistic hits were first presented, including *The Farm Show* and *1837*. After productions in various churches and spaces around town, the theatre was able to buy this space in the late seventies—thanks to obscenity charges laid by the police against another company's production, *I Love You Baby Blue*, making it the biggest profit centre of any Passe Muraille play.

Immediately north is **24 Ryerson**, for about two decades now the home of several writers' organizations. These have varied over the years, but tenants of several years include the Writers' Union of Canada, the Writers' Development Trust, the League of Canadian Poets, the Canadian Authors' Association, Periodical Writers Association of Canada, PEN English-Canadian Centre, and the national offices of the Word on the Street Festival. The Playwrights Union of Canada was formerly housed in this building too, but moved around the corner into offices at **54 Wolseley Street** in the late 1980s.

One block to the east is **Denison Avenue**. Just north of the intersection of Grange and Denison, on the east side, row houses once stood, now replaced by dreary city housing. What was **No.117 Denison** was the first home in Toronto of the author and legendary book reviewer Ken Adachi. He came here for a about a year in 1945 after release from the internment camp to which he had been forced during WWII. The home of Ms. Jane Porter used to be located from Confederation Year to c. 1880 on **Grange Street** when Grange Street extended west of Denison—the house and street were absorbed as part of the Alexandra Park Housing Co-op. Porter was a music teacher and poet from Montreal who published a text in 1865 titled *Six Weeks Tour in Western Canada* in which she describes a visit to Toronto. The careful reader will thus note that prior to Confederation Toronto was considered in western Canada. Miss Porter moved to Toronto in 1867 and taught music until at least 1895—but as with so many women until approximately 1970, her biographical data are arduous to find or non-existent. She wrote poems personally addressed to the Pope, the Turkish Sultan, and the Crown Princess of Prussia, but these eminences seem to have remained oblivious to her talents.

Taking footpaths through the housing development, one reaches **Augusta Avenue**. Charles Pelham Mulvaney (1835-85) died at his residence, **No.69**, to which he had moved but three years before. Mulvaney's first profession was medicine. His second was the church; he was an ordained Anglican minister. Having spent most of his time in Quebec since arriving in Canada in 1860, for some reason he moved to Toronto c. 1878. Once here, he abandoned the clerical life for the literary life. He also became a devotee of the city's history, writing *Toronto: Past and Present*, a text (1884) which, despite its errors of fact, remains seminal to anyone studying any branch of the city's history. His first book (1880) was a collection of poems. Even granting that obituaries are flattering, the *World's* summation of his poetry—"He has written verses that will rank with Tennyson and equal Swinburne"—is clearly excessive, but that such a statement could be made at the time of his death indicates the regard with which he was held locally.

It is worth the ambulatory difficulty of getting to **52 Vanauley Street** (next street to the east; runs south from Dundas) because it was the home of Marjorie Pickthall (1883-1922). Critic Donald Precocsky writes of her, "Probably no other Canadian writer has suffered such a plunge in reputation as Marjorie Pickthall. Once she was thought to be the best Canadian poet of her generation. Now her work, except for two or three anthologized pieces, goes unread." Since that assessment was written, however, Pickthall has made something of a comeback in academia where feminist literary criticism views her life and work more kindly. This, the first address in Toronto I've been able to find for her and her family, was their home from 1892 (and possibly earlier) until 1899.

Marjorie Pickthall (left) and May Skinner at entrance to what is now Birge Carnegie Library, and was then the Victoria College Library, 1910

The urban planning disaster (along the south side of Dundas between Spadina and Bathurst) masquerading as social housing makes for many impossible connections to Kensington Market to the north. The reader has the option of returning to Spadina Avenue for the scenic route north or of walking the labyrinth of the housing complex directly to Dundas. Either way, we recommence the Kensington tour on the northeast corner of Dundas and Kensington Avenue.

No author of note has lived on **Kensington Avenue**. However, it leads us to **St. Andrew Street** which has one address of interest. At **No.13** lived Laura Elizabeth McCully (1886-1924), a poet and key member of what has been termed the first wave of feminism in Canada. Locally, in her time, she was considered a writer of promise rather than of inspiring accomplishment. But her engagement with politics interests scholars today. A UofT graduate, she had a direct manner of speech and feisty tongue. For example, she said there was "no particular reason why a woman whose life is spent between child-bearing under adverse circumstances and labour in a sweatshop should be either too refined or timid to throw stones at windows." Sir Charles G.D. Roberts maintained in a flattering profile of McCully that "she is known as the first woman to have held an open-air meeting in the interests of the suffrage movement in Canada, the gathering taking place in High Park, Toronto, in August 1908." Although a leading suffragette, she was no pacifist, being a vocal supporter of the Allies in WWI, actively supporting recruitment, and organizing the Women's Home Guard. She lived at this address from 1907-9 before travelling to Yale University for graduate study. Sadly, a combination of diabetes and mental illness at the end of her life reduced her to murmuring to herself and rambling dishevelled on Queen Street. Ultimately she was committed to the Hospital for the Insane, and died there. Refusing to take any insulin, the miracle treatment for diabetes discovered only a few blocks away, she wasted away. Her last home before commitment was an unheated room nearby at **3 Fitzroy Terrace**.

Walk west on Baldwin to **Augusta Avenue**. At **No.116** poet Joe Rosenblatt passed three years of his boyhood (1938-41). And at **No.194** Eva Rose York lived c. 1911, having earlier resided at **No.52** for some years. Ms. York (1858-c.1938) authored two novels and what the magazine *Canadian Baptist* politely described as "fugitive verse." On the surface, she might seem to be nothing more than one of the thousands of religious poetasters who peopled the edges of the Toronto literary scene in the decades either side of 1900. But as we shall discover later she was no ordinary woman, being an expert with whips and rifles, as well as a Mother Theresa-like figure to hundreds of babies born out of wedlock.

Curiously, I could find no authorial connections to Nassau Street, whereas **Oxford Street**, the next street to the north, offers at least six. **No.9** was the home (c. 1882) of E.S. Caswell, the editor of the popular anthology *Canadian Singers and Their Songs*. A century later, the science fiction author and renowned SF editor Judith Merril lived next door at **No.11**. Shortly after arriving in this city from New York, Merril (1923-97) donated her personal accumulation of science fiction material to the Toronto Public Library, instantly giving it one of the best SF collections in this and probably neighbouring galaxies. The collection was formerly known as the Spaced-Out Library but is now known as the Merril Collection in her honour. **No.20** was home to Sarah Anne Curzon for about a year in the mid-1870s. Curzon (1833-98), born in England, came to Canada with her new husband in 1862. She was "one of the first English-Canadian playwrights to dramatize Canadian historical subject matter and public social issues of the day." In 1876 she wrote her blank verse drama about Laura Secord's famous walk but could not find a publisher for it until 1887. Curzon was possibly better known as an author and feminist in Toronto than her near neighbour Laura McCully (see above), in large part because every week she wrote a column on matters of import to women for a local periodical. But like McCully she dedicated her adulthood to fighting for rights we take for granted: the right to vote, for example, or the right to attend university.

Vincent Starrett (1886-1974) wrote more than 100 books in several fields, including biography, fiction, and poetry. Moreover, in his time, he was one of the best-known men of letters in America. Yet few Americans were aware that he was born in Toronto. Of course, the same charge could be made against Canadians. In fact, despite the mistaken address he offers in his own autobiography, Starrett was born at **46 Oxford Street** and lived there until c. 1890. In his *Canadian Anecdotes*, Douglas Fetherling relates that Starrett's birth was "beset with complications. To those attending, it appeared that the baby had been born dead and that the mother might not survive. As a temporary measure, the infant was wrapped in a newspaper and placed under the bed until the body could be disposed of properly. The newspaper was the *Globe*. 'Can any of my colleagues of the typewriter,' Starrett would ask in later years, 'point to an earlier appearance in print?'"

The poet William Albert Sherwood (1859-1919) was better known as a painter, especially of Canadian genre scenes, and of portraits, including portraits of fellow writers Alexander McLachlan, Pauline Johnson, Rev. Dr. Scadding, and W.D. Lighthall—all of which were purchased by the National Gallery. He is considered one of the two or three key people behind the formation of the Ontario College of Art and Design. His death came as a shock to the many who knew him in Toronto. Otherwise in fine health, he casually lanced a boil on his foot, and within hours was so sick he was taken to Toronto General Hospital where he died before the night was done. He lived in a staggering number of Toronto addresses, including **111 Oxford Street** in 1889.

Backtrack to **Bellevue Avenue** and stop in front of **No.99**. From 1927 to 1958 this was the home of Rev. James Ward (1883-1958). Interestingly, when he died, all of the daily newspapers emphasized his literary connections over his clerical role in the headlines to their obituaries, even though he was well known in Toronto as having been the rector of St. Stephen's Church for 31 years. This was because he recognized the power of radio to reach a mass audience and for that medium he wrote plays with a strong religious element. As the editor of the weekly drama series "The Way of the Spirit" on CBC Radio, he reached tens of thousands of people in a way that no stage playwright could. He died from complications suffered when he was hit by a truck 18 months before.

No.96 has been the home of three authors. Robert Fones, now better known for his work in the visual arts, was writing poetry when he lived here in the late 1970s. Then he and his wife gave the apartment to Sarah Sheard and David Young in 1980 and that couple stayed at this address until 1983.

Frontiersman, Soldier, Adventurer

Roger Pocock as seen on his last visit to Toronto as part of a world tour to promote the Legion of Frontiersmen

M&E, November 27, 1935

The adventurer Roger Pocock (1865-1941) lived at **60 Bellvue** in 1886-87 while he was recovering from wounds suffered during the Riel Rebellion. English by birth, Pocock came to Canada in 1880, working first on train gangs building the trans-Canada CPR line, and then, once in the west, working as a Mountie in the prairie detachments. Earlier, he claimed to have been a cowboy, missionary to head-hunters, pirate, prospector, peddler, photographer, telegraph operator—and poet. Once recuperated, he returned to the west and would later boast that he "rode from Fort Macleod at the foot of the Rockies to the city of Mexico, 3600 statute miles. The ride was done on three horses, not including pack animals, and occupied 200 days." Later, he led an expedition to the Klondike. These and other adventures are told in his autobiographies, and as historian Norah Story wrote about one of them, *(The Frontiersman)*, "When allowance is made for the bantering style with which he attempted to reconcile his admiration for law and order and his sense of fellowship with rogues and ruffians, and the further conflict between his egoism and his self-deprecation, this book vividly recreates moments of stress during the development of the west."

The final literary address worth noting on this street belonged to Sarah Anne Curzon who lived at **41 Bellevue Avenue** from 1882-88.

At the foot of Bellevue is a T-junction with **Wales Avenue**. **No. 62** was home to novelist Martin Waxman from 1986-87. Here he wrote much of his second novel, and a screenplay still hoping to see the light of the cinema.

Running south from Wales is the northern end of **Denison Avenue**. Two authors of note lived at the same address: **No.153**. Vincent Starrett (1886-1973) is described in one of the leading mystery reference books as "among the more versatile talents to grace the world of detective fiction. His major contributions to the mystery genre are his Sherlock Holmes writings, with his remarkable *The Private Life of Sherlock Holmes* (1933) the first biographical study of a fictional detective hero." In his memoir, Starrett tells how he was rummaging through the attic of his home at this address when "one day—a day of gilt and glory—I found a battered copy of *The Adventures of Sherlock Holmes*. I have no idea what edition it was. I don't remember what it looked like. I didn't recognize the author's name. I turned a few pages tentatively, reading at random, and felt my heart begin to thump under my ribs. It was a warm sunny afternoon, possibly in July or August, and I was perhaps ten years old, a small boy in an

Vincent Starrett, 1940.

old attic in Toronto. I carried the book outdoors and sat down with it on the front steps in a blaze of summer sunshine. My aunts came and went on the porch above me but, in the words of the old Biblical writers, I heard them not. I was still reading Sherlock Holmes when the lamps were lit inside the house and I was called to dinner. 'Oh yes,' said Aunt Lilian when I told her what I had been reading, 'we read that last summer at Muskoka. Isn't it exciting!' And then, as her sister entered the room, she added, 'Charlie's discovered Sherlock Holmes and thinks he'd like to be a detective.'

"I had indeed discovered Sherlock Holmes; and it seems strange to me now that so many years were to pass before I pursued the discovery and read the other available

titles in the great saga of the Detective and the Doctor. It did not occur to me, I suppose, that there could be another such book in the world. Probably I accepted it as something unique and miraculous that could never happen again." Starrett lived at this address from c. 1891 until c. 1904.

The other author who lived at **153 Denison Avenue** was the most notorious drama critic in the history of the country, Nathan Cohen (1923-71). He was so famous for the brutal authority of his performing arts reviews in the *Star* that it is easy to forget that when he first came to Toronto in 1945 he freelanced wherever there was work and then joined the CBC as its drama critic in 1947. A decade later he worked as a television story editor for the Corporation before joining the *Telegram* as its weekly theatre columnist. It was only in 1959 that he joined the *Star* and there became internationally known for his acid tongue—and when the occasion called for it, informed praise. Mordecai Richler immortalized him (albeit unflatteringly) as Seymour Bone in his novel *The Incomparable Atuk*. To non-intimates he always seemed gruff and unapproachable, but to his closest friends he was congeniality itself. His death at the age of only 47 came as a shock to his readers and the theatre world. Cohen wrote one play which was not a success. Another little-known aspect of his life is that he enjoyed translating Yiddish poetry and folktales into English. He had rooms at this address in 1947 shortly after he arrived in Toronto from the Maritimes.

FORT YORK & CNE

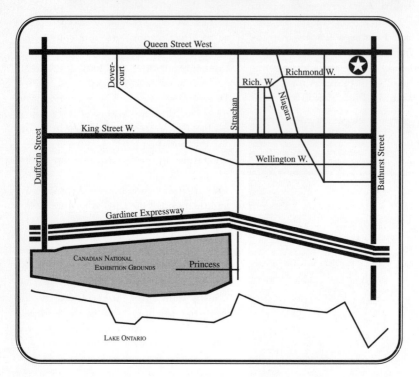

The tour begins at the southwest corner of Queen Street and Bathurst Street.

Walking west on **Queen Street West** we pass **No.799**, home to the Broadway playwright Charles W. Bell (1876-1938) discussed at length. He had the apartment over the current store from 1900-2, and it was here that he wrote his first plays while simultaneously starting his rocket-like ascendancy as a criminal lawyer.

Just to the west is **Niagara Street** descending towards the Lake, following the bank of what used to be Garrison Creek. It was this Creek (with its constant supply of fresh water) which induced the military planners to build Fort York at the point where Garrison debouched into Lake Ontario. Noted haiku poet Chusaburo Ito (b.1910) lodged at **65 Niagara** from 1948-49, his first address in this city. He had immigrated to

Toronto in 1927. **No.109** was an unusual factory with lofts for rent on the upper floors. One of the tenants was poet Diane Keating (b.1950). She had arrived in Toronto in 1975 and almost at once joined poetry workshops, learning her skills until she felt ready to write as a professional. As she said in a letter, "Since Toronto is where I evolved as a poet, I have been imprinted by it emotionally and visually. Perhaps that's why I remember so vividly my first studio space in 1977—a small pine room in a former coffin factory on Niagara Street." The smell from the nearby abattoir greatly aided her decision to move the following year. In 1993 the novelist and playwright David Young (b.1946) sublet an apartment here and worked intensively on his play *Glenn*, a study of pianist Glenn Gould.

Within a stone's throw of Niagara Street is **686 Richmond Street West**. Poet, publisher, and bookseller Nelson Ball (b.1942) moved into a second-floor unit of this commercial building in June 1973 and remained until March 1985, when he transferred his antiquarian business to Paris, Ontario. The final Weed Flower Press poetry books were issued from this apartment.

To the west, the next main north-south route is Strachan Avenue, named in honour of the imperious Anglican bishop responsible for Trinity College, once located at the top of Strachan Avenue. At its southern end are Toronto's only triumphal arches, widely known as the "Princess Gates," although their proper name is the "Princes' Gates." Another misconception common among Torontonians is that these gates have always marked the main entrance to the Canadian National Exhibition. In fact, until the nineteen-twenties, the principal approach to the fairgrounds was via a wide meadow along the northern boundary of the CNE stretching to the Lunatic Asylum and Trinity College (which is why, for example, the front door of the Coliseum is found on its north façade). Since the hospital and the school also had wide open spaces of their own, the abundant green space was most pleasant for walking or riding, a frequent pastime of our Victorian forebears.

A number of authors have either worked or spoken formally—and in a few cases have actually lived—on the fairgrounds. The buildings have been burned or razed so many times, however, that it is impossible to specify an address.

The most famous author was Margaret Atwood, who found a part-time job here during the annual Sportsman's Show when she was in her final year of high school. She has wryly commented on the demands of her occupation: "They wanted a girl and one that could help the customers get the arrow on the string and pointed the right way. What they shot at was balloons pinned to straw targets, and sometimes, by mistake or for a joke, me, when I was up there collecting the arrows. The worst moment was when you turned your back. On my break I would drink Honey Dew and eat hot dogs and watch Miss Outdoors, in her hipped waders and checked shirt tucked in tight, doing a few casts, or wander into the arena to hear Sharky the Seal play the national anthem on a set of pipes, which calmed the nerves."

Crime novelist Jack Batten (b.1932) had a summer job in 1954 working as a cashier at the CNE midway Freak Show. And the novelist Pierre Salinger (b.1925), long admired as a correspondent for ABC News and as the

Provincial Lunatic Asylum, Toronto

Canadian Illustrated News, May 21, 1870

Press Secretary for President John F. Kennedy, played the piano here. His father was a mining engineer who had been hired by a Canadian firm based in Toronto. The Salingers moved to the city in 1929, and it was in Canada that his musical talent was first taken seriously by his parents. In short order they realized he was a musical prodigy and enrolled him in the Toronto Conservatory of Music under the tutelage of the great Clement Hambourg. Salinger underwent the severe regimen of all prodigies, and by the age of six was ready to make his concert debut. He did so during "Music Day" at the CNE, September 3, 1931, when he played the *Sonata in D Major* by Haydn in the Women's Building.

One of the bestselling authors of cowboy westerns was Frederick Faust (1892-1944), better known by his pseudonym Max Brand. Like many Americans during WWI, unhappy that the USA was not fighting, he travelled to Toronto in February 1916 to join the American battalion, a group of approximately 1,200 men who were hoping to be part of the Canadian Expeditionary Force. The Americans were quartered in the Machinery Building, located immediately to the east of where the Dufferin Gate is today. Here he was given Morse code, semaphore, and gunnery lessons. Faust was anxious to get to Europe and fight. He wrote to a friend: "One thing I want to do is jazz a couple of the Deutschers. I've talked with a bunch of returned soldiers and they say there's no sport in the world like a bayonet charge. I believe them. Anyway, I'm damn eager to try it out."

At this time, the American Battalion was becoming a political hot potato and so its overseas departure was delayed, extending Faust's time in Toronto. He put the extra days to good use, finishing a long poem on which he placed high hopes, and learning the skills of a storyteller that would later stand him in good stead. His biographer has commented on the men with whom Brand shared the Machinery Building and how he used them to learn to be a storyteller: "It was the broad slice of humanity that would later be his chief audience. He found that the best way to hold its interest during barracks bull sessions was to 'lie back on your elbows and tell every lie you ever heard from your chest out. If you're interesting, no questions asked. If you're not interesting

The Entrance, Toronto Exhibition, Canada

Bird's eye view of Toronto Exhibition, 1914

they go to sleep. It's a great test.' So he perfected his narrative style."

Sometime c. May or June of 1916, the Battalion was sent to Nova Scotia where its departure once again was delayed. Tired of waiting, Max Brand deserted the Canadian Army and went to New York where he joined an ambulance service and finally got to Europe.

The first extant poem of another soldier, Frank Prewett (1893-1962), was written in February 1915 in Stanley Barracks while he was in training with the Timothy Eaton Machine Gun Battery.

Hugh Garner (1913-79) enlisted in the Royal Canadian Artillery in September 1939 and took his gunnery training in the Government Building of the CNE (still standing). Good math skills are a big asset for an artilleryman, but arithmetic was not Hugh's long suit. This lack of proficiency coupled with his socialist utterances led to his discharge from the unit in March of 1940.

Poet Al Purdy (b.1918) learned first hand the armed force's golden rule, Hurry Up and Wait, when he was sent to the CNE to help win the war in fall 1941. Or, as he put it in his memoirs, "In a dull and depressed mood I was domiciled at the Toronto Exhibition grounds 'Horse Palace' for the next week, along with a few hundred other airmen. I made some casual friends there, with whom I roamed Sunnyside Amusement Park on the Lake Ontario beach, and drank beer with a few times. But my spirits were too black and dismal to enjoy anything much. Having been married for several months, I was used to that condition and resented being deprived of it.

"Eurithe and I talked long-distance on the phone a few times. She said she'd try to get to Toronto, although I didn't really expect that to happen. But it did. And I went AWL (Absent Without Leave) when she got a room in a beachfront lodging house, where we spent a couple of blissful nights.

"Of course, it had to end, with me placed on charge for the nth time it seemed, getting

paraded before yet another bored officer and listening to the prescribed ritual."

Authors who gave well-attended public speeches during the Canadian National Exhibition include John Buchan, Lady Byng, Buckminster Fuller, Watson Kirkconnell, and Marshall Saunders.

Exit Exhibition Place via the Dufferin Gate and walk north on **Dufferin Street**. **No.236** was novelist Charles Templeton's home during the years of WWII. Continue north to Queen and then walk east. The poet and teacher Alexander Muir (who was the principal of a school near here) had his home at **72 Dovercourt Road** just south of Queen from 1884-85. Poet and editor Victor Coleman had the entire top floor of the building at **1087 Queen Street West** a century later. While here, Coleman finished the writing of his book *From the Dark Wood*.

Utter the phrase "nine ninety-nine" to Torontonians of a certain age (or older) and they know instantly that the speaker is referring to the address of the Lunatic Asylum, formerly found at **999 Queen Street West**. Today the institution goes by politer names, and, in part to remove the stigma of irrevocable madness associated with the old number, the new hospital on this site changed its street numbering to **No.1001**. One of the authors connected overtly to this site is James Algie (1857-1928), who was the hospital's assistant resident physician as of 1908. Earlier he had written three well-received novels, but why he stopped writing is unknown. Daniel Clark (1835-1912) was the Medical Superintendent of the entire institution for a full 30 years (1875-1905), author of numerous books on mental health—and the writer of one novel, *Josiah Garth*, a book about the Farmer's Revolt of 1837. Clark lived on the grounds during his three-decade reign. Ezra Stafford (1865-1912?] worked for Daniel Clark as the resident physician at the Asylum from 1894-1900. He also published at least two novels as books, and several stories in leading magazines.

PARKDALE

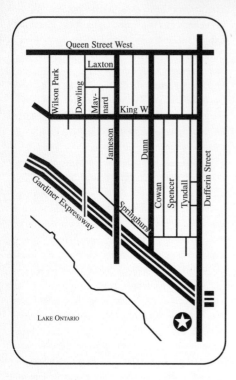

The tour begins at the Dufferin Gate of the CNE.

Walk north to **Springhurst Avenue** just north of the Gardiner Expressway, and turn west. **22 Springhurst** was the last home in Toronto of fiction writer Raymond Knister (1899-1932). While he was resident here from November 1928 to March 1930, his writing career reached a peak—if a life cut short by drowning can be said to have a peak. His work was regularly published in the *Star Weekly* and other good-paying journals; his stories appeared frequently in the most prestigious outlet for stories at the time, Edward O'Brien's annual *Best Short Stories*; and his novel *White Narcissus* (1929) was published in Canada, the USA, and in Britain to reviews that ranged from warm to warmer. Also published while he lived here was his justly praised anthology, *Canadian*

Short Stories (1928), the first such selection in Canadian history. In the last decade or so interest in Knister has increased as new depths in his work are plumbed by readers and critics from a variety of viewpoints.

Tyndall Avenue runs north from Springhurst. The Governor General's Award-winning novelist and poet M.T. Kelly (b.1946) lived with his mother in three different apartments at **60 Tyndall** between 1960-69: apts. 304, 708, and 901. Kelly was born in Toronto and, although he has lived in many neighbourhoods, this district has on his writing. Fighting and struggle, whether between people or the forces of Nature are everywhere in his work. The dominant theme may stem from his own fights as a teenager: "In Parkdale there were fights as well. It was very important. My best friend there was Jack Moore, from Cape Breton, who died violently. I met him when I beat his brother up. Jack came and beat me up. I went to fight him again, having read books of animals fighting to inspire myself, but made friends with him instead, and he didn't admit, or know, it was me he had beat up. We pretended we were 'tied' in fighting. I didn't have to fight the guys he had 'taken.' The permutations of this system were unending, but I remember them. I wrote about Parkdale and its fighting, and glue sniffing, and ambience in my play *The Green Dolphin* (1982)."

Kelly and his mother moved here from The Junction because his father had died and money became even tighter than it had been. When he arrived, Kelly wrote, "Parkdale was a construction site. All the Victorian houses, including the one next door to where my best friend lived, were being torn down for apartment houses. The great trench of the Gardiner went through, further cutting us off from the Lake. While it was being built, we played there, pretending we were wolves; the ramp led up and fell off, as eerie and windswept as a desert . . . There were the blocks of streets, Tyndall, Cowan, Dunn, Jameson, and a changing world. We never had the lingering, plum-blue evenings of European cities, but at six o'clock, above the apartments, shadow and mineral purity; the sky of the North came down for a while."

Journalist and author Augustus Bridle (1869-1952) spent the years 1927-32 at **31 Spencer Avenue**. At this time he was the regular music critic of the *Star* as well as the editor of an excellent general-interest magazine, *Canadian Courier*. This summary does not indicate, however, the central role he played in animating the literary scene. He was everywhere—in the best sense of the expression, supporting artists and artistic endeavours. He also wrote the first history of the Arts & Letters Club of which he was a founding member. His novel *Hansen* was published a year or so prior to his move to this address.

Norma West Linders's first two novels were published in Canada and in Britain in the early 1970s. Before that, she had been living out of suitcases (including during her Toronto years 1947-53), because her husband was a drummer for a dance band and his job demanded they had to travel fast and far on a moment's notice. Naturally, they lived in places that didn't require long leases: one of them was **43 Cowan Avenue** in 1949. Poet, crime writer, and former romance novelist Rosemary Aubert (b.1950?) provided this description of her home in this area: "My first address in Toronto was **46 Cowan Avenue** . . . Though I once walked out the front door to the sound of gunshots on the neighbouring street, I associate this address only with the supreme pleasure of having left the Vietnam War-torn United States (1970) and having arrived in Toronto which then, and still now, seemed a kind of heaven." A very young Victor Coleman (b.1944) lived at **No.109** from November 1965 to September 1967 and here wrote his second book of poems, the first to garner serious attention from other authors: *one/eye/love*.

There must be a special ring in Dante's Inferno for the politicians who approved, and for the planners who designed, the exit from an expressway directly into a quiet and established residential neighbourhood. In the history of Toronto, it is the only neighbourhood so debased. The **Dunn Avenue** exit of the Gardiner Expressway cut off the foot of Dunn, which was the only north-south side street in Parkdale to stretch right down to the marshes which used to line the shore. Mazo de la Roche lived at **157 Dunn** for about six years at the end of the 19th c. and was able to reminisce about this very spot: "Where there is now the lakeshore, a railway line, and apartment houses there were fields of tall feathery grass and daisies which we children called marguerites . . . My grandfather's house was one of [only] five that stood on a tree-shaded street that ended in a kind of wooden terrace with seats, overlooking the lake." The house was the first that de la Roche could call a home. It was also where her cousin Caroline first came to live with her and her family, and the two women remained lifelong companions ever after.

The west side of Dunn Avenue has always been the grounds of a hospital. Originally, it was the site of the Home for the Incurables, **130 Dunn Avenue**, an institution so far ahead of its time architecturally that experts came from as far away as Europe to marvel at its healthful innovations. That building was razed and replaced by the current structure which, until 1998, was known as the Queen Elizabeth Hospital. At least two authors, for reasons of health, lived at this newer version of the address: poet Earle Birney (August to November 1987), and poet E.A. Lacey (April to August 1994). Residents of the earlier building were pioneer feminist and author Alice Chown (died here 1949), and poet Amy Parkinson (c.1859-1938), who was bedridden for more than 60 years. Another resident from September 1932 to May 1933 was

Jack Millar, father of Kenneth, better known as Ross Macdonald, one of the greatest detective novelists. Kenneth visited his father often at this institution, watching him waste away until he died. The deathwatch was to haunt Millar for the rest of his life, and the abandonment of son by father is one of the most predominant themes in Macdonald's Lew Archer novels.

143 Dunn was the home of Wilfred (1901-86) and Magdalena Eggleston (b.1907) in the late 1920s. He always aspired to be known as a poet, but his success as a journalist and author of non-fiction eclipsed what little creative writing he did publish. He began to work for the *Star* in 1926 and after a few years was promoted to Ottawa correspondent. He rarely left the capital after that. Within a few years of the end of WWII he founded the Carleton University School of Journalism. His novel *High Plains* was published in 1938, but his *Literary Friends* (1980), a memoir of notable Canadian authors he had known is at least as important for its unique insights into G.D. Roberts, D.C. Scott, Bliss Carman *et al*. His other memoirs are also engaging, insightful, and full of rich historical information. His wife, Magdalena, whom he married in 1928, was also a novelist and occasional poet as well as an author of radio plays.

One day they awoke to find they had a new authorial neighbour, as Wilfred explained in *Literary Friends*: "My wife recalls how we first found out who our new neighbours were. There was a ring at the door, and when she went to answer it, she saw a 'slight, dark, very intense young man, who stuttered badly.' It was in the middle of the morning. My impression is that he came to see if he could borrow something—was it a pair of pliers, which we didn't have—and that he went on to talk about Wilfred who was at work down town in the *Star* office. He had seen Wilfred's name in the *Star*: was his new neighbour the *Star* writer? When I heard that evening that our new neighbours were the Knisters we were both excited and lost no time in getting better acquainted. We were both young newly-married couples and had plenty to talk about. In the next four months there was much coming and going between the two apartments. My wife's diary reports an invitation to the Knisters for tea, early in the New Year, and they came and had dinner with us soon afterwards. Then we went back for dinner and spent the evening . . . One evening we called up on the telephone and invited them down for a return engagement, playing bridge; but they explained they had a guest. Would we come up instead? We did. The guest was Charles G.D. Roberts . . . I envied Knister's literary successes and prophesied a rosy future as one of Canada's outstanding novelists. He had already won widespread critical acclaim; but I could not help contrasting the hard times the Knisters were going through in the meantime. His wife Myrtle went out every morning to work in a nearby textile factory. Even with this help they were in financial straits. I have some dim recollections of bill collectors hanging around and a brush with the bailiff while they were living above us."

Jameson Avenue was named for the Family Compact member married to Anna Jameson, the wonderful writer. Now one of the uglier streetscapes in Toronto, thanks to the destruction of the Victorian homes which used to line its blocks, the street has been home to a surprising number of authors, although the careful reader will note that all but one of the authors did so before the high-rises blighted the area.

Shortly after she arrived in Toronto, novelist Sylvia Fraser (b.1935) lived in apt. 104 at **87 Jameson Avenue** in 1960 and 1961. Then she moved to apt. 304 at **No.165** and remained there until she took up abode in the Colonnade on Bloor Street West in 1965. The poet Waclaw Iwaniuk (b.1915) emigrated from Poland to Toronto in 1948 and worked as a courtroom translator for most of his life in this city. He lodged at **No.94** in 1952. The aviation novelist Spencer Dunmore (b.1928) called

Toronto home from 1954-63 and lived in apt. 204 at **No.95** in the late 1950s. He remarked that "I moved to an apartment on Jameson Avenue—then quite an attractive street; I believe it was from this location that I made my first sale to the CBC."

Writer Lilian Waters McMurtry died at her home at **No.98 Jameson** in 1934, a fact noted by most of the major dailies which treated her passing as an important news story. Locally she was known as a poet, but at least one of her plays was good enough to be accepted for production by David Belasco, the legendary Broadway producer. Watson Griffin (1860-1952) was another author who died at his Jameson Avenue home. He had lived at **No.196** since at least 1942. Appointed the News Editor of the *News* when he was only 19, Griffin spent most of his life in journalism, although he found time to pen two novels—quite spaced apart in time. The first was published in 1884 and the second in 1927. Before his death, Griffin was festooned with many honours.

Across the street sits one of Toronto's oldest educational institutions, Parkdale Collegiate. By my reckoning there have been two authors who taught here: literary biographer Lois Darroch and playwright Ken Gass. Authors who attended classes as students include David Donnell, Norah Holland, Grace Irwin, M.T. Kelly, Frank Prewett, and Charles Templeton. Basil King gave a 40-minute speech to an entire assembly of the school in 1921.

Walk west on King Street. Gwendolyn MacEwen moved into an apartment at **1512 King Street West** in early 1965 and seems to have kept this as her base (while travelling extensively) until 1968. It was while living here that her love life unravelled, the broken love affair inspiring some of her best poems. This building was also the home of playwright Herman Voaden (1903-91) in 1937.

Playwright Dora Conover (1897-1985) had, like Voaden, tried to foment an English-Canadian theatre scene in the 1930s in a city that seemed indifferent to Canadian plays. She lived at **No.1540** from 1949-57. And novelist Raymond Knister lived at **No.1544** in 1926.

Walk east on Queen Street. At **Wilson Park Road** we head south to pause before **No.63**, where novelist Cynthia Holz (b.1950) lived (1978-81) not long after she arrived in Canada from the USA. While at this address she began to write the stories that appeared in her 1989 collection, *Home Again*. At this time, she joined Joe Rosenblatt's writing workshop at the now-defunct Three Schools of Art. Coincidentally so did a fellow American woman writer living in Parkdale, Rosemary Aubert.

Two blocks further east is **Dowling Avenue**. Playwright Erika Ritter (b.1948) had an apartment at **No.146** from 1977-79. While living here she wrote her second play, *Splits*, a hit that catapulted her to national attention. One of the reasons she chose this apartment was its proximity to the White Eagle Nursing Home, "which I figured would be an easy move in the fullness of time, although I didn't live there long enough to cash in." Two women authors who did inhabit the White Eagle in their last years were Anne Merrill, who was 100 years old when she died in 1971, and novelist Gladys Lewis, whose birthdate and birthplace remain as unknown as her death date. She lived at this address in 1976, but not before or after. Pioneering theatre director and visionary Roy Mitchell (1884-1944) had a house at **No.98** from 1913-17, years that correspond to his augmented involvement with Theosophy (along with scores of other artists and intellectuals in Toronto at that time) and his work as Director of Motion Pictures for the federal government. At his death, the *G&M* remarked, "During his days on the Toronto World, he advanced the cause of a native theatre in Canada; devoted his energies to the establishment of the Little Theatre movement; and publicized the cultural importance of a community centre devoted to the drama. He wrote several books dealing with the theatre."

Novelist and Vancouver native John Cornish (b.1914) was a clerk in the Toronto Post office from 1947 to 1952 before, apparently, returning to B.C. The Toronto stay was long enough, though, to inspire him to write his best-known work, the novel *Sherbourne Street* (1968). He did indeed reside on that street but he also lived at **7 Laxton Avenue** in 1948.

Despite its shortness, **Maynard Avenue** (between Leopold and King) has accommodated four authors. When Fred Bodsworth (b.1918), the author of the much-respected and bestselling novel *Last of the Curlews*, first came to Toronto in March 1943 to work at the *Star*, he lived in a boarding house at **No.3** until the following year when he married. **No.7** was the 1908 home of John D. Logan (1869-1929) when he was the Literary Editor at the *World*. The mystery writer Keith Edgar had digs at **No.27** c. 1943. And closer to our own time, fiction writer Christine Slater (b.1960; her first collections of stories, *Stalking the Gilded Boneyard*, occasioned a flood of praise), passed her girlhood with her family at **No.32**.

A few blocks to the east we return to **Dunn Avenue**. J.D. Logan, just mentioned above, roomed at **220 Dunn Avenue** in 1907. Two doors away, at **No.216**, Augustus Bridle (1869-1952) was installed from 1917-26. In his book *Literary Friends* the novelist and journalist Wilfred Eggleston gives a lovely pen-portrait of Bridle as he saw him in the mid-1920s: "The music and drama critic for the *Star* in those days was Augustus Bridle. Around the newsroom he was called Gus. Most of his work was done in the evenings and he would turn in his copy in the middle of the night, so that we saw little of him. But he was a legendary figure, with a crown of unruly white hair, framing a lined and wrinkled face of distinguished appearance, a 'character' certainly. I was variously told that he was a Scandinavian, or that he was a Barnardo boy who had come over in the steerage from London, or some such tale . . . The more I learned about his background

John D. Logan

and talents, the more he interested me. Bridle would appear in the newsroom at odd hours, unheralded, almost ghost-like, find an unused desk in some corner or brush aside the untidy clutter and set to work filling endless pages of copy-paper with cryptic hieroglyphics which only one linotype operator in the composing room could decipher. I don't think I ever saw him use a typewriter. His writing style was uneven. Sometimes it would soar 'into the Empyrean', as old-fashioned critics would have written. Sometimes it bogged down into almost formless sentences. But it had character . . . His novel and two books of biographical sketches can still be read with pleasure and considerable profit. He showed rare insight into the texture and flavour of Canadian political and cultural life in the period 1880-1920."

PALMERSTON BOULEVARD

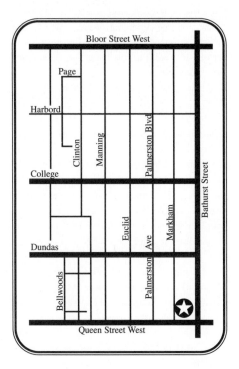

The tour begins at the northwest corner of Bathurst Street and Queen Street West.

Go north on Bathurst. Sarah Anne Curzon (1833-98), who lived at **282 Bathurst Street** in 1880 and 1881, was a pioneer Canadian playwright and feminist. Born and raised in England, she received a first-class education from private tutors and even as a young woman was publishing poetry and stories in British literary periodicals. She moved with her new husband to Toronto in 1862 where she found ready acceptance of her writing. She was not shy about making declarations on women's issues in print, and lambasted the authorities for refusing to allow women the vote, and for refusing to allow women to attend the UofT. The magazine *Grip* commissioned her to write a drama on women's issues. She complied with a comedy wherein a woman, disguised as a man, attends university, graduates at the top of his/her class, thereby exposing the Establishment myth about the alleged intellectual inferiority of women. Her later writing celebrated Canadian history with shameless pride. In fact, her play about Laura Secord was a major factor in the heroine of 1812 becoming well-known throughout the land.

When the distinguished Estonian poet Hannes Oja (b.1919) first arrived with his wife and children in Toronto in April 1951, the entire family lived in just one room for some months at **No.450**. Through hard work and the kindness of friends and relatives, they soon had their own home and he began to write and publish.

Langston Hughes (1902-67), one of the greatest voices of black America, made two visits to Toronto. During the first visit (over a weekend in April 1943), he gave a speech on "Race Relations" at what was known as the Negro Community House, **556 Bathurst Street**. The following day he returned to this address to give a poetry reading. The *Telegram*, alone among the Toronto dailies, reported on the visit: "Both Negroes and white people need to be educated to a greater appreciation of the contribution to American life that Negroes have made in the fields of literature, music, science, industry and political and social thought, in the opinion of Langston Hughes, Negro poet . . . Great hope for the future was expressed by the speaker, for leaders in every country are recognizing the need for racial and class unity. Sunday supper in his honour was followed by a meeting at which he read many of his poems and discussed Negro literature." Hughes was one of the first authors to incorporate black speech patterns and traditions into literature, and is now seen to be the leader of the literary facet of the Harlem Renaissance. Although he wrote fiction and drama (including the lyrics for the 1947 Broadway hit, *Street Scene*, with music by Kurt Weill, book by Elmer Rice), and helped to found theatres in Chicago, New York, and Los Angeles it was his poetry which had the widest following—he was known to both blacks and whites as the Negro Poet Laureate as early as the 1930s. *The Reader's Encyclopedia of American Literature* sums up his career this way, "His populism, encouraged early by the examples of Whitman and Sandburg, has affected his critical reputation. Middle-class Afro-American reviewers often condemned his work in blues and jazz as exposing the worst element of the race: these and other critics also sometimes found Hughes insufficiently intellectual. But he was committed to an art that both reflected the realities of Afro-American culture and was accessible to a large section of the community. In general he succeeded. Especially among black Americans, his body of work continues to appeal to a surprisingly wide audience."

Poet and publisher Nelson Ball (b.1942), with his wife, the artist Barbara Caruso, moved into apt. 2 at **756-A Bathurst Street** in September 1968 and lived there until June 1973. This was their first home sufficiently large for them both to indulge their professions. His Weed/Flower Press, begun a year earlier when he lived around the corner at 501 Markham Street, went into high gear (if any small press can be said to be in high gear) at this address. Among the books he printed in this apartment were bp Nichol's *The True Eventual Story of Billy the Kid* (1970) which, to almost everyone's amazement, won the Governor General's Award for Poetry. The surprise was due, in part, to the fact that this marked the first time a book produced by a tiny literary press had ever won the country's highest literary prize. Other titles produced here were Ball's own *The Pre-Linguistic Heights* (1970), *Points of Attention* (1971), and most of the poems in *The Concrete Air* (1996). Ball was a frequent host to authors from out of town,

many of whom crashed in his place, and among the literary celebrities who climbed these steps were Allen Ginsberg, Victor Coleman, Diane Wakoski, Earle Birney, Mike Doyle, George Bowering, Gerry Gilbert, and bill bissett. In May 1972, he began his renowned antiquarian book business from this location.

Although playwright Charles Tidler (b.1946) has lived on the west coast of Canada for almost 30 years, he spent an important half-year in Toronto from October 1983 to April 1984. During that time he spent some months at **520 Markham Street** while overseeing production of *The Farewell Heart* at the Tarragon Theatre. He also wrote most of a radio play for the CBC while he had lodgings in the city, as well as another full-length drama for the stage, *Startle the World, Release the Rose*.

The most notorious drama critic in the history of Toronto was Nathan Cohen (1923-71). He was infamous because his commentary was frequently uttered in extraordinarily acerbic terms and because he firmly believed that Canadian productions should be held to the same high standards as foreign efforts. When they attained those standards, Canuck and foreigner alike would be bathed in his praise. But fail to attain those standards and the barbs were merciless. Born in Sydney, Nova Scotia, he first came to Toronto to study at Osgoode Hall, but poor health caused him to return to the Maritimes to begin work as a newspaperman. In 1945 he returned to Toronto where he, in his own words, "bummed around" for about 12 months before gaining enduring employment at the CBC. One of the places he lived during 1945 was **507 Markham Street**. From January 1971 to the autumn of 1975, Ludwig Zeller (b.1927) rented a studio at **No.501,** where he went to work on his surrealist poems and collages almost every day. One fruit of that labour was *When the Animal Rises from the Deep the Head Explodes* (1976). Four years before Zeller began to work at this address, poet Nelson

Ball moved into an apartment in the same house. Here he wrote the poems of his book *Sparrow* (1968), and produced the last two issues of his literary magazine *Weed*, and a number of titles by his small press house Weed/Flower Press. The poet and journalist Jean Blewett (1862-1934) occupied **No.492** from 1906-11. In addition to writing poems, and editing the "Homemaker's Page" for the *Globe*, she penned a novel, *Out of the Depths* (1890).

Poet Susan Glickman (b.1953) describes her stay on **Markham Street**: "The history of my time here is in large part the history of my literary life. I grew up in Montreal, but when I returned to Canada in 1977 after 7 years abroad . . . the English-language publishing community was not doing much hiring, the Parti Quebecois victory having unnerved everyone just a tad. I got a job as an assistant editor with a small firm, NC Press, in Toronto, and moved into an apartment at **436 Markham Street** where I was to remain for seven years. Peter Such, who was publishing a book on the Beothuk Indians with NC Press, bought a house up the street from me. That summer he organized a poetry reading as part of a local street festival and invited me to participate. . . . The summer and fall of 1978 were when I started writing the poems for *Complicity* (1983). That book really represents my Markham Street life to me, and the section called 'From The Balcony' commemorates all the time I spent observing neighbourhood activity."

Sir Beverley Baxter (1891-1964) was born in Toronto and worked for the Nordheimer Piano Company when he lived at **No.397** from 1909-14. Sent to England to fight in WWI, he stayed on after the war as a reporter for the *Daily Express*, a newspaper owned by another Canadian, Lord Beaverbrook. The latter remained Baxter's patron, endorsing his elevation through the ranks, ultimately editor-in-chief of the *Daily Express* for the years 1929-33. Baxter then left fulltime newspaper work to sit as an MP in the British House of Commons, a post he held for several elections. He kept contact with Canada, in part via his "London Letter," a regular column in *Maclean's* magazine, and in part via frequent trips home. Although knighted for his services to journalism, Baxter was proud of his creative writing which included short stories (the first were published in *Maclean's* while he lived at this address), novels, and plays. He was also a noted drama critic of the London stage.

William A. Sherwood (1859-1919) was one of those painters who, like Lawren Harris or J.E.H. Macdonald, also published a little poetry. Sherwood occasionally sought out writers as subjects and thanks to him we have wonderful portraits of, among others, Alexander MacLachlan and Pauline Johnson. He lived at **385 Markham Street** in 1906.

Playwright Joan MacLeod (b.1955) wrote to me, "In August 1986 I moved to **378 Markham Street**. That fall I became a playwright-in-residence at the Tarragon. I performed and wrote my one woman show *Jewel* at the Tarragon in April '87 and *Toronto, Mississippi* premiered there in September '87." Her play *Amigo's Blue Guitar* (Governor General's Award, 1992) also opened at Tarragon and all of these works were either written or polished at her Markham Street address. She continued, "The apartment I live in is unquestionably the ugliest on the block but it's a great place to live and is full of other writers and actors . . . I like Toronto. I never thought I'd stay this long. I like living in an artistic community. That never happened in Vancouver." It was a sad loss when this talented dramatist left Markham Street (and Toronto) for her native Vancouver in 1992. Coincidentally, this same building was the home of another writer, Paul A.W. Wallace, who lived in apt. 3-A from 1922-24. Wallace (b.1891) published stories for young adults as well as those of an older bent. Some of them are retellings of French Canadian legends.

When novelist Ian Adams (b.1937) lived at **No.367** from August 1974 to July 1978, he wrote two of his best-known works: *End Game* *in Paris* (1979) and *Bad Faith* (1983). Nathan Ralph Goldberg (1919-60) published two books of poetry and a play in his short life. After WWII, he enrolled at the UofT and roomed at **No.353** for his three undergraduate years, 1945-48, which is when he began to write and publish. Archie McKishnie's first address in Toronto seems to have been **No.347½** from 1909-14. McKishnie (1876-1946) was a veteran news reporter as well as a fiction writer with a special fondness for outdoors and nature writing.

Philip Kreiner (b.1950?) seems to have published nothing in English since he moved to Japan in the late 1980s. However, the fiction he did publish in that decade harvested glowing reviews, and one book, *People Like Us in a Place Like This* (1983), was nominated for the Governor General's Award. He lived at **No.335 Markham** from 1983-87. Ethelbert Cross (b.1872) published just one book, *Fire and Frost* (1898), but one noted critic described it as "the work of a reflective, well-read man with some skill in giving his thought imaginative expression." His residence from 1906-7 was at **No.315**.

Edward S. Caswell (1861-1938) was the Assistant Librarian of Toronto for the last three decades of his life, and the compiler of the first poetry anthology in our history to include portraits of the contributors—thereby allowing readers to put faces finally to their favourite authors. His book, *Canadian Singers and Their Songs*, had its first edition in 1902, a revised edition in 1919, and another in 1925. His home for the first decade of the century (during which his anthology was first published) was **No.245 Markham**. Across the street at **No.241**, the poet and journalist Jean Blewett undoubtedly would have waved good morning to Mr. Caswell, because it was here she kept rooms from 1900-2. Another poet, Joe Rosenblatt (b.1933), spent a brief part of his boyhood (1937) at **No.211**, and five years later his family was living at **No.121**. The writing of Marjorie Pickthall (1883-1922) was hugely popular in her own time and then, until recently, was sneered at by most critics. However, in academia at least, feminist critics are making new claims for Pickthall's importance, seeing her struggles to make a living as a writer in Victorian and Edwardian Canada as positively heroic. They make a good case. Most of her life was spent in Toronto, and the years 1900-6 (when she was writing novels for juveniles) were spent at **No.169 Markham**. By the way, she did appear in Mr. Caswell's anthology.

The next street to the west is **Palmerston Avenue**. The nomenclature of this road is unnecessarily confusing in that it begins as Avenue then becomes Boulevard, only to become Avenue again at its northern end. One of the stretches should be re-named. Dare we hope, named after a Torontonian?

The novelist Charlotte Vale Allen (b.1941) spent a large part of her youth living on this street, as did novelist Gerald Lampert (1922-78); his family resided at **No.182** for most of the 1930s. Before William Talbot Allison (1875-1941) became a famous professor of English at the University of Manitoba, he worked for some years as a reporter at the Toronto *News*. Before that he was both an undergrad and grad at the UofT. And before that, he lived at **No.229** for two years from 1891-92. Allison published a book of poems, but he was most admired for his voracious reading and supportive reviews of Canadian authors. The reviews were syndicated in newspapers from Halifax to Victoria. He was literary editor of the *Winnipeg Tribune* for more than two decades

James Hogg Hunter (b.1890), a native of Scotland, came to Canada as a young man where he worked at the *Globe* before joining the editorial team of the *Evangelical Christian* (also based in Toronto). His novels usually appeared in serial form first and were extremely popular with readers throughout North America who had a taste for detective mysteries crossed with fundamentalist Christianity. He kept his home at **332 Palmerston Boulevard** from 1935-40.

Ray Levinsky is one of the many mystery women I encountered in my researches. Her play, *The Other Woman*, was presented at Massey Hall on January 7, 1915 to what was described as "a large and enthusiastic audience"—this at a time when the hall seated more than 4,000 people. The play was a four-act comedy and Ray Levinsky took one of the lead roles. Among the few biographical facts I could find about her was that she was well known as a suffragette and that she managed her own theatre company for a while—but what company, and where, and when remain unknown. The play was presented under the auspices of the Political Equality League in "aid of the unemployed." This makes the event sound as if it were sponsored by Marxists—but then how can one explain the presence of an Establishment audience along with leading arts figures such as Professor James Mavor, J.W. Bengough, Wyly Grier, Verna Sheard, Katherine Hale, A.E.S. Smythe and Professor DeLury (all of whom we meet elsewhere in this book, and none of whom could be described as having shown Marxist sympathies)? The play was given extensive advance publicity and all but one of the five dailies reviewed the production favourably, and they also reported that the audience showered the performers in flowers and ovations. One report implied that Levinsky still lived with her parents around this time. The only address I could find anywhere in the city for her father was **397 Palmerston Avenue** in 1919.

A playwright whose political sympathies are better known is Rick Salutin (b.1942). He moved into an apartment in the old Garfield Weston house at **469 Palmerston Boulevard** in October 1972 and stayed until the summer of 1979. This proved to be a productive address for him, in that he wrote more plays here than at any of his other Toronto addresses to date. Among his dramatic labours were *1837, Les Canadiens, The False Messiah*, and *Nathan Cohen: A Review*. He also wrote here *1837: A History/A Play* which included a full-dress history of the event, along with the script and a production diary. On top of this creative writing, he found time to write *The Organizer: A Canadian Union Life*, a biography of labour leader Kent Rowley.

Rick Salutin during a rehersal for the stage version of Ian Adam's *S: Portrait of a spy*, at Toronto Workshop Productions, Fall, 1984

A few paces to the north was one of two homes on this street of feminist poet Betsy Warland (b.1946). In 1976-77 she lived at **No.480**, and in 1978-79 she lived at **No.512**.

The playwright John Gray (b.1946) moved to Toronto in 1975 to be a director of Theatre Passe Muraille. While in the city his artistic tasks including writing the music score for two plays by Rick Salutin (*1837* and *The False Messiah*) and writing all of his own musical, *18 Wheels*. This latter play has been produced at major theatres across Canada and is almost as popular as the next play he wrote, *Billy Bishop Goes to War*. *Billy* premiered in Vancouver, to which Gray had returned, but much of the play was written while he lived at **627 Bloor Street West** for the first six months of 1976.

Moving one block west we discover **652 Euclid Avenue**, the home (1894-96) of Ezra Hurlburt Stafford (1865-1912?). Stafford had an exotic life. Born near Sarnia, he studied arts at McGill before enrolling in Law in Winnipeg. His legal training was interrupted by the Northwest Rebellion (his unit was the Prince of Wales Rifles). With Riel's demise, he left the prairies, signing on as an ordinary seaman in the merchant marine. After a few years of pelagic travel he settled in Toronto and worked as a reporter before finding himself attracted to Medicine in 1886. He pursued studies in that field at the UofT and graduated as an MD, although he was fond of pointing out that he always regarded himself, above all else, as a writer. No doubt he found plenty of background material in his daytime duties, for much of his medical practice was devoted to mental diseases at the Ontario Medical College for Women and at the Toronto Hospital for the Insane. He returned to the sea in 1900, serving as the onboard surgeon for the sealer *Neptune* but hurried back to Toronto to continue a more traditional practice the following year. He disappears from the public record c. 1912.

Poet and social critic Brian Fawcett (b.1944) occupied **638 Euclid** from June 1992 until April 1997. Although his first books were poetry, he has since abandoned that form for fiction and polemical essays. At this address he wrote some of his best-known works in these latter categories including *Gender Wars*, *The Disbeliever's Dictionary* and *Guide to the Intellectual Low Road*. Since then he has lived elsewhere on the street.

At **286 Harbord Street** between Euclid and Manning lies Harbord Collegiate. This is one of the oldest of Toronto secondary schools, and as a result can count some important Canadian authors among those who have sat in its classrooms:

William Talbot Allison
Edward Ashworth
Lereine Ballantyne
Beverley Baxter
Ethel Hume Bennett
Nathaniel Benson
Dionne Brand
David Donnell
Kathleen Coburn
David French
Basil King
Henry Kreisel
Gerry Shikatani
Joan Skelton
David Lewis Stein
Helen Weinzweig

Franco-Manitoban writer Paul Savoie moved to Toronto in August 1986 and first settled "into a house on **543 Euclid** with my wife, her cousin and two cats. It was a charming, narrow, slightly dilapidated house in dire need of repair but quite conducive to creative writing . . . While there I completed *The Meaning of Gardens* (Black Moss, 1987). I also wrote the first three stories of *Cosmic Picnic*, a book of horror and science fiction stories, and began work with Marie-Lynn Hammond on *Mimi's Bar & Grill*, a futuristic musical." He left this address as his marriage was disintegrating c. November 1987. Marjorie Pickthall, whom we met earlier in this tour on Markham Street, also lived at **537 Euclid** from 1907-10. While ensconced here she wrote one of her books for young adults, *Billy's Hero, or The Valley of Gold* (1908) and undoubtedly some of the poems that appeared in her most famous single volume, *The Drift of Pinions* (1913).

Before Franklin Davey McDowell (1888-1965) became a novelist, and director of the Public Relations Dept. of the CNR, he worked as a reporter for the *M&E*. While employed as a journalist he lived at **No.512** (1917-18). His first novel, *The Champlain Road* (1939), won the Governor General's Award. Playwright Allan Stratton (*Nurse Jane Goes to Hawaii*) inhabited the second floor of **No.496** from September 1973 to April 1974 while completing his master's degree in Drama at the UofT. The author of two well-received works of fiction, Helen Weinzweig (b.1915) passed her youth alone with her mother, a hairdresser, first in rooms at **No.428** (1926-77), and then at **No.344** (1928-c.1933). In an interview, she recalled her arrival at the age of nine from Poland: "I had never been to school, and I had to learn to read and write. English was my first written language, and it had a tremendous impact. I remember leaving the room when anybody spoke Yiddish or Polish. The associations of both were very traumatic for me."

Also spending part of his youth on this street was playwright David French (b.1939). He and his parents lived at **No.355** for about three years in the middle of the 1950s. Artist and poet Robert Fones had digs at **No.352** for the last three years of the 1970s. While here he wrote much of *House Viruses* and *Butter Models*, and worked on visual art he showed at the Carmen Lamanna Gallery.

When Montreal native Beatrice Redpath (1886-1937) married in 1910, she moved to Toronto with her husband and lived at **No.352** for a few years. She wrote poems and stories. To see how one's man's meat is another man's poison one need only compare the critical vocabulary used to describe her work in 1922 ("we know of no writer of the period who has a greater power of evoking a sense of the poignancy of great beauty than Mrs. Redpath") with that used in 1989 ("a slick writer of mindless romances"). When poet Libby Scheier (b.1946) came to live in Toronto from New York in 1975 she settled at **No.119** for her first five years.

Albert Durrant Watson (1859-1926) lived at **10 Euclid Avenue** for most of his adulthood (1886-1926). He was a poet of note, a doctor of note, and a Theosophist of note. In his life, Watson published more than 20 books, including a large *Poetical Works* in 1924. He was also extremely interested in the next life, and a few of his books "explore" the possibilities of knowing what comes after death: *The Twentieth Plane: A Psychic*

Albert Durrant Watson

Revelation, *Birth Through Death: The Ethics of the Twentieth Plane*, and *Mediums and Mystics: A Study in Spiritual Laws and Psychic Forces*. Whether Watson and his fellow believers were dupes or savants depends, I suppose, on your predilection for believing in the reality of mythology. Watson held many séances at his Euclid home with the American medium Louis Benjamin, and the spirit-sessions were of a distinctly literary bent. The poet John Robert Colombo is an expert on the history of psychic research in this country, and in his book *Mysterious Canada* he outlines how the ghosts operated: "The Twentieth Plane is or was a place that abounded in good spirits with familiar names. For instance, Benjamin contacted the poetic spirit of Samuel Taylor Coleridge and was able to communicate with him. The deceased English poet was impressed with the seriousness shown by Watson and Benjamin, and he offered to contribute a preface to the second volume of their findings. The offer was accepted, the words were transmitted and transcribed, and the preface was duly published. So this little-known volume came complete with a hitherto-unknown prose work signed by S.T.C. . . . Not only did the spirits of the dead approve Watson's plans to publish their privileged communications, they set up a Publication Committee on the Twentieth Plane. The committee consisted of four notables: Abraham Lincoln, Ralph Waldo Emerson, Walt Whitman, and Robert G. Ingersoll.

"It is a comforting thought to realize that Canadian literature, although it may be ignored on the earthly plane, is widely read on the Twentieth Plane. It seems that John Keats enjoys reading the poems of Robert Norwood, whose writing is now entirely out of fashion and out of print. Tennyson, though regrettably unfamiliar with the poems of W.W. Campbell, is familiar with Bliss Carman's poetry." It would be wrong to leave the reader with the sense that Watson was a fool in other matters. He was not. In addition to being a medical doctor held in high standing by his colleagues, he was a former President of the Royal Astronomical Society, and held a variety of posts on social welfare committees of the Methodist Church of Canada. Whenever he could, he would promote contemporary Canadian writers among those who did not know them. In this vein, he published the first critical study of his friend, poet Robert Norwood.

Novelist and poet Margaret Atwood (b.1939) kept an office at **82 Manning Avenue** from 1980-85. Among the books she wrote in whole or in part at this address were *True Stories* (1981), *Bodily Harm* (1981), *Interlunar* (1984), and *The Handmaid's Tale* (1985). This block has also been the home of novelist Christine Slater (b.1960) since 1996. A few metres to the north, at **No.180**, sculptor and poet Eldon Garnet (b.1946) passed his earliest years.

Nathaniel Benson (1903-66) was born at **No.222** and lived here until c. 1912 when the family moved next door to **No.224**. Nat remained at this address until 1932. By this latter date he had already won the Jardine Prize for poetry at the UofT. (It's worth noting how good a barometer of future poetic talent the Jardine Prize was. Among others who won it and who went on to high standing as poets were Dorothy Livesay and Robert Finch.) In addition to publishing six volumes of his own poetry, Benson did noble duty as editor of *Canadian Poetry Magazine*, 1937-43. For *Saturday Night* he was a frequent contributor of drama criticism, a field he was qualified to write about because he wrote three one-act plays (all produced at Hart House). Benson's work was held in high esteem by senior poets; for example, when he gave his first major public reading in December 1928 (he was only 26 years old) for the Canadian Authors' Association, he attracted to the event Charles G.D. Roberts, Wilson MacDonald, J.M. Elson, and E.J. Pratt.

Poet George Whipple was born in New Brunswick in 1927 but came with his family to Toronto the following year. In 1950 he moved to the top floor of **No.381** and lived there for the next three decades. It was at this address that he wrote his first volume, *Life Cycle* (1984).

Evan MacColl died at his home, **453 Manning Avenue**, in 1898. Born in Strathclyde Scotland in 1808, MacColl was fluent in both English and Gaelic but preferred to write and publish in the Gaelic tongue. In 1850 he came to Canada to visit relatives but decided to remain. Due to the widespread prevalence of Scottish immigrants in Victorian Canada (and their nostalgia for the old country) his Robbie Burns-like poetry found a large following and he soon was regarded as the most important Gaelic poet in the country. The Marquis of Lorne, Governor General of Canada and himself a writer, intervened personally to ensure that MacColl was made a charter member of the Royal Society of Canada in 1882. Despite MacColl's high profile and the fact that he lived to be 90, biographical data are hard to come by. He was extensively eulogized by the newspapers at his death (the *M&E* described him as "the oldest and probably the best-known poet in Canada" regardless of language) yet they could not agree on when he had moved to Toronto. It seems he moved to the USA for a couple of years when he was in his eighties, and probably returned to live in Toronto at Manning Avenue c. 1892.

Near where Manning Avenue intersects with Bloor Street West was once the home of Hubert Evans (1892-1986), an author usually associated with the west coast. Evans is a legendary figure in British Columbia. He was a logger, fisherman, fisheries inspector, trapper, boat-builder, beachcomber—and author. The empathy he showed with native culture was extraordinary for its time (see especially *Mist on the River*, 1954), and his other writing about life on the coast clearly appeals to something amorphous but powerful to those who live in the region. Wanting badly to be a writer, he moved from his native Galt, Ontario, to Toronto when quite young (c. 1910) to work as a reporter, first at the *M&E*, then the *World*. He certainly roomed at **659 Bloor Street West**, just west of Manning, in 1913 and this may have been his address for the first six years he spent here (the standard sources for addresses do not list him otherwise). The literary historian Alan Twigg, writing while Evans was still alive (Evans died aged a venerable 94), described an episode from the first of his Toronto stays: "Hubert Evans has received a great many accolades in his writing career, the most recent his honorary doctorate from Simon Fraser University in 1984, followed in 1985 by the decision of the B.C. Book Prize committee to name the province's annual non-fiction award after him. One of the honours he remembers most fondly remains the standing ovation he received from the news staff of the *Toronto World* in June 1914 when, as a 22-year-old reporter, he returned from his world-shared coverage of the sinking of the *Empress of Ireland*, a CPR liner that collided with a Norwegian ship during a fog on the St.

Lawrence on May 29. Over 900 lives were lost in this tragedy. The majority of the 1,476 passengers on board the *Empress of Ireland* were from Toronto. Evans' interviews with the survivors—under the initially misspelled byline of Herbert R. Evans—and his reportage on the legal aftermath of this unprecedented marine disaster, earned him overnight respect as a journalist." Evans enlisted in 1915 and was shipped overseas. Demobbed, he returned to Toronto and worked at the *World* for a few months, a changed man. As Twigg relates, "He was offered a job as City Hall reporter for the *World*. 'I looked at the old grey faces there. Some of the old desk men that I had worked under were getting on. And I'm not a city person . . . ' It was late March [1919]. The city was covered with dirty snow. He took his press pass and went, via an army transport train, to visit his parents who had moved to New Westminster." He remained on the coast for the rest of his life, apart from the winter of 1924-25 when, on a leave of absence from his civil service job, he returned to Toronto to write fiction and renew contacts with editors, friends, and fellow scribes.

Clinton Street is relatively devoid of literary connections, although apt. 1 at **330 Clinton** deserves a glance as having been the home of fiction writer Philip Kreiner (b.1950?). Both his *People Like Us in a Place Like This* (1983; nominated for the Governor General's Award) and *Heartlands* (1984) were written when he lived here 1980-83. The short-story writer Don Bailey lived a few paces north at **No.336** for a year or two in the early 1970s, and Paul Savoie whom we met on our exploration of Euclid Avenue above, also lived at **No.344** from 1987-88.

Page Street is a small artery near the top of Clinton. **18 Page Street** was the home of novelist Robert Mirvish (yes, younger brother of Honest Ed) for two decades starting in 1939. Mirvish, born in 1921, lived in this duplex with his mother. Before this (1924-39), Mirvish had lived nearby over the family grocery store at 788 Dundas Street West. Economic circumstances and his father's poor health forced him to leave school (aged 13) to help out in the shop. In a magazine profile, novelist Jock Carroll recounted: "The Mirvish store remained open from 6 a.m. until 2 a.m. the following day by using all hands. Bob found himself, in his early teens, working from 9 p.m. to 1 a.m. when business was slack. Sitting at the counter, he began to write. At first it was stories for the pulps, but by the time he was fifteen he had completed his first novel. It was first titled *Saga of a Tribesman* (later changed to *Because of Women*) and was the story of three generations of a family living in the Khyber Pass. It was written, as Mirvish ruefully says now, 'from my years of experience in the grocery business.' It was typed out by Bob's sister Lorraine. Feeling that local publishers might be prejudiced against a 15-year-old author, he had his older brother [Honest Ed] carry it into local publishing offices—from which it returned almost immediately." He left the family business to become a radio operator in the merchant marine and his extensive travels to exotic places provided much of the fare for his writing, although it was some time before his work was accepted. In fact, he was on the high seas in 1952 when he had the unusual pleasure of taking down a morse message for himself, informing him that his first book had been accepted for publication. He found being onboard ship, with long stretches of free time, to be ideal for writing. Later, during shore leave at home, he sat at a portable typewriter on a folding bridge table and refined the novels. Among the books he wrote at this address are *The Eternal Voyagers*

(1953), *The Long Watch* (1954), *Red Sky at Midnight* (1955), *Texana* (1954), and *Woman in a Room* (1959).

The most significant literary address on **Clinton Street** is **No.23** where poet and publisher John Imrie (b.1846) died in 1902. A Glaswegian by birth, and a devout Presbyterian by upbringing, Imrie emigrated to Toronto in 1871 where he continued his labours as a printer, and as a proselytizer for his church. Most of his life was devoted to celebrating things Caledonian, and he made his living in part by publishing periodicals such as the weekly *The Scottish-*

Robert Mirvish, Spring 1939, standing in front of 18 Page Street

Canadian and anthologies such as *The Scottish-Canadian Collection of Poetry*. His own poetry book of devotional and patriotic verses, *Songs and Miscellaneous Poems,* was first published in 1888, but demand was so high there were continually enlarged editions published in 1891 (with an Introduction by G. Mercer Adam), 1894, 1902, and 1906—a formidable printing history indeed.

The leader of the painters known as the Group of Seven, J.E.H. Macdonald, (1873-1932) was not, alas, one of our best poets, but write and publish poetry he did, following a nervous breakdown in 1917. For three years (1896-98) he lived at **113 Bellwoods Avenue**.

Canon Frederick George Scott (1861-1944) was both an Anglican cleric and a poet. Most of his life and career were spent in Montreal but late in his life he made highly public and popular visits to Toronto to lecture. During WWI he was the senior chaplain with the main body of Canadian troops and he was renowned among the troops for his courage at the front. In fact, he was mentioned in dispatches on many occasions, and was wounded near the end of the war. He published several volumes before and after the war, and even tried his hand at fiction with a novel in 1892. Scott's writing was conservative in theme and style yet his politics were socialist, even radical, even with old age, and no doubt had heavy influence on his better-known son, F.R. Scott. On October 21, 1923, he gave the guest sermon at the seven o'clock service at St. Matthias' Church at **45 Bellwoods**.

When C.H.J. Snider (1879-1971) died, the obituaries in the Toronto newspapers emphasized his 65-year affiliation as a senior editor with the *Telegram*. His books were mentioned almost as afterthoughts. Now, it is his books that are of continuing interest to historians and history buffs, especially those that deal with Great Lakes shipping. The short stories inspired by his maritime interests were published in 1913 as *In the Wake of the Eighteen-Twelvers,* and some of these stories were written when he lived at **39 Robinson Street** from 1898 to 1908.

Novelist Susan Swan (b.1945) rented the second-floor apartment at **21 Bellwoods Avenue** for the six years covered by 1983-88. It was at this address that she penned her controversial novel, *The Last of the Golden Girls* (1989).

Sylvia Fraser (b.1935) is now as well known for her non-fiction as for her novels. On January 1, 1988 she moved into apt. 2 at **762 Queen Street West** and there wrote the film-script based on her book about incest, *My Father's House.*

TRINITY BELLWOODS

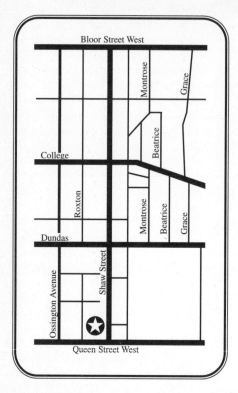

The tour begins at the northwest corner of Queen Street West and Shaw Street.

The anchor for this area—and this tour—is paradoxically no longer standing. Trinity College was razed to the ground in 1956. This destruction of a magnificent complex of collegiate Gothic buildings must rank as one of the worst acts of civic vandalism in Toronto history.

Bishop Strachan, the chief Anglican cleric in Toronto for much of the 19th c., was outraged in 1850 that the government, responding to pressure from non-Anglicans, had made the University of Toronto a secular institution, thereby removing the Anglican Church from its privileged position. To Strachan such a decision was a godless act, and partly for religious reasons and partly to show that he was a man not to be dealt with lightly, he raced to England and there obtained cash for the construction of a new college, and a charter allowing it to grant degrees. Trinity College (as it was named) was built in stages, and even a man as powerful as Strachan found that he could not raise the funds necessary to build the perfect Anglican post-secondary school. So the College gained a chapel, for example, only several decades after it had already opened its classrooms to students. Nonetheless, in part because of the use of blonde brick throughout all phases of construction, and in part because later architects were sensitive to what had been built before, the whole seemed greater than the sum of the parts. Architectural historian William Dendy noted that "Trinity was romantically picturesque

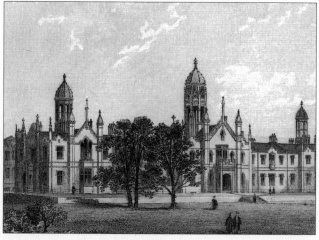

Trinity College, Queen Street West at Strachan Avenue, 19th c. engraving

rather than sternly religious in character. Designed to be seen slightly elevated on a grassy terrace, surrounded by mature trees and approached by a broad avenue from Queen Street, the building proclaimed the lineage and importance of the new college. From a distance, the central bell tower and the flanking turrets, chimneys and pinnacles, shining white against the clear blue sky, caught the eye and the imagination." Trinity College finally amalgamated with the UofT and moved to its current location on Hoskin Avenue in 1925. Its former buildings and grounds were sold to the City but the edifices were destroyed through years of deliberate neglect—and then their poor state of repair was the specious argument used to condemn them. All that remains of the original college are the gates on Queen Street at the top of Strachan Avenue, gates that marked the entrance to the original drive and sidewalk leading to the College's front door.

Several authors attended Trinity College on Queen Street as students. Gilbert Parker (1862-1932) lived and studied at Trinity (residence on campus was compulsory for students) in 1882 and then, to augment his income, from 1883-85 he continued his divinity studies while teaching Elocution. He was so poor at this time that once he had to borrow a pair of pants in order to attend a college dance. During this period he was writing a poem every few days. In 1886 his health failed him and he set sail for Australia and its warmer climes. There he wrote plays that had remarkable success, and published his first book of prose. Convinced he could make it in England, he moved to Britain and began to publish the historical novels, such as *The Seats of the Mighty* (1896), for which he would become world famous. He made a number of return trips to Toronto throughout his life, and on two occasions he returned to his alma mater on Queen Street to speak. The first was on June 1, 1898 at 4:00 p.m. when he gave a lecture on "The Art of Fiction"; his second was to speak at the convocation of March 1923.

Henry Bedford-Jones (1887-1949), like Gilbert Parker, was both a graduate of Trinity (B.A. 1908) and an extremely popular historical novelist. His literary path through the world began with short stories published while he was still an undergrad. It seems he left Toronto immediately upon gaining his degree, heading first for the USA and then Europe. He wrote so much fiction, especially for pulp magazines, that he became a millionaire at a relatively young age. He admitted to writing more than 100 books under at least 15 pseudonyms. Wealth did not protect him from scandal, however. At the height of the Depression his first wife sued the second Mrs. Bedford-Jones for stealing her husband away—and was awarded $100,000 (U.S.) as "heart-balm" by the jury. Within weeks, Bedford-Jones's 17-year-old daughter accused her father of writing libellous comments about her in *Liberty*, a mass-circulation magazine, and this incident too was widely reported in newspapers across the English-speaking world. In addition to the pulp fiction, some of it set in Canada, Bedford-Jones published two books of poetry which, as a student of type design, he himself hand-set.

Charles W. Bell (1876-1938) led a charmed life: he became one of the most famous criminal lawyers in Upper Canada, a hugely popular Member of Parliament, an Ontario amateur champion in at least two sports, the author of 11 plays that ran on Broadway, and the writer of musicals that featured music and lyrics by the Gershwin brothers.

Philip Child (1898-1978) was a poet and novelist who is remembered today primarily for his novel *The Village of Souls* (1933), although another novel, *Mr. Ames Against Time*, won the Governor General's Award for 1949. He enrolled at Trinity in 1915 and completed his studies after serving overseas in the WWI. After holding a variety of jobs elsewhere, Child returned to Trinity (by now removed to Hoskin Avenue) to teach English in 1942 and remained with the faculty until he retired.

Archibald Lampman (1861-99) has long been regarded as one of the finest Canadian poets of the 19th c. He arrived at Trinity from Port Hope in 1879 and at once settled into the section of the east wing reserved for freshmen, tellingly known as "The Wilderness." Although students had individual rooms, they were Spartan, as his biographer Carl Conner delineates: "Most of the rooms had fireplaces with an accompanying woodbox. The thick walls were undecorated. The windows were high and narrow; lighting was by gas. The furniture was of the most meagre description— a chair, a bench, a table, a bookcase, a bed and a washstand—all of them bearing obvious evidence of the usage of former occupants." The students were summoned to chapel at 7:15 in the morning (in the academic gowns they were to wear all day), followed by a breakfast of porridge. Lectures consumed the morning; the afternoons were supposed to be for reading and study. Evening chapel after dinner was compulsory. And so to bed.

Despite this near-monastic existence, Lampman enjoyed his undergraduate years. As a sophomore, he was an occasional contributor of critical essays—but no poetry—to the school's just-born literary magazine. But not much later he would devote so much time to this college periodical that it affected his marks. That, and beer-drinking and poetry talk in town with Charles G.D. Roberts, his contemporary. Lampman left an account of the strong emotions he felt on first looking into Roberts's *Orion* when both poets were only 20 years old: "Like most of the young fellows about me, I had been under the depressing conviction that we were situated hopelessly on the outskirts of civilization, where no art and no literature could be, and that it was useless to expect that anything great could be done by any of our companions, still more useless to expect that we could do it ourselves. I sat up most of the night reading and re-reading *Orion* in a state of the wildest excitement and when I went to bed I could not sleep. It seemed to me a wonderful thing that such work could be done by a Canadian, by a young man, one of ourselves. It was like a voice from some new paradise of art, calling to us to be up and doing. A little after sunrise I got up and went out into the college grounds. The air, I remember, was full of the odour and cool sunshine of the spring morning. The dew was thick upon the grass, all the birds of our Maytime seemed to be singing in the oaks, and there were even a few adder tongues and trilliums still blooming on the slope of the little ravine. But everything was transfigured for me beyond description, bathed in an old world radiance of beauty, the magic of the lines was sounding in my ears, those divine verses as they seemed to me, with their Tennysonian-like richness and strange earth-loving Greekish flavour. I have never forgotten that morning, and its influence has always remained with me." Lampman graduated in 1882 with an Honours degree in Classics and within a few months was a civil servant in Ottawa. As the years progressed, his reputation as a poet became larger and ever more impressive.

John Plummer Llwyd (1861-1933) obtained two degrees from Trinity: a

Archibald Lampman

Bachelor of Divinity in 1905, and a Doctor of Divinity three years later. He was a church rector in three western states of America before returning to Trinity to be its Vice-Provost in 1909. He published ambitious books of poetry, including *The Vestal Virgin: A Dramatic Poem* (1920).

Knox Magee (1877-1934) made his living as a journalist but found time to write two historical novels, both published in Toronto around the turn of the century. Literary history assigns a higher value to his editorship of *Moon*, a periodical modelled on the British magazine *Punch*. *Moon* was eclipsed after less than two years (1902-3), but it was one of the first magazines in Toronto to try to cultivate a Canadian approach to humour. Magee claimed to have studied at Trinity, but if he did, the records of when he was here have vanished.

There is little of literary significance immediately to the west of Trinity-Bellwoods Park on this tour. But north of Dundas there are a number of literary connections. For example, Morley Callaghan lived at his in-laws' house at **191 Roxton Road** for some months during 1931-33 while coming to terms with the Depression and a Toronto very different from the Paris he had just left behind. While here he put the finishing touches on his novel *A Broken Journey*. Another novelist, Nino Ricci (b.1959), lived at **No.241** from 1993-97. The third novel of his trilogy, *Where She Has Gone* (1997), was written at this address. That book was published a year later in the USA and was nominated as a Book of the Year by *Time*. This street has been home to a third novelist: Helen Weinzweig (b.1915) lived for half a decade at **No.360** with her new husband, the composer John Weinzweig, immediately after they were married in 1940. Weinzweig did not begin to write until she was 45 years old. She then published two books that garnered much applause: *Passing Ceremony* (1973) and *Basic Black with Pearls* (1980). Her third volume, *A View from the Roof* (1990), a collection of stories,

was nominated for the Governor General's Award.

The daring playwright Herman Voaden (1903-91) supported his writing habit by teaching during the day. Most of his time as a pedagogue was spent at Central Commerce, **570 Shaw Street**. He taught English here from 1928 to 1964. Voaden was never a popular playwright but he was a thinking man's dramatist. His works had larger themes than those of his contemporaries in Canada and he was singular in welcoming the influence of foreign specialists such as Antonin Artaud into Canadian theatre. Voaden was also a politically *engagé* writer: he ran on the CCF ticket for the Trinity riding in four federal elections, losing every time to Lionel Conacher, one of the most popular sports figures in Canadian history. He later quit the party over its support for state funding of Catholic schools. He was given the Order of Canada in 1974. At his death, he was remembered for his commitment to Canadian art, landscape, and images, and for his advocacy of the creation of the Canada Council.

Cary Fagan, born in Toronto in 1957, moved into the second-floor flat at **684 Shaw Street** in April 1988 and remained for about two years. It was here that he wrote three of the five stories of his first collection, *History Lessons* (1990). Before the book was published, he and his wife printed, sewed, and bound one of the stories in a deluxe limited edition in this apartment— one of the first titles to appear under their Shaw Street Press imprint.

Novelist Margot Livesey (b.1953) came to Canada from her native Scotland in the 1970s. At first, while waiting for her citizenship papers to come through, she worked at a variety of odd jobs, including the selling of roses in restaurants and packing incense in a Hare Krishna factory. Such work did not allow her much time for writing, so in the little time she did have she wrote stories. "When I finished work late at night, I often hitch-hiked home through the city and my first published story was about a man who gives a young woman a lift." The place she would come home to was **No.723**, where she lived from 1977-79. "Growing up in a remote part of Scotland [as I did], Toronto was the first city I knew well and what better place to discover the pitfalls and possibilities of urban life. Poised between the new world and the old, the conservative and the radical, Toronto taught me to look both ways at once. During the decade I lived there, the city gave me my first tantalising glimpses of living writers and, gradually, painfully, turned me into a writer." Livesey's novels and stories have been praised in the USA, UK, and Canada. She remains a Canadian citizen although she has been living and teaching in the USA since 1982.

Two streets to the east is **Montrose Avenue**. **492 Montrose Avenue** was the first Toronto home of the critically acclaimed British novelist Patrick McGrath (b.1950), who actually started his writing career in this city. McGrath's five novels have been called brilliant and chilling by the leading critics of three continents and have been translated into more than a dozen languages. When he landed in Toronto, he was still trying to decide if he wanted to be an academic or a full-time author. Of that time he has said: "October 1972 to May 1973 I lived in an apartment on Montrose Avenue across Bloor from Christie Pits . . . I wasn't a writer of any description then, though I did have an unusual job. I worked as a gofer on a movie being made at Kleinburg called *The Poseidon Adventure* with Ernest Borgnine and I don't know who else. They built a pool for the underwater sequences, then covered the bottom of the pool with gravel. But the gravel was dusty and made the water cloudy which made it impossible to film in. Somebody had to wash the dust off the gravel.

"Enter our hero. A bitterly cold winter; a mountain of dusty gravel on a desolate film lot; a hosepipe; a sieve. I couldn't wear gloves because they got soggy then froze. So with

bare hands, in subzero temperatures, for several weeks I hosed that gravel sievefull by icy sievefull, like some Jack London character in the Klondike; and all in the cause of world cinema. What a miserable job."

When playwright Rick Salutin was born in 1942, his parents were dwelling in the middle unit of a triplex at **No.490**, and the family stayed there until 1950. A few steps further south, poet and novelist Joy Kogawa (b.1935) lived from 1982 to 1994 at **No.447**. Many readers know her for one book only, the internationally acclaimed *Obasan* (1982), but at this address she wrote a volume of poems, *Woman in the Woods* (1985) and the much-admired children's book *Naomi's Road* (1986). Kogawa is a Member of the Order of Canada. Poet Miriam Waddington (b.1917) lived at **No.339** from 1937-38.

Novelist Isabelle Hughes (b.1912) was born at **15 Beatrice Street**. In addition to being a regular reviewer of books in the *G&M* in the 1950s, she authored four well-received novels of her own, the best known of which was *Serpent's Tooth* (1947), a tale of two rebellious daughters in a well-to-do Toronto family. Poet Gerry Shikatani (b.1950) was born and raised in Toronto but currently lives in Montreal. He last lived in this city from 1987-90 at **No.54**. Another poet also had a flat at **No. 54** as her last Toronto address: Jan Conn (b.1952) lived there from July 1985 until she left for Latin America in 1988 in order to pursue her post-doctoral studies on various species of flies. "Nathan Ralph" was the *nom de plume* of Montreal native Nathan Ralph Goldberg (1919-60). After serving overseas in WWII with the RCAF, he moved to Toronto to finish his university undergraduate work and lived at **No.61** from 1949-56. He produced one play and two books of poetry in the 1940s. **No.102** was one of only two addresses I could find for the mysterious Urias Katzenelenbogen. He was the subject of a small profile in the *Star* in 1935. The article began, "Illegal songs which brought whipping, jail or death to those who sang them are the subject and content of an excellent volume, *The Daina: An Anthology of Lithuanian and Latvian Folk Songs* just published by the young Lithuanian poet and scholar who has been making his home in Toronto." He was cited at this address in the city directory for 1935.

Myrna Kostash at a "Love-in", Toronto, 1967

The author Myrna Kostash lived at **No.163** for three years (July 1972-June 1975) and wrote her section of the anthology of feminist essays titled *Her Own Woman* in this house. Also during this period she was one of the first employees in the then very experimental Women's Studies Program at the UofT. As Myrna wrote: "You could tell it was experimental because it hired someone like me—a working magazine writer, not an academic or activist." Her residence on

Beatrice was her last in Toronto before she returned to her native Alberta. Yet her time here was vital in some ways. "I first lived in Toronto in the late 1960s before prairie regionalism had become an identity; by the time I moved back to Alberta, in 1975, regionalism was in full, hot flower but I was already pretty much formed by my Toronto cultural experience—Canadian left nationalism, anti-Americanism, and international feminism, and have never quite got over it. In fact, it was several years before I overcame my anxiety in Edmonton that I was 'missing' vital affairs by being away from Toronto.

"In any case, I have never completely left Toronto as I come and go frequently in order to attend conferences and the like. Unlike some of my prairie compatriots, I do not consider this a sinister exercise; it is in fact normal for freelance writers to have connections with their country's cultural and economic centre. The truth is, having lived most of my adult life under right-wing governments in Alberta, the chance to travel and work and lollygag in Toronto has been a blessed relief (until, that is, Ontario itself elected a right-wing government in 1995).

"At the same time, I have never wanted permanently to return to Toronto. Even in 1975 I felt that, had I stayed on as a full-time freelance, I would soon have become absorbed like so much fibre into the digestive tract of Toronto media, indistinguishable from the mush. In Edmonton I stood out. There were so few full-time writers, and we all had only just begun the project of being 'young, gifted, and western Canadian' as a film of the time put it. But it's a project that would have been nonsensical without the Toronto-based achievements of the independent publishers, artists' organizations and left-liberal clout in Ottawa. No, I don't hate Toronto."

A bookstore worth noting used to be found nearby. Milton Cronenberg ran a bookshop under his own name at **696 College Street** (between Beatrice and Montrose), starting in the mid-1930s. By 1942 the damage wrought by the Depression was exacerbated by the disappearance of much of the population overseas, and the business was forced to fold. Cronenberg's son, David, has achieved international acclaim as a director of feature films. He proudly keeps his father's business diary from the Depression years, complete with a tote of each day's sales—all cash at that time, of course. Even though it is a fascinating document, the income statements (some days he grossed less than two dollars) make for sad reading.

Milton Cronenberg standing in front of his bookshop at 696 College Street c. 1939.

weeks in the summer of 1970 shortly after leaving prison (where he served time for armed robbery) and while commencing a rehabilitation that has seen him publish a number of well-received tomes. British-born Peter Robinson (b.1950) has become well known as a detective writer, but his literary career started with poetry: "I first came to Toronto in August 1976 and lived in a top-floor flat at **128 Grace Street**, just opposite the big Catholic church south of College Street. The house was owned by a Portuguese family who lived downstairs. I lived there until May 1977 and wrote there some of the poems that went into my first collection, *With Equal Eye*, including 'Ezra Pound at St. Elizabeth's' and 'The Edge.'"

Playwright Charles Tidler (b.1946) lived at three addresses in Toronto between October 1983 and April 1984, the last of them **312 Grace Street**. During this period he saw his play *The Farewell Heart* produced at the Tarragon Theatre, and a radio play, *The Blue Devil*, produced on CBC. He also found time to write another full-length drama for the stage. Fiction writer Don Bailey (b.1942) touched down at **No.286** for a few

RUSHOLME

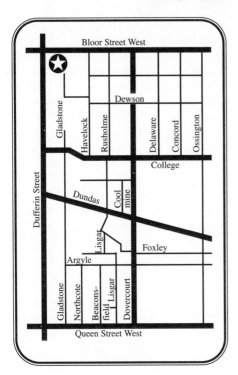

The tour begins at the southeast corner of Bloor Street West and Dufferin Street.

Walk one block east along Bloor to **Gladstone Avenue** and to where Jesse Edgar Middleton lived at **427 Gladstone Avenue** from 1912 to 1942, longer than at any other of his Toronto residences. Originally a teacher, Middleton (1872-1960) came to Toronto as a young man and lived by his pen for the rest of his life. Most of his writing was for newspapers: he had, for instance, a column for over 20 years in the *News*, and he was the music critic for the *M&E*. As a creative writer, he had an astonishing range: books of poetry, history, plays, novels, and biography. His three-volume history of Toronto was an ambitious effort and although published in 1923 it is still used by local and national historians. Middleton was a fixture in the city's cultural

politics. In 1921 he agreed to be the first head of the Toronto branch of the Canadian Authors' Association and he nurtured the organization through its infant years. His novel *Green Plush* was published in London by Methuen in 1932. In 1942 he was appointed literary editor of *Saturday Night*, succeeding Robertson Davies in the post. During the years 1904-11 he kept rooms around the corner at **1073 Bloor Street West**.

Jesse Edgar Middleton

Lereine Ballantyne (1891-1962), a once popular novelist and poet, lived at **196 Havelock Street** from 1944-54, at which time she seems to have moved to Hamilton. The acclaimed playwright George F. Walker (b.1947) began life at **349 Gladstone Avenue** and lived with his family at this address until 1950. Another internationally famous author and near-contemporary, William Gibson (b.1948), lived at more

273

than a dozen places when he was in Toronto 1967-71, but he said that he could recall only two of them, and one of those was the rear coach house of **257 Rusholme Road** (between Dewson and Hepbourne). Gibson has since gone on to become one of the best-known science fiction authors of his generation, and one of the few to break beyond the bounds of the genre to attract readers of more literary fiction. His first novel, *Neuromancer* (1984), made a spectacular debut, being the first novel ever to win the three most important SF prizes: the Philip K. Dick, the Hugo, and the Nebula. Gibson is also known, correctly, as the man who coined the word "cyberspace," a term used by millions who may never have read his work. He did no writing when he was in this city. That honour belongs to Vancouver to which he moved in 1971. The distinguished poet George Johnston (b.1913) lived briefly with his parents at **245 Rusholme Road** in 1938-39 before being sent overseas with the RCAF. Takeo Nakano (b.1943) was a haiku poet, interned by the Canadian Government during WWII. He was allowed to depart for Toronto to perform essential war work in 1943 and has lived in the city ever since. One of those addresses was **No.216** (1950-76).

Cross College Street on **Gladstone Avenue** and continue south. Another author who spent her infancy in this area is poet and novelist Phyllis Gotlieb (b.1926) who lived at **265 Gladstone Avenue** from 1927-28. Alexander Muir (1830-1906), author of "The Maple Leaf Forever" and many other poems, made his living as a teacher and then as a principal of several schools. He was the principal of Gladstone Avenue School at **No.108** from 1889 until he died in 1906. So popular a principal was he that, not long after his death, the school was renamed in his honour. In fact, there are two elementary schools named in his honour—the other is in Scarborough.

Glasgow native John Imrie kept rooms at **60 Gladstone** for a couple of years in the mid-1880s. Imrie (1846-1902) wrote and acted almost as if he never left Scotland. He edited a periodical in Toronto called *The Scottish-Canadian*, wrote poems in Scots dialect, and led the drive for a bronze statue to Robert Burns in Toronto. The success of that drive can be seen in the life-sized sculpture of the famed Scottish bard in Allan Gardens. The success, or at least the popularity of Imrie's writing can be gauged by the fact that his *Sacred Songs, Sonnets, and Miscellaneous Poems* (1886) went through at least four editions, the last in 1906, a full 20 years after the first.

The leader of the Group of Seven, J.E.H. MacDonald (1874-1932) is renowned as a landscape painter, but his fans are often surprised to learn that he fancied himself a poet of some talent. He has one book of verse to his credit. Where he lived after arriving in Toronto from England in 1887 as a young man remains cloudy, but we do know he was at **100 Northcote Avenue** in 1893 and 1894 while completing his studies at the Central Ontario School of Art and Design, forerunner of the Ontario College of Art. MacDonald then moved two blocks east to **119 Lisgar Street** where he kept rooms in 1895 and began working for Grip Printing.

West-coast playwright Joan MacLeod (b.1955) wrote in a letter: "My first year in Toronto [1985] I lived at **166 Beaconsfield Avenue**. A few months after moving in I slipped on a floor at Casa Loma and ripped up my knee. So I spent my first winter here on Beaconsfield in a tiny apartment on top of a very old house with no money, few friends and my leg up in the air. This started me off as a full-time writer. I wrote the first draft of *Toronto, Mississippi* that winter. I was a member of the Tarragon Playwrights Unit. I also wrote a poem about being single in this neighbourhood called 'When I Am Married and Portuguese,' and I think it's a pretty good testament to being a newcomer in T.O. During this time I also wrote the libretto for a chamber opera version of *The Secret Garden* (December '85 for Comus

MusicTheatre at TWP) and won the Dora Award for Best New Musical. It was at a publicity function for this opera at Casa Loma that I ripped my knee ligaments. . . . '

Alexander Muir, principal of the nearby Gladstone Avenue Public School lived at **148 Lisgar Street** 1888-89, and then at **No.254** from 1890-91.

Foxley Street runs east off Dovercourt Road. **8 Foxley Street** was the home from 1880-88 of one of the few butcher-poets in Toronto's history. When Robert Awde (1838-1921) arrived in Toronto as a young man from his native England, he worked at a meat stall on Queen Street West. The knowledge gained there qualified him for a job as a city meat inspector. That task in turn led to his promotion as the Dept. of Health's chief inspector of food and he held this position for 30 years, retiring in 1914. During that time he served under 17 different mayors of Toronto. In his lifetime he published two books of verse. The second was prefaced with a statement in which he declares his talents to be modest as a poet. This is a refreshingly different boast than one usually hears from versifiers, and in his case a boast distinguished, alas, by its accuracy. After his residence on Foxley, Awde moved around the corner to **194 Dovercourt Road** and resided there from 1889 to at least 1914.

Goldwin Smith (1823-1910) was known as the Sage of the Grange. When he first came to Toronto in 1871, he lived with relatives on Dundas Street West near the intersection with Lisgar (the records regarding the exact location are vague), and then seems to have bought—or possibly had constructed—a large house on what was part of the Rusholme Estate, namesake of the street. Given Smith's fame, and that of J.E.H. MacDonald for that matter, it is unfortunate that the early whereabouts in Toronto of these men have not proven traceable with certainty. I mention this so that the reader can have some idea of how much work yet needs to be done just to document our history—much less interpret it. My best guess is

that Goldwin Smith stayed with his relatives (who were described as poor) from 1871-72, and then moved into his large house at **1 Rusholme Road**. It was while living here that he met the widow Boulton who was to become his bride in 1875 and with whom he would then live at the Grange (at Dundas and Beverley Streets) as of October 1875. Knowing these early addresses is more than pedantry. Smith was the dominant intellectual force in the city for 40 years, and it was while in residence at Rusholme that he made the decision to stay in Canada and to become intensely involved with both national and local politics.

Smith was a brilliant student at Oxford and it was there he began writing letters to the editor and some journalism—both were to remain his passions for the rest of his life. His Huguenot background may have accounted for his college criticisms of the Church of England and its undue privileges and influence on education. Regardless, the criticisms brought him to the positive attention of the authorities and he found himself at a young age appointed to royal commissions investigating matters on which he had pontificated. By the time he was 35 he was Regius Professor of History at Oxford and fully engaged with the major debates of his day. Throughout this time he continued to write verse in Latin and translate the classical poets.

In 1867 his father committed suicide, an act for which Goldwin Smith assumed partial blame. Looking for a complete change in his life after this shock, he accepted an invitation from Cornell University. He stayed a mere two years and to this day no one is quite sure why he left upstate New York to settle in Toronto. Ithaca's brutal weather and Cornell's co-education policy have been cited as possible reasons. Regardless, the gain was certainly Toronto's, for he brought not only an air of sophistication, but real sophistication to the level of discourse attached to many topics. This is not to suggest that he was the great white bwana bringing

Enlightenment and the scientific method to the colonials. Rather, it is to say that Smith had met with, argued with, and agreed with the progenitors of many of the leading intellectual debates of the late 19th c., and his insights and connections, and, it must be emphasized, his encouragement did much to make Torontonians and Canadians feel that they were at the centre of these debates and that they had every right to participate in them, and if so inclined and properly equipped, make helpful contributions to them.

In 1873, while based at **1 Rusholme Road**, Smith declared to an English audience urging him to return to Britain that he was now committed to Canada. Or, in the words of his biographer Elisabeth Wallace: "Goldwin Smith rejected [their pleas] on the ground that the remainder of his life was too short to be divided between two countries. In Canada, he said, literary use was made of him for a variety of odd jobs . . . Moreover, he had formed ties with relatives in Toronto which he was unwilling to break, and was already involved in political journalism in Canada, so that if he left the country he would feel like a deserter leaving his friends in the lurch. In the Dominion, even a single pen was difficult to replace. The comment was characteristic of his modesty. No one in Canada ever wrote like Goldwin Smith. To the comparative magnitude of fields of action in Britain and the Dominion he was indifferent. In Canada he found ample scope, believing that what the country lacked in importance it made up in hopefulness . . . When in 1874, the National Club was founded, Goldwin Smith was chosen as its first president. He told a dinner meeting of its stockholders that, although he had lived only a few years in Canada, no native Canadian could be more loyal or more interested in its future He appreciated the kind reception given newcomers like himself who meant to cast in their lot with the country."

A few paces to the east is **Coolmine Road. No.64** was the home of poet Norah

Holland (1876-1925) from 1893 to 1902. Earlier she had roomed at **152 Argyle Street** and later she would abide briefly at **234 Dovercourt Road. 70 Coolmine Road** used to be the home of poet and novelist John Mebourne Elson (1880-1966). In fact, it was to this address he moved in 1922 when he ceased to be mayor of St. Catharines, Ontario. He remained here until 1929, during which time he published his novel *The Scarlet Sash* (1925).

At the southeast corner of Dovercourt Road and Dewson Street is **75 Dewson Street**, home from 1909-17 of James Algie (1857-1928). He studied medicine at Trinity University when it was on Queen Street West and practised medicine in small-town Ontario until 1908 when he joined the staff of the Queen Street Insane Asylum. Later, he would be the head physician at the Mercer Reformatory. Before he settled into these institutional positions, he published three novels under a pseudonym, but I have not been able to determine why he stopped writing once he came to Toronto.

Delaware Avenue has been a friendly street to authors over the years. **125 Delaware** was the only Toronto address ever held by a young poet, Alma Frances McCollum (1879-1906), who died at this address in March 1906. She and her mother had come to the city from Peterborough in September 1905. In her short life she published only one book, but that book attracted serious praise from major writers of the time including William Henry Drummond (best known for his "Little Bateese" and other *habitant* poems), Charles Mair, and Jean Blewett. By coincidence the same house was the home of John Garvin not long afterwards from 1909-10. Garvin was not himself a creative writer but was an ardent and important expositor of Canadian authors. He was the editor of *The Collected Poems of Isabella Valancy Crawford*, and the editor of an important pioneering anthology, *Canadian Poets* (1916; revised edition 1926). Other titles included *Canadian Poems of the Great War* (1918) and some of the volumes in the series *Masterworks of Canadian Literature*. His wife was the well-known author Katharine Hale, whom he married a couple of years after he quit this address.

W.W.E. Ross and Mary Lowry Ross on the back steps of their home, 62 Delaware Avenue

62 Delaware Avenue was the home for several years of W.W.E. Ross (1894-1966) and his wife, Mary Lowry Ross (1891-1984). Eustace Ross was the most important Imagist poet ever produced by Canada. He graduated from the UofT in 1914 with a degree in Chemistry and was a geophysicist with the Dominion Magnetic Observatory for all of his professional life. Much of his work was in deliberate opposition to the kind of writing favoured by McCollum and Garvin; Ross preferred the spare, clean image and line, unadorned by flowery romanticism. His best work is a literary equivalent of the hard-edged landscape painting of Lawren Harris. Indeed, he travelled through the same countryside that so affected the Group of Seven. Ross was an extremely private person, rarely given to public appearances of any kind. He and his

wife (a journalist, and close friend of Ernest Hemingway) were regular bridge partners with Morley Callaghan and his wife. Other than that, his contacts with the book world appear to have been nil. The Rosses moved to this address shortly after they were married in 1924. He died here of cancer in 1966.

Novelist Gerald Lampert (1922-78) spent part of his boyhood (1936-40) living at **18 Delaware**. In addition to writing novels, Lampert organized the first important writing seminars in Canada. These took place at Glendon College as well as at Ryerson and the UofT. David French and Wendy Lill were just two students of these courses who have gone to national renown.

Among the authors who have attended Dewson Street Public School at **108 Concord Avenue** are playwright Rick Salutin (1948-51) and poet David Knight (1932-36). Playwright Guillermo Verdecchia (b.1962) lived on the third floor of **121 Concord** for most of 1991, and while there wrote much of his play *Fronteras Americanas* (1993), winner of the Governor General's Award for Drama. The esteemed historian and novelist Donald Creighton (1902-79) lived the first decade of his life at **No.262**. His two-volume biography of Sir John A. Macdonald has been the standard ever since it was published.

BROCKTON

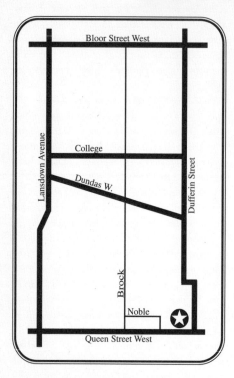

The tour begins at the northwest corner of Dufferin Street and Queen Street West.

Poet Elizabeth Woods (b.1940) lived at **No.1282 Queen Street West** from August 1974 until May 1979, her longest stay at any one address during her Toronto period. The poems in *Men* (1979) were written entirely at this address.

The eminent British novelist Patrick McGrath actually began his writing career in Toronto. He arrived in the city in October 1972, a young immigrant finding his way in the world. When summer arrived the following year he went to British Columbia where he remained until July 1980. Then he returned to Toronto to live until December 1981, first, for a few months in a loft at **50 Noble Street**, and then in an apartment around the corner at **1340**

Queen Street West. This was an important time in his professional life as he explained in a letter: "I had only just recently made the decision to become a writer, and was unpublished. I had a teaching diploma and worked as a substitute teacher, mostly in Scarborough. This I supplemented with a much more interesting job writing curriculum materials for an educational publisher . . . I was also taking graduate courses at OISE in sociology, philosophy and education. But I was hanging out, not with students, or other writers but with Toronto artists, the group that showed at Mercer

Elizabeth Rhett Woods

Union and other downtown spaces . . . Being so much around artists in Toronto was important to my writing in those days, and my first published work was in a Canadian art magazine. I also saw my first fiction published in this period, in a literary magazine called *Writ*, edited by Roger Greenwald, out of Innis College.

"This I guess is what Toronto means to me, as a writer: the place where I first published, and where the first inchoate attempts to develop a voice, a style, a way of working as a fiction writer, bore fruit. It was a strange time. My sense of identity was fragile—I had no roots—I was in transit—I was embarking on an ambitious adventure—that is, becoming a writer—with no sort of guarantee of it amounting to anything. This is not so unusual, but I was thirty years old and painfully aware of having, as I saw it then, wasted much time . . . I began to forge an identity as a writer, as important a process at the time as the slow and gradual acquisition of technique. This is what happened in Toronto, and very valuable to my development as a writer it was."

At the Sunnyside Clinic, **1437 Queen Street West,** the Irish playwright Brendan Behan had one of the longest dry spells of his life: a fortnight's worth of alcohol-free days in the private hospital still located at this address. His incarceration was not voluntary and he hated every second he had to stay here.

Behan was in town in March 1961 as the star of a jazz musical having its premiere at the O'Keefe Centre (as the Hummingbird Centre at Yonge and Front streets was then known). He was obviously inebriated at the opening performance and even more obnoxiously drunk afterwards in the nightclubs from which he was bounced. Back in his room at the Royal York Hotel, he demanded more drink, but the hotel refused to meet his request either because he was drunk or because closing time had passed. Enraged, he assaulted the house detective sent to calm him, and then further assaulted one of the police officers sent to apprehend him for the attack on the detective. He was arrested on several charges and remanded on bail. The next day, when his arrest was all over the front pages of the papers, he was fired from the musical. Released on bail, a few days later he failed to show for his trial on the assault charges because he had resumed his heavy drinking—so heavy, in fact, that the alcohol actually reached toxic levels in his body. His desperate friends checked him into the Sunnyside Private Hospital (acclaimed for treating alcoholics), with the hope that he might be saved from killing himself with booze. He arrived here on the night of March 26 and was released on April 13, 1961. Upon release, he was re-arrested for failing to make his first trial appearance. A new trial date was set, Behan posted bail, fled Canada for New York, and returned (sober) on April 27 to be fined two hundred dollars by

—Globe and Mail, John Young, Loubé.

Shackled to Officer, Irish Playwright Brendan Behan Is Brought Into Court
He faces charges of assault and causing a disturbance in Toronto hotels.

Brendan Behan, handcuffed to a policeman on his way into court to face charges of assault and causing a disturbance

G&M, March 23, 1961

the judge. He paid immediately, and as he left Toronto that day for the last time, he described the city in architectural terms: "a not too picturesque lunatic asylum."

Queen intersects a few steps to the west with Lansdowne Avenue. **219 Lansdowne Avenue** was the household of poet Verna Harden (b.1904) for about three years (1924-26). Harden was a better poet than obscurity would have her. One of her poems, "Post Mortem," is as poignant today as when it was written in the 1940s and could easily describe many of the homes found near Queen and Lansdowne:

This is the shack where the old man died;
Not unhappy, not afraid,
But weary of the long, long day
And aching from the effort of living.

This is the table where his last meal lay
Long untouched, when they found him,
The thick-sliced bread shrinking into the
   crust,
The tea stone cold,
The sugar being carried laboriously away
By small black ants.

This mended chair creaked under him
Though he weighed less each year;
That sweater hanging on the back of the
   door
Was far too wide for his shoulders.

He had only one cup and saucer.
His dog died years ago.
He never had a wife.

Let us go outside now.
The old man was not used to visitors
And he might resent our curiosity.

A renaissance man lived at **58 Brock Avenue** in Confederation Year and probably longer. William Hodgson Ellis (1845-1921) was a medical graduate who practically invented forensic chemistry in Canada. From 1876-1907 he developed the techniques in the lab and in the courtroom which form so much a part of detective thrillers today. Historian Jesse Middleton wrote: "No other circumstances threw into more prominent relief his outstanding qualities than the investigation of some suspected case of poisoning. No pains were too great, no precaution was too trivial when the laboratory examination was under way, and in the witness box his evidence was so clear, direct and unmistakable that it was never shaken by counsel." In addition to his work in science (for which he was made a Fellow of the Royal Society of Canada), he wrote lyric poems, some of which were published in a volume in 1913.

HIGH PARK EAST

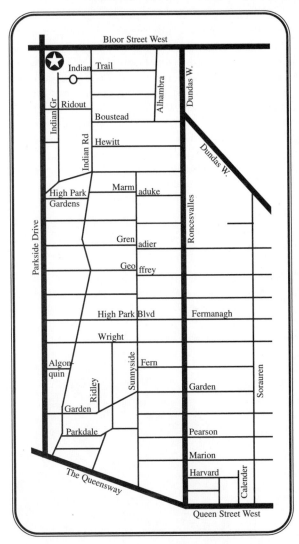

The tour begins at the southeast corner of Parkside Drive and Bloor Street West.

For almost 60 years (1912-71), a span roughly equivalent with the time he held various high-level editorial posts at the *Telegram*, C.H.J. Snider (1879-1971) lived at **499 Parkside Drive**. Outside of the newspaper world, he was acclaimed for his knowledge of, and books on Canadian ships. He wrote, for example, about his involvement in the unearthing of—and the restoration of—the valiant *Nancy*, a schooner burned and sent to the bottom of the Nottawasaga River by the Americans during the War of 1812. His other titles are noted for their professional attention to detail. But it is his meticulous drawings and paintings of Great Lakes ships and boats which have won the undying admiration of historians and buffs. Less celebrated (although perhaps of interest to those same buffs—or any students of that era) are his short stories published in the volume *In the Wake of the Eighteen Twelvers* (1913 and 1969), tales addressing various nautical incidents on the lakes from an overtly Canadian vantage.

Snider would certainly have known Kim Beattie, his colleague at the *Telegram* for several years, who lived around the corner at **25 Ridout Street**. Earlier in life, at the outbreak of WWI, Beattie (1900-63) had run away from his Guelph home—at the age of 14—to fight overseas. The authorities claimed not to have known that he had been underage until he was wounded four years later. He put his time in the trenches to good use writing poems that were later published in the book *And You* (1930). His military experience was of help when he came to write *Dileas* (1959), a history of the famous 48th Highlanders. A little further up the street, at **No.5**, can be found one of the last homes of the Victorian author Jean Blewett (1862?-1934). She was an early female contributor to the *Globe*. Ill health forced a premature end to her journalism career in 1925 as editor of the paper's Homemaker's Department. For several years she hosted an evening for the Women's Art Association wherein she introduced new Canadian writing and authorial stars. In 1925, when she was unable to prepare the annual literary occasion, others stepped in (including Florence Randal Livesay) and the night was publicly named in Blewett's honour. Jean Blewett wrote the kind of poetry the public loved and knowledgeable critics despised. In the words of one commentator, "She does not attempt wild flights of rhapsody or deep philosophical problems. It is an everyday sort of poetry, simple in theme and treatment . . . In sentiment and morals her poems are wholesome. . . ." Blewett lived here from 1922-24.

A block or so away, in an apartment at **89 Indian Grove,** Gwendolyn MacEwen (1941-87) spent a few months in 1953 with her mother. Indian Trail intersects at this point. Playwright Herman Voaden boarded from 1929-31 and possibly earlier at **28 Indian Trail.** At this time Voaden (1903-91) had started to teach English at Central High School of Commerce and was already working on the large, singular plays that were never popular with the public but which would eventually win the admiration of professional scholars of drama. While living at this address, Voaden published *Six Canadian Plays* (1930). Next door, at **No.30,** feminist author Betsy Warland (b.1946) lived for a couple of years in the mid-1970s, not along after she had emigrated to Canada from the USA. She reports that it was effectively at this address she began her writing career.

Indian Trail intersects with **Indian Road** near here and it's worth making a tiny detour a few steps north to look at **435 Indian Road,** for it was here that Mazo de la Roche (1879-1961) lived with her family for a few

summers around the turn of the century and for possibly all of 1902. The house belonged to her art teacher, G.A. Reid, the renowned narrative painter. He, presumably, was away in the summer months on sketching expeditions, but why Mazo's family was the beneficiary of his palatial largesse is unknown. As are the exact times they were here. That she was here we do know because she used **435 Indian Road** as the return address for some of the stories she wrote at this address and which she sent to various magazines in Canada and the USA.

Indian Trail ends at **Alhambra Avenue. 26 Alhambra Avenue** was the last home of poet Nora Holland (1876-1925) who died here, a victim of tuberculosis. She had been single for all but the last three years of her life, two of those years spent at this address. Her poetry was mystical but hardly in the same league as her famous cousin William Butler Yeats, although Yeats was fond of visiting her during his Toronto stops. Prior to her final illness she had worked as an editor at Macmillan of Canada.

Norah Holland

12 **Alhambra Avenue** was the only home in Toronto Thomas Barwell Gleave (1882-1971) ever had. Born in England, he had come to this city in 1919 to head the Canadian arm of his family's agricultural feed empire. A Toronto historian, writing in 1923, remarked, "In connection with their business the concern has operated, in both England and the United States, experimental farms which fill the purpose of demonstration, and they plan to inaugurate a similar enterprise in Canada. Personally, Mr. Gleave is doing efficient educational work among the farmers of the Dominion, particularly with reference to poultry, through lectures to poultry associations, farmers' clubs, etc., and he is considered a leading authority on all questions relating to poultry." All was going well until something terrible—and unnamed—happened to him. In the autumn of 1946, Gleave wrote in the Foreword to his third book of poetry, "Seven years ago, in the midst of an intensely active life, engaged in scientific research, I was suddenly laid aside with a disability which has more or less confined me to my bed. The window of my room faces north and the only things visible through it are the branches of a maple tree, very little of the sky and nothing of the street below or of those who pass along it. The first three weary years seemed endless . . . Then one day my thoughts took the form of a verse, and, surprised (for I did not read or write poetry, and do not know one note of music), I wrote the words down. They formed a poem . . . Today this invisible world—this world of poetry—has become the real world to me. . . ." Gleave seems never to have left his bed until he died in 1971. Yet if he was depressed, it did not show in his writing. Indeed, it is inspirationally cheerful. It was certainly popular with the public. One of his poems, "The Bells of Peace," had over 600,000 copies printed and distributed near the end of WWII.

Alhambra ends at **Boustad Avenue**. No.31 was briefly home to the science fiction maven Judith Merril in 1987. Running parallel, one block south, is **Hewitt Avenue**. **No.12** was the first home of novelist John Norman Harris after he returned in 1945 a hero from Stalag Luft III. Harris had been one of the planners of the notorious "wooden horse" escape from the camp. Once he found his feet, he was hired as a reporter by the *G&M*. A few years later he worked in public relations for the Bank of Commerce. It was during this period that he wrote his first play and eventually, his best novel, *The Weird World of Wes Beattie* (1963), a mystery tale much praised by Howard Engel among others. Decades earlier, historian and novelist Donald Creighton spent most of his youth at **32 Hewitt Street**. His time here (1912-28) coincided with his secondary and university education and the start of his legendary career teaching history at the UofT. Two blocks south is Howard Junior School at **30 Marmaduke Street** from which he graduated.

The poet, playwright, journalist, and publisher C.H. (Marty) Gervais (b.1946) lived in a number of Toronto addresses in the 1960s, most in this area. His final stop was **40 High Park Gardens**. He remembered exactly when he moved here: November 7, 1968: "I know this date because it is the date of my anniversary. Moved in there on the wedding night. Grand place with lots of marble and tile and high ceilings and a four poster bed. Lovely woodwork. We had a Christmas tree up until the end of January. Till the landlord [entered] the apartment and took it down. Lived there until February/March 1969, then back to Windsor," the city in which he has lived ever since. The literary significance of this locale, Gervais explains, is that "it was there that I really began to plot out Black Moss Press, and from there began to gather up poems from people like George Bowering, Margaret Atwood, bp Nichol, Victor Coleman, Charles Bukowski, etc."

209 Grenadier Road was the first home of Toronto-born novelist James Houston (b.1921), who lived here until his parents moved in 1926. Houston later became known as one of the pre-eminent novelists writing about the Arctic. He has been credited with introducing silkscreening to Inuit artists, and was a major player in making all of their arts better known around the world. To a *New Yorker* journalist he described his Scottish Presbyterian upbringing here: "Boy, never did a kid have more support than I. My sister, Barbara, and I were devoted to our parents and they to us. I had the happiest childhood—I didn't have to overcome a damn thing. My father sold English yard goods for men's suiting in central and western Canada. He was away four or five months of the year, and on his selling trips he'd loop through Canada, going to places that amused him—particularly Indian places like Prince Rupert, the Queen Charlottes, Fort Churchill. He was fascinated with Indians. Once when I was seven or eight, a box the size of a grand piano without legs arrived at home, causing wild excitement on the part of me and my sister. We tried to guess what was in the box and finally Mother said to us, 'No, there will be bones in that box,' and, sure enough, there were dinosaur bones. Nowadays, no one would dare move dinosaur bones, but this was in the twenties. The big thrill when we were little kids was when Mother would drive us to Toronto's Union Station late at night to meet my father's train. Father would get off, with a little leather grip, homburg, beautiful necktie—spiffily dressed, smiling and laughing. The next morning, we'd run in and jump on our parents' bed, and Father would say, 'Reach in my grip, Jimmy.' Out would come two pairs of delicious-smelling soft moccasins made of smoked moosehide, with huge beaded vamps. The smell and the feel of those moccasins is still with me. Then he'd get out a pad of order forms and start drawing all the unusual Indian things he'd seen, and telling us all about them."

As we walk easterly along Grenadier Road we pass near **353 Sunnyside Avenue**. This was the home of novelist and journalist Archibald McKishnie from 1915-46.

McKishnie (1876-1946), a native of New Scotland, Ontario, came to Toronto as a young man to be a reporter. Before he left newspapers for a freelance career he worked as the drama critic for the *Sunday World*. In addition to articles for leading magazines in Canada and abroad, he wrote stories and novels, largely concerned with our wildlife, a subject he knew well from his frequent nature trips across the country—trips during which, according to noted critic Clara Thomas, he "learned to speak Indian dialects fluently, and he gained from his companions a knowledge of the wilds that was truly Indian-like in its thoroughness." Thomas also notes that "for many years, Mr. McKishnie lived by his pen alone, and most of his work was published in Canada—no mean accomplishment for an author of the first quarter of this century." To supplement his writing income—a necessity during the Depression—he became the director of the first well-known creative writing school in Canada, part of the Shaw School empire. He was quite close to his older sister who lived and published under her married name, Jean Blewett (1862-1934). In fact, they often lived only blocks apart when she, a widow, was not actually inhabiting his house. For example, she lived at **399 Parkside Drive** from 1914-20 before moving into **353 Sunnyside** for about a year. After 1925, she was quite ill, and until her death in 1934 divided her time between her brother's residence and the home of her children in Alberta, according to the season. Jean Blewett published one novel and several books of poetry. It was her fame as a poet that led the *Globe* to hire her as its response to the pioneering success of the *Mail & Empire's* Kit Coleman, the latter now seen as not only the greatest female journalist of her era but also as the person who fought to have women reporters regarded as worthy enough to report on any topic in a newspaper, not just the homemaker's page. Kit Coleman's biographer describes what happened when the contest in print of the two well-known ladies finally took place: "It was no contest. Blewett lacked Kit's humour, punch, and sheer show-business pizzaz, and if the *Globe* editors hoped for a weekly, circulation-building catfight between the two, they were disappointed. Kit and the poet became fast friends and were forever tossing bouquets to each other in print. It was Blewett who crowned Kit 'the Queen of Hearts.' In a *Globe* column she wrote that Kit 'not only writes of the affairs of the heart when she renders romantic advice, but she touches our hearts with everything she does. She is the Queen of Hearts, the supreme monarch of our emotions.'" Jean Blewett's reputation was truly national: a town southeast of Weyburn, Saskatchewan, was named Blewett in her honour. When she died, her passing was given page-one treatment by Toronto newspapers.

Returning to Grenadier Road, we continue walking east. **No.43** was a childhood address of novelist, Grace Irwin (b.1907). In her memoir, *Three Lives in Mine*, Irwin ruminates on this place and some of its memories for her: "The first house of my more-than-fragmentary remembrance, **43 Grenadier Road**, smaller than my birthplace on Robert Street, had four bedrooms, so that, unless relatives were visiting, my eldest brother had a room to himself.

"How my mother managed it, I do not know, but I never saw her or my father inadequately clothed; and in spite of freedom and considerable rough house among us children, the basics of the male physique remained unknown to me. I recall a vague impression, gleaned from modest textbook illustrations, that the male torso terminated in a fig leaf; and only the statues viewed in a classical archaeology course at university dispelled, without traumatic effect, this concept. So much for the universal application of Freud's first fundamental regarding the girl child; that she is the victim of penis envy. As well say I envied a turtle his shell. More plausible. I had seen a shell and knew its use; I had never seen a penis and [I] did

not know its use. I do not even recall ever hearing the word used in conversation, and then from the lips of an 'advanced child', until I was over thirty."

Frank Prewett

When poet Frank Prewett (1893-1962) left home to fight in WWI he left from **19 Grenadier Road**, and, when forced in 1920 to repatriate by the Canadian Army, it was to this same address he returned. He may have been happy when he departed for war, but he was decidedly unhappy when he returned to Toronto. In England, he had been introduced to a literary world of a richness such as he had never dreamed, a world where his talent had been welcomed, indeed praised by some of the most famous authors in the language, including Thomas Hardy, Virginia Woolf, Siegfried Sassoon, D.H. Lawrence, and Robert Graves. In post-war Toronto, he found no equivalent Valhalla. There were serious authors about; two of them even, W.W.E. Ross and A.R.M. Lower, had been his classmates at University College. But the ether in Toronto seemed pinched and thin compared to the air he had breathed at Lady Ottoline Morrell's Garsington estate.

It was when Prewett was living on Grenadier that Sassoon made a lecture stop in Toronto. As the two walked about the city, Sassoon warned Prewett that the Canadian had been (and would be) much happier back in England, and not long after that visit, Prewett took Sassoon's advice and left Canada forever. That Prewett did not become as famous as his colleagues has little to do with his decision to leave his native land. But it is regrettable that, talented as he was, Prewett is not better known here.

Nearby is **Geoffrey Street**. At **No.4** we pause before the house that was, from 1953-56, the home of the Polish-language poet Waclaw Iwaniuk (b.1915). He came to Toronto c. 1950 and worked as a court interpreter for decades during the day while writing and translating poetry at night. His poems have been Englished and are known to a few cognoscenti in Canada and elsewhere but his biggest following by far remains with Polish-speakers. When he first arrived in Toronto he roomed for a few months at **135 Geoffrey Street**. The Great Lakes historian and short-story writer C.H.J. Snider (whom we met earlier in this tour at 499 Parkside Drive) kept rooms at **No.88** from 1908 to 1911. Visual artist and writer Robert Fones lived for about a year at **No.91** in the mid-1970s.

Where Geoffrey Street intersects with Sunnyside Avenue is approximately where Charles Christopher Jenkins (1882-1943) lived from 1927 to 1938. The exact address was **315 Sunnyside Avenue**. Jenkins was another of the many journalists at Toronto daily newspapers in the first half of the century who turned his hand to fiction. He joined the *Globe* in 1922 and he died while in its employ in 1943. Over the years he had worked at a variety of tasks; his posts included radio editor, literary editor, day editor, and author of the hugely popular "Bystander At The Window" column. In retrospect, perhaps his most interesting claim to fame as a journalist is that he was the newspaper's expert on television. The new medium had

debuted in the USA only minimally in 1941, and the first programs did not air in Canada until nine years after Jenkins had died. Jenkins wrote two novels and several short stories. In 1918, three of them were included in Edward J. O'Brien's prestigious *Best Short Stories of the Year*. He returned to this street later in life. He moved into **No.234** c. 1941. It was his last home on earth.

Three blocks to the south is **Wright Avenue**. The award-winning playwright Jason Sherman (b.1962) lived on the third floor of **306 Wright Avenue**, although at this point he was not writing plays but rather co-editing and writing the saucy but exceptional periodical *what*. At **No.241** Maud Irene Robertson apparently lived from 1932-33 (records are ambiguous); she published stories in Canadian and UK periodicals and published two novels.

Down the street at **174 Wright Avenue** lived a much more important author, Emily Murphy. Although often thought of as an Albertan through and through, she spent much of her early life in Toronto. Murphy is important to Canada, of course, for several reasons. As critic Donna Coates has noted, "It is difficult to say whether Emily Murphy, née Ferguson, is best known as the first woman appointed police magistrate in the British Empire, the woman who instigated the lengthy struggle to have Canadian women declared 'persons,' the author of the first comprehensive book on drug addiction in North America, or as 'Janey Canuck,' a writer with a considerable literary reputation for her books of travel sketches." She was born in Cookstown, Ontario in 1868, but was sent as a boarding student to Bishop Strachan School in Toronto. In 1887 she married a missionary minister and spent some time in the UK before returning to Toronto around the turn of the century. Soon after they settled into **No.174**. The address was significant in many ways. It was here that she put the finishing touches to her first book, *Impressions of Janey Canuck Abroad*, published in 1901. It was here, too, amid the comfort of her surroundings and daily visits to High Park with her youngest child, Doris, that severe illness and then death visited her home. The first to fall was her husband, Arthur. Bitten by a mosquito, his subsequent "flu" quickly revealed itself to be typhoid. As if that weren't bad enough, his employer, the Church Parochial Mission, due to financial cutbacks, laid him off, leaving the family in its own dire straits. While Arthur lingered near death for weeks, Emily increased her workload not only by nursing her husband at home but by writing more and more for magazines in the small hours of the night. This stress probably reduced her own resistance and she herself succumbed to typhoid in the fall of 1902. Both husband and wife recuperated slowly, and when she was able, and to assist with the formidable medical bills, she resumed her writing, including the article "Loose Leaves from the Diary of a Typhoid Patient." In it she described her return to this address: "There was a sortie from the front door, a precipitate attack on the ambulance—kisses, little secrets, greetings, stored-up grievances and more kisses all in one breath. Then the big ambulance policeman carried me in. How gentle he was. Only a giant can be gentle. Tenderness is an inflection of strength . . . Someone was playing and singing 'When Janey Canuck Comes Home'. It was a homecoming that overbalanced the pain." Her relief was to be shortlived. Less than a month later, Doris, only six, was diagnosed with diphtheria. Mother sat by child but to no avail, and Doris died in her arms. The loss was so devastating, Emily confirmed to a few intimate friends, she never fully recovered from it, despite the passage of decades. Under the circumstances, it is not surprising that Emily and her husband wished to move, and it was with the hope of a fresh start together that he took up timber-farming in western Canada and she agreed to accompany him. They waited for the first sign of spring, and in April 1903 she said goodbye to this house. One of her biographers captures the moment, "On the last night in her Toronto home she sat to write on top of a huge up-ended trunk. She was turning her back on her own world which had collapsed about her . . . The house was hollow and echoing. The relatives had gone home; the family was asleep. Praise be, there was an hour in which she could write. This was the end of a phase; and there could be no turning back. 'To move means a review of your whole life,' she wrote. 'Inside one little hour you laugh, swell with pride, cry, grovel with humility and burn with indignation as the fingers of still-born projects, dead joys or foolish frolics reach out and touch you from the past . . . There are compensations, though. Things get cleaned up. You lose fifteen pounds of absolutely useless flesh. There is the secret and blissful consciousness of removing mountains and making things happen.' *Removing mountains and making things happen.* In saying farewell to one phase of her life, she was hailing the next, with a phrase which was to prove her fundamental motif in all the years ahead."

The last addresses to note on this street are **No.65** where poets Kim Maltman and Roo Borson lived from 1986 to 1987, and **No.41** where Frank Prewett lived with his parents from 1900 to 1902.

Walk along Fern Avenue to **Roncesvalles Avenue**. In the building that used to exist at **222 Roncesvalles** a major South African poet once had an apartment. Arthur Nortje (1942-70) had little fame in his day, but with the posthumous publication of his work his reputation has grown, especially with younger generations in South Africa. As a schoolboy he was lucky to have Dennis Brutus as an English teacher. Brutus, of course, would go on to become one of the most vocal critics of apartheid. Forced into exile, Brutus continued his attacks on the racialist government while augmenting his own formidable reputation as a poet. Later he would edit *Dead Roots* (1973), the first important collection of Nortje's poems, although, to ensure it could be distributed in their native country, the name of Brutus, a banned person, could appear nowhere on the book. Nortje was a brilliant student. He won a scholarship to Oxford, after which he chose, for reasons that remain obscure, to become a high-school teacher in Hope, British Columbia, in July 1967. The combination of weather, exile, and the beginnings of the clinical depression which would lead to his early death, made him distinctly unhappy in Hope. By July 1968 he was in Toronto and that fall began teaching English at Aldershot Collegiate, itself now defunct. In January 1970 he took sick leave, and by July of that year he had moved back to England. He died in December 1970 from an overdose of barbiturate pills—although whether this was a deliberate suicide as most believe, or "death by misadventure" as the coroner reported, is moot. Regardless, his death at 27 years of age was a blow to South African letters.

Nortje's papers are spread over three continents and determining exactly where and when he lived has proved impossible. Despite corresponding with Nortje experts around the world, and further hours reading his journals at Northwestern University in Evanston, I found next to nothing concerning his relatively lengthy stay in this city. However, that he lived at **No.222** from his arrival in the summer of 1968 until March 1970 seems most likely (he lived at only one other address in Toronto, on Balsam Street for just a few months before quitting the city). Some of the best poems he ever wrote were written during this Parkdale period, including one titled "A House on Roncesvalles."

Across the street, on the east side of **Roncesvalles** is **No.157**, the second floor of which was home to Peter Donovan in 1914 and 1915. Donovan (b.1884) was the literary editor of *Saturday Night* from 1909 until 1920, at the time the most important such editorship in Canadian journalism. He also wrote comic pieces for the magazine and these were published as books that had large followings.

Little known is his novel *Late Spring* (1930), set in a very thinly disguised Toronto. Donovan was lured to England in 1920 by another Torontonian, Beverley Baxter, who, with Canadian Lord Beaverbrook's help, was already one of Britain's best-known newspapermen. But how Donovan ended his days is a mystery. Even his death date remains elusive.

Continue south to Garden Avenue and then proceed west. Heading towards High Park, we pass **Ridley Gardens. No.37** was for two years the home of the once popular author of sea yarns, Commander William J.G. Carr (1895-1959). Born in England, he served with its submarine navy during WWI, an experience he put to use in his book *By Guess and by God* (1930). He emigrated to Toronto after the Great War and in the interbellum published several books on martial and naval topics, including *A Century of Sea Stories* (1934). He fought with the Canadian Navy during WWII, retiring in 1945 as a full commander.

Elisabeth Harvor in her Toronto apartment, March 1988

The next street to the west is **Indian Road**. The noted short-story author Elisabeth Harvor (b.1936) lived twice on this street during her seven-year stay in Toronto. In 1989 she wrote to me that this was her favourite part of the city in part because she "suffered a bit of culture shock. I had been living for five years in a very English section of Montreal where I seldom even heard French spoken and I arrived in a city that seemed to be situated on a lake somewhere in eastern Europe." Her first abode was apt. 505 at **109 Indian Road** from September 1987 to 1990. She then moved to **83 Indian Road**, where she stayed for about a year. While here she wrote much of the volume of stories titled *Our Lady of All the Distances* (1991). She has since returned to Montreal. Poet Chris Dewdney (b.1951) lived in between these addresses at **96 Indian Road** from 1980-83. During this residence he penned most of his poetry collection *Predators of the Adoration* (1983), a nominee for the Governor General's Award.

Garden Avenue ends near **167 Parkside Drive** where André Alexis (b.1957) lived from 1991-95 and where he started to write fiction professionally. At this house he wrote four stories for his debut collection *Despair* (1994), and also wrote his play *Lambton, Kent and Other Vistas*. Just a few paces north is **4 Algonquin Avenue**, the dwelling of poet Owen McGillicuddy 1922-42. McGillicuddy was a reporter all his life, working first for the *Star*, then the *M&E*, and then the *G&M*. The *Star* graciously ran an editorial on his passing. The *G&M* did likewise. His poetry volume was published in 1918.

Backtrack a few steps along Garden Avenue, then descend Indian Road to Parkdale Road. A second-floor apartment at **50 Parkdale Road** was Roy MacSkimming's home after he returned to Canada from Europe in August 1969. During his nine-month stay here MacSkimming (b.1944) continued to work on his first novel, *Formentera* and also joined with Jim Bacque and Dave Godfrey in the formation of "new press," one of the more influential literary small presses of the 1970s in Canada.

Parkdale Road jogs at Sunnyside and becomes **Pearson Avenue**. At **236 Pearson Avenue** the mystery writer James Powell

(b.1932) spent eight of his peripatetic youthful years (1950-58) while attending St. Michael's College High School, and then the UofT (B.A. 1955). Powell is renowned for his many short stories, a form he prefers to novels, but this approach to fiction has meant that, since short-story collections are allegedly hard to sell, his work remains unknown to all but those who read mystery mags. His only book to date is *A Murder Coming* (1990). One critic has called him "the S.J. Perelman of the mystery story." Powell

Christopher Dewdney (left) and bp Nichol, in the loft of Coach House Press, during the shooting of a documentary film about poetry

described how, while living here, he decided to become an author:"After my second year of high school while working as a stock clerk for Simpson's department store on Queen Street I met a co-worker, an Englishman who had some experience in films and radio in London before emigrating to Canada. He wanted to write comedy for Wayne and Shuster, liked my sense of humour and suggested we write some scripts together, hoping perhaps to add a Canadian flavour to the product. Though nothing came of this collaboration I suddenly realized that someone actually wrote the things I read or heard on the radio or saw on the screen. I tried writing on my own for the CBC without success . . . After graduation I spent three years in France writing a great deal of material which hasn't seen the light of day. In July 1958 I returned to **236 Pearson Avenue** until October 1958 when I went to work in New York City."

The first student uprising in Canada of more than intramural import took place at the UofT in 1895. The editor of the *Varsity*, the university's newspaper, was an undergrad named James A. Tucker (1872-1903). Tucker oversaw and wrote many of the words in a *Varsity* issue which, amazingly for the time, severely criticized the manner by which faculty appointments were made. In his day, faculty appointments were sometimes made, not on the basis of the scholarship of the applicant, but on the applicant's connections—with little or no regard for his teaching ability or academic seriousness. Tucker led the respectful protest in print against this policy, and for his temerity and for refusing to publish a full apology was instantly expelled. This gesture led to a mass meeting of students who compiled a list of grievances which the *Globe* deigned to publish. Sides were taken. Tempers flared. The furor left the public astounded. The students thrilled at their first taste of power. One of the rebel student leaders was Arthur Meighen. A mere three students refused to join the strike. One of them was William Lyon Mackenzie King. The issue became so public the government was forced to intervene and

appointed a commission to investigate the student complaints. As one later observer put it, "it is probable that the revision of the manner of appointment which came with the federation of the colleges was a result of the sentiments so noisily expressed by Tucker." However, to help the University administration save face, the commission upheld Tucker's expulsion. It is a measure of his popularity with his fellow students, however, that they raised among themselves the funds necessary for his travel costs to, and tuition at, an American college from which he did graduate. Not long afterwards he returned to the city to become, in 1899, the assistant editor of *Saturday Night*, a post he held until his heart gave out and he died of a seizure just before Christmas 1903. After his death, a selection was made from the many poems he had written and the volume was published by William Briggs in 1904. He resided at **163 Pearson Avenue** for the last two years of his life.

One block south is **Marion Street.** The poet and detective novelist Peter Robinson (b.1950), author of the many Inspector Banks mysteries, wrote to me, "In September 1979 I went to live at **73 Marion Street** which is where the Gabbro Press people, the now defunct small handpress that published my two volumes of poetry, also lived." He left here in January 1980. Near where Marion crosses Sorauren can be found **46 Sorauren Avenue**, notable because its basement apartment was novelist Richard

James A. Tucker

Wright's first home in Toronto when he came here in 1956. He stayed at this address for about a year. Later he would work for Oxford University Press as well as Macmillan before quitting to become a teacher and novelist. His first work, *The Weekend Man* (1970), had a tremendous reception at home and abroad, and his subsequent novels, while not engendering as much thunder perhaps, have certainly offered substantial literary humour, rumination, and insight. His 1995 novel, *The Age of Longing*, was nominated for both the Giller Prize and the Governor General's Award.

Harvard Street can be found in the next block south. **No.66** was poet David Donnell's dwelling for three years in the mid-1970s. A few steps down, at **No.74**, can be found the former abode of Norman Reilly Raine (1895-1971). Raine is well-known to most North Americans in that they have heard of his most famous character, Tugboat Annie. An American, he fought with the Canadian Army in WWI. After hostilities, he lived in Toronto where he was an assistant editor at *Maclean's Magazine* and he seems to have stayed here until he was married in 1928. If so, **74 Harvard** was his last address (1927-28) in Toronto. From Toronto he went to the USA, where he published more short stories in the *Saturday Evening Post* and wrote plays—experiences that enabled him to work easily in Hollywood where he wrote several screenplays, mostly for Warner Brothers, including *The Life of Emile Zola*, for which he won an Oscar for best screenplay. His own novel *Sea of Lost Ships*, was also translated into feature film.

Harvard ends at **Callender Street**. Poet and poetry critic Fraser Sutherland (b.1946) moved to an apartment at **1 Callender Street** in October 1983, where "our landlord [was] a Yugoslavian dentist whose office was below us, and whose family had recently occupied our new premises. (Yugos with toothaches would appear at the foot of our stairs calling up to me, 'Zoran! Zoran!') I thought then, and still do, that Parkdale is Toronto's most interesting neighbourhood: Filipinos, West and East Indians, Yugoslavs, the Phoenix Colombian-Chinese restaurant, the miscellaneous crazed from 999 Queen farmed out into rooming houses, streetcorner hookers and fisticuffs at the Parkdale Hotel, the poor white trash on whom Terry Kelly (who spent his high school years in the area) is an authority—as he is on the Green Dolphin greasy spoon recreated in his Theatre Passe Muraille play of the same name. Not far away was Roncesvalles, with its strips of Polish delis, and the cake-shop of Maria Granowski, baker to the Pope." Sutherland lived here until February 1986.

SWANSEA

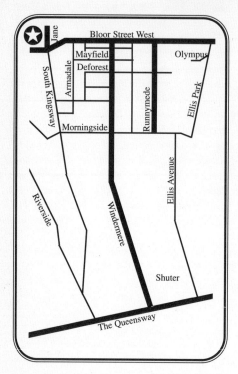

The tour begins at the northwest corner of Jane Street and Bloor Street West.

Walk to the south side of Bloor Street and then a few steps east where you will find **Armadale Avenue**. Poet, soldier, and veteran newspaperman Kim Beattie (1900-63) lived at **371 Armadale** in 1931. Across the street at **No. 376**, the poet Paul Dutton (b.1943) spent his first six months on the planet. Speaking of matters planetary, Dutton was a member of the Vancouver sound poetry group, The Four Horsemen. They were active in the 1970s and 1980s and were hailed by cognoscenti around the globe.

Armadale crosses **Mayfield Avenue**. **No. 28** was long the home of poet and publisher Raymond Souster (b.1921). In an autobiographical essay, he discusses its discovery and the matrimonial delights that happened in the living room on the day he moved in: "I'd become engaged to Rosalia Geralde, and we decided to marry June 24 [1947]. Lia was then living in rooms with her mother. The momentous decision was made to buy a house; the two of us immediately began reading the real-estate ads. After a weary round of house-hunting we made a lucky find. We bought a semi-detached, six-room house in the village of Swansea, located directly south of my old Runnymede district. Here we would live for the next seventeen years.

"Lia and her mother moved into the new house on June 1; I visited them after supper every night, cleaning and polishing floors, stripping off old wallpaper. Then, on the twenty-fourth, with my brother as best man and Lia's father a surprise visitor from the West, we were married by the family minister." During his residency here, Souster published his first novel, *The Winter of Time* (1949), and much more importantly, his first significant poetry book, *Cerberus* (with Irving Layton and Louis Dudek, 1952), which was also the first book published by the legendary Contact Press—itself an outgrowth of *Contact Magazine*. The two Montreal-based poets in the book feared reprisals from the Duplessis regime in Quebec, so **28 Mayfield Avenue** was chosen as the publishing address to appear on the copyright page. As it happened, it remained the mailing address of the press until 1958, although most of the administration and order fulfilment duties were handled elsewhere. Souster has the editing gene, so he found himself in 1956 starting another literary magazine, *Combustion*, featuring work by many celebrated authors including Lawrence Ferlinghetti, Margaret Avison, Robert Duncan, Allen Ginsberg, and Leroi

Jones (Amiri Baraka). Also while living here he began the Contact Readings (1957-62) in conjunction with art gallery owner Av Isaacs, the first regular poetry readings in the history of Toronto. Souster wrote and published 13 volumes of his own poetry during his tenure on Mayfield, and edited the important anthology *Poets '56: Ten Younger English-Canadians* (1956). And he undertook all of this literary activity while holding down a full-time job in the Securities Department of the Canadian Imperial Bank of Commerce at King and Bay.

A block to the south, humorist and novelist Max Braithwaite (1911-95) lived at **34 Deforest Road** from 1944-46, an address that, more than one could ever suspect, became a psychic destination for him. "When I was teaching school in Saskatchewan during the 'Hungry Thirties' (the title of a book I wrote many years later) in one-room rural schools and in miserable little villages I longed to be in Toronto. For I was spending all my spare time writing and I knew that Toronto was the place! The place where magazines and books were published and where radio plays originated. *Liberty Magazine* was there and *Liberty* paid one thousand bucks (twice my yearly salary) for a short short story of one thousand words. And *Maclean's* to which I had managed to sell a piece about the horrible condition of education on the prairies. And Buckingham Theatre to whom I had submitted more than one script. And, of course, the CBC. I had tried writing for all these markets without much success. I was married and had one child, and both my wife and I knew we were in the wrong place. We had to be in or near Toronto. But it seemed hopeless. Then came the war and I quit teaching and joined the RCNVR in Saskatoon and in the spring of 1944 I was posted to H.M.C.S. York, the naval division in Toronto, as head schoolmaster. And there I met my first real-life editor . . . Jim Harris of *Liberty Magazine*, and he actually asked me to write an article for *Liberty*, which I did. And later I met Arthur Irwin and Ralph

Allen and Scott Young of *Maclean's* and they asked me to write articles for them, which I did. . . . There was a great shortage of writers after the war and I was willing and (because of the time I'd spent learning the craft in Sask.) able. At last we were in the right place at the right time. Our address in Toronto from early 1944 to June 1946 was **34 Deforest Road** in Swansea. That's what Toronto meant to us. . . . Moving to Toronto was the turning point in our lives. Up until then, we'd had mostly bad luck; after moving to Toronto and the Toronto area we've had nothing but good luck. I see Toronto, of course, from the point of view of a writer and for a writer it is the only place to be. Apart from that, Toronto is a great city: a great entertainment city, great sports city, a clean civilized city . . . ." Braithwaite's best-known book, *Why Shoot the Teacher* (1965), was made into a popular feature film in 1977. His *The Night We Stole the Mountie's Car* (1972) won the Leacock Medal for Humour.

Melbourne Australia native Albert Munday (1896-1957) had a life that would fill several adventure novels. He was educated on the playing fields of Eton, and later at Columbia University in New York, so he was not wanting in quality education. After serving as the Trade Commissioner of the Bahamas in Canada, he changed careers to become a reporter in Moose Jaw. At some undetermined time he moved to Toronto where he worked on several newspapers and magazines, including the *News*. He was overseas in WWI (where he was mentioned twice in dispatches and attained the rank of Wing Commander), following which he began to write fiction and non-fiction about flying and airplanes. From 1939-41 he lived in apt. 2 of **306 South Kingsway**. This street intersects with **Morningside Avenue** where poet and critic Ronald Bates, long associated with the University of Western Ontario, lived at **No.118**, while working on his master's and doctoral degrees at the UofT.

Morningside intersects with **Ellis Avenue**. The writer John D. Robins (1884-1952)

lived at **No.257** for two decades, 1932-52. Robins began his teaching career at Victoria College, at first in the German dept. and then in the English—in fact, he was head of the English dept. for several years until he died. He was mad about fishing, and yet wrote humorously about its foibles: *The Incomplete Angler* (1943), the first tome, won the Governor General's Award. It was followed by a gently satiric account of a summer fishing vacation, *Cottage Cheese* (1951). He also edited two important anthologies: *A Pocketful of Canada* (1946) and *A Book of Canadian Humour* (1951).

At its eastern end, Morningside merges into **Ellis Park Road**. **No.60** was the home of the Master Gatherer, John Robert Colombo (b.1936) from 1965-68. He is called this because, in addition to poetry, early in his career he published collections of quotations and books of facts (about Canada) which most cultures have, but which Canada lacked until Colombo compiled them. While living at this address he sustained himself and family by working as a freelance book editor. As an author, he investigated the limits of "found poetry" and the results were published as *John Toronto:*

John Robert Colombo relaxing at Villa Colombo (no relation), August 1998

New Poems by Dr. Strachan (1966), and *The Great Wall of China* (1966). According to him, "This has to be the most scenic street in Metro, overlooking as it does the western boundary of High Park. We rented this modest house. Many books were edited here, including *Black Night Window* by John Newlove, Judy LaMarsh's bestselling memoirs *Bird in a Gilded Cage*, and W.W.E. Ross's *Shapes and Sounds* with Raymond Souster. I associate the *Tamarack Review* with this address, as some of the mailings took place here (though the real address for it was the Owens' house on Balmoral). Ray [Souster] wrote a poem about the Colombos moving their books out of Ellis Park Road . . . An important meeting that brought into existence the League of Canadian Poets took place here with Ray and Earle Birney in attendance. In fact, I regard it as the 'birthplace' of the League as I distinctly recall sending letters (to Seymour Mayne and others) and signing them 'Provisional Coordinator' of the League with the concurrence of all."

Ellis Park Road ends at **Olympus Avenue** where, at **No.10**, Ethel Hume Bennett (b.1881) spent more than a quarter of a century, 1924-50. Born in Toronto, Bennett was an early female graduate of Victoria College. She was head of the boarding school at Havergal for a number of years. She put that experience to good use when writing her four popular books for girls and young women, all of which were published by Houghton Mifflin in the States and Allen in Toronto. For Macmillan of Canada she edited *New Harvesting: Contemporary Canadian Poetry 1918-1938* (1938), an anthology of interest because it restricted itself to authors alive at the time of compilation.

There is no easy way to walk to **Riverside Drive**; access is either from Bloor or from near the Queensway. The street is worth the walk, however, because it was home to three writers, two of them among Canada's most famous. Albert Munday whom we met above, lived at **No.518** in 1936. Of more import is **No.316**, where Morley Callaghan (1903-

1990) lived when he returned in the autumn of 1929 from his memorable stay in Paris, where he matured as a writer and developed friendships with some of the most famous authors of the century including Hemingway and Joyce. Morley remained in his apartment on Riverside about a year and during that time worked on his books *It's Never Over* (1930) and *No Man's Meat* (1931).

Lucy Maud Montgomery outside her home, 210 Riverside Drive, circa 1940

Most importantly, **210 Riverside Drive** was the only home in Toronto of Lucy Maud Montgomery (1874-1942), the beloved author of *Anne of Green Gables* and many other novels especially popular with girls and young women. Montgomery was married to a minister, Rev. Ewan Macdonald, who had continuing mental illnesses. His absences from work due to ill health coupled with small-town feuding forced the Macdonalds to leave Norval, Ontario (where they had lived for years) and move to Toronto. A real-estate agent convinced them they could afford to buy a house; until then they had

only rented. So at the age of 60 Montgomery sold all her stocks and pooled her assets in order to afford this large and expensive home in what has always been an upscale street for housing. Lucy, Ewan, and their two sons Chester and Stuart, took possession in March 1935. Fighting anxieties over her husband's health, her sons' inabilities to find proper wives, and worries about her financial vulnerability (she was effectively the sole breadwinner), Lucy Maud began to write *Anne of Windy Poplars*. The new premises must have placated her muse because she finished the book, according to her biographers, in record time. And her next books now began to feature Toronto in a prominent way. "Opening in Toronto, *Jane of Lantern Hill* reflects Montgomery's joy in the new house on Riverside Drive: in the novel, Jane glories first in a perfect house on Prince Edward Island and later in a small house in 'Lakeside Garden's' in Toronto." After this novel, however, the skies in Montgomery's life began to darken. Her husband slipped in and out of insanity, WWII approached, and with it the likely draft of her sons to the front. Yet she managed amidst this turmoil to write *Anne of Ingleside*. However, the stress and strain caused a nervous breakdown in 1940. Her creative writing essentially ceased at this point, and as one scholarly commentary on Montgomery has phrased it, "In 1942, Montgomery's physical and mental health continued to decline, despite regular medication from her doctor and frequent visits from friends. Her husband had become too senile to function rationally; she brooded that the war would take her only 'good' son, as she called Stuart; she had wasted away to the point that visiting friends barely recognized her. Much of the time she was bedridden, too weak and unsteady to hold a pen: she was unable to write letters or journal entries, let alone fiction. The will to live was apparently gone. Death came in the spring of 1942, on 24 April, seven months before her sixty-eighth birthday."

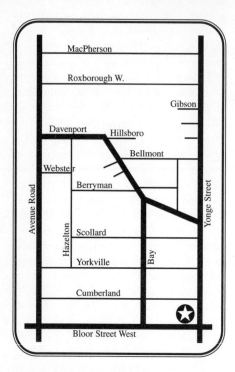

The tour begins on the northwest corner of Yonge Street and Bloor Street West.

At **2 Bloor Street West**, the Toronto Ladies' Club was located in the Traders Bank Building for many years. Near here one day (c. 1940) a very young Timothy Findley came face to face with the first famous writer he ever met: "My mother and I were walking along Bloor Street, near where the Ladies' Club used to be, and a big black car with a chauffeur stopped and Mazo [de la Roche] was let out and she looked something like the character actress in the movies—Edna May Oliver—tall, angular, not pretty. But she had presence—she had style and absolute grace. My mother said to me— I was still a child—'Look, and remember this. That is Mazo de la Roche!' As though one were seeing God." Findley later said, "True to the nature of Canadian being, the entire population of that intersection— including my mother—greeted the sight of such an arresting and famous figure not with loud exclamations or even a buzz of excitement—but with a sudden diminished level of conversation. It was definitely a 'hushed tones' moment."

Cumberland Avenue, the next block north, currently houses row after row of élite boutiques, but look carefully and one can decipher the original Victorian houses behind the façades. It was in such houses that two writers, long associated with the city, lived as young men. E.J. Pratt (1882-1964), as an undergraduate, had purchased some houses on Atlas Avenue, and the rental income from these, coupled with his modest salary as a teaching assistant allowed him to rent better digs at **159 Cumberland** as of 1911, the same year he began his studies for a master's degree. He remained at this address until 1915. In what used to be a house at **No.164**, the eminent Canadian crime writer Eric Wright (b.1929) had lodgings from July 1958 to June 1960, the year he made his first appearance in *The New Yorker* with a short story.

Near here is the rear entrance to the flagship operation of Chapters, the first and largest book superstore chain in Canada. The official address is **110 Bloor Street West**. The store, which opened November 1996, hosts numerous author events almost every day throughout the year, including occasional readings by poets and fiction writers. The store also houses a coffee shop. A number of sofas and stuffed chairs encourage customers to preview the approximately 150,000 available titles at their own pace before deciding whether to purchase.

At the western end of Cumberland there was once a small apartment building,

Hampton Court, **21 Avenue Road**, which was the home of a trio of authors over the years. Greg Hollingshead (b.1947), winner of the 1995 Governor General's Award for his *The Roaring Girl*, had an apartment here from September 1966 to May 1968 while finishing his B.A. at Victoria College. The owners of the building had poetically named his wing of the building "Dolphintorn," but tenants who were not enamoured of the site called it "Porpoise-rift." He shared this flat with poets Charles Douglas and Ian Carruthers (d.1970). Novelist and actor Anthony Quogan (b.1937) lived here for exactly the same length of time but there is no indication that he knew Hollingshead or vice-versa. Quogan, relatively new to Canada, had just resigned from a career in advertising to join a travelling theatre company. He would later study for his doctorate in theatre under Robertson Davies, and become a drama professor at York University as well as a detective writer.

The third author to live at Hampton Court was Joseph Easton McDougall (b.1901) who published a book of poetry in 1929 and another in 1936. However, he will be remembered instead for his remarkable editorship of *The Goblin*. This magazine of humour, articles, and cartoons began as a UofT undergraduate exercise in 1921 but its immediate sales success soon meant it moved off campus, taking its surprised founding editors with it. Joe McDougall was one of them. The others drifted away, but McDougall and his financial backers continued to improve the magazine both in editorial content and in design—although it had been handsome from the beginning. Which may account in part why its first printing of 1,000 copies sold out in a mere 24 hours. That issue contained an article by Stephen Leacock and others soon after other issues had articles by Merrill Denison and Peter McArthur, two of the best-known journalists of the day. In the mid-twenties, McDougall was the literary editor, as well as general dogsbody, doing anything that needed to be done to put the magazine to bed. As of October 1925 he was the editor-in-chief and remained so until the magazine's undocumented death in 1930, a victim of the Depression. McDougall lived at **21 Avenue Road** in apt. 6 in 1924 and 1925.

Novelist Brian Moore (1921-1999) lived in Toronto only once, when he was writer-in-residence at the UofT for the fall term of 1982. From September to December of that year he occupied apt. 303 in Hazelton Lanes, **55 Avenue Road**. Novelist Susan Swan also lived in Hazelton Lanes from 1973 to 1974. Since the mid-1980s this complex of buildings has been the headquarters of HarperCollins Canada which has been publishing Canadian authors for several years. Among the more eminent Canadians on its list are Barbara Gowdy and Timothy Findley.

Yorkville Avenue is named after the village annexed to the City of Toronto in the 19th c. **No.148** was the headquarters of Little Brown Canada from 1990 until it ceased operations in 1998. Throughout this period it published a number of distinguished Canadian authors, including Barry Callaghan and Kildare Dobbs.

142 Yorkville was The Book Cellar from 1968 to 1997, a shop popular with many writers, and also with movie stars who frequented the Four Seasons Hotel across the street. A few writers of note worked as sales clerks in this store, including playwright John Krizanc, novelist Paul Quarrington, and novelist Barbara Betcherman. Opposite the store was an apartment building, The Chetwynd, at **No.135**, where playwright Erika Ritter lived in 1970. Her main memory of this period is, in the days before cable, that the cars driving by to stare at the hippies on Yorkville played havoc with her television reception. One of the reasons the hippies were first attracted to Yorkville was the leading-edge coffee houses. They presented the first protest singers to be heard in the city. The best-known was The Riverboat, but the Penny Farthing had thousands of admirers, in part because it featured poet-balladeers such as Leonard Cohen (b.1934), who first sang here for a number of nights in late July 1966, and Joni Mitchell (b.1943).

Novelist Timothy Findley had not yet published a novel when he lived at **No.91** during 1961 and 1962. In those years he was working full-time as an actor and also working on his divorce.

Mazo de la Roche (1879-1961) moved to **No.86** in late 1926 with her cousin Caroline. One of Mazo's biographers described their new home: "The women occupied a light airy room, crammed with family heirlooms and heavy furniture, in which they would entertain small groups of friends. As the modest place became a part of the story surrounding the spectacular success, they became a little self-conscious about it. Offended when William Arthur Deacon called it 'a bed-sitting room,' Caroline carefully explained that it was an apartment. Edward Weeks, describing his first meeting with de la Roche, tactfully called it a 'studio-apartment.' It was the first really satisfactory place they had found for the winter months. After deciding that the upkeep of a rented house was impractical, they had been plagued by under-heated rooms, but this one was warm, with a large fireplace and a chimney that 'drew well'; it was also close to the Parliament buildings where Caroline worked, and there was a small garden for [their dog] Bunty."

Once unpacked, Mazo immediately put the finishing touches to her novel *Jalna*. She submitted the work for a best-novel contest run by *Atlantic Monthly*. In April 1927 she was announced as the winner of the $10,000 prize, a goodly amount today but, of course, a fortune back then. The Toronto newspapers splashed the story across their front pages and the next day did "follow-up" stories.

Less than a month after she won the prize, a huge banquet was held in her honour at the Queen's Hotel. Charles G.D. Roberts was in the chair, and Bliss Carman, B.K. Sandwell, Ralph Connor, Pelham Edgar, Katherine Hale, and Marshall Saunders made toasts or speeches. The Mayor of Toronto attended the banquet and presented the author with a silver tea service on behalf of the citizenry. A Justice of the Supreme Court of Ontario also made an address in her honour, as did the President of the UofT, and even the Premier of the Province attended the banquet in order to deliver his plaudits. A week later, another banquet was hosted at Casa Loma by the Local Council of Women, attended by more than three hundred people, all paying honour to Mazo and her success. One of the ironies of these celebrations is that the participants believed they were honouring a Toronto girl made good. Mazo, born in Newmarket, could not bring herself to correct the impression (which she herself had spawned) that she was a Toronto native. In her acceptance of the tea-service, for example, she began her expression of gratitude by saying, "This gift, coming as it does from the city of my birth. . . ."

Marriage proposals came by the dozens, as did other crackpots with their suggestions of how to spend her money, so in late 1927 Mazo and her companion packed up and reluctantly left the apartment that had brought them such good luck, that had so changed their lives. By the time she passed away, nearly nine million copies of the Jalna novels had been sold in hardcover, many millions more in paperback. In 1937, in *Atlantic Monthly*, she published a tale, "Electric Storm," set in this apartment.

The short-story specialist Norman Levine (b.1923) lived in an apartment at **11 Yorkville** when he returned to Canada to live in 1980. He arrived on March 12 and would have stayed beyond the end of June except for the fact that he found a new companion and moved into her house, later marrying her. A house existed at this address before it was an apartment. Literary critic and memoirist Hector Charlesworth lived in it in 1898.

Norman Levine in front of the Flatiron
Building, Church and Front Streets
Star, October 11, 1980

William Tyrrell was as old as Canada, born
in 1867, and came to this country as a very
young man. After working for other booksellers in Toronto, he opened his first bookshop in 1894 on King Street and sold books
in that area until he moved to **820 Yonge
Street** in 1925. After more than 60 years as a
Toronto bookseller, he died in 1945, but the
business remained at this location until 1961.
Thus, for several decades, the two most important retail bookshops in the city, Tyrrell's
and Britnell's, faced each other in friendly
competition. William Arthur Deacon in his
eulogy in the *Globe* gave a wonderful sense of
the man and of his importance: "Mr.
Tyrrell had a nice taste in reading and his
advice to his customers was valued by them
and had an enormous effect on the reading
habits of this city during the years of its
growth into a metropolis. With experience
accumulating through decades, and possibly
on account of the respect with which his
judgements were received, he became quite
positive in his opinions . . . As he grew older
there were more and more titles he refused
to handle for moral or political reasons . . .

One can dissent from his views and honour
his character for standing by his principles
to his own financial loss on each transac-
tion. . . .Being born much later, I regarded
some of his views as Victorian prejudices but
he was such a dear old gentleman, so really
tolerant and kind, that he never allowed our
differences of outlook to interfere with a
friendship I greatly prized. The tolerance
was his, not mine, since I regarded his prejudices as harmless whereas he must have felt
mine to be sinister. Few citizens ever have
the opportunity, the will, or the ability to
confer on their communities the cumulative
benefits bestowed by William Tyrrell on
Toronto. Through half a century this quiet
little man of good taste influenced beyond
measure the literary awareness of two generations of readers."

The fifth and final series of poetry readings organized by Contact Press with the
support of Av Isaacs took place at his new
gallery space, The Isaacs Gallery, **832
Yonge Street**. The poets were selected by a
committee: Padraig O Broin, Kenneth
McRobbie, Raymond Souster, and John
Robert Colombo. The Contact readings was
the first program of organized readings by
important poets in the history of the city.
The authors invited to speak in the last
round were:

October 21, 1961: Robert Creeley
(substituting for Allan Ginsberg)
November 11, 1961: Peter Miller
and Miriam Waddington
December 9, 1961: Louis Dudek
February 3, 1962: Gael Turnbull
February 24, 1962: Charles Olson
April 7, 1962: Frank O'Hara
April 28, 1962: James Reaney

Speaking of important readings, before
proceeding down Scollard Street we should
detour slightly to pause before the Masonic
Hall at **888 Yonge Street** (northwest corner
of Davenport). Here, some of the biggest
names in literature of the first half of the

20th c. gave readings or talks. Among them were: G.K. Chesterton (twice), Aldous Huxley, Sir Henry Newbolt, Sir Gilbert Parker, and Hugh Walpole (twice).

The term "avant-garde" is not misplaced when used to describe Roy Mitchell (1884-1944), the collaborator with Vincent Massey on the design of Hart House Theatre, and the theatre's first artistic director. It was Mitchell who convinced Massey to subsidize a space presenting new plays of high artistic merit, regardless of commercial potential. He lived at **113 Scollard Street** in 1912.

Hazelton Avenue has long been popular with writers—especially poets—and can make a good claim for being the most poetical street in Toronto. Barker and Margaret Fairley had a home at **16 Hazelton** from 1944-52. Barker (1887-1986), the better known of the couple, made his living as a professor in the German dept. at the UofT, but he was no ivory-tower academic. Quite the contrary. Writers who knew him always spoke of him warmly, describing him as a congenial host and a man keenly interested in contemporary writing by Canadians as well as others. His critical texts on Goethe were known around the world (Thomas Mann was a fan) and late in life he proudly published his own translation of *Faust* (1970). After he retired from teaching in 1956, he spent more time on his painting and his poetry. Authors were among his favourites for portrait studies, and someday someone will mount an exciting exhibition of his painted views of fellow artists. His poetry volumes include *Poems* (1977) and *Wild Geese and Other Poems* (1984).

The former church (built in 1875) at **No.35** has been the home of the Heliconian Society since 1923. The group was founded in 1893 as a place where women interested in the arts could gather once a month to discuss artistic topics, with literature and music being the dominant disciplines. The name was suggested to the founders by Goldwin Smith, and refers to Mount Helicon in Greece, home of the Muses. Given the well-to-do ambience of the area today, it bears

remembering that in the Depression street urchins and the poor were the main tenants of the district. E.J. Pratt was frequently invited to read in this building, but as his biographer noted, "worshippers at the shrine of letters often found their rituals disturbed by the shouts and jeers of young infidels outside." A partial list of the authors who have given talks here includes:

> Bliss Carman
> Ralph Connor
> Mazo de la Roche
> Mabel Dunham
> John Murray Gibbon
> Katherine Hale
> Basil King
> Michael Macliammor
> Robert Norwood
> E.J. Pratt
> Charles G.D. Roberts
> George Russell ("A.E.")
> B.K. Sandwell
> Elizabeth Sprigge
> Arthur Stringer
> Constance Davies Woodrow

40 Hazelton Avenue was an extremely important address in the life of Earle Birney (1904-95), one of our best poets, because it was here in 1940 that he wrote his most famous work, "David." Birney had been at this address since 1940, working as an assistant professor at University College and he remained here until his May 1943 departure overseas with the Canadian Army. "David" became an albatross for Birney, because it was often the only poem with which he was associated. Studied to death in thousands of schools across the country, it led otherwise decent people to ask Birney if he really killed his best friend by pushing him over a cliff. No poet, no writer, wants to be known exclusively for something he or she published decades earlier, yet it remains a staple of the Canadian literary canon. Not as popular but still having wide currency is a most attractive lyric, "From the Hazel Bough," written for one of his many lovers, a neighbour on Hazelton. The title is a coded reference to their shared street as well as a shared bed.

Another wonderful poet, Margaret Avison (b.1918), lived briefly at **No.51** in 1960. Poet Wilson MacDonald's fame has faded since his passing, but he was among the best-known versifiers in Canada during his long lif. primarily because he was so aggressive about obtaining reading engagements in schools across the nation. He was the only Canadian writer known to, or seen by, tens of thousands of students in the 1930s and 1940s. MacDonald (1880-1967) lived in a room at **No.74** in 1905. Still other top-echelon poets lived on this street. After they were married in 1962, Gwendolyn MacEwen (1941-87) and Milton Acorn (1923-86), eschewing a honeymoon, moved from Dupont Street to their first large apartment at **No.93** The landlord was the brother of famed poet bp Nichol. When bp first came to Toronto in 1963, he stayed with his older brother at this address. When his brother asked him what he was going to do with his life, bp told him he was going to be a full-time poet. His brother rolled his eyes, leaned back in his chair, stared at the ceiling, and let out a quiet, "Oh my God, no!" Apparently the only poets he had ever known were Acorn and MacEwen—and it seems they had not been, with their shouting matches and heavy drinking, ideal tenants.

Near here, **Berryman Avenue** is worth a detour for fans of Margaret Atwood, for it was at **No.15** that she lived in 1960, house-sitting for some months for its owner, poet Jay Macpherson, who was a don at Victoria College. This was a brief but important respite for Atwood, as her biographer Rosemary Sullivan explains: "The house was practically empty. Jay bought a few sticks of furniture from the Salvation Army, but when Margaret moved in in the spring of her final year, she was virtually camping out. She stayed after graduation, and, through that summer, Jay came to fix up the house. She

remembered them scraping off the horrible wallpaper of wild horses that seemed to fill the kitchen (together they called it 'the vanishing prairie').

"Sitting at the kitchen table over endless cups of coffee, they would talk books. Jay stored some of her books in the house, and of course Margaret had permission to read them. Jay remarks, 'I think she chose the Jung part of the shelf and Graves' *White Goddess*, and all the modern Canadian poetry.'

"There was a wonderful creative symbiosis between them. Jay became one of Margaret's early readers, seeing drafts of a novel she had started titled *Up in the Air So Blue* and reading the manuscript of *Double Persephone*."

At the top of Hazelton is **164 Davenport Road**, where the offices of 68 Publishers, the samizdat press for Czech literature operated by Zdena Skvorecky with assistance from her husband, the novelist Josef Skvorecky, were located from 1984-91. The fall of the Soviet empire, combined with the freedom of the press that came with Havel's rise to power meant the main purpose of 68 Publishers (to keep Czech history and literature alive) was no longer necessary. In Prague shortly after the return of democracy, I was curious to know how influential the house had been. Was it just a footnote in Czech literary history, or had it really made a difference? I was soon convinced of the latter. Cab drivers, for example, on discovering I was from Toronto, would ask if I happened to know a fellow call Skvorecky. When I said he was a friend, they turned off the meter and insisted the ride was free. Waiters in beer halls, on learning I knew Skvorecky, would insist that the first round was free. In Brno as well as Prague, intellectuals were frank in their assessments of the house's importance, and to a person they rated that importance very highly.

I was delighted to discover the code-words used between Czech citizens to determine if a new 68 Publishers book was available for reading. The books had to be smuggled into the country, of course. It seems friends would approach friends in the street and ask, "Have you had any postcards from Toronto lately?" If the answer was affirmative, the two would arrange to meet and secretly exchange the forbidden text. The first exhibition in The National Library of Czechoslovakia, after the removal of the communist censors, was a complete retrospective of the hundreds of titles published out of Toronto by the determined husband and wife team.

Running west from near the top of Hazelton is **Webster Avenue**. The poet and noted translator of Japanese literature, David Aylward (b.1942), spent his youth at **No.20** from 1946-61. Just to the south of the junction of Webster and Avenue Road is the Venture Inn, **89 Avenue Road**, in whose coffee shop Margaret Atwood worked in the summer of 1962 after her first year of grad study at Harvard. Harvard, alas, taught her skills other than how to pour coffee and make change. She described the experience: "Immediately I was caught in the Lunchtime from Hell. Milkshakes and spilled coffee puddled on the counter. My hair unravelled. A line of irate customers formed behind the cash register, waiting for their change, while I fruitlessly pushed buttons and the little drawer shot in and out, locking itself at will. From time to time my boss would stop by with regular customers to show me off. 'She has an M.A.,' he would say proudly, as I frazzled around like a trapped June bug, shedding hairpins, dropping cloth or filthy plate in hand."

Edward Douglas Armour was described by the *Globe* at his death as a "great lawyer and educator." For more than three decades, Armour (1851-1922) was the head of his own eminent law practice, and for ten years was a Bencher of the Law Society of Upper Canada. He founded—and for almost 20 years edited—the *Canadian Law Times*. In addition to his legal life, he published poetry extensively, and in 1922, the year of his death, published his translations of the *Odes of Horace*. He passed away from pneumonia at his home, **103 Avenue Road**.

Walk east along Davenport Road on the north side. The first left is **Hillsboro Avenue**. The poet and diplomat Douglas LePan (1914-98) was a resident of **No.30** from 1971-78, and during this period wrote the memoir of his life as a public servant, *Bright Glass of Memory* (1979). *The Oxford Companion to Canadian Literature* comments, "In this book, which gives us fresh insight into some of the most significant moments in recent Canadian history, we see the man of letters and the man of affairs as one man, single and indivisible." The novelist Marika Robert has been off the CanLit radar screens for almost three decades but in 1964 when her novel *A Stranger and Afraid* appeared, she was a national sensation. The book was the first S&M novel in Canadian history to be published by a mainstream house. That the author was the founder of one of Toronto's most popular haunts, The Coffee Mill on Bloor Street, only added to its piquant appeal. The book shot onto the bestseller lists. But after that book, the rest was silence.

Return to Davenport and look south to the stoplights at **Belmont Street**. When playwright and man of the theatre Mavor Moore (b.1919) lived at **25 Belmont** from 1966-69, he was the General Manager of the newly opened St. Lawrence Centre for the Arts. He was also writing short works for television and radio, as well as the dramas that were later published as *Six Plays by Mavor Moore*. Married to him at the time and also living at this address was the acclaimed literary biographer Phyllis Grosskurth (b.1924).

Playwright John Herbert (*Fortune and Men's Eyes*) moved to **1050 Yonge Street** in 1974 and remained until 1986. During the early part of his stay he helped to form the Playwright's Co-op (which later became the Playwrights' Union of Canada), while also serving as associate editor of *Onion*, a biweekly newspaper of the arts that lasted until 1982. In addition to writing reviews of plays, art openings, and dance, he drew cartoons and illustrated articles for the paper.

Herbert (b.1926) was a writing and theatre teacher at the Three Schools of Art in the Annex, and regarded this as the best job he ever held: "Several of my students from this school became professional writers, not because I was their teacher, but because they were talented and needed only encouragement . . . I presented theatrical productions at the Poor Alex Theatre under the label Maverick Theatre Company. We did plays, revues, and even a full-length musical. It was all, for me, the ideal situation." Throughout his years at this address he continued to write plays which were produced by Maverick, Autumn Leaf, and other theatre companies.

John Herbert, in costume as the "Dazzling Dowager" at the Coronation Ball, Colony Hotel, Toronto, October 12, 1996

Another pioneering playwright was Leslie Hart Reid (b.1896), alleged to have been the first Canadian author to have a work produced at Hart House Theatre. From 1927-28 he dwelt at **14 Gibson Avenue**. The street is currently the home of yet another dramatist, Erika Ritter (b.1948).

Novelist Katherine Govier (b.1948) moved into the unit on the main floor of **22 Roxborough Street West** in the fall 1979, writing much of her book *Going Through the Motions* over the next year before setting up house elsewhere with her new husband, John Honderich. The same house was Erika Ritter's home from 1981-93. While here she wrote the play *Murder at McQueen* (1986), won an ACTRA Award for her radio writing, and published two collections of essays, *Urban Scrawl* (1984), and *Ritter in Residence* (1987).

The year 1929 marked the beginning of the Depression and the start of many financially-stressed moves by the famed historian Donald Creighton (1902-79) and his wife Luella, (b,1901). In that year they shared a flat at **No.39**. He had just joined the History dept. at the UofT. His reputation rests on his books of Canadian history, but he began his university life as an Honours English student, and throughout his life exemplified a care for word use and delicacy of phrasing more usually associated with novelists than academics. In fact, at the end of his life, finding factual writing too constricting for some of the things he wanted to say about Canada, he published a novel. He may have asked his wife for counsel on fiction writing, since she had been publishing novels all her life.

W. Gordon Mills (1886-1960) was, for most of his early life, a senior executive of the T. Eaton Company. Among his duties were helping the Eaton family in its work with the Art Gallery of Ontario and the Margaret Eaton School of Expression and Literature. In 1935, however, due to a nervous breakdown, he resigned from the firm, left Toronto, and following recovery, became serious about his painting. Yet he needed a day job, so he moved to Ottawa and during WWII rose through the ranks, becoming Deputy Minister of Defence in 1947. He had been writing poetry since the 1920s, and a posthumous selection was published in 1985. From 1917-19 he made his home at **151 Roxborough Street West**.

During the last eight years of her life, Irene McElheran (1879-1955) lived at **No.157**. She was born in Toronto, the daughter of the founder of the Great-West Life Assurance Co. She attended the UofT, but left the city, not to return until 1930 when her husband was appointed principal of Wycliffe College. Presumably they lived on campus because they do not appear in city directories until 1948. In addition to books of poetry, she published an account of her husband's life, *That's What I'm Here For* (1955). Among her accomplishments was the fact she was invited by the Primate of the Church of England in Canada to be the first woman in the country to speak from an Anglican pulpit.

When Newton MacTavish was made the editor of *Canadian Magazine* in 1906, he moved to **127 Macpherson Avenue**. He remained until 1910, when he moved to **No.131** and stayed at the new address until 1918. Among his many titles was an early attempt to authoritatively document our higher culture in his *The Fine Arts in Canada* (1925). Fiction writer David Helwig (b.1938) moved back to his native Toronto in 1974 to work as the Literary Manager of CBC-TV. He found a small apartment at **No.130** from 1974-76, and while he lived there, wrote the earliest draft of his book *A Sound Like Laughter* (1983). One of the little oddities of life is that, unaware of Helwig's proximity, I happened to be living in another apartment in the same building reading and very much enjoying his book *The Street of Summer* (1969).

Husband-and-wife novelists Clark Blaise (b.1940) and Bharati Mukherjee (b.1940) "moved to Toronto (**45 Macpherson Avenue**) in June 1978 and left on October 15, 1980. We immediately began remodelling, which meant we lived with debris and plaster dust and gaping holes right up to the time of moving. While there I wrote only a few stories ('Prying' and 'Man And His World') . . . For Bharati, it was a most unsettled time. She was pushed around on subway platforms, not served in stores, and it was a time of a great many assaults on Indians all over the city. We had no idea such backwardness was rampant, and it left us unable to cope. It seems to us unforgivable that something so medieval as racism should destroy one's life in a modern, self-consciously progressive city like Toronto. She wrote 'Isolated Incidents' which was published in *Saturday Night*, 'The World According to Su' which won the *Chatelaine* Fiction contest, and laboured long and hard on a novel, 'The Father of His Country' which thus far has yielded only stories which were published in *Darkness* and *The Middleman*. Much of our time was spent on human rights causes, interviewing assault victims, attending zoning meetings in East York, and slowly becoming political people, disenchanted with everything we saw going on around us. When Skidmore College offered her a visiting professorship in 1979, she took it. They offered the same to me in 1980, which facilitated our escape from the worst two years of our life . . . Had we never left Montreal, we would not have been so disturbed, nor, perhaps, so agitated. In that sense only, Toronto was a beneficial experience. We of course continue to count many friends in Toronto, and we sincerely recommend it to any white people who ask."

Playwright John Krizanc lived at **No.42** from the fall of 1985 to 1988. During this period, he "reworked, rethought, rewrote *Tamara* for New York—then sat on my ass, then fell asleep, not necessarily in that order."

Mavor Moore and Phyllis Grosskurth bought a house at **19 Macpherson** and Moore lived here from 1970 until 1976 when he and Grosskurth separated. During this period his musicals *Johnny Belinda* and *Fauntleroy* were produced.

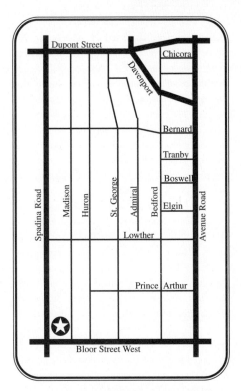

The our begins at the northeast corner of Spadina Road and Bloor Street West.

Walk north on **Spadina Road**. 41 **Spadina Road** has been the home address of at least three authors. The translator of the classic Canadian novel *Maria Chapdeleine*, William Hume Blake, lived in apt. 9 for only about a year (1913-14). B.K. Sandwell (1876-1954), in contrast, lived in apt. 5 from 1942-51—longer than at any other of his Toronto residences. Sandwell is more important to our literary history as a man of letters than as a creative writer. For example, in 1932 he succeeded Hector Charlesworth as the editor of *Saturday Night*, when that periodical was far more influential than it is today, especially in its promotion of Canadian authors. He was also a key member in the founding of the Canadian Authors' Association. And he was active in lobbying the government to make needed changes to the Copyright Act to assist Canadian authors and publishers. Unusually for a literary man, his roots were in the financial sector. Early in the century he was editor of *Financial Times*. Thanks to the intervention of Stephen Leacock, Sandwell joined the faculty of the Economics dept. at McGill University in 1919 for a few years, and over a longer period he contributed hundreds of columns to the *Financial Post*. He left this address in 1951, the same year he retired as editor from *Saturday Night*.

Mort Forer (1922-81) spent the last three years of his life at **No.41**. He and his wife had immigrated to Toronto from New York in 1967. In 1970, he published his only novel, *The Humback*, a book scarcely known today but which Margaret Laurence said was the kind of book that "sinks without a trace at the time of publication only to surface years later as a classic."

Fiction writer Matt Cohen lived at **75-A Spadina Road**, 1967-68, while commuting to McMaster University to lecture in Religious Studies. Within the year he would publish his first novel, Korsoniloff, to wide acclaim. He little realized that the house had earlier been the home of novelist Graeme Gibson (b.1934). The young Gibson and his mother had moved into this house in 1941 while his father, a General in the Canadian Army, was fighting overseas. Graeme and his mother remained at this address until 1946 when his father returned. This building has also been the home of filmmaker and writer Myrna Kostash. She inherited Cohen's apartment from Matt, and lived in it for nearly a year.

The playwright Ken Gass, better known today as the artistic director of the revitalized

Factory Theatre Lab, in 1968 lived at **No.71**. Three decades earlier, the much revered poet Margaret Avison also lived at this same address for about five years. From 1950 to 1966 the remarkable short-story writer, George Elliott (1923-96) was based at **73 Spadina Road** and finished his too-little known collection *The Kissing Man* at this address.

Filmmaker and writer Myrna Kostash inherited Cohen's apartment at **75-A Spadina** and lived in it for approximately a year. Before he lived at this address, Matt Cohen, living the peripatetic life of the grad student and young writer, had kept house just up the street at **No.87** for about 12 months in the mid-1960s. Cohen reminisced about this block of Spadina in a recent *Toronto Life* personal essay: "January 1, 1966: I wake up at noon, pull on my jeans, light a cigarette. I'm twenty-three years and two days old, which means I still have almost two more years of being immortal. I walk to the window, layered in several centuries of Toronto pollution, and look out to see what's happening.

"This little patch of the world is Spadina Road, a couple of blocks north of Bloor Street. Spadina is Toronto central, the cosmic spine. On its southern stretch, you can breakfast at the Crest Grill, lunch at Switzer's, dine, drink beer and listen to jazz at Grossman's Tavern. You can shoot pool on Spadina. . . . I myself have already lived at three Spadina addresses, dressed in Spadina-bought clothes, even gone to my grandfather's funeral at a Spadina Avenue funeral chapel. One day I will be walking through the snow toward this very apartment, looking at my car parked on the front lawn. While I'm watching, another car, speeding south, will slide off the road and into my car."

Novelist Joan Barfoot came to Toronto in 1969 and rented an apartment in a high-rise on Davisville Avenue. Its charms quickly fatigued her, and, as she wrote in a letter: "I figured if I had to live with a bunch of people, they might as well be people I knew and liked. So a group of us rented **101 Spadina Road** in the Spring of 1970, in a cooperative arrangement. The house was a grand three-storey, with glorious wooden floors and stairs and banisters, and stained glass windows, and fireplaces. It had been expropriated by Metro for the doomed Spadina Expressway and cost us a total, I believe, of $300 a month." Barfoot, working on suburban weekly newspapers as a reporter/editor, was quickly coming to the realization that to be a creative writer she would have to write fiction rather than talk about it. Not long after she left here in 1972, she began to write, *Abra*, which won the *Books in Canada* First Novel Award. In 1992 she was awarded the Marian Engel Prize for her body of work.

Musician Marcus Adeney was 97 when he died in 1998. He had settled in Toronto in 1927 (fresh from deportation from the USA; he had been playing without a green card), and had purchased a house in the Beaches, where he and his wife lived for more than half a century. Even though he was principal cellist with the Toronto Symphony for many years, and taught music at the Toronto Conservatory until he was 84, he maintained that he was always more interested in Marcel Proust than the cello, and clearly regarded himself as a "literary gent." His novel, *The New Babylon*, was given second prize in 1931 in a notorious contest organized by Graphic Press of Ottawa. Alas, the Depression curtailed Graphic's operations before Adeney's book could be published; it was sixty years before it finally found another publisher. He moved to **123 Spadina Road** in 1990 and lived here until 1994 when failing health finally forced him into a nursing home.

W.J. Alexander resided at **155 Spadina Road** from 1921 until he died in 1944, and he lived here longer than at any other of his Toronto addresses. Alexander was one of the most celebrated professors in the history of the English dept. at the UofT, and the prestigious annual Alexander Lectures were created in his honour. His literary anthologies were used in English departments across the country. Compared to his contemporaries, he was vigorous in supporting Canadian authors, and among his students can be numbered Arthur Stringer, Norman Duncan, and Harvey O'Higgins. Alexander was that unusual combination: an academic much respected by his colleagues, yet an academic who relished speaking to the general public in plain English whenever opportunities arose. Although his standards were high, his style was avuncular, and thus popular. Even a decade after he had retired from teaching, his utterances were considered sufficiently newsworthy to receive front-page treatment in the *Star*.

Silver Donald Cameron (b.1937) is a journalist with many books to his credit, including *Conversations with Canadian Novelists* (1973) and the novel *Dragon Lady* (1981). Four of his 45 radio dramas have been ACTRA Award finalists, and many have been produced in France, New Zealand, Ireland, and other nations. He was born in Toronto and lived for the first year of his life at **215 Spadina Road**, while his father studied for his doctorate. Just paces away, poets Roo Borson and Kim Maltman lived at **225 Spadina Road** in 1980-81.

At Dupont Street turn right and walk east to **Madison Avenue**. Novelist Matt Cohen lived briefly at **No.162** in 1965. Brief residencies also characterize the following: poet Kenneth Radu at **No.148** (1967-68); novelist M.T. Kelly at **No.135** (1980); Cary Fagan at **No.121** (1980-81); and Matt Cohen again at **No.115** (1964-65).

No.104-A was the home of Adrienne Clarkson (b.1939) from 1964-66. While nationally known today as one of our leading television journalists, she was, in the seventies, a novelist of some repute. When she and her then-husband, Stephen Clarkson, departed this address, they handed the keys to playwright and theatre administrator Tom Hendry (b.1929), who also lived here for about two years. Hendry was the head of the triumvirate who founded the Toronto Free Theatre. Earlier, he had helped to found the Manitoba Theatre Centre, and had worked at the Stratford Festival as Literary Manager. One critic has stated that "Hendry's career in Canadian theatre is perhaps unmatched in its breadth." While living at this address, he transformed the Canadian Theatre Centre into a fully professional organization.

Another important man of Canadian theatre, playwright Herman Voaden (1903-91), lived at **103 Madison** for part of 1933. Crime writer and CBC producer John Reeves (not to be confused with the famous portrait photographer of the same name) lived in the mid-fifties at **No.99**, while UofT philosophy professor and poet Francis Sparshott (b.1926) lived at **No.98** for three years in the early sixties.

Gerald Noxon (1910-90), who spent his boyhood years at **88 Madison**, was a radio producer and radio dramatist. In the 1940s, he helped to give the CBC its international reputation for producing plays of the highest quality. He was an intimate friend of Conrad Aiken and Malcolm Lowry—so close to the latter, in fact, that Lowry took to calling him brother, as in "long-lost." The editor of the Lowry/Noxon letters, Paul Tiessen, comments, "Lowry desperately needed an editor and a brother in 1940, and the letters . . . attest to Noxon's energy and purpose in fashioning himself as the willing recipient of the roles Lowry offered him. In 1940, Noxon became Lowry's connection with the world beyond the wilderness. During the process of Lowry's transforming *Under the Volcano* into its final form, Noxon was willing to become not only Lowry's 'brother' but also his 'White Man,' his 'Man from the East.' So when the Lowrys finally travelled east to the Toronto area . . . their acceptance of Noxon's standing invitation to visit was doubly significant: they were going in search of last minute help with *Under the Volcano*, and they were going to visit 'family' to get that help."

The legendary literary producer Robert Weaver started working at the CBC in 1948.

By the time he moved to **No.83 Madison** in 1951, he was preparing a 15-minute weekly series titled "Canadian Short Stories," which eventually became, under Weaver's stewardship, and quite justifiably, the most famous literary program in the history of Canadian radio, "Anthology."

When the UofT Classics professor and short-story writer Gilbert Norwood first came to Toronto from his native England in 1926, he lived at **No.72**, and stayed until 1930. Did he know that the painter and writer Arthur Heming had lived in the same house just a few years before (1920-24)? Closer to our end of the 20th c., Christine Slater lived on Madison, **No.64** in the 1980s.

When he died, Frederic Davidson (c.1870-1945) was described by the press as a language expert well known for his literary work. Indeed, the *G&M* reported in its obituary that his literary work in France had been recognized by the French Government in the form of the honorific title: "L'Officier de l'Academie de France." He was a graduate in languages from the UofT, and after study abroad he returned to that school to teach for the rest of his life. He spoke several languages, as one might expect from such a professor, yet the list is daunting: French, German, Italian, Greek, Latin, and Arabic. He wrote a novel titled *Old Wine in New Bottles*, with Toronto as its setting. Apparently it had a wide sale in Europe but it remains an obscure and little-read title in Canada. He lived at **22 Madison Avenue** from 1903 until 1915.

No.17 has been home to three important authors. The earliest inhabitant was Theodore H. Rand (1835-1900), who moved to this address in 1893 and lived here for the few years left to him. Rand came to Toronto after a full career in Nova Scotia where he had been first a teacher, then superintendent of education for the province, then a professor at Acadia University. He was invited to Toronto in 1885 to be among the first faculty of the new Baptist college called

McMaster, and in 1892 he became its Chancellor. McMaster University later moved to Hamilton, but the original building is still around the corner at 273 Bloor Street West (now the Royal Conservatory of Music). While living at this address, he published *At Minas Basin and Other Poems*, which became so popular that another edition was published within the year. The book is still a fixture of recommended reading lists for those studying Canadian poetry. As an

Theodore Harding Rand

administrator, Rand had hired Canadian academics whenever he could. And he showed similar zeal for his fellow scribblers by publishing in the year he died *A Treasury of Canadian Verse*, a widely praised anthology.

Walter Bauer (1904-76) arrived in Toronto on September 17, 1952, and after a brief stay in the High Park area he settled into a room at **No.17** on October 16, 1952 and stayed here until July 4, 1954. Bauer was said to have left Germany because of his disgust for the political direction the country had been taking after the war, but as he confessed to his friend, the writer Herman Hesse, there were other reasons, including problems with his marriage and with his creative life. "When Bauer finally made up his own mind [to leave], his decision rested, to some extent, on the illusion that a fresh start in a new country could possibly save his broken marriage." During his residency here he worked as a dishwasher until he had saved enough money (and learned enough English) to study at the UofT. After graduation in 1958 he was hired by the German dept. as a lecturer and he taught there until his retirement. He died within months of retiring. In his lifetime he wrote six dozen books in German including novels, poetry, biographies—and a short-story collection tellingly called *A Stranger in Toronto.*

Tomson Highway (b.1951) moved to Toronto in October 1978, and has become one of the nation's best-known playwrights. As with many writers, his early years in the city were marked by frequent moves from apartment to apartment. His third residence in Toronto was at **No.17** from June to October 1979.

Estelle Kerr was a prominent visual artist and journalist in Toronto when she shocked her colleagues in 1918 by volunteering to be a non-combatant volunteer with the Canadian troops in the front lines. Her time in Europe changed her life. The horror of actual combat affected her perceptions, of course, but European, especially French culture, also changed her viscerally, and when she returned from overseas she wrote about her time there in ways which proved popular, especially with children. She lived at **No.14** with her father from the beginning of the century until 1914.

Montreal native Alan Sullivan (1868-1947) attended the UofT's Engineering School but failed to graduate. This, however, did not hinder him from securing jobs in engineering with the CPR. After WWI he settled in England, where he continued to write and publish more than 40 novels that brought him such renown that whenever he returned to Toronto he was treated as a literary celebrity. Early in his career, from 1909-12, he lived at **10 Madison Avenue.**

At Bloor Street, turn east and walk to **Huron Street.** This street has been home to more authors (59 by my count) than any other stretch of road of similar size in Toronto—no doubt, in part, because of its proximity to the UofT and the bohemian life of the undergraduate community.

Helena Coleman (1860-1953) lived at only one address in Toronto: **476 Huron Street.** Born in eastern Ontario, Coleman contracted polio at 11. She could walk with the aid of two crutches for all but the last 20 years of her long life, when she was finally forced to use a wheelchair full-time. Yet she managed to study music in Berlin and loved travelling so much that at her death it was said that few Canadian women were as intimately acquainted with European and American cities. Back in Canada she wrote many songs and books of poetry, and extended her travels to include Alberta where, despite her disabilities, she frequently rode horseback and even went mountain climbing. The literary biographer Elsie Pomeroy wrote of Coleman: "From the standpoint of financial success Miss Coleman's stories were vastly more important than her poetry. For many years her work appeared in all the leading American magazines but always under a pen name. That fact that Paul Reynolds was her agent speaks for itself. He was only interested in authors whose stories commanded top prices." Helena lived here with her brother, the internationally acclaimed geologist A.P. Coleman, from 1906 until her death nearly five decades later.

The Italian Cultural Institute has been located at **No.496** since 1982, and in that time has become by far the most active of all the cultural missions based in the city. Just the list of visual artists who have exhibited here would make any museum proud. Under the direction of its dynamic director, Francesca Valente (b.1943), the Institute has been a remarkable influence for good with the Canadian Opera Company, the Royal Ontario Museum, the Art Gallery of Ontario, and certainly with the Harbourfront Reading Series. Almost all of the Italian authors who have read at Harbourfront have been presented with some support from, and in conjunction with, the I.C.I. Valente is also a literary translator of wide repute. She has translated a number of Canadian authors and has arranged for their work to be published in Italy. Among the Canadians she has thus helped are Margaret Atwood, Northrop Frye, Irving Layton, Gwendolyn MacEwen, Marshall McLuhan, Anne Michaels, P.K. Page, and Leon Rooke. She also translated two anthologies of Canadian short stories, *Musica silente* (1992) and *Altre terre* (1996), the first ever to be published in Italy. She translated poetry books by Giorgio Bassani and Patrizia Cavalli from Italian into English. Her husband Branko Gorjup (b.1944), living and working at the same address, has done similar stellar service for Canadian authors in Croatia as well as in Italy. Here he edited several anthologies of Canadian short fiction; edited and translated into Croatian one book by Leon Rooke (*Selected Stories*, 1997), and two books by Barry Callaghan (*Selected Stories*, and *Hogg Poems*, 1998). He also edited for publication in Europe bilingual volumes of poetry by Irving Layton, P.K. Page, Gwendolyn MacEwen, and Al Purdy.

Before the Italians arrived to renovate the building, it housed very small and inexpensive apartments, at least one of which was home from 1962-64 to novelist Richard B. Wright (b.1937). His first novel, *The Weekend Man*, was published to nearly unanimous rave reviews, not just in Canada, but around the world. His subsequent fictions

have cemented his reputation. Wright clearly enjoyed his years here: "My most vivid memories of the city centre on the Annex area . . . As a bachelor, I had a ball in a house on **Huron Street** . . . Back in the mid-sixties, another fellow and I (he's now one of Canada's leading geophysicists) had the top flat overlooking Huron Street for about three years. The place was filled with Australian women and other party types."

504 Huron was poet Robert Fones's home from 1971-72, and playwright Erika Ritter lived at **No.528** from 1969-70. Montreal novelist Ray Smith (*Cape Breton Is the Thought Control Centre of Canada*) tried writing fiction in Toronto for some years in the 1960s. One of those years, 1965-66, was at **No.534 Huron**.

In the literary history of Toronto there have been several eminent painters who took themselves seriously as poets, and, more importantly, were taken seriously as poets by literary folk. One thinks of Barker Fairley. Or Arthur Heming. Or W.A. Sherwood. But the most famous painter/poet of them all is Lawren Harris. We will discuss his literary life when we arrive at his houses, but as we pass Huron Public School, at **No.541**, we should note that he attended this school from 1894-99. Other graduates were Ethel Hume Bennett (b.1881), the poet, anthologist, and one-time head of Havergal College, and the late Douglas LePan, poet and distinguished diplomat.

Novelist Percy Janes (1922-99) spent his last year as a graduate student (1949-50) at **542 Huron**. Norman Ward (1918-90) won the Leacock Medal for Humour in 1960 for *Mice in the Beer* and wrote two other books of fiction poking fun at academics and politicians. As a Professor of Political Science in Saskatchewan he wrote seminal texts on the House of Commons and Canadian government. For his writing he was elected a fellow of the Royal Society of Canada and given the Order of Canada. When starting his grad studies at the UofT, 1942-43, he lived at **No.544**.

Frank Yeigh was the first literary impresario in Toronto. He organized the city's first gala reading of Canadian authors in 1892. Others had presented foreign writers as solo acts, but none had had the faith, until Yeigh, to believe that Canadians would come in droves to listen to Canadian authors read their work. The *M&E* noted that "his status as an authority on all things Canadian was undisputed, and his writings for magazines and newspapers over a long period of years established him as foremost among the men who devoted their lives to the political, social and economic history of the Dominion." He died in 1935 at **No.588**, where he had been living since 1913.

Like Norman Ward, A.G. Bailey (b.1905) was both a member of the Order of Canada and a fellow of the Royal Society of Canada. The two men spent their adult lives as professors but also had active creative writing lives. Bailey, a New Brunswicker, published his first poetry book in 1927. However, it was only when he arrived in Toronto that he was introduced to modernism by poets he met here such as Earle Birney. He lived at **598 Huron** during 1930-31, and continued living in the university area while obtaining his master's degree and doctorate.

David Young lived in the coach house at the rear at **No.603** from 1991-92. It was here that he began to write his remarkable play, *Glenn*, based on the life of the extraordinary Canadian pianist Glenn Gould. Not much has been heard of late from Rolf Harvey, but in the early 1970s when he lived at **No.620** he was considered an important up-and-coming poet. Another writer whose pen has been muted recently is the former President of the League of Canadian Poets, Henry Beissel (b.1929). From 1959-61, while writing plays and following a master's program at the UofT, he had rooms at **654 Huron**.

Walk one block east along Dupont Street to **St. George Street** and head south. Anna Durie (whom we met at 8 Spadina Road), after losing her luxurious home and pampered life, took a few years to regain her feet but once she did, she lived at **306 St. George** from 1913-32. It was here that she started to write and publish books of her poetry. Another poet, Anthony Frisch (b.1921), apparently lived in Toronto for some years but I could connect him with only one address—and that for just one year: **No.298** in 1954. He wrote several books, but he will be remembered most for having edited an anthology. William Arthur Deacon in 1956 described the project: "Anthony Frisch who teaches at Pickering College wishes to ensure an adequate crop of Canadian writers for 1975 and years following. To this end he has promoted, through the provincial departments of education, an anthology of verse and prose by high school students from sea to sea. After regional weedings out, 5,300 contributions went to the final judges who selected 155 items to fill a book of 224 pages entitled *First Flowerings* and to be published in Toronto June 1. Of the 155 selections, 61 are from Ontario. The book will certainly stimulate teen-agers with literary leanings. Somebody should follow the careers of the 155 for the next 20 years to find out what percentage become first rate adult writers." A check of the contributors' list reveals the name of Dennis Lee, his first publication in a book.

The under-rated poet Robert Finch (1900-95) lived briefly at **292 St. George**, and may have met his literary neighbour Pelham Edgar, who resided at **No.286** from 1917-46.

In his day, Edgar (1871-1948) was the brightest star in the UofT English dept.'s firmament in the same way that Northrop Frye was after him, or as W.J. Alexander before him. Pelham Edgar was at first mentor, then friend to Frye. Frye's biographer, John Ayre, wrote of the mentor: "At the still-strongly-Methodist [Victoria] College, Edgar was an anomaly. He was an Anglican who looked like a British major with moustache and correct air. His father, Sir James Edgar, had been Speaker of the House of Commons in

Pelham Edgar

literature was vast, and included the contemporary work of D.H. Lawrence and Eliot, which was spurned as degenerate at other colleges. He also had a weird ability to push people in exactly appropriate directions . . . Very early, he sensed something Coleridgian about Kay Coburn, and sent her on her way to pre-eminence as editor of Coleridge's notebooks. When he saw Frye he thought Blake.

"In class, he had a diffuse air about him and often wandered off into areas—particularly in contemporary literature—that had nothing to do with the lecture . . . In one lecture, Edgar began a discussion about Blake that was exciting enough to involve Frye a little further in Blake's work. Above all, Frye admired the depth of Edgar's knowledge. Edgar once electrified him when he impatiently told a student talking about an obscure poet to sit down. He then launched into an amazingly detailed analysis, starting with, 'The facts about Crabbe are these.'"

Pelham Edgar was born in Toronto and sent to Upper Canada College. Later he would return to UCC as a teacher. One of his fellow students, and also one of his fellow teachers at the private boys' school, was a life-long friend, Stephen Leacock. When other eminent authors came to Toronto, they would sometimes stay with Edgar at his house on St. George Street. Among such visitors were Duncan Campbell Scott and Vachel Lindsay.

Another was the English poet Siegfried Sassoon who wrote about his only Toronto visit: "On the evening of March 30 [1920] I arrived in Toronto, after twenty-three hours in the train, which was five hours late. Dishevelled and greatly overdue, I went straight to a big dinner party which was being given for me by Vincent Massey, who, by his high intelligence and wealth has done so much to foster the arts in Toronto. I was staying with Professor Pelham Edgar, a charmingly friendly but rather fatiguingly talkative man, who was in a flutter of excitement about my performance, which would be the central

Ottawa. Edgar was not wealthy but inherited the family mansion. There was an illusive rakishness about him and one inaccurate legend had him taking a corner so fast in his car that he pitched a visiting duchess out of her seat and over a hedge. His close friend was E.J. Pratt whom Edgar rescued out of a minor instructor's job in psychology on the premise that Pratt seemed to know something about literature, though his PhD, improbably, was on speculative theology. Together, Pratt and Edgar played golf and drank liquor with a clear conscience that was positively idiosyncratic at the Methodist Vic.

"The professors at University College who ran the English department considered Edgar a dilettante. He hadn't, in fact, published much except for a pioneering study of Henry James, and his area of interest, the Romantics, was unpopular in academe. Another of his problems was his first wife who made him miserable and insomniac with her severe attacks of depression. But Edgar had two unusual qualities. His knowledge of ingredient of a 'Benefit' for the poet Bliss Carman. I had casually assumed that I should be giving the usual reading to a moderate-sized audience, so I was horrified when Pelham Edgar told me that I was expected to lecture for not less than half an hour on contemporary English poets, in addition to reading my war poems. He had taken it for granted that I had some such lecture prepared. So after receiving a couple of newspaper men, being motored all round the town, and conspicuously entertained to luncheon at the Arts and Letters Club, I retired to my bedroom with the prospect of delivering, to about twelve hundred people, within a few hours, an as yet unwritten lecture. Overtired as I was, the desperate situation seemed irretrievable. At this juncture, however, a helping hand arrived in the shape of my friend 'Toronto' Prewett who had returned to his native place for a time after studying English literature at Oxford during 1919. I explained the plight I was in, and between us we vamped up a superficial conspectus of living British bards—Toronto Prewett's providential collaboration converting what had previously appeared an inevitable catastrophe into a light-hearted tour de force. I went to the Convocation Hall rather queasily sustained by his assurance that I should 'get away with it' more successfully by being bright and chatty than if I had composed a serious academic discourse. Fortunately for me, the audience was indulgent, and my impudently unconsidered remarks were accepted as Toronto Prewett had predicted. As usual, my war poems proved themselves extremely effective. One of the newspapers compared me to 'an avenging angel through whom the voice of the slaughtered youth was speaking.' This was rather how I had seen myself, for I was becoming a conscious performer, enjoying the sense of playing on the emotions of my hearers, though aware of a dangerous allurement towards histrionic artifice."

Dennis Lee lived in a second-floor flat at **273 St. George Street** from June 1961 until August 1962, his last address before tackling the big poetry projects for which he is renowned. At **No.224** novelist Paul Vasey (b.1945), author of *The Failure of Love* (1991), arrived in 1972 in Toronto (with his new bride) to work as an editor on the night shift at Canadian Press. He described his home: "If you look at the building from St. George, the door is on the left and the right half of the front wall is glass and you can see the stairs snaking up to the ninth floor which is where we lived and which stairs we had to climb, more than once, when the damned elevators refused to work. We were there a year, Marilyn going to Teacher's College, and I working the night shift. During the day—the apartment to myself—I wrote what turned out to be a dreadful novel—lots of waves crashing and women wailing and so on. Its title was *And Wounded They Fall*—which tells you all you need to know about its contents."

The Oxford Companion to Canadian Theatre described John Thomas McDonough's *Charbonneau & Le Chef* as "a landmark in Canadian theatre for its treatment of an important event in Canadian history and its appeal to both French- and English-speaking audiences." The author spent much of his life (c.1935-54) with his family at **No.221**. He would later join the Catholic priesthood, but his decision to leave the clerical life in 1968 was so shocking that it was front-page news in the Toronto newspapers. He settled happily in Scarborough and taught philosophy at Centennial College.

A pioneer of Canadian radio and television drama, Andrew Allan (1907-74) lived at **193 St. George Street** during the Depression. Forty years later, and having lived in other Toronto locales in the meantime, he came full circle and moved into apt. 303 of the adjacent building, **No.191**, and lived here from 1969 until he died. In his memoir, Allan gives a sense of the hardness of the Depression years while at home here: "To avoid starvation, I had swallowed pride, and had borrowed the bus-fare back to Toronto, where at least I had a friendly roof in the house the family had rented on St. George Street. I had tried selling feature stories to the *Daily Star*, with marked lack of success. I had looked disconsolately at all the darkened theatres. People had even stolen the lightbulbs out of the marquees."

He learned that CFRB was looking for a new announcer, and the job opportunity gave him his unwitting start in writing and producing radio drama. "When I went to the auditions, there appeared to be hundreds of young men present—all, I presumed, with experience; and all apparently with more confidence than I had. The only things I knew about radio announcing were that you had to be clear and you had to be friendly, and you had to be able to say Rimsky-Korsakoff and things like that. After my turn was over, they took my name, address, and phone number, and said they'd be in touch. A young man with red hair and an impressive grey suit was being treated with great tenderness. Obviously, he had the job—so that was that.

"Well, it wasn't quite that. I went home and glued my head to the loudspeaker. I listened to everything that came over the air, no matter how depressing. I took notes. I decided that some of the stuff must be written down for the announcer to say; and there were even little plays, sometimes, that clearly had to be written by someone. So I went to the typewriter and wrote scripts for every kind of show I had heard, and a few I hadn't heard but I thought might be heard if a man played his cards right. I returned to CFRB and delicately placed the wad of typescript on the desk of the man who seemed to be in charge. I said that when I was doing the announce audition I had forgotten to mention that I was also a writer, and here was proof. The man looked startled, but he thanked me. I went away. Somewhere in the three months that followed, I decided that *really* had been that. . . .[However] I got the job. I was to be junior announcer, open the station in the morning, and close it after midnight. I was to do anything the mind of

an unsympathetic senior announcer could devise for me. And I was to write all sustaining programmes . . . I made over the top floor of the St. George Street house as my own apartment . . . In Canadian radio then, there was no such creature as a 'producer' or 'director.' Whoever was handy—usually the announcer—threw the programme on the air, after little, if any, rehearsal. Nobody owned a stopwatch. However, when I wrote the first Canadian soap-opera, and sold it to a pill company, some production and timing became necessary—so I supplied that."

From CFRB, Allan worked at a variety of legitimate theatre jobs. Then he joined the CBC where he became the executive director of radio dramas during their heyday—when, the *G&M* declared, "they were among the best of their kind in the world." Allan was committed to the older classics of literature but also to newer Canadian writers. Under his aegis were developed the radio talents of Fletcher Markle, Len Peterson, Lister Sinclair, and Tommy Tweed. Lister Sinclair said of him in 1974: "The idea that our plays should feel Canadian, that they should have social content and should be abrasive—these are commonplace now, but they weren't when he started. The whole climate was set by Andrew Allan . . . He represented the spearhead of Canadian culture." Novelist and biographer Lois Darroch also lived at **No.193** from 1939-40.

For some years the house at **No.186 St. George** has been the home of Hillel, the Jewish community and cultural club of the university. Hillel has sponsored readings by many excellent writers of fiction and poetry over the decades, but usually at other venues on campus. Eli Mandel, in contrast, actually read in the clubhouse itself, on March 4, 1973. This place was also the home of novelist Henry Kreisel during his second year (1943-44) of undergraduate study at the UofT.

Gwendolyn MacEwen came to an apartment at **No.149** in 1975 and stayed for about four years. Her residence overlapped with that of another poet in another apartment, David Donnell. He lived here from 1978-85.

New Zealand native Wallace Reyburn (b.1913) lived in Toronto for only a few years at the end of the 1930s. After a successful career as a journalist in his birth country, he moved to Toronto in 1937 to work for Maclean Hunter and then the *Telegram* before he moved permanently to England, initially as the UK correspondent for the *Telegram*, and then as an editor and writer for *Queen* magazine. His second and last address in our city was **145 St. George Street**. Reyburn was a study in contrasts. Most of his time in Toronto was spent as the editor of *Chatelaine*. Yet he was the author of several books and articles on rugby. His imaginative writing took the form of novels (all published by Cassell in London). For his writing he was awarded the Order of the British Empire by the Queen.

This address was also the first home in Toronto (1964-65) of the distinguished French-language author Cécile Cloutier (b.1930). Madame Cloutier had moved to Toronto to join the French dept. of the UofT. In addition to her writing in French, she has made formal studies in other languages as diverse as Sanskrit, Chinese, Eskimo, Greek, Polish, and Spanish.

The York Club at **No.135** has long remained aloof from the city and university life swirling around it. On rare occasions it has housed authors during their Toronto stays. The most famous of these was Sir Henry Newbolt (1862-1938), who had a room here for about 10 nights when he was in town to lecture at Convocation Hall and other venues in February 1923. The ties to Britain were still so strong in the 1920s that the visit of Newbolt was treated as a major event by the press. Newbolt's may be one of those names you recall from your school years but whose actual writing remains elusive. A single line may refresh your memory. His most famous is the one where he treats war like a schoolyard football match: "Play up! play up! and play the game!" Such affection for the martial, no matter what cost the carnage, is an unfashionable emotion today, but it held powerful sway over intelligent people in the first decades of this century. Stanley Kunitz, a wonderful poet and astute critic, had this to say of Newbolt: "Newbolt's novels are already forgotten but he produced much verse which, though it never reached great imaginative heights, has its place in the second order of poetry by reason of its metrical music and breezy heartiness. . . . His historical writings have solid worth, and he wrote much sagacious and scholarly criticism."

Another knight of the pen, Sir Steven Runciman (b.1903), also stayed at the York Club. In December 1952 he was in Toronto to give five lectures over the period of a fortnight and the Club was his base for much of that time. He returned for about a week in 1957 while lecturing at the UofT. I am aware of only two creative writers who were members of the York Club: Robertson Davies and E.J. Pratt.

Backtrack one block north to **Prince Arthur Avenue**, then turn right and walk east. Poet Theodore H. Rand lived at **75 Prince Arthur Avenue** from 1890-92 while Chancellor of McMaster University, then located around the corner on Bloor Street. The Royal Conservatory of Music is located in what used to be McMaster's main building. Rand had had an unblemished career as an educator in the Maritimes when he was called upon by Ontario Baptists to act as a calming influence on some of the factional squabbles then plaguing the Baptist Church.

At least three authors have lived in the high-rise at **50 Prince Arthur**. Phyllis Brett Young made apt. 506 her home from c.1969 until c.1981—indeed, this is the last known address for this often untraceable woman. Her profile as a novelist was extremely high in the brief period 1959-64 when she published five novels to huge acclaim. One Toronto newspaper suggested without contradiction that her works (which had been translated into French, German, Swedish, and Norwegian and had been published in British and American editions as well as Canadian), had a readership of over ten million. Yet in 1964, after all that activity—silence. She was married to a prominent management consultant and, assuming they remained married, their last listing in either telephone or city directory is for this building in 1981.

Lloyd Abbey (b.1943), another author who lived in this building, hung his hat and wrote a book of poetry (*Braindances*, 1979) in apt. 1602 between 1977 and 1980 while he taught English at the UofT. Here, too, he began the writing of his best-known book, the novel *The Last Whales* (1989). Finally, it should be noted that distinguished critic, essayist, and editor Kildare Dobbs (b.1923) lived here from 1983-87.

The venerable poet Robert Finch (1900-95) resided at **No.33** during WWII. Finch was one of the longest-lived authors in the history of the country, and was writing poetry until he died.

Frontiersman Roger Pocock (1865-1941) recuperated in Toronto from wounds he suffered in the Northwest Rebellion. Assuming he arrived in the city in early 1886 (travel would not have been easy from the prairies after the Rebellion's end in late 1885), his father's home at that time was **30 Prince Arthur**. His father moved elsewhere in town a year later, and Roger went with him. Pocock may have started to write during this period of recovery, for his adventures in the Canadian West haunt the many popular novels and memoirs he penned over the next decades.

When Stan Obodiac (1922-84) first arrived in Toronto from Saskatchewan in 1959, he stayed for a year at **25 Prince Arthur**. He began his writing career, at the suggestion of novelist and hockey fan Scott Young, by composing publicity releases for Maple Leaf Gardens. Soon, he was Publicity Director for the arena, and by 1978 was also in charge of media for the Maple Leaf hockey

team. During this time, he wrote 12 books, including the novel *Cashmir of the RCAF* (1955).

Robert Cecil Cragg (b.1905) is another long-lived author who has made this street his home. His dwelling from 1934-45 was **No.22**. Here he wrote his formidable *Canadian Democracy and the Economic Settlement* (1947) and his first novel, unpublished, on which he worked for 17 months—and then burned. In addition to writing, he worked his way through three degrees at the UofT, getting his doctorate in 1945. Since then he has lived on the west coast, where he has been writing and publishing a ten-volume comic novel with the overall title, *Sheep May Safely Graze*.

A trio of writers has lived at **No.21**. Blodwen Davies (1897-1966) is one of the many women authors about whom documentary and biographical information is difficult to find. We do know she lived here from 1929-33, a period not long after her arrival in Toronto. She had come specifically to meet the Group of Seven. Through them she was introduced to the work of Tom Thomson and a formal study of that painter was her first book—a book she typeset and printed herself. After that, she made her living as a freelance writer, publishing a variety of titles including a modest history of Toronto, *Storied York*. Her novel *Ruffles and Rapiers* appeared with Ryerson Press in 1930.

Playwright David French also lived at this address from 1967-68. Alice Boissonneau did as well from 1953-54 while working on her first novel, *Eileen McCullough* (1976). She reminisced: "I lodged in private at 21 Prince Arthur Avenue. A white plaster building, (now frame) which seemed contained under a distilled light or come upon as a page turned, with its long carved windows and dark dignified entrances, the impact of its chalky bulk austere and Bronté-like. I lived in a large room to the right at the top of the stairs, with windows opening vertically from a sill where you could lean, staring out into the leaves of elms, inches away. At that time, a long porch at the back through a creaking door gave onto a large garden, now a parking lot, with a central elm . . . To walk at night along Prince Arthur—all houses then—beneath the elms' floating chlorophyll bounty was like being ushered through a magic grove . . . I had started into social work as an outsider to Toronto during a time when the welfare department allotted one orange a month to the family baby, and people lived above dusty fur-stores on Queen, often without heat and overrun by rats. Many had done without teeth (lost through malnutrition). . . . All these were not 'the poor' as was popularly imagined, but about sixty percent of the Canadian population.

"During the day, while passing the streets with rotting doorways, images sprang full-fledged and unasked into my head, forming themselves into short stories or sketches, some of which were published. I wanted to show this world in a whole novel and examine the divisions of the city—to describe the contrasts miles from Prince Arthur. . . ."

The English suspense writer Peter James (b.1948) lived in Toronto for a number of years, four of them at **No.20** (1970-73). Here, as part of his literary apprenticeship, he wrote numerous episodes of the children's television program "Polka Dot Door" for TVO. He also wrote television commercials for Edam and Gouda cheeses, and for Eaton's department store. He now has a large international readership for his novels of the supernatural, including *Possession* (1988), *Sweet Heart* (1991), and *Host* (1993). When asked if he ever went to school here, he replied: "The only educational institution I attended in Toronto was in fact the most helpful thing I ever did in my life! I attended a speed reading course at the University of Toronto over a six month period in 1971. If I can honestly say one thing changed my life that was it—it gave me a tremendous ability to consume data, something which has helped in the enormous research I do now for each book beyond measure." About 50 years before, **No.20** was also the home of Henry Fane

Sewell (1870?-1944), for the first three decades of the century the manager of the Bank of Commerce branch at College and Spadina—the same bank over which writer Gordon Hill Grahame lived in an apartment as a child. Sewell lived at **No.20** from 1915-41. Because I have uncovered for this book few bankers who published books of poetry, I include Sewell here for historical reasons. But to be honest, he was a bit player as a literary figure—or as one learned commentator put it, "he was much addicted to writing occasional verses, and he published [one] volume."

Anne Langton (1804-93) was a middle-class arrival in the Sturgeon Lake area of Upper Canada in the mid-1830s. As critic Clara Thomas has pointed out, Anne Langton and her husband were willing settlers in Canada, and her accounts of her life after her arrival in Ontario "have a constant ring of irrepressible good humour, adaptability and high hopes that make them unique in the literature of settlement." Both husband and wife were well educated and it is touching to read in her journals again and again the care with which they build shelves for their books, and the pride they take in the care and the reading of books—despite the fact that they live in the wilderness and have little time but to make or grow things to survive. He eventually became the first auditor of both the Canadas and, after Confederation, the first auditor of the entire nation. For most of their later years they were based in Toronto, and Anne died in the city. We shall meet her again on Beverley Street, but let us note now that this cheerful pioneer (whose writing for too long has been eclipsed by her much more dour compatriot, Susanna Moodie), lived at **9 Prince Arthur** from 1880 to c. 1884. She may also have lived at **No.23** in 1884—the documentation is insecure. It was at the former or both of these addresses that she wrote the manuscript which would be published posthumously as *A Gentlewoman in Upper Canada*.

Our final stop on this street is **No.4**, where the Merrill sisters, Anne (1871-1971) and Helen (1866-1951), lived for many decades. Helen was well enough known as a poet by 1892 that she was invited to the first gala reading of Canadian authors in Toronto organized by Frank Yeigh. She shared the bill with Pauline Johnson, Wilfred Campbell, Duncan Campbell Scott and William Douw Lighthall, all of whose reputations have survived more intact than hers. Her sister Anne lived to be one hundred years old. After WWI Anne moved to Toronto to be the women's editor of the *M&E* and it was in that paper that she published her first poems. In her day, she was best known for her weekly bird column in the *G&M*, a column that ran for years and had a large, passionate following. Anne lived at this address from the late 1920s until at least 1950. Her sister Helen lived here from 1905 to c.1938.

Return along Prince Arthur to **Bedford Road**, and walk north. Tom Marshall (1938-93) had an apartment at **25 Bedford Road** from the summer of 1974 to summer 1977. It was his first permanent residence in a city to which he had been paying extended visits all his life. While at this address he wrote most of his first novel, *Rosemary Goal* (1978), the poetry volume *The White City* (1976), and a book of literary criticism, *Harsh and Lovely Land* (1979).

The famous Nova Scotia novelist Ernest Buckler (*The Mountain and The Valley*) came to Toronto in 1929 to study for his master's degree. Although he was offered a scholarship to complete a PhD, he declined, choosing instead to move from the academic world to the actuarial, working for the Manufacturer's Life Insurance Company from 1931-36. For the first three of those six years he had lodgings at **No.84**, but whether he did any writing there is unknown.

Turn right at **Lowther Avenue** and head east. **12 Lowther Avenue** was home during most of the Depression to Lois Reynolds Kerr (b.1908), a UofT grad who came to the attention of the literary world in 1931

when her one-act play *Open Doors* premiered in Toronto. One year previously her drama had won a competition sponsored by the IODE, usually regarded as a conservative organization. However, the *M&E* said, "*Open Doors* reaches a high note of human interest, depicting the suffering of the unemployed labourer which reaches the breaking point with the importation of 120 foreigners willing to work on non-union wages." (In 1980 Anton Wagner included the play in his landmark anthology, *Canada's Lost Plays*.) Kerr, who later became a reporter in the women's section of the *Globe*, joined fellow female playwrights Dora Smith Conover, Leonora McNeilly, and Rica McLean Farquharson in forming in 1933 the Playwrights' Studio in an effort to produce Canadian plays at a time when foreign fare was not just the staple diet but pretty well the only diet of theatregoers in Toronto.

One of the most important Ukrainian-Canadian authors, Vera Lysenko, lived at **No.37** in 1948. Earlier (1888-89), this same house had been the home of Theodore H. Rand, poet and Chancellor of the first McMaster University, then located on Bloor Street West. **72 Lowther** was one of the many homes in the area of the eminent poet Margaret Avison. She had a room here from 1938-39. The Coleridge scholar and novelist Kathleen Coburn lived for the last five years of the 1950s at **No.79 Lowther**.

Walk a few paces backward to reclaim the intersection with **Admiral Road**, then walk north. George Elliott (1923-96) began writing as a cub reporter for small-town papers but eventually joined MacLaren Advertising in Toronto where he ultimately became vice-president. In between he wrote fiction, especially short stories, including his masterpiece, *The Kissing Man* (1962). He had strong connections to the Liberal party and for some time he worked closely with Pierre Trudeau when the latter was Prime Minister. Elliott's last address in this city was **10 Admiral Road**, where he lived from 1967 to 1975.

The next address to the north, **No.12**, was long the home of W. Stewart Wallace, librarian at the UofT from 1920 until 1954, at which point he became the owner of the Dora Hood Book Room, the most famous antiquarian bookshop in Canadian history. Wallace will always be cherished by cultural historians because he did so much—when others did not—to document our past: his *Dictionary of Canadian Biography* in 1926 went through several editions, and his six-volume *Encyclopaedia of Canada*, published at the height of the Depression, was positively quixotic. Regardless, it was a masterpiece, especially given the few resources available, and of such quality that it formed the basis of the *Encyclopaedia Canadiana*. His *Dictionary of North American Authors Deceased Before 1950* was the product of years of research and is often the only source of biographical data about many authors. He was the editor of the Champlain Society for more than 30 years, and the editor of the *Canadian Historical Review* for the ten years after he founded the periodical in 1920. More than most professional historians in Canada, Wallace paid attention to creative writers, and his own writing reflects his care for language. He lived from 1947-58 at **No.12**. Earlier in his life, while teaching at McMaster University on Bloor Street West from 1910-15, he lived at **No.94 Admiral**.

Detective novelist Eve Zaremba lived at **No.52** when the house was subdivided into four apartments; she lived on the top floor from 1978-85 and wrote *Work for a Million* and *Beyond Hope*. From May to September 1979 she sublet this apartment to New Brunswick novelist Kent Thompson, who had come to Toronto to study drama-writing at a workshop run by the CBC.

Two of The Four Horsemen, the greatest group of sound poets anywhere ever, lived in this area. Paul Dutton made his home at **55 Admiral** from 1975-78, **No.82** (1972-75), **No.98** (1969-70), and **No.105** (1970-72), while bp Nichol lived at **No.59** (1966-69), **No.61** (1971-74), **No.98** (1980-86), and **No.131** (1978-80). Detective novelist,

and current book columnist of the *Star*, Philip Marchand made his home at **No.82** from 1976-77. In all likelihood these buildings were affiliated with Therafields, a spiritual organization to which these men belonged in that era.

Stop at **Bernard Avenue** and walk west. A number of important literary folk have lived on **Bernard Avenue**. Poet David W. Harris (who wrote under the pseudonym "David UU") lived for a few months during 1966-67 at **No.73** and wrote parts of his books *Gideon Music* and *Touch* at this address. The house was previously the home of short-story writer Hilda Ridley, who lived here with her sister for a couple of years just before WWII. Both made their livings as freelance journalists but only Hilda (c.1890-1960) published imaginative writing.

The apartment building on the northeast corner of Bernard and St. George is **88 Bernard Avenue**. Kim Maltman and Roo Borson are husband and wife and lived together in apt. 708 (1978-79) and then, after some time outside Toronto, returned to apt. 406 (May 1979 to May 1980). Maltman wrote two books while here: *Branch Lines* (1982) and *The Sickness of Hats* (1982). About a decade before Borson and Maltman, the edifice was home to J.A. Wainwright for about a year, and David UU lived here for some months (1966-67) before moving across the street to **No.73**. The notorious *S: Portrait of a Spy*, authored by Ian Adams, was written at **No.96** when he lived there from May 1972 to July 1974. This novel contained an unsavoury character alleged to have been based on a real figure, and the subsequent legal action marked the first time in Canada that a work of fiction was put on trial for libel. The case attracted international attention and was a milestone in our jurisprudence.

Rosemary Sullivan lived at **No.112** from 1981-82 just before she wrote her first poetry book and certainly before she had thought of becoming a biographer—now she is one of Canada's pre-eminent literary biographers.

The novelist Basil Partridge (b.1900?) came to Toronto in 1921 and his first home seems to have been **No.117**. Certainly he was here from 1924-29. When he left his Halifax home to move to Toronto, he worked for a while as a classified-ad salesman at the *Star* before the joys of penning advertising copy lured him away. He remained with ad agencies until June 1951, when he quit to write fiction full-time. His novel *The Penningtons* was but the first in a series he produced in the fifties documenting the humorous incidents in the lives of a pastor's family in New Brunswick.

Reclaim **Admiral Road**. The profession of *diseuse* has disappeared from our lives and our vocabulary, but a century ago, if a woman was good at reciting the verses and "deep thoughts" of others, she could make a handsome living. Jessie Alexander (1864-1955) was such a woman—one of the best according to her contemporaries. She began her elocution performances when she was a young woman, at first on a part-time basis. After her husband died in 1907, in order to support her family, she became a full-time platform speaker, reciting famous poems, and on occasion her own poems. At her death, one newspaper said she was "more universally loved than any other entertainer in the Dominion." In her native Toronto she had to rent large halls such were the crowds that wanted to hear her recite. She inhabited **No.108 Admiral** for the decade 1909-19.

Our last stop on this street is **151 Admiral Road**. It was here that the poet and playwright Wilfred Watson (b.1911) had lodgings from 1946-49 while doing his PhD at the UofT. Watson was married to novelist Sheila Watson (*The Double Hook*) at this time, but she may not have lived with him at this time; both spent most of their careers in Canada's west. He won the Governor General's Award for Poetry in 1955. Wilfred and Sheila were the first people hired by Marshall McLuhan when the latter established his Centre of Culture and Technology on the UofT

Campus in 1951, and Wilfred co-authored *From Cliché to Archetype* with McLuhan in 1970.

Admiral Road ends at St. George Street. Walk north to Dupont, then walk east to where it intersects with **Davenport Road**. Turn right and follow Davenport southeast. The distinguished diplomat and poet Douglas LePan was born at **267 Davenport Road** and lived there for the first two years or so of his life. Another *éminence grise* was B.K. Sandwell, the son of a minister. The Rev. Sandwell served many parishes when his son was young, and hence they lived at a variety of addresses in town, including, briefly, **No.226**, in 1892.

Consider a side trip south on **Bedford Road**. The Wallace family home was located at **95 Bedford Road** and it was here that Paul A.W. Wallace, author and Victoria College graduate, lived from infancy until he enlisted and was shipped overseas in 1916. Not long after the war Wallace (b.1891) joined the English faculty of his alma mater. While he did write *Twist and Other Stories* (1923), he is remembered more for his editing of early Canadian literary texts when such editing was neither fashionable nor career-enhancing. In the same year that he published his short-story collection he also published one of the first edited versions of Anna Jameson's *Winter Studies and Summer Rambles* and Thomas C. Haliburton's *Selections from Sam Slick* (the reviews of the latter assumed that no ordinary readers had ever heard the name Sam Slick, much less read the work). His contributions to Canadian letters might have been substantial had he not been lured away in 1926 to a better-paying academic post in the USA.

Throughout its history, Toronto has been home to writers who were important literary figures in their homelands but who emigrated to Canada either for personal reasons or too frequently because they were fleeing for their personal safety. But once here, they had no status as artists in mainstream Canada, and too often they toiled at menial jobs, sometimes for years, and usually had no contact with the local literary community. Within their own ethnic or linguistic communities they were revered however, and that is certainly true of Hermann Boeschenstein (1900-82). Already the author of books of fiction, he first arrived in this country in 1926, travelling with other Swiss students by rail, working at odd jobs to cover his expenses, until he reached the Pacific. He liked what he saw. After returning to Switzerland to marry, he brought his bride to Toronto in 1928 and attached himself to the university, labouring at the Banting Institute as well as the UofT Library while studying philosophy with G.S. Brett. In 1930 the German dept. discovered Boeschenstein in their midst and hired him as a professor (he succeeded Barker Fairley as Chair in 1956). He remained with the faculty until he retired in 1972, at which point he dedicated himself again to full-time creative writing. He purchased **103 Bedford** in 1935 from an academic colleague and lived here until his death in 1982.

Poet Dennis Lee had a room on the third floor of **No.110** from July 1963 until August 1964. This was the first address in Toronto where he began to write the poems that comprise his first book, *Kingdom Of Absence* (1967). Novelist Mary Quayle Innis (1899-1972) lived for a few months at **No.112** in 1955 after her husband, the great Canadian historian Harold Innis, had died.

Walk north to **Dupont Street** via Bedford Road. **No.93 Dupont** was playwright Larry Fineberg's home from 1975-78, and **No.91** next door was briefly the home of poet and publisher Barry Callaghan in 1969. East of Bedford, at **31 Dupont Street**, one can see where the Toronto Women's Bookstore had its beginnings in 1973. Finally, we note that it was to **No. 20**, apt. 4, that Milton Acorn and Gwendolyn MacEwen returned when they were married at the Old City Hall on February 8, 1962. Acorn had been living here for a few weeks, and it's possible MacEwen had as well. It was from this unit that they issued the sixth issue of their maga-

zine, *Moment*. By the summer of 1962 they had moved to Ward's Island.

Carry on to **Avenue Road**. The thoroughfare is hostile to pedestrians so we will confine our exploration for the moment to the west side and then duck into the small streets running west from Avenue Road. Walk south.

The upper half of **19 Chicora Avenue** was the penultimate address of the man of letters Newton MacTavish (1875-1941), who lived here from 1939-40. In the last decade of his life he was in poor health and did little writing, but when younger he was one of the best known litterateurs in the land. His journalism career began at the *Globe* in 1898 and by 1906 he was the editor of *Canadian Magazine*, an excellent journal. A charter member of the Arts & Letters Club, he authored half a dozen books including *The Fine Arts in Canada* (1925) and his short stories were published abroad as well as nationally.

Selwyn Dewdney attended the Ontario College of Education in Toronto 1931-32 after graduating from the UofT, and during the year he was learning to be a teacher he lived at **No.21**. The celebrated writer James Reaney wrote of Dewdney that he "is probably more widely known as an authority on aboriginal Canadian art and culture than he is as a novelist. But although his reputation may endure longer with such definitive works as *Indian Rock Paintings of the Great Lakes* . . . it is to the novels that students of Canadian culture will have to turn not only to explain the drives behind the Indian research but also to map that stage in Canadian cultural history when, for the first time, those of European descent began to depict the way the native people had of looking at the world."

The biographer of Sigmund Freud, Ernest Jones, lived for a few months in 1908-9 at **35 Chicora** as he was learning about the extraordinary sexual prudery of Torontonians. **No.38** from 1944-48 was the residence of John Morgan Gray (1907-78), novelist and publisher. Gray had joined Macmillan of Canada in 1930 and in 1946 he was made the general manager of the firm. During his reign, Macmillan was arguably the most important house for the best Canadian authors: included in his stable were Morley Callaghan, Grey Owl (no relation), and Donald Creighton. J.M. Gray himself published stories in magazines, and the novel *The One-Eyed Trapper* in 1941.

Michael Hollingsworth (b.1950) came to Toronto in 1956 from England. When he left the parental nest in 1969, he took an apart-

Michael Hollingsworth and Deanne Taylor on the roof of the Cameron House, 408 Queen Street West, 1997

ment at **No.41** and while here researched and wrote much of his first play, *Strawberry Fields*, and part of his second, *Clear Light*. The premiere run of *Clear Light* at Toronto Free Theatre was closed by the police on the grounds that it was obscene. Much of his literary energy in the past 15 years has been expended on the writing of a series of plays about various facets of Canadian history. The cycle goes under the general title *The Village of Small Huts*, and has been called by the *Oxford Companion* "a major contribution to Canadian theatre."

When crime novelist Eve Zaremba first came to Toronto in 1963, she lived over a laundromat at **134-A Avenue Road** until 1972.

Continuing south on Avenue Road, we come to **Bernard Avenue**, where Emily Poynton Weaver (1865-1943) resided at **No.26** from 1907 until her death. She was a novelist and historian who focused her work in both disciplines on Canadian subjects. Robert Weaver (b.1921), creator of fondly recalled literary programming on CBC, was her nephew, and he lived on one floor of the house from 1940-50, a period covering some of his university years, his war service, and his beginnings as a radio producer.

Poet Joe Rosenblatt, from 1960-66, had his abode at **No.32**, while playwright, journalist, and fiction writer Rick Salutin had a brief residency of about a year at **No.46** in 1972, shortly after he had returned to Toronto from New York.

Few other stretches of older Toronto have been so transmogrified as have been the blocks of Avenue Road north of Bloor Street. At **120 Avenue Road** there used to be a building called the Prince Arthur Apartments. In 1953-54, two of Canada's best known novelists lived here as flatmates: Hugh Hood and Timothy Findley. Hood was finishing up his academic studies at the UofT and Findley, working as an actor in a CBC-TV version of Leacock's *Sunshine Sketches*, was preparing to go to Stratford for its first season.

When poet Rhea Tregebov arrived in Toronto in May 1978, her first residence was an apartment over what was then an antique store at **No.110**. While here she wrote much of her first book, *Remembering History*, and worked as an editorial assistant at Oxford University Press. The building had once been the home (1894-1906) of the eminent UofT English professor W.J. Alexander, a man who bestrode the Canadian literary scene of his day in the way that Northrop Frye recently bestrode ours. The most prestigious lecture series hosted by the English dept. of the UofT has been the annual Alexander Lectures, to which only the finest scholars of literature are invited to speak (locals invited to be Alexander Lecturers include Robertson Davies and Northrop Frye). The series was created in his honour in 1927 and continues to this day.

26 Tranby Street was Norman Duncan's home from 1891-92 while he was studying for his bachelor's degree at the UofT. His reports in *McClure's* magazine were largely responsible for making Sir Wilfred Grenfell (and his Labrador hospital ships) a household name throughout North America. The seacoast villages and people provide the background for Duncan's most successful fiction, the Billy Topsail series. After

Duncan left Toronto in 1895, he never returned. He died of a heart attack when he was 45 years old.

Rhea Tregebov moved to the second floor of **No.31** in October 1979. Here she finished her poetry book *Remembering History*, and wrote almost all of another, *No One We Know*. I say "almost" because she lived in Europe from July 1982 to January 1983, during which another poet, Carolyn Smart, lived in the apartment. Tregebov sublet the apartment again (September 1986 to January 1987) to another author, Brian Shein (d.1988). Tregebov left the building in May 1988.

The great British poet W.H. Auden visited **No.64** on three occasions because it was the home of his friend Peter Salus. Auden stayed here once in 1970 and twice in 1971 when in town to give readings at the UofT and York University. Professor Salus described the photo of Auden, "[it] was taken in the front room of **64 Tranby** where Auden was reading Forster's *Alexandria*. His god-daughter, Emily Wystan Salus, at that time about 15 months old, traded a jar of

W.H. Auden speaking to his goddaughter, Emily, at 64 Tranby Street, 1970

bouillon cubes for the book. When I snapped the photo, Wystan had just said, 'But I was reading that, Emily'. . . . Wystan enjoyed Toronto. He liked the (original) buildings at Scarborough College and commented to me and Anne Brown (who worked for John Brown, the architect) that the siting was well effected. . . .he did not enjoy his trip to York [University]."

Paul Hiebert (1892-1987) lived for just one year in Toronto, and he did so during 1916-17 at **No.73** while obtaining his master's degree in Gothic and Teutonic Philology. Hiebert spent most of his adult life as a professor of chemistry in Winnipeg but he is included in this *Guide* because he authored the wickedly funny satire (and Leacock Medal winner) *Sarah Binks* (1947). Sarah was a poet like no other in Canada—and yet was like far too many poetasters in Canada in the first half of the twentieth c.

> . . . in my little book,
> I write verses,
> Sometimes they don't rhyme—Curses!

A crisp summary of the book's importance is given by critic Louis MacKendrick: "Sarah Binks is a burlesque of literary biography and a satire of literary critics and criticism, contrasting a fervent hagiographic manner with a subject of low degree . . . By the time the book appeared—it is cast as anthology and biography, using the verse to interpret the life and vice-versa—it was clear that Hiebert's targets included provincialism, presumptiveness, sentimentality, academic enthusiasm (too often clouded by local pride), academic method (too often cluttered by attention to minutiae at the expense of common sense) and the 'simple' failure to distinguished between good and bad writing." Sarah Binks was, according to Hiebert, the Sweet Songstress of Saskatchewan and the winner of that province's highest literary prize, The Wheat Pool Medal. His satire was so accurate that many people even today believe that Sarah once

lived. Certainly his book does. It would be too cruel to leave what was Hiebert's Toronto home without another little taste of Sarah:

> A little blade of grass I see
> Its banner waving wild and free
> And I wonder if in time to come
> 'Twill be a great big onion.

Despite its literary name, **Boswell Avenue** cannot rival Tranby for literary connections. Nonetheless, we should note that novelist and playwright David Young spent the winter of 1992-93 at **No.23**, writing screen and teleplays. Story writer Hilda Ridley inhabited **No.32** in 1937, and playwright and theatre founder Ken Gass had an abode at **No.38** from 1973-74. **No. 46-A** was the home of Leslie Hartley Reid in 1924 when he was studying for his Forestry degree at the UofT. Reid (b.1896) was said to be the first contemporary Canadian to write a play and have it produced at Hart House Theatre. Regardless, his main claim to fame was as a novelist, especially for his first book, *Rector of Maliseet*, a Gothic romance written at this address. Still resident in Toronto, he published his last novel in 1928 to fine reviews—and then disappeared from the public record.

At least ten authors have lived on **Elgin Avenue**. Novelist Cynthia Holz arrived in Toronto in March 1976 and moved into a coach house behind **1 Elgin** before the building was razed for more upscale development. During the two years she had a dwelling here, she studied writing with Joe Rosenblatt at the now defunct Three Schools, and was also involved with the Innis College Writers' Workshop. The *bon-vivant* professor Pelham Edgar showed broad hospitality to anyone interested in good writing at his home at **No.21**, where he held court from 1901-14. No doubt he passed Gerald Noxon's mother pushing a pram on the street, because Noxon was born at **No.26** in 1910 and spent the first three years of his childhood here. Noxon would later become an important writer of radio plays and a close friend to Malcolm Lowry and Conrad Aiken.

Novelist Roy MacSkimming (b.1944) brought his new bride to **No.30**, "a two-bedroom apt. on the second and third floors of this lovely Victorian house right at the height of the coffee-house culture on Yorkville a couple of blocks away." It was at **30 Elgin** that he began writing his first novel, *Formentera*.

Tom Hendry, one of the founders of the Manitoba Theatre Centre and Toronto Free Theatre, and himself a playwright, lived at **No.34** for most of his time in Toronto: he arrived here on July 10, 1968 and left on July 9, 1997. In addition to the important work he has done as an arts administrator and consultant in Toronto, he wrote *Hogtown: Toronto the Good* (1981), *Satyricon* (1969), and all but one of his other plays while at this address.

Novelist and Coleridge scholar Kathleen Coburn had a home at **39 Elgin** for the decade of the 1960s. Vernal House (b.1905) was a wizard with Morse code and after WWII he worked in the telegraph office of the *G&M* handling stories and breaking news from around the world. Perhaps to counterbalance that hectic pace, he also wrote poetry, and for many years was the primary poetry reviewer at the *G&M*.

Poet and translator David Aylward (b.1942) lived twice at **No.44**: in the basement flat in 1968, and again in 1974, by which time he had graduated to the first floor. While here he began his impressive translations of Basho, probably the most famous haiku poet ever. **45 Elgin** was briefly the home (1905-6) of Peregrine Acland (1891-1963), author of the novel *All Else Is Folly*, a book praised by Bertrand Russell and Ford Madox Ford among many others. Acland, when a teenager, moved with his family from this address to Ottawa where his father later became the King's Printer. This house was also the home of novelist Susan Swan (b.1945), who was in residence here from 1975-78. She told me that at the time this was a co-op, a necessary refuge for her, a single mother recently divorced. "I began researching the novel *The Biggest Modern Woman of the World* here. I also wrote poetry as well as wrote and performed most of my performance work from this base. Choreographers and filmmakers lived in the co-op and we often planned our next piece of theatre there. *Queen of the Silver Blades*, my theatre piece about the 1940s figure skater Barbara Ann Scott, was conceived in its mouldy old kitchen. So was a piece about self-pity called *Down and In*, a piece about size called *Balloon Slices*, and various other performance pieces."

80 Avenue Road was a boyhood home of Hector Charlesworth (1872-1945). In his autobiography published in 1925, he relates how much this area had changed even in his time. "The environs of the University of Toronto when we moved to the neighbourhood in 1880 were very different from now. A large tract now covered by the buildings of Victoria College, Annesley Hall and the Domestic Science edifice was rented out by the bursar of the University as a cow pasture; for many residents in the vicinity kept their own cows which was considered the safe course for families with young children, in those days when typhoid fever was rife. As a boy of nine or ten it was my duty to bring our cow home with me on my way from school . . . Below the knoll where Victoria College stands was a marshy patch where dragon flies of myriad hues were to be seen on summer days . . . I distinctly remember as a little boy in the seventies a stagnant pond which submerged the valley in which Hart House stands in its chaste beauty. It was a disgusting place, but was drained before 1880; long after, a stream ran through the valley beside the present Royal Ontario Museum, and dispersed itself I know not where . . . The quiet parochial life of Yorkville and the college district was even then shot through with the spirit of growth and there were prophets seemingly rash who predicted that Toronto would some day be a city of 200,000. But to most people this seemed ridiculous commercial optimism. Whenever I read one of Booth Tarkington's later novels like *The Magnificent Ambersons* and *The Midlander*, which have as their underlying motif the growth and mutability of cities, I am reminded of the processes which have taken place in Toronto within my own experience; and which have extinguished the old professional and academic aristocracy of my boyhood." Charles was primarily a journalist, but one with an unapologetic fondness for the arts, and for many years he was one of the leading critics of drama, music, and art in Canada. His three volumes of memoirs, full of vignettes and anecdotes about celebrity writers and others, still make for fascinating reading decades after they were written.

Novelist Morley Callaghan lived in apt. 3 at **46 Avenue Road** from 1932-34 and here wrote one of his most famous novels, *Such Is My Beloved*, and some of the stories that appeared in his collection *Now That April's Here*. This was also his home when *A Broken Journey* was published. At **No.40** there used to be a building called The Bryn Mawr Apartments. One of its residents from 1939-40 was the much revered poet Margaret Avison (b.1918).

Continuing south we encounter the bulk of the Park Hyatt, formerly known as the Park Plaza Hotel. Among the authors who have stayed here are Vladimir Nabokov, Vera Brittain, Walter Allen, John Cheever, James T. Farrell, Alberto Moravia, and Thomas Raddall. The master scholar of Henry James's, Leon Edel, described his happy stay at this hostelry: "My third stay [in Toronto] was in the sixties, in 1967 when Canada was celebrating Confederation. I was invited by Claude Bissell to be a Centennial Visiting Professor. I had a bedroom and sitting room in the Park Plaza, worked mornings, and enjoyed Toronto, gave seminars and lectures; met the old journalistic crowd—and the new—fraternized with the *Time* people (Serrell Hillman and co.) but also saw much of my UofT friends, Kathleen Coburn, Pat Rosen-baum with whom I had a shared interest in Bloomsbury, Phyllis Grosskurth, who was trying to learn as much as possible about biography etc. It was a fruitful stay and I wrote several essays, and chapters, and above all came to know the more cosmopolitan Toronto, which has replaced the uptight town I knew in the thirties. You could call my story *Toronto in three decades*. It had always been a contrasted town as you may imagine—the Montreal I knew with its bilingual problems, and McGill, where I graduated and which could not be compared with Toronto in any way. McGill was old Canadian ivy league, and very much in the hands of dons from England. I was fond of Toronto University and its scholars—from Pelham Edgar long ago, E.K. Brown who was an extraordinary critic and a remarkable personality, A.S.P. Woodhouse, E.J. Pratt, Kathleen Coburn and the others. McGill had no such individuals to match them; it was charmingly provincial."

The Roof Top Bar has been famous for decades as having been *the* literary haunt of creative writers in the second half of the 20th c. Like many legends, this one is extremely short on documentary or even anecdotal evidence. The bar has certainly been popular over the year with reporters. Publisher Jack McClelland was a famous *habitué* and authors have certainly been seen imbibing in its precincts. Regardless, it is a wonderful place to have a drink, look over the skyline of the city, and contemplate the literary tour of the East Annex which is now concluded.

THE ANNEX

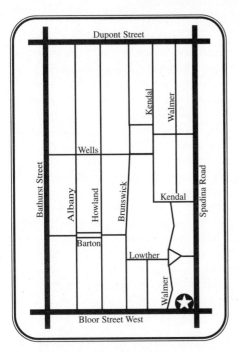

The tour begins at the northwest corner of Bloor Street and Spadina Road.

Novelist Paul Quarrington lived in a basement apartment at **No.2 Spadina Road** after he dropped out of the UofT in 1973. In the year or so that he lived here he began and finished his first novel, *The Service*. According to Paul: "I had a succession of roommates, including one fellow who owned a boa constrictor. The snake escaped one night and disappeared, presumably into the walls of the apartment. I decided to vacate."

Anna Durie (1856-1933) lived in comfortable circumstances in continental Europe for most of her formative years. When she married Col. Durie (after whom Durie Street is named) in 1880, the couple settled at **No.8** in a large house known as "Craigluscar" (razed). Here she held gatherings of many of the city's literati. But after a mere half-decade of marriage, her husband suddenly died.

Sir Charles G.D. Roberts, writing after Anna's own death, believed the "first five years of her marriage were the happiest she knew." In 1895 she was forced to sell this home due to mounting debt. She wrote several books of poetry, and in 1930 she became one of the first writers in Canada to read her work on radio.

66 Spadina Road was home to poet David McFadden (b.1940) in the early 1980s. The building that once stood at **No. 70** was briefly (1942-43) the residence of poet, biographer, and music critic Ronald Hambleton (b. 1917). The litterateur B.K. Sandwell (1876-1954) made **No.72** his home for the second half of the 1930s. Classics professor Gilbert Norwood (1880-1954) wrote texts such as *The Acting Edition of the Aristophanes' Acharians* and *The Riddle of the Bacchae*, but he also found time to write amusing sketches and short stories published as *Spoken in Jest* and *The Wooden Man*. **74 Spadina** was his home from 1933-37. Novelist Charles Israel (b.1920) also lived in this same building (apt. 102) from 1978 to 1979.

Estelle Kerr (1879-1971), already established as an author and artist, made a splash in the Toronto newspapers in January 1918 when she left her job as the women's editor of *Canadian Courier* to be a chauffeur-mechanic in the Canadian Army during WWI. The overseas job was no soft posting: her main duty was to drive a truck between the front lines and the supply depots—and too often, to drive from the front lines to hospitals or morgues. After the war she wrote and illustrated books for children (published in New York) based on her European experiences. For most of her life (1925-66) she lived at **No.78**. Earlier (1918-24) she had lived next door at **No. 80**.

Windsor native Andrew Jackson Elliott (1899-1965) made **90 Spadina Road** his domicile in the late 1940s. Elliott spent the last three decades of his life helping others, primarily as the director of the Good Neighbours Club which he founded during the Depression as a day-centre for homeless men, and as the executive director of Kingsley Hall, a men's shelter. His highly-regarded novel, *The Aging Nymph* (1948), was based on his experiences in both world wars.

Hugh Hood (b.1928) has not lived in Toronto since 1955, perhaps tellingly the very year in which he started to write about the city. Toronto continues to fascinate him and several of his books and stories are set here. He has lived throughout the town,

A Peep Behind the Curtains of Time

JOHN MEBOURNE ELSON

NOW

SIX YEARS

Two views of John Mebourne Elson
Telegram, April 25, 1927

including, in 1950-51, shared digs at **98 Spadina Road**. Half a decade later he returned to this area and lived for a few months at **No. 154**.

John Mebourne Elson (1880-1966) moved to Toronto in 1905 to be a reporter for the *Globe* but was such a remarkable journalist that, in 1907, still in his twenties, he was appointed editor of the *Sunday World*, a newspaper far ahead of its rivals in design and attitude. Within a few years he left the city to become the publisher of the main newspaper in St. Catharines, and in 1919 he used that position to launch a successful campaign for mayor, the youngest in the Dominion. He returned to Toronto in 1921 as managing editor of various Maclean Hunter business publications, only to join the editorial staff of the *Star* shortly thereafter. During the Depression he taught writing and journalism at the night school at the UofT. Among his students who felt singled out for encouragement was poet Bertram Warr. Elson was constantly active in local literary politics. One week, for example, would find him organizing a huge testimonial dinner for Mazo de la Roche, while another week he would be helping to found the Canadian Authors' Foundation. His books included a history of the movie industry in Canada (given that it was written in the early 1930s, it must surely be the first of its kind), a volume of poetry, and his best-known novel, *The Scarlet Sash*, set during the War of 1812. His home for the last 21 years of his life was **No.136**.

Walmer Road has been home to over 40 writers. Paul Quarrington (b.1953), novelist and screenwriter, lived at **No.176** from 1977 to 1980. The narrator of his book *Home Game* lives in this area in a rooming house amazingly like this one. Across the street, **No.171** has been home to two women authors: Marlene Nourbese Philip (b.1947), while here in 1976 worked on her first poetry book, *Thorns*. This same address was later the home of poet Carolyn Smart (b.1952), who lived on the second floor c.1982-83. This was her last residence in the city. "I was two blocks from the scene of the kidnapping and murder of Sharin Morningstar Keenan and deeply affected by it. The central image of the main sections of *Stoning the Moon* (1986) deals with violence in various forms, and Sharin's death figures largely in one of the long poems, as do a series of brutal rapes that occurred in or near the Annex that same year."

Crime novelist Philip Marchand (b.1946) (the *Star* book critic for the past decade) has lived on Walmer Road on three different occasions. On the second of these he lived at **No.133** from 1971-75 where he wrote most of the essays published in his first book, *Just Looking, Thank You* (1976).

Poet Dorothy Livesay (1909-96) lived at home (**No.132**) with her parents from 1926-29, during which time she began classes for her B.A. in Modern Languages at Trinity College. Her father, J.F.B. Livesay, was a famous journalist and manager of Canadian Press. Her mother, Florence Randal Livesay (1884-1953), was a poet as well, although of lesser renown than her daughter. Here Dorothy wrote her much-lauded first book, *Green Pitcher* (1928), and the poem that won her the Jardine Prize in 1929. That same year she went to France for further study. Her father and her mother, the latter also a skilled translator, continued to live at this address for another year.

Matt Cohen (b.1942) made one of his many brief Annex area stops at **128 Walmer** from 1966-67. Greater literary import attaches to a house across the street. **No.123** has been the home of three of our novelists: Morley Callaghan, Barry Callaghan, and Philip Marchand, and of a sound poet, Paul Dutton.

Morley Callaghan (1903-90) brought his family here in 1940 when the building was a fourplex. They lived in the upper half on the south side. While Barry (b.1937) was attending St. Peter's school on Bathurst St., Morley was entering a decade relatively meagre of productivity, although he was still writing at a pace that most others would regard as substantial. For the Canadian magazine *New World* he started to contribute essays every month, and did so for eight years. He penned *Luke Baldwin's Vow* (1948), a novel for young adults. To help the UofT's fundraising campaign he produced a book called *The Varsity Story* (1948). And he worked on the production of his first play in Toronto, *Going Home*, presented at the Museum Theatre by the New Play Society in March 1950. In addition, he was reaching a mass electronic audience for the first time by appearing weekly on national radio quiz shows and other programs. And in the late 1940s he made a hefty start on his major novel, *The Loved and The Lost* (the author's photo on the jacket flap of this book shows Morley leaning against the lamppost in front of 123 Walmer). He also found time to go to sea with the Canadian Navy during WWII. But the decade produced few short stories of note, and at a personal level, he lost his brother, father, and mother between 1946 and 1950.

The address carries far happier recollections for his son Barry. The photo on the front jacket of his memoir, *Barrelhouse Kings*, shows him as a boy in front of this house. But in 1950, Morley felt the time had come to move, and his fiction genes stirring again, he packed his family and headed to what would be his last domicile, 20 Dale Avenue.

Philip Marchand was unaware that **123 Walmer** had once been the home of the Callaghans on either occasion when he lived here (but since we don't put historical plaques on our literary landmarks, how could Marchand have known?). Marchand's first tenure at this address was 1970-71, when he had just become a permanent resident of Canada; his second here was longer: 1977-80. It was during this second stay that he wrote the initial drafts of his first murder mystery, *Deadly Spirits*. During his earlier residence another tenant in the building (albeit only for the summer of 1970) was Paul Dutton, who would later become one of The Four Horsemen, an internationally acclaimed sound poetry quartet. Just prior to Dutton's arrival, another member of that group, bp Nichol, had lived next door at **No.121** for about a year.

During the latter part of WWII, one of our most celebrated poets, Margaret Avison (b.1918), lived at **85 Walmer** for approximately a year. A contemporary of Avison's, Douglas LePan (1914-98), spent most of his youth living at **82 Walmer** from 1918 until he departed for graduate studies at Oxford in autumn 1935.

Poets Dorothy Livesay and her parents lived at **No.77** from 1922-25. During this period Dorothy was attending Glen Mawr School for Girls on Spadina Avenue. In one of her memoirs, she cast her mind back to life in the Annex: "Those streets of the Annex still exist, although many blocks of houses have been demolished by the growth of the UofT. Willcocks Street, where painter and scholar Barker Fairley lived, has the same red brick semi-detached houses, small and discreet with pocket handkerchief lawns. But where are the overhanging elms that I remember being astonished by, so much taller they were than Winnipeg trees? In the Toronto Annex there were always two places to play: the backyard with its high wooden fence, apple, plum or pear tree, green patch of lawn and rhubarb plot; or the street, not yet overtaken by automobiles and so still the territory of schoolchildren.

"In those days boys and girls did not mix or meet in twos. On Albany Avenue, where we spent part of our first year, I stole glances across the street at the doctor's son, Evan Withrow; on Walmer Road, I watched John Pennyfather and his brother playing catch, and I watched them watching me. They were different because they were Catholics. Even though I was a friend to their younger sister, we would never mingle. So the valentine I received that February when I was home with the mumps was not a love letter from a boy. I dreamed that it was, but I knew it wasn't. I was just a tomboy without any skills of attraction: plump, freckled, wearing glasses, able to hold

my own only with the younger boys and, in summer, go fishing off the dock at Sparrow Lake.

"At **77 Walmer Road** I sought compensation by creating dramatic games for the younger children on the street. After school, half a dozen would come over to our place to play a complicated fairy-tale routine called Old Witch. In the winter I created a five-pin show in which the neighbouring children did a dance and a play under my direction, their parents sitting on the stairs to watch. The children living in the other half of the duplex at that time were Madge and Than Shaw, whose father, Professor Shaw, taught Italian at the university. My mother, always feeding my ambition, told me the professor enjoyed watching the games I made up. She told me he thought I would be an actress or go to university.

"When we settled in Toronto our parents made the decision to send us to a private school. Immediately, one had to be dressed properly, books had to be bought, school lunches were put on the bill. Every month when that school account arrived, my mother would go over it groaning, saying that we'd have to cut out the extras, wondering if maybe last year's winter coat might still fit, if Sophie could wear my old tunic. My father seemed to take all this lightheartedly. On payday he handed out housekeeping money, and, presumably, he paid the rent and the Simpson's bill. But there seemed nothing my mother could do about emergencies: the doctor, the dentist, the plumber. It came to be that we felt guilty about asking her for things. We were supposed to get a weekly allowance, but often it was not forthcoming. If I simply had to have stockings or underwear, I was given a slip to go down to Simpson's and put it on the bill. I was never given the opportunity to budget or learn how to buy for myself.

"In consequence, I think, I felt deprived, mean, drably dressed; the word poor became a real word. We were poor. And yet we lived in a middle-class neighbourhood and were supposed to be comfortably off. Although I continued to accept funds for my education, I felt 'kept,' and longed to earn my own living."

Immediately to the south (**75 Walmer**) Hector Charlesworth (1872-1945) passed a few of his mid-teenage years. Charlesworth is described in *The Oxford Companion to Canadian Literature* as "a notable force in the arts. As a drama critic he survives only as a brief portrait in Robertson Davies' novel, *World of Wonders* . . . his criticism of the Group of Seven gave him a peculiar place in Canadian art history. Though he admired many of their paintings he criticized them often enough ('the hot, mush school'), to become, in the 1920s, the new movement's most notorious enemy." A conservative in most matters artistic, it's a sure bet that Charlesworth would not have liked the poetry of bp Nichol who lived at **No.70** in 1970. Many others do, however, including Michael Ondaatje who early in his career made a feature-length film about Nichol.

Three authors have lived at **44 Walmer.** Poet and librarian David Aylward (b.1942) has lived here since 1975 (in the 1960s he worked together with bp Nichol in the stacks

Elizabeth Smart (left) with her biographer, Rosemary Sullivan, at 192 Lowther Avenue, 1983.

of the Sigmund Samuel Library at the UofT). For most of his adult life, Aylward has been interested in the Far East, particularly Japanese culture. Since he moved here he has published *A Darkening Sea* (20 translations from Basho) and *Paper Doors*, an anthology of Japanese-Canadian poetry, co-edited with Gerry Shikatani. As well, he translated and published (with Kodansha) four novels by the great Japanese novelist Masuji Ibuse. Another resident of this apartment building was romance writer Charlotte Fielden (b.1932) who was here for a dozen years in the 1980s and 1990s. And poet George Whipple (b.1927) also rented an apartment here from 1980-84.

Most literary critics would place Dennis Lee and Barbara Gowdy among the best of the living Canadian authors. Lee (b.1939), renowned as much as a poet for children as for adults, lived in the ground floor, rear right apartment at **No.40** from January to September of 1972. Gowdy (b.1950) lived here longer, 1991-96, and in that time wrote her novel, *Mr. Sandman.*

The street swells at this point to a circle intersecting with Lowther. In 1996 this treed oasis was named Gwendolyn MacEwen Park. It was a favourite stopping place of the popular poet.

A detour onto **Lowther Avenue** handily introduces us to three addresses worth noting. Poet Richard Outram (b.1930) resided from 1958-66 at **171 Lowther**, where he wrote almost all of his highly regarded *Exsultate, Jubilate.* At the Walmer Road Baptist Church (**No.188**), novelist Ralph Connor, although a Presbyterian minister (and, by the way, the first bestselling novelist in Canada), was invited by his ecumenical hosts to give a sermon. He agreed, and on February 3, 1918 he spoke on the war and its "progress" to an overflow congregation. A little further west on Lowther, we encounter **No.192** where, in the top-floor apartment, the Canadian expatriate author Elizabeth Smart resided during her relatively short tenure in Toronto, June 1983 to May 1984.

Back to **Walmer Road: No.35** has also been home at different times to three noted authors. The first Toronto home of the first winner of the Giller Prize, M.G. Vassanji (b.1950), was in this building from 1980-85. Here he wrote most of *Uhuru Street* (1992) and much of *The Gunny Sack* (1989). The latter won the Commonwealth Prize for Best First Novel. Poet Mary di Michele also lived here, although only in 1979. A seventh floor apartment was Neil Bissoondath's final home in Toronto before he settled permanently in Quebec. During the three years he lived at **35 Walmer** (February 1986 to February 1989), he wrote most of the stories that appeared in the collections *A Casual Brutality* (1988) and *On the Eve of Uncertain Tomorrows* (1990).

The screenwriter and novelist Charles Israel made his home at **31 Walmer Road** from 1979-83, while earlier in the 1970s, dramatist David French lived at **No.30**.

Charles Israel, March, 1964

Finally, many commentators declare Cécile Cloutier (b.1930) a Quebec writer—indeed, one of the best from that province. Admittedly she writes in French but surely the time is overdue to celebrate her as well as a Toronto writer since she has been here since 1966. For two years at the end of the 1960s she lived at **No.2** and there wrote *Paupières* (1970), an early distinguished book of poems.

Nearby is **378-A Bloor Street West** where the respected dramatist Hrant Alianak (b.1950) lived from 1978-83 and wrote his popular play *Lucky Strike* (published 1989).

Kendal Avenue deviates from the normal city grid system, so it will be easier to examine it by retracing our steps up Walmer Road a couple of hundreds meters to where it intersects with **Kendal Avenue**.

Ken Adachi (1928-89) had many strengths as a reviewer when he was the book critic of the *Star* in the 1980s, but he was at his best when reviewing fiction. Frankly, I don't believe the country has ever been blessed with anyone better at the task. He lived at **No.14** for almost three decades, 1961 until his death in 1989.

In the 1970s the poet and Japanese translator David Aylward lived at **No.22**. So did Margaret and Barker Fairley from 1920 to 1925. Barker Fairley (1887-1986) is the better known of the couple. A professor of German at the UofT for most of his life, he was also a painter of note, and an *engagé* writer, anxious to change a social order that seemed to him to care little about the disadvantaged. The year he moved to this address was significant for him in two ways. First, it marked the formal organization of the Group of Seven, artists with whom he painted when they were in Toronto. He had been on the best of terms with them since his own arrival in Toronto in 1915. Second, in 1920, the local counterculture magazine, *The Rebel*, with which he and Margaret had been increasingly involved, was transformed into a national journal, *The Canadian Forum*. Over the next five years at **22 Kendal** he continued to write reviews, essays, and poems for its pages. Margaret (1885-1968) was even more left-leaning in her politics than her husband. Her best book was *Spirit of Canadian Democracy* (1945). Despite a title that makes it seem a political science textbook, it was the first, easily-available Canadian anthology of poetry and prose selected from a Marxist viewpoint. It was a daring book to publish immediately after the end of WWII when anti-Communist feeling was quickly starting to flare across the continent. Later she edited the prose of William Lyon Mackenzie, a fellow firebrand.

Novelist M.T. Kelly (b.1947) has lived on this street since 1984, and poet Paul Dutton (b.1943) since 1980. **No.63** was home to the fantasy and SF author Garfield Reeves-Stevens (b.1953) in the early 1980s. The next house north (**No.65**) was the brief abode of poet and anthologist J.A. Wainwright (b.1946) in the late 1960s. He probably passed crime novelist Alison Gordon (b.1943) frequently on the street (although neither had published a book at that point) because she lived at **No.75** in the same period. From 1988 to 1990, the playwright John Krizanc (b.1956, best known for his award-winning *Tamara*) was spending part of his days at **No.91**, occasionally writing his drama *The Half of It*. His friend, novelist Paul Quarrington (b.1953), whom we encounter many times in these walks of the Annex area, lived at **95 Kendal** from 1974-76. Poet Victor Coleman (b.1944), who was involved with Coach House Press in its earliest years, has returned to the press in its reincarnated version, Coach House Books. From 1973 to 1976 he and his family lived in a triplex at **No.101**. For the last two of those years, the top floor was rented to David Young (b.1946). Several American authors of note were house guests here at this time, among them Kathy Acker, Robert Creeley, Ed Dorn, Fielding Dawson, and Robert Duncan.

Continuing north on Kendal takes us to Dupont Street. After turning left but before reaching Brunswick Avenue, we pass on the north side **374 Dupont Street**. Today it is nothing remarkable to look at. Indeed, 30 years ago it was nothing special either, having been a candle factory and then an autobody shop. But at this address, on the second floor, Factory Theatre Lab began in 1970 under the direction of playwright Ken Gass (b.1945). The story of Factory has been told well and at length in Denis Johnston's splendid history of the alternative theatre movement, *Up the Mainstream*. However, it's worth quoting Gass from 1974 to remind ourselves how exciting this theatre was when it burst onto the scene with its seemingly reckless and, at the time, unheard of policy of producing only Canadian plays: "The policy did not stem from any passionate nationalism. Rather it was a simple and arbitrary way of escaping the Canadian theatrical rut of following fashion. Regional playhouses were (and, largely, still are) shaping their seasons to reflect the fashions of Broadway and the West End . . . By limiting the Factory to only new Canadian plays, we forced ourselves to abandon the security blanket of our colonial upbringing. We found ourselves in a vacuum, without roots and, indeed, without playwrights. The plays soon surfaced happily, many of them bouncing to life after years of neglect. We also discovered to our surprise that the country was indeed ready for a surge of nationalism in many fields and that we were on the crest of a timely wave." Gass put so much of his own energy and money into establishing the theatre that he was soon broke and had to live in the theatre itself for a while. But week by week the plays drew increasing attention, and early successes with playwrights such as John Herbert, Beverley Simons, Herschel Hardin, and especially with David Freeman's *Creeps* meant that the theatre's importance was ensured. Director Bill Glassco worked full-time at Factory in its first year before establishing his own theatre, Tarragon, a few blocks away in 1971. And it was at this address, in the summer of 1971, that George F. Walker's first play was produced, beginning a long and fruitful relationship with Factory that continues to this day.

We now head south from Dupont Street onto **Brunswick Avenue**. Standing at **535 Brunswick** we behold the former residence of playwright John Krizanc (b. 1956), author of the hugely successful *Tamara* and other dramas. Finding addresses for Juan Butler (1942-81) has been almost impossible. As an adult, he moved frequently from rented room to rented room, and left next to no paper trail of his whereabouts. I could discover only two residences for him. One was **No.500** where he lived for about two years, 1973-74. Fortunately his three novels survive, including *Cabbagetown Diary* (1970) and *Canadian Heating Oil* (1974), part of which he wrote at this address. When they were published, his books were much at odds with the mood of the city, and as a result they gained notoriety for their sociological rage as much as for their literary merit. He still has his passionate admirers among the literati. Butler hanged himself in Toronto after a long battle with his psychological illnesses.

Poet bp Nichol lived at **No.477** on two occasions: in 1964, when he began Ganglia Press here, and again in 1974. Dennis Lee lived at **No.474** from August 1967 until December 1971. Much of *Civil Elegies and Other Poems* (1972), which won the Governor General's Award, was written here. This block has proven popular with poets—yet another was here: Eldon Garnet (b.1946) lodged at **No.473** from 1973-75. Garnet is less well known for his writing than he is for his art. He has created several popular sculptures in the city, including the statues outside the police headquarters on College Street.

Morley Callaghan wrote or published three of his most famous books in the mere trio of years (1935-37) he and his young family occupied the second floor of **456 Brunswick**: *They Shall Inherit the Earth* (1935); *Now That April's Here and Other Stories* (1936); and *More Joy in Heaven* (1937). Despite the relative brevity of the stay, this is an impressive display by anyone's reckoning. Excellent as it obviously was for writing, the apartment proved too small when son Barry was born in 1937, so that year the Callaghans moved to a larger unit on the second floor of the adjacent building, **32 Wells Street**, and

were there until 1939 when they moved, again within the Annex, to 123 Walmer Road. One of Barry Callaghan's oldest and best friends is the novelist Austin Clarke (another author who ran for office; Clarke has run for mayor of Toronto, as well as for the House of Commons). In the late 1970s Clarke (b.1934) resided at **432 Brunswick**.

An author of much applauded fantasy novels for young adults, O.R. Melling (b.c. 1955), passed most of her life in Toronto before beginning long commutes between Ireland and Canada. She lived at **No.431** at the end of the eighties.

The Bible of this street is surely *Fables of Brunswick Avenue* (1985), the short-story collection by Katherine Govier (b.1948) which so neatly and humorously reflects the *zeitgeist* of the Annex and its denizens. Govier herself has spent time at three Brunswick locales. The most important was the second floor of **No.411** (c.1975 to fall 1977) where she started *Fables* and where all of her novel *Random Descent* (1979) was written. Earlier, she had rented a third-floor apartment one door south (**No.409**), from 1973-75. Sections of the novel *Going Through the Motions* (1982) were first put down on paper here. Her first place on Brunswick was another third-floor flat (**No.398**) where she lived for most of 1971 and a little of 1972 while finishing her studies at York University. Govier had inherited **No.411** from another writer, Karen Mulhallen (b.1942), who while here began to edit *Descant*, the vaunted literary journal. Mulhallen lived in the unit from 1969 to c. 1975 and in addition to her *Descant* duties wrote parts of her books *Modern Love* and *Sheba and Solomon*, as well as her PhD on William Blake. Earlier, she had lived briefly down the street at **No.334**. When Mulhallen first moved to **411 Brunswick**, poet Gary Geddes (b.1940) was her neighbour (for 1969 at least) at **No.409**. Geddes is known to almost every university student of CanLit because his anthology *15 Canadian Poets* has been one of the standard textbooks since the late 1960s.

No.407 was the main address in Toronto for Ernest Jones (1879-1958), long famous as the first authorized biographer of Freud (whom he knew well). Thanks to the recommendation of Sir William Osler, Jones was appointed Director of the Toronto Psychiatric Clinic—later transmogrified into the Clarke Institute of Psychiatry. Upon first arriving in September 1908, Jones wrote to Freud that he found the town "very charming." Later he noted that, "I have some beautiful cases here, with very pretty results in the analysis. I can certify that hysteria is just the same here as in Vienna, and probably at least as common." After staying in a series of apartments, he wrote the Master from 407 Brunswick on February 17, 1909: "I have at last got a house of my own, and am happy in that I shall soon be able to get at my beloved books once more." Apart from pornographers, I suppose psychiatrists are the only professionals who hope that sex will actually rear its ugly head. But a Freudian such as Jones found few like-minded souls at the beginning of the 20th c. in Orange, repressed—and anally retentive—Toronto. He later described to Freud what he was up against: "the attitude in Canada towards sexual topics has, I should think, hardly been equalled in the world's history: slime, loathing, and disgust are the only terms to express it." Sadly, he was delineating the feelings—not of the general citizenry—but of his colleagues in the psychiatry department! Jones's own biographer shakes his head in disbelief, "One man he [Jones] failed to win over was crucial to his future in Canada—Dr. C.K. Clarke, Jones's boss at the Toronto Hospital for the Insane. After reading Freud's Clark University lectures he informed Jones that 'any ordinary reader would gather Freud advocates Free Love, removal of all restraints and a relapse into savagery'—as wildly inaccurate an account of the lectures as unbridled prejudice could produce. The impermeability of Canada to the rapidly growing new approach to psychological medicine, sex and morality, which had begun far back in the 1880s with the work of Krafft-Ebing and Havelock Ellis, was remarkable." Ernest Jones lived at this address from 1909 to January 1913. Shortly after, he fled to England.

Toronto-born novelist Marion Quedneau (b.1934) lived at 398 Brunswick during 1973-74, her third year at the UofT, just after Katherine Govier (b.1948) had finished her residence here. Next door, the third storey of No.396 was the home and writing office of playwright Judith Thompson (b.1954) for the years 1981-84. Here she finished her play *White Biting Dog* (1984) and the teleplay *Turning to Stone*. Judith is convinced that her landlady at this time was the model for the character "Ivy" in Govier's *Fables of Brunswick Avenue*. The poet Mary di Michele (b.1949) passed the mid-eighties at No.386. A longer stay (1975-84) was mustered by novelist Sylvia Fraser (b.1935) in the first-floor flat at No.382. At no other address has she been such a fruitful writer of fiction. Three of her novels came from this house: *A Casual Affair* (1978), *The Emperor's Virgin* (1980), and *Berlin Solstice* (1984).

After he was released from an internment camp in 1941 to which he had been sent in error 18 months earlier, novelist Henry Kreisel (1922-91) headed to Toronto to restart an education begun in Austria. During his first year at the UofT he roomed at No.366.

Professional creative writers who were also electrical engineers are few in this world. But there was at least one in Toronto. "Johnson Abbott" was the pseudonym of Edward Ashworth (1880-1954) when he wrote the novels *La Roux* and *The Seigneurs of La Saulaye*. In 1924 (the year he published *La Roux*), after decades as an employee, he was appointed the general manager of the entire Toronto Hydro-Electric System—and he kept the top post until he retired in 1952. His memoirs of his electrical life were published posthumously under his own name. He made his home at No.348 from 1912-26, and earlier in the century lived for some years at No.332.

Howard (b.1931) and Marian (1933-85) Engel were married and living together at **No.338** from 1971-74. During this era, she wrote her internationally notorious novel *Bear*. He worked as a producer in the literary department at CBC-Radio. She stayed at this address for one more year, i.e., until 1975, when she moved to Marchmount Road. Around the same time, another couple was getting together across the street: David Young (b.1946) and Sarah Sheard (b.1953) had never met until each rented a room at **No.329**. Not long after, their friendship blossomed into love, and they married. Both are novelists: she the author of the much praised *Almost Japanese* and *The Swing Era*; he of *Incognito*. Both worked for several years as editors at Coach House Press. Robert Fones (b.1949), better known today for his visual art than for his writing, was better known in the seventies for his writing than his visual art, in part because of poetry books like *The Forest City* (which he wrote when for some months he too lived at **No.329**— just prior to Young and Sheard). G.A. Kingston (1876-1943) was a noted lawyer with a poetic bent. He published *Legendary Lyrics*, and wrote a number of hymns used in various hymnals across Canada. After a few years of residency, he died at **No.329**.

Although he began life as a poet, Peter Robinson (b.1950) has become internationally acclaimed for the sophistication of his detective novels. But in January 1980 when he moved to the top floor of a rooming house at **No.322**, he was still thinking lyrically and wrote *Nosferatu*, his only volume of published poetry.

Once you reach Bloor Street, it is worthwhile to cast an eye in an easterly direction, for at **390 Bloor West**, a young Jack Cole (c.1920-97) dropped out of Harbord Collegiate in 1938 to help his brother Carl operate a store where they sold used school books. In 1939 they expanded the business to include **No.370**, and by now the bookselling firm was known as Cole & Company. Their first retail store selling new as well as remaindered titles did not open until 1950, at the southwest corner of Yonge and Charles. The operation quickly became the largest book chain in Canada by far, and Jack Cole ran the company quite profitably until 1978. Later Coles merged with W.H. Smith Books of Canada to form the Chapters superstore empire. Reversing direction and walking towards Howland, we pass **420 Bloor Street West** where your humble guide lived for about 15 years (1978-93), at first on the second floor and then on the third. While ensconced here, I wrote *Growing Still* (1981, poems) and *Whales: A Celebration* (1983) and in 1989 won the City of Toronto Arts Award for contributions to Literature.

At **1 Howland Avenue** lived a noted author of detective fiction who few realize is still a Canadian, because he has been living in the USA for so long. James Powell (b.1932) has an impressively long entry in the *Encyclopedia of Crime & Mystery Writers*. Among its accolades is this: "In an era when generally only [mystery] authors of the status of Sara Paretsky and Mary Higgins Clark have their short fiction collected, it says a great deal about the reputation of James Powell that 14 of his best stories were collected in 1990 in *A Murder Coming*." While his father was in the Army during WWII, Powell and his mother lived in many places across town. This was their home c.1941-42.

William Henry Moore (1872-1960) was a popular Member of Parliament and the author of many tomes, including *The Clash* (1918), an outrageous book about Quebec and Canada that still has a cult following among the cognoscenti of PoliSci. His novel *Polly Masson* (1919) is one of the earliest of Canadian political novels. In 1893 his home was **No.18**. Novelists Aviva Layton (b.1933) and Leon Whiteson (b.1930) lived as husband and wife at **No.33** in the early 1980s before leaving the city permanently for California.

Graham McInnis (1912-70) was from a most literary family. His mother was the novelist Angela Thirkell and his brother Colin also published fiction. Graham was the art critic of *Saturday Night* from 1935-41 (a fitting role, since he was the great-grandson of the famed English painter Edward Burne-Jones). During that same period he was a frequent arts commentator on national radio. The Dept. of External Affairs became his employer as of 1948 and he served in many diplomatic posts with distinction. Among these was as Canada's permanent representative at UNESCO. McInnis had arrived in Canada from Australia in 1934 and lived in Toronto only until c. 1942 before the charms of Ottawa lured him away. His last home here was at **47-A Howland**.

Immediately north (**No.49**) lived R.E. Knowles (1868-1946), a blustering, full-of-himself journalist, famed for his interviews with celebrities in which he talked about himself more than the person being interviewed. Novelist Jock Carroll noted that, as a minister, Knowles "electrified his congregation with fiery sermons in which he strode about the platform, thumped the Bible and tore off his collar. As too often happens, this excessive energy led to the writing of novels. He turned out six and they brought him fame and fortune." Knowles lived at **49 Howland** in 1910, later returning to live at **No.57** for most of the period 1911-23.

Alice Chown (1866-1949) was a pioneer feminist who lived at **No.53** from 1938 to 1944. Once her primary battle for women's suffrage was won, she turned her formidable energies to union organizing of female labour. Her novel, *The Stairway*, was published in 1921 in Boston.

We first met John Mebourne Elson on this tour at 136 Spadina Road. The journalism *wunderkind* was a great booster of Canadian literature in the 1920s when the numbers in the chorus were many fewer than today. During the last world war he taught popular Extension Courses in Journalism and in Writing at the UofT. While doing so he lived at **No.66**.

At the intersection with **Barton Street** it would be profitable to digress from Howland to note that Brian Doherty (1906-74) lived in 1919 (and possibly earlier) at **15 Barton Street**. Doherty, trained as a lawyer, began his literary career as a dramatist with a bang. His play *Father Malachy's Miracle* opened on Broadway in 1937 to rave reviews (Brooks Atkinson of *The New York Times* called it "an original, genuinely humorous play that shines like a good deed in this naughty neighbourhood"). Despite the play's commercial as well as critical success, he kept his day job and continued to practise law in Toronto while keeping his hand in the drama scene. In the 1960s he began to dream of a festival for Shaw such as Shakespeare had at Stratford, and not long afterwards, as the founder of the Shaw Festival, his dream was realized. Across the street, writer Roberta Morris rented **No.16** from Dr. and Mrs. Wasserman (whom she describes rightly as two unsung heroes of the arts) for a decade, 1973-83.

The literary toil of Charles Israel (b.1920) has been mostly in radio and TV, although his novels continue to have their fans. **113 Howland Avenue** was his home for most of the 1980s. Man of letters Douglas Fetherling (1949) resided at **No.134** from 1972-77 and his early years there overlapped with the arrival at **No.147** by playwright David French (b.1939). **No.152** was briefly the home of bp Nichol in 1964. However, it had a more important tenancy, 1918-29, with Newton MacTavish (1875-1941). MacTavish spent most of his life in Toronto and used his position as editor (as of 1906) of the excellent but too little known *Canadian Magazine* (not to be confused with the anemic Saturday supplement of the 1970s) to educate Canadians about their culture and artists.

At **Wells Street** take a brief detour to **No.106** to observe the second and final Toronto home of Toronto-born Silver Donald Cameron (b.1937) (he left the city at the age of two for the Maritimes). His first book was *Faces of Leacock* (1967) and his second was *Conversations with Canadian Novelists* (1973). He has written many other books of labour and social history—and two novels.

Silver Donald Cameron with his father at their home, 106 Wells Avenue, 1938

Joy Kogawa's (b.1935) creative writing career began as a poet but when she published her first novel, *Obasan*, in 1981 while living at **169 Howland**, her fame became international as country after country bought rights to the book. While living on the first floor of **No.190** from August 1964 to August 1965, poet Dennis Lee (b.1939) was writing much of his first book, *Kingdom of Absence* (1967).

There is something appropriate about a mystery writer being slightly mysterious. That is certainly the case with L.A. Morse (b.1945), whose novels (such as *The Big Enchilada*) were admired by buffs when they were published in the 1980s. But since then he has published no books, and he is—or was—rarely under the spotlight of the media. He lived in rooms at **No.208** in the early 1970s while working at the UofT. Barbara Betcherman (1948-83), immediately after her divorce in 1980, also lived at **No.208**—

the very year in which she had such success in the USA with her first novel, the thriller *Suspicions*. This was her last Toronto address. From here she moved to California. Not long after, she was struck by a car and killed in front of her home in Malibu.

Playwright Allan Stratton (b.1951) lived in the vicinity: The Howland Court Apartments at **No.245** from May 1974 until late spring 1976. At this time he was an actor more than an author, using this abode as a base while touring Ontario in the collective play *The Farm Show*. Not long after, he gained a large national audience with his comic drama *Nurse Jane Goes to Hawaii*.

At the top end of the street, at **No.344**, politico and author William Henry Moore lived during most of his undergraduate years at University College (1890-92). Our final stop on Howland, **No.359**, was the home of poet sean o'huigin (b.1942) from 1968 until 1985. His last name, pronounced "oh-hay-geen," is much better known to children than adults. One book alone, *Scary Poems for Rotten Kids* (1982), has sold tens of thousands of copies around the world and remains the bestselling title of his long-time publisher Black Moss Press.

As we walk west on Dupont towards Albany Avenue, we pass an apartment building at **399 Dupont Street** in which the great Canadian poet E.J. Pratt (1882-1964) resided 1918-21 with his new bride, Viola. At this time, Pratt was yet not the legendary teacher at Victoria College, nor even a poet with any reputation. Rather, "his new work for the Toronto City Health Department proved to be, initially at least, far less an arid drudgery than he had feared. For one thing, he found that the nature of the project had been changed. Instead of making widespread visits to Toronto schools to investigate reputed cases of mental defectiveness and retardation, at the suggestion of C.K. Clarke, the Health Department and Board of Education had agreed that he should first conduct a 'vitally necessary pilot project': a comprehensive 'psychological survey' of the entire population of a single public school." C.K. Clarke, here an enlightened fellow, was the victim of the bad press from the Freud biographer Ernest Jones (and his biographer) we encountered earlier in this tour.

At **354 Albany Avenue** the novelist (and acclaimed Coleridge scholar) Kathleen Coburn prepared for her undergraduate studies at Victoria College from 1922-23. Just down the road, at **No.337**, the American poet Burton Raffell (b.1928) wrote much of his collection *Four Humours* from 1972-73. The previous academic year he had just arrived from the USA to be Dean of the Ontario College of Art. He had been hired by its new president, Roy Ascott, himself only recently arrived from the Slade School in England. The reign was, to be generous, tumultuous. Within the year, Ascott re-signed. Raffell jumped at the chance to be a visiting professor in the humanities at York. He recalled his stint at OCA as "brawling, divisive, unpleasant." Albany Avenue must have seemed an oasis to him.

Mystery writer and journalist Jack Batten (b.1932) lived at **No.199** from 1967 to 1979. In addition to being the managing editor of *Saturday Night* for part of this period, he began his book career with modest tomes such as *The Honest Ed Story* (1972) and *The Leafs in Autumn* (1975). His novels and more substantial non-fiction books were to come later—including *Bloody York: Tales of Mayhem, Murder, and Mystery in Toronto* (1996). John Robert Colombo wrote in *The Oxford Companion to Canadian Literature* that Batten "writes with ease and insight" on a wide variety of subjects, and the same assessment can easily be made of Douglas Fetherling's non-fiction books and articles. This street has also been Fetherling's home since 1977.

The next block has seen little permanent residence by writers. Pit stops included those of the hack R.E. Knowles in 1909 at **No.186**; novelists Aviva Layton and Leon Whiteson at **No.144** c. 1980; and Jean Graham (d.1936), the poet and *Saturday Night* editor, at **No.128** in 1925. One author is an exception. Phyllis Brett Young (c.1917-81?) passed her childhood and early adulthood at **No.127**. Her father, G.S. Brett, whose house this was, had literary connections of his own. Morley Callaghan, Hugh Hood, and Ernest Buckler all refer to him flatteringly (albeit briefly) in their writing, such was his profile in Toronto as the head of the Dept. of Philosophy at the UofT. The father, at least, once had inclusion in *The Oxford Companion to Canadian Literature*. Phyllis, though, is an excellent example that the glory of the world is fleeting. Her novels *Psyche* (1959), *The Torontonians* (1960), and *Undine* (1964) were the talk of the town—indeed, of the country—and Canadian bestsellers to boot. Her work was serialized in *Chatelaine*, and the books had large printings in the USA as well as Canada . In addition, they were translated and published overseas. In October 1960, arts journalist Robert Fulford reported that "W.H. Allen, the firm which bought the English rights to *Psyche* has now also purchased *The Torontonians* and will bring it out next year. *Psyche* is appearing there this season after serialization in a British paper." Her papers were purchased in the mid-1970s by the Library of Boston University, whose director in 1998 still regarded her as "hugely talented." Yet she has not only completely disappeared from all literary discussion in Canada, she has neatly disappeared from the public record. Even with the help of research librarians in three countries, I could not determine if the author is alive or dead, and if dead, when she died. Even her birth year is uncertain. What is known is that she lived with her parents at **127 Albany** from 1917 until 1940 and while here attended both Havergal and Bishop Strachan.

James Wetherell (1851-1940) was a minor poet but his literary tastes influenced generations because he was the general editor of textbooks for Ontario from 1917 to 1924. For much of his professional life he was a pedagogue: at first a teacher, then principal, then Inspector. He was a UofT grad, but student records for the years he attended do not exist, so the first sure address for him in Toronto is **98 Albany**, where he resided from 1910-14. Much to his credit, Wetherell ensured that textbooks included healthy amounts of Canadian literature and history. This is in sad contrast to our own time when, in Ontario and many other provinces, the study of Canadian literature is merely optional, even for those who are university bound.

Montreal novelist Ray Smith (b.1941), author of *Cape Breton Is the Thought Control Centre of Canada*, lived for a few years in Toronto, usually in frat houses, since razed, bordering Robarts Library. But in 1967 he kept lodgings at **84 Albany Avenue**. Gwendolyn MacEwen's (1941-87) penultimate residence (1978-83) was the bottom flat at **No.73**, a dark place where Gwen (1941-87) kept the drapes drawn, enhancing the gloom and reflecting her declining spirits. Her work on her novel *Noman's Land* was progressing haltingly and the only bright spot in this period seemed to be the adaptation of some her poems to music. However, even this event had a shadow cast over it, for at the end of the world premier by the Toronto Symphony in October 1978 the orchestra, conductor, and composer were warmly applauded and hailed—but the organizers forgot to call MacEwen onto the stage to share in the glory.

The Crackwalker, provocatively titled, provoked strong reaction when it was first produced in Toronto in 1981. Its author, Judith Thompson (b.1954), has since become one of the best-known dramatists of her generation in Canada. From May 1979 to July 1980 she wrote the play in the attic room of **No.44** on a door laid horizontally as a desk while she "listened to the subway come in and out of the Bathurst Station." Across the street, **No.43** was the first Toronto home of poet Dorothy Livesay (1909-96) and her family, including her mother, the poet Florence Randal Livesay (1874-1953). They lived here for only two or three years (c.1920-22)

before settling into a larger home on Walmer Road.

Poet C.H. (Marty) Gervais has lived in Windsor, Ontario, for so long and from there has so effectively run his small literary house, Black Moss Press, that it is understandably forgotten that both the press and the poet got their professional starts in Toronto. In fact, the first book published under the Black Moss imprint was issued while Gervais was living at **34 Albany** from about the middle of 1967 to June of the following year. At the time, in addition to writing, he was working at the UofT Medical Library along with many other less celebrated poets, including David UU. The ur-Black Moss book caught the attention of bp Nichol, who wrote enthusiastically about it in *Quarry*, one of the most important Canadian literary journals. Gervais lived in Toronto from 1965 to 1969.

WEST ANNEX

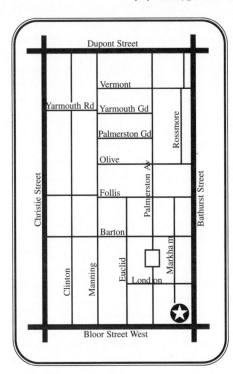

The tour begins at the northwest corner of Bloor Street West and Bathurst Street.

Walk one block west to **Markham Street** and then proceed north.

The West Annex is also known as Seaton Village, named in honour of Lord Seaton who was once Lieutenant Governor of Ontario.

The Markham Street Public School at **700 Markham Street** can count the esteemed mystery writer James Powell (b.1932) among its graduates. Fantasy writer O.R. Melling (b.1956), who now lives in Ireland, had a flat from 1981-82 at **No.721**. Detective novelist and long-time city alderman Horace Brown (1908-96) had rooms at **No.761** at the end of the Depression. This was his first abode in Toronto and while here he worked in the Script Dept. of CBC Radio. At this time he would have still been beaming because a poem he had composed about Remembrance Day was read by Boris Karloff to a gigantic audience over the NBC network in the USA in 1937.

42 Barton Street was the home for half a century (1940-88) of Oscar Ryan (1904-88), playwright, critic, and activist. Ryan came to Toronto from Montreal in 1926 and worked at everything from woodworking to the writing of advertising copy. It was during his Toronto years that his politics came into focus and, in addition to writing poetry for several left-leaning periodicals, he edited other such journals, including the *Daily Clarion*, for which he wrote a theatrical news and reviews column.

Oscar Ryan was determined to organize a theatre and theatrical movement that would not only involve the working class but articulate its frustrations and its dreams. To that

Oscar Ryan, Toronto, 1959

end, he was the driving force in 1931 behind the founding of the Progressive Arts Club, a group of primarily theatrical folk (but including, as well, Dorothy Livesay and Stanley Ryerson) dedicated to examining the causes of the Depression and possible solutions to its end.

However, it is for his involvement with the play *Eight Men Speak* that Ryan will be most remembered. The best example of agitprop in Canadian history, the work was inspired by the Bennett Government's promulgation of Section 98 of the Criminal Code outlawing communist activity of any sort, and the subsequent 1931 arrest of eight communist leaders, including Tim Buck, general secretary of the Communist Party of Canada, for no other reason than that they were communists. They were sentenced to long terms in Kingston Penitentiary. Oscar Ryan reported on the trials for one of his periodicals and was thereby inspired to write *Eight Men Speak*. The play is usually described as having been a collective creation, but few are in doubt that the writing was predominantly Ryan's. His play was only loosely based on the actual trial. Rather, he expanded its view to include a look at the country's treatment of immigrants, and (for what surely must have been the first time on any stage in Canada) a look at how the mainstream press consciously or unconsciously colluded with the authorities. Critic Rose Adams describes what happened next, "The production had a cast of thirty-five, mostly unemployed men with little or no acting experience. Rehearsals began in October and the performance premiered 4 December 1933 at the Standard Theatre on Spadina Avenue [at Dundas] before an enthusiastic Toronto audience of 1,500. Audience reaction was ecstatic, with cheers, boos and wild applause. The final curtain brought a sustained ovation.

"Reviews of the play in the mainstream press were scant, while its success with its intended audience was unmistakable. Consequently, the importance of its subject matter did not go unnoticed. The Toronto Police Commission threatened to cancel the licence of any theatre offering to rent its hall to the Progressive Arts group. This caused the cancellation of a second performance in Toronto, and a performance in Winnipeg was prevented by a similar edict. Prime Minister Bennett is said to have received an RCMP stenographer's report of the script and to have strongly approved of banning the play. The Progressive Arts Club continued to organize mass protests against Section 98 as public opinion gradually shifted in their favour. In the federal election campaign of 1935, William Lyon Mackenzie King promised to repeal Section 98 if he became prime minister. In June 1936, with Mackenzie King in office, the law was finally repealed and the Kingston 8 were released. *Eight Men Speak* had played an active role. . . . " *Eight Men Speak* was revived in 1982 in Toronto—with Oscar Ryan sitting in the audience. The play itself was published as a book in 1976.

Markham Street ends at Follis Avenue. Turn left and walk to **Palmerston Avenue**. Once there, turn left (south). Daniel Richler (b.1957) arrived in Toronto in 1981 to work in television but quit his high-profile jobs in order to write a novel. The reviewers described *Kicking Tomorrow* in generally favourable terms and most stated they were looking forward to his next novel—which has yet to appear. Richler moved into **715 Palmerston Avenue** in 1991, the year his novel was published, and he left it for nearby digs in December 1997.

Milton Acorn left the Waverley Hotel in 1978 in order to be a flatmate of another poet, James Deahl. They shared **No.555** from September 1978 to February 1981, although Acorn kept a room at the Waverley as a kind of writing office. Deahl said that Acorn had three typewriters: one at the hotel and two at their Palmerston abode, but Deahl could never get Milton to explain why he needed so many machines.

Near here, Palmerston intersects with **London Street**. The American feminist author Valerie Miner (b.1947) lived in

Toronto for the first half of the 1970s when she supported herself as a freelance journalist by day and worked on her fiction at night. She moved into a second-floor flat at **94 London Street** in 1971 and stayed until January 1974. She said of that time: "My years in Toronto were provocative, stimulating and unsettling in very good ways. People were extraordinarily tolerant of and generous to this rather wide-eyed young American. . . . I often think about moving back to Toronto—then I remember those grim, grey, cold days in March." While living at this address she co-authored *Her Own Woman* (1975), a collection of profiles of Canadian women.

Continue west on London towards Euclid Avenue. But before proceeding north on Euclid, take a little detour and walk a block south to where Euclid meets Bloor. Nearby, at **618-A Bloor Street West**, lived two young men in 1968-69 who were finishing their undergraduate studies at the UofT. One of them, Bob Rae, would become the premier of the province of Ontario in the early 1990s; his flatmate, Michael Ignatieff (b.1947) would eventually move to England, where he finished his formal studies and then began to publish books examining social and economic aspects of history and their contemporary relevance. These were books with a very limited readership, and in the 1980s he chose to aim at a wider audience. He hosted several highbrow interview television programs and wrote a popular column in *The Observer*. His book *The Russian Album* (1987) won the Governor General's Award. To date he has published two novels. The first, *Asya* (1991), was crucified by the British critics but was relatively well received in Canada. The second novel, *Scar Tissue* (1993), was poorly received by Canadian reviewers and warmly embraced in Britain. His most recent book, *Blood and Belonging* (1993), won the $50,000 Lionel Gelber Prize as the best book published anywhere in English on the subject of international relations.

Walk north on Euclid. Oddly, given the many authors who have lived in this area, not a single writer of note lived for any notable time on the Seaton Village portion of Euclid, but it makes a pleasant walk to **Follis Avenue** at its top. A house on **Follis Avenue** has been home to the renowned poet Dennis Lee (b.1939) since 1985. **No.75** was award-winning novelist's Paul Quarrington's (b.1953) dwelling from 1981-83, a period when he was more interested in exploring corporeal pleasures than in writing. Fortunately for literature, the period was relatively short. Quarrington also lived nearby at **27 Rossmore Road** for some months in 1984.

Walk west on Follis Avenue to **Manning Avenue** and turn south. **No.775** was the home of poet Rosemary Sullivan 1982-87. Here Sullivan (b.1947) wrote her first book of poetry, and did the initial work on her biography of Elizabeth Smart. This successful effort was followed by her Governor General's Award-winning biography of Gwendolyn MacEwen, and a history of the life and times of Margaret Atwood.

Montreal poet Sharon Nelson (b.1948) has lived twice in Toronto, the first time during the winter of 1970-71 at **755 Manning Avenue**. She recalled that stay: "I was trying to work on a novel and wisdom had it that a change of scene and an environment supportive of artistic accomplishment would ease the transition to fiction. The Manning Avenue house was full to overflowing with theatre people and artists, some of whom were doing shows. That meant that they worked evenings, unwound until the middle of the night, and slept most of the mornings, a time when it was not kind to be banging away at a noisy old typewriter. Between the lengthy unwinding and the household needs for quiet, there seemed to be so much cooking to do for so many people that there was never any left for working on the novel . . . I managed to convince the few writers I knew in Toronto at that time, Fred Cogswell and Irving

Layton, to trek out for dinner, so I managed to continue cooking.

"The moral of the story is probably clear to you, but it took me a bit longer to figure out for myself that I'd rather cook than write fiction. By the time I left Toronto, I suspected that I was not going to be successful at novel-writing. . . ."

Move to the next street to the west, **Clinton Street** and walk north. Playwright Judith Thompson (b.1954) has lived on **Clinton Street** since 1992. **No. 550** was once the home of Toronto-born Cary Fagan (b.1957). Here, in the basement and first floor which they rented, he and his wife started Shaw Street Press, a limited-edition house that published four literary titles in its first few years, including work by Ralph Gustafson. As a writer, Fagan has published mostly fiction, although he has compiled two books about Toronto: the first, *City Hall and Mrs. God: A Passionate Journey Through a Changing Toronto* (1990), was nominated, appropriately enough, for the Toronto Book Award; the second, *Streets of Attitude: Toronto Stories* (1990), an anthology which did win the Toronto Book Award.

Carry on to Follis Avenue. Go east one block and then proceed north on **Manning Avenue. 820 Manning** was briefly the home at the start of the Depression of Ida Fitch Baker (1858-1948) and her twin sister, Eva Rose York (1858-1938?). Both were writers, and Eva Rose in particular was a fascinating character. After a colourful career in the USA, she returned to Toronto and helped establish a philharmonic society while maintaining her reputation as a crack shot and woman of literary accomplishment.

Playwright Judith Thompson moved to the second and third floors of **No.867** in July 1980. She described her literary time this way: "I wrote *White Biting Dog* at a child's school desk at the large window facing Manning Avenue—while watching a man in the window opposite, who I later found out to be a professor of English at York, writing

his book. I would sip tea and he would drink beer. The Weston bread factory up the street on Dupont filled my head with the sometimes sweet, sometimes nauseating aroma of cheap bread and jelly rolls." She lived here until September 1981. In January 1985, the mother of a new baby girl, she sought larger accommodation and found it around the corner at **16 Yarmouth Road**. She stayed at this new address until 1992 and during her residency wrote the play *I Am Yours* (produced at Tarragon), as well as many film and television scripts.

Proceed north to **Dupont Street**. The Warr family, including Bertram (1917-1943), lived in 1918 at **623 Dupont Street**. His family was poor and unable to send him to university during the Depression so he worked as a clerk during the day and took writing classes from the UofT Extension dept. at night. His main teacher was John Mebourne Elson. Just prior to WWII, Warr went overseas, not as a soldier but as a stowaway. In 1941 he was drafted into the RAF—paradoxically, just as he was writing poetry that tried to incorporate socialist and pacifist ideas. This was the period of his best poetry—inspired by both the ugliness and the courage he witnessed during the Blitz. A small group of these poems were published in London in 1941 and Robert Graves wrote to him in flattering terms, calling him a true poet. Earle Birney said Warr would have been "a leading poet of his generation," but Warr's was a promise unfulfilled. His bomber was shot down in 1943.

Walk east to **Palmerston Avenue**, then proceed south. **No.854 Palmerston** was briefly home to poet Gail Fox (b.1942) in 1979, yet her stay was long enough that she was able to write many of the poems in her book *In Search of Many Things* (1980). The novelist and Coleridge scholar Kathleen Coburn also had a brief stay on this street. She lived at **No.818** in 1921. A longer residence was that of playwright and novelist Rick Salutin (b.1942) who kept house at **No.792** from 1979 to 1986. Here he wrote

344

the script of *S: Portrait of a Spy* along with Ian Adams, based on Adams's novel, and compiled the collection of some of his best essays: *Marginal Notes: Challenges to the Mainstream* (1984).

While descending this part of Palmerston Avenue we pass some small side streets. The first of these is **Vermont Avenue. No.2** was the home of Kenneth Porter Kirkwood (1899-1968) while he was studying at the UofT. After graduation, Kirkwood worked first for the Student Christian Movement in Smyrna, Turkey, and then for the Dept. of External Affairs, eventually reaching the rank of ambassador to Egypt, and High Commissioner in Pakistan and then New Zealand. All the time that he worked as a diplomat he wrote poetry, publishing a number of volumes in the 1930s. He also wrote books about foreign relations, as well as about the countries he visited, including *Turkey*, co-authored with Arnold Toynbee (1927). This same house was later the home of novelist and story writer Austin Clarke (b.1934) in the early 1960s. Clarke came to Toronto from Barbados in 1955 and has since established himself as one of the most respected fiction writers in the country.

Olive Avenue has seen inhabitancies by three authors. Poet Christopher Dewdney lived at **No.1** from 1992-96. John Mebourne Elson (1880-1966), newspaper *wunderkind*, lived at **No.66** from 1908-10. Later he would write a novel and a book of poems while working for the leading Toronto papers as one of their youngest editors ever. The Governor General's Award for Drama was awarded to Guillermo Verdecchia (b.1962) in 1993, and his other plays have attracted substantial acclaim. From 1985-86 he lived at **No.98**.

CHRISTIE PITS

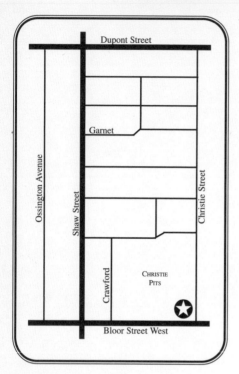

Dupont Street

Garnet

Ossington Avenue

Shaw Street

Christie Street

Crawford

CHRISTIE PITS

Bloor Street West

The tour begins at the northwest corner of Bloor Street West and Christie Street.

Walk west along Bloor, past Christie Pits, to **Crawford Street**. Poet Libby Scheier (b.1946) lived for two years (1982-84) at **796 Crawford Street** and while there wrote part of the ms that later became her book *Second Nature*.

784 Shaw Street was home from 1984-87 to another poet, Ross Leckie (b.1953)—not to be confused with another Toronto writer, Keith Ross Leckie, also born in 1953. The latter is primarily a fiction writer and author of teleplays, while the former has a day job in academe. The most recent book of "Ross Leckie the Poet" was *The Authority of Roses* (1997). Yet another poet, Helen Fairbairn (b.1864), lived at **No.810** from 1922-29 while working at the UofT. She was on the library staff there from 1908-36.

From Dawn to Dusk, an accomplished book of poems adhering to French metrical forms, was published in 1945, but whether that was posthumously is not known. Helen Fairbairn is one of those women writers who just disappears from public view and public records. Even the library where she worked, otherwise a marvellous and helpful repository, has no information about her—not even a death year.

Shaw Street certainly attracted poets. **No.907** was home to both Gail Fox (b.1942) and Joy Kogawa (b.1935) in 1979-80. Kogawa began her publishing career with verse, but is known around the world for her novel *Obasan*.

The final stop in this tour is **44 Garnet Avenue**, the last home in Toronto of the novelist and distinguished journalist Pierre Van Paassen (1895-1968). Van Paassen came from Holland to Canada in May 1911. He had been sent (with his brother) by his parents to scout the land for the best place for the family to settle and start a new life. A chance meeting with a chaplain onboard his ship led him to choose Toronto. His first job was working as a packer in the Christie bread and cookie company (coincidentally, Christie Pits is named after property owned by the same Mr. Christie, the baker). A local clergyman tried to induce Pierre to join the Anglican priesthood. However, he was more attracted to the Methodist faith, and began studies at Victoria College. To pay his tuition, he took a job as a streetcar conductor. Because he was Dutch, the local Orangemen in charge of scheduling ensured that his hours of duty "fell from 5 in the morning till 9, and then once again in the evening from 8 till 11:30, leaving me ample time to attend classes in the daytime."

Near the end of his life, Van Paassen reflected on how Canada had treated him as an immigrant: "I can scarcely find adequate words of appreciation for Canada's educational system which allowed a total stranger to enter college and work his way through without being held up or embarrassed by financial considerations or tests of class, caste, race, or religious affiliation. Such a system was then unheard of in Holland. . . . In Canada I made acquaintance with an honest attempt to put democracy into practice. As a result of that first encounter my admiration and affection for the country and its people have never waned. Toronto was a good city to me."

Pierre soon graduated from Vic, and was sent to western parishes as part of his clerical apprenticeship. Returning to Toronto after the start of war, he remarked, "Toronto was a changed city. Recruiting rallies were being held every noon hour on the steps of city hall . . . Troops filled the buildings at the exhibitions grounds and trained in the parks. On Yonge and Bay Streets one saw men and boys hobbling around on crutches, legless and armless fellows, the first fruit of the gory harvest in Flanders' fields. The newspapers published casualty lists, exercising great caution in order to camouflage the magnitude of the losses suffered in the first battle of Ypres when the Princess Patricia Light Infantry and the Canadian First Division had been heavily engaged."

Van Paassen soon came to work for two of those same newspapers: first the *Globe* and then the *Star*. For the *Star*, he was a foreign correspondent based in Europe, one of the most celebrated that newspaper has ever featured on its staff. His early success, in fact, led to his departure: "I was busy at the *Globe* office, writing a series of articles . . . when a letter arrived from Clark Howell, the owner and publisher of *The Atlanta Constitution*, inviting me to come to Georgia and work as a feature writer . . . I told [my editor] that I would be back shortly, since I considered Canada my country and Toronto my home. Atlanta was to be a mere interlude. But this is not the way things turned out. I never returned to Toronto except to lecture in that same Massey Hall where I had heard so many others." Just before Van Paassen returned to give that lecture at Massey Hall, the *Star* ran full-page ads announcing the upcoming talk. No other employee in the history of the *Star* ever received such adulatory advance press, or so much lineage advertising his return.

DOVERCOURT PARK

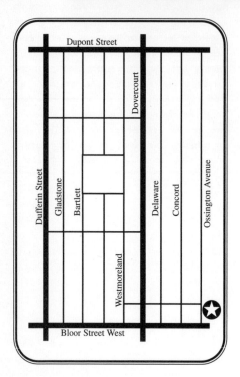

The tour begins at the corner of Bloor Street West and Ossington Avenue.

Prize-winning poet and novelist Dionne Brand (b.1953) had her residence at **806 Ossington Avenue** from 1988-93. Here she wrote the long poem *Bread out of Stone* (1994) and *No Language Is Neutral* (1990), nominated for the Governor General's Award. Her collection *No Burden to Carry: Narrative of Black Working Women* (1991) was also prepared while she lived at this address.

On the next street to the west, **Concord Avenue**, stop at **No.393**, once home to novelist Matt Cohen in 1981-82. Some of the stories in his collection *The Expatriate* (1982) were written here; the title story is set in Toronto. Cohen was the 1998 winner of the City of Toronto Arts Award for Literature.

J. Hunt Stanford (d.1935?) lived in this area for as long as he could be located in the

public record. Most of his Toronto life was spent on Westmoreland Avenue, but he did live at **267 Delaware Avenue** for a couple of years, 1905-6. Stanford published a book of poems in 1908 that was politely received, but his larger claim on our literary past is as one of the longest-serving presidents of the largest Dickens Fellowship in the world. By day, Stanford practised as an architect but he read, thought, drank, ate, and slept Charles Dickens, and the Dickens Fellowship attracted hundreds of Torontonians as members in the first half of the 20th c. The Club had several public meetings and lectures throughout the year, including an annual pageant in which members dressed up as Boz's characters and acted out scenes from his books. Stanford claimed that Dickens came to Toronto twice, but that is incorrect. He was here only once, in 1842—an odd mistake for the head of the Dickens Fellowship to make, but such is the knowledge of our literary past. The Toronto branch of the Fellowship seems to have had its start in the 19th c. and was active into the 1960s, but its current profile, if it still exists, has diminished greatly.

Hannes Oja (b.1919) is a poet who writes in Estonian and is an important scribe in that community. Like many immigrants he had a less than cushy landing, as he recalled: "I came to Toronto in April 1951. My first experience was in finding a place for me, my wife and our two small children. Nobody in the city appeared to like children. We lived in a series of places—first, all of us together in just one room in a house on Bathurst Street, then in a two-room place on Afton Avenue. When a friend bought a house on Broadway Avenue, we were invited to live with them. A different family lived in every room in that house! Shortly thereafter (c.1953) my brother-in-law bought a house on **Delaware Avenue** and we moved again. I wrote some poems while living in that house which were published in my first book *Koputused eneses* ("Inward Beats," 1955). The house was **No.360**. Writer Bev Daurio (b.1953) lived at **No.380** from 1981 to 1984 while working as the fiction editor for *Cross-Canada Writers' Quarterly*. Later she would start her own small literary house, Mercury Press.

The stretch of **Dovercourt Road** delimited by this tour is barren of literary associations except for **No.811** where the noted Newfoundland author Percy Janes (1922-99) (*House of Hate*) lived in 1945-46 while completing his second-year studies at UofT.

Poet and Charles Dickens fan J. Hunt Stanford had his longest residence in Toronto at **17 Westmoreland Avenue**, 1907-35. Born, raised, and trained in England as an architect, he managed to win at least one commission with literary associations: he claimed to have restored Thomas Carlyle's old Chelsea home in London. In Toronto he would recall for friends a friendly walk he once took through London's streets with Matthew Arnold.

Douglas Glover (b.1947), editor of *Best Canadian Stories* (1996, 1997), is himself the author of award-winning stories, and a novelist held in high regard (*The South Will Rise at Noon*, 1988; *The Life and Times of Captain N.*, 1993). He has been working in the USA for some years now, but he lived in Toronto over a 12-year span in the 1960s and 1970s. He was nominated for the Books In Canada First Novel Award (*Precious* 1984), and for the Governor General's Award in 1991 for his collection *A Guide to Animal Behaviour*. His early years in Toronto were spent as a student at York University. While he loved books, his real love at the time was competitive long-distance running, and he discovered Toronto at a speed, literally, that few others have. "I roamed that city for three years, loping fifteen or twenty miles at a stretch, all the way down to the lake and back, or north past the rail yards at the top of the city and into the farms beyond, threading the golf courses and parks along the city's ravines. Mostly by myself, but also with a series of running buddies." After York he travelled to Europe to study but continued to train, with realistic hopes of making the Canadian national team. Then injuries accumulated and the dream of a gold medal died. But by the 1970s his fiction writing became more important and he returned to Toronto in November 1977, to an upstairs apartment at **245 Westmoreland**, where he stayed until April 1978, part of a year in which he hoped to refine the fiction that, until then, had been rejected by most magazines and all book publishers. Disappointments as an author, however, were ameliorated by running—now mostly for unmedalled pleasure. In a letter, he recollected, "When I lived on Westmoreland, I ran with the Toronto Olympic Club. We'd meet at the indoor track which was set up in one of the buildings at the Exhibition at the foot of Bathurst and then run out along the lakeshore to the Humber and circle back and up into High Park before returning along the lakeshore again. This was winter and at night and the weather could be stunningly vile and beautiful at the same time."

Poet Victor Coleman (b.1944) wrote most of his book *Honeymoon Suite* while living at **300 Westmoreland Avenue** from June 1987 to May 1988.

Two blocks to the west is **Bartlett Street**. At **No.269** from 1990-91 playwright and novelist Guillermo Verdecchia (b.1962) wrote much of his Governor General's Award-winning play, *Fronteras Americanas* (1993). Verdecchia's performance in this one-man show was so moving that it won him the Dora Mavor Moore Award that year. Earlier, with his flatmate Daniel Brooks, he had written a large segment of the unusual drama *The Noam Chomsky Lectures* (1991) while living here.

Writer and sculptor Eldon Garnet (b.1946) worked at home in 1972-73 when he resided at **617 Gladstone Avenue**. Where Gladstone meets **Dupont Street**, the novelist

Dionne Brand (b.1953) lived at **No.1155** with her sister shortly after she arrived in Canada from her native Trinidad. During her four years she lived at this address in the early 1970s she finished her secondary schooling at Harbord Collegiate and then attended Erindale College.

The name of Hugh Eayrs (1894-1940) is still heard occasionally in the conversations of those who know the book trade in Canada. He came from England in 1912, and after a variety of jobs, he started to work at Macmillan c. 1917. By 1921 he was president of the Canadian arm—yes, he was only 26 years old when he was made head of the large firm. This promotion made him the most influential publisher of the era, and, because of his open personality, the best-known book publisher in the land. His successor in the job, John Morgan Gray, in his autobiography, portrayed his mentor Eayrs in frank terms: "One of the young [Eayrs'] first decisions after taking over was to publish W.H. Blake's translation of Louis Hémon's *Maria Chapdelaine*. Neither his sales manager nor the formidable president of the Macmillan Company in New York liked the decision or thought the book would sell; and at first it appeared they were right. Then, suddenly, the book took off, to become a brilliant success in Canada, Britain, and the United States, and young Hugh Eayrs took off with it.

"To have started with so striking a success, to have been right where greater experience was wrong, conferred both prestige and immense confidence. At the core of his confidence was a belief in his luck; a belief all gamblers—and publishers—must have, but none should have too much; at once a great and dangerous gift. I was to see it make him by turns unbeatable and intolerable, and to see it contribute to his destruction long before his time."

But that was all in the future. Before Eayrs started at Macmillan, one of his jobs had been selling ads for *Bookseller and Stationer* magazine produced by Maclean Hunter. No doubt it was in the corridors of the periodical giant that he met another young up-and-coming editor, Thomas B. Costain, himself to become a bestselling author of novels. The two became friends, and then collaborators. Together they co-authored one of the bibliographic rarities of Canadian literature, a novel titled *The Amateur Diplomat*. Earlier, Eayrs had written a biography of General Sir Isaac Brock. The first available address for Hugh Eayrs is **1206-A Dufferin Street**. He was here in 1914 and this is likely to have been his home for the first three years of his life in this country. Before leaving this discussion of Eayrs it's worth noting the title of the magazine he worked for. It is often not realized by many readers today that it is only in the last few decades that bookstores have sold only books. For almost a century and a half before then, selling stationery and concomitant supplies was the norm for bookshops in Toronto and other Canadian centres.

This house may have been Eayrs' first in Toronto but it was the last of novelist Juan Butler (1942-81). He certainly lived here in 1979 and may have done so until he next appears as a patient at the Clarke Institute of Psychiatry in 1991. During his short life, Butler wrote only three novels, but they caused a sensation when they were published in the early 1970s (the best known is *Cabbagetown Diary*, 1970). Sadly, he was afflicted by what seems to have been paranoid schizophrenia, and died by his own hand.

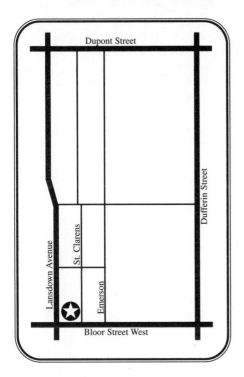

Dupont Street

Lansdown Avenue

St. Clarens

Emerson

Dufferin Street

Bloor Street West

The tour starts at the northeast corner of Lansdowne Avenue and Bloor Street West.

The northeast corner was once the locale of a remarkable theatrical experiment. This was the site of the Lansdowne Theatre, a thousand-seat emporium originally built for vaudeville c. 1911—although why a vaudeville theatre was built so far from downtown is puzzling. Regardless, not long after it was built it was converted to a cinema and was kept that way until 1958, when playwright Len Peterson and business partners spent a lot of money to restore the space to a legitimate theatre. The official address of The Playhouse was **683 Lansdowne Avenue**. The principals had ambitious plans for the first season: a mix of original Canadian plays and off-Broadway shows. Not only the scheduling

was ambitious. In the words of one of the founders of the company, "One of Playhouse's chief aims is to try to bring in the Elia Kazans, the Jose Quinteros and the cream of Broadway directors to work with promising Canadian writers." Peterson and his colleagues were not short on optimism. A previous venture of theirs, Jupiter Theatre, begun in 1951 at the theatre of the Royal Ontario Museum, had featured original productions of plays by Bertolt Brecht, Lister Sinclair, Eugene O'Neill, Ted Allan, Jean-Paul Sartre, Christopher Fry (starring Christopher Plummer, with sets by Harold Town)—and even a play by the drama critic Nathan Cohen. But after four enterprising and sophisticated seasons, the financial strains of live theatre caught up to them and Jupiter folded.

The Playhouse opened with a bang on October 1, 1958: the world premiere of Sean O'Casey's own favourite among his later plays, *Cock-A-Doodle Dandy*. Just prior to the opening, the author was interviewed by phone from his home in England: "Mr. O'Casey said he had no fear that the Toronto opening meant his play would premier in the sticks before a hick audience. 'I know more about Toronto than that,' he said, 'although I have never been to Canada. I am very, very pleased by this [premiere] because I would like to be more acquainted with the Canadian people and I would certainly like them to be more acquainted with me. I don't think any of my plays have ever been offered in Canada professionally before. I am very old but I am still trying very hard to find out how people all over the world think. I am more interested in Canada because it is part of the Commonwealth and belongs to us. Or rather, it is joined to us by political and economic ties.'

Mr. O'Casey said he had even contributed a number of articles to a Toronto magazine in which he suggested a national flag for Canadians. Canada . . . is a very important country with a very important part to play. We must reckon with Canada now and I hope I can get to know a little about it."

The production was mounted with an almost entirely New York cast. All the right people were seen to be at the theatre in its first week—and some who were not so right. The *G&M* reported that key moments in the drama "were punctured by shouts of 'It's a lie!' 'Blasphemy!' at the Playhouse Saturday night until ushers ejected two men who apparently considered the play anti-Catholic." This, of course, is publicity that impresarios die for. But extensive as the coverage was of a world premiere by one of the world's great playwrights, it was not enough to save The Playhouse, and the production closed early—in fact, after just two weeks. It wasn't the house that was jinxed, though. According to critic Herbert Whittaker, less than a month later The Playhouse "was jammed to the doors last night for the performance of a visiting troupe from Paris. Despite the bad weather and theories that Bloor and Lansdowne was an impenetrable area, Toronto's French audience turned out en masse for the sole appearance here by Le Theatre du Vieux-Colombier in Racine's *Britannicus*." Despite this French success, The Playhouse English-language company seems never to have materialized. It was to be another 20 years before such an erudite program would be artistically and financially feasible in Toronto.

In early 1976, the hall had another name change: it became The Radio City Theatre (having been an Italian-language cinema for some years) and presented very short runs of imported productions of musicals. *Hair* ran for a week, and *Godspell* for two, but whether it was the area, or the fatigued quality of the plays presented, the theatre was not long for this world, and was razed soon after the cast of *Godspell* limped out of town.

Further up the street is **No.731**, the home of John Mitchell (1880-1951) who, as "Patrick Slater" wrote *The Yellow Briar* (1934), a novel that is still enjoyed by sophisticated readers. Mitchell lived in this house in 1906 and 1907 when still a student, and then lived the next year at **No.811**. After Victoria College, he went to Osgoode, and then practised law quietly while writing fiction at night. *The Yellow Briar* was greeted by enthusiastic reviews and had three quick printings. But then something snapped. Lawyer John Honsberger recounts what happened: "Shortly after *The Yellow Briar* was published, Mr. Mitchell became obsessed with the idea that he had misused trust funds in connection with his practice. He requested that he be arrested and charged with theft. If there was any misuse of money on his part, it would appear from the maze of contradictions and scanty records that it was more from his incompetence as a bookkeeper than from any attempt at theft. Although he claimed that he had used some $20,000 of clients' money, only two persons whose claims were small could be found to testify against him. Mr. Mitchell's self accusation was contained in a letter which he wrote to the Crown attorney. . . .

"Ultimately, Mr. Mitchell was charged as he had requested. His friends rallied to his aid. A John Mitchell Fund was organized by a committee of prominent persons from the profession, the staff of Victoria College and from the field of arts and letters. His trial was unusual. Magistrate Jones (the presiding magistrate), and the Crown attorney attempted to minimize the crime of which Mr. Mitchell had accused himself. On the other hand, Mr. Mitchell demanded that he be convicted and severely punished. He was, in the end, convicted and sentenced to eighteen months in the reformatory. Following his conviction, he was disbarred and struck off the rolls in November of 1935. When Mr. Mitchell became eligible for parole he resisted it, saying that others needed it more badly. When he was released, he was greeted by his creditors who—again in a turnabout role—threw a party for him. In the years that followed, he paid back most of the money he had misused. The farm that he had owned, of which he wrote about in *The Yellow Briar* and which had meant so much to him, he sold to help pay what he believed were his debts."

While in jail at Langstaff, Mitchell wrote a book of poems, *The Water Drinker* (1937), and an odd novel, *Robert Harding* (1938), but after that, little more. He was so poor that he lived in a shack, and when the rent for that became too much, he moved into the cheapest rooms imaginable in the area where he had spent his youth—in other words, this area and slightly to the east of Wallace-Emerson. Mitchell is such a pathetic soul that I wanted to ensure his last home was properly commemorated in this *Guide*. Alas, while the three Toronto dailies carried obits immediately following his death in 1951, they differed wildly on his final residence. The *Star* said he died in Streetsville, the *Telegram* said Port Credit, and the *G&M* said in Toronto, in a room on McCaul Street. I suspect that the *Globe*'s is the true reference because William Arthur Deacon, the *Globe*'s book critic, would occasionally take Mitchell out for a modest lunch of soup and sandwiches. But no directory cites him as a resident, and I could not find a probated will or even a death certificate which would cite his last residence. Somehow (appropriately I suppose for a self-hating lawyer), at the end he left no legal paper trail whatsoever.

Marian Keith lived for four years (1911-14) at **No. 891 Lansdowne**. Her real name was Mary Esther MacGregor (1876-1961). She wrote popular novels set among the Scots of southern Ontario. While living at this address she met Lucy Maud Montgomery at a meeting of the Toronto Women's Press Club and the two were friends for life—and later co-edited the book *Courageous*

Women in 1934. Critic Marilyn Rose writes of Marian Keith in the latest edition of *The Oxford Companion to Canadian Literature*: "In all, MacGregor wrote fourteen novels—the last, *A Grand Lady* (1960), was published a year before her death. Although overly didactic and sentimental by modern standards, and slim and formulaic in plot, her books retain some value as regional idylls rich in quotidian detail regarding life in small Ontario communities before the turn of the century."

Frank Prewett (1893-1962) is a Canadian poet who has been brought back from obscurity and neglect by his compatriots, thanks largely to the sleuthing efforts of another Canadian poet and scholar, Bruce Meyer. Prewett's *Collected Poems* was edited and introduced by none other than Robert Graves in 1964—just two years after Prewett's death. Despite this attention from one of the century's most famous poets, and many other accolades besides, Prewett appeared in no anthologies of Canadian verse until 1997.

He was born in 1893 near Mount Forest, Ontario, the son of a cobbler. By 1900 the family was living in Toronto, in Parkdale, and then moved in 1902 to **425 St. Clarens Avenue** and stayed there until some time in 1905. From here the family moved one block east, to **59 Emerson Avenue** (1905-8). Soon after WWI began, he interrupted his University College studies to enlist and was shipped overseas. His parting from his homeland seems to have prompted him to write his first poem. Near the war's end, due to injuries, he returned to England from the front lines. Because of shell shock, Prewett was receiving psychological help and a fellow patient was another war poet, Siegfried Sassoon. Sassoon later wrote of their first encounter, "But the greatest luck I had was finding among my fellow convalescents one who wrote poetry. His name was Frank Prewett. Everyone called him 'Toronto,' that being his home town. He was a remarkable character." Thanks to Sassoon, Prewett soon came to the attention of Wilfred Owen, another English poet forever linked with WWI, and to the Woolfs, and then to William Heinemann. These, in turn, introduced Prewett to other leading literary lights such as John Masefield, Edmund Blunden, T.E. Lawrence, H.G. Wells, Thomas Hardy, Katherine Mansfield, the Sitwells, and Robert Graves. In his Introduction to Prewett's posthumous collection Graves wrote: "I met him in 1920 . . . He had privately published a small pamphlet of poems with the Hogarth Press, Richmond, sent me by Siegfried Sassoon. Three of these stuck in my memory, and despite my disappointment with *A Rural Scene* (1924) . . . I still reckoned him among the few true poets . . . Dedicated poets like Frank Prewett are few in any age; and lamentably so in this."

In late 1919, the Canadian Army ordered him home for repatriation, and for a kid from Parkdale the enforced departure from daily intercourse with the luminaries was an unhappy experience. Meeting Sassoon during the latter's lecture stop in Toronto in 1920 only heightened Prewett's sense that he was living in a cultural outpost, and within a year he was back in England, enrolled at Oxford. Shortly after he returned to Britain, Virginia Woolf typeset and published his first book and in 1924 Heinemann published his second. A decade later he published a novel that may be the earliest socialist novel by a Canadian. After serving in a variety of high commands in WWII, he stayed with the Royal Air Force in England until 1954, and then retired to a modest cottage in the Cotswolds. He died alone, in Scotland, in 1962, and his gravestone is marked simply, "Frank Prewett —Canadian Poet."

Alexander Muir (1830-1906), author of "The Maple Leaf Forever" and other poems, made his living as a teacher and later as a principal. When he lived at **387 Clarens Avenue** in 1886 and 1887 he was principal of nearby Shirley Street Public School.

Further south, at **No.199**, we see what was once the home of Clara Field from 1917 to 1923. Ms. Field was a woman of many talents.

A later newspaper account maintained she was the first woman undertaker in Toronto, a claim which has to date withstood all attempts at breach. In addition, the *Star* said she had established quite a reputation as stage director, elocutionist, bird caller—and playwright.

EAST JUNCTION

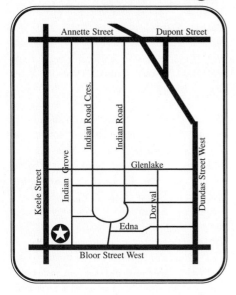

The tour begins at the northeast corner of Keele Street and Bloor Street West.

Walk east along Bloor Street one block to **Indian Grove** and head north.

301 Indian Grove was the home in 1950 of the mystery writer Keith Edgar whose life is also something of a mystery. He published at least four novels in the genre (*I Hate You to Death*, 1944) and 21 of his short stories appeared in the *Star Weekly* alone between 1943-52, probably a record for that journal. He edited an aviation magazine, which is ironic because the only newspaper reference I could find for him reported his crash-landing a small plane in Brockville in 1946, with the loss of only his two front teeth (and his plane, of course). The article mentions that his wife, who fractured her elbow in the crash, was a writer as well, but where or when they were born—or died—is unknown.

Raymond Souster (b.1921), for many the ultimate Toronto poet because so much of his subject matter is centred on the city, lived as a boy at **No.359**. He wrote, "Almost

the first memory I have of childhood is of the great endless rooms of our Indian Grove house. Or so they seemed to a child first crawling, then slipping, then struggling to his feet only to crash down with a thud a few steps later. Another impression that's remained is being wheeled in a stroller by my mother to nearby High Park where apparently I was fascinated by ducks on the pond . . . At age three I made friends with the boy next door. His name was Joe Spring, and he was every bit as curious and over-energetic as I was. One day we fought; he swung his toy shovel in a rage and came close to slicing into my left eye. I still have the scar to prove it. Another day we wandered off to see the trains at West Toronto Station where police and distraught parents found us hours later."

Souster attended kindergarten at Indian Road Public School one block to the east, just north of Humberside Avenue. Just south of the school at **217 Indian Road Crescent** lived (1946-51) another pulp mystery writer of mid-century, Tedd Steele (b.1922). As well as typing novels at this address with appropriately lurid titles (*Artists, Models and Murder*, 1946, or *Trail of Vengeance*, 1950), Steele illustrated comic strips and books issued by Bell Features of Toronto (samples of his drawing are included in *The Great Canadian Comic Book*, 1971). Scholar and novelist Kathleen Coburn lived at **No.60** from 1924-34. It was while at this address that she was just beginning her monumental researches into Samuel Taylor Coleridge at the UofT. Because of his opium addiction, and the strict moral lens through which literary critics viewed the work and the life, the author of "The Rime of the Ancient Mariner" was considered up to that point an interesting but definitely minor author. Thanks in large part to Coburn's digging and analyses, Coleridge's reputation was salvaged. For her scholarly labours, Coburn was awarded the Order of Canada.

Indian Road Crescent curves north to intersect with **Indian Road**. **No.557** was home to poet and long-time *Tamarack Review* editor Janis Rapoport (b.1946).

From July 1979 until November 1983 Keith Leckie (b.1953) resided at **No.610**. According to him, his novel *Seventh Gate* "began as a story of two Canadian brothers in the Spanish Civil War. That story I began researching when I lived at 312 Quebec Avenue, but then the Soviets invaded Afghanistan and I decided to place the story in a romantic environment I could experience first hand. I went to Pakistan/Afghanistan for a couple of months, travelled and did research and filed some stories for Canada News Syndicate. One interesting thing that occurred on Indian Road was a few days after my stories (very anti-Soviet in approach) appeared in the newspapers the house was firebombed. I can't prove it had anything to do with the articles but it sure was weird. I wrote the first few chapters of the book at **610 Indian Road**." Leckie's most recent work to gain national prominence was his script for the CBC-TV special on the Avro Arrow, starring Dan Ackroyd.

Indian Road intersects with **Glenlake Avenue**. **42 Glenlake Avenue** was home to Barbara Betcherman (1948-83) from 1973 to 1976 while she was studying for her bar exams. She was called to the bar in 1976 but soon gave up her law practice because of the international success of her first novel, a thriller. She was killed in a car accident before she could publish another book, although two works were published posthumously.

At the eastern end of Glenlake we find **Dundas Street West**. Near the T-junction with Glenlake is **No.2360**, where the esteemed short-story writer Elisabeth Harvor (b.1936) lived from 1992-93 as part of a five-year experiment at living in Toronto.

She has now returned to Montreal where she spent her formative years as an author.

Prince Rupert runs south from Glenlake. Novelist and writer of radio plays Rachel Wyatt (b.1929) lived at **40 Prince Rupert Avenue** from 1985-93. Her stay here overlapped with that of her neighbour, novelist Charles Israel, who inhabited **No.42** in 1991.

Continuing south, the reader reaches **25 Dorval Road**, home for several decades to Wilmot Lane (1872-1960), a professor of Ethics at Victoria College. Lane came to Toronto in 1912 after having spent some years teaching at Cornell and other American colleges. From 1913-40 he taught Ethics and his prose writings were on that subject. But when Lane lived at this address (1914-40), he also wrote poetry and saw several volumes of it published in his lifetime.

In 1961 Gwendolyn MacEwen (1941-87) had published her first book of poetry and, although only 19, was invited to Montreal to read from it. This was also the year she became the lover of poets, first of David Donnell, and then of Milton Acorn, whom she would eventually marry. Following her visit to Montreal in the summer of 1961 she moved in with her sister's family at **159 Edna Avenue** and seems to have stayed here for about half a year until she and Acorn were married.

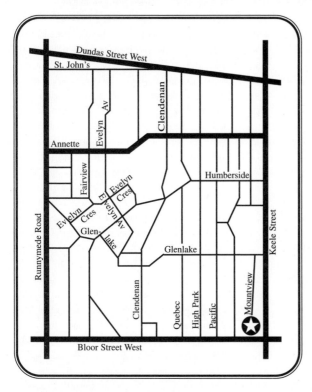

The tour begins at the northwest corner of Keele Street and Bloor Street West.

Poet Gwendolyn MacEwen (1941-87) was born at **38 Keele Street**. Her biographer, Rosemary Sullivan, describes what the house was like: "[It] stood in odd isolation from the rest of the street; it was a large, three-storied red brick structure up to which one had to climb by three staggered flights of forty-two steps from the street. Because of its elevation the local children used to make up stories about seeing bats circling it at night and claimed that it was haunted. On both sides of the house were open fields: on the south a small field that the city had divided up into Victory gardens for local residents to cultivate their own vegetables against the war rationing; on the north a huge expanse where the kids gathered to

sleigh and toboggan, and, in the summer, build castles in the sand pits. West, along Bloor Street, behind the old Rome Apart-ments between Quebec and Gothic avenues, were the Mineral Baths. Originally built as a spa fed by mineral springs. . . ." Construction of the subway led to the destruction of the house and substantial changes to the look of the area.

Walk one block west along Bloor Street to **Mountview Avenue**. Walking north on **Mountview Avenue** we pass **No.99**, Keele Street Public School, attended by poets Janis Rapoport and Gwendolyn MacEwen in the early 1950s. The school they attended was razed and replaced by the current building.

Mountview ends at **Glenlake Avenue**. Walk west on Glenlake. Jason Sherman (b.1962) won the Chalmers Award in 1993 for best new play for his *League of Nathans*. Since then, his star as a playwright has only risen. His productions have been seen in major theatres across Canada and he is becoming increasingly well known in the USA. From 1985 to 1990 he edited a sassy periodical called *what*, which, from its beginnings, operated at a level of discourse substantially more sophisticated than almost all other such alternative outlets for criticism by the young. Since he arrived in Toronto from Montreal he has lived in the city's western half, including a short residency (September 1992-February 1993) at **No.254**.

When Raymond Souster's mother returned from the hospital with Ray in swaddling clothes, she brought him to **No.263**. However, Ray's father decided the home wasn't large enough for the family's recent growth in size, and so they soon settled at **359 Indian Grove**, east of Keele.

At **Pacific Avenue** turn north and pause briefly **No.180**, the home of William Wesley Walker, clergyman and poet who lived at this address longer than at any other in the city, 1925-46. Walker, like many clergymen of his epoch, wrote and published his verse but Walker had unusual success. His *Hymns, Poems and Notes* went through at least five editions in just a few years. Pulp mystery writer and comic-book artist Tedd Steele (b.1922) spent the years of the middle 1940s at **No.204**. But our real goal on this street is **No.370**. This spot, alas now a supermarket parking lot, marks approximately where "Aikenshaw" once stood, the birthplace manor of E.W. Thomson (1849-1924). The house was built by his father in 1844. One of the early historians of Toronto, John Ross Robertson, included a drawing of the residence in his book *Landmarks of Toronto* and described it as a "large red brick house," and as late as 1929 literary historian E.J. Hathaway noted, "What was once a fine old mansion still stands on Dundas Street at the corner of Pacific Avenue, but it is now hidden behind a row of stores." The house was the manse of a 200-acre farm, said to have been cultivated "until the 1870s by the labour of escaped slaves."

Thomson would eventually become one of the best-known writers in Canada. But before that glory arrived, he led a life of some adventure, striving to emulate the military triumphs of his grandfather and other tale-telling ancestors. At the age of 14 or 15 (sources differ) he was visiting an uncle in Philadelphia and there met Abraham Lincoln. Thomson told a later correspondent that he was standing in front of a pastry store eating a piece of cheesecake when a tall man put a hand on his shoulder and asked "Good, sonny?" The two apparently chatted for a while and then Lincoln moved on. The fortuitous encounter inspired Thomson to join the Union Army and although he was underage, and a British subject, he saw action in the Virginia campaigns of 1864 and fought with Ulysses S. Grant at the Battle of Petersburg. His worried parents finally tracked their son down and forced the Americans to return him to Toronto. But he was no sooner back, it seemed, than the Fenians were invading Canada, and once again he took up arms, this time with the Queen's Own Rifles, and fought at the Battle of Ridgeway in 1866. He then went west with writer and politician Joseph Howe and worked as a land surveyor, then returned east to work in Ottawa as a civil engineer on a major canal project. By December 1878 he was back in Toronto to work with George Brown at the *Globe* becoming the journal's chief editorial writer. He worked at that newspaper for a dozen years. He would have stayed longer but for the *Globe's* increased leanings to political integration with the USA. Paradoxically, he then left for a job as editor of *Youth's Companion* in Boston. He wrote to fellow creative writer Ethelwyn Wetherald with much bitterness about the Toronto he had just left, "No, I have no wish to see a stone of Toronto again. You know I always detested the narrow, bigoted, canting spirit of that active Belfast, where I had the misfortune to belong to a political crew whose personnel I always detested. It was the misfortune of my life to like the Tories individually and their general way of thinking, while believing their politics to be in the main idiotic and ill calculated. And being a *Globe* man cut me off from nearly all the people in the world for whom I cared a cuss."

While in Boston he published his most famous book, *Old Man Savarin and Other Stories*, a tome that is frequently found on reading lists for those studying early Canadian literature. But just as Toronto got on his nerves, so did Boston, and after a decade there he returned to Canada—to Montreal, and then in 1902 to the nation's capital where he was the Ottawa correspondent for a major Boston newspaper for 20 years. In Ottawa he refreshed his connections with the leading political men of the day, including his old friend Wilfrid Laurier. He also continued his creative writing, and published books of translations, poetry, and fiction for boys. His reputation was not limited to Canada. He was published in both the USA and UK—and election to Britain's Royal Society of Literature came in 1909. Arthur Quiller-Couch included Thomson in *The Oxford Book of Victorian Verse*. M.O. Hammond, at one time the book editor of the *Globe*, knew Thomson in Ottawa, and wrote of him in 1931, "His impaired hearing limited his intercourse, but among intimates he was a welcome addition to any circle, where his wit, stories and reminiscences added immediately to the gaiety of the company."

Thomson was in a car accident in 1924 and never fully recuperated. One of the most progressive Canadian litterateurs of his day, he was a man whose "political views, reversing the usual course, moved steadily towards radicalism as he grew older." Thomson died at his son's home in the United States. Hammond, noting the irony of a nationalist Canadian dying in the USA, reminded his readers of a Thomson poem illuminating the man's attachment to Canada—a singular pride of country born and nourished at this intersection of Pacific Avenue and Dundas Street West:

> When the swallows slant curves
>   of bewildering joy
> As the cool of the twilight descends,
> And rosy-cheek maiden and
>   hazel-hue boy
> Listen grave while the Angelus ends
> In a tremulous flow from the bell
>   of a shrine.
> Then a faraway mountain I see,
> And my soul is in Canada's
>   evening shine,
> Wherever my body may be.

Lawrence Garber and his mother on the lawn of 25 Rostrevor Road, c. 1952

Also nearby, and a little closer in time, is the building where fiction writer Lawrence Garber was born in 1937. The author of such books as *Tales from the Quarter* (1969) and *Sirens and Graces* (1983) conveys the splendour of his boyhood in this area: "I am, in fact, a Toronto boy—more specifically a Junction kid, since that's where I was born, at **2998 Dundas Street West**. My mother had a millinery store at that address—called Morgan's (she simply saved costs by not removing the sign of the previous business) and we lived in the flat upstairs. I lived the first ten years of my life in the Junction, from May 1937 until the summer of 1947. Indeed, although I have lived elsewhere in the city since, I still consider myself a West Toronto kid, familiar with its parks and railway tracks and sudden ponds and ravines. I attended Annette Street Public

School and went to the local branch library (Annette Street Public Library) where an elderly librarian named Miss Loveheart read us stories in a small turret room every Saturday morning illuminated only by natural sunlight. My experience of Dundas West (my mother's store was located between Keele St. and Pacific Avenue)—at least in memory—is tied to the War years: rationing at the neighbourhood market, my Uncle Jack's surprise furloughs from England where he was a bombardier on a Lancaster, the hum and flash of music and uniforms across the street at Liberty Hall where serviceman dances were held on weekends, etc. My childhood stamping grounds in the Junction were High Park—a fair hike from our store but a paradise for a child—the back lanes of the district where the milk companies stabled their horses and the rats were the size of tumescent pintos, and the railway tracks themselves on which (to the incredulous horror of my parents) I played hopscotch with other Junction urchins till dusk. I went to Saturday matinées at the fabulous Beaver theatre a couple of blocks away, thought for years that the Victoria Day fireworks display in High Park was in my honour (since my birthday was also May 24), and wrote my first and only poem one evening under my bedroom skylight in 1945. I was hit by a truck on Dundas Street in front of my mother's store when I was 3 and a half years old, dragged 150 feet, and suffered a fractured skull and pelvis . . . I was in a coma from that accident, unconscious for nine days and nights—a Toronto *Star* human interest story, in fact, with photos of me on the back pages in my little sailor suit—but resurrected intact. We lived in a block of clothing businesses, most of them owned by Jews like ourselves, so that—although there was an undertaste of anti-Semitism in that area of the city in those days—a certain ethnic fellowship existed too: Gang's furs, Kaufman's, Klyman's, the Walsh family next door: Mr. Walsh a frustrated artist who worked in oils but made his living as a cut-

ter. My father was a compositor at Trader's Printing Co and I can remember waiting for his streetcar to bring him home to the Junction every night at 6 p.m. . . . And who knows what might have been had not my father gone into business for himself, had we then not abandoned the Junction for more affluent plains? Maybe I would have become a Junction historian—I revisit that part of Toronto every five years or so and wax nostalgic as I walk from Keele Street to Runnymede and along Annette Street and the wide avenues that form the city apron of High Park."

Walk one block west and descend **High Park Avenue**. When Margaret Avison (b.1918) came from Galt with her family, they lived at **246 High Park Avenue** from 1930-38. Her father was pastor of the nearby High Park Avenue United Church. Margaret said: "My parents once lived in a house owned by the church and I lived there briefly—away at school and for summer as much as possible." While living here she began her studies at Victoria College (B.A. 1940). She later went on to become one of the most respected and honoured poets in Canada. Her friend, fellow poet, and near equal in age, Raymond Souster (b.1921), lived on the third floor at **No.229** from 1964-66. During his first year at this address he won the Governor General's Award. And it was at this address that he and the young poet Victor Coleman selected and then edited the poets to be included in one of the most important anthologies ever published in this country, *New Wave Canada*. The collection marked the first time that several young writers were brought to a large national audience (and the prescience of the editors was outstanding): Michael Ondaatje, Roy MacSkimming, Daphne Marlatt, George Bowering, bp Nichol, Frank Davey, and David McFadden to name just a few. Sadly, this was the last book published by Contact Press, the amazing house created by Souster with substantial help from his partners Peter Miller and Louis Dudek.

Another important poet born slightly earlier than Souster and Avison, George Johnston (b.1913), also lived on this street in an apartment at **220 High Park Avenue** for a year and a half (1946-47) shortly after he was married and while doing graduate studies at the UofT. By adding W.J. Alexander's name to the list of those who have lived on this street (at **No.178** from 1910-20), we confirm that it is an important street indeed. Alexander (1855-1944) one of the most beloved professors in any discipline ever to teach at the UofT was in that institution's Dept. of English from 1889 to 1926. He was the friend and teacher of many of the authors mentioned in this book. When he retired, the university established the Alexander Lectures as a tribute to his contributions. The lectures are reserved for only the best critics of literature and it is a singular honour to be invited to deliver them. One wishes the university did a better job of alerting the general public to the occasion of the lectures. W.J. Alexander was never one to shy away from communion with the great unwashed and it is a shame that those who would enjoy these talks cannot do so for want of information about their happening.

Toronto is also poorer for the recent loss of poet Douglas LePan (1914-98), who in his retirement spent his last 20 years in apt. 704 at **80 Quebec Avenue**. It was while living at this address that he published *Something Still to Find* (1982), in which he hinted that the subject of his love poems was male, and then made the revelation overt in his 1989 collection *Far Voyages*. This was hardly shocking to a younger generation, but for some older people who had known LePan during his long career as a distinguished diplomat, scholar, husband, and father the news was unsettling. In his obituary, writer Alberto Manguel noted that LePan's "apartment on Toronto's west side was unpretentious, full of the tidy mementoes of a long life. Books lined the living room, where, on his dining-table-cum desk, he kept pictures of his

sons, Nick and Don, and a folder with notes for the poems he still hoped to write." LePan had a stroke in 1995, and whenever I spoke to him on the phone he was always quick to apologize for the slowness of his speech, which, in fact, was nowhere near as slurred as he believed. We spoke about matters relating to this book and the literary history of Toronto generally. He was happy to know that the photo of himself beneath the portrait by Wyndham Lewis would be included in this book. The picture was taken at this address c. 1987. The portrait itself was made in the summer of 1941 when LePan was in Toronto for a few months on his way from Harvard to join the Canadian Army in England. He sat for it in Lewis's Toronto studio.

Douglas LePan sitting under a drawing of himself by Wyndham Lewis, at LePan's apartment, 80 Quebec Avenue, 1987

The paintings of the Group of Seven are the best known in Canada but what is not so well known is that two of its members thought of themselves as poets. Lawren Harris was one and the other was J.E.H. Macdonald. Both men also claimed other authors among their closest friends, especially literary folk who liked to paint, such as Barker Fairley.

J.E.H. Macdonald (1874-1932) certainly lived on **Quebec Avenue** but where is confusing. I have found four different addresses for him on this street but whether he actually moved four times to separate abodes or whether the numbering of the street changed four times is not clear (this area was a relatively late annexation to the City of Toronto, and thus its records prior to that time are deficient). For example, for 1900-2, he is listed at **No.512**. He does not appear in the 1903 directory, but does in 1904 at **455 Quebec Avenue**. In 1907 he is listed at **No.105**, but at **No.475** for the following two years before allegedly returning to live at **No.105** for 1910-11. His correspondence that survives from that era does not clarify matters either. Suffice to say that he liked the street and lived on it for most of the first dozen years of the 20th c. His poems were often published in *Canadian Forum*, and a book of them, *West by East and Other Poems*, prepared and illustrated by his son Thoreau Macdonald, was published in 1933 by Ryerson Press.

The resilient children's author and infrequent writer for adults, Ella Bobrow (b.1911), arrived in Toronto with two children and two suitcases in 1950. Originally she was supposed to go to Saskatoon but never left Toronto. After passing from pillar to post like most immigrants after the war had to do, she had finally saved enough money by 1954 to buy her first house at **No.245** and kept it until 1969. She remembers this address with fondness because it was only here that she had, for the first time in her life, the time necessary to write. She received her first commission to write for children while living here, and here wrote her first work for adults, *Irina Istomina*, a long narrative poem first published in Russian and much later in English translation. Her writings have also been published in Germany and France.

Over the years, a few authors of note have attended Humberside Collegiate at **No.280**

Quebec. They include Donald Creighton, Lois Darroch, John Norman Harris, Violet May King, Margaret Avison, and Raymond Souster. Avison was three years ahead of Souster. The novelist Grace Irwin taught Latin and Greek here from 1931 until her retirement in 1969. Grace Irwin's presence was vital for another reason: it was she who led the campaign to stop the Board of Education from destroying a mural painted by Arthur Lismer for the school's auditorium. Incredibly, the mural was to be discarded during renovations. Most of the original mural was saved when it was moved to another location in the school, but were it not for Irwin's efforts, this the largest surviving painting by any member of the Group of Seven (the original was over sixteen feet high), would have been taken to the dump. Lismer's first biographer was a student at the school, Lois Darroch.

If you follow Glendonwynne Road which runs southwest from Humberside Collegiate, within three blocks you pass Western Technical School whose official address is **125 Evelyn Crescent**. Gwendolyn MacEwen (1941-87) studied here from 1954-58. Lady Byng, widow of the Governor General and herself a novelist paid a visit to the school in September 1944 to speak to the students. Tedd Steele (b.1922), the mystery novelist, also went to school here.

Ella Bobrow, whom we met just a few paragraphs ago, lived at **224 Evelyn Avenue** from 1969-79. Michael Coren, literary biographer and controversialist, currently lives on **Clendennan Avenue**. The novelist Eliza Clark (b.1963) wrote her second novel, *What You Need*, while living at **480 Clendennan** from Spring 1991 to August 1995.

Novelist Grace Irwin (b.1907) holds the record for longest residence at one address of any author I have encountered in my researches. With the exception of a two-year hiatus, she has lived at **33 Glenwood Avenue** since 1920. Irwin's father was a Methodist lay preacher who died when Grace was just entering her teens. Her mother was resourceful, however, as Grace recounts in her own words: "When I was twelve my mother made a brief essay in the business world. A post-war boom in the building trade was stretching into the open country north of Bloor Street between the Village of Swansea on the west and the southern fringe of Toronto Junction on the east. In 1911 my father had bought, for two thousand dollars, two lots on [nearby] Beresford Avenue. In 1919, on the advice of a friend also speculating in building, Mother sold our two Grenadier Road houses and built two houses there. Moving into one before it was completely finished, she invested in four lots on Glenwood Avenue and had houses erected on two of these. Selling the Beresford house over our heads, we moved into **33 Glenwood Avenue** six months after our first move . . . Undaunted, she purchased more property on the upper reaches of Forest Hill Road, and on Douglas Avenue. If our new house had sold (as I fervently prayed it would not), we should have moved again. But to my joy and relief, the market slowed. So we settled down, and, but for a two year absence, it has been my home ever since."

While Irwin's family was more religious than most, it would not have been considered extreme at the time, because its beliefs and practices were not that far removed from the mainstream. She relates how being a good Methodist, though, could lead to transportation challenges living in what was then the edge of the city: "For a family that attended at least three services every Sunday in the same church—and the degree to which social life and contacts centred on that church is almost unknown to our free-ranging, week-ending society—moving to a new neighbourhood presented a problem. For our family the problem was complicated, and not merely by the fact that we owned no car. Few of our friends owned one, and most of them 'put it up' for the winter—literally, removing the tires and propping the frame on supports in the garage, a new, but by no means common addendum. But few

urban dwellers were out of reach of the Toronto Street Railway; and though the final westerly limit at the time [1920] was a half mile from our house, and connecting buses were still several years in the future, the streetcar was available for us. But on Sunday we would not use it. I do not think we ever discussed the possibility."

Grace Irwin, who never married, was close to all of her siblings and especially her brother John. He had been working at the publishing company Macmillan in Toronto for only a year before he established with his brother-in-law, William Clarke, the house known as Clarke, Irwin & Co. The firm was famous for enforcing its strict morality on the part of the book-publishing world it controlled. Just how strict could border on the severe. I recall a joint reception in 1976 celebrating a gallery opening of paintings by Robert Bateman and the simultaneous publication of a book of his paintings by Clarke Irwin. When one of the senior Clarkes arrived at the hotel reception, she was mortified to find more than 100 people smoking and drinking. She ordered the publicity manager of her firm to inform each person in the room that the "beverage alcohol being served tonight is courtesy of the Moos Gallery, not Clarke Irwin."

That quirk aside, the house published a number of important Canadian authors, and for many years Grace Irwin sat on its board of directors. Most of her own novels, though, were published in Canada by McClelland and Stewart (her books were also published in the UK, USA, Norway, Germany, China, and Sweden). They are distinguished by their heroes, generally a person confronting grave and devotional doubts within the strictures of organized religion. Her first novel, *Least of All Saints* (1952), is still considered her best by literary critics. One of them, Barbara Pell, wrote: "It is the story of Andrew Connington, a cynical agnostic who enters the ministry in order to exercise his considerable intellectual and rhetorical gifts. Successful and admired in a prestigious church on the strength of his deception. He nevertheless is challenged by several spiritual crises and the influence of his devout fiancé and finally comes to genuine faith. The hero's intellectual tensions, the love story, and his final conversion are convincing and unsentimental. Irwin also vividly re-creates the setting of Toronto in the 1920s. The novel, published fifteen years after its inception, and after many publishers' rejections, made Irwin an instant bestseller and popular lecturer."

Grace Irwin, at age 91, is still writing, and still the co-pastor (since 1974) of the Emmanuel Christian Congregational Church she helped to found in 1953.

Glenwood Avenue ends at Fairview Avenue. Take Fairview north to **St. John's Road**. St. John's Hospital at **274 St. John's Road** is the last place where the remarkable pulp author Thomas P. Kelley (1905-82) spent his last months. His best-known book by far is *The Black Donnellys* (1954), which has sold hundreds of thousands of copies, and is one of the few books that bears his name on the cover. He used more than 30 pseudonyms when writing most of his material—which he estimated at over eight million words by 1970. He bragged that he could produce three stories (of 4,000 words each) in a single day, a credible claim because he had to write for the maws of such magazines as *True Confessions* and a myriad of trashy detective periodicals. Sometimes, he bragged, he wrote an entire magazine, cover to cover, using aliases to give the reader the impression that several writers were contributors. Fellow writer Scott Young "recounted how he and Kelley were walking along Wellington Street in the late 1940s when an editor of a pulp magazine rushed up to Kelley saying he needed a story immediately for a confessional magazine. Kelley was offered $200 if he could do it before noon. 'So I walked in' Kelley said, 'and he sat me down at a typewriter and I said "What's the title?" and the editor said "Type this at the top, *I Was a Love Slave*."' Before lunch Kelley had rejoined Young, the money in his pocket." Kelley, alas, was an alcoholic and when his wife and landlady could no longer care for him he was brought here around the end of 1981 and died without ever leaving.

St. John's Road crosses **Runnymede Road**. The Runnymede Public School at **357 Runnymede** can count poet Raymond Souster among its illustrious graduates. Another nearby resident was sound poet Paul Dutton (b.1943) who spent his boyhood (1944-69) living at **No.333**. At this address he wrote his first poems, a few of which appeared in his first book, *Right Hemisphere, Left Ear* (1979). Another poem written here appeared in *Horse d'Oeuvres*, the first widely available book of the amazing sound poetry group The Four Horsemen, of which Dutton was one-quarter.

BLOOR WEST VILLAGE

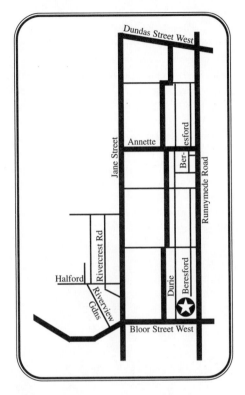

The tour begins at the northwest corner of Runnymede Road and Bloor Street West.

The Runnymede United Church, at **432 Runnymede Road**, once had the best-selling novelist Ralph Connor (1860-1937) as guest preacher. The *M&E* reported that on October 14, 1934 Connor gave "an impassioned plea for men and women and boys and girls to see the futility in the pursuit of wealth and power at the expense of all else." By this date the dailies had stopped their decades-long practice of reporting the sermons of better-known ministers. Yet Connor was so important a writer and a preacher in his day that what he had to say from the pulpit was considered news.

After his release from prison in 1969 for armed bank robbery, fiction writer Don Bailey (b.1942) became serious about his writing. His earliest residences in Toronto in the years immediately after jail were generally in rooming houses and were stays of short duration. For the first three months of 1972 he lived at **452 Runnymede Road**. From this address he seems to have moved to Vancouver, and apart from a year-long interlude about a decade later, he has not lived in Toronto, the city where he was born.

Biographer and novelist Lois Darroch (b.1912) lived one block to the west at **271 Beresford Avenue** beginning in 1924. She described what living at this time was like: "Harry Lauder and the Dumbells sang for the troops overseas and then for us at home. Charlie Chaplin and Mary Pickford played in that new wonder, the moving pictures, and the apes in a Tarzan film wore shoes. When the war was over my mother bobbed her hair long and abandoned her corsets. My father built a house on Beresford Avenue in the West End.

"We walked a mile to Humberside Collegiate, newly expanded. One day in the auditorium we heard Wilson MacDonald read his poetry. Eight of us formed a Poetry Club to indulge our new-found delight—write a poem every week or pay a dime fine. A dime was big money. The thrill of seeing our poems and short stories in the school magazine was incalculable . . . William Butler Yeats read in the Eaton Auditorium, the Stratford-on-Avon players performed in the Royal Alexandra Theatre. The Chicago Opera sang in that unlikely place, Maple Leaf Gardens, but you could hear a pin drop when Lily Pons sang the Flute Song.

"It was the height of the Depression. One year piece work, three years teaching high school in the sterile environment of small towns, then back to Beresford Avenue and a city collegiate job. The West End was now the sticks for one who still wanted to write. It was proper for an unmarried young woman to remain at home."

At **No.292**, poet Raymond Souster (b.1921) lived from 1942-47. Although he was away fighting the war for most of the early years here, this was his home when his first appearances between book covers took place, including the milestone anthology, *Unit of Five* (1944), and his first solo volume, *When We Are Young* (1946). **No.310** was briefly (1919-20) the home of novelist Grace Irwin (b.1907) before she moved to her house on Glenwood Avenue.

Playwright Allan Stratton (b.1951) reports that Bloor West Village is still his favourite part of town, although he now lives elsewhere. However, the area was home when he lived here from the Spring of 1981 until Spring 1987 at **No.494**. He wrote all of his play *Joggers* (1982) at this address and did major revisions to *Papers* (1985), *The 101 Miracles of Hope Chance*, and *Friends of a Feather* (1984), his Shaw Festival adaptation of the French farce *Célimare* by Labiche and Delacour.

W.O. Mitchell (1914-98) is usually associated with the prairies (especially because of his enduring novel *Who Has Seen the Wind*), but he lived in Toronto on three occasions. In the 1970s, already a well-established author, he was a writer-in-residence at the UofT, and then he taught at York University. But his first stay in the city was 1948-51, when he came from Alberta to be the fiction editor at *Maclean's* magazine. After residence in a friend's cottage on Hanlan's Point, and then Springdale Boulevard, Mitchell and his wife settled in the upper half of a duplex at **450 Durie Street** in 1950 and lived here until May 1, 1951, when the adventure with *Maclean's* came to an end and he returned to Alberta.

Walk back down Durie to Bloor Street West and turn right, to Jane Street. A few metres north of Bloor on the west side of Jane is **Rivercrest Road. 15 Rivercrest Road** was home for about two years to the Australia-born writer Albert Munday (1896-1957).

Munday came to Canada originally as the Trade Commissioner of the Bahamas in Ottawa. Deciding to stay, he worked as a newspaperman in Moose Jaw before arriving in Toronto in the middle of the Depression. He held reporting or editing jobs with the *News*, *Star*, and *Telegram*, and then was associate editor of *Maclean's* magazine for a year. His experience as an ace in WWI was put to good use in both his fiction and his non-fiction, much of which is devoted to flying (he was First Vice-President of the Toronto Flying Club). He was most acclaimed in his day for the novel *No Other Gods* (1934). Further up the street (**No.95**) is found the boyhood home of writer Karl Jirgens (born c. 1955). The greater part of his best-known fiction, *Strappado*, was written here.

W.O. Mitchell in his office at *Maclean's*, June 1948

One block west is **Halford Avenue**. Norma Harrs (b.1936) arrived in Winnipeg from Belfast in 1958 and there began to write plays and fiction, but it was not until she settled in Toronto in 1972 at **34 Halford Avenue** that she penned a novel, *A*

Certain State of Mind (1980). She also wrote two plays here: *Essential Conflict* (1984) and *The 40th Birthday Party* (1986).

The reigning poet laureate of the Ukraine lives not in Kiev but Toronto. Lydia Palij (pronounced paul-ee) came to Canada in 1948. Palij (born c. 1930) studied at the Ontario College of Art and then at the UofT. To pay the rent she has worked as a commercial artist for most of her life, but her first love is writing, especially poetry, although she has published fiction and art criticism. In addition to writing which has been of singular importance to Ukrainians, she has translated contemporary Ukrainian poets into English and Canadian poets into Ukrainian. Dorothy Livesay (whose mother translated several Ukrainian poets long before Lydia Palij came to Canada) listened to Lydia's attempts to render her own poems in English translation, and Livesay encouraged Palij to continue her translation projects. Since the collapse of the Soviet Union and the Soviet stranglehold on Ukrainian politics, Palij's writing has found a huge new audience in what was her homeland. Previous to 1990 her fiction and verse, while not overtly political, were unacceptable to the censorious authorities. She lived at **29 Halford Avenue** from 1974-95.

26 Halford Avenue was the only Toronto address of novelist Arthur Mayse (b.1912), who lived in the city from 1945-51. Mayse was born on the Peguis Indian Reserve in Manitoba but left for the B.C. coast as soon as he could, deeply in love with its landscape and challenges. He worked in logging camps to save money for his schooling in Vancouver and it was there he started his journalism career specializing in outdoor assignments. After service in WWII, he moved to Toronto, where his tales of life on the coast or in the mountains found favour with major magazines in the USA as well as Canada. He worked on a variety of Maclean Hunter trade journals before preceding W.O. Mitchell in the fiction editor's chair at *Maclean's* (1945-47). In 1951 he returned to the west coast, earning his living as a freelance. His novels include *Perilous Passage* (1949), serialized first in *Saturday Evening Post*, as was his second novel, *The Desperate Search* (1952), and his third, *Morgan's Mountain* (1960). His daughter, Susan Mayse (born c. 1948), spent her infant years also at this address until 1951. She has authored two books; the first was the novel *Merlin's Web* (1987).

At the south end of Halford Avenue turn right and walk a few metres to **Riverview Gardens**. Gladys Joy Tranter (1902-72) was an immigrant from Ireland in 1919 who settled originally in western Canada and came to Toronto in 1939. She was no sooner in the city, it seems, than she left it temporarily to be present at the rehearsals of her play *Around the Flagstone* at the Pasadena Playhouse, then the leading theatre west of the Mississippi. She played one of the leads. Tranter may have lived at **45 Riverview Gardens** as early as 1939 but I can place her here definitely for two years only: 1942 and 1943. A few years later she published *Ploughing the Arctic* (1945), an account of the *St. Roch*'s sail through the Northwest Passage, and had the odd experience of seeing the book published in the UK, as well as in the French and Scandinavian languages before the book was available in Toronto. Even then, she did not have a Canadian publisher; copies of the British edition had to be imported a full season after the book was published abroad. It later found a publisher in Canada, and then in Holland. Also successful was her CBC radio serial *Bridget and Pat* that ran from 1932-38. The narrative poem *A Soldier's Legacy* was serialized in the popular American magazine *Good Housekeeping* and was shortly thereafter published in Finland. She was a popular speaker at literary gatherings in Toronto in the 1940s and 1950s. At some point in the 1960s she moved to Vancouver, but returned to our city a few years before she died at Toronto General Hospital on April 25, 1972—popular while alive and almost completely forgotten after death. No Toronto newspapers ran obituaries.

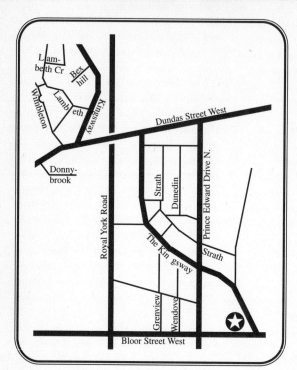

The tour begins at the
Old Mill Subway Station.

Walk about six blocks west to **Wendover Road**. Head north. When novelist Paul Vasey (b.1945) was born in Toronto he and his parents lived at **8 Wendover Road** for the first year or two of his infancy.

Wendover ends at The Kingsway. Follow The Kingsway northwest for one block and take the first street on the right (Grenview Boulevard) which leads to **Strath Avenue**. Turn right. The celebrated Canadian novelist Carol Shields (b.1935) lived in Toronto twice. The first time was 1957–59. The second was after she and her husband had returned from a three-year stop in England. They bought the house at **41 Strath Avenue**. Carol describes her stay here: "I enclose a snap by the front door. Notice white gloves. I can tell from the size

of the children that this was taken in 1968, just a few months before we packed up and moved to Ottawa . . . By this time I had published a few more short stories, written some poems which had been published in *The Canadian Forum* (payment was a free subscription, or perhaps it was half a subscription), and had been one of the winners in the CBC Young Writers Competition. Young was under-30 and I just slipped in under the wire. These were interesting days in Toronto, all the controversy over the Archer, and the new City Hall design. I was astonished to be downtown one summer evening, 1964 I think, and see a genuine love-in in Nathan Philips Square. In 1966 I went to the Parliament Street library one stormy night to hear Irving Layton read his poetry. He was not particularly well known then; I remember that occasion with great warmth. Also went about the same time to hear Gwen MacEwen read at the Classics Bookstore in the Colonnade. I knew no writers.

"This is heresy for a Winnipegger to say, but I love Toronto. I'm there quite often, and now have two daughters who live there. I love the domestic side of the city, the houses and neighbourhoods, and the street life along west Bloor on a Saturday afternoon."

To date, Shields is best known for her novel *Stone Diaries* (1993), which won both the Governor General's Award and the Pulitzer Prize (she has dual Canadian/American citizenship). Two of her earlier works are set in Toronto: *The Box Garden* (1977) and *Swann: A Mystery* (1987). The latter

Carol Shields on the front doorstep of 41 Strath Avenue, 1968

reporter in Moose Jaw. After some years there he came to Toronto to work in editorial positions for most of the dailies before joining *Maclean's* magazine. In the *Canadian Who's Who* he said his favourite pastimes included big-game hunting, horseback riding, and Arctic exploration. No sedentary author he—although he did die relatively young in 1957. His passing went unnoticed by the newspapers for whom he once worked.

Further north we find **88 Dunedin Drive,** where poet and critic Dennis Lee (b.1939) spent the first 20 years of his life. From here he would travel to the UofT and later, to international acclaim as one of our most respected poets for adults—and for children.

The Kingsway North crosses Royal York Road at Dundas and, if you're driving, continues north a couple of hundred metres west of Royal York Road. However, if you are walking or biking, continue north directly on Royal York until Lambeth Road (the first street north of Dundas on the west side). This intersects with the re-continued Kingsway. Take The Kingsway and go north about a hundred metres to **Bexhill Court.**

5 Bexhill Court is the first address in Toronto I've been able to find for a woman who wrote under the name Jan Hilliard but whose real was name was Kay Grant (1910-96). She is generally unknown today—but in her time she was a highly regarded Canadian writer, winner of the Leacock Medal for Humour in 1952 for *The Salt Box*, and literary praise from *The New Yorker*. In all she published four novels, two memoirs, and two biographies: one on Samuel Cunard, reminding us that she was a Bluenose, born in Yarmouth, Nova Scotia. Kay Grant informed William Arthur Deacon in 1951, apparently in all seriousness, "I've had quite an uneventful life. I've found as other women writers have

won the Arthur Ellis Award, given annually to the best work of mystery fiction published by a Canadian.

Going northwest on Strath it is possible, by a mildly circuitous route, to arrive at **Dunedin Drive. No.11** was home from 1942-53 to Albert Munday (1896-1957), the longest of any of his residencies in Toronto. Munday was a Fellow of the Royal Geographic Society and a writer of novels concerned largely with flying and with western Canada, although his first book was a volume of poetry published by Briggs in Toronto in 1916. A native of Melbourne, Australia, he travelled extensively and somehow became Trade Commissioner of the Bahamas to this country—a diplomatic position. For some reason he abandoned that job to work as a cub found, that scrubbing floors and writing make a good team. Housework is good exercise but such a disenchanting occupation that one must think of something else while doing it—and what better way than making up stories?" She lived at this address from 1955-58, and then moved nearby to Royal York Road and Richview where she lived until at least 1970. I'm not able to give a more exact location because, incredibly, as late as 1970, this intersection was still a postal rural route and specific numbers for homes were not used. Looking at this area now with its urban sprawl and postwar design, it's hard to believe it was ever bucolic. However, in a 1959 letter to an editor at the *Star Weekly*, Grant/Hilliard described her house's setting as "outside Toronto" and blessed with a wildflower garden, an adjacent forest and plenty of pheasants!

Moose Jaw, already linked to Albert Munday above, was the birthplace of playwright Jack Winter (b.1936), who lived just a couple of blocks to the north of Bexhill at **308 The Kingsway** from 1952-54. He came to this city initially to commence his doctoral studies at the UofT, then to do postgraduate study at York University. At the same time he was busy writing dramas, and became playwright-in-residence (1963-67), at Toronto Workshop Productions on Alexander Street. *Hey Rube!* is the best known of the plays emerging from that era. He also made time to write scripts for radio and TV. A short movie for which he had written the script, *Selling Out* (1971), was nominated for an Academy Award. Although he was very much at the centre of the magnificent decade-long storm in Toronto that saw so many plays—and theatres—emerge (1967-77), he left it all behind to travel to England to pursue the literary life there, mostly as a poet. Of late, no one knows where he is. McMaster University Library has many of his papers, but their correspondence to him is returned as "Current Whereabouts Unknown" and their further efforts to find him have failed. As have mine.

Fans of Albert Munday will want to note that he lived elsewhere in this area: at **145 Wimbleton Road** from 1954-57. The street runs roughly parallel to the Kingsway north of Dundas.

Our final stop on this tour is just south of Dundas and is related to novelist Margaret Drury-Gane (b.1926). Born in the centre of the city, she moved to this westerly area after she was married. She lived at **31 Donnybrook Lane** from 1954-65. In 1967 she moved to an older house just a few blocks away and has lived there ever since. It was here that she wrote her one novel published to date, *Parade on an Empty Street* (1978), as well as her 12 published short stories and several articles for Canadian, American and Australian magazines. When asked what Toronto meant to her, good or bad, as an author, she replied, "Wherever an author lives is bound to affect both the perception and realization of her work, fiction or factual. And the impact is two-fold, I think: personal circumstances and the climate of childhood deeply influence writing. Then there is the general 'feel' of a particular city—what Jan Morris refers to as *fizz* and *sizzle*—whether it's old grandeur, sleaziness, brashness, quaintness, whatever. The Toronto in my novel was a stubbornly British, insular, often puritanical cluster of villages compared to the Toronto I wrote about later on. But certainly 1939 and the onset of the last war marked the beginning of those changes. Obviously everyone is deeply affected by the environment in which they live—but probably writers, who absorb, observe, and obey the inner compulsion to write it all down, must be the ones to preserve what they've seen. It's a *private* accuracy, of course which we can only hope touches readers in the same way."

DE LA SALLE/OAKLANDS

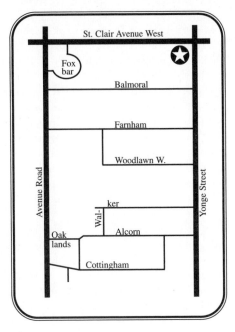

The tour begins at the southwest corner of Yonge Street and St. Clair Avenue West.

Walk west on the south side of St. Clair until you reach Deer Park United Church at **129 St. Clair Avenue West.** Two noted authors have been guests of honour here. Lloyd Douglas (1877-1951), author of *The Robe* and other mega-sellers, lived for a number of years as the pastor of a huge congregation in Montreal. He travelled to Toronto infrequently, but when he did, the churches where he spoke were packed. His first visit to Toronto was occasioned not by a sermon but by a speech he gave, "Writing For Profit and Reading for Fun," at Deer Park United Church on November 22, 1932. There was much publicity in the media before the talk, and the event was considered important enough that the *Star* reported it on page one.

A speech delivered at this church on November 8, 1935 by novelist and belletrist

Nellie McClung (1873-1951) was also given front-page treatment by the *Star* under the inimitable hand of R.E. Knowles. His first question to her gives a good sense of his feminist credentials, "Mrs. McClung, is it possible for a lady to be a successful writer—and still be stylish?"

Foxbar Road nearby runs south off St. Clair Avenue. The playwright Herschel Hardin (b.1936) reported: "I lived on the top floor of a three-storey house at **32 Foxbar Road** from the fall of 1961 to the spring of 1962. Part of that time was spent doing a finished draft of *The Great Wave of Civilization* while my wife supported us by work at the UofT Library. Alas, the inspiration of Avenue Road and St. Clair which form a triangle with Foxbar did not add much to my play about the liquor trade in northern Montana and southern Alberta. Nor did the alcoholic in a 'suite' (actually a room) on the second floor, although he drank enough liquor to support a trade in hooch all by himself. On the other hand, the kitchen in our apartment was a converted closet without a window. The kitchen sink was the washbasin on the other side of the large single room. Best of all, the sloping ceiling genuinely qualified me as an unsung literary genius working in a garret. What more, other than a higher ceiling, could a young writer ask for?" The play he refers to was first produced at Festival Lennoxville under the direction of Paul Thompson. Another man of the theatre, Timothy Findley (b.1930), passed part of his boyhood living with his paternal grandmother at **No.27** from 1935-36.

Crime novelist Howard Engel (b.1931) spent the last months of 1974 trying his hand at poetry rather than prose when he lived at **136 Balmoral Avenue**—apparently without success, for none has been published. Fiction writer Alice Boissonneau (*Stories From Ontario*, 1974) was ensconced from 1954-55 at **No.102**, as she described: "Pitch dark under the two slanted ceilings of the front and back rooms shared with a friend, Joan. A sink, a tiny gas stove, what a luxury. Water brought up in pails from the bathroom below . . . As you entered from the porch on Balmoral, the face of the bleached blonde landlady would appear through the doorway of the downstairs parlour, darkened for television, still new then, tears damp in her eyes over some soap opera . . . In our high location during that fall's unprecedented heatwave, we wore dressing gowns and ran the electric fan. This caused feelings of quick alarm below. On returning through the dark door after grocery shopping . . . the landlady's voice shrilled from below, 'This is a high class respectable neighbourhood!' She then cut off our electricity for lights—and the fan." Playwright Ken Gass (b.1945), the founder of Factory Theatre Lab and its current Artistic Director, lived at **No.94** from 1989 until 1991.

Some of the world's best science fiction writers have called Toronto home: William Gibson, A.E. Van Vogt, Robert Sawyer among them. In addition, the city has produced a battalion of excellent writers in the genre who are much respected by cognoscenti but who are not so well known to mainstream readers. Among these is S.M. Stirling (b.1954): "I settled in Metro in September of 1976—Downsvoid, actually; I was at Osgoode Hall Law School, part of York University—and have lived here ever since. Earlier residences included Ottawa, Nairobi, and Metz, France where I was born. For most of the period 1979-87 I lived in an apartment complex [**1348 Yonge Street**] right across from CHUM on Yonge Street. There I wrote the manuscript of my first novel, *Snowbrother,* which was published by NAL/Signet in 1985, and *The Sharpest Edge* (written in collaboration with Shirley Meier) published by NAL/Signet in 1986."

Tedd Steele (b.1922), the pulp fiction novelist, had a flat at **4 Farnham Avenue** in the last three years of the 1950s. Novelist and journalist Colin Sabiston (1893-1961) also dwelt here for a couple of years upon retirement from the editorial board of the *G&M* and remained until his death.

Charles Bruce (1906-71) moved to Toronto in 1933 to work for Canadian Press. Before he retired he was the General Superintendent of the company. In 1941 he and his family moved to **40 Farnham** and he stayed here until his death in December 1971. For some reason, Bruce's only novel has attracted until now more attention than all of his poetry books combined. This is odd, because he is a more interesting poet than he is a writer of fiction. Regardless of discipline, almost all of his creative work is concerned with, or inspired by, his native Maritimes. He came into his own as a writer at this address after the traumas of WWII. *The Flowing Summer* (1947) is a long narrative poem about a Toronto boy who returns to his ancestral home in Nova Scotia. A better book is *The Mulgrave Road* (1952), winner of the Governor General's Award for Poetry. And it was here he typed his novel, *The Channel Shore* (1954).

Louis MacKay (b.1901) graduated from the UofT a Rhodes Scholar. Upon his return

Louis A. MacKay

from Oxford he began a distinguished career as an academic and was regarded, along with Leon Edel and W.E. Collin, as one of Canada's best literary critics. But he is also included here because he published *The Ill-Tempered Lover and Other Poems* (1948), as well as a play written first in French and then translated by the author into English. Under the pseudonym John Smalacome he published the small poetry book *Viper's Bugloss* (1938). From 1933-41 he made his home at **45 Farnham Avenue** with his wife, the daughter of Hector Charlesworth, and for most of this stretch he was the associate editor of *Canadian Forum*.

Playwright John Krizanc (b.1956) lived at **No.50**. He described the house as "my wife Carolyn's family home. Apparently it was used as a police station in the 1800s—it certainly is one of the nicer homes on the street—and we lived here from about November 1982 until May 1983. I re-wrote *Tamara* for its Los Angeles opening here, and also began work on *Prague*." Whether by luck or by fate, immediately before living on Farnham, Krizanc lived from 1980-82 just around the corner at **1404-A Yonge Street** in a one-room bachelor where he "scribbled the first draft of *Tamara*, first performed at the Toronto World Stage Theatre Festival in May 1981."

The husband and wife team of John Garvin (1859-1935) and Katherine Hale (1878-1956) were highly visible in the Toronto literary scene in the first decades of the 20th c., he especially as an anthologist, and she as a poet and book-page editor. From 1914-16 they made their home at **117 Farnham**.

De La Salle Oaklands at **No.131** has taught three novelists who, for one reason or another, are well known in our own time. Pierre Salinger (b.1925) came to Toronto with his parents in 1929 and was quickly recognized as a child prodigy at the piano. He was enrolled at the Conservatory to study for half-days under the internationally acclaimed Clement Hambourg, and the other half-days he studied at De La Salle. The family returned to the USA c. 1933. In 1960, Salinger became the Press Secretary of President John F. Kennedy. He is now retired as the Chief Foreign Correspondent of ABC News. His novel *On Instructions of My Government* was published in 1971, and much more controversially, he wrote the Introduction to the 1998 English translation of short stories by Muammar Qaddafi, the dictator of Libya.

Hugh Hood (b.1928) attended grades seven to thirteen at De La Salle from 1938-45. And M.T. Kelly (b.1946), although he found De La Salle unpleasant, did have his life changed there: "My first literary experience—it's an inexact label, but comes close; perhaps I should say self-conscious epiphany—occurred in the corner of the De La Salle library. This library stressed such books as the Hardy Boys mysteries, there wasn't much, but they had *The Old Man and The Sea* by Ernest Hemingway, perhaps thinking it was a safe book. I clearly remember holding the book and reading the opening. That moment. Here, I must have felt, was dignity. Later I argued with my mother about the part where the fisherman urinates over the side of the boat; but any shock value to me must have surely been that here was life—here was how to be in the world."

On August 8, 1918, Miss Florence Deeks set out from her home, **140 Farnham Avenue**, to deliver her manuscript (which she titled *The Web*) to the Macmillan Company of Canada. Macmillan had not asked to see the work. It was an over-the-transom submission. The tome was a general history of the world. As is the way of publishers, it lingered on the shelves until someone thought to return it to the author six months later, along with a rejection slip. Which should have been the end of the matter. Except that H.G. Wells published his *Outline of History* not long after with the same publisher, albeit the Macmillan based in New York. To Ms. Deeks this was not synchronicity, but rather blatant plagiarism and she launched a lawsuit that dragged on for years, rising from the legal doldrums every once and a while to claim a place on the front pages of newspapers in Canada, the USA, and UK. The case was absurd and that it lasted as long as it did is surely as astounding as the initial credibility given to any of Deeks's claims. She maintained, for example, that during the half-year her manuscript was with Macmillan for consideration, the house sneaked a copy to Wells so that he could steal its structure and insights. That Deeks herself had based her unpublished work almost exclusively on an already published outline of history seemed not to bother her. The case was finally put down like a sick dog, but not before it had cost all parties a great deal—and more than just cash. In 1937 Hector Charlesworth made observations about the matter which could as well be made today: "It may be noted here that newspapers everywhere treat charges of plagiarism, always easy to formulate, with too much levity; a sort of 'may-the-best-man-win-and-the-devil-take-the-hindmost' attitude. Even when Mr. Wells emerged with his reputation unscathed, and publishing firms accused of gross acts of perfidy were completely exonerated, the matter was treated casually, as though the decision might very well have gone the other way, with nobody the worse off. An action more or less unique, claiming half a million dollars in damages and demanding other penalties, does not arise every day and newspapers naturally exploited it, but few gave consideration to the feelings and reputation of honourable men, who over a period of some years, had to face the accusation that they had been guilty of disgraceful conduct."

Three authors have lived at **No.150**. The radio playwright, producer, and director Andrew Allan (1907-74) lived in apt. 210 from 1957-68. Another acclaimed veteran of radio drama, Len Peterson (b.1917), had an apartment here from 1952-54. And novelist and evangelist Charles Templeton (b.1915) was here even earlier, 1947-48.

Woodlawn Avenue runs south from the middle of Farnham. **93 Woodlawn Avenue West** was where E.K. Brown was born in 1905 and where he spent his earliest years. Brown's importance rests in the fact that he established—with erudite authority—the first canon for the study of Canadian literature. His study *On Canadian Poetry* (1943) remains compulsory reading for serious students of our literary culture. He died far too early in 1951.

John Morgan Gray (1907-78) began to work at the publishing firm Macmillan in 1930 and was managing director by 1946. Three years later he moved to **60 Woodlawn** and lived at this address until he died. During the time he lived here, he became president of the firm, and had the pleasure of seeing a number of eminent authors added to the Macmillan list, including Grey Owl and Morley Callaghan. Undoubtedly it was also here that he listened in 1953 to the 13-episode, CBC radio adaptation of his own novel, *The One-Eyed Trapper*.

The playwright William S. Milne (1902-79) made his living as the head of the English dept. at Northern Secondary School for 34 years. He specialized in one-act plays, all of which were produced. And most were published by Samuel French. He won the Canadian Drama Award in 1958 while living at **No.41** between 1956 and 1965.

A "bad boy" of CanLit in the 1960s was novelist Scott Symons (b.1933). One of the reasons he was regarded as an outsider, apart from the singular nature of his fiction (and the exotic manner in which it was designed and printed), was his public declaration of his homosexuality. This may not seem unusual today, but at the time the practice was still illegal in Canada. And tongues wagged as well because Symons was married. All of which tended to obscure appreciation of his work, although a younger generation is now celebrating his writing. From 1979-81, during an infrequent return to Canada from his home in Morocco, he lived at **20 Woodlawn**.

1238 Yonge Street holds large significance for fiction writer and journalist David Lewis Stein (b.1937): "We moved to a cigar store lunch counter my father had somehow managed to rent [c.1941-47] at the corner of Yonge and Walker Street. We were there for another seven years, living on top of the store. Those years were the most important for me. I think my fascination with cities and the way streets work comes from sitting on a stool in the lunch counter my parents ran. . . . That little store, which was known then as Murray's Smokeshop, although I never did know who Murray was, was certainly the beginning of my literary education. I was allowed to read anything on the floor to ceiling magazine rack. I started with the comic books which were then all black and white because of the war, and worked my way up to *Argosy* and *True*, the men's adventure magazines, and on to *Time Magazine* and *Photoplay* which used to novelize the latest movies . . . Class lines at that time were sharply drawn. Walker Avenue, which had larger houses with gables and front lawns, was strictly middle class . . . Alcorn Avenue, one block to the south, was dominated by the factory that supplied all the Hunt's Bakery Stores. The houses on Alcorn were small row-houses right on the street with no front lawns at all. The children from Alcorn went to Cottingham School. Today, both Alcorn and the complex of streets around Cottingham have all been gentrified but at that time, they were the working class streets while Walker and the streets above it, going up to St. Clair, were for the middle class. We lived there until 1947 when the owner of the store sold it out from under my parents . . . ."

Novelist Fred Bodsworth (b.1918), author of *The Last of the Curlews* (1954), came to Toronto to work as a reporter at the *Star* and just before he married in 1944 lived for about half a year at **20 Walker Avenue**, where he tried his hand at nature writing and fiction, but also where he "was unpopular because I often kept my typewriter clacking until late in the night." Mazo de la Roche (1879-1961) lived at **No.29** in 1924, and at **No.121** in 1926, just two of the many places in Toronto where she stayed for a year or less. She was writing stories at these addresses, and at **No.121** was also undoubtedly working on *The Whiteoaks of Jalna*, the novel which, the following year, would launch her onto the world stage as a bestselling writer. Another bestselling woman author, Barbara Betcherman (1948-83), lived at **No.39** in 1977. Following the big international success of her thriller *Suspicions*, she moved to California where she was killed, struck by a car. The poet Gary Geddes (b.1940) is known to tens of thousands of university students as the editor of *Fifteen Canadian Poets*—the standard textbook for CanLit courses since the 1960s. While recuperating from a broken marriage in 1968, he lived first at **No.94** and then at **No.62**. Crime novelist and literary radio producer Howard Engel found accommodation at **No.127** from 1975-76.

No writers of renown have lived on **Alcorn Avenue**, the next street to the south, but in the 1990s **No.10** became the new headquarters of Penguin Books of Canada, a firm well into its second decade of publishing eminent Canadian authors, including Audrey Thomas and Roch Carrier.

The address of the store at the east end of Alcorn is **1224 Yonge Street**, the second home in this area of short-story writer David Lewis Stein. He explained how his family came to settle here in September 1949 after a disastrous interlude in California: "There were only four launderettes in the city at the time and my parents had the idea that this would be an ideal location for a launderette. But my father had lost his nerve as well as his money in California and he began to gulp sleeping pills and stay in bed all day. Lou __ , and Harry Tepperman, his closest friends came and wanted to send him to a nursing home. My mother told them if they put my father in a nursing home he would die there. So what could they do to help? Get me a plumber, my mother said.

"Washing machines are solid little machines now but in 1949 the Bendix machines were not really suitable for the hard use they got in launderettes and they required special plumbing and had to be held down with four-foot-long steel bolts, or else they would shake loose during the spin cycles and take off on their own. The floor of our store had been ripped up to make room for all the plumbing but nobody seemed to know how to do it properly. For months we had been crossing the floor on a narrow bridge of boards. It looked like we were going to lose this place too. But the next morning we heard a loud banging at the front door. A little man with a toothbrush moustache and an overcoat that, in my memory, hung down to his ankles, was waiting for us. We came to know him simply as Mr. Baum. He was a plumbing contractor who had been sent to my mother by Lou __. Mr. Baum and my mother set up the launderette and when it was up and running my father got out of bed and began to run it. It became a neighbourhood attraction. My mother hung pictures on the wall and advertised it as the first combination launderette and art gallery in the city."

Pedestrians can reach **Cottingham Street**, two blocks to the south, via the school grounds. The poet R.G. Everson (1903-92) had rooms at **135 Cottingham** during his first year at the UofT, 1923-24. Soon after graduating, Everson would start to publish the books that secured him a place among the best poets of his generation in Canada. The distinguished writer Arthur S. Bourinot (1893-1969) spent most of his life in Ottawa, but did his undergraduate degree at the UofT. The only records that survive from that era show him living at **152 Cottingham** from 1914-15, after which he went overseas to fight (he was captured and was a POW for the last two years of the war). In 1939 he won the Governor General's Award for Poetry. In addition, he was one of the leading critics of Canadian verse, publishing many books on the subject, and was an extremely active and helpful member of the major national literary organizations. Another UofT graduate who has spent most of her adult life elsewhere is Toronto-born Marian Quedneau (b.1952), winner of the *Books in Canada* First Novel Award for *The Butterfly Chair* (1988). During her second year at university she roomed at **No.162**.

Robertson Davies had two homes in his later years. One was in Caledon, a village north of Toronto. The other was in Toronto proper. From 1981 until his death in 1995 he lived on **Oaklands Avenue**.

Poplar Plains

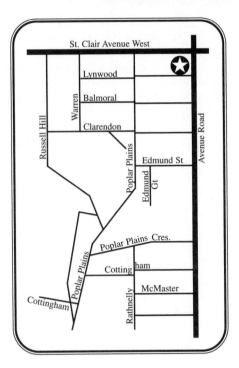

The tour begins at the southwest corner of St. Clair Avenue West and Avenue Road.

The Unitarian Church at **175 St. Clair Avenue West**, just west of Avenue Road, has invited a few notable speakers into its embrace through the decades. Authors who have addressed congregations here include John Kenneth Galbraith, Sir Julian Huxley, Irving Layton, Wilson MacDonald, Alan Paton, and J.B. Priestley. Usually, authors combine many lecture engagements into one tour, but in the case of Alan Paton (*Cry the Beloved Country*) he was flown all the way from South Africa to Toronto by the Committee of Concern for South Africa to talk on "Current South African Problems." More than 700 people listened to his speech on October 18, 1960.

Return to **Avenue Road** and head south about a block. Fiction writer David Lewis

Stein (b.1937) went to Brown School at **454 Avenue Road** for grades six to eight but, as he reported: "I grew to loathe the place. It wasn't just that I was the only Jew in the school; it was the mean, ugly class structure that was imposed on us. After a few fights, I didn't have much trouble being accepted as a Jew. But I was definitely lower class, living at the bottom of the Yonge Street hill and over a launderette . . . My best friend in grade seven and eight at Brown School was Bill Berney, who was a great athlete and always stood at the top of the class without ever opening a book. He was a natural at everything. The teachers called his father in and said Bill would really be happier at Jesse Ketchum or Cottingham, the schools below the Avenue Road hill. Bill's father asked a few questions and although his English wasn't very good he caught on pretty quickly to what the game was. They were telling him they didn't think the son of a Sicilian stonemason really belonged in Brown School—even if he was at the top of the class. The old man told them Bill was in the Brown School district and he was staying in the school. Period. But that was the kind of place Brown School was. Beginning in grade six, the good kids—the ones whose parents had money—were siphoned off to Upper Canada and Ridley and private school. By grade eight only the dregs were left. In my gang in grade eight, I was the only one who went to a collegiate high school with the vague idea of going to university. The rest all went to trade schools . . . Some of those boys were bright and capable and might have done almost anything. But the class system of Toronto in the 50s closed off opportunities for them. So I have little nostalgic feeling for the Toronto I grew up in."

Another noted journalist, Robert Fulford (b.1932), has lived on **Lynwood Avenue** for almost two decades. Lynwood ends at **Warren Road** where poet bp Nicol lived at **No.48** from 1975-78 he wrote and published *Journal* (1977), one of his rare forays as a novelist. He became actively involved as an editor with Coach House Press during this period, the house that published most of his writing before and after his death. For those who care about sound and concrete poetry, Barry Nichol was one of the best, known and respected internationally. In his later years, he published more straightforward free verse which attracted thousands of new readers who were indifferent to, or frightened by, his more marginal experimentation.

Painter Lawren Harris (1885-1970), while best known as a leader of the Group of Seven, was also a poet of some talent and his volume *Contrasts* was published in 1922 by McClelland and Stewart. When Harris married in 1910, he and his wife moved to **176 Balmoral Avenue**, where they remained until moving to Cottingham Street about three years later. This was a crucial period in Harris's life. In 1911 he met Arthur Lismer, and in 1912 he sold his first painting to the National Gallery of Canada. It was also in 1912 that he put up a large part of the money for the construction of the Studio Building on Severn Street, where the Group could paint in proper conditions.

Phyllis Brett Young lived in apt. 1004 at **160 Balmoral** from 1961 to 1967. It was while living here that her novels *Anything Could Happen*, *The Ravine*, and *Undine* were written and published, and that Boston University began to collect her papers, obviously holding her work in higher regard than did her compatriots—although her second novel, *The Torontonians* (1960), sold thousands of copies in Toronto alone and had a good reception among reviewers.

Novelist and noted translator Joyce Marshall (b.1913) resided at **450 Avenue Road** from 1949-50.

Frances Shelley Wees (1902-82) wrote and published her second mystery novel, *Under the Quiet Water* (1948), while living at **8 Clarendon Avenue** from 1947-52. Wees published stories, poems, and articles in many of the slick magazines in the 1940s and 1950s, as well as other well-received mystery novels. She also ran the Canadian Chautauquas for a number of years while making a living as a public-relations professional. Lawren Harris, the painter and poet, lived at **18 Clarendon** in 1913 and 1914, years that corresponded to his supervision of the construction of the Studio Building, a structure that was originally intended to include a theatre and art gallery but which, even simply by providing studio space for painters such as Arthur Heming, A.Y. Jackson, and J.E.H. Macdonald, had a huge influence on Canadian cultural life.

Nearby is **224 Poplar Plains Road** where the bestselling novelist Sam Llewellyn (b.1948) wrote large parts of his first two novels. His books deal with various aspects of sailing and seafaring and are hugely popular around the world. He arrived in Toronto in March 1976 and moved in 1978 to this address, his last before departing for his native Britain in June 1979. He is refreshingly unpretentious about his work, despite its commercial success: " . . . at Poplar Plains Road I wrote first *Gurney's Revenge*, a saga of violence, passion, lust and navigation in the Chinese Opium Wars, and its sequel, *Gurney's Reward*. Both these books were published by Arlington, Corgi and Bantam. They are entirely without literary merit but possess a certain hectic vigour . . . my memories of this seminal three year period are what in medical circles is called a bit of a blur. I have to say that Toronto has had no great direct bearing on my literary life, probably because I do not write a hell of a lot of literature . . . Recently, I have written some seafaring murder mysteries. Many of the savage bastards between their pages are based on people I came across in RCYC evening races in Toronto harbour, continuing the day's dirty dealings in the stock exchange and their law offices by other means."

Another mystery novelist who settled in this area after arriving from the UK is Anthony Quogan (1937). He had rooms at **7 Edmund** from 1965-66. His stay overlapped with that of novelist Leo Simpson (b.1934), who also lived here 1964-66 while employed at Macmillan as an editor and publicity director.

When novelist and playwright David Young (b.1946) moved into a two-room apartment on the second floor of **342 Avenue Road** in 1969, he was determined to become a serious author. He described his two and half years at this address: "My windows faced the Benvenuto. Massive cooking smells in the hall, everything slathered with thick layers of lime green. I painted my place red, white and blue. Installed industrial lighting. My first official writing desk was set up. A series of short stories produced during this period were cordially rejected by House of Anansi. Hadn't yet met my first Canadian author."

As we walk along **Cottingham Street** to get to Poplar Plains Road, note **No.200**, where Colin Sabiston, former drama critic of the *G&M* (and author of one novel) lived throughout the 1950s.

Cottingham Street leads to the southern stretch of **Poplar Plains Road**. W. Stewart Wallace (1994-1970) lived at **No.59** from the end of one world war to another: 1919-46. The longer one studies our literary history, the more one is impressed by Wallace's pioneering work and his love of his country. For his general editorship of the six-volume *The Encyclopedia of Canada* alone he deserves ongoing applause, but of course he wrote or compiled several other essential tomes. Wallace's textbooks on Canadian history were used in schools for decades. He was the founder of the *Canadian Historical Review* in 1920 and for more than 30 years he was an editor of the Champlain Society. While living at this address in 1936, he was awarded the Tyrrell Gold Medal from the Royal Society of Canada, one of the country's highest honours given to historians.

Poet James Reaney (b.1926) and his wife Colleen Thibaudeau (b.1925) had rooms at **No.51** for about three years in the late 1950s, while another husband-and-wife writing team, Donald and Luella Creighton, also lived in the area in 1954, just a few steps away at **36 Poplar Plains**.

The crime novelist Eve Zaremba wrote *Privilege of Sex: A Century of Canadian Women*, her only non-fiction book to date, while living at two addresses on nearby **Cottingham Road**: **No.184** in 1972 and **No.200** from 1973-74.

10 Rathnelly Avenue has provided accommodation to three writers this century. The poet Helen Merrill Egerton dwelled here from 1921 until c. 1925 and probably longer. The dramatist John R. Gray (b.1927), who was here from 1956-59, quit his job as assistant editor at *Maclean's* in 1957 in order to write his first play, *Bright Sun at Midnight*, produced at the Crest Theatre that same year. The play was a treatment of the alleged suicide in Cairo by the Canadian diplomat Howard Norman. The following year he wrote the lyrics for the musical *Ride a Pink Horse*—again produced at the Crest. Before he left Rathnelly he had written a large part of *The Teacher*, which was produced at the Stratford Festival in 1960. The cultural critic and journalist Robert Fulford (b.1932) was resident here from 1962 to 1974. He began his editorship of *Saturday Night* while living here. For two years before moving here he had lived around the corner at **1 McMaster Avenue**.

Brian Vallee's thriller *Pariah* (1991) won him an international following, but his first book was a non-fiction bestseller in Canada, *Life with Billy* (1986), revealing how a battered woman finally turned on her husband and murdered him. Vallee came to Toronto in 1973 to work as the first Queen's Park columnist for the newly created *Sun*, a job he held for about six months before moving to the *Star*. A few years later he switched media and began working at CBC-TV's investigative program "the fifth estate." His home from 1973 until 1987 was **13 McMaster Avenue**.

When the comic novelist Donald Jack (b.1924) lived with his new bride at **No.20**, he had his first success as an author. He recounted its origins: "By now married, I was to be found at **20 McMaster Avenue**, off Avenue Road, Nancy and I in one ground-floor front room of a house owned by a Chinese couple and their three delightful girls . . . I had a baby of my own by then . . . At the time I was earning a living as a proof machine operator with the Canadian Bank of Commerce (as it was then) from five to eleven p.m., and attending the Canadian Theatre School [at Bay and College Streets] during the day. But it was while I was at McMaster that I wrote my first success, a play called *Minuet for Brass Band* which was put on by the theatre school and received high praise from the newspapers, magazines and radio. As a result of its success, I was offered a job as script writer with Crawley Films Ltd., which took me to Ottawa for two years."

After Barker Fairley moved from Alberta to Toronto in 1915 to teach in the German dept. at the UofT, he and his wife settled into **No.21 McMaster**, and it remained their home until 1919. It was a momentous time for them, in that they came immediately under the sway of two mentors. One was J.E.H. MacDonald who introduced him to the other members of the Group of Seven with whom he became fast friends. The other was Sam Hooke, a professor at Victoria College who edited the left-leaning campus magazine *The Rebel*. Fairley became heavily involved with the periodical which evolved, in 1920, to become *Canadian Forum*. Barker Fairley was the *Forum*'s first literary editor.

CASA LOMA

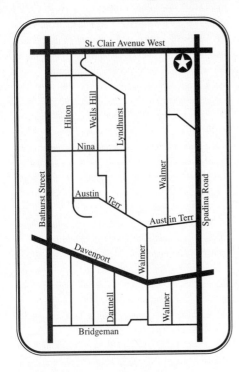

St. Clair Avenue West

Hilton · Wells Hill · Lyndhurst · Nina · Walmer · Bathurst Street · Austin Terr · Austin Terr · Spadina Road · Davenport · Walmer · Dartnell · Walmer · Bridgeman

The tour begins on the southwest corner of Spadina Road and St. Clair Avenue West.

Toronto-born Florence Westacott (born c. 1895?) began publishing her short stories in the *Star Weekly* and other Canadian magazines around the time she moved to **345 St. Clair Avenue West** in 1927, her home until 1933. This address was also home to another woman creative writer, Eva-Lis Wuorio, from 1941-55. Wuorio (b.1918) was a native of Finland who came to Toronto in 1929 as a journalist, first for the *G&M*, then the *Telegram* and then for *Maclean's,* where she became the first full-time female on the editorial staff. Her premier novel, *Return of the Viking*, was published in 1955 just as she left this address—and apparently Toronto, for thereafter, while she remained a frequent contributor to Canadian journals, her residences were cited as Andorra or the Channel Islands, or Ibiza. All of her novels found success abroad and were translated into several languages.

Florence Westacott moved from her St. Clair apartment to a flat at **342 Spadina Road** in 1934 where she stayed for a year, during which time her first plays were produced in Toronto.

320 Spadina Road was long the home of Franklin McDowell (1888-1965), winner of the Governor General's Award in 1939 for his first novel, *The Champlain Road*, a narrative of the Jesuit Huron mission. Most of McDowell's later professional years were spent as a senior public relations representative of the CNR and he was shameless about using his position to assist authors whenever he could, either by granting them complimentary tickets so that they could attend a meeting, or so that they might find inspiration in another part of the land. Many of the city's best writers were among his friends, and frequently they would read new work to each other. As a result of one such reading given by McDowell, E.J. Pratt was galvanized into writing his revered *Brébeuf and His Brethren*. McDowell worked as a reporter for most of the city's dailies in his early years, and in his later years was rewarded with an Honorary Lifetime membership in the Canadian Authors' Association, and with a D.Litt from the University of Western Ontario.

Peregrine Acland (1891-1963) lived at **No.292** from 1952 to 1956. Acland was born in Toronto, the son of Frederick Acland, the former King's Printer. Peregrine's novel *All Else Is Folly* (1929) was praised energetically by Bertrand Russell—he called it "beautiful and original." Ford Madox Ford liked the book so much he wrote an Introduction for it. Knowledgeable readers have compared it to another Canadian war novel, Humphry Cobb's *Paths of Glory*.

Mazo de la Roche was honoured at a banquet in Casa Loma, **1 Austin Terrace**, on May 18, 1927, shortly after it was announced she had won the *Atlantic Monthly* Prize for her novel *Jalna*. This merits mention only because, apart from a gala birthday party held for poet Irving Layton (b.1912) on his 65th birthday (at which he had a public reconciliation with poet A.J.M. Smith), few other literary events of a public nature have taken place here. Of course, there are many places in Toronto where readings or talks by authors have been held, but it does seem strange that one of the few distinctive buildings in Toronto has been so neglected by the book trade for almost a century. Maybe someday someone will write a novel in which Casa Loma features as prominently in the plot as it does on the skyline.

Author and CBC producer Robert Zend (1929-85) lived with his family at **2 Austin Terrace** from April 1970 to June 1973. While here, he wrote at least one (untranslated) book in Hungarian, his mother tongue. His poetry collection, *From Zero to One*, published in 1973, was an English translation undertaken by Zend in collaboration with John Robert Colombo. One of his biggest fans was Northrop Frye. At the instigation of several authors, I organized a memorial tribute at the Harbourfront Reading Series for Zend shortly after his death. When the roster of speakers was almost complete, Frye telephoned and, most uncharacteristically of him, asked if he could be a speaker as well. Because I had not been aware of his interest, I had not called on Frye to speak. Of course, we found space for him on the bill.

Playwright Jack Winter (b.1936) lived in apt. 3 at **344 Walmer Road** while teaching at Victoria College from 1960-62. It was at this address that he started to write his first play *Before Compeigne*, produced at Toronto Workshop Productions in 1963, winner of the *Telegram* Prize for Best New Canadian

Play. Over the next decade several of his plays were presented by TWP. **No.377** was the home of the poet Louise Morey Bowman (1882-1944) who spent her last three years in Toronto (1921-23). A fan of her work was Dorothy Livesay, as was poet and critic Anne Cimon, who notes of Bowman: "her work now suffers neglect. Yet Bowman left an important legacy, a provocative vision of the sacredness of life, a powerful, honest exploration of woman's nature. Much of her work remains contemporary in message and technique." Bowman was a transitional figure. Her books had titles made from treacle (*Dream Tapestries*, or even worse *Characters in Cadence*), yet she wrote in free verse and was published in the famous magazine *Poetry Chicago*, the standard-bearer for Modernism in poesy. In contrast, Horace Brown (1908-96) lived most of his life in the city, becoming one of its most notorious aldermen when he was on city council 1960-72. If he is remembered today as a politician it is usually for slapping the face of another alderman, John Sewell, when Sewell (who later became Mayor) allegedly called him a liar. But long before he entered politics, Brown was an author, publishing several mystery novels (*The Corpse Was a Blonde*) in the thirties and forties. He made his home at **No.355** in the mid-sixties.

Davenport Road follows the shore of the ancient glacial lake which once covered all of Toronto south of this line. Thousands of years ago, runoff from retreating glaciers in the last Ice Age formed the body of water known to geologists as Lake Iroquois. Toronto's richest families built gigantic houses on the upper brim of this geologic feature in order to have an endless supply of summer breezes and to have, of course, spectacular views of the city and of Lake Ontario. As the fortunes of these families declined, their properties were subdivided, but the absence of numerous uninterrupted north-south streets through this line is a legacy of the single ownership of large land parcels which prevented the creation of such thoroughfares. Thus, to get to Bridgman and Dartnell Avenues, we must descend Walmer Road to Davenport Road, then turn right along Davenport to Howland Avenue. Make a left turn down Howland to **Bridgman**, where the Tarragon Theatre is located at **No.30**.

Tarragon was founded in 1971 by director Bill Glassco and his wife, theatre manager Jane Glassco. Bill had been working with Ken Gass at Factory Theatre Lab but artistic differences drove Glassco to start his own theatre. Despite a search throughout the city for a suitable space, they settled on a former metalcasting plant just a few blocks and a short walk away from Factory Theatre Lab. The first production in October 1971 was a remount of David Freeman's *Creeps*. It was a hit with the audience and with reviewers, and the theatre seemed well launched. (Curiously, because Nathan Cohen had died suddenly, the *Star's* new drama critic that evening was Urjo Kareda—the man who, in 1982, would succeed Glassco as Tarragon artistic director.) Subsequent productions of other plays were not so well received, and it appeared the theatre would have to close. But a new playwright came along to save the day. David French (b.1939) came to the theatre to show his first script to Glassco. Like all new writers, supersensitive to criticism, French reacted angrily to what Glassco had intended only as helpful suggestions. French reminisced: "We had a fierce fight. Bill told me that he liked the play, but that it hadn't realized its full potential. I grabbed the script. I called him names and left the theatre. Bill came after me saying, 'I'm your friend.' I went back in and we talked. That was the only fight we ever had." The play was *Leaving Home* and its critical and financial success allowed the Tarragon dream to continue.

Since then, Tarragon has produced dozens of world premieres of plays by Canadians, and original productions of contemporary plays by American and other dramatists. Notable Canadian authors closely associated with the theatre include David French, Judith Thompson, Michel Tremblay, and more recently, Jason Sherman.

In 1974, Tarragon created a playwrights-in-residence program to allow up to ten writers the opportunity to study all aspects of play production. The worthy program continues to this day, albeit with reduced numbers due to cuts in funding.

Playwright Allan Stratton (b.1951) in a letter had this to say about his home just east of the Tarragon Theatre: "From spring 1976 to spring 1981, I was based at **32 Dartnell Avenue**, a residence which I fear caused my mother a few grey hairs. The drywall was shot, and through the cracks and holes it was clear the walls were insulated with old, yellowed newspapers. This was a cause of some concern, as the wiring was not what it might be and the walls were hot to the touch. During this period, I spent time out of town acting with The Globe Theatre, Regina. I also spent, important note, two years working at the Bathurst Street Theatre [in Toronto] with the NDWT Company on new plays by James Reaney, *Baldoon and the Dismissal*—in the latter of which I played a young W.L.M. King as a student politico . . . While living at **32 Dartnell** I also acted on CBC, playing a young muckraking W.L.M. King on an episode of "A Gift To Last"; I mention this as it was the second time I acted King before writing *Rexy!*, my play about the Great Waffler's wartime years . . . I also wrote, had my first productions and published *Nurse Jane Goes to Hawaii* and *Rexy!*"

Return via Davenport Road and Walmer Road to **Austin Terrace**. Albert Einstein's collaborator and friend Leopold Infeld (1898-1968) moved to Toronto in 1938, living first in Forest Hill. In 1940 he moved to **61 Austin Terrace**, where he wrote his autobiographical novel *Quest* (1942), which received warm praise in several countries when it was published. It was also while living here that he became a Canadian citizen. This commitment to Canada proved awkward for him in 1950 when he was exhorted by the Communist Government of Poland to return to Warsaw. As he said at the time, "I am a Canadian. I am happy in Canada. I have come to love and admire its democratic spirit and its sense of fair play and British justice . . . I will not go to Poland if my government thinks I am doing a wrong." That democratic spirit, of course, was what allowed him to leave. On his return to Poland he was showered with academic honours, but his ongoing pleas to the regime to permit more freedom for its people met with silence and then quiet reprimand. Circa 1943, Infeld and his wife had moved to **87 Lyndhurst Avenue** and remained at this address until their return to Europe at mid-century.

Poet and critic Frank Davey (b.1940) occupied **104 Lyndhurst** on September 1, 1976 and stayed there until he joined the faculty of the University of Western Ontario in June 1990. Davey was one of the first creative writers in Canada to embrace cyberspace. In a letter, he outlined his wired commitment: "I had a computer room that in 1980 was hard-wired by Bell Canada to the Coach House Press computers, about twenty blocks away . . . I edited *Open Letter* here, using the dedicated computer link to Coach House to transfer files to that press and to edit and correct them in the Coach House computer. The link was extremely useful in keeping me on top of editorial developments at Coach House (where from 1976-96 I was on the editorial board)." While inhabiting this house on Lyndhurst, he published several books of poetry with Coach House and a number of non-fiction works with other firms.

The most famous author to live on **Lyndhurst** was Ernest Hemingway (1899-1961). He arrived in Toronto in early January 1920 to be the paid companion of the son of Mr. and Mrs. Ralph Connable. The elder Connable was the manager of the Woolworth chain in Canada. In 1915, he built a large house—a mansion really—for his family at **153 Lyndhurst**, overlooking the ravine. About a week after his arrival in

Toronto, Hemingway was anxious to further his budding journalism career by writing for the biggest paper in the country, so he asked Mr. Connable to arrange an introduction to the right people at the paper. Because Woolworth was a major advertiser in the *Star*, Mr. Connable was able to arrange a meeting between Hemingway and the *Star's* director of advertising, Arthur Donaldson. Donaldson introduced Hemingway to Greg Clark, at that time the features editor of the *Star's* weekend newspaper, known as the *Star Weekly*. Clark passed Ernest along to the editor, J.H. Cranston. Cranston reluctantly offered freelance work to Hemingway—but at a maximum rate of ten dollars per article.

The amount did not deter Hemingway, partly because he was being well paid by the Connables for doing next to nothing, and because he was anxious to be published. His first article appeared in mid-February, around the time the senior Connables left for a Florida vacation, appointing Ernest the head of the household—including chauffeur with luxury car, butler and maids. He was only 21 years old.

Before he left Toronto in mid-May 1920, Hemingway had written 11 articles for the *Star Weekly*, and possibly more. Just as importantly, he had established good connections with the senior editorial staff of one of the biggest and most aggressive papers on the continent. The association between Hemingway and the *Star* would mature to the point that in 1921 he was hired to be one of its European correspondents, a job that paid him more than enough to indulge his creative writing and his wanderlust, and allowed him to return to Toronto, a journalistic hero, in 1923.

From 1982-83 novelist Susan Swan (b.1945) and her boyfriend at the time "rented a large house, **64 Wells Hill Avenue** (it had a large indoor swimming pool—he paid most of the rent). I finished the novel *The Biggest Modern Woman of the World* here." By coincidence, playwright Rick Salutin (b.1942) recalls that he had an apartment at this same address for most of 1971, but he had just returned to Canada and was yet to write his first play.

A few strides to the south takes us to **29 Wells Hill Avenue**, where Marshall McLuhan (1911-80) made his home from 1955-68. Biographer Terrence Gordon remarks: "After more than nine years of living on the St. Michael's campus, the McLuhans moved to a comfortable, Tudor-style house . . . But the McLuhans were not living in baronial splendour at **29 Wells Hill**. With six children between the ages of thirteen and three, on a salary that had driven some of his friends out of university teaching, McLuhan was concerned constantly about providing for his family. It was at this time that he got the idea for Idea Consultants—a company for the development, processing, and promotion of schemes and dreams." When he moved from here to Wychwood Park in 1968, his library consisted of 4,000 volumes.

Margaret Atwood at the International Festival of Authors at Harbourfront, October 1993

Wells Hill is connected to **Hilton Avenue** by Nina Street. Novelists Margaret Atwood and James Polk (b.1939) had met at Harvard and, newly married, they returned to Toronto in August 1971. Atwood was about to begin an academic year as an assistant professor at York University. They bought **27 Hilton Avenue**, renting the top floors to students in order to make ends meet. In addition to her teaching load, Atwood was up to her elbows editing manuscripts and doing whatever jobs that needed to be done at House of Anansi. Yet somehow she managed to find the time to write *Survival* here, her bestselling guide to Canadian literature. On top of this, her novel *Surfacing* was published at this time, greatly elevating her profile in Canadian letters. Despite this success, she was not especially happy: her marriage was disintegrating and her workload was frightful. Polk and Atwood separated in the summer of 1972; he left, she stayed, but they remained friends and colleagues, for he was becoming more and more involved with Anansi, eventually assuming the post of chief editor. Atwood moved from this address c. September 1973.

The esteemed poet and journalist Charles Bruce (1906-71) made his first home in Toronto at **146 Hilton** when he arrived from the Maritimes in 1933. The family remained here until 1936.

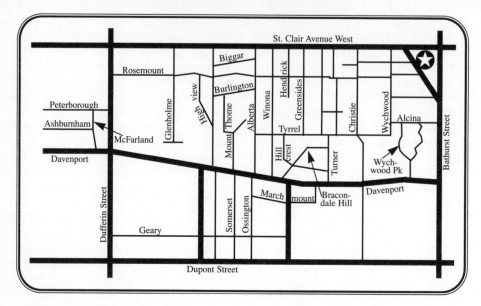

The tour begins at the southwest corner of Bathurst Street and St. Clair Avenue West.

Walk south on Bathurst to **Alcina Avenue** where Margaret Bullard lived at **No.67** from c. 1947-50. She mounted a vicious attack against Toronto in her novel *Wedlock's the Devil* (1951). Bullard had come from England with her husband when he accepted an appointment to the Physics dept. at the UofT in the late 1940s. They returned to the UK c. 1950 where she published one more novel, *Perch in Paradise* (1952).

When Timothy Findley (b.1930) left his parents' home in Rosedale in 1959 to live on his own, his first address for about a year was **80 Alcina**. The house has been razed and replaced by a new structure.

Alcina leads to **Wychwood Avenue** which, in turn, descends into **Wychwood Park**, a private district originally intended as an artist's enclave but well beyond the financial means of almost any artist, then and now. When the CBC producer and crime novelist John Reeves (b.1926) first came to Toronto

from Vancouver in 1952, he lived in a series of apartments, but in 1960 he moved to a house at **2 Wychwood Park** in 1960; he remained until 1986. Here he wrote *Triptych* (1972), *The Arithmetic of Love* (1975), and his first three detective novels, starting with *Murder by Microphone* (1978). When asked what Toronto had meant to him, he replied: "It's not easy to give a succinct answer to your question, but here goes anyway. It's a truism, but nevertheless true, to say that a writer's business is the human condition. After leaving Canada at the age of three to live in England, I was raised in the worst British tradition of disconnection from other people in general, and in particular (and especially) from people on another rung in the class-ladder. To return to Canada twenty years later was to discover the human race: first, briefly in Vancouver; afterwards here in Toronto. This has been an immeasurable boon to me as a man and as a writer; it is one for which I will be forever grateful."

Louise Morey Bowman (1882-1944) is little read today, which is odd in that her poetry was praised by some leading American verse experts, including Amy Lowell and Harriet Monroe. The latter was editor of *Poetry*, the leading magazine in the USA for contemporary verse and Monroe included Bowman's work in her periodical. Lowell discovered Bowman while judging a poetry contest, and awarded her special notice in her judge's remarks. During her only lecture in Canada, Amy Lowell again singled out Bowman among Canadian writers as someone on whom laurels should descend. One reason her work may not have flourished is that she celebrated women at a time when that was a sure way to be relegated to inconsequentiality by most of the male reviewers. Also, her first book, *Moonlight and Common Day* (1922), did not appear until she was 40, well past the age when she might have been more aggressive about promoting her writing. Whatever the reason, the near complete obscurity of her work is undeserved. From 1917-20 she lived at **3 Wychwood Park**.

3 Wychwood Park was also the home of Marshall McLuhan (1911-80) from 1968 until his death in 1980. While living here he published two of his best-known books: *Counterblast* (1969) and *From Cliché to Archetype* (1970).

Mark Abley (b.1955) is the former book editor of the Montreal *Gazette* and the author of books of poetry, literary travel, and reportage. He was a Rhodes Scholar in 1975, and other awards include the Fiona Mee Prize for excellence in literary journalism. Despite his long association with Montreal, Toronto has been his home twice, once when he worked at the CBC and the second time when he worked as an editor at *Saturday Night* from May to September 1986. During this latter stay he lived at **91 Wychwood Park**. His residencies have been long enough for him to remark about the city: "In certain moods I take delight in its generosity, its tolerance, and the glorious diversity of its citizens. In other moods, I chafe at its snobbishness towards the 'regions', i.e., all the rest of the country. And perhaps Canada gets the Toronto it deserves: unfortunately, there is

no such thing as Queen Street without a Bay Street as well."

3 Wychwood was also the home of Alan Sullivan from 1913-20. Sullivan (1868-1947) had been an engineering student at the UofT but left before getting his degree to work for the CPR at a variety of engineering jobs. William Arthur Deacon reports from a conversation he had with Sullivan that "it was during this period that Mr. Sullivan ran the Canadian rapids [at Sault Ste. Marie] and

Alan Sullivan

nearly drowned them both." As an author, Alan Sullivan published more than 40 novels, some under the *nom de plume* Sinclair Murray. His first novel, *Blantyre Alien* (1914), was set in the Toronto of his day and many others are set throughout Canada. In 1911 Sullivan bought the land on which the Wychwood house stands and had a keen hand in its design. It was finished in 1913 and today the exterior is much as it was when it was first occupied. One of the literary guests entertained by Sullivan at this address was the American novelist Winston Churchill (1871-1947), who was in town in 1915 to give a speech. It may be hard to credit but the

American Winston Churchill was more famous than the British Winston Churchill at the end of the 19th and beginning of the 20th c. In fact, after a friendly exchange of letters, the British Churchill agreed to add his middle initial to his name on all publications so as to diminish confusion in the public mind about which man had written what. When the American Churchill arrived in Toronto, his visit was covered extensively by all the dailies—the *Star* gave it front-page treatment, and the *News* even ran an editorial which was, in effect, an essay of literary appreciation coupled with a greeting of warm welcome.

Poet and publisher James Deahl (b.1945) lived at **165 Wychwood Avenue from** 1982-86, while novelist Marlene Nourbese Philip (b.1947) made her home briefly at **No.200** in 1978.

Benson Avenue runs west from Wychwood Avenue. The poet David Zieroth (b.1946), formerly known as Dale Zieroth, arrived in Toronto in October 1968 and was settled at **105 Benson** until August 1969. He explained how he happened to come to the city: "Living in Manitoba in 1968 and wanting to be a writer meant at the time I either had to go west to Vancouver or east to Toronto in order to find the milieu I thought I needed. Vancouver seemed far away and rainy, and Toronto was in fact the destination of the woman I had fallen in love with and whom I later married there in March 1970. So Toronto had a romantic glow to it. When I arrived there I went around to the publishers and asked for work and in my wonderful naivete I was welcomed by Doug Gibson at Macmillan (among other editors and publishers) who suggested I try the smaller presses. Which led me to Ann Wall, Dennis Lee and others at Anansi, and where I found the climate and excitement I was looking for. Perhaps most important, Toronto allowed me the distance to look back and see where I had come from and who I had been. Such a perspective was an entryway into my writing life."

Another poet on this street was Mark Abley, met with above in Wychwood Park, who wrote to me, "I lived at **131 Benson Avenue**, corner of Arlington, from Septem-ber 1978 to August 1979. I lived upstairs; the downstairs flat was occupied by a couple of graduate students, one of whom put up a small wooden sign over the front door: BLOOMSBURY WEST. In that time, I began the long poem that became 'Asian Mass'; it was eventually broadcast on CBC Radio and published in my book *Blue Sand, Blue Moon* (1988)."

Take Arlington Avenue south to **Tyrrel Avenue**. Poet and politician True Davidson (1901-78) was living in rooms at **2 Tyrrel** when her writing career was given a boost with the winning of the first prize for poetry awarded by the Women's Canadian Club. The $100 award was a fortune, of course, to a young woman in the Depression. The presentation took place in a grand ceremony at the King Edward Hotel. Her biographer noted the significance of the timing of the award and the growth it gave to her self-confidence: "True continued to regard herself as being first and foremost a writer for the rest of her life. Charlotte Maher told me that True always 'saw herself as a researcher and writer. What she was, was one terrific politician, but that wasn't part of her image of herself.' Doris Tucker remembered a time when all municipal candidates had to list their occupation. True first wrote down 'Mayor' but, when Doris told her she couldn't do that, changed it to writer. True talked about how, after leaving public life, she had moved 'into the field of study and writing, where I have always felt I really belonged.'"

The man many consider the finest Yiddish poet ever to practise in Canada, Peretz Miransky (1908-93), lived at **No.46** for the last three years of the 1950s. He came to Canada in 1948 and worked at menial jobs before becoming the Canadian agent for leading Yiddish newspapers. His first book was published in 1951, but it wasn't until he retired from his day job that he found the time to write as much as he wanted.

The novelist Margaret Drury-Gane (b.1926) reported: "I was born in Toronto at **137-A Tyrrel Avenue**, used as the setting in my novel *Parade on an Empty Street* (1978) . . . The Toronto in my novel was stubbornly British, insular, often puritanical cluster of villages compared to the Toronto I wrote about later on."

Turner Road, running south from Tyrrel, leads to **Bracondale Hill Road. No.8** was long the home of playwright Herman Voaden (1903-91). His occupancy of this house began in 1954 and he remained until he died. Voaden's importance to Canadian cultural life is less in what he wrote and more in what he aspired to. His plays were so grand in ambition that they were rarely presented, but the very fact that he thought so grandly was pioneer thinking in Canadian theatre of the first half of the century. His conviction that grand theatre could also be about Canadian subjects transcended the pioneering and moved into the revolutionary. Voaden wanted an expressionist theatre which incorporated choruses, orchestras, professional dancers, individual singers, and actors, along with innovative lighting and set design. Such additions to the normal demands of stage-craft are in short supply at the best of times, but were especially so in the Depression. Nonetheless, he lived to see productions of his plays mounted, and their presentation respectfully treated by critics such as Augustus Bridle.

When poet George Johnston (b.1913) returned from duty at the end of WWII, he lived for a few months with his parents at **38 Bracondale Hill Road**. At this time his poetic mentor was E.J. Pratt under whom he had studied English at the UofT in the thirties. Both before and after the war, Johnson said, "Ned accepted me as a writer and used to invite me around to his house sometimes to literary parties. This was very generous of him [Johnston's first book would not appear until 1959]. I did not think nearly so much it at the time as I do now. I met Morley Callaghan there and Ralph Bates

among others. He also had me to two or three of his big stag parties at the York Club. They were munificent affairs all right, ceremonious, lots to eat and drink, good cigars and good company. I guess there were always at least thirty men. I confess I was awed by them, though I always enjoyed them too."

James Elgin Wetherell (1851-1940) died at his residence at **60 Hillcrest Drive** when he was in his 90th year. He was famous in his own century as one of the leading educationists in the province, and his anthologies of literature were used in schools for decades. One of his anthologies had a wide currency among adults: *Later Canadian Poems* (1893), an early but influential compendium celebrating Canadian verse. His time at this address was 1915-40. **No.82** was also the last Toronto address of another poet, Robert Zend (1929-85), who moved here in 1973. Here he published books in his native Hungarian as well as in English, including *My Friend Jeronimo* and The Three Roberts Series. The poet Greg Cook (b.1942), when he was president of the Writers Union of Canada in 1990, lived at **No.84**.

Hillcrest ends at Tyrrel and is quite close to the south end of **Greensides Avenue**. Poet Joe Rosenblatt (b.1933) described his stay on Greensides: "My most stable address was **15 Greensides Avenue** from 1973-80 where I did most of my drawings and my poems in the seventies were produced on Greensides (*Virgins & Vampires,* 1975), and so was a book of drawings, *Doctor Anaconda's Solar Fun Club* (1978) . . . I think my years on Greensides were my happiest and most productive years, and I look back on them with some nostalgia." He moved to British Columbia in the fall of 1980. Poet Dennis Lee (b.1939) was just up the street at **No.97** from September 1981 to October 1985, working on such books for children and adults as *Jelly Belly* (1983) and *Riffs* (1982).

The headquarters of publishers Clarke, Irwin were located at **791 St. Clair Avenue West** (at the junction with Greensides) until the firm went into receivership in 1983. It was rescued by John Irwin, brother of the novelist Grace, and eventually entered the Stoddart/General Publishing family of smaller houses.

Poet Bertram Warr (1917-43) was killed in WWII just as his talent was coming to fruition. Critic Keith Garebian has commented: "After his death, Warr's poems attracted the attention of Oscar Williams, Earle Birney, Lorne Pierce, A.J.M. Smith, Ralph Gustafson and Alan Crawley—not purely on the basis of sentiment but because these eminent men felt that, had Warr survived, he could have been, as Birney put it, 'a leading poet of his generation.'" He lived with his parents on **Hendrick Avenue**: at **No.59** from 1927-29, and at **No.64** from 1930-38. It was in 1938 that, fed up with working in an office, he stowed away on a passenger ship headed to Liverpool. From there he hitchhiked to London, took a series of petty jobs, and wrote poetry that attracted the attention of renowned poet Robert Graves. Warr was shot down behind enemy lines and regrettably the location of his grave is unknown.

Tim Wynne Jones (b.1948) has established an impressive reputation as an author of books for children, but his creative writing career began with novels for adults. His second novel, "*The Knot* was set in Cabbagetown, though, by then [1981], we had moved to **142 Winona Drive**. I think I can generally say I have to have some distance from where I'm writing about even if it's only a street car, a subway ride, and another street car away. I liked Winona. It means 'first born' in Ojibway and we moved into little 142 to have our first born. Winona was an ethnic neighbourhood and always has been: Jews in the forties, Italians later, and increasingly West Indians nowadays . . . I left Toronto in September of 1988—fifteen years of it under my fingernails and coating my lungs. By then I'd written a third novel, *Fastyngange*, which, like any good romance, starts in Somerset, England in a crumbly castle and ends up on Queen Street West . . . I left Toronto because

[the mayor] and his cronies had divvied up the city and were hell-bent to make it as attractive as any old American city, say, St. Louis, for instance. I left when the density of BMWs was suffocating, although the drivers of same have improved. After all, it's hard to drive aggressively when you're talking on your cellular phone and changing your compact disc. I left because the loonies on the street car were no longer an inspiration but a pain in the heart. I left Toronto to get away from my generation who put real estate above everything—whose brains have been Remaxxed, maybe at the same place they got their hair done. I left Toronto because succour is spelt with a K and an E there. I left for air, for my children, for sun. I now live in the country, outside of Ottawa. People here are amused at my Volvo, especially mechanics. What do I miss? Real Chinese food. Bagels. Hell, maybe it's worth going back!"

Daniel Elisha Hatt (1869-1942) was a Baptist minister born and educated on the east coast, who also had pastorates on the west coast. For three years (1922-25) he touched down in Toronto to be the manager of the American Baptist Publication Society. He published volumes of poetry based on his experiences on the Pacific shore (*Sitka Spruce*, 1918) and the Atlantic shore (*Digby Chickens*, n.d.). The latter title is Maritime slang for herring. He lived at **139 Alberta Avenue**.

Ida Emma Fitch Baker (1858-1948) and Eva Rose York (1858-1938?) were twin sisters who shared a love of the arts and literature but in other ways were like oil and water. Ida Baker was a conventional Victorian wife, in that she indulged the masculine pastimes of her husband without obvious complaint and obeyed him whenever he issued uxorious commands. Among the latter was his insistence that she vote when women were granted suffrage. She complied, but as her son noted, "she often remarked that she recalled her visit to the polls as one of the most unpleasant experiences of her life." Late in life the Bakers owned a ranch in British Columbia. She decided to accompany her husband,

and—at the age of 70—taught herself to ride and somehow survived her tumbles. It was also in her last years that she took up writing with renewed energy (her first poetry book had been published in 1882). At her death in her 90th year, her son found two books of plays, four religious treatises, and six volumes of poetry from which a selection was made and published by Ryerson Press in 1951.

The life of Eva Rose York has been summarized by her nephew: "Left a widow in her twentieth year, 'Auntie York,' as she was always called, had studied at the New England Conservatory of Music, then at the height of its reputation, and had become one of the most popular musicians of her time. As vocalist, organist, composer, editor, and conductor, she received wide acclaim. After she returned from Boston she organized one of the first philharmonic choruses and one of the first philharmonic orchestras in the Province of Ontario. One of her songs 'O Morning Land,' possesses a noble melody which has kept it alive. Auntie York, however, was more than a musician. Like my mother she was interested in literature, and she wrote two novels as well as several religious treatises and much occasional verse. One of her poems, 'In Life,' beginning with the well-known lines, 'I shall not pass this way again,' has been widely translated and has been enshrined in numerous anthologies. Unlike my mother, who was impervious to its demands and pretensions, she played her part in society with consummate ease and elan. A graceful swimmer, an expert shot, and accomplished horsewoman, she seemed to my brother and to me like a creature from another sphere when she arrived for her semi-annual visits with her pistols and her riding crops. On these occasions she took charge of us and thus released my mother for other affairs. For everyone concerned this was a happy arrangement. When many years later, Auntie York abandoned the world of music and of fashion to succour the unfortunate and to test the Providence of God, she and

my mother became inseparable. Eventually she took up residence in an apartment constructed for her in our home, and the two sisters were as one: Auntie York, with her selflessness and her tolerance for human frailty, and my mother with her high-minded determination to improve the lot of her neighbours and to shape their lives to fit her own standards." Ida Baker lived at **77 Alberta Avenue** from 1930 until her death in 1948; Eva York was here from 1930-38.

Playwright Guillermo Verdecchia (b.1962) lived at **65 Alberta** from September 5, 1988, until early 1990, during which time he worked on *The Noam Chomsky Lectures* (1991) with his flatmate and co-author, Daniel Brooks. The play won the Chalmers' Canadian Play Award in 1992.

The novelist and wonderful memoirist Gordon Hill Grahame (born c. 1893) lived at **No.42** from the end of WWII until 1950. After that he disappears from telephone and city directories, although it is possible he lived here until he died.

Alberta ends at Davenport Road. Walk east to Ossington Avenue, then south to **Marchmount Road**. David [Dale] Zieroth lived at **No.32** from September 1970 until May 1971, at which point he left Toronto for good to live in western Canada. Novelists Sarah Sheard (b.1953) and David Young (b.1946) were wife and husband when they lived at **No.34** from c. 1984 until they separated in 1991. It was at this address that Young wrote his first plays, *I Love You, Ann Murray*, and *Fire* (1989). He spent most of his time here writing for television in order to pay down the mortgage. At this address Sarah Sheard wrote much of her first novel, *Almost Japanese* (1985).

Fiction writer Margot Livesey (b.1953) inhabited **63 Marchmount** in 1979 and 1980, using her free time to write several of the short stories which appeared in her first book, *Learning by Heart* (1986). Novelist and poet Beatrice Redpath (1886-1937) had considerable commercial success with her stories in the slicks. A native of Montreal, she married in 1910 and moved that year to Toronto with her husband, an optician. In 1913 they settled into **No.80**, but since the grass is always greener just down the road, they moved down the road to **No.68** in 1918 and were there until they disappear from Toronto records in 1922.

Marian Engel (1933-85) moved into **No.70** in 1975 and was here until her much-mourned death a decade later. In this house she wrote the novels *The Glassy Sea* (1978) and *Lunatic Villas* (1981) and the story collection *The Tattooed Woman* (1985). *My Name Is Not Odessa Yarker* (1977), a children's book, was also written here.

A couple of blocks to the west of Marchmount, the poet Colleen Thibaudeau (b.1925) was born in the upper half of the duplex at **102 Somerset Avenue**. Her family was here until 1927.

Walk north on Somerset to its northern end and continue along Mount Thome to **Burlington Crescent**. Tommy Tweed (1908-71) kept lodgings at **No.9** in 1946 and 1947 while establishing himself as an actor and literary critic, and especially as a radio playwright. By this time he was working regularly with Andrew Allan and was also becoming involved with the New Play Society.

Take Alberta Avenue north to **Biggar Avenue**. A resident of this street more than four decades ago was novelist Robert Walshe (*Wale's Work*, 1985). Walshe (born c. 1930) briefly chronicled his residency: "My experience of Toronto spans a five-year period from 1951 to 1956 throughout which time I lived in a welcoming if small basement apartment at **21 Biggar Avenue**, which was far more a street than an avenue; I remember it mainly for the wealth of trees . . . During those years I began a novel that I completed in Vienna during the winter of 1957. It was accepted by Curtis, Brown and rejected by Heinemann and Knopf. I put it away in a box and have not read it since. Education did not come into [his Toronto time]. If I was in any way open to the spoonfeeding for which universities are famous, the spoon

would have to be held by Northrop Frye. I very much regret having missed him. I worked at MacLaren Advertising Company in Richmond Street: liked the people and loathed the job.

"Toronto remains in my memory as one of the better places in my life story. My friends were mainly musicians; one of my girlfriends was a painter. Mazo de la Roche was the only writer I knew: I found myself in a tête à tête with her on two or three occasions and was grateful to have met her. By that time she must have been seventy years young and was fascinating in a way that twenty-year-olds can only dream of becoming."

Walter Bowles (1889-1967) was born in Toronto and attended Harbord Collegiate and Victoria College. He returned to the UofT for employment, becoming the Warden of Hart House for its first three years (1919-21). Later he worked in Toronto for Oxford University Press for eight years, then changed direction again and became a radio broadcaster, initially for private radio then nationally for the CBC for more than 30 years. It was for radio broadcast that he wrote his first poems but they became so popular there was demand for them in printed form, and thus was born his book *Verse and Verse* (1956). He lived at **22 Biggar** for a very long time—from 1914 until he died in 1967.

The poet Dorothy Livesay (1909-96) was studying abroad for intermittent periods during 1930-35, but when she was home she stayed with her parents at **20 Rosemount Avenue**. During this interval she published her second poetry volume, *Signpost* (1932), and completed her studies at the Dept. of Social Science in 1934. Her mother, Florence Randal Livesay, herself a minor poet and translator, was permanently at this address over the same era, 1930-35.

Writers like to leave no experience unused, if they can help it, and Tom Marshall (1938-93) was no exception, as he explained: "I spent the winter and spring of 1944 at my grandfather's house, **48 Highview Crescent**, before returning to my birthplace, Niagara

Falls, after four years in Tennessee and Missouri where my father was doing war work. I attended kindergarten in Toronto . . . My novel *Voices on the Brink* (1989) briefly describes this Toronto interlude."

Two blocks to the west is **Glenholme Avenue**. The writer Charlotte Fielden (born c. 1932) passed her youth and early adulthood at **15 Glenholme Avenue** from 1945 until she married in 1956. Fielden is a UofT grad who studied drama at schools in Toronto, Montreal, and at the Marcel Marceau School of Mime in France. Her bilingualism allowed her to do the translated subtitles for Claude Jutras's film *Kamouraska* and other films from Quebec. Her published creative writing includes one novel, and Centaur Theatre in Montreal has produced one of her plays.

There have been two Margaret Lawrences in our literary history. The author of *The Diviners* and *The Stone Angel* spelled her last name with a "u," not a "w." Also, she regarded herself as a feminist. The other Margaret Lawrence (1896-1973) was not a feminist. In fact, her most popular book, *A School of Femininity* (1936), argues that women are clearly inferior to men in several fields solely because they are women, and the sooner women face that fact the happier they will be. She further argued that women, unlike men, need "to bind themselves to something or someone" and unless they came to terms with this need they would never be truly happy. Despite these beliefs, Lawrence supported herself as a journalist, sometimes working at *Saturday Night*, sometimes freelance, and was a frequent reviewer of novels for Toronto newspapers.

Just how extraordinary her book was can be gauged by R.E. Knowles's description of the tome and its author (on the front page of the *Star*, no less): "In Miss Margaret Lawrence we have a new writer who has, at a single bound, in her *A School of Femininity*, won a separate place as having written a book which, in point of psychological penetration and clarity of thought, transcends any volume thus far presented to the world from a Canadian pen." Six months later she was still hugely popular. The organizers of the annual Toronto Book Fair made her one of their stellar attractions along with E.J. Pratt, and their judgement was borne out when she drew a capacity audience (approximately 2,000 people) to the Crystal Ballroom of the King Edward Hotel and held the audience spellbound. William Arthur Deacon reported her as "commending to their attention the fiction now being written by women as more interesting than it would be fifty years hence. She said this was because, while women have discovered fictional expression, for which they have a special aptitude, they are still suffering from memories of ancient frustrations and are at the height of personal revelation." She was such a hit at the 1936 Book Fair she was invited back as a keynote speaker the next year. The crowds were just as large the second time round.

Margaret Lawrence finally found someone to bind herself to in 1929: Baruch Greene, the publisher of *Who's Who in Canada*. Unfortunately for her, he was married—albeit unhappily, but still married. And rather than offend his aged father's sense of decency, he refused to divorce his wife. Nonetheless, he carried on an affair with Lawrence until 1937, when he ended the relationship. Following this trauma she converted to Catholicism and was about to join a nunnery when, in 1942, Baruch appeared in her life again after his wife had died. Now daddy could possibly have no objection to his marrying Lawrence. They married and lived happily ever after. Many of her letters to her husband, both before and after their marriage, were published by Musson in 1973 as *Love Letters to Baruch*. From 1926 until her wedding in 1943 she lived at **101 Glenholme Avenue**.

Near where Glenholme intersects with **St. Clair Avenue** is Oakwood Collegiate, **991 St. Clair Avenue West**. Authors who attended this school include Margaret Drury-Gane, David French, Isabelle Hughes, and Bertram

Warr. An event of some literary importance took place here on Monday, February 21, 1921: the poet Bliss Carman (1861-1929) made his first public appearance in Toronto—indeed, it marked the first time he had ever read his poems in public anywhere.

Those who love Oscar Wilde should walk west along St. Clair to Dufferin, south on Dufferin to Peterborough, and west to **McFarland Avenue**. Here lived Robert Ross (1869-1918), the man usually credited with being Wilde's first male lover, and certainly his longest and most loyal friend. He was the son of John Ross, a prominent lawyer in Toronto with an active political career. The father was a member of the Legislative Council in 1848. Then, at Confederation, he was one of the first appointed to the Senate, and in 1869 he was made Speaker of the upper chamber. In 1851 he married Augusta, the daughter of Robert Baldwin. (Robert Baldwin was, if not a Father of Confederation, then certainly a Grandfather.

It was Robert Baldwin, for example, who first proposed responsible government for Canadians in 1841. He died in 1858.)

Due to ill health, John Ross spent extended periods in France and it was there that, on May 25, 1869, his wife gave birth to Robert. On the family's return to Toronto, the elder Ross discovered his business partner was a cheat and had besmirched the partnership's name with bad debts. Feeling honour bound to make restitution, the elder Ross did what he could to assuage the anger of the embezzled and to make good the defrauded amounts. The effort exacerbated his frail health, and he died prematurely in 1871.

Once all her husband's business debts had been discharged, Augusta Ross left Toronto for England with her children in April 1872, and neither she nor Robert Ross ever returned to this city. This means that Robert Ross was almost three years old when he left Toronto. I mention this because one of the

Leading Canadian authors at an undated literary function in Toronto. Back row, left to right: Charles G.D. Roberts, Lorne Pierce, unidentified; front row, left to right: Bliss Carman, Annie Dalton, A.M. Stephen

anomalies of my research was trying to reconcile how Ross could speak with a Canadian accent (according to persons who encountered him in adulthood) when it seems he was here hardly long enough to acquire one. That said, he never tried to disguise the fact he was a Canadian, and his mother would certainly have made sure he was aware of his fiercely Canadian grandfather.

Robert Ross met Oscar Wilde at Oxford in 1886. Ross was 17, Wilde was 32, yet both told intimates it was Ross who seduced Wilde. After some months they ceased being lovers but their friendship deepened. In 1895, when Wilde was on trial and abandoned by almost all of his friends, Robert Ross was his constant ally and support. Two years later, it was Ross who was at the dock in France to welcome Wilde as he began his exile. Wilde made Ross his literary executor, and in 1899, when Oscar's most famous play, *The Importance of Being Earnest*, was finally published, he dedicated the work "To Robert Baldwin Ross, in appreciation, in affection." Ross attended Wilde throughout the latter's long dying and was with him at his death in 1900. Thereafter, he looked after Wilde's two sons (their mother had predeceased Oscar), forsaken because of their father's disgrace. He helped the boys partly by securing for them the copyrights to the Wilde opus—and partly by acting as a surrogate father. In 1905, he arranged for the publication of *De Profundis*, and in 1908 oversaw the publication of the *The Collected Works of Oscar Wilde* in 14 volumes. In his later life Ross was heavily involved in the visual art world as a dealer, valuator, and finally, trustee of the Tate Gallery in London. When he died in 1918, Ross asked in his will that his ashes be interred with Oscar's at the Père Lachaise Cemetery in Paris. His family, horrified, refused. But the wish was finally fulfilled a half-century later, in 1950.

In the 1840s John Ross had built for his family a mansion on top of the cliff which once formed the shoreline of an ancient glacial lake. Casa Loma, Spadina House,

Oaklands, and the mansions of other very rich people were also constructed on the same clifftop. (Spadina House—now a museum—was Robert Baldwin's house.) The location of "Earlscourt," as the Ross house was now named, was chosen for its view and for its breezes, the latter no small mercy in Toronto's hot and humid summers. The actual site of the house was about one block west of Dufferin and one block north of Davenport, but since Ross owned the acres around his house, there were no blocks or streets, of course, apart from the muddy track of Davenport, an old Indian trail.

The estate was later purchased by a Major Foster. In 1910, his descendants made the first proposal to subdivide the property. In that year the placement of the streets was decided, and it is clear from the blueprints that the front door of "Earlscourt" would have been found where **56 McFarland Avenue** is today. Apart from the name Earlscourt, which describes a neighbourhood, there is not a single vestige of the original building or wooded estate left—except for McFarland Avenue itself whose curves follow the original stream which supplied fresh water to the Ross family.

Poet Christopher Dewdney lived at **107 Ashburnham** for the last seven years of the eighties. While at this address he wrote *The Immaculate Perception* (1986) and *The Radiant Inventory* (1988). Both books were nominated for the Governor General's Award.

West of this point, in the strip between Dupont/Annette and St. Clair West, there are no significant authorial connections.

ORIOLE PARKWAY

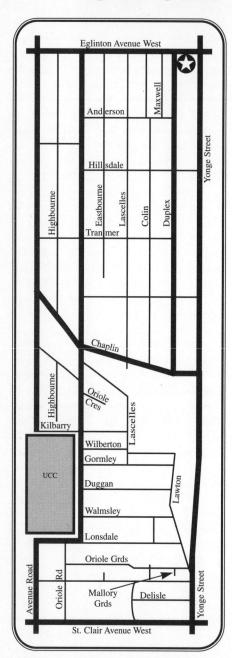

Terrence Green

The tour begins at the southwest corner of Eglinton Avenue West and Yonge Street.

Two blocks west of Yonge Street is **Maxwell Avenue. No.55** was the home of Terrence M. Green (b.1947) from February 1947 until he left the family home to live on his own in December 1968. Green is widely regarded as being in the top echelon of science fiction writers in Canada, and he is developing a following in other lands.

On **Eglinton Avenue**, between Maxwell and Colin, was the home of Luke Allan, the most common of the pseudonyms used by William Lacey Amy (1877-1962). Allan wrote more than 40 books, over half of them the Blue Pete series of cowboy westerns—quite popular in their day. He lived out his days (1953-62), not on a ranch, but in Toronto, in the very un-prairie-like apt. 14 at **119 Eglinton Avenue West**. By 1942 he seems to have stopped writing fiction. He rode off into the sunset in 1962, his passing hardly noted by the Toronto newspapers. They ran tiny—or no—obituaries at all.

In 1929 Bert Case Diltz (1894-1992) lived briefly at **178 Colin Avenue**, and then returned to the street in 1941 to live at **No.92** for more than half a century. He died in July 1992 at the venerable age of 98. For many years he was associated with the Ontario College of Education, and became its Dean in 1958. Hundreds of thousands of students in Ontario throughout the 20th c. have had to study his grammar textbooks as well as his texts on English literature and English composition. In addition to these teaching tools, he wrote the novel *The Barnardo Boys* (1982), the story of European orphans shipped to Ontario in the early part of the century to work on farms across the province. Also quite late in life he began to publish his poetry: *A Flurry of Voices* (1978) and *Fleeting Fantasies for Fellow Travellers* (1981).

Hillsdale Avenue West crosses Colin Avenue near here. Paul Wallace had a home from 1924-25 at **41 Hillsdale**; in fact it was his last home in Toronto. Wallace (b.1891) published short stories of his own, but his real legacy is his editing and promotion of pioneer Canadian authors Thomas Chandler Haliburton (*Selections from Sam Slick*, 1923) and Anna Jameson (*Winter Studies and Summer Rambles*, 1923). He was himself a pioneer in translating French-Canadian stories into English (*Baptiste Laroque: Legends of French Canada*, 1923). Sadly, he moved to the USA and seems never to have returned. Wallace emigrated. Kurt Palka immigrated. Palka (b.1941) came to Canada in 1965 and worked for the three main television networks as a reporter and producer. His novel *Rosegarden* was published by McClelland and Stewart in 1982 while he was living at **83 Hillsdale** from 1979-90, as were the books *The Chaperon* (1983) and *Scorpio Moon* (1988).

Back on **Colin Avenue**, **No.74** was the residence of Napier Moore (1893-1963) from 1929 to 1937. Moore became the editor of *Maclean's* in 1926 and over the next two decades built its circulation from 50,000 to a quarter of a million. At the end of WWII, he was promoted to the editorial directorship of all Maclean Hunter periodicals. At *Maclean's* he fostered the careers of and became friends with authors such as Marjorie Wilkins Campbell, Norman Reilly Raine, and W.O. Mitchell. Moore himself authored several short stories and plays. He had the knack of creating deep loyalty among his friends and nose-holding contempt among his critics. Fraser Sutherland, a poet and historian of magazines in Canada, had this to

Anna Jameson

say about Moore: "A small, dapper, talkative man with a protruding lower lip, he had contributed to the magazine [*Maclean's*] since 1922. Impatient and sometimes sarcastic, he would, at times, seem to be more concerned about rising in the Maclean Hunter hierarchy than leaving his mark on *Maclean's*. To some, Moore was a far from infallible editor. In 1928, for example, he rejected the gifted historical novelist Thomas Raddall's early story 'Tit for Tat.' It was snapped up by *Blackwood's* magazine in Britain, and was the beginning of a long relationship between the Nova Scotian writer and the British magazine. In November 1939, Raddall learned to his fury that without his knowledge, a self-appointed agent had resold his stories—including 'Tit for Tat'—to Napier Moore. Having forgotten that he'd contemptuously rejected it, he was 'now impressed by its publication in a world-famous magazine.' It was to be the first of many Raddall stories *Maclean's* reprinted from *Blackwood's*. In fairness to Moore, it should be added that the magazine *had* published Raddall's first short story in the 28 January, 1938 issue, though it did change a line about a barometer dropping 'like a gull's dung.'"

Fans of Barbara Gowdy (b.1950) may want to take a small detour from the grid of streets we are exploring at this point to go to **1930 Yonge Street**, between Imperial Street and Chaplin Crescent. She lived there from June 1972 to May 1975, although the building has since been razed.

Another national magazine editor with a literary bent who lived near here was Newton MacTavish (1875-1941). He died at his residence, **163 Lascelles Boulevard**, where he had been living for less than a year. A journalist most of his life, he was also intimately involved with the worlds of Canadian literature and Canadian visual art. For a while he was a trustee of the National Gallery, and he was one of the founders of the Arts and Letters Club. He was able to combine his two interests, journalism and art, when he was made editor of *Canadian Magazine* in 1906. Founded in 1893, it was a wonderful periodical celebrating all aspects of Canadian life, and from the beginning dedicated itself to "cultivating Canadian patriotism and Canadian interest, and of endeavouring to add in the consolidation of the Dominion." Under MacTavish's editorship particularly, it published large amounts of Canadian fiction. He is remembered in our time as the editor of the ambitious *Fine Arts in Canada* (1925).

One of Canada's most esteemed poets, Margaret Avison (b.1918), was installed at **117 Lascelles** from 1971-84. During this period she worked in the archives of the CBC and later for the Mustard Seed Mission in Toronto. This latter job reflects her passionate commitment to Christianity, a religious engagement reflected in the book she wrote at this address: *Sunblue* (1978). Two of her six volumes of verse have won the Governor General's Award. Napier Moore, mentioned above, made his home at **No.77** for about three years in the mid-1920s.

Hillsdale Avenue traverses Lascelles here. **136 Hillsdale** was the home of John Norman Harris (1915-64) for the last seven years of the 1950s. Harris was a bomber pilot shot down behind enemy lines in 1942. He spent the duration of WWII in Stalag Luft III, and was instrumental in planning the biggest POW breakout of the war, the "Wooden Horse Escape," so called because of the wooden exercise horse the airmen used to hide the entrance to their tunnel. Fifty of the 75 men who escaped were later captured and shot by the Gestapo. He used his military experience when writing his radio play *One of These Men Is Guilty*. And, in a more comic vein, wrote the novel *The Weird World of Wes Beattie* (1963).

The next street westward is **Eastbourne Avenue**. Fiction writer Joyce Marshall

Newton MacTavish   *Star*, August 18, 1941

(b.1913) has never been a prolific author, but it seems some of the writing in her novel *Lovers and Strangers* was composed while she resided at **118 Eastbourne** from 1951-54. Poet George Johnston, born in the same year as Joyce Marshall, moved to **No.134** in 1925. He described his house: "Dad bought a new house on Eastbourne Avenue near Eglinton; my third floor bedroom looked out on Oriole Parkway; fields at first and a farm with an orchard on the skyline. Soon built up." He returned to live in this house from 1950-51 before moving permanently to Ottawa. Poet, translator and publisher Barry Callaghan (b.1937) also lived in this house. His tenure was from July 1965 to September 1969. During this period he was the literary editor of the *Telegram*, managing within a very short time, to make the book pages of that newspaper the most exciting and unpredictable—and the best designed—in Canadian history.

Ruth Massey Tovell (1889-1961), after returning from a year in Europe in fall 1936, settled into **307 Oriole Parkway** and stayed there until spring 1941. She published only three books, and all deal, in one way or another, with painting. Her first was a murder mystery set amidst the galleries of Paris, *The Crime in the Boulevard Raspail* (1932), the second and third were tomes of art history: *Flemish Artists of the Valois Courts* (1950) and *Rogier van der Weyden* (1955). Another author very much interested in painting who lived on this street was Lawren Harris (1885-1970). From 1929-31 his residence was **289 Oriole Parkway**. Although his stay here was short, it was during this period that he painted two of his best-known canvases: *Bylot Island* (now in the National Gallery) and *North Shore, Baffin Island II* which he gave to the National Gallery. His poetry book, *Contrasts*, had been published in 1922. The comic novelist Seymour Blicker (b.1940) (*Schmucks*) tried living in Toronto for a second time in the early 1990s at apt. 804 of **240 Oriole Parkway** (he has since returned to live in Quebec).

Tranmer Avenue cuts across Oriole Parkway. Take Tranmer one block west to **Highbourne Avenue**. Sol Allen (1902-68) was the son of the man who established the first movie theatre chain in Canada. Allen had the benefits of a well-to-do upbringing, graduating from the UofT and Osgoode, but chose to spend much of his youth at blue-collar jobs such as lake-boat stoker and shoeshiner, tasks which may account for the socialist slant to his fiction. His first novel was *They Have Bodies* (1929) but his most controversial novel was *Toronto Doctor* (1949). When he lived at **14 Highbourne Road** from 1942-50, he was the manager of the Hollywood Theatre on Yonge Street, just north of St. Clair.

The noted French-Canadian poet and essayist Cecile Cloutier (b.1930) came to Toronto to live in 1964; part of her stay (September 1969 to July 1978) was at **20 Highbourne**, during which time she published the volumes *Paupières* (1970) and *Câblogrammes* (1972) and wrote *Chaleuils*, published later in English translation as *Springtime of Spoken Words* (1979) Her work has been honoured with the Governor General's Award. Renowned Classics scholar Gilbert Norwood (1880-1954) died at his home, **90 Highbourne**, after having lived there since 1942. He was acclaimed in his day for his translations and treatments of many Greek and Roman poets, notably Euripedes, Plautus, Terrence, and Pindar. In 1926, Heinemann published in London Norwood's short stories, *The Wooden Man*, and in 1938, Macmillan of Canada published a book of his humorous essays, *Spoken in Jest*. The award-winning journalist and all round man of letters, Barry Callaghan, had digs in the top left unit of the four-plex at **No.156** from July 1963 to July 1965 while establishing himself as a reporter and poet.

On the east side of **Avenue Road**, in a flat between St. Clair and Eglinton, the renowned CBC literary producer Robert Weaver (b.1921) has been making his home for more than two decades. Also on this side of the street, the radio playwright and actor

Tommy Tweed lived at **No.923** from 1960-62. While here he wrote one of his best works for radio (produced by Andrew Allan), *Full Speed Sideways* (1961), a dramatic study of the Riel Rebellion. In all, he wrote 60 plays and even more adaptations of novels for radio.

Wine expert and crime novelist Tony Aspler (b.1939) uncorked a vintage bottle or two during his residence in the ground-floor apartment at **No.883** from 1992-93. All was not wine and song while he lived here, however, for he also wrote three books: *Cellar & Silver* (with Rose Murray); *Aligoté to Zinfandel*, and *The Beast of Barbaresco* (an Ezra Brant mystery). Just next door, the thriller writer Barbara Betcherman (*Suspicions*, 1980) lived at **No.881** throughout 1976.

Take Chaplin Crescent to Avenue Road and walk south. Two blocks south of Chaplin is a tiny street, **Oriole Crescent. No.4** was where Lois Reynolds Kerr lived from 1943-47. The winner of a national playwriting contest in 1930, Kerr (b.1908) was one of the small group of women in the early decades of the 20th c. who, exasperated with the absence of opportunities for Canadian playwrights to see their work produced in their own city, conjoined their efforts in 1932 to form the Playwrights' Studio Group. Others in the band included Leonora McNeilly, Rica Farquharson, and Dora Smith Conover. Their energy was impressive, in that they oversaw the production of more than 60 plays, mostly at Hart House Theatre, and most of them comedies—an economic necessity, perhaps, during the Depression. Since the women made next to nothing from their plays, they had day jobs as journalists with the Toronto dailies. *Open Doors*, the play that won the national competition for Kerr, was selected by Anton Wagner for inclusion in his important anthology, *Canada's Lost Plays* (1980).

Walk another block south on Avenue Road to Kilbarry Road and turn east. Kilbarry terminates at the lower end of **Lascelles Boulevard**. Czech-born Marika Robert (born c. 1930) caused a sensation in Toronto when she published her novel *A Stranger and Afraid* (1964), an unabashed examination of a loving S&M relationship. In an interview with the *Telegram*, the author said, "I try to show how the heroine gets into a conflict because she could not be like everyone else. The question is, can she conform to a conventional life or accept the complexity of her nature, but I don't try to give a pat answer." About Toronto she said, "I like it now. At first I was unhappy because it seemed a loveless place, so cold, but now I wouldn't want to live anywhere else. Now it has everything that was missing at first. The cafés, coffee houses, theatres, galleries." She lived at **25 Lascelles Boulevard** from 1962-64 and was at this address when her book was published. Another writer who had an apartment in this building was the distinguished poet Eli Mandel (1922-92). While he occupied his flat from September 1967 to January 1969 he edited *Five Modern Canadian Poets* (1970) and wrote many of the poems in *Stony Plain* (1973).

Joseph McDougall's last address in Toronto before he (and the magazine he edited, *The Goblin*) moved to Montreal was **26 Wilberton Road**. New business administrators had convinced McDougall that his humour magazine would survive only if it moved to Quebec where ads for beer and spirits were not illegal as they were in Ontario—indeed, liquor ads were a lucrative source of income for a periodical. But McDougall liked living in Toronto and he only moved out of province with the greatest reluctance—and at some cost to the energy and spirit of the magazine. What the move did not destroy, the Depression did, and its last issue appeared in 1932.

Lascelles continues south on **Gormley Avenue**. Crime novelist Eric Wright (b.1929) has made his home on this street for almost four decades. The other major creative writer who has lived here was Ulster-native John Coulter (1888-1980), who inhabited **69 Gormley** between 1942 and 1947. Coulter was easily among the most important playwrights in Canada in mid-century. When he arrived in this country in 1936 he came with several drama successes in London already to his credit. He also immigrated with a broad sophistication about theatre, which he generously shared with others. During the period when he lived on Gormley he composed a number of important works: *Transit Through Fire* (1942); *Mr. Churchill of England* (1942), *Deirdre of the Sorrows* (1944), *Turf Smoke* (1945), *Oblomov* (1946), and *The Blossoming Thorn* (poetry, 1946). His researches for the Churchill play induced him to later write a biography of the man, *Churchill* (1944). *Transit Through Fire* was his first libretto on a Canadian theme; the music was composed by Healy Willan, and many regard it as the first all-Canadian opera ever professionally mounted. *Oblomov*, based on the 19th c. Russian novel of the same name, began life as a stage play. He reworked it for broadcast on the BBC, and in 1961 rewrote it again for CBC-TV.

The great Group of Seven painter J.E.H. MacDonald (1875-1932) died at his home, **40 Duggan Avenue**, on November 26, 1932. His passing was a front-page story in Toronto. Curiously, in almost all of the press coverage, his role as principal of the Ontario College of Art rated more attention than his career as a painter. He moved to this house in 1926. Friends posthumously collected the poems he had written over the years and published them in a volume *West By East* (1933). The most perceptive obituary was written by long-time art critic Pearl McCarthy in the *M&E*: "A fine artist is dead . . . Cleavages between artistic ideas meant nothing yesterday. All men mourned the death, at his home on Saturday, of a man they honoured and loved. J.E.H. MacDonald died while there yet hung on the walls of the Royal Canadian Academy exhibition, at the Toronto Art Gallery, paintings which perhaps the finest mountain subjects he ever did, and which were among the most beautiful canvases of that assemblage which made Canadians proud . . . Few knew that the artist and pedagogue was also a poet in words. Some of his poems have been published in the *Canadian Forum*, and in anthologies, and he hoped to publish them in book form." MacDonald not only wrote poetry; he savoured books. He counted many of the town's scribblers among his friends, and he illustrated the title pages and book jackets of several authors, including poets Isabel Ecclestone Mackay, Marjorie Pickthall, and Pauline Johnson.

When Kildare Dobbs (b.1923) arrived in Toronto in 1952 he worked at Macmillan as an editor for about a decade before beginning a long career as a literary journalist and belletrist. In 1956, with Robert Weaver, he co-founded one of the most important literary periodicals in our history, *The Tamarack Review*. Most recently, he has published a book of poetry. From 1957-58, he had lodgings at **126 Lawton Boulevard**. In the following four years he lived at **10-A Gormley Avenue**.

Playwright and performing arts specialist Mavor Moore's (b.1919) 1929-30 tenure at **112 Lawton Boulevard** was the last time his family lived together—thereafter, his father was not in the picture, but his mother, Dora Mavor, very much was. Across the street, **No.111** was the final residence of the novelist George H. Sallans (1895-1960). He was a senior writer at the *G&M* during the last decade of his life (during the war years he was Director of Public Relations for the Army). His novel, *Little Man* (1942), won the Ryerson Fiction Award amidst as much fanfare as WWII would allow, and then it won the Governor General's Award. A footnote of interest concerning this book is that 6,000 copies of the title were ordered for sale in Australia once it was announced as the prize-winner. Poet and playwright Joseph McLeod (b.1929) dwelt at **101 Lawton** from 1988-92.

Mavor Moore and his truncated family moved from Lawton to **38 Walmsley Boulevard** in 1931, where they remained until 1938. Moore described this as "our first real home." It was while living here he saw his first plays produced and made his debut as an actor. The same house was purchased less than three years later by the novelist Basil Partridge (born c. 1900) and was his home until the 1980s, after which point he disappears from the public record, presumably deceased. It was at this address he wrote the humorous Pennington trilogy about life in the household of a Maritime parson: *The Penningtons* (1952), *Larry Pennington* (1954), and *Chaplet of Grace* (1956). Kildare Dobbs lived at **No.100** from 1954-56.

The novelist Gwethalyn Graham (1913-65) spent the first two years of her life at the family home, **2 Lonsdale Road**. She would become one of the most respected novelists of her generation in Canada, even though she published only two novels in her lifetime: *Swiss Sonata* (1938) and *Earth and High Heaven* (1944). Both books were among the

Earle Birney (left) with Gwethalyn Graham and E.J. Pratt at the Canadian Authors Association Conference, Toronto, June 1946

few in that era by a Canadian to be simultaneously published by major houses in London and New York. Both books also won the Governor General's Award. She was the daughter of F. Erichsen Brown, a leading lawyer, and her sister became a well-known author of non-fiction, Isabel LeBourdais.

8 Lonsdale Road was Brian Doherty's last address in Toronto before he moved to

Niagara-on-the-Lake in 1955. There he would eventually found the Shaw Festival. During the day, Doherty (1906-74) practised law, but, when he was younger, he had had a second career as a playwright. His drama, *Father Malachy's Miracle*, was presented on Broadway in 1937 and was greeted with quite flattering reviews. To the *Canadian Forum* he contributed theatre reviews throughout the thirties and forties. He had lived on Lonsdale since 1951.

Pierre Salinger (b.1925) has written in his memoir, "With the Wall Street crash signalling the start of the Great Depression, my father, like so many other Americans, lost his job. Fortunately, he was offered a position in Canada and in 1929 we moved to Toronto. The next few years, while tough, were far easier for us than for many of my parents' friends and neighbours back in San Francisco." The Salingers moved into **37 Lonsdale Avenue** and remained until some time in 1932-33. Salinger's prodigious music gifts were brought to the attention of his parents who then placed their child under the tutelage of pianist Clement Hambourg at the Conservatory. The family returned to the USA where Salinger eventually became the Press Secretary of President Kennedy and then of Lyndon Johnson. His first novel, *On Instructions of My Government*, not surprisingly, given his background, deals with politics.

Another man who knew a lot about both politics and writing was Douglas LePan (1914-98). During the 1964-71 period when he lived at **No.44**, he was the principal of University College during the most radical student years in the institution's long history. While he undoubtedly had trying moments, he was bound to recall that he too had been a rambunctious undergraduate at the same college. The 1964-71 period also saw important honours conferred on him. In 1968 he was inducted as a Fellow into the Royal Society of Canada, and was awarded an Honorary Doctorate from Queen's in Kingston.

Bestselling novelist Joy Fielding (b.1945) lived at **No.83** for about three years at the end of the seventies. During her occupancy of this place she wrote *Kiss Mommy Goodbye* (1980), winner of the Book of the Year Award from the Periodical Distributors of Canada.

Most Canadians have heard of Farley Mowat (b.1933) and the sales of his books testify that many have read him. But few Canadians know that his father, Angus Mowat (1892-1977), was also a novelist. His two books of fiction were *Then I'll Look Up* (1938) and *Carry Place* (1944). Both men lived in Toronto at **90 Lonsdale Road** for about a half-year, over 1939-40, shortly after Angus became Inspector of Public Libraries for all of Ontario. Al Purdy wrote about Angus affectionately in an essay published in his *Starting from Ameliasburgh* (1995). Neither Farley nor his father were celebrated for their love of cities, so it was not surprising when Farley wrote to me that he was "incarcerated" for five months in Toronto. "I spent most of my time down at Ashbridge's Bay wading around in the sewage looking at birds. Toronto's main influence on me was my connection with the Royal Ontario Museum and its department of ornithology. Through this connection, I met many fascinating naturalists and my bent for living in the natural world was enormously strength-ened. Many people from 'away' find very little good to say about Toronto and, for the most part, neither do I. I hate cities! However, I have to give Toronto credit for having encouraged my connection with the natural world at a critical time in my life." He also said that his home was "a stone's throw from Upper Canada College—at which I used to throw stones."

The official address of Upper Canada College is **220 Lons-dale Road**. The school was orig-

inally built on the 200 block of King Street West (approximately where the Royal Alexandra Theatre stands today) but the encroaching city forced the school to larger, greener pastures, and it formally opened at its current location on October 14, 1891. About a dozen of its graduates have become respected creative writers, and, reversing the coin, some creative writers have been among its teaching staff. Authors who were students of the school at this location include:

> Peregrine Acland
> James Bacque
> Robertson Davies
> Brian Doherty
> Robert Flaherty
> Graeme Gibson

Stephen Leacock, a young teaching master at UCC on Lonsdale, circa 1895

David Gilmour
John Reid
Stanley Ryerson
B.K. Sandwell
Archibald Sullivan

Authors who taught and lived on this site were:

Pelham Edgar
George Washington Johnson
Stephen Leacock
Edward McCourt

Robert Flaherty (1884-1951) is now regarded as the father of documentary movie-making because of the unique brilliance of his film *Nanook of the North*. He came to UCC because his father, who was the manager of a mine in Rainy Lake, had had the boy in his care for two years, and felt the time had come for Robert to have some formal schooling. Flaherty described his urban adventure: "I was packed out to 'civilization'—to Upper Canada College—English masters, Eton suits and collars and English games, Rugby and cricket. All of which to me was even more strange than I, wild and woolly as I was, must have seemed to the other boys, who spent a great deal of time plying me with questions. There was one boy from Australia who boasted a cattleman's whip which, I did concede, he could crack like a rifle. But didn't I have gold nuggets and Indian moccasins? And besides, I knew a few pidgin Indian words, quite enough to make everyone believe that I spoke real Indian. Chequered were those school years of mine, as they must always be to anyone born with the instincts of a wanderer. By seventeen I broke away from it all and drifted back to the frontier."

Edward McCourt (1907-72) was also a trailblazer in his way. Born in Ireland, he came to UCC to teach (just after finishing his Rhodes scholarship at Oxford) from 1936-38. Eventually he taught in the Maritimes as well, but it is his writing about the west that makes his readers associate him with the prairies. His first novel, *Music at the Close*, was a crucial, liberating watershed for western writers, as critic Paul Denham explains: "*Music at the Close*, in addition to its own merits, is a work which stands squarely at a significant turning point in the development of prairie literature. The fiction which preceded it . . . presented the prairie as a place with a lot of geography, but no history. For subsequent writers of poetry, fiction and drama such as Margaret Laurence, Rudy Wiebe, Robert Kroetsch, John Newlove, Andrew Suknaski and Sharon Pollock, geography has receded in importance, and the prairie is more defined as a place with a distinctive history. The shift is signalled in *Music and the Close*."

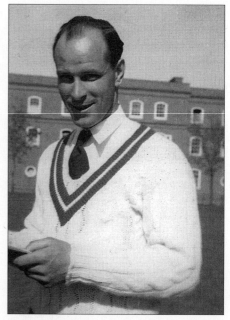

Edward McCourt on the playing field at UCC, c. 1937

Television host, polemicist, and novelist Michael Ignatieff (b.1947) spent two of his teenage years living with his family at **82 Oriole Road** in 1960 and 1961. Near here, **Oriole Gardens** ends. Andrew Jackson Elliott (1899-1965) spent the last four years of his life in a flat at **73 Oriole Gardens**.

He had been a social worker all his life, specializing in the care of homeless or unemployed men in the inner core of the city. His novel, *The Aging Nymph*, had wide popularity in the USA as well as Canada when it was first published in 1948. He came by his name honestly: he was the grand-nephew of U.S. President Andrew Jackson.

Another relatively unknown author whose final years were spent on this street was Charlotte Beaumont Jarvis (1843?-1927). Charlotte and her family fell on hard times c. 1886, at which point they had to sell their lovely Rosedale mansion known as Glen Hurst, built for them in 1866. The building still stands at the core of Branksome Hall School for Girls, although it is hard to see it beneath the subsequent additions. Charlotte became a piano teacher to help keep her large family afloat, and lived at a bewildering variety of addresses, a testament to a constant shortage of funds. She had a small apartment at **58 Oriole Gardens** from 1926-27. Her poetry book, *Leaves from Rosedale*, was published by Briggs in 1905.

Just paces away, at **No.27**, the journalist and pioneer historian of literary Toronto E.J. Hathaway (1871-1930) lived from 1925-30. Eva-Lis Wuorio (b.1918) seems to have lived in only two places in Toronto before setting off to live in Andorra, the Channel Islands, and Ibiza. She was at the first of her Toronto addresses, **10 Oriole Gardens**, from 1939-40. In the fifties she published novels for adults and for young adults, the latter having particular success with foreign publishers, and her 1968 book, *The Land of Right Up and Down*, was illustrated by the eminent artist Edward Ardizzone. Novelist and poet Michael Ondaatje (b.1943) was ensconced at **1 Oriole Gardens** from 1983-85 where part of his poetry book, *Secular Love* (1984) was written. This same house had been cultural critic Hector Charlesworth's home from 1938-45, and it was where he died in December, 1945—having just filed a review of a Toronto Symphony performance for his employer, the *G&M*. His passing was front-page news, and all of the dailies carried warm tributes from colleagues. As the *G&M* noted in its editorial: "The influence of Hector Charlesworth on Canadian journalism and cultural life went far beyond his actual status in either sphere. It lasted so long, for one thing. His technical ability as a reporter and editor helped to set standards which are commonplace today but were not so frequent before his time . . . His home was for many years . . . a cultural focus and centre in inspiration and encouragement to untold numbers of young artists."

The last Toronto address I could find for Maida Parlow French (b.1901) was apt. 48 at **8 Mallory Gardens**, where she lived from 1964-69. Until 1938, she was a painter, and then she changed disciplines and began writing professionally with her first novel, *Boughs Bend Over* (1943). Thereafter she published short stories, biography, and other novels.

Timothy Findley (b.1930) lived at **32 Delisle Avenue** from 1936-38. He had his earliest literary experiences in this house, albeit vicariously: "My father adored reading, and so the houses were always filled with books. And one of the guests at my parents' dinner parties . . . was Charles G.D. Roberts. At the age of five or six, I used to peer over the banister at him—an imposing and vaguely cantankerous man in a dark cloak. He had a loud voice and an impassioned manner of speaking, and I used to think he was always arguing—although from anything I actually heard him saying as I leaned down into the hall, he was actually complaining about his own hard luck, and how nobody really understood him!

"While we lived on Delisle and Crescent Road, a lot of time (both real and mythological) was spent in the Don Valley. My father had been brought up on Mark Twain and Ernest T. Seton, and so the Don Valley, apart from being a favourite playground for me (it was still in a relatively wild state, then), was also filled with landmarks and animal species from *Two Little Savages* and *Wild*

Animals I Have Known. I think my attitudes to animals were shaped by what I saw in, and read about the Don Valley—which was filled with rabbits and raccoons and grouse, etc.— and certainly those damned rabbits keep cropping up in my stories."

Journalist and belletrist B.K. Sandwell (1876-1954) succumbed to cancer at his home, **58 Delisle**. Unusually for someone so closely affiliated with the fine arts, he was also a specialist in finance—indeed, in 1911 he was appointed editor of the *Financial Times*, and later taught economics at McGill. From there he went to Queen's to teach English until 1932, when he became editor of *Saturday Night*. He was the last surviving charter member of the Canadian Authors' Association. A citation, given when he won an award, read in part: "He has for more than the past 30 years belonged to Canada as the Bayard of journalism in this country, as a speaker, as a publicist, and as a luminous figure in public affairs . . . True to a few great central loyalties, Sandwell has moulded and enriched the life of this country. He has used an English vocabulary but has assisted in creating a Canadian language."

Sandwell was born in England but came to Toronto as a young man. Although he spent many years in Montreal, he was, as he told the Canadian Club of Toronto in 1924, "inescapably a Toronto product, although I was not born here, but I spent the four most important years of my school life here, and the four years of my university career here; and were it not for the presence of some gentlemen who participated in the business of educating me, and whom I should not like to embarrass, I might pause here to pay a few tributes to the educational facilities which I enjoyed." It was he who hired the very young Robertson Davies to be the literary editor of *Saturday Night*, and as Davies's biography notes: "Sandwell set high standards. Despite frail health, he worked long hours, steadily writing or dictating pieces distinguished by an air of civilized argu-

ment. He was a convinced libertarian who reigned courteously, appreciatively, judiciously, undogmatically. But, as Davies once commented, he could also 'cut a man's head off so neatly and so swiftly that the victim did not realize what had happened until next time he sneezed.'"

Near the end of Delisle is **Oriole Road**. Novelist Barbara Gowdy (b.1950) lived with poet Christopher Dewdney (b.1951) in the third-floor flat at **56 Oriole Road** from 1990-91. The distinguished literary critic E.K. Brown (1905-51) passed his youth while living at **No.44** from 1908-20.

Near the foot of Oriole Road is **150 St. Clair Avenue West**. One of our most highly praised poets, Margaret Avison (b.1918), lived in apt. 104 between 1964 and 1970. During this period she wrote some of the poems that form *The Dumbfounding* (1966), her second collection. Another resident of the building (1983-85) was playwright John Krizanc (b.1956) who described his flat as "a great apartment. I worked on *Prague* here." Among the neighbours with whom he would exchange greetings was the mystery novelist L.A. Morse (b.1945), who lived in apt. 202 from 1976-87. Morse reported: "That which is laughingly referred to as my writing career began at the St. Clair apartment. Actually, to be more precise, it began in the small park right next to the building. Occupying the northeast corner of St. Clair and Avenue Road, this is called Amsterdam Square, and it was there that large portions of each of my books were written (and *The Big Enchilada* was entirely written). I would move out to the park with my notebook and clipboard on the first vaguely mild day in early spring and stay out until it grew too cold in the fall, subtracting or adding clothes as the seasons progressed. Since this went on for about ten years, I became one of the park's fixtures, considerably more reliable than the fountain, which only worked sporadically. As I've not written any novels since leaving St. Clair, the park thus remains the source for all my fiction."

FOREST HILL

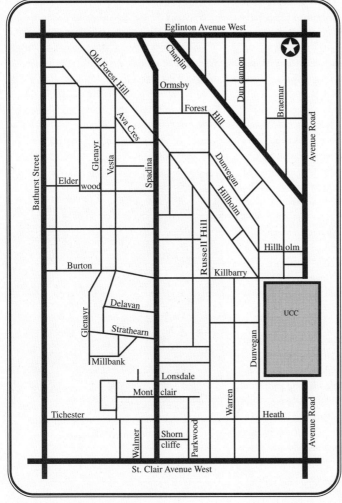

The tour begins at the southwest corner of Eglinton Avenue West and Avenue Road.

D avid Wevill (b.1935) has been living in the USA for so long that most connoisseurs of poetry believe he is an American. But, although he was born in Japan, he is a Canadian who arrived in Toronto with his parents in 1941. His father worked for Canadian Pacific which, until WWII, had been doing a lot of business in Japan. The

Wevills left Toronto in 1943, but in their short interval, managed to enrol their son in Oriole Park School at **80 Braemar Avenue**, just west of Avenue Road.

Alice Munro has consistently described Robert Weaver as crucial for the aid and encouragement he gave to her when she was beginning as a professional. Weaver (b.1921) was the founding producer in 1953 of "Anthology," the most important literary program of the CBC in the latter half of the 20th c. He ran the program until 1985, and in that era produced poems, stories, and commentary of an astonishing range for broadcast on radio every week. He took the time to correspond at length with many authors, including Alice Munro. His letters, even when he was rejecting material, were like life-rings to authors who often felt they were swimming alone, or swimming against a hostile current. His residence for the decade following 1966 was **27 Braemar Avenue**.

Braemar connects with **Chaplin Crescent**. **197 Chaplin** was the home from 1941 to 1954 of poet and science fiction writer Phyllis Gotlieb, born in Toronto in 1926. Like another Toronto novelist, Sol Allen, her father started a movie-theatre chain in the city. She lived here before the appearance of her first substantial book *Within the Zodiac* (1964). Her next book, *Ordinary, moving*, was nominated for the Governor General's Award for Poetry (1969).

Take Chaplin Crescent northwest to **Duncannon Drive. No.67** was where Luke Allan wrote at least one of his popular westerns: *Blue Pete's Dilemma* (1945) and probably several other novels. "Luke Allen" was the pseudonym reserved for his Canadian stories by William Lacey Amy (1877-1962). He admitted to publishing more than 50 novels. Amy travelled the world frequently, but Toronto was always the base to which he returned. However, finding where he lived in the city before 1942 has proved impossible. The son of a peripatetic Methodist minister, from birth he lived in a number of towns and villages across Ontario. His Victoria College records indicate he had to repeat his first year, and then repeat his second, which may be why he wasn't invited to return for the third. At that point he seems to have started to work for *Dry Goods Review*, part of the Maclean Hunter empire of trade journals. With that schooling in journalism under his belt, he bought the newspaper in Medicine Hat, Alberta, and edited it, all the time absorbing western colour and characters that he used in his novels when he returned east sometime before WWI. We next encounter him in London in 1916 as the London correspondent for various Canadian papers. From London he went to France as a war reporter. London, England, seems to have been his home after the war and for the next seven years, following which he spent time on the Continent and in Africa. According to the Canadian literary historian Clara Thomas, "in 1939 he began an ill-fated trip around the world which ended in Tahiti with the French capitulation in 1940. He made his return to Canada with some difficulty." Amy told Napier Moore, editor of *Maclean's*, that between 1923 and 1932 he and his wife

had lived in 20 different countries. What those nations were I do not know. But I do know that between 1942 and 1950 he was at **67 Duncannon**.

Walk west on Eglinton from Chaplin Crescent, and just past Vesta Drive arriving at "The Roycroft," **707 Eglinton Avenue West**, the home of playwright John Coulter (1888-1980). This was officially his home address from 1938-42, but since he was in New York for most of 1938-40, it was his home only from 1940-ish until he moved to Gormley Avenue in 1942. His consequential work for the stage was done at his other addresses.

John Coulter on the back steps of his father-in-law's home, 50 Forest Hill Road

However, it's an innocent pleasure to wonder if he knew Herman Voaden at that time: surely he must have. Voaden (1903-91), almost a next-door neighbour at "The Croften," **No.717**, from 1941 to 1950, was well known for his "symphonic theatre" productions. The mystery writer Frances Shelley Wees (1902-82) also lived at **No.717** for part of this time: in apt. 201 from 1941-43.

Return to Spadina Road and walk south one block on the east side to **Ormsby Crescent**. When Alice Munro (b.1931) was a high-school student, she came to Toronto in the summer of 1948 to work as "an all-purpose servant . . . At the time it was thought

Morley Callaghan (left) talking to Alice Munro at a book launch, 1988. Robert Weaver is partially visible in the background

that country girls made good servants which they *did*. I knew how to *do* a lot of things that most sixteen-year-old girls didn't know how to do. I was fetched down from the country. I worked all summer in this environment. I didn't like it . . . I saw all sorts of class things. I thought I knew a lot because I had read a lot, but I really had hardly any experience. I was a very naïve person in some ways. Being a servant in a household, for one thing, you see things about you and them—the barrier—which totally surprised me. Then you see things about them they don't show to people who are their equals because the ideal servant has no eyes or ears. But I had them! . . . I wrote a story about that [experience] in *Dance of the Happy Shades*. I think the story's called 'Sunday Afternoon.'" The house where she worked was **23 Ormsby Crescent**.

A block to the south **Forest Hill Road** begins. Novelist Sol Allen (1902-68) inhabited **282 Forest Hill Road** from 1951 until his death on January 7, 1968. "Letters in Canada," the annual round-up review in the

University of Toronto Quarterly, described Allen as "a Zola in Canadian corduroy" because his novel *Toronto Doctor* (1949) seemed to the reviewer to be a belated offshoot of French Naturalism. I guess that's a compliment. Certainly the book remains his best known, although he published over a wide range of years: his first novel, *They Have Bodies: A Realistic Novel in Twelve Chapters*, came out in 1929, while his last, *The Gynecologist*, appeared in 1965. Amabel King (b.1899), born in Toronto, published books of her own poetry and during WWII edited a patriotic poetry anthology. At the launch of her first book in 1943, she managed to attract a stellar guest-list: E.J. Pratt made a speech, as did John Mebourne Elson, and others in attendance included Charles G.D. Roberts, W.A. Deacon, Nat Benson, and Franklin D. McDowell. She frequently entertained local and visiting writers in her home at **179 Forest Hill Road** from 1940 until 1970, when she disappears from the public records. Cultural critic Robert Fulford (b.1932) lived at **No.153** from 1975-79.

Crossing nearby is **Hillholm Road**. The mystery writer and Flemish art expert Ruth Massey Tovell (1889-1961) was the chatelaine at **5 Hillholm** from 1947-61. Before living here she had published a mystery novel set in the Paris art world. After moving to this address she issued her two books of Flemish art studies aimed at the layperson as well as the specialist: *Flemish Artists of the Valois Courts* (1950), and *Rogier van der Weyden* (1955). Robert H. Lindsay (1910-62) published his first novel, a mystery, in 1941, the year he moved to New York. In Toronto he had written several radio plays, an experience he put to use in the USA where he wrote several television plays, some of which were spoken of as more than ephemeral, and one of which, *Miracle at Potter's Farm* (1956), won a major TV award. His home from 1931 until 1941 was **40 Hillholm**.

Hillholm crosses **Dunvegan Road**. Follow **Dunvegan** north towards Spadina Road, noting **No.187**, the house where poet Carolyn Smart (b.1952) lived with her family while attending Bishop Strachan School. Cross Spadina Road and go south one short block to Robinwood, with **Ava Crescent** as the ultimate destination.

2 Ava Crescent was Lawren Harris's last home in Toronto. He designed it himself in collaboration with architect Alexandra Biriukova, and moved in with his family in 1931. Harris (1885-1970) at this time was one of the best-known painters in Canada and widely regarded as the uncrowned leader of the Group of Seven. He was also heavily involved in Theosophy and a search for a higher meaning to existence. This elevated vocabulary was how he initially described his relationship to Bess Housser. Theirs was a friendship based on a mutual quest for intellectual enlightenment and the mystical joy to be found from exploring higher spiritual planes. Unfortunately, as they spent more and more time with each other, their spouses did not regard this mutual exploration in quite the same platonic light, and on June 13, 1934, Harris left his family forever—and thus, this home—to cohabit with Ms. Housser. Harris's biographer believes that the artist still intended to live in Toronto, but conventional morality in Toronto was so powerful a social force that many of their friends cut them completely, describing them as sinners, home-wreckers, and threats to the status quo. Not long afterwards, he and Bess left Toronto for the USA.

Mazo de la Roche and her companion, Caroline Clement, occupied **3 Ava Crescent** from 1953 until de la Roche died in 1961, a relatively long stay at one address for this restless duo. Despite her old age, de la Roche was as productive as ever, writing three novels at this address: *Variable Winds at Jalna* (1954), *Centenary at Jalna* (1958), and *Morning at Jalna* (1960), and an autobiography, *Ringing the Changes* (1957), heavily laced with fiction. She also found time to publish two books for children—her only books for children—*The Song of Lambert* (1955) and *Bill and Coo* (1958). De la Roche's death was treated as a major news story, and both the *Star* and the *G&M* ran appreciative editorials in addition to their reportage. While she lived here, she continued to receive visitors from around the world, and seemed to be as happy as she had ever been. Sadly for history, it was in the fireplace of this house that her companion obeyed de la Roche's last request and burned every page of every one of her diaries.

Moving south from Ava down Vesta Drive, we reach **Elderwood Drive**. The novelist Cecil J. Eustace (1903-1983?) spent most of his life in Forest Hill. The years 1955-61 were passed at **8 Elderwood Drive**, one of the few periods when he did not write novels. This may have been due to his preoccupation with executive duties at J.M. Dent; from 1953-61 he was the vice-president of the large publishing firm, and was its president from 1963-68. Eustace was a religious author who once said that "my whole life has been dominated by my interest in religion and philosophy, sometimes to the detriment, I fear, of my creative work."

Publishers disagreed, and continued to publish his novels as late as 1974. Toronto-born Isabelle Hughes (b.1912), author of four novels, wrote her first, *Serpent's Tooth* (1947), while living at **10 Elderwood** from 1938 to 1947. The novel is the story of two rebellious daughters from an upper-middle-class Toronto family.

Continuing south on Vesta, turn west at Burton to reach **Glenayr Road**. Near here is **50 Glenayr**, where novelist Jack Batten (b.1932) spent the final years of his youth. When novelist Susan Swan (b.1945) lived at nearby **19 Millbank Avenue** between 1967 and 1969, she was a reporter on the Education beat at the *Telegram*, spending most of her time covering student activism on Canadian campuses.

John M. Elson (1880-1966) lived at **14 Vesta Drive** for most of the Depression, and he made his living by directing for several years the first writing and journalism extension course in the history of the UofT. In 1925 he published *The Scarlet Sash*, a romantic novel about the War of 1812 on the Niagara frontier. While at this address he wrote a volume of poems, *Riders of the Dawn* (1934). One of his students in the creative writing program was also a neighbour, Amabel King (b.1899), who owned the house around the corner at **15 Strathearn Boulevard** from 1935-39. Her book *The New Crusaders and Other Poems*, with illustrations by poet Wilson MacDonald, was published in 1943. She will be remembered for other things.

Poet Irving Layton (b.1912) and novelist Aviva Layton (b.1933) were husband and wife when they lived at **22 Delavan Avenue** in 1977 and 1978, but it was the last time the couple shared a home. By the end of 1978, Irving was married to another woman, and had just retired from York University after a lifetime of teaching. Around this time, the Montrealer in him yielded slightly, allowing him to admit, "Toronto may not be Paris or Athens but it's interesting in a heartless sort of way. I lived there for over a decade and quite grew to like it. It's changed a great deal

because of the influx of non-Wasp Poles, Italians and Coloureds. Some really wonderful restaurants and here and there some evidences of a decadence still unsure of itself and stiff around the edges." During his time in this house Irving Layton wrote most of the poems that appear in his book *The Tightrope Dancer* (1978).

Delavan intersects with **Spadina Road**.

Irving Layton   *Star*, April, 1979

Nearby is **476 Spadina Road** where whodunit author Frances Shelley Wees dwelt from 1936 to 1940. Her mysteries betray the commonly held belief that detective novelists did not set their mysteries in Toronto until the 1970s. Many of hers were.

When Mona Gould's husband joined the army in WWII, she and her son moved to Toronto where she began to work for MacLaren Advertising as a copywriter. Mother and son settled into apt. 24 at **464 Spadina Road** in 1940, their home for the duration of the war. A dynamic women given to flashing red nails, bright red lipstick, and wide-brim hats, she quickly entered into the poetry world of Toronto and found encouragement from two of its biggest guns: E.J. Pratt and B.K. Sandwell. Thanks to their exhortations, she persevered with her writing, and Macmillan published two volumes of her lyrics while she was at this address: *Tasting the Earth* (1943) and *I Run with the Fox* (1946). It was at this building, as well, that she learned her brother had been killed in the raid on Dieppe, a shock that inspired her most famous poem, "This Was My Brother," a work that quickly travelled the world and is still read at Remembrance Day ceremonies by veterans moved by its honest poignancy. After the war, Gould became a radio broadcaster and interviewer of almost every celebrity who came to town in the 1950s. Thereafter she moved about; her final home was in Collingwood. She died at the age of 91.

Mathematician and physicist Leopold Infeld (1898-1968) was a friend and colleague of Albert Einstein, and like Einstein had been forced to flee Europe because of the Nazis. Working with Einstein at Princeton, Infeld was hoping to obtain a tenured position at an established faculty anywhere on the continent. The UofT, showing astuteness, was the first to invite him, initially for a one-year lectureship which both parties were confident would soon become a permanent arrangement. Infeld knew that the UofT had an excellent reputation but he clearly knew nothing of the city. Shortly after he arrived at **404 Spadina Road** in the fall of 1938, his high hopes were dashed: "Toronto is a curious mixture of a town in the United States and one in England. Externally it is like the United States. The same drug stores with milk shakes and sodas, the same cars, tourist homes, cabins, advertisements. But it is different if one looks beneath the surface. The silence, the reserve, the slow tempo, are those of an English town. In the evenings streets are empty, and their deadly silence is oppressive. On Saturday afternoons a new spark of life frightens the town, only to die out completely on Sundays. For one day the town becomes lifeless, only to show a slow, scarcely perceptible pulse on Monday. It must be good to die in Toronto. The transition between life and death would be con-

tinuous, painless, and scarcely noticeable in this silent town. I dreaded the Sundays and prayed to God that if he chose for me to die in Toronto he would let it be on a Saturday afternoon to save me from one more Toronto Sunday . . . In Toronto I heard my voice amplified by the persistent silence; my gestures seemed to me spectacular against this calm background. The dignified, tranquil way in which everything was accepted redoubled my efforts to shatter this unresisting poise. I felt that I must be shocking to my surroundings, but my surroundings refused to show that they were shocked." Infeld's irascibility and impatience may be partially explained (apart from the verisimilitude of his observations) if the reader discovers that he had had to leave his fiancée behind in New York, meaning that he was able to see her only once a month on average, and only for a weekend at that. In Toronto, he wrote both an autobiography, and a highly praised novel titled *Whom the Gods Love* (1948).

When dramatist John Coulter (1888-1980) first came to Canada from Belfast via London, he made **345 Spadina Road** his home from 1936 to 1939. Here he wrote three plays: *The Family Portrait, The House in the Quiet Glen,* and *Radio Drama Is Not Theatre.* In his day, Coulter was called the "dean of Canadian playwrights." Critic Geraldine Anthony sums up the impact his arrival had on our moribund theatre scene: "Coulter brought to Canada the rare talent for perfection of style in playwriting. He also brought the farsightedness of the mature supporter of the arts to a culturally underdeveloped country, and he plunged immediately into needed organization, co-founding the Canadian Conference of the Arts, and supporting, with others, the Stratford Shakespeare Festival. Through radio, the press, and finally television, Coulter was persistent in his appeal to young Canadians to produce Canadian drama."

The Cedarvale Ravine forces us to make a little detour here to Bathurst Street. It begins with a jaunt along Tichester Road to

St. Michael's College High School at **1515 Bathurst Street**. The school was founded in 1852 but did not have permanent quarters until 1856, when it moved to Clover Hill, the site today of St. Basil's Church at Bay and St. Joseph Street. The need for expansion drove the school north and in 1950 it transferred operations to Bathurst Street. Students at this Bathurst address who went on to become creative writers include Barry Callaghan, Paul Dutton, Terrence M. Green, and James Powell.

A couple of blocks to the north is **1599 Bathurst Street** where Ernest Hemingway (1898-1961) spent his last weeks in Toronto. The building is easy to find now because the owners actually changed the name of the apartment from "Cedarvale Mansions" to "The Hemingway." The building is also one of the very few literary landmarks in the city that sports an official historical plaque. Quite why this spot—and this author—rate such recognition, while others do not, is not clear.

Hemingway had been lured by the *Star* back to Toronto to be a feature reporter based in the city. This meant he would not have to travel for out-of-town stories, a vital consideration now that his wife, Hadley, was pregnant with their first child. Unfortunately, between the time he accepted the offer and the time he returned, there was a change in the editor to whom he would report. And the new editor, Harry Hindmarsh, had no idea how to deal with a man of Hemingway's talent. In fact, he seems to have gone to great pains to show that he was singularly unimpressed with Hemingway's abilities. So almost from the moment Ernest returned to Toronto at the beginning of September 1923, his life at the paper was hell—even though he was the second highest paid reporter on staff.

Hadley and Ernest settled into the Selby Hotel to get their bearings and look for a suitable apartment. Hemingway soon found one in a new building facing onto the ravine he had discovered during his first stay in the city three years before. This one-bedroom apartment at **1599 Bathurst Street** came with a Murphy bed and a sunroom overlooking the Cedarvale Ravine.

Apart from being assigned to local stories usually given to cub reporters, Hemingway was sent to cover stories in Kingston (an escaped convict), the Sudbury Basin (to expose a fraudulent coal operation), and New York City (failed attempt to interview Lloyd George). Over the next few months his rage intensified at Hindmarsh's manner. One ray of light that broke into his gloom was his new companionship with a UofT student working part-time for the paper. Morley Callaghan described the development of their friendship: "That summer, one of the desk men, Jimmie Cowan, the only man in the editorial room I had talked to about writing, mentioned that a fine newspaperman named Ernest Hemingway, a European correspondent for the *Star*, was coming to Toronto to join the staff . . . I had never heard of him. Since I was the youngest member of the staff and still going to school I didn't expect I would get to know him now.

"A few weeks later, one noon time, crossing the street to the *Star* building, I saw a tall, broad-shouldered, brown-eyed, high-coloured man with a heavy black moustache, who was wearing a peak cap. He smiled at me politely. He had a quick, eager, friendly smile. He looked like a Latin. No other Toronto newspaperman would be wearing that peak cap, and I knew he must be the new man from Europe, Ernest Hemingway. . . .

"He was suddenly moved downstairs to enjoy the more leisurely life on the *Star Weekly*. At this time I went back to school for the fall term. But three times a week I came down to the editorial room where I got my assignment, then I would go downstairs to the library and sit writing my story. One afternoon I looked up and there was Hemingway, watching me. I imagine he had time on his hands and was looking for someone to talk to. Though years have passed, I still wonder what brought him to me.

"He was sitting across from me, leaning close, and there was real sweetness in his smile, and a wonderful availability, and he made me feel he was eagerly and deeply involved in everything. He told me that he had come to Toronto because his wife was having a baby and he had heard the Toronto doctors were good. As soon as possible he said vehemently, he'd go back to Paris. He couldn't write in Toronto . . . He had come to Toronto with good expectations and now he seemed to feel smothered, though he had good friends here. I could see that it wasn't only the job that was bothering him. I didn't know what it was . . .

"On Wednesday, I was waiting in the library with my story, and within five minutes Hemingway appeared. He had some proofs in his hand. 'Did you bring the story?' he asked. I handed it to him. 'I brought these along,' he said, handing me the proofs. They were the proofs of the first edition of *In Our Time*, the little book done in Paris on special paper with hand-set type. 'I'll read your story,' he said, 'and you read these.' . . .

"When he saw that I had finished with his proofs he put down my story and said quietly, 'You're a real writer. You write big-time stuff. All you have to do is keep on writing.'

"He spoke so casually, but with such tremendous authority that I suddenly couldn't doubt him. Without knowing it, I was in the presence of that authority he evidently had to have in order to hold his life together. He had to believe he knew, as I found out later, or he was lost. Whether it was in the field of boxing, or soldiering, or bullfighting, or painting, he had to believe he was the one who knew, and he could make people believe he did. 'Now what about my proofs?' he asked. Fumbling a little, and not sounding like a critic, I told him how impressed I was. 'What do your friends in Paris say about this work?' I asked.

"'Ezra Pound says it is the best prose he has ready in forty years,' he said calmly."

After this auspicious beginning, the two men met almost every day that Hemingway was here. But he wasn't to be here for long. Hemingway always believed Hindmarsh sent

him on the long trek to New York to interview Lloyd George out of a petulant wish that Ernest not be at his wife's bedside for the birth of his son. Despite his rush back to Toronto, Hemingway was not here when Hadley had her baby at St. Michael's Hospital on October 10th. This forced absence only augmented his antipathy to his boss and the *Star*. In December 1923, he gave notice, effective the end of the month. This meant that he had to skip out on the six-month lease he had signed for the apartment at **No.1599**. Rather than advertise the fact that he was going to unlawfully break the lease by openly packing his goods into boxes, Hemingway invited friends to the apartment and had them smuggle out clothes, books, and other small items under their coats as they left.

On January 13, 1924, the Hemingways left Toronto from Union Station, on their way to New York and a passenger ship which took them to Europe. The night before their departure, the Connables (the family who introduced him to Toronto in 1920) held a farewell party in Hemingway's honour at their home on Lyndhurst Avenue.

Return to Spadina Road via Tichester Road. Before you reach Spadina is the northern end of **Walmer Road**. The influence of what is now termed Modernism in poetry (i.e., the movement led by Pound and Eliot) was slow to reach Canada and the poetry anthologies published in the first half of the 20th c. betray little or no awareness of the exciting developments in verse happening in Europe and in the USA. One of the last of these regressive anthologies was edited by Alan Creighton (b.1903) and Hilda Ridley in 1938. Stop in front of **446 Walmer** and berate or celebrate his conservatism—for this was briefly (in 1942) Mr. Creighton's home.

Towards the end of his life, man of letters Newton MacTavish (1875-1941) lived in apt. 2 of **No.425**. His importance has been neatly summarized by another poet and man of letters, Fraser Sutherland, in *The Monthly Epic*, his superb history of Canadian magazines:

"Newton MacTavish had been a reporter and editor on the *Globe* and a frequent contributor to magazines in Canada, the United States and Britain. One of the founders of the Arts and Letters Club, he would twice become president of the Canadian Authors' Association. His connections in the art and literary worlds were many: he was on the executive of the Toronto Art Gallery and from 1923 was a trustee of the National Gallery; among his friends he numbered poets Bliss Carman, Duncan Campbell Scott and E.J. Pratt, politicians like Mackenzie King and painters like James Wilson Morrice. He collected paintings and first editions. In many ways, MacTavish was a transitional figure. With his spectacles on a ribbon, he looked like Sir Charles G.D. Roberts, the very picture of the studious yet sensitive late Victorian; and his collection of short pieces, *Thrown In*, presents gently amused recollections of Ontario village life and Methodist upbringing—others appear in the *Canadian Magazine* under the heading 'Thrown Out.' But for his day he was aesthetically forward-looking and his daughter Maxine married the cartoonist Richard Taylor who became a fixture on *The New Yorker*, that Manhattan emblem of a new, more sophisticated generation."

Return to Spadina Road at Tichester, then go south one block to **Shorncliffe Avenue** which runs east from Spadina Road. Poet and essayist Dennis Lee (b.1939) spent his days at **1 Shorncliffe Avenue** from October 1972 to July 1973. The house was demolished and replaced by the current building. While at this address he worked on his two books for children, *Alligator Pie* (1974) and *Nicholas Knock* (1974) and the early drafts of *Savage Fields* (1977) were penned here as well.

The last home in Toronto of Donald (1902-79) and Luella Creighton (b.1901) was **11 Parkwood Avenue**. This was their home from 1955-61. From here they moved to the village of Brooklin, about 50 kilometres from the Toronto border. It was while he lived at **11 Parkwood** that Donald Creighton saw, in 1955, the publication of the second and final volume of what most regard as his magnum opus, the life of Sir John A. Macdonald. Both volumes won the Governor General's Award for Non-Fiction in the years they were published (1952 and 1955). Just how deserving he was of a literary award is suggested by a student of Creighton's, who, in a profile, after quoting from a section of the biography, comments rightly, "It illustrates Creighton's belief that history was literature of a special kind, but grounded in the same canon, with form, plot, structure, that details would come into afterward; the shafts of light and life that Creighton imbued with the *zeitgeist*, could evoke almost at a touch." Creighton also wrote during this period *Harold Adams Innis: Portrait of a Scholar* (1957), a tribute to his mentor, colleague, and friend, as well as *The Story of Canada* (1959).

Parkwood ends at **Montclair Avenue**. Playwright John Coulter lived at two spots on this streets: at **No.9** from 1947-71, and at **No.36** from 1971-76. At the former he wrote *The Drums Are Out*, which in 1948 had its world premiere at Dublin's Abbey Theatre. Other plays dealing with Irish political strife followed. So too did his dramatic exploration of Canadian political strife—as personified by Louis Riel. Coulter eventually wrote a trilogy about the Métis leader. He was also busy with plays about Edmond Kean and François Bigot: subjects to whom he was attracted because of their rebellious pasts.

William Alexander Fraser (1859-1933) was known in his day as "the Kipling of Canada" because so many of his stories were set in what seemed exotic locales and because they were so popular. A Nova Scotia native, he spent about a decade in India, Burma, and Afghanistan before becoming a prospector in the Canadian north. These experiences were frequently put to use as background for his fiction. Illness forced him to turn to writing to make a living, and after a stint in Georgetown, Ontario, he moved to **10 Montclair Avenue** c. 1915, and remained until just before his death. A magazine profile from 1927 described the house as "cosy and ivy-covered" while in his upstairs study there was "a low, plain, wooden table set by the south window" where Fraser wrote most of his more than a dozen novels and 250 short stories. "In close proximity to the table—for the author likes 'to sleep near the evolving mss'—is a large wooden bed. Opposite the foot of the bed is a stone fireplace over which is a mantelpiece with an ashtray, books, pictures, and a box of cigars. Around the walls—oil paintings (by W.A. Fraser) of fruits and animals."

It was Kipling himself who gave Fraser's career a boost by alerting Frank Munsey (who had one of the largest-circulation magazines in the world) to Fraser's talent. Munsey's interest led to the *Saturday Evening Post* and Fraser never again wanted for paying outlets for his stories.

Fraser was not interested in writing as art, and as late as 1927 claimed he had never heard of James Joyce or D.H. Lawrence, much less read them. The works of Elinor Glyn and Aldous Huxley he thought were "absolutely filthy." Theodore Dreiser he described as "laborious, sexually morbid and the result of a fad." Indifferent to academics, he was interested in down-to-earth readers of commercial fiction who sent flattering letters—such as the one he received from Theodore Roosevelt: "You have done as Kipling has done, given us true tales of animal life frankly told as fiction; not as some have done, given us fiction told as true stories."

Fraser seems to have sold his house c. 1932 to John de Navarre Kennedy (b.1888), a lawyer who, on a bet, wrote a convincing novel about Russia without ever visiting the country. His *In the Shadow of the Cheka* (1935) proved to be a very popular spy thriller. Four years later, he published another mystery, *Crime in Reverse*. Both books were written while he resided at **10 Montclair** from 1933-52, at which point he retired to Peterborough.

The next street to the north is **Lonsdale Road**. Just west of Spadina can be found

No.349, where Thomas Guthrie Marquis passed the years 1931-32. At this time Marquis (1864-1936) was still referred to as a freelance writer; he had been a teacher until 1901. In addition to his history books, much lauded in their day, he authored *Marguerite de Roberval: A Romance of the Days of Jacques Cartier* (1899). With Agnes Machar he retold *Stories of New France* (1890). Late in life he turned to poetry, and published a volume in 1936 with a foreword by Charles G.D. Roberts. **348 Lonsdale** was the last address in Toronto of Frances S. Wees before she retired to Stouffville. While on Lonsdale (1953-55) she wrote her most applauded novel, *M'Lord, I Am Not Guilty* (1954). In all she published 27 books, the last in 1965.

When WWII was declared, the American novelist Mary Lee Settle (b.1918) believed it was wrong for her country not to be fighting the fascist threat, so she and her husband moved to Toronto where he joined the Canadian Army. She remained at their home at **320 Lonsdale** to look after their son just born in the city. In 1942, when the USA finally entered WWII, she returned to her native land. Although she did not publish her first novel until the mid-fifties, she told me that she decided in Toronto that she was going to be a writer, and she inscribed my copy of her 1966 book, *All the Brave Promises*, "The book that started in the time of Toronto."

The poet and anthologist Gary Geddes (b.1940) also lived at **No.320** from 1964-65. He described his earliest Toronto years: "I spent my most formative years, intellectually, in Toronto, so I have a great affection for the city. I arrived in 1964, after a year of study in England at Reading University. Frank Watt, in the Graduate English Department at the UofT, took one look at me and advised me to get rid of the Cavalry twills and tweed jacket or the summer would kill me—if the faculty didn't first! I took his advice. In fact, I spent that first summer on roller-skates at Longman's warehouse, zooming along the aisles making up orders. Those were the days when Longman still handled the Penguin list and I was overwhelmed by the volume of books at my disposal. To this day, I still have a selection of those damaged or coverless books which fell into my hands."

On the other side of Spadina Road, playwright Rick Salutin (b.1942) moved with his family into the lower duplex of **309 Lonsdale Road** in 1950 and remained until 1957. Bishop Strachan School opened at **298 Lonsdale** in 1915, having earlier operated from 1870 on a large lot at the southwest corner of Yonge and College. Authorial graduates of the school at its Forest Hill location include Isabelle Hughes, Carolyn Smart, and Phyllis Brett Young.

336 Russell Hill Road was the last home of John P. Clare (1911-91). He had been here since 1960. After WWII, Clare became the managing editor of *Maclean's*. From 1952-56 he was the editor of *Chatelaine*. Later he would work as an executive editor at the *Star*. All the while he worked as a journalist, he was writing stories for the slicks in the USA, *Collier's* and *Saturday Evening Post* among them. He published at least one novel, *The Passionate Invaders* (1965).

322 Russell Hill Road has been the home of two great Canadian publishers: John McClelland, founder of McClelland and Stewart, and his more famous son, Jack (b.1922). John McClelland started his publishing house in partnership with Frederick Goodchild in 1906. The two had met when both were sales reps for the Methodist Book Room at 299 Queen Street West. McClelland, a devout Methodist, dissolved his partnership with Goodchild when he discovered the latter cavorting with naked women in the company offices. The partnership might have survived this bacchanalia had Mr. Goodchild not been transgressing on Sunday, the Lord's Day. The firm had financial ups and downs throughout the Depression and WWII. Nonetheless, it did publish some Canadian authors such as Constance Beresford-Howe and Stephen Leacock, although its primary income came

from distributing American and British books.

After studies at the University of Toronto Schools and at St. Andrew's College in Aurora, Ontario, Jack McClelland attended the UofT for only one year before enlisting in the Canadian navy to fight overseas. After serving with distinction as captain of a motor torpedo boat, he returned to Toronto to finish his degree, determined to follow in his father's footsteps. He also tried to write fiction, starting and then abandoning serval novels, at least one of which was set in Toronto. Post-war housing was in such short supply that, even after his marriage in December 1945, Jack McClelland and his bride Elizabeth had to live on the third floor of the house in which he had been raised, **332 Russell Hill Road**, until the housing crunch eased three years later.

Jack officially joined McClelland and Stewart in the fall of 1946. His father started him in the warehouse, insisting that Jack work in every department so as to learn all aspects of the business before being named General Manager. Six years later, Jack's apprenticeship was complete, and he took effective control of the firm in November 1952.

A few years earlier, it was Doubleday, an American publishing house, that had decided to establish its office in Toronto. Until then, Doubleday's titles had been distributed by M&S, and the deal was the most lucrative agency contract held by the firm. The inability to control one's destiny because of irrevocable decisions made in a foreign country was not lost on Jack McClelland, and he declared that, because of the Doubleday decision to abandon M&S, "a Canadian nationalist was born overnight." As he assumed more and more control of the company, he made certain that at least half of the company's catalogue was comprised of Canadian authors (e.g., Merrill Denison, Robert Finch, Henry Kreisel, Roger Lemelin, Thomas Raddall, and Gabrielle Roy). After his father stepped down as head in 1952, Jack McClelland pursued his nationalist dream by adding to the company's list new, or nearly new, authors such as Pierre Berton, Earle Birney, Irving Layton, Brian Moore, Farley Mowat, and Mordecai Richler. They were to be followed by Margaret Atwood, Leonard Cohen, Marian Engel, and Margaret Laurence. From the 1950s and into the early 1980s, these and other M&S authors benefited greatly from Jack McClelland's singular gifts for marketing and publicity.

By the late 1960s, financial woes started to become too serious to ignore. Despite government loans and unheralded private support, fiscal burdens accumulated as the company's fame increased. In 1982, 30 years after he had become publisher, Jack McClelland resigned as president of the company. In 1985, he sold the firm to Avie Bennett, and in February 1987 he severed all connections to the house. Since then he has lived in relative seclusion. The Order of Canada was conferred on him in 1976. In 1993, an award was created in his name (The Jack Award) to celebrate those who have made a major contribution to the promotion of Canadian books. And in 1998, the UofT announced that the writer-in-residence position would henceforth be named in his honour.

Mazo de la Roche lived a little further south, at **307 Russell Hill**, from 1945-52. No sooner had she settled in when her companion, Caroline Clement, became seriously ill for months, and, for the first time, de la Roche was forced to look after the quotidian chores ordinarily assumed by Caroline. She found herself unable to write until April 1947, but then she returned to fecundity and wrote *Mary Wakefield* (1949), *Renny's Daughter* (1951), and the novella *A Boy in the House* (1952).

With a well-reviewed Broadway play under his belt in 1937, Brian Doherty (1906-74) looked as though he would follow in the footsteps of that other successful Toronto lawyer-playwright, Charles W. Bell. But for reasons apparently never explained, Doherty wrote no more plays, although he kept his

hand in the theatre by writing reviews. Instead, he pursued his law practice in Toronto until 1955 when he moved to Niagara-on-the-Lake, and there fulfilled his dream of creating the Shaw Festival. From 1931-50 his home was located at **293 Russell Hill Road,** and it was here presumably that he wrote his drama, *Father Malachy's Miracle,* so warmly greeted on Broadway in New York City.

During the 1922-31 period in which John A. Currie (1862-1931) lived at **158 Warren Road**, he became embroiled in a sensational libel trial. Sir Arthur Currie (no relation) was suing two gentlemen for aspersions they had cast on his generalship during the Battle of Ypres in WWI, a battle in which John Currie had participated with the rank of Captain. The poor General's lawyers were so ill-prepared they seemed not to realize that the Captain, whom they had called to support their case, held the General in just as low regard as his accusers. At the time, John Currie was also an MPP, so his witness-box remarks were distinguished by the abruptness and acidity usually reserved for parliamentary debate. The judge, increasingly furious with Currie's testimony, finally exploded and screamed "Get out of that witness box, or I'll have the Sheriff remove you!" a quote that was splashed across the front page of the *Globe* as its lead story. John Currie came within a hair of being arrested for contempt. Determined to make his point, he returned to the courtroom the next day, and, called to the witness box once more with the judge glowering at him, was but a sentence or two into his peroration when the magistrate ordered the marshals to evict him from the courthouse, not just the courtroom.

Currie began life as a reporter but switched professions in 1897 to become a mining broker. He was elected to the House of Commons in 1908 and held his seat until 1923 when he ran for the Provincial Legislature. He retained his Toronto seat until 1930. Currie was one of the founders of the venerable Toronto regiment, the 48th Highlanders. The *Standard Dictionary of Canadian Biography* reports, "He was perhaps the first officer of high rank who had engaged in actual combat to return to Canada and graphically inform the country of the conditions overseas. Because of his journalistic career and his special parliamentary training he was peculiarly fitted for this task." In 1892 he published a book of poems, *A Quartette of Lovers*.

Pioneer playwright Leonora McNeilly was lodged at **100 Dunvegan Road** from 1950-56. During the twenties and thirties she and Raymond Card, Nat Benson, Rica Farquharson, and a few others strove to create a Toronto theatre scene by producing their plays at Hart House Theatre. They believed that Canadians had every right to see themselves on stage as any other country—radical thinking, of course, at the time in Toronto.

When Mary Quayle Innis moved to **92 Dunvegan Road** in 1943, she published that year her first collection of short stories, *Stand on a Rainbow* (sometimes called a novel). In 1952, with the death of her famed husband, historian Harold Innis, her own talents seemed to gain wider recognition. Books published while she lived here were *Unfold the Years: A History of the YWCA in Canada* (1949), and *Changing Canada* (1951-52).

Gwethalyn Graham (1913-65) was the daughter of one of the leading lawyers in Toronto, and her parents were vigorous champions of the arts. Their home, first on South Drive and then, from the early thirties to 1947 at **66 Dunvegan**, was frequently visited by many of the leading theatre and literary people of the day. Graham, while happy to acknowledge the richness of this environment, seems to have been extraordinarily sensitive as a teenager about her height and good looks and felt like an outsider—or was made to feel like an outsider—throughout her youth. When she was only 19, following a couple of years at a Swiss finishing school, she shocked her parents and friends by eloping with a man who, the moment his wife became pregnant, took up with another woman. Divorce promptly ensued. Graham returned to live with her parents on Dunvegan and was definitely in Toronto when her first novel, *Swiss Sonata*, was published in 1938. It won the Governor General's Award for the 25-year-old author. According to one commentator, "Following the publication of *Swiss Sonata*, Graham spent some six months in Europe, where she witnessed and was deeply moved by the plight of the homeless victims of Hitler's *Anschluss* . . . In Toronto in the fall of 1938, she wrote two well-documented articles for *Saturday Night*, arguing for the admission of refugees into Canada, and she gathered petitions and made speeches on the refugees' behalf. In the course of these activities, she met and became emotionally involved with a Jewish-Canadian lawyer whom her father declined to meet."

This refusal by her father stunned her, and shaken, she set about writing her most famous novel, *Earth and High Heaven*, a thinly disguised account of the motives and effects of anti-Semitism amidst a family that regards itself as cultured and liberal. Published in 1944, this book too won the Governor General's Award. But unlike its predecessor it had a wide international sale. There were translations into the major languages of Europe. In English the book sold more than one million copies.

For reasons about which one can only speculate, Graham never published fiction again. She did publish an unusual book in 1963: *Dear Enemies*, an exchange of letters with Solange Chaput-Rolland, about English-French tensions in Canada. But no more novels, no more stories. Cancer killed her when she was but 52.

VAUGHAN ROAD

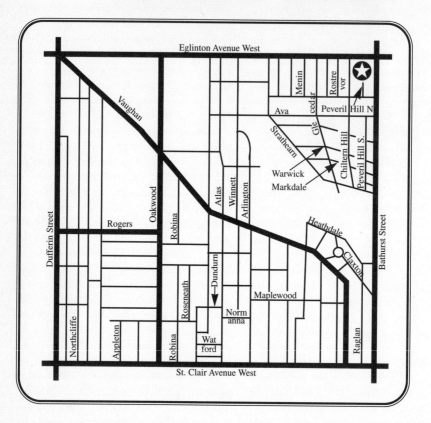

Eglinton Avenue West

Menin | Rostre vor | Cedar | Ava | Peveril Hill N | Gle | Chiltern Hill | Peveril Hill S | Strathearn | Warwick | Markdale | Vaughan | Atlas | Winnett | Arlington | Dufferin Street | Rogers | Oakwood | Robina | Heathdale | Bathurst Street | Claxton | Dundurn | Roseneath | Norm anna | Maplewood | Northcliffe | Appleton | Robina | Wat ford | Raglan

St. Clair Avenue West

The tour begins on the southwest corner of Bathurst Street and Eglinton Avenue.

Walk west on Eglinton five blocks to **Glen Cedar Road**. The last residence of the legendary drama critic Nathan Cohen (1923-71) can be found at **169 Glen Cedar Road**. Cohen aroused passionate rage and admiration in a way that no Canadian cultural reviewer had before—or has since. He was only 47 when he died of complications from heart-surgery. At his death, tributes came from across the continent: Clive Barnes called Cohen one of North America's most knowledgeable critics, and reminded people that it was Cohen who got Barnes his job at the *New York Times*. Herbert

Whittaker, his opposite number at the *G&M*, wrote one of the more perceptive obituaries, and in it noted: "The force of Nathan Cohen's criticism bears witness to the present maturity of theatre in Canada. In taking from him the unrelenting discipline he administered to it, it learned to be strong. He was a good teacher—stern, consistent, quotable, and memorable. As I was often opposed to his points of view, I cannot say that Nathan was never wrong. For me he was generally wrong but his kind of wrongness was one I appreciated more than anybody else."

Nathan Cohen had—has—a reputation of being an unrelenting ogre whose instincts bordered on the mean. But as Whittaker remarked, his "kindness and helpfulness to people in the theatre, which extended from his colleagues to the youngest apprentice, was so widely known that it almost undermined his cherished reputation as a dread supercritic, approaching every performance in full battle array." And in a radio interview with another theatre reviewer, Jeremy Brown, Cohen himself said, "I'm a very soft critic. That's one of my weaknesses, and I'm not joking. I mean it. I think it's not my duty to tell bad actors they can be less bad. I don't think it's my duty to tell half-competent actors or playwrights that they're competent or brilliant. I don't think it's my job to lie." With the possible exception of Whittaker himself, no other reviewer had so much power in establishing the minimum standards for professional theatre (including writing, acting, design) in Canada. Nathan Cohen, the man and the reputation, became the subject of a play by Rick Salutin, first performed at Theatre Passe Muraille in 1981.

In November 1946 fiction writer and urban-affairs journalist David Lewis Stein (b.1937) moved with his parents to **17 Menin Road**. Stein recounted his memory of the area: "My parents rented a flat, the second floor of a brand new, two-storey house. That area was then so new that Menim Road had not even been paved yet and in the spring turned into a mud hole. Many years later I met Nathan Cohen . . . and offered to drive him home, which turned out to be [nearby]. Nathan was then suffering from the heart disease that shortly after did him in . . . I hadn't been in Cedarvale for many years and it had become a neighbourhood of neat, well-kept, two-storey houses, a fine expression of Jewish middle-class respectability. Look, we have made it. The scrawny sticks I remembered stuck in the mud fields had become fine shady trees. I told Nathan that I had once lived around the corner from where he was living now. He told me that was the difference between us. For him, [the area] was a place to get to, while for me it had been a place to get away

from. Actually, I would have loved to have stayed in Cedarvale, but we only lasted there from November to June [1947]."

The novelist Lawrence Garber (b.1937) may have just passed David Stein on the street. Both were the same age, but one was arriving as the other was leaving. Garber explained his arrival from The Junction this way: "I would have attended Humber Collegiate had we not moved 'North' in 1947 to the Eglinton-Bathurst area—probably the second greatest Exodus of Jews since Moses. Instead, I attended John R. Wilcox Public School and then Vaughan Road Collegiate Institute on Vaughan Road. My parents bought a house at **25 Rostrevor Road**. Indeed, I lived at this address myself—with various random experiments elsewhere—well into my university days. I wrote the second and mostly definitive draft of *Tales from the Quarter* in that house, situated at my typewriter before the artificial fireplace of its wood-panelled rec room. When we first moved up to this area, Eglinton was still considered a boundary line above which existed a socially unmapped frontier of fields and golf courses and random housing projects. I played hockey on the lots adjacent to our house, ankling over the knotty ice to the accompaniment of my own Foster Hewitt play-by-play. I managed to save money for Europe by living on Rostrevor Road long beyond the normal incubation period; but then Paris, France, had become a sort of necessary lifeline for me and I kept going back for summers and whole years all through the sixties."

Go east one block to Chiltern Hill Road, then go south three blocks to Avenal Drive. Turn left on Avenal to **Peveril Hill Road South** and pause before **25 Peveril Hill Road South**. From 1965 to 1975, this was the home during her adolescence (1965-75) of novelist and poet Anne Michaels (b.1958). This area has been vital to her writing as she explained in a letter: "Toronto—its architecture, the islands, its prehistory—has exerted a considerable and direct influence on my work, in terms of form as well as content. I was born and raised in downtown Toronto, and my mother was too, so I feel I've known the city a long time, because of her stories, as well as my own—what she remembers. And her memory has made me look further back, back past the early history of the city to the prehistory of the area. This idea of archeological or geological layers of any *specific place or personal moment* has become integral to everything I write—not just in terms of the content (explicit in 'Lake of Two Rivers' or 'Miner's Pond' or 'Old Lakes' which is specifically about Toronto history)—but this is also the reason I began to write long poems with a continual narrative. I think of every poem I write as a cross-section. It seems natural that this aesthetic would rise out of the experience of having always lived in the same city—I must have a memory for every block of the down-town—and also having the benefit of overlapping memories. Also, most simply, when a city changes as you are changing, one ends up, often, documenting both . . . When we moved to Peveril Hill Road South, I wrote my first 'literary work'—an autobiography—documenting my 'childhood' on Springmount Avenue."

Nearby is **1950 Bathurst Street**, Holy Blossom Temple. The original synagogue of this name was located at 115 Bond Street but in the late 1930s, as the congregation moved north, the synagogue moved with it. At least four creative writers have given speeches here that were widely advertised to the general public and not just to the congregation. None of the four is widely read today, but that is more a reflection of fashion than of substance.

Phyllis Bottome (1884-1963), the English novelist, made the second of her two Toronto visits to the Temple in 1938, and spoke about Hitler's persecution of the Jews and the British government's lack of vigorous response to same.

Vera Brittain (1893-1970) made three trips to Toronto over the years; her second

was in this building in 1940 to speak about the war and literature. The speech was well-publicized in advance but reports on it were eclipsed by war news. However, her first visit caused an uproar. Like many professional public women, she was known and promoted as "Miss Vera Brittain" even though she was married. However, when a publicity photo showing her with her two

Vera Brittain in the office of her Canadian publisher, Macmillan of Canada

children ran in the *M&E* just prior to her 1934 Toronto speech, the howls of moral outrage from the Toronto righteous was formidable. The protectors of public virtue were aghast that the newspapers would publish a picture of such a brazen hussy showing off her two illegitimate (they presumed) children, and they were not quiet in making their displeasure known. They seemed little mollified when hastily informed by the paper that the children had been born very much in wedlock. The indignant smelled a cover-up. Otherwise, the speech went smoothly.

Maurice Hindus (1891-1969), novelist and specialist on Soviet affairs, also made several speaking visits to Toronto. His February 1939 speech at Holy Blossom was on the inevitability of a second world war.

Erika Mann (1905-69) was a better novelist than she was a political analyst if the reports on her 1940 speech at this synagogue were accurate. In an interview with the *Star*, she declared, "I have a pretty good idea of what is going on inside the country [Germany], and I'd say Germany is starting this war in almost the same condition she ended the last one. You know what that was like—complete exhaustion."

A little more than a block to the south is the Beth Tzedec Synagogue, **1700 Bathurst Street**. Two novelists who have given public addresses here are Leon Uris (b.1924) and Elie Wiesel (b.1928). Uris spoke in October 1959, riding the tidal wave of publicity and goodwill that was given his book *Exodus* (1958).

Walk west on either Warwick or Avenal to **Chiltern Hill Road**. The poet Janis Rapoport (b.1946) passed her adolescence at **90 Chiltern Hill Road** from 1953-67. When novelist Gerald Lampert (1922-78) inhabited **14 Markdale Avenue** from 1957-

60 he was leading the first of the annual Summer Writers' Workshops, then housed at the Ryerson Institute of Technology. The workshops were the first large-scale creative writing classes in Toronto, and featured an impressive group of teachers including Hugh Garner, Graeme Gibson, Austin Clarke, John Colombo, and Marian Engel. Lampert was also writing his first novel at this address: *Tangle Me No More* (1971).

Walk across the Cedarvale Ravine to **Heathdale Road**. At **No.61** we see Gerald Lampert's last residence. Lampert moved here in 1960. While at this address, he continued to operate his Summer Writing Workshops. In 1971 and 1972 they took place at Glendon College, and from 1973-78 they were held at New College, UofT. Lampert also wrote two books during this period: *The Great Canadian Beer Book* (1975), and *Chestnut Flower Eyes of Venus* (1978). Poets across the nation mourned his sudden death at 54 because he had been the organizer of the trans-Canada reading tours throughout the seventies that allowed hundreds of poets for the first time to explore and write about all of

Gerald Lampert's summer writing workshop faculty relaxing between classes, circa 1969. Left to right: unknown, Kildare Dobbs, Sean Mulcahy, Hugh Garner, Marian Engel, John Robert Colombo, Austin Clarke, Gerald Lampert

Canada—and gave tens of thousands of students and older Canadians the opportunity to meet Canadian writers face to face.

His neighbour for much of this era was Philip Child (1898-1978), who made his home at **40 Heathdale** from 1946-70, and then at **No.59** from 1970-75. Child has a minor but secure place in the CanLit canon because of his novel *The Village of Souls* (1933). Unlike many historical novels where the writer seems more concerned with showing historical detail than providing well-rounded characters, Child's novel about a voyageur forced to choose between two women representing two worlds conveys the moral dilemmas of real people. The legitimate knock against Child's writing is its didacticism—not surprising, perhaps, in someone who was a university teacher all his life, most of it at Trinity College, Toronto. Child wrote other novels of lesser importance, and poetry that some admire. One of his poems, *The Victorian House*, (1951), was undoubtedly inspired by elements of his home at **40 Heathdale**.

Scriptwriter and novelist Charles Israel (b.1920) had his home at **54 Heathdale** from November 1961 until September 1969, a period during which he wrote the novels *Shadows on a Wall* (1965) and *The Hostages* (1966).

Continue south on Heathdale to **Raglan Avenue**. Waclaw Iwaniuk (b.1915) came to Canada from Poland via war-torn routes in 1948. For most of his adult life here he worked during the day as an interpreter in the courts and his nights were given to writing poetry in Polish which, because his work was banned by the Communists, had to be published by émigré houses in Europe. Two volumes were published in English translation with the assistance of John Robert Colombo. Between 1957 and 1964 he lived at **207 Raglan Avenue**, at which point he moved to **100 Raglan** and remained there until 1966.

Claxton Boulevard crosses tangentially here. Its imposing gates were built as part of a grand property development scheme headed by Sir Henry Pellat, who had dreams of building houses throughout the Cedarvale region. Financial setbacks and an economic recession put paid to the subdivision, and the gates now stand as testament to the dangers of land and building speculation. **19 Claxton** was the home of Toronto-born playwright Stanley Mann (b.1928) from 1953-56. While Mann had moderate success with his stage plays in the 1950s, he seems to have found the world of television and film more congenial. In London he wrote several teleplays, but it is his screenplays which have brought him the largest audiences. Among them are *The Mouse That Roared*, *High Wind in Jamaica*, and *The Collector*. For several years his home has been in Los Angeles.

This is a propitious spot from which to detour slightly to a block of **Bathurst Street** which has associated with it a number of high-echelon names attached to some of its addresses. The first is **No.1600**, where the fiction writer Christine Slater (b.1960) wrote much of her first book, *Stalking the Gilded Boneyard* (1993) when she lived here from 1992-94 with Sam Hiyate, publisher of Gutter Press. Next door at **No.1598** André Alexis (b.1957) was living for a couple of years (1988-90) just prior to the commencement of his writing *Despair and Other Stories* (1994), his much-lauded debut. Herman Voaden (1903-91), the groundbreaking playwright of the thirties, made a home at **No.1594** in 1932. Northrop Frye (1912-91), the internationally acclaimed literary critic, lived at **No.1574** for all of the WWII years. And while his personal life was in some disarray, the legendary poet Irving Layton (b.1912) found shelter at **No.1560** throughout 1981-82.

Return to **Raglan Avenue**. Since 1989 Philip Marchand (b.1946) has been the book columnist of the *Star*. In that same year he moved to **124 Raglan**, where many of the essays in his controversial collection, *Ripostes* (1998), were written. His neighbour for most of this period (although neither knew the other at the time) was the poet and novelist Anne Michaels (b.1958). Her tenure at

120 **Raglan** spanned the years 1983-88, during which she wrote the first drafts of her internationally bestselling novel *Fugitive Pieces* (1996), and most of the poems in her notable volume *The Weight of Oranges* (1985).

Another poet who has recently turned to novel-writing with success is Dionne Brand (b.1953). From 1978 to 1985 she lived and worked in apt. 27 at **No.50**, where she wrote all of the poems in her book *Winter Epigrams* (1983).

The next thoroughfare to the west is **Vaughan Road**. Just north of St. Clair Avenue at **101 Vaughan Road**, the poet and novelist Cary Fagan (winner of the Toronto Book Award) settled into apt. 8 in 1982, and spent the next two years writing a novel that he then put aside. He left this building when he was married in August 1984. Anne Michaels (*Fugitive Pieces*), whom we have already met on this tour, inhabited apt. 115 at **120 Vaughan** between 1979-83 where she began to write poetry as a professional and where some of the poems of her first publication, *The Weight of Oranges*, were composed.

Nova Scotia writer Greg Cook (b.1942) gave up the Maritimes to live in apt. 2 at **203 Vaughan** from 1992-97. The poet Robert Billings (1949-87) spent the last two years of his life in apt. 11 at **205 Vaughan**. In addition to writing seven books of poetry, Billings did far more than most in promoting poetry and poets in Toronto. For years he held the thankless jobs of editing *Poetry Canada Review* and *Poetry Toronto*.

Poet Gail Fox (b.1942) also lived at **No.205** for the first half of the eighties. These were fruitful writing years, in that she produced *Houses of God* (1983) and *The Deepening of the Colours* (1986).

Take Maplewood Avenue to its western end, then descend Arlington Avenue to Normanna Avenue. Go one short block west to **Atlas Avenue**. Joe Rosenblatt was a freight handler for the CPR when his abode was **63 Atlas** from 1953-57. It would be several more years before he was able to quit the railroad and write full-time.

A small street crossing near here is **Dundurn Crescent**. Between 1965 and 1973 the current Poet Laureate of the Ukraine, Lydia Palij (born c. 1920), made her home at **20 Dundurn**, although she did not start to write material that would be published until later in life.

One block south lies **Watford Avenue**. The Cuban-born playwright René Aloma (1947-86) lived at **No.4** for a couple of years before he died. His first drama, *Once a Family* (1975), was one of the first productions of Tarragon Theatre. Later works were presented at the St. Lawrence Centre, the Charlottetown Festival, and in the USA.

David Carpenter, c. 1983

Fiction writer David Carpenter (b.1941) described his "two-year stay in Toronto (November 1982 to May 1984) . . . I began life in Toronto at the Victoria Hotel and stayed there until New Year's Eve, 1983. It was too expensive so I moved from there to an attic at **22 Watford** . . . There I wrote all of 'Luce' which is the novella in *Jokes for the Apocalypse* (1985). This is perhaps my favourite story, certainly of all the early work, so I have a fondness for that attic. The house itself was in a state of spiritual and legal chaos at the time, and things got so bad there I may someday write about it. In the first four months of 1984, I wrote early drafts of three of the stories that appeared in *God's Bedfellows* (1988): 'The Father's Love,' 'The Elevator,' and 'God's Bedfellows', and a story I turned into a narrative poem entitled 'Toronto Eschatology.' This last piece was based on the rape and murder of a Toronto girl about 1983 and came out in *Heading Out* (1986). The story 'God's Bedfellows' was published in *Saturday Night* about the time I left Toronto.

"I loved Toronto, but almost too much. There was so much going on (restaurants, readings, low budget movies, art galleries, etc.) that my output slowed somewhat. Toronto began to absorb, then replace, my imaginative needs . . . Toronto is not beautiful like Old Montreal or scenic like Victoria. And its winters are even worse than Vancouver's winters. But Toronto is surely the most fascinating city I've ever lived in. Not the WASP enclave I was told to expect, but an ethnically rich, flourishing place that was good to work in, and even better to eat in."

By coincidence, **22 Watford** was also the home (1992-95) of another noted fiction writer, Olive Senior (b.1941). While here she worked on *Discerner of Hearts* (1995) and a book of poetry, *Gardening in the Tropics* (1994). Before coming to Canada in 1991, Senior edited a number of scholarly journals in her native Jamaica, and is still highly regarded there, especially for her reference book *An A to Z of Jamaican Heritage* (1983).

Harold Sonny Ladoo (1945-73) arrived in Toronto in 1968 to study at Erindale College. His first novel, *No Pain like This Body* (1972), had strong advocates in Peter Such (who had taught Ladoo at Erindale) and Dennis Lee, and the book did collect a number of good-to-excellent reviews but its fate was that of most literary first novels: benign

neglect at the sales counter. Before Ladoo could celebrate the publication of his second book, *Yesterdays* (1974), he was murdered during what was supposed to have been a brief visit to his native Trinidad. Ladoo is an example of how quickly the facts of our literary history can disappear. Writers who knew him remember him living for a while in an apartment on Jane Street. But none can recall the street number—or even the block where the apartment stood. The jobs by which he supported himself were menial (he was briefly a dishwasher at Fran's Restaurant on St. Clair, for example) and such jobs do not lend themselves to permanent records complete with home addresses. The city directories and the telephone books are either unhelpful or contradictory. So even though he lived for almost six years in Toronto within the memory of dozens of people still alive, where he actually lived is a mystery—except in one case: **21 Roseneath Gardens**. Peter Such helped him move his furniture to this address and recalls that Ladoo lived here for about 18 months c. 1972-73, and it was here that he wrote much of his first novel. The author's talent (and his murder) inspired Dennis Lee to write a confessional and moving poem, *The Death of Harold Ladoo* (1976).

To the west, poet James Deahl (b.1945) lived for a year 1981-82 at **22 Robina Avenue**, the same building where novelist and journalist Scott Young (b.1918) lived, also for a year, from 1940-41, having just arrived in Toronto with his new bride to begin work at Canadian Press. In his memoirs, Young describes a Toronto that is no more, and highlights the simple pleasures accruing to newlyweds: "When Rassy and I arrived at Toronto's Union Station on a cuttingly damp November morning in 1940, 36 hours after we boarded the train in Winnipeg, we were met by my uncle Jack Paterson. Over the years he had sold articles and fiction to *Maclean's* magazine and had recently moved to Toronto as its assistant editor. He loaded our luggage into his car and took off through a Toronto that bore little resemblance to the city of today—streetcars running on Bay and Yonge, businesses long since gone, no subway, no parking meters. Jack told us that good apartments were getting scarce because of the influx of war workers, but there was one near where he and Ruth lived. It was no Taj Mahal, he said, but might do for starters. He drove us there to look at it and we took it. It was one room, a kitchen and bathroom, furnished with a card table, three folding chairs, a bed that folded into the wall and not much else.

"He and I left Rassy with Ruth and drove back downtown to the CP newsroom, which at the time occupied the eleventh floor of the Metropolitan building at the southwest corner of Victoria and Adelaide. I was introduced to men at various levels of bossdom and was told that, after a couple of days to get settled, I would work on the day rewrite desk, learning the ropes, and then probably would be moved to night rewrite. That was my introduction to the kind of newsroom bedlam that I'd live in for the next couple of years.

"I learned from the beginning that it was a dirty place to work. Fresh copy from a dozen or more teletype machines tended to smear when handled. So did the carbons on each 'book' of multiple flimsies on which we typed. We were all fast, even though the typing styles varied all the way from expert to my own technique, two forefingers and one thumb. At the end of each of my 'books' of rewrites, I'd pull the carbons (as many as ten) in one big yank. This would free the flimsies, which were then delivered by copy boys to the several wire editors, who either threw them away or added them to the pile waiting to be sent by teletype on the west wire, Ontario wire, Canadian wire or New York wire (this only if a story had a U.S. angle that our allies at Associated Press might wish to use). With all the machines going, spewing out news from around Canada and the world, the noise was considerable. Bedlam was not too strong a description. On top of all this—the hammering of teletype machines, editors yelling advice or insults or comments on the incoming news—there was one extra: sometimes many or all of the men around the newsroom would break into song, never missing a beat in punching out news being relayed across the country. The songs might be from musicals, but most popular, words and music best known, were hymns . . . I can recall news editor Ab Fulford (father of writer Robert Fulford, who was a child at the time) leaning in his office doorway to listen with a smile, as did Charles Bruce, the fine writer, novelist and poet who was CP's general superintendent when I arrived . . . My eight-hour shift on night rewrite started each day at 6 pm and ended each morning about 2, allowing me to catch a northbound streetcar up Yonge Street, then a westbound one on St. Clair. I got off at Oakwood and after a few minutes' walk would be with Rassy, telling her the day's happenings. Besides the card table, which we ate on, and the folding chairs, soon we had a chesterfield that Rassy had found in the hall, about to be thrown out. It had been painted orange with ordinary house paint by its previous owner. Rassy asked the janitor if we could have it, and he helped her carry it in; a surprise for me when I got home that night. . . . Streetcar wheels screeched under the single kitchen window, which, when left open, gave pigeons a warm place to forage and shelter from cold rain. A few years later I sold a short story based on that place. It made honourable mention in the annual Martha Foley Short Story Collection."

Across the street, the novelist and *G&M* fiction reviewer Isabelle Hughes (b.1912) was at home at **33 Robina** for the first seven years or so of the thirties during which she studied at UofT. The fiction writer and activist Marlene Nourbese Philip (b.1947), winner of the Toronto Arts Award for Literature, has lived on this road since 1979, and all of her published creative writing was composed here.

Three blocks to the west, running north from St. Clair is tiny **Appleton Avenue**. The poet Eva Tihanyi (b.1956) reported: "I lived in Toronto at **39 Appleton** from May 1981 to January 1985 (during which time my first book *A Sequence of the Blood* was published [1982], and my second, *Prophecies Near the Speed of Light*, published by Thistledown in 1984, was largely written). Then, from January 1985 to April 1989 I was at **68 Appleton**."

Moving towards Dufferin Street we encounter **Lauder Avenue** where J.D. Robins occupied **No.187** from 1920-31. Robins was an immensely popular professor of English at Victoria College and Northrop Frye always cited Robins as one of the major influences on his education. Frye's biographer John Ayre states it was Robins who "pointed his students, most of them ominously ignorant about art, to the Toronto Art Gallery's small but growing collection of Group of Seven paintings. In his college office, he had his own J.E.H. MacDonald painting, *Montreal River*." When he lived on Lauder, Robins seems not to have done any creative writing, but in the following decades his humorous sketches would win him many fans, and a Governor General's Award.

The most westerly street we explore on this particular tour is **Northcliffe Boulevard**. Poet Afua Cooper resided from 1985-96 at **No.105**, where she wrote *Memories Have Tongue* (1992) and *Black Teachers in Canada West* (1991). Up the street, poet Colleen Thibaudeau (b.1925) lived with her parents at **No.167** for the two years of 1933-34, and it was here she distinctly remembers starting to write verse—some of it was published at the time in the *Star*. Another few metres to the north is **No.354** where, in apt. 2, James Hogg Hunter (b.1890) passed most of the WWII years. Hunter wrote evangelical mystery novels which apparently sold thousands and thousands of copies in Canada and the USA. At least one of them, *The Great Deception* (1945), was written at this address. Internal and other evidence suggest he was born in Scotland, came to Canada in 1915, and worked as a journalist for most of his life. From c. 1926-36 he was a reporter for the *Globe*, but by the fifties he was the editor of the *Evangelical Christian*.

CALEDONIA & ROGERS

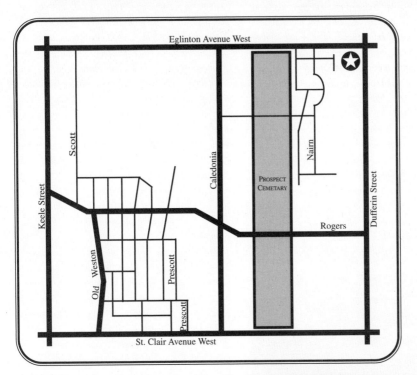

The tour begins at the southwest corner of Dufferin Street and Eglinton Avenue West.

Walk south on **Dufferin Street** to **No.1854**. From 1958-59, this was one of the many Toronto homes lived in by the noted Canadian playwright David French (b.1939). In these years, having just graduated from Oakwood Collegiate, he took his first steps to a professional theatre career by enrolling in acting classes which eventually led him to the Pasadena Playhouse in 1959. He seems to have done no creative writing here, but in the 1970s he would become a nationally-known author for dramas such as *Leaving Home* (1972), *Of the Fields Lately* (1973) and *One Crack Out* (1975).

Nairn Avenue runs parallel to Dufferin and is about five blocks to the west. Poet and fiction writer David Helwig (b.1938) moved

David Helwig at 274 Nairn Avenue with his dog, Buddy, circa 1945

c. 1941 to "**274 Nairn Avenue**, a tiny, yellow-brick house in York Township. I went to Rawlinson Public School at the same time as David French, but we didn't know each other, though we both remember the same fierce and frightening Kindergarten teacher. She was named Miss French and David was apparently worried that she might be related to him." In 1948, Helwig and his family moved back to Niagara-on-the-Lake, but it was not long before he returned to Toronto to enrol at University College.

The easiest way to cross Prospect Cemetery is via Rogers Road. Given the age of this burial ground, I was surprised in my research to determine only two authors who are interred here: the leader of the Group of Seven, J.E.H. MacDonald, and the literary journalist and novelist Jesse Edgar Middleton.

Gail Bowen in her father's arms, 84 Prescott Avenue, circa 1943

To the west of Prospect Cemetery is **Prescott Avenue**. **No.84** was the home of crime novelist Gail Bowen, creator of the sleuth Joanne Kilbourne (*Deadly Appearances*, 1990; *Verdict in Blood*, 1998). She was raised from her birth in 1942 at **84 Prescott Avenue**, the house built by her grandfather, Nathaniel Bartholomew. The house is found just north of St. Clair about three blocks west of Caledonia Road. Here, sharing the premises with her parents, aunt and uncle, and grandparents, she remained until 1955. She described the area as "working class, overwhelming British, and a great place to grow up." Now living in Saskatchewan where she has written all of her books, she still recalls her years here with much fondness: "I've been working on an adaptation of *Peter Pan* for the Globe Theatre here, and the address I've given the Darling family is **84 Prescott Avenue**."

Walk several blocks west to **Scott Road**. The disingenuous novelist Violet May King (dates unknown) published only one novel, *Better Harvest* (1945), a tale set during the Mackenzie Rebellion of 1937. The book, J.M. Dent's lead title that year, received glowing reviews across Canada when it was published, but the author chose not to publish again. For all of her life, it seems, she lived alone with her father. They resided at **171 Scott Road** from 1936 until 1961. William Arthur Deacon contacted her at the time of the book's publication: "Miss King, when located, explained that she is not a professional writer, but a time clerk in the Acme Screw and Gear Company, having first gone to work for that organization in February 1941 as a stockroom worker. 'When I wrote *Better Harvest* I was working sixty hours a week in two ten-hour shifts.' She wrote the novel in her spare time by way of relaxation which is a novel way to rest up after two ten-hour shifts. In contrast to the importance her publisher evidently attaches to the book, Miss King was strikingly modest about its quality. 'The story was written in a rather haphazard fashion just to please myself,' she said, and, as a novice, she believes there may be some better way of doing it."

HEATHER STREET

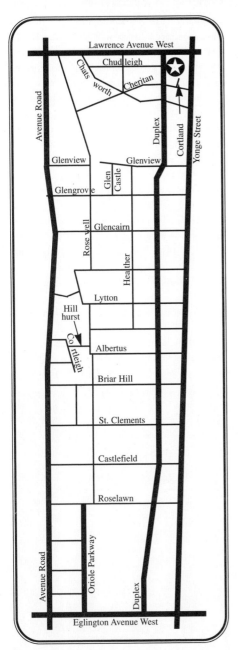

The tour begins at the southwest corner of Lawrence Avenue West and Yonge Street.

Walk west on Lawrence to Cortland and go south a few paces to **Chudleigh Avenue**. Don Coles (b.1928), a winner of the Governor General's Award for his poetry, is a UofT graduate who has been teaching at York University since 1965. For the first few years of his teaching he and his family rented a variety of houses, but "the first house of our own was at **36 Chudleigh Avenue** and we were there from the summer of 1968 until 1979 when we moved . . . the manuscripts for my first three books (*Sometimes All Over; Anniversaries; The Prinzhorn Collection*—all Macmillan of Canada books) were written in part at the **36 Chudleigh Avenue** address ('in part' because some of each of these books was written while on sabbatical or unpaid leave-of-absence . . .)." He explained what Toronto has meant to him as a writer: "Initially and, well, uninterruptedly, too, it meant a workplace (York University) which allowed me near-total liberty to follow out in my teaching whatever interests I was developing . . . By now the city has become valuable in other and quite typical ways; its familiar images have shown themselves to me often enough and over enough years that they can get into a poem in what might be a more natural, a more organic way than if the acquaintanceship between us were briefer. As an example, last month I finally managed a poem in which the guy who for ten years has driven the Zamboni up and down the outdoor rink I can see from my workroom window made the kind of appearance he has been demanding of me for a long while; he's been too busy to have known about this demand but it had begun to matter a lot to me, and if it has now been responded to as well as I hope, then it, and in a way he too, will matter to whoever reads the poem. Of course I am not totally

431

unaware that he has mattered all these years in more important ways than anything that has to do with me."

The popular novelist Jane Urquhart (b.1949) described the years 1955-61: "While I was in public school I lived with my parents and two older brothers at **107 Chudleigh Avenue**, in a square, red-brick, middle-class house that must have been built in the late twenties or early thirties. It had a small back garden surrounded by one of those wonderful, slightly ornamental wire fences that one rarely sees anymore . . . Toronto of the late fifties and early sixties was, I think, the perfect city for a child like me. It was small enough to be known and understood and large enough to continue to explore. The cultural activities that I engaged in were stimulating but not stressful in any way. I never felt pressured by my teachers (music, drama, etc.) to win prizes or to compete with the other children I knew who were interested in the arts. The great plea-sure came from the experience of making something happen: a play, a poem, a con-cert. There were no special public schools for the arts so children who showed special interests or talents were not segregated from ordinary life or looked upon as oddities. Now Toronto is a place I visit once or twice a month to do business (see my editor or agent) or for pleasure (to see friends, go to parties, attend readings or the theatre). The growth of the city in all ways is staggering; sometimes exciting, sometimes disturbing. I keep having to readjust my response to it."

Mary Quayle Innis (1899-1972) and her husband, the renowned historian Harold Innis, settled into **128 Chudleigh** in 1927 and kept it theirs until 1943. During this period she was busy raising a large family, but found enough time to write stories that found outlets in leading magazines such as *Canadian Forum*, and wrote the primer *An Economic History of Canada*, published in 1935.

Close to where Chudleigh ends is Lawrence Park Collegiate, **125 Chatsworth Drive**. Published creative writers who attended the

school include David J. Knight, Caroline Llewellyn, and Joan Skelton.

The novelist Wayne Johnston (b.1958), originally from Newfoundland , has lived in Toronto since 1989, and lived at **121 Cher-itan Avenue** between September 1991 and August 1992, during which he worked on the novel *Human Amusements*, published in 1994.

Cheritan forms a T-junction with Rosewell Avenue. At this point we can see the back of Havergal College. The school, founded in 1894, and originally located in the 300 block of Jarvis Street, opened here in the mid-1920s. The school was named after a British poet, Frances Ridley Havergal (1836-79), to emphasize the school's connections to Wycliffe College and the evangelical tradition of Anglicanism. The official address of the school is **1451 Avenue Road**. Authors who studied here include Claire Mowat, Susan Swan, Jane Urquhart, and Phyllis Brett Young.

Head south on Rosewell to **Glengrove Avenue West**. The John Ross Robertson Public School at **130 Glengrove** was the pri-mary school for two novelists: Joan Skelton (b.1929) and Jane Urquhart (b.1949). A

Douglas Lochhead relaxing in his backyard, 315 Rosewell Avenue, circa 1971

stone's throw away was the home of poet and Massey College librarian Douglas Lochhead (b.1922) from 1961-75: **315 Rosewell Avenue**. At this address he wrote four books: *Poet Talking* (1964); *A&B&C&: An Alphabet* (1969); *Prayers in a Field* (1974), and *The Full Furnace: Collected Poems* (1975). Lochhead retired in the mid-seventies and moved to the Maritimes.

Proceed east on Glengrove to Glen Castle, then north to **Glenview Avenue**. A number of writers have lived in these two short blocks. **111 Glenview** was the last Toronto home of Lois Reynolds Kerr (b.1908) before she moved permanently to British Columbia. A UofT grad, Kerr won a prize when she was only 22 for her play *Open Doors*, an award that led to the play's production in Toronto and her appointment to the *Globe* as a reporter. The newspaper job brought her into contact with other journalists, mostly women, who had formed a group (The Playwrights' Studio Group) determined to present Canadian fare as a counterweight to the mass of British and American theatre which dominated the professional Toronto stages. Her subsequent plays were almost all comedies. She lived at this address from 1948-50.

Bertram Brooker (1888-1955) is one of about half-a-dozen people in this book who met acclaim in the disciplines of writing and visual art (others include Arthur Heming and Lawren Harris, for example). He first came to the attention of the art world in 1927 with an exhibition of his paintings at the Arts and Letters Club—the first abstract work by a Canadian to be shown in this country. It's worth noting that Brooker had only begun to paint the year before the exhibition opened. An adroit wordsmith, Brooker wrote a syndicated column in which he expressed his opinions about individuals as well as movements in Canadian culture: painting, of course (although an early advocate of abstract art, he was also a pioneer booster of the Group of Seven), but fiction, theatre, poetry, and music also came within his purview. Whereas in our time a career in the fine arts

seems to preclude a career in the power corridors of the corporate world, Brooker embraced that world, working at the MacLaren Advertising Agency from 1940 onwards, eventually becoming a vice-president of the firm, and a kind of walking god to advertising folk who marvelled at his ad skills.

Brooker was born in England and came to Canada when he was 17. To the best of my knowledge, he is the only author, besides Margaret Laurence, who ever lived in Neepawa, Manitoba—he owned the movie theatre there around the time of WWI. In 1921, he made his move to Toronto. At this point, according to one profiler, "he entered the advertising business, first editing *Marketing Magazine* and then buying it." His first books, in fact, were not novels but rather texts on merchandising (e.g., *Layout Technique in Advertising*, 1929).

Bertram Brooker at his home, 107 Glenview Avenue, circa 1935

However, he did eventually write fiction, and was very good at that too. His first novel, *Think of the Earth* (1936), was also the first winner of the Governor General's Award. Brooker's daughter told me her father was tickled pink to receive the award in person from a man he had read when a kid in Britain: John Buchan, Lord Tweedsmuir.

His 1949 novel, *The Robber* (an historical, almost religious deliberation upon the significance of Barabbas) is even more highly regarded by critics and scholars.

It is thanks to Brooker's singular energy and drive that we have two valuable compendiums of essays by Canadian artists ruminating on and explicating their own work: *Yearbook of the Arts in Canada* was published first in 1929, and the second, because of economic conditions, did not appear until 1936. They still make for fascinating reading, and make one lament we do not have something similar today.

During the thirties, two of his plays were produced by Herman Voaden as part of his Drama Workshop at the school where Voaden taught, Central High School of Commerce. The plays (published in 1985) closely reflect Brooker's intense, life-long involvement in Theosophy and mysticism. As if all of these accomplishments were not enough, he also tried his hand at commercial fiction (under a pseudonym), and more seriously, to poetry. The latter has many admirers.

The Brookers moved to **107 Glenview Avenue**, and Bertram lived there until he died on March 21, 1955.

Poet and novelist David Knight (b.1926) (*Farquarharson's Physique and What It Did to His Mind*, 1971) reported that "once my father was well re-established (in 1938) he bought **94 Glenview Avenue** on the ravine. And having been the first member of the family into the house (through a back basement window) in August 1938, I became the last member to leave (through the front door this time), 31 years later when my mother died. By then, of course, I had lived in a lot of places on my own." It was while living at **Glenview** that Knight began to write, although everything he has published thus far was written elsewhere.

Poet Anne Elizabeth Wilson (1901-46), who was *Chatelaine's* first editor, came to Toronto from the USA c. 1923 and boarded at **19 Glenview Avenue** throughout 1924 while working for the book publisher Musson.

At the eastern end of the street, **2 Glenview**, the ghosthunter R.S. Lambert (1894-1981) lived in apt. 615 from 1948-49. In his native England, Lambert had had a fine career with the BBC. Among other accomplishments, he was the founding editor of *The Listener*. He immigrated to this country with his family just before the start of WWII and worked for the CBC. Before he died, he could claim more than 40 books to his credit. They include volumes of travel, history, visual art, fiction, and especially the paranormal. According to John Robert Colombo, a specialist in Canadian parapsychology, Lambert was an expert on poltergeists. Lambert won the Governor General's Award in 1949 for his book, *Franklin of the Arctic*, a book for juveniles.

Just to the north of the point were Glenview meets Yonge is **2904 Yonge Street,** where the poet Wilson MacDonald (1880-1967) had an apartment from 1945 to c. 1957. Wilson was probably the most aggressive poet in the history of the country, in the sense that he was bold about being a poet and nothing but a poet and that was how he made his living thank you very much. But also in the way he sold his poetry. Older writers described with a mixture of envy and disdain how Macdonald would scout the venue where he was about to give a reading, arrange for all exits but one to be blocked, and then stand at that open exit at the end of his reading so as to shake the hands of his listeners—and coerce them with guilty looks into buying his books which just happened to be stacked on a table next to him. He was also assertive about reading in schools, and from the thirties into the fifties he was probably the only Canadian writer the students ever saw—indeed, was probably the only Canadian author many students ever heard of. One of the schools at which he spoke was Leaside Collegiate when Margaret Atwood was a pupil there: "Once a year a frail old man would turn up and read a poem about a crow; afterward he would sell his own books . . . autographing them in his thin, spidery handwriting. That was Canadian poetry."

When he lived at this address, MacDonald was the subject of a tribute at the Great Hall of Hart House in 1955. The moderator of the event was Pierre Berton, and the 350 people present were reminded of the kind of praise MacDonald received for his work from his earliest days. Sir Gilbert Parker said, "I am certain in days to come no poet will have a greater fame. To my mind, and I say this carefully, there is an unending day for Wilson MacDonald." Another fan, incredibly, was Albert Einstein: "The greatest thing I discovered in Canada was Wilson MacDonald. Canada must be proud of this great genius writing in her midst." Well, 350 people were proud of him that night but the number was nowhere near the figure MacDonald felt should be admiring his work. One place where his work was admired by large crowds was Russia. In 1957, MacDonald received an invitation from the Soviet Government to travel to Moscow—all expenses covered by the Soviets. He was given the kind of treatment usually reserved for heads of state: VIP status at the Bolshoi Ballet, the Moscow Circus, and Red Square military parade, followed by a reception at the Kremlin where he was introduced to Khruschchev, and the then Soviet Premier Bulganin (who apparently was a fan and had asked specifically to be introduced to MacDonald). In subsequent days, MacDonald gave readings to adoring fans in Moscow and discovered "he rivalled Stephen Leacock as the best known Canadian author."

With each decade of the century that elapsed, MacDonald's approach to poetry (and the lyrics themselves) seemed old fashioned, then antique, and finally embarrassing. To be frank, they often are. But he was no fool. Some poems are quite good. And from this distance, one cannot help but admire his determination and his tenacity to survive as a poet in a city, in a land where the occupation is frequently ignored, and often derided. Amabel King founded the Wilson MacDonald Poetry Society in 1953 to discreetly channel modest sums to him so as to allow him to keep this residence, and to coordinate the activities of the hundreds of people who really did passionately admire his work.

Another famous poet of rather more talent who lived in this neighbourhood was E.J. Pratt (1882-1964). He and his wife moved into half of the duplex at **47 Glencairn Avenue** in 1953, immediately following his retirement from Victoria College. According to his biographer, Donald Pitt, "having much less space in the new quarters, they had no choice but to dispose of many items . . . He would also have less backyard for a vegetable patch, but he was glad to have 'a small garden where I can put a steamer chair and have a snooze in the middle of the day.' Once settled there in late April, and the old house sold for a satisfactory sum, he soon adjusted to the transition and by the end of May seems to have been happily anchored once more. One complaint only was recorded in subsequent letters . . . a greater volume of outdoor noise at night." The Pratts remained here until 1960. Two years before, he had had the pleasure of overseeing the publication of *The Collected Poems of E.J. Pratt* with an Introduction by Northrop Frye. The poet Ralph Gustafson (1909-95) relates an anecdote about a night he spent with Pratt at this address, which reiterates the loathing most poets feel for those who try to burden their work with meanings it cannot support: "I remember Ned in his chair at **47 Glencairn Avenue** in 1957 with a cigar talking to me about symbolism in poetry. John Sutherland's book, *The Poetry of E.J. Pratt*, had appeared some months previously. We talked of the subconscious symbolic meanings that good, virtuous critics excavate from the poems to the poet's utter amazement. The book by John Sutherland appeared under tragic circumstances. John was dying. Ned was circumspect in comment, saying, at first, that the religious symbolism tacked onto his poem *The Cachalot* by John was 'remote.' We eased into the comedy which all life should be moved into if we are to keep any sanity in our course through it—an ability preeminent in Ned. 'Ned,' I asked, 'do you suppose the squid and the kraken in your poem really imply a re-enactment of the Divine Mysteries?' 'Jesus,' said Ned quietly."

Novelist Wayne Johnston, after brief residencies at a number of apartments, settled into apt.B at **811 Duplex Avenue** in September 1992 and kept it as his home and workplace until Sep-tember 1996. The unit seemed conducive to him and his muse in that here he finished his novel *Human Amusements* (1994), wrote his contribution to the anthology *Original Six*, and word-processed most of *The Colony of Unrequited Dreams* (1998), his international hit.

Belletrist and poet Kildare Dobbs (b.1923) was installed at **776 Duplex** from 1962-75, a period which saw the publication of his first book, *Running to Paradise* (1962), an auspicious beginning—the book won the Governor General's Award. Two years later he published *Canada*, a paean of sorts to his new country, and four years later he oversaw the publication of a collection of his urbane essays, *Reading the Time* (1968). In 1970 he collaborated with artist Ronald Searle on a history of the Hudson's Bay Company, *The Great Fur Opera*.

When Kim Beattie (1900-63) lived at **116 Glencairn** from 1932-35, he was the aviation editor at the *Telegram*, a newspaper for which he had been writing since 1919. His books included a history of the 48th Highlanders, another of Ridley College, and a book of poems published just prior to his move to this address. He seems to have sold the house to Nat Benson (1903-66), whom he would have known personally since Benson was also a poet and journalist (he was once, for example, the drama critic of *Saturday Night*). For the years he lived here (1936-43), Benson was the editor of *Canadian Poetry Magazine*. While in his home on **Glencairn**,

Wayne Johnston in front of his home, 811 Duplex Avenue, circa 1995

Benson wrote the poetry volume *The Glowing Years* (1937).

Toronto-born Dorothy Jane Goulding (b.1923) lived at **No.135** from 1952-58. In addition to being a drama consultant and editor at the CBC for many years, she wrote a number of popular books for young people, and became a specialist in the uses of theatre in education, writing some fundamental Can-adian texts for the field. She also wrote the copy accompanying Boris Spremo's photographs in the book *Boris Spremo and His Camera Look at Toronto* (1967).

In his excellent history of Canadian magazines, Fraser Sutherland summarizes changes at *Maclean's*: "In January 1914, the magazine had a new size . . . and by October a new editor. Born in Brantford, Ontario in 1885, Thomas Bertram Costain had written four rejected novels by the time he was seventeen. After a small-town newspaper career, he toiled for several of Maclean's trade journals. He shaped a more consistent, visually appealing magazine: the illustrations were larger and the ads distributed among the editorial copy rather than bunched at the front and back. Sworn to uphold Maclean's Canadianism, Costain made even greater use of C.W. Jefferys, Arthur Heming and the embryonic Group of Seven, and there were short stories by Arthur Stringer, Alan Sullivan and Sir Gilbert Parker. He even printed the twenty-three-year-old Beverley Baxter. Writers like Stephen Leacock, H.G. Wells, and Jack London could now get as much as $100 an article. Another contributor was Hugh Eayrs, the future Macmillan publisher, who was then an editor of the Maclean company trade magazine *Men's Wear*. A quiet, unflustered man with a luxuriant head of hair, Costain wrote fiction for the magazine, and his wife, Ida Spragge, contributed verse." In 1920 Costain moved to the USA, where he worked first, as a successful magazine editor, and second, as a successful story editor for 20th Century. Fox. It was not until the 1940s that he published his first novel, but after that his productivity was enormous—as were his sales, especially *The Silver Chalice* (1952). He died in 1965. For about three years (1916-18) he and his wife dwelt at **156 Glencairn**. When they first arrived in Toronto in 1914 they lived not far away at **16 Lytton Boulevard** for about half a year, and for some reason abandoned their Glencairn home to spend their last couple of years in Toronto at **22 Lytton Boulevard**.

Moving south via Rosewell Avenue, we pass **Cortleigh Boulevard. No.21** was E.J. Pratt's home between 1932 and 1953. Apart from the poetry that was written here, the house has other literary significance, for it was here that Pratt, Deacon, Pelham Edgar, and a few others met to concoct the very idea of national literary awards, and then drew up the terms and conditions of the Governor General's Awards. Fittingly, Pratt won the award in 1937 for his *The Fable of the Goats*, in 1940 for *Brébeuf and His Brethren*, and in 1952 for *Towards the Last Spike*. His *Collected Poems* appeared in 1944.

Another national institution founded, at least in part, within these walls was the *Canadian Poetry Magazine*, which Pratt agreed to edit from 1936-43. He also joined the editorial board of *Saturday Night* when he lived here.

Pratt just missed being the neighbour of another mid-century Canadian writer almost as celebrated as himself: Laura Goodman Salverson (1890-1970). One critic has called Salverson "one of the pioneers of Canadian prairie fiction, perhaps Canada's first native prairie novelist." Her first book, *The Viking Heart* (1923), addresses the problems and challenges faced by Icelandic immigrants to the Manitoba-Minnesota region. On a recent trip to Iceland I was surprised to discover among the literary folk there an ongoing guilt about how Iceland treated—or, in their words, "discarded"—these people. Salverson is still very much read in translation in Iceland, but there she is not considered a Canadian author but rather a "west Icelander." A later novel won the Governor General's Award, and she won another G.G. Award for her autobiography, *Confessions of an Immigrant's Daughter* (1939). By the time she moved to Toronto in 1950, she had stopped writing books. However, she was certainly writing stories and articles extensively for the *Star Weekly* in the 1950s, including the years when she lived at **11 Hillhurst Boulevard**, 1955-57.

Samuel Alexander White (1881-1956) published his first novel, *The Foreign Correspondent*, before 1910, and thereafter published at least 15 more novels, all of them written to be popular and consumed quickly. Most are set in the wilds of Canada. As early as 1912 he had to resign his high-school teaching post to keep up with the demand, particularly from the USA, for his fiction. He spent the last two decades of his life at **108 Albertus Avenue**.

The playwright John Herbert (*Fortune and Men's Eyes*) was born at **31 Briar Hill Avenue** in 1926 and passed the first four years of his life here. Wayne Johnston has lived at **No.148** since 1996. It was in this house that he put the finishing touches to the first of his novels to have a large international success, *Colony of Unrequited Dreams* (1998). And the journalist and novelist R.E. Knowles (1868-1946) roomed for some months in 1918 at **200 Briar Hill**.

St. Clements School at **21 St. Clements Avenue** can count at least three creative writers amongst its graduates: Suzanne Butler, Caroline Llewellyn, and Julia McGrew.

Poet, newspaperman, and war hero Kim Beattie (1900-63) made his home at **79 St. Clements** for the years 1949-53. The term "war hero" is unofficial, in that the government could not bring itself to admit that it had allowed Beattie to enlist when he was only 15 years old. It then shipped him overseas to fight, and somehow he survived in the trenches for four more years. He was sent home only after he had been seriously wounded, at which time the army said it was shocked—*shocked!*—to discover someone so young had been allowed to sign up.

The most celebrated literary figure to live on this street was the irrepressible Irving Layton (b.1912) and his wife at the time, novelist Aviva Layton (b.1933). The Laytons inhabited **122 St. Clements** (demolished) from 1970-76, and Irving rented **No.120** next door for much of this period as an office in which to write poetry. This was a fructiferous address for Irving; the books published or written while he lived here include his second *Collected Poems* (1971), *Nail Polish* (1971), *Engagements: The Prose of Irving Layton* (1972), *Lovers and Lesser Men* (1973), The

Pole Vaulter (1974), *The Darkening Fire: Selected Poems* (1975), and *For My Brother* (1976). These books contain Layton's most political and many of his most controversial poems, lyrics in which he makes large accusations and hurls spears of attack in all directions—doing what he believes a poet must do: raise hell and challenge the status quo. The libidinous Layton is certainly there in these poems, although by the last book there are the first hints that the alpha-male in him is conscious of the appearance of time accelerating. Aviva Layton published her first work while living here: a children's book, *How the Kookaburra Got His Laugh* (1975).

CBC producer and mystery novelist John Reeves (b.1926) lived at **No.286** for a little more than two years (1986-88). Still, the stay was long enough for him to write his fourth detective novel, *Death in Prague* (1988).

Maida Parlow French (b.1891) and her husband Donald French (1873-1945) moved to **36 Castlefield Avenue** in 1941. She had been a serious oil painter until she moved to this address, but something happened, and she abandoned painting and took up writing. Within two years she was publishing her first book, *Boughs Bend Over* (1943), and in 1947 published her second, *All This To Keep*. She was one of the main reviewers of fiction for the *G&M* throughout the fifties. Her husband had been the book editor of the *Sunday World* during WWI. Later he joined McClelland and Stewart, and some years before his death in 1945 had been named a vice-president of the firm. His own books included *The Appeal of Poetry* (1923) and several other tomes devoted to poetry appreciation. With J.D. Logan he edited an anthology important in its day and for some years afterwards: *Highways of Canadian Literature* (1924), a synoptic introduction to Canadian letters. The two men issued a revised edition in 1928. Donald French was a Canadian literature enthusiast at a time in our history when such a passionate stance was unusual. One of his most important contributions to Toronto's literary history specifically was his foundation of the Canadian Literature Club in 1915. When it began the fellow enthusiasts met every two weeks to discuss Canadian books, because there was no other place in Toronto where such a discourse was taking place. Over time, the meetings became more elaborate, and major figures, including authors of course, but also publishers and critics from time to time, were asked to give speeches. The meetings seemed to have always been open to the public. The Club's activity eventually dwindled to nothing in the early 1970s, its goal achieved of making CanLit a matter of daily consciousness to the general public, and in 1973 it formally ceased to exist. Maida continued to live at this address until 1963.

Poet and journalist Ronald Hambleton was moving into **78 Castlefield** in 1953 just as Ryerson was publishing his book *Object & Event*. Hambleton notes wryly in his autobiography that Lorne Pierce, the boss of Ryerson had written to him, "'I hope very much that we can take on other books of yours and go on to immortality together as publishing house and author.' He rejected everything else I submitted."

John Reid (b.1915), the quiet, Volkswagen salesman in North York who earlier in his life had been a friend of Pound, Eliot, and Wyndham Lewis, resided at **No.169** from 1969 until his death in 1982. Born in Guelph, he departed for Europe soon after he graduated from Upper Canada College in 1936. He spent almost a year studying with Pound at Rapallo, Italy, before returning to Toronto where he fell in with Marshall McLuhan and Hugh Kenner, themselves to become two of the most famous literary critics of the century. Kenner dedicated his first book to John Reid. Reid is now known for only one novel: *Horses with Blindfolds* (1969). The art historian Robert Stacey is at work on a biography of Reid and reports that the man left several unpublished novels and stories with recognizable Toronto settings, along with a correspondence rich in letters from Pound and other members of the European literary Valhalla.

Playwright Tomson Highway (b.1951) spent the first half of 1979 living at **84 Roselawn Avenue**. By this time he had worked with James Reaney in London and had graduated in Theatre from the University of Western Ontario but was yet to compose the plays, such as *The Rez Sisters* (1987), for which he has become internationally celebrated. Another author who lived in this neighbourhood just prior to writing books that would make him a national figure was Charles Bruce (1906-71). He based himself at **94 Roselawn** from 1937-40. His job as head of Canadian Press kept him working at other than literary writing, but almost as soon as the war stopped his creative writing flourished. He won the Governor General's Award in 1951 for *The Mulgrave Road*.

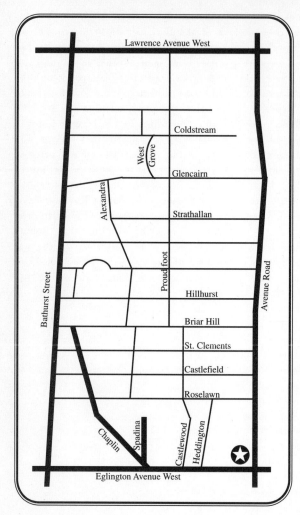

Lawrence Avenue West

Coldstream

West Grove

Glencairn

Alexandra

Strathallan

Proud foot

Bathurst Street

Hillhurst

Avenue Road

Briar Hill

St. Clements

Castlefield

Roselawn

Chaplin

Spadina

Castlewood

Heddington

Eglinton Avenue West

The tour begins at the northwest corner of Eglinton Avenue and Avenue Road.

W alk west on Eglinton two blocks to **Heddington Avenue**. Jack Batten (b.1932), a crime novelist and author of notable books about the law, although born in Montreal, was brought to Toronto when quite young and lived at **94 Heddington** until 1938.

When John Morgan Gray (1907-78) moved into **75 Castlewood Road** in 1937 he

was rising through the ranks of Macmillan of Canada, on his way to the presidency of the company. Shortly after arriving at this address, he published one of his first books, *A.W. Mackenzie, The Grove, Lakefield: A Memoir* (1938). Within a year he was writing his first work of fiction, *The One-Eyed Trapper* (1941), and even though he worked in a major publishing house, he found the process of circulating the manuscript to other publishers for considera-tion as thrilling and as depressing as any author. The delays in pub-lishers' respon-ses he also found educational, and in his memoirs he was honest enough to admit: "I sent off my manuscript like a mother sending off her child to his first school. I was to learn a good deal about the writing trade from those dealings, including one simple law: every publisher should write at least one book and try to find a publisher for it."

Jack Winter (b.1936) was one of the most prominent play-wrights in Toronto during the sixties and seventies—yet now he has com-pletely disappeared from our theatrical radar. For the first years of his 1963-71 occu-pancy of **125 Castlewood** he was the play-wright-in-residence at Toronto Workshop Productions, where he had several hits: *Before Compeigne*, *The Death of Woyzeck*, *Hey Rube!*, and *Ten Lost Years* among them. These successes awakened the interest of the CBC, and they convinced him to join the writing staff of "The Bruno Gerussi Show" and to work on other television projects. His plays travelled across the nation, and were popular beyond Toronto (the National Arts Centre, for example, commissioned him to write the play with which they opened the arts complex). And then in 1977 he moved permanently to England and seems not to have returned to Toronto, at least professionally.

Poet Don Coles (b.1928) made **415 Roselawn Avenue** one of his relatively brief stops (September 1966-May 1967) shortly after arriving in Toronto to teach at York University. He did little writing here; the poems that comprise his much respected collections were written at a later address on Chudleigh Avenue.

Playwright and novelist Patricia Joudry (b.1921) lived at **351 Castlefield Avenue** between 1943 and 1946. Her best-known work is a play, *Teach Me How to Cry* (1955). It opened in New York, transferred successfully to London, and was made as a feature film in 1959 by Universal under the title *The Restless Years*. She arrived in Toronto in 1940 via Montreal but after her stay on Castlefield headed to New York City where she was employed by NBC. Her earliest work for radio was done at the CBC on a series known as "Penny's Diary," a sitcom in which she also starred. Her work on that project overlapped with her stay at this address.

One of the youngest authors cited in this book is Lydia Millet (b.1968), author of the novel *Omnivores* (1996). Born in Boston, she moved to Toronto when her father, an Egyptologist, was hired by the Royal Ontario Museum. Following a traditional education at University of Toronto Schools, she had a most untraditional series of post-secondary jobs: "Worked in Hollywood for a valium-popping, aging TV producer who threw bottles at my head, moonlighting as a caterer and picnic clown. Finally got a job at Larry Flynt Publications Inc. where I worked for about two years. Was copy editor of two right-wing weapons magazines: *S.W.A.T. (For the Prepared American)* . . . and *Fighting Knives: America's Most Incisive Cutlery Publication.* Then I was 'promoted' to Larry Flynt's flagship magazine: worked for a year and half as copy editor of *Hustler*." She quit the Flynt empire when she received the publishing contract for her first novel, and moved, first to North Carolina, then Rio de Janeiro, then New York City. Before she was 30 she had lived in Berlin, Germany; Montpelier, France; London, England; Tucson, Arizona; Los Angeles, California. And Toronto, where she lived at **524 Castlefield** from April 1972 until 1986.

Poet and poetry publisher David J. Knight lived at **391 St. Clements Avenue** for the last four years of the Depression—and for the two years before that he was at **No.460**. A block or so away lived one of the most honoured children's authors of mid-century: John F. Hayes (1904-80). While dwelling at **448 St. Clements** from 1931-49, Hayes published his first books: *Buckskin Colonist* (1947) and *Treason at York* (1949). Later titles would win two Governor General's Awards and a Vicky Metcalf Award. All of his novels for youths deal with various locales and pivotal moments in Canadian history. They are noted for their attention to detail and historical authenticity.

Isabelle Hughes (b.1912) wrote four novels about the same fictional Toronto family, and the last two of them, *Lorena Telforth* (1952) and *The Wise Brother* (1954), were published while she lived at **428 Briar Hill Avenue** from 1952-62. These years also saw her extensively publishing reviews of fiction in the *G&M*.

The first four of humorist Morley Torgov's (b.1928) books were written at **208 Hillhurst Avenue** where he lived from 1964-96. Those books are: *A Good Place to Come From* (1974), *The Abramsky Variations* (1977), *The Outside Chance of Maximilian Glick* (1982), and *St. Farb's Day* (1990). He won the Leacock Medal for Humour on two occasions: for *A Good Place* and for *Maximilian Glick*. He described Toronto in this way: "In my lifetime I've had two affairs with the same woman. The first occurred when she was old, a corseted matron whose sons wore tweed suits in July and worked in head offices—the grey imitations of the Parthenon. On Mother's Day they dutifully took her to lunch at Murray's. I courted her because of her reputed influence, but she offered me nothing except Sabbath bleakness and the emptiness of her winters.

"That was thirty-five years ago. By what miracle she grew young, only God knows, but today she stands before me unbuttoned, a hint of carnality in her smile. She speaks half-a-hundred languages, and wherever she chooses to take her Lord's Day lunch, she insists on wine and to hell with what day of the week it is! Her name is Toronto. Once again I find myself courting her. But there's a difference: this time we are lovers."

Abutting Hillhurst is **Alexandra Wood**. Jack Batten spent much of his adolescence at **5 Alexandra Wood** from 1938-47.

Jane Urquhart (b.1947) has had the good fortune to write novels which attain magnificent critical success as well as bestseller status. She first lived in this neighbourhood as a little girl at 107 Chudleigh, but then suddenly: "About the time I entered Havergal (Grade 8), we moved to **209 Strathallan Boulevard**; a larger house which reflected my father's moderate good fortune in the Toronto Stock Exchange." By her own admission, Jane was a "bad girl," and she fled Toronto for Vancouver at the age of 18, returning to Toronto not long after—not to respectability, but to live in Rochdale College at the peak of its disrepute. This might suggest that her Strathallan years were unhappy, but, as she confirmed, the years were far from unhappy: " . . . the city seemed to grow as I did—not in size but in accessibility. I remember that after the age of twelve my best friend and I used to celebrate spring by walking all the way down Yonge Street from what was then the city limits (just above Hogg's Hollow) to the Lake, passing through district after district, eating at various greasy restaurants, visiting Gerrard Street, and later the Yorkville Village. I also remember singing with my school choir at Massey Hall and at

Jane Urquhart standing next to her portrait painted by Mieke Bevelander, at the Bau-Xi Gallery, Toronto, 1989

Convocation Hall with the St. George's United Church Youth Choir. I was lucky enough to take acting lessons with Dora Mavor Moore at the New Play Society, and to study piano at the North Toronto Branch of the Royal Conservatory of Music, and to borrow books from the North Toronto Branch of the Toronto Public Library."

Primarily known as the author of biographies on Canadian subjects and short stories for children, Fred Swayze (1907-67) occasionally wrote poetry books aimed at an adult audience. But when he lived at **319 Glencairn Avenue** from 1955 until his death, he concentrated on books for juveniles, including *Frontenac and the Iroquois* (1959). He had been the supervisor of high-school inspectors in Ontario, and at his death was in charge of the history curriculum for the province. He authored at least four textbooks used in our schools.

When Margaret Laurence (1926-87) was writer-in-residence at the UofT from September 1969 until April 1970, she lived at **9 West Grove Crescent** (at the corner of Glencairn)—quite a distance from Massey College for someone who did not drive and was terrified of taking a bus to work. As she recalled in her memoir, "I took possession of the house . . . sight unseen. It had been recommended to me by a person at the university and belonged to a married couple, both academics, who were on a year's sabbatical. I later realized that I could have rented a small apartment within walking distance of Massey College, but at the time, the thought of looking for somewhere to live in a city I scarcely knew was too much for me to handle. It was a pleasant house, but too much for my needs and full of what I was told was priceless Italian antique furniture. I rented the downstairs study, bedroom, and bathroom and use of the kitchen to a young woman, Eleanor, who was doing publicity work for several publishers. Hers was a cheering presence in the house. We often laughed about our reluctance to even touch the furniture. I never used the living room and very seldom the dining room, much less the good china and crystal. I mostly lived upstairs in the study which was less intimidating. I don't think I had friends in for dinner more than two or three times during the whole year."

Near where Glencairn meets Bathurst is **2601 Bathurst Street**. Apt. 206 in this building was the first Toronto home of the eminent Hungarian poet George Faludy (b.1910) after he arrived in the city in 1967 as a political émigré. It was at this address that he wrote one of his major studies, *Erasmus of Rotterdam* (1970). Once this work was finished, he concentrated on writing poetry and on entering Canadian literary society. Poets such as John Colombo and Robin Skelton became friends and collaborators in the translation of his work into English. With the fall of the Soviet regime in 1989, he returned to Budapest.

MARLEE AVENUE

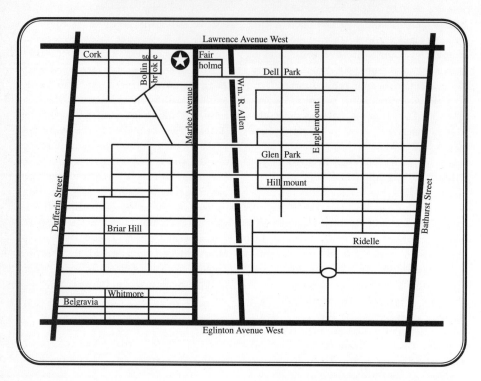

The tour begins at the southwest corner of Marlee Avenue and Lawrence Avenue West.

No Toronto playwright in our time has had the success on Broadway that Charles W. Bell or Edgar Selwyn had in the first decades of this century, but the author who comes closest is Bernard Slade (b.1930). His play *Same Time, Next Year* (1975) was a hit with critics and public, and was quickly followed by two other plays that, if not long-running hits, made respectable showings: *Tribute* (1978), and *Romantic Comedy* (1979).

Slade was born in St. Catharines, Ontario, but spent most of his childhood and teenage years in England. The family returned to Canada c. 1948; within a year or so Slade went to work as a clerk at the Customs and Excise Building on Front Street next to Union Station. "During the next eighteen months I wrote weekly mournful letters to my friends in England, saw countless movies, attended a series of dismal dances at the YMCA in the almost always unsuccessful quest for female companionship . . . I didn't acknowledge that I was lonely and it was only sometime later, when someone pointed out that my first seven television plays were all about loneliness, that I realized how traumatic this period had been." In 1951, around this unhappy time, he lived at **178 Fairholme Avenue**, just south of Lawrence Avenue.

Novelist Lisa Herman (born c. 1947) was born in California but did not remain there long: "My formative years were all spent in Toronto. I arrived here with my family who sought a more reasonable political climate— my father was Canadian, my mother is American—in 1950 from Los Angeles and lived in Mimico. We then moved to Winette Street and then **112 Dell Park Avenue** which is the setting for the beginning of my book *Bourgeois Blues* . . . I've spent a good part of my life running away from things. Toronto seems to force me to face them. I have been both dulled to numbness and excited to passion by this city and its people. I've been nurtured and excluded, charmed and repulsed, honoured and ignored. As a writer, I'd say growing up and now living in Toronto helps me explore my own extremities." She and her family lived on **Dell Park** from 1953-61.

Our next stop involves a small hike, but any fan of Mordecai Richler will happily make the walk to see his first residence (albeit a relatively short one) in Toronto. Follow Dell Park Avenue west to its end. Go north on Marlee to Lawrence, then west on Lawrence to Bolingbroke Road. Go south on Bolingbroke a few steps to **Cork Avenue**, and pause before **44 Cork Avenue**, the unlikely home of Mordecai Richler (b.1931) from November 1960 until June 1961. Mordecai described this as "a perfectly dreadful little apartment," and when asked why, of all places, he chose this one, he replied that he and his wife had just returned from Europe after a long absence from Canada, and, being a little homesick, they wanted to get to know some other parts of the country. At the time, Mordecai was waiting to hear whether he would receive a Guggenheim Foundation grant—the grant would allow him to live and write in London. The Richlers asked friend and writer Ted Allan to help find a place to live in a city they did not know well, and Allan found this place. Mordecai had severe culture shock. Recently he reminisced, "When I lived among those ROC natives for six perplexing months in 1960, a latter-day Llemuel Gulliver, I discovered that in order to buy a quart of single malt I required a passport, and that each of my bottled sins was entered therein, like a rebuke, by a sour official of the Ontario Liquor Control Board."

The literary significance of this apartment, apart from the fact it was Richler's home, is that he wrote most of his novel *The Incomparable Atuk* in it, a novel poking substantial fun at Toronto and its pretensions. The only spot to "scape whipping" was the Roof Top Bar of the Park Plaza Hotel, where Mordecai, by his own account, did a lot of research. The place remains his favourite in Toronto, as he explained in an article in *Toronto Life*: "For more than twenty years now, the Park Plaza has been my Toronto hotel, the Park Plaza Roof Lounge the bar where I meet to drink with cherished Toronto friends. I have tried, unavailingly, some of the other T.O. albergos. The Four Seasons, all of them concrete-grim, Sutton Place, and out there where nobody but highways meet, the Inn on the Park, a drummers' commune.

"I'm fussy. I spend too much time in hotels here and there. So, over the years, I have refined a set of my own prejudices. I will not, out of choice, stay at any inn where the embarrassed doorman is obliged to dress up like a voyageur or an eighteenth-century French footman or a Chelsea Pensioner or the Jack of Hearts. Dining rooms where there is a simulated waterfall or where the velvet-covered menu trails a gaudy fringe are out. Their waiters are bound to be so misinformed as to heat your cognac glass, so that you sear your unsuspecting lips on the first swallow. Also to be avoided are hotel bars where the waitresses are squeezed into anything like bunny costumes or, honouring their Etobicoke heritage, saris . . . What first attracted me to the Park Plaza was the Roof Lounge, surprisingly well lit. I should explain that that was in the early '60s, when I was still rooted in London, accustomed to drinking in cheery, well-lit pubs. In those days, to fly home and venture out of the afternoon sun into a bar in Montreal or Toronto was to stumble through all but total darkness or, at best, a very dimly lit place. But in the Park Plaza Roof Lounge it was possible to read a magazine or a newspaper while you waited for Jack McClelland to turn up, late as usual."

Return east along Lawrence to Englemount and walk south to **Meadowbrook Road**. The man many consider the finest Yiddish poet ever to have lived in Toronto, Peretz Miransky (1908-93), lived at **1 Meadowbrook Road** from 1977 until his death on July 11, 1993. He won almost every Yiddish literary prize possible, including the J.I. Segal Award in Canada, and the National Jewish Book Award (twice) in the USA. The *Canadian Jewish News* noted that "his Meadowbrook Avenue duplex was filled with birds and flowers made from sea shells, and animals from driftwood, a hobby that grew out of his love for nature, a love reflected in much of his writing." Earlier in his life he had lived a few blocks to the south at **177 Hillmount Avenue** from 1960-66.

Literary evening at the Zionist Centre, 788 Marlee Avenue, May 1, 1977. Left to right: Peretz Miransky, Miriam Scneid-Ofseyer, Sam Simchovitch

Arved Viirlaid (b.1922) arrived with his wife and children in Canada on Boxing Day, 1953, strangers in a strange land. But friends in the Estonian community found them temporary shelter until the Viirlaids could find their own accommodation—which they did, at **640 Glengrove Avenue**.

They came to this address in April 1954 and stayed until August 1955. Working hard at his day job, coupled with the shock of the move to a new continent, meant he was not able to write either fiction or poetry until another year had elapsed and he was settled into another home. Since then, his writing has established him as one of the major cultural figures in the Estonian language. Regrettably, only one of Viirlaid's many books has been published in English, the novel *Graves Without Crosses* (1972).

The most distinguished literary figure ever to visit the Jewish Public Library at **22 Glen Park Avenue** was the Nobel laureate Isaac Bashevis Singer (1904-91). Singer gave an address in English and Yiddish titled "Trends in Contemporary Yiddish Prose" on the evening of December 3, 1962—the first of his seven official visits to Toronto. And the first since his semi-humorous, unofficial visit (escapade is perhaps a better word), when he sneaked into Canada in 1936 to come to Toronto to renew his American visa at the USA Consulate. Before setting out from New York on this clandestine mission, he became friendly with a young woman he had met on the ship that brought them from Europe to the New World. She, looking for adventure, was anxious for Singer to take her to Toronto and, there, deflower her. He agreed. But once in Toronto his heart was not interested in sex, and, stalling for time, he wandered over to the garment district where he daydreamed about what life would be like were he to stay in Toronto: "I was told that Spadina Avenue was the centre of Yiddishism in Toronto, and there we went. I again strolled on Krochmalna Street—the same shabby buildings, the same pushcarts and vendors of half-rotten fruit, the familiar smells of the sewer, soup kitchens, freshly baked bagels, smoke from the chimneys. I imagined that I heard the singsong of cheder boys reciting the Pentateuch and the wailing of women at a funeral. A little rag dealer with a yellow face and a yellow beard was leading a cart harnessed to an emaciated horse with short legs and a long tail. A mixture of resignation and wisdom looked out of its dark eyes, as old and as humble as the never-ending Jewish Exile . . .

"Although it was too late for lunch and too early for dinner, the restaurant we entered—a kind of Jewish Polish coffeehouse—was crowded with young men and women. They all conversed—or rather, shouted—in Yiddish. The tables were strewn with Yiddish newspapers and magazines. I heard the names of Jewish writers, poets, and politicians. This place was a Canadian version of the Warsaw Writers' Club. Its patrons engaged in the same kind of conversations one always hears among Yiddishists: Could literature ignore social problems? Could writers retreat to ivory towers and avoid the struggle for justice? I didn't have to listen to their talk—their faces, voices, and intonations told me what each of them was: a Communist, a Left Poalei Zionist, or a Bundist. Hardly anyone here spoke with a Litvak accent. These were boys and girls from Staszow, Lublin, Radom, each one hypnotized by some social cause. I could tell by the way they pronounced certain words from which bank of the Vistula the speaker came, the left or the right. I imagined that even their gestures had unique meanings. Zosia and I found a table and sat down. She said, 'Here you are in your element.'

"'Not really.'

"It was odd that having crossed the Atlantic and smuggled myself over the border I found myself in a copy of Yiddish Poland. I told myself that there had been no need to consider suicide when Zosia vanished with my passport. All I would have had

to do was come to Spadina Avenue. Here, I could have become a teacher, a writer for the local periodical, or at least a proofreader. The Yiddishists would have hidden me here, provided me with documents, and sooner or later obtained Canadian citizenship for me. One of the girls sitting at these tables and smoking cigarettes would probably have become my wife and, like Lena had long ago, would have tried to persuade me to harness my creative powers to the struggle for a better world."

In the summer of 1938 Dora Mavor Moore took possession of **2600 Bathurst Street**—later renumbered **8 Ridelle Avenue**. Her son Mavor and his then-wife Dilly lived there c. 1946-47 after they returned to the city following WWII. In his valuable memoir, *Reinventing Myself*, Mavor Moore recalled the house and its environs: "The house that [my mother] bought in the summer of 1938 on the outer edge of Forest Hill Village was one of the oldest in Toronto. Built in 1815, it stood at the corner of what is now Bathurst Street and Ridelle Avenue, several blocks north of Eglinton Avenue (unpaved west of Spadina), with only one other roof in sight. Without electricity, gas, plumbing, or water supply other than the hand pump in the backyard, it had been the farmhouse for the area, and was said, on firm if minimal authority, to be the house where William Lyon Mackenzie, fleeing his failed 1837 rebellion, disguised himself as woman to reach the U.S. border and freedom . . . It had a wood stove in the kitchen, three fireplaces on the main floor, and no heat on the second. West of the house there still towers the ancient elm tree, with one branch, according to local legend, bent horizontal by the Mohawks as a trail marker. The property cost us $3,500 . . . Beside it, on a lot we neither owned nor could afford to buy, stood a small barn, sheltering, for as long as anyone living could remember only a two-holer outhouse. Despite its lack of everything conducive to public use, including accessibility, it was this abandoned barn that Dora Mavor

Moore recognized as the theatre of her dreams . . . By 1946 the old house with its well on one side and its septic tank on the other was being crowded by fashionable brick homes with swimming pools . . . The postwar shortage of housing led developers to snap up every vacant suburban lot, including the one between us and Bathurst Street that we could never afford to buy. Now relegated to a side street, the grandly numbered **2600 Bathurst Street** became the lowly **8 Ridelle Avenue**. Soon even its view of the thoroughfare was blocked by a characterless high-rise apartment building. Then we learned that our beloved barn, half of it encroaching on an adjacent lot to the north, would have to be demolished if that lot were sold. Within a month, the barn came down, its yellow planks of weathered pine sold for reincarnation as designer furniture."

The log house was dismantled in 1994 and is being reconstructed in Cobourg. The house and especially the adjacent barn were odd but essential landmarks in the development of Canadian theatre, for it was here that Dora Mavor Moore launched a troupe of neophyte semi-professional actors known as The Village Players. The troupe eventually became the New Play Society in 1946, the first company in Canada to produce new Canadian plays as part of its annual repertoire. It is because of Dora Mavor Moore's unparalleled commitment to, and belief in Canadian theatre (begun at this address) that the country's highest awards for drama are called The Doras in her honour. Her son relates in his memoir: "A more unpromising launching pad for the revival of professional theatre would have been hard to find. It was miles from the city's centre and hard to reach. The stage (formerly the stables, transitionally an outhouse, then a storage space for scenery) was eighteen feet across, eight feet deep, two feet off the floor, and about three feet higher than the tall actors. The rest of the small barn held about eighty spectators, counting those draped among the rafters of the

hayloft. Our first lighting, supplied by coal oil lamps and candles, was as hazardous as it was dramatic; but once the house was electrified in 1942—the year after we got indoor plumbing—we ran lines out to the barn . . . Since it was unheated, the place was unusable in winter. Legally speaking, it was unusable as a public theatre at all, which was why passed hats replace tickets."

The final three stops on this tour are to the west of Marlee Avenue. Begin at the most southerly of these stops, **101 Belgravia Avenue**, the home from 1945-57 of novelist Helen Weinzweig (b.1915). She would later write three books of fiction that earned high praise from reviewers: *Passing Ceremony* (1973), *Basic Black with Pearls* (1980), and *A View from the Roof* (1989). The latter was nominated for the Governor General's Award; the second book won the City of Toronto Book Award in 1981. She lived here with her husband, the noted composer John Weinzweig. In a *G&M* interview she related how she met her husband (when both were high-school students at Harbord Collegiate), and the romantic, seductive line he used to win her heart: "I had been away for two years at a sanatorium because of tuberculosis. Just after I got back, I was waiting for a streetcar outside Jack's house, and he came out and saw me there and said, 'Helen! I thought you were dead.'"

Novelist Joy Fielding (b.1945) wrote her first novel (*The Best of Friends*, 1972) while living at **123 Whitmore Avenue**. This was her home from 1957 until 1974. At the time, she was pursuing a career as an actress. Her books have been big sellers in the USA and other countries. Her success stems in part from a pastime she undertook while living at this address: "I played with cut-out dolls until I was fourteen years old, long past the age my friends played with theirs. That's what I feel like I'm doing when I'm writing— playing with my cut-outs. Everybody says what I tell them to say, and does what I want them to do, unlike life, which is not so easily constructed."

The final stop on this tour is the former home of A.E. Van Vogt (b.1912) and his wife, writer E. Mayne Hull (1905-75), at **997 Briar Hill Avenue** (at the corner of Times Road). Van Vogt was born in Winnipeg, raised on the prairies, and had his life changed when, at the age of 14, he discovered the magazine *Amazing Stories*. He devoured every issue he could find of that periodical and others like it. Then, in his twenties, he himself began to write science fiction and fantasy short stories. In 1939, three momentous events took place in his life. He married Mayne Hull in May. In July, he made his publishing debut with the short story "Black Destroyer" in the magazine *Astounding Science Fiction* (coincidentally Isaac Asimov's first story appeared in the same issue). And in November, after WWII began, and because he was nearsighted and excused from military duty, he and his bride moved to Ottawa where he worked at an army desk job by day and tried to write at night.

Unfortunately the demands of the job allowed him no time for his creative work, so he resigned, and c. September 1941 moved to Toronto. At first, they lived in a duplex (address unknown) in a suburb he called "Thistletown." Then, as he writes in his autobiography: "Early in '43 we made a downpayment on a small house on **Briar Hill Drive** in north Toronto. And I sat in the second bedroom of that dwelling until, in November 1944, we sold it and with the proceeds migrated to Los Angeles." This short description gives no indication that at this Briar Hill home he wrote, in addition to some of his best short stories, the novel *Slan* (1946), universally regarded as one of the masterpieces of science fiction. Van Vogt claimed that his wife decided to become a writer of SF stories while typing his manuscripts when they lived in Ottawa. Her first story was also published in *Astounding Science Fiction* in 1942.

Amazingly, neither could officially see their stories in print because all pulp mag-azines and comics from the USA were pro-hibited in Canada throughout the war. But by unofficial means they received issues in which their own work appeared. Nonethe-less, one of the reasons they moved to the USA was because all other SF material was denied to them for the duration.

Both authors stopped writing in 1950 when they converted to Dianetics—a "reli-gion" founded by another science fiction writer, L. Ron Hubbard.

BROOKE AVENUE

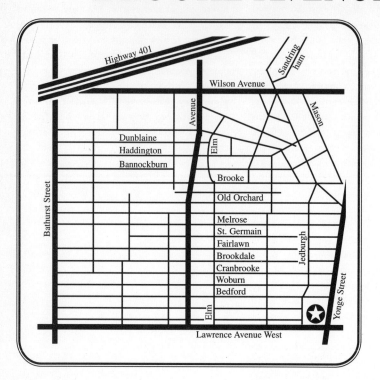

The tour begins at the northwest corner of Lawrence Avenue West and Yonge Street.

Walk north on Yonge Street one block to **Bedford Park Avenue. No.41** was the home of playwright Jason Sherman (b.1962) for only a year (July 1991 to August 1992), yet at this address he managed to complete two of his most important dramas to date: *The League of Nathans* (1996) and *Three in the Back, Two in the Head* (1995). No other Canadian playwright of similar age has been as heralded as Sherman for his work. Though relatively young, he has already won the Governor General's Award (1995, for *Three in the Back, Two in the Head*) as well as a Dora Prize, and a Chalmers Award. His 1998 play *Patience* has been optioned by Hollywood producers.

Next block to the north is **Woburn Avenue**. Since 1985 this thoroughfare has

been the home street of writer M.G. Vassanji and of his wife, the literary publisher Nurjehan Aziz. When asked why he moved here from the Annex, he admitted that the area was less exciting than the Annex but in its favour was the less expensive housing, and he and his wife felt the district was a preferable one in which to raise their children. Most of his novel *The Gunny Sack* (1991) was written here, and all of his novel *The Book of Secrets* (1994) saw composition here. This latter novel won the inaugural Giller Prize for best Canadian novel.

The poet Robert Billings (1949-87) was based at **166 Woburn** in 1980 and 1981, during which period he wrote *The Elizabethan Trinities* (1980). He made his living as a freelance editor. Given that he died by his own hand, a statement he made about a poem written at this address is especially poignant:

"'Chest Wounds' demonstrates my interest in contemporary affairs and was written during the organization of The Writer and Human Rights: A Congress in Aid of Amnesty International in Toronto, 1981, for which I did voluntary work . . . I realize that from Toronto it is almost immoral to imagine the horrors in Argentina, Lebanon, El Salvador, etc., etc., but some statement must be made, some awareness of the various powers which contribute to the death of compassion. It's a slow death: like a beautiful animal caught in a fur-trap."

Lydia Millet (b.1968) was born in Boston but came with her parents to **278 Woburn Avenue** in 1970 and remained here for a couple of years until moving to a new home a few blocks south of Lawrence. Millet has worked in Hollywood, as well as for Larry Flynt's *Hustler* magazine, and in an astonishing variety of other exotic locales for one so young. Her novel *Omnivores* was published in 1996, and the author is currently residing in New York City.

Laura Goodman Salverson

By the time Laura Goodman Salverson (1890-1970) arrived in Toronto in 1950 she had effectively ceased writing novels. Why this was so, no one seems to know. The cause was not writer's block, because she continued to write stories and articles for *The Star Weekly* throughout the fifties. And there was certainly interest among publishers in her books, for they sold well and had garnered serious review attention since her first, *The Viking Heart*, was published in 1923 in Canada and the USA. All of her books dealt, in one way or another, with her Icelandic heritage. The first novels addressed the crises faced by Nordic immigrants of her parents' generation; the later novels probed further back into the history of the land of the sagas. She was a two-time winner of the Governor General's Award. In 1954, she resided at **588 Woburn Avenue**.

Morris Winchevsky (1856-1932) was born in Lithuania but attended a Russian government school during the day. At night, his parents ensured he had excellent schooling in Hebrew language and culture. As a young man he was active in both political and poetry circles (often they were the same circle), activity which led to his arrest and imprisonment in Prussia. His sentence completed, he was told to leave the country. He went to Copenhagen, but his socialist political activity led to his deportation from Denmark. He tried Paris next, but soon settled in London where he joined a group founded by Marx and Engels. He is credited with starting the first socialist periodical written in Yiddish (1884). A decade later he moved to New York where he edited a more mellow weekly aimed at a broader audience. It was only after his move to the USA that his writing, especially his poems, elevated him into the highest echelon of Yiddish writers. Just before he died, he had the pleasure of seeing his *Collected Works* published in Yiddish as a ten-volume set. The Winchevsky Centre at **585 Cranbrooke Avenue** is named in his honour, but as far as I know he never came to Toronto.

Novelist Joan Skelton (*The Survivor of the Edmund Fitzgerald*), who lived at **153 Cranbrooke** from 1934-47, was adamant about Toronto having no influence on her writing. "Although born [1929], raised, and educated exclusively in Toronto, Joan Skelton's spiritual home was not, and is not there. She knew from childhood she would be a writer but it was not until she moved away from the large urban setting that she found her subject matter in the people and country of northern Ontario."

Barker Fairley, poet and painter (and head of the German dept. at the UofT), made a portrait in oils of writer Walter Bauer (1904-76). Fairley also gave a succinct word-portrait of this quiet man: "Walter Bauer was a German author resident in Toronto. He wrote extensively in his native tongue—verse, biography, autobiography. I feel sure that he wrote daily, almost compulsively. This may not always produce the best results, but it must have been for him part of the act of living. I think of him, now that he is gone, as having existed, as it were, on that plane. This made him a different person, less mundane, less worldly than others, though not less friendly . . . He was a refugee from Nazi Germany. This is my second key to his character. I don't believe a day passed without his feeling a sense of shame that Hitler spoke the same language as he did. If I wanted companionship in my outlook on the world, I used to drop in on Walter for a chat. He was easy for me to reach because he spent his later years as a member of the German department in my old college. Happily on the whole, I trust. Prior to that he had made a living as best he could, part of the time as a dishwasher, about which experience he afterwards wrote amusingly." He was certainly doing undergraduate studies at the UofT, and may have been working as a dishwasher, when he lived in the home of a friend at **149 Cranbrooke** from July 5, 1954 to December 19 of the same year.

One of the schools attended by Joan Skelton (above) was John Wanless Public School at **250 Brookdale Avenue**. This school was also the elementary school of Toronto-born novelist James Houston (b.1921). Each year the school presents to a deserving student the "James Houston Prize" for an adjudicated work of art.

Alice Ann Dorey was a poet of modest accomplishment and talent who did yeoman duty as the Head of the Toronto Poetry Group for many years after WWII. The Group was open to anyone, and was one of the few places in Toronto where someone could go for criticism of his or her verses, and be among people who read widely in the field. Her home was **396 Fairlawn Avenue** for the entire decade of the 1950s.

James Houston moved with his parents to **148 St. Germain Avenue** in 1927 and this was his home until he left to go overseas with the Toronto Scottish Regiment in September 1940. After attending John Wanless, Houston went to Northern Vocational, and then to the Ontario College of Art where he studied under Arthur Lismer. Houston was stunned by Lismer's love of African art, and by Lismer's magnificent methods of teaching: "I was hooked forever on primitive peoples. Lismer changed everything for me. I was going to travel and draw." After the war, Houston returned to **St. Germain Avenue** and it was from here he set out on his first trip to the North, the region with which he is most associated in the public mind, in part because some of his novels are set in the Arctic. Of greater social significance was his introduction of silkscreening to the Inuit— a technique with which many of their artists fell in love immediately. The best Inuit prints are in major art museums around the world. Similarly, it was Houston who began the organized marketing of Eskimo soapstone carvings. In the sixties he left the Arctic for New York in order to work as an artist at Steuben Glass, and it was in the same decade he began to write for both old and young. His first book for children, *Tikta'liktak: An Eskimo Legend* (1965), was selected Canadian Children's Book of the Year. Several subsequent books for children, most of which he illustrated himself, have also won major prizes. His adult novels centre around the conflict between native and non-native cultures, and Houston's ability to convey the aboriginal sense of magic and wonder can make the book compelling and simultaneously frightening to read.

James Hogg Hunter's last address in Toronto before he moved to Gravenhurst was **283 Jedburgh Road** (near St. Germain Avenue). Hunter (b.1890) was the author of several religious mystery novels that, in their day, were quite popular with the devout in the USA and Canada. When he lived in this house, 1945-53, Hunter wrote *Banners of Blood* (1948), *Bow in the Cloud* (1948), and *Thine Is the Kingdom* (1951). This last volume was described by literary historian Vernan Rhodenizer as "winner of the first prize in the Zondervan Second International Christian Fiction Contest, contrasting the enduring quality of Christian principles with the destructiveness of communistic ideology in a Toronto and Muskoka setting." Just up the street, at **No.309**, novelist Sarah Sheard (b.1953) passed part of her childhood in the mid-fifties.

Since his arrival in Toronto c. 1907, Guy Morton (1884-1948) had rented the same house for more than 40 years. Then the house was sold and he had to move. It seems he died of a broken heart, because he had no sooner moved to **100 Melrose Avenue** than he passed away. After a brief stint at the *Star*, he joined the *Globe* as a financial reporter, rising to the editorship of the section in the 1920s. Throughout his life he published popular adventure and mystery novels of no literary pretension—more than 20 altogether. They were big sellers in Britain and Australia particularly. One of the books was called *The Black Robe* (1927). It is mentioned here, not because it has anything to do with Brian Moore's novel of the same name (they have nothing in common), but because it was the first murder mystery ever set in Vancouver. Morton's last novel, *Mystery at Hardacres*, was published in 1937.

Novelist Eric Koch (b.1919) arrived in Canada in 1935 and after studies at the UofT began to work at the CBC, which was his employer until he retired. He has published a play, but is best known for his fictions, which include *The French Kiss* (1969) and *The Last Thing You'll Want To Know* (1976). Another novel was published in Germany but has not yet found an English-language publisher. His most recent work is a history of the Hambourgs, the most important musical family in Toronto in the 20th c. Koch's home from 1953-56 was **169 Melrose Avenue**.

Eric Koch strolling in Chorley Park, Rosedale, 1995

When they met on the street, Harry Boyle (b.1915) and Eric Koch would no doubt discuss the CBC and television industry from time to time, for Koch was a senior producer and administrator at the Corp and Boyle was the CBC Program Director for the Ontario region. Boyle lived at **174 Melrose** from June 1942 to April 1968, a period corresponding exactly to his years with the public broadcaster. Harry wrote to me, "When I was with CBC from '42 to '68 I wrote a lot. I had an agreement with the management that I could keep on writing when I joined."

Among the books he wrote during his Melrose years were *Mostly in Clover* (essays, 1961), *Homebrew and Patches* (essays, 1963), *A Summer Burning* (novel, 1964), *With a Pinch of Sin* (novel, 1966), *The Great Canadian Novel* (novel, 1972), and *Straws in the Wind* (essays, 1969). Boyle was awarded the Leacock Medal for Humour in 1964 for *Homebrew*, was also the winner of several eminent awards for his career in radio and television, and has been given a number of honorary doctorates for both his writing and broadcasting.

Another veteran journalist who lived in this area was Owen McGillicuddy. In August 1954, he died at his home, **332 Elm Road**, where he had lived for about a dozen years. McGillicuddy (b.1888) had been with *G&M* for decades, and was the city's most famous crime reporter, equally respected by his colleagues in the newspaper world for his photo scoops. He was proud of his friendship with Prime Minister Mackenzie King and of the book he had written about King's early career. He also authored a book of poems in 1918.

Sports writer and novelist Scott Young (b.1918) lived for about a year in a two-storey house at **49 Old Orchard Grove** in 1958. At the time, he was a columnist for the *G&M*, happy that *The Flood*, his first novel for adults (following three books for children), had been published in England and in Canada to good reviews—and unhappy because his marriage was disintegrating, a fact which led to his move into smaller quarters on his own the next year. It was around this time that he wittily replied, when asked the difference between professional and amateur writers: "The difference is about thirty hours of work a week."

John Linnell's birth and death dates are as unknown as his place of birth, and in John Morgan Gray's memoir, *Fun Tomorrow*, Linnell comes painfully close to being the Willy Loman of Canadian publishing. After years in the ranks, Gray eventually became the very popular head of Macmillan of Canada: "John Linnell, nominally manager of the Educational Department, had not been in the position long. He was a scholar and a poet, newly arrived from England and employed on impulse by Hugh Eayrs on the recommendation of Professor E. J. (Ned) Pratt. Linnell found himself struggling to understand the Canadian educational system, to learn publishing and the whole craft of editing in between trips to Quebec and the Maritime Provinces as a traveller. I watched him with a mixture of sympathy and impatience, having little notion of his problems; watched him go home at night, his case bulging with proofs, and watched him in the morning red-eyed as he lugged them back corrected. By late spring 1931 he was gone, fired, a married man with one child, who had been pushed in at the deep end in publishing, and too hastily judged not a good enough swimmer. Though the depression had not yet bitten deep, employers were becoming very cautious and for some weeks John Linnell walked the streets in search of work, a picture of growing despair." He had been at **150 Old Orchard Grove** for only a few months when he was fired. No longer able to afford to live in this area, he next appears in the directories of 1932-33 at 97 Ossington Avenue as a labourer at Southern Auto Gear—and then he disappears from the Toronto records altogether. What John Gray did not mention was that Linnell's poetry book, *Youth and Other Poems*, had been published by Macmillan of Canada in 1929, about the very time Linnell began to work at his star-crossed job.

Another publisher, Oxford University Press, was the employer of Richard Wright (b.1937) when he lived at **375 Elm Road** from the summer of 1967 to the following summer. His experiences at Oxford, and those of his earlier employer, Macmillan of Canada, inspired the background for his remarkable first novel, *The Weekend Man* (1970).

A stone's throw up the street, poet and critic Frank Davey (b.1940) lived at **395 Elm** during the years 1970-76, his first residence in Toronto. He recalled for me what (and where) he had written at this address: "I wrote *Earle Birney* in the summer of 1970 (at the dining room table, 1971); *King of Swords* (at night in the large bedroom over the garage) in 1970-71 (1972); *Griffon* (1972); *The Clallam* (1973); *From There to Here* in the summer of 1973 (also at the dining room table) (1974); and *Louis Dudek and Raymond Souster* throughout 1974-75 (1981). I edited various issues of *Open Letter* at this address, which served as the editorial address of the journal."

Old Orchard Grove leads to **Yonge Boulevard** (near Yonge Street). Yet another CBC producer *cum* author in this neighbourhood was George Jonas (b.1935) whose home was at **8 Yonge Boulevard** from 1961-62. At this time he had yet to publish a book; books of poetry came from his pen in the late sixties-early seventies, followed by libretti, essays, and a stellar book of non-fiction, *By Persons Unknown* (1977), co-authored with his then wife, Barbara Amiel.

Two blocks to the east is **Mason Boulevard**. David Wevill (b.1935) is one of the most highly regarded poets active in the USA, yet he remains a Canadian. He came

David Wevill

to Toronto with his parents in 1941. They had been evacuated from Japan where Wevill's father had been working for Canadian Pacific. After staying at a Toronto hotel for a few weeks, they moved into a furnished apartment near Oriole Park School for just a few months before settling into **56 Mason Boulevard** for approximately two years. The family left the city permanently in late 1943.

The adventuresome may want to walk to the northern end of Mason and cross Wilson Avenue to get to **Sandringham Drive**. **No.74** was the home of novelist and military man Richard Rohmer (b.1924) over the years 1964-70. When he lived here, he worked on his first book, *The Green North* (1970), and was just about to begin a career as a bestselling author of books about American military invasions of Canada.

Yet another CBC veteran on this tour was Walter Kanitz (1910-86). Born in Austria where he trained as a journalist, he managed to flee the country during the opening weeks of WWII. He joined the fighting as a member of the French Foreign Legion, but eventually moved to Canada by the end of the war and almost immediately began to broadcast on the CBC. When he moved to Toronto he worked for CHUM, then CFRB, and finally CKO, all of these positions helping to make his one of the most recognizable voices on the airwaves. In addition to two non-fiction books about the French Foreign Legion, he published the thriller *Close Call* in 1979. **97 Sandringham** was his home from 1966 until his death two decades later.

If you want to skip the Sandringham detour, proceed along Mason to **Brooke Avenue** and walk west until you reach **No.351**. This spot was the home of Luke Allan (1877-1962) for the first two years of the 1950s. Allan was one of the most successful writers of westerns in Canadian history. Once Allan had graduated from Victoria College, he became a world traveller *par excellence*, but Canada seemed to remain his favourite country. The foreign countries provided backdrops for

Four of the participants at the 1989 PEN World Congress, Toronto. Left to right: Anita Desai, Arthur Miller, Claribel Alegria, Margaret Atwood

books he wrote under another name, but the Luke Allan adventures were set in our North and West. By the time Allan moved back to Toronto, he had published more than 50 novels and had retired from writing this popular fare.

Once he was discharged from wartime service with the Navy in 1945, Scott Young bought the house at **355 Brooke** and occupied it until mid-1948 when he and his family (including his son Neil, the world-renowned pop singer) left Toronto for the Ontario countryside. In between, he was working as an assistant editor at *Maclean's* by day and by night was writing short stories he was able to sell to the American slicks.

West of Avenue Road, the next street to the north is **Bannockburn Avenue. No.12** was the site of the Duke of York School attended by a young Margaret Atwood during the years 1946-48. The school was stripped of its blue-blood status in 1950 and thereafter called simply Bannockburn Public School—until 1983 when it was closed. Atwood herself lived just a couple of blocks away at **111**

Haddington Avenue, also for the 1946-48 period.

Robertson Davies was replaced as literary editor of *Saturday Night* in 1942 by Jesse Edgar Middleton (1872-1960). Middleton began his working life as a teacher but soon switched to journalism and writing. His first book was a volume of poems, *Sea-dogs and Men-at-Arms* (1918), but he found his real calling as an historian of Toronto, and to a lesser degree of Ontario. His three-volume *The Municipality of Toronto* (1923) remains compulsory reading for anyone doing professional research into the city. Also frequently consulted is his *Toronto's Hundred Years* (1934), published to mark the city's legal centenary. During the Depression he published two novels of modest accomplishment: *Green Plush* (1932), and *The Clever Ones* (1936). Both are set in Toronto. In addition, Middleton wrote a number of plays which were produced at Hart House or at Herman Voaden's theatre at Central Commerce. From 1948 until his death, Middleton lived at **19 Dunblaine Avenue.**

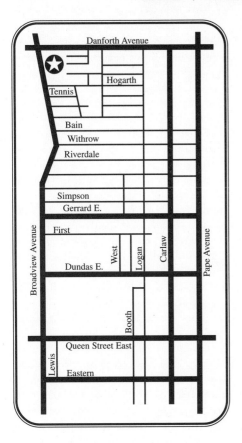

The tour begins at the southeast
corner of Danforth Avenue
and Broadview Avenue.

F or many of his last years Bernard McEvoy
(1842-1932) claimed that he was the oldest working journalist in the world—a claim
that seems never to have been challenged or
contradicted. At the age of 90 he still went
to his newspaper desk every day and filed his
copy, just as he had done since landing in
Canada in 1888. Born in England, he had
trained as a mechanical engineer, and came
to Canada when promised work on a new
railroad in northern Ontario. But no sooner
had he arrived, than the job was cancelled
for want of funds. But rather than despair,

he gave up engineering to work full-time on
a newspaper. He had dabbled in journalism
in the old country, but his job at the *M&E*
was his first permanent position. McEvoy
quickly established himself as one of the most
competent reviewers of the arts in Canada,
although, as was the custom of the time, his
work was rarely bylined. Sometimes it
appeared under the nom de plume "Redbarn
Relates." His creative side was represented
by *Away From Newspaperdom and Other Poems*
(1898), illustrated by the noted artist G.A.
Reid. He left the *M&E* in 1898 to work as an
editor at the Morang book publishing company. While living at **27 Danforth Avenue**
from 1901-2 he published another volume
of verse, *From the Great Lakes to the Wide West*
(1902). That year he moved to Vancouver,
which remained his home until he died. He
published a number of non-fiction books
there, as well as more poetry titles.

A few paces to the east is **179 Danforth**,
where Gwendolyn MacEwen opened her
coffee house, The Trojan Horse, with her
husband, Nikos. The space was not large,
and was very dark, more like a Quebec *bôite-
à-chanson* than a typical Toronto night spot.
I know, because I was invited to the opening
night. I was told that the festivities would
begin at nine, and, ever a good Canadian, I
showed up at nine to discover I was the only
customer there—Gwen, Nikos, and others
were frantically cooking in the back or
putting finishing touches to the décor. It
seems that when Gwen said nine o'clock, she
meant Greek nine o'clock, which is not as
exact as Canadian nine o'clock. I sat on the
huge corduroy cushions bunched against
the walls and sipped a coffee. I thought to
myself, Well, I'll just sit here for a few minutes until other mutual friends appear.
Alas, no mutual friends appeared until

midnight, by which time it seemed the night owls were just getting ready to party but, bloated on the 18 or so cups of coffee I had drunk to occupy the intervening three hours, I headed home.

Gwen and Nikos worked like dogs to make the coffee house a success but without a liquor licence, and lacking sufficient capital to hire extra staff, they were soon exhausted, and broke. The Trojan Horse opened in September 1972 and was sold at a loss by the couple in July 1973.

Walk east to Logan and then proceed three blocks south on Logan Avenue to **Wolfrey Avenue**. Novelist Barbara Gowdy (b.1950) made her home at **122 Wolfrey** from May 1975 to January 1976 while she was working as an editor at book publisher Lester & Orpen Dennys. John Garvin (1859-1935), long the champion of poets and one of the most important literary editors in Victorian and Edwardian Canada, lived at **No.98** for about two years, 1911-12. His anthology *Canadian Poets* (1916) became the standard text for studying our verse writers, and demand was sufficiently strong that a revised edition was published in 1926. He remained at this address until November 1912, when he married Amelia Beers Warnock who, as "Katherine Hale" was herself one of Toronto's pre-eminent women of letters.

Morley Callaghan (1903-90) moved as a boy with his family to **No.43** in 1908 and this was effectively his home for his entire youth and young adulthood. Even when he travelled, he gave this as his home address. It was while living here that he entered journalism—curiously, thanks to his prowess in baseball. Morley prided himself on being a formidable pitcher. To help pay his way through university he had been working in a lumber yard but found the heavy lifting was taxing his muscles and stealing strength from his pitching arm. So, in 1923, in order to save the arm, he decided to try to find a job in journalism. He went to the *Star* and asked, brazenly, to speak with the senior editor. Perhaps the effrontery worked because the senior editor "a man named Johnson came to see me. I told him 'You're always in need of a first-class reporter. Here I am.' Johnson said "No." Morley said, "In that case, I'm willing to work one week for free to show you I can do the job." And after one week he was hired. His first task was scalping obits from other newspapers. Then, after some days, he received his first news assignment: to report on a druggists' convention being held in town. Not having the faintest idea of what exactly to do, he asked the *Globe* reporter sitting next to him at the convention press table what he should do. The *Globe* reporter, realizing Callaghan was a rookie, took pity and showed Callaghan his notes. Realizing the insufficiency of that, he actually wrote the brief article for Callaghan. Callaghan submitted the story under his own name but he couldn't recall if the story was actually printed. He would, of course, write all his own material thereafter, including the novels and stories which made him our most internationally celebrated author for almost four decades. Books actually written at this address or published during his tenure here

Morley Callaghan's home, 35 Wolfrey Avenue, 1912-29 (replaced by apartment buildings in the 1950s)

were *Strange Fugitive* (1928) and *A Native Argosy* (1929). He remained at home until his marriage in April 1929.

Near where Wolfrey meets Broadview Avenue is **671 Broadview Avenue**, the home of James Lewis Milligan from 1923-36. A native of England, Milligan (1876-1961) came to Canada in 1911, first to Peterborough, and to Toronto in 1914 when he signed on as a reporter at the *Globe*, a position he kept until 1922. A few years later he worked for the *M&E*. Always interested in religion, he eventually became a lay preacher of the United Church. His creative writing reflects his religious interests. He wrote a number of hymns used by Baptists and Methodists, as well as books of poetry, the play *Judas Iscariot*, and even the libretto for a light opera produced in Britain in 1938.

The playwright Hrant Alianak (b.1950) lived for some years (1983-92) at **629 Broadview**, during which time his best-known play *Lucky Strike* was published, as were two other works: *The Blues* and *Passion and Sin*. He wrote two more plays while ensconced here: *The Big Hit* and *Four Grim Men*.

This area was full of dedicated newspapermen. Another reporter who worked at his desk six days a week for decades was Guy Morton (1884-1948). He came to Toronto c. 1906 and rented **70 Hogarth Avenue**, where he lived for the next 40 years. He would have lived there longer had the house not been sold, and the shock of the move to another address seems to have killed him, for he died within weeks of his departure from his old home. After working at the *Star* for a few months, he joined the staff of the *M&E* and then, when that paper merged with the *Globe*, he stayed with the new newspaper as the financial editor until he passed away. Morton published a large number of adventure and mystery novels with foreign publishers. He did not seek a Canadian publisher, he said, because he was friends with all of them and did not want to submit a manuscript whose acceptance would excite envious murmurings, and whose rejection would be awkward. According to Morton's obituaries, the books were big sellers in Australia and Britain; titles include *Rangy Pete*, *Black Gold*, and *The Perrin Murder Case*. David Skene-Melvin, the reigning specialist in Canadian crime-writing history, has noted of Morton, "I don't think he left Ontario in his life and yet every one of his books was set in New York or London. You'd never know the man was a Canadian."

A mystery writer who is proud to set her books in Toronto is Alison Gordon (b.1943), granddaughter of another Toronto author of note, Charles Gordon, better known as Ralph Connor. Alison Gordon had lodgings at **84 Hogarth** from 1981-88, during which time she worked as a sports reporter for the *Star*. The experience inspired her to write her first book, *Foul Balls: Five Years in the American League* (1984), a popular treatise on the beginnings of the Toronto Blue Jays, the antics of players, and on the business of sport. She also wrote her first mystery (featuring her amateur sleuth Kate Henry) at this address: *The Dead Pull Hitter* (1988). When asked to comment briefly on Toronto, Alison wrote, "Toronto, to me, is my neighbourhood. When I moved here, it was on the wrong side of the Don River to be fashionable, but that has changed. Part of me deplores the gentrification now under way, but I appreciate the changes it has brought. When I moved here, the closest thing to a bookstore was the paperback rack at the variety store. Now we have two within walking distance of the streets of Riverdale (or Danforth by the Valley as it is now, obnoxiously called), pondering plots while I do my rounds of shopping at the wonderful stores along the Danforth . . . The Toronto of 'world-class' pretensions—stretch white limos and celebrity chefs is as foreign to me as Wawa or Minnesota. I appreciate the energy of being able to live a small-town life in my neighbourhood, and others I have annexed as part of mine: the St. Lawrence Market, the SkyDome. I can work in my garden all morning, then hop a streetcar to be downtown in fifteen minutes for lunch. And I cherish the cosmopolitan nature of Toronto, which I usually experience through eating at cheap restaurants representing every conceivable nationality."

Three authors have lived in the apartment building at **9 Tennis Crescent**. The poet and science fiction writer Phyllis Gotlieb (b.1926) passed part of her childhood here from 1935-40. The playwright Ted Allan (1916-95) moved from Montreal to Toronto in 1982, and after a stint on Logan moved to apt. B-24 at **9 Tennis** in 1986 and made it his home until 1993. He is best known for his book *The Scalpel, The Sword: The Story of Dr. Norman Bethune* (1952), and he wrote the screenplay based on that book at this address. The film was produced in 1990 as *Bethune: The Making of a Hero*. Another film for which he wrote the screenplay, *Lies My Father Told Me*, was nominated for an Academy Award. Ted was also a novelist. His first book, in fact, was the novel *This Time a Better Earth* (1939). The adjacent apartment (B-25) was Brian Flack's home for January and February of 1980; then he moved upstairs to C-25 and that flat was his home until October 1983. In both places he worked on his novel *With a Sudden and Terrible Clarity* (1985).

Three blocks south is **Bain Avenue**. Both Morley Callaghan and Phyllis Gotlieb were once students at Withrow Public School at **25 Bain**.

No.37 was the home of a woman who is scarcely known in her native city, yet who was long the love-interest of Nobel laureate Sinclair Lewis, and a novelist in her own right. Edith Summers Kelley (1884-1956) lived at this address from at least 1895 until her graduation from the UofT and almost immediate departure for the USA in 1903. Her great marks at Jarvis Collegiate had earned her a scholarship to University College, and she was the top student in her class for four years straight. While she had published a few poems in newspapers and college journals, she left no obvious record in Toronto of the fierce determination she had to enter the world of books. In New York, she toiled for Funk and Wagnall's Dictionary factory for a few years before becoming in 1906 the private secretary of Upton Sinclair at the socialist community he had founded at Helicon Hall in New Jersey. By this date, Upton Sinclair was already notorious (and rich) from his novel *The Jungle*, an attack on unregulated capitalism. The book forced massive improvements in the meat-packing industry and changes in how food was sold to the public. At Helicon Hall he attracted a number of leading (and not so leading) artists, thinkers, and politicos to his experiment with communal living. Predictably, it lasted only a few months, but in that time, Kelley was introduced to a wide range of alternative art and political philosophy given short

Edith Summers Kelley's entry in the University of Toronto yearbook, 1903

shrift in the mainstream. Also in that time she met Sinclair Lewis and was actually engaged to him for some weeks, until they decided it would be better if she married instead one of his good friends, also a novelist. She did. They lived at Helicon Hall until it burned, and then they lived in Hell's Kitchen where she wrote pulp fiction to keep the wolf from the hovel door. This marriage lasted until 1914, when she moved in with (but seems not to have married) the sculptor Fred C. Kelley, whose name she added to her own. Turning her back on the city, she and her new man became tobacco farmers in Kentucky, the setting of her first novel *Weeds*, published in 1923. After tobacco they tried growing alfalfa in California, the setting of her second novel, *The Devil's Hand* (1974), which went unpublished in her lifetime. In fact no one knows why she never published anything after *Weeds*. She had major supporters in writers such as Upton Sinclair and Sinclair Lewis, and two of the best houses in the world had happily published her fiction. Her silence may be due simply to fatigue. She and her husband failed at farming and at one point she was earning cash as a cleaning woman. Her work was rediscovered by the American literary critic and historian Matthew Bruccoli in 1972, and he was instrumental in having it republished and re-reviewed. The *New York Times* then said of *Weeds* that it was "unquestionably a major work of American fiction."

Bain leads east to **Logan Avenue. 720 Logan** was the home of fiction writer Don Bailey (b.1942) for some months in the early 1980s. Another novelist, Susan Swan (b.1945), had her home at **609 Logan** from 1988-93, where she wrote her novel *The Wives of Bath* (1993). Her neighbour a block away at **639 Carlaw** from 1991-93 was novelist Paul Quarrington (b.1953). While living on this street he concentrated less on fiction and more on screenplays. His story *Perfectly Normal* (1991), written here, won a Gemini Award. Another playwright, Jason Sherman (b.1962), started his brassy arts magazine

what at this address and he edited it out of this building while this was his home between July 1985 and April 1986. Yet another dramatist, Ken Gass (b.1945), lived near here. He bought his first house at **256 Withrow Avenue** in 1977 while he was the Artistic Director of Factory Theatre (which he had founded just a few years earlier). This was his home for approximately the next half-decade, a period that saw the writing and production of his most notorious play, *Winter Offensive*. **No.70** was poet Libby Scheier's (b.1946) place of abode from 1984-85, and the novelist Michael A. Gilbert (b.1945) (*The Office Party*) has had a house on this street since 1983.

After her time on Withrow, Libby Scheier moved a block south to **165 Riverdale Avenue** and made it home until 1987. Another resident of the street was poet Betsy Warland (b.1946), who came to Toronto from the USA in 1972. Warland was involved in the seventies in the founding of the Toronto Women's Writing Collective, a body important to some female writers because they could get solid criticism of their work in what they felt was a mutually supportive ambience. Warland was also the chief organizer of the Women and Words Conference held in 1983 and of the three Writers In Dialogue events held at Hart House. These featured one American and one Canadian woman author in conversation and then both read their work aloud. The pairings were conscientious: Audrey Thomas and May Sarton (1978), Margaret Atwood and Marge Piercy (1980) and Nicole Brossard and Adrienne Rich (1980). Over 1974-75 Warland lived at **120 Riverdale**, and it was in this flat that she began her creative writing.

Mystery writer Alison Gordon, met above, also lived at **20 Simpson Avenue** from 1978-81. No doubt she made occasional use of the public library located a stone's throw away at **370 Broadview Avenue**. Paul Stuewe, the biographer of Hugh Garner, has written about how this particular branch was important to Garner: "In the early part of 1936, Hugh and his friend George Young who went on to become an Anglican minister, worked part-time at the Gerrard and Broadview branch of the public library, reshelving books for fifteen cents an hour . . . The book-shelving job, although it only lasted a few weeks, symbolized how much Hugh had changed since the days when the library had primarily been a place for his gang to hang out. Although he had always been a reader and had his own library card at the age of twelve, it was the crystallization of his desire to be a writer that really started him reading in earnest. At the Gerrard and Broadview branch, he spent much of the winter and spring of 1936 devouring everything he could find on politics and economics, reading Marx and Engels dutifully and Shaw's *An Intelligent Woman's Guide to Capitalism and Socialism* with great pleasure. At the same time he applied himself to the serious study of contemporary fiction, adopting Dos Passos and Hemingway as his mentors in the writing of realistic narratives but reserving a soft spot for the sentimental effusions of J.B. Priestley and the didactic messages of H.G. Wells.

"He was no more successful at creating his own fictional stories than he had been earlier in New York, but he did make a major breakthrough in the writing of non-fiction. In the spring of 1936 he printed, in pen and ink and on lined notepaper, an essay entitled 'Toronto's Cabbagetown' and sent it off to *The Canadian Forum*. This journal was at the time under the control of the League for Social Reconstruction, a loose alliance of reformist intellectuals instrumental in the founding of the CCF. Someone at the magazine would likely have known of Garner through his presidency of the CCF youth club, or he may have mentioned the fact in a covering letter, but whatever the circumstances of his article's acceptance, he found himself being published in the same pages as the likes of E.J. Pratt, F.R. Scott, Frank Underhill and A.J.M. Smith."

First Avenue is the first block south of Gerrard Street. It has been the home of Paul Quarrington since 1994. In that time he published *Fishing with My Old Guy* (1995), a humorous meditation on sport-fishing, edited *Original Six: True Stories from Hockey's Classic Era* (1996), and wrote *The Boy on the Back of the Turtle* (1997). Down the street at **No.82** was novelist Hugh Garner's home for a few months in 1933, one of several he shared with his mother in this area. He was broke, and one of millions of unskilled men looking for work during the Depression. He took any part-time job he could find—including the selling of ice-cream cones to people waiting to see the King and Queen during their royal visit to Toronto in 1939, a year when poverty again forced him to have live with his mother for a few months at 82 First Avenue

Running south from First is **West Avenue**, once the home of the poet and *engagé* Christian Tim Lilburn (b.1950). He wrote in a letter, "I lived at **67 West Avenue** from the summer of 1984 until the spring of 1985. I had a small room at the top of a very narrow semi-detached house. West Avenue is in south Riverdale not far from the Don Jail where I did some pastoral visiting. The house itself then contained a community of Roman Catholic religious trying to live a simple life with the poor—a task hurt by the rapid gentrification of the area. While living there I wrote *Names of God*, my first book of poems.

"Before moving to Toronto I had been living on a farm near Guelph. I found the closeness of the city oppressive—no green, living stretches; millions of sleeps, lusts, daydreams pressing in on one; the hustle of glib wealth everywhere. Life had no amplitude, no lazy generosity for me. I missed the farm with a longing that verged on depression. One night, after supper, walking into the falling sun across the Don Valley Parkway, I saw ahead in the shadows of some tall grass what appeared to be a herd of Ayrshires grazing along a slope. I thought I had received a vision, but in fact had stumbled upon the

Riverdale Zoo. The traffic kept on with demonic obsession either side of the median while the cows ahead on the shores of receding light flicked tails and ate in great calm."

Walk east on Dundas Street under the railway bridge to Logan Avenue. A few dozen metres south of Dundas is **272 Logan**, where novelist M.T. Kelly (b.1947) had a room in 1979 and where he worked on his novella *The More Loving One* (1980), its title taken from the Auden couplet "If equal love cannot be/Let the more loving one be me." Continuing a few steps further takes us to **194 Logan** where Hugh Garner had, for him, a long residence, 1928-30. In February 1929, he quit school to become the youngest copyboy at the *Star*, the beginning of his lifelong connection to journalism. Garner, who was fatherless at the time, related in his memoirs an unfortunate incident connected to this address that sourly affected his thinking for years: "I had a record as a juvenile delinquent and I became the natural prey of another type of 'social worker,' the gentlemen of the Big Brother Movement. One day, when I was fifteen, I was visited on lower Logan Avenue where we then lived, by one of those guys. He told me he was going to get me a season ticket for the Broadview YMCA (which he did), and then he pulled me onto his knee and kissed me on the cheek. I was having no part of that caper and I broke away. I guess I'd been aware of homosexuals since my preteens, and if anyone *was* one, he was. I used him as my model for Mr. Gurney in *Cabbagetown*."

Walk west on Queen Street from Logan. The next block is **Booth Avenue** where at **No.170** poet Bev Daurio (b.1953) lived for the last three years of the eighties. This was a productive address for her. In this brief era she was the editor-in-chief of Aya Press, the main editor of *Poetry Canada Review*, the editor of the anthology *Love and Hunger* (1988), and one of two editors of *Ink and Strawberries: An Anthology of Quebec Women's Fiction* (1988).

About five short blocks to the west is **Lewis Street**. Hugh Garner and his mother lived twice on this short road: at **No.63** in the summer of 1921, and at **No.42** from 1930-33. While living here he had his first of many encounters with the police and the courts, as he explained in his autobiography: "Until my on-the-road days years later, my only brush with the law came one winter day when we lived at **42 Lewis Street** in lower Riverdale. A small gang of us used to go down to the empty lots north of the ship channel and play touch football in the sand . . . Anyhow, on this particular day we tired of playing in the sand, and decided to board one of the tied-up lake boats which were wintered along the ship channel. These ships were usually guarded by a watchman who made his quarters on one of them for the winter. Whether the watchman was around or not that day I don't remember, but we broke into the galley and crews' mess and proceeded to have a throwing fight with the ship's chinaware, ending up by spraying the ship's interior, and ourselves, with fire extinguishers.

"A few days later a special constable, who combed the East End beaches on a never-ending safari against fornicators, vagrants, rubbydubs, and, especially, youthful deprecators, knocked on our door and handed me a summons inviting me to Juvenile Court to face a charge of malicious damage to property. . . . Because I was the oldest of the group by a couple of months, I bore the brunt of Judge Mott's wrath. I remember that at one stage of the proceedings he threatened to place me in the Working Boys' Home for a couple of months, 'to straighten you out and give you a realization of the seriousness of the charge you face.' I was the only boy not accompanied by his mother, for my mother couldn't afford to take a day off from work. We were each fined $10 and costs, and my fine (which I later repaid) was taken care of by one of the boys' mothers."

LESLIEVILLE

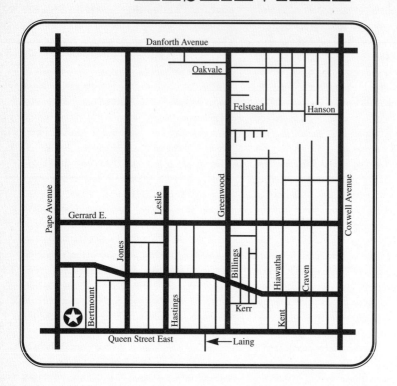

The tour begins at the northeast corner of Pape Avenue and Queen Street East.

Walk east on Queen about a block to **1054 Queen Street East**, once the site of a cottage where school teacher and author of "The Maple Leaf Forever," Alexander Muir (1830-1906), lived for a number of years while he taught at the one-room Leslieville School (itself originally located nearby at the northeast corner of Queen and Curzon streets) from 1863-70. City historian John Ross Robertson was able to communicate with a contemporary of Muir's while both lived here: "Mr. Muir was then a magnificent specimen of manhood, tall, robust, and every inch an athlete, and as I often saw him on a winter morning striding along to school, his clear skin and rosy cheeks, no one could help but admire him as he greeted you with a merry smile and

a cheery good morning. As I attended his school for three winters I have vivid recollections of his manners and methods of teaching, and many a fact of useful importance to me in after life was first received from Alex Muir. He was to us boys and girls a continual surprise from his original ideas, and looking backwards after forty years, I can clearly see how advanced he was above his fellows, towering in his individuality.

"As you say, he was very fond of singing, and school was always opened with prayer and hearty singing . . . He loved singing and always led it himself. He had a good baritone voice . . . Alex Muir's method of teaching was his own. He followed no monotonous stereotyped form, and that was the charm. Children loved to go to school because he made them love him by his kind and entertaining disposition. Some days he would treat us to some chemical experiments

. . . Another time he would send several boys outside on the road to dance and kick up, while inside he would, with the camera and a ray of light through the keyhole, show the amazed scholars, on the white wall beyond, the figures of their dancing playmates outside . . . .These experiments the children would practice at home to the wonder of their friends and parents so that Alex Muir not only taught a school but a whole countryside. The pupils to Leslieville School came from Todmorden, The Plains, East Toronto, Norway, and as far away as Scarboro town line [Victoria Park Avenue]."

The next block is **Bertmount Avenue**. The Rev. William Wesley Walker lived at **103 Bertmount** between 1921 and 1924. He was born in Toronto in 1858, graduated from McGill, but did not enter the ministry until he was 30—apparently because he had been fighting on the American side in the Spanish-American War. He published a number of books that reflected his wide travelling, including a novel, *Occident and Orient* (1905), "in which Herbert Cameron, the central character, is born in the wilds of Algoma, northern Ontario, and becomes the president of a university." Another novel, *Alter Ego*, is described as a tale of the Far East.

Return to Queen Street, and walk east to **Leslie Street**. Nearby is **173 Leslie** where the prominent Canadian playwright George F. Walker lived from 1957-58, one of several homes he had in this district during his youth. Walker (b.1947) has one of the longest entries of any dramatist in the latest issue of the *Oxford Companion to Canadian Literature*. He began writing plays by answering a plea for scripts posted on a telephone pole by Factory Theatre Lab in 1970. His first play was produced there in 1971. By 1978 he was so closely associated with the Factory that he became its Artistic Director for a year. He remains artistically affiliated with the Factory, although his work has also been seen on other stages in town, including Tarragon and Canadian Stage. His accumulation of drama prizes is unsurpassed in Canada. He has won the Chalmers Award more than once, the Dora Mavor Moore Award more than once, and the Governor General's Award twice. He has also had more success in the USA than any other Canadian dramatist of his generation. His works have been staged at the Mark Taper Forum in Los Angeles and at Joe Papp's Shakespeare Festival Theatre in New York. And countries other than the USA have also admired his work. Many of Walker's plays have been translated into other languages and produced overseas.

According to Canadian critics, his most recent writing is his best to date. *Criminals in Love* is the best known of these gritty dramas. They are known as the "East End plays" because they are set in the very streets you will walk through on this tour.

Where Leslie meets Gerrard is Riverdale Collegiate, **1094 Gerrard Street East**. Two distinguished writers were students at this school: Morley Callaghan and George F. Walker. The fiction writer Roger Burford Mason (1943-98) taught here in the late 1980s shortly after he arrived in Canada. And Basil King (1859-1928), the once popular author of novels about the emerging power of the middle class, gave a speech to the assembled students here at nine o'clock on November 24, 1921, one of four speeches he gave that day in Toronto secondary schools.

After living on Leslie Street, the Walker family moved to **152 Hastings Avenue** (the next street to the east) for the year 1959.

Near the foot of Hastings, on the south side of Queen is **1333 Queen Street East**, where the celebrated playwright Tomson Highway lived from October 1979 until October 1982. At this point he had withdrawn from actively producing his plays in traditional theatres, but in a few years would write the works which have made him internationally renowned, including *Dry Lips Oughta Move to Kapuskasing* (1990), one of the few local plays ever to appear in the Royal

Alexandra Theatre (where it had a most successful run). Just around the corner at **62 Laing Street** is the tree alleged to have been the one to inspire Alexander Muir to write "The Maple Leaf Forever" in 1867 while he lived a few blocks west of here. There are no documents stating categorically that this was the tree (assuming there even was one specific tree) which motivated Muir, so its authority comes from the long-held belief of local Torontonians that this tree—and no other—is the one. To its credit the Toronto Parks Department has taken seeds from the tree and nursed them as seedlings so that when the tree finally succumbs, one of its immediate descendants can take its place on this spot. One wonders why the City hasn't done something about the derelict house on whose property the tree sits. Its condition as a backdrop for such a national symbol is a disgrace.

Walk back to Queen Street, travel east to Greenwood, north on Greenwood to Kerr Road, then east to **Billings Avenue**. John Steffler (b.1947) was born at Women's College Hospital and lived the first year or so of his life at **57 Billings Avenue**. Steffler has written highly regarded collections of poetry, and a book for children, but it was his novel, *The Afterlife of George Cartwright* (1992), which attracted the highest praise and the most attention. The most attention because we live in a culture that values the writing of novels as a far more worthy occupation than the writing of poetry, and because the book won the Books in Canada Best First Novel Award, a literary prize with an excellent track record at discerning fine talent. After their experiment in urban living, the Stefflers moved to a farm in what was then open countryside north of Toronto.

Continuing east, using Queen Street as our conduit, we reach **Kent Road**, where George F. Walker and his family lived at **No.7** from 1951-54.

At the top of Kent Road, take a step or two to the left and enter **Hiawatha Road**. **23 Hiawatha Road** was the home of the minor poet Kathryn Tupper (1885-1964) in the middle years of the Depression.

For those of us who knew novelist Hugh Garner in his later years, and knew the damage years of cigarette-smoking had done to his vocal chords, it may seem incredible to know that Garner was once a choirboy at St. Monica's Anglican Church, **No.79**, in 1923, and again in 1926. Just up the street is **No.151**, Roden Public School, one of the several schools in this district in which Hugh Garner was enrolled. This street has also been the home since 1990 of the noted playwright Allan Stratton (b.1951). He lives in a house that once belonged to a descendant of the Ashbridges (whose property enclosed much of the acreage covered by this tour plus all of the land down to the lake and Ashbridge's Bay). When asked for a few thoughts on what Toronto has meant to him, he replied, "Like all long-term relationships, my relationship with Toronto has changed significantly over the years. I'm not sure to which degree my reactions are an objective barometer of the city and to which a function of the life stages at which I experienced them.

Allan Stratton in front of the historic Ashbridge Farmhouse, near his home, 1998

466

"When I first moved here thirty years ago to go to university, Toronto was like a candy store. Although I'd spent the previous year, my grade thirteen year, studying at Neuchatel, Switzerland, Toronto was the first place I called 'home' that didn't include a parent. It was a great place to go wild on the cheap. The range of experiences available was an especial eye-popper for a kid who was raised in London, Ontario.

"In the eighties, Toronto felt like a fishbowl. Leaving the city was like escaping to freedom and worlds where all things were still possible. Returning brought creative and emotional constriction; I recollect an oppressive sense of heavy clouds descending.

"Those feelings of claustrophobia have gone now, and I'm back to loving Toronto for its variety, its civility, and its spark. It's a great place to live and work. But I do worry about what I have seen happening around me over the past few years. I lived in New York as the Reagan cuts to social infrastructure gutted the heart out of the city in the mid-to-late eighties; greed was tangible and I watched the entrances to subways and streets filled with the homeless, and communities of people living in cardboard boxes that sprang up around the Port Authority and other venues. I worry that, in the same way, the past few years and the present are seeing the heart ripped out of the Toronto that I love and value."

Two blocks to the east we discover the home of another author who wrote from the inside about the lives of working-class people

living east of Yonge: Hugh Garner (1913-79). As a young child, Garner came to Canada with his mother expecting to find a father who had been working to compile a little nest—and nest-egg—for his family arriving from England. Instead, the mother found him living with another woman and indifferent to his first family's plight. Mrs. Garner raised her children in Toronto at a time, especially during the Depression, when social agencies for women in her position were few. Poverty kept her in this area, changing rooms frequently. Hugh Garner, therefore, spent most of the first half of his life living in the same streets played in and used by George F. Walker. Garner, in fact, spent far more time in these streets than he ever did in Cabbagetown, the area with which he is most associated in the public mind—although he had plenty of friends in Cabbagetown and in an age before the Don Valley Expressway, it was easy to walk there from here. From January to June 1924, the Garners lived at **273 Craven Road**.

Yet another author who writes about people generally ignored in mainstream fiction is novelist Margaret Gibson (b.1948). A native of Toronto, Gibson had a troubled

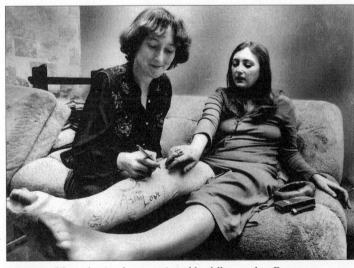

Margaret Gibson having her cast signed by fellow author Rosemary Allison prior to the gala booksigning known as the "Night of 100 Canadian Authors" at the Park Plaza Hotel, April 2, 1979

childhood. Her first treatment for mental illness came when she was 15 and the following years were often tormented. One of her short stories from this period of her life, "Making It," was the basis of the feature film *Outrageous*, starring the female impersonator Craig Russell, her friend and occasional flatmate. The film was considered scandalous and sensational when it was released in the seventies. In 1976 she won the City of Toronto Book Award for her first collection of stories, *The Butterfly Ward*, and her subsequent collections have all dealt in one way or another, with varying degrees of success, with mental illness. In 1997 she published her first novel, *Opium Dreams*, the same year which saw the distinguished literary publisher List Verlag of Germany purchase, for a record sum, five of her books for translation. She lived at **440 Coxwell Avenue** (just north of the railway tracks) from 1987 to 1990, and continues to live elsewhere on the same street.

Hanson Street intersects near here. Walk west on Hanson a couple of blocks until it merges into **Felstead Avenue. 152 Felstead** was the home of Frank J. Tate from 1928-31. Tate (1902-c.1987) graduated with a degree in Semitics from the UofT, yet almost all of his professional life was spent teaching mathematics to high-school students. He began a long association with Danforth Tech in 1929. In 1938 he published his only novel, *Red Wilderness*. The main value of that book today is historical, in that it is a superb example of the kind of Depression-era, right-wing fiction which proclaimed the reality of the international communist conspiracy and the evil of unions. The author's belief in the inherent goodness of the professional classes and of Ontario logging companies is amazingly genuine in its sincerity. This is one case where an author has absolutely no empathy with those who live on the other side of the tracks—in this case literally, since the CNR line just to the south is still considered a class boundary.

Felstead ends at Greenwood Avenue. Take Greenwood north for three short blocks to **Oakvale Avenue** on the west side. **15 Oakvale** (since razed) was the home of poet George Whipple (b.1927), who came with his family to Toronto when he was one year old, and stayed until 1947. Whipple came to some national prominence as a writer when he was one of eight authors featured in the anthology *Poets '56* published by Contact. Thereafter he published little until his first collection appeared in 1984. Some people think it wise not to rush into print.

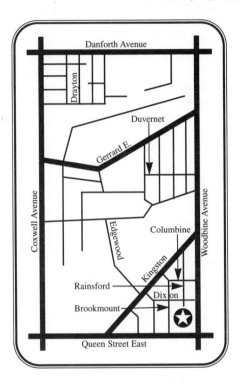

The tour begins at the northwest corner of Queen Street East and Woodbine Avenue.

Walk west on Queen Street one block to **Rainsford Road**. Norah Mary Holland (1876-1925) was a poet whose death was treated as major news by all Toronto dailies. One gets a hint of the kind of poetry she wrote from the *Globe's* straight-faced headline, "Frail Singer of Fairy Songs Passes Smiling To Her Rest." The reference to fairies was not misplaced. She was the cousin of William Butler Yeats, and the great Irish author made a point of visiting her on each of his visits to Toronto. She lived at **22 Rainsford** from 1914-22. At her passing she was buried in nearby St. John's Cemetery, Norway at **256 Kingston Road**.

Near the north end of Rainsford is **Columbine Avenue**. The poet Blanche Elmore, born sometime in the latter half of the 19th c., published a number of small poetry books in the 1890s in which blindness is the main theme. She was born without sight. **36 Columbine** was her home for two decades at least, 1922-41, but after that she disappears from the public record.

M.T. Kelly (b.1947) had just published his first novel, *I Do Remember the Fall* (1977), when he was living at **37 Brookmount Road** for about a year. The book's humour and pathos quickly brought him a national audience, except in Moose Jaw, which did not look kindly on Kelly's characterization of the town, thinly disguised as "Elk Brain, Saskatchewan" in the novel.

Running northwest from Kingston Road near Dixon is **Edgewood Road**. The distinguished English poet and critic A. Alvarez (b.1929) first came to Toronto in 1966 to visit his prospective parents-in-law, for he was engaged to a woman from Toronto who had grown up in the Beaches. Apparently he passed the inspection of the prospective in-laws, for in April 1966 the marriage took place—in fact, it took place in the home of the bride's parents at **59 Edgewood Road**. At the time, Alvarez was a visiting professor at SUNY in Buffalo, and frequently came to Toronto for private visits. This was the period when he was writing his most famous book, *The Savage God* (1971), a brilliant monograph on Sylvia Plath and suicide.

Edgewood terminates at Eastwood Road. Follow Eastwood east three short blocks to **Normandy Boulevard**. Jeni Couzyn (b.1942) and David Day (b.1947) were a married couple when they moved to Toronto from the west coast on October 1, 1976 and settled into the second-floor flat at **84 Normandy**. They remained here until February 12, 1978, when they left the city for Britain. Day has recently returned to Toronto with a new bride. While at this address Couzyn wrote many of the poems that appeared in her collections *House of Changes* (1978) and *Life by Drowning* (1983). The central theme of David Day's opus has been humanity's treatment of animals, an idea that colours all his poetry, as well as his bestselling anthologies, including one he was working on at this address, *The Doomsday Book of Animals: A Natural History of Vanished Species with a Foreword by HRH the Duke of Edinburgh* (1981).

The playwright Michael Hollingsworth (b.1950) first came to prominence as the author of *Clear Light* (1973), the last play in Toronto to be closed by the police on the grounds of obscenity. His more mature work includes the ambitious series of plays addressing the entire history of Canada, *The History of the Village of Small Huts*. Hollingsworth was born in Wales but came to Canada with his parents when he was five, and he lived with his family at **33 Kingsmount Park Road** until 1969, when he moved into a flat of his own.

Padraig O Broin with his landlady, 1962

Another author who arrived in Toronto from Europe when he was five was poet Padraig O Broin (1908-67) who went by the name Patrick Byrne until 1957 when, in deference to his Irish roots, he legally changed the spelling to O Broin and was always insistent that, properly spelt, Irish last names, including his, have no apostrophe. Despite his Irish heritage, he always claimed he was uninterested in poetry until he was 24 years old when, out of boredom, he tagged along with a friend to a St. Patrick's Day event where someone read aloud excerpts of a long poem by Yeats. Indeed, stretching credulity, he always claimed he had never heard of Yeats until that night. Regardless, something about the work bowled him over and he trolled the city's bookshops the next day, buying everything he could afford by the Irish master. Reading Yeats led to the reading of other poets and soon O Broin was writing his own work, initially under the tutelage of Donald French (v.p. of McClelland and Stewart and husband of writer Maida Parlow French), and then on his own. He edited alone or with others Gaelic-language poetry magazines in Toronto, surely among the most quixotic of our literary enterprises. A massive coronary killed him in 1967. His work in English is hardly read today, but those who knew him, such as Al Purdy, John Colombo, and Joe Rosenblatt, always cite his name with much fondness, and Gwendolyn MacEwen wrote a touching poem in his memory, "Reviresco." For the last three years of the 1940s he had rooms at **87 Glenmore Road**.

Glenmore is intersected by DuVernet Avenue. Take Duvernet to Woodbine then proceed north to **666 Woodbine Avenue**, once the home of Hans and Ed Jewinski, brothers and poets. Hans (b.1946) was known throughout the 1970s and 1980s as the "Poet Cop," not coincidentally the title of his 1975 mass-market paperback bestseller. That book was comprised of popular poems he had published earlier with small presses. Hans was deeply troubled by the public and media reaction to the book.

People marvelled that a policeman could have feelings, or seemed astonished that a cop could write something other than a ticket. Stung that few commentators paid serious attention to the poems as poems, he has published nothing since. His younger brother, Ed (b.1948), published one book of poems with Black Moss in 1979 but subsequent publications have been of an academic nature, including studies of Joe Rosenblatt and Michael Ondaatje. The brothers lived here after arriving in Canada from Germany with their parents in 1956 and stayed for three years.

Patrick Lane
1997

John Newlove (left), Alden Nowlan, Ralph Gustafson (right) at the Bond Place Hotel, Toronto, for the annual meeting of the League of Canadian Poets, February 28, 1977

By happenstance, **666 Woodbine** was where poet John Newlove (b.1938) lived from 1978-79 when he was in Toronto working as an editor at McClelland and Stewart. In the 1960s and 1970s he was a major literary figure, and Dennis Lee told me once that he regarded Newlove as "frighteningly good" and potentially the best poet of his generation in Canada. However, Newlove has been largely silent as a poet since then, although in 1993 he did publish the appropriately titled *Apology for Absence: Selected Poems.*

The last stop on this tour is the home shared by poets Patrick Lane and Lorna Crozier in 1989-90 when they were both writers-in-residence at the UofT. Take Woodbine to Danforth then proceed west seven blocks to **Drayton Avenue**. Their home from August 1989 to May 1990 was **149 Drayton**. Crozier (b.1941) is one of the most popular poets in Canada, her books regularly reaching sales in the five figures, a number almost all other poets can only fantasize about. While at this address she wrote many of the poems that appeared in her book *Inventing the Hawk* (1992), winner of the Governor General's Award. Patrick Lane (b.1939) is also an immensely popular and respected author (he, too, has won the Governor General's Award). While at this address he put the finishing touches to his much-lauded poetry book *Winter* (1990).

THE BEACHES

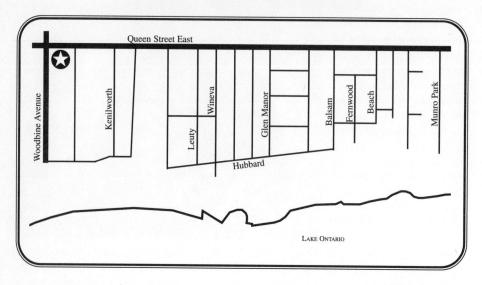

The tour begins at the southeast corner of Queen Street East and Woodbine Avenue.

The first-wave feminist and poet Laura McCully (1886-1924) seems to have lived with a brother or cousin named Kenneth McCully, first at **24 Kenilworth Crescent** from 1913-14, and then at **172 Kenilworth** for the last two years of the decade. Born in Toronto, Laura McCully had an extraordinary education for a woman of the time, gaining her M.A. from the UofT in 1909, but even before she finished her graduate degree she was publicly arguing passionately for women's rights. She would later become a reporter at the *World*, although most of her energies until her illness took control were dedicated to the women's suffrage movement. Unlike most of her sisters in the movement, however, she was a fierce supporter of Canada's involvement in WWI, and even among prominent suffragettes who supported the Allied position, she was almost unique in demanding that women have the right to bear arms and fight in the front lines. By the time she moved to **172 Kenilworth**, she was stricken with the first symptoms of the disease that would eventually lead to her incarceration in the Hospital for the Insane: paranoid schizophrenia. It makes for depressing reading to follow her long descent into madness and the awful inadequacy of the treatment afforded her. Despite her years-long divorce from reality, the obituaries were generous in their praise of her integrity and of her poetry, and she was clearly mourned by many people.

A young Hugh Eayrs (1894-1940) lived at **27 Kenilworth** in 1916 and 1917 shortly after arriving in Canada from Britain. He was living at this address when he entered the book trade in two ways: first, by writing a short biography of General Isaac Brock aimed at the school market, and second, by joining Macmillan of Canada, where he became president not long afterwards at the age of only 26. He also tried his hand at writing fiction, co-authoring the novel *The Amateur Diplomat*, with another young Torontonian who would also go on to do rather well in the book business, Thomas B. Costain.

Three blocks to the east is **Leuty Avenue**, once the home of the comic novelist Donald Jack (b.1924), as he outlined in a letter: "[in 1970] we moved to our favourite part of the city, the Beaches, to **41 Leuty Avenue**. We lived there for three years, and there I wrote many TV plays, and *Bandy II, That's Me in the Middle*, and started volume III. We were driven out of the house by noise pollution—an amplified guitar next door." *That's Me in the Middle* (1973) won the Stephen Leacock Medal for Humour—one of three that Jack has won for his writing. No other author has won more.

Donald Jack at the Toronto Island Airport, circa 1972Donald Jack, early 1970's

56 Wineva Avenue was Lorne Pierce's domicile from 1921-25. Pierce (1890-1961) was one of the three or four greatest literary publishers in our history. During his reign as editorial director of Ryerson Press from 1922-60 he published more Canadian literary writers by far than any other house, and for his entire life was passionate in his restrained way in the espousal of Canadian authors.

After divinity studies at various schools (including Victoria College) he was ordained a minister in the Methodist faith in 1916, and immediately took on pastoral duties associated with the war. A speech on literature he gave at a religious conference in Ottawa so impressed the leaders of the church that he was offered a position as the assistant to the Book Steward of the Methodist Book and Publishing House in Toronto—known as The Ryerson Press after 1918. Within two years after his first day on the job he was head of the entire publishing operation.

Almost immediately upon entering the field, he did not wait for authors to come to him but rather he sought them, and urged them to send him their manuscripts. Because the press had the backing of a major church, he did not have to make every title a profit-centre, and thus published poetry, essays, and criticism which he knew in advance were unlikely to sell many copies but which he also knew were essential to the development of a national literary culture. As early as 1925, he was making sage remarks about what the country's literature needed and where it should be going: "A national literature must be fostered in order that Canada may make a spiritual contribution to the nations of the world," he said to the Women's Press Club in Toronto. The *Globe* report of the speech continued, "'It is well to be a creator but it is well also in the present day to be a critic,' said Dr. Pierce, deploring the insincere, untruthful adulation that Canadian literature had received in the past from the pens of mediocre critics. 'We require a new race of critics in Canada who will hold up the world's best literature and then challenge us,' was Dr. Pierce's assertion."

Pierce was an innovator in packaging. In the interests of reaching as wide an audience as possible, he issued a number of controversial religious books in a paperback size, with a modest hardcover binding, and at a low price. Their success induced him to issue poetry in the same format, and the Ryerson Poetry Chapbooks (as they were called) were often the first books of several well-known

Canadian writers. He contracted leading Canadian artists, including members of the Group of Seven, to make woodblock illustrations for the bindings or to illustrate the pages. With the Toronto poet Albert D. Watson he edited the first Canadian anthology to feature poetry and prose from both languages: *Our Canadian Literature* was published in 1922. The following year, he published a biographical appreciation of his co-editor, A.D. Watson, and continued his research, editing, and writing about Marjory Pickthall and William Kirby, and before he left **56 Wineva Avenue** in 1925 (where he had lived since 1920), he also published another book, *Fifty Years of Public Service: A Life of James L. Hughes* (1924), a study of the Toronto poet and educationist.

Macmillan publisher John Gray in his autobiography recounts an intimate moment shared with Lorne Pierce revealing something of Pierce's manner: "Because we were still working with the Ryerson Press on a revision of the reading series developed fifteen years before, I made part of the trip with Lorne Pierce, Editor of the Ryerson Press and a national figure. It was very different from the travels with Hugh Eayrs, and yet it had some pleasant similarities. We had the same long talks in the evenings, after the last dinner-guest had gone; the publishing shoptalk that made me forget the war and the uncertainties. Conversation wasn't easy because Lorne was deaf, but it was worth the effort.

"On one of these occasions Lorne startled and flattered me by suggesting that I join the Ryerson Press and train as his successor. . . . In the rather high-pitched, hard voice that came from his deafness he said, 'I have the finest job in publishing in Canada. I plan my own list, do the things I think are needed, ask no one's permission.' I knew this appeared to be true and that his list was the most ambitious and idealistic in Canada—or anywhere—if a bit dull and probably not very successful in business terms. And then he put the question to which this

had led without my recognizing it. 'How would you like my job?'

"It was only at the last minute that I somehow guessed where this was tending and couldn't prepare myself for it. Perched on a radiator with a drink in my hand, I sat transfixed. It was a fine, prestigious job, and a compliment I had not earned, but it was no place for me. Lorne was watching me closely. Slowly, and smiling my appreciation, I shook my head. I said he did me great honour, but it wouldn't work. Cupping his hand around his ear he leaned forward, 'What's that?' 'I'm not the type,' I roared. 'Why not?' again sharply. Thinking of the stiff rectitude of the United Church legend—easy to respect but hard to love—I could only hold up my glass and my cigarette. 'I drink,' I said, 'I smoke.' Lorne himself had a drink in is hand, but it was a very small Scotch and a rare indulgence, when he was tired, or to keep me company. 'Do you have to do these things?' I answered, 'No, but I intend to.' He left it there and said goodnight."

Three blocks east again is **Glen Manor Drive**. Novelist Maud Petit (1877-1959) lived at **No.66** from 1938-44, at which point she moved to Glendale, California. Hill wrote plays in the 1920s, an interesting book of travel reflections in 1942, and a novel, *Keep Your Quilt, Mary Ann* (1944), about Canadian-American social relations, which was written at this address.

After a very brief stint in Forest Hill, poet and anthologist Gary Geddes (*Fifteen Canadian Poets*) moved to this street from the west coast for about two years starting in 1965 while completing his doctorate at the UofT. He wrote, "I moved to the Beaches, to **42 Glen Manor Drive**. It was a great spot for me, as it felt coastal and brought back some of my Vancouver feelings about the sea. It was also quite a quiet, almost English neighbourhood, which was a plus for me. The lower duplex was somewhat sterile, but the setting and trees made it all quite magical, especially as I was embarking on an exciting new academic career."

Novelist Scott Young (b.1918) spent his second summer (1941) in Toronto in an apartment at **15 Hubbard Boulevard**, while he struggled to make a living by writing short stories and by working as a journalist. His brief interlude at this address revealed an ugly but real facet of Toronto's history, as he divulged in his memoirs: "One sunny spring weekend . . . we went downtown and took an eastbound Queen streetcar to Hammersmith, where CP's west wire editor, big, balding, witty Eric Dunn, off that day as well, had invited us for coffee. He lived a few houses from the lakeshore. Leaving the Dunns a little later we headed for the lake and strolled along the wide boardwalk. Waves were rolling in from a passing tugboat. Leaves were beginning to show along the well-treed stretch of grassy parkland between us and a row of solidly built duplexes. Kids were playing baseball and soccer. Somehow it wasn't at all like the Robina streetcar loop.

"Near the east end of the boardwalk we turned and passed a three-storey apartment building called Hubbard Court. A sign read: Vacancy. As far as I can recall, the decision was made not in words but more like a meeting of eyes, no more. We went inside and found the janitor, who led us upstairs to a third-floor one-room apartment. There was a tiny bathroom in one corner and a kitchenette (fridge and stove) behind lattice doors near the entrance. But what captured us was the lake view, and all that action outside. We were sold even before the janitor gave his spiel.

"The building, he informed us, was owned and administered by the city's property department, closed that day but open again Monday. First thing Monday I was at City Hall filling out the necessary forms. These mainly concerned my willingness to sign a one-year lease, which I did on the spot. One provision I scarcely noticed at the time, was that I could not sublet without City Hall approval.

"Our time in the apartment was brief, however. Later that happy and carefree summer, Rassy became pregnant and we decided that with a baby we should have a home with a separate bedroom. I checked with the man at the Property Department, who said it was okay as long as we found another tenant. We advertised. An attractive young couple answered the ad and loved the place. We told them to go to the Property Department and do the paperwork. Certain that they would be considered perfect tenants and that the sublet would go through without problems, we went apartment hunting once again and found a plain one-bedroom apartment in a building called Blythwood Manor in the north part of the city.

"A day after we signed that new lease our new sublet tenant phoned to say that the Property Department had turned them down. At first I thought they might have changed their minds and were blaming it on City Hall, but he insisted that was not the case.

"'We're heartbroken,' he said.

"'But what reason could they possibly give?' I asked.

"'The man in the Property Department said he was sorry, and really didn't have to explain anything, but I insisted and it turns out it's because we're Jewish,' he said.

"I was shocked and offered to raise hell—even to write something for the paper on the lines that Hitler wasn't so far away after all.

"'No, please don't,' he said. 'We don't want a fuss. Our families, our jobs. . . We have a line on something else and don't want to go there as the people who. . .'

"I called the Property Department. The man there, when pressed, said—not apologetically at all—that in east Toronto, the Beaches area, there was an understanding about who could buy or rent, and that no Jews were allowed. The city Property Department could not go against the long-held will of the majority, he said. 'You'll just have to find another tenant. Shouldn't be hard, but it's got to be someone we accept, as your lease says.'"

Follow Hubbard to Balsam and then jump a block to **Fernwood Park Avenue**. Surprisingly, the only address I could find for Charles Langton Clarke (1859-1936) was the home where he died, **2-A Fernwood Park**. This had been his home since the start of the Depression. I say "surprisingly" because he had been a prominent newspaperman all his life. The *Mail* was his first employer, but then he switched to *Saturday Night*. After a few years he became the cable editor of the *World* and, with its demise, he found himself again working for the *M&E*. During all of this newspaper writing, he also wrote verse and fiction, selling the latter frequently to *Argosy* in the USA.

Clarke perpetrated one of the most notorious newspaper hoaxes in Canada in the first decades of the century. The *M&E* recounted it with glee: "The pros and cons of fundamentalism were being waged when Mr. Clarke in an idle moment wrote a mythical European cable reporting that two German scientists, Dr. Schmierkasse and Dr. Butterbrod had discovered the fossilized remains of a huge fish, not only large enough for a man to have lived 'quite comfortably in its belly for three days' but also possessed of a remarkable trap-door aperture in its back, connected by a canal to the stomach, and covered by a sort of cartilaginous lid which the whale could have opened and closed at will by muscular action.

"Mr. Clarke submitted the report to the *Christian Guardian* which, however, turned it down. For some months it lay in his desk until, during an international conference of fundamentalists in Toronto, he recalled the despatch and mailed it in a plain envelope to one of the leading delegates at the conference.

"The conference was electrified next day when the leading delegate read out the despatch to the meeting as scientific proof of the existence of a species of whale such as could have housed Jonah. An evening paper carried large headlines featuring the revelation, and the delegate in an interview assured

the public at large of the eminence of the scientists Schmierkasse and Butterbrod, and that he had long been aware of their researches . . . The *Mail & Empire* exposed the hoax, pointing out that the names of the alleged scientists mean Dr. Cheese and Dr. Buttered Bread."

Another literary journalist, J.V. McAree, in recalling Clarke's life, told of another escapade: "*Collier's* magazine had a Canadian edition . . . A prize was offered for the best English verses to be sung with 'O Canada.' Hector Charlesworth was one of the judges. The verses poured in, the award was made, and published in *Collier's*. The lady who had won received her cheque.

"A week later to the horror of the editor and judges a letter was received which pointed out that practically every line of the verses had been lifted. The writer then produced what purported to be the original lines culled from a dozen or so seventeenth century poets, and it was plain enough that the lady had perpetrated a monstrous fraud. The editor of *Collier's* was on the point of denouncing her in public and demanding a return of his cheque and a re-opening of the contest when Clarke admitted that so far as he knew the only hoax was his invention of the seventeenth century poets and their works."

The creator of the character Tugboat Annie lived at **4-A Fernwood Park** in 1927. Norman Reilly Raine (1895-1971) served with the Canadian Army in WWI, and then worked as an editor at *Maclean's* before he began to send his short stories to the slicks. Once Tugboat Annie appeared in the *Saturday Evening Post* in a serial, his fame and fortune were secured, for she was an instantly likeable creation. Two films based on the character were made in 1933 and 1940. He seems to have left the city in the late 1920s, and this Beaches address may have been his last in Toronto. He headed to Hollywood, where he was a successful screenwriter. He wrote movies that were upmarket by Hollywood standards, and one of them, *The Life of Emile Zola* (1937), won him an Academy Award for best screenplay.

Novelist and Macmillan publisher Hugh Eayrs (met above) found accommodation at **No.50** from 1918-21. Having been promoted to the presidency of the company in 1921, he moved to larger quarters, more suitable for entertaining.

Radio playwright and broadcaster Lister Sinclair lived at **15 Beech Avenue** from 1961-64. While at this address he wrote much of *Democracy in America: Scripts of Fourteen Dramatizations by Lister Sinclair and George E. Probst Based on the Classic Work by Alexis de Tocqueville* (1962).

Lister Sinclair in the "Ideas" studio of CBC Radio, 354 Jarvis Street, 1989

Roy Mitchell (1884-1944) was the first Artistic Director of Hart House Theatre, and had a large hand in the design of the hall and a large influence on the philanthropic thinking of Vincent Massey regarding the purpose of this particular theatrical space. His experiments with staging, with music, with costumes—indeed, with just about everything—seemed to have been far ahead of their time, certainly Toronto's time, and he left the city in 1927, disappointed at its preference for commercial theatre and indifference to art-theatre. While living at **17 Munro Park Avenue** over

1925-26 he was writing the first drafts of his book *The Creative Theatre* (1929), which many scholars now agree is of such import that, when discussing leading theorists of the stage, Mitchell can easily be spoken of in the same breath as Antonin Artaud, Jerzy Growtowski, and Peter Brook.

Just around the corner is **2465 Queen Street East** where poet Sharon Nelson (b.1948) endured from June to September 1973, as she painfully recalled: "My summer in the Beaches has to be the noisiest I have ever experienced. A Montrealer accustomed to the pastoral charms of the Laurentian mountains during summer, I was constitutionally unsuited for the heat and humidity of a Toronto summer. The noise of the streetcars was a constant torment, and when it stopped the noisy breathing of the neighbour's asthmatic dog replaced it. I took the first secretarial job I could find in an air-conditioned downtown office, and by Labour Day I was on the 401 heading to Montreal. What particular poems I may have been working on at the time I don't remember, but if any of my poems seem to have the cadences of laboured breathing or the grinding sounds of streetcars, they probably date from that period."

NORTH BEACHES

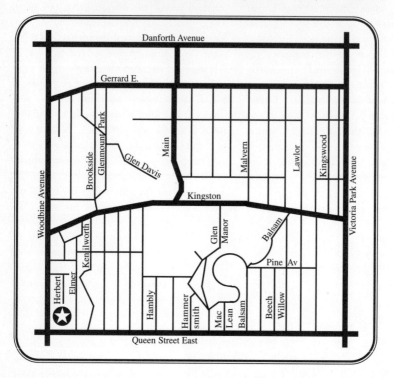

The tour begins at the northeast
corner of Woodbine Avenue
and Queen Street East.

W alk one block east on Queen to **Herbert
Avenue**. The Regina writer Ken
Mitchell (b.1940) has lived in Toronto on
two occasions. The first was for the academic year 1958-59 when he studied Journalism
at the Ryerson Institute of Technology and
lived at **63 Herbert**. Unfortunately it seems
he did not study hard enough, because he
failed the course and returned to Saskatchewan. Journalism's loss was literature's
gain, because Mitchell went on to become
one of the prairie's best-known authors. He
has written for both the stage and the page,
but regards theatre as the pre-eminent discipline. One of his early plays, *Davin, The
Politician* (1979), examines the life of a
Toronto author who moved to the prairies

and, although successful as an author, with
no forewarning, took his own life. When living in Toronto Ken Mitchell did no writing.

Florence Randal Livesay (1874-1953) has
long lived in the shadow of her daughter,
poet Dorothy Livesay, but Florence in her
time was nationally known as an author, and
widely respected as a literary translator. She
was included in two major anthologies: Bliss
Carman's *Canadian Poetry in English* (1954) and
John Garvin's *Canadian Poets* (1926). Around
the same time that Dorothy was publishing
her first books, Florence published two collections of her own: *Shepherd's Purse* (1923)
and *Savour of Salt* (1927). Her first book, however, had been a selection of her translations,
Songs from Ukrainia (1916). She published two
more books of Ukrainian translations (one
was posthumous). Despite all of this literary
activity, and despite her husband having been
the head of Canadian Press for years, a job

which had seen them living in Toronto since 1920, she died in almost complete obscurity after a bus accident. She had been living at **149 Elmer Avenue** for about a year at the time of her death.

On **Queen Street East** between Kenilworth and Waverley, the poet Rienzi Crusz (b.1927) lived at **No.1966½** from July 1965 to June 1967. While he wrote nothing that was published at this address, he did make "the greatest discovery of my life: that I could write or had the sensibility to write poetry . . . As a new immigrant, I took the first job that came my way: as an assistant cataloguer at the UofT Library. Here I had to produce 500 edited catalogue cards by 4:30 in the afternoon. The job was anathema to my latent creative spirit. After six months of what I called corporate slavery, I got my agony to sing and wrote my first poem which I titled 'The Unhappy Cataloguer.' . . . I then passed the poem to my friend Gordon Hodgins who sat next to me in the office doing the same mindless job. Gordon had a look at the poem and said 'Rienzi, this is very good. How long have you been writing?' I laughed in utter disbelief. 'You should read Yeats and Eliot and keep on writing,' Gordon continued. Gordon Hodgins was a graduate student in English at the UofT and so, at the back of my mind I thought he may have something in the back of his remarks. A month later, I left UofT and joined the University of Waterloo Library . . . where within three weeks I wrote three new poems and had the audacity to send them to Irving Layton who was then the writer-in-residence at the University of Guelph. Layton's reaction? 'These are very good indeed . . . ' It was Toronto that first fashioned the crucible that produced my first poem and set the environment that resulted in the later major theme of my early poetry: the immigrant encounter in human colours. Twenty-seven years ago, Toronto was not the dynamic city it is today. I hardly saw another brown or black face on the streets. It was a cold city

with a Puritan face. In a strange and ironic way, however, it was these very conditions that set me on my writing career."

The poet Laura McCully (1886-1924) lived at **24 Kenilworth Avenue** from 1913-14, and then moved up the street to **No.172**, her home until 1919. Where she lived after that is unclear. McCully was a woman of some literary talent, but this review published in the *Canadian Bookman* in 1924 gives an indication of the level of poetry reviewing in Canada in the first half of the century: "It is no exaggeration to say that this remarkable woman ranks immeasurably high among the really few true poets whose names are brightly and inseparably associated with Canadian literature. There are many who have been called Canadian poets. There is really only a limited number of persons who deserve that exalted and meritorious designation. In the past, everyone in Canada who has displayed a facility in composing verses, or in evolving rhymes, has been accustomed to pass unchallenged into the mystic realm where only the true poet should be permitted to enter." Her literary merit aside, she is increasingly discussed by feminist critics for her trailblazing work in the suffrage movement. And during WWI, "she was the pioneer woman recruiter and organizer in the world of a woman's battalion. Had she been permitted, she, like Joan of Arc, would have led a female army into battle." The publisher of Macmillan of Canada (and himself an author), Hugh Eayrs (1894-1940), lived at **No.27** for the years 1916 and 1917.

Kenilworth exits onto Kingston Road. Go east a few steps to find Brookside Drive and then take Brookside for a very short block to **Glenmount Park Road. No.83** was the home of poet Bill Howell from 1979-84. During this time he wrote and published *In a White Shirt* (1982). Howell is not prolific; in fact, he is a painstaking poet whose carefully constructed lyrics, many of them about the Beaches, have devoted admirers.

Running east from the middle of Glenmount Park Road is **Glen Davis Crescent** on which the novelist Arved Viirlaid (b.1922) has been living since March 1956. Here he finished his novel *Seven Days of Judgement*, as well as at least six other novels, all written in his native Estonian, and, until recently, all published in the Nordic countries because his work was banned in Estonia under the Communist rule. Regarding Toronto, Arved wrote: "Having lived in various countries after escaping the land of my birth twice (once from the Nazis, then from the Soviet regime), I chose Toronto as the best place available for me. There were warnings, of course. Friends, who had preceded us, cautioned me before I left England, describing Toronto as a big village without 'culture.' Still, we came as did so many others from all parts of the world and Toronto welcomed us with open arms. From the day I arrived until now I have never regretted my choice. The travels in different countries (and through many cities) have made me appreciate the uniqueness of Toronto.

"To a writer our fair city can be many things. Kind, exciting, dynamic, ever-changing, occasionally maybe boring and dull (it depends on where your travels take you and what you choose to see), but never nonchalant. One has only to explore the various neighbourhoods to experience the different faces—the vivid colours of a huge mosaic. Toronto is the world in miniature. It is the poor man's rich world. To a writer, the journey through the city is like fertilizer for the mind and soul. And yes, 'culture' too is now part of Toronto . . . and corruption and crime."

Return to **Kingston Road** and head east. **474 Kingston Road** was Hugh Garner's address for a decade—a near record for him in terms of duration at one spot. It was also the place where his alcoholism nearly killed him. Yet, as he related in his memoir, he fooled himself into thinking the drinking made him a better author: "After leaving the Island for an apartment on **Kingston Road** in East Toronto, I would occasionally drink myself into various states of ill-health. Twice I ended up vomiting copious amounts of blood while drinking, which scared the daylights out of my wife. The first time I was rushed by ambulance to Sunnybrook Veterans Hospital where I complicated things by having an alcoholic seizure . . . The second time I haemorrhaged was a couple of years later . . . I had the DTs in the East General, of an auditory nature mainly, in which I heard beautiful symphonic music . . . as I'd had the DT's before I'd learned not to be afraid of them but to lie back and enjoy them. I think that having had the delirium tremens, which started in my case in my apartment on **Kingston Road** when I held a conversation with our refrigerator, has helped me in my writing. I found I could write knowledgeably about a psychotic, as I did in a short story, 'The Sound of Hollyhocks,' and about Lightfoot's delirium tremens in *Silence on the Shore*."

Science fiction novelist Phyllis Gotlieb passed part of her childhood at **520 Kingston Road** from 1929-34.

About two blocks east of Main Street is Malvern Collegiate, **55 Malvern Avenue**, a high school attended by at least four authors over the decades: Langford Dixon, O.R. Melling, George Miller, and Ian Young.

Running south from Malvern Collegiate towards the lake is Glen Manor Drive. As you descend Glen Manor Drive, look for Williamson Road on the right. Take it two blocks west to **Hambly Avenue**. **28 Hambly** was the residence of cleric and novelist Thomas York (1940-88), for the last two years of the seventies. Tom was no ordinary minister. While he did not deliberately seek controversy, he did not flee from it when it came. Even by the liberal standards of his United Church he was a free-spirited padre—on one occasion, in British Columbia, his congregation tried to have him defrocked. And Tom was never apologetic about the fact that women found him mesmerisingly attractive. He relished their company, and welcomed their intimacy. His chaplaincies were far flung: he had pastorates in Yellowknife, Bella Bella, the Queen Charlottes, and, in sharp contradistinction, Thorncliffe Park, Toronto. A draft resister as of 1964, he was pursued aggressively by the FBI for more than a decade, an experience he put to good use in his novel *Trapper*, based on the life of the Mad Trapper of Rat River, the first absconding criminal in Canada to be chased by air as well as on the ground. His other novels promised much, so it was a shock to everyone who knew him to learn that he had been killed; the car he was driving was demolished from behind by a tractor trailer.

Return to Queen Street and walk two blocks east to **Hammersmith Avenue**. Fans of the superb short-story writer George Elliott (*The Kissing Man*) will want to know that he and his novelist-father, Thomas Rose Elliott, lived at **170 Hammersmith** from 1934 to c. 1940, although neither seems to have written fiction at this address: George (b.1923) was still studying, and his father published nothing during the Depression or WWII.

Two blocks further east is **MacLean Avenue**. The poet Jan Conn (b.1952) wrote most of her collection *Red Shoes in the Rain* (1984) while living at **103 MacLean** from September 1982 to September 1984. At the same time, she was working on her doctorate in cytogenetics (in case your dictionary is not handy, that is the study of blackflies).

E.S. Caswell (1861-1938) lived at two spots on the next street to the east: in 1913 he lived at **16 Balsam Avenue**, and in the following year he moved to **No.122**, which was his home until he passed away. His main literary importance lies in the anthology he first produced in 1912. *Canadian Singers and Their Songs* was not only a judicious selection of the best poets then working in Canada, it was the first to include photographs of the authors, and would have allowed most of their readers to put a face to the poems for the first time (photos of Canadian authors in newspapers and magazines were almost unheard of in that era). The book went through several printings and three editions. Caswell, early in his career, had worked for the Ryerson Press, but from 1909 onwards he was the Assistant Librarian of Toronto. He died in that post, and every library in the city flew its flag at half-mast on the day of his funeral.

The South African author Arthur Nortje (1942-1970) probably lived at **106 Balsam** from March until June 1970. His movements in Toronto are impossible to trace with exactitude, but it seems he lived in rooms at this address before finally quitting Canada to return to Britain, ostensibly to study but more pressingly to flee from his demons. Nortje wrote several poems in Toronto, some probably written here. In the new South Africa he is regarded as an essential poet for study.

Two blocks to the east is **Beech Avenue**. **No.15** was the home of radio playwright, actor, and recipient of the Order of Canada, Lister Sinclair (b.1921) from 1961-64. In recent years his creative writing has diminished in quantity, but he will remain nationally known as the longtime host of CBC-Radio's "Ideas." He is the winner of the George Foster Peabody Award, one of the most coveted—in the world—in radio, and has been given honorary doctorates by many universities.

In a house elsewhere on this street, Fred Bodsworth (b.1918) the author of *The Last of the Curlews* (1954), one of the best-loved books in Canada, continues to live and work, as he has since March 1947. Shortly after he arrived here, he wrote: "I free-lanced for *Maclean's Magazine* for a year or so and then went on the *Maclean's* staff in 1949. *Maclean's* and Maclean Hunter were then at University and Dundas. Meanwhile at home at nights I was trying to write short stories and in 1954 one of them grew into my first book, *Last of the Curlews*. It was fairly success-ful and in 1955 I left *Maclean's* to write books full-time. All my subsequent books—*The Strange One* (1959), *The Atonement of Ashley Morden* (1964), *The Sparrow's Fall* (1967) and

The Pacific Coast (1970)—were written at **Beech Avenue** . . . I was influenced more by Toronto people than Toronto places, especially the scientists at the Royal Ontario Museum in the 1950s and 1960s who gave me an impromptu science education and guided me into life-science writing."

Near where Beech cuts across Pine Avenue can be found Balmy Beach Public School, **14 Pine Avenue**. Langford Dixon and George M. Elliott were two of the best-known creative writers to attend.

Langford Dixon (b.1915) was an engineer by training, and a navy man by disposition. He did not begin to write poetry until long after his war service, but as he told an interviewer in 1965: "I think it was then, seeing what war does to people, rather than war itself, I began to think and feel with a new kind of emotional intensity." Before he began to publish books of poetry, Dixon, a graduate of the Academy of Radio Arts, had written plays for radio broadcast, and had acted in productions of the National Film Board and the CBC. He became well-known for his recitations of his own work and that of other Canadian poets, and that, in turn, led to evening programs comprised of his readings interspersed with musical interludes.

One of Dixon's finest contributions to our culture was not what he wrote but what he did. In 1952, six members of the Toronto Symphony Orchestra were banned from entering the USA (as part of the Symphony's first tour to that country) on the grounds that they might be Communists. The TSO replaced the six for the duration of the tour, a disquieting decision certainly. What is beyond debate, however, was what happened next. On its return to Canada, the TSO, infected with the McCarthyism then rampant in the States, fired without cause the six who had been left behind. The six, of course, appealed to the Musicians' Union for aid, only to find that the head of the local was even more rabidly McCarthyite than most politicians. People who might

have been expected to speak out about this matter remained silent, including the Conductor, Sir Ernest Macmillan. It was at this point that Langford Dixon, disgusted by what he seen, formed a committee to publicly protest the actions of the TSO. Among those he convinced to join were Lawren Harris and A.Y. Jackson. They did not succeed in having the musicians reinstated, but they did show that not all Torontonians were willing to remain quiet-before orthodox thundering. From the year of his birth until 1925, Dixon lived at **57 Willow Avenue**, and from 1926 until c. 1948 the family lived up the street at **No.165**.

Another resident of **Willow** as of 1973, was the comic novelist Donald Jack (*The Bandy Papers*). As he explained: "We bought a beautiful house on **Willow Avenue**, the house I loved most of all, but funnily enough I can't remember the number [**No.246**]. It's a big detached house with a distinctive mansard roof a few houses above Pine . . . I had started to improve the properties we occupied . . . and continued this at **Willow Avenue**, because it was such a beautiful house, a noble house as a friend called it. I landscaped the back with its great oak trees, converted a veranda into a beautiful bathroom, extended the kitchen, restored woodwork damaged by dogs, cigarette ends, and neglect. I had a big office at the back and there I wrote *It's Me Again* (1975), *Me Bandy You Cissie* (1979), the radio history *Sinc Betty, and the Morning Man* (1977), and started the great medical history *Rogues, Rebels and Geniuses: The Story of Canadian Medicine* (1981). But by 1977 the house was becoming too expensive for my writer's income, and that was when we left for Lindsay."

At the top of Willow, cross Kingston Road and, after a few steps to the east, proceed north on **Lawlor Avenue**. The detective novelist Peter Robinson (b.1950), acclaimed for his Inspector Banks mysteries, moved to a self-contained, second-storey flat at **30 Lawlor Avenue** in May

1988. The novels *Caedmon's Song* (1990), *Past Reason Hated* (1991), and *Wednesday's Child* (1992) were all written here, and Robinson also started the novel *Final Account* (1994) at this address. When asked what Toronto has meant to him as a writer, Peter, who came to Canada from Britain in 1976, answered: "It's very hard to say how much a place means to you as a writer, especially as an *émigré* writer. There are too many levels. On the most practical level, Toronto has enabled me to support myself, one way or another, while I pursued a writing career, and it has also given me a lively literary community, people I can meet with and discuss writing problems or projects. But that could also have happened in London, or even Leeds, perhaps. On a more complex level, it has also given me somewhere to be homesick from, but even that's not the full story. Homesickness was certainly *one* stage of having become an immigrant here, but the more this place becomes home, the more the nostalgia becomes muted. I don't think my books would have had such a strong sense of the Yorkshire place as they do if I hadn't lived here, and I don't think I would have been able to distance myself so much from my tangled roots in the English class system, either, if I hadn't moved away."

The fantasy writer O.R. Melling (b.1955) passed about five years of her youth at **293 Kingswood Road** from 1965-70, while down the street at **No.65** lived one of the few Canadian novelists to overtly address the stresses caused by the Depression. The eminent Canadian critic Desmond Pacey, writing about Canadian novels of the 1930s in the *Literary History of Canada*, noted, "A much more glaring example of didacticism, however, but still interesting because of its unusualness in the context of Canadian fiction of this period, is the work of Claudius Gregory (1889-1944). Gregory was born in England, came to Canada at the age of seventeen, and lived in Toronto and Hamilton. He was the author of three novels: *Forgotten Men* (1933), *Valerie Hathaway*

(1933), and *Solomon Levi* (1935). All of these novels are much too long—by judicious pruning they could have been cut down at least by half—and much too obviously propagandist. They are, however, among the few items of Canadian fiction which attempt to deal seriously with the social problems of the depressed era of the 1930s . . . we might have expected these conditions to provoke a large number of novels of social protest. Canadian poets had reacted quickly to these conditions, and such verse writers as F.R. Scott, A.M. Klein, Leo Kennedy, and Dorothy Livesay produced many poems of social protest in the period. Novels of this kind, however, were rare." *Forgotten Men* was written at **65 Kingswood** when Claudius Gregory lived here from 1927-32.

O.R. Melling spent the first year or so of the 1970s living with her parents at **24 Victoria Park Avenue**, whereas radio playwright Lister Sinclair spent the last year or so of the fifties at **No.66**. Short-story writer George Elliott (*The Kissing Man*) lived as a child at **No.332½** with his father from 1931-34. George Elliott (1923-96) eventually became a better fiction writer than his father; the latter is now almost forgotten. Thomas Rose Elliott (dates unknown) began writing as a journalist in the Goderich-London area before joining MacLaren Advertising in 1930. In 1942 he was named the public relations manager of General Motors of Canada. While serving the corporate world during the day, he wrote Canadian history adventure novels at night, the best known of which, *Hugh Laval, A Romance of the Up-Country* (1927), addresses the conflicts between trappers and early settlers in the Red River region.

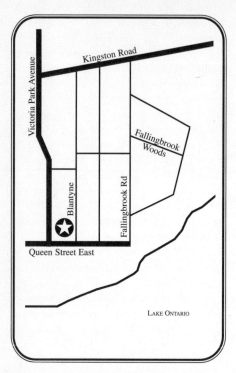

Kingston Road

Victoria Park Avenue

Fallingbrook Woods

Blantyre

Fallingbrook Rd

Queen Street East

LAKE ONTARIO

The tour begins at the northeast corner of Queen Street East and Victoria Park Avenue.

Walk one block east to **Blantyre Avenue**. Novelist Fred Bodsworth (*Last of the Curlews*) wrote: "I got married in 1944 and we moved into a second-floor flat at **71 Blantyre Avenue**. I got bumped from the *Star* at the end of the war when servicemen began coming home and reclaiming their old jobs. I switched to magazine freelance writing out of **71 Blantyre** for another couple of years and then, in March 1947 moved to Beech Avenue where I have lived ever since." Bodsworth was born in a small fishing port on the north shore of Lake Erie in 1918.

Poet Ian Young (b.1945) has lived in the east end ever since his arrival in Canada from England around 1951. From 1964-88

he made his home at **315 Blantyre**. It was out of this house that he ran his small publishing house, Catalyst Press. Young was one of the first openly gay writers to publish in Canada His book of poems *Year of the Quiet Sun* (1969) was also one of the first to include obviously homophiliac lyrics, and is considered a milestone in gay letters in this country.

Two blocks east of Blantyre is **Fallingbrook Road. No.18** was the home of Marcus Adeney (1900-98) from 1931-89. Adeney holds one record in this book: no other author was 91 years old when he published his first novel. To be accurate, the novel had been written 65 years before. *New Babylon* had been submitted to a 1929 contest run by a daring new publisher in Ottawa called Graphic Press, which was determined to publish only Canadian books. The company was doing good business until the Depression came, at which point it collapsed into bankruptcy. Adeney's book had won second prize in the contest, but he was able to collect only half the prize money before Graphic went under. The book sat unpublished until the author's son decided to give the novel another chance, and found a publisher for the tome in 1991.

Adeney was raised in the area of Paris, Ontario, mostly by his mother, because his father had gone off to fight in 1914 and never returned, presumed dead. However, after the war, when Adeney went to England to study cello, he discovered his father was still very much alive, and living with another woman—an unearthing sadly similar to that made by Hugh Garner when he came from England to this city around the same time.

By 22, Adeney was playing in the Detroit Symphony but his lack of a green card eventually led to his deportation from the USA in 1927. At that point he and his new bride returned to Toronto and converted the former stable at **18 Fallingbrook** into a salon for artists from across the city. In Toronto, Adeney played for the TSO from 1928-48, but not content with that, also founded the Beaches Concert Orchestra, was a music teacher at the Royal Conservatory, and passionately involved in music-making whenever he got the chance. Because he always had a yen for writing, he wrote music criticism for *Canadian Forum* and *Saturday Night* in the thirties and wrote poetry and essays for publication in Canada and abroad. Only old age forced him from his home here. In 1995 he moved to a senior's residence.

1995 was also the year in which Toronto-born novelist Jock Carroll died after living at **74 Fallingbrook Road** for 52 years. Carroll (b.1919) worked as a journalist and photographer for most of his life. When photographing celebrities he would keep notes about the occasion, frequently expanding the notes into lengthy captions, articles, profiles, or, in one case, into a novel, *The Shy Photographer* (1961), a bawdy satire of newspaper and magazine life published by the notorious Olympia Press in Paris. The book has sold more than half a million copies in more than a dozen languages.

Running east from the middle of Fallingbrook Road is **Fallingbrook Woods**. The bestselling novelist Arthur Hailey (b.1920) lived at **No.11** from spring 1961 until he left Canada to live in the Bahamas in December 1965. Like many authors in this book, he came to Canada from Britain as a young man and worked as an editor for trade journals of the Maclean Hunter empire. His creative writing career began with plays for television. His first hit was *Flight into Danger* (1956), broadcast by the CBC and later translated into a novel of the same name (1958). However, it was not until 1965, when he published *Hotel*, that he became globally known, and since then he has published a large number of extremely popular novels that combine deep research with edge-of-the-seat drama. Among them: *Airport* (1968), *Wheels* (1971), *The Money-Changers* (1975), and *Detective* (1997). To date, only one of his novels has a Canadian setting: *In High Places* (1962). Both *Hotel* and *Airport* were written at **11 Fallingbrook Woods**. As for what Toronto means to him now, he stated, "Toronto is a major part of my life because that is where I met my wife Sheila, where our three children were born, and where I began my writing career."

WEST ROSEDALE

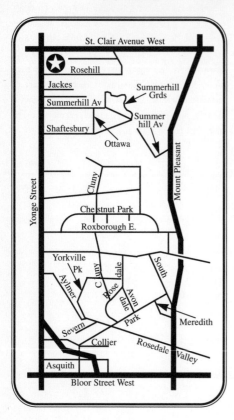

The tour begins at the southeast corner of St. Clair Avenue East and Yonge Street.

Walk two blocks south on Yonge Street to **Rosehill Avenue**. **No.24** was the last home of the pioneer women's leader Alice Chown (1866-1949) who had lived here from the end of WWII. Although born in Kingston, and a graduate of Queen's in Political Science and Economics, she had made Toronto her home for the last decades of her life. A passionate commitment to women's issues, especially suffrage, and to trade-union matters marked her entire adult career. From 1918-27, for example, she taught at a trade-union college in New York, after which she returned to Toronto to work for better understanding between Jews and Gentiles. A regular columnist with the *United Church Observer*, she wrote one novel, *The Stairway* (1921).

Novelist Joyce Marshall (b.1913) lived at **No.52** from 1956-67. This was her home when her second novel, *Lovers and Strangers*, was published in 1957. The book is set in Toronto in the 1940s.

The British writer Peter James (b.1948) made his start as an author in Toronto at **44 Jackes Avenue**. The author of such bestselling supernatural novels as *Possession* and *Dreamer* described his stay here: "At **44 Jackes Avenue** I wrote the original story for *Spanish Fly*, a film I subsequently produced with Terry Thomas and Leslie Philips. During this period I was director of Quadrant Films, and was involved in the creative and production sides of several feature films. At **44 Jackes** I also began my first novel, *Dead Letter Drop*, published in 1980 in England by W.H. Allen." James lived here from 1973-75, at which point he returned to the UK, his image of Canada and Toronto quite changed: "In the late 1960s, ads were shown on television in England, in cinemas, and there were colour ads in magazines, for Canadian Club whisky. The image was the same in each: trendy young people in a snug cabin, seated in front of a roaring fire, drinking Canadian Club. It was the image of Canada itself. The young country of opportunity, adventure, and it conjured up rugged beauty and opportunity together in a heady cocktail.

"When I arrived in Toronto in 1969, I found a grubby mixture of high-rise and low-rise buildings, seedy bars either with topless girls or no girls at all, dull food and feeling like a criminal when I bought booze. I was fresh from swinging sixties London, and the culture shock was horrific. Canadian culture seemed to be a case of Labatts in front of ice hockey on television. But when I left, five years on, I left a country that would haunt me forever. I left a great, pulsing, energetic city; tough, warm, people—I miss fall in Ontario every year—I miss the beat, the rhythm, the swinging contrasts of brashness and elegance . . . and I miss Labatts in front of the hockey game on TV. Toronto gave me my start in life. Like in Yevtushenko's Xima Junction, go, it said. I went, and I'm still going."

One of Canada's most respected short-story writers, Norman Levine (b.1923), lived at **103 Summerhill Avenue** from July 1, 1980 until 1991. He had returned to Canada in 1980 from a self-imposed exile in Britain of many years. Almost all of the stories which appeared in *Something Happened Here* (1991) were written at this address, inspired by his new wife, Anne. "I enjoyed living in Toronto because of Anne. Her house, right opposite the park, was also close to the ravine where we would walk the dog. And where Sarah, our young cat, would come up the little park to meet us. There were good bookstores, good libraries, close by. And a vast cemetery laid out like a botanical garden . . . Toronto in the 1980s was a new Toronto I was getting to know. It had a lot of vitality. Often at a dinner every person there came from a different country . . . Towards the end of the 1980s, Anne's health could not take another Canadian winter. She decided to move to France . . . I came later, after the publication of *Something Happened Here*."

During the years 1922-32 when Hector Charlesworth lived at **No.105**, he was made the editor of *Saturday Night*. He kept the post until 1932, when he was appointed to the Chair of the National Radio Broadcasting Commission In Ottawa. Charlesworth was the first important theatre critic in Canada, and was, for the first three decades of the 20th c. one of the most widely-read reviewers of all of the arts in this country. His three volumes of memoirs are full of readable and effusive anecdotes about various people of culture he encountered.

Dennis Lee's inhabitancy of **107 Summerhill** lasted from April 1975 to August 1980. Lee (b.1939) is highly regarded in two branches of literature: poetry for adults and poetry for children. At this address he wrote one volume in each: *Garbage Delight* (1977) and *The Gods* (1980). He also penned some of the poems that later appeared in another book for kids, *Jelly Belly* (1983), and put the finishing touches to *Savage Fields: An Essay on Literature and Cosmology* (1977).

Summerhill Gardens is found at the east end of Summerhill Avenue. John De Navarre Kennedy (b.1888) lived at **14 Summerhill Gardens** from 1927-32, just prior to the period when he wrote his first novel on a bet. A friend had wagered that Kennedy could not write a convincing novel about a place he had never visited. The result was the sensational *In the Shadow of the Cheka* (1935), succinctly described by one reviewer as adventures under Soviet despotism. Novelist and short-story writer Hugh Hood (b.1928) lived in rooms with his father at **39 Summerhill Gardens** from 1946-50. When poet Richard Outram (b.1930) resided at **No.44** from 1968-74, he wrote his book *Turns* (1975) and some of the poems that were published in *The Promise of Light* (1979).

The longest stay at any one Toronto address by Joe Wallace (1890-1975) was from 1956-60 at **No.48**. Wallace was born in Toronto, but thereafter his chronology is vague. In the preface to a book of his poetry he says he was in a reformatory before enrolling at a technical college. At some point he drifted to Nova Scotia where he attended but did not graduate from St. Francis Xavier University. Soon afterwards he started his own ad agency, and simultaneously became active in the Liberal Party. But he found the Liberal Party insufficiently socialist for his ideals, so he bid the Party adieu in 1919. By 1921 he was a member of the Communist

Joe Wallace, Toronto, 1953

Party, although, amazingly in retrospect, the corporations for which he created ad campaigns did not tire of his Marxist connections until 1933, when they gave him an ultimatum: forget the commie speech-making or forget their contracts. At the height of the Depression, he chose the Party—and thereby joined the unemployed. He returned to Toronto in 1936 to write for Party newspapers for the next four years, after which he was interned as a threat to the security of the country. About two years later, he was released and almost immediately published his first book of poems, *Night Is Ended* (1942). This book contains some poems of startling poignancy, far superior to the doggerel about workers' imminent overthrow of their capitalist bosses which he had written before WWII. Take, for example, a little gem that Barker Fairley was especially fond of:

My prison window is not large,
Five inches high, six inches wide,
Perhaps seven.
Yet it is large enough to show
The whole unfettered to and fro

Of heaven. How high, how wide is heaven?
Five inches high, six inches wide,
Perhaps seven.

Just as he was a contradiction as a poet, Wallace was something of an oddity in his spiritual life. A devout Communist, whose books were published by the leading presses of Moscow, and who travelled as a V.I.P. guest in several communist bloc countries, he was also a devout Roman Catholic at a time when the rift between his Church and the Soviet Union was at its widest. Joe Wallace died in a nursing home in Vancouver.

Anthologist and poet Garry Geddes's (b.1940) last home in Toronto was a basement flat at **62 Summerhill Gardens**. He remained here from 1970-72 while finishing his doctoral studies at the UofT. During this residency he met book editor Phyllis Bruce and together they compiled the first edition of *Fifteen Canadian Poets* (OUP, 1970), one of the bestselling college-level English texts in Canadian history.

Around the corner is **118 Shaftesbury Avenue**, where the novelist Chris Scott (b.1945) made his home from 1971-73. While here he published his inimitable work *Bartleby* (1971), a novel within a novel within a novel (within a novel, etc.) written long before anyone had heard of the term "postmodern." During this time he was teaching at York University, but in 1973 he quit, separated from his wife, and moved to the country where he has since re-married and publishes with long stretches of time between books. His ex-wife became Dennis Lee's companion, which is how Dennis Lee came to live at **No.118** from July 1973 to April 1975. Here Lee wrote parts of his major critical book, *Savage Fields* (1977), and completed two of his most famous books for children, *Alligator Pie* (1974) and *Nicholas Knock* (1974).

Running between Summerhill and Shaftesbury Avenues is **Ottawa Street**. The distinguished American novelist Don DeLillo (b.1936) lived at **13 Ottawa Street** from June

1976 until the end of the calendar year. He wrote in Toronto while his wife, who is a business executive, worked on an 18-month contract with a local firm. It was at this address that DeLillo wrote a large part of his novel *Running Dog* (1978).

Head south on Yonge three blocks to Roxborough Street East, then walk a few paces to find **Chestnut Park Road**. George Allen Kingston (1870-1943) lived for most of his life in Toronto where he was a lawyer specializing in liability law. He wrote several hymns which had wide currency in Canada. His poems, too, were published in many magazines, and in a volume, *Legendary Lyrics* (1938), written while he lived at **25 Chestnut Park Road** from 1908-39.

A more important poet who lived on this street was Earle Birney (1904-95). After a 20-year absence from the city, Birney returned to Toronto in May 1965 to be the first writer-in-residence in the history at the UofT. Part of his time was to be spent at Scarborough College, and part in an office at the main campus. He settled into an apartment at **35-A Chestnut Park**, his home until he moved to the University of Waterloo in July 1967. In a letter to poet George Bowering, Birney described this address as "a really swell pad in Rosedale, in the one decaying house in a kind of British Properties surroundings. That is, there are huge elms, curving streets; quiet; expensive neighbours, but our house is part of a minute re-zoning area and is divided into six broken-down but huge flats with catsmells in the corridor and a young tart upstairs & happy drunks across the hall."

Playwright David Young (b.1946) house-sat **55 Chestnut Park** for several consecutive months over 1993-94. This was an active period for him: for the CBC he began the radio adaptation of *Swann* by Carol Shields, and also while here he began and completed the radio adaptations of two of Michael Ondaatje's books, *The English Patient* and *In the Skin of a Lion*.

Intersecting Chestnut Park is **Cluny Drive**. At its north end can be found **114**

Cluny, the last address I could find for the poet (and former manager of the Old Favourites Bookshop) Alan Creighton (b.1903). He lived in this house from 1964-66. Throughout the forties and fifties, Creighton was an associate editor of *Canadian Forum*.

Return to **Roxborough Street East. No.7** was poet Nathaniel Benson's home for about two years, 1949-50. Benson (1903-66) was born in this city and graduated from University College and the Faculty of Education. The latter degree allowed him to teach high-school English in Toronto, a task he performed for a few years at Danforth Tech and at R.H. King Collegiate. In between these teaching positions, he worked full-time as a journalist and ad-copy writer (he also served a stint as the drama critic of *Saturday Night*). His literary output included volumes of poetry, and he was one of the small noble band who wrote plays and actually had them produced in Toronto during the Depression. The last secondary school where he was employed was Sir Winston Churchill in Scarborough.

Judith Kelly is something of a mystery woman. She was born in Toronto in 1908 and passed her first five years at **93 Roxborough East**. She lived with her family elsewhere in the city during her late high-school years when she was sent to a school in Boston. There she met the man she would marry in 1933. The Toronto newspapers took more than a passing interest in her second novel, *Marriage Is a Private Affair* (1941), because it was selected as the winner of the $10,000 Harper Prize from among hundreds of manuscripts submitted to Harper & Row, the giant American publisher. Perhaps the Toronto papers were hoping she would follow the trail of Mazo de la Roche, who had similar beginnings. Among the judges for the prize were two quite distinguished American men of letters, Louis Bromfield and Clifton Fadiman. According to Morley Callaghan, Bromfield was so highly regarded even Scott Fitzgerald was envious of his standing. The winning novel was extensively and positively reviewed in the Toronto press, and Kelly did publish one more novel in 1949—but after that, silence.

Playwright John Herbert (*Fortune and Men's Eyes*) had intentions of living at **No.101** longer than he did, but fate intervened: "When I reached Toronto in June 1972 [after residence in London, England] I wanted to find an apartment, flat or studio that would not be too different from the flat I enjoyed in London. I wanted privacy, seclusion, a garden and trees. Yet I did not want to be too far from shopping places, cafes, and transportation. **101 Roxborough Street East** seemed ideal . . . I took a second-floor front flat in the old three-storey house and liked the big windows and lawn with a couple of large trees . . . I was enjoying my residence at this address until one day, seated at a desk near the front window, I glanced out to see [a man] with a rather cherubic face and wearing powder-blue summer shorts, standing at the large old tree on the front lawn, near the sidewalk, holding a medium-sized dog on a leash. The dog had raised its leg and was pissing on the huge tree . . . " I would like to include John Herbert's description of the man but the laws of libel prevent me from doing so. Suffice to say that the man with the dog turned out to be a critic whom Herbert believed hated his work. Worse, the critic lived just a few doors away. Herbert continued, "The performance on the front lawn with the dog that had marked its territory and with the master who was doing the same in his own way was repeated every few days during the summer and fall. At some point I decided that I would not continue to dread looking out of my front window and decided to move. I was tired of the disrespectful neighbour, the only flaw in an otherwise pleasant location. Before leaving the house, I made up my mind to make my disapproval known to neighbours. On a fairly warm day, when my front windows were open and many neighbours were coming and going from the front of their houses [the man] hovered into

sight, led by his Airedale. Standing behind the sheer curtains of my window, which was wide-open, I waited until the dog was in full pee against the tree, then in the loud, rasping voice of a very old woman, I screamed, 'Get that filthy beast away from my herbage, and you get out of here, too, Dog!' [The man] toddled away at remarkable speed . . . My neighbours stared in disbelief, laughing in shock, for Rosedale is a quiet, uneventful place. My longtime tenseness slipped away and I burst into wild laughter at the strange scene. Farewell to Rosedale!"

Joyce Marshall's first novel *Presently Tomorrow* (1946) was published when she was residing at **105 Roxborough East** from 1946-48. The novel is set in Quebec, which is where Marshall was born. However, Toronto has been her home since 1937.

The German immigrant Walter Bauer worked at a number of menial jobs after arriving in Canada in 1952 before Barker Fairley met him, recognized his formidable talent, and had a large hand in having Bauer appointed to the German dept. at the UofT. Thanks to Bauer's extensive correspondence, we can date his move to a rented apartment at **No.143**: December 20, 1954. He quit this place several years later on January 11, 1967. His arrival on **Roxborough East** coincides fairly closely with the commencement of his association with the German dept. Just before that he had been working as dishwasher at a restaurant. During his stay at this address he published about one book a year, much of it Canadian in content. The volumes included poetry, fiction, children's literature, and biography. The title of one of the short stories hints at one facet of his feelings about his place here: "Stranger in Toronto." Yet it would be wrong to state he was friendless or disliked the city. He had many friends here, and several people translated his poetry into English.

The eminent Canadian novelist Timothy Findley (b.1930) lived with his parents at **27 Crescent Road** from 1938-45. "This is the house I remember best: only half of it remains—the other half was taken down for the construction of the Rosedale Subway Station and that half's place is now taken by **25 Crescent Road** . . . .When we lived on Crescent Road and I was attending Rosedale Public School, someone who lived on the way to school was Scott Symons, who was about three years younger than me. My uncle Tif (my father's elder brother—the writer of letters home from the front of WWI) and Aunt Dodie were inseparable friends with Scott's parents. But of more striking memory is Scott's grandfather, Perkins Bull. He was another wearer of cloaks—a gigantic man who was bearded rather like God. I swear he deliberately played the role of neighbourhood terror, grimacing and growling if any of us approached him. He certainly was the focus of all kinds of rumours—none of them, I'm sure, true: that he kept a woman locked up in the basement; that he was involved in *murder*. I do know that once, as my brother and I were passing his house, he emerged and bristled at us—and we literally screamed and ran away down the street.

Timothy Findley (far right): "March 1944. My father prepares to go overseas. He was a member of the RCAF. Michael is 15; mother and dad are 42; I am 13 years old. We are standing in the backyard of our Crescent Road house. Two minutes later, mother bursts into tears."

"Naturally, the environs of my childhood have found their way into my writing. In *The Last of the Crazy People*, the 'small town' the Winslows live in is really Rosedale. In the novella *Lemonade*, the milieu is Crescent Road. (In one of my short stories, 'Stones,' the narrator lives just across Yonge Street from Crescent Road and contrasts the two sides of Yonge in terms of class and income. This is the mirror image of my life in Rosedale.)"

The historian and poet Edgar McInnis lived at **80 Crescent** for about three years in the middle of the 1950s. George Allen Kingston, met above, lived across the street at **No.83** from 1906-7. This house later became the home of poet Elizabeth Rhett Woods (b.1940), when she first moved to Toronto in September 1966. It remained her home until January 1967. Colin Sabiston (1893-1961), newspaper veteran of 40 years and author of one novel, *Zoya* (1932), lived in a rented flat at **No.88-A** for the last seven years of the 1940s. **No.90** was playwright and novelist Rick Salutin's base for a few months when he returned to Canada in 1970 from studies in the USA.

Toronto-born George Doran (1869-1956) eventually became one of the greatest publishers in the United States during the first half of the 20th c. His ascent began as an office boy in a religious publishing house on Yonge Street when he was 14 years old. When 23 he headed to Chicago for larger opportunities in the religious book trade, quickly becoming a vice-president of the Fleming Revell Company. By the time he was 39, Doran was ready to launch his own publishing operation, and through clever deal-making with British houses, he had enough distribution agreements in place that he could return to Toronto to hang his own shingle: George H. Doran Company Limited. It seems that he always intended to return to the USA (New York this time), to conquer America with a savvy blend of religious texts and bestselling novels having literary pretensions or accomplishments. He succeeded masterfully, ultimately merging his company with another of about the same size: Doubleday. While he was with this newly created firm it was known as Doubleday, Doran & Co. When Doran returned to Toronto in 1908 to start his own company, he made his home at **112 Crescent Road**.

Kenneth Dyba moved to Toronto in 1975 and settled into **120 Crescent Road** in October 1981. The address remained his home until June 1989, at which point he left Toronto for Burlington. While inhabiting this spot he wrote *Pet Theories* (1985; a series of five linked radio plays), *Lilly, Alberta* (1989; stage play), *Betty Mitchell* (1986, theatre biography), *Peggy's Miranda* (1988, children's play), and a myriad of short stories published in most of the leading literary magazines of the country.

Running south from Crescent Road is **South Drive. No.22** has been the site of Rosedale Public School for many decades. Among the authors who attended classes here as children were Pierre Berton, Timothy Findley, Gwethalyn Graham, Ann Ireland, Sarah Sheard, and Scott Symons.

Scott Symons (b.1933) returned to Toronto from King's College, Cambridge, in 1957, lived with his parents again at their large home, **45 South Drive**, and began working as a reporter for the *Telegram*. Here, at this time, he marked the formal start of his writing life. He especially recalled a treasured letter from Albert Camus encouraging him to continue typing away and to have faith in his talent. Symons had lived here from 1950-55 when his father, Harry, bought the house at mid-century. It was constructed on part of the back lot of the estate of Scott Symon's grandfather, Perkins Bull. The address of Bull's house was **3 Meredith Crescent**, but since the two homes were separated by just a couple of steps across the rear lawn, Scott told me that while he slept at his parent's home, he was living in his grandfather's house almost as much as at **45 South Drive**.

Symons described his grandfather: "William Perkins Bull wrote some ten books centred around or about Peel County, but in effect a macrocosmic history of pioneer Ontario. He was one of the few Canadians ever elected to the Mark Twain Society. His electors included Compton Mackenzie, Stephen Leacock, Sir Winston Churchill and Booth Tarkington. He must have been the only Canadian Protestant (he was a Methodist in origin) and Grand Pajundrum of the Orange Lodge, to receive a signed letter from the Pope congratulating him on his history of Roman Catholicism in the Toronto area. I commend him to your attention [as well] for his amazing wedding gift to his son Michael Bull and bride Noreen Hennessy: an entire library of books signed by Canadian authors! So many books that the list of them was published as a hardback in its own right."

Scott Symons, March 6, 1998, standing on the front steps of 3 Meredith Crescent, the former home of his grandfather, Perkins Bull.

Harry Symons (1893-1962) was a real-estate consultant by day and a humour writer by night. In fact, his book *Ojibway Melody* won the first Stephen Leacock Medal for Humour in 1946. Symons was living at 45 South Drive when he passed away in 1962.

Two playwrights of modest renown roomed in sequence at **47 South Drive**. Tommy Tweed (1908-71) was here from 1944-45, and Fletcher Markle (1921-91) made this his home in 1946.

Park Road ends at South Drive near here. Novelist Ann Ireland (b.1953) was a popular winner of the $50,000 Seal First Novel Award in 1985. Since then she has published only one novel, *The Instructor* (1995). **108 Park Road** was her home from birth until she left for Vancouver in 1971. During her childhood and adolescence one of her best friends was Sarah Sheard (b.1953), who lived around the corner at **4 Meredith Crescent** from 1957-71. In their teens, both girls became admiring neighbours of Seiji Ozawa, conductor of the Toronto Symphony Orchestra, who lived equidistant from their homes for about two years. His presence and occasional chats induced in the young women a long bout of Japanophilia—worth noting because affection for things Japanese infuses both of their first novels. Curiously, as adults, while still friends, and while both women knew that the other was writing a novel, neither knew that their subject matter would be essentially the same. Ann Ireland's first novel was called *A Certain Mr. Takahashi* (1985). Sarah Sheard's first novel was titled *Almost Japanese* (1985).

Philosopher and poet Francis Sparshott (b.1926) made **17 Meredith Crescent** his home from 1955-60. Here he completed the poetry manuscript that became *A Divided Voice* (1965) and most of *A Cardboard Garage* (1969). He also finished a philosophy book, *An Enquiry into Goodness* (1958) and most of *Looking for Philosophy* (1972). **17 Meredith** then became the home of Eric Wright (b.1929) from July 1960 to February 1961. Wright has since gone on to become one of

the pre-eminent authors of police-procedurals in Canada.

Rosedale Road runs north from about the middle of Park Road. The literary historian and long-time librarian of the UofT, W. Stewart Wallace (1884-1970), spent the last decade of his life in apt. 608 at **16 Rosedale Road**. By the time he had moved here in 1961, he had left the university behind him and was first the owner and then the adviser to the Dora Hood Book Room, an antiquarian shop famous for the quality of the Canadian historical material it handled. Poet and playwright Marian Osborne (1871-1931) lived for three years at **41 Rosedale**, but in 1912 she moved down the street to **21 Rosedale**, her last home in Toronto before she and her husband retired to Ottawa in 1920. While at this Toronto address she published her first of four books of poetry, *Poems* (1914). One of her plays was produced at Hart House and was included in an anthology of Hart House plays compiled by Vincent Massey. Apparently this house was a popular spot with artists in the first decades of the century. Certainly she impressed Charles G.D. Roberts for he wrote, "Mrs. Osborne made her Rosedale house famous for its musical and literary gatherings. Her social talent was unsurpassed, and would alone have sufficed to make her memory endure with those who had enjoyed a hospitality that was in itself an act of genius. Her assured position made her impatient with the arts of the newly arrived or the just arriving, and she could afford to gather about her people whose artistic instincts were as responsive as her own. These were perhaps her happiest days, when health and hope were in full tide."

Comic author Harry Symons, met above, lived at **No.39** for the first five years of the thirties, and this is where his son, novelist Scott Symons (b.1933) passed his earliest years as well. In 1936, the Symons clan moved just a couple of doors up the street to **45 Rosedale**, their home until mid-century. It was at this latter address that Harry Symons wrote *Ojibway Melody* (1946), humorous sketches about life in cottage country, that was the very first winner of the annual Leacock Medal for Humour. This house was important to Scott Symons as well: "The home that was 'most vital' to me in all my later writing and imagination was that at **45 Rosedale Road**. It is illustrated and commented upon in Patricia McHugh's architectural guide to Toronto. The house was filled with books, several thousands of them—in the main living room also called 'the library,' in the sun-room, and in most of the seven children's bedrooms! In my own bedroom I had about 800-1,000 books.

"That home is what I really drew upon in writing my piece about Rosedale for *Toronto Life*, published in 1972 . . . [My novel] *Civic Square* was written in Rosedale and in Yorkville, but its sense of Rosedale comes right out of my years at **45 Rosedale Road**— vital inspiration and knowledge indeed. Indeed my years as curator at the Royal Ontario Museum are a predicate of Rosedale Road specifically."

By coincidence, this house had earlier been the home of another novelist, Basil Partridge (b.1900?). He was writing for pulp magazines by night and writing ad copy for an advertising agency by day when he lived here 1932-34. In the fifties he would publish his more literary wares, a series of humorous novels about a chaplaincy.

Cluny Drive runs north from about the middle of Rosedale Road. From June to September of 1946, poet Colleen Thibaudeau was a summer governess for M.P. Harry Jackman's children at **3 Cluny Drive**. Across the street at **No.4** was the final home of poet Anne Wilkinson (1910-61). After the collapse of her marriage she bought this house in June 1952. Before moving in with her children, she had the place completely renovated, a necessity perhaps, but one that added substantially to the stress evoked by her marital difficulties, as she described in her journal: "The work to be done seems

endless. I can't believe it will someday be finished, furnished and inhabited. Will it be lived in and loved? I have been so involved in the trivia of moving and settling and buying a house and planning the alterations and preparing the children's clothes for camp that there has been no interval long enough in which to stop and listen—certainly no stretch of peace in which to organize what I hear into words." By the end of July, the renovations were far from complete but she remained optimistic that happiness would come with this house: "The painter is a flop but the house will be liveable, cheery, and, after all the growing pains, very much ours."

Anne Wilkinson in Toronto, 1948, with her children (left to right): Jeremy, Heather, and Alan

While living at this house, Wilkinson became in 1956 one of the founding editors—and the chief patron—of *The Tamarack Review*, one of the most important literary magazines in Canadian history. She also penned *Lions in the Way*, the history of the famous Osler family, her family. It was around this time that she was diagnosed with the cancer that would eventually kill her. Paradoxically, this news seems to have liberated her writing, and scholars are agreed that her most important work was written at **4 Cluny**. *Tamarack* published her prose account of her childhood, "Four Corners of My World," in the year of her death. In the year before, she published a fable for children, *Swann and Daphne*, and in 1955 she composed her second poetry volume, *The Hangman Ties the Holly*.

When the eminent French author Paul Claudel (1868-1955) was his country's ambassador to Washington, Vincent Massey arranged for him to be given an honorary doctorate by the UofT. So, in November 1928, Claudel travelled to this city with his daughter and stayed at **8 Cluny Drive** as the guest of Sir William Mulock for a week. The Empire Club took advantage of his presence to have him make a speech during which he said all the right diplomatic things but nothing of real substance. From his diary, however, we know that what most fascinated about Toronto was not the pomp and circumstance, but rather the splendour of the Chinese art and artifacts at the Royal Ontario Museum.

Take Yorkville Park Drive from Cluny to **Aylmer Avenue**. After he became literary editor of *Saturday Night* in November 1940, Robertson Davies moved in to a two-storey row house once at **25 Aylmer Avenue** [demolished], his home for a year or so before he quit Toronto in 1942 to become editor of the *Peterborough Examiner*.

The Studio Building at **25 Severn Street** was co-financed by painter and poet Lawren Harris in 1912 as a building that would allow the Group of Seven and like-minded painters to work in near-ideal studios. Harris (1885-1970) worked—and, during his marital difficulties, sometimes slept for days—in his studio until he left Toronto in the mid-thirties. Poet and painter J.E.H. MacDonald (1874-1932), usually regarded as the unofficial leader of the Group, was also known to sleep over in his studio in this building. Arthur Heming (1870-1940) lived and worked in a studio here from 1916-1919, and novelist Wyndham Lewis rented space here for some months in 1941 in order to paint.

In its early years, the Studio Building had a ramshackle former cabinetmaker's shop on its grounds. Beginning in 1915, Tom Thomson inhabited the shack until he died mysteriously in July 1917. Twenty years later, poets Roy Daniells and Earle Birney called the shanty their home. Birney had just returned to Toronto from scholarly researches in the UK in early 1936 when Daniells invited him to share the building. "I think Daniells and I stuck it out in the

Roy Daniells, circa 1936, in front of the shack he shared with Earle Birney, next to the Studio Building of the Group of Seven

shack for all of March and most of April and then (the undergrads having moved out of their digs) we got reduced rent in the men's residence of Emmanuel College." They were constantly cold in the shack: it was not properly insulated, and the only heat came from a wood stove which they fed by scrounging wooden boxes from the street and backs of stores. Unfortunately, the heat brought the rats to life, and they watched as the vermin "began to eat the place." When asked if he was conscious of the art historical significance of the rickety structure, Birney replied, "Sure we knew about the Group of Seven—there was a book about them in '27 and we'd seen plenty of their work in Hart House. Daniells had met somehow the man who owned the shack who arranged to let us live in it rent free. I remember we were somewhat surprised to find some of the board panels on the kitchen walls had Group-like paintings (but no signatures) but it never occurred to us that they were of any marketable value—even Thomson's stuff wasn't selling that early on, so far as I can recall."

Fiction writer and biographer Roger Burford Mason (1943-98) moved to apt. 301 of **120 Rosedale Valley Road** in November 1997 and remained there until he died of cancer the following year. Regrettably, he was too ill at this point to do any creative writing. Barry Callaghan (b.1937) lived at **130 Rosedale Valley Road** on two occasions. Apt. 109 was his home from January 1970 to spring 1973. He then lived on Church Street for three years before returning in May 1976 to live in apt. 108 which had been, all along, the home of the woman he was dating and who soon afterwards became his companion for the following decades, artist Claire Weissman Wilks. The couple remained at this address until October 1983. During his residence in this building, Callaghan founded *Exile Magazine* in 1972. In 1976 he began his internationally acclaimed literary publishing company, Exile Editions. It was also at this address where he wrote many of the poems that were published in his first book, *The Hogg*

Poems and Drawings (1978), and nearly all of the poems included in his second book, *Seven Last Words* (1983). Barry Callaghan is an adroit fiction author as well, and in apt. 108 he wrote *The Black Queen Stories* (1982).

Bestselling novelist Martyn Burke (b.1942) is also prominent in Hollywood as a film director (*Power Play*, 1978; *The Last Chase*, 1981) and as a screenwriter (*The Second Civil War*, 1997). From 1968-72 he was learning his craft as a screenwriter and producer at the CBC; his home during this half-decade was **40 Park Road**. Since then he has divided his time equally between Los Angeles and a home in the Annex.

Poet and music critic Ronald Hambleton (b.1917) bought **148 Collier Street** in April 1963 and it remained his home until the middle of June 1970. During this era he worked as a literary producer at CBC-Radio. There is something fitting about Hambleton living on this road, because it was just a few steps away from two of the homes of his most famous biographical subject, Mazo de la Roche.

Following the death of her father, Mazo de la Roche (1879-1961) moved to Toronto and lived with her mother and cousin Carolyn Clement at **89 Collier Street** from May 1916 to 1923. Then followed one of their typical brief removals to another address, followed by a return to this street, **No.125**, for most of 1925. The **Collier Street** years saw her writing flourish, in part because her mother died in 1920, allowing Mazo and Caroline to live their life together—finally free of parental eyes. Her first book, a collection of short stories, *Explorers of the Dawn* (featuring a Foreword by the prominent New York author Christopher Morley) was published in 1922, and her first novel, *Possession* (1923), was also written at **No.89**. Because these were the pre-Jalna years, money was frequently in short supply, so to augment the household income Mazo took on freelance writing assignments. Among these were the writing of book reviews for the Eaton's ads on the back pages of Toronto newspapers (the department store book-shops were among the most important in the country for the first six decades of the century). At. **No.125** she also wrote part of her second novel, *Delight* (1926).

Asquith Avenue is now dominated by the Toronto Public Reference Library, opened in 1977 to mixed reviews from architecture critics and to huzzahs from the general public. This is the main reference library for Toronto, and the repository of many of the library system's special collections, including the Conan Doyle Room, Toronto theatre archives, and the Baldwin Room. The last is where much of the research for this book was undertaken. The Baldwin's holdings of early Toronto material are the finest in the world. A number of highly-respected Canadian creative writers have been authors-in-residence in this building: among them have been Matt Cohen, Paul Savoie, M.T. Kelly, and Katherine Govier.

At the base of the eastern façade of the library building can be found the Marian Engel Memorial Garden. Timothy Findley described its origins: "It was an idea I had and I simply petitioned the library to provide the space, and then solicited some of Marian's friends and relatives to donate either plants or money. (The donations included plants from Marian's own garden.) I then commissioned Matthew Mackery, a friend from Stratford who works as a landscape designer and gardener, to plan and implement the Garden accordingly. Everyone was extremely supportive and helpful—including Charlotte and William, Marian's children—but most people have stipulated that their support be anonymous . . . I can say that the Writer's Development Trust is administering a small maintenance fund that has been set up—largely from donations from two of Marian's publishers—and this money will be used to replace plants as required, and to do the 'twice a year' bit of work that is needed to keep the Garden going. Otherwise, the Library is responsible for watering and weeding."

Muriel Denison (1885-1954) lived with her parents at **No.96** from 1908-12, when **Asquith Avenue** was still known as Bismark Avenue (WWI led to the name change). At this time she was pursuing music studies quite seriously at the Toronto Conservatory. Only later, when ill health forced her to seek other careers, did she take up writing. In the mid-twenties she was one of the dramatists trying to establish a Canadian theatre—and theatrical industry—via the Hart House Theatre. During the Depression she turned her hand to writing juvenile fiction and here she had spectacular success with her Susanna books, including *Susannah, A Little Girl with the Mounties* (1936), *Susannah of the Yukon* (1937) and *Susannah Rides Again* (1940). The books were translated into the major languages of Europe, and enjoyed great success—due in part to the 1939 film version of the first Susanna novel, starring Shirley Temple. Muriel Denison (née Goggin) married playwright Merrill Denison in 1926 and after some years helping him to manage the Bon Echo Inn (later donated by Merrill to form a provincial park) she followed him to New York in 1932 where he worked in radio. All of her writing was done in New York, including her non-fiction, published under the name Frances Newton. The severe symptoms of Parkinson's Disease afflicted her in 1943, after which she did no more writing. She returned to Toronto to die in 1954.

Poet Gerry Shikatani (b.1950) had rooms at **88 Asquith** from 1971-72, while another contemporary author, novelist Michael Hale (b.1949) lived at **No.87** from 1969-70. Harvey O'Higgins (1876-1929), who lived at **No.72**, was born in London, Ontario, but stayed in Toronto after graduating from the UofT in 1897. He was a city hall reporter for the *Star* until he left Toronto c. 1900 to seek fame and fortune in Manhattan. He found both. His first novel, *Don-a-dreams*, a story of student life in Toronto, was published by Century in New York in 1906. Other novels soon followed, published by Century and other major houses such as Harper and

Doubleday. In our time, O'Higgins is still well regarded for his contributions to the detective genre. He lived at **72 Asquith**. The *Encyclopedia of Mystery and Detection* declares that his novel *Detective Duff Unravels It* (1929) "represents the first serious approach to psychoanalytical detection." Mystery buffs also rate highly O'Higgins's short stories featuring a boy detective.

"'Gad' was the hero's name, and whenever Gad spoke he said something so dazzlingly witty that the paper suspended publication while the staff leaned back and roared. 'Jawn' had the second lead. He sat with his hat on the back of his head and smoked a corn-cob and wrote the editorials that were stolen by the country journals. After the paper went to press he put his feet in the top drawer of his desk, lifted his pipe, and ruthlessly defeated the government policies which he had been upholding in his editorials.

"The real editor, who was at once managing editor, exchange editor, financial editor, the staff copy reader and the make-up man, was a tyrant called 'Bowzer' because his bark was worse than his bite. He did the work of seven men and expected his reporters each to do as much. Whenever Gad paraded up and down Yonge St. for a morning, swinging the tails of his paddock overcoat and smoking his after-breakfast cigar, instead of working on his assignment, the paper was scooped and Bowzer shut himself up in his sanctum and kicked his overshoes around the room. He seemed to think a reporter was paid for gathering news. That was Bowzer's great fault.

"Bilk was the low comedian of the office. He wrote an article on the state of the egg market and it was copied in all the papers on the continent and generally credited to Mark Twain, who was so flattered that he did not repudiate it. The others were Davie and Bant and Lou and they were clever enough to make any ordinary paper famous.

"Gad had a vocabulary so large that even he himself did not know what all the words meant. And Jawn's editorials were so fearfully potent that he had to write some parts of them in what he called Chinese script so the printers would not be able to set them up. It was generally understood that if the whole of one of Jawn's arguments ever got printed the entire edifice of society would fall in ruins.

"The really incredible thing about the paper was the fact that it paid its wages regularly every Friday afternoon and this was so miraculous that the operation always drew a crowd."

Playwright and novelist Maud Pettit (1877-1959) was a newlywed when she lived at **52 Asquith** from the time of her marriage in 1913 until 1924. The later years of this period saw her involved with other women playwrights such as Dora Conover and Rica Farquharson at the Hart House

Three members of the Playwrights Studio Group just prior to the premieres of their one-act plays at Hart House Theatre. Left to right: Dora Conover, Leonora McNeilly, Rica McLean Farquharson

M&E, January 25, 1933

Theatre. Before moving to **Asquith** she had published what must be the first novel by a woman about life at the UofT. *Beth Woodburn* (1897) is set in Victoria College shortly after its move from Cobourg to Toronto.

Comic novelist Donald Jack (b.1924) returned to Canada from England in 1967, at which time, he "rented a house at **48 Asquith Avenue**. I did a lot of good work in the years we lived there, writing TV plays, theatre plays, and starting the second novel in the Bandy series (the first had been written in Oakville). It was an exciting time in the city, with the hippies and flower children thronging Yorkville just three or so minutes' walk from the house, and of course, there were the Centennial celebrations. We were thrilled to be back in a city which when I first arrived had been so staid and uptight but which now, with every year that was passing, was growing more cosmopolitan and sophisticated, filled with interesting people who had come here from all over the world. I think 1967 marked the major change in the citizen's change of attitude to the city. Before it had been defensive. Now it began to have an attitude of pride in the city, its increasingly handsome look, and its civilized behaviour. I think I contributed to this changed outlook by writing a letter to the *Star*, urging journalists to stop calling it Hogtown and other epithets like that—that it no longer deserved it. The Asquith Avenue house was taken over by its owner, Crown Life [in 1969], and that was when we moved."

His neighbour for about two years would have been fiction writer Austin Clarke (b.1934,) who lived next door at **No.46** from 1964-68. It was at this address that he wrote much of the material comprising his first three books of fiction: *Survivors of the Crossing* (1964), *Amongst Thistles and Thorns* (1965), and *The Meeting Point* (1967).

The Second Floor Club, at **No.33**, a precursor of the Bohemian Embassy, was a coffee house with occasional readings by locals poets c. 1960.

Just south of where Asquith meets Yonge was **765 Yonge Street**, the location of Albert Britnell Books from 1928 until February 28, 1999. The shop was regarded by some as the finest bookstore in Toronto—certainly it was unique. For decades the books were arranged on a shelf not alphabetically but by size. Thus the largest book was placed at the extreme left and the smallest at the extreme right. Antiquarian collectors marvel even today at the used-book treasures which Albert Britnell used to sell at extremely modest prices—often only to people whom he knew would appreciate the rarity of the item being sold. Britnell's had a friendly rivalry for years with Tyrrel's bookstore across the street, although the Rosedale carriage trade much preferred the shop at **No.765**.

In 1930 the *Star Weekly* described Arthur Heming (1879-1940) as "Canada's best-known artist-writer," just after he had left his lodgings at **771 Yonge Street** where he had dwelt for half a decade. When he moved to this address in 1924, he published his third and final book—and his most renowned—*The Living Forest*, which he illustrated himself. It was also at this address where Heming sued another Canadian novelist, Arthur Stringer. Heming (or Heming's publisher Doubleday) had sent Stringer for advance comment a draft of a Heming novel-in-progress. Stringer, however, expropriated much of the outdoor material in the book for use in his own novel-in-progress, *Empty Hands*. Stringer yielded to temptation because Heming's novel was well-written, and because Heming, internationally famous for his wildlife painting and word descriptions, was far more knowledgeable about the subject than Stringer. Matters came to a head when Stringer's novel was bought by Hollywood and Stringer thereby stood to make a lot of money. By way of compensation Heming received from Stringer an amount said to be $7,000, a tidy sum in the mid-twenties, but minuscule when compared to what Stringer earned from his novels and movie options.

EAST ROSEDALE

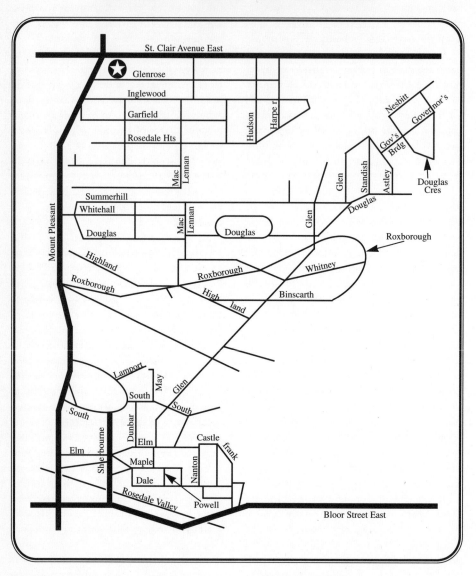

The tour begins at the southeast corner of St. Clair Avenue East and Mount Pleasant Road.

Walk one block south on Mount Pleasant to **Glenrose Avenue. No. 110** was long the home of visual artist and poet Florence Wyle (1881-1968) and her lifelong compan-

ion Frances Loring, also a sculptor. The two women bought this house-cum-studio in 1920, and Florence lived in it until the year before her death in 1967. Their home was originally a school house built in 1881 as part of a complex of Anglican buildings built on the property between Yonge and Lawton Boulevard. As the congregation grew, it needed new premises. For some reason, the schoolhouse was saved from demolition in 1910 and moved to what was then open ground at **110 Glenrose**. Its high ceilings and sturdy floors were perfect for the needs of sculptors, although the building was modified slightly when they lived there, and has been much modified since. Like Lawren Harris, J.E.H. MacDonald, and Arthur Heming, Wyle was a visual artist first and a writer second. Nevertheless, as with the others, she took her writing seriously—as did her publisher, Ryerson Press, which issued *Poems* in 1956, the collection of lyrics she wrote at this address.

Edgar McInnis

Historian and poet Edgar McInnis (1899-1973) was on the faculty of the UofT when he lived at **No.132** from 1931-34. His poetry was published when he was younger; in his later life he lent his writing skills to some of the most respected history texts produced in Canada. Another of the country's most distinguished historians, Donald Creighton (1902-79), turned to creative

writing at the end rather than the start of his adult life, finding in fiction the freedom to say what he could not say in monographs. His wife Luella (b.1901) also wrote fiction. Both lived at **No.161** from 1942-44.

Ralph Allen (1913-66), a native of Winnipeg, was born with printer's ink in his veins. No university for him after high school; he immediately began to write for a Winnipeg newspaper, but looking for larger opportunities, moved to Toronto in 1938 where he signed on with the *G&M*. During WWII he distinguished himself as a war correspondent, and his martial experiences were the background for his first novel, *Home-Made Banners* (1946). Not long afterwards, Arthur Irwin, editor of *Maclean's*, finally induced Allen to join the writing staff of the magazine, a remarkable team of journalists which included Pierre Berton, W.O. Mitchell, Eva-Lis Wuorio, John Clare, and Scott Young—all of whom also published fiction. Indeed, it was in order to write fiction full-time that Allen quit the magazine in late 1948. However, when Arthur Irwin resigned the following year, Ralph Allen found the offer of the editor's chair too tempting to resist, and he returned to the magazine's offices at University and Dundas to become the most popular editor in *Maclean's* history. A decade later he resigned again in order to find time for his novels, despite the fact that throughout the fifties he had published four novels, including what has remained his best-known, *The Chartered Libertine* (1954). But his second attempt to write full-time was as inefficacious as his first, and he became the managing editor of the *Star* in 1964. The world of book publishing and of journalism was stunned by his sudden death in December 1966.

In his history of Canadian magazines, Fraser Sutherland quotes Allen's wife as saying, "There isn't any doubt in my mind that what Ralph wanted was to be a full-time writer, a novelist, but he had a family to support and he didn't want us to go through the kind of financial hardship he experienced as a child." Later, Sutherland notes, "The reverence with which this freckled, red-haired, pudgy, pipe-smoking man is regarded is probably unique in the history of Canadian journalism." We get some sense of that reverence from Peter Gzowski's opinion of Ralph Allen, under whom Gzowski worked at the *Star*: "On December 2, to everyone's shock, he died. I stayed at the *Star* for a little while after, but quickly realized that, salary or not, I had gone to work not so much for the paper as for the man. I turned to other things. Twenty-one years later, I cannot write a paragraph or consider how to cover a story without thinking he might be looking over my shoulder, trying to make sure I do it as well as I can." From 1941 to 1952 he lived at **253 Glenrose**. In 1953 he moved to **No.229** and it remained his home until his passing.

When fiction writer Rachel Wyatt (b.1929) moved to Toronto in 1975, she lived at **No.241** and here wrote *The Rosedale Hoax* (1977) and started *Foreign Bodies* before moving elsewhere in Rosedale in 1978.

One block south is **Inglewood Drive. No.52** was where E.K. Brown (1905-51) lived from 1924 until 1926 (when he left for study at the Sorbonne), and then from June 1929 until September 1935 (when he went to teach at the University of Manitoba). Two years later he was back at **No.52** where he stayed until obtaining a job at Cornell University in the USA in 1941.

Brown was one of the first scholars to try to establish a Canadian canon which others could either teach or rebel against. His book *On Canadian Poetry* (1943) remains compulsory reading for any serious student of CanLit. E.J. Pratt's biographer gives a wonderful brief portrait of E.K. Brown, a description that nicely conveys the informed confidence that so marked his writing—intelligent criticism that tantalizingly hints at the further insights lost to us by his early death at 46: "[Pratt] still needed, and would until his declining years, the psychological as well as

intellectual sustenance of 'surrogate brothers.' This other new friendship was with a young man of rare intellectual gifts and personal radiance, whose influence on Pratt's public career as poet was probably as great as the private and personal fascination and attraction he held for Pratt during two decades of his life. This was E.K. (Eddie) Brown, who in 1931 at the age of twenty-six, after two years English at University College, Toronto, his alma mater, had been confirmed an Assistant Professor, a peer among some of the most notable, seasoned scholars in Canadian academe. He was a tall, well-built, broad-shouldered man, with a boyish smile and hearty laugh, with deep and penetrating eyes (though usually bespectacled in the 1930s he often wore pince-nez which he had a habit of frequently removing and replacing), always impeccably dressed and groomed, and the epitome of self-assurance and savoir-faire. Fond of walking, he loved to hit a brisk, confident stride, which when Pratt first knew him was usually measured with an elegant cane. Said never to have even tried his hand at any form of 'creative writing,' he was none the less a scholar and critic to the fingertips, between which a nonchalant cigarette seemed to burn forever. Pratt had known him slightly as a student, before he had embarked on postgraduate studies in Paris, and on his return in 1929 had lured him to a few poker evenings with mutual friends from University College. Instantly attracted to one another, he and Pratt had by the autumn of 1931 become fast friends as Eddie and Ned, the younger man half the age of the elder—a surrogate son rather than a brother—but intellectual and emotional soul-mates all the same. When a decade later Brown moved to Cornell University, Pratt was quite bereft, describing his going as 'the greatest personal loss I have ever had in the University circle.'"

E.K. Brown's biographer nicely sums up his singular importance to the formal study of CanLit: "Brown was a genuine pioneer. He found himself championing a literature for which there was no appreciation and, in order to do so, he had to make critical evaluations in a vacuum both social and historical: there was no critical tradition devoted to Canadian literature on which he could rely. He carved out a tradition, depending solely on his own judgement, a task as formidable as his second undertaking, that of evaluating the contemporary, much of it not yet published in book form. That his judgements strike us today for the most part as obvious is a tribute to his outstanding taste and ability. It is also to some extent a measure of the powerful effect he had as teacher and critic in shaping the views of subsequent generations. The Canadian poetic tradition remains almost exactly as he defined it some fifty years ago. 'No one, I think, in his generation,' said B.K. Sandwell, 'made a more lasting imprint upon Canadian literary taste.'"

Journalist and novelist Scott Young (b.1918) and his new wife settled into **280 Inglewood** in 1961 and stayed there until the end of the decade. Although for much of this time Young dreamed of moving to the countryside near Peterborough, he found this Rosedale address conducive to creative writing. He published a book a year, including several juveniles and a short-story collection, *We Won't Be Needing You, Al* (1968). A large number of sports books joined his bibliography during this era. He lost this house when he abruptly quit his columnist's job at the *G&M*.

Before Jack Batten became the author of more than 30 books, he wrote for *Maclean's*, and before that, he practised law. The switch from law to journalism took place in the middle of his stay at **91 Hudson Drive**, his home from 1960-66. Batten is a member of an informal body known as the Bookmen's Club (although, in recent years, a few women have become members), and one of the authors with whom he shares its luncheon table is novelist Jack MacLeod (b.1932). MacLeod earned his PhD at the UofT. He was appointed to the to Dept. of Political Science in 1972 and he remained until the

mid-1990s. His first books of fiction and non-fiction were all written when he lived at **71 Harper Avenue** from 1966-83. These include the novels *Zinger and Me* (1979), and *Going Grand* (1982). He continues to live in this area.

An author who has not lived in this area for decades but whose writing continues to be infused with memories of his residencies in its streets is Hugh Hood (b.1928). As a child, he attended classes (Kindergarten to Grade 6) at Our Lady of Perpetual Help, **1 Garfield Avenue**.

Scott Young told me, "After changing newspapers from the *G&M* to the *Telegram*, I bought a lovely house (five bathrooms, three fireplaces) at **17 Rosedale Heights Drive**. Here I had a fine study with fireplace, and wrote parts of a novel called *Face-Off* (a collaboration with George Robertson)." Young remained in this house until 1976 when his second marriage dissolved and he moved to a hundred-acre lot in Omemee.

Fiction writer and publisher James Bacque (b.1929) passed his infancy and youth at **40 Rosedale Heights Drive** (1930-55). "In that house I wrote my first professional work, which was a very funny short story published in the Toronto *Star* when I was about twelve." Bacque attended Whitney Public School, **119 Rosedale Heights Drive**, for three years. Another famous literary student of this institution is Margaret Atwood (b.1939). Her family lived just north of St. Clair.

The playwright Rica McLean Farquharson (c. 1900-55) lived at **No.147** for the decade 1943-53 while her husband was the managing editor of the *G&M*. By the time she was living at this address, Farquharson had stopped publishing for reasons unknown. In the thirties, as part of the Playwrights Studio Group, she had written eight plays, all of them produced at Hart House Theatre when it was a fully professional operation. Earlier, she had been a journalist of wide experience, having been a general reporter for the *News*, features writer for the *Sunday World*, Canadian correspondent of *Time Magazine*, and movie critic of the *Star Weekly*.

Thanks to the CPR tracks, the only way to get to the rest of Rosedale is via Mount Pleasant Road. Just beyond the railway underpass is **Whitehall Road**. **No.85** was the home of J.F. Hendry (d.1986) from 1984-85. Born and educated in Scotland, Hendry came to Canada in the sixties. Establishing himself in Sudbury, he then founded the School of Translating and Interpreting at Laurentian University. He divided his time between northern Ontario and Scotland until the mid-eighties when he settled in Toronto. He published fiction and poetry of limited distinction, and is now remembered for the anthology he edited, *Scottish Short Stories* (1978).

From 1948-55, Timothy Findley (b.1930) was based at his parents' home, **97 Whitehall Road**. But, as he wrote: "I was away at Stratford and then England for part of this time, and in the winter of 1952-53 I lived with Hugh Hood (in his final year of university) and three other UofT students in an apartment building . . . I was then working as an actor." The writing of his award-winning and internationally acclaimed novels would come later.

Take Gregory Avenue north to **Summerhill Avenue**. Hugh Hood's (b.1928) earliest years were spent at the family home, **430 Summerhill**. Although the Hoods quit this address in 1937, memory of its grounds has remained vivid and powerful with Hood, and has infused much of his writing, particularly *The Swing in the Garden*.

Poet Francis Sparshott (b.1926) was at **44 Standish Avenue** from 1964-67. While ensconced here she published a book of philosophy, *The Concept of Criticism* (1967), a tome reflecting his status as a Philosophy professor at the UofT. Jack MacLeod, another Varsity prof and creative writer, lived for a year or two at **50 Standish** in the mid-sixties. His first novel was not published until a dozen years later. The street has been Eric Koch's (b.1919) home since

1977. In addition to his novels, Koch recently published *The Brothers Hambourg* (1997), a history of a family of classical musicians who, by their teaching and playing, exerted an enormous influence on Toronto music for more than five decades. Willa Cather stayed at the home of one of the Hambourg brothers when she lived in Toronto. Timothy Findley (b.1930) was just a teenager when he and his parents inhabited **No.90** from 1946-47.

Although Morley Callaghan (1903-90) lived in one-half of a duplex at **58 Astley Avenue** for only a year over 1930-31, he managed to write an entire book, the novel *Broken Journey* (1932). Callaghan and his wife had returned to Toronto from a life-changing residence in Europe the year before. But after a few months in Canada, they headed to Pennsylvania. Less than six months later they were back in Toronto, and it was to this address they migrated. All of the travelling obviously charged Morley's creative batteries because the thirties would become one of the most productive decades of his long career.

Cross the Governor's Bridge which stems northeast from Astley Avenue. The bridge leads to three streets: Nesbit Drive, **Governor's Road**, and **Douglas Crescent**. Two authors lived on **Douglas Crescent**. Elsie Mack (b.1909) seems to have lived in Toronto only during her undergraduate years at the UofT. But she is worth noting because in the forties and fifties, under the pseudonym Frances Sarah Moore, she published in the United States at least 22 light romances which met with much favour among her legions of readers. During her freshman and sophomore years (1928-30) she lived at **37 Douglas Crescent**.

Judy LaMarsh (1924-1980) was the first woman ever appointed to a federal Liberal cabinet post. As Minister of Health and Welfare she oversaw the implementation of national medicare as well as the Canada Pension Plan. Later, as Secretary of State, she created a Royal Commission on the

Status of Women, one of the few such commissions whose conclusions actually affected subsequent legislation and political thinking. She left politics in 1968 with the rise of Pierre Trudeau and decided to try her hand at writing books. Her first effort was a controversial memoir of her years in politics. But her next two books were novels: *A Very Political Lady* (1979), trashed by the critics but a bestseller nonetheless was followed in 1980 by *A Very Honourable Lady*, also a bestseller and a book more generously treated by reviewers. She lived at **77 Douglas Crescent** from 1975 until she passed away from cancer at her home in 1980.

Eric Koch (b.1919), encountered above, made his home at **17 Governor's Road** from 1956-71, during which he rose through the ranks of the CBC, first in production and then in administration. A 1971 appointment to the directorship of English-language services in Montreal led to his departure from this abode. During his stay at this address he wrote and published his first novel, *The French Kiss* (1969). Earlier, in 1961, he had collaborated with Vincent Tovell on the play *Success of a Mission*.

Re-cross the Governor's Bridge, and descend Astley Avenue to **Douglas Drive**. The park at the foot of Astley is all that is left of what used to be Chorley Park, the grounds and official residence of the lieutenant-governor. Rising like a duke's chateau in France, the building was larger and grander than Rideau Hall in Ottawa. Construction was finished in 1915 and was complemented with landscaping by one of the leading New York architects. Among the authors who were guests of the government here during their Toronto visits were John Masefield, Winston S. Churchill, and Vita Sackville-West. Unbelievably, successive provincial governments allowed the building to decay through niggardly maintenance, and then used that decay as the excuse for razing the building in 1959.

Novelist Claire Mowat (b.1933) lived at **167 Douglas Drive** from 1950 until her marriage to novelist Farley Mowat in 1963. Ethel Smith Wilcox (1890-1944) published poems and short stories usually on ecumenism and cohabitation, the same theme as the non-fiction books of her husband who was director of the Canadian Conference of Christians and Jews. They lived at **166 Douglas** from 1931-40. The peripatetic mystery writer Jack Batten (b.1932) was practising as a lawyer when he resided at **No.119** from 1958-60.

John Masefield (right) being greeted upon his arrival at Union Station *Telegram*, July 25, 1933

One of our finest historians, Edgar McInnis (b.1899-1973), was a prize-winning poet as a young man but it is as a Governor General's Award-winning historian that he is remembered today. When he was installed at **11 MacLennan Avenue** from 1948-52, he was on the faculty of the UofT's History dept.

Return to **Glen Road** via Douglas Drive. Novelist (*Formentera*) and a co-founder of new press, James Bacque lived at **306 Glen Road** for the last three years of the 1950s. Fred Jacob (1882-1928) came to Toronto from Elora in 1898. In 1903 the *M&E* hired him to edit and write and by 1910 he was the drama critic for the paper. Five years later he became its popular literary critic. And he was one of the first broadsheet reviewers to review movies as if they were something more than star vehicles. Not content with writing about other people's work, he also wrote poetry, fiction and plays. At least five of his one-act dramas were mounted at Hart House Theatre during its era as a professional house. One might think that a drama critic's efforts to write for the boards would invite calumny but his stage-work was warmly received. Macmillan published an assortment of his plays under the odd title *One Third of a Bill* (1925). And his two novels gave promise of what his pen might have produced had he not died so young from a heart attack. His funeral was attended by a who's who of Canadian cultural figures. From 1917-23 he occupied **196 Glen Road**.

Lloyd Douglas (1877-1951), author of *The Robe* and other religious bestselling novels, was based in Montreal for many years. On a fews occasions he travelled to Toronto at the invitation of local churchmen to give talks from their pulpits. Because of his popularity as an author, these sermons were always "sold-out," although admission to services was free of charge obviously. In January 1933, he spoke at Rosedale United Church, **159 Roxborough Drive** (corner of Glen Road). A little over a year later, novelist Ralph Connor (in real life, Presbyterian minister Rev. Charles Gordon) chastised the Christian church for its lack of involvement with the unemployment crisis evident everywhere in the Depression. "Work or employment is not a consideration for economists alone, but for all Christian-thinking men. The lack of work in this country is making five million persons unhappy and two million very unhappy. It is driving them from the church."

When Anne Wilkinson's husband was finishing his advanced medical studies in New York, he received an appointment to the staff of the Hospital for Sick Children and so the family returned to Toronto just prior to the outbreak of WWII. They chose to live at **267 Roxborough Drive** and this was officially their home until their marriage dissolved in May 1952—although Anne had quit and then returned to the house as part of a series of moves and separations beginning in 1951.

This was an important address in Anne Wilkinson's life, for it was here that she began to write. The initial spur seems to have been the need to come to terms with her grief over the death of her second baby in 1943. As well, this period corresponds to her realization that her marriage was in declining health. So she started to write poems, and then, in 1947, began a journal. *Canadian Poetry Magazine* and *Reading* were the periodicals where her first verse publications appeared in 1946. Slowly but with increasing frequency her poems were published in other important outlets and her reputation as a poet of a high order began to emerge. Much as she loved her Toronto homes, past and present, she always had a troubled relationship with the idea of Toronto. On May 11, 1948, she confided to her journal: "A test of true love for a Torontonian: If you can walk down Yonge Street with your beloved and still think man's world is a thing of beauty, it's love. I can't." Her first book was not published until she had moved elsewhere in Rosedale.

Sculptor and poet Florence Wyle (1881-1968), encountered above, was born in Illinois and it was while studying at the Art Institute of Chicago that she met her life-long lover Frances Loring. It was Loring who chose to move to Toronto first, in part because her father (her main source of funds) had moved here as a pioneer mining engineer, and in part, as she said later, because she preferred to be part of an emerging art scene in Toronto than a small fry in the established scene in New York. Florence Wyle joined Loring in Toronto in early 1913 and the two lived at **315 Roxborough Drive** until they found the home studio on Glenrose discussed above. Wyle's book, *Poems* was published by Ryerson Press in 1959.

Nearby is the eastern end of Whitney Avenue. Financier Christopher Ondaatje is not as famous a writer as his brother Michael, but his books documenting his extensive and unusual travels have been lavish productions generally well-received by reviewers. What is not well known is that Christopher Ondaatje has published at least one novel under a pseudonym: *Fool's Gold: The First $1,000,000* appeared under the name Simon Marawille in 1974. From 1965 until just before the novel was published he lived at **10 Whitney Avenue**.

Novelist and freelance journalist Stephen Franklin (1922-85) moved to Toronto in 1963 when he won a major Southam Fellowship. He settled into **5 Binscarth Road** and it was his home until he died of a heart attack in 1985. His most widely-reviewed novel was *Knowledge Park* (1972) although his non-fiction books about Stephen Leacock and other Canadian heroes undoubtedly sold better. Apart from a number of programs he produced for the CBC, he also worked as the executive director of the Leacock Centennial celebrated in 1969.

Toronto has been the home of two men named John Gray, and to confuse matters further, both were playwrights. The older of the two was called Jack Gray by his friends. He was born in Detroit in 1927 but came to Toronto as a child, only to be moved shortly thereafter to a number of towns throughout the province. He attended classes at the UofT in 1951 and a decade later moved to England (1960-68) to pursue theatre studies in London. During the fifties he worked as an assistant editor at *Maclean's* in order to support his stage activities and then worked in summer stock in Muskoka.

In the 1950s there was little original Canadian writing seen on Toronto stages, so Gray's *Bright Sun at Midnight*, produced at the Crest Theatre in 1957, received hefty advance publicity, and elevated his status as a Canadian writer. He wrote the libretto for a musical, *Ride a Pink Horse*, that the Crest produced the following year and then Stratford came calling. His play *The Teacher* appeared as part of the 1960 season of the Shakespearean Festival. Following this flurry in the Toronto area, there were productions of his work at Neptune in Halifax, the Crest mounted one more play in 1965, and he wrote dramas for CBC television. However, his work was ignored by the Canadian theatres which exploded on the Toronto scene c. 1970. Around the same time he decided to finish his formal education, getting a B.A. in 1972 and M.A. the next year from the UofT. This was followed by various occupations in cultural administration, most notably as the president of ACTRA from 1977-82. From 1969-84 he lived at **32 Binscarth Road**.

Binscarth begins at **Highland Avenue**. The poet and cartoonist J.W. Bengough (1851-1923) was curtailing his writing substantially by the time he moved to **68 Highland** in 1913, but he continued to give his humorous lectures known as "chalk-talks" throughout the time this was his home. Nearby is **71 Highland**, the house which was nominally Anne Wilkinson's home from 1929-31, although she was abroad for almost all of this period, travelling in the Mediterranean countries. She returned to this address in 1931 but left when she was married on July 21, 1932.

Follow Glen Road south over the ravine bridge to **South Drive**. Immediately to the west of the intersection of Glen and South is **122 South Drive**. This was the home of Marjory MacMurchy, journalist and novelist, from 1916 until her death in 1938. MacMurchy (1880?-1938) was born in Toronto. Her father was the principal of the Toronto Grammar School, later known as Jarvis Collegiate. She attended the UofT but seems not to have graduated, preferring to enter journalism as soon as possible. At a time when a long book review in Toronto newspapers was just three hundred words, and the weekly book-review section had no personality, MacMurchy joined the *News* in 1903 as literary editor and immediately injected her own self into the columns—and gave extensive attention to Canadian books. She kept the post until 1917 to further develop her interest in feminist issues—suffrage, of course, but also the economic aspects of women's lives. Her first book, *The Woman—Bless Her* (1916), and her second, *The Canadian Girl at Work* (1919), were both ruminations on the place of woman in society and the need for improvements in that place. Her novels such as *The Child's House* (1923) were clearly aimed at a young female audience. In 1926 she married Sir John Willison, whom she had known since he edited the *News* at the turn of the century. As an ur-feminist, she continued to publish articles and stories under her own name, but publicly she was referred to as Lady Willison.

CANADIAN AUTHOR DIES
Lady Willison, who died yesterday at her home. She was born and educated in Toronto. An author of merit, her works include "The Child's House" and "Famous Treasury of Famous Books."

Marjory MacMurchy (Lady Willison)

Star, December 16, 1938

120 South Drive was the home of novelist Graeme Gibson (b.1934) and his then-wife, Shirley, from 1967 until their marriage dissolved and he departed the premises c. 1972—but not before writing his second novel, *Communion* (1971).

Shirley Gibson (1927-1997) was a native of Toronto who once thought she would be an actor. Shortly after marrying, she and Graeme lived in England where he wrote his first novel *Five Legs* (1969). On their return to Toronto, the novel was published by Anansi to rave reviews and large sales. Through Graeme, Shirley became involved in Anansi, eventually becoming its publisher for five years starting in 1970. It was then through Anansi that Shirley met the Maritime poet John Thompson (1938-76), who moved in with her at **120 South Drive** from the spring of 1974 until summer 1975. His work inspired some of the poetry she published as *I Am Watching* (1973), but most commentators agree she wrote much better poems after Thompson's sudden death in 1976. These poems were published in *The Tamarack Review* but have yet to appear in a book.

John Thompson was plagued by alcoholism and manic depression (for some weeks during his Toronto year he was hospitalized at the Clarke Institute). He could be both charming and bizarrely hostile, as author and Anansi editor James Polk (b.1939) recalls: "The first time I met John Thompson, I was outraged. In the winter of 1974, a year after we had published his first book, *At the Edge of the Chopping There Are No Secrets*, House of Anansi Press had flown the poet to Toronto for a small party [at 120 South Drive]. We could scarcely wait to meet the man responsible for so many insightful letters, such radiant, passionate poetry. There John sat, his back squared against the wall, tense and surly, a much smaller, grimmer man than the woodsman-hero who welcomes us into the open spaces on his back-cover photo. He gave short shrift to our polite questions, and began to bark out insults into the polite, embarrassed silence about mean publishers and a gutless Toronto literati that did not understand or value poetry. After less than an hour of this, the guests began to slip away.

"The next day, I got another version—a lively, vigorous intelligence, a wry Lancashire humour, a firm integrity, and a breathtaking knowledge of world poetry: Neruda, Roethke, Lorca, Trakl, Yeats. Animatedly, Thompson talked of his life in the British army, of graduate school in the States, of teaching at Mount Allison University and the Dorchester Penitentiary where he had made the prisoners analyze Satan in *Paradise Lost* with touching results. By daylight, he looked hale and ruddy as he explained the appeal of rock-climbing and spelunking, the exploration of caves; later I heard that he was all but a professional in these hard, demanding sports.

"Then that night, bottle of Jack Daniels at hand, he turned on me. He took a hunting knife from his khaki jacket, dropped it like a stone on the table, and asked if I had ever seen blood drawn. I couldn't read the voice or the smile, and simply ducked this challenge, or threat, or whatever it was. I know now that John was fascinated with any kind of gear—fishing tackle, rifles, mountaineering axes—and possibly he was showing off a good steel blade. Still, like any gutless Toronto literati, I took my leave, wondering about Jekyll and Hyde, about the conflict of selves in the creative personality."

Novelist Gwethalyn Graham (1913-65) published only two novels in her abbreviated life but both were winners of the Governor General's Award. Her father was one of the most prominent lawyers in Toronto which meant the family lived in substantial comfort at **106 South Drive** from 1916 until the fall of 1929 when Gwethalyn left Toronto for a Swiss finishing school. She scandalized her parents—and Toronto—when she eloped, aged 19, with a bounder who quickly dropped her for another woman when he realized Gwethalyn was pregnant. Her father placed her on a fixed allowance which allowed her to write full-time while still caring for her son. The result was *Swiss Sonata* (1938), one of the first Canadian novels to tackle anti-Semitism (although the book is set in pre-WWII Switzerland). The book received good reviews in the USA, UK, and Canada; all three countries published their own editions. The Nazis banned the book. Her second novel, *Earth and High Heaven* (1944), addressed anti-Semitism of a subtler kind than that practised by Hitler; a well-to-do WASP family refuses to have anything to do with a daughter involved with a Jew—a tale reflecting aspects of Graham's troubled relationship with her own parents because of her liaison with a Jewish lawyer in Montreal. The novel caused a sensation, was translated into the major languages of Europe and at last count had sold well over a million copies. She died of brain cancer, aged 52.

Poet Peter Miller (b.1920) worked in the head office of the Bank of Commerce in downtown Toronto when c. 1957 he discovered that another employee working in the same building, Raymond Souster, was also a poet on the side. After a few months, knowing that Souster was one of the principals of Contact Press, then the major outlet for leading edge poetry in Canada, Miller showed Souster a manuscript of his poems. Impressed, Souster sent them to his co-editor, Louis Dudek, in Montreal, and Louis Dudek concurred with Souster's enthusiasm. So Contact published *Meditation at Noon* in 1958. The following year they published another volume of Miller's lyrics. It was around then that Miller realized Contact's marketing and distribution were less than perfect. In a history of the press, one of the most important literary presses in Canadian history, Miller notes, "On September 13, 1959, Ray wrote to Louis that I had moved into a large apartment and had offered to use it to stock Contact Press books and from it to ship orders sent to Ray's address. If Louis agreed, we would need to open a bank account in Toronto and keep records . . . ." This gesture was more important than any of the men could have known, for it marked the formal move of the centre of gravity of Canadian poetry from Montreal to Toronto. After Louis agreed to the reorganization, Miller continues, "My apartment [apt. 109], from which the administration would proceed, was at **10 Lamport Avenue** in Rosedale. It was secluded from the downtown hurly-burly. It surveilled an expanse of lawn ruled over by a lordly elm. This address was never officially used by the Contact Press but it was here that the operations were reformed and became intense and continuous." Miller remained at this address from 1959 to March 1964, and in addition to his Contact distribution duties, found time to write another poetry book, *A Shifting Pattern* (1962), to translate *Sun-stone* (1963), a book of verse by Nobel laureate Octavio Paz, and to translate the *Selected Poems* of Alain Grandbois (1964).

Toronto-born Wilfrid Heighington was only 47 when he died of pneumonia in his native city in 1945. He was an eminent lawyer and a former member of the Legislature, winning twice in St. David's riding but losing in 1937. During the Depression he twice ran for the Tory party leadership in Ontario. Perceived by his colleagues as a polished dresser and speaker, the *G&M* remarked at his death (in what I interpret as a left-handed compliment at best), "His suits were models of what a rising young Conservative politician should wear, and his speeches were said to have been models of what the rising young Conservative politician should say." Heighington published a book of light verse *Whereas and Whatnot* (1934), and a novel with more serious goals, *The Cannon's Mouth* (1943). This latter is highly regarded by novelist Scott Symons who tells me that Heighington was so close a friend to his father that Scott called him Uncle Wilf: "A close friend of Dad's was Wilfrid Heighington (he was my godfather). Uncle Wilf's books have been wrongly forgotten. At the least they have a place in the Toronto literary story. His novel growing out of WWI,

and carrying through the twenties, happens to have a wondrously humorous depiction of Perkins Bull (named Sir Leo Hunter in the novel, as I recall)." Heighington lived at **8 May Street** from 1925-30.

Susie Frances Harrison (1859-1935) lived in three houses on **Dunbar Street**. From 1893-1902 she was based at **13 Dunbar**; from 1903-13 at **No.21**; and from 1914-22 at **No.25**. Born in Toronto, Harrison was a trailblazer in that, like Isabella Valancy Crawford, she attempted from earliest adulthood to make a living in Toronto solely as an author. A few years in Ottawa in the early 1880s awakened in her a fascination with Quebecois culture, and much of her writing after she returned to Toronto addressed facets of French-Canadian folklore and literature. In 1887 she published *The Canadian Birthday Book*, one of the first anthologies to include a broad sampling of Quebec poetry in translation. A few years later she gave popular lectures on *habitant* folksongs, and then published two novels focusing on life in French Canada: *The Forest of Bourg-Marie* (1898) and *Ringfield* (1914), the latter published by Hodder & Stoughton in London. While living on this street she also published *In Northern Skies and Other Poems* (1912). Poet Richard Outram (b.1930) lived at **9 Dunbar** from 1966-68.

One of our great poets, E.J. Pratt (1882-1964) spent his last years in an apartment at **5 Elm Avenue**. Pratt, his wife Viola, and their daughter Claire (also a poet of modest accomplishment) moved to this address in spring 1960 where his physical decline hastened to such a degree that he was too weak to write, and for the last months, too weak to leave his bed. Only intimates of long standing were allowed to visit, among them the poets Ralph Gustafson and George Johnston. Another was a fellow student from his days at Victoria College, Prime Minister Lester Pearson. Poet Ralph Gustafson flew from Quebec to attend the funeral and interment, and was appalled to see that no other poets were in attendance.

He wrote to Earle Birney, "Not a poet there to lower Ned into the soil. I thought Trawna was lousy with poets? Or I suppose they thought Ned didn't rate."

Left to right: Claire Pratt, Viola Pratt, E.J. Pratt, Ralph Gustafson, outside the Pratt apartment, 5 Elm Avenue, 1961

Poet Charlotte Beaumont Jarvis (1843?-1927) and her husband, Edgar Jarvis, bought acres of property in this area and, at its centre, in 1866 constructed Glen Hurst, their home which still stands as the heart of Branksome Hall, **10 Elm Avenue**. (A decade later, Edgar Jarvis built an even larger house in the area, presumably as a capital venture. He sold the building, Craigleigh, to financier Sir Edmund Osler, and it would later become the home of poet Anne Wilkinson. See below.) Authors who attended Branksome Hall include Judith Kelly, Sarah Sheard, and Dora Olive Thompson.

With his bestselling novels *Ultimatum* (1973), *Exoneration* (1974), and *Exodus/UK* (1975) Richard Rohmer effectively captured the fear of Americans prevalent in the Canadian zeitgeist of the 1970s. All three books were published when Rohmer, a retired Brigadier General, lived at **23 Sherbourne Street North** from 1971-75. He also chaired, during his residence here, the Ontario Royal Commission on Book Publishing (1971-72), which produced land-mark documents and policies instrumental in allowing Canadian book publishers the chance to nurture the Canadian authors who have since gone on to international acclaim. Since 1975, Rohmer has continued to publish commercial fiction as well as non-fiction addressed to his favourite topics, the Arctic and military history.

Stephen Vizinczey (b.1933) came to Toronto in 1962 and after inhabiting an apartment hotel for some months, moved to **38 Sherbourne North** (at South Drive) in September 1963, his home until October 1965. It was here that he wrote all of his first and most famous novel, *In Praise of Older Women* (1965), while working by day as a CBC producer. Since 1965 he has lived in Europe, making occasional but extended visits to Toronto. *In Praise of Older Women* was rated a dirty book by some (which only helped its sales, of course). Public murmurings by the police that they would have to confiscate the book for its obscenity then guaranteed its infamy and bestseller status. But just as the public and press mocked the police for harassing poets who were reading poetry in Allan Gardens around the same time, so too did the publication of Vizinczey's book mark a maturing of Toronto. Those who wanted to be outraged were outraged. But the vast majority of readers savoured its humour and understood its value in aerating the closed-attic stuffiness enveloping so much of Toronto's public discourse and arts scene.

Poet Ronald Hambleton lived at **46 Elm Avenue** (1971-86)—longer than at any other address in Toronto—during which he published his intriguing memoir *How I Earned $250,000 As a Freelance Writer—Even If It Did Take Thirty Years* (1977). Despite its inflation-dated title, it remains a valuable document of literary history, being concerned with poetry circles, literary bookshops, and the escapades of authors as well as with journalism.

The British maritime thriller writer Sam Llewellyn (b.1948) spent a few years in Toronto in the latter half of the seventies. From June to December 1979 he rented accommodation at **No.49**. Susie F. Harrison ("Seranus") dwelt at **No.53** from 1923-27. Poet and historian Edgar McInnis (1899-1973) passed the last 15 years of his life at **No.83** in quiet retirement.

Poet Anne Wilkinson once stood near **152 South Drive** looking over the park that was all that remained of Craigleigh, the mansion owned by her grandfather, Sir Edmund Osler, president of the Dominion Bank (as in Toronto-Dominion), where she had spent so many years of her youth: "I stood where the house had stood and tried to build it up again in my imagination, brick by brick. Nothing happened. It was as if I had gone to a looking-glass expecting to meet my own image and had found no self reflected back to me. Green grass grew over the labyrinth of cellars. Green grass carpeted the floors of what I had believed to be eternal rooms. In vain I papered the air dark red, as were once the walls of the long wide hall, but it would not hold, nor the pictures in their heavy gilt frames. And the curving stair kept tumbling down." Fortunately for posterity, she left a detailed account of the house, its occupants, and of her years there in another book, *Lions in the Way* (1956), a personal history of the Oslers, her mother's family.

Wilkinson was actually born in Craigleigh in 1910, although her parents soon moved to London, Ontario. Her father died when Anne was nine. Her grandfather quickly wrote to his daughter, reminding her that there were plenty of rooms at Craigleigh where she could live in comfort with Anne and her other children. Anne's mother accepted the offer, and returned to the family palace in 1918. Life was relatively idyllic until Sir Edmund himself died in 1924, at which point Craigleigh was sold. The house was demolished by its new owners in 1932, the same year that Anne was married. An academic specialist in Wilkinson, writing about the poet's life

at Craigleigh, comments: "Although membership in this large family carried with it many privileges which Anne Wilkinson greatly enjoyed, it sometimes created in her a sense of claustrophobia. As her poem 'Summer Acres' implies, she was proud of her ancestry but also felt restricted by her inheritance of particular qualities of character and a clearly defined social role."

In the Epilogue to *Lions in the Way* Wilkinson gives a remarkable account of a way of life which seems to hail from some Dickensian world in Britain. But in fact it salutes us from the heart of our own city within near-living memory: "To say we moved from London, Ontario, to Toronto would not be a lie but it would certainly be no more than a half truth; more accurate to say that after our father's death we moved from London to Craigleigh, a relic of the earlier town and the Principality of our maternal grandfather, Sir Edmund Osler.

"The house stood in the middle of thirteen acres bordering a Rosedale ravine. The front gates opened on to South Drive; the tradesmen's entrance faced Elm Avenue as did two neat brick houses, one occupied by Mr. Allen, the head gardener, the other by the family of the deceased coachman. A large house on a corner of the property belonged to an uncle and aunt and completed our community. We had no other neighbours.

"Beyond the gates we could not go unless escorted by Lizzie, the old Craigleigh nurse, or by our governess. All very well for those to the manner born but we came from London, Ontario.

"The Craigleigh nursery had four barred windows. The two facing south gave us a distant view of street life. We knew our elders lied when they told us how lucky we were, with thirteen acres at our disposal, while the Nanton Avenue children were confined to city sidewalks. But they lied in innocence for they believed that by having too much we had everything.

"Every afternoon as the grandfather clock struck five we were prepared for the downstairs world—washed, brushed and buttoned into dresses stiff with starch. Supper in the billiard room (the billiard table had vanished but the name remained) was followed by an hour or two in the company of the grandfather, mother and resident or non-resident aunts and uncles.

"The governess of the moment presided over supper. If other grandchildren were staying in the house their nanny ruled opposite. The second parlour-maid waited at table. She travelled through two kitchens, the maids' sitting-room, a large pantry and a long corridor before she reached her destination, . . . For some reason, vague and never defined, supper was a joyless meal. Governess and visiting nannies seldom saw eye to eye; the preserved fruit bit like vinegar. In memory it is linked with the smell of linoleum in the back halls and up the back stairs, a lost Victorian smell produced by daily scrubbings with yellow soap.

"After an hour with the family we retired from their adult world but not before we had said our goodnights, a formidable procedure when the room was lined with relations. Each must be addressed, each kissed. The grandfather and one uncle were bald except for their curling back fringes, the others baldish. As they usually received our salutations from the comfort of chairs, we chose their shining domes as targets for our lips. A man seemed over-decorated if his head produced a normal crop of hair. Kissing was a pursuit that only the passing of time taught us to appreciate. We marvelled when we read of its delights, accustomed as we were to counting heads—how many to give and receive before we left the room and climbed the stairs to bed . . .

"We were forbidden the warm kingdom of kitchens and their comforting smells, but the pantry was another matter. The parlour-maids ignored us, William made us welcome. He was referred to as William-the-butler to distinguish him from the many Williams in the family. Behind the scenes he called us Missy which we preferred to the stiff Miss Anne and Miss Betty used by the rest of the staff; a form of address that jarred until our ears adjusted to the sedate measure of Craigleigh tunes. Sometimes William took time off to play with us under the oak trees a long way from the house. He could swing a child higher than any man we knew. When he married a daughter of the deceased coachman and settled in an apartment above the stable-garage the family approved, thankful he had made no foreign alliance.

"The younger children lived on the third floor. My sister and I slept in the old day nursery, a long room often shared with one or two visiting cousins. Lizzie's reign as family nurse had started before our mother's birth and despite competition from a succession of governesses and nannies she kept her crown. Her room was papered with photographs of three generations of Oslers. In curly gilt frames they covered walls and bureaus and small spindly tables. Victorian babies, Edwardian babies and the latest batch of Georgian babies, big boys and girls and little girls and boys and dozens of lacey brides kept her company as she sat with her mending in the long evenings.

"Lizzie and Queen Victoria merged in our minds and became indistinguishable. The resemblance did not end with the physical. They shared common interests. History would read the same if Lizzie had ruled the Empire for sixty years. Church, Throne and Family were mutual and dominant passions."

Mazo de la Roche (1879-1961) and her companion Caroline Clement lived in many rooms and apartments in Toronto. Despite de la Roche's wealth they were never able to settle in any one place long until late in life. After being in England for a couple of years de la Roche was anxious to return home in 1933, but by bad luck and timing, the intimate friends with whom she expected to fraternize in Toronto themselves had headed for Europe on vacation. As de la Roche biographer Ronald Hambleton has commented about her year (1933-34) at **74 Castle Frank Road**, "In the summer Caroline and Mazo were happily settled . . . when Caroline was badly injured in an automobile accident. Not long after her partial recovery from that she tumbled on the river bank and broke her leg. Winter in Toronto in a furnished house overlooking the ravines of the Don River was a convalescence period for Caroline; and for Mazo it was a time for the first attempts at Young Renny, a book that was to bring about the first real differences of opinion between her and her publishers. Her involvement with Caroline's well-being was very deep, and without Caroline's support, Mazo's writing, too, went on crutches."

The Master Gatherer, John Robert Colombo (b.1936) wrote about his year at **78-A Dale Avenue**: "Ruth and I lived in the attic eyrie here, in Rosedale, next door to [magazine editor] Arnold Edinborough, down the street from Morley Callaghan from 1959 to 1960. The apartment was small but large enough to entertain A.J.M. Smith and F.R. Scott one memorable afternoon, and to permit the operation of an Adana hand press and California job cases of imported type. Some Hawkshead Press publications were issued here, including two broadsheets: *Lines for the Last Day*, apocalyptic poems by yours truly illustrated by William Kurelek, his first commission; and Phyllis Gotlieb's *Who Knows One?*, illustrated by Michael Snow. At the time I was a graduate student, and the organizer of the Bohemian Embassy readings."

Running north from the middle of Dale Avenue is **Nanton Avenue. No.19**, when it was an apartment building, was home to three authors over the years: Colin Sabiston (1893-1961) journalist and author of the novel *Zoya* was in the last year of his residence here (1925-33) when his novel appeared. Poet and woman of letters Katherine Hale (1878-1956) spent her last four years as a widow in apt. 31. Such was her affection for Toronto that just a few hours before she died at St. Michael's Hospital, she signed the contract for what obviously would be her last book, *Toronto, Romance of a Great City*, the manuscript of which she had recently completed at this address. And mystery novelist L.A. Morse (*The Big Enchilada*) lived here from 1973-75, just prior to the start of his writing career.

Novelist Graeme Gibson (b.1934) and his wife Shirley (1927-1997) moved to Toronto in 1962 and settled into **25 Nanton**. They lived here for about two years, after which time they chose to live in Mexico for a year before returning to Toronto. Both authors would later publish books that attracted national attention—Graeme especially for his novels *Five Legs* (1969) and *Communion* (1971)—but nothing they wrote at this address seems to have been published.

Man of letters and novelist Augustus Bridle (1869-1952) had shifted his gaze to music by the time he came to live at **33 Nanton** in 1932. For the dozen years this was his home he was intimidatingly active, organizing choral concerts and music extravaganzas while still writing a weekly column of music reviews and arts commentary for the *Star*. He died from injuries suffered when he was hit by a truck on Bloor at Sherbourne.

Marie McPhedran (b.1900) was presented with the Governor General's Award in 1953 for *Cargoes on the Great Lakes*, just one of many books for young adults she published after a life filled with colourful travel. Born in Sault Ste. Marie, she graduated in Modern History from University College, then returned to the north where she worked on the *Sault Star*. She then lived in Flin Flon when it was still a primitive mining camp. Married in 1936 to a doctor, she accompanied him on long canoe and airplane trips of actual exploration and mapping throughout northern Ontario, Manitoba, and Saskatchewan. For her prize-winning novel, she signed onto a lake freighter and sailed the Great Lakes on her. From 1936 until 1973 she lived at **35 Nanton**, but where she lived thereafter and when she died are unknown.

John Harris's last four years were divided between Europe and his Toronto home, **No.45**. In WWII Harris (1915-64) had been a pilot. Shot down behind enemy lines in 1942, he was sent to a stalag where, in March 1944, he helped to orchestrate one of the largest P.O.W. escapes of the war. Of the more than 75 pilots and crew who crawled through a tunnel over 100 metres long, only three made it to freedom. Fifty were murdered by the Gestapo. After the war, Harris worked as a reporter for the *G&M* then joined the public relations arm of the Bank of Commerce. He also wrote television drama for the CBC and wrote the novel *The Weird World of Wes Beattie* (1963) while living in this house.

Under new owners, the third floor of the same building then became the home of playwright Tom Hendry (b.1929) who, in the year that he lived here (1965-6) wrote the final drafts of his drama *Fifteen Miles of Broken Glass*, a winner of the Governor General's Award in 1970. Then the house was transformed again in 1969, and became, until 1988, the home of Kati Rekai, a noted author of books for children.

A granddaughter of Henry Scadding, Mabel Sullivan Johnston (1870-1945) too was an ardent student of Toronto history and literature. Under the pseudonym Suzanne Marny she published *Tales of Old Toronto* (1906). She and her husband seemed to have ordered the construction of **53 Nanton**. They took possession of the new house in 1905 and it was her home until she died 40 years later.

William Hume Blake (1861-1924) also seems to have ordered construction of his home. In this case, it appears he lived at **5 Powell Avenue** in 1905-6, during which he supervised the building of a new house on the property immediately to the south. When that building was finished c. 1906, he took possession of the new place (with its address of **30 Dale Avenue**) and then sold his previous home. He stayed here for only half a dozen years before moving again, this time to the Annex. Blake published two collections of literary essays, but he is now recalled for his confident and felicitous translation of two classics of French Canada: *Maria Chapdelaine* (1921) by Louis Hémon and *Chez Nous* (1924) by Adjutor Rivard.

Television arts broadcaster Adrienne Clarkson (b.1939) wrote two novels while she lived at **9 Powell** between 1966 and 1974. McClelland and Stewart published *A Lover More Condoling* (1968), *Hunger Trace* (1970), and the non-fiction *True to You in My Fashion: A Woman Talks to Men About Marriage* (1971).

The apartment building at **21 Dale Avenue** has housed a number of authors. Radio playwright Fletcher Markle (1921-91) was based here in 1962-63 just after he had returned to Canada from the USA to direct the film version of *The Incredible Journey* for Walt Disney Pictures. This was the same year he learned he had diabetes and so he abandoned film directing for the allegedly less stressful task of producing a television interview series for the CBC. Man of the theatre and crime novelist Anthony Quogan (b.1937) was finishing his grad studies at UofT when he rented apt. 931 between 1960 and 1964. Bestselling novelist Richard Rohmer (b.1924) had his home here from 1976-83, during which he wrote and published the thrillers *Periscope Red* (1980), *Separation II* (1981), *Triad* (1981), *Retaliation* (1982), and the controversial military history, *Patton's Gap* (1981).

Betty Jane Wylie (b.1931) took over apt. 701 in 1975. One of the reasons she bought this co-op unit was because it had both indoor and outdoor swimming pools and she swam 50 laps a day for most of the 11 years she had accommodation here. Recently widowed, and nearly broke, she began to make a living as a freelance features-journalist writing for an astonishing variety of periodicals. Many of these assignments inspired her creative writing. *The Horsburgh Scandal* remains her best-known play, a collective work she created for Paul

Thompson at Theatre Passe Muraille. Playwright and composer John Gray (*Billy Bishop Goes to War*) wrote the incidental music. At this address she wrote plays for children, another drama for adults, *A Place on Earth* (TWP, 1982), and, as a result of the sudden death of her own husband, *Beginnings: A Book for Widows* (1977), a bestseller in Canada, the USA, and UK. To date she has written more than 20 plays.

Apt. 808 of **21 Dale** was Lovat Dickson's (1902-87) home for the last 20 years of his life. Dickson had been working in England since 1929 when he left Canada after a number of unhappy tries at other occupations to become an editor of *The Fortnightly Review* in London, with what he called a "side-occupation" as a book scout for Macmillan in New York. Not long afterwards, he had established his own book publishing company which was instrumental in introducing Grey Owl to the British public, and thereby to the whole world.

Lovat Dickson, in front of his apartment, 21 Dale Avenue, circa 1980

Eventually, he chose to work for Macmillan London where he was the *éminence grise* among the city's literary editors. Throughout WWII and for many years after, he ran the company while its nominal head, Harold Macmillan, was embroiled in British political life. Dickson tried his hand at writing fiction, a novel called *Out of the West Land* (1944), and in 1959 he published the first of his two much-lauded autobiographies, *The Ante-Room*. When he retired from Macmillan in 1967, Dickson returned to Canada, to Toronto, but did not live a retired life. He published a biography of H.G. Wells in 1969; a biography of the man who had deceived him, *Wilderness Man: The Strange Story of Grey Owl* (1973); and in 1975 he published yet another biography of a literary figure he had known, *Radclyffe Hall*. Somehow he also found the time to write a history of the Royal Ontario Museum: *The Museum Makers* (1986). An active supporter of the PEN Canadian Centre when it formed in Toronto in 1983, his august appearance, which was always offset by a charming smile and open friendliness, reminded us that he had been a member of the British PEN centre since 1930 and had rubbed shoulders frequently with Shaw, Wells, and other famous members.

His sunset years did not mark, however, his first residence in Toronto. Shortly after arriving in Canada from his native Australia, he moved to Toronto to enlist in the air force (nearly three years underage) in March 1918. WWI ended before he could obtain his wings, so after nine months in uniform in Toronto, he set out to conquer the world with whatever jobs he could find. Heart disease soon had him bedridden and near death. But as he explained in *The Ante-Room*, life had to reach bottom before he could rise again: "When I came out of hospital it was quite clear that I could never do heavy work again, and once more I dreamt of the possibility of working for a newspaper or a magazine. But I had no experience and no introductions, and I did not know how to begin to go about finding such a job. While I was convalescing at home, Jack Bickell came on a visit to the mine. He talked to me from time to time, and knowing that he was a rich and influential man, I exercised all the charm and intelligence I had at command—and it wasn't much—to earn his interest and help. Miraculously it worked. He was President of Paramount Pictures Corporation in Canada. He said he would speak to the General Manager. A few days later I got a letter from Paramount offering me a job in their sales department at $25 a week, commencing immediately, and I left for Toronto, feeling that at last I was to get a foothold in the world of imagination and art.

"I little guessed what was in store for me, some of the most interesting as well as the most painful months in my life. In 1920 there were ninety-two churches in Toronto and ninety-five picture theatres. Our business was with the latter; our job to persuade the managers of those theatres to exhibit our films in preference to those of Metro-Goldwyn, Warners and Fox. The business was highly competitive, and it was conducted entirely in Yiddish, the managers of the theatres and the salesmen who sold the films being Jews. I was attached for the purpose of learning the ropes to Jake Berman, the senior salesman, a fat, jolly Jew with pendulous cheeks and rotund paunch, who had sold films all his life and knew the business backwards. We had our stars, now long set but in those days objects of profound passion to a public who had no other entertainment except vaudeville . . . After a month Jake said 'Ready to try it on your own, kiddo?' and I was given some small suburban theatres of Toronto to cut my teeth on . . . For three months until Christmas-time I was engaged in this unenlightening work. The week before Christmas was the last booking, and two days before the holiday I returned to Toronto, glad to be free of a distasteful job, and positively looking forward to the New Year and to taking up my work of selling films again. I felt I had reached a low ebb in my struggle to get on in the world, but I had not quite reached the depths. In my pay envelope was an extra week's wages, and a

Morley Callaghan (left) and his son Barry on the front porch of 20 Dale Avenue, 1988

517

typed notice to say that my services would not be required after December 31st. I had $50 in hand; I had failed again. It was midwinter, and I was out of work."

Morley Callaghan bought **20 Dale Avenue** in 1950 and it was to be his home until he died in 1990. When he purchased the building it was still operating under wartime regulations as a rooming house and it took him almost a year to negotiate the removal of the owner and her roomers He and his family did not take possession until spring 1951. Many authors write their best stuff in their twenties and thirties but Callaghan (1903-90) continued to write top-drawer fiction right up to the end of his life—in his ground-floor study until 1985, and then in a second-floor den after that. Among the distinguished novels he wrote here were *The Many Colored Coat* (1960), *A Passion in Rome* (1961), *A Fine and Private Place* (1975), *Close to the Sun Again* (1977), *The Enchanted Pimp* (1978), *A Time for Judas* (1984), *Our Lady of the Snows* (1985), and *A Wild Old Man on the Road* (1988). In addition to fiction, he also penned *That Summer in Paris* (1963), an account of his time amidst the Lost Generation in France in the twenties—the finest recounting of that era by any writer.

Also published while he lived here were several volumes which gathered material Callaghan had written mostly at other locations, although late additions and revisions were made by him at **20 Dale**. These books include *Morley Callaghan's Stories* (1959), *No Man's Meat* (1978), *The Lost and Found Stories of Morley Callaghan* (1985), and *The Man with the Coat* (1987).

A number of prizes and awards were bestowed on Morley, almost all of them while he lived in Rosedale. These include the Governor General's Award in 1951 for *The Loved and The Lost*, the Lorne Pierce Medal for Literature from the Royal Society of Canada in 1971, the Molson Prize (1970), and the Royal Bank Award (1970), these latter two accompanied by large amounts of cash. Quite notoriously in 1967 he declined one

honour: the Order of Canada. He argued publicly, rightly it seems to me, that if political party bagmen and antique politicians were to be given the Order of Canada at its highest of three levels (along with the truly deserving), then as Canada's pre-eminent novelist he was entitled to the same courtesy. The federal government had offered him the lowest level of the award. To punish him for his effrontery, the government did not offer Callaghan the Order again until many years later—this time at the highest level. and this time he accepted.

It was through my conversations with Morley Callaghan that I became alive to the literary history of Toronto. Again and again he would bring me up short by mentioning his encounter in a Toronto café or party with internationally celebrated authors. He was always willing to talk to me about "what it was like in Toronto when . . . " or "what was such-and-such a Toronto author really like . . . " But I hasten to say that our conversations were much more than my simply asking him questions about the past and he answering. In fact, when we talked about authors, most of our time was given to discussion of living writers and what they were producing. It has been my experience that as authors age, they read fewer and fewer of their contemporaries and revert to reading the classics of the long-dead. Morley was certainly conversant with the classics, but he never failed to surprise me by the breadth of his reading of contemporary fiction. A typical conversation might begin with his asking me for my opinion of the latest novel by X, an author in his early thirties. I replied that I enjoyed the book. He then said that he too had enjoyed the book—but not as much as the two earlier novels by X, written when X was in his twenties (and Callaghan in his eighties). Although I have met many elderly and famous authors, I have never met one who came close to Morley Callaghan for intellectual curiosity about the present in all its senses, including the younger generations of writers.

Does Toronto fully embrace Morley Callaghan? The answer is debatable. No school is named in his honour. The City only reluctantly agreed to the placement of a small memorial plaque and garden at the foot of Dale Avenue after a group of private individuals agreed to raise the funds for their maintenance. And Toronto's muted response to Callaghan always mystifies erudite outsiders. The silent deprecation was what led American critic Edmund Wilson to speculate in *The New Yorker* in 1960, "whether the primary reason for the current underestimation of Morley Callaghan may not be simply a general incapacity—apparently shared by his compatriots—for believing that a writer whose works may be mentioned without absurdity in association with Chekhov's and Turgenov's can possibly be functioning in Toronto."

Morley's son Barry (b.1937) is also an internationally acclaimed and translated author. He lived with his parents at **20 Dale** until 1957 when he left to study at Assumption College in Windsor. He returned to the family household in 1959 and remained until 1963 when he graduated from the UofT. Morley willed the house to Barry, and, after extensive renovations, it became his home once more in 1991. From this address he continues to edit his long-running literary magazine *Exile*, and edit the books published by his Exile Editions. His own writing has been fruitful here. Among the volumes he has written or anthologies edited are *Barrelhouse Kings: A Memoir* (1998); *Hogg: The Poems and Drawings* (1997); *The Austin Clarke Reader* (1996); *This Ain't No Healin' Town: Toronto Stories* (1995); *A Kiss Is Still a Kiss* (1995); *The Poetry of Gwendolyn MacEwen* [co-edited with Margaret Atwood](1994); and *When Things Get Worst* (1993).

In *Barrelhouse Kings*, Barry Callaghan recalled a poignant moment that took place at this address: "When I stood alone at night on the footbridge over the ravine I felt that I was in the arms of the trees. I could feel the dew and hear the dong of the Old City Hall clock bell and muffled foghorns from the lake . . . As I turned up our street, heading home, the overhead street lights were like wind lamps hidden in the maple leaves. Everything was in shadows . . . All the houses and clumsy mansions were dark, except for Clery's upstairs window and my father's front window where he sat into the early hours, a writer working at his desk, the floor lamp shedding light over his shoulders, staring into the dark outside the window, an oblong of amber light.

"I often stood out on the lawn at the edge of a flower bed, watching him, sometimes moving in so close I could reach out and touch the glass, yet he could not see me—lost as he was in the little confessions his characters were making —and since the glass was like a mirror, silvered by the night, I was standing on the other side of the mirror, watching as he mouthed a phrase, bringing a voice, a plea, secretly to life in the open view of anyone passing on the street . . . My father was back sitting in his box of amber light, his head cocked to the side, listening, with only the glass between us. I wanted to knock on the glass and tell him that I realized even the police have secret stories, little healing confessions they want to make while standing in the dark. I felt that I knew something a young man does not often know, and I knew it with the kind of innocence I could see in my father's eyes as he sat hearing his voices, staring into my eyes, unaware that I was there."

PLAYTER ESTATES

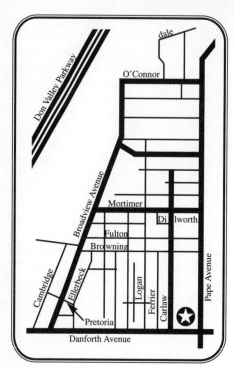

The tour begins at the northwest corner of Danforth Avenue and Pape Avenue.

Walk three blocks west to **Ferrier Avenue**. **No.12** was the home of noted science fiction writer Michelle Sagara from 1990-96. Sagara (b.1963) was once the manager of the Bakka Books when it was on Queen Street (the oldest surviving SF bookshop in the world), and was inspired to write in the genre by what she read in the store. On Ferrier Sagara had her first baby, which affected the time she could devote to writing. Nonetheless she managed to finish *Hunter's Oath* at this address, and then wrote all of *Hunter's Death* and about half of *Broken Crown* before moving to another house in this area.

Norman Williams (b.1923) was born at **922 Logan Avenue** and seems to have lived at the same address for his entire life—an honour no other author in the *Guide* can claim as far as I know. Williams began writing dramas in high school and had several plays broadcast on the CBC but felt that his real beginning as a playwright happened when Norman Corwin directed his play *Homecoming* on CBS in February 1946. He did not write stage plays until the 1950s and they were all of the one-act persuasion. These latter were praised and taken most seriously by eminences such as Herbert Whittaker, Robertson Davies, and Herman Voaden—Whittaker even wrote a Preface for *World's Apart: Six Prize-Winning Plays by Norman Williams* (1956). A *Montreal Star* reviewer, commenting on the book, wrote: "In a most perceptive Preface to the collected one-act plays of Norman Williams, Herbert Whittaker says that because no native son has written a fine play for the theatre, Canadian theatre-goers who are disturbed by this national shortcoming lift their heads like deer in the forest at the first indication of a new and talented playwright. After reading these six one-act plays my head will in future be raised like a giraffe on the veld at the mention of this Toronto playwright's name, scanning the horizon to see whether he has produced his first big three-act drama, so whetted is my appetite by the samples in this volume." Norman Williams never seems to have written a three-act drama and, rather mystifyingly, seems to have completely disappeared from our contemporary theatre's radar. There is one play of his which, based solely on a publisher's intriguing outline, I hope someone produces in the near future: *He Didn't Even Say Goodbye* is described thus: "Ben locks himself into a room and refuses to go to the office. His wife Alice panics when she learns that, in Ben's mind, all other people have vanished."

Although long associated with Montreal, Ted Allan (1916-95) spent almost a dozen of his later years living in Toronto. When he arrived in 1982, he settled into **927 Logan**, his home for the next four years. Here he wrote and published the story collection *Don't You Know Anybody Else?* (1985), the stage version with music of *Lies My Father Told Me* (1984), and the novel *Love Is a Long Shot* (1984).

Poet Gwendolyn MacEwen (1941-87) and her husband, a Greek-Canadian musician, moved into an apartment at **13 Browning Avenue** in the fall of 1970. Their home was but a block away from the heart of Greektown where her husband hoped to find work, and where, soon after, he and Gwen would open their own club, The Trojan Horse. In her wonderful biography of MacEwen, poet Rosemary Sullivan discusses a telling incident that involved Gwen at this time: "Gwendolyn loved the Danforth. Her Greek was by now very good and she came to know many of the Danforth's characters. What she most liked about the Greeks was their uninhibitedness, their exuberance. They seemed transparent; in what they said or did there seemed no hidden agenda. They had a particular kind of insanity she admired 'You live life; you think you know what you're doing; but you look at it from another perspective and it's all suddenly absurd.' But there was still a chauvinism to contend with. In its public persona at least, this was a male world.

"Her old friend from the Toronto Island days the sculptor Mac Reynolds remembers visiting one of the nightclubs with Gwen. When the strains of the *zembekiko* began to play, Gwen got up to dance. She danced with a brilliant fierceness, playing intricate variations with her body on the strict and complex rhythm of the music. She loved the dance: it was, she said, 'both a fight against gravity and a kind of flirtation with the earth.' She danced it defiantly. On the sidewalk afterwards Reynolds remembers a fierce argument, entirely in Greek, with one of the men who had followed Gwen out. She had violated their tradition. In 1970, the *zembekiko* was still a dance danced only by men."

In order to be free of distraction—to have time to write—Gwen gave this Browning address to intimates only, meeting people elsewhere if she had to meet them face to face. She worked on a short-story collection here (*Noman*), and the poetry books *The Armies of the Moon* (1972), as well as *Magic Animals: Selected Poems Old and New* (1974). Some of the poems in *The Fire-Eaters* (1976) were probably written at this address as well.

Poet Ralph Cunningham (b.1932) has lived at **20 Browning Avenue** since 1943—in other words for most of his life. Many of his poems deal with Toronto's topography in one way or another, and have been published in leading literary magazines across the country. His one poetry volume, *Lovesongs*, appeared in 1962.

Crime novelist Alison Gordon (b.1943) first moved to the Broadview-Danforth district when she settled into **89 Browning** in the autumn of 1976. It was to be her home for the next two years. Since then, she has lived just south of the Danforth, and currently lives just north of it. While installed on Browning she worked at the CBC. Immediately after her residency here, she joined the sports department of the *Star*, and her experiences there and at the CBC provided her with much of the material for her internationally popular books.

Near the west end of Browning is **Ellerbeck Street**. **No.60** was the first home in Toronto, 1972-75, of Suniti Namjoshi (b.1941). Born in India, she worked in that country's civil service until (by her own admission bored to tears), she went to the USA and then to Montreal to do graduate work in English at McGill. She was hired by the UofT in 1972 (as soon as she got her PhD) to teach at Scarborough College, and this was her day job until 1987. After three years on Ellerbeck, she moved a few blocks to the north, to **53 Mortimer Avenue** and remained there until 1987, at which point she emigrated to Britain. Books that were partly written in Toronto were *The Jackass and the Lady* (1980), *Flesh and Paper* (1986), and *The Blue Donkey Fables* (1991). In 1979, she declared to the world and to her readers that she was a lesbian, and the year marks a watershed in her work, critics agreeing that the writing after this date is "qualitatively different, presenting an artist who has found her own voice." Books she wrote entirely in Toronto (mostly at the Mortimer domicile) were *Feminist Fables* (1981), *The Authentic Lie* (1982), *From the Bedside Book of Nightmares* (1984), *The Conversations of Cow* (1985), *Aditi and the One-Eyed Monkey* (1986).

Walk south on Broadview Avenue to Pretoria, then west to **Cambridge Avenue**. Playwright Brad Fraser (b.1959) has lived in Toronto off and on many times, but his first residency was crucial to his writing career in that it directly led to the creation of his most notorious and, to date, best-known play: "I lived and worked in Toronto from 1981 until 1984. I was initially lodged in a number of sumptuous residences by Theatre Passe Muraille. These lovely places included The Wheat Sheaf Hotel, chosen for the prairie images it evokes, no doubt, certainly not for its bathrooms . . . I finally settled into a smart, five-bedroom home in the Bloor/Danforth area with various out of work actors and writers. The address was **100 Cambridge Avenue**, although many of us simply referred to it as 'One Hun Came' which pretty much summed up the tenor of the place and my demeanour at the time.

"While living at **100 Cambridge** one of my room mates was the erstwhile, and highly entertaining actress and playwright Carol Sinclair. Carol is, in many ways, the person the character of Candy in *Unidentified Human Remains and the True Nature Of Love* is based on. I guess you could say that of the concerns dealt with in that play, as well as the genesis of a number of characters, began at this locale."

Return to Broadview via Pretoria and walk north two blocks to **Fulton Avenue**. When the poet George Johnston (b.1913) was a ten-year-old child he and his family moved from Hamilton to Toronto and spent their first three or four years in the city at **21 Fulton**. George reminisced: "The city ended one street north of us and there was a county school on Broadview at the end of Fulton. There were occasional skirmishes with the county kids along the street to and from school; I avoided them. I went to Kitchener school at Fulton and Pape. It was a teacher's college. . . ." Playwright George F. Walker (b.1947) was about the same age as Johnson when he lived at **No.183** in 1960. Scottish-born John Herries McCulloch (b.1892) came to Canada as a young man but returned to Scotland at the height of the Depression in 1933. He had been the assistant editor of the *Star Weekly* for the years 1929-31. One of his only two appearances in the directories cites him at **No.203** in 1929. Although he was in Canada for about a decade at most, it seems, he wrote a number of novels set in Canada after his return to the UK, including *Dark Acres* (1935), a story addressing the effect of the Depression on prairie wheat farmers. Of a brighter nature is his tale about the Caribou titled *North Range* (1954). In his later years, McCulloch became an expert on the training of sheep dogs.

One of the greatest—and one of the most unsung—heroes of 20th c. letters in Toronto is William Arthur Deacon (1890-1977), who bought his first home at **36 Dilworth Crescent** in 1924 and remained until the fall of 1936. **Dilworth** is found by taking Fulton to Carlaw and walking north one short block.

Although he had trained as a lawyer in Winnipeg, Deacon was unique in the Canada of his time in craving to be the nation's first full-time reviewer of books. His wish was fulfilled when he was hired in 1922 to be the literary editor of *Saturday Night*, a Toronto weekly, to be sure, but one read across the country. The magazine had not hired Deacon on a whim. He had established his credentials in Winnipeg by publishing literary essays and reviews in an impressive assemblage of American and Canadian outlets including *Canadian Magazine*, the *New York Times*, the *Manitoba Free Press*, and *American Mercury*. These were eventually gathered and published again as books; one of them, *Poteen, a Pot-Pourri of Canadian Essays* (1926), was published after he had moved to Playter Estates. The essays reveal the passions and traits which would absorb Deacon all his life: a sense of wry humour, a love of country, a judicious exhortation to others to read the best Canadian writing, and a singular combination of pride somehow melded with self-effacement. This last characteristic comes through in the confidence with which he said—in 1921—"I want to be an anonymous herald announcing the great ones."

William Arthur Deacon

The sense of humour comes through clearly in his most famous and yet, in some ways, slightest book: *The Four Jameses* (1927), a satiric look at four poets whose first name was James. The strength of the book lies not so much in its mockery of the poets themselves (their awfulness makes that easy) as in its ridicule of the pretentious, nationalist reviewing of the time which tried to equate the poetasters of early Canada with the literary titans of much older cultures.

As the Depression became a fixture of national life, Deacon penned at this address what turned out to be his last book: *My Vision of Canada* (1933). This is a remarkably prescient work. In addition to espousing support for the creation of a national culture (a groundswell that would not happen for 40 more years), he pushed for the cutting of ties to the mother country, saying that Canada would never achieve its full destiny unless it relied solely on its own strengths and stopped camouflaging its global insecurity with over-the-top displays of monarchical loyalty.

Although he published no more books, his influence only grew with age. His weekly columns, full of news of author travels, health, and successes, allowed Canadian authors from coast to coast to feel they were part of a national community, and I think did much to make organizations such as the Canadian Authors' Association viable. The CAA members met annually, but it was Deacon's columns which uniquely helped to sustain their sense of worth and purpose. As if the reviewing (and pleading for ad support from publishers) were not enough, Deacon was constantly active in a number of literary organizations in Toronto: the CAA (he had joined its Winnipeg branch when the only national organization for authors at the time had formed in 1921, and in the 1940s would serve as its national president), the Writers' Club, the Arts and Letters Club, the Association of Canadian Bookmen, the Whitman fellowship, the Canadian Literature Club and the PEN Club. He was a key player in the formation of the Governor General's Awards, the Leacock Medal for Humour, and much more quietly, of the Canadian Writer's Foundation, established to discreetly provide financial assistance to writers in dire financial straits.

About four years after Deacon had moved to **36 Dilworth**, Fred Jacob, the playwright and literary editor of the *M&E* died in June 1928. The paper, anxious to find a replacement promptly offered the post to Deacon and he quickly accepted. It was an important move, for the paper had a much bigger circulation than *Saturday Night* and, perhaps surprisingly, was much less restrictive than the weekly about what he wrote and what he reviewed. Both his job at the *M&E* and his tenure at this house ended in late 1936.

Dilworth feeds into **Mortimer Avenue**. **No.25** was the home of mystery novelist Ted Wood (b.1931) shortly after he arrived in Canada from Britain in 1954 to join the Toronto Police Force. One of his earliest Canadian memories is "being hauled out on the night of Hurricane Hazel to go to the Court Street Police Station where I sat and drank coffee with my fellow new coppers in

Ted Wood, Spring 1956, directing traffic on Yonge Street

reserve." Perhaps this watery experience explains why he moved to higher ground in Scarborough less than a year later. He stayed with the police until 1957, when, like many writers, he joined MacLaren Advertising, initially as a copywriter and then eventually as creative director. During this advertising age he wrote plays broadcast on CBC, and then went completely freelance in 1974, publishing hard-edged crime novels that have won acclaim in Canada, the USA, UK, as well as Holland, Germany, France, Italy, and Japan. Under the pseudonym Jack Barnao he writes a second series of crime novels which feature a bodyguard who lives at 60 Clifton Road, an in-joke of sorts in that this is a property he himself owns in Moore Park.

About a kilometre north of Mortimer is a small enclave of streets tucked away in the pocket formed by Pape Avenue, O'Connor Drive, and the Don Valley. One of these streets, **Hopedale Avenue**, has been home to two noted Canadian authors. Playwright Tomson Highway (*Dry Lips Oughta Move to Kapuskasing*) occupied **No.28** from September 1986 to April 1987, a period in which he received his first Dora nomination, for the Toronto production of his remarkable play *The Rez Sisters*.

Novelist Claire Mowat (b.1933) was born in Toronto and spent her earliest years (1933-49) living at **No.78**. She described her time in the city, "I lived there and nowhere else for the first twenty-eight years of my life. I attended William Burgess School in East York, Havergal College, and the Ontario College of Art.

"During my student years my dearest ambition was to leave Toronto behind. It was a dreary, prosaic city for those of us who had ambitions to do something other than move to the new suburbs and drive a car with chrome-plated tail fins. I wanted to live in England—and I did, for a while—but in the end I grudgingly conceded that Toronto was my home, and, for better or worse, I came back. When I married [novelist Farley Mowat], I moved to a small community . . . I do visit Toronto often. The place is in my blood. As big cities go, it isn't half bad. The narrow, Orange-lodge mentality which I so loathed back in 1950 has all but disappeared now. Other problems have appeared but despite them Toronto has grown up admirably. It shines like a jewel in comparison with virtually every American city. It lags way behind Melbourne, Australia, if you compare their public transportation network with ours. It doesn't even come close to Helsinki, Finland, when we compare their exquisitely restored heritage buildings and their remarkable new buildings with ours. Yet Toronto does have tolerance, friendliness, and a lot of energy and daring. For all its faults, it's still a humane place. I do intend to write about it, but I know that I will never live in Toronto again. If I had remained there, I would never have written one word for publication. The distractions and entertainments of the city, along with the complications and competition of mere survival in the midst of three million people, would have drained me of any creative energy. Writing is solitary, self-disciplined work. I love small towns now, but perhaps it is because they remind me of the old Toronto neighbourhoods of the 1940s, grim places in a lot of ways but the communities which nurtured me and shaped me."

DONLANDS AVENUE

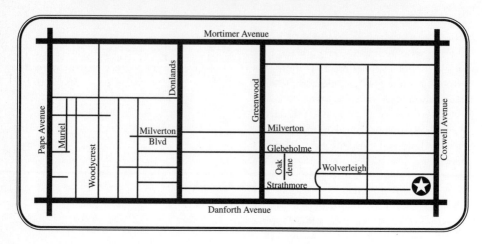

The tour begins at the northwest corner of Danforth Avenue and Coxwell Avenue.

The relative age of this part of Toronto is revealed by the presence of Susie Frances Harrison (1859-1935) who lived at **212 Strathmore Boulevard** from 1928 to 1933. Harrison usually published under her pseudonym "Seranus," derived apparently from a typesetter's misreading of the name "S. Frances" by which she signed an early publication. The daughter of a Toronto innkeeper, Seranus was married in 1879 and moved with Mr. Harrison to Ottawa for some years before returning permanently to Toronto in 1886. Shortly after her return she worked for *The Week*, first as music critic and later as acting editor. While at *The Week* she had the unpleasant task of informing Isabella Valancy Crawford that she could not pay what Crawford wanted for her poems, a fact worth mentioning because Harrison herself in later life had to struggle to make a living from her pen. Her novels were published in Britain and Canada, her journalism appeared in the USA, and her poetry was published in Canada. While she lived at this address, she had to subsidize the publi-

cation of her own book *Later Poems and New Villanelles* (1928). She died in Toronto, and the *Telegram* considered her passing so important that it placed news of her death on the front page.

Novelist Paul Quarrington (b.1953), during a rough patch in his life, moved into the home of a buddy whose wife had just left him. Misery loves company. Their abode was **95 Wolverleigh Boulevard** and what was intended to be a short residency lasted almost three years, during which Quarrington wrote, ironically, one of his funniest books, *King Leary* (1987). The book won the Stephen Leacock Medal for Humour.

A libel suit drove Rosemary Aubert (b.1950) to **Glebeholme Boulevard**. At her previous address she had written a novel to which a neighbour took grave exception and launched legal action. Since seeing the neighbour every day was not a pleasant prospect, Rosemary fled to **250 Glebeholme** "to escape the consequences of the libel suit. Here I hid out, terrified to write a single word, lest I again offend. I did, however, work on a novella called *Terminal Grill* . . . I remember this basement as a place of refuge. I began *Free Reign* there as notes and musings. I don't remember, but I rather suspect that I worked on a lot of things, but always with the feeling that my writing career was done." Her career was far from done. Her latest mystery novel, *Free Reign* (1997), set in the Don Valley, has been published to excellent reviews in the USA, France, and Japan. Her romance fiction has sold millions of copies in those countries as well as in Brazil, Italy, Spain, Australia, and Holland.

When the painter and writer Bertram Brooker (1888-1955) moved to Toronto from Manitoba in 1921, he settled into **44 Oakdene Crescent**. He had come to the city to be the editor of *Marketing Magazine*, an important trade journal. He bought the magazine not long after he had moved around the corner to **707 Greenwood Avenue** in 1923. During the next four years he was at this address he busied himself writing articles and books about the techniques of advertising and importance of type and page design. His very first book, *Subconscious Selling* (1923), was just the first of some of his texts on advertising which were read with admiration and profit for years by those in the trade.

While at **No.704**, Brooker also expanded his involvement with visual art. Two members of the Group of Seven, Lawren Harris and Arthur Lismer, became especially close friends, and through them he moved to the centre of the arts world in Toronto. In 1926, he became much more serious about his own painting, and, as a recent catalogue for a touring show of his art states, "In 1927 he burst onto the Canadian scene with an exhibition of abstract painting at the Arts & Letters Club in Toronto. These were the first abstract pictures to be exhibited in Canada by a Canadian."

Two playwrights lived within a few blocks of Brooker's house. George F. Walker (b.1947; *Criminals in Love*; *Nothing Sacred*) passed part of his youth at **26 Milverton Boulevard** during 1961-65. A little to the north at **902 Greenwood** lived the one-act play specialist William S. Milne (1902-79)

from 1922-33. For the first few years of his stay here he was an undergrad at the UofT, followed by grad work for an MA and BEd. He then began a long career as a high-school teacher of Drama and English. In his spare time, Milne devoted himself whole-heartedly to what has become known as the Little Theatre Movement in Canada. He acted in plays at Hart House throughout the twenties, and later for such noted directors as Mavor Moore and Leon Major. Milne directed for an astounding number of amateur, semi-professional, and professional companies and his work ranged from Shakespeare to the Canadian premiere of John Coulter's *The Drums Are Out*. His theatre experience was even wider than this. From 1925-26 he was the property master of the Margaret Eaton Theatre, and later he was the electrician for stage productions at the Arts and Letters Club.

Historian and novelist Pierre Berton (b.1920) lived in Toronto for about a year when he was eleven, but his first residency as an adult began just after the war when, in order to pursue his journalism career, he dwelt at **379 Donlands Avenue** for about a year and a half. The city did not impress him as it had when he was a boy: "I moved to Toronto in 1947. What a dreadful one-horse town this was! The WASP elite and the Orange Lodge ran the city. Fun was a no-no. Sunday was a horror. There was literally nothing to do on your one day off (for we worked half a day Saturday); no entertainment of any kind, no sports, no movies. You couldn't even window shop at the Methodist temple of Eaton's because the blinds were tightly drawn. That explains why so many people were willing to suffer the banality of a Toronto church service . . . When I arrived, George's on Yonge Street was the only seafood restaurant in town. The Canadian Way of Life was symbolized by the all-Canadian beer parlour, with the sexes separated, and no laughing or singing allowed . . . When I first came to Hogtown there was no home-grown ballet, no opera, no theatre save for Dora Mavor Moore's struggling New Play Society. Ernie Rawley imported threadbare touring companies for his Royal Alex and finally gave up. If Rawley couldn't make a go of it, the WASPs said, nobody could. They laughed when the son of an immigrant storekeeper, Ed Mirvish, took it over. He turned it into a howling success.

"Yes, the immigrants did destroy the old way of life and I say thank God they did."

Three blocks west of Donlands and running north from Danforth is **Woodycrest Avenue. No.37** has been Lesley Krueger's (b.1954) base since 1982, although most of the eighties were spent in travel abroad. Her first appearance between hardcovers came in 1986 in *Coming Attractions 4*, a collection of new voices (which also featured the first book appearance by Rohinton Mistry) published by Oberon. Subsequent fictions include *Hard Travel* (1989) and *Poor Player* (1983).

Michael Ondaatje (b.1943) and Linda Spalding (b.1943) moved to **99 Woodycrest** in 1988 and this was their home until 1993. While ensconced here Ondaatje published a book of poetry, *The Cinnamon Peeler* (1992), and his world-famous novel, *The English Patient* (1992). The latter won the Governor General's Award and was a co-winner of the Booker Prize. Playwright and movie director Anthony Minghella translated the novel into a feature film which won several Oscars, including Best Motion Picture. Spalding was also busy here, publishing her novel *Daughters of Captain Cook* (1988), and co-editing with Ondaatje *The Brick Reader* (1991), an anthology of highlights in the magazine *Brick* which they jointly edit.

Ondaatje and Spalding undoubtedly passed Lesley Krueger on the street, and those three at some point, while shopping on the Danforth, probably bumped into Eliza Clark (b.1963), then a young author writing her first novel (*Miss You Like Crazy*, 1991) just two blocks away at **56 Muriel Avenue.** This was her address from 1986-91.

MOOREPARK

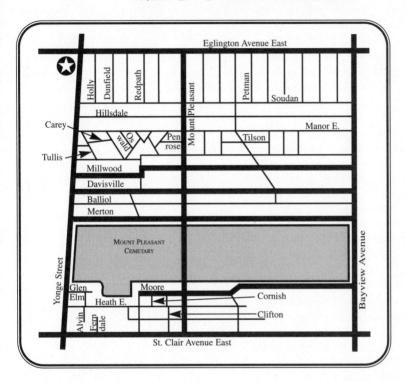

The tour begins at the southwest corner of Eglinton Avenue East and Yonge Street.

Walk one block east to **Holly Street**. When novelist Wayne Johnston (b.1958) moved to Toronto from his native Newfoundland in August 1989, his first abode was apt. 1606 at **30 Holly Street**. He remained at this address just long enough to finish his first novel, *The Divine Ryans* (1990). They moved at the end of March 1990.

Australian poet Craig Powell (b.1940) came to Canada in 1972 for a decade of advanced studies in psychoanalysis. He now runs a private practice in Sydney. As a poet he is well known in Australian literary circles, and his work appears in most of the major anthologies. One of his books is dedicated to David Brooks, another Australian poet who, by chance, was also living in Toronto at the

time. From 1975-78, Powell and his family occupied apt. 803 at **40 Soudan Avenue**. One book of poems was published while he lived in Toronto: *Rehearsal for Dancers* (1978).

Following a libel action that froze her novelist's pen for some years, Rosemary Aubert (b.1950) lived in three apartments at **45 Dunfield Avenue** between 1990 and 1997: apts. 613, 2512, and 2320. She wrote: "Here I gained a second (now also former) husband. Here I became a writer again by the grace of God. I assisted a police officer to write his autobiography [*Copperjack: My Life on the Force*, 1991] and was stunned and thrilled when the first publisher to see it bought it. It got good press and I felt I might be on the road again as a writer. But I had also returned to university and was working as a criminologist from the late 1980s on. At **45 Dunfield**, and I think just about every place I've ever lived, I wrote poems, including some which were to become *Picking Wild Raspberries* (1995). I also wrote *A Thousand to One*, a little romance novel that had the distinction of having been read only by me prior to having been accepted for publication in New York." Here she also wrote much of her first crime novel, *Free Reign*, praised by reviewers around the world, and a nominee for the Arthur Ellis Award as Best Novel in 1998.

Walter Bauer (1904-76) remains a largely unknown author in Canada, the country he adopted in 1952 after quitting his native Germany, primarily because he continued to write in German and, although much of his work addresses Canadian topics, little of it has been translated. German speakers, however, rate his work highly. When he immigrated, he worked at a variety of low-paying jobs in factories, and as a dishwasher. Then, after enrolling as a student at the UofT he was "discovered" and invited to join the faculty of the German dept. From January 12, 1967, until his death on December 23, 1976, his home was made at apt. 15-A at **95 Redpath Avenue**.

Walk east along Soudan Avenue for six blocks to **Petman Avenue**. By the time Laura Goodman Salverson (1890-1970) moved into **56 Petman Avenue** in 1958 she had lapsed into silence as an author. She remained in this house until she died in her sleep here on July 13, 1970. All of her work is heavily infused with her experience as the daughter of Icelandic immigrants living in Manitoba where she was born. Although her writing is rococo by today's standards, it was highly regarded in her time (for example, she won the Governor General's Award for her 1937 novel *The Dark Weaver*). Her opus is still regarded by scholars as a watershed of prairie realist fiction and of immigrant literature in Canada.

Toronto-born Tedd Steele (b.1922) called **507 Soudan Avenue** his home from 1962 to 1978. As far as I can determine, all of his books were published by a remarkable firm known as Export Books. The firm was founded in 1949 by some daring Canadians who felt there should be a Canadian-owned mass-market paperback company competing with the likes of Penguin and Pocket Books. Those foreign houses controlled all of the paperback titles sold in this country through sheer want of rivals. Due to wartime shortages of paper, there was hunger everywhere for new paperbacks, and so business prospects appeared fine. However, although the owners planned to publish Canadian fiction suitable to the format, next-to-no Canadian hardback publishers issued mysteries or shamelessly commercial fiction which could be sold for reprinting in the more ephemeral binding. Worse, the few Canadian mysteries extant were insufficient to meet the quantity needed by Export. So the company hired an editor whose task was to find authors who would write original fiction appropriate for the house. Thus authors as distinguished as Raymond Souster, Hugh Garner, and Ted Allan made some much-needed money writing novels under colourful pseudonyms.

Tedd Steele published at least four books, two of them under his own name. In its short life of 18 months, Export published an amazing 150 titles, almost all westerns or mysteries. The business was undone by a disastrous fire in December 1950 which entirely destroyed its plant and all of its stock. Historian Paul Stuewe interviewed Tedd Steele for a 1977 article in which Steele recounted the apogee of his career with Export: "One day I got onto the Bloor streetcar and noticed that the motorman was reading one of the books I had written, *Trail of Vengeance*. He was so absorbed in it that he tried to keep reading it between stops, and I thought to myself that this was the highest compliment anyone would ever pay me."

Walk south one block to **Hillsdale Avenue**. Novelist and historian Heather Robertson (b.1942) came to Toronto from the prairies in the mid-seventies, and as she related: "I lived in Toronto at **379 Hillsdale Avenue East** from August 1974 until

October 1982. While at Hillsdale I published *Salt of the Earth* (1974), researched and edited *A Terrible Beauty: The Art of Canada at War* (1977), wrote and published *The Flying Bandit* (1981), and wrote most of [the novel] *Willie: A Romance* (1983). I also wrote a great deal of journalism, including a column for *Maclean's* until 1975."

Further west along **Hillsdale**, poet and Coach House editorial director Victor Coleman (b.1944) made his home at **No.74** from June 1982 to October 1985, during which time he wrote and published *Corrections: Rewriting Six of My First Nine Books* (1985).

Fiction writer Margaret Gibson (b.1948) shared an apartment with the female imper-

Victor Coleman, ignoring the elements on his back porch, 74 Hillsdale Avenue, 1983

sonator Craig Russell from 1968 to 1972 near the start of Hillsdale at **2101 Yonge Street**. Some of her experiences here were background for her famous short story "Making It," which was translated into the notorious feature film *Outrageous* (starring Craig Russell).

A stone's throw to the south is **2005 Yonge Street**, the address since 1987 of Writers & Company, a bookshop which, as the name suggests, is frequented by many authors. The store was originally located across the street at **2094½ Yonge Street** in September 1982, and from its inceptions has specialized in hard-to-find literary fiction from around the world, and in baseball books, two areas reflecting the passionate interests of the original owner, Irene McGuire.

Take nearby Glebe Road East to Tullis Drive. A few paces away is **Carey Road**. Dora Conover (1897-1985) was one of the founding members of the Playwrights Studio Group, a band of mostly women dramatists who tried to cultivate a body of Canadian work sufficiently good and sufficiently large to supply the critical mass needed for a Canadian theatrical explosion. That they did not succeed should not distract us from the nobility of their attempt nor from the nearly impossible circumstances under which they made the attempt. Conover was raised from infancy in China where her parents were missionaries. When she was eight she was sent back to Canada to be raised by relatives. After graduating from the UofT she made journalism her career, working for the *World*, and from 1925—and for 40 years thereafter—she wrote for the *Farmer's Advocate*. Her earliest plays were produced in the late 1920s, and by the mid-thirties she was thought of as one of the leading Canadian playwrights, that being, admittedly, a very small group. The dictates of the Depression and the demands of WWII put an end to the Playwrights Studio activities and the Group folded in 1940. Dora Conover and her husband (he was the Sheriff of York) lived at **24 Carey Road** from 1929-48. By coincidence, the house was later briefly occupied by another specialist in one-act plays, the author W.S. Milne (1902-79) from 1967-68.

On **Tullis Drive** itself, the great Canadian poet E.J. Pratt lived from 1923-32 at **No.25**. He had just settled into the house in

April when he hosted a party to mark the publication of his first poetry book, *Newfoundland Verse*. Before more than half a hundred of Toronto's literati, he collapsed from what seems to have been a mild cardiac arrest, a precursor of the heart disease that would later kill him. After a month in bed he regained his old spirits. It was while living on **Tullis** that his career really began to soar. He entered fully into the literary life of the city and with each book he published his stature rose, not just among writers but among the society at large: *The Witches'Brew* (1925), *Titans* (1926), *The Iron Door* (1927), *The Roosevelt and the Antinoe* (1930), and *Many Moods* (1932). Demand was high for him to give speeches because he was a very good talker and could make audiences laugh. Newspaper coverage of his public remarks, even to small groups, was regular and prominent. On the academic side of his life, he was appointed to the rank of Professor at Victoria College in 1930, the same year that the Royal Society of Canada made him a Fellow.

The profession of elocutionist has disappeared from our culture, but in the Victorian and Edwardian periods there were

E.J. Pratt speaking to students at Jarvis Collegiate, 1953

dozens of women who made their livings by reciting sections of novels, poems, and prose homilies to large and appreciative audiences across the continent. One of the best elocutionists (often called *diseuses*, with the hope that the concocted foreign phrase would elevate their status) was Jessie Alexander (1864-1955). From 1921 until she died in her sleep on March 14, 1955, she lived at **13 Oswald Crescent**. Unfortunately, because public speaking of this kind was woman's work, it is poorly documented and has received paltry attention from academics. So it is not clear how much of a typical program was recited from memory and how much was read from a book or script mounted on a lectern. Nor could I find any evidence to document how much an elocutionist's stage patter between selections was crucial to the success of a performance. That Alexander was successful is beyond doubt. Her appearances were hardly limited to Canada. She appeared frequently throughout the USA and was popular in Great Britain as well, as this excerpt from a review in a June 1894 issue of the Edinburgh *Scotsman* testifies: "The dramatic and musical entertainment at Queen's Hall last evening . . . attracted a large and fashionable assemblage, the Marchioness of Tweeddale . . . being among the audience. Miss Jessie Alexander, the distinguished Canadian elocutionist was the central figure which magnetized the audience, and her appearance was greeted with unmistakable enthusiasm. Her Scotch and Irish selections were beyond criticism, but the number that crowned her success was 'The Royal Bowman' a recitation that few ladies would attempt, and fewer still accomplish with any degree of satisfaction, and where others would have signally failed in such a heavy production, Miss Alexander shone most brilliantly. In gentle pleading or in stern rebuke, in portraying the simplicity of childhood, or reproducing the idiosyncrasies of human life in every phase, in pathos or humour, in dialect or otherwise, Miss Alexander is a perfect mistress of the art of elocution."

In Toronto, Alexander made annual appearances at Massey Hall for a number of years around the turn of the century, regu-

THE DISTINGUISHED READER

Jessie Alexander, promotional brochure (detail), 1895

larly drawing more than 3,000 paying customers. This would be an impressive figure on its own, but it becomes even more so when one learns that she also made several other appearances in Toronto around the same time. In the 1895-96 season, for instance, she gave 20 other performances in Toronto at other venues, and yet was still able to attract thousands to her Massey Hall program.

A *diseuse* was not an actress. She was something between an author giving a reading and an actress performing roles. The nuanced difference is vital. In that epoch, had she been perceived as an actress, thousands of people would not have attended her performances because, well, because everyone knew what actresses were—and what they were was not what polite society associated with. Actresses were guttersnipes who worked in theatres. Elocutionists were ladies who recited in halls. As the *Star Weekly* noted

approvingly in 1914: "The laughter she inspires is wholesome and sweet and pure-hearted, like the little artist herself."

Alexander was born and educated in Toronto but did her graduate work at the National School of Elocution in Philadelphia. From there she went to New York to perform and take yet more lessons from elocution teachers. One of them she married in 1901, but her husband died unexpectedly in 1907 and Jessie, now a mother, had to support her family by reciting full-time. She returned to her native city and it remained her base. Unlike many of her colleagues in the profession, Alexander used a lot of her own writing in her programs, and the reviews indicate that these were often the most popular elements—no small feat given that she was also reciting passages from Shakespeare, Dickens, and the other classic authors. Her writings were published by McClelland and Stewart in 1916.

A couple of blocks to the east is **Penrose Road. No.19** was the Toronto abode of New Brunswick novelist and playwright Kent Thompson (b.1936). In addition to the five novels for which he is best known, he has authored two collections of short stories, two books of poems, and a number of radio plays for the CBC. He came to Toronto for an education: "From the summer of 1980 to the summer of 1981 I lived on **Penrose Road**, off Mount Pleasant Road near the old Crest Theatre. What I did that year was the same as I'm trying to do this year: learn stuff. For example, I tried to cure my musical illiteracy by taking lessons in how to read music at what was then the Skills Exchange. I even took some flute lessons. I did not become a musician, of course, but I learned how to listen to music. Well worth the effort and cash—in fact, it was a real bargain.

"More particularly, I suppose, I participated in a CBC workshop on radio drama that year, and wrote *What Does the Winner Get?* (produced in March 1982), and *A Passion for Young Girls* (produced in December 1982). I also participated in a directors' workshop . . .

at Tarragon Theatre, and as a result of that—together with the experience of seeing *Tamara* at the Toronto Theatre Festival that year—came *Victoria's Return*, a piece of environmental theatre I wrote and directed at the King's Landing Historical Village, New Brunswick in the summer of 1984. Truth to tell: I do like Toronto: the theatres and bookstores, the great places to run (the Island, the Belt Line) and skate, and the movies."

The Crest Theatre, **551 Mount Pleasant Road**, was founded in 1953 by two actors, the brothers Donald and Murray Davis, as a place to feature both foreign art theatre and original Canadian drama in repertory. This is a noble but financially risky proposition at any time, but in the Toronto of the early fifties it was extraordinarily brave if not quixotic. The building they bought had been a cinema since 1927. After substantial renovations, the curtains were pulled back on the first production in January 1954. When the final curtain fell 13 years later, the Davises could boast that well over 100 plays had been presented, including a daring number of world premieres by such Canadian authors as Robertson Davies, Bernard Slade, Ted Allan, and John (Jack) Gray. Despite its many successes and its trailblazing, the Crest was never able to pin its financial ogres to the ground, and mounting debts finally forced it to close.

One of the more important events to take place here was the world premiere of a play by J.B. Priestley (1894-1984). In 1956, during one of his many visits to Toronto to lecture, Priestley had been the dinner guest of Robertson Davies. Invited to join the dinner were the two Crest founders, Murray and Donald Davis, and their sister Barbara Chilcott, also an actor. Priestley later admitted that he was enthralled by the physical similarities of the Davis trio. Excited by the theatrical possibilities offered by their joint appearance on stage, he decided within days of meeting the three actors to write a new play for them, and then further decided to let them have the world premiere in their own theatre. The result was *The Glass Cage*. With much fanfare it opened at the Crest on March 5, 1957. Priestley, who had been in town for several weeks prior to the opening in order to attend rehearsals, did not, as was his custom, answer the calls of "Author! Author!" on opening night. Indeed, some newspaper accounts suggested he was not even in the theatre. Despite his absence, the opening night—and the production—were judged a success and the play did very good business for the Crest over several weeks.

When dramatist and Member of Parliament Wendy Lill (6.1950) lived in Toronto throughout the seventies, she wrote nothing that has since been produced (although her first play was publicly workshopped at Phoenix Theatre.This play, *3 Star*, was the story of a bag lady in Allan Gardens). However, she did work at a number of jobs, all of which have productively fed her work. She was a cocktail waitress as well as a YMCA community counsellor at a birth-control clinic. Since then, she has become one of Canada's most respected authors for the stage and is a winner of the Governor General's Award, a Chalmers Award, a Gemini, and several ACTRA prizes. From 1971-73 she made her home at **14 Tilson Road**, just a couple of blocks east of the Crest Theatre site. A few months later she lived for a brief time around the corner at **162 Manor Road East**.

Near where Manor Road meets Bayview is **1600 Bayview Avenue**, the current home of Canada's best-known shop for mystery buffs, The Sleuth of Baker Street Bookstore. The store was started in 1979 at **1543 Bayview** by Judy Lelkes. After three years the business was purchased by J.D. Singh and Marian Masters, who moved it to **1595 Bayview** in 1989, and to its current location in 1994.

Follow Bayview south to **Millwood Road**. Poet Dennis Lee (b.1939) resided at **440 Millwood** from August 1966 to June 1967 while working as a Lecturer at Victoria College. This was an important address for CanLit in that it was here that Lee finished his first book of adult poetry, *Kingdom of Absence* (1967), here that he began writing one of his most famous poetry volumes, *Civil Elegies* (1968), and here that he began to write his two most famous books for children, *Alligator Pie* (1974) and *Nicholas Knock* (1974).

New Brunswick poet Douglas Lochhead's relatively brief stay on this thoroughfare was sufficient to inspire a book of poems. Lochhead (b.1922) made his home at **249 Millwood** from June 1960 to June 1961 and penned the collection *Millwood Road Poems* (1970) when he was not busy as the founding Librarian of York University. One of his neighbours would have been a young John Robert Colombo (b.1936) who lived down the street from 1960-62 in the lower left unit of the fourplex at **No.195**. At this address Colombo wrote many of the poems which appeared in his first two books: *The Mackenzie Poems* (1966) and *The Great Wall of China* (1966). At the time, he was working as an editor at Ryerson Press during the day, and by night was managing his tiny literary operation, Hawkshead Press. Another significance attached to this spot is that it was here where Margaret Atwood printed (from type set by Colombo) her first book, *Double Persephone*, now one of the most expensive rarities in all of Canadian literature.

Novelist and polemicist Brian Fawcett moved to Toronto from British Columbia in 1990 and first settled at **No.180**. Over the two years he dwelt here he wrote part of *Unusual Circumstances* (1991), *The Compact Garden* (1992), and the first draft of *Gender Wars* (1994).

When Earle Birney returned to Toronto in 1936, a housing shortage (and his poverty) meant that he and his wife had to scramble to find rooms. After living for a few months on Gloucester they found a place at **90 Millwood** which was: "owned by an elderly woman painter. Her name was Montgomery. She has a certain reputation with painting enthusiasts. That was before we had our baby. But because Esther had decided to have a baby, we had to move out of there and

we found a flat near Yonge Street still on **Millwood Road [No.26]**. Another reason we moved in there was because we were now beginning to get some of Esther's Polish refugee cousins. They had hair-raising escapes out of Poland."

Fiction writer André Alexis (b.1957) was a child when his father brought the family from Ottawa to Toronto for a year while he interned at Toronto Western Hospital as a surgeon. During that year they lived at **43 Millwood Road**. Alexis returned to Toronto in January 1987 and the city has been his home since.

Another internationally celebrated young novelist associated with this street is Douglas Coupland (b.1961). Coupland came to Toronto from B.C. in 1988 to pursue his dream of becoming a visual artist. At the time he had yet to do any creative writing. A job as a fact-checker at a magazine provided the airfare, and the salary covered his rent. For the first six months he lived in Cabbagetown, but after the magazine collapsed, he needed cheaper digs. So in March 1989 he moved to **22 Millwood Road**. He took intermittent freelance writing assignments while he continued his development as a sculptor. Until one day, outside the Golden Griddle Restaurant at Yonge and Davisville, he decided he wanted to write fiction rather than sculpt. He therefore dates his beginnings as a writer to his time at **No.22**. Coupland claims that he quite likes Toronto and would probably have stayed here were it not for the coldness of our winters. Among the city's attractions for him are its bicycle paths (he rode his ten-speed all over Toronto), and its tough laws on smoking. It was thanks to those laws that he was finally able to quit.

Broadcaster Daniel Richler (b.1956) lived in a penthouse at **55 Davisville Avenue** from 1989-91, where he wrote his first (and to date only) novel, *Kicking Tomorrow* (1991). Novelist Stephen Vizinczey (b.1933) sublet Earle Birney's apartment on Balliol for the summer of 1980 and then moved to an apartment at **111 Davisville**, where he stayed until March 1982. At this address he finished his epic novel *An Innocent Millionaire* (1983).

When novelist Joan Barfoot (b.1942) was asked about her Toronto experiences, she replied, "I moved to Toronto from Windsor in September 1969. Never having lived in a high-rise before, I tried a bachelor apartment on **Davisville Avenue** (I know it was apt. 404 but I can't for anything remember the street number of the building itself [the street number was **No.225**]). That lasted over the winter until the eggshell-white walls of the apartment closed in like some Poe story, and the swimming pool and sauna lost their charm, along with the gazillions of singles, each of whom apparently was locked into a different (but uniformly loud) radio station during communal activities."

The noted science fiction author Edward Llewellyn (1918-84) lived at **67 Balliol Street** from 1971-83. He and his family had come to the city via Singapore, Montreal, and Nova Scotia. For most of his Toronto period he was, by day, a Professor of Biomedical Engineering at the UofT as well as Assistant Dean of the Faculty of Medicine. Much of his free time he gave to the writing of his novels. The first, *The Douglas Convolution*, written at this address, appeared in 1979, and for each year thereafter he published one novel more; two appeared posthumously. According to his widow, his academic papers "were the taking off point for his fiction. Tommy got tremendous excitement and enjoyment out of writing his science fiction and much of that enjoyment came from the fact that in fiction he was able to communicate his ideas to a more general audience. So many of the notions in his stories were a sort of imaginative extrapolation of the varied subjects of his scientific papers—plus an expression of his keen appetite for adventure."

His daughter Caroline Llewellyn (b.1948) is also a novelist. She lived at **No.67** until 1973 when she departed for the UK. Before becoming a writer, she was a librarian who began to write, as she notes: "when I had the

least time for it, after the birth of my first son, inspired at last by the examples of my father and my grandmother . . . She [F.H. Dorset] supported her family with her short stories and novels which appeared in England and the U.S. in the thirties." Caroline Llewellyn's first novel, *The Masks of Rome* (1988), was published by Collins in Canada, Scribners in the USA, and Simon & Schuster in the UK.

Earle Birney, 1966

Earle Birney moved to apt. 2201 at **200 Balliol Street** in July 1975 following a round-the-world tour he had made with his new wife, Wailan Low. These were some of the happiest years in Birney's life, although his residency here got off to a rocky start when he had a ten-metre fall from a friend's tree he was trying to prune. He hobbled around in a cast and on crutches for months in substantial pain, but once mended, began to write some of his finest poems. Books published while at this address include *Ghost in the Wheels: Selected Poems* (1977), *Fall by Fury* (1978), *Big Bird in the Bush* (essays, 1979), *Spreading Time* (memoirs, 1980), and *Copernican Fix* (1986).

As one of the most popular senior poets in the country, he was invited to give an impressive number of public readings (close to 100 in the dozen years he lived here). He worked with John Cage while both were temporarily working at the University of Western Ontario, and back in Toronto Birney continued his experiments with musicians when he produced three remarkable albums with the internationally distinguished percussion group Nexus. Honorary doctorates were bestowed on him as one of the grand old men of Canadian poetry. In January 1987, Birney and Low left this apartment for a country home in Uxbridge. Two months later, Birney had a heart attack, and began a long period of hospitalization and removal from the world.

Fiction writer Katherine Govier (b.1948) bought the house at **443 Balliol** in the Spring of 1977 but lived in it for less than a year before renting it to Tim Heald, the British novelist who was in town for a working vacation Another major Canadian novelist who has lived on **Balliol** since 1988 is Anne Michaels (b.1958). Almost all of her novel *Fugitive Pieces* (1996) was written while living on this street.

When Howard Engel (b.1931) and Marian Engel (1933-85) lived at **503 Merton Street** from 1968-71, neither had yet to write a book. His sleuth Benny Cooperman would be born at another address in 1980. Marian's first two novels were published while she lived here: *No Clouds of Glory* (1968) and *The Honeyman Festival* (1970).

Take Mount Pleasant Road south through Mount Pleasant Cemetery. This burial ground is the final resting place of several writers, including:

Nathaniel Benson
John Coulter
John Currie
Sarah Anne Curzon
John Mebourne Elson
John Imrie
Laura Elizabeth McCully
Alexander Muir
bp Nichol
James M. Oxley
E.J. Pratt
W.W.E. Ross
James E.Wetherell
Frank Yeigh

Short-story writer and novelist Hugh Hood (b.1928) passed approximately three years of his adolescence (1943-46) at **17 Moore Avenue**. Man of the theatre Mavor Moore's last home in Toronto was appropriately on **Moore Avenue, No.176** to be exact. He lived here from 1980-84, after which he set out for B. C. During this period he was busier acting than writing, appearing in feature films (including the Hollywood picture *The Killing Fields*) and hosting a CBC television program. He was also busy as Professor of Theatre at York University. While living on **Moore**, Moore received the John Drainie Award, given for a lifetime's contribution to broadcasting.

Walk west on Moore to **Cornish Road**. Hugh Hood spent three childhood years at **29 Cornish** from 1937-39. **No.43** was novelist John Reid's house from 1943-62, a period during which he was a regular correspondent with Ezra Pound, Hugh Kenner, and Wyndham Lewis, among others. Reid (1915-82), with high aspirations , had studied with Pound in Italy before WWII, and later in London was on speaking terms with T.S. Eliot and Wyndham Lewis. With war looming, he returned to Canada in 1939 and continued to write, but after a few years seems to have had little intercourse with the main literary and publishing circles. For many of his last years he was a car salesman. His first novel, *Horses with Blindfolds*, was published in 1968, and his second and last novel, *The Faceless Mirror*, appeared in a self-published limited edition in 1974.

110 Heath Street East was the home of Cecil John Eustace (b.1903) from 1931-45. Eustace worked for the Canadian branch of the British firm J.M. Dent for most of his life, first as an editor (when he lived on **Heath**), then as an executive, until finally he was named president in 1963. A deeply committed Catholic, he wrote a number of non-fiction books about aspects of his faith. And he also wrote novels, including the tale *Damaged Lives* (1934) written at this address. Until 1955, Dent operated from a lovely building at **224 Bloor West** known as Aldine House.

In a third floor flat at **100 Heath Street East**, author Terence Green, encountered above, wrote the novel *Children of the Rainbow* (1992) when he found accommodation here from 1985-88.

The towering literary critic Northrop Frye (1912-91) lived for almost four decades at **127 Clifton Road**. His biographer, John Ayre, describes the 1945 purchase which came on the heels of Frye's learning that his *Fearful Symmetry* had just been accepted by Princeton University Press: "The home . . . was Frye's first real material luxury, accomplished only by means of a stiff mortgage . . . The Fryes initially let out the attic bedroom—which would eventually become Frye's permanent workroom."

During the time this was his home, Frye published the books that made him one of the three or four most highly regarded literary critics of his age. His writing won him many national honours, including the Lorne Pierce Medal in 1958 from the Royal Society of Canada, and two decades later the Royal Bank Award.

Long before many of his colleagues at the UofT, Frye took Canadian writing seriously. Throughout the fifties, for example, he read every book of poetry published in Canada and wrote an annual, often harsh critical summary of the verse he encountered for the *UofT Quarterly*. He was not interested in coddling egos, or saluting those who wrapped themselves in maple leaf flags. Rather, he held Canadian poets to the same standards by which the poets he admired in other lands were judged, and he did much to cleanse Canadian verse reviewing of its kid-glove treatment of mediocre wares. In 1971 he published *The Bush Garden*, a collection of his critical thoughts on and evaluations of CanLit.

Frye's authority came from more than just wide reading of Canadian authors, however. As George Woodcock remarked in the *Oxford Companion to Canadian Literature* (1997), "not only was he a pioneer of systematic criticism in Canada, but his writings had a scope that extended far beyond the purviews of a national literature." He followed the international triumph of *Fearful Symmetry: A Study of William Blake* (1947) with *Anatomy of Criticism* (1957), which garnered him even higher standing in the minds of scholars. In subsequent years, he published more than a dozen books, pleased to have lived long enough to see the publication of what he regarded as his magnum opus, *The Great Code: The Bible and Literature* (1982). Somewhat laughably, the only Governor General's Award he won was for what may be his slightest book, *Northrop Frye on Shakespeare* (1986), a collection of his lectures on the Bard to undergraduates.

Take Clifton to St. Clair and then head west for a few paces. Poet Phyllis Webb lived at **170 St. Clair Avenue East** in 1968 and 1969. She had come to Toronto from Montreal in 1965 to be a producer at CBC and left the city from this address for the west coast where she has lived ever since. Phyllis did little writing in Toronto, "being extremely preoccupied with my work at CBC." Part of her radio legacy from that period is a program she created which continues to run: "Ideas."

At **23 Ferndale Avenue** is Deer Park Public School where at least three authors attended classes: Ann Ireland, Sarah Sheard, and Laura Elizabeth McCully. Novelist Franklin Davey McDowell (1888-1965) won the Governor General's Award for his first novel, *Champlain's Road* (1939). After some years as a reporter with Toronto newspapers he joined the Toronto office of the CNR as a public relations executive, and was singularly instrumental in sending dozens, probably hundreds of Canadian authors across the country on free passes, so that they could explore their own land and write about its glories. From 1926 to 1936 his home was **9 Ferndale Avenue**.

Historian Donald Creighton (who published one novel at the end of his life) and his wife, Luella, were lodged at **63 Alvin Avenue** from 1934-40. While here, Creighton wrote and published his first book, *The Commercial Empire of the St. Lawrence 1760-1850*, which immediately marked him as a successor to Harold Innes, and one who could write more felicitous prose than the master.

At the north end of Alvin Avenue, turn west on Glen Elm Avenue to the handsome Yorkminster Baptist Church, **1585 Yonge Street**. In the earlier part of the 20th c. the church invited a number of eminent persons to speak from its pulpit, and at least three creative writers of note were among them: Edgar Guest, Maurice Hindus, and John Cowper Powys.

On **Glen Elm** itself, the great editor of Ryerson Press, Lorne Pierce, ended his days. Pierce (1890-1961) had assumed the editor's chair in 1922 and from the moment he took on the job he dedicated himself to promoting Canadian writers, and to creating a critical mass of publications sufficient to provide a canon which could either be applauded or reviled. He moved into apt. 309 of **49 Glen Elm Avenue** in 1955 and remained here until he died in 1961, only months after he had retired from his job at Ryerson.

The last Toronto residence of fiction writer Timothy Findley (b.1930) was **27 Glen Elm**. He moved into this place early in 1962 with his new companion, William Whitehead. The two are still together, in part because they agreed life would be better living outside Toronto, so they quit this address—and the city—near the end of the year.

LEASIDE

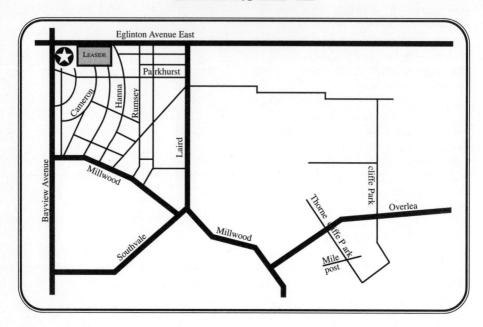

The tour begins at the southeast corner of Eglinton Avenue East and Bayview Avenue.

Walk east on Eglinton Avenue to Hanna Road. At **200 Hanna Road**, near the intersection with Eglinton, is Leaside High School. Two students of the school graduated to become noted writers. One is the poet Richard Outram (b.1930). The other is Margaret Atwood (b.1939), who studied here from 1952-57 (Grades 9-13). Atwood has described the collegiate as "located in the middle of the middle class, in the mid-fifties, which were themselves in the middle of the century. It was a school of medium size, and was in fact so middling that the kids who went to Jarvis (cosmopolitan) and Forest Hill (rich) sneered at it. Leaside was not then the area of trendy boutiques and apparently desirable bijou houses that I'm told it is now. On the contrary. The walk home from it to my house—which was not located in Leaside proper, I would then

hasten to add—led past such things as the Woolworth's where girls who were indiscreet in the back seats of cars had to go to work after they quit school, and IDA drugstores and Aikenhead hardwares, and shops that sold discouraging women's clothing of middle quality."

At this school the only Canadian author encountered by Atwood and her fellow students was Wilson MacDonald, who included Leaside among the schools he visited each year for readings. Despite the absence of role models, it was here that Atwood knew she would become a professional author. She described her epiphany this way: "The day I became a poet was a sunny day of no particular ominousness. I was walking across the football field, not because I was sports-minded or had plans to smoke a cigarette behind the field house—the only other reason for going there—but because this was my normal way home from school. I was scuttling along in my usual furtive way, suspecting no ill, when a large invisible thumb descended from the sky and pressed down on the top of my head. A poem formed. It was quite a gloomy poem; the poems of the young usually are. It was a gift, this poem—a gift from an anonymous donor, and, as such, both exciting and sinister at the same time."

Richard Outram with Irene McGuire, the then owner of Writers & Co., c.1987

Richard Outram lived with his family in the next block east, at **175 Rumsey Road** from 1939-54. Then he went by himself to England. When he decided to come back to Canada, he returned to the family home at **No.175** in the fall of 1956 and stayed here until he was married in April 1957.

At **207 Rumsey Road** was begun one of the most under-heralded short-story collections in Canadian literature. George Elliott (1923-96) "started writing *The Kissing Man* in a loathsome basement apartment— $200 a month—at **207 Rumsey Road** in what was known as Leaside in 1948. The landlord with a heart of gold . . . would often tippy-toe through the 'apartment' to fiddle with the furnace."

Fiction writer Terence M. Green (b.1947) had rooms at **9 Parkhurst Boulevard** from July 1978 to July 1982, at which point he

moved down the street to **159 Parkhurst**, which was his home until October 1985. At the latter address he wrote his first novel, *Barking Dogs* (1988), and in both homes on Parkhurst he penned the short stories which appeared in his first book, the collection *The Woman Who Is the Midnight Wind* (1987). Green has since become one of the better-known authors of literary SF in Canada, and has an impressive international following.

Shortly after arriving at **66 Parkhurst**, William Arthur Deacon, the literary critic of the *G&M*, had the satisfaction of seeing the first presentation of the Governor General's Awards. The ceremony was a grand occasion at Convocation Hall, UofT, in November 1937, and Deacon more than anyone had the right to beam for, more than anyone, he was the driving force behind the creation of the national literary prizes. While living in Leaside he also put his legal training to use, helping to put the Canadian Authors' Association (then the only national organization for writers in the country) onto solid footing financially and administratively. Through his intervention, the major writers' organizations finally found proper headquarters; thus, the C.A.A., the Writers' Club, the PEN Club and the Women's Press Club shared accommodation and expenses at 99 Yonge Street as of 1939. Over the 1951-52 academic year he taught at Ryerson Institute of Technology the earliest course on Canadian Literature in Toronto. Following the death of Stephen Leacock in 1944, Deacon was instrumental in establishing the Leacock Medal to honour the humorist's memory. Almost alone, he lobbied against the creation of the Canada

Council if it meant (as it did in the beginning) that most of the grant money would be given to academics rather than artists. And while engaged in all of this meritorious labour on behalf of authors, he somehow found the time to write reviews for the *G&M* book page, as well as solicit ads from publishers to supplement those same pages. No.66 was his home until 1954.

The novelist Constance Beresford-Howe (b.1922) described her move from Montreal: "I have lived in Toronto since August 1970 when, like many other Quebeckers dismayed by the political tension in Montreal, we uprooted ourselves from the province. As a born and bred Montrealer, I found the decision hard to make, but it was expedited in the end by a number of unpleasant incidents. One evening I came home to find our apartment cordoned off by police because a bomb had been planted in a corner mailbox. It was a new and rather grim experience, too, to have my briefcase searched by a security guard whenever I went into McGill's Arts Building . . . So we packed up our goods, our three-year-old son, and the family cat and came to Toronto.

"On arrival, we bought a house in Leaside, at **16 Cameron Crescent** . . . It was here in a study my husband converted for me from an upstairs sun-room that I wrote *The Book of Eve*, published in 1973. Two of my subsequent books were also written here: *Night Studies* (1985) and *Prospero's Daughter* (1988).

"I did not visit Toronto until the mid-fifties. At that point I was mildly appalled by the Sunday-school atmosphere and general lack of piquancy in every field, from the cultural to the gastronomic. Since then, of course, things have changed for the better in every way, and I've grown greatly to like and admire what has so quickly grown into a great cosmopolitan city." Beresford-Howe moved to Britain in the mid-nineties.

Take Rumsey Road south to **Millwood Road**. The lower right-hand unit (while facing the building) at **No.727** was the home of novelist Barbara Gowdy (b.1950) from September 1982 to August 1983. During this period she was yet to write her first fiction. Rather, she was working as an editor for Harlequin Books. Appropriately, while blue-pencilling tales of exotic romance for the publishing house, Gowdy met another editor hired to supervise Harlequin's audacious Mack Bolan, Super-Executioner fiction series (aimed at macho male wannabes)—and married him.

Novelist and academic Peter Such (b.1939) came to Canada from the UK in 1953. After obtaining his B.A. in 1960 from the UofT he went on to pursue a master's degree, after which he began a brief peripatetic year teaching hither and yon until he began teaching full-time at York University, his employer up to the present. In 1971 he became the founding editor of *Impulse* which was, for a decade or so, one of the more invigorating of the literary magazines which burst into national bloom in the immediate post-Centennial years. Such published three novels in the 1970s but since then he has not published any novels. From 1962-64 he inhabited **841 Millwood Road**.

Thorncliffe Park is a hefty walk from the streets of Leaside but there is no easier way to get there from any other part of town. Take Millwood Road to Overlea Boulevard to **Thorncliffe Park Drive. No.16**, Chapel-in-the-Park, was one of the churches in Toronto where novelist Thomas York (1940-88) was pastor. He was the chaplain here from 1976-77. York came to Canada as a Vietnam War draft resister and almost immediately enrolled at the UofT, from which he obtained his Bachelor of Divinity degree in 1967. As a minister of the United Church, he followed clerical assignments which took him to B.C., the Northwest Territories, and New Brunswick—all areas in which he set his fictions. Usually considered his finest writing is *Trapper* (1981), a fictionalized account of the true story of the murdering trapper of Rat River. While serving at this chapel, Thomas York lived in apt. 516 at **71 Thorncliffe Park Drive**.

Ethel Granger Bennett (1891-1988) died in the same year as Tom York and lived on the same street at the same time, although I have no evidence that they knew each other. Bennett lived in apt. 504 at **No.27** from 1961 until c. 1980 when she entered a seniors' home and lived to be 96. A scholarship student at the UofT, her speciality was French, a subject she was able to marry to her love of history to produce novels about New France and Quebec. She was predeceased by her husband, who had been for many years the president of Victoria College. Granger Bennett lived with him on campus during this period and taught French to the undergrads.

Poet and fiction writer Kristjana Gunnars (b.1948) was an immigrant from Iceland in 1969. Since then she has published several volumes of lyrics and a number of story collections. She was nominated for the Governor General's Award in 1991. She came to Toronto in 1972 because her husband at the time had been accepted into a doctoral program at the UofT. "We drove from the west in our old VW station wagon with a reservation for the UofT married student housing. Our apt. was No.1202 at 35 Charles Street West. Right downtown. But when I saw the apartment I felt it was just a matchbox and we couldn't move in it. And I couldn't take the kid out to play on the corner of Yonge and Charles. So after a brief life on Charles Street we moved to **[52] Thorncliffe Park Drive**, a suburban complex of apartment buildings which are quite unpalatable and depressing in nature . . . We were on the third floor. That is all I remember, except that we had much more room and absolutely no furniture to fill it with.

"We were there for the academic year. We arrived in August 1972 and I left in the Spring of 1973. That was the year the volcanic island of Heimaey erupted in Iceland. I was waiting on tables for a living and customers regularly asked me where I was from. When I told them Iceland, which was much in the news then, they always left very large tips. I cashed in on the eruption to such an extent that I took a plane to Iceland and volunteered as a crisis helper during the evacuations of the homes in Heimaey. . . .[In Toronto] I did not write. I had a one-year-old child whom I looked after all day and I worked at the Boulangerie Restaurant of the Inn On The Park all night. I conceived of a great desire to write about the Four Seasons establishment as a microcosm of the world. But I did not start writing until five years later."

The distinguished French-Canadian author Cécile Cloutier (b.1930) lived at **2 Milepost Place** for a couple of years while teaching in the French dept. at the UofT. Her exact dates at this home were September 1965 to September 1967, during which she wrote her book *Canelles et Craies* (1969).

LAWRENCE PARK

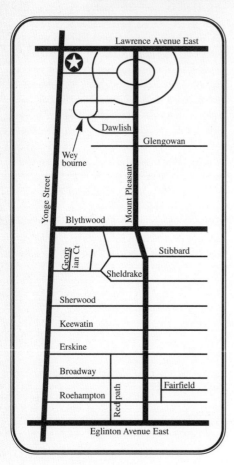

The tour begins at the southeast corner of Yonge Street and Lawrence Avenue East.

Walk east along Lawrence Avenue, then south on Weybourne Crescent to **Dawlish**. Ethel Granger Bennett (1891-1988) lived to be 96 years old but published only three novels within a short period. She and her impoverished family came to Canada from England when she was quite young. A brilliant high-school student, she won sufficient scholarships to allow her to attend and graduate in French from the UofT in 1911. A keen interest in Canadian

history coupled with her fluency led to her writing her first historical novel while living at **151 Dawlish Avenue** from 1934-55. *Land for Their Inheritance* (1955) is the story of Champlain and the early attempts to found settled outposts in the New World against the objections of the fur traders. Her third novel, *Short of the Glory* (1960), won the Ryerson Fiction Award in the year of publication, but after that book, silence.

Barker Fairley (1887-1986) was another long-lived author connected to this street. He and his wife, Margaret (1885-1968), resided at **No.197** from 1926 until they quit Toronto for a teaching post in England in mid-1932. Both were born in Britain and both had emigrated from England c. 1910. They married in 1914, drawn together by a deep commitment to politics of the left. By day Barker taught German at the UofT and became renowned in Canada and in German-speaking countries for his Goethe criticism and translations. But when free of university duties he wrote poetry, painted, and was an astute art critic for *Canadian Forum* with which he was involved for many years after its founding. The Fairleys returned to Toronto in 1936. Barker became head of the German dept. and Margaret became actively involved with Marxist arts activity, producing *New Frontiers*, a magazine which tried to meld social protest and anti-fascist ideology with fine writing. In later life, Barker turned to portrait painting, and an astonishing number of authors are included in his *oeuvre*.

The author of *Beautiful Joe*, Marshall Saunders (1861-1947), spent her last years at **62 Glengowan Road**, just south of Dawlish. Saunders was a Nova Scotian who published an apprentice novel in 1889 before writing the book for which she is still remembered a century later. *Beautiful Joe* (1893) is a fictional re-creation of the life of a real dog who belonged to friends of the Saunders family. A previous owner of the animal had mutilated the pet. Saunders chose to tell the story, in typical Canadian fashion, from the point of view of the dog. Incredibly, she had trouble finding a publisher, but eventually it was published and almost immediately became a bestseller. It is book-trade lore that Saunders's novel was the first by a Canadian to sell over one million copies. By 1929, she claimed, without contradiction by others, that the book had sold over seven million copies. One of the obvious reasons for the book's success was the author's ability to make an unspoken link between the inferior position of animals and a child's awareness that he or she, too, has no power, has only to obey.

At the end of the 19th c. Saunders moved to New England for a couple of years, then to California for a couple more and set fictional works in these varied parts of the world. But the works written after she settled in Toronto in 1914, have lost favour with readers in our time, and only *Beautiful Joe* remains in print. Despite that, Saunders was hailed as a major literary citizen by Torontonians. In 1931, several organizations banded together to honour her on her 70th birthday with what the *Telegram* described as "the biggest birthday party ever held

in the city." All of the newspapers reported that nearly 500 people attended the banquet at the Royal York Hotel, including the principal Toronto literati. For reasons yet to be uncovered, Saunders published no books after she moved to **Glengowan Road** c. 1929.

Walk south on Mount Pleasant to **Blythwood Road**. Reading the newspapers of June 4, 1928, one catches only a glimmering of the extraordinary shock that hundreds experienced when they learned that 46-year-old Fred Jacob had died of a heart attack the night before at his home, **139 Blythwood**. He was the drama, music,

Hans Andersen wrote fairy tales, Marshall Saunders has lived them. For seventy years she has been making friends of birds, beasts and people. In all of them she has found the magic which makes people in fairy tales so delightful. We see her here in her garden spoon-feeding a little lost baby robin. Fiji, the Boston terrier, looks on approvingly; he knows there is love enough for both of them. Tuesday afternoon, with the Canadian Women's Press Club as sponsors, Miss Saunders will tell the story of her life. Her sister, Miss Grace Saunders, will show pictures snapped when the author of "Beautiful Joe" was not posing. The address will be in the Eaton Auditorium at 3 o'clock, and following it those who attend—and it is open to the public at a nominal fee—will have the privilege of meeting Miss Saunders in the tea room.

Marshall Saunders

M&E, November 28, 1932

and literary critic of the *M&E*, but unlike many reviewers, he was immensely popular with those who worked in the arts. Hugh Eayrs, Pelham Edgar, Arthur Lismer, E.J. Pratt, Hector Charlesworth, and Augustus Bridle were just a sampling of prominent persons in the book trade at the funeral. One of the reasons for his acceptance among arts colleagues was that he was also a creator. His plays were highly regarded and showed greater promise than any other dramatist of the time in Canada, with the exception of Merrill Denison. He published poetry and was the author of two novels, the latter completed just before he died.

Mavor Moore (b.1919), playwright, actor, and arts administrator bought his first house at **168 Blythwood** in 1948 and it remained his home until 1966. It was at this address that he wrote, "hundreds of radio and television shows." More enduring works composed here were the early *Spring Thaws*, as well as his most popular play, *The Ottawa Man* (1958), and the libretto for one of the finest Canadian operas to date, *Louis Riel* (1967), with music by Harry Somers. For the last three years of the fifties, Moore was the drama critic of the *Telegram*.

When the poet Don Coles (b.1928) moved to Toronto in September 1965, his first address was **No.182**. He reports that he wrote nothing publishable here, and in May 1966 moved to Roselawn Avenue. When novelist Mort Forer (1922-81) came to Toronto in 1967, he too chose to live on **Blythwood**, at **No.359**, and it was while living here that M&S published his only novel, *The Humback*, in 1969. As with Fred Jacob, so too with Mort Forer when he died suddenly of a heart attack: hundreds with whom he worked in the arts were stunned by his death. By way of commemoration, a group of writers within ACTRA solicited support from his many admirers and convinced the Toronto Parks Dept. to plant an oak tree in Clarence Square where he loved to walk. The tree was supposed to be the first of many in what was going to become a writer's

grove. However, no other trees have been planted since this worthy idea was conceived.

The next block to the south is **Stibbard Avenue**. Radio and television playwright Fletcher Markle (1921-91) housed himself at **86 Stibbard** between 1968 and 1972, possibly longer, although by 1976 he had left Toronto permanently. During this period he worked for CBC-TV, writing and producing arts-interview programs as well as adaptations of novels such as Brian Moore's *The Feast of Lupercal*. He was aggressive in promoting Canadian writers and drama, and his vigour in this regard is in stark relief with the poverty of Canadian stories appearing on so-called Canadian television networks today. For the academic year 1974-75 he was writer-in-residence at the UofT.

The final years of Nathaniel Benson (1903-66) were spent at **210 Stibbard**. When he died, he was an English teacher at R.H. King Collegiate. Benson was a highly regarded poet in his day and the six volumes he published before death were all warmly welcomed by the reviewers. History plays for radio were also part of his bibliography, as were dramas written (and published) for the theatre. Never an aloof author, he acted as president of the Canadian Literature Club in the thirties and forties, and took on the thankless task of editing the *Canadian Poetry Magazine* (a job also held by E.J. Pratt and Earle Birney) for a number of years at the same time. Earlier in his life, Benson had abandoned teaching to be an ad copywriter in New York, but by 1950 he was back in Toronto where he resumed teaching. While in Manhattan he reviewed stage events for *Saturday Night*.

Yet another author in this area who worked extensively in radio was Harry Boyle (b.1915). His career at the CBC began in 1942, and from the beginning his employment contract allowed him time to write essays and fiction. Three collections of the essays were published, but as a writer he is better known for his novels, including *The*

Great Canadian Novel (1972) and *Memories of a Catholic Boyhood* (1973). Unfortunately, since he moved to **12 Georgian Court** (near the intersection of Yonge and Sheldrake) in 1977 he has published no creative writing.

Frank Tate (1902-86?) was a high-school math teacher at Danforth Tech who had majored in Semitics at the UofT. Quite why a degree in ancient languages allowed him to teach arithmetic is one of the research mysteries yet to obsess scholars. In some reference books, Tate's one novel, *Red Wilderness* (1938), is referred to simply as an adventure novel. This does not *quite* do justice to the book's singular nature. Before describing it, the reader should know the book was hailed by more than one reviewer as the best novel of the year. Playwright W.S. Milne, for example, went even further, when he wrote in *Saturday Night*, "It really does seem that the very profitable mantle of the late Ralph Connor has descended upon Mr. Tate . . . Of its merits as an interesting yarn, with excellent characterization, humour, and suspense, I am convinced." The plot centres on a young doctor who is sent to a northern logging camp by a lumber company just prior to the closing of the roads and rivers due to winter. The reader learns the medical man has also been sent as a company spy to report on a communist conspiracy alleged to be operating in the region. Sure enough, for reasons that are never given the credit of logic, the forestry workers, puppets in the hands of their commie manipulators, decide to block all shipment of trees in order to bankrupt the company. The loggers are also striking for higher wages, an obvious sign, according to the author, of their moral weakness and ingratitude. The happy ending sees the strike broken, and the company flourishing. What is curious about this book is not its blatant politics—good books have been written by authors who are passionate believers at either end of the political spectrum—but that such a poorly written book should receive such supportive reviews. That

such a virulently anti-communist book was published before WWII, rather than after, is also of historical interest. Frank Tate lived at **275 Sheldrake Boulevard** from 1932 until 1986.

The creator of the popular Flashman novels, George MacDonald Fraser (b.1925), was newly married when he came to Canada in the autumn of 1949, looking to broaden his horizons. He did so literally when he went to work at the *Regina Leader Post* later in the year, but when he first arrived in this country he lived for two months (September 1 to October 31, 1949) at **175 Sherwood Avenue** while scouting journalism opportunities here. He found the job prospects in Toronto dim for an immigrant reporter so he moved to the prairies where he had better luck. Eventually, he returned to his native Britain where, in 1969, he published *Flashman*, the first in a series of droll picaresque military novels about the bully from *Tom Brown's Schooldays*.

Another novelist who writes about reds is Tony Aspler, oenophile. Aspler (b.1939) is Canada's best-known writer on wine and a noted writer of mysteries, many with a wine theme. He purchased **202 Keewatin Avenue** in October 1977 and not long after published his first novel, *Chain Reaction* (1978; co-authored with Gordon Pape). Other books originiated here include *Tony Aspler's International Guide to Wine* and the novel *Blood Is Thicker Than Beaujolais* (the first in a series featuring his sleuth Ezra Brant). He remained at this address until April 1992.

J. Robert Janes (b.1935), better-known and better-reviewed abroad than he is in Canada, revealed just how important his childhood residence at **320 Keewatin Avenue** from 1935-58 has been to his fiction: "Our backyard gave out onto the top of Sherwood Park which, very early on, became both haven and refuge for me. As a kid I loved that park and had so many, many adventures there. But when sad, when in tears and fighting the world, I ran there too, and it sort of soaked me up. We were one.

"I grew up in the last half of the Depression and through the Second World War (of which I seem to write constantly now) and those two huge sociological disasters permeated the life of our street and every household on it. We weren't well off, but there were others far poorer than us and they 'lived down the hill' in tenements, rented houses, and some they owned themselves. But though less than half a block away I went there in fear of my life. At the tender age of five or six I saw my first knife fight and it was a very grim, life-threatening struggle . . . I saw and heard my first Colt .45 semiautomatic being fired into the air on May 24th (fire-cracker night) and my first .38 Smith & Wesson revolver. Again, in Sherwood Park, right behind our house.

"Although it was years after I had left the city before I began to write full-time, *Theft of Gold* (1980) uses the Royal Ontario Museum and a robbery I experienced while an undergraduate. I always knew who had done it, and in *Theft* I had the opportunity to use the information. *Danger on the River* (1982) used the Don River Valley I knew as a boy and the back of Sherwood Park as much as it did the Twelve Mile Creek in St. Catharines . . . *Gypsy* (1997) has, among its characters, the prospector I met as a boy of about ten while down in Sherwood Park at 5:00 a.m. I often went there very early in the morning. A dog had broken through the ice on the pond which was next to the graveyard's dump, and after discussing the problem with the prospector, it was agreed that I should rescue it. I then received an invitation to visit him and his son (a student of mining engineering). Fifty years later I used that most kind-hearted of men [in a novel]. *The Third Story* (1983) used one of the old Eaton estates which was at the back of Sherwood Park (on land E.P. Taylor later bought). For a while I delivered the *G&M* to them, but they never paid me, and still owe me for six months!"

In November 1966 Hugh Garner moved to apt. 1006 at **33 Erskine Avenue**, where he would spend his last years despite complaints from the neighbours to the landlord about his drunken escapades. He was sober in stretches and still able to show signs of the street-hustling kid he had once been, as his biographer outlines: "The frustrations with publishers . . . came to a head when he learned that almost a thousand copies of his short-story collection *Men and Women* were languishing in Ryerson's warehouse. He kept bugging the company to do something with the books and finally offered to buy the whole lot if they were priced as remainders. As a result, the basement storage cubicle allotted to the Garners at **33 Erskine Avenue** was soon crammed with 970 copies of *Men and Women* and Hugh made his entry into the wholesale end of the book business.

"For a more ivory-tower sort of author, this impulsive purchase could have been a disaster; but for someone who had sold men's clothing, groceries and soap-flakes—the last door-to-door to Depression era housewives —selling books was a piece of cake. Carting the books around town in the trunk of his car, he made major sales to the Toronto library system, the Readers' Club of Canada, and a local high school, and during his summer stint at the Ryerson Polytechnical Institute's creative-writing workshop he sold his students autographed copies for one dollar each. The approximately 200 copies left over went to the Coles bookstore chain for slightly more than what he had paid for them, and by the time he was finished, he had made a substantial profit, enjoyed himself immensely, and reinforced his conviction that he knew more about selling books than did any of his publishers."

Around this same time, he was given the Toronto Civic Award of Merit for his writing which, if anything, picked up in pace while he lived at this address. Among the books he penned here were: *A Nice Place to Visit* (1970); *The Sin Sniper* (1970), which sold over 50,000 copies in paperback; *Violation of the Virgins* (1971); *Death in Don Mills* (1975); and his autobiography, *One Damn Thing After Another* (1973).

Sad to relate, these and the other books he wrote at this address have none of the élan of his earlier work. They were written quickly, with a quick buck as their primary motive, and had to be composed in between ever-increasing battles with the bottle.

J. Robert Janes attended John Fisher Public School at **40 Erskine**. Novelist Marika Robert (*A Stranger and Afraid*, 1964) moved immediately after the extensive publicity surrounding the launch of her first novel to **No.55** and lived here until 1969. Despite the book's selling well in Canada, she published no other books. The same building housed the pulp novelist and cartoonist Tedd Steele (b.1922) throughout the eighties.

SF specialist Terence M. Green (b.1947) passed his adolescence in the fifties at **14 Broadway Avenue**. Irish-born Father James Dollard (1872-1946) was the parish priest of St. Monica's at **44 Broadway** from c. 1912 to 1921. Dollard published a short-story collection *The Gaels of Moondharig* (1907), but was internationally renowned for his poetry: *Irish Mist and Sunshine* (1901), *Poems* (1910), and *Irish Lyrics and Ballads* (1917). He wrote poetry that is far too saccharine for modern taste but there is no denying his extensive popularity in his own day. Joyce Kilmer wrote of his last volume, "Here is some genuine Celtic magic—a beautiful blend of melody and fancy. It should be set to music—the words almost carry a tune with them—and sung by John McCormack."

Hugh Garner tried to settle into a flat at **66 Broadway** in 1964 but the other tenants quickly came to despise the author because of his obnoxious public inebriation. Eventually they signed a petition demanding Garner's eviction and presented it to the landlord. The landlord, who respected Garner's literary talent, complied with the demand in 1966 by moving Garner and his wife to an apartment building he owned at 33 Erskine.

Another resident of this building has been the novelist and publisher Anna Porter (b.1947?). She has published non-fiction, but has captured international success with her sophisticated murder mysteries, all written at her home in Moore Park, not here. She first came to Toronto in 1968, having been transferred to Collier Macmillan Canada by the London head office. After some dreadful weeks in a hotel, she found a "truly dingy little apartment which I shared with two other people" at **No.66** and it remained her home during the start of her employment at McClelland and Stewart and until her marriage to the prominent lawyer Julian Porter in 1972. Anna said, "When I first arrived, my general impression of the city was that it was heartless and mean, but then I arrived late in the year, was broke and had nowhere to live. Later I discovered that many of the residents had some generosity and kindness . . . Having tried numerous capitals and non-capital cities around the world prior to coming to Toronto (Auckland, Wellington, Christchurch, Sydney, Lima, Mexico City, Rome, London, Stockholm, Budapest, and Vienna) I continue to find this to be the most liveable city in the world. This, notwithstanding that there is a general meanness of spirit when Canadians seek to celebrate their own. I mean they don't."

Poet Nathaniel Benson, met above, resided at **No.71** throughout the 1950s, a decade during which he returned to teaching high-school English. Books written by him at this time include a biography, and his final book of poems, *One Man's Pilgrimage* (1962). He was the editor of Volumes I and II of *Canadian Tales of Action and Humour* (1955-57) and a frequent contributor of articles to *Forbes* business magazine. The same building was home (1946-50) to the one-act play specialist W.S. Milne (1902-79).

When Laura Goodman Salverson (1890-1970), twice winner of the Governor General's Award for Fiction moved to Toronto in 1950, she and her husband chose to live in apt. 2 at **82 Broadway**. By this time, her health was in decline and her writing curtailed. Nonetheless, she wrote a number of short stories for the *Star Weekly*, and finished here her last novel, *Immortal Rock* (1954). She had the further satisfaction of seeing it win a major literary prize of that time, the Ryerson Fiction Award.

North Toronto Collegiate, **70 Roehampton Avenue**, can boast novelist J. Robert Janes and poet George Johnston among its graduates. Wilson MacDonald, reciting his poems, was a frequent annual visitor, and likely the only Canadian author encountered by generations of students here and elsewhere.

When Edmonton writer Myrna Kostash (b.1935) came to Toronto to do graduate studies at the UofT starting in 1969, part of her Toronto stay was spent at **125 Roehampton** (September 1971-June 1972). She did a little writing at another Toronto address; otherwise, all of her books were written in Alberta.

Novelist and Arctic expert James Houston (b.1921) attended Northern Vocational School (as it was known) at **813 Mount Pleasant Road**. Many years later, Houston would have mixed feelings about his time at this school. On the one hand, he is immensely grateful that his talent for writing and for visual art were indulged by the teachers—an indulgence that led to his studying under Arthur Lismer at the Ontario College of Art immediately after leaving Northern. On the other hand, as he told a journalist for *The New Yorker*, he felt his education was so unbalanced he actually considers himself uneducated.

While he did write plays produced in Toronto, Des McAnuff (b.1952) is much more celebrated for his feats on Broadway and in Hollywood. For example, he directed the film *Cousin Bette* (based on a novel by Balzac), starring Jessica Lange and Bob Hoskins. In Manhattan he directed the two-and-a-half year run of *The Who's Tommy*, for which he won the 1993 Tony Award as Best Director. That Tony joined the one he won in 1985 for his direction of the musical *Big*

River. He was also nominated in 1995 for directing *How to Succeed in Business Without Really Trying*. McAnuff spent almost all of his childhood (1954-73) at **8 Fairfield Road**, which runs between Roehampton and Broadway east of Rawlinson.

By coincidence, another Canadian who has had success on Broadway and in Hollywood—and who lived nearby—is playwright Bernard Slade (b.1930). In 1958 and in 1959 Slade lived at **197 Redpath Avenue**, a period which saw him writing variety scripts for the CBC, and writing his first drama, *The Prizewinner*, broadcast on the CBC. Slade was nominated for a Tony in 1975 for his play *Same Time Next Year*. In Hollywood in the late 1960s he created some legendary sitcoms, of which *The Flying Nun* remains the best known.

SUNNYBROOK

York University (Glendon College)

Lawrence Avenue East

Bayview Avenue

Donlea

Laird

Eglinton Avenue East

The tour begins at the northeast corner of Eglinton Avenue East and Bayview Avenue.

Walk east on Eglinton to **Donlea Drive**. Eli Mandel (1922-92) is one of the most important prairie poets to have made the trek to Toronto. His importance stems not just from his own creative writing, but from his labour as an anthologist and as an accessible critic of his poetic contemporaries. Mandel was born and raised in Estevan, Saskatchewan, and his geographical roots and ethnic background were prominent but hardly exclusive themes in his work. Following action in WWII, he returned to Saskatchewan for his bachelor's and master's degrees, then came to Toronto in 1950 to pursue his doctorate. At the time he was married to Miriam Mandel (1930-82) who, although she published nothing while in Toronto, later won the Governor General's Award for Poetry for her volume *Lions at Her Face* (1973). The Mandels remained in Toronto from 1950 until the end of the school year in 1953, at which point both returned to the prairies. Their residence for most of 1950-53 was **16 Donlea Drive**. Eli was clearly taken with what he saw in Toronto. He returned a decade later to teach at York University, and the city remained his home thereafter.

Marika Robert (born c.1930) began the writing of her sensational success (but to date only novel) *A Stranger and Afraid* (1964) when she lived in apt. 109 at **970 Eglinton Avenue East**.

Glendon College, **2275 Bayview Avenue**, is now one of several colleges within the federation of York University, but in 1960, when York was founded, Glendon was the original and only campus of the institution. When the large campus at Keele and Steeles was opened in 1964, the decision was made to take advantage of Glendon's isolation and satellite status by making it a bilingual and bicultural liberal arts undergraduate centre. The aim was to produce Canadians who were not only fluent in the other official language but comfortable in the culture of the other solitude. Generous scholarships were offered to high-school graduates in Quebec in order to beef up the francophone side of the equation, and until separatist sympathies won over most of the French-speaking students, the Glendon experiment was a noble effort to put into practice a Canadian ideal. A few of the Glendon students have become published creative writers. Among them are J.D. Carpenter, M.T. Kelly, Greg Gatenby, Larry Krotz, and Lawrence Scanlon. Authors who taught at Glendon include Eli Mandel and Michael Ondaatje. In the late seventies, Glendon was also the base of the Scottish writer participating in the annual Canada-Scotland Writers' Exchange. Caledonian authors who had offices here for one year each were Liz Lochhead and Cliff Hanley.

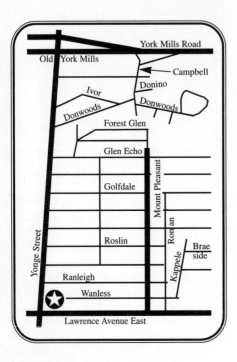

The tour begins at the northeast corner of Lawrence Avenue East and Yonge Street.

Walk north on Yonge Street to **Wanless Avenue**. The author of the novel *The Survivor of the Edmund Fitzgerald* (1985), Joan Skelton (b.1929), passed her youth and young womanhood at **No.245** from 1947-54.

Intersecting with Wanless is **Ronan Avenue**. **No.11** was Rica Farquharson's home from 1931-35, a period during which she was active in the Playwrights Studio Group. The Group consisted mostly of women journalists who really wanted to write plays for a living but, in the absence of even a single theatre in Toronto committed to Canadian production, could not fulfil their dreams. Rather than mope and curse the darkness, however, these women raised money and pooled resources, allowing them to mount their plays using professional staff, albeit in most cases for only a single night.

Farquharson was married to Robert A. Farquharson, editor of the *G&M*, and one of the leading cultural nationalists during the Depression years. Mr. Farquharson argued that to foster its own independence, including economic independence, Canada had to aggressively promote its own artists, its own culture, a lesson, alas, too many people in power still have not learned. His editorial stance, like the funding of the Playwrights Studio Group, was undone by the exigencies of WWII.

The first street east of Ronan running north from Wanless is **Kappele Avenue**. Take Kappele to get to **Braeside Road**, noting on your way **50 Kappele**, where novelist John Reid (1915-82) (*Horses with Blindfolds*) lived from 1962-63. Carol Coates (b.1906) was born and raised in Tokyo, the child of a Methodist missionary. She lived most of her life in Japan until the eve of WWII, at which point she came to Toronto and lived here for the duration. Following the war, she moved to New York for a couple of years and then settled in England. While in Toronto she published her first and second books, *Fancy Free* (1939) and *Poems* (1942), two volumes that clearly show the influence of Japanese literary forms and imagery. In 1940 and 1941 she occupied **50 Braeside Road**.

Regain Ronan Avenue and walk north one block to **Ranleigh Avenue**. **No.139** was novelist Barbara Gowdy's home from March to September 1982. At this period of her life Gowdy (b.1950) was an editor at Harlequin Books and had not yet started to write the novels (*Falling Angels*, 1989; *Mr. Sandman*, 1995; *The White Bone*, 1998) which have won her so much critical distinction (and bestseller status) in Canada, Europe, and the USA.

Bedford Park Public School, **81 Ranleigh**, can boast at least two noted creative writers among its alumni: Richard Outram and Caroline Llewellyn. Outram (b.1930), a highly regarded poet, lived just down the street at **No.42**, between 1934 and 1939.

Perhaps no other gesture epitomizes the self-destructive streak in the Briton Archie Belaney, better known as Grey Owl, than his four-month-long lecture tour of England when he went out of his way to speak in the places where he was most likely to be recognized as an imposter by friends from his youth. The stress of awaiting discovery was immense, only partially alleviated by the alcoholic drinking binges in which he indulged. Those in England who may have recognizied him chose not to publicly, perhaps because they valued his proto-environmentalist message and homilies more than the damage that would ensue if his fraud were exposed.

Because Grey Owl was a gigantic hit in Britain, he was, of course, treated as an even greater hero in Canada. On his way back to his place in the northern woods, he stopped over in Toronto for a few days to meet with old friends and with the press. During his stay, he was the guest of a confidant at **260 Roslin Avenue**.

What was intended to be a quiet period of repose became anything but as the clergy erupted in rage at remarks he made to a local interviewer suggesting that Christianity had nothing to teach aboriginals. His old friend William Deacon, then with the *M&E*, gave Grey Owl a chance to rebut the squeals from the clerics. Deacon's report began, "Grey Owl . . . last night replied that 'civilization' contained so much that was repulsive, and with which the Christian church seemed incapable of coping, that 'uncivilized' Indians had difficulty in understanding the 'superiority complex' which coloured most efforts to induce them to switch to Christianity. 'In the many attempts that have been made to

Christianize me,' Grey Owl said last night, 'the chief platform has been that my religion was all wrong. The Indian has been asked to throw aside his art, his language, and some beautiful conceptions, to make room for a religion that has not yet proved its case to many untutored minds. Since I entered civilization, I have been astounded and repulsed by the perversions, the insincerities, and evidences of self-interest as justification for almost any act."

What makes this tempest of literary historical interest is that half a year later, thanks to Deacon's intervention, Grey Owl appeared as a key speaker at the big Toronto Book Fair, and was welcomed by more than 2,000 people giving him a standing ovation. In other words, his tirade against the reigning religious dogma did not drastically hurt his public image or his book sales in Toronto. Rather, it marked a milestone in the loosening of the grip of the churches in dictating the rectitude with which people should behave in public. Had the harangue against Christianity occurred a decade before, the public reaction would likely have been very different, for the sway of the pulpit over the public mind and conventional response was far more powerful then, and Grey Owl's ostracism would have been much more likely.

When the science fiction novelist and bio-medical professor Edward Llewellyn (1918-84) and his family settled in Toronto in 1959 after some years in Nova Scotia, they bought a house at **152 Golfdale Road** and remained there for a decade. He published half a dozen highly regarded SF novels starting in 1979. His daughter Caroline (b.1948) lived at **No.162** as well. She began her writing career after she left Canada in 1973.

Crime novelist Jack Batten (b.1932) was pursuing his legal studies at Osgoode Hall when he lived at **6 Glen Echo Road** from 1956-58.

British-born Napier Moore (1893-1963) was appointed editor of *Maclean's* in 1929 and kept the post until November 1945, when he was promoted to an amorphous

Caroline Llewellyn with her father, Edward, and siblings in front of 152 Golfdale Road

position as editorial director of Maclean Hunter publications, a post he held until 1954. Then he retired to the Bahamas. From 1939 until he left for sunnier climes he lived at **20 Forest Glen Crescent**. As an editor, Moore was constantly at war with his staff over their attempts to feature Canadian writers writing about Canadian subjects, with Canadian artwork on the covers of every issue. Moore never seemed to grasp the muted but strong desire of some Canadians to forge an identity independent of England. For Moore, Canada's greatness lay in its connections to Great Britain, and there were few tears shed when he was kicked upstairs. No one bristled more under Moore's anglophilia than William Arthur Irwin, the associate editor (that is, the number two man of the magazine), who succeeded to the editor's chair on Moore's departure. Irwin's biographer relates that one of the reasons Irwin quit the Arts and Letters Club was the Englishness of the place—and the eternal presence, it seemed, of Napier Moore who loved the Club

for that very reason. The biographer comments, "Soon after joining the *Maclean's* staff, Irwin was sponsored for membership . . . Napier Moore joined shortly after Irwin, and he quickly became a prominent club member and producer of the annual spring show, which included the best acts of the previous year. Moore often starred in the revues, while Irwin usually served as a stagehand . . . Legend has it that Moore dominated the shows from start to finish and could be a tough taskmaster. Once, during a difficult and noisy dress-rehearsal, he was heard to shout, 'How many sons of bitches are directing this show?' In the silent moment that followed, a lone voice replied: 'Only one, Napier.'"

Not everyone disliked Moore, of course. The American fiction writer and critic Christopher Morley, for example, was apparently quite fond of him, and after a healthy night of male ribaldry and excess with E.J. Pratt and Moore, Morley sent them a limerick written in their honour:

If I don't get drunk in Toronto
It's not because I don't want to
For Napier and Ned
Will put me to bed
So give me another drink pronto!

Poet Peter Miller (b.1920) joined Ray Souster and Louis Dudek in the running of Contact Press in 1959 and stayed with the firm until it folded of its own volition in 1967. His Toronto residences were the storerooms, mailing centres, and production offices of what is now seen to have been among the most important poetry publishing operations of the post-war years in Canada. In 1964, Miller moved to **9 Ivor Road**. While working for the Canadian Banking Association during the day, he edited Contact books by night, and personally handled all of the distribution of Contact titles out of his kitchen and living room. Several of Contact's seminal publications bear the **9 Ivor Road** address, including its most famous anthology, *New Wave Canada*, which helped to launch the careers of several poets, including Michael Ondaatje. Miller lived on **Ivor** until 1983 when he retired to Oakville.

Ivor Road leads east to Donwoods Drive and Donino Avenue. Walk north on Donino over the bridge where the street becomes **Campbell Crescent. No.5** was the home of one of Canada's great editors and publishers, Lorne Pierce (1890-1961), from 1935-54. By the time he took possession of this property (which he named La Ferme) he was already a nationally known figure.

As the head of Ryerson Press, he was respected for the idealism of his list, and his lifelong championing of Canadian writers. While he is rightly remembered for his advocacy of other writers, it should not be forgotten that he himself authored 18 books. Books he wrote or edited while living on **Campbell Crescent** include: *Our Canadian Literature* (1935), *A Postscript on J.E.H. MacDonald* (1940), *Thoreau MacDonald* (1942), *A Canadian People* (1945), *A Catalogue of Canadian Manuscripts* (1946), *The Armoury in Our Halls* (1946), *Christianity and Culture in Our Time* (1947), *On Publishers and Publishing* (1951), *Canadian Poetry in English* (1954), and *Bliss Carman: Selected Poems* (1954).

West Don Mills

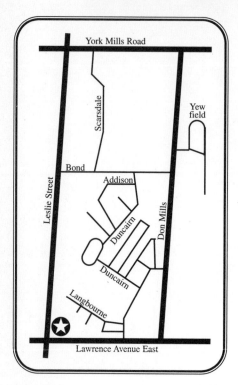

The tour begins at the northeast corner of Lawrence Avenue East and Leslie Street.

Proceed east to The Donway, then walk north two short blocks to **Langbourne Place. 32 Langbourne** was novelist Paul Quarrington's home from his birth in 1953 until 1964. Quarrington has since become one of the country's leading comic novelists (*Home Game*, 1983; *Logan in Overtime*, 1990), an obvious fact confirmed when he won the Leacock Medal for his novel *King Leary* (1987). About the only writing discipline to which Quarrington has not turned his adroit hand is poetry, for he has won a Gemini for one of his screenplays (*Perfectly Normal*, 1991), and warm reviews for his play *The Invention of Poetry* (1990).

From 1959-65 he attended Norman Ingram Public School, **50 Duncairn Road**.

Another noted author who attended the school is novelist Garfield Reeves-Stevens (b.1953), author of *Children of the Shroud* (1987) and with his wife, Judith, wrote a Star Trek novel *Memory Prime* (1988).

Just east of The Donway is **1065 Don Mills Road**, where novelist Rohinton Mistry lived when he first came to Canada from his native India in 1975. This was his home until 1981. During this time he worked during the day in a bank at 150 Eglinton Avenue East (razed) and by night attended classes at the UofT. Since then he has published a collection of short stories and a series of novels which have won substantial international renown. Canadian honours accrued to *Such a Long Journey* (1991), which won the Governor General's Award, and *A Fine Balance* (1995), which won the Giller Prize. In 1999 he was given an honorary doctorate by the UofT.

The bestselling novelist Richard Rohmer (b.1924) lived at **3 Addison Crescent** from 1955-63. During this period he was practising law and had yet to write any of his thrillers (*Ultimatum*, 1973; *Death by Deficit*, 1995) or any of his highly regarded nonfiction histories (*Patton's Gap*, 1981; *Rommel and Patton*, 1986).

Novelist C.J. Eustace worked his way up through the ranks of the J.M. Dent (Canada) publishing company. By the time the firm had moved to **100 Scarsdale Road** in 1957, he was a vice-president. In 1961 he became the managing director, and from 1963-68 he was president of the company. His fictions are marked by a strong concern with moral questions. His first book was a novel published in 1927, and his last was also a novel, *Forgotten Music* (1974). He also wrote tomes such as *Developments in Canadian Book Production and Design* (1972).

Poet Miriam Waddington (b.1917) lived at **32 Yewfield Crescent** from 1965 until 1992, when she left Toronto to reside in B.C. She had studied social work at the UofT and, after plying that trade in other cities, returned here in 1960, where she worked for a branch of the social services of what was then the Borough of North York. Five years later she was appointed to the English dept. of York University and taught there until she retired in 1983. She published almost all of her books while living at this address; among them, *The Glass Trumpet* (1966) and *Collected Poems* (1986).

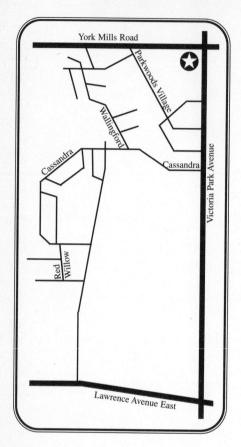

York Mills Road

Parkwoods Village

Wallingford

Cassandra

Cassandra

Victoria Park Avenue

Red Willow

Lawrence Avenue East

The tour begins at the southwest corner of York Mills Road and Victoria Park Avenue.

Walk south on Victoria Park one long block to **Parkwoods Village Drive**. Novelist Hugh Garner (1913-79) met the landlords who would tolerate his obnoxious drunken phases when he moved from Kingston Road to **51 Parkwoods Village Drive** in 1962. Initially he and his wife lived in what was called a maisonette, but after some weeks, finding the place too large, settled for a one-bedroom at the same address. After a couple of years he found the removal from downtown action too stressful, so he

gave notice. The Perkells (the landlords) offered him accommodation in a new apartment building they were constructing on Erskine Avenue, but as Garner says in his memoir, "I've always been a quick-decision, quick-move guy and I couldn't wait." So he moved to a unit on Broadway Avenue. "I made the mistake of moving into a place whose denizens were elderly church-goers and teetotallers, and some of the neighbours, with the help of their 'Christian' ethics, had me turfed out for excessive drinking."

Fortunately for Garner, by the time he was evicted, the new apartment building was ready, and the Perkells made one of the penthouses available to him. It remained his home for the rest of his life. While living in Don Mills, Garner published two books: *Hugh Garner's Best Stories* (1963), a compendium of old short stories peppered with a few previously unpublished tales. The book won the Governor General's Award. And in 1964 he published a selection of his journalism features, *Author, Author!*, with Ryerson Press. In essence, he wrote nothing original while in this suburb and would later term his two years here as "the most unproductive of my life." However, I hasten to point out that his book *Death in Don Mills* is not an account of his time in this part of the city— but rather fiction.

Poet Robert Billings (1949-87) lived for about a year from the fall of 1978 to early summer 1979 in apt. 305 of **76 Parkwoods Village Drive**.

Return to Victoria Park Avenue and proceed south two blocks to Cassandra Boulevard. Turn right (west) and the first street on the north side is **Wallingford Road**. Poet and novelist Michael Ondaatje (b:1943) made his home at **26 Wallingford** from 1972-81. He was, during this era, an English professor at Glendon College. Two

Susan Swan (left), Michael Ondaatje, Sarah Sheard at an editorial meeting of Coach House Press, circa 1991

of Ondaatje's best-known volumes of poetry were written while he lived at this address: *Rat Jelly* (1973) and *There's a Trick with a Knife I'm Learning to Do* (1979). The autobiographical *Running in the Family* (1982) was also composed while he lived here, as was the novel *Coming Through Slaughter* (1976). As if he were not productive enough in this decade, he also edited a short-story anthology, *Personal Fictions* (1977), and *The Long Poem Anthology* (1979).

Victoria Park Secondary School, **15 Wallingford**, can count prize-winning novelist and screenwriter Paul Quarrington (b.1953) among its graduates. From 1965-71, Quarrington lived a few blocks to the southwest of the school at **47 Redwillow Drive**.

TORONTO ISLANDS

The tour begins at Ward Island and progresses west to the other islands.

Take the ferry from the docks at the foot of Yonge Street (hidden behind the Harbour Castle Hotel) to Ward Island.

Novelist Peter Robinson (b.1950), author of the Inspector Banks mysteries (e.g., *Final Account*, 1994; *Dead Right*, 1997), began his first attempts at writing in the mystery genre while living at **8 First Street** on Ward Island in the summer of 1979. Until then, his creative writing was confined to poetry, the writing of which he also continued while living here. Since then, his police procedural novels have garnered some of the highest praise conferred on a Canadian mystery author.

When poets Gwendolyn MacEwen (1941-87) and Milton Acorn (1923-86) were married in February 1962 they moved soon after to a small, four-room cottage at **10 Second Avenue** on Ward Island. One of the reasons they moved here is that both were trying to live on their incomes as poets—a paltry sum in total, of course, and at the time the Island mini-houses represented some of the cheapest rents in town. Also, Acorn, a native of PEI, liked the idea of living on an island. His affection for the insular lifestyle could not overcome, however, the inescapable fact that his marriage to MacEwen had been a huge mistake. Cohabitation revealed that neither was suitable for the other, and by July 1962 MacEwen had left the Island, had left Acorn, indeed had left Toronto temporarily to discover Israel.

Immediately after he finished Grade 12 at Jarvis Collegiate, poet Victor Coleman (b.1944) took a job as an office clerk at the headquarters of the Thomson newspaper chain on Bay Street and moved to **24 Bayview Avenue** on Ward Island. It was his home for the next 18 months, but even after he returned to the mainland, he hoped to live again on the Island. His wish was fulfilled in October 1970 when he was able to take possession of **25 Third Street**, his home until June 1973, and again from November 1976 to September 1980. Coleman entered fully into the life of the Island community, and found his time here good for his poetry. During his first stint at **25 Third** he wrote two books, *Stranger* and *Speech Sucks*, and during the second tenure he finished *Captions for the Deaf*.

Poet and children's author Penn Kemp (b.1944) made a home at **11 Third Street** from 1971-74, during which time she wrote her first book, *Bearing Down* (1972), and edited the women's issue of the literary magazine *IS*. She then moved to **14 Fourth Street** and remained here until 1979. This is a most literary cottage for two reasons. First, Kemp wrote a number of books here: *Trance Form* (1976), *Clearing* (1977), *The Epic of Toad and Heron* (1977), *Angel Makers* (1978), *Toad Tales* (1980), *Some Talk Magic* (1986), and *Travelling Light* (1986). Second, after she left, the cottage passed into the hands of two other writers. In 1984, novelist Peter Such (b.1939) bought the cottage and made it his home from that date until 1988 when he moved back to the Annex. During the decade 1969-79 he published three novels that hinted at large possibilities, but since then he has published no books of creative writing. He teaches at York University.

Between the Kemp and Such years, poet Robert Sward (b.1933) developed a taste for island life when he lived in the same cottage from 1979-80. He then transferred to **3 Wyandot** on Algonquin Island and that was his home to February 1984. So taken with the islands was Sward that he wrote their history in the book *The Toronto Islands, An Illustrated History* (1983), and was inspired to

Milton Acorn and Gwendolyn MacEwen at a party at Raymond Souster's c. 1960, just prior to their marriage

finish two books of poetry: *Twelve Poems* (1982) and *Poems New and Selected* (1983). In a recent autobiographical essay, Sward recounts how, visiting from B.C., he came to discover the Island: "One day, Coach House Press editor Victor Coleman invited me to a party. Victor lived in a community of about seven hundred people on the Toronto Islands, a mile-and-a-half ride from downtown Toronto . . . The residents, a unique mix of writers, painters, musicians, workers in Canada's business and entertainment industries all commuted to the city together on a ferry boat. A number of American expatriates live on the Islands, along with people from England, France, Germany, and Switzerland. The Coach House party went on late into the night. It was two days before I got back to Toronto and, by that time, I had made up my mind to move to the Big City, and to live in the island community."

Thanks to the intervention of a girlfriend of the time, novelist and playwright David Young was able to obtain a fall-to-spring-only sublet at **1 Willow Avenue** from 1971-75. David tells me, "I cleared out in the summer to travel in Europe. This was a sweet little hidey-hole, a Peter Rabbit cottage hidden behind a high hedge. The place was uninsulated and fiercely cold in winter. I was writing in earnest now. Here I met Victor Coleman and thus began my long association with Coach House Press. The island house was a hub for frenzied, nonstop socializing with Coach House authors such as Matt Cohen, Ed Dorn, Allen Ginsberg, General Idea, Billy Hutton, bp Nichol, David McFadden, Michael Ondaatje, *et al*. Here I wrote my first screenplay, *125 Rooms of Comfort*. Also here my first publication: *Rifle News*, a *faux* tabloid newspaper which I wrote, designed and printed at the Coach House Press. And I began work on *Agent Provocateur* (1976)."

Novelist Phil Murphy (b.1925) was a fifth-generation Torontonian, the only child of the noted visual artist R.W. Murphy, a member of the Royal Canadian Academy. The first six months of Phil's life were spent on a hammock in his parents' yacht, soon after which they bought The Moorings, a house at **118 Lake Shore Avenue** on Ward Island. The home appears on the cover of Murphy's story collection, *Summer Island* (1984). For the next years, this was to be his main residence, the family returning to various rented houses only for the three or four worst months of winter, and his youthful memories of the island provide the background for his only published volume.

Novelist and short-story writer Hugh Hood (b.1928) lived at the Manitou Hotel, **320 Lake Shore Avenue**, Centre Island, from 1939-43. In a letter he remarked, "I should note that while I lived at the island, I *iceboated* on Toronto Bay, *walked across the Bay many times* during the winters, and *rode across in a car* once, terrified, when a drunk offered me a ride after the [ferry] Ned Hanlan had made its last crossing for the day. Almost no Torontonians can make that statement."

Norma West Linder (b.1928) was born in Toronto but spent most of her childhood and youth on Manitoulin Island. Because her husband was a dance-band musician, the couple were forced to live out of suitcases for much of their married life, including the post-war decade when Toronto was their home as much as any place. In 1947 she lived at **7 Mohawk Street** on Centre Island: "Centre Island was my favourite spot. I loved taking the ferry back and forth to work. At that time, I made the notes for a book of poems called *The Rooming House*. I learned something important with the publication of that collection. Never trust anybody to proof for you! Toronto will always mean a great deal to me—creatively and emotionally. I used it as the setting for my first novel, *The Lemon Tree*. It was released simultaneously in England and Canada in 1973. With that, I was thoroughly hooked on writing."

By the time Herman Voaden (1903-91) spent a year, 1939-40, living at **15 St. Andrew's Avenue** on Centre Island, he was well-known in the Canadian arts community for his accomplishments as a playwright. For almost 20 years by this point he had been espousing a singular vision of what theatre should be, a symphonic blend of all the arts certainly more ambitious than anything else being proposed in the country. That it was also successful the few times it was presented was beyond doubt. His scale of production was difficult to produce in a nation which was largely indifferent to the absence of stages on which Canadian voices could be heard. And the economic woes of the Depression certainly made the task almost impossible. Yet he persevered in doing what he could to see his own plays—and those of others—professionally performed, and he remains an undersung hero of Canadian drama.

Toronto-born Vancy Kasper (b.1930) is a poet, novelist and was also for most of the 1950s a features writer at the *Star*. During the decade 1955-65 she lived in since-razed rooming houses [addresses unknown] on either Ward Island or Centre Island from March 1 to December 1 of each year. She would have happily lived year-round on the Island, but in the off-months the ferry did not leave early enough for her to get to the *Star* office by the required 7 am starting time.

Raymond Knister's brilliant promise was cut short when he drowned in 1932, at the age of 33. Adept at poetry, he was more highly regarded in his time, and now, as a fiction writer of wonderful adroitness. Macmillan recognized his talent early and in 1927 commissioned him to make a selection of Canadian short stories for the first anthology dedicated to the form to be published in this country. Knister's introduction to the collection is still regarded as a milestone assessment of the Canadian approach to short-story writing. Much of the reading and editing for that book was done while he lived at The Poplars, a cottage on the Western Sandbar at **23 West Island Drive** [demolished] to which he had moved immediately after his marriage on June 18, 1927. When not absorbed with his work on the Macmillan project, he finished his first novel, *White Narcissus* (1929), at this address. Morley Callaghan wrote an appreciation of the book for the New Canadian Library edition. In a July 1, 1927 letter to a friend, Knister described his island home: "We have a nice cottage here, on the beach with neighbours only on one side, and a sort of wild little park on the other, and while I sit here I can see Lake Ontario on one hand, and an islet on the other. On which latter they are prosecuting regatta races at this moment, in celebration of the glorious first [July 1]. Except on such occasions, it is quite secluded here, though you can see the city, and hear the City Hall clock strike. It is nearly opposite the Exhibition grounds, and the domed and fancy roofs of those buildings are finely lit up in the mornings. Myrtle and I went over to the Rodeo the other afternoon, and wished we could swim home instead of going all the way round in sweltering street cars. No cars of any sort over here, and only one horse, the garbage man's. Eaton's and Simpson's deliver with two-wheeled carts pulled by men. So, behold me at established length and happier already than I have succeeded in being for any length of time before, feeling rich in everything but money, and even rather assiduously working. In June I re-wrote with much addition about 120 pages of *White Narcissus*, one story, and two articles. Not so bad for a honeymoon?" The Knisters remained here until January 1928, when they moved to a flat in Parkdale.

Novelist Hugh Garner lived in three furnished flats on Centre Island [addresses unknown] from 1950-53, probably near the Manitou Hotel where he was a frequent visitor to the beer parlour. In his autobiography, he describes how he wrote fiction in those days: "During the summer of 1951 I drank myself broke, and my $75 monthly rent day was less than a week away. I had to write a saleable story fast, and at eight o'clock one evening after the children had been put to bed, I dreamed up a story about a little old lady, an old-age pensioner who was determined to take a summertime trip on a train . . . By three the next morning the story was written, and after a few hours sleep I typed a corrected copy of it." The story was purchased the next day by *Chatelaine*'s editor Byrne Hope Sanders for publication in their October issue. Garner was able to pick-up his payment for the story a mere 24 hours later. He lived this way, from hand to mouth, for much of the 1950s. One of his ongoing financial saviours was Jack Kent Cooke, later famous as a tycoon and owner of leading sports franchises in the USA, but in the fifties a rising entrepreneur of magazines and radio. During one bad patch, Garner went to see Cooke and convinced the millionaire to hire him as Public Relations Director. The job provided Garner with a steady income, but left him little time for any original writing while the Island was his home. It was only after he had moved to the mainland that he wrote an article for *Saturday Night*, a piece that includes his own odd assessment of his former fellow citizens across the bay: "Although living conditions and lifestyles are Bohemian in the extreme, very few writers or painters make their homes there for long; they can't stand the social pace and there are too many diversions popping up between themselves and their Muse. Many of the inhabitants belong to a half-world that includes chronic alcoholics, wife and husband deserters, beachcombers, deadbeats and spinsters-on-the-make. The majority of these live on Centre Island, the biggest of the chain, and one given over to a peculiar type of Edwardian architecture that is a hodge-podge of widows' walks, wings, cupolas and closed-in porches added to the houses as if thrown at them by a demented tent-maker. The normal fringe of the population is in a minority on Centre Island, as it is on Hanlan's Point, while Algonquin Island is settled by a peculiar stuffy type of water-borne suburbanite who tries to pretend that the less-inhibited Centre Islanders do not exist."

One other notable author lived on the Island but I have not been able to determine where. Len Deighton cannot recall the address of where he lived, and none of the oldtimers or archives on the Island have a record of his whereabouts. Deighton (b.1929) discussed his Toronto days and plans for a novel to be set in the city with the *Star* when he was passing through town on a promotional tour in 1978: "Don't be surprised if you see a shoot-out scene on a Toronto Island ferry . . . And how about a winter chase sequence, with the spy on the run from Toronto to Ottawa to Quebec and on up to the snowy wastelands of the Canadian Arctic?" Those are some of the images running through Deighton's mind for a projected thriller that will use Toronto Island as its main locale.

"'I like using actual spy cases in an authentic setting as a springboard for my fiction,' he said in an interview. 'Canada has all the ingredients for the sort of suspense story I like to write and I can't understand why its setting hasn't been used more often.'

"'You've got a lakeside proximity to the American border, an exotic dual language situation, a unique relationship with Russia, an historical background of Gouzenko-style espionage, and all that fantastic scenery running up to the North Pole . . . At this stage, all I know is it [the proposed novel] will contain the word spy. It ought to convey the idea of winter. And somewhere in the title there should be the 49th Parallel—a powerful image that epitomizes Canada to me.' But why Toronto Island? 'Because that's where I lived for four months back in the summer of 1956. I loved the ferries and the mixed community there. And it's a terrible, terrible shame they intend throwing out the Islanders and making it an arid sort of vacation park.'"

EASTERN SUBURBS

The tour begins at St. Clair Avenue East and O'Connor Drive.

In 1952, when Jack McClelland (b.1922) assumed control of the publishing house founded by his father in 1906, he immediately made plans to move the company's office and warehouse from its expensive and crammed premises downtown to roomier and cheaper facilities to what was then regarded as the edge of the world, **25 Hollinger Road**. The actual move took place about a year and a half later, and this remained the headquarters of "The Canadian Publishers" as the firm liked to be called, until it moved back downtown in 1986.

Unfortunately for those who worked there in summer, the building was not air conditioned—except, for some reason, the "editorial compound," a small warren of semi-divided offices where most of the editors read unsolicited manuscripts or blue-pencilled forthcoming tomes. Oddly enough, if an editor were promoted to senior editor, he or she was also promoted out of the compound to a west-facing window office—a nice perk in winter and hell in summer. When the heat and humidity combined on the worst days, Jack McClelland was known to strip to his undershirt and carry on publishing—a delightfully casual approach to business dress that freed the staff to be nearly as informal.

It was from this building that Jack McClelland built the list that made his house the most important for Canadian literature in the 1950s and 1960s. Among the authors he fostered (almost all of whom made the trek to this place to meet with Jack or with their editors) were Margaret Atwood, Pierre Berton, Earle Birney, Leonard Cohen, Margaret Laurence, Irving Layton, Farley Mowat, Peter Newman, Al Purdy, and Mordecai Richler.

The New Canadian Library was launched from this site in 1958, a paperback series which made—and continues to make—high points of Canadian literature available to hundreds of thousands of students who otherwise would scarcely have known their country did have a literary history.

Over the years, a few authors of varying celebrity toiled as editors at McClelland and Stewart when it was on Hollinger; among them: Greg Gatenby, Sam Llewellyn, Philip Marchand, Lily Miller, Frank Neufeld, John Newlove, Anna Porter, Peter Taylor, and J.A.Wainwright.

Tucked away in the triangle formed by the intersection of O'Connor and St. Clair is **Joanith Drive. No.25** was the home of Chusaburo Ito (b.1910), one of the country's most distinguished *haiku* and *tanka* poets, from 1960-86. Born in Japan, Ito came to Canada in 1927 and has lived in Toronto since 1947.

The next stop is Don Mills. Take Don Mills Road north of Eglinton to Barber Greene Road. Turn west on Barber Greene and go five blocks to **Broadpath Road**. Novelist Morley Torgov (b.1927) lived at **35 Broadpath** from 1955-64, during which time he practised law and dreamed of becoming a novelist. He would write most of his award-winning humorous novels while living at his next address.

A block to the east is **Southill Drive**. When poet and critic Eli Mandel (1922-92) returned to Toronto in mid-1963 to live permanently in the city (he had obtained a job teaching English at Glendon College), he and his first wife, Miriam (1930-82), also a poet, settled into **85 Southill Drive** and remained here for about a year. They separated not long afterwards.

About equidistant from Don Mills Road on the other side of the thoroughfare is

North Hills Terrace, where at **1 North Hills Terrace** novelist Barbara Gowdy (b.1950) passed her childhood and early adolescence from 1954 to 1963. Gowdy's novels are now among the best-known by a Canadian in Europe, and in Canada and the USA she is consistently rated in the front rank of fiction writers working in this country. Her books include *Falling Angels* (1989), *Mr. Sandman* (1995), and *The White Bone* (1998).

Return to Eglinton Avenue and head east. Just past the Don Valley Parkway is Wynford Drive. Take it north to **Concorde Place**. Apt. 1704 at **3 Concorde Place** was the home for a year (September 1990 to August 1991) of novelist Wayne Johnston (b.1958). Part of his book *Human Amusements* was composed at this address.

Return to Eglinton and proceed east to the next street running north, Swift Drive. Swift ends quickly at **Ecclestone Drive** where, in apt. 417 at **48 Ecclestone Drive**, novelist and poet Rosemary Aubert had a literary epiphany of sorts, as she explained in a letter: "This is a building near Victoria Park and Eglinton. It figures in my mystery novel, *Free Reign*, as one of the places near the Don Valley lived in by Ellis Portal, the hero. It is also the home of a police character who will appear in the third Ellis Portal mystery, but that may change. I must have written poems here because I lived here during my very first days as a poet in Toronto, and I recall having had a poem published in a magazine and bringing it into the bedroom to show my then (first) husband, and I remember that he was not as pleased as I had hoped, thus beginning a recurring theme in my life as a writer and a wife . . . It must have been while I was living at this address that I made the most important decision of my writing life: I went to Harbourfront and met other poets and became one and left the marriage and the suburban life forever."

Take the Don Valley Parkway north to York Mills Road, and then proceed west on York Mills past Leslie Street to the first street west of Leslie, Banbury Road. Take Banbury to Pinnacle. Take Pinnacle to **Mossgrove Trail**. **No.31** was the home of comic novelist Seymour Blicker (*Schmucks*) from August to December 1977. Blicker (b.1940) and his wife had been living in Los Angeles when they decided that L.A. was not the best place to raise their children. But rather than return to their native Montreal, they decided to give Toronto a try. Blicker had thought he would write fiction at this address, but as he said in a letter, "Not long after our arrival, I was contracted to write an episode for the CBC detective drama series *Sidestreet*, and wrote the first draft of the script while I was in Toronto . . . In any event, we didn't stay very long in Toronto mainly because we missed Montreal, and particularly the Laurentian Mountains. As much as I liked Toronto, I felt as though an important piece of my life was missing by being away from Quebec, and I didn't want to give it up, so home we went."

Return to Banbury Road. Two blocks to the north is Heathcote Avenue. Five blocks to the west, running south from Heathcote is **Honeywell Place**. **No.7** was where the literary phenomenon Edna Jaques (1891-1978) spent her last years living with her daughter and her family. Born in Collingwood, Jaques spent the first half of her life living north of Moose Jaw. Her family was so poor that, as an adolescent, when she ran out of scribblers in which to write poems, she borrowed used wrapping paper from any source she could find in order to placate her muse. By the age of 14 she was selling poems to the famous evangelist Billy Sunday, who converted them into hymns used at his revival meetings. Her unsophisticated poetry became immensely popular with housewives across North America, and as Nellie McClung said of her work, "When poems are cut out of newspapers, pinned above the sink, and committed to memory by busy women in house dresses as they peel potatoes or wash dishes, has not such a poet achieved fame?" By the 1950s, Jaques was certainly famous: a national poll in 1952 stated she was one of the most popular women in Canada. And by the end of the

1960s, she claimed she had earned more than eighty thousand dollars solely from the poems she sold to serials, or from her books. Before she died, her ten volumes had sold more than a quarter million copies worldwide. She published her disingenuous autobiography in 1978, the year she died peacefully at her daughter's home.

Take Bayview Avenue north to Sheppard Avenue. Turn east and proceed about five blocks to **Bessarion Road. No.36** was the home of playwright Hrant Alianak (b.1950) when he moved to Toronto from Montreal in 1968. He stayed here until 1978. In his first years, Alianak pursued grad studies at York University in Downsview, but in the 1970s he became active writing dramas and as a director of his own plays and those of others. Most of his own writing has been produced at Theatre Passe Muraille. Plays written at Bessarion which were also presented and published (including one-act plays) were *Tantrums* (1972), *Western* (1972), *Mathematics* (1972), *Brandy* (1973), *The Violinist and the Flower Girl* (1972), *Christmas* (1973), and *Mousetown* (1974).

Proceed north on Bessarion to Sheppard Avenue. Cross Sheppard and on the north side find Burbank Road nearby. Go north on Burbank about ten blocks to Candida Gate. Candida Gate leads to **Ravenscroft Circle. No.31** was the home of Broadway playwright and Hollywood screenwriter Bernard Slade from 1959-61. It was at this address that Slade conceived and wrote his first stage play, *Simon Says Get Married*. The play was produced at the Crest Theatre. In an autobiographical essay, Slade reminisced about his writing of the play: "While writing it I became nervous that the audience wouldn't respond and this apprehension caused me to inject a laugh line about every ten seconds. It was rather like, 'If you don't like this one, wait a minute!' When the play opened, the audience laughed at everything but, because I had sacrificed character and believability for jokes, left the theatre feeling somewhat dissatisfied. The reviews were devastating . . . but the experience was not without its rewards, some immediate, some delayed. The show played to capacity houses for its six-week run, and the script, surprisingly, was instrumental in helping my later career."

Proceed east on Sheppard Avenue a few kilometres past Pharmacy Avenue one block to Bridlewood Boulevard. Go north on Bridlewood one block to **Ravencliff Crescent. No.32** was Barbara Gowdy's home throughout her teenage years and early womanhood, 1963-71. She attended high school at Sir John A. Macdonald Collegiate at **2300 Pharmacy Avenue**.

Proceed east on Sheppard Avenue a few kilometres to Kennedy Road. Go north on **Kennedy Road. No.2775** is less than a block south of Finch. This was the home of the internationally celebrated surrealist poet and collagist Ludwig Zeller (b.1927). His daughter Beatriz, also an author, recalled the family's years here: "From late October 1971 to September 1975 we lived at **2775 Kennedy Road**. It was a bungalow

Ludwig Zeller (far right) and his wife Susanna Wald entertain Colombian novelist Alvaro Mutis (left) and Hungarian poet George Faludy at their home in Toronto, 1987

surrounded by a marvellous orchard of pear trees, right at the corner of Finch and Kennedy. In the winter the wild pheasants would come down and feed on the fruit buried under the snow. Ludwig's poem 'The White Pheasant' is inspired in part by that. Ludwig always says that if it hadn't been for the beauty of that space, the peace of that garden, he would never have survived the first few years of life in Canada. He wrote one of his greatest poems in that house: 'Woman in Dream.'"

Our final stop on this tour is **3590 Bayview Avenue**, just south of Steeles Avenue. The advent of WWII had forced Mazo de la Roche (*Whiteoaks of Jalna*) to return to Canada. One of the reasons novelist de la Roche (1879-1961) bought this property in April 1939 was that she craved privacy more than ever, now that she was one of the most popular novelists in the English language, not just in Canada. At the time, this property was considered a country estate and went by two different country-house names: "Windrush Hill," and "Singing Pines." For the first four years she lived here she was as prolific as ever, finishing the novel *Whiteoak Heritage* (1940), and writing all of *Wakefield's Curse* (1941). The war inspired a non-Jalna book, *The Two Saplings* (1942). She also finished at this address her novel *The Building of Jalna*, worth singling out because it was the first book since she had become a money machine to receive a negative reaction from all three of her publishers in Canada, the UK, and the USA. The author stuck to her guns, in part because the publishers could not agree on what were the best bits and what were the parts needing drastic revision. As it happened, the book was selected as the main selection of the Literary Guild in the USA, a sure sign that her popularity was as strong as ever with readers. Fuel rationing because of the war made even occasional trips to downtown Toronto difficult. However, when Mazo's chauffeur was drafted, she realized that she would have to move again, this time closer to the city centre, if she were to have any contact with friends and book-trade acquaintances. She sold this house in mid-1945 and moved to Russell Hill Road. But she did so with mixed feelings: "I have missed my study at Windrush which was a complete sanctuary from the outside world. When I closed that door behind me, I felt safe and happy."

WESTERN SUBURBS

The tour begins at the Queensway and Park Lawn Road, about one kilometre west of the Humber River.

Go north on Park Lawn Road about six blocks to **Berry Road**. **No.158** was the home of Broadway playwright Bernard Slade (b.1930). In 1955 he lived in apt. 27, and in 1956 he moved to apt. 8. At the time, Slade was trying to make a full-time career for himself as an actor with the CBC and on the boards. The year before, he had worked as a flight attendant for Air Canada in order to support his thespian dreams, but as he explained to a journalist in 1972, he was not really cut out to be a flight steward: "I thought it would give me a chance to see the world, so of course they gave me the Toronto-Winnipeg run. I remember my first night flight. Your first sight of those exhaust flames belching out of the old North Stars . . . well, it was unsettling. Actually, I panicked. Picked up the phone in the galley and yelled at the pilot, just about to take off, 'The engine's on fire!' 'Really?' he said, 'Which one?' 'All of them!' A long pause, then he said very quietly, considering, 'Just sit down. And once we've taken off, I'm coming back *to talk to you*.'"

By the end of the fifties, he started to write for television, and in 1960 he graduated to the legitimate stage with his first comedy. Seeing a slim future for himself as a dramatist in Canada, he moved to Hollywood in 1964 and had great success writing TV sitcoms such as "The Flying Nun" and "The Partridge Family."

In the middle of the next decade he had his first Broadway hit, *Same Time Next Year* (1975), nominated for a Tony Award for Best Play. Other humorous works on Broadway followed: *Tribute* (1978) and *Romantic Comedy* (1979) were hits; *Special Occasions* (1982) was not. More recent work includes *Fatal Attraction* (1986) and *Same Time Another Year* (1995).

Another playwright who lived in this area was Jack Winter (b.1936). To find his home go east on Berry Road to **Stephen Drive**, then proceed north to **177 Stephen Drive** where Winter lived in apt. 103 from 1959-60 while attending the School of Graduate Studies at the UofT. Within three years of living here, Winter became the playwright-in-residence at Toronto Workshop Productions, producing such critically successful plays as *Hey Rube!* and *The Golem of Venice*. Following a successful career in Toronto in TV as well as theatre, he felt larger opportunities were available in London and he left for England.

Yet another author from this region who had success in Toronto and then in Hollywood is Martyn Burke (b.1942). From 1954-68 his home, as a teenager and in between his travels as a young adult was **157 Prince Edward Drive**, found by taking Berry Road west to the start of Prince Edward and then going north about six blocks to Kirk Braden. While still living at this address, Burke went far afield as a correspondent, covering the Vietnam War, and then returned to Canada to write novels. Since that did not pay well, he also worked at the CBC, quickly rising through the ranks to become a senior producer. His best-known work for television in this country is *Connections*, a legendary exposé of the Mafia. Among his novels are *The Commissar's Report* (1984), *Ivory Joe* (1981), and *Tiara* (1995), all published in Canada and the USA. As a writer for television and the big screen his credits include *The Second Civil War* (TV, 1997) and *Power Play* (feature film, 1978). Burke has also directed three, as they say in Hollywood, major motion pictures: *The Clown Murders* (1975), *Power Play* (1978), and *The Last Chase* (1981). He told me that it is discretion alone which forces him not to wax enthusiastic about his memories of "growing up while cruising Canada's version of *American Graffiti*: The Queensway. And how to stage a drag race at midnight in the parking lot of the Stonegate Shopping Mall. Or playing hockey on the Humber without falling through the ice."

Return to the Queensway and proceed west to Royal York Road. Go north on Royal York about six short blocks to Yorkview Drive. Take Yorkview and head west for two blocks to **Uno Drive. No.109**, just to the south, was the home of novelist Hugh Garner in April 1946 and for about two years thereafter, thanks to a veteran housing program for which Navy man Garner was eligible. During the day, he worked at the War Assets Corporation offices downtown, and then trudged home to his rented typewriter to work on what would become his most famous novel, *Cabbagetown*: "Every evening after supper I would retire to our unfurnished dining room, close the door so as not to awaken the children who were sleeping upstairs, and place my typewriter on the top of our treadle sewing-machine. On my left would be the slowly diminishing pile of the original typescript, and on my right the slowly thickening pile of revision, this time double spaced on white bond paper. I worked on it most evenings, and always tried to do twenty pages before quitting for the night. It was sheer bull labour now, for there was not the élan of creation that had carried me through the winter before."

Proceed west on The Queensway to Kipling Avenue. Go north a few kilometres to the third street north of Bloor Street: **Mattice Avenue. No.62** was the childhood home of novelist Christine Slater (b.1960). She lived here with her family from 1968 until she married in 1989, and this was where she wrote most of the stories that appeared in her first book, *Stalking the Gilded Boneyard* (1993). Her other critically well-received fictions include *The Small Matter of*

Getting There (1994) and *Certain Dead Soldiers* (1995). She did not have far to walk to school: She attended Our Lady of Peace School at **70 Mattice** for Grades 3 to 8.

Around the corner, at **36 Botfield Avenue**, the poet (and publisher of Mercury Press) Bev Daurio (b.1953) lived from 1976-77 while she was the assistant editor of the Toronto alternative arts newspaper *The Onion*. In recent years her Mercury Press has become one of the leading poetry book publishers in the country. Earlier, from 1955-66, the house had been the family home of author David Halliday (b.1948). He too attended Our Lady of Peace School.

Proceed west on Bloor Street about one kilometre past Highway 427. Here you will find **Mill Road. No.222** is Millwood Public School which can boast Steven Heighton among its alumni; he took Grades 1 to 6. Heighton (b.1962) is considered by most literary critics as being easily in the top rank of his generation in Canada. In 1989 he won the Air Canada Award, given annually to a

Martyn Burke (left) with his father and younger brother on the back porch of their home, 157 Prince Edward Drive, 1955

young author showing exceptional promise. The following year he won the Gerald Lampert Award for his book *Stalin's Carnival*. And the year after that, the National Magazine Award Gold Medal for best short story. His short stories have appeared in several distinguished anthologies and periodicals in Canada, the UK, and USA. Early in his career he published more poetry than fiction, but of late the pattern has been reversed. From 1967 until he departed for Queen's University in Kingston in 1980, Heighton lived two blocks to the northeast at **26 Winsdale Road**. For Grades 7 and 8, he went to Bloordale Public School at **10 Toledo Road**, and his five high-school years were spent at Silverthorn Collegiate, **291 Mill Road**.

Follow Rathburn Road several blocks east to Islington Avenue. Go north on **Islington Avenue**. The stretch of this thoroughfare between Rathburn and Eglinton has been the home of the playwright Len Peterson for almost half a century: 1955 to the present. Even though Peterson (b.1917) came to Toronto at the end of WWII, the themes that dominate much of his writing were shaped by the geography of his native Saskatchewan and the bleak economy of the Depression. He came to this city to work with Andrew Allan and the CBC drama department, and his radio plays and scripts remain the work for which he is best known. That said, poetry is about the only discipline of creative writing in which he has not shown an adept hand. His first publication was a novel (1949), soon followed in 1950 by a collection of his radio plays published by McClelland and Stewart. His output in various fields remained steady throughout the decades, and his bibliography includes original plays (legitimate and radio) for adults and children, adaptations for radio of plays and novels by other authors, and texts for films and musicals.

Further up the street is Richview Collegiate, **1738 Islington Avenue**, which was Janice Kulyk Keefer's school for Grades 9 to 13. Her home from 1956 until 1970 was **5 Kingsfold Court,** which is found by following Prince George Drive west from about the middle of this stretch of Islington to Princess Anne Crescent. Go south on Princess Anne one short block to **Kingsfold Court**. Keefer (b.1953) has published books of poetry and fiction, although it is the nature of the beast that she is much better known for her stories than for her verses. *The Paris-Napoli Express* (1986), her first collection of tales, was followed by another collection in 1987, and then in 1988 appeared her first novel, *Constellations*. Recently, she has been exploring in her fiction and non-fiction her Ukrainian roots.

Return to Prince George Drive. Go west one block to The Kingsway. Follow The Kingsway south past Islington for a few blocks to **Hartfield Road**. John Ballem (b.1925), author of several thrillers including *The Devil's Lighter* (1973), *Oilpatch Empire* (1985), and *The Barons* (1991), reported, "I lived in Toronto for two years—from July 1952 to July 1954, and resided at **1 Hartfield Road**. At the time, I was employed as a lawyer by Imperial Oil Limited in their old head office at King and Church . . . Toronto has played a rather important role for me as a writer in a philosophical rather than geographical sense. A number of my novels have been set in the western Canadian oil patch, which inevitably involves the 'hinterland-metropolis' economic model which is so typical of Canada. While Toronto as a place has appeared in only one of my books (*The Dirty Scenario*, 1974), its spirit is represented in the tension between the consuming East and the producing West. There is nothing evil or bad about this; it is simply a fact of Canadian life, but it does create an interesting conflict."

Go east on Eglinton Avenue for several kilometres to Trethewey Drive (which is one block west of Keele Street). Take Trethewey north two blocks to **Greentree Court**. The award-winning comic novelist Donald Jack (b.1924) said in a letter, "We returned, all three of us, to Toronto thankfully in 1957

(Ottawa didn't have a single decent bakery), and from then on I was a full-time freelance professional writer. We lived first at **9 Greentree Court** off Trethewey Avenue in the northwest of the city, and I did well enough in writing for radio and selling a novelette to *Maclean's* (written in Greentree Court) to enable us to buy a house in Oakville [the following year]."

Return to Eglinton Avenue. Go west on Eglinton to Weston Road. Proceed north on Weston for two short blocks, looking for **Locust Street** on the right. **No.11** was the home of poet Gwendolyn MacEwen (1941-87) in the summer of 1968 following her return to Canada. Actually, the house belonged to her sister, who also lived there with her children. Because of a family crisis, Gwen volunteered to help with expenses and chores. According to her biographer, Rosemary Sullivan, MacEwen's living conditions were Spartan: she "lived on the screened-in back porch with only a simple bed and a small table for her typewriter." After a year of trying to write poetry and fiction in a house full of children, Gwen found a house nearby on **Weston Road** [address unknown] in the summer of 1969.

Go north on Weston Road about eight blocks to **Nickle Street** (at Jane Street). Playwright John Herbert (b.1926) described his years on this street from 1939-47: "My family lived at **29 Nickle Street**, Mount Dennis. We moved to this address the year I started secondary school. I wrote my first published short stories here: 'A Boy and His Queen,' (aged thirteen) published in *Wee Wisdom Magazine*, Kansas City, Mo., USA (1940), and 'The Chinese Proverb,' (aged fourteen) also published in *Wee Wisdom Magazine* (1941) . . . I was sent to Guelph Reformatory from this house in 1946, a convicted homosexual." After his release from incarceration two years later, he returned to live with his family who had moved around the corner to **1329 Weston Road**, corner of Rutherford Avenue. He lived elsewhere after 1949.

Proceed north on Jane Street a few kilometres to **Heathrow Drive**, located three blocks north of Wilson Avenue. Novelist Peter Such (b.1939), author of *Fallout* (1966) and *Riverrun* (1973), made his home at **55 Heathrow Drive** from 1957-58. This was his first year living in Toronto, and his first year as an undergrad at Victoria College.

The western end of Heathrow Drive is intersected by Datchet Road. Follow Datchet north for one block to find **Monclova Road**. The novelist Adele Wiseman (1928-1992) (*The Sacrifice*, 1956; *Crackpot*, 1974) moved to Toronto for the first time in 1969 but was no sooner settled into a house than the landlord forced them to move. She wrote to her old friend Margaret Laurence in September 1970 about **29 Monclova**: "We found a place just in the nick, a really great place, though it's just got a bare open backyard & we'll have to manufacture some privacy and garden next year. But it's only about 4¹/₂ years old and it's got *eleven* rooms! . . . This place will cost us slightly less to rent than the old one, mainly because the Italian owner has rented it on condition that we won't rent out rooms. I guess he's afraid that just about anybody would be tempted to rent a room or two. What else would you do with eleven rooms? There's even an extra kitchen downstairs, a big one. Apparently that's a feature of Italian-built homes around here; upstairs for show, downstairs to live in. So we've plenty of space to spread out in, though the family has diminished." A year and a half later, she and her husband were still unpacking, as she told Laurence in a letter of January 31, 1972: "Myself am fine, dithering about as usual. We're finally getting our books unpacked. Dimitry's knocking up a few shelves in the library. We figure even if they sell this place in the next few months, it'll be just as easy for us to pack them anew as to repack those collapsed cartons. And meanwhile we'll have them around. Such a pleasure to see one's tattered old friends." By the end of October Wiseman had to move again, and she and her family headed for Kleinburg.

Return to Heathrow Drive. Go east on Heathrow one block to Chesham Drive. Follow Forthbridge Crescent one short block to **Calvington Drive**. Novelist Carol Shields (b.1935) is unique in Canadian Literature in being the only novelist to win both the Governor General's Award and the Pulitzer Prize. She was eligible for the latter because she was born and raised in the USA. Although long a resident of Winnipeg, she has twice lived in Toronto, as she said in a letter: "Toronto: I arrived in November 1957, a young bride aged 22 from Chicago. We lived for some months in an apartment on **Wilson Avenue** just west of Jane [**1770 Wilson Avenue**], and in the summer of 1958 bought a tiny house, **252 Calvington Drive** in Downsview. We lived there two years, and during that time I wrote a few stories, one of which was actually sold to the CBC, to the John Drainie program."

EARLY LITERARY VISITORS

The earliest literary mention of Toronto belongs to the Belgian author, Father Louis Hennepin (1626-c.1705), who seems not have set foot on our shores but mentions us—literally—in passing, while on his way in a brigantine from Quebec to Niagara in 1678. Actually, rather than Toronto *per se*, he cites the Indian village of Teieiagon (at the mouth of the Rouge River) as one among many villages on the north shore of Lake Ontario he saw from his ship during the voyage. Hennepin recorded his extensive travels, amazing exploits, daring escapes, and anthropological discoveries in a book he published in 1683 once he was back in France. The work became a best-seller in its time, and was quickly translated into the leading languages of Europe.

The first literary description of Toronto (as opposed to Hennepin's mere listing of the name) appears in the work of the Scottish poet George Heriot (1759-1839). After the standard education and jobs typically obtained by the gentry of that time, he found himself posted to Canada in 1799 as the postmaster-general. Heriot took the post seriously, and from the beginning endeavoured to improve the country's mail-delivery system. His job entailed touring to various parts of the country, and he recorded his impressions in his 1807 work, *Travels Through the Canadas*. Given that he saw the city in the years immediately after the turn of the century when the population was a mere few hundred people—at most—it is not surprising that it is the bay and the Island which capture his imagination: "York, or Toronto, the seat of government in Upper Canada, is placed . . . near the bottom of a harbour of the same name. A long and narrow peninsula, distinguished by the appellation of Gibraltar Point, forms and embraces this harbour, securing it from the storms of the lake and rendering it the safest of any around the coast of that sea of fresh waters. Stores and block-houses are constructed near the extremity of this point . . . The advancement of this place to its present condition has been effected within the lapse of six or seven years and persons who have formerly travelled in this part of the country are impressed with sentiments of wonder on beholding a town which may be termed handsome, reared as if by enchantment in the midst of wilderness . . . The scene from this part of the basin is agreeable and diversified . . . The left side of the view comprehends the long peninsula which incloses this sheet of water, beautiful on account of its placidity, and rotundity of form; the distant lake, which appears bounded only by the sky, terminates the whole."

A few pages later in his book he makes the first reference in a book to Toronto's most western suburb, Etobicoke: "To the westward of the garrison of York are the remains of an old French fort, called Toronto, adjoining to this situation is a deep bay, receiving into it the river Humber between which are the head of Lake Ontario, the Tobyco, the Credit and two other rivers with a number of smaller streams."

The next literary visitor was Lieutenant Francis Hall (d.1833). He penned a description of Toronto—unusually sardonic for the era—in his *Travels in Canada and the United States* (1818): "There is a good bridge over the rocky bed of the Humber, and large mills near it. The surface of the whole country seems flat; I did not observe a single hill, or inequality, but such as have been evidently formed by streams, descending over a soil little tenacious; and as the banks of all these are very lofty, there is probably a considerable, though gradual, slope of the whole country down to the lake, the shores of which have no elevation worthy of notice. From the Humber to York is a uniform tract of sandy pine-barren, unsusceptible of culture; a change of feature, probably connected with the ancient history and revolutions of the lake. York being the seat of government for the upper province, is a place of considerable importance in the eyes of its inhabitants; to a stranger, however, it presents little more than about 100 wooden houses, several of them conveniently, and even elegantly built, and I think one, or perhaps two, of brick. The public buildings were destroyed by the Americans; but as no ruins of them are visible, we must conclude, either, that the destruction exceeded the desolation of Jerusalem, or that the loss to the arts is not quite irreparable. I believe they did not leave one stone upon another, for they did not find one. Before the city, a long flat tongue of land runs into the lake, called Gibraltar Point, probably from being very *unlike* Gibraltar. York, wholly useless, either as a port or military outpost, would sink into a village and the seat of government transferred to Kingston but for the influence of those whose property in the place would be depreciated by the change."

Short-story writer John Howison (1797-1859) had just turned 21 when he was in Toronto the year after Francis Hall. He passed through town on his way from Quebec to St. Catharines, where he practised medicine for a couple of years. With this experience he returned to Scotland and there he published his impressions, first in instalments in *Blackwood's* magazine (one of the leading periodicals of Great Britain) and then in a book, *Sketches of Upper Canada* (1821). The book was hailed in the UK as the best account of life in the New World yet published, and its popularity (including translations in Europe) meant that if any overseas reader had an impression of Toronto it was most likely to have come from Howison's tome. And how did Toronto strike him?: "The town of York is situated on the shore of Lake Ontario and has a large bay in front of it, which affords good anchorage for small vessels. The land all around the harbour and behind the town is low, swampy, and apparently of inferior quality; and it could not be easily drained, as it lies almost on a level with the surface of the lake. The town, in which there are some good houses, contains about 3000 inhabitants. There is but little land cleared in its immediate vicinity, and this circumstance increases the natural unpleasantness of its situation. The trade of York is very trifling; and it owes its present population and magnitude entirely to its being the seat of government, for it is destitute of every natural advantage except that of a good harbour.

"York is nearly defenceless at present, and the character of the surrounding country precludes the possibility of its ever being made a place of strength. There is no eminence or commanding point of land suitable for the erection of a battery; and the fort, which was lately built, is so incapable, from its low situation, of effectually annoying an enemy, that a single frigate might lay the town in ruins without any difficulty. From this circumstance, it is evident that York is not at all calculated for the seat of government, which, in colonies particularly, should be either situated in the interior, or, if in an exposed situation, nearly impregnable.

"I believe it was once proposed by parliament that the seat of government should be removed to Kingston, which town, although not altogether unexceptionable, has, from its position and resources, many more claims to this distinction than York; but it seems that the government officers, residing in the latter place, estimated the depreciation which their property would suffer, and the loss which they themselves would necessarily incur, if this arrangement took place, at such an immense amount, that the project was abandoned. It was likewise urged as an objection, that were the seat of government removed to Kingston, the members of parliament for the western parts of the province would suffer much inconvenience, in being obliged to travel a distance of four or five hundred miles every time the legislature met . . . After strolling around York for an hour or two, I re-embarked on board the steamboat, in company with the greater number of my former fellow-passengers."

Captain Basil Hall (1788-1844) joined the British Navy when he was a boy and rose through the ranks with dispatch. Most of his sailing was for exploration or for scientific purposes, and following his voyages he published a bestselling account detailing the journeys. For 14 months in 1827-28 Hall (no relation to Lt. Francis Hall above) travelled throughout North America and that trip too resulted in a book the following year. Part of his tour included a brief visit to Toronto, officially known as York until 1834. In addition to his literary travel books, Capt. Hall published a book of poems, and in 1836 a novel—it was not long afterwards that mental illness overtook him and he died, aged 55, in a lunatic asylum. His description of the fledgling Toronto antedates Anna Jameson's by nearly a decade. Curiously, he missed encountering in Toronto his fellow Scot, novelist John Galt, by only a few days.

Because there was so little urban Toronto to describe, he spends most of his few paragraphs reserved for the city for the bay and Island : "Our dinner was laid under the fly of a tent, on the rich green-sward of a dressed piece of ground, sloping gently towards the lake. We sat on the eastern side of the house so that by five o'clock the shadow fell upon us. The deep sea-blue face of old Ontario was now quite smooth; for morning breeze had fallen, except where a straggling catspaws, as we call them, here and there, breathed on the face of the calm mirror, and straightway disappeared. The harbour, or, more properly speaking, the bay of York, formerly called Toronto—a name which it was a sin to change—is formed by a long spit, or low projecting point of wooded land, with a light-house at the end of it, round which one or two schooners

were slipping with the last faint puffs of the sea-breeze, just enough to fill their upper sails, but without rippling the water. The air had become deliciously cool, and more grateful than I can describe, after the sultry day to which we had been exposed. The wine was plunged into a large vessel filled with ice, close to the table; but the water was cooled in a goblet, or unbaked earthen pitcher, brought from Bengal . . . On the 19th of July [1827], instead of proceeding, as we had intended, straight along the great road to the eastward, we made a sharp turn to the left, and travelled for some thirty miles directly north towards Lake Simcoe, one of those numerous sheets of water with which Upper Canada is covered; and destined, no doubt, in after times, to afford the means of much valuable intercourse from place to place, when their banks are peopled and cultivated."

The great American novelist Henry James (*The Portrait of a Lady; Daisy Miller; The Turn of the Screw*) came to Toronto in 1871 and left a flattering account, not of the city (which did not register on his imagination), but of the lake that he saw from the deck of the steamboat that was going to carry him from Toronto to Niagara Falls: "[Lake Ontario] has the merit, from the shore, of producing a slight ambiguity of vision. It is the sea, and yet not just the sea. The huge expanse, the landless line of the horizon, suggest the ocean; while an indefinable shortness of pulse, a kind of fresh-water gentleness of tone, seem to contradict the idea. What meets the eye is on the scale of the ocean but you feel somehow that the lake is a thing of smaller spirit. Lake-navigation, therefore, seems to me not especially entertaining. The scene tends to offer, as one may say, a sort of marine-effect missed. It has the blankness and vacancy of the sea, without that vast essential swell which, amid the belting brine, so often saves the situation to the eye."

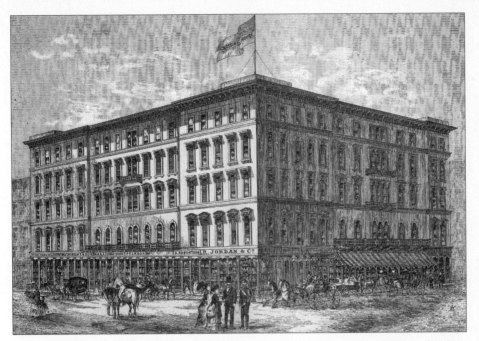

19th c. engraving of The Rossin House, formerly at the corner of King and York Streets, a hotel popular with literary visitors during the Victorian Age

Canadian Illustrated News, May 13, 1871

APPENDIX A:

York University

What is now the main campus of York University opened at this location in 1965, after operating for four years at Glendon College. The university was founded in 1959 to accommodate the expanding needs of the geographically expanding city. Its name, an unfortunate choice, was intended to reflect the legal name of Toronto for the first forty-one years of its existence under the British. However, given that the world is full of Yorks thanks to the energy of British explorers, and also given that there is a York University in England, one wishes more thought had been given to naming the institution after something more distinctively Canadian.

From its beginnings, York has been strong in its teaching of liberal arts and humanities, and as a result, a number of young or about-to-be creative writers were attracted to its newness, and its aura of taking chances—especially when York was compared with the UofT which appeared staid and hidebound, and not interested in Canadian letters to the same degree.

York does have a college system but none of them has developed the personality, religious affiliation, or prejudices long evident at the city's oldest university. The possible exceptions to that statement are Glendon College (with its French-language aspect), and Atkinson College (with its informal and cross-disciplinary approach to night school and extension teaching). Therefore, rather than cite authors by college affiliation, the following list gives those who attended classes and in almost all cases graduated from York, or pursued grad studies here:

Hrant Alianak	Katherine Govier	Bp Nichol
Barbara Betcherman	Barbara Gowdy	Niyi Osundare
Eliza Clark	Rolf Harvey	Nino Ricci
Bev Daurio	Lisa Herman	Peter Robinson
True Davidson	Frances Itani	Sarah Sheard
Christopher Dewdney	Wendy Lill	Jason Sherman
Brian Flack	Toby Maclennan	Ken Sherman
Eldon Garnet	Kim Maltman	Martin Waxman
Douglas Glover	Daniel David Moses	

Some creative writers of note have been on the fulltime faculty of York University at this campus. They include:

Clark Blaise	Eli Mandel	Susan Swan
Barry Callaghan	Edgar McInnis	Richard Teleky
Don Coles	Mavor Moore	Miriam Waddington
Frank Davey	Anthony Quogan	Jack Winter
Michael Gilbert	Burton Raffel	
Dave Godfrey	Chris Scott	
Douglas Lochhead	Peter Such	

York was one of the first universities in Canada to have a degree program in Creative Writing. While a number of prominent authors have taught part-time in that dept. for a year or two, it remains a modest influence on the literary life of Toronto.

APPENDIX B

Authors registered at UofT for Undergraduate
Studies (College affiliation unknown):

Peregrine Acland
Andrew Allan
Edward M. Ashworth
Barbara Betcherman
Gail Bowen
Afua Cooper
Bev Daurio
Frederick Davidson
Muriel Denison
Brian Doherty
Sharon Drache
Evelyn Durand
Thomas Rose Elliott
Charlotte Fielden
Joy Fielding
Robert Finch
Pearl Foley
David Fujino
Eldon Garnet
Phyllis Gotlieb
John Morgan Gray
John R. Gray
Terence Green
John Norman Harris
Isabelle Hughes
Grace Irwin
Percy Janes
Henry Kreisel
Robert H. Lindsay
Elsie Mack
Archibald MacMechan
Marjory MacMurchy
Laura McCully
Joseph E. McDougall

Irene B. McElheran
W.S. Milne
Robert Mirvish
Roy Mitchell
Mavor Moore
William H. Moore
Harvey O'Higgins
Lydia Palij
Quarrington, Paul
Nathan Ralph
Stanley Ryerson
Michele Sagara
B.K. Sandwell
John Steffler
Fred Swayze
Harry Symons
Frank Tate
Paul A.W. Wallace
W.S. Wallace
Bertram Warr
Eva-Lis Wuorio
Eve Zaremba

APPENDIX C

*Authors who were enrolled in Graduate Studies
at UofT:*

Lloyd Abbey
Margaret Avison
A.G. Bailey
Ronald Bates
Barry Callaghan
Matt Cohen
Jan Conn
Beaumont Cornell
Alexander W. Crawford
Rienzi Crusz
Merrill Denison
Cary Fagan
Lawrence Garber
Gary Geddes
Susan Glickman
Phyllis Gotlieb
William G. Hardy
Paul Hiebert
Greg Hollingshead
Hugh Hood
Grace Irwin
J. Robert Janes
Percy Janes
Robert Smith Jenkins
George Johnston
Ed Kleiman
Eric Koch
Myrna Kostash
Henry Kreisel
Wilmot Lane
Ross Keckie
Dennis Lee
Douglas Lochhead
Jay Macpherson
Eli Mandel

Robin Mathews
Laura McCully
Jack MacLeod
Kenneth McRobbie
Roberta Morris
Karen Mulhallen
C.J. Newman
E.J. Pratt
Anthony Quogan
James Reaney
Erika Ritter
Kenneth Sherman
Evan V. Shute
Lister Sinclair
Lionel Stevenson
Orlando J. Stevenson
Allan Stratton
Colleen Thibaudeau
Paul A.W. Wallace
W.S. Wallace
Norman Ward
James Wreford Watson
Sheila Watson
Wilfred Watson
Bruce Whiteman
Jack Winter
William H. Withrow
Eric Wright
Robert Zend

ACKNOWLEDGEMENTS

This book took much longer to research and to write than I ever expected. That it has appeared at all seems a small miracle. However, it was not divine intervention but rather the hard work of the patient staff at McArthur & Company that made it possible. I thank everyone at the house, especially the eponymous Kim, for their forbearance in the face of a manuscript delivered late—and rather larger than anyone expected. Mary Adachi took on the burden of editing the book while swamped with other commitments, yet performed the task with her legendary thoroughness. For this generous favour—and for her essential attention to deail—she has my sincerest appreciation. My agent, Jan Whitford of Westwood Creative, adroitly helped me pilot this project over the years past more than one whirlpool, and for her guidance I am most indebted. My staff at the Harbourfront Reading Series, led by Geoffrey Taylor, has shown remarkable patience before my distractions, and I offer them all gratitude for their stoicism.

The paths I took to discover where authors lived in Toronto were many. The first route was to ask living writers to cite their former addresses. Unless an author gave me permission to do otherwise, no current addresses are given for reasons of privacy. Because the human memory is fallible, many of the home addresses given by the respondents were checked against other sources.

For more than two years, I travelled to the fourth floor of the Toronto Reference Library to examine the city directories, telephone directories, and maps of Toronto in order to ascertain the thousands of addresses belonging to more than twelve hundred authors. This Library also has an excellent collection of well-indexed biographical scrapbooks which contain profiles of several authors from the first half of the 20th c. These periodical clippings often proved the only source for determining what X did for a living, or whether Y was still a resident of the city, or what was the married name of Z. The adjacent Baldwin Room contains the finest collection of historical Toronto material in the world, and it was here that I was able to inspect unique examples of old newspapers, magazines, and photos of the city. The Baldwin Room also holds histories of buildings, families, and societies and, painfully slow as these often were to devour (19th c. handwriting is not an easy read), they were frequently the only source for some of the information in this book. The archives of the Performing Arts Dept. of the same Library were a unique and often surprisingly rich source of information about matters relating to Toronto theatres and playwrights. David Kotin and his staff at the History Dept. of the Toronto Public Reference Library were models of patience and cooperation, handling my hundreds of queries (which ranged from the basic to the recondite) with equipoise and professionalism. His staff, especially Alan Walker, were inventive in finding solutions to challenges that seemed to have no answers, and I am most grateful for their assistance over the years. Lee Ramsay of the Theatre Dept. at the same library was always particularly willing to help with my questions about dramatists, theatres, and and theatrical productions. Apart from the high level of service, the Baldwin Room and History Dept. of the TPL feature a high level of cataloguing of their unique holdings. Without those detailed catalogues, which I used extensively, most of their holdings would be unknown and therefore unexploited by myself or any other historian of the city.

My other principal source of information was the Robarts Library of the University of Toronto. For nearly two decades, I examined Toronto newspapers and magazines on microfilm, looking for announcements—or coverage—of literary events. Of course, while looking for this coverage I would find reports of events or visits that were previously unknown to me. Such moments of eureka were common, even at the end of my years of looking, and suggest to me that this vein of literary ore is far from exhausted. The stacks of Robarts Library were my principal source for biographies of, and autobiographies by, authors cited in the *Guide*. Just a short walk from Robarts is the Archives Dept. of the UofT, sometimes the only source for an author's address if the author (frequently a woman) had been a student or professor. The nearby Thomas Fisher Rare Book Library has an inimitable collection of papers of Canadian authors, and examination of its holdings yielded many nuggets, some deliberately sought, others fortuitously found. Richard Landon and his staff at Thomas Fisher Rare Book Library were also models of cooperation, always patient with my queries and willing to suggest solutions to questions or research problems. Harold Averil of the UofT Archives was an endless font of knowledge who on many occasions always believed—thankfully—there must be some way to find information about the university that had otherwise eluded me and others. He also introduced me to the unique resources of the Gay and Lesbian Archives.

Leon Warmski and his staff at the Archives of Ontario helped me to find otherwise inaccessible information about companies and organizations These archives were also my main source for census data.

Some of Canada's finest antiquarian book dealers are based in Toronto and a few of them were consistently helpful in working with me to locate authors or bibliographic info about those authors. Their catalogues, too, proved to be an excellent source of bio- and biblio-graphic information. I especially want to thank Hugh Anson-Cartwright, Nick Brumbolis, Janet Inksetter, David Mason, and Steven Temple.

Over the past two decades and more I have corresponded with, or had direct assistance from many people regarding authors in Toronto. Sincerest thanks to the following scholars, librarians, authors, researchers, and history-lovers for their help in this regard:

Ken Adachi, John C. Adams, Keith Aldritt, Helen Anderson, Prof. Arnold Armin, H.E. Ashley, John Atteberry, John Ayre, Judy Baeckman, Nelson Ball, Paul Banfield, Christopher Barnes, Ana Bayefsky, Isabel Bayley, Mary Anne Beamish, Knut S. Beck, Murray Beck, Mary P. Bentley, Henk Bernlef, Lita-Rose Betcherman, Michael Betcherman, Alan Bishop, Robert Bjork, Gertrude Boeschenstein-Knighton, Patricia Boland, Laura Boone, John Boutilier, Christine Boyanoski, Brian Boyd, Janice Braun, George Brendak, Patrick Brode, Evan Brooker, Harry Bruce, Phyllis Bruce, Dennis Brutus, Ronald Bryden, Phil Bunker, Helen Burkes, Nancy Butler, Robert Calder, Barry Callaghan, Cameron Campbell, Mary Cannings, Louise carpentier, Alessandro Carrera, Glen Cavaliero, Diana Chardin, D.A. Christopher, Linda Cobon, Marie Coetzee, John Robert Colombo, Judith Colwell, Ivan A. Conger, J. Conway, Sarah Cooper, Rosemary Corbett, Michael Coren, Clare Coulter, Robert Crew, Philip Cronenwett, Bernard Crystal, Ron Csillig, Sarah Culpepper, Anne M. Cuningham, Glen W. Curnoe, Eleanor Darke, Brenda Davies, Jo Ellen McKillop Dickie, Sandra Djwa, Gail Donald, Jeffrey Donaldson, James Doyle, Douglas Dunn, Laura A. Endicott, Dorothy Farmiloe, Douglas Fetherling, George Wallis Field, Barbara Filipac, Mark Finkelstein, Bejamin Franklin Fisher IV, Shawna Fleming, Cindy Forbes, Marian Fowler, C.J. Fox, Robert L. Fraser, Jane French, Robert Fulford, Albert Fulton, Ernst Gallati, David Gardner, Pat Garrow, Carole Gerson, Sir Martin Gilbert, Mollie Gillen, Doris Giller, Ted Goossen, Judith Skleton Grant, Richard Graves, Roger Greenwald,

Laura Groening, Chris Gudgeon, Betty Gustafson, Sheila Hailey, Brian Hall, Geoffrey Handley-Taylor, Simon Harris, Rupert Hart-Davies, Cathy Henderson, George Henderson, Gunter Hess, Linda Hoad, Cameron Hollyer, John Honderich, William Howarth, Sara Hudson, Susan Hummer, Molly Hutton, Janet Irving, Vivienne James, Denis Johnston, Donald Jones, Leonie Jones, Austen Kark, John Kelly, Catherine Kerrigan, David B. Kesterson, J.F. Kidd, Kathleen Stewart Kidd, Kathleen E. Kier, David H. Kirk, Bernard R. Kogan, Goerge J. Kovtun, Rev. Richard Knight, Maddellena Kuitunen, Arlene Lampert, Patrice Landry, Peter Larisey, Diana Lary, Maurice Lebel, Hermione Lee, Mark Le Fanu, John Lennox, Stephen Lewis, Susan Lewthwaite, Frank Ligtvoet, Charles Lock, Wailan Low, Townsend Ludington, Sylvia Lustgarten, John Lutman, Sverre Lyngstad, Cheryl MacDonald, Paul R. Magocsi, Ann Mandel, Alberto Manguel, Philip Marchand, Lois Lyon Mattox, Francis O. Mattson, Margaret McBurney, Bennett McCardle, Thomas McCarthy, Janet McDonough, John Metcalf, Bruce Meyer, E.H. Mikhail, Keith, M.O. Miller, Michael Millgate, John C. Moran, Janet Morgan, A.F. Moritz, Sheridan Morley, Ellen Morrison, Martin Moskovits, Barbara Myrvold, Vera Nabokov, Harald Naess, Moses Nagy, Mary Anne Neville, William H. New, Eleanor Nichol, Mary-Anne Nicholls, Nigel Nicholson, Sonja Noble, Kelly Nolin, Hugh Noyes, Richard W. Oram, Lydia Palij, John Pearce, Pat Perelli, Catherine Peters, Chris Petter, Cahtherine Phillips, Marilyn Pilling, Henry Pilon, David G. Pitt, Richard Plant, Doina Popescu, Donald M. Powell, Michael Power, Gerald Pratley, Viola Pratt, Judith Priestman, Susan Rainville, Benedict Read, Chris Redmond, Dennis Reid, Kati Rekai, Beth Rodger, Janice Rosen, Val Ross, Phyllis A. Roth, Toby Gordon Ryan, Peter Salus, Rick Salutin, Peter Sanger, Robert J. Sawyer, Fred H.W. Seliger, Margaret Shannon, Ellen Shea, S.M. Simpson, Robin Skelton, W.J. Slater, Beverley Slopen, Frank L. Smith, Colin Smythe, Helen Southwick, Carl Spadoni, Stephen Speisman, Robert Stacey, David Stafford, David Staines, Apollonia Steele, Helga Stephenson, Ricardo Sternberg, Audrey Sutherland, Fraser Sutherland, Thomas H.B. Symons, Aivars Tannis, Beverly Tansey, Peter Taylor, Brendan Teeling, Thomas Tenney, Clara Thomas, Claire Thompson, Ann Thwaite, Paul Tiessen, Amber Timmons, Vincent Tovell, George Tremlett, Mary Jane Trimble, Alan Twigg, Rosemary Ullyot, Francesca Valente, Amanda Valpy, George A. Vanderburgh, Arved Viirlaid, Tom Vincent, Susan Walker, Ethel Warren, George R. Warren, Jacqueline Wassermann, Margaret G. Watermen, Elizabeth Waterston, Robin Wear, Crocker Wight, Alan Wilkinson, Carol Wilson, Pat Wilson, Ruth Wilson, Theresa Winkler, Ruth Wisse, Bill Wood, James Woodress, Hilda Woolnough, Beatriz Zeller, Janine Zend, Moses Znaimer.

Special thanks to Peter LaRocca, Dennis Lee, Branko Gorjup and Francesca Valente for their unique contributions. Mike Devries gets a big thanks as well for his solution to my database challenge.

Small grants from the Ontario Heritage Foundation and the Ontario Arts Council more than a decade ago helped me to continue my research at a crucial time.

All errors in this book are my responsibility. Persons who can correct errors with supporting documentation are urged to contact me via the publisher. Every effort has been made to locate the holders of copyrighted material. Persons with further information are urged to contact me via the publisher.

PHOTO ACKNOWLEDGEMENTS

Photographs of authors in Toronto are not common. Few living authors have snapshots of themselves at their homes, and when they do, the pictures are often out of focus, or undatable, or not identifiably in Toronto. Photos of resident (or visiting) authors in Toronto from eras earlier than our own are even scarcer. In choosing photos, I have preferred the picture showing an author in Toronto—no matter how poor the original, often a newspaper reproduction—rather than a better-quality glossy taken elsewhere in the world. It is worth remembering that these poor quality (by our standards) newspaper reproductions were frequently the only means by which Torontonians of the day could put a face to an author's name. My thanks to the following for their courtesy in providing illustrations for this book:

30 National Library of Canada/neg. no. C54336
31 private collection
34 Thomas Fisher Rare Book Library
35 private collection
40 private collection
45 Toronto Public Library
46 National Archices of Canada/neg. no C6720
53 private collection
57 from Seton, *Trail of an Artist-Naturalist* (New York, 1940)
61 New York Historical Society
64 Toronto Public Library
65 Toronto Public Library
74 Toronto Public Library
76 Toronto Public Library
77 Joyce Marshall
82 Toronto Public Library
83 Toronto Public Library
88 Toronto Public Library
91 Toronto Public Library
99 Toronto Public Library
100 Thomas Fisher Rare Book Library/ Deacon Papers
102 Josef Skvorecky
105 Toronto Public Library
110 University of Witwatersrand Archives
113 private collection
116 City of Toronto Archives
118 private collection
117 Toronto Public Library/Theatre Dept.
120 Toronto Public Library
121 Toronto Public Library
125 Toronto Public Library
131 Toronto Public Library
135 Toronto Public Library
136 Charlotte Engel
138 private collection
139 private collection
143 Howard Engel
145 National Archives of Canada/neg. no. C7043
147 Toronto Public Library
151 Toronto Public Library
154 Academy of Motion Picture Arts and Sciences
156 McCrae House
160 Toronto Public Library
161 private collection
165 private collection
168 private collection
169 Andreas Schroeder
170 Toronto Star Syndicate
172 James Bacque
177 University of Toronto Archives/A74-0003/28
185 Audrey Sutherland
193 private collection
196 private collection
198 University of Toronto Archives/*Torontoensis* 1944
203 private collection
207 Canadian War Museum/70-220
213 Toronto Public Library
216 University of Toronto Archives
220 private collection
221 Brenda Davies
231 York University Archives & Special Collections
238 James Reaney
242 private collection
244 Toronto Public Library
245 private collection
248 private collection
254 private collection
259 Rick Salutin

BIBLIOGRAPHY

1. Toronto Newspapers and Magazines:

Saturday Night,
Start Weekly
The Empire
The Examiner
The Globe
The Globe and Mail
The Irish Canadian
The Mail
The Mail and Empire
The News
The Star
The Telegram
The World
Varsity

2. Books Cited in Endnotes:

Allan, Andrew, *A Self-portrait* (Toronto: 1974)

Ayre, John, *Northrop Frye* (Toronto: 1989)

Baker, Ida Fitch, *Selected Poems* (Toronto: 1951)

Ballstadt, Carl, Elizabeth Hopkins, and Michael Peterman, eds., *Letters of Love and Duty: The Correspondence of Susanna and John Moodie* (Toronto: 1993)

Baraness, Marc and Larry Richards, *Toronto Places* (Toronto: 1987)

Barr, Robert: *The Measure of the Rule* (Toronto: 1973)

Baxter, Beverley, *Strange Street* (New York: 1935)

Belford, Barbara, *Bram Stoker* (New York: 1996)

Benson, Eugene and L.W. Conolly, *Encyclopedia of Post-Colonial Literatures in English* (London: 1994)

Benson, Eugene and L.W. Conolly, *Oxford Companion to Canadian Theatre* (Toronto: 1989)

Benson, Eugene and William Toye, *Oxford Companion to Canadian Literature* (Toronto: 1997)

Berton, Pierre, *Starting Out* (Toronto: 1987)

Bissell, Claude, *University College: A Portrait 1853-1953* (Toronto: 1953)

Blackwood, Algernon, *Episodes Before Thirty* (London: 1923)

Blain, Virginia et alia, eds., *The Feminist Companion to Literature in English* (New Haven: 1990)

Brady, James J., *Life of Denman Thompson* (New York: 1888)

Bratton, Daniel, *Thirty-two Short Views of Mazo de la Roche* (Toronto: 1996)

Brome, Vincent, *Ernest Jones: Freud's Alter Ego* (London: 1982)

Brown, E.K., *On Canadian Poetry* (Toronto: 1944)

Bruccoli, Matthew J., *Kenneth Millar/Ross Macdonald: A Checklist* (Detroit: 1971)

Byers, Mary, *Havergal: Celebrating a Century* (Toronto: 1994)

Callaghan, Barry, *Barrelhouse Kings: A Memoir* (Toronto: 1998)

Cameron, Elspeth, *Earle Birney: A Life* (Toronto: 1994)

Carroll, Jock, *The Life and Times of Greg Clark* (Toronto: 1981)

Charlesworth, Hector, *Candid Chronicles* (Toronto: 1925)

Christie, Agatha, *An Autobiography* (London: 1997)

Clever, Glen, *The E.J. Pratt Symposium* (Ottawa: 1977)

Colombo, John Robert, *Mysterious Canada* (Toronto: 1988)

Connor, Carl: *Archibald Lampman* (Toronto: 1929)

Cooke, Nathalie, *Margaret Atwood: A Biography* (Toronto: 1998)

Darke, Eleanor, *Call Me True* (Toronto: 1997)

Davidson, Cathy and Linda Wagner-Martin, *The Oxford Companion to Women's Writing in the United States* (New York: 1995)

de la Roche, Mazo, *Ringing The Changes* (Toronto: 1957)

Dendy, William, *Lost Toronto* (Toronto: 1993)

Dendy, William and William Kilbourn, *Toronto Observed* (Toronto: 1986)

Dickens, Charles, *American Notes* (London: 1842)

Dickson, Lovat, *The Ante-Room* (Toronto: 1959)

Disraeli, Benjamin, *Lothair* (London: 1975)

Donegan, Rosemary, *Spadina Avenue* (Vancouver: 1985)

Doran, George, *Chronicles of Barabbas* (New York: 1952)

Easton, Robert, *Max Brand* (Norman, Oklahoma: 1970)

Edgar, Pelham, *Across My Path* (Toronto: 1952)

Eggleston, Wilfred, *Literary Friends* (Ottawa: 1980)

Fairley, Barker, *Barker Fairley Portraits* (Toronto: 1981)

Farmiloe, Dorothy, *Isabella Valency Crawford* (Ottawa: 1983)

Fetherling, Douglas, *The Broadview Book of Canadian Anecdotes* (Peterborough, Ont.: 1988)

Fetherling, Douglas, *Travels By Night* (Toronto: 1994)

Fetherling, Douglas, *Way Down Deep in the Belly of the Beast* (Toronto: 1996)

Galt, John, *Autobiography* (London: 1833)

Galt, John, *Bogle Corbet* (Toronto: 1977)

Garner, Hugh, *One Damn Thing After Another* (Toronto: 1973)

Gatenby, Greg, *The Very Richness of That Past* (Toronto: 1995)

Gatenby, Greg, *The Wild Is Always There* (Toronto: 1993)

Gingell, Susan, *E.J. Pratt on his Life and Poetry* (Toronto: 1983)

Givner, Joan, *Mazo de la Roche: The Hidden Life* (Toronto: 1989)

Gleave, T.B., *Beyond Our Walls* (Toronto: 1946)

Gordon, Charles, *Postscript to Adventure* (Toronto: 1975)

Gordon, W. Terrence, *Marshall McLuhan* (Toronto: 1997)

Grahame. Gordon, *Short Days Ago* (Toronto: 1972)

Gray, John Morgan, *Fun Tomorrow* (Toronto: 1978)

Griffith, Richard, *The World of Robert Flaherty* (New York: 1953)

Groening, Laura Smyth, *E.K. Brown, A Study in Conflict* (Toronto: 1993)

Gudgeon, Chris, *Out of This World* (Vancouer: 1996)

Gzowski, Peter, *The Private Voice* (Toronto: 1988)

Hale, Katherine, *Isabella Valency Crawford* (Toronto: 1923)

Hall, Capt. Basil, *Travels in North America* (Edinburgh, 1829)

Hall, Lt. Francis, *Travels in Canada and the United States* (Boston: 1818)

Hambleton, Ronald, *How I Earned $250,000 as a Freelance Writer...Even If It Did Take 30 Years!* (Toronto: 1977)

Hambleton, Ronald, *Mazo de la Roche of Jalna* (New York: 1966)

Harris, Robin, *English Studies at Toronto* (Toronto: 1988)

Harte, G.B., ed., *The Letters of Bret Harte* (London: 1926)

Heriot, George, *Travels Through The Canadas* (Edmonton: 1971)

House, Madeline, et alia, Eds., *The Letters of Charles Dickens* (Oxford: 1974)

Howells, Mildred, *Life in Letters of William Dean Howells* (Garden City, NY: 1928)

Howison, John, *Sketches of Upper Canada* (London: 1821)

Irwin, Grace, *Three Lives in Mine* (Toronto: 1986)

James, Henry, *Portraits of Places* (London: 1883)

Johnston, Denis, *Up The Mainstream* (Toronto: 1991)

Jones, Alun, *The Life and Opinions of T. E. Hulme* (Boston: 1960)

Keller, Betty, *Black Wolf: The Life of Ernest Thompson Seton* (Vancouver: 1984)

Keller, Betty, *Pauline: A Biography of Pauline Johnson* (Vancouver: 1981)

Kingston, W.H.G., *Rob Nixon, The Old White Trapper* (Edmonton: 1983)

Kingston, W.H.G., *Western Wanderings* (London: 1856)

Kirkconnell, Watson, *A Slice of Life* (Toronto: 1967)

Klinck, Carl F., ed., *Literary History of Canada* (Toronto: 1965)

Kunitz, Stanley and Howard Haycraft, *Twentieth Century Authors* (New York: 1961)

Larisey, Peter, *Light for a Cold Land* (Toronto: 1993)

Laurence, Margaret, *Dance on the Earth: A Memoir* (Toronto: 1998)

Layton, Irving, *Wild Goodberries* (Toronto: 1989)

Lennox, John and M. Lacombe, eds., *Dear Bill: The Correspondence of William Arthur Deacon* (Toronto: 1988)

Lennox, John and Ruth Panofsky, eds., *Selected Letters of Margaret Laurence and Adele Wiseman* (Toronto: 1997)

Livesay, Dorothy, *Journey With My Selves* (Vancouver: 1991)

Livesay, Dorothy, *Right Hand, Left Hand* (Erin, Ont.: 1977)

Longfellow, Henry Wadsworth, *Journals and Letters* (Boston: 1886)

Lorne, Marquis of, *A Trip to the Tropics and Home Through North America* (London: 1867)

Lucid, Robert, ed., *Journal of Richard Henry Dana* (Cambridge, Mass.: 1968)

Macdonald, Ross, *Archer in Hollywood* (New York: 1967)

Macdonald, Ross, *Self-Portrait* (Santa Barbara: 1981)

MacKenzie, David, *Arthur Irwin* (Toronto: 1993)

Marchand, Philip, *Marshall McLuhan* (Toronto: 1989)

Marryat, Capt., *A Diary in America* (New York: 1962)

Marryat, Florence, *Life and Letters of Capt. Marryat* (London: 1872)

Martyn, Lucy Booth, *Toronto* (Toronto: 1984)

McKellar, Duncan, *Poems* (Toronto: 1922)

Middleton, Jesse Edgar, *Municipality of Toronto* (Toronto: 1923)

Moore, Mavor, *Reinventing Myself* (Toronto: 1994)

Morgan, Henry, *Canadian Men and Women of the Time* (Toronto: 1898)

Morgan, Henry, *Canadian Men and Women of the Time* (Toronto: 1912)

Morris, Clara, *Life on the Stage* (New York: 1901)

O'Brien, Kevin, *Oscar Wilde in Canada* (Toronto: 1982)

Paskauskas, R. Andrew, *The Complete Correspondence of Sigmund Fried and Ernest Jones 1908-1939* (Cambridge, Mass.: 1993)

Pitt, David, *E.J. Pratt, The Master Years* (Toronto: 1987)

Pitt, David, *E.J. Pratt: The Truant Years* (Toronto: 1984)

Purdy, Al, *Reaching for the Beaufort Sea* (Maderira Park, B.C.: 1993)

Redmond, Christopher, *Welcome to America, Mr. Sherlock Holmes* (Toronto: 1987)

Rex, Kay, *No Daughter of Mine: The Women and History of of the Canadian Women's Press Club* (Toronto: 1995)

Rhodenizer, Vernon, *Canadian Literature in English* (Montreal: 1965)

Riedel, Walter, ed., *The Old World and the New* (Toronto: 1984)

Robertson, John Ross, *Landmarks of Toronto: A Collection of Historical Sketches of the Old Town of York from 1792 until 1833, and of Toronto from 1834 to 1914* (Toronto: 1894-1914)

Rose, W.K., ed., *Letters of Wyndham Lewis* (London: 1962)

Rubio, Mary and Elizabeth Waterson, *Writing A Life: L.M. Montgomery* (Toronto: 1995)

Saddlemyer, Ann, ed., *Early Stages: Theatre in Ontario 1800-1914* (Toronto: 1990)

Salinger, Pierre, *P.S.: A Memoir* (New York: 1995)

Sanders, Byrne Hope, *Emily Murphy* (Toronto: 1945)

Sassoon, Siegfried, *Siegfried's Journey 1916-1920* (London: 1945)

Seton, Ernest Thompson, *Trail of an Artist-Naturalist* (New York: 1940)

Singer, Isaac Bashevis, *Lost in America* (New York: 1981)

Skelton-Grant, Judith, *Robertson Davies: Man of Myth* (Toronto: 1994)

Starrett, Vincent, *Born in a Bookshop* (Norman, Oklahoma: 1965)

Story, Norah, *Oxford Companion to Canadian History and Literature* (Toronto: 1967)

Stuewe, Paul, *The Storms Below* (Toronto: 1988)

Sullivan, Rosemary, *Shadow Maker* (Toronto: 1995)

Sullivan, Rosemary, *The Red Shoes* (Toronto: 1998)

Sutherland, Fraser, *The Monthly Epic* (Toronto: 1989)

Thomas, Clara and John Lennox, *William Arthur Deacon* (Toronto: 1982)

Thomas, Clara, *Canadian Novelists: 1920–1945* (Toronto: 1946)

Thompson, Samuel, *Reminiscences of a Canadian Pioneer* (Toronto: 1968)

Thomson, E.W., *Old Man Savarin and Other Stroies* (Toronto: 1974)

Tiessen, Paul, ed., *Letters of Malcolm Lowry and gerald Noxon 1940–1952* (Vancouver: 1988)

Tippett, Maria, *Emily Carr: A Biography* (Toronto: 1979)

Trevelyan, Janet, *The Life of Mrs. Humphry Ward* (London: 1923)

Trollope, Anthony, *North America* (New York: 1862)

Twigg, Alan, *Hubert Evans* (Maderira Park, B.C.: 1985)

van Paassen, Pierre, *To Number Our Days* (New York: 1964)

Wachtel, Eleanor, *Writers & Company* (Toronto: 1993)

Waddington, Miriam, *Apartment Seven* (Toronto: 1989)

Walker, Frank, *Sketches of Old Toronto* (Toronto: 1965)

Walker, Hugh, *The O'Keefe Centre* (Toronto: 1991)

Wallace, Elisabeth, *Goldwin Smith: Victorian Liberal* (Toronto: 1957)

Wallace, W. Stewart, *A History of the University of Toronto 1827–1927* (Toronto: 1927)

Wallace, W. Stewart, *Macmillan Dictionary of Canadian Biography* (Toronto: 1978)

Wilkinson, Anne, *Lions in the Way* (Toronto: 1956)

Wilkinson, Anne, *The Tightrope Walker* (Toronto: 1992)

Willan, Brian, *Sol Plaatje* (London: 1984)

Woodress, James, *Willa Cather* (Lincoln, Nebraska: 1987)

Young, Scott, *A Writer's Life* (Toronto: 1994)

ENDNOTES

Author note: quotations by authors without attribution are taken from personal letters to Greg Gatenby by those same authors, in response to a standard query letter as research for this book.

22 "all the leading" *Examiner*, May 11, 1842, p.3.

22 "Beverley House faced" Martyn, *Toronto*, p.46

22 "the wild and rabid" House, *The Letters of Charles Dickens*, v.3, p.236

23 "The country round" Dickens, *American Notes*, 202-3.

24 "I am not in" Florence Marryat, *Life and Letters of Capt. Marryat*, pp.30-31.

24 "Toronto, which is" Frederick Marryat, *A Diary in America*, pp.116-7.

25 "The Canadian Literature" "The Fly Leaf" *G&M*, February 3, 1940, p.8.

26 "The Punch in Canada" Walker, *Sketches of Old Toronto*, pp.265-295.

27 "We had to flit" Morris, *Life on the Stage*, p.3.

27 "Thereafter, season" *Dictionary of American Biography*, v.7, p.204.

27 "The wet eyes" quoted in *Dictionary of American Biography*, ibid.

30 "one of the largest" "The Political Morality" *Globe*, September 18, 1858, p.2

30 "The Mechanics' Institute" Dendy, *Lost Toronto*, p.137.

31 "with a coved" ibid, p.137.

31 "Mr. McGee's lecture" "Mr. McGee's Lecture" *Globe*, February 5, 1862, p.2.

33 "When asked to name" Kingston, *Rob Nixon, The Old White Trapper*, pp.xi-xii.

33 "Toronto faces south-east" Kingston, *Western Wanderings*, v.1, pp.114-127.

35 "I do not wish" ibid, v.2, pp.30-53.

37 "[my husband]" Christie, *An Autobiography*, pp.303-4.

38 "Not only is" Quoted in theBartlett entry of the *National Reference Book* (Montreal, n.d.) p.45.

38 "Amongst business men" "The Hub Wine Company" *World*, November 26, 1891, p.2.

41 "In a small" Galt, *Autobiography*, pp.50-51.

41 "The Steamboat Hotel" Galt, *Bogle Corbet*, pp.53-54.

41 "We had given" Walker, *The O'Keefe Centre: Thirty Years of Theatre History*, p.1.

41 "We Now Rate" *Star*, April 1, 1961, p.21.

41 "In our enjoyment" "Road Town Status" *G&M*, November 26, 1960, p.11.

42 "The poetry reading" Robert Fulford, "Books" *Star*, May 5, 1961, p.36.

43 "They failed, but" "Probe Is Requested" *Telegram*, May 18, 1943, p.13.

43 "In the spring of 1916" van Paassen, *To Number Our Days*, pp.121-3.

44 "A man of more" "Ian Maclaren Tonight" *World*, November 9, 1896, p.2.

45 "much of what was" "Life Reflected" *M&E*, March 14, 1921, p.4.

46 "She was no sooner unpacked" Farmiloe, *Isabella Valancy Crawford*, p.50.

48 "This is why" Dendy and Kilbourn, *Toronto Observed*, p.140.

49 "a round of characters" *National Cyclopedia of American Biography*, p.45.

49 "As might be expected" James J. Brady, *Life of Denman Thompson* (New York: 1888) pp.32-3.

51 "the preeminent intellectual" *The Oxford Companion to Women's Writing in the United States*, p.348.

54 "His pen name" Louis MacKendrick, Intro. To Robert Barr, *The Measure of the Rule* (Toronto:1973) p.viii.

54 "In his last illness" Duncan Mckellar, *Poems* (Toronto:1922) p.9.

54 "During the week or so" Garner, pp.49-50.

55 "In 1872 the book committee" *DCB*, v.13, p.1103.

56 "took a taxi downtown" Garner, pp.48-9.

57 "It was on one of these" ibid, pp.57-8.

57 "One day, after I had been" Seton, pp.152-3.

62 "The advent of Mark Twain" *Mail*, December 9, 1884.

62 "Well, I'd kept that" *Globe*, December 9, 1884.

62 "the audience these two drew" *World*, December 9, 1884.

63 "the practical application" *Mail*, May 25, 1882, p.5.

63 "It is probable that" *Mail*, May 26, 1882, p.8.

64 "In this condensed report" *News*, May 26, 1882, p.1.

64 "I suppose that the poet" *News*, May 29, 1882, p.4.

64 "The bust was exhibited" Kevin O'Brien, *Oscar Wilde In Canada* (Toronto: 1982) p.110. O'Brien's is the most exhaustive treatment to date of Wilde's Toronto visit.

66 "probably based his story" Christopher Redmond, *Welcome To America, Mr. Sherlock Holmes* (Toronto: 1987) p.137.

66 "I fancy you will find" Howells, p.200-201.

67 "Matthew Arnold, for example" *DCB*, p.989.

67 "His letters, stamps" *DCB*, p.990.

68 "One Saturday morning" Doran, *Chronicles of Barabbas* (New York: 1952), pp.5-13.

72 "Most of Cabbagetown" Garner, pp.4-5.

74 "deserves a much better" "The Fly Leaf" *G&M*, May 28, 1949, p.10.

75 "In 1940" Waddington, *Apartment Seven*, p.9.

75 "During my field work" ibid, pp.19-20.

78 "Mrs. Harrison is" "Literary Notes" *Mail*, November 20, 1891, p.5.

80 "In case anyone" *Star*, October 25, 1930, p.1.

80 "In the foyer" Fetherling, *Travels By Night*, p..208-9.

81 "Elizabeth Woods" ibid, pp.205-6.

83 "In his time Dent" *DCB*, v.11, p.249.

83 "While reviewing" *Canadian Bookman*, April 1939, p.16.

84 "She was admitted" Sophia Sperdakos, "For the Joy of Working" *Ontario History*, December 1992, p.308. This is, by far, the fullest treatment of Laura McCully's life and work in print.

85 "The famous 'iron curtain'" "Not Iron" *Star*, June 13, 1946, p.1

85 "By naming the" Byers, *Havergal: Celebrating A Century*, p.10.

88 "E.E. Sheppard" Fetherling, *Way Down Deep In The Belly of the Beast*, p.83.

89 "I don't think it occurred" Berton, *Starting Out*, pp.54-69.

91 "To the amazement" *Christian Science Journal*, June 1989, pp.20-21.

91 "in the arrangement" ibid.

92 "They had tea" Tippett, *Emily Carr: A Biography*, pp.145-6.

93 "introduced her to artists" *DLB*, v.68, p.56.

93 "Two days later" ibid, pp.150-1.

95 "to recognize and foster" Shesko, intro. to Thomson, *Old Man Savarin and Other Stories*, p.xii.

97 "Critic Mary Lu MacDonald" *DLB*, v.99, p.97.

98 "After the winter" Rose, ed., *The Letters of Wyndham Lewis*, p.282.

98 "It is an apartment hotel" ibid, p.281.

98 "The city is said" ibid, p.283.

98 "A prominent bookseller" ibid, pp.293-4.

99 "Novelist-Artist Loses" "60 Driven to Icy Streets" *Star*, February 15, 1943, p.1.

99 "On January 31, 1885" Seton, p.279.

101 "Toronto has failed" *Canadian Magazine*, October 1927, p.39.

103 "In his years in the west" Thomas and Lennox, *William Arthur Deacon*, p.26 and p.31.

107 "Take Don Bailey." "Lonely living" *G&M*, April 16, 1970, p.43.

108 "I got a small room" Don Bailey, "Down and Out in Toronto" *Canadian Forum*, April/May 1970, p.65.

108 "a Briton to his" Morgan, *Canadian Men and Women of the Time* (1912).

110 "the first South African" Benson, *Encyclopedia of Post-Colonial Literatures in English*, p.1223.

110 "The best index" "Welcome to Plaatje" *Negro World*, February 5, 1922.

115 "although neither gift" Willan, *Sol Plaatje*, pp.259-264.

115 "It was at this time" Katherine Hale, *Isabella Valancy Crawford* (Toronto:1923) p.10.

115 "at the time of his death" *Dictionary of American Biography*, v.6, p.569

116 "Other visitors from the" "The Empire's Big Four" *News*, October 19, 1907, p.25

116 "Never had the Canadian Club" "Poet of Empire" *World*, October 19, 1907, p.1.

117 "'was well advanced when" "Proclaimed Kipling" *Star*, October 19, 1907, p.2.

117 "There is an eager, biting" *News*, October 19, 1907, p.6

119 "No young Boswells?" "An Uncomplicated Man" *Telegram*, October 18, 1958, p.32.

119 "Stoker was the first" Barbara Belford, *Bram Stoker* (New York: 1996) p.100.

120 "even players so high" Robertson Davies, "The Nineteenth Century Repertoire" in *Early Stages* (Toronto: 1990) p.93.

121 "that genius of melodrama" ibid, pp.101-2.

121 "Why do you allow" "Canada Should", *News*, April 13, 1905, p.9

121 "Emerson lectured in Toronto" *The Reasoner*, April 10, 1859, p.117. See also "Mr. Emerson's Lecture", *Globe*, December 23, 1858, p.2.

122 "I served my first literary" Algernon Blackwood, *Episodes Before Thirty* (London: 1923) pp.6-9.

123 "The sail across Lake Ontario" Robt. Lucid, Ed., *The Journal of Richard Henry Dana* (Cambridge, Mass: 1968) pp. 314-5.

124 "Josh Whitcomb, the plain" *National Cyclopedia of American Biography*, p.46

124 "It was a great success" "With Canadian Authors", *World*, January 18, 1892, p.3

126 "June 9th: Niagara" Henry W. Longfellow, *Journals and Letters* (Boston: 1886) p.12.

128 "In the publishing house" Charles Gordon, *Postscript to Adventure* (Toronto: 1975) pp.149-150.

129 "Tall, straight as a ramrod" "Publisher Introduced" *G&M*, January 9, 1956, p.4.

131 "The weather at Toronto was" Lorne, Marquis of, *A Trip To The Tropics And Home Through North America* (London: 1867) pp.344-5.

131 "Had Francis Bond Head" *DCB*, v.10, p.345

133 "is one of the first" Peter Hinchcliffe, "Isabella V. Crawford" in *Profiles in Canada Literature*, v.5 (Toronto, 1986) p.57.

133 "Crawford seems to have" ibid, p.58.

133 "Isabella had no income" Dorothy Farmiloe, *Isabella Valancy Crawford* (Ottawa: 1983) p.51.

133 "From the back of" ibid, p.63.

130 "I began to write plays" quoted in *The Canadian Magazine*, October 1927, p.17.

135 "It is to be hoped" ibid, p.17.

135 "Among the older playwrights" ibid, p.17.

136 "an astounding majority" *Dictionary of Hamilton Biography*, v.3, p.10

136 "If you want to be constructive" quoted in *DHB*, v.3, p.10

140 "People's Poet Award" the fullest treatment to date of the People's Poet Award is found in Chris Gudgeon, *Out Of This World* (Vancouver, Arsenal Pulp Press, 1996) pp 136-143.

141 "I painted my face" letter to GG, Feb 3, 1989. See also Jack Batten, "The bizarre Boogie Dick rocks with super-straight working class" *G&M*, May 23, 1970.

141 "one of the finest" Rosemary Donegan, *Spadina Avenue* (Vancouver, D&M, 1985) p.110.

141 "His name may not mean" *Star*, Nov. 4, 1933, p.1

145 "he asked me for a copy" Ballstadt, *Letters of Love and Duty: The Correspondence of Susanna and John Moodie*, p.292.

145 "generally acknowledged" *DCB*, v.13, p.248.

145 "It is delightful" "Finds Palestine" *Star Weekly*, December 1, 1934, p.1.

147 "In the field of periodical" quoted in Sutherland, *The Monthly Epic*, p.32

148 "From the commercial" Vernon Bogdanor, intro. to Disraeli, *Lothair*, p.ix.

148 "When I returned" Fetherling, *Travels By Night*, pp.247-8.

150 "...all this while the world" Baxter, *Strange Street*, pp.34-6.

152 "each volume appeared" Thompson, *Reminiscences of a Canadian Pioneer*, p.155.

152 "Literary historian Mary Lu MacDonald" Mary Lu MacDonald, "Three Early Canadian Poets" *Canadian Poetry*, No.17 (Fall/Winter 1985) p.79.

154 "in a shed" "Will Spend Summer" *Star*, May 23, 1925, p.6.

155 "It was serviced by" Keller, *Black Wolf*, pp.40-1.

155 "Our daily associates" Seton, *Trail of an Artist-Naturalist*, p.54.

155 "Woodcuts of letters" Seton, pp.61-2.

156 "Not far, a quarter mile" Seton, p.62.

156 "one of the neglected" *DLB*, v.99, p.99.

157 "found here...more" Sanders, *Emily Murph*, p.21.

157 "the fine finish" Dendy, *Lost Toronto*, p.201.

158 "Seldom has a visiting writer" "The Fly Leaf" *G&M*, March 11, 1939, p.11.

159 "His beautiful blurred" "Yeats Tells of Rise" *M&E*, November 24, 1932, p.4.

159 "All night the lecturer" *Telegram*, November 24, 1932, p.39

161 "His audiences were" B.B. Opala, *Matthew Arnold in Canada* (unpublished M.A. thesis, McGill, 1968) p.27.

162 "At Toronto the audience" Harte, ed., *The Letters of Bret Harte*, p.19.

164 "Prices were higher" John Robert Colombo, *Contemporary Authors Autobiography Series*, v.22 (Detroit: 1994), pp.40-1.

164 "he was part of Toronto's" Keller, *Pauline*, p.56.

166 "The northernmost residence" Grahame, *Short Days Ago*, pp.3-4.

166 "was a woman who" Grahame, pp.14-5.

170 "She had covered the chest" Sullivan, *Shadow Maker*, p.361 and p.342.

172 "read an essay in" "The Fly Leaf" *G&M*, October 6, 1945, p.8

174 "the pioneer voice" *G&M*, February 8, 1941, p.11.

176 "In early June" Macdonald, *Self-Portrait*, pp. 29-31.

177 "My main market was" Bruccoli, *Kenneth Millar/Ross Macdonald: A Checklist*, p.xiii.

177 "Many of these were" Jerry Tutunjian, "Interview with Ross Macdonald" *Tamarack Review*, No. 62 (1974) p.72.

173 "I don't know Robertson" Tutunjian, p.73.

177 "He was the Canadian" Tutunjian, pp.73-4.

178 "I'm not and never" Ross Macdonald, *Archer In Hollywood*, p.ix.

178 "...Toronto, I like it now" Tutunjian, p.73.

179 "something unprecedented" quoted in Fetherling, *Travels By Night,* p. 108.

179 "Among the authors" the full history of Anansi has yet to be written. Until then, the reader can get a glimmering of the excitements and personal costs of the press by reading Roy MacSkimming's summary history, *Making Literary History: House of Anansi Press 1967-1997* (Toronto: Anansi, 1997).

179 "When we settled" Livesay, *Journey With My Selves*, p.60.

180 "What must be done' de la Roche, *Ringing The Changes*, pp.146-8.

181 "McNeilly's one-act plays" "Flyleaf" *G&M*, October 28, 1939, p.12

181 "He practiced criminal law" Morgan, *Canadian Men & Women Of The Time* (1898) p.502.

181 "A brief spasm" Kirkconnell, *A Slice Of Life*, pp.85-6.

183 "Thomas Guthrie Marquis" "A Great Canadian Historian" *Star*, April 3, 1936, p.4.

185 "He was, for ten years" Bruce Whiteman, "John Sutherland" *Poetry Canada Review* (Summer 1987), p.10

187 "while in Toronto he" Alun Jones, *The Life And Opinions of T.E. Hulme* (Boston: 1960) p.23.

187 "The first time I ever felt" from "A Lecture on Modern Poetry" quoted in Jones.

191 "with the possible exception" Robin Harris, *English Studies At Toronto* (Toronto: 1988) p.103

191 "George W. Russell's" *Star*, February 25, 1928.

194 "what Canadian writing" *Oxford Companion to Canadian Literature* (Toronto: 1997) p.492.

195 "The Department" John R. Colombo, "On Meeting Jorge Luis Borges" *Canadian Forum*, April 1968, p.7.

195 "[It] was one of the most interesting" *News*, May 18, 1908, p.5

196 "Mrs. Ward's gown was" "Famous Novelist Visits Toronto" *M&E*, May 18, 1908, p.4

192 "who made a short speech" "The Countryman in Literature" *News*, May 19, 1908, p.6

196 "Among modern writers" "Peasant's Place in Literature" *Star*, May 19, 1908, p.7

197 "of leaf-green satin" "On Dit" *M&E*, May 20, 1908, p.7

197 "Toronto is less exciting" Janet Trevelyan, *The Life of Mrs. Humphry Ward* (London: 1923) p.216

197 "Toronto seems to be a vast" from a letter in MS, Pusey House, Oxford. My thanks to The Rev. M.R. Knight, Custodian of the Library, for making this letter available to me.

198 "Dr. Van Dyke ingratiated" "Diplomat and Orator" *World*, October 26, 1919, p.6.

198 "Women ought to stay women" "Women Should Stay" *Star*, October 27, 1919, p.8.

199 "I wasn't very alert" G. Gatenby conversation with Earle Birney at his home, December 1982.

200 "At the University of Toronto" Andrew Allan, *A Self-portrait* (Toronto: 1974), p.55.

200 "There were red faces" Allan, pp.58-60.

201 "the job was menial" Ayre, pp.61-2.

204 "as members of my generation" Austin Clarke, *Contemporary Authors Autobiography Series*, v.16, p.77.

204 "By the age of eighteen" D. Livesay, *Right hand Left Hand* (Erin, Ont: Press Porcepic, 1977) p.22

205 "In my fourth university year" Livesay, pp.32-3.

207 "And in his two best novels" For a detailed discussion of Faulkner's time in Toronto, see my *The Wild Is Always There* (Toronto: Knopf Canada, 1993), pp.1-20.

209 "Before the fire" W. Stewart Wallace, *A History of the University of Toronto 1827-1927* (Toronto:1927) p.146.

211 "He said that the façade" discussed in Claude Bissell, *University College, A Portrait 1853-1953* (Toronto: 1953) p.89.

211 "In 1883 we graduated" Ralph Connor, *Postscript to Adventure* (Toronto: 1975) p.45.

212 "From Prescott we went on" Anthony Trollope, *North America*, (New York, 1862), pp.73-4.

213 "Illustrating his points" "Checkhov Style" *Varsity*, October 26, 1950, p.3.

214 "Buchan had been asked" Clara Thomas, *William Arthur Deacon*, p.196.

214 "*O Canada* was played" for a full report on the event, see William Arthur Deacon, *Canadian Authoir and Bookman* (December 1937) pp.6-7.

215 "Who but a Frenchman" Merrill Denison, "Canada Traslates Poetry" , *Star*, November 8, 1928.

216 "We are exposed" "Dr. Leacock Adddresses Lit" *Varsity*, January 15, 1912, p.1 & p.4.

218 "If it was an evening visit" Pelham Edgar, *Across My Path* (Toronto: 1952), p.34

218 "I was intimidated" quoted in Rosemary Sullivan, *The Red Shoes* (Toronto: 1998), p.77

218 "I thought at the time" quoted in Nathalie Cooke, *Margaret Atwood: A Biography* (Toronto: 1998), p.58

219 "I and another fellow" Susan Gingell, *E.J.Pratt On His Life and Poetry* (Toronto: 1983) p.51

219 "He was probably" quoted in David Pitt, E.J. Pratt, *The Truant Years* (Toronto: 1984) p.87.

220 "one of which was" Pitt, p.102

220 "It wasn't until my" *The Open Room*, vol. 1, no. 1 (1989), p.19

220 "As long as Canada's" quoted by Donald Jones, "Unmistakably Canadian Poet" *Star*, May 1, 1982, p.G14.

220 "Robins, who was" John Ayre, *Northrop Frye* (Toronto: 1989) p.59.

221 "When they returned" Ayre, pp.73-4.

222 "His 1936 arrival" I am indebted to Professor Ted Goossens of York University for the biographal data about this author.

223 "an early, worthwhile" Sutherland, p.202

223 "It was spring, 1945" Hambleton, pp.67-73

225 "Between our house" Pelham Edgar, Across My Path (Toronto: 1952) pp.15-16.

225 "I remember our last" Morley Callaghan, "Hemingway" *Star Weekly*, October 7, 1961, p.4.

227 "the most beautiful" *Canadian Courier*, February 23, 1907, p.16

227 "*The Oxford Companion*" *Oxford Companion to Canadian Theatre*, p.399

227 "Mr. Yeats is" "Artist Less Emotional" *Star*, February 14, 1914, p.4.

230 "he planned to start" W.

Tewrrence Gordon, *Marshall McLuhan* (Toronto: 1997) p.135.

230 "Across the road" Terrence Gordon, *Marshall McLuhan* (Toronto: 1997) p.165.

232 "Just before New Year's" Hugh Garner, *One Damn Thing After Another* (Toronto: 1973) pp.38-9

233 "established a pattern" Paul Steuwe, *The Storms Below* (Toronto: 1988) p.93.

234 "It was also a force" J.R. Colombo, *Contemporary Authors Autobiography Series*, v.22, p.40

235 "it looked as if" James Woodress, *Willa Cather* (Lincoln, Nebraska: 1987) p.319.

236 "while the 350 lovers" "Noted Author" *Globe*, November 6, 1936, p.15

237 "Mr. Heming's studio" "Famous Author" *Star Weekly*, March 1 [?], 1930.

239 "The Islington Jersey Dairy" Algernon Blackwood, *Episodes before Thirty* (London: 1923) p.10-14.

240 "I must say that" Ibid, p.122.

240 "Mr. Sheppard had" Hector Charlesworth, *Saturday Night*, Jan 1, 1938, p.15.

241 "She wrote poems personally" see Carole Gerson, *Canadian Notes & Queries*, No.40, pp.4-5.

241 "Probably no other" Donald A. Precosky, "Marjorie Pickthall" in *Dictionary of Literary Biography*, v.92, p.285.

242 "no particular reason" quoted in Roberts, *Standard Dictionary of Canadian Biography*, v.1, p.340

242 "she is known as" ibid, p.340

242 "Her last home" for a full discussion of McCully see S. Sperdakos, *Ontario History*, December 1992, pp.283-314.

243 "one of the first" Anton Wagner, "Sarah Anne Curzon" in *Dictionary of Literary Biography*, v.99, p.82

243 "beset with complications" Fetherling, *Canadian Anecdotes*, pp.97-8

244 "When allowance is made" Story, *Oxford Companion to Canadian Literature and History*, p.639

244 "among the more versatile" *St. James Guide To Crime & Mystery Writers* (Detroit: 1996) pp.953-4.

244 "one day—a day" Vincent Starrett, Born In A Bookshop (Norman, Oklahoma: 1965) pp. 12-13.

247 "'They wanted a girl" quoted in Sullivan, p.63.

248 "'It was the broad" Robert Easton, *Max Brand* (Norman, Oklahoma: 1970) p.37.

249 "In a dull and depressed" Al Purdy, *Reaching For The Beaufort Sea* (Madeira Park, B.C.: 1993), pp.95-6.

250 " In Parkdale there were" M.T. Kelly, *Contemporary Authors Autobiography Series*, v.22, p.110.

250 "Parkdale was a" Marc Baraness and Larry Richards, editors, *Toronto Places* (Toronto:1987) p.10.

251 "'Where there is now" quoted in Ronald Hambleton, *Mazo de la Roche of Jalna* (New York: 1966) pp.99-100

253 "During his days on the" "Active Backer" *G&M*, July 28, 1944, p.5.

254 "The music and drama" Eggleston, pp.22-23.

255 "Both Negroes and white" "Negro Contribution Lacks Appreciation" *Telegram*, April 19, 1943, p.17

256 "His populism," *Benet's Reader's Encyclopedia of American Literature* (New York: 1991) p.497

258 "the work of a reflective" Rhodenizer, *Canadian Literature in English* (Montreal: 1965) p.868

259 "a large and enthusiastic" "Miss Ray Levinsky" *News*, January 8, 1915, p.4

261 "I had never been" H.J. Kirchoff,

"Quirky Imagination" *G&M*, March 7, 1990.

261 "we know of no writer" "New Volume" *Canadian Bookman*, February 1922, p.35

261 "a slick writer of" Fraser Sutherland, *The Monthly Epic* (Toronto: 1989) p.146.

261 "The Twentieth Plane" John R. Colombo, *Mysterious Canada* (Toronto: 1988), p.247.

262 "Benson's work was held" *Canadian Bookman* (January 1929) p.29

263 "the oldest and probably" "Evan MacColl Died Yesterday" *M&E*, July 25, 1898, p.

263 "Hubert Evans has" Alan Twigg, *Hubert Evans* (Madeira Park, BC: 1985) p.89.

263 "He was offered a job" Twigg, p.10.

264 "The Mirvish store" Jock Carroll, "Bob Mirvish" *Telegram Weekend Magazine*, Nov.17, 1962.

266 "Trinity was romantically" William Dendy, *Lost Toronto* (Toronto, 1993) p.159.

268 "Most of the rooms" Carl Connor, *Archibald Lampman* (Toronto: 1929)

268 "Like most of the" quoted in E.K.Brown, *On Canadian Poetry* (Toronto, 1944) pp.91-2.

270 "Illegal songs" "Wrote Fine Volume of Baltic Folk-Lore" *Star*, November 2, 1935, p.5.

276 "Goldwin Smith rejected" Elisabeth Wallace, *Goldwin Smith: Victorian Liberal* (UofT Press, 1957) p.55

278 "No other circumstances" J.E. Middleton, *Municipality of Toronto*, v.3, p.316.

282 "She does not attempt" quoted in John Maclem, "Jean Blewett" *Canadian Bookman* (April 1927) p.99

283 "In connection with" J.E. Middleton, *Municipality of Toronto* (1923) p.362

283 "Seven years ago" Foreword to T.B. Gleave, *Beyond Our Walls* (Toronto, 1946)

284 "Boy, never did a kid" Mary Kierstead, *New Yorker*, August 29, 1988, p.33.

284 "for many years," Clara Thomas, *Canadian Novelists: 1920-1945* (Toronto, 1946), pp.86-7.

285 "When she died" For an amusing sidelight on Blewett, see *Canadian Author & Bookman*, December 1945, p.17.

286 "It is difficult to say" Donna Coates, "Emily Murphy" *Dictionary of Literary Biography*,v.99, p.255

287 "There was a sortie" *National Monthly*, November 1902

287 "On the last night" Byrne Hope Sanders, *Emily Murphy, Crusader* (Toronto, 1945) p.75

288 "the S.J. Perelman" *Twentieth Century Crime & Mystery Writers* (Detroit: 1985) p.723.

290 "it is probable" *Standard Dictionary of Canadian Biography*, p.448

292 "I'd become engaged" Raymond Souster, *Contemporary Authors Autobiography Series*, v.14, p.313

295 "The new premises" Mary Rubio and Elizabeth Waterston, *Writing A Life: L.M. Montgomery* (Toronto, 1995) p.103.

295 "Opening in Toronto" ibid, p.107.

295 "In 1942, Montgomery's" ibid, pp.116-7.

296 "My mother and I" Daniel Bratton, *Thirty Two Short Views of Mazo de la Roche* (Toronto:1996) p.159.

298 "The women occupied" Joan Givner, *Mazo de la Roche: The Hidden Life* (Toronto: 1989), p.116.

298 "By the time she passed away" Ronald Hambleton, *Mazo de la Roche* (New York: 1966) p.50.

299 "Mr. Tyrrell had" "The Fly Leaf" *G&M*, January 20, 1945, p.8.

300 "worshippers at the shrine" David G. Pitt, *E.J. Pra t: The Master Years*

1927-1964 (Toronto:1987), p.194.

300 "Yet, the fact is it remains" Elspeth Cameron, *Earle Birney: A Life* (Toronto: 1994) p.240.

301 "Sitting at the kitchen table" Rosemary Sullivan, *The Red Shoes* (Toronto: 1998), pp.96-7.

302 "Immediately I was caught" quoted in Nathalie Cooke, *Margaret Atwood: A Biography* (Toronto: 1998) p.106.

304 "Among her accomplishments" see "Pastor's Wife" *G&M*, October 1, 1955, p.5.

306 "January 1, 1966" Matt Cohen, "The Tunnel of Endless Pleasure" *Toronto Life* (Nov.1996) p.102.

307 "Even a decade after" "Retired Professor Finds Joy" *Star*, June 22, 1936, p. 1.

307 "Hendry's career in Canadian" Johnston, *Up The Mainstream*, p.173.

307 "Lowry desperately needed" Paul Tiessen, editor, *Letters of Malcolm Lowry and Gerald Noxon 1940-1952* (Vancouver, UBC Press, 1988) pp.4-5.

309 "When Bauer finally" Gunter Hess, "The German Immigrant Writer Walter Bauer" in Walter Riedel, editor, *The Old World And The New*, p.62

309 "From the standpoint" *G&M*, Dec.12, 1953, p.13.

311 "his status as an authority" "Eminent Historian" *M&E*, Oct 28, 1935, p.4.

311 "Anthony Frisch who teaches" *G&M*, "The Fly Leaf" April 7, 1956, p.8

312 "In class, he had a diffuse" John Ayre, *Northrop Frye* (Toronto: Random House, 1989) pp.63-4.

312 "On the evening of March 30th" Siegfried Sassoon, *Siegfried's Journey, 1916-1920* (London: 1945) p.199.

314 "When I went to the auditions" *Andrew Allan: A Self-Portrait* (Toronto: Macmillan, 1974) pp.67-70.

314 "they were among the best" *G&M*, obituary, Jan 17, 1974, p.10.

314 "The idea that our plays" ibid

315 "Newbolt's novels are" Stanley Kunitz, *Twentieth Century Authors* (New York, 1961) p.1017.

317 "he was much addicted" W. Stewart Wallace, *Macmillan Dictionary of Canadian Biography*, p.759.

321 "is probably more widely known" James Reaney, "Selwyn Dewdney" in *Dictionary of Literary Biography*, v.68, p.120.

322 "a major contribution" Robert Wallace, "Michael Hollingsworth" in *Oxford Companion to Canadian Theatre*, p.273.

324 "Sarah Binks is a burlesque" Louis MacKendrick, "Paul Hiebert" in *Dictionary of Literary Biography*, v.68, pp.180-6.

325 "The environs of the University" Charlesworth, *Candid Chronicles*, p.42.

327 "first five years" *Standard Dictionary of Canadian Biography*, v.1, p.337.

330 "Those streets of the Annex" Dorothy Livesay, *Journey With My Selves* (Toronto: 1991) pp.26-7.

333 "The policy did not" quoted in Denis Johnston, *Up The Mainstream* (Toronto, UofT Press, 1991) pp.79-80.

335 "I have at last" R. Andrew Paskauskas, *The Complete Correspondence of Sigmund Freud and Ernest Jones 1908-1939* (Cambridge, Mass: 1993) p.18

335 "the attitude in Canada" quoted in Vincent Brome, *Ernest Jones: Freud's Alter Ego* (London, 1982) p.68.

335 "One man he [Jones] failed" Vincent Brome, *Ernest Jones: Freud's Alter Ego* (London, 1982) p.78.

337 "electrified his congregation" Jock Carroll, *The Life and Times of Greg Clark* (Toronto: 1981) p.174.

338 "his new work for" David G. Pitt, *E.J. Pratt: The Truant Years* (Toronto, UofT Press, 1984) p.178.

339 "W.H. Allen" " Fulford on Books" *Star*, October 31, 1960.

342 "The production had a cast" Rose Adams, "Oscar Ryan" in *Dictionary of Literary Biography*, v.68, pp322-3. See also Toby Gordon Ryan, *Stage Left: Canadian Theatre in the Thirties* (Toronto, 1981).

346 "fell from 5 in the morning" ibid, p.89.

347 "I can scarcely find" ibid, p.91.

347 "Toronto was a changed city" ibid 101.

347 "I was busy at the *Globe*" Ibid, pp.232-3.

349 "I roamed that city" Doug Glover, *Contemporary Authors Autobiography Series*, v.23, p.88.

350 "One of the young" Gray, *Fun Tomorrow*, p.138.

351 "One of Playhouse's" Herbert Whittaker, "New Theatre" *G&M*, July 21, 1958, p.28.

351 "Mr. O'Casey said" Morris Duff, "Sean O'Casey" *Star*, September 27, 1958, p.28.

352 "The Playhouse "was jammed"" Whittaker, *G&M*, November 14, 1958, p.8.

352 "Shortly after *The Yellow*" John Honsberger, *Gazette* (Law Society of Upper Canada), v.25 (1991) pp 267-8.

353 "In all, MacGregor" Marilyn Rose, "Marian Keith" in Benson, *Oxford Companion to Canadian Literature*. p.700

354 "I met him in 1920" Robert Graves, intro.to *The Collected Poems of Frank Prewett* (London: Cassell, 1964) pp. vii-viii.

354 "He died alone" I am indebted to Dr. Bruce Meyer for the biographical facts concerning Prewett. See his helpful Introduction to *Selected Poems of Frank Prewett* (Toronto: Exile Editions, 1987).

354 "In addition, the *Star*" "First Woman Undertaker" *Star*, January 6, 1934, p.3.

355 "He edited an aviation" for information regarding Edgar's publications I am indebted to Nelson Ball. The *G&M* article "Author and Wife Slightly Hurt" appeared July 10, 1946, p.2.

356 "Almost the first" Raymond Souster, *Contemporary Authors Autobiography Series*, v.14, pp.305-6.

356 "As well as typing novels" I am indebted to Nelson Ball for much of the publication data on Ted Steele.

357 "[It] stood in odd isolation" Sullivan, *Shadow Maker*, p.2.

358 "What was once" The Robertson description is on p.734 of *Landmarks of Toronto*. Hathaway's is found in his *Star Weekly* article "Why Not Literary Shrines in Toronto?" March 23, 1929, pp.9-10.

358 "until the 1870s" Linda Shesko, intro. to Thomson, *Old Man Savarin and Other Stories*, p.vii.

358 "No, I have no wish" quoted by Shesko, *ibid*, p.x

359 "His impaired hearing" M.O. Hammond, "Edward William Thomson" *Queen's Quarterly*, v.38 (1931), p.124.

361 "apartment on Toronto's" Alberto Manguel, "Lives Lived" *G&M*, December 7, 1998, p.A20.

362 "When I was twelve" Irwin, *Three Lives In Mine*, p.60.

363 "For a family that attended" ibid, p.61.

359 "It is the story of Andrew" Barbara Pell, "Grace Irwin" in *DLB*, v.68, pp.185-6.

364 "recounted how he" Obituary, "Thomas P. Kelley" *Star*, February 17, 1982

369 "I've had quite an" "Flyleaf" *G&M*, February 24, 1951, p.10

373 "My first literary experience" M.T. Kelly, *Contemporary Authors Autobiography Series*, p.113

382 "'her work now suffers" *DLB*, v.68, p.29.

383 "We had a fierce fight" quoted in Johnston, *Up The Mainstream*, p.152.

384 "I am a Canadian" "Noted mathematician" *Star*, January 17, 1968, p.7.

385 "After more than nine years" Gordon, *Marshall McLuhan*, p.168.

387 "it was during this period" "Alan Sullivan" *G&M*, May 18, 1946, p.8.

388 "True continued to regard" Darke, *Call Me True*, p.31.

389 "Ned accepted me" quoted in Pitt, *E.J. Pratt, The Master Years*, p.116.

390 "she often remarked" Baker, *Selected Poems*, p.xii.

391 "Left a widow" ibid, pp.xiii-xiv.

393 "'In Miss Margaret Lawrence" "Toronto's New Authoress" *Star*, April 18, 1936, p.1.

393 "commending to their" "Book Fair Talks" *M&E*, November 11, 1936, p.3.

397 "A small, dapper" Sutherland, *The Monthly Epic*, p.148.

400 "I try to show how" "But Not Enough Romance" *Telegram*, April 20, 1964, n.p.

401 "A fine artist is dead" "Group of Seven" *M&E*, November 28, 1932, p.1.

401 "A footnote of interest" "The Bookshelf" *Satuday Night*, November 2, 1946, p.20.

402 "With the Wall Street" Salinger, *P.S.: A Memoir*, p.4.

404 "'I was packed out to" quoted in Griffith, *The World of Robert Flaherty*, p.xviii.

404 "'Music At the Close" DLB, v.88, p.211.

405 "'The influence of Hector" *G&M*, December 31, 1945, p.6

406 "He has for more" "Author, Teacher" *G&M*, December 9, 1954, p.16.

406 "inescapably a Toronto" *Proceedings of the Empire Club of Canada*, 1924, p.31.

406 "Sandwell set high" Skelton-Grant: *Robertson Davies: Man of Myth*, p.237.

408 "'in 1939 he began" Thomas, *Canadian Novelists 1920-1945*, pp.1-2.

408 "Amy told Napier" "In The Editor's Confidence" *Maclean's*, September 1932.

408 "an all-purpose servant" Wachtel, *Writers & Company*, pp.101-12.

409 "'a Zola in Canadian" "Letters in Canada" *UofT Quarterly*, Winter 1949, p.270.

410 "Harris's biographer believes" Larisey, *Light For a Cold Land* , p.118.

410 "'my whole life has been" *Contemporary Authors*, vols. 49-52, p.173.

411 "'Toronto may not be" Layton, *Wild Gooseberries*, p.342.

412 "Coulter brought to Canada" Geraldine Anthony, "John Coulter" in *DLB*, v.68, p.78.

413 "That summer, one" Morley Callaghan, "Hemingway" *Star Weekly*, October 7, 1961, pp.2-4.

415 "Newton MacTavish" Sutherland, *The Monthly Epic*, p.102.

415 "It illustrates Creighton's'" P.B.Waite, "Donald Creighton" *The Beaver*, February-March, 1998, p.31.

416 "laborious, sexually morbid" T.K. Farah, "Fraser—The Heathen Idol" *The Canadian Magazine*, January 1927, pp.33-4.

419 "He was perhaps the first" *Standard Dictionary of Canadian Biography*, v.1, p.137.

419 "Following the publication" Barbara Opala, "Gwethalyn Graham" *DLB*, v.88, pp.89-90.

420 "kindness and helpfulness" "A Missionary Zeal" *G&M*, March 27, 1971, p.25.

421 "'I'm a very soft critic" "Society Treated Me" *Star*, March 27, 1971, p.59.

423 "I have a pretty good idea" "Nazis

are Desperate" *Star*, January 15, 1940, p.2.

428 "pointed his students" Ayre, *Northrop Frye*, p.59.

430 "'The story was written" "The Fly Leaf" *G&M*, September 22, 1945, p.21.

433 "he entered the advertising" Evan Brooker, "A Canadian Gadfly" *G&M*, November 23, 1996, p.C10.

434 "Once a year" quoted in Cooke, *Margaret Atwood*, p.35.

434 "The greatest thing" see "Wilson MacDonald Day" *G&M*, October 21, 1955, p.6.

435 "he rivalled Stephen Leacock" Donald Jones, "Historical Toronto" *Star*, October 22, 1983, p.F6. Most of my information about MacDonald's visit to Russia comes from Donald Jones.

435 "having much less space" Pitt, *E.J. Pratt: The Master Years*, pp.452-3.

435 "I remember Ned" Ralph Gustafson in Clever, *The E.J. Pratt Symposium*, p.6.

436 "In January 1914" Sutherland, *The Monthly Epic*, p.142.

437 "the house has other literary significance" Pitt, *E.J. Pratt: The Master Years*, pp.182-3.

437 "one of the pioneers" Paul Hjartson in *DLB*, v.92, p.319.

439 "I hope very much" Hambleton, *How I Earned etc*, p.107.

440 "'I sent off my manuscript" Gray, *Fun Tomorrow*, p.226.

444 "'During the next eighteen months" Bernard Slade, *Contemporary Authors Autobiography Series*, v.9, p.240.

527 "In 1927 he burst" Deidre Chilsholm, catalogue notes for *Assembling Sounds: The Drawings and Illustrations of Bertram Brooker* (Barrie, Ontario: 1997), p.1.

527 "I moved to Toronto" Pierre Berton, "I Won't Wax Nostalgic" *Star*, August 20, 1994.

530 "One day I got onto" Paul Stuewe, "Export, Eh?" *Books in Canada*, May 1977, pp.8-10. Steele later told poet and antiquarian Nelson Ball that he was never an employee of Export—simply a contracted author. He also told Ball that the covers were not racy, certainly not in comparison to the lurid American covers. And the press did not spend time tinkering editorially with manuscripts. Steele recalled an occasion when he and others at the press spent twenty minutes to find a title for a book. According to Steele, this happened only once, and it was a record for time spent improving a text.

532 "The dramatic and" Quoted from a promotional brochure distributed by Jessie Alexander in my possession.

533 "The laughter she inspires" "Jessie Alexander Roberts" *Star Weekly*, May 9, 1914.

538 "The home...was Frye's" John Ayre, *Northrop Frye* (Toronto: 1989) pp.196-7.

540 "located in the middle" Quoted in Cooke, *Margaret Atwood*, p.33.

540 "The day I became" Quoted in Sullivan, *The Red Shoes*, pp.66-67.

545 "the biggest birthday" "Ten Organzations" *Telegram*, April 14, 1931, p.8.

547 "It really does seem" "Ralph Connor's Mantle" *Saturday Night*, January 7, 1938.

548 "For a more ivory-tower" Paul Stuewe, *The Storms Below*, pp.181-2.

549 "Here is some genuine" Quoted in Hector Charlesworth, *Encyclopedia of Canadian Biography*, p.184.

550 "On the other hand" Mary Kierstead, "James Houston" *New Yorker*, August 29, 1988, p.34.

553 "Grey Owl" "Grey Owl Answers, *M&E*. March 3, 1936, p.11.

554 "Soon after joining" David MacKenzie, *Arthur Irwin* (Toronto: 1993) p.96.

558 "I've always been" Garner, p.209.

558 "the most unproductive" Stuewe, p.162.

561 "One day, Coach" *Contemporary Authors Autobiography Series*, v.13, pp.296-7.

563 "We have a nice" Raymond Knister, *Collected Poems*, ed. by Dorothy Livesay (Toronto: 1949) p.xxviii.

563 "Although living conditions" Hugh Garner, *One Damn Thing After Another* (Toronto: 1973) p.122.

564 "Don't be surprised" "Novelist plots" *Star*, February 10, 1978, p.D1.

566 "When poems are cut" quoted in Kay Rex, *No Daughter of Mine: The Women and History of the Canadian Women's Press Club* (Toronto: 1995), p.27.

567 "While writing it" *Contemporary Authors Autobiography Series*, v.9, p.243.

568 "I have missed my" Hambleton, *Mazo de la Roche of Jalna*, p.163.

569 "I thought it would" David Cobb, "If You Can Make It," *Canadian Magazine*, June 17, 1972, p.8.

570 "Every evening after" Stuewe, p.95.

572 "lived on the screened-in" Sullivan, *The Shadow Maker*, p.225.

572 "We found a place" John Lennox and Ruth Panofsky, Editors, *Selected Letters of Margaret Laurence and Adele Wiseman* (Toronto:)p.309.

572 "Myself am fine" ibid, p.321.

574 "York, or Toronto" George Heriot, *Travels Through the Canadas* (Edmonton: 1971) pp.138-9.

574 "There is a good bridge" Lieutenant Francis Hall, *Travels in Canada and the United States* (Boston: 1818), pp.131-2.

575 "The town of York" John Howison, *Sketches of Upper Canada* (London: 1821) pp.55-7.

576 "Our dinner was laid" Captain Basil Hall, *Travels In North America* (Edinburgh: 1829) v.1, pp.262-3.

576 "[Lake Ontario] has" Henry James: *Portraits of Places* (London: 1883), pp.364-5.

INDEX